EVERYMAN'S LIBRARY

EVERYMAN,
I WILL GO WITH THEE,
AND BE THY GUIDE,
IN THY MOST NEED
TO GO BY THY SIDE

THE BABUR NAMA

TRANSLATED, EDITED AND ANNOTATED
BY ANNETTE SUSANNAH BEVERIDGE

WITH AN INTRODUCTION
BY WILLIAM DALRYMPLE

EVERYMAN'S LIBRARY
Alfred A. Knopf   New York   London   Toronto
399

THIS IS A BORZOI BOOK
PUBLISHED BY ALFRED A. KNOPF

First included in Everyman's Library, 2020

First published in two volumes in 1921 under the title *The Bābur-nāma
in English* (*Memoirs of Babur*), *translated from the original Turki Text
of Ẓahiru'd-dīn Muḥammad Bābur Pādshāh Ghāzī* by
Annette Susannah Beveridge

www.randomhouse.com/everymans
www.everymanslibrary.co.uk

ISBN: 978-1-101-90823-5 (US)
978-1-84159-399-9 (UK)

A CIP catalogue reference for this book is available from the
British Library

Typography by Peter B. Willberg

Book design by Barbara de Wilde and Carol Devine Carson

Typeset in India by SPI Global, Pondicherry
Front matter typeset in the UK by Input Data Services Ltd,
Isle Abbotts, Somerset

Printed and bound in Germany by GGP Media GmbH, Pössneck

GENERAL CONTENTS

———

THE BABUR NAMA

vi

INTRODUCTION

At the end of 1525, Zahiru'd-din Muhammad Babur, a Timu-rid poet-prince from Farghana in Central Asia, descended the Khyber Pass with a small army of hand-picked followers; with him he brought some of the first modern muskets and cannon seen in India. With these he defeated the Delhi Sultan, Ibrahim Lodhi, and established his garden-capital at Agra.

This was not Babur's first conquest. He had spent much of his youth throneless, living with his companions from day to day, rustling sheep and stealing food. Occasionally he would capture a town – he was fourteen when he first took Samarkand and held it for four months. Aged twenty-one, he finally managed to seize and secure Kabul, and it was this Afghan base that became the springboard for his later conquest of India. But before this he had lived for years in a tent, displaced and dispossessed, a peripatetic existence that had little appeal to him. "It passed through my mind," he wrote, "that to wander from moun-tain to mountain, homeless and houseless ... had nothing to recommend it."[1]

Babur died in 1530, only four years after his arrival in India, and before he could properly consolidate his new conquests. He regarded himself as a failure for having lost his family lands in Central Asia and was profoundly ashamed that his generation of Timurids, thanks to their squabbles and rivalries, had failed to defend their ancestral inheritance after holding Oxiana for more than a century. He could not have imagined that his new Indian conquests would grow to be the greatest and most populous of all Muslim-ruled empires with, by 1650, around 150 million sub-jects – five times the number ruled by their Ottoman rivals. At this point, his family's lands were producing about a quarter of all global manufacturing: the Mughal Empire had become the world's industrial powerhouse and its greatest producer of man-ufactured textiles. In comparison, England then had just five per cent of India's population and was producing under three per cent of the world's manufactured goods.[2] A good proportion of the profits of these Indian manufactures found their way to the Mughal exchequer in Agra, making Babur's successors, with incomes of around £100 million, by far the richest monarchs in the world.

In Milton's *Paradise Lost*, the great Mughal cities of Agra and Lahore are revealed to Adam after the Fall as future wonders of God's creation. This was no understatement: by the age of Milton, Lahore had grown larger even than Constantinople, and, with its two million inhabitants, dwarfed both London and Paris. From the ramparts of the Fort, Babur's descendants ruled over most of India, all of Pakistan and Bangladesh, and great chunks of Afghanistan. Their army was all but invincible; their palaces unparalleled; the domes of their many mosques quite literally glittered with gold. The Mughals were really rivalled only by their Ming counterparts in China. For their grubby contemporaries in the West, stumbling around in their codpieces, Babur's descendants, dripping in jewels, were the living embodiment of wealth and power – a meaning that has remained impregnated in the word "mogul" ever since.

If the dynasty Babur founded represented Islamic rule at its most powerful and majestic, it also defined it at its most aesthetically pleasing: this was, after all, the Empire that gave the world Mughal miniatures, Mughal gardens and the spectacular architectural tradition that culminated in the Taj Mahal. The great Mughal Emperors were also, with one notable exception, tolerant, pluralistic and eclectic. Their Empire was effectively built in coalition with India's Hindu majority, particularly the Rajputs of Rajasthan, and succeeded as much through conciliation as by war.

This was particularly true of Babur's grandson, the Emperor Akbar (1542–1605), who issued an edict of universal religious toleration, forbade forcible conversion to Islam and married a succession of Hindu wives. At the same time that Jesuits were being hanged, drawn and quartered in London, and when much of Catholic Europe was subject to the Inquisition, in India Akbar was summoning Jesuits from Goa, as well as Sunnis and Shia Muslims, Hindus of both Shaivite and Vaishnavite persuasions, Jews from Cochin, Parsis from Gujarat and groups of Hindu atheists, to come to his palace and debate their understanding of the metaphysical, declaring that "no man should be interfered with on account of religion, and anyone is to be allowed to go over to a religion that pleases him".

Babur not only established this extraordinary dynasty and set the tone for its future political, economic, aesthetic and humanistic triumphs; he also produced one of the most fascinating autobiographies ever written to record exactly how he did it. The *Babur Nama* does much more than merely keep the memory of his conquests alive. In its pages Babur opens his soul with a frankness and lack of inhibition comparable to Pepys. Typical is his description of falling in love with an adolescent boy from the camp bazaar: "Up till then I had had no inclination for anyone, indeed of love and desire," he wrote. "In that frothing-up of desire and passion, and under that stress of youthful folly, I used to wander bare-headed, bare-foot, through street and lane, orchard and vineyard. I shewed civility neither to friend nor stranger, took no care for myself or others."[3]

Throughout his memoir, we are admitted to Babur's innermost confidence as he examines and questions the world around him. He compares the fruits and animals of India and Afghanistan with as much inquisitiveness as he records his impressions of falling for men or marrying women, or weighing up the differing pleasures of opium, hashish and alcohol. Profoundly honest and unusually articulate, at once emotionally compelling and profoundly revealing, the *Babur Nama* is in many ways an oddly modern text, almost Proustian in its self-awareness. It presents the uncensored fullness of the man, a human life perfectly pinned to the page in simple, direct and unpretentious prose.

The uniqueness of the *Babur Nama* was immediately recognized by all Babur's contemporaries as it was by his Mughal successors, who quickly had it translated from Babur's colloquial Turki to literary Persian; from Persian it was first translated into English in 1826 by William Erskine and John Leyden, and became a favourite text of the Orientalists of the British Raj who had replaced the Mughals in India, and who saw many echoes of their life and thoughts in his. According to the Victorian administrator and Persian scholar Henry Beveridge, husband of the translator of this volume, Annette Beveridge (their son, William Beveridge, was instrumental in the formation of the British Welfare State) the *Babur Nama* "is one of those priceless records which are for all time, and is fit to rank with the confessions of St Augustine and Rousseau, and the memoirs of Gibbon and Newton. In Asia it stands almost alone."[4]

This last sentence is not quite accurate: there was in fact a wonderfully rich tradition of Islamic autobiography out of which the *Babur Nama* grew, and which includes such masterworks as the witty and urbane *Memoirs of Usamah Ibn-Munqidh*, a Syrian Arab landowner from the time of the Crusades, and the wise, measured and ironic *Mirror for Princes* of Kai Ka'us Qabus, an eleventh-century Seljuk vassal of the Ziyarid dynasty, whose grandfather built the great Gunbad-i-Qabus tomb tower on the Caspian steppe, and had his corpse suspended halfway up in a rock crystal coffin.[5] What is true, however, is that the *Babur Nama* is the culmination and climax of that Islamic autobiographical tradition as much as the Taj Mahal is the climax of its architectural legacy.

It is not just that the book is so very long and fabulously detailed: it extends to six hundred pages in the latest Turki critical edition, even with fifteen Afghan years of the story now missing and lost forever. This means that Babur's life is more fully documented than that of any figure in the entire pre-colonial Islamic world. What makes it stand out and remain relevant and moving today is its universal humanism, and its unusual honesty, sensitivity and self-understanding. As his latest scholarly biographer, Stephen Dale puts it:

Babur transcended the narrative and historical genres of his culture to produce a retrospective self-portrait of the kind that is usually associated with the most stylishly effective European and American autobiographies. No other author in the Islamic world – or in pre-colonial India or China – offers a comparable autobiographical memoir, a seemingly ingenuous first-person narrative enlivened with self-criticism as well as self-dramatization and the evocation of universally recognizable human emotions. Not only does Babur make himself seem engaging and personally approachable to modern readers, he also creates a three-dimensional picture of his world otherwise known mainly from traditional, stylized political narratives and dazzlingly colourful but two-dimensional miniature paintings.[6]

The *Babur Nama* is also, as generations of readers from different cultures have found, an unusually charming text: a warm-hearted, romantic and deeply engaging record of a highly cultured and honestly self-critical man: "His literary work delivers to us everything," writes Jean-Paul Roux, the French historian of the Mughals, "with his qualities and faults, especially his daily inner self, in his most casual moods, in his most profound thoughts, which often could have been our own."[7]

From the opening page, Babur's love of nature and the fineness of his descriptive eye are immediately apparent as he evokes his lost homeland, the Farghana Valley. Passage after passage lovingly describes the things he adored and now, writing in Indian exile, misses: spring mornings spent in hillsides dotted with wild violets, tulips and roses; cold running water, passing through "a shady and delightful clover-meadow where every passing traveller takes a rest"; "beautiful little gardens with fruit trees and almond trees in the orchards"; "pomegranates renowned for their excellence", "good hunting and fowling", pheasants which "grow so surprisingly fat that rumour has it four people could not finish one they were eating with its stew".[8]

Throughout the text, Babur's eye is alert for natural beauty and inquisitive about its curiosities. He is, for example, delighted by the idea of the flying squirrels that he "found in these mountains, an animal larger than a bat and having a curtain, like a bat's wing, between its arms and legs . . . it is said to fly, downward from one tree to another . . . Once we put one to a tree; it clambered up directly and got away, but, when people went after it, it spread its wings and came down, without hurt, as if it had flown."[9]

Paragraphs are devoted to the different varieties of many-coloured tulips growing wild in the Hindu Kush or to the smell of holm oak when used as winter firewood, "blazing less than mastic but like it, making a hot fire with plenty of hot ashes, and nice smell. It has the peculiarity in burning that when its leafy branches are set alight, they fire up with amazing sound, blazing and crackling from bottom to top."[10] He goes into raptures about the changing colours of a flock of geese on the horizon, "something as red as the rose of the dawn kept shewing and vanishing between the sky and the water".[11] Elsewhere he rhapsodizes about the brilliant colours of an Afghan autumn.

Above all, he loved books. His first act after a conquest was to go to the library of his opponent and raid its shelves. Whenever he visited a new city he would go to poetry meetings and listen to the verses being recited by its poets, joining in where appropriate, and criticizing whenever he disliked a particular couplet. Bad poets were a particular source of irritation to the connoisseur in Babur. One uncle he admired for his table and administration – "everything of his was orderly and well-arranged" – but castigated for kidnapping beautiful boys for his bed ("that vile practice") and even more so for his "flat and insipid" verse – "not to compose is better than to compose verse such as his".[12]

His sensibilities sharpened by wide reading, Babur had a great gift for producing these witty and often piquant word-portraits of his contemporaries. His own father he described as

short and stout, round-bearded and fleshy-faced . . . He used to wear his tunic so very tight that to fasten the strings he had to draw his belly in and, if he let himself out after tying them, they often tore away. He was not choice in dress or food . . . In his early days he was a great drinker, later on used to have a party once or twice a week. He was good company, on occasions reciting verses admirably . . .[13]

The *Babur Nama* is an intriguingly mixed bag of such character sketches mixed with musings on a wide variety of subjects: it is at once a diary, a history, a collection of nature notes, a gazetteer, a family chronicle and book of advice of a concerned father to a slightly hopeless son. It is divided into three parts. The first tells of his childhood and the adolescent failures that led to the loss of his patrimony. The second tells of his early twenties and his time spent homeless and wandering beyond the Oxus. This is followed by the lucky capture of Kabul, which he then uses as a base to rally his exiled and scattered Timurid relatives. The third tells the story of his final years and the conquest of India, a triumph tainted in its author's eyes by the ever-present pain of exile and loss. History may remember him as the first Mughal Emperor, but in his own eyes he was always a refugee.

Much of the text is a record of Babur's restless energy and

ambition, his struggles in a world that is inevitably profoundly male, military and feudal: fighting, riding, polo, drinking, swimming, fishing and hawking occupy many more pages than more peaceful pursuits such as chess, painting, calligraphy, romance, versifying or love-making. But even the most relentlessly masculine passages are redeemed by Babur's personal modesty and his awareness of his own failures, which he depicts as leading directly to the displacement and the exile of his people. He gives as much space for battles lost as he does to battles won, and he takes full responsibility for his youthful failures: "These blunders," he writes, "were the fruits of inexperience."[14]

He is also frank about his capacity for grief and depression, and open about the great tragedies of his life, and the way that they brought about his darkest moments. He writes with palpable feeling about his mother's death from fever, and the death of his comrades-in-arms: "His death made me strangely sad," he writes at one point, "for few men have I felt such grief; I wept unceasingly for a week or ten days."[15]

He sets out at the beginning that he intends to hide nothing, however badly it may reflect on him, and he remains strikingly true to this undertaking: "In this History," he writes, "I have held firmly to it that the truth should be reached in every matter, and that every act should be recorded precisely as it occurred."[16] Partly as a result of this, the *Babur Nama* also records much that is to our eyes unflattering. In this way it provides evidence for those in India, particularly from the Hindu Right, who today look on Babur as a barbarous and bloodthirsty jihadi invader.

For all the examples of his intense sensitivity towards botany, his love of poetry and calligraphy and painting, he also records himself ordering the slaughter of captives, the bloody torture and impaling of rebels and the enslavement of the women and children of his enemies. He even records building pyramids of skulls. These were, after all, extremely violent times. Like Alexander the Great, Rajaraja Chola, a Florentine prince of the age of Machiavelli, or an Elizabethan poet-privateer contemporary of Sidney or Drake, Babur was a man of ruthless, even pitiless action as well as one of extraordinary sensitivity. As Stephen Dale puts it, Babur shares with his Renaissance contemporaries, "the cultivation and refinement of aesthetic sensibility amidst a brutal life of constant political and social violence".[17]

The parallel with the Italian Renaissance also struck Salman Rushdie. "The Western thinker whom Babur most resembles is his contemporary, the Florentine Niccolò Machiavelli," he wrote in his brilliant essay on the *Babur Nama*:

In both men, a cold appreciation of the necessities of power, of what would today be called *realpolitik*, is combined with a deeply cultured and literary nature, not to mention the love, often to excess, of wine and women. Of course, Babur was an actual prince, not simply the author of *The Prince*, and could practise what he preached; while Machiavelli, the natural republican, the survivor of torture, was by far the more troubled spirit of the pair. Yet both of these unwilling exiles were, as writers, blessed, or perhaps cursed, with a clear-sightedness that looks amoral; as truth often does.[18]

Babur, in short, was at once the most refined of aesthetes, personally warm and loyal, with a sophisticated and sensitive mind; and also what we today might regard as a war criminal: casually violent and quite capable, when necessary, of overseeing acts of mass murder. As Rushdie concludes, "Who then was Babur – scholar or barbarian, nature-loving poet or terror-inspiring warlord? The answer is to be found in the *Baburnama*, and it's an uncomfortable one: he was both."

Amid so much in his memoir that is deeply human and which speaks to us with so much immediacy, it is this interplay of the sophisticated and warmly familiar with the alarmingly foreign and brutal that, more than anything else, gives the *Babur Nama* its compelling complexity.

*

The Farghana Valley is the Kashmir of Central Asia. The Soviets tried to turn it into an industrial zone, the focus of several Five Year Plans, intending to create a mass regional monoculture of industrialized cotton. But the cotton business died along with the USSR, and the region is now quickly reverting to the beautiful, high-altitude Eden it was at the time of Babur.

The valley is reached from the steppe around Tashkent by

a winding mountain road which climbs steeply through alpine meadows. Then, at the top of the pass, you pass through a rain shadow – a high-altitude desert, declining, as you descend, into scrubby, arid steppe grassland. Then quite suddenly, at the bottom, the desert blossoms and beyond the first green fields of rich spring wheat you see the bubbling irrigation runnels, muddy with fresh snow-melt from the Kyrgiz Pamirs, that have brought about the transformation. Beyond these fields, framed by jagged snow-peaks, lies the fertile fruit basket of Babur's beloved Farghana.

As you drive along avenues of poplar, rolling meadows full of poppies and wild tulips flank an expanse of apple, mulberry, apricot and almond orchards, all heavy with ripening fruit. In the distance, on the higher ground at the edge of the valley, are vineyards. Next to some of the larger irrigation runnels – bubbling streams from the Tien Shan – men sit cross-legged on wooden charpoys in the shade of poplars, eating tent-flaps of naan and long skewers of shashlik. Flocks of fat-tailed sheep are grazing amid the meadows. Donkeys rest by the roadside. An old man casts a fishing-line from a bridge.

The green intensifies as you progress, until eventually the poplars mass into thickets around the ox-bow meanders of the Amu Darya, Alexander's Oxus. Directly above its banks rise the precipitous mud-brick walls of the greatest fortress of Farghana, and its ancient capital, Akshi. The sun sets behind the snow-peaks; below, waterfowl call to roost. There is no one about. The town was destroyed and left deserted by a catastrophic earthquake of 1621, but even in complete ruination, you can sense the massive grandeur and might of this place in its Timurid glory days.

Babur was born here in Akshi in 1483. The cataclysmic thirteenth-century conquests of Chingiz Khan (most active between 1218 and 1221) followed in the late fourteenth century by those of Timur, had between them destroyed the old global order and utterly changed the complexion of the world between the Mediterranean and India; but they left Central Asia one of the richest regions on earth, and Akshi as one of its most imposing and impregnable fortresses.

Timur had hauled back to Samarkand the greatest craftsmen, artists and intellectuals from every region he conquered, and through their captive labour turned his steppe-land capital into one of the great cities of the world. A major cultural renaissance followed, as the Timurids – dubbed "the Oriental Medici" by the aesthete and travel writer Robert Byron – transformed themselves into refined littérateurs, connoisseurs of painting and poetry and calligraphy, as well as scientists, mathematicians and astronomers. This moment of cultural efflorescence reached its height in Herat under Timur's son Shahrukh (1377–1447) – whose own sons argued over the superior literary talents of Khusraw or Nizami, comparing their poems "line by line"[19] – and continued throughout Babur's early years under Sultan Husain (1438–1506), a Timurid of the elder branch of Baiqara, who presided over a court of extraordinary talent where Bihzad painted his masterpieces.

Babur was directly descended from both of the great world conquerors: from Chingiz (1162–1227) and his son Chaghatai (1183–1242) on his mother's side, and from Timur (1336–1405) on that of his father, who was one of Timur's great-great-grandsons. But the cultural achievements of Babur's generation were not matched by political or military triumphs. Instead Timur's many descendants fought among themselves over his inheritance, and each campaigning season brought another round of internecine family feuds: an endlessly repeating cycle of raids and invasions, alliances and betrayals. As E. M. Forster noted in his essay on Babur, "there were too many kings about, and not enough kingdoms. Tamerlane and Genghis Khan . . . had produced between them so numerous a progeny that a frightful congestion of royalties had resulted along the upper waters of the Jaxartes and the Oxus, and in Afghanistan. One could scarcely travel two miles without being held up by an Emperor."[20] Babur put the same thought more succinctly: "Ten darwishes can sleep under one blanket," he wrote, quoting a proverb, "but two kings cannot find room in one clime."[21]

The *Babur Nama* opens with a panorama of the final years of Timurid Central Asia, just before the rule of Babur and his cousins was snuffed out for ever. Babur tells how his father died, in a fall from his pigeon-house in 1494, when his heir was eleven years old. Immediately, two uncles, one Timurid, one Chaghatai Mongol, invaded his lands, while several of his father's nobles tried to replace him with his more malleable younger brother. Babur saw off both threats, and it was this that occasioned his first capture of Samarkand at the tender age of fourteen.

But a new and much more formidable enemy soon appeared on the horizon. Taking advantage of Timurid infighting, the disciplined cavalry of the Uzbek warlord Muhammad Shaibani Khan (1451–1510) swept into Oxiana, taking Bukhara and Samarkand without even a fight in 1500. One by one, in a startling short time, he was to overthrow each of Babur's feuding cousins and kinsmen, none of whom seemed to realize the seriousness of the Uzbek threat until too late.

Babur claims he tried to raise the alarm:

I represented . . . that now such a foe as Shaibaq Khan had made his appearance, Mughul and Turk alike must guard against him; that thought about him must be taken while he had not well-mastered the horde or grown very strong, for as they have said; –

> To-day, while thou canst, quench the fire,
> Once ablaze it will burn up the world;
> Let thy foe not fix string to his bow,
> While an arrow of thine can pierce him.[22]

He himself had scored a considerable success in swiftly recovering Samarkand in a surprise attack, but the following year Shaibani took it back again, easily outmanoeuvring and defeating his inexperienced teenaged opponent in open battle. Babur made another stand at his birthplace of Akshi in 1502. His outnumbered men – he claims they were only one or two hundred strong – were unable to staunch the relentless attack of Shaibani's ally, the Mongol Sultan Ahmad Tambal. Many were killed and his half-sister, Yadgar Sultan Begim, was captured. By evening Babur was leading his last companions through the east gate, fleeing for their lives through the orchards below as the enemy pursued them on horse. "That was no time to make a stand or delay," he wrote later. "We went off quickly, the enemy following and unhorsing our men."[23] By sunset, Babur found himself with only eight men, one of whom offered him his horse. Finally he was left with just one companion whose horse was flagging and who insisted on Babur's continuing without him. "It was a miserable position for me," wrote Babur. "He remained behind. I was alone."[24] Babur hid and was soon discovered, but somehow managed to convince his enemies that he would reward them handsomely if they helped him escape. In June 1503 he was with his Chaghatai Mongol uncles making an unsuccessful last stand against Shaibani at the battle of Archian. His uncles were captured, and Tashkent was lost. Babur again escaped.

"Mughul and Turk alike" had not heeded his advice, and had failed to unite. Of these years spent wandering forlornly between relatives, looking for opportunities to make a comeback, Babur wrote sadly: "I endured much poverty and humiliation. No country or hope of one! Most of my retainers dispersed, those left, unable to move about with me because of their destitution!"; "It came very hard on me. I could not help crying."[25] Worse was to follow in the next few years as his cousins north of the Oxus were, one by one, defeated, captured or killed. Babur and his extended family had lost everything: "For nearly 140 years," he wrote, these lands had belonged to "our dynasty".[26] Now he and his people were reduced to utter destitution.

Babur wrote this first section with all the elegiac love of an exile for a world he knows he has lost forever and will never see again. As a result, it is also the part of his book that is most challenging to read – charmingly nostalgic in small doses, it is also at times a bewilderingly, even numbingly, detailed record of the lost world of Timurid Central Asia, and the annihilated Timurid nobility that once peopled it. It was as if setting it down minutely on paper could somehow preserve a fragment of what had been lost.

*

The second part of the *Babur Nama* is, in literary terms, the most successful. Fugitive, homeless and utterly bewildered, "not knowing where to go or where to stay, our heads in a whirl", Babur was forced to turn to brigandage.[27] His ragged party headed south, eventually, sadly, taking the ferry over the Oxus, knowing what little chance there was of their ever returning to their homeland. Then they crossed the high passes into the Hindu Kush. They had no plan or no destination, other than to put as much space as possible between themselves and the

Uzbeks. "Those who, hoping in me, went with me into exile, were small and great, between 2 and 300; they were almost all on foot, had walking-staves in their hands, brogues on their feet, and long coats on their shoulders. So destitute were we that we had but two tents amongst us; my own used to be pitched for my mother."[28]

But as things fell apart behind him in Farghana, help arrived from an unexpected quarter, as "one man after another came in" to join Babur's party from the Mongol army of Khusrau Shah, ruler of Badakhshan, whose territory was also being threatened by the Uzbeks.[29] Throughout, Babur remained active and resilient, realizing that he could not afford to give way to despair: "As there was in me ambition for rule and desire of conquest, I did not sit at gaze when once or twice an affair had made no progress."[30] What began as a sprawling refugee column slowly grew into a new army, as more Mongol horsemen and heads of households joined his ranks. By October 1504 Babur's column had swelled to a staggering 20,000 armed men.

It was then that Babur finally had a lucky break. The rich and cosmopolitan city of Kabul, centre of the lucrative caravan trade between India and Central Asia, was controlled by an unpopular ruler, widely considered a usurper. The local Afghan chiefs were ready for a change. To their own surprise, Babur's men took the city without a battle, after Babur lined them up in disciplined ranks below the Bala Hisar: "Those in the fort becoming much perturbed," he wrote, "Muqim made an offer through the begs, to submit and surrender the town."[31]

Once inside the battlements, Babur quickly called in more of his fractious Timurid cousins to bolster his numbers. These were joined by other refugee tribes and clans who had also been displaced by the Uzbek advance. Babur also made a coalition of alliances with those Afghans who were prepared to accept his rule, while using brutal terror tactics – raids, impaling and enslavement – on those, such as the independent Hazara Turkmen of Bamian, who refused to do so.

Before long, Babur was laying out *charbagh* Persian gardens and remodelling his new base according to his tastes, introducing bananas and sugar cane into the area, and setting up a new Timurid court-in-exile within the walls of the Bala Hisar. Later in life, Babur looked back on this time in Kabul as his happiest moments since childhood. His years of wandering and anxiety were over, and while he distrusted and sometimes despised the Afghans he now ruled, he greatly loved the reassuringly familiar climate and landscape of their country. Many of his most inspired descriptive passages are devoted to the beauties of his new Afghan safe haven. It was, moreover, the first time in years that he was able to relax. He hunted, fished, hawked and held parties on the green hills around the city. He found time to write poetry and work on his memoirs. He even developed his own form of calligraphy, the *khatt-i-Baburi*. It was at this period too that he fathered his children, including, in 1508, his son, Humayun.

For Babur, it was also a time of experimentation in life's different pleasures. He investigated the differing effects of opium and hashish and recorded that while under the influence of drugs "wonderful fields of flowers were enjoyed. In some places sheets of yellow . . . in others sheets of red . . . We sat on a mound near the camp to enjoy the sight."[32] On another occasion in 1519, he took a party of nobles on a boating trip, not realizing that at one end of the boat his friends were eating hashish, while at the other they were drinking wine: "A *majun* party never goes well with a *araq* or wine-party," he wrote.

The drinkers began to make wild talk and chatter from all sides, mostly in allusion to *majun* and *majunis*. Baba Jan even, when drunk, said many wild things. The drinkers soon made Tardi Khan mad-drunk, by giving him one full bowl after another. Try as we did to keep things straight, nothing went well; there was much disgusting uproar; the party became intolerable and was broken up.[33]

There was now only one other Timurid court left, and this was the greatest of them all: that of Herat, in western Afghanistan, ruled by Husain Baiqara, a distant cousin. In May 1506 the elderly sultan died. Babur had already set out for Khurasan in response to his pleas for help against the Uzbeks; he decided to continue his journey and pay Husain's sons a visit. In Herat for the first time in his life, he found himself feeling like an unsophisticated, mud-booted provincial. His cousins paid little attention to the unfashionable new arrival and seemed unimpressed by his new conquests – so much so that he had, humiliatingly, to complain to them that "to be laggard in shewing me respect was unreasonable".[34] To the young warlord who only two years previously had been a vagrant, the clothes and fashions of his Herati cousins seemed dazzling, their manners elegant, their tastes refined. At one party, they served roast goose, which Babur did not know how to eat:

As I was no carver or disjointer of birds, I left it alone. "Do you not like it?" inquired the Mirza. Said I, "I am a poor carver." On this he at once disjointed the bird and set it again before me. In such matters, he had no match. At the end of the party he gave me an enamelled waist-dagger.[35]

On another occasion, his cousins were listening to the music of flutes and dulcimers, singing, dancing and drinking wine, something Babur had so far never tasted: "I knew nothing of its cheer and pleasure."[36] His cousins mocked him for his abstemiousness:

The party was altogether elegant ... The social cups were filled ... the guests drank down the mere wine as if it were water-of-life; when it mounted to their heads, the party waxed warm ... It crossed my mind now, when the Mirzas were so pressing and when too we were in a town so refined as Herat, "Where should I drink if not here? here where all the chattels and utensils of luxury and comfort are gathered and in use." So saying to myself, I resolved to drink wine; I determined to cross that stream ...[37]

Babur was thoroughly dazzled by the court at Herat and the brilliant Persianate cultural world Husain Baiqara had created during his long reign: "His was a wonderful Age," he wrote in his diary, looking back. "In it Khurasan, and Herat above all, was full of learned and matchless men ... It is the sad nuisance of Herat that a man can't stretch his leg without its touching a poet's backside."[38] Babur toured the sights, visiting the shrine of the Gazur-gah and relished the beauty of a pavilion decorated with murals depicting the heroic deeds of Abu-sa'id Mirza.[39]

Babur enjoyed himself so much that he lingered too long into autumn, and nearly died in the terrible blizzards that dogged his return to Kabul over the passes of the Hindu Kush. But it was as well he did not stay on: the following spring, at the very beginning of the campaigning season, Shaibani Khan and his Uzbeks stormed Herat, slaughtering Babur's cousins. He even "behaved badly . . . to the wives and children of its rulers". (These included Babur's aunt Payanda-sultan Begim, who fled to Iraq where she died "in great misery".)[40] According to the historian Khwandamir, "the delicate beauties of the inner sanctum of inviolability were taken captive and tormented by the merciless Uzbeks, and Venuses of the chambers of chastity were left by ravaging [Mongols] to wander destitute in the lanes and bazaars".[41] Once again the Timurids had vacillated and paid the price. They "could not act, collect troops, array those they had. Dreamers, they moved in a dream!"[42]

These events not only saddened Babur, they left him the last Timurid ruler standing. In 1508, in recognition of this, he decided formally to take on Timur's legacy and adopt his Persian title, Padshah. Kabul was now full of refugee Timurid nobility looking to him for leadership. In 1511, with Shaibani now dead, Babur made one last attempt at recapturing Samarkand, in alliance with the Persian Shah Isma'il Saffawi, the founder of the Safavid dynasty. This was a humbling episode during which Babur briefly abjured orthodox Sunni Islam and took on the clothing of the Shias, including the twelve-pointed hat, as the price of Persian support – but without any lasting result. He was forced to abandon the city the following year. Finally, giving up on Oxiana, he turned his gaze southwards, to Hindustan.

As early as 1505 Babur had descended the Khyber Pass and made his first exploratory raids on Kohat and Bannu, near Peshawar: "The sun being in Aquarius . . . we rode out of Kabul for Hindustan . . . Another world came to view, – other grasses, other trees, other animals, other birds, and other manners and customs of clan and horde." (The change continued to strike him when he repeated the journey in later years: "Once the water of Sind is crossed, everything is in the Hindustan way.")[43] In February 1519 he crossed the Indus and raided deep into the Punjab. He had by this time acquired a set of the latest muskets, cannon and mortars, as well as a skilled Ottoman Turkish artilleryman, Ustad 'Ali-quli, to work them. He made good use of them, en route, to storm the fortress of Bajaur (Khahr). "Ever since we came to Kabul," he wrote, "it had been in my mind to move on Hindustan."[44] Increasingly, however, he did not just intend to plunder Hindustan but to rule it. Timur had conquered the Delhi Sultanate and the successors of the defeated Tughluks had, for several generations, acknowledged the Timurids as overlords. Babur needed to create an empire rich enough to support his family and to save his dynasty from extinction. Timur's overlordship of Delhi, he felt, gave him the right to claim what he felt was rightfully his. In March he formally made his request to the new Delhi sultan, Ibrahim Lodhi. For the sake of peace, "I sent him a goshawk," he wrote, "and asked for the countries which from of old have depended on the Turk."[45] Ibrahim gave the envoy no reply. Babur returned to Kabul and began to make preparations for launching a further series of plundering raids into the Punjab the following year.

Then, in 1522, an irresistible opportunity presented itself. Daulat Khan was a disgruntled Indo-Afghan nobleman whom Ibrahim Lodhi had appointed governor of Lahore. Angered at the brutal and autocratic sultan's violent treatment of his nobility, many of whom he had arrested and killed, and afraid that he might be next, Daulat Khan sent his son to Kabul to seek an alliance. The timing was perfect.

At the dawn of the day . . . Babur prayed in the garden for a sign of victory in Hindustan, asking that it should be a gift to himself of mango or betel, fruits of that land. It so happened that Daulat Khan had sent him, as a present, half-ripened mangoes preserved in honey; when these were set before him, he accepted them as the sign, and from that time forth . . . made preparations for a move on Hindustan.[46]

The expedition resulted in the defeat of a Lodhi army sent from Delhi, though Daulat Khan proved an unreliable ally and Babur occupied Lahore himself before returning to Kabul. The final assault was still to come.

*

In 1525, India, like Central Asia, was undergoing a period of political fragmentation. This diffusion of authority, like that in Oxiana, was caused by the vacuum left by Timur's conquests. The collapse of the paramount power in South Asia, the Tughluk Delhi Sultanate, which at its peak extended from the Indus southward through most of India, had left the subcontinent fragmented and vulnerable to further invasion.

In the south, Vijayanagar, the great Hindu City of Victory, was then approaching the peak of its power, and controlled almost all the lands of peninsular India beyond the river Tungabhadra. It was much the richest kingdom in India. In 1443, eighty years before Babur began dreaming of an Indian empire, it had been visited by the ambassador of Timur's son, Shahrukh. Abdur Razzak Samarqandi enthused:

The city of Vijayanagar is such that the pupil of the eye has never seen a place like it, and the ear of intelligence has never been informed that there existed anything to equal it in the whole world . . . a place extremely large and thickly peopled, and a king possessing greatness and sovereignty to the highest degree, whose dominion extends . . . more than a thousand parasangs [leagues]. The country is for the most part well cultivated, very fertile, and contains about three hundred harbours. One sees there more than a thousand elephants, in their size resembling mountains, and in their forms resembling devils . . . This empire contains so great a population that it would be impossible to give an idea of it . . .[47]

Abdur Razzak was astonished at the extraordinary personal wealth visible everywhere – especially the profusion of jewellery worn by men and women of every social class, and the sophistication of the jewellers: stalls selling pearls, rubies, emeralds and diamonds were, he says, doing strong business, drawing in traders from across the globe.[48]

Vijayanagar was not the only kingdom of dazzling wealth in India. North of the City of Victory, the Deccan was fragmented into a patchwork of small but culturally dynamic Shia Muslim Sultanates, the most cosmopolitan of which was Bijapur. The *Nujum al Ulum*, or *Stars of Science*, is a typical Bijapuri production of the period. It is a grimoire, or book of spells, which brings together the astrology of the medieval Islamic and Hellenistic worlds and the mystical Indic astrology of Vijayanagar. The *Nujum* is full of invocations of spirits and demonesses as well as esoteric musings on such subjects as the celestial levels, the nature of angels, sorcery and the signs of the Zodiac. It blends astronomy, mysticism and politics in a text that gives a remarkably heterodox vision of medieval Indian courtly culture. Hindu goddesses are placed next to Muslim astronomical symbols. Tantric methods of summoning gods into mandala diagrams are crossed with Middle-Eastern techniques for summoning djinns. There follows a concluding section of love spells, one for each day of the week.

In the embattled north, once the centre of power and patronage, scholarship and high Indo-Islamic culture, there was nothing to match this. A much diminished and culturally unremarkable Delhi Sultanate, now controlled from Agra by the Lodhis, squatted amid the ruins of earlier more impressive dynasties. Their energies were spent battling with rival Afghan claimants to the throne, such as the Sharquis of Jaunpur, many of whose clans had taken advantage of the defeat of the Lodhis to descend into the Indian plains like "ants and locusts".[49] In the 1520s the paranoid and notably brutal Ibrahim Lodhi unwisely began alienating his nobility by murdering any he suspected of plotting against him: "[He] has put twenty-three of them . . . to death, without any cause . . . He suspended some from walls, and has caused others to be burned alive." One group he blew up by placing charges of gunpowder under the building in which they were feasting.[50] The reports that reached Babur were that few outside the Lodhi inner circle would be prepared to die for this unpopular tyrant.

Babur's fifth and final expedition into Hindustan began in the autumn of 1525, when he was forty-two years old. He rode south at the head of an army of 8,000 men, including his Turkish matchlock- and artillerymen. Crossing the Indus at Attock in mid-December, he advanced slowly forward, capturing Lahore without resistance. In February he was ready to advance on his foe. "I put my foot in the stirrup of resolution," he wrote, "set my hand on the rein of trust in God, and moved forward against Sultan Ibrahim, son of Sultan Sikandar . . . whose standing-army was called a *lak* (100,000), whose elephants and whose begs' elephants were about 1000."⁵¹ It was only in April that he came face to face with Ibrahim Lodhi, on the fields of Panipat, a little over fifty miles north of Delhi.

Ibrahim certainly outnumbered him – though probably by about four to one – but Babur was now an experienced general and used on Ibrahim the same flanking cavalry movement that had led to his own defeat by Shaibani Khan outside the walls of Samarkand a quarter of a century earlier. Moreover, he had Ustad 'Ali-quli's artillery, which he had mounted on 700 farm carts placed bound together into a barricade at the front of his forces. Cannon had been known in the Deccan for some time, but these were far more sophisticated than anything currently available in northern India. Babur provoked Ibrahim Lodhi to attack his position, and then unleashed his firepower. The artillery wiped out the cream of Ibrahim's cavalry and panicked his elephants. Babur then unleashed his own cavalry who rolled up the Afghan wings and rained arrows down on the Lodhi army from both flanks. By midday, 20,000 Indians were dead, including Sultan Ibrahim.

Babur indicated his desire to rule rather than plunder his new conquests when, unusually for the time, he gave orders to his disappointed troops that they could not sack the Delhi they had just conquered. Instead, he guaranteed the safety of its population and toured the city's celebrated Sufi shrines, especially those of its two patron saints, Qutb'ud-din Bakhtiyar Kaki in Mehrauli, and Nizamu'd-din Auliya to the north of the city, in the area named after his shrine. Head bowed, he sought the blessings of both. "Having done this," he wrote, "we dismounted at the camp, went on a boat, and there [afloat on the Yamuna] *'araq* was drunk."⁵²

Humayun, meanwhile, was sent straight ahead to Agra. As Babur noted, when his son took the surrender of the family of Bikramajit, Raja of Gwalior, who were in Agra at the time, "They made him a voluntary offering of a mass of jewels and valuables amongst which was the famous diamond which [Sultan] Alau'ud-din [Khalji] must have brought. Its reputation is that every appraiser has estimated its value at two and half days' food for the whole world. Apparently it weighs 8 *misqals*.

Humayun offered it to me when I arrived in Agra; I just gave it him back."[53]

Another contemporary source, a small treatise on precious stones dedicated to Babur and Humayun, also refers to Babur's diamond: "No private individual has ever seen such a diamond, or heard of it, nor is there any mention of it in any book."[54] These two mentions are often assumed to be early references to the Koh-i-Noor. They may well be – or not: the description is too vague to be certain, and there were clearly several very large diamonds circulating in India at this time, including a truly massive one set in the throne of Vijayanagar. But these were just two highlights of the vast fortune that now passed into Babur's possession. "The treasures of five kings fell into his hands," wrote his daughter Gulbadan. "He gave everything away."[55]

Arriving in the middle of the dry and dusty summer heats, Babur was initially unimpressed by his new kingdom, although he was thrilled by its riches: "The towns and country of Hindustan are greatly wanting in charm," he grumbled. "Its towns and lands are all of one sort; there are no walls to the orchards, and most places are on the dead level plain."[56] This was not his only complaint. "Its people have no good looks; of social intercourse, paying and receiving visits there is none; of genius and capacity none; of manners none; in handicraft and work there is no form or symmetry, method or quality; there are no good horses, no good dogs, no grapes, musk-melons or first-rate fruits, no ice or cold water, no good bread of cooked food in the *bazars*, no Hot-baths, no Colleges, no candles, torches or candlesticks."[57] Worst of all were jackfruits, which tasted like the "revolting intestines of sheep".[58] On the plus side, Hindustan "is a large country and has masses of gold and silver".[59]

Babur began to try and make Hindustan more like his much-missed Central Asia and built several *charbagh* gardens, one with a cascading fountain and a *hammam* – while encouraging his nobles to do likewise. The first was in Agra where he established his "Garden of Eight Paradises", with canals and raised walkways on the Persian plan, and where he planted reassuringly familiar Afghan grapes and melons.

But he had little leisure to really explore or enjoy his new conquests. In 1527, less than one year after his great victory,

Babur was forced to fight an even more formidable coalition of enemies. Mahmud Lodhi, brother of Ibrahim, had fled west into the deserts of Rajasthan following the defeat at Panipat, and there he formed an alliance of convenience with a former enemy, Rana Sanga, the leader of the Rajput Sisodiya clan.

This time, the Indian army advancing towards him was much larger than that he had faced at Panipat, and Babur's own forces had shrunk after many of his Timurid, Mongol and Afghan *begs* had departed for Afghanistan in response to the heat, taking their winnings with them. With his back now firmly against the wall, and terrified at the prospect of defeat so far from home, Babur made a vow to give up the alcohol to which he was now strongly addicted, and announced to his troops that this would be a battle of religion. His men, he said, were *ghazis* fighting for the faith against an army of infidels – even though half Mahmud Lodhi's troops were Indo-Afghan Muslims, of the same faith as themselves, and whose leader had never abjured Sunni Islam for Shi'ism as Babur had briefly done. At Kanwa, west of Agra, Babur's Timurids and their superb artillery again carried the day; but the fight this time was much closer, and Babur's losses much more substantial than they had been at Panipat.

Babur's framing of Kanwa as a battle of religion against idolatrous non-Muslims, along with the erection, the following year, of a small mosque allegedly built by one of his generals on the birthplace of the Hindu deity, Lord Ram, has led to the widespread impression in modern India, that Babur was some sort of fanatical jihadi who saw himself as the scourge of the infidels. This is clearly a gross misrepresentation of a man who throughout his memoirs had boasted of his love of alcohol and partying, and whose life revolved far more around pleasure than piety. Although he certainly regarded himself as an observant Muslim, and was more than happy to unite his wavering troops in the name of religion, in reality he was far from devout, and in his memoirs talks much more about time spent in gardens than in mosques: indeed in the entire vast text, he hardly mentions a single place of worship, less still the act of praying in one. Least of all does he lay claim to ordering the construction of the mosque for which he is most famous in modern India – the Babri Masjid in Ayodhya.[60]

Babur was clearly a fairly unorthodox sort of Muslim. In 1512, when he was required to wear Shia dress as the price for Persian assistance to regain his Samarkadi throne, he had no hesitation doing so, even though this horrified orthodox Sunnis who regarded the Safavids as dangerously heterodox and their leader, Shah Isma'il, as an outright heretic. Moreover, in the original Turki text of the *Babur Nama*, Babur does not even use the Arabic word 'Allah' for God, but instead talks of the Almighty as Tengri, the name of the pre-Islamic Mongol sky deity.[61]

Likewise, Babur was always deeply pragmatic in his politics. Just as he was willing to ally with the Shia Safavids in his attempt to regain Samarkand, and just as in Afghanistan he had accommodated a wide range of ethnic groups into his army – Baluch, Chaghatai Mongols, Afghan Hindus, even his Uzbek enemies – so after the battle of Kanwa, Babur went out of his way to reach a political settlement with Rana Sanga's defeated Rajput Sisodiya clan, as well as other non-Muslim landowning groups such as the Purbias of Malwa.[62] He always attempted to conciliate those whom he defeated, to share power with the vanquished and create open coalitions of self-interest with them. It was one of the most important lessons he passed on to his children.

Although Babur had spent much of his adult life dreaming of a rich empire, his triumphant conquest of India, the culmination of his life's work, seems to have brought him little happiness. After Kanwa, Babur spent most of the rest of his life on campaign, marching back and forth from Rajasthan to Bengal, from the Punjab to the banks of the Narmada. In 1528 he brought the women of his harem down from Kabul and he continued to try and order his new conquests according to his tastes, building more gardens, surveying the landcape and commissioning milestones to line the road between Kabul and Agra. He also developed a passion for mangoes. But India always remained strange and foreign to him.

He hated the heat and hated the rains even more: "While it rains . . . the air beomes very soft and damp," he moans. "A bow . . . after going through the Rains in Hindustan, may not be drawn even; it is ruined; not only the bow, everything is affected, armour, book, cloth, and utensils all; even a house does not last long."[63] Perhaps more than anything he hated the abstinence to which he was condemned by his vow to abjure alcohol before Kanwa.

The longer he stayed in India the more he looked back fondly on his hard-drinking Afghan glory days. To his old friend Khwaja Kalan in Kabul, Babur asked, "with whom canst thou now associate? with whom drink wine?" "How should a person forget the pleasant things of those countries, especially one who has repented and vowed to sin no more? How should he banish from his mind the permitted flavours of melons and grapes? [Recently] a melon was brought to me; to cut and eat it affected me strangely; I was all tears!"[64]

I am grief-stricken at abandoning wine.
Darkening my heart, I am always in a confused state.

Frozen in grief I am lost.
With wine I am cheerful and smiling.[65]

Everybody regrets drinking and then takes the oath
But I have taken the oath and now regret it.[66]

In exile this month of abstinence ages me.
Separated from friends exile has affected me.

I deeply desired the riches of this Indian land.
What is the profit since this land enslaves me?[67]

To one correspondent he even wrote, "Shall we return to Kabul, poverty-stricken?"[68] But Babur never had the chance to return to his beloved Afghan mountains. In 1530, Humayun became ill, and lay languishing in his bed with a violent fever, close to death. Humayun's sister Gulbadan wrote that when the seriousness of the illness became clear, his mother, Maham, went to fetch Humayun from his camp in Sambhal and "the two, mother and son, like Jesus and Mary, set out [by boat] for Agra".[69]

Babur had always had an uneasy relationship with Humayun. Throughout his diaries, Babur had shown a mixture of pride and extreme irritation with regard to his brave and intelligent but unfocused, unambitious and perennially unpunctual son; even an undertaking as important as the invasion of India was delayed by Humayun failing to present himself on time in Kabul. He eventually turned up, three weeks late, which meant that the climax of the invasion had to take place in the heat of summer.

Both in his rule and during his exile Humayun demonstrated the same dreamy and somewhat unreliable nature. One of Babur's last letters was written to his son complaining about his style, handwriting and syntax:

Thou hast written me a letter, as I ordered thee to do . . . Though by taking trouble it can be read, it is very puzzling, and who ever saw an enigma in prose? Thy remissness in letter-writing seems to be due to the thing which makes thee obscure, that it is say, elaboration. In future write without elaboration; use plain, clear words. So will thy trouble and thy reader's be less.[70]

Now, however, Babur was horrified to see how ill his son was. According to Gulbadan, Maham said, " 'Do not be troubled about my son. You are a king; what griefs have you? You have other sons. I sorrow because I have only this one.' His Majesty rejoined: 'Maham! although I have other sons, I love none as I love your Humayun.' "[71] Babur sought the advice of a Sufi saint and was told that in order to save Humayun he should give up the most valuable thing he possessed. Babur said, "I am the most valuable thing that Humayun possesses . . . I myself shall be his sacrifice. He is in extremity and I have lost the power to behold his powerlessness, but I can endure all his pain."[72] "O God! if a life may be exchanged for a life, I who am Babar, I give my life and my being for Humayun."[73] Babur then said his prayers and three times circled his son's bed. "When his prayer had been heard by God," Abu'l Fazl writes, ". . . he felt a strange effect upon himself and cried out 'We have borne it away. We have borne it away.' Immediately a strange heat of fever surged upon his Majesty and there was a sudden diminution of it in the person of his Highness . . ."[74]

From that moment Babur became ill while Humayun recovered. He died two months later, on 26 December 1530, at the age of only forty-seven. He left instructions that he wished to be buried on a high terrace in his favourite garden in Kabul where he loved to sit and admire the view.

Ironically, for a man who prided himself on his valour in the field, his greatest moment of heroism was not displayed on the battlefield, but at home.

*

Among the Uzbeks today, perhaps ironically, Babur is regarded as something of a hero.

"Bobor", as the Uzbeks pronounce him, has an avenue and a park named after him in the diplomatic quarter of Tashkent as well as a memorial garden and library commemorating him in Andijan, the capital of Farghana. His grave in Kabul has recently been beautifully restored by the Aga Khan after years of war damage, and his beloved hillside garden there has been replanted. It is now a favourite place for Kabuli couples to court and for Kabuli families to picnic. A rather lovely craft bazaar selling Afghan carpets and blue Herati glass now fills the cara-vanserai complex at its entrance. Babur would approve.

In South Asia, Babur's memory has a more complicated legacy. In Pakistan, the Mughals are remembered as heroes, but there are no monuments there associated with Babur, so there is little opportunity or excuse for public memorializing. In India, his memory is, to put it mildly, less revered. When BJP politi-cians today refer to Indian Muslims as "the children of Babur" they mean it as an insult.

Today, if you visit Babur's old garden-capital of Agra, you will see the roundabouts are full of statues of the Rani of Jhansi (who led the resistance to the British in 1857) and two to Shivaji (who led the resistance to Aurangzeb, the last of the six Great Mughals.) But not one image of any Mughal emperor has been erected anywhere in the city since Independence, despite the fact that Mughal monuments bring in all of its tourist income. Although a Bahadur Shah Zafar road still survives in Delhi, for many Indians today, rightly or wrongly, the Mughals are still perceived as it suited the British to portray them in the Imperial propaganda that they taught in Indian schools after 1857: as sensual, decadent, temple-destroying invaders – some-thing that was forcefully and depressingly demonstrated by the whole episode of the demolition of the Babri Masjid at Ayodhya in 1992.

The profoundly sophisticated, liberal and plural civilization championed by Babur's descendants has limited resonance for the urban middle class in modern India, many of whom are now deeply ambivalent about the idea of the Mughals, even if they will still happily eat a Mughal meal, flock to the cinema to watch a Bollywood Mughal epic, head to the Red Fort to hear their Prime Minister give the annual Independence day speech from the battlements.

But Babur's book remains in print in a huge variety of languages, and his masterpiece is more read today than ever. His right-wing Hindutva detractors can certainly pick selectively at his text to find material to bolster their case that Babur was a jihadi barbarian; but few who read the book in its entirety have ever been able resist its charm.

For although the *Babur Nama* records extraordinary, world-changing events, today, as in previous ages, it is still read for its humanity. As much as any pre-modern text it is a reminder that while some things change from age to age, much remains universal. To read Babur waxing on the beauty of a spring-time garden, or the perils of mixing drink and drugs, is still as resonant and pleasurable in the twenty-first century as it was in the early twentieth, when this translation was produced, or in the sixteenth, when it was first written.

It is remarkable above all for the picture it provides of an extraordinary man, one of the very few in history who combined dexterity with both sword and pen. It remains, without doubt, one of the greatest memoirs, in any language and of any age, and presents us with one of the most complex, complete and satisfying self-portraits in world literature.

William Dalrymple
Mira Singh Farm, New Delhi

NOTES

1 *Babur Nama* folio 99b, p. 153

2 Angus Maddison, *Contours of the World Economy, 1–2030 AD: Essays in Macro-Economic History* (Oxford, 2007), pp. 116–20, 309–11, 379; Shashi Tharoor, *Inglorious Empire: What the British Did to India* (New Delhi, 2016), pp. 2–3

3 *Babur Nama*, folios 75b, 76, pp. 120–21

4 Quoted in Stanley Lane Poole, *Babar* (Oxford, 1909), p. 12

5 *An Arab-Syrian Gentleman and Warrior in the Period of the Crusades: The Memoirs of Usamah Ibn-Munqidh*, tr. Philip K. Hitti (New York, 1929; new edition 2000); *A Mirror for Princes: The Qabus Nama by Kai Ka'us ibn Iskandar, Prince of Gurgan*, tr. Reuben Levy (London, 1951). The Gunbad-i-Qabus was immortalized by Robert Byron in *The Road to Oxiana* (London, 1937). Byron thought it the finest of all Islamic tomb towers.

6 Stephen F. Dale, *The Garden of the Eight Paradises: Babur and the Culture of Empire in Central Asia, Afghanistan and India, 1483–1530* (Leiden, 2004), pp. 23–4

7 Jean-Paul Roux, *Histoire des Grands Moghols: Babur* (Paris, 1986), p. 19

8 *Babur Nama* Section 1: Farghana, folios 2b–4, pp. 3–8

9 *Babur Nama* folio 135, p. 213

10 *Babur Nama* folio 136, p. 215; folio 141b, p. 223

11 *Babur Nama* folio 153, p. 240

12 *Babur Nama* folios 25b–26, pp. 45–6

13 *Babur Nama* folios 7–7b, pp. 14–15

14 *Babur Nama* folio 111b, p. 173

15 *Babur Nama* folio 98b, p. 152

16 *Babur Nama* folio 201, pp. 317–18

17 Stephen F. Dale, *The Garden of the Eight Paradises*, op. cit., p.13

18 Salman Rushdie, "*The Baburnama*". In *Step Across This Line: Collected Nonfiction 1992–2002* (London, 2002), pp. 188–94

19 C. P. W. Gammell, *The Pearl of Khorasan: A History of Herat* (London, 2016), pp. 86–7

20 E. M. Forster, "The Emperor Babur". In *Abinger Harvest* (London, 1936)

21 *Babur Nama* folio 121, p. 190

22 *Babur Nama* folio 101b, pp. 157–8

23 *Babur Nama* folio 113b, p. 176

24 *Babur Nama* folio 115, p. 178

25 *Babur Nama* folio 101, p. 157; folio 55b, p. 91

26 *Babur Nama* folio 85, p. 134

27 *Babur Nama* folio 60, p. 99

28 *Babur Nama* folio 120, pp. 187–8

29 *Babur Nama* folio 122b, p. 192

30 *Babur Nama* folio 55b, p. 92

31 *Babur Nama* folio 127b, p. 199

32 *Babur Nama* folio 232, p. 393

33 *Babur Nama* folios 227b–228, p. 386

NOTES

34 *Babur Nama* folio 187, p. 299

35 *Babur Nama* folio 191, p. 304

36 *Babur Nama* folio 189, p. 302

37 *Babur Nama* folio 187, p. 299; folios 189–189b, pp. 302–3

38 *Babur Nama* folio 177b, p. 283; folio 180, p. 287

39 What was left of this extraordinary monument was immortalized by the great English travel writer Robert Byron during his visit in the 1930s. In *The Road to Oxiana*, Byron brilliantly described his excitement at his discovery of the city and its great Timurid ruins: "Stepping out on to a roof adjoining the hotel, I see seven sky-blue pillars rise out of the bare fields against the delicate heather-coloured mountains. Down each the dawn casts a highlight of pale gold. In their midst shines a blue melon-dome with the top bitten off . . . On closer view, every tile, every flower, every petal of mosaic contributes its genius to the whole. Even in ruin such architecture tells of a golden age. Has history forgotten it? . . . Strolling up the road towards the minarets, I feel as one might feel who has lighted on the lost books of Livy or an unknown Botticelli . . . These Oriental Medici were an extraordinary race . . ." Robert Byron, *The Road to Oxiana* (London, 1937), pp. 89–90

40 *Babur Nama* folio 206, p. 328; folio 169, p. 268

41 Ghiyas al-Din Muhammad Khwandamir, "Habib al-Siyar", *Century of Princes*, 232–3. Quoted in Lisa Balabanlilar, *Imperial Identity in the Mughal Empire: Memory and Dynastic Politics in Early Modern South and Central Asia* (London, 2012), p. 21

42 *Babur Nama* folio 205b, p. 327

43 *Babur Nama* folio 145, p. 229; folio 272, p. 484

44 *Babur Nama* folio 222, p. 377

45 *Babur Nama* folio 226b, p. 385

46 *Babur Nama* para c (translator's note), p. 440, source Ahmad Yadgar, *Tarikh-i-Salatin-i-Afghana* in H. M. Eliot & J. Dowson, *The History of India, as Told by Its Own Historians*, vol. 5 (London, 1873), pp. 24–5

47 *Narrative of the Journey of Abd-er-Razzak* in R. H. Major, *India in the Fifteenth Century, Being a Collection of Narratives of Voyages to India* (London, 1857), pp. 22–6

48 Ibid., pp. 23–5

49 Quoted in Richard M. Eaton, *India in the Persianate Age, 1000–1765* (London, 2019), p. 110

50 Ahmad Yadgar, op. cit., p. 24, p. 14

51 *Babur Nama* folio 261, p. 463

52 *Babur Nama* folio 268, p. 476

53 *Babur Nama* folio 268b, p. 477

54 Quoted by Henry Beveridge in "Babar's Diamond: Was It the Koh-i-Nur?", *Asiatic Quarterly Review*, April 1899. I have written at length on the question of when the Koh-i-Noor entered Mughal hands in William Dalrymple and Anita Anand, *Koh-i-Noor* (London, 2016)

55 Gulbadan, *The History of Humayun* (*Humayun-Nama*), tr. Annette Beveridge (London, 1902), p. 94

56 *Babur Nama* folio 274, p. 487

57 *Babur Nama* folio 290b, p. 518

58 *Babur Nama* folio 284, p. 506. I go here with the translation of Annemarie Schimmel. Annette Beveridge for once seems to miss the point when she translates the taste of jackfruit as being like "haggis".

59 *Babur Nama* folio 291, p. 519

60 This structure, probably built by Babur's general Mir Baqi Beg Shighavul in 1528–9, was finally destroyed by Hindu mobs in 1992, who believed they were righting a major historical injustice, and revenging the destruction by Babur of a temple deliberately built to mark the birthplace of Lord Ram – the Ranjanmabhoomi. The truth about this matter is elusive. It is firstly unclear if the modern town of Ayodhya is on the same site as the Ayodhya celebrated as the capital of Lord Ram in the great Hindu epic, the *Ramayana*. It is also unclear if Mir Baqi's mosque was built on the orders of Babur – the section of the *Babur Nama* dealing with the period of its construction is missing. And while recent excavations have established that the mosque was indeed built on the site of an earlier structure that was most probably a Hindu temple, it is unclear if that temple was standing when the mosque was built or even if the temple was Vaishnavite: it was circular, which could mean that it is Shaivite. The dispute has become central to Indian politics and was one of the issues that led to the rise of the current Indian political dispensation led by Narendra Modi's BJP. Following a controversial judgment by the Indian Supreme Court in 2019, the site is to be handed over to the Hindu community to build a temple to mark the site of Lord Ram's birth. The Chief Justice who made the decision was subsequently elevated by the BJP government to the Raja Sabha, the Upper House of the Indian Parliament, in a move that was widely interpreted in the Indian media as a reward for his services. See Stephen F. Dale, *The Garden of the Eight Paradises*, op. cit., pp. 442–4. See also the nuanced excavation report by B. R. Mani of the Archaeological Survey of India who dug the site.

61 Stephen F. Dale, *The Garden of the Eight Paradises*, op. cit., pp. 170–72; Richard M. Eaton, *India in the Persianate Age*, op. cit., p. 200

62 Munis D. Faruqui, *The Princes of the Mughal Empire, 1504–1719* (Cambridge, 2012), p. 51

63 *Babur Nama* folios 291–291b, pp. 519–20

64 *Babur Nama* folio 361, p. 648; folio 359, pp. 645–6

65 Stephen F. Dale, *Babur: Timurid Prince and Mughal Emperor, 1483–1530* (Cambridge, 2018), p. 176

66 Francis Robinson, *The Mughal Emperors* (London, 2007), p. 119

67 Stephen F. Dale, *Babur*, op. cit., p. 176

68 Quoted in Lisa Balabanlilar, *Imperial Identity in the Mughal Empire*, op. cit., p. 35

69 Gulbadan, *The History of Humayun*, op. cit., p. 104

70 *Babur Nama* folio 349b, p. 62

71 Gulbadan, *The History of Humayun*, op. cit., p. 104

72 *The Akbarana of Abu'l Fazl*, tr. Henry Beveridge, vol. 1 (London, 1907), p. 276

73 Gulbadan, *The History of Humayun*, op. cit., p. 105

74 *The Akbarana of Abu'l Fazl*, tr. Henry Beveridge, vol. 1 (London, 1907), p. 276

NOTE ON THE
TRANSLATION

Annette Susannah Beveridge (1842–1929), the first translator of the *Babur Nama* into English from the original Turki, was a most unusual memsahib.

On arrival in India in 1872 at the age of thirty, far from drowning under a tidal wave of pink gins or disappearing into a vortex of bridge parties, Annette Ackroyd, as she then was, threw herself straight into the cause of Indian women's education. She herself was a graduate – in the days before women were officially awarded their degrees – of Bedford College, one of the earliest institutions of higher education for women in Britain, which later morphed into Royal Holloway College of the University of London. By the age of only twenty-two, she had helped found the Working Women's College in Queen Square, London. Eight years later, she arrived in India, determined that Indian women should have the same right to education she herself had enjoyed.

Within three years she had become involved in a major scandal. In 1875, she publicly took on the conservative Hindu patriarchy of Calcutta, insisting on the right of Indian women to higher education and fighting to found the Hindu Mahila Vidyalaya, one of the first girls' school in India, where she insisted that her pupils should be allowed to learn subjects previously considered "unladylike", such as mathematics, philosophy and science. The school closed after her departure but a successor institution survived and merged with Bethune College, now part of the University of Calcutta.

Annette's radical views attracted the attention of the Orientalist and district judge, Henry Beveridge of the Indian Civil Service, a passionate reformer and avowed agnostic, who had been in India since he arrived in Bengal in the immediate aftermath of the Mutiny of 1857. After they married, it was he who nourished her growing interest in Indian history and languages. In her fifties, and back in England, Annette learnt Persian and

Turki for what she described as "linguistic entertainment" and to distract herself from the grief of losing two of her four children. Of the surviving pair, the elder, William turned out every bit as radical and idealistic as his parents. In time, he went on to become the noted Left-leaning economist who gave his name to the celebrated report which in turn led to the formation of the National Health Service and the British Welfare State. Annette began working on the Mughal manuscripts, and her translation of the *Humayun Nama* – written by Babur's daughter Gulbadan – was published in 1902, the *Babur Nama* in its entirety not until 1921 when she was nearly eighty years old.

The *Babur Nama* had been written by Babur in Turki – Chaghatai Turkish – the language of Timurid Central Asia; but ever since Akbar's reign it had almost always been read in the 1589 Persian translation of Abdu'r-rahim Mirza (1556–1627). It took the Beveridges some years of research to locate a Turki manuscript of similar quality, the so-called Haidarabad Codex, which Annette described as "the *grande trouvaille* of my search for the Turki text". This had been copied directly from Babur's autograph copy, probably in the Red Fort scriptorium in Delhi, during the reign of Aurangzeb, around 1700. Even so, despite its vast size – running to 600 pages in modern printed Turki – it was still missing large portions of the text, in this resembling the Persian translation.

According to Babur's most recent biographer, Stephen Dale, "More than two-thirds of the text that covers the years between 1504 and 1526 is missing, most pages probably lost when Babur's son Humayun was driven from India by resurgent Afghan forces in 1540." Even in its incomplete state, however, the Haidarabad Codex represented a remarkable find. Read in its original form, the autobiography has, as Beveridge noticed, "the rare distinction of being contemporary with the events it describes, is boyish in his boyhood, grows with his growth, matures as he matured. Undulled by retrospect, it is a fresh and spontaneous recital of things just seen, heard or done."

WD

SELECT BIBLIOGRAPHY

BALABANLILAR, LISA, *Imperial Identity in the Mughal Empire: Memory and Dynastic Politics in Early Modern South and Central Asia* (London, 2012).

DALE, STEPHEN F., *The Garden of the Eight Paradises: Babur and the Culture of Empire in Central Asia, Afghanistan and India, 1483–1530* (Leiden, 2004).

EATON, RICHARD M., *India in the Persianate Age, 1000–1765* (London, 2019).

FARUQUI, MUNIS D., *The Princes of the Mughal Empire, 1504–1719* (Cambridge, 2012).

GASCOIGNE, BAMBER, *The Great Moghuls* (London 1971).

FORSTER, E. M., "The Emperor Babur". In *Abinger Harvest* (London, 1936).

KOCH, EBBA, *Mughal Architecture: An Outline of its History and Development, 1526–1858* (Munich, 1991).

LANE POOLE, STANLEY, *Babar* (Oxford, 1909).

LENTZ, THOMAS W., and LOWRY, GLENN D., *Timur and the Princely Vision: Persian Art and Culture in the Fifteenth Century* (Los Angeles, 1989).

ROUX, JEAN-PAUL, *Histoire des Grands Moguls: Babur* (Paris, 1986).

RUSHDIE, SALMAN, "The Baburnama". In *Step Across This Line: Collected Nonfiction 1992–2002* (London, 2002).

CHRONOLOGY

DATE	AUTHOR'S LIFE	LITERARY CONTEXT
1368		
c. 1370		
1390		Death of Persian poet Hafez in Shiraz.
1398–9		
1405		
1420		Contruction begins of Ulugh Beg's observatory at Samarkand.
1450		
1453		
1467		
1469		Thomas Malory: *Le Morte Darthur* (to 1470).
1478		
1483	Birth of Babur (14 Feb) at Akhsi in the Timurid principality of Farghana (in modern Uzbekistan).	Nawa'i: *Khamsa* (to 1485). Matteo Maria Boiardo: *Orlando Innamorato* (to 1495). Birth of Raphael.
1484		Palazzo Medici, Florence, completed.
1485		Ivan III brings Italian architects to Russia to design and rebuild the Kremlin. (*c*.) Botticelli paints *The Birth of Venus*.
1486		Jami: *Haft Awrang* (Seven Thrones) completed. Sultan Ali Mashhad illustrates Sa'adi's *Gulistan* in Herat. Pico della Mirandola: *De dignitate hominis* (On the Dignity of Man).

Ming dynasty in China (to 1644), displacing Mongol Yuan dynasty.
Timur at Samarkand: proclaims himself sovereign of the Chaghatai line of
khans and restorer of the Mongol empire.

Timur's invasion of India.
Timurid capital moves to Herat under Timur's son Shahrukh.

Johannes Gutenberg sets up first moveable type printing press in Europe.
Fall of Constantinople to Ottoman Sultan Mehmet II.
Outbreak of Onin War in Japan, ushering in Warring States period (to 1615).
Uzun Hasan (leader of Aq Qoyunlu or "White Sheep" Turkoman tribal
confederation) defeats Timurid sultan Abu-sa'id Mirza (Babur's paternal
grandfather) at the battle of Qarabagh and has him executed. Having
annexed Azerbaijan and much of Iran, Uzun Hasan sets up his capital
in Tabriz; Timurid resistance is led by Sultan Husain Baiqara who takes
control of Herat (to 1506). Weakened Timurid empire splits into two: Sultan
Husain Baiqara rules Khurasan, to the east; Babur's father and uncles divide
Transoxiana, to the west, between them.
Spanish Inquisition founded.
Conquest of Herzegovina by Sultan Bayezid II.
England: death of the young Edward V and his brother in the Tower of
London; accession of Richard III.

Yunas Khan (Babur's Chaghatai Mongol grandfather), khan of Mughulistan,
takes advantage of his Timurid sons-in-law's squabbling over Tashkent to
appropriate the city for himself and make it his capital.
Ottoman–Mamluk war (to 1491).
Fall of Vienna to Matthias Corvinus of Hungary (recovered by Habsburgs
in 1490).
Battle of Bosworth Field, death of Richard III; Henry Tudor becomes king
of England as Henry VII.
Birth of Bengali guru, Chaitanya Mahaprabhu, founder of Gaudiya
Vaishnavism tradition which proclaims Krishna as the supreme god.
Marriage of Henry Tudor with Elizabeth of York.

DATE	AUTHOR'S LIFE	LITERARY CONTEXT
1487		Daulat-shah Samarqandi finishes his *Tadhkirat al-shu'ara*, a biographical dictionary of poets and a history. Jami: *Baharestan*.
1488	Taken to Samarkand for betrothal to his Timurid cousin Ayisha-sultan Begim.	Bihzad illustrates Sa'adi's *Bustan*. Japanese poets Sogi, Shohaku and Socho meet at Minase and compose finest example of linked verse or *renga*.
1489		
1491		Final recension of Jami's *divan*.
1492		Death of Jami. Nawa'i's *divan* in four sections (to 1498).
1493		Nuremberg Chronicle: illustrated encyclopedia of world history.
1494	Around this time, made governor of Andijan. Accidental death of his father, 'Umar Shaikh Mirza; Babur becomes ruler of Farghana (June). Advised by his maternal grandmother Aisan-daulat Begim, he fights off incursions of his male relatives.	Isfizari's *Rawdat*, a historical geography of the Herat region, completed. Herat edition of the *Khamsa* of Nizami, probably illustrated by Bihzad (to 1495). Sebastian Brant: *Das Narranshift* (Ship of Fools).
1495		Aldine Press (Venice) prints first Greek Aristotle (to 1498).
1496	Babur joins in the succession struggle in Samarkand, and lays siege to the city with his cousin Sultan 'Ali Mirza.	

CHRONOLOGY

Death of Yunus Khan.

Death of Chenghua emperor in China; Zhu Youtang becomes the
Hongzhi emperor.

Extension of Inca empire: second capital established at Quito.

Portuguese explorer Bartolomeo Dias becomes the first European to round
the Cape of Good Hope.

Sikandar Lodhi becomes Delhi Sultan.

Catherine Cornaro, Queen of Cyprus, is forced to abdicate; the Republic of
Venice takes control.

Death of Kwaja Ahrari, prominent Naqshbandi Sufi. Babur's father was a
disciple and he was a lifelong influence on Babur.

(*c.*) Victory of 12-year-old Vallabhacharya at Vijayanagar court in debate
on the dual nature of god; three years later embarks on 20-year pilgrimage
around India, and founds the *Pushtimarg* ("path of grace") sub-tradition of
Vaishnavism.

Rodrigo Borgia becomes pope as Alexander VI. Death of Lorenzo de'
Medici ("the Magnificent").

Fall of Granada: reconquest of Spain from Moors completed by Ferdinand
of Aragon and Isabella of Castille. Alhambra decree expelling Jews from
Spain; many migrate to Ottoman empire.

Christopher Columbus reaches the Caribbean.

Death of Sultan Ahmad Mirza, Babur's uncle, father-in-law and ruler of
Samarkand since 1469; Sultan Mahmud Mirza succeeds his brother.

Alauddin Husain Shah gains control of Bengal and extends the sultanate
(to 1519).

Italian Wars (to 1559). Charles VIII leads French invasion of Italy. Medicis
expelled from Florence; dictatorship of Savonarola.

Death of Sultan Mahmud Mirza in Samarkand; his three sons dispute the
succession.

Death of Cem, exiled brother of the Ottoman Sultan Bayezid II, at the
papal curia in Rome.

Bartholomew Columbus establishes first secure Spanish colony at Santo
Domingo.

DATE	AUTHOR'S LIFE	LITERARY CONTEXT
1497	Siege resumes in spring. Babur enters Samarkand (Nov) and occupies it for 100 days.	Leonardo da Vinci paints *The Last Supper* (to 1498).
1498	Leaves Samarkand after Mongol chieftain Sultan Ahmad Tambal deserts him and seizes Andijan in the name of Babur's younger brother Jahangir; murder of Babur's former tutor Khwaja Maulana-i-qazi. Period of Babur's "vagabondage" begins.	Nawa'i's *Majalis al-nafa'is* (Assemblies of Distinguished Men): biographies of 459 poets (Herat). "Seven Earlier Masters" active in Beijing, led by poets Li Meng-yang and Ho Ching-ming (to 1507). (*c.*) John Skelton: *The Bowge of Court.*
1499	Andijan and Akhsi recovered. Campaign against Tambal. Wins his first ranged battle as commander at Khuban.	Nawa'i: *The Trial of the Two Languages* asserts claims of Turki over Persian.
1500	Forced to come to terms with Tambal by Mongol chieftain, 'Ali-dost Taghai; surrenders Akhsi and returns to Andijan. Babur's marriage to Ayisha-sultan Begim consummated. His infatuation with Baburi. Sultan 'Ali Mirza surrenders Samarkand to Uzbek warlord Shaibani Khan. Babur recaptures the city with a small force. Correspondence with Turki poet Nawa'i in Herat.	Erasmus's first collection of classical proverbs, *Collectanea adagiorum*. (*c.*) Birth of Ottoman architect Sinan.
1501	Birth and death of his first child (a daughter). Loses battle of Sar-i-pul to Shaibani Khan; besieged in Samarkand. Abandons the city, taking a few troops and his mother; his elder sister Khanzada Begim is left, possibly by negotiation, and is obliged to marry Shaibani Khan. Babur, again throneless, spends winter in village of Dikhkat. Visits his Chaghatai Mongol uncle Sultan Mahmud Khan in Tashkent.	Death of Nawa'i. Nilakantha Somayaji's astronomical treatise, *Tantrasangraha*. Michelangelo's *David* (to 1504).
1502	Arrival of Ahmad Khan, Mahmud's brother from Khitai (north China); the khans'	

CHRONOLOGY

John Cabot reaches mainland Newfoundland from Bristol.

Nanak founds Sikh religion.

Vasco da Gama reaches Calicut, India, by sea; beginning of Portuguese empire.

Execution of Savonarola in Florence; Piero Soderini leader of the republic (Machiavelli serving under him).

Louis XII king of France (to 1515).

Ottoman–Venetian war (to 1503).

Louis XII invades Italy; Ludovico Sforza driven from Milan.

Uzbek expansion into Transoxiana. Bukhara and Samarkand fall to Shaibani Khan without a fight; khanate of Bukhara established.

14-year-old Isma'il seizes Tabriz and proclaims himself shah, founding the Safavid dynasty of Iran (to 1722); declares Shi'ite sect of Islam the established religion and executes Sunni leaders.

Amerigo Vespucci's voyage to South America (to 1502).

Death of Ulugh Beg Kabuli, Babur's uncle and Timurid ruler of Kabul since 1461; his heir is a minor and control is eventually seized by his son-in-law Muqim Arghun (displaced by Babur in 1504).

xlv

DATE	AUTHOR'S LIFE	LITERARY CONTEXT
1502 *cont.*	expedition against Tambal; Tambal allies with Shaibani. Khans' failure to retake Andijan. Babur enters Akhsi but is defeated by Tambal, and forced to flee. His capture and escape.	
1503	The khans defeated by Shaibani (June) at battle of Archian. Babur's wanderings resume, accompanied by his mother and two younger brothers. His first wife returns to her family.	Earliest surviving poem of Michelangelo. Vespucci: *Mundus novus.* William Dunbar: *The Thissil and the Ros.* Heironymus Bosch paints *The Garden of Earthly Delights.*
1504	Babur's party leaves Farghana, moving southward across the Hisar Mountains (June). Reinforced by Mongol army of Khusrau Shah of Badakhshan, marches on Kabul and takes its surrender from Muqim Arghun without a battle. Supplies troops and imposes Timurid authority on the region by raiding surrounding countryside.	Li Tung-yang: *Ballads in the Style of Antiquity.* Babur's first garden project in Kabul, a *charbagh* outside the city gates. Cortile del Belvedere gardens at the Vatican Palace, Rome, designed for Julius II by Donato Bramante (to 1513).
1505	First raid into Hindustan. Death of his mother, Qutluq-nigar Khanim, from fever. Death of his grandmother Aisan-daulat Begim. Earthquake in Kabul area.	Leonardo's *Mona Lisa.*
1506	Learns of death of Husain Baiqara as Babur marches to his assistance against Shaibani; entertained by Sultan Husain's sons (Oct) at their camp; frustrated by their failure to engage Shaibani; returns with them to Herat where he remains for a month. Marries Mahim (or Maham) Begim, who becomes his chief consort (the first of four marriages in the course of the next two years).	Pope Julius II lays foundation stone of Bramante's St Peter's Basilica in Rome.
1507	Dangerous return journey through snow. Death of his	

CHRONOLOGY

Shah Isma'il defeats White Sheep Turkoman army.
Piero Soderini elected Gonfalionere for life in Florence.

Having defeated Babur and his Mongol uncles, Shaibani Khan takes possession of Tashkent. Shah Isma'il takes Shiraz from the White Sheep Turkomans.
Portuguese take over the kingdom of Cochin, creating first European settlement in India.
Giuliano della Rovere becomes pope as Julius II (to 1513) – patron of Michelangelo, Bramante and Raphael.
Marriage of James IV of Scotland to Margaret Tudor.

Death of Hongzhi emperor in China; 14-year-old Zhu Houzhao becomes the Zhengde emperor; a group of eunuchs, the "Eight Tigers", introduced as fiscal and military intendants, come to wield despotic powers.
Portuguese trading in Sri Lanka. Portuguese–Mamluk naval war (to 1517).

Death of Husain Baiqara, Timurid ruler of Herat; succeeded by two of his sons, ruling jointly. Uzbeks take Khiva (a dependency of Khurasan) after a ten-month siege, followed by the Balkh, an important city and fortress. Lisbon massacre of Jews.

Shaibani Khan takes Herat; the joint rulers are put to death. Uzbek conquest of Timurid lands almost complete.

DATE	AUTHOR'S LIFE	LITERARY CONTEXT
1507 cont.	brother Jahangir. Promptly quells rebellion in Kabul on arrival. Battle of Qandahar: Babur defeats Arghun brothers and takes the Afghan city, installing his brother Nasir Mirza there. Marries Ma'suma-sultan Begim (half-sister of his first wife), whom he had asked for in Herat. Temporarily flees Kabul when Shaibani lays siege to Qandahar; returns when siege abandoned.	
1508	Takes the imperial Iranian title of *Padshah*. Birth of son Humayun (to Mahim Begim). Death in childbirth of Ma'suma-sultan Begim. Mutiny amongst his Mongol troops crushed. Hiatus in biography until 1519.	Azeri Turkish poet Fuzuli writing in Baghdad under Safavid patronage. Babur lays out the *Bagh-i Wafa* (Garden of Fidelity), near the fortress of Adinapur, and extends another garden made by his uncle Ulugh Beg on the Istalif hillside 20 miles northwest of Kabul. Michelangelo paints ceiling of Sistine chapel (to 1512).
1509	Sultan Mahmud Khan and six sons murdered by Shaibani. Birth of Babur's second son Kamran (to Gulrukh Begim). Takes in his cousin Haidar Dughlat Mirza, his future biographer, then an 11-year-old refugee from the Uzbeks.	Death of Necati, lyric and panegyric writer, in Istanbul. Death of Shen Zhou, leading painter – also a poet – of the Ming Dynasty, and founder of the Wu school.
1510		Meeting of devotional poet Surdas with guru Vallabhacharya at Gaughat; Surdas went on to write the *Sur-sagar*, songs in honour of Krishna. *The Travels of Ludovico di Varthema of Bologna from 1502 to 1508* (including Mecca, Persia, India and Burma).
1511	Following his defeat of Shaibani, Shah Ismai'il sends back Babur's sister Khanzada. Babur swears	Erasmus: *Moriae Encomium* (The Praise of Folly).

CHRONOLOGY

HISTORICAL EVENTS

Two German humanists are the first to recognize the discovery of an entirely new continent; Matthias Ringmann publishes in Lorraine his *Introduction to Cosmography* which proposes the name "America" after Amerigo Vespucci; Martin Waldseemüller produces the accompanying map – the largest ever printed and the first to show and label the new continent.

Shah Isma'il conquers Baghdad, putting an end to the White Sheep dynasty; Sunni sites destroyed.
Julius II conquers Perugia and Bologna as part of campaign to restore Papal States. League of Cambrai against Venice.

Krishna Deva Raya becomes emperor of Vijayanagar; expansion reaches a peak (to 1529).
Naval battle of Diu: Portuguese defeat Mamluk fleet.
Henry VIII king of England (to 1547); marries Catherine of Aragon.
Birth of Jean Calvin.

Shah Isma'il defeats Shaibani at battle of Merv (Dec); Shaibani is killed trying to escape (Shah Isma'il converts his skull into a golden drinking goblet). Safavids now control the whole of Iran; Herat relegated to a provincial capital.
Fall of Liu Jin, chief eunuch, in China; sentenced to death by a thousand cuts.
Portuguese capture Goa from Bijapur sultanate and make it the capital of their Indian territories.

Portuguese admiral Afonso de Albuquerque captures port of Malacca.
Pope Julius II proclaims Holy League against France.

xlix

DATE	AUTHOR'S LIFE	LITERARY CONTEXT
1511 cont.	"loyalty and submission" to Shah Ismai'l to obtain military support. Defeats Uzbeks at Hisar. Takes Samarkand (for the third time) and Bukhara but obliged to embrace publicly Shia Islam in return for Safavid help. Babur's half-sister Yadgar Begim, captured at Andijan in 1502, also restored to him.	
1512	Defeated by Uzbek army near Bukhara (battle of Kul-i-malik); withdraws from Samarkand to Hisar. Joined by a Safavid army; unable to prevent them massacring the inhabitants of Karshi; when his Safavid allies are defeated at battle of Ghajdavan, Babur plays a minimal role.	
1513	Wanderings in Qunduz region of northern Afghanistan.	Machiavelli completes *Il Principe* (The Prince).
1514	Returns to Kabul. Occupied with Afghan affairs. Impressed by Ottoman victory over Safavids, Babur around this time requests and receives canon foundry and artillery experts from Selim I.	Albrecht Dürer's engravings *Saint Jerome in his Study* and *Melencolia I* (Nuremberg). Cardinal Wolsey begins to build Hampton Court Palace.
1515	Death of his brother Nasir Mirza, governor of Ghazni; suppresses rebellion in Ghazni.	Ho Ching-ming and Li Meng-yang correspond on the nature of poetry. *Ballads of an Era of Lasting Peace* (Chinese anthology of popular songs). King's College Chapel, Cambridge, completed.
1516	Babur's son 'Askari born, full brother of Kamran.	Ludovico Ariosto: *Orlando Furioso*. Thomas More: *Utopia*. Erasmus: *Institutio Christiani Principis* (The Education of a Christian Prince). First Greek New Testament printed at Basle. Skelton: *Magnyfycence*.

1

Selim I becomes Ottoman sultan.
French defeat Holy League at Ravenna but withdraw from Italy; return of
Medicis to Florence and Sforzas to Milan.
'Ubaidullah Khan's victory against the Safavids at Ghajdavan ensures
survival of Shaibanid power in Central Asia.

Mongol raids on China under Dayan Khan (to 1526).
Giovanni de' Medici becomes pope as Leo X.
Scots defeated at Flodden; death of James IV.
Ottomans under Selim I defeat Isma'il (battle of Chaldiran) and take
Tabriz; later withdraw but annexe Safavid lands in Eastern Anatolia and
Northern Mesopotamia; humiliated Shah Isma'il fights no more battles and
takes to drink.
By 1514 Copernicus's *Commentariolus*, privately circulated, has put forward his
theory of heliocentrism, later developed in *De revolutionibus orbium coelestium*
(1543). He draws on the work of a number of earlier Islamic astronomers.
Chaitanya Mahaprabhu in Vrindavana; he dispatches poet Rupa Goswami
and others to rescue the holy places there.
Leo X renews decree allowing sale of indulgences.
Francis I king of France (to 1547); defeats Swiss and Venetian armies at
battle of Marignano and reoccupies Milan.
Cardinal Wolsey becomes Lord Chancellor of England.
Spanish conquest of Cuba complete.

Muhammad-i-zaman, Timurid kinsman of Babur, takes power in Balkh,
ending a short period of Safavid control; he governs as Babur's feudatory.
Selim I attacks Mamluk Syria; wins decisive victory at battle of Aleppo.
Death of Ferdinand II of Aragon; accession of his grandson, of the house of
Habsburg, as Charles I of Spain. First use of "ghetto" in Venice as an area
where Jews are confined.

DATE	AUTHOR'S LIFE	LITERARY CONTEXT
1516 cont.		Raphael designs garden for the Villa Madama, Rome (completed 1534).
1517	Marries his nine-year-old daughter Ma'suma-sultan Begim to Muhammad-i-zaman Mirza, governor of Balkh in northern Afghanistan.	Death of Persian poet Afasi in Herat. Skelton: *The Tunnyng of Elynour Rummyng*.
1518		Erasmus: *Colloquia*. Tomb of Sikandar Lodhi, Delhi.
1519	Siege of Bajaur (use of firearms and artillery) and subsequent massacre. Raid into Hindustan (Feb–March); takes Bhirah; claims "territories that have been dependent on the Turk". Birth of his youngest son Hindal ("the taking of Hind"), to Dildar Begim. Spends the rest of the year partying, punctuated with usual raids against rebellious Afghan tribes, once passing through the Kyber Pass again (Sept). Three-day trip to view the autumn colours in the Istalif mountains. First collection of verse complete.	Death of Persian lyric poet Baba Fighani of Shiraz.
1520	Memoirs break off (Jan) until 1525. Another raid further into India. Returns to make an attempt on Qandahar (back in Arghun hands).	Luther's three Reformation Treatises. Death of Raphael.
1521	Siege of Qandahar continues. His 13-year-old son Humayun installed as governor of Qunduz in Badakhshan.	Hilali (Sufi poet): *Shah u gada* (The King and the Beggar). Machiavelli: *Dell'arte della guerra* (The Art of War). Chateau de Chenonceau built in French Loire Valley.
1522	Gains possession of Qandahar; instals Kamran there. Writes *Dar fiqa mubaiyan*, a poem on Islamic law, dedicated to Kamran.	Bizhad appointed head of the royal library in Safavid capital Tabriz. Shah Isma'il commissions

CHRONOLOGY

Ibrahim Lodhi becomes sultan of Delhi.
Ottoman Turks conquer Palestine and Egypt; Mamluks become their vassals. Baghdad, Medina and Mecca occupied: Abbasid Caliph recognizes Selim as rightful sultan of the faithful.
Isma'il expands northwest into present-day Georgia.
Start of the Reformation in Germany: Luther's 95 Theses.
Portuguese ships arrive at Canton in southern China. Dayan Khan's Mongol army threatens Beijing.
Rana Sanga of Mewar extending territory into north Rajasthan; defeats Ibrahim Lodhi.
Huldrych Zwingli people's priest at Zürich.
Heyreddin Barbarossa, Algerian ruler, becomes Ottoman vassal.
Prince of Ning rebellion in China.
On the death of his grandfather Maximilian I, Charles I of Spain succeeds to the Habsburg Monarchy and is elected Holy Roman Emperor as Charles V.
Spanish conquistador Hernando Cortés lands in Mexico; captures Aztec ruler Montezuma.
Ferdinand Magellan embarks on voyage round the world (to 1522).

Suleyman the Magnificent becomes Ottoman sultan.
Field of the Cloth of Gold: stage-managed meeting of Francis I and Henry VIII near Calais with accompanying tournament.

Uzbeks invade Khurasan (throughout the 1520s).
Turks besiege and capture Belgrade.
Battle of Tunmen: Ming forces expel a Portuguese fleet.
Diet of Worms condemns Luther's teachings.
Italian War (to 1526).
Magellan killed in the Philippines.
Rhodes capitulates to Turks.
Death of Zhengde emperor: Jiajing emperor succeeds (to 1567).
Conquest of Mexico completed.

DATE	AUTHOR'S LIFE	LITERARY CONTEXT
1522 cont.	Dilawar Khan arrives in Kabul; his father, Daulat Khan Lodhi, disaffected governor of Lahore, invites Babur to join attack on Sultan Ibrahim Lodhi.	a new edition of Firdausi's *Shamana* (Book of Kings) "the apogee of Persian miniature painting", completed under Shah Tahmasp *c.* 1537. Prominent miniaturists who worked on it include Sultan Muhammad and Mir Musavvir. Luther publishes first vernacular translation of the New Testament. Historical novel *The Romance of the Three Kingdoms* (attrib. Luo Ghuanzhong) first printed in China.
1523	Babur heads for India in autumn (fourth expedition). Birth of his daughter Gulbadan Begim (to Dildar Begim).	
1524	Occupies Lahore; breaks with Daulat. Returns north to relieve Uzbek siege of Balkh.	Khwandamir completes *Habib al-Siyar*, a continuation of his grandfather Mirkhond's history of the Timurid dynasty. Rupa Goswami: *Vidagdhamadhava* (drama about the pastimes of Krishna). Philippe de Commynes: *Mémoires* (to 1528). Luther's German hymnbook printed in Wittenberg.
1525	Back in Kabul. Fifth expedition to Hindustan (Nov), joined by Humayun. By the end of the year they are at Lahore.	Haidar Mirza Kurkan Dughlat completes first part of his *Tarikh-i-rashidi*.
1526	Humayun defeats a subsidiary Lodhi army (Feb); Babur's army defeats Sultan Ibrahim Lodhi at battle of Panipat (20 April); Agra and Delhi taken and treasuries confiscated. Extends control by seizing towns and fortresses. Saddened by the return of his friend Khwaja Kalan to Kabul, where he becomes governor.	Thomas Wyatt's early poems ("Whoso list hunt"?). Hans Holbein in England (to 1528). William Tyndale's translation of the complete New Testament in English printed in Cologne. Clément Marot: *L'Enfer*. Babur begins constructing

Zwingli's 67 Theses.

Death of Shah Isma'il; succeeded by his son, Shah Tahmasp, a minor.

Uzbek army lays siege to Herat (unsuccessfully, to 1526).
Battle of Pavia: Francis I captured by Emperor Charles V.
Muslims in Spain obliged to convert or leave the kingdom.

While Babur and Humayun are in India, Balkh is lost permanently to the Uzbeks.
Battle of Mohács – Suleyman I defeats and kills Louis II of Hungary.
Bohemia and Slovakia come under Habsburg control.
First copies of Tyndale burnt in England. Henry VIII's pursuit of Anne Boleyn becomes public.
Spanish explorer Francisco Pizarro lands in South America and discovers Inca empire.

DATE	AUTHOR'S LIFE	LITERARY CONTEXT
1526 *cont.*	Poisoned by Sultan Ibrahim's mother (Dec).	formal garden in Agra (*Hasht Bihisht Baghi*: Garden of the Eight Paradises). Hindu Beg (one of Babur's nobles) builds mosque at Sambahl.
1527	Moves against Rana Sanga, Rajput of Mewar. Loses preliminary skirmishes and begins to lose hold of territories secured in 1526. Resolves to renounce alcohol. Victorious at battle of Kanwa (17 March). Adds *Ghazi* (holy warrior) to his titles. Subjugates Miwat. Humayun and others return to Kabul. Babur suffers first bout of illness which frequently afflicts him in Hindustan.	Kabuli Bagh mosque in Panipat built. Construction of Babur's *Bagh-i Fath* (Victory Garden) at Sikri. François I transforms Fontainebleau into a palace.
1528	Campaign against Rana Sanga's allies: successfully storms fortress of Chandiri. Called away to fight with Afghan supporters of the Lodhi sultanate; fails to defeat them decisively. Visits Gwalior palaces and temples. Constructs reservoir at Dulpur. Orders road between Agra and Kabul to be measured; sets up relay stations. Formally celebrates foundation of new Timurid empire (Dec). Second collection of verse complete.	Baldassare Castiglioni: *Il libro del cortegiano* (The Book of the Courtier). Francisco Delicado: *Portrait of Lozana: The Lusty Andalusian Woman.* Tyndale: *The Obedience of a Christian Man.* Possible construction of Baburi mosque in Ayodhya.
1529	Sultan Mahmud Lodhi takes Bihar; Babur puts him to flight. Appoints his son-in-law Muhammad-i-zaman Mirza governor of Bihar. Defeats Mahmud Lodhi in battle of Ghaghra (5 May). Babur's sister Khanzada, wife Mahim Begim, daughter Gulbadan and other female relatives join him in Agra. Humayun's arrival and establishment at Sambahl. Memoirs break off (Sept).	Poet Hilali executed in Herat by Uzbeks. Rupa Goswami: *Lalitamadhava.*

HISTORICAL EVENTS

Buda falls to Turks.
Imperial troops sack Rome while Pope Clement VII takes refuge in the
Castel Sant'Angelo (valiantly defended, according to artist Benvenuto
Cellini's *Autobiography*, by Cellini). Medicis expelled from Florence and a
republic declared.
Henry VIII applies to the pope for an annulment of his marriage.

Death of Rana Sanga, Rajput of Mewar, in Chittor (thought to be poisoned
by his own chiefs).
Battle of Jam: Shah Tahmasp defeats Uzbeks.

Uzbeks under Shaibani's nephew 'Ubaidu'llah take Herat.
Siege of Vienna by the Turks. Habsburg–Persian alliance.
Muslim Somalis fight Holy War against Christian Ethiopia, destroying
churches and shrines (to 1543).
Fall of Cardinal Wolsey; Thomas More Lord Chancellor in England.
Peace of Cambrai between France and the Emperor.

DATE	AUTHOR'S LIFE	LITERARY CONTEXT
1530	Illness (April) and recovery of Humayun; illness of Babur (Sept); names Humayun his successor. Death of Babur (21 Dec) at Agra.	Tyndale's English translation of the Pentateuch published in Antwerp. Otto Brunfels publishes *Living Images of Plants*, first serious natural history with illustrations.

CHRONOLOGY

Safavids take back Herat.

Confession of Augsburg presented to imperial Diet by Philip Melanchthon, defining Lutheran faith.

Florence is restored to the Medici after a siege by imperial forces. Pope Clement VIII crowns Charles V as Holy Roman Emperor.

Death of Wolsey. Persecution of reformers in England. Thomas Hitton burnt at the stake – regarded as first English Protestant martyr of the Reformation.

EDITORIAL NOTES

Annette Beveridge explained at some length the history of the various MSS of the *Babur Nama* in her original Preface, omitted here. The following is a brief summary which will clarify the frequent references made to these MSS in her footnotes.

Elphinstone Codex: Purchased by British diplomat Mountstuart Elphinstone at Peshawar in 1810, donated in 1826 to the Advocates' Library in Edinburgh where AB's researches led to its rediscovery in 1906. She dated it to between 1556 and 1567 and identified it as a copy made from an earlier codex (now lost). The earlier codex had been ordered by Humayun, Babur's son and successor, and annotated by him, the annotations causing some confusion to the copyist. Comparing the two Turki MSS, AB found this Codex rather less complete than the Haidarabad Codex, but verbally almost identical.

The Haidarabad Codex: See Note on the Translation. Found by Henry Beveridge in 1900. AB arranged for its publication in facsimile by the Royal Asiatic Society in 1905.

The Kehr MS: The transcription by Georg Jacob Kehr in St Petersburg in 1737 of a Turki text (subsequently lost) from Bukhara. Long considered to be a reproduction of the authentic *Babur Nama*, it was re-edited and published as such by Nikolai Ilminsky in Kazan in 1857 and used as a basis for the first French translation – *Mémoires de Baber* – by Abel Pavet de Courteille in 1871. AB discovered that the Bukhara text had been produced as recently as 1709 for a forthcoming tsarist mission to the city. It was a confusing compilation from various sources, and the first part of the *Babur Nama*, when pieced together, turned out to be a retranslation into Turki from the Persian. However, she found the Hindustan section largely compatible with the other two Codices and useful for filling in their lacunae.

EDITORIAL NOTES

The Leyden and Erskine translation: The first translation of the *Babur Nama* into English (or indeed, the first into any European language). William Erskine and John Leyden had been friends as students in Edinburgh; both were employed by the East India Company, one in Bombay, the other in Calcutta. Leyden died in 1811 and AB credits Erskine with the lion's share of the translation, which he had already made from the Persian before being sent by Elphinstone in 1813 Leyden's very partial unfinished translation from the Bukhara text, and later the Elphinstone Codex as well. Erskine made what use of these he could, but was unfamiliar himself with Turki. The pioneering work was published in 1826 as *Memoirs of Zehir-ed-din Muhammed Baber*, Erskine modestly according his friend top billing, and was the only English translation before AB's. It is viewable online at Archive.org.

The Everyman edition of AB's translation follows the format of the Luzac edition of 1921: folio numbers of the Haidarabad MS appear in the margins (b refers to verso pages); the Hijri dates (from the original MSS) appear in the running heads ('AH' is the westernized form, 'Anno Hegirae'), followed by the corresponding dates for that year in the Julian calendar (the Islamic Hijri calendar is a 12-month lunar calendar of 354 or 355 days). The useful subheadings are AB's, the Turki MSS being continuous text. A decision has been taken to omit diacritical marks as unnecessary for specialists and offputting for the general reader. All AB's footnotes and appendices are included and two of her detailed indices.

AB explains her system for transliteration on page 2. Her scrupulous following of the Turki lettering sometimes results in English spellings now unfamiliar – Auzbegs for Uzbeks, for example, or Ludi for Lodhi. For place names she follows Babur's usage – Heri/Hiri rather than Herat, for example – but also gives more familiar versions where necessary for identification.

Secondary Bibliography

Full bibliographical citations are not always present in the footnotes due to the omission of some of AB's endmatter. The more frequently recurring abbreviated references are expanded below:

Waqi 'at-i-baburi (Babur's Acts), often abbreviated W.-i-B., First or Second, refers to the two sixteenth-century Persian texts of the *Babur Nama*. The first, privately commissioned by two Mughals in Hindustan (1583) is now fragmentary (and in the British Museum); for the second (1589), see Note on the Translation.

The *Tarikh-i-Rashidi of Mirza Muhammad Haidar, Dughlat*, ed. N. Elias, tr. E. Denison Ross, London, 1895 (often abbreviated T. R.) This is viewable at Archive.org, as are all the following.

The *Ain i Akbari*, tr. Heinrich Blochmann (Books I and II, 1873) and Colonel H. S. Jarrett (Book III, 1891; Books IV and V, 1894). The *Ain i Akbari* forms part of the *Akbarnama* and was written by the sixteenth-century historian Abu'l-fazl at the court of the Emperor Akbar. Henry Beveridge translated the rest of the *Akbarnama* in 3 volumes (1902–39). All the above were first published in Calcutta.

HENRY ELLIOT and JOHN DOWSON, *The History of India As Told by Its Own Historians* (8 vols, London, 1867–77).

ROBERT BARKLEY SHAW, *Sketch of the Turki Language as Spoken in Eastern Turkistan* . . . (Lahore, 1875).

GODFREY THOMAS VIGNE, *A Personal Narrative of a Visit to Ghuzni, Kabul, and Afghanistan and of a Residence at the Court of Dost Mohamed* . . . (London, 1840) and *Travels in Kashmir, Ladak, Iskardo* . . . (2 vols, London, 1842).

CHARLES MASSON, *Narrative of Various Journeys in Balochistan, Afghanistan, the Panjab, & Kalat* . . . (3 vols, London, 1842) and *Narrative of a Journey to Kalat* . . . (London, 1843).

MAJOR-GENERAL ALEXANDER CUNNINGHAM, *The Ancient Geography of India* (London, 1871).

MAJOR H. G. RAVERTY, *Notes on Afghanistan and Part of Baluchistan* . . . (London, 1888).

EUGENE SCHUYLER: *Turkistan: Notes of a Journey in Russian Turkistan, Khokand, Bukhara, and Kuldja* (2 vols, London, 1876).

COL. L. F. KOSTENKO'S 3-volume Russian-language *The Turkestan Region: Being a Military Statistical Review of the Turkestan Military District of Russia or Russian Turkestan Gazetteer* (St Petersburg, 1880), translated by British military intelligence in Simla 1882–4, and viewable at Pahar.in/central-asia.

THE BĀBUR-NĀMA
IN ENGLISH
(Memoirs of Bābur)

Translated from the original Turki Text of
Ẓahiru'd-dīn Muḥammad Bābur Pādshāh *Ghāzī*
by Annette Susannah Beveridge

This work
is dedicate to
Babur's
fame.

TABLE OF CONTENTS

SECTION I.—FARGHANA

[END OF TRANSLATOR'S NOTE.]

SECTION II.—KABUL

[END OF TRANSLATOR'S NOTE.]

[END OF TRANSLATOR'S NOTE.]

SECTION III.—HINDUSTAN

[END OF TRANSLATOR'S NOTE.]

APPENDICES

THE MEMOIRS OF BABUR

SECTION I. FARGHANA

IN the name of God, the Merciful, the Compassionate.

In[1] the month of Ramzan of the year 899 (June 1494) and in the twelfth year of my age,[2] I became ruler[3] in the country of Farghana.

Haidara-bad MS. fol. 1b.

(a. Description of Farghana.)

Farghana is situated in the fifth climate[4] and at the limit of settled habitation. On the east it has Kashghar; on the west, Samarkand; on the south, the mountains of the Badakhshan border; on the north, though in former times there must have been towns such as Almaligh, Almatu and

---

1 The manuscripts relied on for revising the first section of the Memoirs, (i.e. 899 to 908 AH.—1494 to 1502 AD.) are the Elphinstone and the Haidarabad Codices. To variants from them occurring in Dr. Kehr's own transcript no authority can be allowed because throughout this section, his text appears to be a compilation and in parts a retranslation from one or other of the two Persian translations (Waqi'at-i-baburi) of the Babur-nama. Moreover Dr. Ilminsky's imprint of Kehr's text has the further defect in authority that it was helped out from the Memoirs, itself not a direct issue from the Turki original.

Information about the manuscripts of the Babur-nama can be found in the JRAS (Journal of the Royal Asiatic Society) for 1900, 1902, 1905, 1906, 1907 and 1908.

The foliation marked in the margin of this book is that of the Haidarabad Codex and of its facsimile, published in 1905 by the Gibb Memorial Trust.

2 Babur, born on Friday, Feb. 14th 1483 (Muharram 6, 888 AH.), succeeded his father, 'Umar Shaikh who died on June 8th 1494 (Ramzan 4, 899 AH.).

3 pad-shah, protecting lord, supreme. It would be an anachronism to translate padshah by King or Emperor, previous to 913 AH. (1507 AD.) because until that date it was not part of the style of any Timurid, even ruling members of the house being styled Mirza. Up to 1507 therefore Babur's correct style is Babur Mirza. (Cf. f. 215 and note.)

4 See Ayin-i-akbari, Jarrett, p. 44.

Yangi which in books they write Taraz,[1] at the present time all is desolate, no settled population whatever remaining, because of the Mughuls and the Auzbegs.[2]

Farghana is a small country,[3] abounding in grain and fruits. It is girt round by mountains except on the west, *i.e.* towards Khujand and Samarkand, and in winter[4] an enemy can enter only on that side.

Fol. 2.

The Saihun River (*darya*) commonly known as the Water of Khujand, comes into the country from the north-east, flows westward through it and after passing along the north of Khujand and the south of Fanakat,[5] now known as Shahrukh-iya, turns directly north and goes to Turkistan. It does not

1 The Hai. MS. and a good many of the W.-i-B. MSS. here write Autrar. [Autrar like Taraz was at some time of its existence known as Yangi (New).] Taraz seems to have stood near the modern Auliya-ata; Almaligh,—a Metropolitan see of the Nestorian Church in the 14th century,—to have been the old capital of Kuldja, and Almatu (var. Almati) to have been where Vernoe (Vierny) now is. Almaligh and Almatu owed their names to the apple (*alma*). *Cf.* Bretschneider's Mediæval Geography p. 140 and T.R. (Elias and Ross) *s.nn.*

2 *Mughul u Auzbeg jihatdin.* I take this, the first offered opportunity of mentioning (1) that in transliterating Turki words I follow Turki lettering because I am not competent to choose amongst systems which *e.g.* here, repro-duce Auzbeg as Uzbeg, Özbeg and Euzbeg; and (2) that style being part of an autobiography, I am compelled, in pressing back the Memoirs on Babur's Turki mould, to retract from the wording of the western scholars, Erskine and de Courteille. Of this compulsion Babur's bald phrase *Mughul u Auzbeg jihatdin* provides an illustration. Each earlier translator has expressed his meaning with more finish than he himself; 'Abdu'r-rahim, by *az jihat 'ubur-i (Mughul u) Auzbeg*, improves on Babur, since the three towns lay in the tide-way of nomad passage (*'ubur*) east and west; Erskine writes "in consequence of the incursions" etc. and de C. "*grace aux ravages commis*" etc.

3 Schuyler (ii, 54) gives the extreme length of the valley as about 160 miles and its width, at its widest, as 65 miles.

4 Following a manifestly clerical error in the Second W.-i-B. the *Akbar-nama* and the Mems. are without the seasonal limitation, "in winter." Babur here excludes from winter routes one he knew well, the Kindirlik Pass; on the other hand Kostenko says that this is open all the year round. Does this contradiction indicate climatic change? (*Cf.* f. 54*b* and note; A.N. Bib. Ind. ed. i, 85 (H. Beveridge i, 221) and, for an account of the passes round Farghana, Kostenko's *Turkistan Region*, Tables of Contents.)

5 Var. Banakat, Banakas, Fiakat, Fanakand. Of this place Dr. Rieu writes (Pers. cat. i, 79) that it was also called Shash and, in modern times, Tashkint. Babur does not identify Fanakat with the Tashkint of his day but he identifies it with Shahrukhiya (*cf.* Index *s.nn.*) and distinguishes between Tashkint-Shash and Fanakat-Shahrukhiya. It may be therefore that Dr. Rieu's Tashkint-Fanakat was Old Tashkint,—(Does Fana-kint mean Old Village?) some 14 miles nearer to the Saihun than the Tashkint of Babur's day or our own.

join any sea[1] but sinks into the sands, a considerable distance below [the town of] Turkistan.

Farghana has seven separate townships,[2] five on the south and two on the north of the Saihun.

Of those on the south, one is Andijan. It has a central position and is the capital of the Farghana country. It produces much grain, fruits in abundance, excellent grapes and melons. In the melon season, it is not customary to sell them out at the beds.[3] Better than the Andijan *nashpati*,[4] there is none. After Samarkand and Kesh, the fort[5] of Andijan is the largest in Mawara'u'n-nahr (Transoxiana). It has three gates. Its citadel (*ark*) is on its south side. Into it water goes by nine channels; out of it, it is strange that none comes at even a single place.[6] Round the outer edge of the ditch[7] runs a gravelled highway; the width of this highway divides the fort from the suburbs surrounding it.

Andijan has good hunting and fowling; its pheasants grow   Fol. 2*b*.

1 *hech darya qatilmas*. A gloss of *digar* (other) in the Second W.-i-B. has led Mr. Erskine to understand "meeting with no other river in its course." I understand Babur to contrast the destination of the Saihun which he [erroneously] says sinks into the sands, with the outfall of *e.g.* the Amu into the Sea of Aral.

Cf. First W.-i-B. I.O. MS. 215 f. 2; Second W.-i-B. I.O. MS. 217 f. 1*b* and Ouseley's Ibn Haukal p. 232-244; also Schuyler and Kostenko *l.c.*

2 Babur's geographical unit in Central Asia is the township or, with more verbal accuracy, the village *i.e.* the fortified, inhabited and cultivated oasis. Of frontiers he says nothing.

3 *i.e.* they are given away or taken. Babur's interest in fruits was not a matter of taste or amusement but of food. Melons, for instance, fresh or stored, form during some months the staple food of Turkistanis. Cf. T.R. p. 303 and (in Kashmir) 425; Timkowski's *Travels of the Russian Mission* i, 419 and Th. Radloff's *Réceuils d'Itinéraires* p. 343.

N.B. At this point two folios of the Elphinstone Codex are missing.

4 Either a kind of melon or the pear. For local abundance of pears *see* *Ayin-i-akbari*, Blochmann p. 6; Kostenko and Von Schwarz.

5 *qurghan*, *i.e.* the walled town within which was the citadel (*ark*).

6 *Tuquz tarnau su kirar, bu 'ajab tur kim bir yirdin ham chiqmas.* Second W.-i-B. I.O. 217 f. 2, *nuh ju'i ab dar qila' dar mi ayid u in 'ajab ast kah hama az yak ja ham na mi bar ayid.* (*Cf.* Mems. p. 2 and *Méms.* i, 2.) I understand Babur to mean that all the water entering was consumed in the town. The supply of Andijan, in the present day, is taken both from the Aq Bura (*i.e.* the Aush Water) and, by canal, from the Qara Darya.

7 *khandaqning tash yani.* Second W.-i-B. I.O. 217 f. 2 *dar kinar sang bast khandaq.* Here as in several other places, this Persian translation has rendered Turki *tash*, outside, as if it were Turki *tash*, stone. Babur's adjective *stone* is *sangin* (f. 45*b* l. 8). His point here is the unusual circumstance of a high-road running round the outer edge of the ditch. Moreover Andijan is built on and

so surprisingly fat that rumour has it four people could not finish one they were eating with its stew.[1]

Andijanis are all Turks, not a man in town or bazar but knows Turki. The speech of the people is correct for the pen; hence the writings of Mir 'Ali-shir *Nawa'i*,[2] though he was bred and grew up in Hiri (Harat), are one with their dialect. Good looks are common amongst them. The famous musician, Khwaja Yusuf, was an Andijani.[3] The climate is malarious; in autumn people generally get fever.[4]

Again, there is Aush (Ush), to the south-east, inclining to east, of Andijan and distant from it four *yighach* by road.[5] It has a fine climate, an abundance of running waters[6] and a most beautiful spring season. Many traditions have their rise

---

of loess. Here, obeying his Persian source, Mr. Erskine writes "stone-faced ditch"; M. de C. obeying his Turki one, "*bord extérieur.*"

1 *qirghawal ash-kinasi bila. Ash-kina*, a diminutive of *ash*, food, is the rice and vegetables commonly served with the bird. Kostenko i, 287 gives a recipe for what seems *ash-kina*.

2 b. 1440; d. 1500 AD.

3 Yusuf was in the service of Bai-sunghar Mirza *Shahrukhi* (d. 837 AH.-1434 AD.). *Cf.* Daulat Shah's *Memoirs of the Poets* (Browne) pp. 340 and 350-1. (H.B.)

4 *guzlar ail bizkak kub bulur.* Second W.-i-B. (I.O. 217 f. 2) here and on f. 4 has read Turki *guz*, eye, for Turki *guz* or *goz*, autumn. It has here a gloss not in the Haidarabad or Kehr's MSS. (*Cf.* Mems. p. 4 note.) This gloss may be one of Humayun's numerous notes and may have been preserved in the Elphinstone Codex, but the fact cannot now be known because of the loss of the two folios already noted. (*See* Von Schwarz and Kostenko concerning the autumn fever of Transoxiana.)

5 The Pers. trss. render *yighach* by *farsang*; Ujfalvy also takes the *yighach* and the *farsang* as having a common equivalent of about 6 *kilomètres*. Babur's statements in *yighach* however, when tested by ascertained distances, do not work out into the *farsang* of four miles or the *kilomètre* of 8 kil. to 5 miles. The *yighach* appears to be a variable estimate of distance, sometimes indicating the time occupied on a given journey, at others the distance to which a man's voice will carry. (*Cf.* Ujfalvy *Expédition scientifique* ii, 179; Von Schwarz p. 124 and de C.'s Dict. *s.n. yighach.* In the present instance, if Babur's 4 y. equalled 4 f. the distance from Aush to Andijan should be about 16 m.; but it is 33 m. 1¾ fur. *i.e.* 50 versts. (Kostenko ii, 33.) I find Babur's *yighach* to vary from about 4 m. to nearly 8 m.

6 *aqar su*, the irrigation channels on which in Turkistan all cultivation depends. Major-General Gérard writes, (Report of the Pamir Boundary Commission, p. 6,) "Osh is a charming little town, resembling Islamabad in Kashmir, —everywhere the same mass of running water, in small canals, bordered with willow, poplar and mulberry." He saw the Aq Bura, the *White wolf*, mother of all these running waters, as a "bright, stony, trout-stream;" Dr. Stein saw it as a "broad, tossing river." (Buried Cities of Khotan, p. 45.) *Cf.* Réclus vi, cap. Farghana; Kostenko i, 104; Von Schwarz *s.nn.*

in its excellencies.[1] To the south-east of the walled town (*qurghan*) lies a symmetrical mountain, known as the Bara Koh;[2] on the top of this, Sl. Mahmud Khan built a retreat (*hajra*) and lower down, on its shoulder, I, in 902 AH. (1496 AD.) built another, having a porch. Though his lies the higher, mine is the better placed, the whole of the town and the suburbs being at its foot.

The Andijan torrent[3] goes to Andijan after having traversed the suburbs of Aush. Orchards (*baghat*)[4] lie along both its banks; all the Aush gardens (*baghlar*) overlook it; their violets are very fine; they have running waters and in spring are most beautiful with the blossoming of many tulips and roses.   Fol. 3.

On the skirt of the Bara-koh is a mosque called the Jauza

---

1 *Aushning fazilatida khaili ahadis warid dur.* Second W.-i-B. (I.O. 217 f. 2) *Fazilat-i-Aush ahadis warid ast.* Mems. (p. 3) "The excellencies of Usb are celebrated even in the sacred traditions." *Méms.* (i, 2) "*On cite beaucoup de traditions qui célèbrent l'excellence de ce climat.*" Aush may be mentioned in the traditions on account of places of pilgrimage near it; Babur's meaning may be merely that its excellencies are traditional. *Cf.* Ujfalvy ii, 172.

2 Most travellers into Farghana comment on Babur's account of it. One much discussed point is the position of the Bara Koh. The personal observations of Ujfalvy and Schuyler led them to accept its identification with the rocky ridge known as the Takht-i-sulaiman. I venture to supplement this by the suggestion that Babur, by Bara Koh, did not mean the whole of the rocky ridge, the name of which, Takht-i-sulaiman, an ancient name, must have been known to him, but one only of its four marked summits. Writing of the ridge Madame Ujfalvy says, "*Il y a quatre sommets dont le plus élevé est le troisième comptant par le nord.*" Which summit in her sketch (p. 327) is the third and highest is not certain, but one is so shewn that it may be the third, may be the highest and, as being a peak, can be described as symmetrical *i.e.* Babur's *mauzun.* For this peak an appropriate name would be Bara Koh.

If the name Bara Koh could be restricted to a single peak of the Takht-i-sulaiman ridge, a good deal of earlier confusion would be cleared away, concerning which have written, amongst others, Ritter (v, 432 and 732); Réclus (vi. 54); Schuyler (ii, 43) and those to whom these three refer. For an excellent account, graphic with pen and pencil, of Farghana and of Aush *see* Madame Ujfalvy's *De Paris à Samarcande* cap. v.

3 *rud.* This is a precise word since the Aq Bura (the White Wolf), in a relatively short distance, falls from the Kurdun Pass, 13,400 ft. to Aush, 3040 ft. and thence to Andijan, 1380 ft. *Cf.* Kostenko i, 104; Huntingdon in Pumpelly's *Explorations in Turkistan* p. 179 and the French military map of 1904.

4 Whether Babur's words, *baghat, baghlar and baghcha* had separate significations, such as orchard, vineyard and ordinary garden *i.e.* garden-plots of small size, I am not able to say but what appears fairly clear is that when he writes *baghat u baghlar* he means *all sorts of gardens*, just as when he writes *begat u beglar*, he means *begs of all ranks*.

Masjid (Twin Mosque).¹ Between this mosque and the town, a great main canal flows from the direction of the hill. Below the outer court of the mosque lies a shady and delightful clover-plain (*maidan*) where every passing traveller takes a rest. It is the joke of the ragamuffins of Aush to let out water from the canal² on anyone happening to fall asleep in the meadow. A very beautiful stone, waved red and white³ was found in the Bara Koh in 'Umar Shaikh Mirza's latter days; of it are made knife handles, and clasps for belts and many other things. For climate and for pleasantness, no township in all Farghana equals Aush.

Again there is Marghinan; seven *yighach*⁴ by road to the west of Andijan,—a fine township full of good things. Its apricots (*auruk*) and pomegranates are most excellent. One sort of pomegranate, they call the Great Seed (*Dana-i-kalan*); its sweetness has a little of the pleasant flavour of the small apricot (*zard-alu*) and it may be thought better than the Semnan pome-

granate. Another kind of apricot (*auruk*) they dry after stoning it and putting back the kernel;⁵ they then call it *subhani*; it is very palatable. The hunting and fowling of Marghinan are good; *aq kiyik*⁶ are had close by. Its people are Sarts,⁷ boxers,

---

1 Madame Ujfalvy has sketched a possible successor. Schuyler found two mosques at the foot of Takht-i-sulaiman, perhaps Babur's Jauza Masjid.

2 *aul shah-ju'idin su quyarlar.*

3 Ribbon Jasper, presumably.

4 Kostenko (ii, 30), 71¾ versts *i.e.* 47 m. 4½ fur. by the Postal Road.

5 Instead of their own kernels, the Second W.-i-B. stuffs the apricots, in a fashion well known in India by *khubani*, with almonds (*maghz-i badam*). The Turki wording however allows the return to the apricots of their own kernels and Mr. Rickmers tells me that apricots so stuffed were often seen by him in the Zar-afshan Valley. My husband has shewn me that Nizami in his Haft Paikar appears to refer to the other fashion, that of inserting almonds:—

> "I gave thee fruits from the garden of my heart,
> Plump and sweet as honey in milk;
> Their substance gave the lusciousness of figs.
> In their hearts were the kernels of almonds."

6 What this name represents is one of a considerable number of points in the *Babur-nama* I am unable to decide. *Kiyik* is a comprehensive name (*cf.* Shaw's Vocabulary); *aq kiyik* might mean *white sheep* or *white deer*. It is rendered in the Second W.-i-B., here, by *ahu-i-wariq* and on f. 4, by *ahu-i-safed*. Both these names Mr. Erskine has translated by "white deer," but he mentions that the first is said to mean *argali i.e. ovis poli*, and refers to *Voyages de Pallas* iv, 325.

7 Concerning this much discussed word, Babur's testimony is of service. It seems to me that he uses it merely of those settled in towns (villages) and

noisy and turbulent. They are notorious in Mawara'u'n-nahr for their bullying. Most of the noted bullies (*jangralar*) of Samarkand and Bukhara are Marghinanis. The author of the Hidayat[1] was from Rashdan, one of the villages of Marghinan.

Again there is Asfara, in the hill-country and nine *yighach*[2] by road south-west of Marghinan. It has running waters, beautiful little gardens (*baghcha*) and many fruit-trees but almonds for the most part in its orchards. Its people are all Persian-speaking[3] Sarts. In the hills some two miles (*bir shar'i*) to the south of the town, is a piece of rock, known as the Mirror Stone.[4] It is some 10 arm-lengths (*qari*) long, as high as a man in parts, up to his waist in others. Everything is reflected by it as by a mirror. The Asfara district (*wilayat*) is in four sub-divisions (*baluk*) in the hill-country, one Asfara, one Warukh, one Sukh and one Hushyar. When Muhammad *Shaibani* Khan defeated Sl. Mahmud Khan and Alacha Khan and took Tashkint and Shahrukhiya,[5] I went into the Sukh and Hushyar Fol. 4. hill-country and from there, after about a year spent in great misery, I set out (*'azimat*) for Kabul.[6]

Again there is Khujand,[7] twenty-five *yighach* by road to the

---

without any reference to tribe or nationality. I am not sure that he uses it always as a noun; he writes of a *Sart kishi*, a Sart person. His Asfara Sarts may have been Turki-speaking settled Turks and his Marghinani ones Persian-speaking Tajiks. *Cf.* Shaw's Vocabulary; *s.n.* Sart; Schuyler i, 104 and note; Nalivkine's *Histoire du Khanat de Khokand* p. 45 n. Von Schwarz *s.n.*; Kostenko i, 287; Petzhold's *Turkistan* p. 32.

1 Shaikh Burhanu'd-din 'Ali *Qilich:* b. *circa* 530 AH. (1135 AD.) d. 593 AH. (1197 AD.). *See* Hamilton's *Hidayat.*

2 The direct distance, measured on the map, appears to be about 65 m. but the road makes *détour* round mountain spurs. Mr. Erskine appended here, to the "*farsang*" of his Persian source, a note concerning the reduction of Tatar and Indian measures to English ones. It is rendered the less applicable by the variability of the *yighach*, the equivalent for a *farsang* presumed by the Persian translator.

3 Hai. MS. *Farsi-gu'i*. The Elph. MS. and all those examined of the W.-i-B. omit the word *Farsi*; some writing *kohi* (mountaineer) for *gu'i*. I judge that Babur at first omitted the word *Farsi*, since it is entered in the Hai. MS. above the word *gu'i*. It would have been useful to Ritter (vii, 733) and to Ujfalvy (ii, 176). *Cf.* Kostenko i, 287 on the variety of languages spoken by Sarts.

4 Of the Mirror Stone neither Fedtschenko nor Ujfalvy could get news.

5 Babur distinguishes here between Tashkint and Shahrukhiya. *Cf.* f. 2 and note to Fanakat.

6 He left the hill-country above Sukh in Muharram 910 AH. (mid-June 1504 AD.).

7 For a good account of Khujand *see* Kostenko i, 346.

west of Andijan and twenty-five *yighach* east of Samarkand.[1] Khujand is one of the ancient towns; of it were Shaikh Maslahat and Khwaja Kamal.[2] Fruit grows well there; its pomegranates are renowned for their excellence; people talk of a Khujand pomegranate as they do of a Samarkand apple; just now however, Marghinan pomegranates are much met with.[3] The walled town (*qurghan*) of Khujand stands on high ground; the Saihun River flows past it on the north at the distance, may be, of an arrow's flight.[4] To the north of both the town and the river lies a mountain range called Munughul;[5] people say there are turquoise and other mines in it and there are many snakes. The hunting and fowling-grounds of Khujand are first-rate; *aq kiyik*,[6] *bughu-maral*,[7] pheasant and hare are all had in great plenty. The climate is very malarious; in autumn there is much fever;[8] people rumour it about that the very sparrows get fever and say that the cause of the malaria is the mountain range on the north (*i.e.* Munughul).

Kand-i-badam (Village of the Almond) is a dependency of Khujand; though it is not a township (*qasba*) it is rather a good

1 Khujand to Andijan 187 m. 2 fur. (Kostenko ii, 29-31) and, helped out by the time-table of the Transcaspian Railway, from Khujand to Samarkand appears to be some 154 m. 5¼ fur.

2 Both men are still honoured in Khujand (Kostenko i, 348). For Khwaja Kamal's Life and *Diwan*, *see* Rieu ii, 632 and Ouseley's Persian Poets p. 192. *Cf.* f. 83*b* and note.

3 *kub artuq dur*, perhaps brought to Hindustan where Babur wrote the statement.

4 Turkish arrow-flight, London, 1791, 482 yards.

5 I have found the following forms of this name,—Hai. MS., M:nugh:l; Pers. trans. and Mems., Myoghil; Ilminsky, M:tugh:l; *Méms.* Mtoughuil; Réclus, Schuyler and Kostenko, Mogul Tau; Nalivkine, "d'apres Fedtschenko," Mont Mogol; Fr. Map of 1904, M. Muzbek. It is the western end of the Kurama Range (Kindir Tau), which comes out to the bed of the Sir, is 26⅔ miles long and rises to 4000 ft. (Kostenko, i, 101). Von Schwarz describes it as being quite bare; various writers ascribe climatic evil to it.

6 Pers. trans. *ahu-i-safed*. *Cf.* f. 3*b* note.

7 These words translate into *Cervus maral*, the Asiatic Wapiti, and to this Babur may apply them. Dictionaries explain *maral* as meaning *hind* or *doe* but numerous books of travel and Natural History show that it has wider application as a generic name, *i.e.* deer. The two words *bughu* and *maral* appear to me to be used as *e.g.* drake and duck are used. *Maral* and duck can both imply the female sex, but also both are generic, perhaps primarily so. *Cf.* for further mention of *bughu-maral* f. 219 and f. 276. For uses of the word *maral*, *see* the writings *e.g.* of Atkinson, Kostenko (iii, 69), Lyddeker, Littledale, Selous, Ronaldshay, Church (Chinese Turkistan), Biddulph (Forsyth's Mission).

8 *Cf.* f. 2 and note.

approach to one (*qasbacha*). Its almonds are excellent, hence its name; they all go to Hormuz or to Hindustan. It is five or Fol. 4*b*. six *yighach*[1] east of Khujand.

Between Kand-i-badam and Khujand lies the waste known as Ha Darwesh. In this there is always (*hamesha*) wind; from it wind goes always (*hamesha*) to Marghinan on its east; from it wind comes continually (*da'im*) to Khujand on its west.[2] It has violent, whirling winds. People say that some darweshes, encountering a whirlwind in this desert,[3] lost one another and kept crying, "Hay Darwesh! Hay Darwesh!" till all had perished, and that the waste has been called Ha Darwesh ever since.

Of the townships on the north of the Saihun River one is Akhsi. In books they write it Akhsikit[4] and for this reason the

1 Schuyler (ii, 3), 18 m.

2 Hai. MS. *Hamesha bu deshtta yil bar dur. Marghinangha kim sharqi dur, hamesha mundin yil barur; Khujandgha kim gharibi dur, da'im mundin yil kilur.*

This is a puzzling passage. It seems to say that wind always goes east and west from the steppe as from a generating centre. E. and de C. have given it alternative directions, east or west, but there is little point in saying this of wind in a valley hemmed in on the north and the south. Babur limits his statement to the steppe lying in the contracted mouth of the Farghana valley (*pace* Schuyler ii, 51) where special climatic conditions exist such as (*a*) difference in temperature on the two sides of the Khujand narrows and currents resulting from this difference,—(*b*) the heating of the narrows by sun-heat reflected from the Mogol-tau, —and (*c*) the inrush of westerly wind over Mirza Rabat. Local knowledge only can guide a translator safely but Babur's directness of speech compels belief in the significance of his words and this particularly when what he says is unexpected. He calls the Ha Darwesh a whirling wind and this it still is. Thinkable at least it is that a strong westerly current (the prevailing wind of Farghana) entering over Mirza Rabat and becoming, as it does become, the whirlwind of Ha Darwesh on the hemmed-in steppe,—becoming so perhaps by conflict with the hotter indraught through the Gates of Khujand—might force that indraught back into the Khujand Narrows (in the way *e.g.* that one Nile in flood forces back the other), and at Khujand create an easterly current. All the manuscripts agree in writing to (*gha*) Marghinan and to (*gha*) Khujand. It may be observed that, looking at the map, it appears somewhat strange that Babur should take, for his wind objective, a place so distant from his (defined) Ha Darwesh and seemingly so screened by its near hills as is Marghinan. But that westerly winds are prevalent in Marghinan is seen *e.g.* in Middendorff's *Einblikke in den Farghana Thal* (p. 112). *Cf.* Réclus vi, 547; Schuyler ii, 51; Cahun's *Histoire du Khanat de Khokand* p. 28 and Sven Hedin's *Durch Asien's Wüsten s.n. buran.*

3 *badiya*; a word perhaps selected as punning on *bad*, wind.

4 *i.e.* Akhsi Village. This word is sometimes spelled Akhsikis but as the old name of the place was Akhsi-kint, it may be conjectured at least that the *sa'i masallasa* of Akhsikis represents the three points due for the *nun* and *ta* of *kint*. Of those writing Akhsikit may be mentioned the Hai, and Kehr's MSS. (the Elph. MS.

poet Asiru-d-din is known as *Akhsikiti*. After Andijan no township in Farghana is larger than Akhsi. It is nine *yighach*[1] by road to
the west of Andijan. 'Umar Shaikh Mirza made it his capital.[2]
The Saihun River flows below its walled town (*qurghan*). This
stands above a great ravine (*buland jar*) and it has deep ravines
('*umiq jarlar*) in place of a moat. When 'Umar Shaikh Mirza made
it his capital, he once or twice cut other ravines from the outer
ones. In all Farghana no fort is so strong as Akhsi. Its suburbs

Fol. 5.   extend some two miles further than the walled town. People
seem to have made of Akhsi the saying (*misal*), "Where is the
village? Where are the trees?" (*Dih kuja? Dirakhtan kuja?*) Its
melons are excellent; they call one kind Mir Timuri; whether in
the world there is another to equal it is not known. The melons
of Bukhara are famous; when I took Samarkand, I had some
brought from there and some from Akhsi; they were cut up at an
entertainment and nothing from Bukhara compared with those
from Akhsi. The fowling and hunting of Akhsi are very good
indeed; *aq kiyik* abound in the waste on the Akhsi side of the
Saihun; in the jungle on the Andijan side *bughu-maral*,[3] pheasant
and hare are had, all in very good condition.

Again there is Kasan, rather a small township to the north
of Akhsi. From Kasan the Akhsi water comes in the same way
as the Andijan water comes from Aush. Kasan has excellent air
and beautiful little gardens (*baghcha*). As these gardens all lie
along the bed of the torrent (*sa'i*) people call them the "fine
front of the coat."[4] Between Kasanis and Aushis there is rivalry
about the beauty and climate of their townships.

---

here has a lacuna) the *Zafar-nama* (Bib. Ind. i, 44) and Ibn Haukal (Ouseley
p. 270); and of those writing the word with the *sa'i musallasa* (*i.e.* as Akhsikis),
Yaqut's Dict. i, 162, Reinaud's Abu'l-feda I. ii, 225-6, Ilminsky (p. 5) departing
from his source, and I.O. Cat. (Ethé) No. 1029. It may be observed that Ibn
Haukal (Ouseley p. 280) writes Banakas for Banakat. For Asiru'd-din *Akhsikiti*,
see Rieu ii, 563; Daulat Shah (Browne) p. 121 and Ethé I.O. Cat. No. 1029.

1 Measured on the French military map of 1904, this may be 80 kil. *i.e.* 50 miles.
2 Concerning several difficult passages in the rest of Babur's account of
Akhsi, *see* Appendix A.
3 The W.-i-B. here translates *bughu-maral* by *gazawn* and the same word is
entered, under-line, in the Hai. MS. *Cf.* f. 3*b* and note and f. 4 and note.
4 *postin pesh b:r:h*. This obscure Persian phrase has been taken in the
following ways:—

In the mountains round Farghana are excellent summer-pastures (*yilaq*). There, and nowhere else, the *tabalghu*[1] grows, a tree (*yighach*) with red bark; they make staves of it; they make bird-cages of it; they scrape it into arrows;[2] it is an excellent wood (*yighach*) and is carried as a rarity[3] to distant places. Some books write that the mandrake[4] is found in these mountains but for this long time past nothing has been heard of it. A plant called *Ayiq auti*[5] and having the qualities of the mandrake (*mihr-giyah*), is heard of in Yiti-kint;[6] it seems to be

Fol. 5*b*.

(*a*) W.-i-B. I.O. 215 and 217 (*i.e.* both versions) reproduce the phrase.

(*b*) W.-i-B. MS., quoted by Erskine, p. 6 note, *postin-i mish burra*.

(*c*) Leyden's MS. Trs., a sheepskin mantle of five lambskins.

(*d*) Mems., Erskine, p. 6, a mantle of five lambskins.

(*e*) The Persian annotator of the Elph. MS., underlining *pesh*, writes, *panj*, five.

(*f*) Klaproth (Archives, p. 109), *pustini pisch breh, d.h. gieb den vorderen Pelz*.

(*g*) Kehr, p. 12 (Ilminsky p. 6) *postin bish b:r:h*.

(*h*) De. C., i, 9, *fourrure d'agneau de la première qualité*.

The "lambskins" of L. and E. carry on a notion of comfort started by their having read *sayah*, shelter, for Turki *sa'i*, torrent-bed; de C. also lays stress on fur and warmth, but would not the flowery border of a mountain stream prompt rather a phrase bespeaking ornament and beauty than one expressing warmth and textile softness? If the phrase might be read as *postin pesh pera*, what adorns the front of a coat, or as *postin pesh bar rah*, the fine front of the coat, the phrase would recall the gay embroidered front of some leathern postins.

1 Var. *tabarkhun*. The explanation best suiting its uses, enumerated here, is Redhouse's second, the Red Willow. My husband thinks it may be the Hyrcanian Willow.

2 Steingass describes this as "an arrow without wing or point" (barb?) and tapering at both ends; it may be the practising arrow, *t'alim auqi*, often headless.

3 *tabarrakluq*. *Cf.* f. 48*b* foot, for the same use of the word.

4 *yabruju's-sannam*. The books referred to by Babur may well be the *Rauzatu's-safa* and the *Habibu's-siyar*, as both mention the plant.

5 The Turki word *ayiq* is explained by Redhouse as *awake* and *alert*; and by Meninski and de Meynard as *sobered* and as *a return to right senses*. It may be used here as a equivalent of *mihr* in *mihr-giyah*, the plant of love.

6 Mr. Ney Elias has discussed the position of this group of seven villages. (*Cf.* T. R. p. 180 n.) Arrowsmith's map places it (as Iti-kint) approximately where Mr. Th. Radloff describes seeing it *i.e.* on the Farghana slope of the Kurama range. (*Cf. Réceuil d'Itinéraires* p. 188.) Mr. Th. Radloff came into Yiti-kint after crossing the Kindirlik Pass from Tashkint and he enumerates the seven villages as traversed by him before reaching the Sir. It is hardly necessary to say that the actual villages he names may not be those of Babur's Yiti-kint. Wherever the word is used in the *Babur-nama* and the *Tarikh-i-rashidi*, it appears from the context allowable to accept Mr. Radloff's location but it should be borne in mind that the name Yiti-kint (Seven

the mandrake (*mihr-giyah*) the people there call by this name (*i.e. ayiq auti*). There are turquoise and iron mines in these mountains.

If people do justly, three or four thousand men[1] may be maintained by the revenues of Farghana.

(*b. Historical narrative resumed.*)[2]

As 'Umar Shaikh Mirza was a ruler of high ambition and great pretension, he was always bent on conquest. On several occasions he led an army against Samarkand; sometimes he was beaten, sometimes retired against his will.[3] More than once he asked his father-in-law into the country, that is to say, my grandfather, Yunas Khan, the then Khan of the Mughuls in the camping ground (*yurt*) of his ancestor, Chaghatai Khan, the second son of Chingiz Khan. Each time the Mirza brought The Khan into the Farghana country he gave him lands, but, partly owing to his misconduct, partly to the thwarting of the Mughuls,[4] things did not go as he wished and Yunas Khan, not being able to remain, went out again into Mughulistan. When the Mirza last brought The Khan in, he was in possession of

Fol. 6.

villages or towns) might be found as an occasional name of Alti-shahr (Six towns). See T.R. *s.n.* Alti-shahr.

1 *kishi*, person, here manifestly fighting men.

2 Elph. MS. f. 2b; First W.-i-B. I.O. 215 f. 4b; Second W.-i-B. I.O. 217 f. 4; Mems. p. 6; Ilminsky p. 7; *Méms.* i. 10.

The rulers whose affairs are chronicled at length in the Farghana Section of the B.N. are, (I) of Timurid Turks, (always styled Mirza), (*a*) the three Miran-shahi brothers, Ahmad, Mahmud and 'Umar Shaikh with their successors, Bai-sunghar, 'Ali and Babur; (*b*) the Bai-qara, Husain of Harat: (II) of Chingiz Khanids, (always styled Khan,) (*a*) the two Chaghatai Mughul brothers, Mahmud and Ahmad; (*b*) the Shaibanid Auzbeg, Muhammad *Shaibani* (Shah-i-bakht or Shaibaq or Shahi Beg).

In electing to use the name *Shaibani*, I follow not only the Hai. Codex but also Shaibani's Boswell, Muhammad Salih Mirza. The Elph. MS. frequently uses *Shaibaq* but its authority down to f. 198 (Hai. MS. f. 243b) is not so great as it is after that folio, because not till f. 198 is it a direct copy of Babur's own. It may be more correct to write "the Shaibani Khan" and perhaps even "the Shaibani." (But *see* index, p. 895 n. 1.)

3 *bi murad*, so translated because retirement was caused once by the overruling of Khwaja 'Ubaidu'l-lah *Ahrari*. (T.R. p. 113.)

4 Once the Mirza did not wish Yunas to winter in Akhsi; once did not expect him to yield to the demand of his Mughuls to be led out of the cultivated country (*wilayat*). His own misconduct included his attacking Yunas on account of Akhsi and much falling-out with kinsmen. (T.R. *s.nn.*)

Tashkint, which in books they write Shash, and sometimes Chach, whence the term, a Chachi, bow.[1] He gave it to The Khan, and from that date (890 AH.-1485 AD.) down to 908 AH. (1503 AD.) it and the Shahrukhiya country were held by the Chaghatai Khans.

At this date (*i.e.*, 899 AH.-1494 AD.) the Mughul Khanship was in Sl. Mahmud Khan, Yunas Khan's younger son and a half-brother of my mother. As he and 'Umar Shaikh Mirza's elder brother, the then ruler of Samarkand, Sl. Ahmad Mirza were offended by the Mirza's behaviour, they came to an agreement together; Sl. Ahmad Mirza had already given a daughter to Sl. Mahmud Khan;[2] both now led their armies against 'Umar Shaikh Mirza, the first advancing along the south of the Khujand Water, the second along its north.

Meantime a strange event occurred. It has been mentioned   Fol. 6*b*. that the fort of Akhsi is situated above a deep ravine;[3] along this ravine stand the palace buildings, and from it, on Monday, Ramzan 4, (June 8th) 'Umar Shaikh Mirza flew, with his pigeons and their house, and became a falcon.[4]

He was 39 (lunar) years old, having been born in Samarkand, in 860 AH. (1456 AD.). He was Sl. Abu-sa'id Mirza's fourth son,[5] being younger than Sl. Ahmad M. and Sl. Muhammad M.

---

1 *i.e.* one made of non-warping wood (Steingass), perhaps that of the White Poplar. The *Shah-nama* (Turner, Maçon ed. i, 71) writes of a Chachi bow and arrows of *khadang*, *i.e.* white poplar. (H.B.)

2 *i.e.* Rabi'a-sultan, married *circa* 893 AH.-1488 AD. For particulars about her and all women mentioned in the B.N. and the T.R. *see* Gulbadan Begim's *Humayun-nama*, Or. Trs. Series.

3 *jar*, either that of the Kasan Water or of a deeply-excavated canal. The palace buildings are mentioned again on f. 110*b*. *Cf.* Appendix A.

4 *i.e.* soared from earth, died. For some details of the accident *see* A.N. (H. Beveridge, i, 220.)

5 H.S. iii, 192, Firishta, lith. ed. p. 191 and D'Herbélot, sixth.

It would have accorded with Babur's custom if here he had mentioned the parentage of his father's mother. Three times (fs. 17*b*, 70*b*, 96*b*) he writes of "Shah Sultan Begim" in a way allowing her to be taken as 'Umar Shaikh's own mother. Nowhere, however, does he mention her parentage. One even cognate statement only have we discovered, *viz*. Khwand-amir's (H.S. ii, 192) that 'Umar Shaikh was the own younger brother (*baradar khurdtar khud*) of Ahmad and Mahmud. If his words mean that the three were full-brothers, 'Umar Shaikh's own mother was Abu-sa'id's Tarkhan wife. Babur's omission (f. 21*b*) to mention his father with A. and M. as a nephew of Darwesh Muh. Tarkhan would be negative testimony against taking Khwand-amir's statement to mean "full-brother," if clerical slips were not easy and if Khwand-amir's

and Sl. Mahmud Mirza. His father, Sl. Abu-sa'id Mirza, was the son of Sl. Muhammad Mirza, son of Timur Beg's third son, Miran-shah M. who was younger than 'Umar Shaikh Mirza, (the elder) and Jahangir M. but older than Shahrukh Mirza.

c. 'Umar Shaikh Mirza's country.

His father first gave him Kabul and, with Baba-i-Kabuli[1] for his guardian, had allowed him to set out, but recalled him from the Tamarisk Valley[2] to Samarkand, on account of the Mirzas' Circumcision Feast. When the Feast was over, he gave him Andijan with the appropriateness that Timur Beg had given Farghana (Andijan) to his son, the elder 'Umar Shaikh Mirza. This done, he sent him off with Khudai-birdi *Tughchi Timur-tash*[3] for his guardian.

d. His appearance and characteristics.

He was a short and stout, round-bearded and fleshy-faced person.[4] He used to wear his tunic so very tight that to fasten the strings he had to draw his belly in and, if he let himself out after tying them, they often tore away. He was not choice in dress or food. He wound his turban in a fold (*dastar-pech*); all turbans were in four folds (*char-pech*) in those days; people

Fol. 7.

---

means of information were less good. He however both was the son of Mahmud's wazir (H.S. ii, 194) and supplemented his book in Babur's presence.

To a statement made by the writer of the biographies included in Kehr's B.N. volume, that 'U.S.'s family (*aumagh*) is not known, no weight can be attached, spite of the co-incidence that the Mongol form of *aumagh*, *i.e. aumak* means *Mutter-leib.* The biographies contain too many known mistakes for their compiler to outweigh Khwand-amir in authority.

1 *Cf. Rauzatu' s-safa* vi, 266. (H.B.)

2 Dara-i-gaz, south of Balkh. This historic feast took place at Merv in 870 AH. (1465 AD.). As 'Umar Shaikh was then under ten, he may have been one of the Mirzas concerned.

3 Khudai-birdi is a Pers.-Turki hybrid equivalent of Theodore; *tughchi* implies the right to use or (as hereditary standard-bearer,) to guard the *tugh*; Timur-tash may mean *i.a.* Friend of Timur (a title not excluded here as borne by inheritance. *Cf.* f. 12*b* and note), Sword-friend (*i.e.* Companion-in-arms), and Iron-friend (*i.e.* stanch). *Cf.* Dict. *s.n.* Timur-bash, a sobriquet of Charles XII.

4 Elph. and Hai. MSS. *quba yuzluq*; this is under-lined in the Elph. MS. by *ya'ni pur ghosht. Cf.* f. 68*b* for the same phrase. The four earlier trss. *viz.* the two W.-i-B., the English and the French, have variants in this passage.

wore them without twisting and let the ends hang down.¹ In the heats and except in his Court, he generally wore the Mughul cap.

e. His qualities and habits.

He was a true believer (*Hanafi mazhablik*) and pure in the Faith, not neglecting the Five Prayers and, his life through, making up his Omissions.² He read the Qur'an very frequently and was a disciple of his Highness Khwaja 'Ubaidu'l-lah (*Ahrari*) who honoured him by visits and even called him son. His current readings³ were the two Quintets and the *Masnawi*;⁴ of histories he read chiefly the *Shah-nama*. He had a poetic nature, but no taste for composing verses. He was so just that when he heard of a caravan returning from Khitai as overwhelmed by snow in the mountains of Eastern Andijan,⁵ and that of its thousand heads of houses (*awiluq*) two only had escaped, he sent his overseers to take charge of all goods and, though no heirs were   Fol. 7b. near and though he was in want himself, summoned the heirs from Khurasan and Samarkand, and in the course of a year or two had made over to them all their property safe and sound.

He was very generous; in truth, his character rose altogether to the height of generosity. He was affable, eloquent and sweet-spoken, daring and bold. Twice out-distancing all his

---

1 The apposition may be between placing the turban-sash round the turban-cap in a single flat fold and winding it four times round after twisting it on itself. *Cf.* f. 18*b* and Hughes *Dict. of Islam s.n.* turban.

2 *qazalar*, the prayers and fasts omitted when due, through war, travel sickness, etc.

3 *rawan sawadi bar idi*; perhaps, wrote a running hand. De C. i, 13, *ses lectures courantes étaient* …

4 The dates of 'Umar Shaikh's limits of perusal allow the Quintets (*Khamsatin*) here referred to to be those of Nizami and Amir Khusrau of Dihli. The *Masnawi* must be that of Jalalu'd-din *Rumi*. (H.B.)

5 Probably below the Tirak (Poplar) Pass, the caravan route much exposed to avalanches.

Mr. Erskine notes that this anecdote is erroneously told as of Babur by Firishta and others. Perhaps it has been confused with the episode on f. 207*b*. Firishta makes another mistaken attribution to Babur, that of Hasan of Yaq'ub's couplet. (H.B.) *Cf.* f. 13*b* and Dow's *Hindustan* ii, 218.

braves,[1] he got to work with his own sword, once at the Gate of Akhsi, once at the Gate of Shahrukhiya. A middling archer, he was strong in the fist,—not a man but fell to his blow. Through his ambition, peace was exchanged often for war, friendliness for hostility.

In his early days he was a great drinker, later on used to have a party once or twice a week. He was good company, on occasions reciting verses admirably. Towards the last he rather preferred intoxicating confects[2] and, under their sway, used to lose his head. His disposition was amorous,[3] and he bore many a lover's mark.[4] He played draughts a good deal, sometimes even threw the dice.

f. His battles and encounters.

He fought three ranged battles, the first with Yunas Khan, on the Saihun, north of Andijan, at the Goat-leap,[5] a village so-called because near it the foot-hills so narrow the flow of the water that people say goats leap across.[6] There he was beaten and made prisoner. Yunas Khan for his part did well by him and gave him leave to go to his own district (Andijan). This fight having been at that place, the Battle of the Goat-leap became a date in those parts.

His second battle was fought on the Urus,[7] in Turkistan, with Auzbegs returning from a raid near Samarkand. He crossed the river on the ice, gave them a good beating, separated off all their prisoners and booty and, without coveting a single thing for himself, gave everything back to its owners.

Fol. 8.

---

1 *yigitlar*, young men, the modern *jighit*. Babur uses the word for men on the effective fighting strength. It answers to the "brave" of North American Indian story; here de C. translates it by *braves*.

2 *ma'jun. Cf.* Von Schwarz p. 286 for a recipe.

3 *mutaiyam*. This word, not clearly written in all MSS., has been mistaken for *yitim. Cf.* JRAS 1910 p. 882 for a note upon it by my husband to whom I owe the emendation.

4 *na'l u daghi bisyar idi*, that is, he had inflicted on himself many of the brands made by lovers and enthusiasts. *Cf.* Chardin's *Voyages* ii, 253 and Lady M. Montague's *Letters* p. 200. *See also* Additional Notes, p. 797.

5 *tika sikritku*, lit. likely to make goats leap, from *sikrimak* to jump close-footed (Shaw).

6 *sikrikan dur.* Both *sikritku* and *sikrikan dur*, appear to dictate translation in general terms and not by reference to a single traditional leap by one goat.

7 *i.e.* Russian; it is the Arys tributary of the Sir.

His third battle he fought with (his brother) Sl. Ahmad Mirza at a place between Shahrukhiya and Aura-tipa, named Khwas.[1] Here he was beaten.

g. His country.

The Farghana country his father had given him; Tashkint and Sairam, his elder brother, Sl. Ahmad Mirza gave, and they were in his possession for a time; Shahrukhiya he took by a ruse and held awhile. Later on, Tashkint and Shahrukhiya passed out of his hands; there then remained the Farghana country and Khujand,—some do not include Khujand in Farghana,—and Aura-tipa, of which the original name was Aurushna and which some call Aurush. In Aura-tipa, at the time Sl. Ahmad Mirza went to Tashkint against the Mughuls, and was beaten on the Chir[2] (893 AH.-1488 AD.) was Hafiz Beg *Duldai*; he made it over to 'Umar Shaikh M. and the Mirza held it from that time forth.

Fol. 8b.

h. His children.

Three of his sons and five of his daughters grew up. I, Zahiru'd-din Muhammad Babur,[3] was his eldest son; my mother was Qutluq-nigar Khanim. Jahangir Mirza was his second son, two years younger than I; his mother, Fatima-sultan by name, was of the Mughul *tuman*-begs.[4] Nasir Mirza was his third son; his mother was an Andijani, a mistress,[5] named Umid. He was four years younger than I.

'Umar Shaikh Mirza's eldest daughter was Khan-zada Begim,[6] my full sister, five years older than I. The second

1 The Fr. map of 1904 shows Kas, in the elbow of the Sir, which seems to represent Khwas.

2 *i.e.* the Chir-chik tributary of the Sir.

3 Concerning his name, *see* T.R. p. 173.

4 *i.e.* he was a head-man of a horde sub-division, nominally numbering 10,000, and paying their dues direct to the supreme Khan. (T.R. p. 301.)

5 *ghunchachi i.e.* one ranking next to the four legal wives, in Turki *audaliq*, whence odalisque. Babur and Gul-badan mention the promotion of several to Begim's rank by virtue of their motherhood.

6 One of Babur's quatrains, quoted in the *Abushqa*, is almost certainly addressed to Khan-zada. *Cf.* A.Q. Review, Jan. 1911, p. 4; H. Beveridge's *Some verses of Babur*. For an account of her marriage *see Shaibani-nama* (Vambéry) cap. xxxix.

time I took Samarkand (905 AH.-1500 AD.), spite of defeat at Sar-i-pul,[1] I went back and held it through a five months' siege, but as no sort of help or reinforcement came from any beg or ruler thereabouts, I left it in despair and got away; in that throneless time (*fatrat*) Khan-zada Begim fell[2] to Muhammad *Shaibani* Khan. She had one child by him, a pleasant boy,[3] named Khurram Shah. The Balkh country was given to him; he went to God's mercy a few years after the death of his father (916 AH.-1510 AD.). Khan-zada Begim was in Merv when Shah Isma'il (*Safawi*) defeated the Auzbegs near that town (916 AH.-1510 AD.); for my sake he treated her well, giving her a sufficient escort to Qunduz where she rejoined me. We had been apart for some ten years; when Muhammadi *kukuldash* and I went to see her, neither she nor those about her knew us, although I spoke. They recognized us after a time.

Mihr-banu Begim was another daughter, Nasir Mirza's full-sister, two years younger than I. Shahr-banu Begim was another, also Nasir Mirza's full-sister, eight years younger than I. Yadgar-sultan Begim was another, her mother was a mistress, called Agha-sultan. Ruqaiya-sultan Begim was another; her mother, Makhdum-sultan Begim, people used to call the Dark-eyed Begim. The last-named two were born after the Mirza's death. Yadgar-sultan Begim was brought up by my grandmother, Aisan-daulat Begim; she fell to 'Abdu'l-latif Sl., a son of Hamza Sl. when Shaibani Khan took Andijan and Akhsi (908 AH.-1503 AD.). She rejoined me when (917 AH.-1511 AD.) in Khutlan I defeated Hamza Sl. and other sultans and took Hisar. Ruqaiya-sultan Begim fell in that same throneless time (*fatrat*) to Jani Beg Sl. (*Auzbeg*). By him she had one or two children who did not live. In these days

---

Fol. 9.

Fol. 9*b*.

---

1 Kehr's MS. has a passage here not found elsewhere and seeming to be an adaptation of what is at the top of Hai. MS. f. 88. (Ilminsky, p. 10, *ba wujud ... tapib*.)

2 *tushti*, which here seems to mean that she fell to his share on division of captives. Muh. Salih makes it a love-match and places the marriage before Babur's departure. *Cf.* f. 95 and notes.

3 *aughlan*. Khurram would be about five when given Balkh in *circa* 911 AH. (1505 AD.). He died when about 12. *Cf.* H.S. ii, 364.

of our leisure (*fursatlar*)[1] has come news that she has gone to God's mercy.

i. His ladies and mistresses.

Qutluq-nigar Khanim was the second daughter of Yunas Khan and the eldest (half-) sister of Sl. Mahmud Khan and Sl. Ahmad Khan.

(j. Interpolated account of Babur's mother's family.)

Yunas Khan descended from Chaghatai Khan, the second son of Chingiz Khan (as follows,) Yunas Khan, son of Wais Khan, son of Sher-'ali *Aughlan*, son of Muhammad Khan, son of Khizr Khwaja Khan, son of Tughluq-timur Khan, son of Aisan-bugha Khan, son of Dawa Khan, son of Baraq Khan, son of Yisuntawa Khan, son of Muatukan, son of Chaghatai Khan, son of Chingiz Khan.

Since such a chance has come, set thou down[2] now a summary of the history of the Khans.

Yunas Khan (d. 892 AH.-1487 AD.) and Aisan-bugha Khan (d. 866 AH.-1462 AD.) were sons of Wais Khan (d. 832 AH.- 1428 AD.).[3] Yunas Khan's mother was either a daughter or a grand-daughter of Shaikh Nuru'd-din Beg, a Turkistani Qipchaq favoured by Timur Beg. When Wais Khan died, the Mughul horde split in two, one portion being for Yunas Khan, the greater for Aisan-bugha Khan. For help in getting the upper hand in the horde, Airzin (var. Airazan) one of the Barin *tuman*-begs and Beg Mirik *Turkman*, one of the Chiras *tuman*-begs, took Yunas Khan (aet. 13) and with him three Fol. 10. or four thousand Mughul heads of houses (*awiluq*), to Aulugh Beg Mirza (*Shahrukhi*) with the fittingness that Aulugh Beg M. had taken Yunas Khan's elder sister for his son, 'Abdu'l-

---

1 This *fatrat* (interregnum) was between Babur's loss of Farghana and his gain of Kabul; the *fursatlar* were his days of ease following success in Hindustan and allowing his book to be written.

2 *qilaling*, lit. do thou be (setting down). With the same form (*ait*)*aling*, lit. do thou be saying, the compiler of the *Abushqa* introduces his quotations. Shaw's paradigm, *qiling* only. *Cf.* A.Q.R. Jan. 1911, p. 2.

3 Kehr's MS. (Ilminsky p. 12) and its derivatives here interpolate the erroneous statement that the sons of Yunas were Afaq and Baba Khans.

'aziz Mirza. Aulugh Beg Mirza did not do well by them; some he imprisoned, some scattered over the country[1] one by one. The Dispersion of Airzin became a date in the Mughul horde.

Yunas Khan himself was made to go towards 'Iraq; one year he spent in Tabriz where Jahan Shah *Barani* of the Black Sheep Turkmans was ruling. From Tabriz he went to Shiraz where was Shahrukh Mirza's second son, Ibrahim Sultan Mirza.[2] He having died five or six months later (Shawwal 4, 838 AH.–May 3rd, 1435 AD.), his son, 'Abdu'l-lah Mirza sat in his place. Of this 'Abdu'l-lah Mirza Yunas Khan became a retainer and to him used to pay his respects. The Khan was in those parts for 17 or 18 years.

In the disturbances between Aulugh Beg Mirza and his sons, Aisan-bugha Khan found a chance to invade Farghana; he plundered as far as Kand-i-badam, came on and, having plundered Andijan, led all its people into captivity.[3] Sl. Abu-sa'id Mirza, after seizing the throne of Samarkand, led an army out to beyond Yangi (Taraz) to Aspara in Mughulistan,

Fol. 10b. there gave Aisan-bugha a good beating and then, to spare himself further trouble from him and with the fitting-ness that he had just taken to wife[4] Yunas Khan's elder sister, the former wife of 'Abdu'l-'aziz Mirza (*Shahrukhi*), he invited Yunas Khan from Khurasan and 'Iraq, made a feast, became friends and proclaimed him Khan of the Mughuls. Just when he was speeding him forth, the Sagharichi *tuman*-begs had all come into Mughulistan, in anger with Aisan-bugha Khan.[5] Yunas Khan went amongst them and took to wife Aisan-daulat Begim, the daughter of their chief, Sher Haji

1 *i.e.* broke up the horde. *Cf.* T.R. p. 74.
2 *See* f. 50b for his descent.
3 Descendants of these captives were in Kashghar when Haidar was writing the T.R. It was completed in 953 AH. (1547 AD.). *Cf.* T.R. pp. 81 and 149.
4 An omission from his Persian source misled Mr. Erskine here into making Abu-sa'id celebrate the Khanim's marriage, not with himself but with his defeated foe, 'Abdu'l-'aziz who had married her 28 years earlier.
5 Aisan-bugha was at Aq-su in Eastern Turkistan; Yunas Khan's head-quarters were in Yiti-kint. The Sagharichi *tuman* was a subdivision of the Kunchi Mughuls.

Beg. They then seated him and her on one and the same white felt and raised him to the Khanship.[1]

By this Aisan-daulat Begim, Yunas Khan had three daughters. Mihr-nigar Khanim was the eldest; Sl. Abu-sa'id Mirza set her aside[2] for his eldest son, Sl. Ahmad Mirza; she had no child. In a throneless time (905 AH.) she fell to Shaibani Khan; she left Samarkand[3] with Shah Begim for Khurasan (907 AH.) and both came on to me in Kabul (911 AH.). At the time Shaibani Khan was besieging Nasir Mirza in Qandahar and I set out for Lamghan[4] (913 AH.) they went to Badakhshan with Khan Mirza (Wais).[5] When Mubarak Shah invited Khan Mirza into Fort Victory,[6] they were Fol. 11. captured, together with the wives and families of all their people, by marauders of Aba-bikr *Kashghari* and, as captives to that ill-doing miscreant, bade farewell to this transitory world (*circa* 913 AH.–1507 AD.).

Qutluq-nigar Khanim, my mother, was Yunas Khan's second daughter. She was with me in most of my guerilla expeditions and throneless times. She went to God's mercy in Muharram 911 AH. (June 1505 AD.) five or six months after the capture of Kabul.

Khub-nigar Khanim was his third daughter. Her they gave to Muhammad Husain *Kurkan Dughlat* (899 AH.). She had one son and one daughter by him. 'Ubaid Khan (*Auzbeg*) took the daughter (Habiba).[7] When I captured Samarkand and

1 *Khan kutardilar.* The primitive custom was to lift the Khan-designate off the ground; the phrase became metaphorical and would seem to be so here, since there were two upon the felt. *Cf.*, however, Th. Radloff's *Réceuil d'Itinéraires* p. 326.
2 *quyub idi*, probably in childhood.
3 She was divorced by Shaibani Khan in 907 AH. in order to allow him to make lawful marriage with her niece, Khan-zada.
4 This was a prudential retreat before Shaibani Khan. *Cf.* f. 213.
5 The "Khan" of his title bespeaks his Chaghatai-Mughul descent through his mother, the "Mirza," his Timurid-Turki, through his father. The capture of the women was facilitated by the weakening of their travelling escort through his departure. *Cf.* T.R. p. 203.
6 Qila'-i-zafar. Its ruins are still to be seen on the left bank of the Kukcha. *Cf.* T.R. p. 220 and Kostenko i, 140. For Mubarak Shah *Muzaffari* see f. 213 and T.R. *s.n.*
7 Habiba, a child when captured, was reared by Shaibani and by him given in marriage to his nephew. *Cf.* T.R. p. 207 for an account of this marriage as saving Haidar's life.

Bukhara (917 AH.-1511 AD.), she stayed behind,[1] and when her
paternal uncle, Sayyid Muhammad *Dughlat* came as Sl. Sa'id
Khan's envoy to me in Samarkand, she joined him and with
him went to Kashghar where (her cousin), Sl. Sa'id Khan took
her. Khub-nigar's son was Haidar Mirza.[2] He was in my
service for three or four years after the Auzbegs slew his
father, then (918 AH.-1512 AD.) asked leave to go to Kashghar to
the presence of Sl. Sa'id Khan.

> "Everything goes back to its source,
> Pure gold, or silver or tin."[3]

People say he now lives lawfully (*ta'ib*) and has found the right
way (*tariqa*).[4] He has a hand deft in every thing, penmanship
and painting, and in making arrows and arrow, barbs and
Fol. 11b.   string-grips; moreover he is a born poet and in a petition
written to me, even his style is not bad.[5]

Shah Begim was another of Yunas Khan's ladies. Though
he had more, she and Aisan-daulat Begim were the mothers of
his children. She was one of the (six) daughters of Shah
Sultan Muhammad, Shah of Badakhshan.[6] His line, they say,
runs back to Iskandar Filkus.[7] Sl. Abu-sa'id Mirza took
another daughter and by her had Aba-bikr Mirza.[8] By this

1 *i.e.* she did not take to flight with her husband's defeated force, but,
relying on the victor, her cousin Babur, remained in the town. *Cf.* T.R. p. 268.
Her case receives light from Shahr-banu's (f. 169).

2 Muhammad Haidar Mirza *Kurkan Dughlat* (*see* Additional Notes, p. 797), the
author of the *Tarikh-i-rashidi*; b. 905 AH. d. 958 AH. (b. 1499 d. 1551 AD.). Of his
clan, the "Oghlat" (Dughlat) Muh. Salih says that it was called "Oghlat" by
Mughuls but Qungur-at (Brown Horse) by Auzbegs.

3   *Baz garadad ba asl-i-khud hama chiz,*
    Zar-i-safi u naqra u airzin.

These lines are in Arabic in the introduction to the *Anwar-i-suhaili.* (H.B.)
The first is quoted by Haidar (T.R. p. 354) and in Field's *Dict. of Oriental
Quotations* (p. 160). I understand them to refer here to Haidar's return to his
ancestral home and nearest kin as being a natural act.

4 *ta'ib* and *tariqa* suggest that Haidar had become an orthodox Musalman
in or about 933 AH. (1527 AD.).

5 Abu'l-fazl adds music to Haidar's accomplishments and Haidar's own
Prologue mentions yet others.

6 *Cf.* T.R. *s.n.* and Gul-badan's H.N. *s.n.* Haram Begim.

7 *i.e.* Alexander of Macedon. For modern mention of Central Asian claims to
Greek descent *see i.a.* Kostenko, Von Schwarz, Holdich and A. Durand. *Cf.*
Burnes' *Kabul* p. 203 for an illustration of a silver *patera* (now in the V. and A.
Museum), once owned by ancestors of this Shah Sultan Muhammad.

8 *Cf.* f. 6b (p. 13) n. 5.

Shah Begim Yunas Khan had two sons and two daughters. Her first-born but younger than all Aisan-daulat Begim's daughters, was Sl. Mahmud Khan, called Khanika Khan[1] by many in and about Samarkand. Next younger than he was Sl. Ahmad Khan, known as Alacha Khan. People say he was called this because he killed many Qalmaqs on the several occasions he beat them. In the Mughul and Qalmaq tongues, one who will kill (*aulturguchi*) is called *alachi*; Alachi they called him therefore and this by repetition, became Alacha.[2] As occasion arises, the acts and circumstances of these two Khans will find mention in this history (*tarikh*).

Sultan-nigar Khanim was the youngest but one of Yunas Khan's children. Her they made go forth (*chiqarib idilar*) Fol. 12. to Sl. Mahmud Mirza; by him she had one child, Sl. Wais (Khan Mirza), mention of whom will come into this history. When Sl. Mahmud Mirza died (900 AH.-1495 AD.), she took her son off to her brothers in Tashkint without a word to any single person. They, a few years later, gave her to Adik (Aung) Sultan,[3] a Qazaq sultan of the line of Juji Khan, Chingiz Khan's eldest son. When Shaibani Khan defeated the Khans (her brothers), and took Tashkint and Shahrukhiya (908 AH.), she got away with 10 or 12 of her Mughul servants, to (her husband), Adik Sultan. She had two daughters by Adik Sultan; one she gave to a Shaiban sultan, the other to Rashid Sultan, the son of (her cousin) Sl. Sa'id Khan. After Adik Sultan's death, (his brother), Qasim Khan, Khan of the Qazaq horde, took her.[4] Of all the Qazaq khans and sultans, no one, they say, ever kept the horde in such good order as he;

---

1 *i.e.* Khan's child.

2 The careful pointing of the Hai. MS. clears up earlier confusion by showing the narrowing of the vowels from *alachi* to *alacha*.

3 The Elph. MS. (f. 7) writes *Aung*, Khan's son, Prester John's title, where other MSS. have Adik. Babur's brevity has confused his account of Sultan-nigar. Widowed of Mahmud in 900 AH. she married Adik; Adik, later, joined Shaibani Khan but left him in 908 AH. perhaps secretly, to join his own Qazaq horde. He was followed by his wife, apparently also making a private departure. As Adik died shortly after 908 AH. his daughters were born before that date and not after it as has been understood. *Cf.* T.R. and G.B.'s H.N. *s.nn.*; also Mems. p. 14 and *Méms.* i, 24.

4 Presumably by tribal custom, *yinkalik*, marriage with a brother's widow. Such marriages seem to have been made frequently for the protection of women left defenceless.

his army was reckoned at 300,000 men. On his death the Khanim went to Sl. Sa'id Khan's presence in Kashghar. Daulat-sultan Khanim was Yunas Khan's youngest child. In the Tashkint disaster (908 AH.) she fell to Timur Sultan, the son of Shaibani Khan. By him she had one daughter; they got out of Samarkand with me (918 AH.-1512 AD.), spent three or four years in the Badakhshan country, then went (923 AH.-1420 AD.) to Sl. Sa'id Khan's presence in Kashghar.[1]

Fol. 12b.

(k. Account resumed of Babur's father's family.)

In 'Umar Shaikh Mirza's *haram* was also Aulus Agha, a daughter of Khwaja Husain Beg; her one daughter died in infancy and they sent her out of the *haram* a year or eighteen months later. Fatima-sultan Agha was another; she was of the Mughul *tuman*-begs and the first taken of his wives. Qara-guz (Makhdum sultan) Begim was another; the Mirza took her towards the end of his life; she was much beloved, so to please him, they made her out descended from (his uncle) Minuchihr Mirza, the elder brother of Sl. Abu-sa'id Mirza. He had many mistresses and concubines; one, Umid Aghacha died before him. Latterly there were also Tun-sultan (var. Yun) of the Mughuls and Agha Sultan.

l. 'Umar Shaikh Mirza's Amirs.

There was Khudai-birdi *Tughchi Timur-tash*, a descendant of the brother of Aq-bugha Beg, the Governor of Hiri (Herat, for Timur Beg.) When Sl. Abu-sa'id Mirza, after besieging Juki Mirza (*Shahrukhi*) in Shahrukhiya (868 AH.-1464 AD.) gave the Farghana country to 'Umar Shaikh Mirza, he put this Khudai-birdi Beg at the head of the Mirza's Gate.[2] Khudai-birdi was

Fol. 13.

---

1 Sa'id's power to protect made him the refuge of several kinswomen mentioned in the B.N. and the T.R.

Here Babur ends his [interpolated] account of his mother's family and resumes that of his father's.

2 Babur uses a variety of phrases to express Lordship in the Gate. Here he writes *aishikni bashlatib*; elsewhere, *aishik ikhtiyari qilmaq* and *mining aishikimda sahib ikhtiyari qilmaq*. Von Schwarz (p. 159) throws light on the duties of the Lord of the Gate (*Aishik Aghasi*). "Das Thür ... führt in eine

then 25 but youth notwithstanding, his rules and management were very good indeed. A few years later when Ibrahim *Begchik* was plundering near Aush, he followed him up, fought him, was beaten and became a martyr. At the time, Sl. Ahmad Mirza was in the summer pastures of Aq Qachghai, in Aura-tipa, 18 *yighach* east of Samarkand, and Sl. Abu-sa'id Mirza was at Baba Khaki, 12 *yighach* east of Hiri. People sent the news post-haste to the Mirza(s),[1] having humbly represented it through 'Abdu'l-wahhab *Shaghawal*. In four days it was carried those 120 *yighach* of road.[2]

Hafiz Muhammad Beg *Duldai* was another, Sl. Malik *Kash-ghari*'s son and a younger brother of Ahmad Haji Beg. After the death of Khudai-birdi Beg, they sent him to control 'Umar Shaikh Mirza's Gate, but he did not get on well with the Andijan begs and therefore, when Sl. Abu-sa'id Mirza died, went to Samarkand and took service with Sl. Ahmad Mirza. At the time of the disaster on the Chir, he was in Aura-tipa and made it over to 'Umar Shaikh Mirza when the Mirza passed through on his way to Samarkand, himself taking Fol. 13*b*. service with him. The Mirza, for his part, gave him the Andijan Command. Later on he went to Sl. Mahmud Khan

---

grosse, vier-eckige, höhe Halle, deren Boden etwa 2 m. über den Weg erhoben ist. In dieser Halle, welche alle passiren muss, der durch das Thor eingeht, reitet oder fahrt, ist die Thorwache placiert. Tagsüber sind die Thore beständig öffen, nach Eintritt der Dunkelheit aber werden dieselben geschlos-sen und die Schlüssel dem zuständigen Polizeichef abgeliefert. ... In den erwähnten Thorhallen nehmen in den hoch unabhängigen Gebieten an Bazar-tagen haufig die Richter Platz, um jedem der irgend ein Anliegen hat, so fort Recht zu sprechen. Die zudiktierten Strafen werden auch gleich in diesem selben locale vollzogen und eventuell die zum Hangen verurteilten Verbrecher an den Deckbalken aufgehängt, so dass die Besucher des Bazars unter den gehenkten durchpassieren müssen."

1 *bu khabarni 'Abdu'l-wahhab shaghawaldin 'arza-dasht qilib Mirzagha chapturdilar.* This passage has been taken to mean that the *shaghawal, i.e.* chief scribe, was the courier, but I think Babur's words shew that the *shaghawal's* act preceded the despatch of the news. Moreover the only accusative of the participle and of the verb is *khabarni.* 'Abdu'l-wahhab had been 'Umar Shaikh's and was now Ahmad's officer in Khujand, on the main road for Aura-tipa whence the courier started on the rapid ride. The news may have gone verbally to 'Abdu'l-wahhab and he have written it on to Ahmad and Abu-sa'id.

2 Measured from point to point even, the distance appears to be over 500 miles. Concerning Baba Khaki *see* H.S. ii. 224; for rapid riding *i.a.* Kostenko iii, cap. Studs.

in Tashkint and was there entrusted with the guardianship of Khan Mirza (Wais) and given Dizak. He had started for Makka by way of Hind before I took Kabul (910 AH. Oct. 1504 AD.), but he went to God's mercy on the road. He was a simple person, of few words and not clever.

Khwaja Husain Beg was another, a good-natured and simple person. It is said that, after the fashion of those days, he used to improvise very well at drinking parties.[1]

Shaikh Mazid Beg was another, my first guardian, excellent in rule and method. He must have served (*khidmat qilghan dur*) under Babur Mirza (*Shahrukhi*). There was no greater beg in 'Umar Shaikh Mirza's presence. He was a vicious person and kept catamites.

'Ali-mazid *Quchin* was another;[2] he rebelled twice, once at Akhsi, once at Tashkint. He was disloyal, untrue to his salt, vicious and good-for-nothing.

Hasan (son of) Yaq'ub was another, a small-minded, good-tempered, smart and active man. This verse is his:—

> "Return, O Huma, for without the parrot-down of thy lip,
> The crow will assuredly soon carry off my bones."[3]

Fol. 14. He was brave, a good archer, played polo (*chaughan*) well and leapt well at leap-frog.[4] He had the control of my Gate after 'Umar Shaikh Mirza's accident. He had not much sense, was narrow-minded and somewhat of a strife-stirrer.

Qasim Beg *Quchin*, of the ancient army-begs of Andijan, was another. He had the control of my Gate after Hasan Yaq'ub Beg. His life through, his authority and consequence waxed without decline. He was a brave man; once he gave some Auzbegs a good beating when he overtook them raiding near Kasan; his sword hewed away in 'Umar Shaikh Mirza's

---

1 *qushuqlarni yakhshi aitura ikan dur.* Elph. MS. for *qushuq, tuyuk. Qushuq* is allowed, both by its root and by usage, to describe improvisations of combined dance and song. I understand from Babur's tense, that his information was hearsay only.

2 *i.e.* of the military class. *Cf.* Vullers *s.n.* and T.R. p. 301.

3 The Huma is a fabulous bird, overshadowing by whose wings brings good-fortune. The couplet appears to be addressed to some man, under the name Huma, from whom Hasan of Yaq'ub hoped for benefit.

4 *khak-bila*; the *Sanglakh*, (quoting this passage) gives *khak-p:l:k* as the correct form of the word.

presence; and in the fight at the Broad Ford (Yasi-kijit *circa* 904 AH.-July, 1499 AD.) he hewed away with the rest. In the guerilla days he went to Khusrau Shah (907 AH.) at the time I was planning to go from the Macha hill-country[1] to Sl. Mahmud Khan, but he came back to me in 910 AH. (1504 AD.) when, after taking Khusrau Shah, we besieged Muqim in Kabul, and I shewed him all my old favour and affection.When I attacked the Turkman Hazara raiders in Dara-i-khwush (911 AH.) he made better advance, spite of his age, than the younger men; I gave him Bangash as a reward and later on, after returning to Kabul, made him Humayun's guardian. He went to God's mercy Fol. 14*b*. about the time Zamin-dawar was taken (*circa* 928 AH.-1522 AD.). He was a pious, God-fearing Musalman, an abstainer from doubtful aliments; excellent in judgment and counsel, very facetious and, though he could neither read nor write (*ummiy*), used to make entertaining jokes.

Baba 'Ali Beg's Baba-quli was another, a descendant of Shaikh 'Ali *Bahadur*.[2] They made him my guardian when Shaikh Mazid Beg died. He went over to Sl. Ahmad Mirza when the Mirza led his army against Andijan (899 AH.), and gave him Aura-tipa. After Sl. Mahmud Mirza's death, he left Samarkand and was on his way to join me (900 AH.) when Sl. 'Ali Mirza, issuing out of Aura-tipa, fought, defeated and slew him. His management and equipment were excellent and he took good care of his men. He prayed not; he kept no fasts; he was like a heathen and he was a tyrant.

'Ali-dost Taghai[3] was another, one of the Sagharichi *tuman*-begs and a relation of my mother's mother, Aisan-daulat Begim. I favoured him more than he had been favoured in 'Umar Shaikh Mirza's time. People said, "Work will come from his hand." But in the many years he was in my presence, no work to speak of[4] came to sight. He must have served Sl. Fol. 15. Abu-sa'id Mirza. He claimed to have power to bring on rain with the jade-stone. He was the Falcone (*qushchi*), worthless

---

1 *Cf.* f. 99*b*.

2 One of Timur's begs.

3 *i.e.* uncle on the mother's side, of any degree, here a grandmother's brother. The title appears to have been given for life to men related to the ruling House. Parallel with it are Madame Mère, Royal Uncle, Sultan Walida.

4 *kim disa bulghai*, perhaps meaning, "Nothing of service to me."

by nature and habit, a stingy, severe, strife-stirring person, false, self-pleasing, rough of tongue and cold-of-face.

Wais *Laghari*,[1] one of the Samarkand *Tughchi* people, was another. Latterly he was much in 'Umar Shaikh Mirza's confidence; in the guerilla times he was with me. Though somewhat factious, he was a man of good judgment and counsel.

Mir Ghiyas Taghai was another, a younger brother of 'Ali-dost Taghai. No man amongst the Mughul mirzadas in Sl. Abu-sa'id Mirza's Gate was more to the front than he; he had charge of the Mirza's square seal[2] and was much in his confidence latterly. He was a friend of Wais *Laghari*. When Kasan had been given to Sl. Mahmud Khan (899 AH.–1494 AD.), he was continuously in The Khan's service and was in high favour. He was a laugher, a joker and fearless in vice.

'Ali-darwesh *Khurasani* was another. He had served in the Khurasan Cadet Corps, one of two special corps of serviceable young men formed by Sl. Abu-sa'id Mirza when he first began
Fol. 15*b*. to arrange the government of Khurasan and Samarkand, and, presumably, called by him the Khurasan Corps and the Samarkand Corps. 'Ali-darwesh was a brave man; he did well in my presence at the Gate of Bishkaran.[3] He wrote the *naskh ta'liq* hand clearly.[4] His was the flatterer's tongue and in his character avarice was supreme.

Qambar-'ali *Mughul* of the Equerries (*akhtachi*) was another. People called him The Skinner because his father, on first coming into the (Farghana) country, worked as a skinner. Qambar-'ali had been Yunas Khan's water-bottle bearer,[5] later on he became a beg. Till he was a made man, his conduct was excellent; once arrived, he was slack. He was full of talk and of foolish talk,—a great talker is sure to be a foolish one,—his capacity was limited and his brain muddy.

1 Wais the Thin.

2 *Cf.* Chardin ed. Langlès v, 461 and ed. 1723 AD. v, 183.

3 n.e. of Kasan. *Cf.* f. 74. Hai MS., erroneously, Samarkand.

4 An occasional doubt arises as to whether a *tauri* of the text is Arabic and dispraises or Turki and laudatory. *Cf.* Mems. p. 17 and *Mêms.* i, 3.

5 Elph. and Hai. MSS. *aftabachi*, water-bottle bearer on journeys; Kehr (p. 82) *aftabchi*, ewer-bearer; Ilminsky (p. 19) *akhtachi*, squire or groom. Circumstances support *aftabachi*. Yunas was town-bred, his ewer-bearer would hardly be the rough Mughul, Qambar-'ali, useful as an *aftabachi*.

(l. Historical narrative.)

At the time of 'Umar Shaikh Mirza's accident, I was in the Four Gardens (*Char-bagh*) of Andijan.¹ The news reached Andijan on Tuesday, Ramzan 5 (June 9th); I mounted at once, with my followers and retainers, intending to go into the fort but, on our getting near the Mirza's Gate, Shirim Taghai² took hold of my bridle and moved off towards the Praying Place.³ It had crossed his mind that if a great ruler like Sl. Ahmad Mirza came in force, the Andijan begs would make over to him   Fol. 16. me and the country,⁴ but that, if he took me to Auzkint and the foothills thereabouts, I, at any rate, should not be made over and could go to one of my mother's (half-) brothers, Sl. Mahmud Khan or Sl. Ahmad Khan.⁵ When Khwaja Maulana-i-qazi⁶

(*Author's note on Khwaja Maulana-i-qazi.*)   He was the son of Sl. Ahmad Qazi, of the line of Burhanu'd-din 'Ali *Qilich*⁷ and through his mother, traced back to Sl. Ailik *Mazi.*⁸ By hereditary right

---

1 Babur was Governor of Andijan and the month being June, would be living out-of-doors. *Cf.* H.S. ii. 272 and Schuyler ii, 37.
2 To the word Sherim applies Abu'l-ghazi's explanation of Nurum and Hajim, namely, that they are abbreviations of Nur and Haji Muhammad. It explains Sultanim also when used (f. 72) of Sl. Muhammad Khanika but of Sultanim as the name is common with Babur, Haidar and Gul-badan, *i.e.* as a woman's, Busbecq's explanation is the better, namely, that it means My Sultan and is applied to a person of rank and means. This explains other women's titles *e.g.* Khanim, my Khan and Akam (Akim), My Lady. A third group of names formed like the last by enclitic *'m* (my), may be called names of affection, *e.g.* Mahim, My Moon, Janim, My Life. (*Cf.* Persian equivalents.) *Cf.* Abu'l-ghazi's *Shajarat-i-Turki* (Desmaisons p. 272); and Ogier Ghiselin de Busbecq's *Life and Letters* (Forster and Daniel i, 38.)
3 *Namaz-gah;* generally an open terrace, with a wall towards the Qibla and outside the town, whither on festival days the people go out in crowds to pray. (Erskine.)
4 *Beglar (ning) mini u wilayatni tapshurghulari dur;* a noticeably idiomatic sentence.
5 Mahmud was in Tashkint, Ahmad in Kashghar or on the Aq-su.
6 The B.N. contains a considerable number of what are virtually foot-notes. They are sometimes, as here, entered in the middle of a sentence and confuse the narrative; they are introduced by *kim,* a mere sign of parenthetical matter to follow, and some certainly, known not to be Babur's own, must have stood first on the margin of his text. It seems best to enter them as Author's notes.
7 *i.e.* the author of the Hidayat. *Cf.* f. 3*b* and note; Blochmann *Ayin-i-akbari s.n. qulij* and note; Bellew's *Afghan Tribes* p. 100, *Khilich.*
8 Ar. dead, gone. The precision of Babur's words *khanwadalar* and *yusunluq* is illustrated by the existence in the days of Timur, in Marghinan, (Burhanu'd-din's township) of a ruler named Ailik Khan, apparently a

(*yusunluq*) his high family (*khanwadalar*) must have come to be the
Refuge (*marji'*) and Pontiffs (*Shaikhu'l-islam*) of the (Farghana) country.

and the begs in the fort heard of (the intended departure), they
sent after us Khwaja Muhammad, the tailor,[1] an old servant
(*bayri*) of my father and the foster-father of one of his daughters.

Fol. 16b. He dispelled our fears and, turning back from near the Praying
Place, took me with him into the citadel (*ark*) where I dismounted. Khwaja Maulana-i-qazi and the begs came to my
presence there and after bringing their counsels to a head,[2]
busied themselves in making good the towers and ramparts of
the fort.[3] A few days later, Hasan, son of Yaq'ub, and Qasim
Quchin, arrived, together with other begs who had been sent to
reconnoitre in Marghinan and those parts.[4] They also, after
waiting on me, set themselves with one heart and mind and
with zeal and energy, to hold the fort.

Meantime Sl. Ahmad Mirza took Aura-tipa, Khujand and
Marghinan, came on to Qaba,[5] 4 *yighach* from Andijan and
there made halt. At this crisis, Darwesh Gau, one of the
Andijan notables, was put to death on account of his improper
proposals; his punishment crushed the rest.

Khwaja Qazi and Auzun (Long) Hasan,[6] (brother) of Khwaja
Husain, were then sent to Sl. Ahmad Mirza to say in effect
that, as he himself would place one of his servants in the
country and as I was myself both a servant and (as) a son, he
would attain his end most readily and easily if he entrusted the
service to me. He was a mild, weak man, of few words who,
without his begs, decided no opinion or compact (*aun*), action

---

descendant of Satuq-bughra Khan (b. 384 AH.-994 AD.) so that in Khwaja Qazi
were united two dynasties, (*khanwadalar*), one priestly, perhaps also regal, the other
of bye-gone ruling Khans. *Cf.* D'Herbélot p. 433; *Yarkand Mission*, Bellew p. 121;
Tazkirat-i Sultan Satuq-bughra Khan Ghazi Padshah and *Tarikh-i-nasiri* (Raverty *s.n.*).
1 *darzi*; H.S. *khaiyat*.
2 *bir yirga* (*quyub*), lit. to one place.
3 *i.e.* reconstructed the earthen defences. *Cf.* Von Schwarz *s.n.* loess.
4 They had been sent, presumably, before 'Umar Shaikh's death, to observe
Sl. Ahmad M.'s advance. *Cf.* f. 6.
5 The time-table of the Andijan Railway has a station, Kouwa (Qaba).
6 Babur, always I think, calls this man Long Hasan; Khwand-amir styles
him Khwaja Hasan; he seems to be the brother of one of 'Umar Shaikh's
fathers-in-law, Khwaja Husain.

or move; they paid no attention to our proposal, gave it a harsh answer and moved forward.

But the Almighty God, who, of His perfect power and without mortal aid, has ever brought my affairs to their right issue, made such things happen here that they became disgusted at having advanced (*i.e.* from Qaba), repented indeed that they had ever set out on this expedition and turned back with nothing done.

One of those things was this: Qaba has a stagnant, morass-like Water,[1] passable only by the bridge. As they were many, there was crowding on the bridge and numbers of horses and Fol. 17. camels were pushed off to perish in the water. This disaster recalling the one they had had three or four years earlier when they were badly beaten at the passage of the Chir, they gave way to fear. Another thing was that such a murrain broke out amongst their horses that, massed together, they began to die off in bands.[2] Another was that they found in our soldiers and peasants a resolution and single-mindedness such as would not let them flinch from making offering of their lives[3] so long as there was breath and power in their bodies. Need being therefore, when one *yighach* from Andijan, they sent Darwesh Muhammad Tarkhan[4] to us; Hasan of Yaq'ub went out from those in the fort; the two had an interview near the Praying Place and a sort of peace was made. This done, Sl. Ahmad Mirza's force retired.

Meantime Sl. Mahmud Khan had come along the north of the Khujand Water and laid siege to Akhsi.[5] In Akhsi was

1 *batqaq.* This word is underlined in the Elph. MS. by *dil-dil* and in the Hai. MS. by *jam-jama.* It is translated in the W.-i-B. by *ab pur hila,* water full of deceit; it is our Slough of Despond. It may be remarked that neither Zenker nor Steingass gives to *dil-dil* or *jam-jama* the meaning of morass; the *Akbar-nama* does so. (H.B. ii, 112.)

2 *tawila tawila atlar yighilib aula kirishti.* I understand the word *yighilib* to convey that the massing led to the spread of the murrain.

3 *jan taratmaqlar i.e.* as a gift to their over-lord.

4 Perhaps, Babur's maternal great-uncle. It would suit the privileges bestowed on Tarkhans if their title meant *Khan of the Gifts* (Turki *tar,* gift). In the *Baburnama,* it excludes all others. Most of Ahmad's begs were Tarkhans, Arghuns and Chingiz Khanids, some of them ancestors of later rulers in Tatta and Sind. Concerning the Tarkhans *see* T.R. p. 55 and note; A.N. (H.B. *s.n.*) Elliot and Dowson's *History of India,* 498.

5 *Cf.* f. 6.

Jahangir Mirza (aet. 9) and of begs, 'Ali-darwesh Beg, Mirza
Quli *Kukuldash*, Muh. Baqir Beg and Shaikh 'Abdu'l-lah, Lord
of the Gate. Wais *Laghari* and Mir Ghiyas Taghai had been
there too, but being afraid of the (Akhsi) begs had gone off to
Kasan, Wais *Laghari*'s district, where, he being Nasir Mirza's
guardian, the Mirza was.[1] They went over to Sl. Mahmud

Fol. 17b. Khan when he got near Akhsi; Mir Ghiyas entered his service;
Wais *Laghari* took Nasir Mirza to Sl. Ahmad Mirza, who
entrusted him to Muh. Mazid Tarkhan's charge. The Khan,
though he fought several times near Akhsi, could not effect
anything because the Akhsi begs and braves made such splendid
offering of their lives. Falling sick, being tired of fighting too,
he returned to his own country (*i.e.* Tashkint).

For some years, Aba-bikr *Kashghari Dughlat*,[2] bowing the
head to none, had been supreme in Kashgar and Khutan. He
now, moved like the rest by desire for my country, came to the
neighbourhood of Auzkint, built a fort and began to lay the
land waste. Khwaja Qazi and several begs were appointed to
drive him out. When they came near, he saw himself no match
for such a force, made the Khwaja his mediator and, by a
hundred wiles and tricks, got himself safely free.

Throughout these great events,'Umar Shaikh Mirza's former
begs and braves had held resolutely together and made daring
offer of their lives. The Mirza's mother, Shah Sultan Begim,[3]
and Jahangir Mirza and the *haram* household and the begs came
from Akhsi to Andijan; the customary mourning was fulfilled
and food and victuals spread for the poor and destitute.[4]

Fol. 18.   In the leisure from these important matters, attention was
given to the administration of the country and the ordering of
the army. The Andijan Government and control of my Gate
were settled (*mukarrar*) for Hasan (son) of Yaq'ub; Aush was
decided on (*qarar*) for Qasim *Quchin*; Akhsi and Marghinan
assigned (*ta'in*) to Auzun Hasan and 'Ali-dost Taghai. For
the rest of 'Umar Shaikh Mirza's begs and braves, to each

---

1 *beg ataka*, lit. beg for father.

2 T.R. *s.n.* Aba-bikr.

3 *Cf.* f. 6b and note.

4 *faqra u masakin*, *i.e.* those who have food for one day and those who
have none in hand. (Steingass.)

according to his circumstances, were settled and assigned district (*wilayat*) or land (*yir*) or office (*mauja*) or charge (*jirga*) or stipend (*wajh*).

When Sl. Ahmad Mirza had gone two or three stages on his return-march, his health changed for the worse and high fever appeared. On his reaching the Aq Su near Aura-tipa, he bade farewell to this transitory world, in the middle of Shawwal of the date 899 (mid July 1494 AD.) being then 44 (lunar) years old.

m. Sl. Ahmad Mirza's birth and descent.

He was born in 855 AH. (1451 AD.) the year in which his father took the throne (*i.e.* Samarkand). He was Sl. Abu-sa'id Mirza's eldest son; his mother was a daughter of Aurdu-bugha Tarkhan (*Arghun*), the elder sister of Darwesh Muhammad Tarkhan, and the most honoured of the Mirza's wives.

n. His appearance and habits.

He was a tall, stout, brown-bearded and red-faced man. He had beard on his chin but none on his cheeks. He had very Fol. 18b. pleasing manners. As was the fashion in those days, he wound his turban in four folds and brought the end forward over his brows.

o. His characteristics and manners.

He was a True Believer, pure in the Faith; five times daily, without fail, he recited the Prayers, not omitting them even on drinking-days. He was a disciple of his Highness Khwaja 'Ubaidu'l-lah (*Ahrari*), his instructor in religion and the strengthener of his Faith. He was very ceremonious, particularly when sitting with the Khwaja. People say he never drew one knee over the other[1] at any entertainment of the Khwaja. On one occasion contrary to his custom, he sat with his feet together. When he had risen, the Khwaja ordered the place he had sat in to be searched; there they found, it may have been, a bone.[2] He had read nothing whatever and was ignorant

1 For fashions of sitting, *see Tawarikh-i-guzida Nasrat-nama* B.M. Or. 3222. Ahmad would appear to have maintained the deferential attitude by kneeling and sitting back upon his heels.
2 *bir sunkak bar ikan dur.* I understand that something defiling must have been there, perhaps a bone.

('ami), and though town-bred, unmannered and homely. Of genius he had no share. He was just and as his Highness the Khwaja was there, accompanying him step by step,[1] most of his affairs found lawful settlement. He was true and faithful to his vow and word; nothing was ever seen to the contrary. He had courage, and though he never happened to get in his own hand to work, gave sign of it, they say, in some of his en-

Fol. 19b. counters. He drew a good bow, generally hitting the duck[2] both with his arrows (auq) and his forked-arrows (tir-giz), and, as a rule, hit the gourd[3] in riding across the lists (maidan). Latterly, when he had grown stout, he used to take quail and pheasant with the goshawks,[4] rarely failing. A sportsman he was, hawking mostly and hawking well; since Aulugh Beg Mirza, such a sporting padshah had not been seen. He was extremely decorous; people say he used to hide his feet even in the privacy of his family and amongst his intimates. Once settled down to drink, he would drink for 20 or 30 days at a stretch; once risen, would not drink again for another 20 or 30 days. He was a good drinker;[5] on non-drinking days he ate without conviviality (basit). Avarice was dominant in his character. He was kindly, a man of few words whose will was in the hands of his begs.

p. His battles.

He fought four battles. The first was with Ni'mat *Arghun*, Shaikh Jamal *Arghun*'s younger brother, at Aqar-tuzi, near Zamin. This he won. The second was with 'Umar Shaikh Mirza at Khwas; this also he won. The third affair was when he encountered Sl. Mahmud Khan on the Chir, near Tashkint

Fol. 19b. (895 AH.-1469 AD.). There was no real fighting, but some Mughul plunderers coming up, by ones and twos, in his rear and laying hands on his baggage, his great army, spite of its numbers,

---

1 *Khwajaning ham ayaghlari arada idi.*

2 *ilbasun,* a kind of mallard (*Abushqa*), here perhaps a popinjay. *Cf.* H.S. ii, 193 for Ahmad's skill as an archer, and Payne-Gallwey's *Cross-bow* p. 225.

3 *qabaq,* an archer's mark. Abu'l-ghazi (Kasan ed. p. 18 l. 5) mentions a hen (*tuquq*) as a mark. *Cf.* Payne-Gallwey *l.c.* p. 231.

4 *qirghicha, astar palumbarius.* (Shaw's Voc. Scully.) *See* Additional Notes, p. 797.

5 Perhaps, not quarrelsome.

broke up without a blow struck, without an effort made, without a coming face to face, and its main body was drowned in the Chir.[1] His fourth affair was with Haidar *Kukuldash* (*Mughul*), near Yar-yilaq; here he won.

q. His country.

Samarkand and Bukhara his father gave him; Tashkint and Sairam he took and held for a time but gave them to his younger brother, 'Umar Shaikh Mirza, after 'Abdu'l-qadus (*Dughlat*) slew Shaikh Jamal (*Arghun*); Khujand and Aura-tipa were also for a time in his possession.

r. His children.

His two sons did not live beyond infancy. He had five daughters, four by Qataq Begim.[2]

Rabi'a-sultan Begim, known as the Dark-eyed Begim, was his eldest. The Mirza himself made her go forth to Sl. Mah-mud Khan;[3] she had one child, a nice little boy, called Baba Khan. The Auzbegs killed him and several others of age as unripe as his when they martyred (his father) The Khan, in Khujand, (914 AH.-1508 AD.). At that time she fell to Jani Beg Sultan (*Auzbeg*).   Fol. 20.

Saliha-sultan (*Saliqa*) Begim was his second daughter; people called her the Fair Begim. Sl. Mahmud Mirza, after her father's death, took her for his eldest son, Sl. Mas'ud Mirza and made the wedding feast (900 AH.). Later on she fell to the Kashghari with Shah Begim and Mihr-nigar Khanim.

'Ayisha-sultan Begim was the third. When I was five and went to Samarkand, they set her aside for me; in the guerilla times[4] she came to Khujand and I took her (905 AH.); her one little daughter, born after the second taking of Samarkand,

---

1 The T.R. (p. 116) attributes the rout to Shaibani's defection. The H.S. (ii, 192) has a varied and confused account. An error in the T.R. trs. making Shaibani plunder the Mughuls, is manifestly clerical.
2 *i.e.* condiment, *ce qu'on ajoute au pain*.
3 *Cf.* f. 6.
4 *qazaqlar*; here, if Babur's, meaning his conflicts with Tambal, but as the Begim may have been some time in Khujand, the *qazaqlar* may be of Samarkand.

went in a few days to God's mercy and she herself left me at the instigation of an older sister.

Sultanim Begim was the fourth daughter; Sl. 'Ali Mirza took her; then Timur Sultan (*Auzbeg*) took her and after him, Mahdi Sultan (*Auzbeg*).

Ma'suma-sultan Begim was the youngest of Sl. Ahmad Mirza's daughters. Her mother, Habiba-sultan Begim, was of the Arghuns, a daughter of Sl. Husain *Arghun*'s brother. I saw her when I went to Khurasan (912 AH.-1506 AD.), liked her, asked for her, had her brought to Kabul and took her (913 AH.-1507 AD.). She had one daughter and there and then, went to God's mercy, through the pains of the birth. Her name was at once given to her child.

s. His ladies and mistresses.

Mihr-nigar Khanim was his first wife, set aside for him by his father, Sl. Abu-sa'id Mirza. She was Yunas Khan's eldest daughter and my mother's full-sister.

Fol. 20b.

Tarkhan Begim of the Tarkhans was another of his wives.

Qataq Begim was another, the foster-sister of the Tarkhan Begim just mentioned. Sl. Ahmad Mirza took her *par amours* ('*ashiqlar bila*): she was loved with passion and was very dominant. She drank wine. During the days of her ascendancy (*tiriklik*), he went to no other of his *haram*; at last he took up a proper position (*aulnurdi*) and freed himself from his reproach.[1]

---

1 All the (Turki) Babur-nama MSS. and those examined of the W.-i-B. by writing *aulturdi* (killed) where I suggest to read *aulnurdi* (*devenir comme il faut*) state that Ahmad killed Qataq. I hesitate to accept this (1) because the only evidence of the murder is one diacritical point, the removal of which lifts Ahmad's reproach from him by his return to the accepted rules of a polygamous household; (2) because no murder of Qataq is chronicled by Khwandamir or other writers; and (3) because it is incredible that a mild, weak man living in a family atmosphere such as Babur, Haidar and Gul-badan reproduce for us, should, while possessing facility for divorce, kill the mother of four out of his five children.

Reprieve must wait however until the word *tiriklik* is considered. This Erskine and de C. have read, with consistency, to mean *life-time*, but if *aulnurdi* be read in place of *aulturdi* (killed), *tiriklik* may be read, especially in conjunction with Babur's '*ashiqliklar*, as meaning *living power* or *ascendancy*. Again, if read as from *tirik*, a small arrow and a consuming pain, *tiriklik* may represent Cupid's darts and wounds. Again it might be taken as from *tiramak*, to hinder, or forbid.

Under these considerations, it is legitimate to reserve judgment on Ahmad.

Khan-zada Begim, of the Tirmiz Khans, was another. He had just taken her when I went, at five years old, to Samarkand; her face was still veiled and, as is the Turki custom, they told me to uncover it.[1]

Latif Begim was another, a daughter's child of Ahmad Haji Beg *Duldai (Barlas)*. After the Mirza's death, Hamza Sl. took her and she had three sons by him. They with other sultans' children, fell into my hands when I took Hisar (917 AH.-1510 AD.) after defeating Hamza Sultan and Timur Sultan. I set all free.

Habiba-sultan Begim was another, a daughter of the brother of Sl. Husain *Arghun*.

t. His amirs.

Jani Beg *Duldai (Barlas)* was a younger brother of Sl. Malik *Kashghari*. Sl. Abu-sa'id Mirza gave him the Government of Samarkand and Sl. Ahmad Mirza gave him the control of his own Gate. He must have had singular habits and Fol. 21. manners;[2] many strange stories are told about him. One is this:—While he was Governor in Samarkand, an envoy came to him from the Auzbegs renowned, as it would seem, for his strength. An Auzbeg, is said to call a strong man a bull (*bukuh*). "Are you a *bukuh*?" said Jani Beg to the envoy, "If you are, come, let's have a friendly wrestle together (*kurashaling*)." Whatever objections the envoy raised, he refused to accept. They wrestled and Jani Beg gave the fall. He was a brave man.

Ahmad Haji (*Duldai Barlas*) was another, a son of Sl. Malik *Kashghari*. Sl. Abu-sa'id Mirza gave him the Government of Hiri (Harat) for a time but sent him when his uncle, Jani Beg

---

1 It is customary amongst Turks for a bride, even amongst her own family, to remain veiled for some time after marriage; a child is then told to pluck off the veil and run away, this tending, it is fancied, to the child's own success in marriage. (Erskine.)

2 Babur's anecdote about Jani Beg well illustrates his caution as a narrator. He appears to tell it as one who knowing the point of a story, leads up to it. He does not affirm that Jani Beg's habits were strange or that the envoy was an athlete but that both things must have been (*ikan dur*) from what he had heard or to suit the point of the anecdote. Nor does he affirm as of his own knowledge that Auzbegs call a strong man (his *zor kishi*) a *bukuh* (bull) but says it is so understood (*dir imish*).

died, to Samarkand with his uncle's appointments. He was
pleasant-natured and brave. Wafa'i was his pen-name and he
put together a diwan in verse not bad. This couplet is his:

> "I am drunk, Inspector, to-day keep your hand off me,
> "Inspect me on the day you catch me sober."

Mir 'Ali-sher Nawa'i when he went from Hiri to Samarkand,
was with Ahmad Haji Beg but he went back to Hiri when
Sl. Husain Mirza (Bai-qara) became supreme (873 AH.-1460 AD.)
and he there received exceeding favour. Ahmad Haji Beg kept
and rode excellent *tipuchaqs*,[1] mostly of his own breeding.
Brave he was but his power to command did not match his
courage; he was careless and what was necessary in his affairs,
his retainers and followers put through. He fell into Sl. 'Ali
Mirza's hands when the Mirza defeated Bai-sunghar Mirza
in Bukhara (901 AH.), and was then put to a dishonourable
death on the charge of the blood of Darwesh Muhammad
Tarkhan.[2]

Fol. 21b.

Darwesh Muhammad Tarkhan (*Arghun*) was another, the
son of Aurdu-bugha Tarkhan and full-brother of the mother
of Sl. Ahmad Mirza and Sl. Mahmud Mirza.[3] Of all begs in
Sl. Ahmad Mirza's presence, he was the greatest and most
honoured. He was an orthodox Believer, kindly and darwesh-
like, and was a constant transcriber of the Qu'ran.[4] He played
chess often and well, thoroughly understood the science of
fowling and flew his birds admirably. He died in the height of
his greatness, with a bad name, during the troubles between
Sl. 'Ali Mirza and Bai-sunghar Mirza.[5]

'Abdu'l-'ali Tarkhan was another, a near relation of Darwesh
Muhammad Tarkhan, possessor also of his younger sister,[6]
that is to say, Baqi Tarkhan's mother. Though both by the
Mughul rule (*tura*) and by his rank, Darwesh Muhammad

1 The points of a *tipuchaq* are variously stated. If the root notion of the name be
movement (*tip*), Erskine's observation, that these horses are taught special paces,
is to the point. To the verb *tipramaq* dictionaries assign the meaning of *movement
with agitation of mind*, an explanation fully illustrated in the B.N. The verb
describes fittingly the dainty, nervous action of some trained horses. Other
meanings assigned to *tupuchaq* are roadster, round-bodied and swift.
2 *Cf.* f. 37b.   3 *Cf.* f. 6b and note.   4 *mashaf kitabat qilur idi.*
5 *Cf.* f. 36 and H.S. ii. 271.   6 *sinkilisi ham munda idi.*

Tarkhan was the superior of 'Abdu'l-'ali Tarkhan, this Pharaoh regarded him not at all. For some years he had the Government of Bukhara. His retainers were reckoned at Fol. 22. 3000 and he kept them well and handsomely. His gifts (*bakhshish*), his visits of enquiry (*purshish*), his public audience (*diwan*), his work-shops (*dast-gah*), his open-table (*shilan*) and his assemblies (*majlis*) were all like a king's. He was a strict disciplinarian, a tyrannical, vicious, self-infatuated person. Shaibani Khan, though not his retainer, was with him for a time; most of the lesser (Shaiban) sultans did themselves take service with him. This same 'Abdu'l-'ali Tarkhan was the cause of Shaibani Khan's rise to such a height and of the downfall of such ancient dynasties.[1]

Sayyid Yusuf, the Grey Wolfer[2] was another; his grandfather will have come from the Mughul horde; his father was favoured by Aulugh Beg Mirza (*Shahrukhi*). His judgment and counsel were excellent; he had courage too. He played well on the guitar (*qubuz*). He was with me when I first went to Kabul; I shewed him great favour and in truth he was worthy of favour. I left him in Kabul the first year the army rode out for Hindustan; at that time he went to God's mercy.[3]

Darwesh Beg was another; he was of the line of Aiku-timur Beg,[4] a favourite of Timur Beg. He was a disciple of his Highness Khwaja 'Ubaidu'l-lah (*Ahrari*), had knowledge of the science of music, played several instruments and was naturally Fol. 22b. disposed to poetry. He was drowned in the Chir at the time of Sl. Ahmad Mirza's discomfiture.

Muhammad Mazid Tarkhan was another, a younger full-brother of Darwesh Muh. Tarkhan. He was Governor in Turkistan for some years till Shaibani Khan took it from him. His judgment and counsel were excellent; he was an unscrupulous and vicious person. The second and third times

1 *khana-wadalar, viz.* the Chaghatai, the Timurid in two Miran-shahi branches, 'Ali's and Babur's and the Bai-qara in Harat.

2 *aughlaqchi i.e.* player at *kuk-bura*. Concerning the game, *see* Shaw's Vocabulary; Schuyler i, 268; Kostenko iii, 82; Von Schwarz *s.n. baiga*.

3 Zu'l-hijja 910 AH.-May 1505 AD. *Cf.* f. 154. This statement helps to define what Babur reckoned his expeditions into Hindustan. For Sayyid Murad *Aughlaqchi*, Yusuf's father, *see* Additional Notes, p. 797.

4 Aiku (Ayagu)-timur *Tarkhan Arghun* d. *circa* 793 AH.-1391 AD. He was a friend of Timur. *See* Z.N. i, 525 etc.

I took Samarkand, he came to my presence and each time I shewed him very great favour. He died in the fight at Kul-i-malik (918 AH.-1512 AD.).

Baqi Tarkhan was another, the son of 'Abdu'l-'ali Tarkhan and Sl. Ahmad Mirza's aunt. When his father died, they gave him Bukhara. He grew in greatness under Sl. 'Ali Mirza, his retainers numbering 5 or 6000. He was neither obedient nor very submissive to Sl. 'Ali Mirza. He fought Shaibani Khan at Dabusi (905 AH.) and was crushed; by the help of this defeat, Shaibani Khan went and took Bukhara. He was very fond of hawking; they say he kept 700 birds. His manners and habits were not such as may be told;[1] he grew up with a Mirza's state and splendour. Because his father had shewn favour to Shaibani Khan, he went to the Khan's presence, but that inhuman ingrate made him no sort of return in favour and kindness. He left the world at Akhsi, in misery and wretchedness.

Sl. Husain *Arghun* was another. He was known as Qara-kuli because he had held the Qara-kul government for a time. His judgment and counsel were excellent; he was long in my presence also.

Quli Muhammad *Bughda*[2] was another, a *quchin*; he must have been a brave man.

'Abdu'l-karim *Ishrit*[3] was another; he was an Auighur, Sl. Ahmad Mirza's Lord of the Gate, a brave and generous man.

(*u. Historical narrative resumed.*)

After Sl. Ahmad Mirza's death, his begs in agreement, sent a courier by the mountain-road to invite Sl. Mahmud Mirza.[4]

Malik-i-Muhammad Mirza, the son of Minuchihr Mirza,

Fol. 23.

---

1 *andaq ikhlaq u atawari yuq idi kim disa bulghai.* The *Shah-nama* cap. xviii, describes him as a spoiled child and man of pleasure, caring only for eating, drinking and hunting. The *Shaibani-nama* narrates his various affairs.

2 *i.e., cutlass,* a parallel sobriquet to *qilich*, sword. If it be correct to translate by "cutlass," the nickname may have prompted Babur's brief following comment, *mardana ikan dur, i.e.* Quli Muh. must have been brave because known as the Cutlass. A common variant in MSS. from *Bughda* is Baghdad; Baghdad was first written in the Hai. MS. but is corrected by the scribe to *bughda*.

3 So pointed in the Hai. MS. I surmise it a clan-name.

4 *i.e.* to offer him the succession. The mountain road taken from Aura-tipa would be by Ab-burdan, Sara-taq and the Kam Rud defile.

Sl. Abu-sa'id Mirza's eldest brother, aspired for his own part to rule. Having drawn a few adventurers and desperadoes to himself, they dribbled away[1] from (Sl. Ahmad Mirza's) camp and went to Samarkand. He was not able to effect anything, but he brought about his own death and that of several innocent persons of the ruling House.

At once on hearing of his brother's death, Sl. Mahmud Mirza went off to Samarkand and there seated himself on the throne, without difficulty. Some of his doings soon disgusted and alienated high and low, soldier and peasant. The first of these was that he sent the above-named Malik-i-Muhammad to the Fol. 23b. Kuk-sarai,[2] although he was his father's brother's son and his own son-in-law.[3] With him he sent others, four Mirzas in all. Two of these he set aside; Malik-i-Muhammad and one other he martyred. Some of the four were not even of ruling rank and had not the smallest aspiration to rule; though Malik-i-Muhammad Mirza was a little in fault, in the rest there was no blame whatever. A second thing was that though his methods and regulations were excellent, and though he was expert in revenue matters and in the art of administration, his nature inclined to tyranny and vice. Directly he reached Samarkand, he began to make new regulations and arrangements and to rate and tax on a new basis. Moreover the dependants of his (late) Highness Khwaja 'Ubaid'l-lah, under whose protection formerly many poor and destitute persons had lived free from the burden of dues and imposts, were now themselves treated with harshness and oppression. On what ground should hardship have touched them? Nevertheless oppressive exactions were made from them, indeed from the Khwaja's very children. Yet another thing was that just as he was vicious and tyrannical, so were his begs, small and great, and his retainers and followers. The Hisaris and in particular the followers of Khusrau Shah

---

1 *irildi.* The departure can hardly have been open because Ahmad's begs favoured Mahmud; Malik-i-Muhammad's party would be likely to slip away in small companies.

2 This well-known Green, Grey or Blue palace or halting-place was within the citadel of Samarkand. *Cf.* f. 37. It served as a prison from which return was not expected.

3 *Cf.* f. 27. He married a full-sister of Bai-sunghar.

engaged themselves unceasingly with wine and fornication.
Once one of them enticed and took away a certain man's wife.

Fol. 24. When her husband went to Khusrau Shah and asked for justice,
he received for answer: "She has been with you for several
years; let her be a few days with him." Another thing was
that the young sons of the townsmen and shopkeepers, nay!
even of Turks and soldiers could not go out from their houses
from fear of being taken for catamites. The Samarakandis,
having passed 20 or 25 years under Sl. Ahmad Mirza in ease
and tranquillity, most matters carried through lawfully and
with justice by his Highness the Khwaja, were wounded and
troubled in heart and soul, by this oppression and this vice.
Low and high, the poor, the destitute, all opened the mouth to
curse, all lifted the hand for redress.

> "Beware the steaming up of inward wounds,
> For an inward wound at the last makes head;
> Avoid while thou canst, distress to one heart,
> For a single sigh will convulse a world."[1]

By reason of his infamous violence and vice Sl. Mahmud
Mirza did not rule in Samarkand more than five or six
months.

1 *Gulistan* Part I. Story 27. For "steaming up," *see* Tennyson's Lotus-eaters
Choric song, canto 8 (H.B.).

THIS year Sl. Mahmud Mirza sent an envoy, named 'Abdu'l-qadus Beg,[2] to bring me a gift from the wedding he had made with splendid festivity for his eldest son, Mas'ud Mirza with (Saliha-sultan), the Fair Begim, the second daughter of his elder brother, Sl. Ahmad Mirza. They had sent gold and silver almonds and pistachios.

There must have been relationship between this envoy and Hasan-i-yaq'ub, and on its account he will have been the man sent to make Hasan-i-yaq'ub, by fair promises, look towards Fol. 24b. Sl. Mahmud Mirza. Hasan-i-yaq'ub returned him a smooth answer, made indeed as though won over to his side, and gave him leave to go. Five or six months later, his manners changed entirely; he began to behave ill to those about me and to others, and he carried matters so far that he would have dismissed me in order to put Jahangir Mirza in my place. Moreover his conversation with the whole body of begs and soldiers was not what should be; every-one came to know what was in his mind. Khwaja-i-Qazi and (Sayyid) Qasim *Quchin* and 'Ali-dost Taghai and Auzun Hasan met other well-wishers of mine in the presence of my grandmother, Aisan-daulat Begim and decided to give quietus to Hasan-i-yaq'ub's disloyalty by his deposition.

Few amongst women will have been my grandmother's equals for judgment and counsel; she was very wise and far-sighted and most affairs of mine were carried through under her advice. She and my mother were (living) in the Gate-house of the outer fort;[3] Hasan-i-yaq'ub was in the citadel.

1 Elph. MS. f. 16b; First W.-i-B. I.O. 215 f. 19; Second W.-i-B. I.O. 217 f. 15b; Memoirs p. 27.
2 He was a *Dughlat*, uncle by marriage of Haidar Mirza and now holding Khost for Mahmud. See T.R. s.n. for his claim on Aisan-daulat's gratitude.
3 *tash qurghan da chiqar da.* Here (as *e.g.* f. 110b l. 9) the Second W.-i-B. translates *tash* as though it meant *stone* instead of outer. *Cf.* f. 47 for an

When I went to the citadel, in pursuance of our decision, he had ridden out, presumably for hawking, and as soon as he had

Fol. 25. our news, went off from where he was towards Samarkand. The begs and others in sympathy with him,[1] were arrested; one was Muhammad Baqir Beg; Sl. Mahmud *Duldai*, Sl. Muhammad *Duldai's* father, was another; there were several more; to some leave was given to go for Samarkand. The Andijan Government and control of my Gate were settled on Qasim *Quchin*.

A few days after Hasan-i-yaq'ub reached Kand-i-badam on the Samarkand road, he went to near the Khuqan sub-division (*aurchin*) with ill-intent on Akhsi. Hearing of it, we sent several begs and braves to oppose him; they, as they went, detached a scouting party ahead; he, hearing this, moved against the detachment, surrounded it in its night-quarters[2] and poured flights of arrows (*shiba*) in on it. In the darkness of the night an arrow (*auq*), shot by one of his own men, hit him just (*auq*) in the vent (*qachar*) and before he could take vent (*qachar*),[3] he became the captive of his own act.

> "If you have done ill, keep not an easy mind,
> For retribution is Nature's law."[4]

This year I began to abstain from all doubtful food, my obedience extended even to the knife, the spoon and the table-cloth;[5] also the after-midnight Prayer (*tahajjud*) was less

Fol. 25b. neglected.

---

adjectival use of *tash*, stone, with the preposition (*tash*) *din*. The places contrasted here are the citadel (*ark*) and the walled-town (*qurghan*). The *chiqar* (exit) is the fortified Gate-house of the mud circumvallation. *Cf.* f. 46 for another example of *chiqar*.

1 Elph. Hai. Kehr's MSS., *aning bila bar kishi bar beglarni tuturuldi*. This idiom recurs on f. 76b l. 8. A palimpsest entry in the Elph. MS. produces the statement that when Hasan fled, his begs returned to Andijan.

2 Hai. MS. *awi munkuzi*, underlined by *sagh-i-gau*, cows' thatched house. [*T. munkuz*, lit. horn, means also cattle.] Elph. MS., *awi munkush*, under-lined by *dar ja'i khwab alfakhta*, sleeping place. [T. *munkush*, retired.]

3 The first *qachar* of this pun has been explained as *gurez-gah, sharm-gah*, hinder parts, *fuite* and *vertèbre inférieur*. The H.S. (ii, 273 l. 3 fr. ft.) says the wound was in a vital (*maqattal*) part.

4 From Nizami's *Khusrau u Shirin*, Lahore lith. ed. p. 137 l. 8. It is quoted also in the A.N. Bib. Ind. ed. ii, 207 (H.B. ii, 321). (H.B.).

5 *See* Hughes *Dictionary of Islam s.nn.* Eating and Food.

(a. Death of Sl. Mahmud Mirza.)

In the month of the latter Rabi' (January 1495 AD.), Sl. Mahmud Mirza was confronted by violent illness and in six days, passed from the world. He was 43 (lunar) years old.

b. His birth and lineage.

He was born in 857 AH. (1453 AD.), was Sl. Abu-sa'id Mirza's third son and the full-brother of Sl. Ahmad Mirza.[1]

c. His appearance and characteristics.

He was a short, stout, sparse-bearded and somewhat ill-shaped person. His manners and his qualities were good, he never neglected the Prayers, his rules and methods of business excellent; he was well-versed in accounts, not a *dinar* or a *dirham*[2] of revenue was spent without his knowledge. The pay of his servants was never disallowed. His assemblies, his gifts, his open table, were all good. Everything of his was orderly and well-arranged;[3] no soldier or peasant could deviate in the slightest from any plan of his. Formerly he must have been hard set (*qatirar*) on hawking but latterly he very frequently hunted driven game.[4] He carried violence and vice to frantic excess, was a constant wine-bibber and kept many catamites. If anywhere in his territory, there was a handsome boy, he used, by whatever means, to have him brought for a catamite; of his begs' sons and of his sons' begs' sons he made catamites; and laid command for this service on his very foster   Fol. 26. brothers and on their own brothers. So common in his day was that vile practice, that no person was without his catamite; to keep one was thought a merit, not to keep one, a defect. Through his infamous violence and vice, his sons died in the day of their strength (*tamam juwan*).

1 *Cf.* f. 6b and note. If 'Umar Shaikh were Mahmud's full-brother, his name might well appear here.
2 *i.e.* "Not a farthing, not a half-penny."
3 Here the Mems. enters a statement, not found in the Turki text, that Mahmud's dress was elegant and fashionable.
4 *n:h:l:m.* My husband has cleared up a mistake (Mems. p. 28 and *Méms.* i, 54) of supposing this to be the name of an animal. It is explained in the A.N. (i, 255. H.B. i, 496) as a Badakhshi equivalent of *tasqawal*; *tasqawal* var. *tashqawal*, is explained by the *Farhang-i-azfari*, a Turki-Persian Dict. seen in the Mulla Firoz Library of Bombay, to mean *rah band kunanda*, the stopping of the road. *Cf.* J.R.A.S. 1900 p. 137.

He had a taste for poetry and put a *diwan*[1] together but his verse is flat and insipid,—not to compose is better than to compose verse such as his. He was not firm in the Faith and held his Highness Khwaja 'Ubaidu'l-lah (*Ahrari*) in slight esteem. He had no heart (*yuruk*) and was somewhat scant in modesty,—several of his impudent buffoons used to do their filthy and abominable acts in his full Court, in all men's sight. He spoke badly, there was no understanding him at first.

d. His battles.

He fought two battles, both with Sl. Husain Mirza (*Baiqara*). The first was in Astarabad; here he was defeated. The second was at Chikman (Sarai),[2] near Andikhud; here also he was defeated. He went twice to Kafiristan, on the south of Badakhshan, and made Holy War; for this reason they wrote him Sl. Mahmud *Ghazi* in the headings of his public papers.

e. His countries.

Sl. Abu-sa'id Mirza gave him Astarabad.[3] After the 'Iraq disaster (*i.e.*, his father's death,) he went into Khurasan. At that time, Qambar-'ali Beg, the governor of Hisar, by Sl. Abu-sa'id Mirza's orders, had mobilized the Hindustan[4] army and was following him into 'Iraq; he joined Sl. Mahmud Mirza in Khurasan but the Khurasanis, hearing of Sl. Husain Mirza's approach, rose suddenly and drove them out of the country. On this Sl. Mahmud Mirza went to his elder brother, Sl. Ahmad Mirza in Samarkand. A few months later Sayyid Badr and Khusrau Shah and some braves under Ahmad

---

1 *i.e.* "a collection of poems in the alphabetical order of the various end rhymes." (Steingass.)

2 At this battle Daulat-shah was present. *Cf.* Browne's D.S. for Astarabad p. 523 and for Andikhud p. 532. For this and all other references to D.S. and H.S. I am indebted to my husband.

3 The following dates will help out Babur's brief narrative. Mahmud *æt.* 7, was given Astarabad in 864 AH. (1459-60 AD.); it was lost to Husain at Jauz-wilayat and Mahmud went into Khurasan in 865 AH.; he was restored by his father in 866 AH.; on his father's death (873 AH.-1469 AD.) he fled to Harat, thence to Samarkand and from there was taken to Hisar *æt.* 16. *Cf.* D'Herbélot *s.n.* Abu-sa'ad; H.S. i, 209; Browne's D.S. p. 522.

4 Presumably the "Hindustan the Less" of Clavijo (Markham p. 3 and p. 113), approx. Qambar-'ali's districts. Clavijo includes Tirmiz under the name.

Mushtaq[1] took him and fled to Qambar-'ali in Hisar. From that time forth, Sl. Mahmud Mirza possessed the countries lying south of Quhqa (Quhlugha) and the Kohtin Range as far as the Hindu-kush Mountains, such as Tirmiz, Chaghanian, Hisar, Khutlan, Qunduz and Badakhshan. He also held Sl. Ahmad Mirza's lands, after his brother's death.

f. His children.

He had five sons and eleven daughters.

Sl. Mas'ud Mirza was his eldest son; his mother was Khan- Fol. 27. zada Begim, a daughter of the Great Mir of Tirmiz. Bai-sunghar Mirza was another; his mother was Pasha Begim. Sl. 'Ali Mirza was another; his mother was an Auzbeg, a concubine called Zuhra Begi Agha. Sl. Husain Mirza was another; his mother was Khan-zada Begim, a grand-daughter of the Great Mir of Tirmiz; he went to God's mercy in his father's life-time, at the age of 13. Sl. Wais Mirza (Mirza Khan) was another; his mother, Sultan-nigar Khanim was a daughter of Yunas Khan and was a younger (half-) sister of my mother. The affairs of these four Mirzas will be written of in this history under the years of their occurrence.

Of Sl. Mahmud Mirza's daughters, three were by the same mother as Bai-sunghar Mirza. One of these, Bai-sunghar Mirza's senior, Sl. Mahmud Mirza made to go out to Malik-i-muhammad Mirza, the son of his paternal uncle, Minuchihr Mirza.[2]

* * *

Five other daughters were by Khan-zada Begim, the grand-daughter of the Great Mir of Tirmiz. The oldest of these,

---

1 Perhaps a Sufi term,—longing for the absent friend. For particulars about this man *see* H.S. ii, 235 and Browne's D.S. p. 533.

2 Here in the Hai. MS. is one of several blank spaces, waiting for information presumably not known to Babur when writing. The space will have been in the archetype of the Hai. MS. and it makes for the opinion that the Hai. MS. is a direct copy of Babur's own. This space is not left in the Elph. MS. but that MS. is known from its scribe's note (f. 198) down to f. 198 (Hai. MS. f. 243*b*) to have been copied from "other writings" and only subsequent to its f. 198 from Babur's own. *Cf.* JRAS 1906 p. 88 and 1907 p. 143.

(Khan-zada Begim)[1] was given, after her father's death, to
Fol. 27*b*. Aba-bikr (*Dughlat*) *Kashghari*. The second was Bega Begim. When Sl. Husain Mirza besieged Hisar (901 AH.), he took her for Haidar Mirza, his son by Payanda Begim, Sl. Abu-sa'id Mirza's daughter, and having done so, rose from before the place.[2] The third daughter was Aq (Fair) Begim; the fourth[3]—, was betrothed to Jahangir Mirza (*aet.* 5, *circa* 895 AH.) at the time his father, 'Umar Shaikh Mirza sent him to help Sl. Mahmud Mirza with the Andijan army, against Sl. Husain Mirza, then attacking Qunduz.[4] In 910 AH. (1504 AD.) when Baqi *Chaghaniani*[5] waited on me on the bank of the Amu (Oxus), these (last-named two) Begims were with their mothers in Tirmiz and joined me then with Baqi's family. When we reached Kahmard, Jahangir Mirza took ——— Begim; one little daughter was born; she now[6] is in the Badakhshan country with her grandmother, Khan-zada Begim. The fifth daughter was Zainab-sultan Begim; under my mother's insistence, I took her at the time of the capture of Kabul (910 AH.–Oct. 1504 AD.). She did not become very congenial; two or three years later, she left the world, through small-pox. Another daughter was Makhdum-sultan Begim, Sl. 'Ali Mirza's full-sister; she is now in the Badakhshan country. Two others of his daughters, Rajab-sultan and Muhibb-sultan, were by mistresses (*ghunchachi*).

g. His ladies (*khwatinlar*) *and concubines* (*sarari*).

His chief wife, Khan-zada Begim, was a daughter of the
Fol. 28. Great Mir of Tirmiz; he had great affection for her and must have mourned her bitterly; she was the mother of Sl. Mas'ud Mirza. Later on, he took her brother's daughter, also called Khan-zada Begim, a grand-daughter of the Great Mir of Tirmiz.

1 The T.R. (p. 330) supplies this name.

2 *Cf.* f. 35*b*. This was a betrothal only, the marriage being made in 903 AH. *Cf.* H.S. ii, 260 and Gul-badan's H.N. f. 24*b*.

3 Kehr's MS. supplies Ai (Moon) as her name but it has no authority. The Elph. MS. has what may be *la nam*, no name, on its margin and over *turutunchi* (4th) its usual sign of what is problematical.

4 *See* H.S. ii, 250. Here Pir-i-Muhammad *Ailchi-bugha* was drowned. *Cf.* f. 29.

5 Chaghanian is marked in Erskine's (Mems.) map as somewhere about the head of (Fr. map 1904) the Ilyak Water, a tributary of the Kafir-nighan.

6 *i.e.* when Babur was writing in Hindustan.

She became the mother of five of his daughters and one of his sons. Pasha Begim was another wife, a daughter of 'Ali-shukr Beg, a Turkman Beg of the White Sheep Baharlu Aimaq.[1] She had been the wife of Muhammadi, son of Jahan-shah (*Barani*) of the Black Sheep Turkmans. After Auzun (Long) Hasan Beg of the White Sheep had taken Azar-baijan and 'Iraq from the sons of this Jahan-shah Mirza (872 AH.-1467 AD.), 'Ali-shukr Beg's sons went with four or five thousand heads-of-houses of the Black Sheep Turkmans to serve Sl. Abu-sa'id Mirza and after the Mirza's defeat (873 AH. by Auzun Hasan), came down to these countries and took service with Sl. Mahmud Mirza. This happened after Sl. Mahmud Mirza came to Hisar from Samarkand, and then it was he took Pasha Begim. She became the mother of one of his sons and three of his daughters. Sultan-nigar Khanim was another of his ladies; her descent has been mentioned already in the account of the (Chaghatai) Khans.

Fol. 28*b*.

He had many concubines and mistresses. His most honoured concubine (*mu'atabar ghuma*) was Zuhra Begi Agha; she was taken in his father's life-time and became the mother of one son and one daughter. He had many mistresses and, as has been said, two of his daughters were by two of them.

h. His amirs.

Khusrau Shah was of the Turkistani Qipchaqs. He had been in the intimate service of the Tarkhan begs, indeed had been a catamite. Later on he became a retainer of Mazid Beg (Tarkhan) *Arghun* who favoured him in all things. He was favoured by Sl. Mahmud Mirza on account of services done by him when, after the 'Iraq disaster, he joined the Mirza on his way to Khurasan. He waxed very great in his latter days; his retainers, under Sl. Mahmud Mirza, were a clear five or six thousand. Not only Badakhshan but the whole country from the Amu to the Hindu-kush Mountains depended on him and he devoured its whole revenue (*darobast yir idi*). His open table was good, so too his open hand; though he was a rough getter,[2]

---

1 For his family *see* f. 55*b* note to Yar-'ali *Balal*. For 'Aimaq', *see* Additional Notes, p. 797.

2 *ba wujud turkluk muhkam paida kunanda idi.*

what he got, he spent liberally. He waxed exceeding great after Sl. Mahmud Mirza's death, in whose sons' time his retainers approached 20,000. Although he prayed and abstained from forbidden aliments, yet was he black-souled and vicious, dunder-headed and senseless, disloyal and a traitor to his salt. For the sake of this fleeting, five-days world,[1] he blinded one of his benefactor's sons and murdered another. A sinner before God, reprobate to His creatures, he has earned curse and execration till the very verge of Resurrection. For this world's sake he did his evil deeds and yet, with lands so broad and with such hosts of armed retainers, he had not pluck to stand up to a hen. An account of him will come into this history.

Fol. 29.

Pir-i-Muhammad *Ailchi-bugha*[2] *Quchin* was another. In Hazaraspi's fight[3] he got in on challenge with his fists in Sl. Abu-sa'id Mirza's presence at the Gate of Balkh. He was a brave man, continuously serving the Mirza (Mahmud) and guiding him by his counsel. Out of rivalry to Khusrau Shah, he made a night-attack when the Mirza was besieging Qunduz, on Sl. Husain Mirza, with few men, without arming[4] and without plan; he could do nothing; what was there he could do against such and so large a force? He was pursued, threw himself into the river and was drowned.

Ayub (*Begchik Mughul*)[5] was another. He had served in Sl. Abu-sa'id Mirza's Khurasan Cadet Corps, a brave man, Baisunghar Mirza's guardian. He was choice in dress and food;

1 Roebuck's *Oriental Proverbs* (p. 232) explains the *five* of this phrase where *seven* might be expected, by saying that of this Seven days' world (qy. days of Creation) one is for birth, another for death, and that thus five only are left for man's brief life.

2 The cognomen *Ailchi-bugha*, taken with the bearer's recorded strength of fist, may mean Strong man of Ailchi (the capital of Khutan). One of Timur's commanders bore the name. *Cf.* f. 21 for *bughu* as *athlete*.

3 Hazaraspi seems to be Mir Pir Darwesh Hazaraspi. With his brother, Mir 'Ali, he had charge of Balkh. *See Rauzatu's-safa* B.M. Add. 23506, f. 242*b*; Browne's D.S. p. 432. It may be right to understand a hand-to-hand fight between Hazaraspi and Ailchi-bugha. The affair was in 857 AH. (1453 AD.).

4 *yaraq siz*, perhaps trusting to fisticuffs, perhaps without mail. Babur's summary has confused the facts. Muh. Ailchi-bugha was sent by Sl. Mahmud Mirza from Hisar with 1000 men and did not issue out of Qunduz. (H.S. ii, 251.) His death occurred not before 895 AH.

5 *See* T.R. *s.nn.* Mir Ayub and Ayub.

a jester and talkative, nicknamed Impudence, perhaps because the Mirza called him so. Fol. 29b.

Wali was another, the younger, full-brother of Khusrau Shah. He kept his retainers well. He it was brought about the blinding of Sl. Mas'ud Mirza and the murder of Bai-sunghar Mirza. He had an ill-word for every-one and was an evil-tongued, foul-mouthed, self-pleasing and dull-witted mannikin. He approved of no-one but himself. When I went from the Qunduz country to near Dushi (910 AH.-1503 AD.), separated Khusrau Shah from his following and dismissed him, this person (i.e., Wali) had come to Andar-ab and Sir-ab, also in fear of the Auzbegs. The Aimaqs of those parts beat and robbed him[1] then, having let me know, came on to Kabul. Wali went to Shaibani Khan who had his head struck off in the town of Samarkand.

Shaikh 'Abdu'l-lah *Barlas*[2] was another; he had to wife one of the daughters of Shah Sultan Muhammad (*Badakhshi*) i.e., the maternal aunt of Aba-bikr Mirza (*Miran-shahi*) and of Sl. Mahmud Khan. He wore his tunic narrow and *pur shaqq*;[3] he was a kindly well-bred man.

Mahmud *Barlas* of the Barlases of Nundak (Hisar) was another. He had been a beg also of Sl. Abu-sa'id Mirza and had surrendered Karman to him when the Mirza took the 'Iraq countries. When Aba-bikr Mirza (*Miran-shahi*) came Fol. 30. against Hisar with Mazid Beg Tarkhan and the Black Sheep Turkmans, and Sl. Mahmud Mirza went off to his elder brother, Sl. Ahmad Mirza in Samarkand, Mahmud *Barlas* did not surrender Hisar but held out manfully.[4] He was a poet and put a *diwan* together.

(*i. Historical narrative resumed*).

When Sl. Mahmud Mirza died, Khusrau Shah kept the event concealed and laid a long hand on the treasure. But

---

1 This passage is made more clear by f. 120b and f. 125b.
2 He is mentioned in 'Ali-sher *Nawa'i's Majalis-i-nafa'is*; *see* B.M. Add. 7875, f. 278 and Rieu's Turkish Catalogue.
3 ? full of splits or full handsome.
4 This may have occurred after Abu-sa'id Mirza's death whose son Aba-bikr was. *Cf.* f. 28. If so, over-brevity has obscured the statement.

how could such news be hidden? It spread through the town at once. That was a festive day for the Samarkand families; soldier and peasant, they uprose in tumult against Khusrau Shah. Ahmad Haji Beg and the Tarkhani begs put the rising down and turned Khusrau Shah out of the town with an escort for Hisar.

As Sl. Mahmud Mirza himself after giving Hisar to Sl. Mas'ud Mirza and Bukhara to Bai-sunghar Mirza, had dismissed both to their governments, neither was present when he died. The Hisar and Samarkand begs, after turning Khusrau Shah out, agreed to send for Bai-sunghar Mirza from Bukhara, brought him to Samarkand and seated him on the throne. When he thus became supreme (*padshah*), he was 18 (lunar) years old.

Fol. 30*b*. At this crisis, Sl. Mahmud Khan (*Chaghatai*), acting on the word of Junaid *Barlas* and of some of the notables of Samarkand, led his army out to near Kan-bai with desire to take that town. Bai-sunghar Mirza, on his side, marched out in force. They fought near Kan-bai. Haidar *Kukuldash*, the main pillar of the Mughul army, led the Mughul van. He and all his men dismounted and were pouring in flights of arrows (*shiba*) when a large body of the mailed braves of Hisar and Samarkand made an impetuous charge and straightway laid them under their horses' feet. Their leader taken, the Mughul army was put to rout without more fighting. Masses (*qalin*) of Mughuls were wiped out; so many were beheaded in Bai-sunghar Mirza's presence that his tent was three times shifted because of the number of the dead.

At this same crisis, Ibrahim *Saru* entered the fort of Asfara, there read Bai-sunghar Mirza's name in the *Khutba* and took up a position of hostility to me.

> (*Author's note.*) Ibrahim *Saru* is of the Mingligh people;[1] he had served my father in various ways from his childhood and had attained the rank of Beg, but later on had been dismissed for some fault.

Fol. 31. The army rode out to crush this rebellion in the month of Sha'ban (May) and by the end of it, had dismounted round

---

1 *mingligh aildin dur*, perhaps of those whose hereditary Command was a Thousand, the head of a Ming (Pers. Hazara), *i.e.* of the tenth of a *tuman*.

Asfara. Our braves in the wantonness of enterprise, on the very day of arrival, took the new wall[1] that was in building outside the fort. That day Sayyid Qasim, Lord of my Gate, out-stripped the rest and got in with his sword; Sl. Ahmad *Tambal* and Muhammad-dost Taghai got theirs in also but Sayyid Qasim won the Champion's Portion. He took it in Shahrukhiya when I went to see my mother's brother, Sl. Mahmud Khan.

> (*Author's note.*) The Championship Portion[2] is an ancient usage of the Mughul horde. Whoever outdistanced his tribe and got in with his own sword, took the portion at every feast and entertainment.

My guardian, Khudai-birdi Beg died in that first day's fighting, struck by a cross-bow arrow. As the assault was made without armour, several bare braves (*yikit yilang*)[3] perished and many were wounded. One of Ibrahim *Saru*'s cross-bowmen was an excellent shot; his equal had never been seen; he it was hit most of those wounded. When Asfara had been taken, he entered my service.

As the siege drew on, orders were given to construct head-strikes[4] in two or three places, to run mines and to make every   Fol. 31b. effort to prepare appliances for taking the fort. The siege lasted 40 days; at last Ibrahim *Saru* had no resource but, through the mediation of Khwaja Moulana-i-qazi, to elect to serve me. In the month of Shawwal (June 1495 AD.) he came out, with his sword and quiver hanging from his neck, waited on me and surrendered the fort.

Khujand for a considerable time had been dependent on 'Umar Shaikh Mirza's Court (*diwan*) but of late had looked towards Sl. Ahmad Mirza on account of the disturbance in the Farghana government during the interregnum.[5] As the

---

1 *qurghan-ning tashida yangi tam quparib sala dur.* I understand, that what was taken was a new circumvallation in whole or in part. Such double walls are on record. *Cf.* Appendix A.
2 *bahadurluq aulush*, an actual portion of food.
3 *i.e.* either unmailed or actually naked.
4 The old English noun *strike* expresses the purpose of the *sar-kob*. It is "an instrument for scraping off" what rises above the top" (Webster, whose example is grain in a measure). The *sar-kob* is an erection of earth or wood, as high as the attacked walls, and it enabled besiegers to strike off heads appearing above the ramparts.
5 *i.e.* the dislocation due to 'Umar Shaikh's death.

opportunity offered, a move against it also was now made.
Mir Mughul's father, 'Abdu'l-wahhab *Shaghawal*[1] was in it; he
surrendered without making any difficulty at once on our
arrival.

Just then Sl. Mahmud Khan was in Shahrukhiya. It has been
said already that when Sl. Ahmad Mirza came into Andijan
(899 AH.), he also came and that he laid siege to Akhsi. It
occurred to me that if since I was so close, I went and waited
on him, he being, as it were, my father and my elder brother,
and if bye-gone resentments were laid aside, it would be good
hearing and seeing for far and near. So said, I went.

I waited on The Khan in the garden Haidar *Kukuldash* had
made outside Shahrukhiya. He was seated in a large four-
doored tent set up in the middle of it. Having entered
the tent, I knelt three times,[2] he for his part, rising to do
me honour. We looked one another in the eyes;[3] and he
returned to his seat. After I had kneeled, he called me to his
side and shewed me much affection and friendliness. Two
or three days later, I set off for Akhsi and Andijan by the
Kindirlik Pass.[4] At Akhsi I made the circuit of my Father's

Fol. 32.

---

1 *Cf.* f. 13. The H.S. (ii, 274) places his son, Mir Mughul, in charge, but
otherwise agrees with the B.N.

2 *Cf.* Clavijo, Markham p. 132. Sir Charles Grandison bent the knee on
occasions but illustrated MSS. *e.g.* the B.M. *Tawarikh-i-guzida Nasrat-nama*
show that Babur would kneel down on both knees. *Cf.* f. 123*b* for the fatigue
of the genuflection.

3 I have translated *kurushub* thus because it appears to me that here and
in other places, stress is laid by Babur upon the mutual gaze as an episode of
a ceremonious interview. The verb *kurushmak* is often rendered by the
Persian translators as *daryaftan* and by the L. and E. Memoirs as *to embrace*.
I have not found in the B.N. warrant for translating it as *to embrace*;
quchushmaq is Babur's word for this (f. 103). *Daryaftan*, taken as to grasp or see
with the mind, to understand, well expresses mutual gaze and its sequel
of mutual understanding. Sometimes of course, *kurush*, the interview does
not imply *kurush*, the silent looking in the eyes with mutual understanding;
it simply means *se voyer e.g.* f. 17. The point is thus dwelt upon because the
frequent mention of an embrace gives a different impression of manners from
that made by "interview" or words expressing mutual gaze.

4 *daban*. This word Réclus (vi, 171) quoting from Fedschenko, explains as a difficult
rocky defile; *art*, again, as a dangerous gap at a high elevation; *bel*, as an easy low pass;
and *kutal*, as a broad opening between low hills. The explanation of *kutal* does not
hold good for Babur's application of the word (f. 81*b*) to the Sara-taq.

tomb. I left at the hour of the Friday Prayer (*i.e.*, about mid-day) and reached Andijan, by the Band-i-salar Road between the Evening and Bedtime Prayers. This road *i.e.* the Band-i-salar, people call a nine *yighach* road.[1]

One of the tribes of the wilds of Andijan is the Jigrak[2] a numerous people of five or six thousand households, dwelling in the mountains between Kashghar and Farghana. They have many horses and sheep and also numbers of yaks (*qutas*), these hill-people keeping yaks instead of common cattle. As their mountains are border-fastnesses, they have a fashion of not paying tribute. An army was now sent against them under Qasim Beg in order that out of the tribute taken from them something might reach the soldiers. He took about 20,000 of their sheep and between 1000 and 1500 of their horses and shared all out to the men.

After its return from the Jigrak, the army set out for Aura-tipa. Formerly this was held by 'Umar Shaikh Mirza but it had gone out of hand in the year of his death and Sl. 'Ali Mirza was now in it on behalf of his elder brother, Bai-sunghar Mirza. When Sl. 'Ali Mirza heard of our coming, he went off himself to the Macha hill-country, leaving his guardian, Shaikh Zu'n-nun *Arghun* behind. From half-way between Khujand and Aura-tipa, Khalifa[3] was sent as envoy to Shaikh Zu'n-nun but that senseless mannikin, instead of giving him a plain answer, laid hands on him and ordered him to death. For Khalifa to die cannot have been the Divine will; he escaped and came to me two or three days later, stripped bare and having suffered a hundred *tumans* (1,000,000) of hardships and fatigues. We went almost to Aura-tipa but as, winter being near, people had carried away their corn and forage, after a few days we turned back for Andijan. After our retirement, The Khan's men moved on the place when the Aura-tipa

Fol. 32*b*.

---

1 *Cf.* f. 4*b* and note. From Babur's special mention of it, it would seem not to be the usual road.
2 The spelling of this name is uncertain. Variants are many. Concerning the tribe *see* T.R. p. 165 n.
3 Nizamu'd-din 'Ali *Barlas*: *see* Gul-badan's H.N. *s.n.* He served Babur till the latter's death.

person[1] unable to make a stand, surrendered and came out. The Khan then gave it to Muhammad Husain *Kurkan Dughlat* and in his hands it remained till 908 AH. (1503).[2]

1 *i.e.* Zu'n-nun or perhaps the garrison.
2 *i.e.* down to Shaibani's destruction of Chaghatai rule in Tashkint in 1503 AD.

(*a. Sultan Husain Mirza's campaign against Khusrau Shah*).

In the winter of this year, Sl. Husain Mirza led his army out   Fol. 33.
of Khurasan against Hisar and went to opposite Tirmiz. Sl.
Mas'ud Mirza, for his part, brought an army (from Hisar) and
sat down over against him in Tirmiz. Khusrau Shah
strengthened himself in Qunduz and to help Sl. Mas'ud Mirza
sent his younger brother, Wali. They (*i.e.*, the opposed forces)
spent most of that winter on the river's banks, no crossing
being effected. Sl. Husain Mirza was a shrewd and experienced
commander; he marched up the river,[2] his face set for Qunduz
and by this having put Sl. Mas'ud Mirza off his guard, sent
'Abdu'l-latif *Bakhshi* (pay-master) with 5 or 600 serviceable
men, down the river to the Kilif ferry. These crossed and had
entrenched themselves on the other bank before Sl. Mas'ud
Mirza had heard of their movement. When he did hear of it,
whether because of pressure put upon him by Baqi *Chaghaniani*
to spite (his half-brother) Wali, or whether from his own want
of heart, he did not march against those who had crossed but
disregarding Wali's urgency, at once broke up his camp and
turned for Hisar.[3]

Sl. Husain Mirza crossed the river and then sent, (1) against
Khusrau Shah, Badi'u'z-zaman Mirza and Ibrahim Husain
Mirza with Muhammad Wali Beg and Zu'n-nun *Arghun*, and

1 Elph. MS. f. 23; W.-i-B. I.O. 215 f. 26 and 217 f. 21; Mems. p. 35.
    Babur's own affairs form a small part of this year's record; the rest is drawn
from the H.S. which in its turn, uses Babur's f. 34 and f. 37*b*. Each author words the
shared material in his own style; one adding magniloquence, the other retracting
to plain statement, indeed summarizing at times to obscurity. Each passes his
own judgment on events, *e.g.* here Khwand-amir's is more favourable to Husain
Bai-qara's conduct of the Hisar campaign than Babur's. *Cf.* H.S. ii, 256–60 and 274.
2 This feint would take him from the Oxus.
3 Tirmiz to Hisar, 96m. (Réclus vi, 255).

(2) against Khutlan, Muzaffar Husain Mirza with Muhammad *Baranduq Barlas*. He himself moved for Hisar.

When those in Hisar heard of his approach, they took their precautions; Sl. Mas'ud Mirza did not judge it well to stay in the fort but went off up the Kam Rud valley[1] and by way of Sara-taq to his younger brother, Bai-sunghar Mirza in Samarkand. Wali, for his part drew off to (his own district) Khutlan. Baqi *Chaghaniani*, Mahmud *Barlas* and Quch Beg's father, Sl. Ahmad strengthened the fort of Hisar. Hamza Sl. and Mahdi Sl. (*Auzbeg*) who some years earlier had left Shaibani Khan for (the late) Sl. Mahmud Mirza's service, now, in this dispersion, drew off with all their Auzbegs, for Qara-tigin. With them went Muhammad *Dughlat*[2] and Sl. Husain *Dughlat* and all the Mughuls located in the Hisar country.

Upon this Sl. Husain Mirza sent Abu'l-muhsin Mirza after Sl. Mas'ud Mirza up the Kam Rud valley. They were not strong enough for such work when they reached the defile.[3] There Mirza Beg *Firingi-baz*[4] got in his sword. In pursuit of Hamza Sl. into Qara-tigin, Sl. Husain Mirza sent Ibrahim Tarkhan and Yaq'ub-i-ayub. They overtook the sultans and fought. The Mirza's detachment was defeated; most of his begs were unhorsed but all were allowed to go free.

(b. Babur's reception of the Auzbeg sultans.)

As a result of this exodus, Hamza Sl. with his son, Mamaq Sl., and Mahdi Sl. and Muhammad *Dughlat*, later known as *Hisari* and his brother, Sl. Husain *Dughlat* with the Auzbegs dependent on the sultans and the Mughuls who had been located in Hisar as (the late) Sl. Mahmud Mirza's retainers, came, after letting me know (their intention), and waited upon me in Ramzan (May-June) at Andijan. According to the

1 H.S. Wazr-ab valley. The usual route is up the Kam Rud and over the Mura pass to Sara-taq. Cf. f. 81b.
2 *i.e.* the Hisari mentioned a few lines lower and on f. 99b. Nothing on f. 99b explains his cognomen.
3 The road is difficult. Cf. f. 81b.
4 Khwand-amir also singles out one man for praise, Sl. Mahmud *Mir-i-akhwur*; the two names probably represent one person. The sobriquet may refer to skill with a matchlock, to top-spinning (*firnagi-baz*) or to some lost joke. (H.S. ii, 257.)

custom of Timuriya sultans on such occasions, I had seated myself on a raised seat (*tushak*); when Hamza Sl. and Mamaq Sl. and Mahdi Sl. entered, I rose and went down to do them honour; we looked one another in the eyes and I placed them on my right, *baghish da.*[1] A number of Mughuls also came, under Muhammad *Hisari*; all elected for my service.

(*c. Sl. Husain Mirza's affairs resumed*).

Sl. Husain Mirza, on reaching Hisar, settled down at once to besiege it. There was no rest, day nor night, from the labours of mining and attack, of working catapults and mortars. Mines were run in four or five places. When one had gone well forward towards the Gate, the townsmen, countermining, struck it and forced smoke down on the Mirza's men; they, in turn, closed the hole, thus sent the smoke straight back and made the townsmen flee as from the very maw of death. In the end, the townsmen drove the besiegers out by pouring jar after jar of water in on them. Another day, a party dashed out from the town and drove off the Mirza's men from their own mine's mouth. Once the discharges from catapults and mortars in the Mirza's quarters on the north cracked a tower of the fort; it fell at the Bed-time Prayer; some of the Mirza's braves begged to assault at once but he refused, saying, "It is night." Before the shoot of the next day's dawn, the besieged had rebuilt the whole tower. That day too there was no assault; in fact, for the two to two and a half months of the siege, no attack was made except by keeping up the blockade,[2] by mining, rearing head-strikes,[3] and discharging stones.

Fol. 34*b*.

1 This pregnant phrase has been found difficult. It may express that Babur assigned the sultans places in their due precedence; that he seated them in a row; and that they sat cross-legged, as men of rank, and were not made, as inferiors, to kneel and sit back on their heels. Out of this last meaning, I infer comes the one given by dictionaries, "to sit at ease," since the cross-legged posture is less irksome than the genuflection, not to speak of the ease of mind produced by honour received. Cf. f. 18*b* and note on Ahmad's posture; Redhouse *s.nn. baghish* and *baghdash*; and B.M. Tawarikh-i-guzida nasrat-nama, in the illustrations of which the chief personage, only, sits cross-legged.

2 *siyasat.* My translation is conjectural only.

3 *sar-kob.* The old English noun *strike*, "an instrument for scraping off what appears above the top," expresses the purpose of the wall-high erections of wood or earth (*L. agger*) raised to reach what shewed above ramparts. Cf. Webster.

When Badi'u'z-zaman Mirza and whatever (*ni kim*) troops had been sent with him against Khusrau Shah, dismounted some 16 m. (3 to 4 *yighach*) below Qunduz,[1] Khusrau Shah arrayed whatever men (*ni kim*) he had, marched out, halted one night on the way, formed up to fight and came down upon the Mirza and his men. The Khurasanis may not have been twice

as many as his men but what question is there they were half as many more? None the less did such Mirzas and such Commander-begs elect for prudence and remain in their entrenchments! Good and bad, small and great, Khusrau Shah's force may have been of 4 or 5000 men!

This was the one exploit of his life,—of this man who for the sake of this fleeting and unstable world and for the sake of shifting and faithless followers, chose such evil and such ill-repute, practised such tyranny and injustice, seized such wide lands, kept such hosts of retainers and followers,—latterly he led out between 20 and 30,000 and his countries and his districts (*parganat*) exceeded those of his own ruler and that ruler's sons,[2] —for an exploit such as this his name and the names of his adherents were noised abroad for generalship and for this they were counted brave, while those timorous laggards, in the trenches, won the resounding fame of cowards.

Badi'u'z-zaman Mirza marched out from that camp and after a few stages reached the Alghu Mountain of Taliqan[3] and there made halt. Khusrau Shah, in Qunduz, sent his brother, Wali, with serviceable men, to Ishkimish, Fulul and the hill-skirts thereabouts to annoy and harass the Mirza from outside also. Muhibb-'ali, the armourer, (*qurchi*) for his part, came down

(from Wali's Khutlan) to the bank of the Khutlan Water, met in with some of the Mirza's men there, unhorsed some, cut off a few heads and got away. In emulation of this, Sayyidim 'Ali[4] the door-keeper, and his younger brother, Quli Beg and

1 Presumably lower down the Qunduz Water.
2 *auz padshahi u mirzalaridin artib.*
3 *sic.* Hai. MS.; Elph. MS. "near Taliqan"; some W.-i-B. MSS. "Great Garden." Gul-badan mentions a Taliqan Garden. Perhaps the Mirza went so far east because, Zu'n-nun being with him, he had Qandahar in mind. *Cf.* f. 42b.
4 *i.e.* Sayyid Muhammad 'Ali. *See* f. 15 n. to Sherim. Khwaja Changal lies 14 m. below Taliqan on the Taliqan Water. (Erskine.)

Bihlul-i-ayub and a body of their men got to grips with the Khurasanis on the skirt of 'Ambar Koh, near Khwaja Changal but, many Khurasanis coming up, Sayyidim 'Ali and Baba Beg's (son) Baba-quli Beg and others were unhorsed.

At the time these various news reached Sl. Husain Mirza, his army was not without distress through the spring rains of Hisar; he therefore brought about a peace; Mahmud *Barlas* came out from those in the fort; Haji Pir the Taster went from those outside; the great commanders and what there was (*ni kim*) of musicians and singers assembled and the Mirza took (Bega Begim), the eldest[1] daughter of Sl. Mahmud Mirza by Khan-zada Begim, for Haidar Mirza, his son by Payanda Begim and through her the grandson of Sl. Abu-sa'id Mirza. This done, he rose from before Hisar and set his face for Qunduz.

At Qunduz also Sl. Husain Mirza made a few trenches and took up the besieger's position but by Badi'u'z-zaman Mirza's intervention peace at length was made, prisoners were exchanged and the Khurasanis retired. The twice-repeated[2] attacks made by Sl. Husain Mirza on Khusrau Shah and his unsuccessful retirements were the cause of Khusrau Shah's Fol. 36. great rise and of action of his so much beyond his province.

When the Mirza reached Balkh, he, in the interests of Ma wara'u'n-nahr gave it to Badi'u'z-zaman Mirza, gave Badi'u'z-zaman Mirza's district of Astarabad to (a younger son), Muzaffar Husain Mirza and made both kneel at the same assembly, one for Balkh, the other for Astarabad. This offended Badi'u'z-zaman Mirza and led to years of rebellion and disturbance.[3]

(d. Revolt of the Tarkhanis in Samarkand).

In Ramzan of this same year, the Tarkhanis revolted in Samarkand. Here is the story:—Bai-sunghar Mirza was not so friendly and familiar with the begs and soldiers of Samarkand as he was with those of Hisar.[4] His favourite beg was Shaikh

1 f. 27b, second.
2 The first was *circa* 895 AH.-1490 AD. *Cf.* f. 27b.
3 Babur's wording suggests that their common homage was the cause of Badi'u'z-zaman's displeasure but *see* f. 41.
4 The Mirza had grown up with Hisaris. *Cf.* H.S. ii, 270.

'Abdu'l-lah *Barlas*[1] whose sons were so intimate with the
Mirza that it made a relation as of Lover and Beloved. These
things displeased the Tarkhans and the Samarkandi begs;
Darwesh Muhammad Tarkhan went from Bukhara to Qarshi,
brought Sl. 'Ali Mirza to Samarkand and raised him to be
supreme. People then went to the New Garden where Bai-
Fol. 36b. sunghar Mirza was, treated him like a prisoner, parted him
from his following and took him to the citadel. There they
seated both mirzas in one place, thinking to send Bai-sunghar
Mirza to the Guk Sarai close to the Other Prayer. The Mirza,
however, on plea of necessity, went into one of the palace-
buildings on the east side of the Bu-stan Sarai. Tarkhanis
stood outside the door and with him went in Muhammad Quli
Quchin and Hasan, the sherbet-server. To be brief:—A gateway,
leading out to the back, must have been bricked up for
they broke down the obstacle at once. The Mirza got out of
the citadel on the Kafshir side, through the water-conduit
(*ab-muri*), dropped himself from the rampart of the water-way
(*du-tahi*), and went to Khwajaka Khwaja's[2] house in Khwaja
Kafshir. When the Tarkhanis, in waiting at the door, took the
precaution of looking in, they found him gone. Next day the
Tarkhanis went in a large body to Khwajaka Khwaja's gate but
the Khwaja said, "No!"[3] and did not give him up. Even they
could not take him by force, the Khwaja's dignity was too
great for them to be able to use force. A few days later, Khwaja
Abu'l-makaram[4] and Ahmad Haji Beg and other begs, great
Fol. 37. and small, and soldiers and townsmen rose in a mass, fetched
the Mirza away from the Khwaja's house and besieged
Sl. 'Ali Mirza and the Tarkhans in the citadel. They
could not hold out for even a day; Muh. Mazid Tarkhan went
off through the Gate of the Four Roads for Bukhara;

1 As the husband of one of the six Badakhshi Begims, he was closely connected with local ruling houses. *See* T.R. p. 107.
2 *i.e.* Muhammad 'Ubaidu'l-lah the elder of *Ahrari's* two sons. d. 911 AH. *See
Rashahat-i-'ain-alhayat* (I.O. 633) f. 269-75; and *Khizinatu'l-asfiya* lith. ed. i, 597.
3 *Bu yuq tur*, *i.e.* This is not to be.
4 d. 908 AH. He was not, it would seem, of the *Ahrari* family. His own had
provided Pontiffs (*Shaikhu'l-islam*) for Samarkand through 400 years. *Cf.
Shaibani-nama*, Vambéry, p. 106; also, for his character, p. 96.

Sl. 'Ali Mirza and Darwesh Muh. Tarkhan were made prisoner.

Bai-sunghar Mirza was in Ahmad Haji Beg's house when people brought Darwesh Muhammad Tarkhan in. He put him a few questions but got no good answer. In truth Darwesh Muhammad's was a deed for which good answer could not be made. He was ordered to death. In his helplessness he clung to a pillar[1] of the house; would they let him go because he clung to a pillar? They made him reach his doom (*siyasat*) and ordered Sl. 'Ali Mirza to the Guk Sarai there to have the fire-pencil drawn across his eyes.

> (*Author's note.*)   The Guk Sarai is one of Timur Beg's great buildings in the citadel of Samarkand. It has this singular and special charac-teristic, if a Timurid is to be seated on the throne, here he takes his seat; if one lose his head, coveting the throne, here he loses it; therefore the name Guk Sarai has a metaphorical sense (*kinayat*) and to say of any ruler's son, "They have taken him to the Guk Sarai," means, to death.[2]

To the Guk Sarai accordingly Sl. 'Ali Mirza was taken but when the fire-pencil was drawn across his eyes, whether by the surgeon's choice or by his inadvertence, no harm was done. Fol. 37*b*. This the Mirza did not reveal at once but went to Khwaja Yahya's house and a few days later, to the Tarkhans in Bukhara.

Through these occurrences, the sons of his Highness Khwaja 'Ubaidu'l-lah became settled partisans, the elder (Muhammad 'Ubaidu'l-lah, Khwajaka Khwaja) becoming the spiritual guide of the elder prince, the younger (Yahya) of the younger. In a few days, Khwaja Yahya followed Sl. 'Ali Mirza to Bukhara.

Bai-sunghar Mirza led out his army against Bukhara. On his approach, Sl. 'Ali Mirza came out of the town, arrayed for battle. There was little fighting; Victory being on the side of Sl. 'Ali Mirza, Bai-sunghar Mirza sustained defeat. Ahmad Haji Beg and a number of good soldiers were taken; most of the men were put to death. Ahmad Haji Beg himself the slaves and slave-women of Darwesh Muhammad Tarkhan, issuing out

1 *i.e.* he claimed sanctuary.
2 *Cf.* f. 45*b* and Pétis de la Croix's *Histoire de Chingiz Khan* pp. 171 and 227. What Timur's work on the Guk Sarai was is a question for archæologists.

of Bukhara, put to a dishonourable death on the charge of their master's blood.

(e. Babur moves against Samarkand).

These news reached us in Andijan in the month of Shawwal (mid-June to mid-July) and as we *(act.* 14) coveted Samarkand, we got our men to horse. Moved by a like desire, Sl. Mas'ud Mirza, his mind and Khusrau Shah's mind set at ease by Sl. Husain Mirza's retirement, came over by way of Shahr-i-sabz.[1] To reinforce him, Khusrau Shah laid hands *(qapti)* on his younger brother, Wali. We (three mirzas) beleaguered the town from three sides during three or four months; then Khwaja Yahya came to me from Sl. 'Ali Mirza to mediate an agreement with a common aim. The matter was left at an interview arranged *(kurushmak)*; I moved my force from Soghd to some 8m. below the town; Sl. 'Ali Mirza from his side, brought his own; from one bank, he, from the other, I crossed to the middle of[2] the Kohik water, each with four or five men; we just saw one another *(kurushub)*, asked each the other's welfare and went, he his way, I mine.

I there saw, in Khwaja Yahya's service, Mulla *Bina'i* and Muhammad Salih;[3] the latter I saw this once, the former was long in my service later on. After the interview *(kurushkan)* with Sl. 'Ali Mirza, as winter was near and as there was no great scarcity amongst the Samarkandis, we retired, he to Bukhara, I to Andijan.

Sl. Mas'ud Mirza had a penchant for a daughter of Shaikh 'Abdu'l-lah *Barlas*, she indeed was his object in coming to Samarkand. He took her, laid world-gripping ambition aside and went back to Hisar.

When I was near Shiraz and Kan-bai, Mahdi Sl. deserted to Samarkand; Hamza Sl. went also from near Zamin but with leave granted.

Fol. 38.

Fol. 38b.

---

1 *i.e.* over the Aitmak Pass. *Cf.* f. 49.
2 Hai. MS. *aralighigha.* Elph. MS. *aral,* island.
3 *See* f. 179b for *Bina'i.* Muhammad Salih Mirza *Khwarizmi* is the author of the *Shaibani-nama.*

(a. Babur's second attempt on Samarkand.)

This winter, Bai-sunghar Mirza's affairs were altogether in a good way. When 'Abdu'l-karim *Ushrit* came on Sl. 'Ali Mirza's part to near Kufin, Mahdi Sl. led out a body of Bai-sunghar Mirza's troops against him. The two commanders meeting exactly face to face, Mahdi Sl. pricked 'Abdu'l-karim's horse with his Chirkas[2] sword so that it fell, and as 'Abdu'l-karim was getting to his feet, struck off his hand at the wrist. Having taken him, they gave his men a good beating.

These (Auzbeg) sultans, seeing the affairs of Samarkand and the Gates of the (Timurid) Mirzas tottering to their fall, went off in good time (*airta*) into the open country (?)[3] for Shaibani.

Pleased[4] with their small success (over 'Abdu'l-karim), the Samarkandis drew an army out against Sl. 'Ali Mirza; Bai-sunghar Mirza went to Sar-i-pul (Bridge-head), Sl. 'Ali Mirza to Khwaja Karzun. Meantime, Khwaja Abu'l-makaram, at the instigation of Khwaja Munir of Aush, rode light against Bukhara with Wais *Laghari* and Muhammad Baqir of the Andijan begs, and Qasim *Duldai* and some of the Mirza's household. As the Bukhariots took precautions when the invaders got near the town, they could make no progress. They therefore retired. Fol. 39.

---

1 Elph. MS. f. 27; W.-i-B. I.O. 215 f. 30*b* and 217 f. 25; Mems. p. 42.

2 *i.e.* Circassian. Muhammad Salih (Sh.N. Vambéry p. 276 l. 58) speaks of other Auzbegs using Chirkas swords.

3 *airta yazigha.* My translation is conjectural. *Airta* implies *i.a.* foresight. *Yazigha* allows a pun at the expense of the sultans; since it can be read both as *to the open country* and as *for their (next, airta) misdeeds.* My impression is that they took the opportunity of being outside Samarkand with their men, to leave Bai-sunghar and make for Shaibani, then in Turkistan. Muhammad Salih also marking the tottering Gate of Sl. 'Ali Mirza, left him now, also for Shaibani. (Vambéry cap. xv.)

4 *aumaq,* to amuse a child in order to keep it from crying.

At the time when (last year) Sl. 'Ali Mirza and I had our interview, it had been settled[1] that this summer he should come from Bukhara and I from Andijan to beleaguer Samarkand. To keep this tryst, I rode out in Ramzan (May) from Andijan. Hearing when close to Yar Yilaq, that the (two) Mirzas were lying front to front, we sent Tulun Khwaja Mughul[2] ahead, with 2 or 300 scouting braves (*qazaq yikitlar*). Their approach giving Bai-sunghar Mirza news of our advance, he at once broke up and retired in confusion. That same night our detachment overtook his rear, shot a mass (*qalin*) of his men and brought in masses of spoil.

Two days later we reached Shiraz. It belonged to Qasim Beg *Duldai*; his *darogha* (Sub-governor) could not hold it and surrendered.[3] It was given into Ibrahim *Saru*'s charge. After making there, next day, the Prayer of the Breaking of the Fast ('*Idu'l-fitr*), we moved for Samarkand and dismounted in the reserve (*qurugh*) of Ab-i-yar (Water of Might). That day waited on me with 3 or 400 men, Qasim *Duldai*, Wais *Laghari*, Muhammad Sighal's grandson, Hasan,[4] and Sl. Muhammad Wais. What they said was this: "Bai-sunghar Mirza came out and has gone back; we have left him therefore and are here for the *padshah*'s service," but it was known later that they must have left the Mirza at his request to defend Shiraz, and that the Shiraz affair having become what it was, they had nothing for it but to come to us.

When we dismounted at Qara-bulaq, they brought in several Mughuls arrested because of senseless conduct to humble village elders coming in to us.[5] Qasim Beg *Quchin* for discipline's

Fol. 39b.

1 *i.e.* with Khwaja Yahya presumably. *See* f. 38.

2 This man is mentioned also in the *Tawarikh-i-guzida Nasratnama* B.M. Or. 3222 f. 124b.

3 H.S., on the last day of Ramzan (June 28th 1497 AD.).

4 Muhammad *Sighal* appears to have been a marked man. I quote from the T.G.N.N. (*see supra*), f. 123b foot, the information that he was the grandson of Ya'qub Beg. Zenker explains *Sighali* as the name of a Chaghatai family. An *Ayub-i-Ya'qub Begchik Mughul* may be an uncle. *See* f. 43 for another grandson. 5 *baz'i kirkan-kint-kisakka bash-siz-qilghan Mughullarni tutub.* I take the word *kisak* in this highly idiomatic sentence to be a diminutive of *kis*, old person, on the analogy of *mir, mirak, mard, mardak*. [The H.S. uses *Kisak* (ii, 261) as a proper noun.] The alliteration in *kaf* and the mighty adjective here are noticeable.

sake (*siyasat*) had two or three of them cut to pieces. It was on this account he left me and went to Hisar four or five years later, in the guerilla times, (907 AH.) when I was going from the Macha country to The Khan.[1]

Marching from Qara-bulaq, we crossed the river (*i.e.* the Zar-afshan) and dismounted near Yam.[2] On that same day, our men got to grips with Bai-sunghar Mirza's at the head of the Avenue. Sl. Ahmad *Tambal* was struck in the neck by a spear but not unhorsed. Khwajaki Mulla-i-sadr, Khwaja-i-kalan's eldest brother, was pierced in the nape of the neck[3] by an arrow and went straightway to God's mercy. An excellent soldier, my father before me had favoured him, making him Keeper of the Seal; he was a student of theology, had great acquaintance with words and a good style; moreover he understook hawking and rain-making with the jade-stone. Fol. 40.

While we were at Yam, people, dealers and other, came out in crowds so that the camp became a bazar for buying and selling. One day, at the Other Prayer, suddenly, a general hubbub arose and all those Musalman (traders) were plundered. Such however was the discipline of our army that an order to restore everything having been given, the first watch (*pahar*) of the next day had not passed before nothing, not a tag of cotton, not a broken needle's point, remained in the possession of any man of the force, all was back with its owners.

Marching from Yam, it was dismounted in Khan Yurti (The Khan's Camping Ground),[4] some 6 m. (3 *kuroh*) east of Samarkand. We lay there for 40 or 50 days. During the time, men from their side and from ours chopped at one another (*chapqulashtilar*) several times in the Avenue. One day when Ibrahim *Begchik* was chopping away there, he was cut on the face;

1 Qasim feared to go amongst the Mughuls lest he should meet retaliatory death. *Cf.* f. 99b.

2 This appears from the context to be Yam (Jam) -bai and not the Djouma. (Jam) of the Fr. map of 1904, lying farther south. The Avenue named seems likely to be Timur's of f. 45b and to be on the direct road for Khujand. *See* Schuyler i, 232.

3 *bughan buyini*. W.-i-B. 215, *yan*, thigh, and 217 *gardan*, throat. I am in doubt as to the meaning of *bughan*; perhaps the two words stand for joint at the nape of the neck. Khwaja-i-kalan was one of seven brothers, six died in Babur's service, he himself served till Babur's death.

4 *Cf.* f. 48.

thereafter people called him *Chapuk* (*Balafré*). Another time, this also in the Avenue, at the Maghak (Fosse) Bridge[1] Abu'l-qasim (*Kohbur Chaghatai*) got in with his mace. Once, again in

the Avenue, near the Mill-sluice, when Mir Shah *Quchin* also got in with his mace, they cut his neck almost half-through; most fortunately the great artery was not severed.

While we were in Khan Yurti, some in the fort sent the deceiving message,[2] "Come you to-night to the Lovers' Cave side and we will give you the fort." Under this idea, we went that night to the Maghak Bridge and from there sent a party of good horse and foot to the rendezvous. Four or five of the household foot-soldiers had gone forward when the matter got wind. They were very active men; one, known as Haji, had served me from my childhood; another people called Mahmud *Kundur-sangak*.[3] They were all killed.

While we lay in Khan Yurti, so many Samarkandis came out that the camp became a town where everything looked for in a town was to be had. Meantime all the forts, Samarkand excepted, and the Highlands and the Lowlands were coming in to us. As in Aurgut,[4] however, a fort on the skirt of the Shavdar (var. Shadwar) range, a party of men held fast, of necessity we moved out from Khan Yurti against them. They could not maintain themselves, and surrendered, making

Khwaja-i-qazi their mediator. Having pardoned their offences against ourselves, we went back to beleaguer Samarkand.

(*b. Affairs of Sl. Husain Mirza and his son, Badi'u'z-zaman Mirza.*)[5]

This year the mutual recriminations of Sl. Husain Mirza and Badi'u'z-zaman Mirza led on to fighting; here are the

---

1 Khorochkine (Radlov's *Réceuil d'Itinéraires* p. 241) mentions Pul-i-mougak, a great stone bridge thrown across a deep ravine, east of Samarkand. *For* Kul-i-maghak, deep pool, or pool of the fosse, *see* f. 48b.

2 From Khwand-amir's differing account of this affair, it may be surmised that those sending the message were not treacherous; but the message itself was deceiving inasmuch as it did not lead Babur to expect opposition. *Cf.* f. 43b and note.

3 Of this nick-name several interpretations are allowed by the dictionaries.

4 *See* Schuyler i, 268 for an account of this beautiful Highland village.

5 Here Babur takes up the thread, dropped on f. 36, of the affairs of the Khurasani mirzas. He draws on other sources than the H.S.; perhaps on

particulars:—Last year, as has been mentioned, Badi'u'z-zaman Mirza and Muzaffar Husain Mirza had been made to kneel for Balkh and Astarabad. From that time till this, many envoys had come and gone, at last even 'Ali-sher Beg had gone but urge it as all did, Badi'u'z-zaman Mirza would not consent to give up Astarabad. "The Mirza," he said, "assigned[1] it to my son, Muhammad Mumin Mirza at the time of his circumcision." A conversation had one day between him and 'Ali-sher Beg testifies to his acuteness and to the sensibility of 'Ali-sher Beg's feelings. After saying many things of a private nature in the Mirza's ear, 'Ali-sher Beg added, "Forget these matters."[2] "What matters?" rejoined the Mirza instantly. 'Ali-sher Beg was much affected and cried a good deal.

At length the jarring words of this fatherly and filial discussion went so far that *his* father against his father, and *his* son against his son drew armies out for Balkh and Astarabad.[3]

Up (from Harat) to the Pul-i-chiragh meadow, below Garzawan,[4] went Sl. Husain Mirza; down (from Balkh) came Badi'u'z-zaman Mirza. On the first day of Ramzan (May 2nd) Abu'l-muhsin Mirza advanced, leading some of his father's light troops. There was nothing to call a battle; Badi'u'z-zaman Mirza was routed and of his braves masses were made prisoner. Sl. Husain Mirza ordered that all prisoners should

Fol. 41*b*.

---

his own memory, perhaps on information given by Khurasanis with him in Hindustan *e.g.* Husain's grandson. *See* f. 167*b*. *Cf.* H.S. ii, 261.

1 *baghishlab tur. Cf.* f. 34 note to *baghish da*.

2 *Bu sozlar aunutung.* Some W.-i-B. MSS., *Faramosh nakunid* for *bakunid*, thus making the Mirza not acute but rude, and destroying the point of the story *i.e.* that the Mirza pretended so to have forgotten as to have an empty mind. Khwand-amir states that 'Ali-sher prevailed at first; his tears therefore may have been of joy at the success of his pacifying mission.

3 *i.e.* B.Z.'s father, Husain, against Mu'min's father, B.Z. and Husain's son, Muzaffar Husain against B.Z.'s son Mu'min;—a veritable conundrum.

4 Garzawan lies west of Balkh. Concerning Pul-i-chiragh Col. Grodekoff's *Ride to Harat* (Marvin p. 103 ff.) gives pertinent information. It has also a map showing the Pul-i-chiragh meadow. The place stands at the mouth of a triply-bridged defile, but the name appears to mean Gate of the Lamp (*cf.* Gate of Timur), and not Bridge of the Lamp, because the H.S. and also modern maps write *bil* (*bel*), pass, where the Turki text writes *pul*, bridge, narrows, pass.

The lamp of the name is one at the shrine of a saint, just at the mouth of the defile. It was alight when Col. Grodekoff passed in 1879 and to it, he says, the name is due now—as it presumably was 400 years ago and earlier.

be beheaded; this not here only but wherever he defeated a rebel son, he ordered the heads of all prisoners to be struck off. And why not? Right was with him. The (rebel) Mirzas were so given over to vice and social pleasure that even when a general so skilful and experienced as their father was within half-a-day's journey of them, and when before the blessed month of Ramzan, one night only remained, they busied themselves with wine and pleasure, without fear of their father, without dread of God. Certain it is that those so lost (*yutkan*) will perish and that any hand can deal a blow at those thus going to perdition (*autkan*). During the several years of Badi'u'z-zaman Mirza's rule in Astarabad, his coterie and his following, his bare (*yalang*) braves even, were in full splendour and adornment. He had many gold and silver drinking cups and utensils, much silken plenishing and countless tipuchaq horses. He now lost everything. He hurled himself in his flight down a mountain track, leading to a precipitous fall. He himself got down the fall, with great difficulty, but many of his men perished there.[1]

Fol. 42.

After defeating Badi'u'z-zaman Mirza, Sl. Husain Mirza moved on to Balkh. It was in charge of Shaikh 'Ali Taghai; he, not able to defend it, surrendered and made his submission. The Mirza gave Balkh to Ibrahim Husain Mirza, left Muhammad Wali Beg and Shah Husain, the page, with him and went back to Khurasan.

Defeated and destitute, with his braves bare and his bare foot-soldiers,[2] Badi'u'z-zaman Mirza drew off to Khusrau Shah in Qunduz. Khusrau Shah, for his part, did him good service, such service indeed, such kindness with horses and camels, tents and pavilions and warlike equipment of all sorts, both for himself and those with him, that eye-witnesses said between this and his former equipment the only difference might be in the gold and silver vessels.

1 Khwand-amir heard from the Mirza on the spot, when later in his service, that he was let down the precipice by help of turban-sashes tied together.
2 *yikit yilang u yayaq yaling*; a jingle made by due phonetic change of vowels; a play too on *yalang*, which first means stripped *i.e.* robbed and next unmailed, perhaps sometimes bare-bodied in fight.

(c. Dissension between Sl. Mas'ud Mirza and Khusrau Shah.)

Ill-feeling and squabbles had arisen between Sl. Mas'ud Mirza and Khusrau Shah because of the injustices of the one and the self-magnifyings of the other. Now therefore Khusrau Shah joined his brothers, Wali and Baqi to Badi'u'z-zaman Mirza and sent the three against Hisar. They could not even get near the fort, in the outskirts swords were crossed once or twice; one day at the Bird-house[1] on the north of Hisar, Muhibb-'ali, the armourer (*qurchi*), outstripped his people and struck in well; he fell from his horse but at the moment of his capture, his men attacked and freed him. A few days later a somewhat compulsory peace was made and Khusrau Shah's army retired.

Fol. 42*b*.

Shortly after this, Badi'u'z-zaman Mirza drew off by the mountain-road to Zu'n-nun *Arghun* and his son, Shuja' *Arghun* in Qandahar and Zamin-dawar. Stingy and miserly as Zu'n-nun was, he served the Mirza well, in one single present offering 40,000 sheep.

Amongst curious happenings of the time one was this: Wednesday was the day Sl. Husain Mirza beat Badi'u'z-zaman Mirza; Wednesday was the day Muzaffar Husain Mirza beat Muhammad Mumin Mirza; Wednesday, more curious still, was the name of the man who unhorsed and took prisoner, Muhammad Mumin Mirza.[2]

1 *qush-khana*. As the place was outside the walls, it may be a good hawking ground and not a falconry.
2 The H.S., mentions (ii, 222) a Sl. Ahmad of Char-shamba, a town mentioned *e.g.* by Grodekoff p. 123. It also spoils Babur's coincidence by fixing Tuesday, Shab'an 29th for the battle. Perhaps the commencement of the Muhammadan day at sunset, allows of both statements.

(*a. Resumed account of Babur's second attempt on Samarkand.*)

When we had dismounted in the Qulba (Plough) meadow,[2] behind the Bagh-i-maidan (Garden of the plain), the Samarkandis came out in great numbers to near Muhammad Chap's Bridge. Our men were unprepared; and before they were ready, Baba 'Ali's (son) Baba Quli had been unhorsed and taken into the fort. A few days later we moved to the top of Qulba, at the back of Kohik.[3] That day Sayyid Yusuf,[4] having been sent out of the town, came to our camp and did me obeisance.

The Samarkandis, fancying that our move from the one ground to the other meant, "He has given it up," came out, soldiers and townsmen in alliance (through the Turquoise Gate), as far as the Mirza's Bridge and, through the Shaikh-zada's Gate, as far as Muhammad Chap's. We ordered our braves to arm and ride out; they were strongly attacked from both sides, from Muhammad Chap's Bridge and from the Mirza's, but God brought it right! our foes were beaten. Begs of the best and the boldest of braves our men unhorsed and brought in. Amongst them Hafiz *Duldai's* (son) Muhammad *Miskin*[5] was taken, after his index-finger had been struck off; Muhammad Qasim *Nabira* also was unhorsed and brought in by his own younger brother, Hasan *Nabira*.[6] There were many other such soldiers and known men. Of the town-rabble,

Fol. 43.

---

1 Elph. MS. f. 30*b*; W.–i–B. I.O. 215 f. 34 and 217 f. 26*b*; Mems. p. 46.

The abruptness of this opening is due to the interposition of Sl. Husain M.'s affairs between Babur's statement on f. 41 that he returned from Aurgut and this first of 903 AH. that on return he encamped in Qulba.

2 See f. 48*b*.

3 *i.e.* Chupan-ata; *see* f. 45 and note.

4 *Aughlaqchi*, the Grey Wolfer of f. 22.

5 A sobriquet, the *suppliant* or perhaps something having connection with musk. H.S. ii, 278, son of H.D.

6 *i.e.* grandson (of Muhammad Sighal). *Cf.* f. 39*b*.

were brought in Diwana, the tunic-weaver and *Kal-qashuq*,[1] headlong leaders both, in brawl and tumult; they were ordered Fol. 43b. to death with torture in blood-retaliation for our foot-soldiers, killed at the Lovers' Cave.[2] This was a complete reverse for the Samarkandis; they came out no more even when our men used to go to the very edge of the ditch and bring back their slaves and slave-women.

The Sun entered the Balance and cold descended on us.[3] I therefore summoned the begs admitted to counsel and it was decided, after discussion, that although the towns-people were so enfeebled that, by God's grace, we should take Samarkand, it might be to-day, it might be to-morrow, still, rather than suffer from cold in the open, we ought to rise from near it and go for winter-quarters into some fort, and that, even if we had to leave those quarters later on, this would be done without further trouble. As Khwaja Didar seemed a suitable fort, we marched there and having dismounted in the meadow lying before it, went in, fixed on sites for the winter-houses and covered shelters,[4] left overseers and inspectors of the work and returned to our camp in the meadow. There we lay during the few days before the winter-houses were finished.

Meantime Bai-sunghar Mirza had sent again and again to ask help from Shaibani Khan. On the morning of the very day on which, our quarters being ready, we had moved into Khwaja Didar, the Khan, having ridden light from Turkistan, Fol. 44. stood over against our camping-ground. Our men were not all at hand; some, for winter-quarters, had gone to Khwaja Rabati, some to Kabud, some to Shiraz. None-the-less, we formed up those there were and rode out. Shaibani Khan made no stand but drew off towards Samarkand. He went right up to the fort but because the affair had not gone as

1 This seeming sobriquet may show the man's trade. *Kal* is a sort of biscuit; *qashuq* may mean a spoon.
2 The H.S. does not ascribe treachery to those inviting Babur into Samarkand but attributes the murder of his men to others who fell on them when the plan of his admission became known. The choice here of "town-rabble" for retaliatory death supports the account of H.S. ii.
3 "It was the end of September or beginning of October" (Erskine).
4 *awi u kipa yirlar. Awi* is likely to represent *kibitkas*. For *kipa yir, see* Zenker p. 782.

Bai-sunghar Mirza wished, did not get a good reception. He therefore turned back for Turkistan a few days later, in disappointment, with nothing done.

Bai-sunghar Mirza had sustained a seven months' siege; his one hope had been in Shaibani Khan; this he had lost and he now with 2 or 300 of his hungry suite, drew off from Samarkand, for Khusrau Shah in Qunduz.

When he was near Tirmiz, at the Amu ferry, the Governor of Tirmiz, Sayyid Husain Akbar, kinsman and confidant both of Sl. Mas'ud Mirza, heard of him and went out against him. The Mirza himself got across the river but Mirim Tarkhan was drowned and all the rest of his people were captured, together with his baggage and the camels loaded with his personal effects; even his page, Muhammad Tahir, falling into Sayyid Husain Akbar's hands. Khusrau Shah, for his part, looked kindly on the Mirza.

Fol. 44b. When the news of his departure reached us, we got to horse and started from Khwaja Didar for Samarkand. To give us honourable meeting on the road, were nobles and braves, one after another. It was on one of the last ten days of the first Rabi' (end of November 1497 AD.), that we entered the citadel and dismounted at the Bu-stan Sarai. Thus, by God's favour, were the town and the country of Samarkand taken and occupied.

(b. Description of Samarkand.)[1]

Few towns in the whole habitable world are so pleasant as Samarkand. It is of the Fifth Climate and situated in lat. 40° 6' and long. 99°.[2] The name of the town is Samarkand; its country people used to call Ma wara'u'n-nahr (Transoxania).

[1] Interesting reference may be made, amongst the many books on Samarkand, to Sharafu'd-din 'Ali Yazdi's Zafar-nama Bib. Ind. ed. i, 300, 781, 799, 800 and ii, 6, 194, 596 etc.; to Ruy Gonzalves di Clavijo's Embassy to Timur (Markham) cap. vi and vii; to Ujfalvy's Turkistan ii, 79 and Madame Ujfalvy's De Paris à Samarcande p. 161,—these two containing a plan of the town; to Schuyler's Turkistan; to Kostenko's Turkistan Gazetteer i, 345; to Réclus, vi, 270 and plan; and to a beautiful work of the St. Petersburg Archæological Society, Les Mosquées de Samarcande, of which the B.M. has a copy.

[2] This statement is confused in the Elp. and Hai. MSS. The second appears to give, by abjad, lat. 40' 6" and long. 99'. Mr. Erskine (p. 48) gives

They used to call it *Baldat-i-mahfuza* because no foe laid hands on it with storm and sack.[1] It must have become[2] Musalman in the time of the Commander of the Faithful, his Highness 'Usman. Qusam ibn 'Abbas, one of the Companions[3] must have gone there; his burial-place, known as the Tomb of Shah-i-zinda (The Living Shah, *i.e.*, Faqir) is outside the Iron Gate. Iskandar must have founded Samarkand. The Turk and Mughul hordes call it Simiz-kint.[4] Timur Beg made it his capital; no ruler so great will ever have made it a capital before (*qilghan aimas dur*). I ordered people to pace round the ramparts of the walled-town; it came out at 10,000 steps.[5] Samarkandis are all orthodox (*sunni*), pure-in-the-Faith, law-abiding and religious. The number of Leaders of Islam said to have arisen in Ma wara'u'n-nahr, since the days of his Highness the Prophet, are not known to have arisen in any other country.[6] From the Matarid suburb of Samarkand came Shaikh Abu'l-mansur, one of the Expositors of the Word.[7] Of the two sects of Expositors, the Mataridiyah

Fol. 45.

---

1 The enigmatical cognomen, Protected Town, is of early date; it is used *i.a.* by Ibn Batuta in the 14th century. Babur's tense refers it to the past. The town had frequently changed hands in historic times before he wrote. The name may be due to immunity from damage to the buildings in the town. *Cf.* Daulat-shah, Browne's ed., *s.n.* Qulaiba p. 443. Even Chingiz Khan's capture (1222 AD.) left the place well-preserved and its lands cultivated, but it inflicted great loss of men. *Cf.* Schuyler i, 236 and his authorities, especially Bretschneider.

2 Here is a good example of Babur's caution in narrative. He does not affirm that Samarkand became Musalman, or (*infra*) that Qusam ibn 'Abbas went, or that Alexander founded but in each case uses the presumptive past tense, resp. *bulghan dur, barghan dur, bina qilghan dur*, thus showing that he repeats what may be inferred or presumed and not what he himself asserts.

3 *i.e.* of Muhammad. *See* Z.N. ii, 193.

4 *i.e.* Fat Village. His text misleading him, Mr. Erskine makes here the useful irrelevant note that Persians and Arabs call the place Samar-qand and Turks, Samar-kand, the former using *qaf* (q), the latter *kaf* (k). Both the Elph. and the Hai. MSS. write Samarqand.

For use of the name Fat Village, *see* Clavijo (Markham p. 170), Simes-quinte, and Bretschneider's *Mediæval Geography* pp. 61, 64, 66 and 163.

5 *qadam.* Kostenko (i, 344) gives 9 m. as the circumference of the old walls and 1⅔ m. as that of the citadel. *See* Mde. Ujfalvy p. 175 for a picture of the walls.

6 *Ma'lum aimas kim muncha paida bulmish bulghai*; an idiomatic phrase.

7 d. 333 AH. (944 AD.). *See* D'Herbélot art. Matridi p. 572.

and the Ash'ariyah,[1] the first is named from this Shaikh Abu'l-mansur. Of Ma wara'u'n-nahr also was Khwaja Isma'il *Khartank*, the author of the *Sahih-i-bukhari*.[2] From the Farghana district, Marghinan—Farghana, though at the limit of settled habitation, is included in Ma wara'u'n-nahr,—came the author of the *Hidayat*,[3] a book than which few on Jurisprudence are more honoured in the sect of Abu Hanifa.

On the east of Samarkand are Farghana and Kashghar; on the west, Bukhara and Khwarizm; on the north, Tashkint and Shahrukhiya,—in books written Shash and Banakat; and on the south, Balkh and Tirmiz.

The Kohik Water flows along the north of Samarkand, at the distance of some 4 miles (2 *kuroh*); it is so-called because it comes out from under the upland of the Little Hill (*Kohik*)[4] lying between it and the town. The Dar-i-gham Water (canal) flows along the south, at the distance of some two miles (1 *shari'*). This is a large and swift torrent,[5] indeed it is like a large river, cut off from the Kohik Water. All the gardens and suburbs and some of the *tumans* of Samarkand are cultivated by it. By the Kohik Water a stretch of from 30 to 40 *yighach*,[6] by road, is made habitable and cultivated, as far as Bukhara

1 See D'Herbélot art. Aschair p. 124.

2 Abu 'Abdu'l-lah bin Isma'ilu'l-jausi b. 194 AH. d. 256 AH. (810-870 AD.). *See* D'Herbélot art. Bokhari p. 191, art. Giorag p. 373, and art. Sahihu'l-bokhari p. 722. He passed a short period, only, of his life in Khartank, a suburb of Samarkand.

3 *Cf.* f. 3b and n. 1.

4 This though 2475 ft. above the sea is only some 300 ft. above Samarkand. It is the Chupan-ata (Father of Shepherds) of maps and on it Timur built a shrine to the local patron of shepherds. The Zar-afshan, or rather, its Qara-su arm, flows from the east of the Little Hill and turns round it to flow west. Babur uses the name *Kohik Water* loosely; *e.g.* for the whole Zar-afshan when he speaks (*infra*) of cutting off the Dar-i-gham canal but for its southern arm only, the Qara-su in several places, and once, for the Dar-i-gham canal. *See* f. 49b and Kostenko i. 192.

5 *rud*. The Zar-afshan has a very rapid current. *See* Kostenko i, 196, and for the canal, i, 174. The name Dar-i-gham is used also for a musical note having charm to witch away grief; and also for a town noted for its wines.

6 What this represents can only be guessed; perhaps 150 to 200 miles. Abu'l-fida (Reinaud ii, 213) quotes Ibn Haukal as saying that from Bukhara up to "Bottam" (this seems to be where the Zar-afshan emerges into the open land) is eight days' journey through an unbroken tangle of verdure and gardens.

and Qara-kul. Large as the river is, it is not too large for its
dwellings and its culture; during three or four months of the   Fol. 45b.
year, indeed, its waters do not reach Bukhara.[1] Grapes, melons,
apples and pomegranates, all fruits indeed, are good in
Samarkand; two are famous, its apple and its *sahibi* (grape).[2] Its
winter is mightily cold; snow falls but not so much as in Kabul;
in the heats its climate is good but not so good as Kabul's.

In the town and suburbs of Samarkand are many fine buildings and gardens of Timur Beg and Aulugh Beg Mirza.[3]

In the citadel,[4] Timur Beg erected a very fine building, the
great four-storeyed kiosque, known as the Guk Sarai.[5] In the
walled-town, again, near the Iron Gate, he built a Friday
Mosque[6] of stone (*sangin*); on this worked many stone-cutters,
brought from Hindustan. Round its frontal arch is inscribed in
letters large enough to be read two miles away, the Qu'ran
verse, *Wa az yerfa' Ibrahim al Qawa'id ali akhara*.[7] This also is a
very fine building. Again, he laid out two gardens, on the

1 See Schuyler i, 286 on the apportionment of water to Samarkand and Bukhara.
2 It is still grown in the Samarkand region, and in Mr. Erskine's time a grape of
the same name was cultivated in Aurangabad of the Deccan.
3 *i.e.* Shahrukhi, Timur's grandson, through Shahrukh. It may be noted here that
Babur never gives Timur any other title than Beg and that he styles all Timurids,
Mirza (Mir-born).
4 Mr. Erskine here points out the contradiction between the statements
(i) of Ibn Haukal, writing, in 367 AH. (977 AD.), of Samarkand as having a
citadel (*ark*), an outer-fort (*qurghan*) and Gates in both circumvallations;
and (2) of Sharafu'd-din *Yazdi* (Z.N.) who mentions that when, in Timur's
day, the Getes besieged Samarkand, it had neither walls nor gates. *See*
Ouseley's Ibn Haukal p. 253; Z.N. Bib. Ind. ed. i, 109 and Pétis de la Croix's
Z.N. (*Histoire de Timur Beg*) i, 91.
5 Here still lies the Ascension Stone, the *Guk-tash*, a block of greyish white
marble. Concerning the date of the erection of the building and meaning of its
name, *see e.g.* Pétis de la Croix's *Histoire de Chingiz Khan* p. 171; Mems. p. 40 note;
and Schuyler *s.n.*
6 This seems to be the Bibi Khanim Mosque. The author of *Les Mosquées de
Samarcande* states that Timur built Bibi Khanim and the Gur-i-amir (Amir's
tomb); decorated Shah-i-zinda and set up the Chupan-ata shrine. *Cf.* f 46 and
note to Jahangir Mirza, as to the Gur-i-amir.
7 Cap. II. Quoting from Sale's *Qur'an* (i, 24) the verse is, "And Ibrahim
and Isma'il raised the foundations of the house, saying, 'Lord! accept it from us,
for Thou art he who hearest and knowest; Lord! make us also resigned to Thee,
and show us Thy holy ceremonies, and be turned to us, for Thou art easy to be
reconciled, and merciful.'"

east of the town, one, the more distant, the Bagh-i-bulandi,[1] the other and nearer, the Bagh-i-dilkusha.[2] From Dilkusha to the Turquoise Gate, he planted an Avenue of White Poplar,[3] and in the garden itself erected a great kiosque, painted inside with pictures of his battles in Hindustan. He made another garden, known as the Naqsh-i-jahan (World's Picture), on the skirt of Kohik, above the Qara-su or, as people also call it, the Ab-i-rahmat (Water-of-mercy) of Kan-i-gil.[4] It had gone to ruin when I saw it, nothing remaining of it except its name. His also are the Bagh-i-chanar,[5] near the walls and below the town on the south,[6] also the Bagh-i-shamal (North Garden) and the Bagh-i-bihisht (Garden of Paradise). His own tomb and those of his descendants who have ruled in Samarkand, are in a College, built at the exit (*chaqar*) of the walled-town, by Muhammad Sultan Mirza, the son of Timur Beg's son, Jahangir Mirza.[7]

Amongst Aulugh Beg Mirza's buildings inside the town are a College and a monastery (*Khanqah*). The dome of the monastery is very large, few so large are shown in the world. Near these two buildings, he constructed an excellent Hot Bath (*hammam*) known as the Mirza's Bath; he had the pavements in this made of all sorts of stone (? mosaic); such

1 or, *buland*, Garden of the Height or High Garden. The Turki texts have what can be read as *buldi* but the Z.N. both when describing it (ii, 194) and elsewhere (*e.g.* ii, 596) writes *buland*. *Buldi* may be a clerical error for *bulandi*, the height, a name agreeing with the position of the garden.

2 In the Heart-expanding Garden, the Spanish Ambassadors had their first interview with Timur. See Clavijo (Markham p. 130). Also the Z.N. ii, 6 for an account of its construction.

3 Judging from the location of the gardens and of Babur's camps, this appears to be the Avenue mentioned on f. 39*b* and f. 40.

4 *See infra* f. 48 and note.

5 The Plane-tree Garden. This seems to be Clavijo's *Bayginar*, laid out shortly before he saw it (Markham p. 136).

6 The citadel of Samarkand stands high; from it the ground slopes west and south; on these sides therefore gardens outside the walls would lie markedly below the outer-fort (*tash-qurghan*). Here as elsewhere the second W.-i-B. reads *stone* for *outer*. For the making of the North garden *see* Z.N. i, 799.

7 Timur's eldest son, d. 805 AH. (1402 AD.), before his father, therefore. Babur's wording suggests that in his day, the Gur-i-amir was known as the Madrasa. See as to the buildings Z.N. i, 713 and ii, 492, 595, 597, 705; Clavijo (Markham p. 164 and p. 166); and *Les Mosquées de Samarcande*.

another bath is not known in Khurasan or in Samarkand.[1]   Fol. 46b.
Again;—to the south of the College is his mosque, known as the
Masjid-i-maqata' (Carved Mosque) because its ceiling and its
walls are all covered with *islimi*[2] and Chinese pictures formed
of segments of wood. There is great discrepancy between the
qibla[3] of this mosque and that of the College; that of the mosque
seems to have been fixed by astronomical observation.

Another of Aulugh Beg Mirza's fine buildings is an observatory, that is, an instrument for writing Astronomical Tables.[4]
This stands three storeys high, on the skirt of the Kohik upland. By its means the Mirza worked out the Kurkani Tables,
now used all over the world. Less work is done with any others. Before these were made, people used the Ail-khani Tables,
put together at Maragha, by Khwaja Nasir *Tusi*,[5] in the time of
Hulaku Khan. Hulaku Khan it is, people call *Ail-khani*.[6]

> (*Author's note.*)   Not more than seven or eight observatories seem to
> have been constructed in the world. Mamum Khalifa[7] (Caliph) made
> one with which the *Mamumi* Tables were written. Batalmius (Ptolemy)
> constructed another. Another was made, in Hindustan, in the time of
> Raja Vikramaditya *Hindu*, in Ujjain and Dhar, that is, the Malwa country,
> now known as Mandu. The Hindus of Hindustan use the Tables of this
> Observatory. They were put together 1,584 years ago.[8] Compared with   Fol. 47.
> others, they are somewhat defective.

---

1 Hindustan would make a better climax here than Samarkand does.
2 These appear to be pictures or ornamentations of carved wood. Redhouse
describes *islimi* as a special kind of ornamentation in curved lines, similar to
Chinese methods.
3 *i.e.* the Black Stone (*ka'ba*) at Makkah to which Musalmans turn in prayer.
4 As ancient observatories were themselves the instruments of astronomical
observation, Babur's wording is correct. Aulugh Beg's great quadrant was 180 ft.
high; Abu-muhammad *Khujandi*'s sextant had a radius of 58 ft. Ja'i Singh made
similar great instruments in Ja'ipur, Dihli has others. *Cf.* Greaves Misc. Works i,
50; Mems. p. 51 note; *Ayin-i-akbari* (Jarrett) ii, 5 and note; Murray's Hand-book
to Bengal p. 331; Indian Gazetteer xiii, 400.
5 b. 597 AH. d. 672 AH. (1201–1274 AD.). *See* D'Herbélot's art. Nasir-i-din p. 662;
Abu'l-fida (Reinaud, Introduction i, cxxxviii) and Beale's Biographical Dict. *s.n.*
6 a grandson of Chingiz Khan, d. 663 AH. (1265 AD.). The cognomen *Ail-khani*
(*Il-khani*) may mean Khan of the Tribe.
7 Harunu'r-rashid's second son; d. 218 AH. (833 AD.).
8 Mr. Erskine notes that this remark would seem to fix the date at which Babur wrote
it as 934 AH. (1527 AD.), that being the 1584th year of the era of Vikramaditya, and
therefore at three years before Babur's death. (The Vikramaditya era begun 57 BC.)

Aulugh Beg Mirza again, made the garden known as the Bagh-i-maidan (Garden of the Plain), on the skirt of the Kohik upland. In the middle of it he erected a fine building they call Chihil Situn (Forty Pillars). On both storeys are pillars, all of stone (*tashdin*). Four turrets, like minarets, stand on its four corner-towers, the way up into them being through the towers. Everywhere there are stone pillars, some fluted, some twisted, some many-sided. On the four sides of the upper storey are open galleries enclosing a four-doored hall (*char-dara*); their pillars also are all of stone. The raised floor of the building is all paved with stone.

He made a smaller garden, out beyond Chihil Situn and towards Kohik, also having a building in it. In the open gallery of this building he placed a great stone throne, some 14 or 15 yards (*qari*) long, some 8 yards wide and perhaps 1 yard high. They brought a stone so large by a very long road.[1] There is a crack in the middle of it which people say must have come after it was brought here. In the same garden he also built a four-doored hall, know as the Chini-khana (Porcelain House) because its *izara*[2] are all of porcelain; he sent to China for the porcelain used in it. Inside the walls again, is an old building of his, known as the Masjid-i-laqlaqa (Mosque of the Echo). If anyone stamps on the ground under the middle of the dome of this mosque, the sound echoes back from the whole dome; it is a curious matter of which none knows the secret.

In the time also of Sl. Ahmad Mirza the great and lesser begs laid out many gardens, large and small.[3] For beauty, and air, and view, few will have equalled Darwesh Muhammad Tarkhan's Char-bagh (Four Gardens).[4] It lies overlooking the whole of Qulba Meadow, on the slope below the Bagh-i-maidan.

Fol. 47*b*.

1 This remark may refer to the 34 miles between the town and the quarries of its building stone. *See* f. 49 and note to Aitmak Pass.
2 Steingass, any support for the back in sitting, a low wall in front of a house. *See* Vullers p. 148 and *Burhan-i-qati*'; p. 119. Perhaps a *dado*.
3 *beg u begat, bagh u baghcha*.
4 Four Gardens, a quadrilateral garden, laid out in four plots. The use of the name has now been extended for any well-arranged, large garden, especially one belonging to a ruler (Erskine).

Moreover it is arranged symmetrically, terrace above terrace, and is planted with beautiful *narwan*[1] and cypresses and white poplar. A most agreeable sojourning place, its one defect is the want of a large stream.

Samarkand is a wonderfully beautified town. One of its specialities, perhaps found in few other places,[2] is that the different trades are not mixed up together in it but each has its own *bazar*, a good sort of plan. Its bakers and its cooks are good. The best paper in the world is made there; the water for the paper-mortars[3] all comes from Kan-i-gil,[4] a meadow on the banks of the Qara-su (Blackwater) or Ab-i-rahmat (Water Fol. 48. of Mercy). Another article of Samarkand trade, carried to all sides and quarters, is cramoisy velvet.

Excellent meadows lie round Samarkand. One is the famous Kan-i-gil, some 2 miles east and a little north of the town. The Qara-su or Ab-i-rahmat flows through it, a stream (with driving power) for perhaps seven or eight mills. Some say the original name of the meadow must have been Kan-i-abgir (Mine of Quagmire) because the river is bordered by quagmire, but the histories all write Kan-i-gil (Mine of clay). It is an excellent meadow. The Samarkand sultans always made it their reserve,[5] going out to camp in it each year for a month or two.

1 As two of the trees mentioned here are large, it may be right to translate *narwan*, not by pomegranate, but as the hard-wood elm, Madame Ujfalvy's "*karagatche*" (p. 168 and p. 222). The name *qara-yighach* (*karagatch*), dark tree, is given to trees other than this elm on account of their deep shadow.

2 Now a common plan indeed! *See* Schuyler i, 173.

3 *juwaz-i-kaghazlar* (*ning*) *su'i, i.e.* the water of the paper-(pulping)-mortars. Owing to the omission from some MSS. of the word *su*, water, *juwaz* has been mistaken for a kind of paper. *See* Mems. p. 52 and *Méms.* i, 102; A.Q.R. July 1910, p. 2, art. Paper-mills of Samarkand (H.B.); and Madame Ujfalvy p. 188. Kostenko, it is to be noted, does not include paper in his list (i, 346) of modern manufactures of Samarkand.

4 Mine of mud or clay. My husband has given me support for reading *gil*, and not *gul*, rose;—(1) In two good MSS. of the W.-i-B. the word is pointed with *kasra, i.e.* as for *gil*, clay; and (2) when describing a feast held in the garden by Timur, the Z.N. says the mud-mine became a rose-mine, *shuda Kan-i-gil Kan-i-gul.* [Mr. Erskine refers here to Pétis de la Croix's *Histoire de Timur Beg* (*i.e.* Z.N.) i, 96 and ii, 133 and 421.]

5 *qurugh.* Vullers, classing the word as Arabic, Zenker, classing it as Eastern Turki, and Erskine (p. 42 n.) explain this as land reserved for the

Higher up (on the river) than Kan-i-gil and to the s.e. of it is a meadow some 4 miles east of the town, known as Khan Yurti (Khan's Camping-ground). The Qara-su flows through this meadow before entering Kan-i-gil. When it comes to Khan Yurti it curves back so far that it encloses, with a very narrow outlet, enough ground for a camp. Having noticed these advantages, we camped there for a time during the siege

Fol. 48b.   of Samarkand.[1]

Another meadow is the Budana Qurugh (Quail Reserve), lying between Dil-kusha and the town. Another is the Kul-i-maghak (Meadow of the deep pool) at some 4 miles from the town. This also is a round[2] meadow. People call it Kul-i-maghak meadow because there is a large pool on one side of it. Sl. 'Ali Mirza lay here during the siege, when I was in Khan Yurti. Another and smaller meadow is Qulba (Plough); it has Qulba Village and the Kohik Water on the north, the Bagh-i-maidan and Darwesh Muhammad Tarkhan's Char-bagh on the south, and the Kohik upland on the west.

Samarkand has good districts and *tumans*. Its largest district, and one that is its equal, is Bukhara, 25 *yighach*[3] to the west. Bukhara in its turn, has several *tumans*; it is a fine town; its fruits are many and good, its melons excellent; none in Ma wara'u'n-nahr matching them for quality and quantity. Although the Mir Timuri melon of Akhsi[4] is sweeter and more delicate than any Bukhara melon, still in Bukhara many kinds of melon are good and plentiful. The Bukhara plum is famous; no other equals it. They skin it,[5] dry it and carry

Fol. 49.   it from land to land with rarities (*tabarruklar bila*); it is an excellent laxative medicine. Fowls and geese are much

---

summer encampment of princes. Shaw (Voc. p. 155), deriving it from *qurumaq*, to frighten, explains it as a fenced field of growing grain.

1 *Cf.* f. 40. There it is located at one *yighach* and here at 3 *kurohs* from the town.

2 *taur. Cf.* Zenker *s.n.* I understand it to lie, as Khan Yurti did, in a curve of the river.

3 162 m. by rail.

4 *Cf.* f. 3.

5 *tirisini suiub.* The verb *suimak*, to despoil, seems to exclude the common plan of stoning the fruit. *Cf.* f. 3b, *danasini alip*, taking out the stones.

looked after (parwari) in Bukhara. Bukhara wine is the strongest made in Ma wara'u'n-nahr; it was what I drank when drinking in those countries at Samarkand.[1]

Kesh is another district of Samarkand, 9 yighach[2] by road to the south of the town. A range called the Aitmak Pass (Daban)[3] lies between Samarkand and Kesh; from this are taken all the stones for building. Kesh is called also Shahr-i-sabz (Green-town) because its barren waste (sahr) and roofs and walls become beautifully green in spring. As it was Timur Beg's birth-place, he tried hard to make it his capital. He erected noble buildings in it. To seat his own Court, he built a great arched hall and in this seated his Commander-begs and his Diwan-begs, on his right and on his left. For those attending the Court, he built two smaller halls, and to seat petitioners to his Court, built quite small recesses on the four sides of the Court-house.[4] Few arches so fine can be shown in the world. It is said to be higher than the Kisri Arch.[5] Timur Beg also built in Kesh a college and a mausoleum, in which are the tombs of Jahangir Mirza and others of his descendants.[6] As Kesh did not offer the same facilities as   Fol. 49b.

1 *Min Samarkandta aul (or auwal) aichkanda Bukhara chaghirlar ni aichar aidim.* These words have been understood to refer to Babur's initial drinking of wine but this reading is negatived by his statement (f. 189) that he first drank wine in Harat in 912 AH. I understand his meaning to be that the wine he drank in Samarkand was Bukhara wine. The time cannot have been earlier than 917 AH. The two words *aul aichkanda*, I read as parallel to *aul (baghri qara)* (f. 280) "that drinking," "that bird," *i.e.* of those other countries, not of Hindustan where he wrote.

It may be noted that Babur's word for wine, *chaghir*, may not always represent wine of the grape but may include wine of the apple and pear (cider and perry), and other fruits. Cider, its name seeming to be a descendant of *chaghir*, was introduced into England by Crusaders, its manufacture having been learned from Turks in Palestine.

2 48 m. 3 fur. by way of the Aitmak Pass (mod. Takhta Qarachi), and, Réclus (vi, 256) Buz-gala-khana, Goat-house.

3 The name Aitmak, to build, appears to be due to the stone quarries on the range. The pass-head is 34 m. from Samarkand and 3000 ft. above it. *See* Kostenko ii, 115 and Schuyler ii, 61 for details of the route.

4 The description of this hall is difficult to translate. Clavijo (Markham 124) throws light on the small recesses. *Cf.* Z.N. i, 781 and 300 and Schuyler ii, 68.

5 The Taq-i-kisri, below Baghdad, is 105 ft. high, 84 ft. span and 150 ft. in depth (Erskine).

6 *Cf.* f. 46. Babur does not mention that Timur's father was buried at Kesh. Clavijo (Markham p. 123) says it was Timur's first intention to be buried near his father, in Kesh.

Samarkand for becoming a town and a capital, he at last made clear choice of Samarkand.

Another district is Qarshi, known also as Nashaf and Nakhshab.[1] Qarshi is a Mughul name. In the Mughul tongue they call a *kur-khana* Qarshi.[2] The name must have come in after the rule of Chingiz Khan. Qarshi is somewhat scantily supplied with water; in spring it is very beautiful and its grain and melons are good. It lies 18 *yighach*[3] by road south and a little inclined to west of Samarkand. In the district a small bird, known as the *qil-quyirugh* and resembling the *baghri qara*, is found in such countless numbers that it goes by the name of the Qarshi birdie (*murghak*).[4]

Khozar is another district; Karmina another, lying between Samarkand and Bukhara; Qara-kul another, 7 *yighach*[5] n.w. of Bukhara and at the furthest limit of the water.

Samarkand has good *tumans*. One is Soghd with its dependencies. Its head Yar-yilaq, its foot Bukhara, there may be not one single *yighach* of earth without its village and its cultivated lands. So famous is it that the saying attributed to Timur Beg, "I have a garden 30 *yighach* long,"[6] must have been spoken of Soghd. Another *tuman* is Shavdar (var. Shadwar), an excellent one adjoining the town-suburbs. On one side it has the range (Aitmak Daban), lying between Samarkand and Shahr-i-sabz, on the skirts of which are many of its villages. On the other side is the Kohik Water (*i.e.* the Dar-i-gham canal). There it lies! an excellent *tuman*, with fine air, full of beauty, abounding in waters, its good things cheap. Observers of Egypt and Syria have not pointed out its match.

Fol. 50.

---

1 Abu'l-fida (Reinaud II, ii, 21) says that Nasaf is the Arabic and Nakhshab the local name for Qarshi. Ibn Haukal (Ouseley p. 260) writes Nakhshab.

2 This word has been translated *burial-place* and *cimetière* but Qarshi means castle, or royal-residence. The Z.N. (i, 111) says that Qarshi is an equivalent for Ar. *qasr*, palace, and was so called, from one built there by Qublai Khan (d. 1294 AD.). Perhaps Babur's word is connected with Gurkhan, the title of sovereigns in Khutan, and means great or royal-house, *i.e.* palace.

3 94 m. 6½ fur. via Jam (Kostenko i, 115).

4 *See* Appendix B.

5 some 34 m. (Kostenko i, 196). Schuyler mentions that he heard in Qara-kul a tradition that the district, in bye-gone days, was fertilized from the Sir.

6 *Cf.* f. 45.

Though Samarkand has other *tumans*, none ranks with those enumerated; with so much, enough has been said.

Timur Beg gave the government of Samarkand to his eldest son, Jahangir Mirza (in 776 AH.-1375 AD.); when Jahangir Mirza died (805 AH.-1403 AD.), he gave it to the Mirza's eldest son, Muhammad Sultan-i-jahangir; when Muhammad Sultan Mirza died, it went to Shah-rukh Mirza, Timur Beg's youngest son. Shah-rukh Mirza gave the whole of Ma wara'u'n-nahr (in 851 AH.-1447 AD.) to his eldest son, Aulugh Beg Mirza. From him his own son, 'Abdu'l-latif Mirza took it, (853 AH.-1449 AD.), for the sake of this five days' fleeting world martyring a father so full of years and knowledge.

The following chronogram gives the date of Aulugh Beg Mirza's death:—

> Aulugh Beg, an ocean of wisdom and science,
> The pillar of realm and religion,
> Sipped from the hand of 'Abbas, the mead of martyrdom,
> And the date of the death is *'Abbas kasht* ('Abbas slew).[1]

Though 'Abdu'l-latif Mirza did not rule more than five or six months, the following couplet was current about him:—

> Ill does sovereignty befit the parricide;
> Should he rule, be it for no more than six months.[2]

This chronogram of the death of 'Abdu'l-latif Mirza is also well done:—

> 'Abdu'l-latif, in glory a Khusrau and Jamshid,   Fol. 50b.
> In his train a Faridun and Zardusht,
> Baba Husain slew on the Friday Eve,
> With an arrow. Write as its date, *Baba Husain kasht* (Baba Husain slew).[3]

After 'Abdu'l-latif Mirza's death (Jumada I, 22, 855 AH.—June 22nd 1450 AD.), (his cousin) 'Abdu'l-lah Mirza, the grandson of Shah-rukh Mirza through Ibrahim Mirza, seated himself on the

1 By *abjad* the words *'Abbas kasht* yield 853. The date of the murder was Ramzan 9, 853 AH. (Oct. 27th 1449 AD.).

2 This couplet is quoted in the *Rauzatu's-safa* (lith. ed. vi, f. 234 foot) and in the H.S. ii, 44 and iii, 167. It is said, in the R.S. to be by Nizami and to refer to the killing by Shiruya of his father, Khusrau Parwiz in 7 AH. (628 AD.). The H.S. says that 'Abdu'l-latif constantly repeated the couplet, after he had murdered his father. *See also* Daulat Shah (Browne p. 356 and p. 366). H.B. *See also* Additional Notes, p. 797.

3 By *abjad, Baba Husain kasht* yields 854. The death was on Rabi' I, 26, 854 AH. (May 9th 1450 AD.). *See* R.S. vi, 235 for an account of this death.

throne and ruled for 18 months to two years.[1] From him Sl. Abu-sa'id Mirza took it (855 AH.-1451 AD.). He in his life-time gave it to his eldest son, Sl. Ahmad Mirza; Sl. Ahmad Mirza continued to rule it after his father's death (873 AH.-1469 AD.). On his death (899 AH.-1494 AD.) Sl. Mahmud Mirza was seated on the throne and on his death (900 AH.-1495 AD.) Bai-sunghar Mirza. Bai-sunghar Mirza was made prisoner for a few days, during the Tarkhan rebellion (901 AH.-1496 AD.), and his younger brother, Sl. 'Ali Mirza was seated on the throne, but Bai-sunghar Mirza, as has been related in this history, took it again directly. From Bai-sunghar Mirza I took it (903 AH.-1497 AD.). Further details will be learned from the ensuing history.

(c. Babur's rule in Samarkand.)

When I was seated on the throne, I shewed the Samarkand begs precisely the same favour and kindness they had had before. I bestowed rank and favour also on the begs with me, to each according to his circumstances, the largest share falling to Sl. Ahmad *Tambal*; he had been in the household begs' circle; I now raised him to that of the great begs.

We had taken the town after a seven months' hard siege. Things of one sort or other fell to our men when we got in. The whole country, with exception of Samarkand itself, had come in earlier either to me or to Sl. 'Ali Mirza and consequently had not been over-run. In any case however, what could have been taken from districts so long subjected to raid and rapine? The booty our men had taken, such as it was, came to an end. When we entered the town, it was in such distress that it needed seed-corn and money-advances; what place was this to take anything from? On these accounts our men suffered great privation. We ourselves could give them nothing. Moreover they yearned for their homes and, by ones and twos, set their faces for flight. The first to go was Bayan Quli's (son) Khan Quli; Ibrahim *Begchik* was another; all the Mughuls went off and, a little later, Sl. Ahmad *Tambal*.

Auzun Hasan counted himself a very sincere and faithful

Fol. 51.

---

1 This overstates the time; dates shew 1 yr. 1 mth. and a few days.

friend of Khwaja-i-qazi; we therefore, to put a stop to these desertions, sent the Khwaja to him (in Andijan) so that they, Fol. 51b. in agreement, might punish some of the deserters and send others back to us. But that very Auzun Hasan, that traitor to his salt, may have been the stirrer-up of the whole trouble and the spur-to-evil of the deserters from Samarkand. Directly Sl. Ahmad *Tambal* had gone, all the rest took up a wrong position.

(*d. Andijan demanded of Babur by The Khan, and also for Jahangir Mirza.*)

Although, during the years in which, coveting Samarkand, I had persistently led my army out, Sl. Mahmud Khan[1] had provided me with no help whatever, yet, now it had been taken, he wanted Andijan. Moreover, Auzun Hasan and Sl. Ahmad *Tambal*, just when soldiers of ours and all the Mughuls had deserted to Andijan and Akhsi, wanted those two districts for Jahangir Mirza. For several reasons, those districts could not be given to them. One was, that though not promised to The Khan, yet he had asked for them and, as he persisted in asking, an agreement with him was necessary, if they were to be given to Jahangir Mirza. A further reason was that to ask for them just when deserters from us had fled to them, was very like a command. If the matter had been brought forward earlier, some way of tolerating a command might have been found. At the Fol. 52. moment, as the Mughuls and the Andijan army and several even of my household had gone to Andijan, I had with me in Samarkand, beg for beg, good and bad, somewhere about 1000 men.

When Auzun Hasan and Sl. Ahmad *Tambal* did not get what they wanted, they invited all those timid fugitives to join them. Just such a happening, those timid people, for their own sakes, had been asking of God in their terror. Hereupon, Auzun Hasan and Sl. Ahmad *Tambal*, becoming openly hostile and rebellious, led their army from Akhsi against Andijan.

Tulun Khwaja was a bold, dashing, eager brave of the Barin (Mughuls). My father had favoured him and he was still in favour, I myself having raised him to the rank of beg. In

1 *i.e.* The Khan of the Mughuls, Babur's uncle.

truth he deserved favour, a wonderfully bold and dashing brave! He, as being the man I favoured amongst the Mughuls, was sent (after them) when they began to desert from Samarkand, to counsel the clans and to chase fear from their hearts so that

Fol. 52b. they might not turn their heads to the wind.[1] Those two traitors however, those false guides, had so wrought on the clans that nothing availed, promise or entreaty, counsel or threat. Tulun Khwaja's march lay through Aiki-su-ara,[2] known also as Rabatik-aurchini. Auzun Hasan and Sl. Ahmad Tambal sent a skirmishing party against him; it found him off his guard, seized and killed him. This done, they took Jahangir Mirza and went to besiege Andijan.

(e. Babur loses Andijan.)

In Andijan when my army rode out for Samarkand, I had left Auzun Hasan and 'Ali-dost Taghai (Ramzan 902 AH.-May 1497 AD.). Khwaja-i-qazi had gone there later on, and there too were many of my men from Samarkand. During the siege, the Khwaja, out of good-will to me, apportioned 18,000 of his own sheep to the garrison and to the families of the men still with me. While the siege was going on, letters kept coming to me from my mothers[3] and from the Khwaja, saying in effect, "They are besieging us in this way; if at our cry of distress you do not come, things will go all to ruin. Samarkand was taken

Fol. 53. by the strength of Andijan; if Andijan is in your hands, God willing, Samarkand can be had again." One after another came letters to this purport. Just then I was recovering from illness but, not having been able to take due care in the days of convalescence, I went all to pieces again and this time, became so very ill that for four days my speech was impeded and they

---

1 Elph. MS. *aurmaghailar*, might not turn; Hai, and Kehr's MSS. (*sar ba bad*) *birmaghailar*, might not give. Both metaphors seem drawn from the protective habit of man and beast of turning the back to a storm-wind.

2 *i.e.* betwixt two waters, the Miyan-du-ab of India. Here, it is the most fertile triangle of land in Turkistan (Réclus, vi, 199), enclosed by the eastern mountains, the Narin and the Qara-su; Rabatik-aurchini, its alternative name, means Small Station sub-district. From the uses of *aurchin* I infer that it describes a district in which there is no considerable head-quarters fort.

3 *i.e.* his own, Qutluq-nigar Khanim and hers, Aisan-daulat Begim, with perhaps other widows of his father, probably Shah Sultan Begim.

used to drop water into my mouth with cotton. Those with me, begs and bare braves alike, despairing of my life, began each to take thought for himself. While I was in this condition, the begs, by an error of judgment, shewed me to a servant of Auzun Hasan's, a messenger come with wild proposals, and then dismissed him. In four or five days, I became somewhat better but still could not speak, in another few days, was myself again.

Such letters! so anxious, so beseeching, coming from my mothers, that is from my own and hers, Aisan-daulat Begim, and from my teacher and spiritual guide, that is, Khwaja-i-maulana-i-qazi, with what heart would a man not move? We left Samarkand for Andijan on a Saturday in Rajab (Feb.-March), when I had ruled 100 days in the town. It was Fol. 53b. Saturday again when we reached Khujand and on that day a person brought news from Andijan, that seven days before, that is on the very day we had left Samarkand, 'Ali-dost Taghai had surrendered Andijan.

These are the particulars;—The servant of Auzun Hasan who, after seeing me, was allowed to leave, had gone to Andijan and there said, "The *padshah* cannot speak and they are dropping water into his mouth with cotton." Having gone and made these assertions in the ordinary way, he took oath in 'Ali-dost Taghai's presence. 'Ali-dost Taghai was in the Khakan Gate. Becoming without footing through this matter, he invited the opposite party into the fort, made covenant and treaty with them, and surrendered Andijan. Of provisions and of fighting men, there was no lack whatever; the starting point of the surrender was the cowardice of that false and faithless manikin; what was told him, he made a pretext to put himself in the right.

When the enemy, after taking possession of Andijan, heard of my arrival in Khujand, they martyred Khwaja-i-maulana-i-qazi by hanging him, with dishonour, in the Gate of the citadel. Fol. 54. He had come to be known as Khwaja-maulana-i-qazi but his own name was 'Abdu'l-lah. On his father's side, his line went back to Shaikh Burhanu'd-din 'Ali *Qilich*, on his mother's to Sl. Ailik *Mazi*. This family had come to be the Religious

Guides (*muqtada*) and pontiff (*Shaikhu'l-islam*) and Judge (*qazi*)
in the Farghana country.[1] He was a disciple of his Highness
'Ubaidu'l-lah (*Ahrari*) and from him had his upbringing.
I have no doubt he was a saint (*wali*); what better witnesses
to his sanctity than the fact that within a short time, no sign
or trace remained of those active for his death? He was a
wonderful man; it was not in him to be afraid; in no other
man was seen such courage as his. This quality is a further
witness to his sanctity. Other men, however bold, have
anxieties and tremors; he had none. When they had killed
him, they seized and plundered those connected with him,
retainers and servants, tribesmen and followers.

In anxiety for Andijan, we had given Samarkand out of our
hands; then heard we had lost Andijan. It was like the saying,
"In ignorance, made to leave this place, shut out from that"
(*Ghafil az in ja randa, az an ja manda*). It was very hard and
vexing to me; for why? never since I had ruled, had I been cut
off like this from my retainers and my country; never since
I had known myself, had I known such annoyance and such
hardship.

(f. Babur's action from Khujand as his base.)

On our arrival in Khujand, certain hypocrites, not enduring
to see Khalifa in my Gate, had so wrought on Muhammad
Husain Mirza *Dughlat* and others that he was dismissed
towards Tashkint. To Tashkint also Qasim Beg *Quchin* had
been sent earlier, in order to ask The Khan's help for a move
on Andijan. The Khan consented to give it and came himself
by way of the Ahangaran Dale,[2] to the foot of the Kindirlik
Pass.[3] There I went also, from Khujand, and saw my Khan
dada.[4] We then crossed the pass and halted on the Akhsi side.
The enemy for their part, gathered their men and went to
Akhsi.

Fol. 54b.

---

1 *Cf.* f. 16 for almost verbatim statements.
2 Blacksmith's Dale. *Ahangaran* appears corrupted in modern maps to
Angren. See H.S. ii, 293 for Khwand-amir's wording of this episode.
3 *Cf.* f. 1b and Kostenko i, 101.
4 *i.e.* Khan Uncle (Mother's brother).

Just at that time, the people in Pap[1] sent me word they had
made fast the fort but, owing to something misleading in The
Khan's advance, the enemy stormed and took it. Though
The Khan had other good qualities and was in other ways
businesslike, he was much without merit as a soldier and
commander. Just when matters were at the point that if he
made one more march, it was most probable the country would
be had without fighting, at such a time! he gave ear to what
the enemy said with alloy of deceit, spoke of peace and, as his
messengers, sent them Khwaja Abu'l-makaram and his own   Fol. 55.
Lord of the Gate, Beg *Tilba* (Fool), *Tambal*'s elder brother. To
save themselves those others (*i.e.* Hasan and Tambal) mixed
something true with what they fabled and agreed to give gifts
and bribes either to The Khan or to his intermediaries. With
this, The Khan retired.

As the families of most of my begs and household and braves
were in Andijan, 7 or 800 of the great and lesser begs and bare
braves, left us in despair of our taking the place. Of the begs
were 'Ali-darwesh Beg, 'Ali-mazid *Quchin*, Muhammad Baqir
Beg, Shaikh 'Abdu'l-lah, Lord of the Gate and Mirim *Laghari*.
Of men choosing exile and hardship with me, there may have
been, of good and bad, between 200 and 300. Of begs there
were Qasim *Quchin* Beg, Wais *Laghari* Beg, Ibrahim *Saru
Mingligh* Beg, Shirim Taghai, Sayyidi Qara Beg; and of my
household, Mir Shah *Quchin*, Sayyid Qasim *Jalair*, Lord of the
Gate, Qasim-'ajab, 'Ali-dost Taghais (son) Muhammad-dost,
Muhammad-'ali *Mubashir*,[2] Khudai-birdi *Tughchi Mughul*, Yarik
Taghai, Baba 'Ali's (son) Baba Quli, Pir Wais, Shaikh Wais,   Fol. 55b.
Yar-'ali *Balal*,[3] Qasim *Mir Akhwur* (Chief Equerry) and Haidar
Rikabdar (stirrup-holder).

It came very hard on me; I could not help crying a good
deal. Back I went to Khujand and thither they sent me my

1 n.w. of the Sang ferry over the Sir.
2 perhaps, messenger of good tidings.
3 This man's family connections are interesting. He was 'Ali-shukr Beg
Baharlu's grandson, nephew therefore of Pasha Begim; through his son,
Saif-'ali Beg, he was the grandfather of Bairam Khan-i-khanan and thus the
g.g.f. of 'Abdu'r-rahim Mirza, the translator of the Second *Waqi'at-i-baburi*.
See Firishta lith. ed. p. 250.

mother and my grandmother and the families of some of the
men with me.

That Ramzan (April–May) we spent in Khujand, then
mounted for Samarkand. We had already sent to ask The
Khan's help; he assigned, to act with us against Samarkand,
his son, Sl. Muhammad (Sultanim) Khanika and (his son's
guardian) Ahmad Beg with 4 or 5000 men and rode himself as
far as Aura-tipa. There I saw him and from there went on to
Sang-zar by way of Yar-yilaq, past the Burka-yilaq Fort, the
head-quarters of the sub-governor (*darogha*) of the district. Sl.
Muhammad Sultan and Ahmad Beg, riding light and by
another road, got to Yar-yilaq first but on their hearing that
Shaibani Khan was raiding Shiraz and thereabouts, turned
back. There was no help for it! Back I too had to go. Again
I went to Khujand!

As there was in me ambition for rule and desire of conquest,
I did not sit at gaze when once or twice an affair had made no
progress. Now I myself, thinking to make another move for

Fol. 56.   Andijan, went to ask The Khan's help. Over and above this,
it was seven or eight years since I had seen Shah Begim[1] and
other relations; they also were seen under the same pretext. After a few days, The Khan appointed Sayyid Muhammad Husain
(*Dughlat*) and Ayub *Begchik* and Jan-hasan *Barin* with 7 or 8000
men to help us. With this help we started, rode light, through
Khujand without a halt, left Kand-i-badam on the left and so to
Nasukh, 9 or 10 *yighach* of road beyond Khujand and 3 *yighach*
(12–18 m.) from Kand-i-badam, there set our ladders up and
took the fort. It was the melon season; one kind grown here,
known as Isma'il Shaikhi, has a yellow rind, feels like shagreen
leather, has seeds like an apple's and flesh four fingers thick. It is
a wonderfully delicate melon; no other such grows thereabout.
Next day the Mughul begs represented to me, "Our fighting
men are few; to what would holding this one fort lead on?" In
truth they were right; of what use was it to make that fort fast
and stay there? Back once more to Khujand!

1 Babur's (step-)grandmother, co-widow with Aisan-daulat of Yunas Khan and
mother of Ahmad and Mahmud *Chaghatai*.

(*f. Affairs of Khusrau Shah and the Timurid Mirzas*).[1]

This year Khusrau Shah, taking Bai-sunghar Mirza with him, led his army (from Qunduz) to Chaghanian and with false and treacherous intent, sent this message to Hisar for Sl. Mas'ud Mirza, "Come, betake yourself to Samarkand; if Samarkand is taken, one Mirza may seat himself there, the other in Hisar." Just at the time, the Mirza's begs and household were displeased with him, because he had shewn excessive favour to his father-in-law, Shaikh 'Abdu'l-lah *Barlas* who from Bai-sunghar Mirza had gone to him. Small district though Hisar is, the Mirza had made the Shaikh's allowance 1000 *tumans* of *fulus*[2] and had given him the whole of Khutlan in which were the holdings of many of the Mirza's begs and household. All this Shaikh 'Abdu'l-lah had; he and his sons took also in whole and in part, the control of the Mirza's gate. Those angered began, one after the other, to desert to Bai-sunghar Mirza.

By those words of false alloy, having put Sl. Mas'ud Mirza off his guard, Khusrau Shah and Bai-sunghar Mirza moved light out of Chaghanian, surrounded Hisar and, at beat of morning-drum, took possession of it. Sl. Mas'ud Mirza was in Daulat Sarai, a house his father had built in the suburbs. Not being able to get into the fort, he drew off towards Khutlan with Shaikh 'Abu'l-lah *Barlas*, parted from him half-way, crossed the river at the Aubaj ferry and betook himself to Sl. Husain Mirza. Khusrau Shah, having taken Hisar, set Bai-sunghar Mirza on the throne, gave Khutlan to his own younger brother, Wali and rode a few days later, to lay siege to Balkh where, with many of his father's begs, was Ibrahim Husain Mirza (*Bai-qara*). He sent Nazar *Bahadur*, his chief retainer, on in advance with 3 or 400 men to near Balkh, and himself taking Bai-sunghar Mirza with him, followed and laid the siege.

Fol. 56b.

Fol. 57.

---

1 Here the narrative picks up the thread of Khusrau Shah's affairs, dropped on f. 44.

2 *ming tuman fulus*, *i.e.* a thousand sets-of-ten-thousand small copper coins. Mr. Erskine (Mems. p. 61) here has a note on coins. As here the *tuman* does not seem to be a coin but a number, I do not reproduce it, valuable as it is *per se*.

Wali he sent off with a large force to besiege Shabarghan and
raid and ravage thereabouts. Wali, for his part, not being
able to lay close siege, sent his men off to plunder the clans
and hordes of the Zardak Chul, and they took him back
over 100,000 sheep and some 3000 camels. He then came,
plundering the San and Char-yak country on his way, and
raiding and making captive the clans fortified in the hills, to
join Khusrau Shah before Balkh.

One day during the siege, Khusrau Shah sent the Nazar
Bahadur already mentioned, to destroy the water-channels[1] of

Fol. 57b. Balkh. Out on him sallied Tingri-birdi *Samanchi*,[2] Sl. Husain
Mirza's favourite beg, with 70 or 80 men, struck him down, cut
off his head, carried it off, and went back into the fort. A very
bold sally, and he did a striking deed.

(*g. Affairs of Sl. Husain Mirza and Badi'u'z-zaman Mirza.*)

This same year, Sl. Husain Mirza led his army out to Bast
and there encamped,[3] for the purpose of putting down
Zu'n-nun *Arghun* and his son, Shah Shuja', because they had
become Badi'u'z-zaman Mirza's retainers, had given him a
daughter of Zu'n-nun in marriage and taken up a position
hostile to himself. No corn for his army coming in from any
quarter, it had begun to be distressed with hunger when the
sub-governor of Bast surrendered. By help of the stores of
Bast, the Mirza got back to Khurasan.

Since such a great ruler as Sl. Husain Mirza had twice led a
splendid and well-appointed army out and twice retired, without taking Qunduz, or Hisar or Qandahar, his sons and his
begs waxed bold in revolt and rebellion. In the spring of this
year, he sent a large army under Muhammad Wali Beg to put
down (his son) Muhammad Husain Mirza who, supreme in
Astarabad, had taken up a position hostile to himself. While
Sl. Husain Mirza was still lying in the Nishin meadow (near

---

1 *ariqlar*; this the annotator of the Elph. MS. has changed to *ashliq*, provisions,
corn.
2 *Saman-chi* may mean Keeper of the Goods. Tingri-birdi, Theodore, is the
purely Turki form of the Khudai-birdi, already met with several times in the B.N.
3 Bast (Bost) is on the left bank of the Halmand.

Harat), he was surprised by Badi'u'z-zaman Mirza and Shah Shuja' Beg (*Arghun*). By unexpected good-fortune, he had been joined that very day by Sl. Mas'ud Mirza, a refugee after bringing about the loss of Hisar,[1] and also rejoined by a force of his own returning from Astarabad. There was no question of fighting. Badi'u'z-zaman Mirza and Shah Beg, brought face to face with these armies, took to flight. Fol. 58.

Sl. Husain Mirza looked kindly on Sl. Mas'ud Mirza, made him kneel as a son-in-law and gave him a place in his favour and affection. None-the-less Sl. Mas'ud Mirza, at the instigation of Baqi *Chaghaniani*, who had come earlier into Sl. Husain Mirza's service, did not stay in Khurasan but started off on some pretext, without asking leave, and went from the presence of Sl. Husain Mirza to that of Khusrau Shah!

Khusrau Shah had already invited and brought from Hisar, Bai-sunghar Mirza; to him had gone Aulugh Beg Mirza's[2] son, Miran-shah Mirza who, having gone amongst the Hazara in rebellion against his father, had been unable to remain amongst them because of his own immoderate acts. Some short-sighted persons were themselves ready to kill these three (Timurid) Mirzas and to read Khusrau Shah's name in the *khutba* but he himself did not think this combination desirable. The ungrateful manikin however, for the sake of gain in this five days' fleeting world,—it was not true to him nor will it be true to any man soever,—seized that Sl. Mas'ud Mirza whom he had seen grow up in his charge from childhood, whose guardian he had been, and blinded him with the lancet. Fol. 58b.

Some of the Mirza's foster-brethren and friends of affection and old servants took him to Kesh intending to convey him to his (half-)brother Sl. 'Ali Mirza in Samarkand but as that party also (*i.e.* 'Ali's) became threatening, they fled with him, crossed the river at the Char-jui ferry and went to Sl. Husain Mirza.

1 *Cf.* f. 56b.
2 known as *Kabuli*. He was a son of Abu-sa'id and thus an uncle of Babur. He ruled Kabul and Ghazni from a date previous to his father's death in 873 AH. (perhaps from the time 'Umar Shaikh was *not* sent there, in 870 AH. *See* f. 6b) to his death in 907 AH. Babur was his virtual successor in Kabul, in 910 AH.

A hundred thousand curses light on him who planned and did a deed so horrible! Up to the very verge of Resurrection, let him who hears of this act of Khusrau Shah, curse him; and may he who hearing, curses not, know cursing equally deserved!

This horrid deed done, Khusrau Shah made Bai-sunghar Mirza ruler in Hisar and dismissed him; Miran-shah Mirza he despatched for Bamian with Sayyid Kamal (or Kahal) to help him.

(*a. Babur borrows Pashaghar and leaves Khujand.*)

Twice we had moved out of Khujand, once for Andijan, once for Samarkand, and twice we had gone back to it because our work was not opened out.[2] Khujand is a poor place; a man with 2 or 300 followers would have a hard time there; with what outlook would an ambitious man set himself down in it?

Fol. 59.

As it was our wish to return to Samarkand, we sent people to confer with Muhammad Husain *Kurkan Dughlat* in Aura-tipa and to ask of him the loan for the winter of Pashaghar where we might sit till it was practicable to make a move on Samarkand. He consenting, I rode out from Khujand for Pashaghar.

> (*Author's note on Pashaghar.*) Pashaghar is one of the villages of Yar-yilaq; it had belonged to his Highness the Khwaja,[3] but during recent interregna,[4] it had become dependent on Muhammad Husain Mirza.

I had fever when we reached Zamin, but spite of my fever we hurried off by the mountain road till we came over against Rabat-i-khwaja, the head-quarters of the sub-governor of the Shavdar *tuman*, where we hoped to take the garrison at unawares, set our ladders up and so get into the

1 Elph. MS. f. 42; W.-i-B. I.O. 215 f. 47*b* and 217 f. 38; Mems. p. 63. Babur here resumes his own story, interrupted on f. 56.

2 *aish achilmadi*, a phrase recurring on f. 59*b* foot. It appears to imply, of trust in Providence, what the English "The way was not opened," does. Cf. f. 60*b* for another example of trust, there clinching discussion whether to go or not to go to Marghinan.

3 *i.e. Ahrari.* He had been dead some 10 years. The despoilment of his family is mentioned on f. 23*b*.

4 *fatratlar*, here those due to the deaths of Ahmad and Mahmud with their sequel of unstable government in Samarkand.

fort. We reached it at dawn, found its men on guard, turned back and rode without halt to Pashaghar. The pains and misery of fever notwithstanding, I had ridden 14 or 15 *yighach* (70 to 80 miles).

After a few days in Pashaghar, we appointed Ibrahim *Saru*, Wais *Laghari*, Sherim Taghai and some of the household and braves to make an expedition amongst the Yar-yilaq forts and get them into our hands. Yar-yilaq, at that time was Sayyid Yusuf Beg's,[1] he having remained in Samarkand at the exodus and been much favoured by Sl. 'Ali Mirza. To manage the forts, Sayyid Yusuf had sent his younger brother's son, Ahmad-i-yusuf, now[2] Governor of Sialkot, and Ahmad-i-yusuf was then in occupation. In the course of that winter, our begs and braves made the round, got possession of some of the forts peacefully, fought and took others, gained some by ruse and craft. In the whole of that district there is perhaps not a single village without its defences because of the Mughuls and the Auzbegs. Meantime Sl. 'Ali Mirza became suspicious of Sayyid Yusuf and his nephew on my account and dismissed both towards Khurasan.

The winter passed in this sort of tug-of-war; with the on-coming heats,[3] they sent Khwaja Yahya to treat with me, while they, urged on by the (Samarkand) army, marched out to near Shiraz and Kabud. I may have had 200 or 300 soldiers (*sipahi*); powerful foes were on my every side; Fortune had not favoured me when I turned to Andijan; when I put a hand out for Samarkand, no work was opened out. Of necessity, some sort of terms were made and I went back from Pashaghar.

Khujand is a poor place; one beg would have a hard time in it; there we and our families and following had been for half a

---

1 *Aughlaqchi*, the player of the kid-game, the grey-wolfer. Yar-yilaq will have gone with the rest of Samarkand into 'Ali's hands in Rajab 903 AH. (March 1498). Contingent terms between him and Babur will have been made; Yusuf may have recognized some show of right under them, for allowing Babur to occupy Yar-yilaq.

2 *i.e.* after 933 AH. *Cf.* f. 46b and note concerning the Bikramaditya era. *See* index *s.n.* Ahmad-i-yusuf and H.S. ii, 293.

3 This plural, unless ironical, cannot be read as honouring 'Ali; Babur uses the honorific plural most rarely and specially, *e.g.* for saintly persons, for The Khan and for elder women-kinsfolk.

year[1] and during the time the Musalmans of the place had
not been backward in bearing our charges and serving us to the
best of their power. With what face could we go there again?
and what, for his own part, could a man do there? "To what
home to go? For what gain to stay?"[2]

In the end and with the same anxieties and uncertainty, we
went to the summer-pastures in the south of Aura-tipa. There
we spent some days in amazement at our position, not knowing
where to go or where to stay, our heads in a whirl. On one of
those days, Khwaja Abu'l-makaram came to see me, he like
me, a wanderer, driven from his home.[3] He questioned us
about our goings and stayings, about what had or had not been
done and about our whole position. He was touched with
compassion for our state and recited the *fatiha* for me before he
left. I also was much touched; I pitied him.

(b. Babur recovers Marghinan.)

Near the Afternoon Prayer of that same day, a horseman
appeared at the foot of the valley. He was a man named
Yul-chuq, presumably 'Ali-dost Taghai's own servant, and had
been sent with this written message, "Although many great
misdeeds have had their rise in me, yet, if you will do me the   Fol. 60b.
favour and kindness of coming to me, I hope to purge my
offences and remove my reproach, by giving you Marghinan
and by my future submission and single-minded service."

Such news! coming on such despair and whirl-of-mind!
Off we hurried, that very hour,—it was sun-set,—without
reflecting, without a moment's delay, just as if for a sudden
raid, straight for Marghinan. From where we were to Marghinan may have been 24 or 25 *yighach* of road.[4] Through
that night it was rushed without delaying anywhere, and on

---

1 *bir yarim yil*. Dates shew this to mean six months. It appears a parallel
expression to Pers. *hasht-yak*, one-eighth.
2 H.S. ii, 293, in place of these two quotations, has a *misra'*,—*Na ray safar
kardan u na ruy iqamat*, (Nor resolve to march, nor face to stay).
3 *i.e.* in Samarkand.
4 Point to point, some 145 m. but much further by the road. Tang-ab seems
likely to be one of the head-waters of Khwaja Bikargan-water. Thence the route
would be by unfrequented hill-tracks, each man leading his second horse.

next day till at the Mid-day Prayer, halt was made at Tang-ab
(Narrow-water), one of the villages of Khujand. There we
cooled down our horses and gave them corn. We rode out
again at beat of (twilight-) drum[1] and on through that night
till shoot of dawn, and through the next day till sunset, and on
through that night till, just before dawn, we were one *yighach*
from Marghinan. Here Wais Beg and others represented to
me with some anxiety what sort of an evil-doer 'Ali-dost was.
"No-one," they said, "has come and gone, time and again,
between him and us; no terms and compact have been made;
trusting to what are we going?" In truth their fears were
just! After waiting awhile to consult, we at last agreed that
reasonable as anxiety was, it ought to have been earlier; that
there we were after coming three nights and two days without
rest or halt; in what horse or in what man was any strength
left?—from where we were, how could return be made? and,
if made, where were we to go?—that, having come so far, on
we must, and that nothing happens without God's will. At
this we left the matter and moved on, our trust set on Him.

At the Sunnat Prayer[2] we reached Fort Marghinan. 'Ali-
dost Taghai kept himself behind (*arqa*) the closed gate and
asked for terms; these granted, he opened it. He did me
obeisance between the (two) gates.[3] After seeing him, we
dismounted at a suitable house in the walled-town. With me,
great and small, were 240 men.

As Auzun Hasan and Tambal had been tyrannical and
oppressive, all the clans of the country were asking for me.
We therefore, after two or three days spent in Marghinan,
joined to Qasim Beg over a hundred men of the Pashagharis,
the new retainers of Marghinan and of 'Ali-dost's following,
and sent them to bring over to me, by force or fair words, such

---

1 *tun yarimi naqara waqtida. Tun yarimi* seems to mean half-dark, twilight.
Here it cannot mean mid-night since this would imply a halt of twelve hours
and Babur says no halt was made. The drum next following mid-day is the
one beaten at sunset.

2 The voluntary prayer, offered when the sun has well risen, fits the
context.

3 I understand that the obeisance was made in the Gate-house, between the
inner and outer doors.

hill-people of the south of Andijan as the Ashpari, Turuqshar, Fol. 61b.
Chikrak and others roundabout. Ibrahim Saru and Wais
Laghari and Sayyidi Qara were also sent out, to cross the
Khujand-water and, by whatever means, to induce the people
on that side to turn their eyes to me.

Auzun Hasan and Tambal, for their parts, gathered together
what soldiers and Mughuls they had and called up the men
accustomed to serve in the Andijan and Akhsi armies. Then,
bringing Jahangir Mirza with them, they came to Sapan, a
village 2m. east of Marghinan, a few days after our arrival, and
dismounted there with the intention of besieging Marghinan.
They advanced a day or two later, formed up to fight, as far as
the suburbs. Though after the departure of the Commanders,
Qasim Beg, Ibrahim *Saru* and Wais *Laghari*, few men were
left with me, those there were formed up, sallied out and prevented the enemy from advancing beyond the suburbs. On
that day, Page Khalil, the turban-twister, went well forward
and got his hand into the work. They had come; they could
do nothing; on two other days they failed to get near the fort. Fol. 62.

When Qasim Beg went into the hills on the south of Andijan,
all the Ashpari, Turuqshar, Chikrak, and the peasants and
highland and lowland clans came in for us. When the Commanders, Ibrahim *Saru* and Wais *Laghari*, crossed the river to
the Akhsi side, Pap and several other forts came in.

Auzun Hasan and Tambal being the heathenish and vicious
tyrants they were, had inflicted great misery on the peasantry
and clansmen. One of the chief men of Akhsi, Hasan-dikcha
by name,[1] gathered together his own following and a body of
the Akhsi mob and rabble, black-bludgeoned[2] Auzun Hasan's
and Tambal's men in the outer fort and drubbed them into the
citadel. They then invited the Commanders, Ibrahim *Saru*,
Wais *Laghari* and Sayyidi Qara and admitted them into the fort.

Sl. Mahmud Khan had appointed to help us, Haidar
Kukuldash's (son) Banda-'ali and Haji Ghazi *Manghit*,[3] the latter

---

1 This seeming sobriquet may be due to eloquence or to good looks.
2 *qara tiyaq*. *Cf.* f. 63b where black bludgeons are used by a red rabble.
3 He was head-man of his clan and again with Shaibani in 909 AH. (Sh. N.
Vambéry, p. 272). Erskine (p. 67) notes that the Manghits are the modern Nogais.

just then a fugitive from Shaibani Khan, and also the Barin *tuman* with its begs. They arrived precisely at this time.

Fol. 62b.   These news were altogether upsetting to Auzun Hasan; he at once started off his most favoured retainers and most serviceable braves to help his men in the citadel of Akhsi. His force reached the brow of the river at dawn. Our Commanders and the (Tashkint) Mughuls had heard of its approach and had made some of their men strip their horses and cross the river (to the Andijan side). Auzun Hasan's men, in their haste, did not draw the ferry-boat up-stream;[1] they consequently went right away from the landing-place, could not cross for the fort and went down stream.[2] Here-upon, our men and the (Tashkint) Mughuls began to ride bare-back into the water from both banks. Those in the boat could make no fight at all. Qarlughach (var. Qarbughach) *Bakhshi* (Pay-master) called one of Mughul Beg's sons to him, took him by the hand, chopped at him and killed him. Of what use was it? The affair was past that! His act was the cause why most of those in the boat went to their death. Instantly our men seized them all (*ariq*) and killed all (but a few).[3] Of Auzun Hasan's confidants escaped Qarlughach *Bakhshi* and Khalil *Diwana* and Qazi *Ghulam*, the last getting off by pretending to be a slave (*ghulam*); and of his trusted braves, Sayyid 'Ali, now in trust in my own service,[4] and Haidar-i-quli and Qilka *Kashghari* escaped. Of his 70 or 80 men, no more than this

Fol. 63.   same poor five or six got free.

On hearing of this affair, Auzun Hasan and Tambal, not being able to remain near Marghinan, marched in haste and disorder for Andijan. There they had left Nasir Beg, the husband of Auzun Hasan's sister. He, if not Auzun Hasan's second, what question is there he was his third?[5] He was an

---

1 *i.e.* in order to allow for the here very swift current. The H.S. varying a good deal in details from the B.N. gives the useful information that Auzun Hasan's men knew nothing of the coming of the Tashkint Mughuls.

2 *Cf.* f. 4b and App. A. as to the position of Akhsi.

3 *barini qirdilar.* After this statement the five exceptions are unexpected; Babur's wording is somewhat confused here.

4 *i.e.* in Hindustan.

5 Tambal would be the competitor for the second place.

experienced man, brave too; when he heard particulars, he knew their ground was lost, made Andijan fast and sent a man to me. They broke up in disaccord when they found the fort made fast against them; Auzun Hasan drew off to his wife in Akhsi, Tambal to his district of Aush. A few of Jahangir Mirza's household and braves fled with him from Auzun Hasan and joined Tambal before he had reached Aush.

(c. Babur recovers Andijan.)

Directly we heard that Andijan had been made fast against them, I rode out, at sun-rise, from Marghinan and by mid-day was in Andijan.[1] There I saw Nasir Beg and his two sons, that is to say, Dost Beg and Mirim Beg, questioned them and uplifted their heads with hope of favour and kindness. In this way, by God's grace, my father's country, lost to me for two years, was regained and re-possessed, in the month Zu'l-qa'da of the date 904 (June 1498).[2]   Fol. 63b.

Sl. Ahmad Tambal, after being joined by Jahangir Mirza, drew away for Aush. On his entering the town, the red rabble (qizil ayaq) there, as in Akhsi, black-bludgeoned (qara tiyaq qilib) and drubbed his men out, blow upon blow, then kept the fort for me and sent me a man. Jahangir and Tambal went off confounded, with a few followers only, and entered Auzkint Fort.

Of Auzun Hasan news came that after failing to get into Andijan, he had gone to Akhsi and, it was understood, had entered the citadel. He had been head and chief in the rebellion; we therefore, on getting this news, without more than four or five days' delay in Andijan, set out for Akhsi. On our arrival, there was nothing for him to do but ask for peace and terms, and surrender the fort.

We stayed in Akhsi[3] a few days in order to settle its affairs

---

1 47 m. 4½ fur.

2 Babur had been about two lunar years absent from Andijan but his loss of rule was of under 16 months.

3 A scribe's note entered here on the margin of the Hai. MS. is to the effect that certain words are not in the noble archetype (nashka sharif); this supports other circumstances which make for the opinion that this Codex is a direct copy of Babur's own MS. See Index s.n. Hai. MS. and JRAS 1906, p. 87.

and those of Kasan and that country-side. We gave the Mughuls who had come in to help us, leave for return (to Tashkint), then went back to Andijan, taking with us Auzun Hasan and his family and dependants. In Akhsi was left, for a time, Qasim-i-ʻajab (Wonderful Qasim), formerly one of the household circle, now arrived at beg's rank.

(d. Renewed rebellion of the Mughuls.)

As terms had been made, Auzun Hasan, without hurt to life

Fol. 64. or goods, was allowed to go by the Qara-tigin road for Hisar. A few of his retainers went with him, the rest parted from him and stayed behind. These were the men who in the throne-less times had captured and plundered various Musalman dependants of my own and of the Khwaja. In agreement with several begs, their affair was left at this;—"This very band have been the captors and plunderers of our faithful Musalman dependants;[1] what loyalty have they shown to their own (Mughul) begs that they should be loyal to us? If we had them seized and stripped bare, where would be the wrong? and this especially because they might be going about, before our very eyes, riding our horses, wearing our coats, eating our sheep. Who could put up with that? If, out of humanity, they are not imprisoned and not plundered, they certainly ought to take it as a favour if they get off with the order to give back to our companions of the hard guerilla times, whatever goods of theirs are known to be here."

In truth this seemed reasonable; our men were ordered to take what they knew to be theirs. Reasonable and just though the order was, (I now) understand that it was a little hasty.

Fol. 64b. With a worry like Jahangir seated at my side, there was no sense in frightening people in this way. In conquest and government, though many things may have an outside appear-ance of reason and justice, yet 100,000 reflections are right and necessary as to the bearings of each one of them. From this single incautious order of ours,[2] what troubles! what rebellions

---

1 *Musalman* here seems to indicate mental contrast with Pagan practices or neglect of Musalman observances amongst Mughuls.
2 *i.e.* of his advisors and himself.

arose! In the end this same ill-considered order was the cause of our second exile from Andijan. Now, through it, the Mughuls gave way to anxiety and fear, marched through Rabatik-aurchini, that is, Aiki-su-arasi, for Auzkint and sent a man to Tambal.

In my mother's service were 1500 to 2000 Mughuls from the horde; as many more had come from Hisar with Hamza Sl. and Mahdi Sl. and Muhammad *Dughlat Hisari*.[1] Mischief and devastation must always be expected from the Mughul horde. Up to now[2] they have rebelled five times against me. It must not be understood that they rebelled through not getting on with me; they have done the same thing with their own Khans, again and again. Sl. Quli *Chunaq*[3] brought me the news. His late father, Khudai-birdi *Buqaq*[4] I had favoured amongst the Mughuls; he was himself with the (rebel) Mughuls Fol. 65. and he did well in thus leaving the horde and his own family to bring me the news. Well as he did then however, he, as will be told,[5] did a thing so shameful later on that it would hide a hundred such good deeds as this, if he had done them. His later action was the clear product of his Mughul nature. When this news came, the begs, gathered for counsel, represented to me, "This is a trifling matter; what need for the padshah to ride out? Let Qasim Beg go with the begs and men assembled here." So it was settled; they took it lightly; to do so must have been an error of judgment. Qasim Beg led his force out that same day; Tambal meantime must have joined the Mughuls. Our men crossed the Ailaish river[6] early next morning by the Yasi-kijit (Broad-crossing) and at once came face to

---

1 *Cf.* f. 34.

2 *circa* 933 AH. All the revolts chronicled by Babur as made against himself were under Mughul leadership. Long Hasan, Tambal and 'Ali-dost were all Mughuls. The worst was that of 914 AH. (1518 AD.) in which Quli *Chunaq* disgraced himself (T.R. p. 357).

3 *Chunaq* may indicate the loss of one ear.

4 *Buqaq*, amongst other meanings, has that of *one who lies in ambush*.

5 This remark has interest because it shews that (as Babur planned to write more than is now with the B.N. MSS.) the first gap in the book (914 AH. to 925 AH.) is accidental. His own last illness is the probable cause of this gap. *Cf.* JRAS 1905, p. 744. Two other passages referring to unchronicled matters are one about the Bagh-i-safa (f. 224), and one about Sl. 'Ali mirza Taghai (f. 242).

6 I surmise Ailaish to be a local name of the Qara-darya affluent of the Sir.

face with the rebels. Well did they chop at one another
(*chapqulashurlar*)! Qasim Beg himself came face to face with
Muhammad *Arghun* and did not desist from chopping at him
in order to cut off his head.[1] Most of our braves exchanged

good blows but in the end were beaten. Qasim Beg, 'Ali-dost
Taghai, Ibrahim *Saru*, Wais *Laghari*, Sayyidi Qara and three
or four more of our begs and household got away but most of
the rest fell into the hands of the rebels. Amongst them were
'Ali-darwesh Beg and Mirim *Laghari* and (Sherim?) Taghai
Beg's (son) Tuqa[2] and 'Ali-dost's son, Muhammad-dost and
Mir Shah *Quchin* and Mirim Diwan.

Two braves chopped very well at one another; on our side,
Samad, Ibrahim *Saru*'s younger brother, and on their side,
Shah-suwar, one of the Hisari Mughuls. Shah-suwar struck
so that his sword drove through Samad's helm and seated
itself well in his head; Samad, spite of his wound, struck so that
his sword cut off Shah-suwar's head a piece of bone as large as
the palm of a hand. Shah-suwar must have worn no helm;
they trepanned his head and it healed; there was no one to
trepan Samad's and in a few days, he departed simply through
the wound.[3]

Amazingly unseasonable was this defeat, coming as it did
just in the respite from guerilla fighting and just when we had
regained the country. One of our great props, Qambar-'ali
Mughul (the Skinner) had gone to his district when Andijan

was occupied and therefore was not with us.

(*e. Tambal attempts to take Andijan.*)

Having effected so much, Tambal, bringing Jahangir Mirza
with him, came to the east of Andijan and dismounted 2 miles
off, in the meadow lying in front of the Hill of Pleasure ('Aish).[4]

---

1 *aiki auch naubat chapqulab bash chiqarghali quimas.* I cannot feel so sure as
Mr. E. and M. de C. were that the man's head held fast, especially as for it to fall
would make the better story.

2 Tuqa appears to have been the son of a Taghai, perhaps of Sherim; his name
may imply blood-relationship.

3 For the verb *awimaq*, to trepan, *see* f. 67 note 5.

4 The Fr. map of 1904 shews a hill suiting Babur's location of this Hill of
Pleasure.

Once or twice he advanced in battle-array, past Chihil-dukhteran[1] to the town side of the hill but, as our braves went out arrayed to fight, beyond the gardens and suburbs, he could not advance further and returned to the other side of the hill. On his first coming to those parts, he killed two of the begs he had captured, Mirim *Laghari* and Tuqa Beg. For nearly a month he lay round-about without effecting anything; after that he retired, his face set for Aush. Aush had been given to Ibrahim *Saru* and his man in it now made it fast.

1 A place near Kabul bears the same name; in both the name is explained by a legend that there Earth opened a refuge for forty menaced daughters.

(a. Babur's campaign against Ahmad Tambal Mughul.)

Commissaries were sent galloping off at once, some to call up the horse and foot of the district-armies, others to urge return on Qambar-'ali and whoever else was away in his own district, while energetic people were told off to get together mantelets (tura), shovels, axes and the what-not of war-material and stores for the men already with us.

As soon as the horse and foot, called up from the various districts to join the army, and the soldiers and retainers who had been scattered to this and that side on their own affairs, were gathered together, I went out, on Muharram 18th (August 25th), putting my trust in God, to Hafiz Beg's Four-gardens and there stayed a few days in order to complete our equipment. This done, we formed up in array of right and left, centre and van, horse and foot, and started direct for Aush against our foe.

On approaching Aush, news was had that Tambal, unable to make stand in that neighbourhood, had drawn off to the north, to the Rabat-i-sarhang sub-district, it was understood. That night we dismounted in Lat-kint. Next day as we were passing through Aush, news came that Tambal was understood to have gone to Andijan. We, for our part, marched on as for Auzkint, detaching raiders ahead to over-run those parts.[2] Our opponents went to Andijan and at night got into the ditch but being discovered by the garrison when they set their ladders up against the ramparts, could effect no more and retired. Our raiders

1 Elph. MS. f. 47b; W.-i-B. I.O. 215 f. 53 and 217 f. 43; Mems. p. 70.
2 From Andijan to Aush is a little over 33 miles. Tambal's road was east of Babur's and placed him between Andijan and Auzkint where was the force protecting his family.

retired also after over-running round about Auzkint without getting into their hands anything worth their trouble.

Tambal had stationed his younger brother, Khalil, with 200 or 300 men, in Madu,[1] one of the forts of Aush, renowned in that centre (*ara*) for its strength. We turned back (on the Auzkint road) to assault it. It is exceedingly strong. Its northern face stands very high above the bed of a torrent; arrows shot from the bed might perhaps reach the ramparts. On this side is the water-thief,[2] made like a lane, with ramparts on both sides carried from the fort to the water. Towards the rising ground, on the other sides of the fort, there is a ditch. The torrent being so near, those occupying the fort had carried stones in from it as large as those for large mortars.[3] From no fort of its class we have ever attacked, have stones been thrown so large as those taken into Madu. They dropped such a large one on 'Abdu'l-qadus *Kohbur*, Kitta (Little) Beg's elder brother,[4] when he went up under the ramparts, that he spun head over heels and came rolling and rolling, without once getting to his feet, from that great height down to the foot of the glacis (*khak-rez*). He did not trouble himself about it at all but just got on his horse and rode off. Again, a stone flung from the double water-way, hit Yar-'ali *Balal* so hard on the head that in the end it had to be trepanned.[5] Many of our men perished by their stones. The assault began at dawn; the water-thief had been taken before breakfast-time;[6] fighting went on till evening; next morning, as they could not hold out after losing the water-thief, they asked for terms and came out. We took 60 or 70 or 80 men of Khalil's command and sent them to Andijan for safe-keeping; as some of our begs and household were prisoners in their hands, the Madu affair fell out very well.[7]

Fol. 67.

Fol. 67b.

---

1 mod. Mazy, on the main Aush-Kashghar road.

2 *ab-duzd*; de C. i, 144, *prise d'eau*.

3 This simile seems the fruit of experience in Hindustan. *See* f. 333, concerning Chanderi.

4 These two Mughuls rebelled in 914 AH. with Sl. Quli *Chunaq* (T.R. *s.n.*).

5 *awidi*. The head of Captain Dow, fractured at Chunar by a stone flung at it, was trepanned (*Saiyar-i-muta'akhirin*, p. 577 and Irvine l.c. p. 283). Yar-'ali was alive in 910 AH. He seems to be the grandfather of the great Bairam Khan-i-khanan of Akbar's reign.

6 *chasht-gah*; midway between sunrise and noon.

7 *tauri*; because providing prisoners for exchange.

From there we went to Unju-tupa, one of the villages of Aush, and there dismounted. When Tambal retired from Andijan and went into the Rabat-i-sarhang sub-district, he dismounted in a village called Ab-i-khan. Between him and me may have been one *yighach* (5 m.?). At such a time as this, Qambar-'ali (the Skinner) on account of some sickness, went into Aush.

It was lain in Unju-tupa a month or forty days without a battle, but day after day our foragers and theirs got to grips. All through the time our camp was mightily well watched at night; a ditch was dug; where no ditch was, branches were set close together;[1] we also made our soldiers go out in their mail

Fol. 68.

along the ditch. Spite of such watchfulness, a night-alarm was given every two or three days, and the cry to arms went up. One day when Sayyidi Beg Taghai had gone out with the foragers, the enemy came up suddenly in greater strength and took him prisoner right out of the middle of the fight.

(b. Bai-sunghar Mirza murdered by Khusrau Shah.)

Khusrau Shah, having planned to lead an army against Balkh, in this same year invited Bai-sunghar Mirza to go with him, brought him[2] to Qunduz and rode out with him for Balkh. But when they reached the Aubaj ferry, that ungrateful infidel, Khusrau Shah, in his aspiration to sovereignty,—and to what sort of sovereignty, pray, could such a no-body attain? a person of no merit, no birth, no lineage, no judgment, no magnanimity, no justice, no legal-mindedness,—laid hands on Bai-sunghar Mirza with his begs, and bowstrung the Mirza. It was upon the 10th of the month of Muharram (August 17th) that he martyred that scion of sovereignty, so accomplished, so sweet-natured and so adorned by birth and lineage. He killed also a few of the Mirza's begs and household.

(c. Bai-sunghar Mirza's birth and descent.)

He was born in 882 (1477 AD.), in the Hisar district. He was Sl. Mahmud Mirza's second son, younger than Sl. Mas'ud M.

1 *shakh tutulur idi*, perhaps a palisade.
2 *i.e.* from Hisar where he had placed him in 903 AH.

and older than Sl. 'Ali M. and Sl. Husain M. and Sl. Wais M.
known as Khan Mirza. His mother was Pasha Begim.   Fol. 68*b.*

(d. His appearance and characteristics.)

He had large eyes, a fleshy face[1] and Turkman features, was
of middle height and altogether an elegant young man (*aet.* 22).

(e. His qualities and manners.)

He was just, humane, pleasant-natured and a most accomplished scion of sovereignty. His tutor, Sayyid Mahmud,[2] presumably was a Shi'a; through this he himself became infected
by that heresy. People said that latterly, in Samarkand, he
reverted from that evil belief to the pure Faith. He was much
addicted to wine but on his non-drinking days, used to go
through the Prayers.[3] He was moderate in gifts and liberality.
He wrote the *naskh-ta'liq* character very well; in painting also
his hand was not bad. He made 'Adili his pen-name and
composed good verses but not sufficient to form a *diwan*. Here
is the opening couplet (*matla'*)[4] of one of them;—

> Like a wavering shadow I fall here and there;
> If not propped by a wall, I drop flat on the ground.

In such repute are his odes held in Samarkand, that they are
to be found in most houses.

(f. His battles.)

He fought two ranged battles. One, fought when he was
first seated on the throne (900 AH.-1495 AD.), was with Sl.
Mahmud Khan[5] who, incited and stirred up by Sl. Junaid
Barlas and others to desire Samarkand, drew an army out,   Fol. 69.
crossed the Aq-kutal and went to Rabat-i-soghd and Kan-bai.
Bai-sunghar Mirza went out from Samarkand, fought him near

---

1 *quba yuzluq* (f. 6*b* and note 4). The Turkman features would be a maternal
inheritance.
2 He is "Saifi Maulana 'Aruzi" of Rieu's Pers. Cat. p. 525. *Cf.* H.S. ii, 341.
His book, '*Aruz-i-saifi* has been translated by Blochmann and by Ranking.
3 *namaz autar idi.* I understand some irony from this (de Meynard's Dict.
s.n. autmaq).
4 The *matla'* of poems serve as an index of first lines.
5 *Cf.* f. 30.

Kan-bai, beat him and beheaded 3 or 4000 Mughuls. In this fight died Haidar *Kukuldash*, the Khan's looser and binder (*hall u'aqdi*). His second battle was fought near Bukhara with Sl. 'Ali Mirza (901 AH.-1496 AD.); in this he was beaten.[1]

(*g. His countries.*)

His father, Sl. Mahmud Mirza, gave him Bukhara; when Sl. Mahmud M. died, his begs assembled and in agreement made Bai-sunghar M. ruler in Samarkand. For a time, Bukhara was included with Samarkand in his jurisdiction but it went out of his hands after the Tarkhan rebellion (901 AH.-1496 AD.). When he left Samarkand to go to Khusrau Shah and I got possession of it (903 AH.-1497 AD.), Khusrau Shah took Hisar and gave it to him.

(*h. Other details concerning him.*)

He left no child. He took a daughter of his paternal uncle, Sl. Khalil Mirza, when he went to Khusrau Shah; he had no other wife or concubine.

He never ruled with authority so independent that any beg was heard of as promoted by him to be his confidant; his begs were just those of his father and his paternal uncle (Ahmad).

Fol. 69b.

(*i. Resumed account of Babur's campaign against Tambal.*)

After Bai-sunghar Mirza's death, Sl. Ahmad *Qarawal*,[2] the father of Quch (Quj) Beg, sent us word (of his intention) and came to us from Hisar through the Qara-tigin country, together with his brethren, elder and younger, and their families and dependants. From Aush too came Qambar-'ali, risen from his sickness. Arriving, as it did, at such a moment, we took the providential help of Sl. Ahmad and his party for a happy omen. Next day we formed up at dawn and moved direct upon our foe. He made no stand at Ab-i-khan but marched from his

1 Cf. f. 37b.
2 *i.e.* scout and in times of peace, huntsman. On the margin of the Elph. Codex here stands a note, mutilated in rebinding;—*Sl. Ahmad pidr-i-Quch Beg ast * * * pidr-i-Sher-afgan u Sher-afgan * * * u Sl. Husain Khan * * * Quch Beg ast. Hamesha * * * dar khana Shaham Khan * * *.*

ground, leaving many tents and blankets and things of the baggage for our men. We dismounted in his camp.

That evening Tambal, having Jahangir with him, turned our left and went to a village called Khuban (var. Khunan), some 3 *yighach* from us (15 m.?) and between us and Andijan. Next day we moved out against him, formed up with right and left, centre and van, our horses in their mail, our men in theirs, and with foot-soldiers, bearing mantelets, flung to the front. Our right was 'Ali-dost and his dependants, our left Ibrahim *Saru*, Wais *Laghari*, Sayyidi Qara, Muhammad-'ali *Mubashir*, and Khwaja-i-kalan's elder brother, Kichik Beg, with several of the household. In the left were inscribed[1] also Sl. Ahmad *Qarawal* and Quch Beg with their brethren. With me in the centre was Qasim Beg *Quchin*; in the van were Qambar-'ali (the Skinner) and some of the household. When we reached Saqa, a village two miles east of Khuban, the enemy came out of Khuban, arrayed to fight. We, for our part, moved on the faster. At the time of engaging, our foot-soldiers, provided how laboriously with the mantelets! were quite in the rear! By God's grace, there was no need of them; our left had got hands in with their right before they came up. Kichik Beg chopped away very well; next to him ranked Muhammad 'Ali *Mubashir*. Not being able to bring equal zeal to oppose us, the enemy took to flight. The fighting did not reach the front of our van or right. Our men brought in many of their braves; we ordered the heads of all to be struck off. Favouring caution and good generalship, our begs, Qasim Beg and, especially, 'Ali-dost did not think it advisable to send far in pursuit; for this reason, many of their men did not fall into our hands. We dismounted right in Khuban village. This was my first ranged battle; the Most High God, of His own favour and mercy, made it a day of victory and triumph. We accepted the omen.

On the next following day, my father's mother, my grandmother, Shah Sultan Begim[2] arrived from Andijan, thinking to beg off Jahangir Mirza if he had been taken.

Fol. 70.

Fol. 70b.

---

1 *pitildi*; W.-i-B. *navishta shud*, words indicating the use by Babur of a written record.
2 *Cf.* f. 6b and note and f. 17 and note.

(j. Babur goes into winter-quarters in Between-the-two-rivers.)

As it was now almost winter and no grain or fruits[1] remained in the open country, it was not thought desirable to move against (Tambal in) Auzkint but return was made to Andijan. A few days later, it was settled after consultation, that for us to winter in the town would in no way hurt or hamper the enemy, rather that he would wax the stronger by it through raids and guerilla fighting; moreover on our own account, it was necessary that we should winter where our men would not become enfeebled through want of grain and where we could straiten the enemy by some sort of blockade. For these desirable ends we marched out of Andijan, meaning to winter near Armiyan and Nush-ab in the Rabatik-aurchini, known also as Between-the-two-rivers. On arriving in the two villages above-mentioned, we prepared winter-quarters.

The hunting-grounds are good in that neighbourhood; in the jungle near the Ailaish river is much *bughu-maral*[2] and pig; the small scattered clumps of jungle are thick with hare and pheasant; and on the near rising-ground, are many foxes[3] of fine colour and swifter than those of any other place. While we were in those quarters, I used to ride hunting every two or three days; we would beat through the great jungle and hunt *bughu-maral*, or we would wander about, making a circle round scattered clumps and flying our hawks at the pheasants. The pheasants are unlimited[4] there; pheasant-meat was abundant as long as we were in those quarters.

While we were there, Khudai-birdi *Tughchi*, then newly-favoured with beg's rank, fell on some of Tambal's raiders and brought in a few heads. Our braves went out also from Aush and Andijan and raided untiringly on the enemy, driving in his

---

1 *tuluk*; *i.e.* other food than grain. Fruit, fresh or preserved, being a principal constituent of food in Central Asia, *tuluk* will include several, but chiefly melons. "Les melons constituent presque seuls vers le fin d'été, la nourriture des classes pauvres" (Th. Radloff. l.c. p. 343).

2 *Cf.* f. 4*b* and note.

3 *tulki* var. *tulku*, the yellow fox. Following this word the Hai. MS. has *u dar kamin dur* instead of *u rangin dur.*

4 *bi hadd*; with which I.O. 215 agrees but I.O. 217 adds *farbih*, fat, which is right in fact (f. 2*b*) but less pertinent here than an unlimited quantity.

herds of horses and much enfeebling him. If the whole winter had been passed in those quarters, the more probable thing is that he would have broken up simply without a fight. Fol. 71 b.

(*k. Qambar-'ali again asks leave.*)

It was at such a time, just when our foe was growing weak and helpless, that Qambar-'ali asked leave to go to his district. The more he was dissuaded by reminder of the probabilities of the position, the more stupidity he shewed. An amazingly fickle and veering manikin he was! It had to be! Leave for his district was given him. That district had been Khujand formerly but when Andijan was taken this last time, Asfara and Kand-i-badam were given him in addition. Amongst our begs, he was the one with large districts and many followers; no-one's land or following equalled his. We had been 40 or 50 days in those winter-quarters. At his recommendation, leave was given also to some of the clans in the army. We, for our part, went into Andijan.

(*l. Sl. Mahmud Khan sends Mughuls to help Tambal.*)

Both while we were in our winter-quarters and later on in Andijan, Tambal's people came and went unceasingly between him and The Khan in Tashkint. His paternal uncle of the full-blood, Ahmad Beg, was guardian of The Khan's son, Sl. Muhammad Sl. and high in favour; his elder brother of the full-blood, Beg Tilba (Fool), was The Khan's Lord of the Gate. After all the comings and goings, these two brought The Khan to the point of reinforcing Tambal. Beg Tilba, leaving his wife and domestics and family in Tashkint, came on ahead of the Fol. 72. reinforcement and joined his younger brother, Tambal,—Beg Tilba! who from his birth up had been in Mughulistan, had grown up amongst Mughuls, had never entered a cultivated country or served the rulers of one, but from first to last had served The Khans!

Just then a wonderful ('*ajab*) thing happened;[1] Qasim-i-'ajab (wonderful Qasim) when he had been left for a time in Akhsi,

---

1 Here a pun on '*ajab* may be read.

went out one day after a few marauders, crossed the Khujand-water by Bachrata, met in with a few of Tambal's men and was made prisoner.

When Tambal heard that our army was disbanded and was assured of The Khan's help by the arrival of his brother, Beg Tilba, who had talked with The Khan, he rode from Auzkint into Between-the-two-rivers. Meantime safe news had come to us from Kasan that The Khan had appointed his son, Sl. Muh. Khanika, commonly known as Sultanim,[1] and Ahmad Beg, with 5 or 6000 men, to help Tambal, that they had crossed by the Archa-kint road[2] and were laying siege to Kasan. Here-upon we, without delay, without a glance at our absent men, just with those there were, in the hard cold of winter, put our trust in God and rode off by the Band-i-salar road to oppose them. That night we stopped no-where; on we went through the darkness till, at dawn, we dismounted in Akhsi.[3] So mightily bitter was the cold that night that it bit the hands and feet of several men and swelled up the ears of many, each ear like an apple. We made no stay in Akhsi but leaving there Yarak Taghai, temporarily also, in Qasim-i-'ajab's place, passed on for Kasan. Two miles from Kasan news came that on hearing of our approach, Ahmad Beg and Sultanim had hurried off in disorder.

(m. Babur and Tambal again opposed.)

Tambal must have had news of our getting to horse for he had hurried to help his elder brother.[4] Somewhere between the two Prayers of the day,[5] his blackness[6] became visible towards Nu-kint. Astonished and perplexed by his elder brother's light departure and by our quick arrival, he stopped short. Said we, "It is God has brought them in this fashion! here they have come with their horses' necks at full stretch;[7]

---

1 *Cf.* f. 15, note to Taghai.

2 Apparently not the usual Kindir-lik pass but one n.w. of Kasan.

3 A ride of at least 40 miles, followed by one of 20 to Kasan.

4 *Cf.* f. 72. Tilba would seem to have left Tambal.

5 *i.e.* the Other (Mid-afternoon) Prayer.

6 *Tambalning qarasi.*

7 *atining buinini qatib. Qatmaq* has also the here-appropriate meaning of *to stiffen.*

if we join hands[1] and go out, and if God bring it right, not a man of them will get off." But Wais *Laghari* and some others said, "It is late in the day; even if we do not go out today, where can they go tomorrow? Wherever it is, we will meet them at dawn." So they said, not thinking it well to make the joint effort there and then; so too the enemy, come so opportunely, broke up and got away without any hurt whatever. The (Turki) proverb is, "Who does not snatch at a chance, will worry himself about it till old age."

Fol. 73.

> (*Persian*) *couplet.*   Work must be snatched at betimes,
> Vain is the slacker's mistimed work.

Seizing the advantage of a respite till the morrow, the enemy slipped away in the night, and without dismounting on the road, went into Fort Archian. When a morrow's move against a foe was made, we found no foe; after him we went and, not thinking it well to lay close siege to Archian, dismounted two miles off (one *shar'i*) in Ghazna-namangan.[2] We were in camp there for 30 or 40 days, Tambal being in Fort Archian. Every now and then a very few would go from our side and come from theirs, fling themselves on one another midway and return. They made one night-attack, rained arrows in on us and retired. As the camp was encircled by a ditch or by branches close-set, and as watch was kept, they could effect no more.

(*n. Qambar-'ali, the Skinner, again gives trouble.*)

Two or three times while we lay in that camp, Qambar-'ali, in ill-temper, was for going to his district; once he even had got to horse and started in a fume, but we sent several begs after him who, with much trouble, got him to turn back.

Fol. 73b.

---

1 *ailik qushmaq, i.e.* Babur's men with the Kasan garrison. But the two W.-i-B. write merely *dast burd* and *dast kardan.*

2 The meaning of *Ghazna* here is uncertain. The Second W.-i-B. renders it by ar. *qaryat* but up to this point Babur has not used *qaryat* for *village.* Ghazna-namangan cannot be modern Namangan. It was 2 m. from Archian where Tambal was, and Babur went to Bishkharan to be between Tambal and Machami, coming from the south. Archian and Ghazna-namangan seem both to have been n. or n.w. of Bishkaran.

It may be mentioned that at Archian, in 908 AH. the two Chaghatai Khans and Babur were defeated by Shaibani.

(o. *Further action against Tambal and an accommodation made.*)

Meantime Sayyid Yusuf of Macham had sent a man to Tambal and was looking towards him. He was the head-man of one of the two foot-hills of Andijan, Macham and Awighur. Latterly he had become known in my Gate, having outgrown the head-man and put on the beg, though no-one ever had made him a beg. He was a singularly hypocritical manikin, of no standing whatever. From our last taking of Andijan (June 1499) till then (Feb. 1500), he had revolted two or three times from Tambal and come to me, and two or three times had revolted from me and gone to Tambal. This was his last change of side. With him were many from the (Mughul) horde and tribesmen and clansmen. "Don't let him join Tambal," we said and rode in between them. We got to Bishkharan with one night's halt. Tambal's men must have come earlier and entered the fort. A party of our begs, 'Ali-darwesh Beg and Quch Beg, with his brothers, went close up to the Gate of

Fol. 74.   Bishkharan and exchanged good blows with the enemy. Quch Beg and his brothers did very well there, their hands getting in for most of the work. We dismounted on a height some two miles from Bishkharan; Tambal, having Jahangir with him, dismounted with the fort behind him.

Three or four days later, begs unfriendly to us, that is to say, 'Ali-dost and Qambar-'ali, the Skinner, with their followers and dependants, began to interpose with talk of peace. I and my well-wishers had no knowledge of a peace and we all[1] were utterly averse from the project. Those two manikins however were our two great begs; if we gave no ear to their words and if we did not make peace, other things from them were probable! It had to be! Peace was made in this fashion;—the districts on the Akhsi side of the Khujand-water were to depend on Jahangir, those on the Andijan side, on me; Auzkint was to be left in my jurisdiction after they had removed their families from it; when the districts were settled and I and Jahangir had

---

1 *bizlar*. The double plural is rare with Babur; he writes *biz*, we, when action is taken in common; he rarely uses *min*, I, with autocratic force; his phrasing is largely impersonal, *e.g.* with rare exceptions, he writes the impersonal passive verb.

made our agreement, we (biz) should march together against Samarkand; and when I was in possession of Samarkand, Andijan was to be given to Jahangir. So the affair was Fol. 74b. settled. Next day,—it was one of the last of Rajab, (end of Feb. 1500) Jahangir Mirza and Tambal came and did me obeisance; the terms and conditions were ratified as stated above; leave for Akhsi was given to Jahangir and I betook myself to Andijan.

On our arrival, Khalil-of-Tambal and our whole band of prisoners were released; robes of honour were put on them and leave to go was given. They, in their turn, set free our begs and household, viz. the commanders[1] (Sherim?) Taghai Beg, Muhammad-dost, Mir Shah Quchin, Sayyidi Qara Beg, Qasim-i-'ajab, Mir Wais, Mirim Diwan, and those under them.

(p. The self-aggrandizement of 'Ali-dost Taghai.)

After our return to Andijan, 'Ali-dost's manners and behaviour changed entirely. He began to live ill with my companions of the guerilla days and times of hardship. First, he dismissed Khalifa; next seized and plundered Ibrahim Saru and Wais Laghari, and for no fault or cause deprived them of their districts and dismissed them. He entangled himself with Qasim Beg and he was made to go; he openly declared, "Khalifa and Ibrahim are in sympathy about Khwaja-i-qazi; they will avenge him on me."[2] His son, Muhammad-dost set himself up on a regal footing, starting receptions and a public table and a Fol. 75. Court and workshops, after the fashion of sultans. Like father, like son, they set themselves up in this improper way because they had Tambal at their backs. No authority to restrain their unreasonable misdeeds was left to me; for why? Whatever their hearts desired, that they did because such a foe of mine as Tambal was their backer. The position was singularly delicate; not a word was said but many humiliations were endured from that father and that son alike.

1 bashlighlar. Teufel was of opinion that this word is not used as a noun in the B.N. In this he is mistaken; it is so used frequently, as here, in apposition. See ZDMG, xxxvii, art. Babur und Abu'l-fazl.
2 Cf. f. 54.

(q. Babur's first marriage.)

'Ayisha-sultan Begim whom my father and hers, *i.e.* my uncle, Sl. Ahmad Mirza had betrothed to me, came (this year) to Khujand[1] and I took her in the month of Sha'ban. Though I was not ill-disposed towards her, yet, this being my first marriage, out of modesty and bashfulness, I used to see her once in 10, 15 or 20 days. Later on when even my first inclination did not last, my bashfulness increased. Then my mother Khanim used to send me, once a month or every 40 days, with driving and driving, dunnings and worryings.

(r. A personal episode and some verses by Babur.)

In those leisurely days I discovered in myself a strange inclination, nay! as the verse says, "I maddened and afflicted myself" for a boy in the camp-bazar, his very name, Baburi, fitting in. Up till then I had had no inclination for any-one, indeed of love and desire, either by hear-say or experience, I had not heard, I had not talked. At that time I composed Persian couplets, one or two at a time; this is one of them:—

> May none be as I, humbled and wretched and love-sick;
> No beloved as thou art to me, cruel and careless.

From time to time Baburi used to come to my presence but out of modesty and bashfulness, I could never look straight at him; how then could I make conversation (*ikhtilat*) and recital (*hikayat*)? In my joy and agitation I could not thank him (for coming); how was it possible for me to reproach him with going away? What power had I to command the duty of service to myself?[2] One day, during that time of desire and passion when I was going with companions along a lane and suddenly met him face to face, I got into such a state of confusion that I almost went right off. To

look straight at him or to put words together was impossible. With a hundred torments and shames, I went on. A (Persian) couplet of Muhammad Salih's[3] came into my mind:—

---

1 *Cf.* f. 20. She may have come from Samarkand and 'Ali's household or from Kesh and the Tarkhan households.

2 *Cf.* f. 26 l. 2 for the same phrase.

3 He is the author of the *Shaibani-nama*.

> I am abashed with shame when I see my friend;
> My companions look at me, I look the other way.

That couplet suited the case wonderfully well. In that frothing-up of desire and passion, and under that stress of youthful folly, I used to wander, bare-head, bare-foot, through street and lane, orchard and vineyard. I shewed civility neither to friend nor stranger, took no care for myself or others.

> (*Turki*)   Out of myself desire rushed me, unknowing
> That this is so with the lover of a fairy-face.

Sometimes like the madmen, I used to wander alone over hill and plain; sometimes I betook myself to gardens and the suburbs, lane by lane. My wandering was not of my choice, not I decided whether to go or stay.

> (*Turki*)   Nor power to go was mine, nor power to stay;
> I was just what you made me, o thief of my heart.

(*s. Sl. 'Ali Mirza's quarrels with the Tarkhans.*)

In this same year, Sl. 'Ali Mirza fell out with Muhammad Mazid Tarkhan for the following reasons;—The Tarkhans had risen to over-much predominance and honour; Baqi had taken the whole revenue of the Bukhara Government and gave not a half-penny (*dang*)[1] to any-one else; Muhammad Mazid, for his part, had control in Samarkand and took all its districts for his sons and dependants; a small sum only excepted, fixed by them, not a farthing (*fils*) from the town reached the Mirza by any channel. Sl. 'Ali Mirza was a grown man; how was he to tolerate such conduct as theirs? He and some of his household formed a design against Muh. Mazid Tarkhan; the latter came to know of it and left the town with all his following and with whatever begs and other persons were in sympathy with him,[2] such as Sl. Husain *Arghun*, Pir Ahmad, Auzun Hasan's younger brother, Khwaja Husain, Qara *Barlas*, Salih Muhammad[3] and some other begs and braves.

Fol. 76b.

---

1 *dang* and *fils* (*infra*) are small copper coins.
2 *Cf.* f. 25 l. 1 and note 1.
3 Probably the poet again; he had left Harat and was in Samarkand (Sh. N. Vambéry, p. 34 l. 14).

At the time The Khan had joined to Khan Mirza a number of Mughul begs with Muh. Husain *Dughlat* and Ahmad Beg, and had appointed them to act against Samarkand.¹ Khan Mirza's guardians were Hafiz Beg *Duldai* and his son, Tahir Beg; because of relationship to them, (Muh. Sighal's) grand-son, Hasan and Hindu Beg fled with several braves from Sl.

Fol. 77.   'Ali Mirza's presence to Khan Mirza's.

Muhammad Mazid Tarkhan invited Khan Mirza and the Mughul army, moved to near Shavdar, there saw the Mirza and met the begs of the Mughuls. No small useful friendlinesses however, came out of the meeting between his begs and the Mughuls; the latter indeed seem to have thought of making him a prisoner. Of this he and his begs coming to know, separated themselves from the Mughul army. As without him the Mughuls could make no stand, they retired. Here-upon, Sl. 'Ali Mirza hurried light out of Samarkand with a few men and caught them up where they had dismounted in Yar-yilaq. They could not even fight but were routed and put to flight. This deed, done in his last days, was Sl. 'Ali Mirza's one good little affair.

Muh. Mazid Tarkhan and his people, despairing both of the Mughuls and of these Mirzas, sent Mir Mughul, son of 'Abdu'l-wahhab *Shaghawal*² to invite me (to Samarkand). Mir Mughul had already been in my service; he had risked his life in good accord with Khwaja-i-qazi during the siege of Andijan (903 AH.-1498 AD.).

This business hurt us also³ and, as it was for that purpose we had made peace (with Jahangir), we resolved to move on Samarkand. We sent Mir Mughul off at once to give rendezvous⁴

Fol. 77b.   to Jahangir Mirza and prepared to get to horse. We rode out

1 From what follows, this Mughul advance seems a sequel to a Tarkhan invitation.

2 By omitting the word *Mir* the Turki text has caused confusion between this father and son (Index *s.nn.*).

3 *biz khud kharab bu mu'amla aiduk.* These words have been understood earlier, as referring to the abnormal state of Babur's mind described under Sec. *r.* They better suit the affairs of Samarkand because Babur is able to resolve on action and also because he here writes *biz*, we, and not *min*, I as in Sec. *r.*

4 For *buljar*, rendezvous, *see also* f. 78 l. 2 fr. ft.

in the month of Zu'l-qa'da (June) and with two halts on the way, came to Qaba and there dismounted.[1] At the mid-afternoon Prayer of that day, news came that Tambal's brother, Khalil had taken Aush by surprise.

The particulars are as follows;—As has been mentioned, Khalil and those under him were set free when peace was made. Tambal then sent Khalil to fetch away their wives and families from Auzkint. He had gone and he went into the fort on this pretext. He kept saying untruthfully, "We will go out today," or "We will go out tomorrow," but he did not go. When we got to horse, he seized the chance of the emptiness of Aush to go by night and surprise it. For several reasons it was of no advantage for us to stay and entangle ourselves with him; we went straight on therefore. One reason was that as, for the purpose of making ready military equipment, all my men of name had scattered, heads of houses to their homes, we had no news of them because we had relied on the peace and were by this off our guard against the treachery and falsity of the other party. Another reason was that for some time, as has been Fol. 78. said, the misconduct of our great begs, 'Ali-dost and Qambar-'ali had been such that no confidence in them was left. A further reason was that the Samarkand begs, under Muh. Mazid Tarkhan had sent Mir Mughul to invite us and, so long as a capital such as Samarkand stood there, what would incline a man to waste his days for a place like Andijan?

From Qaba we moved on to Marghinan (20 m.). Marghi-nan had been given to Quch Beg's father, Sl. Ahmad *Qarawal*, and he was then in it. As he, owing to various ties and attach-ments, could not attach himself to me,[2] he stayed behind while his son, Quch Beg and one or two of his brethren, older and younger, went with me.

Taking the road for Asfara, we dismounted in one of its villages, called Mahan. That night there came and joined us in Mahan, by splendid chance, just as if to a rendezvous, Qasim Beg *Quchin* with his company, 'Ali-dost with his, and Sayyid

1 25 m. only; the halts were due probably to belated arrivals.
2 Some of his ties would be those of old acquaintance in Hisar with 'Ali's father's begs, now with him in Samarkand.

Qasim with a large body of braves. We rode from Mahan by the Khasban (var. Yasan) plain, crossed the Chupan (Shepherd)-bridge and so to Aura-tipa.[1]

(t. Qambar-ʿali punishes himself.)

Trusting to Tambal, Qambar-ʿali went from his own district (Khujand) to Akhsi in order to discuss army–matters with him. Such an event happening,[2] Tambal laid hands on Qambar-ʿali, marched against his district and carried him along. Here the (Turki) proverb fits, "Distrust your friend! he'll stuff your hide with straw." While Qambar-ʿali was being made to go to Khujand, he escaped on foot and after a hundred difficulties reached Aura-tipa.

News came to us there that Shaibani Khan had beaten Baqi Tarkhan in Dabusi and was moving on Bukhara. We went on from Aura-tipa, by way of Burka-yilaq, to Sangzar[3] which the sub-governor surrendered. There we placed Qambar-ʿali, as, after effecting his own capture and betrayal, he had come to us. We then passed on.

(u. Affairs of Samarkand and the end of ʿAli-dost.)

On our arrival in Khan-yurti, the Samarkand begs under Muh. Mazid Tarkhan came and did me obeisance. Conference was held with them as to details for taking the town; they said, "Khwaja Yahya also is wishing for the *padshah*;[4] with his consent the town may be had easily without fighting or disturbance." The Khwaja did not say decidedly to our messengers that he had resolved to admit us to the town but at the same time, he said nothing likely to lead us to despair.

Leaving Khan-yurti, we moved to the bank of the Dar-i-gham (canal) and from there sent our librarian, Khwaja Muhammad ʿAli to Khwaja Yahya. He brought word back, "Let them come; we will give them the town." Accordingly we rode from the Dar-i-gham straight for the town, at night-fall, but

---

1 Point to point, some 90 m. but further by road.
2 *Bu waqiʿ bulghach*, manifestly ironical.
3 Sangzar to Aura-tipa, by way of the hills, some 50 miles.
4 The Sh. N. Vambéry, p. 60, confirms this.

our plan came to nothing because Sl. Muhammad *Duldai's* father, Sl. Mahmud had fled from our camp and given such information to (Sl. 'Ali's party) as put them on their guard. Back we went to the Dar-i-gham bank.

While I had been in Yar-yilaq, one of my favoured begs, Ibrahim *Saru* who had been plundered and driven off by 'Ali-dost,[1] came and did me obeisance, together with Muh.Yusuf, the elder son of Sayyid Yusuf (*Aughlaqchi*). Coming in by ones and twos, old family servants and begs and some of the household gathered back to me there. All were enemies of 'Ali-dost; some he had driven away; others he had plundered; others again he had imprisoned. He became afraid. For why? Because with Tambal's backing, he had harassed and perse-cuted me and my well-wishers. As for me, my very nature sorted ill with the manikin's! From shame and fear, he could stay no longer with us; he asked leave; I took it as a personal favour; I gave it. On this leave, he and his son, Muhammad-dost went to Tambal's presence. They became his intimates, Fol. 79*b*. and from father and son alike, much evil and sedition issued. 'Ali-dost died a few years later from ulceration of the hand. Muhammad-dost went amongst the Auzbegs; that was not altogether bad but, after some treachery to his salt, he fled from them and went into the Andijan foot-hills.[2] There he stirred up much revolt and trouble. In the end he fell into the hands of Auzbeg people and they blinded him. The meaning of "The salt took his eyes," is clear in his case.[3]

After giving this pair their leave, we sent Ghuri *Barlas* toward Bukhara for news. He brought word that Shaibani Khan had taken Bukhara and was on his way to Samarkand. Here-upon, seeing no advantage in staying in that neighbourhood, we set out for Kesh where, moreover, were the families of most of the Samarkand begs.

When we had been a few weeks there, news came that Sl. 'Ali Mirza had given Samarkand to Shaibani Khan. The particulars are these;—The Mirza's mother, Zuhra Begi Agha

---

1 *Cf.* f. 74*b*.
2 Macham and Awighur, presumably.
3 *guzlar tuz tuti*, *i.e.* he was blinded for some treachery to his hosts.

(*Auzbeg*), in her ignorance and folly, had secretly written to
Shaibani Khan that if he would take her (to wife) her son
should give him Samarkand and that when Shaibani had taken
(her son's) father's country, he should give her son a country.[1]
Sayyid Yusuf *Arghun* must have known of this plan, indeed
will have been the traitor inventing it.

1 Muh. Salih's well-informed account of this episode has much interest,
filling out and, as by Shaibani's Boswell, balancing Babur's. Babur is
obscure about what country was to be given to 'Ali. Payanda-hasan para-
phrases his brief words;—Shaibani was to be as a father to 'Ali and when he
had taken 'Ali's father's *wilayat*, he was to give a country to 'Ali. It has
been thought that the gift to 'Ali was to follow Shaibani's recovery of his own
ancestral camping-ground (*yurt*) but this is negatived, I think, by the word,
wilayat, cultivated land.

(*a. Samarkand in the hands of the Auzbegs.*)

When, acting on that woman's promise, Shaibani Khan went to Samarkand, he dismounted in the Garden of the Plain. About mid-day Sl. 'Ali Mirza went out to him through the Four-roads Gate, without a word to any of his begs or unmailed braves, without taking counsel with any-one soever and accompanied only by a few men of little consideration from his own close circle. The Khan, for his part, did not receive him very favourably; when they had seen one another, he seated him on his less honourable hand.[2] Khwaja Yahya, on hearing of the Mirza's departure, became very anxious but as he could find no remedy,[3] went out also. The Khan looked at him without rising and said a few words in which blame had part, but when the Khwaja rose to leave, showed him the respect of rising.

As soon as Khwaja 'Ali[4] Bay's[5] son, Jan-'ali heard in Rabat-

1 Elp. MS. f. 57*b*; W.-i-B. I.O. 215 f. 63*b* and I.O. 217 f. 52; Mems. p. 82.

Two contemporary works here supplement the B.N.; (1) the (*Tawarikh-i-guzida*) *Nasrat-nama*, dated 908 AH. (B.M. Turki Or. 3222) of which Berezin's *Shaibani-nama* is an abridgment; (2) Muh. Salih Mirza's *Shaibani-nama* (Vambéry trs. cap. xix *et seq.*). The H.S. (Bomb. ed. p. 302, and Tehran ed. p. 384) is also useful.

2 *i.e.* on his right. The H.S. ii, 302 represents that 'Ali was well-received. After Shaibaq had had Zuhra's overtures, he sent an envoy to 'Ali and Yahya; the first was not won over but the second fell in with his mother's scheme. This difference of view explains why 'Ali slipped away while Yahya was engaged in the Friday Mosque. It seems likely that mother and son alike expected their Auzbeg blood to stand them in good stead with Shaibaq.

3 He tried vainly to get the town defended. "Would to God Babur Mirza were here!" he is reported as saying, by Muh. Salih.

4 Perhaps it is for the play of words on 'Ali and 'Ali's life (*jan*) that this man makes his sole appearance here.

5 *i.e.* rich man or merchant, but *Bi* (*infra*) is an equivalent of Beg.

i-khwaja of the Mirza's going to Shaibani Khan, he also went.
As for that calamitous woman who, in her folly, gave her son's

house and possessions to the winds in order to get herself a
husband, Shaibani Khan cared not one atom for her, indeed
did not regard her as the equal of a mistress or a concubine.[1]

Confounded by his own act, Sl. 'Ali Mirza's repentance was
extreme. Some of his close circle, after hearing particulars,
planned for him to escape with them but to this he would
not agree; his hour had come; he was not to be freed. He
had dismounted in Timur Sultan's quarters; three or four days
later they killed him in Plough-meadow.[2] For a matter of this
five-days' mortal life, he died with a bad name; having entered
into a woman's affairs, he withdrew himself from the circle of
men of good repute. Of such people's doings no more should
be written; of acts so shameful, no more should be heard.

The Mirza having been killed, Shaibani Khan sent Jan-'ali
after his Mirza. He had apprehensions also about Khwaja
Yahya and therefore dismissed him, with his two young sons,
Khwaja Muh. Zakariya and Khwaja Baqi, towards Khurasan.[3]
A few Auzbegs followed them and near Khwaja Kardzan martyred
both the Khwaja and his two young sons. Though Shaibani's

words were, "Not through me the Khwaja's affair! Qambar Bi
and Kupuk Bi did it," this is worse than that! There is a
proverb,[4] "His excuse is worse than his fault," for if begs, out
of their own heads, start such deeds, unknown to their Khans
or Padshahs, what becomes of the authority of khanship and
and sovereignty?

(b. Babur leaves Kesh and crosses the Mura pass.)

Since the Auzbegs were in possession of Samarkand, we left
Kesh and went in the direction of Hisar. With us started off

---

1 Muh. Salih, invoking curses on such a mother, mentions that Zuhra was
given to a person of her own sort.
2 The Sh. N. and *Nasrat-nama* attempt to lift the blame of 'Ali's death
from Shaibaq; the second saying that he fell into the Kohik-water when
drunk.
3 Harat might be his destination but the H.S. names Makka. Some
dismissals towards Khurasan may imply pilgrimage to Meshhed.
4 Used also by Babur's daughter, Gul-badan (*l.c.* f. 31).

Muh. Mazid Tarkhan and the Samarkand begs under his command, together with their wives and families and people, but when we dismounted in the Chultu meadow of Chaghanian, they parted from us, went to Khusrau Shah and became his retainers.

Cut off from our own abiding-town and country,[1] not knowing where (else) to go or where to stay, we were obliged to traverse the very heart of Khusrau Shah's districts, spite of what measure of misery he had inflicted on the men of our dynasty!

One of our plans had been to go to my younger Khan dada, *i.e.* Alacha Khan, by way of Qara-tigin and the Alai,[2] but this was not managed. Next we were for going up the valley of the Kam torrent and over the Sara-taq pass (*kutal*). When we were near Nundak, a servant of Khusrau Shah brought me one set of nine horses[3] and one of nine pieces of cloth. When we dismounted at the mouth of the Kam valley, Sher- Fol. 81*b*. 'ali, the page, deserted to Khusrau Shah's brother, Wali and, next day, Quch Beg parted from us and went to Hisar.[4]

We entered the valley and made our way up it. On its steep and narrow roads and at its sharp and precipitous saddles[5] many horses and camels were left. Before we reached the Sara-taq pass we had (in 25 m.) to make three or four night-halts. A pass! and what a pass! Never was such a steep and narrow pass seen; never were traversed such ravines and precipices. Those dangerous narrows and sudden falls, those perilous heights and knife-edge saddles, we got through with much difficulty and suffering, with countless hardships and miseries. Amongst the Fan mountains is a large lake (Iskandar); it is 2 miles in circumference, a beautiful lake and not devoid of marvels.[6]

---

1 Cut off by alien lands and weary travel.
2 The Pers. annotator of the Elph. Codex has changed Alai to *wilayat*, and *daban* (pass) to *yan*, side. For the difficult route *see* Schuyler, i, 275, Kostenko, i, 129 and Rickmers, JRGS. 1907, art. Fan Valley.
3 Amongst Turks and Mughuls, gifts were made by nines.
4 Hisar was his earlier home.
5 Many of these will have been climbed in order to get over places impassable at the river's level.
6 Schuyler quotes a legend of the lake. He and Kostenko make it larger.

News came that Ibrahim Tarkhan had strengthened Fort Shiraz and was seated in it; also that Qambar-'ali (the Skinner) and Abu'l-qasim *Kohbur*, the latter not being able to stay in Khwaja Didar with the Auzbegs in Samarkand,—had both come into Yar-yilaq, strengthened its lower forts and occupied them.

Leaving Fan on our right, we moved on for Keshtud. The head-man of Fan had a reputation for hospitality, generosity,

Fol. 82. serviceableness and kindness. He had given tribute of 70 or 80 horses to Sl. Mas'ud Mirza at the time the Mirza, when Sl. Husain Mirza made attack on Hisar, went through Fan on his way to his younger brother, Bai-sunghar Mirza in Samarkand. He did like service to others. To me he sent one second-rate horse; moreover he did not wait on me himself. So it was! Those renowned for liberality became misers when they had to do with me, and the politeness of the polite was forgotten. Khusrau Shah was celebrated for liberality and kindness; what service he did Badi'u'z-zaman Mirza has been mentioned; to Baqi Tarkhan and other begs he shewed great generosity also. Twice I happened to pass through his country;[1] not to speak of courtesy shewn to my peers, what he shewed to my lowest servants he did not shew to me, indeed he shewed less regard for us than for them.

> (*Turki*) Who, o my heart! has seen goodness from worldlings?
> Look not for goodness from him who has none.

Under the impression that the Auzbegs were in Keshtud, we made an excursion to it, after passing Fan. Of itself it seemed

Fol. 82b. to have gone to ruin; no-one seemed to be occupying it. We went on to the bank of the Kohik-water (Zar-afshan) and there dismounted. From that place we sent a few begs under Qasim *Quchin* to surprise Rabat-i-khwaja; that done, we crossed the river by a bridge from opposite Yari, went through Yari and over the Shunqar-khana (Falcons'-home) range into Yar-yilaq. Our begs went to Rabat-i-khwaja and had set up ladders when the men within came to know about them and

1 The second occasion was when he crossed from Sukh for Kabul in 910 AH. (fol. 120).

forced them to retire. As they could not take the fort, they rejoined us.

(*c. Babur renews attack on Samarkand.*)

Qambar-'ali (the Skinner) was (still) holding Sangzar; he came and saw us; Abu'l-qasim *Kohbur* and Ibrahim Tarkhan showed loyalty and attachment by sending efficient men for our service. We went into Asfidik (var. Asfindik), one of the Yar-yilaq villages. At that time Shaibaq Khan lay near Khwaja Didar with 3 or 4000 Auzbegs and as many more soldiers gathered in locally. He had given the Government of Samarkand to Jan-wafa Mirza, and Jan-wafa was then in the fort with 500 or 600 men. Hamza Sl. and Mahdi Sl. were lying near the fort, in the Quail-reserve. Our men, good and bad were 240.

Fol. 83.

Having discussed the position with all my begs and unmailed braves, we left it at this;—that as Shaibani Khan had taken possession of Samarkand so recently, the Samarkandis would not be attached to him nor he to them; that if we made an effort at once, we might do the thing; that if we set ladders up and took the fort by surprise, the Samarkandis would be for us; how should they not be? even if they gave us no help, they would not fight us for the Auzbegs; and that Samarkand once in our hands, whatever was God's will, would happen.

Acting on this decision, we rode out of Yar-yilaq after the Mid-day Prayer, and on through the dark till mid-night when we reached Khan-yurti. Here we had word that the Samar-kandis knew of our coming; for this reason we went no nearer to the town but made straight back from Khan-yurti. It was dawn when, after crossing the Kohik-water below Rabat-i-khwaja, we were once more in Yar-yilaq.

One day in Fort Asfidik a household party was sitting in my presence; Dost-i-nasir and Nuyan[1] *Kukuldash* and Khan-quli and Karim-dad and Shaikh Darwesh and Khusrau Kukuldash and Mirim-i-nasir were all there. Words were crossing from all sides when (I said), "Come now! say when, if God bring it right, we

Fol. 83*b*.

1 This name appears to indicate a Command of 10,000 (Bretschneider's *Mediæval Researches*, i, 112).

shall take Samarkand." Some said, "We shall take it in the heats."
It was then late in autumn. Others said, "In a month," "Forty
days," "Twenty days." Nuyan *Kukuldash* said, "We shall
take it in 14." God shewed him right! we did take it in exactly
14 days.

Just at that time I had a wonderful dream;—His Highness
Khwaja 'Ubaid'l-lah (*Ahrari*) seemed to come; I seemed to go
out to give him honourable meeting; he came in and seated
himself; people seemed to lay a table-cloth before him,
apparently without sufficient care and, on account of this,
something seemed to come into his Highness Khwaja's mind.
Mulla Baba (? *Pashaghari*) made me a sign; I signed back,
"Not through me! the table-layer is in fault!" The Khwaja
understood and accepted the excuse.[1] When he rose,
I escorted him out. In the hall of that house he took hold of
either my right or left arm and lifted me up till one of my feet
was off the ground, saying, in Turki, "Shaikh Maslahat has
given (Samarkand.)"[2] I really took Samarkand a few days
later.

(d. Babur takes Samarkand by surprise.)

In two or three days move was made from Fort Asfidik to
Fort Wasmand. Although by our first approach, we had let our
plan be known, we put our trust in God and made another
expedition to Samarkand. It was after the Mid-day Prayer
that we rode out of Fort Wasmand, Khwaja Abu'l-makaram
accompanying us. By mid-night we reached the Deep-fosse-
bridge in the Avenue. From there we sent forward a detachment
of 70 or 80 good men who were to set up ladders opposite
the Lovers'-cave, mount them and get inside, stand up to those
in the Turquoise Gate, get possession of it and send a man

Fol. 84.

---

1 It seems likely that the cloth was soiled. *Cf.* f. 25 and Hughes Dict. of
Islam *s.n.* Eating.

2 As, of the quoted speech, one word only, of three, is Turki, others may have
been dreamed. Shaikh Maslahat's tomb is in Khujand where Babur had found
refuge in 903 AH.; it had been circumambulated by Timur in 790 AH. (1390 AD.)
and is still honoured.

This account of a dream compares well for naturalness with that in the
seemingly-spurious passage, entered with the Hai. MS. on f. 118. For
examination of the passage *see* JRAS, Jan. 1911, and App. D.

to me. Those braves went, set their ladders up opposite the
Lovers'-cave, got in without making anyone aware, went to the
Gate, attacked Fazil Tarkhan, chopped at him and his few
retainers, killed them, broke the lock with an axe and opened
the Gate. At that moment I came up and went in.

> (*Author's note on Fazil Tarkhan.*)   He was not one of those (Samar-
> kand) Tarkhans; he was a merchant-tarkhan of Turkistan. He had
> served Shaibani Khan in Turkistan and had found favour with him.[1]

Abu'l-qasim *Kohbur* himself had not come with us but had
sent 30 or 40 of his retainers under his younger brother,
Ahmad-i-qasim. No man of Ibrahim Tarkhan's was with us; his
younger brother, Ahmad Tarkhan came with a few retainers
after I had entered the town and taken post in the Monastery. Fol. 84*b.*

The towns-people were still slumbering; a few traders
peeped out of their shops, recognized me and put up prayers.
When, a little later, the news spread through the town, there
was rare delight and satisfaction for our men and the towns-
folk. They killed the Auzbegs in the lanes and gullies with
clubs and stones like mad dogs; four or five hundred were
killed in this fashion. Jan-wafa, the then governor, was living in
Khwaja Yahya's house; he fled and got away to Shaibaq Khan.[2]

On entering the Turquoise Gate I went straight to the
College and took post over the arch of the Monastery. There
was a hubbub and shouting of "Down! down!" till day-break.
Some of the notables and traders, hearing what was happening,
came joyfully to see me, bringing what food was ready and
putting up prayers for me. At day-light we had news that the
Auzbegs were fighting in the Iron Gate where they had made
themselves fast between the (outer and inner) doors. With
10, 15 or 20 men, I at once set off for the Gate but before
I came up, the town-rabble, busy ransacking every corner of the
newly-taken town for loot, had driven the Auzbegs out through

---

1 He was made a Tarkhan by diploma of Shaibani (H.S. ii, 306, l. 2).
2 Here the Hai. MS. begins to use the word *Shaibaq* in place of its previously
uniform *Shaibani*. As has been noted (f. 5*b* n. 2), the Elph. MS. writes
Shaibaq. It may be therefore that a scribe has changed the earlier part
of the Hai. MS. and that Babur wrote *Shaibaq*. From this point my text
will follow the double authority of the Elph. and Hai. MSS.

it. Shaibaq Khan, on hearing what was happening, hurried at sun-rise to the Iron Gate with 100 or 140 men. His coming was a wonderful chance but, as has been said, my men were very few. Seeing that he could do nothing, he rode off at once. From the Iron Gate I went to the citadel and there dismounted, at the Bu-stan palace. Men of rank and consequence and various head-men came to me there, saw me and invoked blessings on me.

Samarkand for nearly 140 years had been the capital of our dynasty. An alien, and of what stamp! an Auzbeg foe, had taken possession of it! It had slipped from our hands; God gave it again! plundered and ravaged, our own returned to us.

Sl. Husain Mirza took Harat[1] as we took Samarkand, by surprise, but to the experienced, and discerning, and just, it will be clear that between his affair and mine there are distinctions and differences, and that his capture and mine are things apart.

Firstly there is this;—He had ruled many years, passed through much experience and seen many affairs.

Secondly;—He had for opponent, Yadgar Muh. Nasir
Mirza, an inexperienced boy of 17 or 18.

Thirdly;—(Yadgar Mirza's) Head-equerry, Mir 'Ali, a person well-acquainted with the particulars of the whole position, sent a man out from amongst Sl. Husain Mirza's opponents to bring him to surprise them.

Fourthly;—His opponent was not in the fort but was in the Ravens'-garden. Moreover Yadgar Muh. Nasir Mirza and his followers are said to have been so prostrate with drink that night that three men only were in the Gate, they also drunk.

Fifthly;—he surprised and captured Harat the first time he approached it.

On the other hand: firstly;—I was in my 19th (lunar) year when I took Samarkand.

Secondly;—I had as my opponent, such a man as Shaibaq Khan, of mature age and an eye-witness of many affairs.

1 In 875 AH. (1470 AD.). Husain was then 32 years old. Babur might have compared his taking of Samarkand with Timur's capture of Qarshi, also with 240 followers (Z.N. i, 127). Firishta (lith. ed. p. 196) ascribes his omission to do so to reluctance to rank himself with his great ancestor.

Thirdly;—No-one came out of Samarkand to me; though the heart of its people was towards me, no-one could dream of coming, from dread of Shaibaq Khan.

Fourthly;—My foe was in the fort; not only was the fort taken but he was driven off.

Fifthly;—I had come once already; my opponent was on his guard about me. The second time we came, God brought it right! Samarkand was won.

In saying these things there is no desire to be-little the reputation of any man; the facts were as here stated. In Fol. 86. writing these things, there is no desire to magnify myself; the truth is set down.

The poets composed chronograms on the victory; this one remains in my memory;—Wisdom answered, "Know that its date is the *Victory (Fath) of Babur Bahadur.*"

Samarkand being taken, Shavdar and Soghd and the *tumans* and nearer forts began, one after another, to return to us. From some their Auzbeg commandants fled in fear and escaped; from others the inhabitants drove them and came in to us; in some they made them prisoner, and held the forts for us.

Just then the wives and families of Shaibaq Khan and his Auzbegs arrived from Turkistan;[1] he was lying near Khwaja Didar and 'Ali-abad but when he saw the forts and people returning to me, marched off towards Bukhara. By God's grace, all the forts of Soghd and Miyan-kal returned to me within three or four months. Over and above this, Baqi Tarkhan seized this opportunity to occupy Qarshi; Khuzar and Qarshi (? Kesh) both went out of Auzbeg hands; Qara-kul Fol. 86b. also was taken from them by people of Abu'l-muhsin Mirza (*Bai-qara*), coming up from Merv. My affairs were in a very good way.

(*e. Birth of Babur's first child.*)

After our departure (last year) from Andijan, my mothers and my wife and relations came, with a hundred difficulties and

1 This arrival shews that Shaibani expected to stay in Samarkand. He had been occupying Turkistan under The Chaghatai Khan.

hardships, to Auratipa. We now sent for them to Samarkand. Within a few days after their arrival, a daughter was born to me by 'Ayisha-sultan Begim, my first wife, the daughter of Sl. Ahmad Mirza. They named the child Fakhru'n-nisa' (Ornament of women); she was my first-born, I was in my 19th (lunar) year. In a month or 40 days, she went to God's mercy.

(*f. Babur in Samarkand.*)

On taking Samarkand, envoys and summoners were sent off at once, and sent again and again, with reiterated request for aid and reinforcement, to the khans and sultans and begs and marchers on every side. Some, though experienced men, made foolish refusal; others whose relations towards our family had been discourteous and unpleasant, were afraid for themselves and took no notice; others again, though they sent help, sent it insufficient. Each such case will be duly mentioned.

Fol. 87.

When Samarkand was taken the second time, 'Ali-sher Beg was alive. We exchanged letters once; on the back of mine to him I wrote one of my Turki couplets. Before his reply reached me, separations (*tafarqa*) and disturbances (*ghugha*) had happened.[1] Mulla Bina'i had been taken into Shaibaq Khan's service when the latter took possession of Samarkand; he stayed with him until a few days after I took the place, when he came into the town to me. Qasim Beg had his suspicions about him and consequently dismissed him towards Shahr-i-sabz but, as he was a man of parts, and as no fault of his came to light, I had him fetched back. He constantly presented me with odes (*qasida u ghazal*). He brought me a song in the Nawa mode composed to my name and at the same time the following quatrain;—[2]

1 'Ali-sher died Jan. 3rd 1501. It is not clear to what disturbances Babur refers. He himself was at ease till after April 20th 1502 and his defeat at Sar-i-pul. Possibly the reference is to the quarrels between Bina'i and 'Ali-sher. *Cf.* Sam Mirza's Anthology, trs. S. de Saçy, *Notices et Extraits* iv, 287 *et seq.*

2 I surmise a double play-of-words in this verse. One is on two rhyming words, *ghala* and *mallah* and is illustrated by rendering them as *oat* and *coat*. The other is on pointed and unpointed letters, *i.e. ghala* and *'ala*. We cannot find however a Persian word *'ala*, meaning garment.

No grain (*ghala*) have I by which I can be fed (*noshid*);
No rhyme of grain (*mallah*, nankeen) wherewith I can be clad (*poshid*);
The man who lacks both food and clothes,
In art or science where can he compete (*koshid*)?

In those days of respite, I had written one or two couplets
but had not completed an ode. As an answer to Mulla Bina'i
I made up and set this poor little Turki quatrain;—[1]

As is the wish of your heart, so shall it be (*bulghusidur*);
For gift and stipend both an order shall be made (*buyurulghusidur*);
I know the grain and its rhyme you write of;
The garments, you, your house, the corn shall fill (*tulghusidur*).

The Mulla in return wrote and presented a quatrain to me in   Fol. 87*b*.
which for his refrain, he took a rhyme to (the *tulghusidur* of)
my last line and chose another rhyme;—

Mirza-of-mine, the Lord of sea and land shall be (*yir bulghusidur*);
His art and skill, world o'er, the evening tale shall be (*samar bulghusidur*);
If gifts like these reward one rhyming (*or* pointless) word;
For words of sense, what guerdon will there be (*nilar bulghusidur*)?

Abu'l-barka, known as *Faraqi* (Parted), who just then had
come to Samarkand from Shahr-i-sabz, said Bina'i ought to
have rhymed. He made this verse;—

Into Time's wrong to you quest shall be made (*surulghusidur*);
Your wish the Sultan's grace from Time shall ask (*qulghusidur*);
O Ganymede! our cups, ne'er filled as yet,
In this new Age, brimmed-up, filled full shall be (*tulghusidur*).

Though this winter our affairs were in a very good way and
Shaibaq Khan's were on the wane, one or two occurrences were
somewhat of a disservice; (1) the Merv men who had taken
Qara-kul, could not be persuaded to stay there and it went
back into the hands of the Auzbegs; (2) Shaibaq Khan besieged
Ibrahim Tarkhan's younger brother, Ahmad in Dabusi, stormed
the place and made a general massacre of its inhabitants before
the army we were collecting was ready to march.

With 240 proved men I had taken Samarkand; in the next   Fol. 88.
five or six months, things so fell out by the favour of the Most
High God, that, as will be told, we fought the arrayed battle of
Sar-i-pul with a man like Shaibaq Khan. The help those

---

1 Babur's refrain is *ghusidur*, his rhymes *bul*, (*buyur*)*ul* and *tul*. Bina'i makes
bulghusidur his refrain but his rhymes are not true *viz. yir*, (*sa*)*mar* and *lar*.

round-about gave us was as follows;—From The Khan had come, with 4 or 5000 Barins, Ayub *Begchik* and Qashka Mahmud; from Jahangir Mirza had come Khalil, Tambal's younger brother, with 100 or 200 men; not a man had come from Sl. Husain Mirza, that experienced ruler, than whom none knew better the deeds and dealings of Shaibaq Khan; none came from Badi'u'z-zaman Mirza; none from Khusrau Shah because he, the author of what evil done,—as has been told,—to our dynasty! feared us more than he feared Shaibaq Khan.

(*g. Babur defeated at Sar-i-pul.*)

I marched out of Samarkand, with the wish of fighting Shaibaq Khan, in the month of Shawwal[1] and went to the New-garden where we lay four or five days for the convenience of gathering our men and completing our equipment. We took the precaution of fortifying our camp with ditch and branch. From the New-garden we advanced, march by march, to beyond Sar-i-pul (Bridge-head) and

Fol. 88b.

there dismounted. Shaibaq Khan came from the opposite direction and dismounted at Khwaja Kardzan, perhaps one *yighach* away (? 5 m.). We lay there for four or five days. Every day our people went from our side and his came from theirs and fell on one another. One day when they were in unusual force, there was much fighting but neither side had the advantage. Out of that engagement one of our men went rather hastily back into the entrenchments; he was using a standard; some said it was Sayyidi Qara Beg's standard who really was a man of strong words but weak sword. Shaibaq Khan made one night-attack on us but could do nothing because the camp was protected by ditch and close-set branches. His men raised their war-cry, rained in arrows from outside the ditch and then retired.

In the work for the coming battle I exerted myself greatly and took all precautions; Qambar-'ali also did much. In Kesh lay Baqi Tarkhan with 1000 to 2000 men, in a position to join us after a couple of days. In Diyul, 4 *yighach* off

1 Shawwal 906 AH. began April 20th 1501.

(? 20 m.), lay Sayyid Muh. Mirza *Dughlat*, bringing me 1000 to 2000 men from my Khan dada; he would have joined me at dawn. With matters in this position, we hurried on the fight!   Fol. 89.

> Who lays with haste his hand on the sword,
> Shall lift to his teeth the back-hand of regret.[1]

The reason I was so eager to engage was that on the day of battle, the Eight stars[2] were between the two armies; they would have been in the enemy's rear for 13 or 14 days if the fight had been deferred. I now understand that these considerations are worth nothing and that our haste was without reason.

As we wished to fight, we marched from our camp at dawn, we in our mail, our horses in theirs, formed up in array of right and left, centre and van. Our right was Ibrahim *Saru*, Ibrahim Jani, Abu'l-qasim *Kohbur* and other begs. Our left was Muh. Mazid Tarkhan, Ibrahim Tarkhan and other Samarkandi begs, also Sl. Husain *Arghun*, Qara (Black) *Barlas*, Pir Ahmad and Khwaja Husain. Qasim Beg was (with me) in the centre and also several of my close circle and household. In the van were inscribed Qambar-'ali the Skinner, Banda-'ali, Khwaja 'Ali, Mir Shah *Quchin*, Sayyid Qasim, Lord of the Gate,—Banda-'ali's younger brother Khaldar (mole-marked) and Haidar-i-qasim's son Quch, together with all the good braves there were, and the rest of the household.

Thus arrayed, we marched from our camp; the enemy, also in array, marched out from his. His right was Mahmud and Jani Beg [Sultan] and Timur Sultans; his left, Hamza and Mahdi and some other sultans. When our two armies approached one another, he wheeled his right towards our rear. To meet this, I turned; this left our van,—in which had been inscribed what not of our best braves and tried swordsmen!—to our right and bared our front (*i.e.* the front of the centre). None-the-less we fought those who made the front-attack on us, turned them and forced them back on their own centre. So far did we carry it that some of Shaibaq Khan's old chiefs said to him, "We must move off! It is past a stand." He however held fast. His right beat our left, then wheeled (again) to our rear.   Fol. 89*b*.

---

1 From the *Bu-stan*, Graf ed. p. 55, l. 246.
2 Sikiz Yilduz. *See* Chardin's *Voyages*, v, 136 and Table; also Stanley Lane Poole's *Babur*, p. 56.

(As has been said), the front of our centre was bare through our van's being left to the right. The enemy attacked us front and rear, raining in arrows on us. (Ayub *Begchik's*) Mughul army, come for our help! was of no use in fighting; it set to work forthwith to unhorse and plunder our men. Not this once only! This is always the way with those ill-omened Mughuls! If they win, they grab at booty; if they lose, they unhorse and pilfer their own side! We drove back the Auzbegs who attacked our front by several vigorous assaults, but those who had wheeled to our rear came up and rained arrows on our standard. Falling on us in this way, from the front and from the rear, they made our men hurry off.

Fol. 90.

This same turning-movement is one of the great merits of Auzbeg fighting; no battle of theirs is ever without it. Another merit of theirs is that they all, begs and retainers, from their front to their rear, ride, loose-rein at the gallop, shouting as they come and, in retiring, do not scatter but ride off, at the gallop, in a body.

Ten or fifteen men were left with me. The Kohik-water was close by,—the point of our right had rested on it. We made straight for it. It was the season when it comes down in flood. We rode right into it, man and horse in mail. It was just fordable for half-way over; after that it had to be swum. For more than an arrow's flight[1] we, man and mount in mail! made our horses swim and so got across. Once out of the water, we cut off the horse-armour and let it lie. By thus passing to the north bank of the river, we were free of our foes, but at once Mughul wretches were the captors and pillagers of one after another of my friends. Ibrahim Tarkhan and some others, excellent braves all, were unhorsed and killed by Mughuls.[2] We moved along the north bank of the Kohik-river,

Fol. 90b.

---

1 In 1791 AD. Muh. Effendi shot 482 yards from a Turkish bow, before the R. Tox. S.; not a good shot, he declared. Longer ones are on record. *See* Payne-Gallwey's *Cross-bow* and AQR. 1911, H. Beveridge's *Oriental Cross-bows.*

2 In the margin of the Elph. Codex, here, stands a Persian verse which appears more likely to be Humayun's than Babur's. It is as follows:

> Were the Mughul race angels, they would be bad;
> Written in gold, the name Mughul would be bad;

recrossed it near Qulba, entered the town by the Shaikh-zada's Gate and reached the citadel in the middle of the afternoon.

Begs of our greatest, braves of our best and many men perished in that fight. There died Ibrahim Tarkhan, Ibrahim *Saru* and Ibrahim Jani; oddly enough three great begs named Ibrahim perished. There died also Haidar-i-qasim's eldest son, Abu'l-qasim *Kohbur*, and Khudai-birdi *Tughchi* and Khalil, Tambal's younger brother, spoken of already several times. Many of our men fled in different directions; Muh. Mazid Tarkhan went towards Qunduz and Hisar for Khusrau Shah. Fol. 91. My highly-favoured beg Qambar-i-ali *the Skinner Mughul*, not acting at such a time as this according to the favour he had received, came and took his wife from Samarkand; he too went to Khusrau Shah. Some of the household and of the braves, such as Karim-dad-i-Khudai-birdi *Turkman* and Janaka *Kukuldash* and Mulla Baba of Pashaghar got away to Aura-tipa. Mulla Baba at that time was not in my service but had gone out with me in a guest's fashion. Others again, did what Sherim Taghai and his band did;—though he had come back with me into the town and though when consultation was had, he had agreed with the rest to make the fort fast, looking for life or death within it, yet spite of this, and although my mothers and sisters, elder and younger, stayed on in Samarkand, he sent off their wives and families to Aura-tipa and remained himself with just a few men, all unencumbered. Not this once only! Whenever hard work had to be done, low and double-minded action was the thing to expect from him!

(h. Babur besieged in Samarkand.)

Next day, I summoned Khwaja Abu'l-makaram, Qasim and the other begs, the household and such of the braves as were admitted to our counsels, when after consultation, we resolved to make the fort fast and to look for life or death within it. I and Qasim Beg with my close circle and household were the

---

Pluck not an ear from the Mughul's corn-land,
What is sown with Mughul seed will be bad.

This verse is written into the text of the First W.-i-B. (I.O. 215 f. 72) and is introduced by a scribe's statement that it is by *an Hazrat*, much as notes known to be Humayun's are elsewhere attested in the Elph. Codex. It is not in the Hai. and Kehr's MSS. nor with, at least many, good copies of the Second W.-i-B.

reserve. For convenience in this I took up quarters in the
middle of the town, in tents pitched on the roof of Aulugh

Beg Mirza's College. To other begs and braves posts were
assigned in the Gates or on the ramparts of the walled-town.

Two or three days later, Shaibaq Khan dismounted at some
distance from the fort. On this, the town-rabble came out of
lanes and wards, in crowds, to the College gate, shouted good
wishes for me and went out to fight in mob-fashion. Shaibaq
Khan had got to horse but could not so much as approach the
town. Several days went by in this fashion. The mob and
rabble, knowing nothing of sword and arrow-wounds, never
witnesses of the press and carnage of a stricken field, through
these incidents, became bold and began to sally further and
further out. If warned by the braves against going out so
incautiously, they broke into reproach.

One day when Shaibaq Khan had directed his attack towards
the Iron Gate, the mob, grown bold, went out, as usual, daringly
and far. To cover their retreat, we sent several braves towards the
Camel's-neck,[1] foster-brethren and some of the close household-
circle, such as Nuyan *Kukuldash*, Qul-nazar (son of Sherim?)

Taghai Beg, and Mazid. An Auzbeg or two put their horses at
them and with Qul-nazar swords were crossed. The rest of the
Auzbegs dismounted and brought their strength to bear on the
rabble, hustled them off and rammed them in through the Iron
Gate. Quch Beg and Mir Shah *Quchin* had dismounted at the side
of Khwaja Khizr's Mosque and were making a stand there. While
the townsmen were being moved off by those on foot, a party of
mounted Auzbegs rode towards the Mosque. Quch Beg came
out when they drew near and exchanged good blows with them.
He did distinguished work; all stood to watch. Our fugitives
below were occupied only with their own escape; for them the
time to shoot arrows and make a stand had gone by. I was shooting with a slur-bow[2] from above the Gate and some of my circle

---

1 This subterranean water-course, issuing in a flowing well (Erskine) gave
its name to a bastion (H.S. ii, 300).
2 *nawak*, a diminutive of *nao*, a tube. It is described, in a MS. of Babur's
time, by Muh. Budha'i and, in a second of later date, by Aminu'd-din (AQR
1911, H.B.'s *Oriental Cross-bows*).

were shooting arrows (*auq*). Our attack from above kept the enemy from advancing beyond the Mosque; from there he retired.

During the siege, the round of the ramparts was made each night; sometimes I went, sometimes Qasim Beg, sometimes one of the household Begs. Though from the Turquoise to the Shaikh-zada's Gate may be ridden, the rest of the way must be walked. When some men went the whole round on foot, it was dawn before they had finished.[1] Fol. 92*b*.

One day Shaibaq Khan attacked between the Iron Gate and the Shaikh-zada's. I, as the reserve, went to the spot, without anxiety about the Bleaching-ground and Needle-makers' Gates. That day, (?) in a shooting wager (*auq auchida*), I made a good shot with a slur-bow, at a Centurion's horse.[2] It died at once (*auq bardi*) with the arrow (*auq bila*). They made such a vigorous attack this time that near Shutur-gardan they got close under the ramparts. Busy with the fighting and the stress near the Iron Gate, we were entirely off our guard about the other side of the town. There, opposite the space between the Needle-makers' and Bleaching-ground Gates, the enemy had posted 7 or 800 good men in ambush, having with them 24 or 25 ladders so wide that two or three could mount abreast. These men came from their ambush when the attack near the Iron Gate, by occupying all our men, had left those other posts empty, and quickly set up their ladders between the two Gates, Fol. 93. just where a road leads from the ramparts to Muh. Mazid Tarkhan's houses. That post was Quch Beg's and Muhammad-quli *Quchin's*, with their detachment of braves, and they had their quarters in Muh. Mazid's houses. In the Needle-makers' Gate was posted Qara (Black) *Barlas*, in the Bleaching-ground Gate, Qutluq Khwaja *Kukuldash* with Sherim Taghai and his brethren, older and younger. As attack was being made on the other side of the town, the men attached to these posts were not on guard but had scattered to their quarters or to the

---

1 Kostenko, i, 344, would make the rounds 9 m.

2 *bir yuz atliqning atini nawak auqi bila yakhshi atim.* This has been read by Erskine as though *buz at*, pale horse, and not *yuz atliq*, Centurion, were written. De. C. translates by Centurion and a marginal note of the Elph.

bazar for necessary matters of service and servants' work. Only the begs were at their posts, with one or two of the populace. Quch Beg and Muhammad-quli and Shah Sufi and one other brave did very well and boldly. Some Auzbegs were on the ramparts, some were coming up, when these four men arrived at a run, dealt them blow upon blow, and, by energetic drubbing, forced them all down and put them to flight. Quch Beg did best; this was his out-standing and, approved good deed; twice during this siege, he got his hand into the work. Qara *Barlas* had been left alone in the Needle-makers' Gate; he also held out well to the end. Qutluq Khwaja and Qul-nazar Mirza were also at their posts in the Bleaching-ground Gate; they held out well too, and charged the foe in his rear.

Another time Qasim Beg led his braves out through the Needle-makers' Gate, pursued the Auzbegs as far as Khwaja Kafsher, unhorsed some and returned with a few heads.

Fol. 93 b.

It was now the time of ripening grain but no-one brought new corn into the town. The long siege caused great privation to the towns-people;[1] it went so far that the poor and destitute began to eat the flesh of dogs and asses and, as there was little grain for the horses, people fed them on leaves. Experience shewed that the leaves best suiting were those of the mulberry and elm (*qara-yighach*). Some people scraped dry wood and gave the shavings, damped, to their horses.

For three or four months Shaibaq Khan did not come near the fort but had it invested at some distance and himself moved round it from post to post. Once when our men were off their guard, at mid-night, the enemy came near to the Turquoise Gate, beat his drums and flung his war-cry out. I was in the College, undressed. There was great trepidation and anxiety. After that they came night after night, disturbing us by drumming and shouting their war-cry.

Fol. 94.

Although envoys and messengers had been sent repeatedly to all sides and quarters, no help and reinforcement arrived from any-one. No-one had helped or reinforced me when I was in strength and power and had suffered no sort of defeat

---

1 The Sh. N. gives the reverse side of the picture, the plenty enjoyed by the besiegers.

or loss; on what score would any-one help me now? No hope in any-one whatever recommended us to prolong the siege. The old saying was that to hold a fort there must be a head, two hands and two legs, that is to say, the Commandant is the head; help and reinforcement coming from two quarters are the two arms and the food and water in the fort are the two legs. While we looked for help from those round about, their thoughts were elsewhere. That brave and experienced ruler, Sl. Husain Mirza, gave us not even the help of an encouraging message, but none-the-less he sent Kamalu'd-din Husain *Gazur-gahi*[1] as an envoy to Shaibaq Khan.

(i. Tambal's proceedings in Farghana.)[2]

(This year) Tambal marched from Andijan to near Bishkint.[3] Ahmad Beg and his party, thereupon, made The Khan move out against him. The two armies came face to face near Fol. 94b. Lak-lakan and the Turak Four-gardens but separated without engaging. Sl. Mahmud was not a fighting man; now when opposed to Tambal, he shewed want of courage in word and deed. Ahmad Beg was unpolished[4] but brave and well-meaning. In his very rough way, he said, "What's the measure of this person, Tambal? that you are so tormented with fear and fright about him. If you are afraid to look at him, bandage your eyes before you go out to face him."

1 He may have been attached to the tomb of Khwaja 'Abdu'l-lah *Ansari* in Harat.
2 The brusque entry here and elsewhere of *e.g.* Tambal's affairs, allows the inference that Babur was quoting from perhaps a news-writer's, contemporary records. For a different view of Tambal, the Sh. N. cap. xxxiii should be read.
3 Five-villages, on the main Khujand-Tashkint road.
4 *turk*, as on f. 28b of Khusrau Shah.

(a. Surrender of Samarkand to Shaibani.)

The siege drew on to great length; no provisions and supplies came in from any quarter, no succour and reinforcement from any side. The soldiers and peasantry became hopeless and, by ones and twos, began to let themselves down outside[2] the walls and flee. On Shaibaq Khan's hearing of the distress in the town, he came and dismounted near the Lovers'-cave. I, in turn, went to Malik-muhammad Mirza's dwellings in Low-lane, over against him. On one of those days, Khwaja Husain's brother, Auzun Hasan[3] came into the town with 10 or 15 of his men,—he who, as has been told, had been the cause of Jahangir Mirza's rebellion, of my exodus from Samarkand (903 AH.—March 1498 AD.) and, again! of what an amount of sedition and disloyalty! That entry of his was a very bold act.[4]

Fol. 95.

The soldiery and townspeople became more and more distressed. Trusted men of my close circle began to let themselves down from the ramparts and get away; begs of known name and old family servants were amongst them, such as Pir Wais, Shaikh Wais and Wais *Laghari*.[5] Of help from any side we utterly despaired; no hope was left in any quarter; our

---

1 Elph. MS. f. 68b; W.-i-B. I.O. 215 f. 78 and 217 f. 61b; Mems. p. 97.

The Kehr-Ilminsky text shews, in this year, a good example of its Persification and of Dr. Ilminsky's dealings with his difficult archetype by the help of the Memoirs.
2 *tashlab.* The Sh. N. places these desertions as after four months of siege.
3 It strikes one as strange to find Long Hasan described, as here, in terms of his younger brother. The singularity may be due to the fact that Husain was with Babur and may have invited Hasan. It may be noted here that Husain seems likely to be that father-in-law of 'Umar Shaikh mentioned on f. 12b and 13b.
4 This laudatory comment I find nowhere but in the Hai. Codex.
5 There is some uncertainty about the names of those who left.

supplies and provisions were wretched, what there was was coming to an end; no more came in. Meantime Shaibaq Khan interjected talk of peace.[1] Little ear would have been given to his talk of peace, if there had been hope or food from any side. It had to be! a sort of peace was made and we took our departure from the town, by the Shaikh-zada's Gate, somewhere about midnight.

(b. Babur leaves Samarkand.)

I took my mother Khanim out with me; two other women-folk went too, one was Bishka (var. Peshka)-i-Khalifa, the other, Minglik *Kukuldash*.[2] At this exodus, my elder sister, Khan-zada Begim fell into Shaibaq Khan's hands.[3] In the darkness of that night we lost our way[4] and wandered about amongst the main irrigation channels of Soghd. At shoot of dawn, after a hundred difficulties, we got past Khwaja Didar. At the Sunnat Prayer we scrambled up the rising-ground of Qara-bugh. Fol. 95b. From the north slope of Qara-bugh we hurried on past the foot of Juduk village and dropped down into Yilan-auti. On the road I raced with Qasim Beg and Qambar-'ali (the Skinner); my horse was leading when I, thinking to look at theirs behind, twisted myself round; the girth may have slackened, for my saddle turned and I was thrown on my head to the ground. Although I at once got up and remounted, my brain did not steady till the evening; till then this world and what went on appeared to me like things felt and seen in a dream or fancy. Towards afternoon we dismounted in Yilan-auti, there killed a

1 The Sh. N. is interesting here as giving an eye-witness' account of the surrender of the town and of the part played in the surrender by Khan-zada's marriage (cap. xxxix).

2 The first seems likely to be a relation of Nizamu'd-din 'Ali Khalifa; the second was Mole-marked, a foster-sister. The party numbered some 100 persons of whom Abu'l-makaram was one (H.S. ii, 310).

3 Babur's brevity is misleading; his sister was not captured but married with her own and her mother's consent before attempt to leave the town was made. Cf. Gul-badan's H.N. f. 3b and Sh. N. Vambéry, p. 145.

4 The route taken avoided the main road for Dizak; it can be traced by the physical features, mentioned by Babur, on the Fr. map of 1904. The Sh. N. says the night was extraordinarily dark. Departure in blinding darkness and by unusual ways shews distrust of Shaibaq's safe-conduct suggesting that Yahya's fate was in the minds of the fugitives.

horse, spitted and roasted its flesh, rested our horses awhile and rode on. Very weary, we reached Khalila-village before the dawn and dismounted. From there it was gone on to Dizak.

In Dizak just then was Hafiz Muh. *Duldai's* son, Tahir. There, in Dizak, were fat meats, loaves of fine flour, plenty of sweet melons and abundance of excellent grapes. From what privation we came to such plenty! From what stress to what repose!

> From fear and hunger rest we won (*amani taptuq*);
> A fresh world's new-born life we won (*jahani taptuq*).
> From out our minds, death's dread was chased (*rafa' buldi*);
> From our men the hunger-pang kept back (*dafa' buldi*).[1]

Never in all our lives had we felt such relief! never in the whole course of them have we appreciated security and plenty so highly. Joy is best and more delightful when it follows sorrow, ease after toil. I have been transported four or five times from toil to rest and from hardship to ease.[2] This was the first. We were set free from the affliction of such a foe and from the pangs of hunger and had reached the repose of security and the relief of abundance.

(c. Babur in Dikh-kat.)

After three or four days of rest in Dizak, we set out for Aura-tipa. Pashaghar is a little[3] off the road but, as we had occupied it for some time (904 AH.), we made an excursion to it in passing by. In Pashaghar we chanced on one of Khanim's old servants, a teacher[4] who had been left behind in Samarkand from want of a mount. We saw one another and on questioning her, I found she had come there on foot.

Khub-nigar Khanim, my mother Khanim's younger sister[5]

1 The texts differ as to whether the last two lines are prose or verse. All four are in Turki, but I surmise a clerical error in the refrain of the third, where *bulub* is written for *buldi*.

2 The second was in 908 AH. (f. 118); the third in 914 AH. (f. 216b); the fourth is not described in the B.N.; it followed Babur's defeat at Ghaj-davan in 918 AH. (Erskine's *History of India*, i, 325). He had a fifth, but of a different kind, when he survived poison in 933 AH. (f. 305).

3 Hai. MS. *qaqasraq*; Elph. MS. *yanasraq*.

4 *atun*, one who instructs in reading, writing and embroidery. *Cf.* Gul-badan's H.N. f. 26. The distance walked may have been 70 or 80 m.

5 She was the wife of the then Governor of Aura-tipa, Muh. Husain *Dughlat*.

already must have bidden this transitory world farewell; for they let Khanim and me know of it in Aura-tipa. My father's mother also must have died in Andijan; this too they let us know in Aura-tipa.[1] Since the death of my grandfather, Yunas Khan (892 AH.), Khanim had not seen her (step-)mother or her younger brother and sisters, that is to say, Shah Begim, Sl. Mahmud Khan, Sultan-nigar Khanim and Daulat-sultan Khanim. The separation had lasted 13 or 14 years. To see these relations she now started for Tashkint. Fol. 96b.

After consulting with Muh. Husain Mirza, it was settled for us to winter in a place called Dikh-kat[2] one of the Aura-tipa villages. There I deposited my impedimenta (*auruq*); then set out myself in order to visit Shah Begim and my Khan dada and various relatives. I spent a few days in Tashkint and waited on Shah Begim and my Khan dada. My mother's elder full-sister, Mihr-nigar Khanim[3] had come from Samarkand and was in Tashkint. There my mother Khanim fell very ill; it was a very bad illness; she passed through mighty risks.

His Highness Khwajaka Khwaja, having managed to get out of Samarkand, had settled down in Far-kat; there I visited him. I had hoped my Khan dada would shew me affection and kindness and would give me a country or a district (*pargana*). He did promise me Aura-tipa but Muh. Husain Mirza did not make it over, whether acting on his own account or whether upon a hint from above, is not known. After spending a few days with him (in Aura-tipa), I went on to Dikh-kat. Fol. 97.

Dikh-kat is in the Aura-tipa hill-tracts, below the range on the other side of which is the Macha[4] country. Its people, though Sart, settled in a village, are, like Turks, herdsmen and

---

1 It may be noted here that in speaking of these elder women Babur uses the honorific plural, a form of rare occurrence except for such women, for saintly persons and exceptionally for The supreme Khan. For his father he has never used it.

2 This name has several variants. The village lies, in a valley-bottom, on the Aq-su and on a road. *See* Kostenko, i, 119.

3 She had been divorced from Shaibani in order to allow him to make legal marriage with her niece, Khan-zada.

4 Amongst the variants of this name, I select the modern one. Macha is the upper valley of the Zar-afshan.

shepherds. Their sheep are reckoned at 40,000. We dismounted at the houses of the peasants in the village; I stayed in a head-man's house. He was old, 70 or 80, but his mother was still alive. She was a woman on whom much life had been bestowed for she was 111 years old. Some relation of hers may have gone, (as was said), with Timur Beg's army to Hindustan;[1] she had this in her mind and used to tell the tale. In Dikh-kat alone were 96 of her descendants, hers and her grandchildren, great-grandchildren and grandchildren's grandchildren. Counting in the dead, 200 of her descendants were reckoned up. Her grandchild's grandson was a strong young man of 25 or 26, with full black beard. While in Dikh-kat, I constantly made excursions amongst the mountains round about. Generally I went bare-foot and, from doing this so much, my feet became so that rock and stone made no difference to them.[2] Once in one of these wanderings, a cow was seen, between the Afternoon and Evening prayers, going down by a narrow, ill-defined road. Said I, "I wonder which way that road will be going; keep your eye on that cow; don't lose the cow till you know where the road comes out." Khwaja Asadu'l-lah made his joke, "If the cow loses her way," he said, "what becomes of us?"

In the winter several of our soldiers asked for leave to Andijan because they could make no raids with us.[3] Qasim Beg said, with much insistence, "As these men are going, send something special of your own wear by them to Jahangir Mirza." I sent my ermine cap. Again he urged, "What harm would there be if you sent something for Tambal also?" Though I was very unwilling, yet as he urged it, I sent Tambal a large broad-sword which Nuyan *Kukuldash* had had made for himself in Samarkand. This very sword it was which, as will

Fol. 97b.

---

1 Timur took Dihli in 801 AH. (Dec. 1398), *i.e.* 103 solar and 106 lunar years earlier. The ancient dame would then have been under 5 years old. It is not surprising therefore that in repeating her story Babur should use a tense betokening hear-say matter (*barib ikan dur*).

2 The anecdote here following, has been analysed in JRAS 1908, p. 87, in order to show warrant for the opinion that parts of the Kehr-Ilminsky text are retranslations from the Persian W.-i-B.

3 Amongst those thus leaving seem to have been Qambar-'ali (f. 99b).

be told with the events of next year, came down on my own head![1]

A few days later, my grandmother, Aisan-daulat Begim, who, when I left Samarkand, had stayed behind, arrived in Dikh-kat with our families and baggage (*auruq*) and a few lean and hungry followers.

Fol. 98.

(*d. Shaibaq Khan raids in The Khan's country.*)

That winter Shaibaq Khan crossed the Khujand river on the ice and plundered near Shahrukhiya and Bish-kint. On hearing news of this, we galloped off, not regarding the smallness of our numbers, and made for the villages below Khujand, opposite Hasht-yak (One-eighth). The cold was mightily bitter,[2] a wind not less than the Ha-darwesh[3] raging violently the whole time. So cold it was that during the two or three days we were in those parts, several men died of it. When, needing to make ablution, I went into an irrigation-channel, frozen along both banks but because of its swift current, not ice-bound in the middle, and bathed, dipping under 16 times, the cold of the water went quite through me. Next day we crossed the river on the ice from opposite Khaslar and went on through the dark to Bish-kint.[4] Shaibaq Khan, however, must have gone straight back after plundering the neighbourhood of Shahrukhiya.

(*e. Death of Nuyan Kukuldash.*)

Bish-kint, at that time, was held by Mulla Haidar's son, 'Abdu'l-minan. A younger son, named Mumin, a worthless and dissipated person, had come to my presence in Samarkand and had received all kindness from me. This sodomite, Mumin, for what sort of quarrel between them is not known, cherished rancour against Nuyan *Kukuldash*. At the time when we, having heard of the retirement of the Auzbegs, sent a man to

Fol. 98*b.*

1 *Cf.* f. 107 foot.
2 The Sh. N. speaks of the cold in that winter (Vambéry, p. 160). It was unusual for the Sir to freeze in this part of its course (Sh. N. p. 172) where it is extremely rapid (Kostenko, i, 213).
3 *Cf.* f. 4*b.*
4 Point to point, some 50 miles.

The Khan and marched from Bish-kint to spend two or three days amongst the villages in the Blacksmith's-dale,[1] Mulla Haidar's son, Mumin invited Nuyan *Kukuldash* and Ahmad-i-qasim and some others in order to return them hospitality received in Samarkand. When I left Bish-kint, therefore they stayed behind. Mumin's entertainment to this party was given on the edge of a ravine (*jar*). Next day news was brought to us in Sam-sirak, a village in the Blacksmith's-dale, that Nuyan was dead through falling when drunk into the ravine. We sent his own mother's brother, Haq-nazar and others, who searched out where he had fallen. They committed Nuyan to the earth in Bish-kint, and came back to me. They had found the body at the bottom of the ravine an arrow's flight from the place of the entertainment. Some suspected that Mumin, nursing his trumpery rancour, had taken Nuyan's life. None knew the truth. His death made me strangely sad; for few men have I felt such grief; I wept unceasingly for a week or ten days. The chronogram of his death was found in *Nuyan is dead*.[2] A few days later we went back to Dikh-kat.

With the heats came the news that Shaibaq Khan was coming up into Aura-tipa. Hereupon, as the land is level about Dikh-kat, we crossed the Ab-burdan pass into the Macha hill-country.[3] Ab-burdan is the last village of Macha; just below it a spring sends its water down (to the Zar-afshan); above the stream is included in Macha, below it depends on Palghar. There is a tomb at the spring-head. I had a rock at the side of the spring-head shaped (*qatirib*) and these three couplets inscribed on it;—

> I have heard that Jamshid, the magnificent,
> Inscribed on a rock at a fountain-head[4]

---

1 *Ahangaran-julga*, a name narrowed on maps to Angren (valley).

2 *Faut shud Nuyan*. The numerical value of these words is 907. Babur when writing, looks back 26 years to the death of this friend.

3 Ab-burdan village is on the Zar-afshan; the pass is 11,200 ft. above the sea. Babur's boundaries still hold good and the spring still flows. *See* Ujfalvy *l.c.* i. 14; Kostenko, i, 119 and 193; Rickmers, JRGS 1907, p. 358.

4 From the *Bu-stan* (Graf's ed. Vienna 1858, p. 561). The last couplet is also in the *Gulistan* (Platts' ed. p. 72). The Bombay lith. ed. of the *Bu-stan* explains (p. 39) that the "We" of the third couplet means Jamshid and his predecessors who have rested by his fountain.

> "Many men like us have taken breath at this fountain,
> And have passed away in the twinkling of an eye;
> We took the world by courage and might,
> But we took it not with us to the tomb."

There is a custom in that hill-country of cutting verses and things[1] on the rocks.

While we were in Macha, Mulla Hijri,[2] the poet came from Hisar and waited on me. At that time I composed the following opening lines;—

Let your portrait flatter you never so much, than it you are more (*andin artuqsin*);
Men call you their Life (*Jan*), than Life, without doubt, you are more (*jandin artuqsin*).[3]

After plundering round about in Aura-tipa, Shaibaq Khan retired.[4] While he was up there, we, disregarding the fewness of our men and their lack of arms, left our impedimenta (*auruq*) in Macha, crossed the Ab-burdan pass and went to Dikh-kat so that, gathered together close at hand, we might miss no chance on one of the next nights. He, however, retired straightway; we went back to Macha.

Fol. 99*b*.

It passed through my mind that to wander from mountain to mountain, homeless and houseless, without country or abiding-place, had nothing to recommend it. "Go you right off to The Khan," I said to myself. Qasim Beg was not willing for this move, apparently being uneasy because, as has been told, he had put Mughuls to death at Qara-bulaq, by way of example. However much we urged it, it was not to be! He drew off for Hisar with all his brothers and his whole following. We for our part, crossed the Ab-burdan pass and set forward for The Khan's presence in Tashkint.

---

1 *nima*. The First W.-i-B. (I.O. 215 f. 81 l. 8) writes *tawarikh*, annals.
2 This may be the Khwaja Hijri of the A.N. (index s.n.); and Badayuni's Hasan *Hijri*, Bib. Ind. iii, 385; and Ethe's Pers. Cat. No. 793; and Bod. Cat. No. 189.
3 The Hai. MS. points in the last line as though punning on Khan and Jan, but appears to be wrong.
4 For an account of the waste of crops, the Sh. N. should be seen (p. 162 and 180).

(*f. Babur with The Khan.*)

In the days when Tambal had drawn his army out and gone into the Blacksmith's-dale,[1] men at the top of his army, such as Muh. *Dughlat*, known as *Hisari*, and his younger brother Husain, and also Qambar-'ali, the Skinner conspired to attempt his life. When he discovered this weighty matter, they, unable to remain with him, had gone to The Khan.

The Feast of Sacrifices ('Id-i-qurban) fell for us in Shahrukhiya (Zu'l-hijja 10th—June 16th 1502).

I had written a quatrain in an ordinary measure but was in some doubt about it, because at that time I had not studied poetic idiom so much as I have now done. The Khan was good-natured and also he wrote verses, though ones somewhat deficient in the requisites for odes. I presented my quatrain and I laid my doubts before him but got no reply so clear as to remove them. His study of poetic idiom appeared to have been somewhat scant. Here is the verse;—

> One hears no man recall another in trouble (*mihnat-ta kishi*);
> None speak of a man as glad in his exile (*ghurbat-ta kishi*);
> My own heart has no joy in this exile;
> Called glad is no exile, man though he be (*albatta kishi*).

Later on I came to know that in Turki verse, for the purpose of rhyme, *ta* and *da* are interchangeable and also *ghain*, *qaf* and *kaf*.[2]

(*g. The acclaiming of the standards.*)

When, a few days later, The Khan heard that Tambal had gone up into Aura-tipa, he got his army to horse and rode out from Tashkint. Between Bish-kint and Sam-sirak he formed up into array of right and left and saw the count[3] of his men.

1 I think this refers to last year's move (f. 94 foot).
2 In other words, the T. preposition, meaning E. in, at, *etc.* may be written with t or d, as *ta* or as *da*. Also the one meaning E. towards, may be *gha*, *qa*, or *ka* (with long or short vowel).
3 *dim*, a word found difficult. It may be a derivative of root *de*, tell, and a noun with the meaning of English tale (number). The First W.-i-B. renders it by *san*, and by *san*, Abu'l-ghazi expresses what Babur's *dim* expresses, the numbering of troops. It occurs thrice in the B.N. (here, on f. 103*b*. and on f. 264). In the Elphinstone Codex it has been written-over into *Ivim*, once resembles *vim* more than *dim* and once is omitted. The L. and E. *Memoirs*

This done, the standards were acclaimed in Mughul fashion.[1]
The Khan dismounted and nine standards were set up in front
of him. A Mughul tied a long strip of white cloth to the
thighbone (*aurta ailik*) of a cow and took the other end in his
hand. Three other long strips of white cloth were tied to the
staves of three of the (nine) standards, just below the yak-tails,
and their other ends were brought for The Khan to stand on
one and for me and Sl. Muh. Khanika to stand each on one of
the two others. The Mughul who had hold of the strip of Fol. 100b.
cloth fastened to the cow's leg, then said something
in Mughul while he looked at the standards and made signs
towards them. The Khan and those present sprinkled *qumiz*[2] in
the direction of the standards; hautbois and drums were sounded towards them;[3] the army flung the war-cry out three times
towards them, mounted, cried it again and rode at the gallop
round them.

Precisely as Chingiz Khan laid down his rules, so the
Mughuls still observe them. Each man has his place, just
where his ancestors had it; right, right,—left, left,—centre,
centre. The most reliable men go to the extreme points of the
right and left. The Chiras and Begchik clans always demand
to go to the point in the right.[4] At that time the Beg of the
Chiras tuman was a very bold brave, Qashka (Mole-marked)
Mahmud and the beg of the renowned Begchik tuman was
Ayub *Begchik*. These two, disputing which should go out to
the point, drew swords on one another. At last it seems to
have been settled that one should take the highest place in the
hunting-circle, the other, in the battle-array.

Next day after making the circle, it was hunted near Sam-

(p. 303) inserts what seems a gloss, saying that a whip or bow is used in the
count, presumably held by the teller to "keep his place" in the march past.
The *Siyasat-nama* (Schefer, trs. p. 22) names the whip as used in numbering
an army (*see* Additional Notes, p. 797).

1 The acclamation of the standards is depicted in B.M. W.-i-B. Or. 3714
f. 128b. One cloth is shewn tied to the off fore-leg of a live cow, above the
knee, Babur's word being *aurta ailik* (middle-hand).

2 The libation was of fermented mares'-milk.

3 *lit.* their one way.

4 *Cf.* T.R. p. 308.

sirak; thence move was made to the Turak Four-gardens. On that day and in that camp, I finished the first ode I ever finished. Its opening couplet is as follows;—

> Except my soul, no friend worth trust found I (*wafadar tapmadim*);
> Except my heart, no confidant found I (*asrar tapmadim*).

There were six couplets; every ode I finished later was written just on this plan.

The Khan moved, march by march, from Sam-sirak to the bank of the Khujand-river. One day we crossed the water by way of an excursion, cooked food and made merry with the braves and pages. That day some-one stole the gold clasp of my girdle. Next day Bayan-quli's Khan-quli and Sl. Muh. Wais fled to Tambal. Every-one suspected them of that bad deed. Though this was not ascertained, Ahmad-i-qasim *Kohbur* asked leave and went away to Aura-tipa. From that leave he did not return; he too went to Tambal.

(*a. Babur's poverty in Tashkint.*)

This move of The Khan's was rather unprofitable; to take no fort, to beat no foe, he went out and went back.

During my stay in Tashkint, I endured much poverty and humiliation. No country or hope of one! Most of my retainers dispersed, those left, unable to move about with me because of their destitution! If I went to my Khan dada's Gate,[2] I went sometimes with one man, sometimes with two. It was well he was no stranger but one of my own blood. After showing myself[3] in his presence, I used to go to Shah Begim's, entering her house, bareheaded and barefoot, just as if it were my own. Fol. 101*b*.

This uncertainty and want of house and home drove me at last to despair. Said I, "It would be better to take my head[4] and go off than live in such misery; better to go as far as my feet can carry me than be seen of men in such poverty and humiliation." Having settled on China to go to, I resolved to take my head and get away. From my childhood up I had wished to visit China but had not been able to manage it because of ruling and attachments. Now sovereignty itself was gone! and my mother, for her part, was re-united to her (step)-mother and her younger brother. The hindrances to my journey had been removed; my anxiety for my mother was dispelled. I represented (to Shah Begim and The Khan) through Khwaja Abu'l-makaram that now such a foe as

1 Elph. MS. f. 74; W.-i-B. I.O. 215 f. 83 and 217 f. 66; Mems. p. 104.
2 It may be noted that Babur calls his mother's brothers, not *taghai* but *dada* father. I have not met with an instance of his saying "My taghai" as he says "My dada."
3 *kurunush qilib*, reflective from *kurmak*, to see.
4 A rider's metaphor.

Shaibaq Khan had made his appearance, Mughul and Turk[1] alike must guard against him; that thought about him must be taken while he had not well-mastered the (Auzbeg) horde or grown very strong, for as they have said;—[2]

> To-day, while thou canst, quench the fire,
> Once ablaze it will burn up the world;
> Let thy foe not fix string to his bow,
> While an arrow of thine can pierce him;

that it was 20 or 25 years[3] since they had seen the Younger Khan (Ahmad *Alacha*) and that I had never seen him; should I be able, if I went to him, not only to see him myself, but to bring about the meeting between him and them?

Fol. 102.   Under this pretext I proposed to get out of those surroundings;[4] once in Mughulistan and Turfan, my reins would be in my own hands, without check or anxiety. I put no-one in possession of my scheme. Why not? Because it was impossible for me to mention such a scheme to my mother, and also because it was with other expectations that the few of all ranks who had been my companions in exile and privation, had cut themselves off with me and with me suffered change of fortune. To speak to them also of such a scheme would be no pleasure.

The Khwaja, having laid my plan before Shah Begim and The Khan, understood them to consent to it but, later, it occurred to them that I might be asking leave a second time,[5] because of not receiving kindness. That touching their reputation, they delayed a little to give the leave.

(*b. The Younger Khan comes to Tashkint.*)

At this crisis a man came from the Younger Khan to say that he was actually on his way. This brought my scheme to

---

1 As touching the misnomer, "Mughul dynasty" for the Timurid rulers in Hindustan, it may be noted that here, as Babur is speaking to a Chaghatai Mughul, his "Turk" is left to apply to himself.

2 Gulistan, cap. viii, Maxim 12 (Platts' ed. p. 147).

3 This backward count is to 890 AH. when Ahmad fled from cultivated lands (T.R. p. 113).

4 It becomes clear that Ahmad had already been asked to come to Tashkint.

5 *Cf.* f. 96b for his first departure without help.

naught. When a second man announced his near approach, we all went out to give him honourable meeting, Shah Begim and his younger sisters, Sultan-nigar Khanim and Daulat-sultan Khanim, and I and Sl. Muh. Khanika and Khan Mirza (Wais).

Between Tashkint and Sairam is a village called Yagha (var. Yaghma), with some smaller ones, where are the tombs of Father Abraham and Father Isaac. So far we went out. Knowing nothing exact about his coming,[1] I rode out for an excursion, with an easy mind. All at once, he descended on me, face to face. I went forward; when I stopped, he stopped. He was a good deal perturbed; perhaps he was thinking of dismounting in some fixed spot and there seated, of receiving me ceremoniously. There was no time for this; when we were near each other, I dismounted. He had not time even to dismount;[2] I bent the knee, went forward and saw him. Hurriedly and with agitation, he told Sl. Sa'id Khan and Baba Khan Sl. to dismount, bend the knee with (*bila*) me and make my acquaintance.[3] Just these two of his sons had come with him; they may have been 13 or 14 years old. When I had seen them, we all mounted and went to Shah Begim's presence. After he had seen her and his sisters, and had renewed acquaintance, they all sat down and for half the night told one another particulars of their past and gone affairs.

Next day, my Younger Khan dada bestowed on me arms of his own and one of his own special horses saddled, and a Mughul head-to-foot dress,—a Mughul cap,[4] a long coat of Chinese satin, with broidering of stitchery,[5] and Chinese

Fol. 102*b*.

---

1 Yagha (Yaghma) is not on the Fr. map of 1904, but suitably located is Turbat (Tomb) to which roads converge.

2 Elph. MS. *tushkucha*; Hai. MS. *yukuncha*. The importance Ahmad attached to ceremony can be inferred by the details given (f. 103) of his meeting with Mahmud.

3 *kurushkailar*. *Cf.* Redhouse who gives no support for reading the verb *kurmak* as meaning *to embrace*.

4 *burk*, a tall felt cap (Redhouse). In the adjective applied to the cap there are several variants. The Hai. MS. writes *muftul*, solid or twisted. The Elph. MS. has *muftun-luq* which has been understood by Mr. Erskine to mean, gold-embroidered.

5 The wording suggests that the decoration is in chain-stitch, pricked up and down through the stuff.

armour; in the old fashion, they had hung, on the left side, a haversack (*chantai*) and an outer bag,[1] and three or four things such as women usually hang on their collars, perfume-holders and various receptacles;[2] in the same way, three or four things hung on the right side also.

From there we went to Tashkint. My Elder Khan dada also had come out for the meeting, some 3 or 4 *yighach* (12 to 15 m.) along the road. He had had an awning set up in a chosen spot and was seated there. The Younger Khan went up directly in front of him; on getting near, fetched a circle, from right to left, round him; then dismounted before him. After advancing to the place of interview (*kurushur yir*), he nine times bent the knee; that done, went close and saw (his brother). The Elder Khan, in his turn, had risen when the Younger Khan drew near. They looked long at one another (*kurushtilar*) and long stood in close embrace (*quchushub*). The Younger Khan again bent the knee nine times when retiring, many times also on offering his gift; after that, he went and sat down.

All his men had adorned themselves in Mughul fashion. There they were in Mughul caps (*burk*); long coats of Chinese satin, broidered with stitchery, Mughul quivers and saddles of green shagreen-leather, and Mughul horses adorned in a unique fashion. He had brought rather few men, over 1000 and under 2000 may-be. He was a man of singular manners, a mighty master of the sword, and brave. Amongst arms he preferred to trust to the sword. He used to say that of arms there are, the *shash-par*[3] (six-flanged mace), the *piyazi* (rugged mace), the *kistin*,[4] the *tabar-zin* (saddle-hatchet) and the *baltu* (battle-axe),

---

1 *tash chantai*. These words have been taken to mean whet-stone (*bilgu-tash*). I have found no authority for reading *tash* as whet-stone. Moreover to allow "bag of the stone" to be read would require *tash* (*ning*) *chantai-si* in the text.

2 lit. bag-like things. Some will have held spare bow-strings and archers' rings, and other articles of "repairing kit." With the gifts, it seems probable that the *gosha-gir* (f. 107) was given.

3 Vullers, *clava sex foliis*.

4 Zenker, *casse-tête*. *Kistin* would seem to be formed from the root, *kis*, cutting, but M. de C. describes it as a ball attached by a strap or chain to a handle. *Sanglakh*, a sort of mace (*gurz*).

all, if they strike, work only with what of them first touches, but the sword, if it touch, works from point to hilt. He never parted with his keen-edged sword; it was either at his waist or to his hand. He was a little rustic and rough-of-speech,   Fol. 103b. through having grown up in an out-of-the-way place.

When, adorned in the way described, I went with him to The Khan, Khwaja Abu'l-makaram asked, "Who is this honoured sultan?" and till I spoke, did not recognize me.

(c. *The Khans march into Farghana against Tambal.*)

Soon after returning to Tashkint, The Khan led out an army for Andikan (Andijan) direct against Sl. Ahmad *Tambal*.[1] He took the road over the Kindirlik-pass and from Blacksmiths'-dale (Ahangaran-julga) sent the Younger Khan and me on in advance. After the pass had been crossed, we all met again near Zarqan (var. Zabarqan) of Karnan.

One day, near Karnan, they numbered their men[2] and reckoned them up to be 30,000. From ahead news began to come that Tambal also was collecting a force and going to Akhsi. After having consulted together, The Khans decided to join some of their men to me, in order that I might cross the Khujand-water, and, marching by way of Aush and Auzkint, turn Tambal's rear. Having so settled, they joined to me Ayub *Begchik* with his *tuman*, Jan-hasan Barin (var. Narin) with his Barins, Muh. *Hisari Dughlat*, Sl. Husain *Dughlat* and Sl. Ahmad Mirza *Dughlat*, not in command of the Dughlat *tuman*,—and Qambar-'ali Beg (the Skinner). The commandant (*darogha*) of their force was Sarigh-bash (Yellow-head) Mirza *Itarchi*.[3]

Leaving The Khans in Karnan, we crossed the river on rafts near Sakan, traversed the Khuqan sub-district (*aurchin*), crushed   Fol. 104.

1 The *Rauzatu's-safa* states that The Khans left Tashkint on Muharram 15th (July 21st 1502), in order to restore Babur and expel Tambal (Erskine).
2 lit. saw the count (*dim*). Cf. f. 100 and note concerning the count. Using a Persian substitute, the Kehr-Ilminsky text writes *san* (*kurdilar*).
3 Elph. MS. *ambarchi*, steward, for Itarchi, a tribal-name. The "Mirza" and the rank of the army-begs are against supposing a steward in command. Here and just above, the texts write Mirza-i-Itarchi and Mirza-i-Dughlat, thus suggesting that in names not ending with a vowel, the *izafat* is required for exact transliteration, *e.g.* Muhammad-i-dughlat.

Qaba and by way of the Alai sub-districts[1] descended suddenly on Aush. We reached it at dawn, unexpected; those in it could but surrender. Naturally the country-folk were wishing much for us, but they had not been able to find their means, both through dread of Tambal and through our remoteness. After we entered Aush, the hordes and the highland and lowland tribes of southern and eastern Andijan came in to us. The Auzkint people also, willing to serve us, sent me a man and came in.

> (*Author's note on Auzkint*.)   Auzkint formerly must have been a capital of Farghana;[2] it has an excellent fort and is situated on the boundary (of Farghana).

The Marghinanis also came in after two or three days, having beaten and chased their commandant (*darogha*). Except Andijan, every fort south of the Khujand-water had now come in to us. Spite of the return in those days of so many forts, and spite of risings and revolt against him, Tambal did not yet come to his senses but sat down with an army of horse and foot, fortified with ditch and branch, to face The Khans, between Karnan and Akhsi. Several times over there was a little fighting and pell-mell but without decided success to either side.

In the Andijan country (*wilayat*), most of the tribes and
Fol. 104b. hordes and the forts and all the districts had come in to me; naturally the Andijanis also were wishing for me. They however could not find their means.

(*d. Babur's attempt to enter Andijan frustrated by a mistake.*)

It occurred to me that if we went one night close to the town and sent a man in to discuss with the Khwaja[3] and notables, they might perhaps let us in somewhere. With this idea we rode out from Aush. By midnight we were opposite Forty-daughters (Chihil-dukhteran) 2 miles (one *kuroh*) from Andijan. From that place we sent Qambar-'ali Beg forward,

---

1 *Alai-liq aurchini.* I understand the march to have been along the northern slope of the Little Alai, south of Aush.

2 As of Almaligh and Almatu (fol. 1b) Babur reports a tradition with caution. The name Auz-kint may be read to mean "Own village," independent, as *Auz-beg*, Own-beg.

3 He would be one of the hereditary Khwajas of Andijan (f. 16).

with some other begs, who were to discuss matters with the Khwaja after by some means or other getting a man into the fort. While waiting for their return, we sat on our horses, some of us patiently humped up, some wrapt away in dream, when suddenly, at about the third watch, there rose a war-cry[1] and a sound of drums. Sleepy and startled, ignorant whether the foe was many or few, my men, without looking to one another, took each his own road and turned for flight. There was no time for me to get at them; I went straight for the enemy. Only Mir Shah *Quchin* and Baba Sher-zad (Tiger-whelp) and Nasir's Dost sprang forward; we four excepted, every man set his face for flight. I had gone a little way forward, when the enemy rode rapidly up, flung out his war-cry and poured arrows on us. One man, on a horse with a starred forehead,[2] came close to me; I shot at it; it rolled over and died. They made a little as if to retire. The three with me Fol. 105. said, "In this darkness it is not certain whether they are many or few; all our men have gone off; what harm could we four do them? Fighting must be when we have overtaken our run-aways and rallied them." Off we hurried, got up with our men and beat and horse-whipped some of them, but, do what we would, they would not make a stand. Back the four of us went to shoot arrows at the foe. They drew a little back but when, after a discharge or two, they saw we were not more than three or four, they busied themselves in chasing and unhorsing my men. I went three or four times to try to rally my men but all in vain! They were not to be brought to order. Back I went with my three and kept the foe in check with our arrows. They pursued us two or three *kuroh* (4-6 m.), as far as the rising ground opposite Kharabuk and Pashamun. There we met Muh. 'Ali *Mubashir*. Said I, "They are only few; let us stop and put our horses at them." So we did. When we got up to them, they stood still.[3]

Our scattered braves gathered in from this side and that, but

---

1 For several battle-cries *see* Th. Radloff's *Réceuils* etc. p. 322.

2 *qashqa atliq kishi*. For a parallel phrase *see* f. 92b.

3 Babur does not explain how the imbroglio was cleared up; there must have been a dramatic moment when this happened.

several very serviceable men, scattering in this attack, went right away to Aush.

The explanation of the affair seemed to be that some of Ayub *Begchik*'s Mughuls had slipped away from Aush to raid near Andijan and, hearing the noise of our troop, came somewhat stealthily towards us; then there seems to have been confusion about the pass-word. The pass-words settled on for use during this movement of ours were Tashkint and Sairam. If

Fol. 105*b*.

> (*Author's note on pass-words.*)   Pass-words are of two kinds;—in each tribe there is one for use in the tribe, such as *Darwana* or *Tuqqai* or *Lulu*;[1] and there is one for the use of the whole army. For a battle, two words are settled on as pass-words so that of two men meeting in the fight, one may give the one, the other give back the second, in order to distinguish friends from foes, own men from strangers.

Tashkint were said, Sairam would be answered; if Sairam, Tashkint. In this muddled affair, Khwaja Muh. 'Ali seems to have been somewhat in advance of our party and to have got bewildered,—he was a Sart person,[2]—when the Mughuls came up saying, "Tashkint, Tashkint," for he gave them "Tashkint, Tashkint," as the counter-sign. Through this they took him for an enemy, raised their war-cry, beat their saddle-drums and poured arrows on us. It was through this we gave way, and through this false alarm were scattered! We went back to Aush.

(*e. Babur again attempts Andijan.*)

Through the return to me of the forts and the highland and lowland clans, Tambal and his adherents lost heart and footing. His army and people in the next five or six days began to desert him and to flee to retired places and the open country.[3] Of his household some came and said, "His affairs are nearly ruined; he will break up in three or four days, utterly ruined." On hearing this, we rode for Andijan.

---

1 *Darwana* (a trap-door in a roof) has the variant *dur-dana*, a single pearl; *tuqqai* perhaps implies relationship; *lulu* is a pearl, a wild cow etc.

2 Hai. MS. *sairt kishi*. Muh. 'Ali is likely to be the librarian (*cf.* index *s.n.*).

3 Elph. MS. *ramaqgha u tur-ga*; Hai. MS. *tartatgha u tur-ga*. Ilminsky gives no help, varying much here from the true text. The archetype of both MSS. must have been difficult to read.

Sl. Muh. *Galpuk*[1] was in Andijan,—the younger of Tambal's cadet brothers. We took the Mulberry-road and at the Midday Prayer came to the Khakan (canal), south of the town. A Fol. 106. foraging-party was arranged; I followed it along Khakan to the skirt of 'Aish-hill. When our scouts brought word that Sl. Muh *Galpuk* had come out, with what men he had, beyond the suburbs and gardens to the skirt of 'Aish, I hurried to meet him, although our foragers were still scattered. He may have had over 500 men; we had more but many had scattered to forage. When we were face to face, his men and ours may have been in equal number. Without caring about order or array, down we rode on them, loose rein, at the gallop. When we got near, they could not stand; there was not so much fighting as the crossing of a few swords. My men followed them almost to the Khakan Gate, unhorsing one after another.

It was at the Evening Prayer that, our foe outmastered, we reached Khwaja Kitta, on the outskirts of the suburbs. My idea was to go quickly right up to the Gate but Dost Beg's father, Nasir Beg and Qambar-'ali Beg, old and experienced begs both, represented to me, "It is almost night; it would be ill-judged to go in a body into the fort in the dark; let us withdraw a little and dismount. What can they do to-morrow but surrender the place?" Yielding at once to the opinion of these experienced persons, we forthwith retired to the outskirts of the suburbs. If we had gone to the Gate, undoubtedly, Andijan Fol. 106b. would have come into our hands.

(*f. Babur surprised by Tambal.*)

After crossing the Khakan-canal, we dismounted, near the Bed-time prayer, at the side of the village of Rabat-i-zauraq (var. ruzaq). Although we knew that Tambal had broken camp and was on his way to Andijan, yet, with the negligence of inexperience, we dismounted on level ground close to the village, instead of where the defensive canal would have protected us.[2] There we lay down carelessly, without scouts or rear-ward.

1 The Hai. MS.'s pointing allows the sobriquet to mean "Butterfly." His family lent itself to nick-names; in it three brothers were known respectively as Fat or Lubberly, Fool and, perhaps, Butterfly.
2 *birk arigh*, doubly strong by its trench and its current.

At the top (*bash*) of the morning, just when men are in sweet sleep, Qambar-'ali Beg hurried past, shouting, "Up with you! the enemy is here!" So much he said and went off without a moment's stay. It was my habit to lie down, even in times of peace, in my tunic; up I got instanter, put on sword and quiver and mounted. My standard-bearer had no time to adjust my standard,[1] he just mounted with it in his hand. There were ten or fifteen men with me when we started toward the enemy; after riding an arrow's flight, when we came up with his scouts, there may have been ten. Going rapidly forward, we overtook him, poured in arrows on him, over-mastered his foremost men and hurried them off. We followed them for another arrow's flight and came up with his centre where Sl. Ahmad *Tambal* himself was, with as many as 100 men. He and another were standing in front of his array, as if keeping a Gate,[2] and were shouting, "Strike, strike!" but his men, mostly, were sidling, as if asking themselves, "Shall we run away? Shall we not?" By this time three were left with me; one was Nasir's Dost, another, Mirza Quli *Kukuldash*, the third, Khudai-birdi *Turkman*'s Karim-dad.[3] I shot off the arrow on my thumb,[4] aiming at Tambal's helm. When I put my hand into my quiver, there came out a quite new *gosha-gir*[5]

Fol. 107.

---

1 I understand that time failed to set the standard in its usual rest. E. and de C. have understood that the yak-tail (*qutas tughi* f. 100) was apart from the staff and that time failed to adjust the two parts. The *tugh* however is the whole standard; moreover if the tail were ever taken off at night from the staff, it would hardly be so treated in a mere bivouac.

2 *aishiklik turluq*, as on f. 113. I understand this to mean that the two men were as far from their followers as sentries at a Gate are posted outside the Gate.

3 So too "Piero of Cosimo" and "Lorenzo of Piero of the Medici." *Cf.* the names of five men on f. 114.

4 *shashtim*. The *shasht* (thumb) in archery is the thumb-shield used on the left hand, as the *zih-gir* (string-grip), the archer's ring, is on the right-hand thumb.

It is useful to remember, when reading accounts of shooting with the Turki (Turkish) bow, that the arrows (*auq*) had notches so gripping the string that they kept in place until released with the string.

5 *sar-i-sabz gosha gir*. The *gosha-gir* is an implement for remedying the warp of a bow-tip and string-notch. For further particulars *see* Appendix C.

The term *sar-i-sabz*, lit. green-head, occurs in the sense of "quite young" or "new," in the proverb, "The red tongue loses the green head," quoted in the *Tabaqat-i-akbari* account of Babur's death. Applied here, it points to the *gosha-gir* as part of the recent gift made by Ahmad to Babur.

given me by my Younger Khan dada. It would have been vexing to throw it away but before I got it back into the quiver, there had been time to shoot, maybe, two or three arrows. When once more I had an arrow on the string, I went forward, my three men even holding back. One of those two in advance, Tambal seemingly,[1] moved forward also. The high-road was between us; I from my side, he, from his, got upon it and came face to face, in such a way that his right hand was towards me, mine towards him. His horse's mail excepted, he was fully accoutred; but for sword and quiver, I was unprotected. I shot off the arrow in my hand, adjusting for the attachment of his shield. With matters in this position, they shot my right leg through. I had on the cap of my helm;[2] Tambal chopped so violently at my head that it lost all feeling under the blow. A large wound was made on my head, though not a thread of the cap was cut.[3] I had not bared[4] my sword; it was in the scabbard and I had no chance to draw it. Single-handed, I was alone amongst many foes. It was not a time to stand still; I turned rein. Down came a sword again; this time on my arrows. When I had gone 7 or 8 paces, those same three men rejoined me.[5] After using his sword on me, Tambal seems to have used it on Nasir's Dost. As far as an arrrow flies to the butt, the enemy followed us.

Fol. 107b.

The Khakan-canal is a great main-channel, flowing in a deep cutting, not everywhere to be crossed. God brought it right! we came exactly opposite a low place where there was a passage over. Directly we had crossed, the horse Nasir's Dost was on, being somewhat weakly, fell down. We stopped and remounted him, then drew off for Aush, over the rising-ground

---

1 *Tambal aikandur.* By this tense I understand that Babur was not at first sure of the identity of the pseudo-sentries, partly because of their distance, partly, it may be presumed, because of concealment of identity by armour.

2 *duwulgha burki; i.e.* the soft cap worn under the iron helm.

3 Nuyan's sword dealt the blow (f. 97b). Gul-badan also tells the story (f. 77) à propos of a similar incident in Humayun's career. Babur repeats the story on f. 234.

4 *yaldaghlamai dur aidim.* The Second W.-i-B. has taken this as from *yalturmaq,* to cause to glisten, and adds the gloss that the sword was rusty (I.O. 217 f. 70b).

5 The text here seems to say that the three men were on foot, but this is negatived by the context.

between Faraghina and Khirabuk. Out on the rise, Mazid Taghai came up and joined us. An arrow had pierced his right leg also and though it had not gone through and come out again, he got to Aush with difficulty. The enemy unhorsed (*tushurdilar*) good men of mine; Nasir Beg, Muh. 'Ali *Mubashir*, Khwaja Muh. 'Ali, Khusrau *Kukuldash*, Na'man the page, all fell (to them, *tushtilar*), and also many unmailed braves.[1]

(*g. The Khans move from Karnan to Andijan.*)

The Khans, closely following on Tambal, dismounted near Andijan,—the Elder at the side of the Reserve (*quruq*) in the garden, known as Birds'-mill (*Qush-tigirman*), belonging to my grandmother, Aisan-daulat Begim,—the Younger, near Baba Tawakkul's Alms-house. Two days later I went from Aush and saw the Elder Khan in Birds'-mill. At that interview, he simply gave over to the Younger Khan the places which had come in to me. He made some such excuse as that for our advantage, he had brought the Younger Khan, how far! because such a foe as Shaibaq Khan had taken Samarkand and was waxing greater; that the Younger Khan had there no lands whatever, his own being far away; and that the country under Andijan, on the south of the Khujand-water, must be given him to encamp in. He promised me the country under Akhsi, on the north of the Khujand-water. He said that after taking a firm grip of that country (Farghana), they would move, take Samarkand, give it to me and then the whole of the Farghana country was to be the Younger Khan's. These words seem to have been meant to deceive me, since there is no knowing what they would have done when they had attained their object. It had to be however! willy-nilly, I agreed.

When, leaving him, I was on my way to the Younger Khan's presence, Qambar-'ali, known as the Skinner, joined me in a friendly way and said, "Do you see? They have taken the whole of the country just become yours. There is no opening

Fol. 108.

---

[1] Amongst the various uses of the verb *tushmak*, to descend in any way, the B.N. does not allow of "falling (death) in battle." When I made the index of the Hai. MS. facsimile, this was not known to me; I therefore erroneously entered the men enumerated here as killed at this time.

for you through them. You have in your hands Aush, Marghinan, Auzkint and the cultivated land and the tribes and the
hordes; go you to Aush; make that fort fast; send a man to
Tambal, make peace with him, then strike at the Mughul and
drive him out. After that, divide the districts into an elder and
a younger brother's shares." "Would that be right?" said I.
"The Khans are my blood relations; better serve them than rule
for Tambal." He saw that his words had made no impression,
so turned back, sorry he had spoken. I went on to see my
Younger Khan Dada. At our first interview, I had come upon
him without announcement and he had no time to dismount,
so it was all rather unceremonious. This time I got even nearer
perhaps, and he ran out as far as the end of the tent-ropes.
I was walking with some difficulty because of the wound in
my leg. We met and renewed acquaintance; then he said, "You are
talked about as a hero, my young brother!" took my arm and
led me into his tent. The tents pitched were rather small and
through his having grown up in an out-of-the-way place, he
let the one he sat in be neglected; it was like a raider's, melons,
grapes, saddlery, every sort of thing, in his sitting-tent. I went
from his presence straight back to my own camp and there he
sent his Mughul surgeon to examine my wound. Mughuls call
a surgeon also a *bakhshi*; this one was called Ataka Bakhshi.[1]

He was a very skilful surgeon; if a man's brains had come
out, he would cure it, and any sort of wound in an artery
he easily healed. For some wounds his remedy was in form of
a plaister, for some medicines had to be taken. He ordered a
bandage tied on[2] the wound in my leg and put no seton in;
once he made me eat something like a fibrous root (*yildiz*).
He told me himself, "A certain man had his leg broken in
the slender part and the bone was shattered for the breadth of
the hand. I cut the flesh open and took the bits of bone out.
Where they had been, I put a remedy in powder-form. That

1 Elph. MS. *yakhshi*. Zenker explains *bakhshi* (pay-master) as meaning also a
Court-physician.
2 The Hai. Elph. and Kehr's MS. all have *puchqaq taqmaq* or it may be *puhqaq
taqmaq*. T. *bukhaq* means bandage, *puchaq*, rind of fruit, but the word clear in the
three Turki MSS. means, skin of a fox's leg.

remedy simply became bone where there had been bone before." He told many strange and marvellous things such as surgeons in cultivated lands cannot match.

Three or four days later, Qambar-'ali, afraid on account of what he had said to me, fled (to Tambal) in Andijan. A few days later, The Khans joined to me Ayub *Begchik* with his *tuman*, and Jan-hasan *Barin* with the Barin *tuman* and, as their army-beg, Sarigh-bash Mirza,—1000 to 2000 men in all, and sent us towards Akhsi.

(*h. Babur's expedition to Akhsi.*)

Shaikh Bayazid, a younger brother of Tambal, was in Akhsi; Shahbaz *Qarluq* was in Kasan. At the time, Shahbaz was lying before Nu-kint fort; crossing the Khujand-water opposite Bikhrata, we hurried to fall upon him there. When, a little

Fol. 109b. before dawn, we were nearing the place, the begs represented to me that as the man would have had news of us, it was advisable not to go on in broken array. We moved on therefore with less speed. Shahbaz may have been really unaware of us until we were quite close; then getting to know of it, he fled into the fort. It often happens so! Once having said, "The enemy is on guard!" it is easily fancied true and the chance of action is lost. In short, the experience of such things is that no effort or exertion must be omitted, once the chance for action comes. After-repentance is useless. There was a little fighting round the fort at dawn but we delivered no serious attack.

For the convenience of foraging, we moved from Nu-kint towards the hills in the direction of Bishkharan. Seizing his opportunity, Shahbaz *Qarluq* abandoned Nu-kint and returned to Kasan. We went back and occupied Nu-kint. During those days, the army several times went out and over-ran all sides and quarters. Once they over-ran the villages of Akhsi, once those of Kasan. Shahbaz and Long Hasan's adopted son, Mirim came out of Kasan to fight; they fought, were beaten, and there Mirim died.

(*i. The affairs of Pap.*)

Pap is a strong fort belonging to Akhsi. The Papis made it fast and sent a man to me. We accordingly sent Sayyid Qasim with a few braves to occupy it. They crossed the river *Fol. 110.* (*darya*) opposite the upper villages of Akhsi and went into Pap.[1] A few days later, Sayyid Qasim did an astonishing thing. There were at the time with Shaikh Bayazid in Akhsi, Ibrahim *Chapuk* (Slash-face) Taghai,[2] Ahmad-of-qasim *Kohbur*, and Qasim Khitika (?) *Arghun*. To these Shaikh Bayazid joins 200 serviceable braves and one night sends them to surprise Pap. Sayyid Qasim must have lain down carelessly to sleep, without setting a watch. They reach the fort, set ladders up, get up on the Gate, let the drawbridge down and, when 70 or 80 good men in mail are inside, goes the news to Sayyid Qasim! Drowsy with sleep, he gets into his vest (*kunglak*), goes out, with five or six of his men, charges the enemy and drives them out with blow upon blow. He cut off a few heads and sent to me. Though such a careless lying down was bad leadership, yet, with so few, just by force of drubbing, to chase off such a mass of men in mail was very brave indeed.

Meantime The Khans were busy with the siege of Andijan but the garrison would not let them get near it. The Andijan braves used to make sallies and blows would be exchanged.

(*j. Babur invited into Akhsi.*)

Shaikh Bayazid now began to send persons to us from Akhsi to testify to well-wishing and pressingly invite us to Akhsi. His object was to separate me from The Khans, by any artifice, because without me, they had no standing-ground. His *Fol. 110b.* invitation may have been given after agreeing with his elder brother, Tambal that if I were separated from The Khans, it might be possible, in my presence, to come to some arrangement

---

1 The *darya* here mentioned seems to be the Kasan-water; the route taken from Bishkharan to Pap is shewn on the Fr. map to lead past modern Tupa-qurghan. Pap is not marked, but was, I think, at the cross-roads east of Touss (Karnan). *See* Additional Notes, p. 798.

2 Presumably Jahangir's.

with them. We gave The Khans a hint of the invitation. They said, "Go! and by whatever means, lay hands on Shaikh Bayazid." It was not my habit to cheat and play false; here above all places, when promises would have been made, how was I to break them? It occurred to me however, that if we could get into Akhsi, we might be able, by using all available means, to detach Shaikh Bayazid from Tambal, when he might take my side or something might turn up to favour my fortunes. We, in our turn, sent a man to him; compact was made, he invited us into Akhsi and when we went, came out to meet us, bringing my younger brother, Nasir Mirza with him. Then he took us into the town, gave us ground to camp in (*yurt*) and to me one of my father's houses in the outer fort[1] where I dismounted.

(k. Tambal asks help of Shaibaq Khan.)

Tambal had sent his elder brother, Beg Tilba, to Shaibaq Khan with proffer of service and invitation to enter Farghana. At this very time Shaibaq Khan's answer arrived; "I will come," he wrote. On hearing this, The Khans were all upset; they could sit no longer before Andijan and rose from before it.

The Younger Khan himself had a reputation for justice and orthodoxy, but his Mughuls, stationed, contrary to the expectations of the towns-people, in Aush, Marghinan and other places,—places that had come in to me,—began to behave ill

Fol. 111. and oppressively. When The Khans had broken up from before Andijan, the Aushis and Marghinanis, rising in tumult, seized the Mughuls in their forts, plundered and beat them, drove them out and pursued them.

The Khans did not cross the Khujand-water (for the Kindirlik-pass) but left the country by way of Marghinan and Kand-i-badam and crossed it at Khujand, Tambal pursuing them as far as Marghinan. We had had much uncertainty; we had not had much confidence in their making any stand, yet for us to go away, without clear reason, and leave them, would not have looked well.

---

1 Here his father was killed (f. 6b). *Cf.* App. A.

(l. Babur attempts to defend Akhsi.)

Early one morning, when I was in the Hot-bath, Jahangir Mirza came into Akhsi, from Marghinan, a fugitive from Tambal. We saw one another, Shaikh Bayazid also being present, agitated and afraid. The Mirza and Ibrahim Beg said, "Shaikh Bayazid must be made prisoner and we must get the citadel into our hands." In good sooth, the proposal was wise. Said I, "Promise has been made; how can we break it?" Shaikh Bayazid went into the citadel. Men ought to have been posted on the bridge; not even there did we post any-one! These blunders were the fruit of inexperience. At the top of the morning came Tambal himself with 2 or 3000 men in mail, crossed the bridge and went into the citadel. To begin with I had had rather few men; when I first went into Akhsi some had been sent to other forts and some had been made commandants and summoners all round. Left with me in Akhsi may have been something over 100 men. We had got to horse with these and were posting braves at the top of one lane after another and making ready for the fight, when Shaikh Bayazid and Qambar-'ali (the Skinner), and Muhammad-dost[1] came galloping from Tambal with talk of peace.

Fol. 111b.

After posting those told off for the fight, each in his appointed place, I dismounted at my father's tomb for a conference, in which I invited Jahangir Mirza to join. Muhammad-dost went back to Tambal but Qambar-'ali and Shaikh Bayazid were present. We sat in the south porch of the tomb and were in consultation when the Mirza, who must have settled beforehand with Ibrahim *Chapuk* to lay hands on those other two, said in my ear, "They must be made prisoner." Said I, "Don't hurry! matters are past making prisoners. See here! with terms made, the affair might be coaxed into something. For why? Not only are they many and we few, but they with their strength are in the citadel, we with our weakness, in the outer fort." Shaikh Bayazid and Qambar-'ali both being present, Jahangir Mirza looked at Ibrahim Beg and made him a sign to refrain. Whether he misunderstood to the contrary

1 'Ali-dost's son (f. 79b).

or whether he pretended to misunderstand, is not known; suddenly he did the ill-deed of seizing Shaikh Bayazid. Braves closing in from all sides, flung those two to the ground. Through this the affair was taken past adjustment; we gave them into charge and got to horse for the coming fight.

One side of the town was put into Jahangir Mirza's charge; as his men were few, I told off some of mine to reinforce him. I went first to his side and posted men for the fight, then to other parts of the town. There is a somewhat level, open space in the middle of Akhsi; I had posted a party of braves there and gone on when a large body of the enemy, mounted and on foot, bore down upon them, drove them from their post and forced them into a narrow lane. Just then I came up (the lane), galloped my horse at them, and scattered them in flight. While I was thus driving them out from the lane into the flat, and had got my sword to work, they shot my horse in the leg; it stumbled and threw me there amongst them. I got up quickly and shot one arrow off. My squire, Kahil (lazy) had a weakly pony; he got off and led it to me. Mounting this, I started for another lane-head. Sl. Muh. Wais noticed the weakness of my mount, dismounted and led me his own. I mounted that horse. Just then, Qasim Beg's son, Qambar-'ali came, wounded, from Jahangir Mirza

and said the Mirza had been attacked some time before, driven off in panic, and had gone right away. We were thunderstruck! At the same moment arrived Sayyid Qasim, the commandant of Pap! His was a most unseasonable visit, since at such a crisis it was well to have such a strong fort in our hands. Said I to Ibrahim Beg, "What's to be done now?" He was slightly wounded; whether because of this or because of stupefaction, he could give no useful answer. My idea was to get across the bridge, destroy it and make for Andijan. Baba Sher-zad did very well here. "We will storm out at the gate and get away at once," he said. At his word, we set off for the Gate. Khwaja Mir Miran also spoke boldly at that crisis. In one of the lanes, Sayyid Qasim and Nasir's Dost chopped away at Baqi *Khiz*,[1] I being in front with Ibrahim Beg and Mirza Quli *Kukuldash*.

---

1 The sobriquet *Khiz* may mean Leaper, or Impetuous.

As we came opposite the Gate, we saw Shaikh Bayazid, wear-ing his pull-over shirt[1] above his vest, coming in with three or four horsemen. He must have been put into the charge of Jahangir's men in the morning when, against my will, he was made prisoner, and they must have carried him off when they got away. They had thought it would be well to kill him; they set him free alive. He had been released just when I chanced upon him in the Gate. I drew and shot off the arrow on my thumb; it grazed his neck, a good shot! He came con-fusedly in at the Gate, turned to the right and fled down a lane. We followed him instantly. Mirza-quli *Kukuldash* got at one man with his rugged-mace and went on. Another man took aim at Ibrahim Beg, but when the Beg shouted "Hai! Hai!" let him pass and shot me in the arm-pit, from as near as a man on guard at a Gate. Two plates of my Qalmaq mail were cut; he took to flight and I shot after him. Next I shot at a man running away along the ramparts, adjusting for his cap against the battlements; he left his cap nailed on the wall and went off, gathering his turban-sash together in his hand. Then again,— a man was in flight alongside me in the lane down which Shaikh Bayazid had gone. I pricked the back of his head with my sword; he bent over from his horse till he leaned against the wall of the lane, but he kept his seat and with some trouble, made good his flight. When we had driven all the enemy's men from the Gate, we took possession of it but the affair was past discussion because they, in the citadel, were 2000 or 3000, we, in the outer fort, 100 or 200. Moreover they had chased off Jahangir Mirza, as long before as it takes milk to boil, and with him had gone half my men. This notwithstanding, we sent a man, while we were in the Gate, to say to him, "If you are near at hand, come, let us attack again." But the matter had gone past that! Ibrahim Beg, either because his horse was really weak or because of his wound, said, "My horse is done." On this, Sulaiman, one of Muh. 'Ali's *Mubashir's* servants, did a plucky thing, for with matters as they were and none constraining him, while we were waiting

Fol. 113.

Fol. 113b.

---

1 *kuilak,* syn. *kunglak,* a shirt not opening at the breast. It will have been a short garment since the under-vest was visible.

in the Gate, he dismounted and gave his horse to Ibrahim Beg.
Kichik (little) 'Ali, now the Governor of Koel,[1] also shewed
courage while we were in the Gate; he was a retainer of Sl.
Muh.Wais and twice did well, here and in Aush.We delayed in
the Gate till those sent to Jahangir Mirza came back and said
he had gone off long before. It was too late to stay there; off
we flung; it was ill-judged to have stayed as long as we did.
Twenty or thirty men were with me. Just as we hustled out of
the Gate, a number of armed men[2] came right down upon us,
reaching the town-side of the drawbridge just as we had
crossed. Banda-'ali, the maternal grandfather of Qasim Beg's
son, Hamza, called out to Ibrahim Beg, "You are always boasting
of your zeal! Let's take to our swords!" "What hinders? Come
along!" said Ibrahim Beg, from beside me.The senseless fellows
were for displaying their zeal at a time of such disaster! Ill-timed
zeal! That was no time to make stand or delay! We went off
quickly, the enemy following and unhorsing our men.

(*m. Babur a fugitive before Tambal's men.*)

When we were passing Meadow-dome (Gumbaz-i-chaman),
two miles out of Akhsi, Ibrahim Beg called out to me. Looking
Fol. 114.   back, I saw a page of Shaikh Bayazid's striking at him and
turned rein, but Bayan-quli's Khan-quli, said at my side, "This
is a bad time for going back," seized my rein and pushed ahead.
Many of our men had been unhorsed before we reached Sang,
4 miles (2 *shar'i*) out of Akhsi.[3] Seeing no pursuers at Sang, we

1 *i.e.* when Babur was writing in Hindustan. Exactly at what date he made this
entry is not sure. 'Ali was in Koel in 933 AH. (f. 315) and then taken prisoner, but
Babur does not say he was killed,—as he well might say of a marked man, and,
as the captor was himself taken shortly after, 'Ali may have been released, and may
have been in Koel again. So that the statement "now in Koel" may refer to a time
later than his capture. The interest of the point is in its relation to the date of
composition of the *Babur-nama*.
   No record of 'Ali's bravery in Aush has been preserved. The reference here
made to it may indicate something attempted in 908 AH. after Babur's adventure
in Karnan (f. 118*b*) or in 909 AH. from Sukh. *Cf.* Translator's note f. 118*b*.
2 *aupchinlik*. Vambéry, *gepanzert*; Shaw, four horse-shoes and their nails; Steingass,
aupcha-khana, a guard-house.
3 Sang is a ferry-station (Kostenko, i, 213). Pap may well have been regretted
(f. 109*b* and f. 112*b*)! The well-marked features of the French map of 1904
allows Babur's flight to be followed.

passed it by and turned straight up its water. In this position of our affairs there were eight men of us;—Nasir's Dost, Qasim Beg's Qambar-'ali, Bayan-quli's Khan-quli, Mirza Quli *Kukuldash*, Nasir's Shaham, Sayyidi Qara's 'Abdu'l-qadus, Khwaja Husaini and myself, the eighth. Turning up the stream, we found, in the broad valley, a good little road, far from the beaten track. We made straight up the valley, leaving the stream on the right, reached its waterless part and, near the Afternoon Prayer, got up out of it to level land. When we looked across the plain, we saw a blackness on it, far away. I made my party take cover and myself had gone to look out from higher ground, when a number of men came at a gallop up the hill behind us. Without waiting to know whether they were many or few, we mounted and rode off. There were 20 or 25; we, as has been said, were eight. If we had known their number at first, we should have made a good stand against them but we thought they would not be pursuing us, unless they had good support behind. A fleeing Fol. 114*b.* foe, even if he be many, cannot face a few pursuers, for as the saying is, "*Hai* is enough for the beaten ranks."[1]

Khan-quli said, "This will never do! They will take us all. From amongst the horses there are, you take two good ones and go quickly on with Mirza Quli *Kukuldash*, each with a led horse. May-be you will get away." He did not speak ill; as there was no fighting to hand, there was a chance of safety in doing as he said, but it really would not have looked well to leave any man alone, without a horse, amongst his foes. In the end they all dropped off, one by one, of themselves. My horse was a little tired; Khan-quli dismounted and gave me his; I jumped off at once and mounted his, he mine. Just then they unhorsed Sayyidi Qara's 'Abdu'l-qadus and Nasir's Shaham who had fallen behind. Khan-quli also was left. It was no time to proffer help or defence; on it was gone, at the full speed of our mounts. The horses began to flag; Dost Beg's failed and stopped. Mine began to tire; Qambar-'ali got off

---

1 In the Turki text this saying is in Persian; in the Kehr-Ilminsky, in Turki, as though it had gone over with its Persian context of the W.-i-B. from which the K.-I. text here is believed to be a translation.

and gave me his; I mounted his, he mine. He was left.
Khwaja Husaini was a lame man; he turned aside to the
higher ground. I was left with Mirza Quli *Kukuldash.* Our

Fol. 115.   horses could not possibly gallop, they trotted. His began to
flag. Said I, "What will become of me, if you fall behind?
Come along! let's live or die together." Several times I looked
back at him; at last he said, "My horse is done! It can't go on.
Never mind me! You go on, perhaps you will get away."
It was a miserable position for me; he remained behind,
I was alone.

Two of the enemy were in sight, one Baba of Sairam, the
other Banda-'ali. They gained on me; my horse was done;
the mountains were still 2 miles (1 *kuroh*) off. A pile of rock
was in my path. Thought I to myself, "My horse is worn out
and the hills are still somewhat far away; which way should
I go? In my quiver are at least 20 arrows; should I dismount and
shoot them off from this pile of rock?" Then again, I thought
I might reach the hills and once there, stick a few arrows in
my belt and scramble up. I had a good deal of confidence in
my feet and went on, with this plan in mind. My horse could
not possibly trot; the two men came within arrow's reach.

Fol. 115b. For my own sake sparing my arrows, I did not shoot; they,
out of caution, came no nearer. By sunset I was near the
hills. Suddenly they called out, "Where are you going in this
fashion? Jahangir Mirza has been brought in a prisoner;
Nasir Mirza also is in their hands." I made no reply and went
on towards the hills. When a good distance further had been
gone, they spoke again, this time more respectfully, dismounting to speak. I gave no ear to them but went on up a glen
till, at the Bed-time prayer, I reached a rock as big as a house.
Going behind it, I saw there were places to be jumped, where
no horse could go. They dismounted again and began to
speak like servants and courteously. Said they, "Where are
you going in this fashion, without a road and in the dark?
Sl. Ahmad Tambal will make you *padshah*." They swore this.
Said I, "My mind is not easy as to that. I cannot go to him.

Fol. 116.   If you think to do me timely service, years may pass before
you have such another chance. Guide me to a road by which

I can go to The Khan's presence. If you will do this, I will shew you favour and kindness greater than your heart's-desire. If you will not do it, go back the way you came; that also would be to serve me well." Said they, "Would to God we had never come! But since we are here, after following you in the way we have done, how can we go back from you? If you will not go with us, we are at your service, wherever you go." Said I, "Swear that you speak the truth." They, for their part, made solemn oath upon the Holy Book.

I at once confided in them and said, "People have shewn me a road through a broad valley, somewhere near this glen; take me to it." Spite of their oath, my trust in them was not so complete but that I gave them the lead and followed. After 2 to 4 miles (1-2 *kuroh*), we came to the bed of a torrent. "This will not be the road for the broad valley," I said. They drew back, saying, "That road is a long way ahead," but it really must have been the one we were on and they have been concealing the fact, in order to deceive me. About half through the night, we reached another stream. This time they said, "We have been negligent; it now seems to us that the road through the broad valley is behind." Said I, "What is to be done?" Said they, "The Ghawa road is certainly in front; by it people cross for Far-kat."[1] They guided me for that and we went on till in the third Fol. 116*b*. watch of the night we reached the Karnan gully which comes down from Ghawa. Here Baba Sairami said, "Stay here a little while I look along the Ghawa road." He came back after a time and said, "Some men have gone along that road, led by one wearing a Mughul cap; there is no going that way." I took alarm at these words. There I was, at dawn, in the middle of the cultivated land, far from the road I wanted to take. Said I, "Guide me to where I can hide today, and tonight when you will have laid hands on something for the horses, lead me to cross the Khujand-water and along its further bank." Said they, "Over there, on the upland, there might be hiding."

Banda-'ali was Commandant in Karnan. "There is no doing without food for ourselves or our horses;" he said, "let me go

1 *Cf.* f. 96*b* and Fr. Map for route over the Kindir-tau.

into Karnan and bring what I can find." We stopped 2 miles (1 *kuroh*) out of Karnan; he went on. He was a long time away; near dawn there was no sign of him. The day had shot when he hurried up, bringing three loaves of bread but no corn for the horses. Each of us putting a loaf into the breast of his tunic, we went quickly up the rise, tethered our horses there in the open valley and went to higher ground, each to keep watch.

Fol. 117.

Near mid-day, Ahmad the Falconer went along the Ghawa road for Akhsi. I thought of calling to him and of saying, with promise and fair word, "You take those horses," for they had had a day and a night's strain and struggle, without corn, and were utterly done. But then again, we were a little uneasy as we did not entirely trust him. We decided that, as the men Baba Sairami had seen on the road would be in Karnan that night, the two with me should fetch one of their horses for each of us, and that then we should go each his own way.

At mid-day, a something glittering was seen on a horse, as far away as eye can reach. We were not able to make out at all what it was. It must have been Muh. Baqir Beg himself; he had been with us in Akhsi and when we got out and scattered, he must have come this way and have been moving then to a hiding-place.[1]

Banda-'ali and Baba Sairami said, "The horses have had no corn for two days and two nights; let us go down into the dale and put them there to graze." Accordingly we rode down and put them to the grass. At the Afternoon Prayer, a horseman passed along the rising-ground where we had been. We recognized him for Qadir-birdi, the head-man of Ghawa. "Call him," I said. They called; he came. After questioning him, and speaking to him of favour and kindness, and giving him promise and fair word, I sent him to bring rope, and a grass-

Fol. 117b. hook, and an axe, and material for crossing water,[2] and corn for the horses, and food and, if it were possible, other horses. We made tryst with him for that same spot at the Bed-time Prayer.

---

1 This account of Muh. Baqir reads like one given later to Babur; he may have had some part in Babur's rescue (*cf.* Translator's Note to f. 118b).

2 Perhaps reeds for a raft. Sh. N. p. 258, *Sal auchun bar qamish*, reeds are there also for rafts.

Near the Evening Prayer, a horseman passed from the direction of Karnan for Ghawa. "Who are you?" we asked. He made some reply. He must have been Muh. Baqir Beg himself, on his way from where we had seen him earlier, going at night-fall to some other hiding-place, but he so changed his voice that, though he had been years with me, I did not know it. It would have been well if I had recognized him and he had joined me. His passing caused much anxiety and alarm; tryst could not be kept with Qadir-birdi of Ghawa. Banda-'ali said, "There are retired gardens in the suburbs of Karnan where no one will suspect us of being; let us go there and send to Qadir-birdi and have him brought there." With this idea, we mounted and went to the Karnan suburbs. It was winter and very cold. They found a worn, coarse sheepskin coat and brought it to me; I put it on. They brought me a bowl of millet-porridge; I ate it and was wonderfully re-freshed. "Have you sent off the man to Qadir-birdi?" said I to Banda-'ali. "I have sent," he said. But those luckless, clownish mannikins seem to have agreed together to send the man to Tambal in Akhsi!

We went into a house and for awhile my eyes closed in sleep. Those mannikins artfully said to me, "You must not bestir yourself to leave Karnan till there is news of Qadir-birdi but this house is right amongst the suburbs; on the out-skirts the orchards are empty; no-one will suspect if we go there." Accordingly we mounted at mid-night and went to a distant orchard. Baba Sairami kept watch from the roof of a house. Near mid-day he came down and said, "Commandant Yusuf is coming." Great fear fell upon me! "Find out," I said, "whether he comes because he knows about me." He went and after some exchange of words, came back and said, "He says he met a foot-soldier in the Gate of Akhsi who said to him, 'The padshah is in such a place,' that he told no-one, put the man with Wali the Treasurer whom he had made prisoner in the fight, and then galloped off here." Said I, "How does it strike you?" "They are all your servants," he said, "you must go. What else can you do? They will make you their ruler." Said I, "After such rebellion and fighting,

Fol. 118.

with what confidence could I go?" We were saying this,
when Yusuf knelt before me, saying, "Why should it be hidden?
Sl. Ahmad Tambal has no news of you, but Shaikh Bayazid
has and he sent me here." On hearing this, my state of mind
was miserable indeed, for well is it understood that nothing in
the world is worse than fear for one's life. "Tell the truth!"
I said, "if the affair is likely to go on to worse, I will make
Fol. 118b. ablution." Yusuf swore oaths, but who would trust them?
I knew the helplessness of my position. I rose and went to a
corner of the garden, saying to myself, "If a man live a hundred
years or a thousand years, at the last nothing..."[1]

TRANSLATOR'S NOTE ON 908 TO 910 AH.—1503 TO 1504 AD.

Friends are likely to have rescued Babur from his dangerous
isolation. His presence in Karnan was known both in Ghawa
and in Akhsi; Muh. Baqir Beg was at hand (f. 117); some of
those he had dropped in his flight would follow him when
their horses had had rest; Jahangir was somewhere north of the
river with the half of Babur's former force (f. 112); The Khans,
with their long-extended line of march, may have been on the
main road through or near Karnan. If Yusuf took Babur as a
prisoner along the Akhsi road, there were these various chances
of his meeting friends.

His danger was evaded; he joined his uncles and was with
them, leading 1000 men (Sh. N. p. 268), when they were
defeated at Archian just before or in the season of Cancer, *i.e.
circa* June (T. R. p. 164). What he was doing between the
winter cold of Karnan (f. 117b) and June might have been

1 Here the Turki text breaks off, as it might through loss of pages, causing a
blank of narrative extending over some 16 months. *Cf.* App. D. for a passage,
supposedly spurious, found with the Haidarabad Codex and the Kehr-Ilminsky
text, purporting to tell how Babur was rescued from the risk in which the lacuna here leaves him.

known from his lost pages. Muh. Salih writes at length of one affair falling within the time,—Jahangir's occupation of Khujand, its siege and its capture by Shaibani. This capture will have occurred considerably more than a month before the defeat of The Khans (Sh. N. p. 230).

It is not easy to decide in what month of 908 AH. they went into Farghana or how long their campaign lasted. Babur chronicles a series of occurrences, previous to the march of the army, which must have filled some time. The road over the Kindirlik-pass was taken, one closed in Babur's time (f. 1b) though now open through the winter. Looking at the rapidity of his own movements in Farghana, it seems likely that the pass was crossed after and not before its closed time. If so, the campaign may have covered 4 or 5 months. Muh. Salih's account of Shaibaq's operations strengthens this view. News that Ahmad had joined Mahmud in Tashkint (f. 102) went to Shaibani in Khusrau Shah's territories; he saw his interests in Samarkand threatened by this combination of the Chaghatai brothers to restore Babur in Farghana, came north therefore in order to help Tambal. He then waited a month in Samarkand (Sh. N. p. 230), besieged Jahangir, went back and stayed in Samarkand long enough to give his retainers time to equip for a year's campaigning (l. c. p. 244) then went to Akhsi and so to Archian.

Babur's statement (f. 110b) that The Khans went from Andijan to the Khujand-crossing over the Sir attracts attention because this they might have done if they had meant to leave Farghana by Mirza-rabat but they are next heard of as at Akhsi. Why did they make that great détour? Why not have crossed opposite Akhsi or at Sang? Or if they had thought of retiring, what turned them east again? Did they place Jahangir in Khujand? Babur's missing pages would have answered these questions no doubt. It was useful for them to encamp where they did, east of Akhsi, because they there had near them a road by which reinforcement could come from Kashghar or retreat be made. The Akhsi people told Shaibani that he could easily overcome The Khans if he went without warning, and if they had not withdrawn by the Khuldja road (Sh. N. p. 262). By that

road the few men who went with Ahmad to Tashkint (f. 103)
may have been augmented to the force, enumerated as his in
the battle by Muh. Salih (Sh. N. cap. LIII.).

When The Khans were captured, Babur escaped and made
"for Mughulistan," a vague direction seeming here to mean
Tashkint, but, finding his road blocked, in obedience to orders
from Shaibaq that he and Abu'l-makaram were to be captured,
he turned back and, by unfrequented ways, went into the hill-
country of Sukh and Hushiar. There he spent about a year
in great misery (f. 14 and H. S. ii, 318). Of the wretchedness of
the time Haidar also writes. If anything was attempted in
Farghana in the course of those months, record of it has been
lost with Babur's missing pages. He was not only homeless
and poor, but shut in by enemies. Only the loyalty or kindness
of the hill-tribes can have saved him and his few followers.
His mother was with him; so also were the families of his men.
How Qutluq-nigar contrived to join him from Tashkint,
though historically a small matter, is one he would chronicle.
What had happened there after the Mughul defeat, was that
the horde had marched away for Kashghar while Shah Begim
remained in charge of her daughters with whom the Auzbeg
chiefs intended to contract alliance. Shaibani's orders for her
stay and for the general exodus were communicated to her by
her son, The Khan, in what Muh. Salih, quoting its purport,
describes as a right beautiful letter (p. 296).

By some means Qutluq-nigar joined Babur, perhaps helped
by the circumstance that her daughter, Khan-zada was
Shaibaq's wife. She spent at least some part of those hard
months with him, when his fortunes were at their lowest ebb.
A move becoming imperative, the ragged and destitute company
started in mid-June 1504 (Muh. 910 AH.) on that perilous
mountain journey to which Haidar applies the Prophet's
dictum, "Travel is a foretaste of Hell," but of which the end
was the establishment of a Timurid dynasty in Hindustan. To
look down the years from the destitute Babur to Akbar,
Shah-jahan and Aurangzib is to see a great stream of human
life flow from its source in his resolve to win upward, his
quenchless courage and his abounding vitality. Not yet 22,

the sport of older men's intrigues, he had been tempered by failure, privation and dangers.

He left Sukh intending to go to Sl. Husain Mirza in Khurasan but he changed this plan for one taking him to Kabul where a Timurid might claim to dispossess the Arghuns, then holding it since the death, in 907 AH. of his uncle, Aulugh Beg Mirza *Kabuli*.

THE MEMOIRS OF BABUR

SECTION II. KABUL[1]

910 AH.—JUNE 14TH 1504 TO JUNE 4TH 1505 AD.[2]

(a. Babur leaves Farghana.)

In the month of Muharram, after leaving the Farghana country Haidarabad MS. Fol. 120. intending to go to Khurasan, I dismounted at Ailak-yilaq,[3] one of the summer pastures of Hisar. In this camp I entered my 23rd year, and applied the razor to my face.[4] Those who, hoping in me, went with me into exile, were, small and great, between 2 and 300; they were almost all on foot, had walking-staves in their hands, brogues[5] on their feet, and long coats[6] on

1 As in the Farghana Section, so here, reliance is on the Elphinstone and Haidarabad MSS. The Kehr–Ilminsky text still appears to be a retranslation from the *Waqi'at-i-baburi* and verbally departs much from the true text; moreover, in this Section it has been helped out, where its archetype was illegible or has lost fragmentary passages, from the Leyden and Erskine *Memoirs*. It may be mentioned, as between the First and the Second *Waqi'at-i-baburi*, that several obscure passages in this Section are more explicit in the First (Payanda-hasan's) than in its successor ('Abdu-r-rahim's).

2 Elph. MS. f. 90*b*; W.-i-B. I.O. 215, f. 96*b* and 217, f. 79; Mems. p. 127. "In 1504 AD. Ferdinand the Catholic drove the French out of Naples" (Erskine). In England, Henry VII was pushing forward a commercial treaty, the *Intercursus malus*, with the Flemings and growing in wealth by the exactions of Empson and Dudley.

3 Presumably the pastures of the "Ilak" Valley. The route from Sukh would be over the 'Ala'u'd-din-pass, into the Qizil-su valley, down to Ab-i-garm and on to the Ailaq-valley, Khwaja 'Imad, the Kafirnigan, Qabadian, and Aubaj on the Amu. See T.R. p. 175 and Farghana Section, p. 184, as to the character of the journey.

4 Amongst the Turki tribes, the time of first applying the razor to the face is celebrated by a great entertainment. Babur's miserable circumstances would not admit of this (Erskine).

   The text is ambiguous here, reading either that Sukh was left or that Ailaq-yilaq was reached in Muharram. As the birthday was on the 8th, the journey very arduous and, for a party mostly on foot, slow, it seems safest to suppose that the start was made from Sukh at the end of 909 AH. and not in Muharram, 910 AH.

5 *charuq*, rough boots of untanned leather, formed like a moccasin with the lower leather drawn up round the foot; they are worn by Khirghiz mountaineers and caravan-men on journeys (Shaw).

6 *chapan*, the ordinary garment of Central Asia (Shaw).

their shoulders. So destitute were we that we had but two tents (*chadar*) amongst us; my own used to be pitched for my mother, and they set an *alachuq* at each stage for me to sit in.[1]

Though we had started with the intention of going into Khurasan, yet with things as they were[2] something was hoped for from the Hisar country and Khusrau Shah's retainers. Every few days some-one would come in from the country or a tribe or the (Mughul) horde, whose words made it probable that we had growing ground for hope. Just then Mulla Baba of Pashaghar came back, who had been our envoy to Khusrau Shah; from Khusrau Shah he brought nothing likely to please, but he did from the tribes and the horde.

Fol. 120b. Three or four marches beyond Ailak, when halt was made at a place near Hisar called Khwaja 'Imad, Muhibb-'ali, the Armourer, came to me from Khusrau Shah. Through Khusrau Shah's territories I have twice happened to pass;[3] renowned though he was for kindness and liberality, he neither time showed me the humanity he had shown to the meanest of men.

As we were hoping something from the country and the tribes, we made delay at every stage. At this critical point Sherim Taghai, than whom no man of mine was greater, thought of leaving me because he was not keen to go into Khurasan. He had sent all his family off and stayed himself unencumbered, when after the defeat at Sar-i-pul (906 AH.) I went back to defend Samarkand; he was a bit of a coward and he did this sort of thing several times over.

(*b. Babur joined by one of Khusrau Shah's kinsmen.*)

After we reached Qabadian, a younger brother of Khusrau Shah, Baqi *Chaghaniani*, whose holdings were Chaghanian,[4] Shahr-i-safa and Tirmiz, sent the *khatib*[5] of Qarshi to me to

---

1 The *alachuq*, a tent of flexible poles, covered with felt, may be the *khargah* (kibitka); Persian *chadar* seems to represent Turki *aq awi*, white house.

2 *i.e.* with Khusrau's power shaken by Auzbeg attack, made in the winter of 909 AH. (*Shaibani-nama* cap. lviii).

3 *Cf.* ff. 81 and 81b. The armourer's station was low for an envoy to Babur, the superior in birth of the armourer's master.

4 var. Chaqanian and Saghanian. The name formerly described the whole of the Hisar territory (Erskine).

5 the preacher by whom the *Khutba* is read (Erskine).

express his good wishes and his desire for alliance, and, after we had crossed the Amu at the Aubaj-ferry, he came himself to wait on me. By his wish we moved down the river to opposite Tirmiz, where, without fear [or, without going over himself],[1] he had their families[2] and their goods brought across to join us. This done, we set out together for Kahmard and Bamian, then held by his son[3] Ahmad-i-qasim, the son of Khusrau Shah's sister. Our plan was to leave the households (*awi-ail*) safe in Fort Ajar of the Kahmard-valley and to take action wherever Fol. 121. action might seem well. At Aibak, Yar-'ali Balal,[4] who had fled from Khusrau Shah, joined us with several braves; he had been with me before, and had made good use of his sword several times in my presence, but was parted from me in the recent throneless times[5] and had gone to Khusrau Shah. He represented to me that the Mughuls in Khusrau Shah's service wished me well. Moreover, Qambar-'ali Beg, known also as Qambar-'ali *Silakh* (Skinner), fled to me after we reached the Zindan-valley.[6]

(c. Occurrences in Kahmard.)

We reached Kahmard with three or four marches and deposited our households and families in Ajar. While we stayed there, Jahangir Mirza married (Ai Begim) the daughter of Sl. Mahmud Mirza and Khan-zada Begim, who had been set aside for him during the lifetime of the Mirzas.[7]

Meantime Baqi Beg urged it upon me, again and again, that two rulers in one country, or two chiefs in one army are a source of faction and disorder—a foundation of dissension and ruin.

---

1 *bi baqi* or *bi Baqi*; perhaps a play of words with the double meaning expressed in the above translation. A third and perhaps here better rendering of *bi baqi* is that of p. 662 (*s.d.* April 10th), "leaving none behind."
2 Amongst these were widows and children of Babur's uncle, Mahmud (f. 27*b*).
3 *aughul*. As being the son of Khusrau's sister, Ahmad was nephew to Baqi; there may be in the text a scribe's slip from one *aughul* to another, and the real statement be that Ahmad was the son of Baqi's son, Muh. Qasim, which would account for his name Ahmad-i-qasim.
4 *Cf.* f. 67.
5 Babur's loss of rule in Farghana and Samarkand.
6 about 7 miles south of Aibak, on the road to Sar-i-tagh (mountain-head, Erskine).
7 *viz.* the respective fathers, Mahmud and 'Umar Shaikh. The arrangement was made in 895 AH. (1490 AD.).

"For they have said, 'Ten darwishes can sleep under one
blanket, but two kings cannot find room in one clime.'

> If a man of God eat half a loaf,
> He gives the other to a darwish;
> Let a king grip the rule of a clime,
> He dreams of another to grip."[1]

Baqi Beg urged further that Khusrau Shah's retainers and
followers would be coming in that day or the next to take
service with the Padshah (i.e. Babur); that there were such
Fol. 121b. sedition-mongers with them as the sons of Ayub *Begchik*,
besides other who had been the stirrers and spurs to disloyalty
amongst their Mirzas,[2] and that if, at this point, Jahangir Mirza
were dismissed, on good and friendly terms, for Khurasan, it
would remove a source of later repentance. Urge it as he would,
however, I did not accept his suggestion, because it is against
my nature to do an injury to my brethren, older or younger,[3]
or to any kinsman soever, even when something untoward has
happened. Though formerly between Jahangir Mirza and me,
resentments and recriminations had occurred about our rule
and retainers, yet there was nothing whatever then to arouse
anger against him; he had come out of that country
(i.e. Farghana) with me and was behaving like a blood-relation
and a servant. But in the end it was just as Baqi Beg predicted;—
those tempters to disloyalty, that is to say, Ayub's Yusuf and Ayub's
Bihlul, left me for Jahangir Mirza, took up a hostile and mutinous
position, parted him from me, and conveyed him into Khurasan.

(*d. Co-operation invited against Shaibaq Khan.*)

In those days came letters from Sl. Husain Mirza, long and
far-fetched letters which are still in my possession and in that
Fol. 122. of others, written to Badi'u'z-zaman Mirza, myself, Khusrau
Shah and Zu'n-nun Beg, all to the same purport, as follows:—
"When the three brothers, Sl. Mahmud Mirza, Sl. Ahmad
Mirza, and Aulugh Beg Mirza, joined together and advanced

---

1 *Gulistan* cap. i, story 3. Part of this quotation is used again on f. 183.
2 Mahmud's sons under whom Baqi had served.
3 Uncles of all degrees are included as elder brethren, cousins of all degrees, as
younger ones.

against me, I defended the bank of the Murgh-ab[1] in such a way that they retired without being able to effect anything. Now if the Auzbegs advance, I might myself guard the bank of the Murgh-ab again; let Badi'u'z-zaman Mirza leave men to defend the forts of Balkh, Shibarghan, and Andikhud while he himself guards Girzawan, the Zang-valley, and the hill–country thereabouts." As he had heard of my being in those parts, he wrote to me also, "Do you make fast Kahmard, Ajar, and that hill–tract; let Khusrau Shah place trusty men in Hisar and Qunduz; let his younger brother Wali make fast Badakhshan and the Khutlan hills; then the Auzbeg will retire, able to do nothing."

These letters threw us into despair;—for why? Because at that time there was in Timur Beg's territory (*yurt*) no ruler so great as Sl. Husain Mirza, whether by his years, armed strength, or dominions; it was to be expected, therefore, that envoys would go, treading on each other's heels, with clear and sharp orders, such as, "Arrange for so many boats at the Tirmiz, Kilif, and Kirki ferries," "Get any quantity of bridge material together," and "Well watch the ferries above Tuquz-aulum,"[2] so that men whose spirit years of Auzbeg oppression had broken, might be cheered to hope again.[3] But how could hope live in tribe or horde when a great ruler like Sl. Husain Mirza, sitting in the place of Timur Beg, spoke, not of marching forth to meet the enemy, but only of defence against his attack?

Fol. 122b.

When we had deposited in Ajar what had come with us of hungry train (*aj aunuq*) and household (*awi-ail*), together with the families of Baqi Beg, his son, Muh. Qasim, his soldiers and his tribesmen, with all their goods, we moved out with our men.

1 Presumably the ferries; perhaps the one on the main road from the north–east which crosses the river at Fort Murgh-ab.
2 Nine deaths, perhaps where the Amu is split into nine channels at the place where Mirza Khan's son Sulaiman later met his rebel grandson Shah-rukh (*Tabaqat-i-akbari*, Elliot & Dowson, v, 392, and A.N. Bib. Ind., 3rd ed., 441). Tuquz-aulum is too far up the river to be Arnold's "shorn and parcelled Oxus".
3 Shaibaq himself had gone down from Samarkand in 908 AH. and in 909 AH. and so permanently located his troops as to have sent their families to them. In 909 AH. he drove Khusrau into the mountains of Badakhshan, but did not occupy Qunduz; thither Khusrau returned and there stayed till now, when Shaibaq again came south (fol. 123). *See* Sh. N. cap. lviii *et seq.*

(e. Increase of Babur's following.)

One man after another came in from Khusrau Shah's Mughuls and said, "We of the Mughul horde, desiring the royal welfare, have drawn off from Taliqan towards Ishkimish and Fulul. Let the Padshah advance as fast as possible, for the greater part of Khusrau Shah's force has broken up and is ready to take service with him." Just then news arrived that Shaibaq Khan, after taking Andijan,[1] was getting to horse again against Hisar and Qunduz. On hearing this, Khusrau Shah, unable to stay in Qunduz, marched out with all the men he had, and took the road for Kabul. No sooner had he left than his old servant, the able and trusted Mulla Muhammad *Turkistani* made Qunduz fast for Shaibaq Khan.

Fol. 123.

Three or four thousand heads-of-houses in the Mughul horde, former dependants of Khusrau Shah, brought their families and joined us when, going by way of Sham-tu, we were near the Qizil-su.[2]

(f. Qambar-'ali, the Skinner, dismissed.)

Qambar-'ali Beg's foolish talk has been mentioned several times already; his manners were displeasing to Baqi Beg; to gratify Baqi Beg, he was dismissed. Thereafter his son, 'Abdu'l-shukur, was in Jahangir Mirza's service.

(g. Khusrau Shah waits on Babur.)

Khusrau Shah was much upset when he heard that the Mughul horde had joined me; seeing nothing better to do for himself, he sent his son-in-law, Ayub's Yaq'ub, to make profession of well-wishing and submission to me, and respectfully to represent that he would enter my service if I would make terms and compact with him. His offer was accepted, because Baqi *Chaghaniani* was a man of weight, and, however steady in his favourable disposition to me, did not overlook his brother's side in this matter. Compact was made that Khusrau

---

1 From Tambal, to put down whom he had quitted his army near Balkh (Sh. N. cap. lix).

2 This, one of the many Red-rivers, flows from near Kahmard and joins the Andar-ab water near Dushi.

Shah's life should be safe, and that whatever amount of his goods he selected, should not be refused him. After giving Yaqʻub leave to go, we marched down the Qizil-su and dismounted near to where it joins the water of Andar-ab.   Fol. 123*b*.

Next day, one in the middle of the First Rabiʻ (end of August, 1504 AD.), riding light, I crossed the Andar-ab water and took my seat under a large plane-tree near Dushi, and thither came Khusrau Shah, in pomp and splendour, with a great company of men. According to rule and custom, he dismounted some way off and then made his approach. Three times he knelt when we saw one another, three times also on taking leave; he knelt once when asking after my welfare, once again when he offered his tribute, and he did the same with Jahangir Mirza and with Mirza Khan (Wais). That sluggish old mannikin who through so many years had just pleased himself, lacking of sovereignty one thing only, namely, to read the *Khutba* in his own name, now knelt 25 or 26 times in succession, and came and went till he was so wearied out that he tottered forward. His many years of begship and authority vanished from his view. When we had seen one another and he had offered his gift, I desired him to be seated. We stayed in that place for one or two *garis*,[1] exchanging tale and talk. His conversation was vapid and empty, presumably because he was a coward and false to his salt. Two things he said were extraordinary for the time when, under his eyes, his trusty and trusted retainers were becoming mine, and when his affairs had reached the point that he, the sovereign-aping mannikin, had had to come, willy-nilly, abased and unhonoured, to what sort   Fol. 124. of an interview! One of the things he said was this:—When condoled with for the desertion of his men, he replied, "Those very servants have four times left me and returned." The other was said when I had asked him where his brother Wali would cross the Amu and when he would arrive. "If he find a ford, he will soon be here, but when waters rise, fords change; the (Persian) proverb has it, 'The waters have carried down the fords.'" These words God brought to his tongue in that hour of the flowing away of his own authority and following!

1 A *gari* is twenty-four minutes.

After sitting a *gari* or two, I mounted and rode back to camp, he for his part returning to his halting-place. On that day his begs, with their servants, great and small, good and bad, and tribe after tribe began to desert him and come, with their families, to me. Between the two Prayers of the next afternoon not a man remained in his presence.

"Say,—O God! who possessest the kingdom! Thou givest it to whom Thou wilt and Thou takest it from whom Thou wilt! In Thy hand is good, for Thou art almighty."[1]

Wonderful is His power! This man, once master of 20 or 30,000 retainers, once owning Sl. Mahmud's dominions from Quhlugha,—known also as the Iron-gate,—to the range of Fol. 124*b.* Hindu-kush, whose old mannikin of a tax-gatherer, Hasan *Barlas* by name, had made us march, had made us halt, with all the tax-gatherer's roughness, from Ailak to Aubaj, that man He so abased and so bereft of power that, with no blow struck, no sound made, he stood, without command over servants, goods, or life, in the presence of a band of 200 or 300 men, defeated and destitute as we were.

In the evening of the day on which we had seen Khusrau Shah and gone back to camp, Mirza Khan came to my presence and demanded vengeance on him for the blood of his brothers.[2] Many of us were at one with him, for truly it is right, both by Law and common justice, that such men should get their deserts, but, as terms had been made, Khusrau Shah was let go free. An order was given that he should be allowed to take whatever of his goods he could convey; accordingly he loaded up, on three or four strings of mules and camels, all jewels, gold, silver, and precious things he had, and took them with him.[3] Sherim Taghai was told off to escort him, who after setting Khusrau Shah on his road for Khurasan, by way of Ghuri and Dahanah, was to go to Kahmard and bring the families after us to Kabul.

---

1 Qoran, *Surat* iii, verse 25; Sale's Qoran, ed. 1825, i, 56.

2 *viz.* Bai-sunghar, bowstrung, and Mas'ud, blinded.

3 Muh. Salih is florid over the rubies of Badakhshan he says Babur took from Khusrau, but Haidar says Babur not only had Khusrau's property, treasure, and horses returned to him, but refused all gifts Khusrau offered. "This is one trait out of a thousand in the Emperor's character." Haidar mentions, too, the then lack of necessaries under which Babur suffered (Sh. N., cap. lxiii, and T.R. p. 176).

(h. *Babur marches for Kabul.*)

Marching from that camp for Kabul, we dismounted in Khwaja Zaid.

On that day, Hamza Bi *Mangfit*,[1] at the head of Auzbeg raiders, was over-running round about Dushi. Sayyid Qasim, the Lord of the Gate, and Ahmad-i-qasim *Kohbur* were sent with several braves against him; they got up with him, beat his Auzbegs well, cut off and brought in a few heads. Fol. 125.

In this camp all the armour (*jiba*) of Khusrau Shah's armoury was shared out. There may have been as many as 7 or 800 coats-of-mail (*joshan*) and horse accoutrements (*kuhah*);[2] these were the one thing he left behind; many pieces of porcelain also fell into our hands, but, these excepted, there was nothing worth looking at.

With four or five marches we reached Ghur-bund, and there dismounted in Ushtur-shahr. We got news there that Muqim's chief beg, Sherak (var. Sherka) *Arghun*, was lying along the Baran, having led an army out, not through hearing of me, but to hinder 'Abdu'r-razzaq Mirza from passing along the Panjhir-road, he having fled from Kabul[3] and being then amongst the Tarkalani Afghans towards Lamghan. On hearing this we marched forward, starting in the afternoon and pressing on through the dark till, with the dawn, we surmounted the Hupian-pass.[4]

I had never seen Suhail;[5] when I came out of the pass I saw a star, bright and low. "May not that be Suhail?" said I. Said they, "It is Suhail." Baqi *Chaghaniani* recited this couplet;—[6]

"How far dost thou shine, O Suhail, and where dost thou rise?
A sign of good luck is thine eye to the man on whom it may light."

---

1 *Cf.* T.R. p. 134 n. and 374 n.

2 *Jiba*, so often used to describe the quilted corselet, seems to have here a wider meaning, since the *jiba-khana* contained both *joshan* and *kuhah*, *i.e.* coats-of-mail and horse-mail with accoutrements. It can have been only from this source that Babur's men obtained the horse-mail of f. 127.

3 He succeeded his father, Aulugh Beg *Kabuli*, in 907 AH.; his youth led to the usurpation of his authority by Sherim Zikr, one of his begs; but the other begs put Sherim to death. During the subsequent confusions Muh. Muqim *Arghun*, in 908 AH., got possession of Kabul and married a sister of 'Abdu'r-razzaq. Things were in this state when Babur entered the country in 910 AH. (Erskine).

4 var. Upian, a few miles north of Charikar.

5 Suhail (Canopus) is a most conspicuous star in Afghanistan; it gives its name to the south, which is never called Janub but Suhail; the rising of Suhail marks one of their seasons (Erskine). The honour attaching to this star is due to its seeming to rise out of Arabia Felix.

6 The lines are in the Preface to the *Anwar-i-suhaili* (Lights of Canopus).

The Sun was a spear's-length high[1] when we reached the foot
of the Sanjid (Jujube)-valley and dismounted. Our scouting
Fol. 125b. braves fell in with Sherak below the Qara-bagh,[2] near Aikari-
yar, and straightway got to grips with him. After a little of some
sort of fighting, our men took the upper hand, hurried their
adversaries off, unhorsed 70–80 serviceable braves and brought
them in. We gave Sherak his life and he took service with us.

(i. Death of Wali of Khusrau.)

The various clans and tribes whom Khusrau Shah, without
troubling himself about them, had left in Qunduz, and also the
Mughul horde, were in five or six bodies (bulak). One of those
belonging to Badakhshan,—it was the Rusta-hazara,—came,
with Sayyidim 'Ali darban,[3] across the Panjhir-pass to this camp, did
me obeisance and took service with me. Another body came
under Ayub's Yusuf and Ayub's Bihlul; it also took service with me.
Another came from Khutlan, under Khusrau Shah's younger
brother, Wali;[4] another, consisting of the (Mughul) tribesmen
(aimaq) who had been located in Yilanchaq, Nikdiri (?), and the
Qunduz country, came also. The last-named two came by
Andar-ab and Sar-i-ab,[5] meaning to cross by the Panjhir-pass; at
Sar-i-ab the tribesmen were ahead; Wali came up behind; they
held the road, fought and beat him. He himself fled to the
Auzbegs,[6] and Shaibaq Khan had his head struck off in the Square
(Char-su) of Samarkand; his followers, beaten and plundered,
came on with the tribesmen, and like these, took service with me.
Fol. 126. With them came Sayyid Yusuf Beg (the Grey-wolfer).

(j. Kabul gained.)

From that camp we marched to the Aq-sarai meadow of the
Qara-bagh and there dismounted. Khusrau Shah's people were

1 "Die Kirghis-qazzaq drücken die Sonnen-hühe in Pikenaus" (von Schwarz, p. 124).
2 Presumably, dark with shade, as in qara-yighach, the hard-wood elm (f. 47b and
note to narwan).
3 i.e. Sayyid Muhammad 'Ali, the door-ward. These bulaks seem likely to have
been groups of 1000 fighting-men (Turki Ming).
4 See Additional Notes, p. 798.
5 In-the-water and Water-head.
6 Wali went from his defeat to Khwast; wrote to Mahmud Auzbeg in Qunduz to
ask protection; was fetched to Qunduz by Muh Salih, the author of the Shaibani-
nama, and forwarded from Qunduz to Samarkand (Sh. N. cap. lxiii). Cf. f. 29b.

well practised in oppression and violence; they tyrannized over one after another till at last I had up one of Sayyidim 'Ali's good braves to my Gate[1] and there beaten for forcibly taking a jar of oil. There and then he just died under the blows; his example kept the rest down.

We took counsel in that camp whether or not to go at once against Kabul. Sayyid Yusuf and some others thought that, as winter was near, our first move should be into Lamghan, from which place action could be taken as advantage offered. Baqi Beg and some others saw it good to move on Kabul at once; this plan was adopted; we marched forward and dismounted in Aba-quruq.

My mother and the belongings left behind in Kahmard rejoined us at Aba-quruq. They had been in great danger, the particulars of which are these:—Sherim Taghai had gone to set Khusrau Shah on his way for Khurasan, and this done, was to fetch the families from Kahmard. When he reached Dahanah, he found he was not his own master; Khusrau Shah went on with him into Kahmard, where was his sister's son, Ahmad-i-qasim. These two took up an altogether wrong position towards the families in Kahmard. Hereupon a number of Baqi Beg's Mughuls, who were with the families, arranged secretly with Sherim Taghai to lay hands on Khusrau Shah and Ahmad-i-qasim. The two heard of it, fled along the Kahmard-valley on the Ajar side[2] and made for Khurasan. To bring this about was really what Sherim Taghai and the Mughuls wanted. Set free from their fear of Khusrau Shah by his flight, those in charge of the families got them out of Ajar, but when they reached Kahmard, the Saqanchi (var. Asiqanchi) tribe blocked the road, like an enemy, and plundered the families of most of Baqi Beg's men.[3] They made prisoner Qul-i-bayazid's little son, Tizak; he came into Kabul three or four years later. The plundered and unhappy families crossed by the Qibchaq-pass, as we had done, and they rejoined us in Aba-quruq.

Fol. 126b.

1 *i.e.* where justice was administered, at this time, outside Babur's tent.
2 They would pass Ajar and make for the main road over the Dandan-shikan Pass.
3 The clansmen may have obeyed Ahmad's orders in thus holding up the families.

Leaving that camp we went, with one night's halt, to the Chalak-meadow, and there dismounted. After counsel taken, it was decided to lay siege to Kabul, and we marched forward. With what men of the centre there were, I dismounted between Haidar *Taqis*[1] garden and the tomb of Qul-i-bayazid, the Taster (*bakawal*);[2] Jahangir Mirza, with the men of the right,

Fol. 127. dismounted in my great Four-gardens (*Char-bagh*), Nasir Mirza, with the left, in the meadow of Qutluq-qadam's tomb. People of ours went repeatedly to confer with Muqim; they sometimes brought excuses back, sometimes words making for agreement. His tactics were the sequel of his dispatch, directly after Sherak's defeat, of a courier to his father and elder brother (in Qandahar); he made delays because he was hoping in them.

One day our centre, right, and left were ordered to put on their mail and their horses' mail, to go close to the town, and to display their equipment so as to strike terror on those within. Jahangir Mirza and the right went straight forward by the Kucha-bagh;[3] I, with the centre, because there was water, went along the side of Qutluq-qadam's tomb to a mound facing the rising-ground;[4] the van collected above Qutluq-qadam's bridge,—at that time, however, there was no bridge. When the braves, showing themselves off, galloped close up to the Curriers'-gate,[5] a few who had come out through it fled in again without making any stand. A crowd of Kabulis who had come out to see the sight raised a great dust when they ran away from the high slope of the glacis of the citadel (*i.e.* Bala-hisar). A number of pits had been dug up the rise

Fol. 127b. between the bridge and the gate, and hidden under sticks and rubbish; Sl. Quli *Chunaq* and several others were thrown as they galloped over them. A few braves of the right exchanged sword-cuts with those who came out of the town, in amongst

1 The name may be from Turki *taq*, a horse-shoe, but I.O. 215 f. 102 writes Persian *naqib*, the servant who announces arriving guests.
2 Here, as immediately below, when mentioning the Char-bagh and the tomb of Qutluq-qadam, Babur uses names acquired by the places at a subsequent date. In 910 AH. the Taster was alive; the Char-bagh was bought by Babur in 911 AH., and Qutluq-qadam fought at Kanwaha in 933 AH.
3 The Kucha-bagh is still a garden about 4 miles from Kabul on the north-west and divided from it by a low hill-pass. There is still a bridge on the way (Erskine).
4 Presumably that on which the Bala-hisar stood, the glacis of a few lines further.
5 *Cf.* f. 130.

the lanes and gardens, but as there was no order to engage, having done so much, they retired.

Those in the fort becoming much perturbed, Muqim made offer through the begs, to submit and surrender the town. Baqi Beg his mediator, he came and waited on me, when all fear was chased from his mind by our entire kindness and favour. It was settled that next day he should march out with retainers and following, goods and effects, and should make the town over to us. Having in mind the good practice Khusrau Shah's retainers had had in indiscipline and longhandedness, we appointed Jahangir Mirza and Nasir Mirza with the great and household begs, to escort Muqim's family out of Kabul[1] and to bring out Muqim himself with his various dependants, goods and effects. Camping-ground was assigned to him at Tipa.[2] When the Mirzas and the Begs went at dawn to the Gate, they saw much mobbing and tumult of the common people, so they sent me a man to say, "Unless you come yourself, there will be no holding these people in." In the end I got to horse, had two or three persons shot, two or three cut in pieces, and so stamped the rising down. Muqim and his belongings then got out, safe and sound, and they betook themselves to Tipa.

Fol. 128.

It was in the last ten days of the Second Rabi' (Oct. 1504 AD.)[3] that without a fight, without an effort, by Almighty God's bounty and mercy, I obtained and made subject to me Kabul and Ghazni and their dependent districts.

DESCRIPTION OF KABUL[4]

The Kabul country is situated in the Fourth climate and in the midst of cultivated lands.[5] On the east it has the

---

1 One of Muqim's wives was a Timurid, Babur's first-cousin, the daughter of Aulugh Beg *Kabuli*; another was Bibi Zarif Khatun, the mother of that Mah-chuchuq, whose anger at her marriage to Babur's faithful Qasim Kukuldash has filled some pages of history (Gulbadan's H.N. *s.n.* Mah-chuchuq and Erskine's B. and H. i, 348).

2 Some 9m. north of Kabul on the road to Aq-sarai.

3 The Hai. MS. (only) writes First Rabi but the Second better suits the near approach of winter.

4 Elph. MS. fol. 97; W.-i-B. I.O. 215 f. 102*b* and 217 f. 85; Mems. p. 136. Useful books of the early 19th century, many of them referring to the *Babur-nama*, are Conolly's *Travels*, Wood's *Journey*, Elphinstone's *Caubul*, Burnes' *Cabool*, Masson's *Narrative*, Lord's and Leech's articles in JASB 1838 and in Burnes' *Reports* (India Office Library), Broadfoot's *Report* in RGS Supp. Papers vol. I.

5 f. 1*b* where Farghana is said to be on the limit of cultivation.

Lamghanat,[1] Parashawar (Pashawar), Hash(t)-nagar and some of
the countries of Hindustan. On the west it has the mountain
region in which are Karnud (?) and Ghur, now the refuge and
dwelling-places of the Hazara and Nikdiri (var. Nikudari) tribes.
On the north, separated from it by the range of Hindu-kush, it
has the Qunduz and Andar-ab countries. On the south, it has
Farmul, Naghr (var. Naghz), Bannu and Afghanistan.[2]

(a. Town and environs of Kabul.)

The Kabul district itself is of small extent, has its greatest
length from east to west, and is girt round by mountains. Its
walled-town connects with one of these, rather a low one known
as Shah-of-Kabul because at some time a (Hindu) Shah of
Kabul built a residence on its summit.[3] Shah-of-Kabul begins
at the Durrin narrows and ends at those of Dih-i-yaq'ub;[4]
it may be 4 miles (2 shar'i) round; its skirt is covered with
gardens fertilized from a canal which was brought along the
hill-slope in the time of my paternal uncle, Aulugh Beg Mirza
by his guardian, Wais Ataka.[5] The water of this canal comes
to an end in a retired corner, a quarter known as Kul-kina[6]

1 f. 131b. To find these tumans here classed with what was not part of Kabul suggest
a clerical omission of "beyond" or "east of" (Lamghanat). The first syllable may be
lam, fort. The modern form Laghman is not used in the Babur-nama, nor, it may be
added is Paghman for Pamghan.
2 It will be observed that Babur limits the name Afghanistan to the countries
inhabited by Afghan tribesmen; they are chiefly those south of the road from
Kabul to Pashawar (Erskine). See Vigne, p. 102, for a boundary between the
Afghans and Khurasan.
3 Al-biruni's Indika writes of both Turk and Hindu-shahi Kings of Kabul. See
Raverty's Notes p. 62 and Stein's Shahi Kings of Kabul. The mountain is 7592 ft.
above the sea, some 1800 ft. therefore above the town.
4 The Kabul-river enters the Char-dih plain by the Dih-i-yaq'ub narrows, and
leaves it by those of Durrin. Cf. S.A. War, Plan p. 288 and Plan of action at
Char-asiya (Four-mills), the second shewing an off-take which may be Wais
Ataka's canal. See Vigne, p. 163 and Raverty's Notes pp. 69 and 689.
5 This, the Bala-jui (upper-canal) was a four-mill stream and in Masson's time,
as now, supplied water to the gardens round Babur's tomb. Masson found in
Kabul honoured descendants of Wais Ataka (ii, 240).
6 But for a, perhaps negligible, shortening of its first vowel, this form of the
name would describe the normal end of an irrigation canal, a little pool, but
other forms with other meanings are open to choice, e.g. small hamlet (Pers. kul),
or some compound containing Pers. gul, a rose, in its plain or metaphorical
senses. Jarrett's Ayin-i-akbari writes Gul-kinah, little rose (?). Masson (ii, 236)
mentions a similar pleasure-resort, Sanji-taq.

where much debauchery has gone on. About this place it Fol. 128b. sometimes used to be said, in jesting parody of Khwaja Hafiz,[1] —"Ah! the happy, thoughtless time when, with our names in ill-repute, we lived days of days at Kul-kina!"

East of Shah-of-Kabul and south of the walled-town lies a large pool[2] about a 2 miles [shar'i] round. From the town side of the mountain three smallish springs issue, two near Kul-kina; Khwaja Shamu's[3] tomb is at the head of one; Khwaja Khizr's Qadam-gah[4] at the head of another, and the third is at a place known as Khwaja Raushanai, over against Khwaja 'Abdu's-samad. On a detached rock of a spur of Shah-of-Kabul, known as 'Uqabain,[5] stands the citadel of Kabul-fort with the great walled-town at its north end, lying high in excellent air, and overlooking the large pool already mentioned, and also three meadows, namely, Siyah-sang (Black-rock), Sung-qurghan (Fort-back), and Chalak (Highwayman?),—a most beautiful outlook when the meadows are green. The north-wind does not fail Kabul in the heats; people call it the Parwan-wind;[6] it makes a delightful temperature in the windowed houses on the northern part of the citadel. In praise of the citadel of Kabul, Mulla Muhammad Talib Mu'ammai (the Riddler)[7]

1 The original ode, with which the parody agrees in rhyme and refrain, is in the Diwan, s.l. Dal (Brockhaus ed. 1854, i, 62 and lith. ed. p. 96). See Wilberforce Clarke's literal translation i, 286 (H.B.). A marginal note to the Haidarabad Codex gives what appears to be a variant of one of the rhymes of the parody.

2 aulugh kul; some 3 m. round in Erskine's time; mapped as a swamp in S.A.War p. 288.

3 A marginal note to the Hai. Codex explains this name to be an abbreviation of Khwaja Shamsu'd-din Jan-baz (or Jahan-baz; Masson, ii, 279 and iii, 93).

4 i.e. the place made holy by an impress of saintly foot-steps.

5 Two eagles or, Two poles, used for punishment. Vigne's illustration (p. 161) clearly shows the spur and the detached rock. Erskine (p. 137 n.) says that 'Uqabain seems to be the hill, known in his day as 'Ashiqan-i-'arifan, which connects with Babur Badshah. See Raverty's Notes p. 68.

6 During most of the year this wind rushes through the Hindu-kush (Parwan)-pass; it checks the migration of the birds (f. 142), and it may be the cause of the deposit of the Running-sands (Burnes, p. 158). Cf. Wood, p. 124.

7 He was Badi'u'z-zaman's Sadr before serving Babur; he died in 918 AH. (1512 AD.), in the battle of Kul-i-malik where 'Ubaidu'l-lah Auzbeg defeated Babur. He may be identical with Mir Husain the Riddler of f. 180b, but seems not to be Mulla Muh. Badakhshi, also a Riddler, because the Habibu's-siyar (ii, 343 and 344) gives this man a separate notice. Those interested in enigmas can find one made by Talib on the name Yahya (H.S. ii, 344). Sharafu'd-din 'Ali Yazdi, the author of the Zafar-nama, wrote a book about a novel kind of these puzzles (T.R. p. 84).

used to recite this couplet, composed on Badi'u'z-zaman Mirza's name:—

> Drink wine in the castle of Kabul and send the cup round without pause;
> For Kabul is mountain, is river, is city, is lowland in one.[1]

(b. Kabul as a trading-town.)

Just as 'Arabs call every place outside 'Arab (Arabia), 'Ajam, so Hindustanis call every place outside Hindustan, Khurasan. There are two trade-marts on the land-route between Hindustan and Khurasan; one is Kabul, the other, Qandahar. To Kabul caravans come from Kashghar,[2] Farghana, Turkistan, Samarkand, Bukhara, Balkh, Hisar and Badakhshan. To Qandahar they come from Khurasan. Kabul is an excellent trading-centre; if merchants went to Khita or to Rum,[3] they might make no higher profit. Down to Kabul every year come 7, 8, or 10,000 horses and up to it, from Hindustan, come every year caravans of 10, 15 or 20,000 heads-of-houses, bringing slaves (barda), white cloth, sugar-candy, refined and common sugars, and aromatic roots. Many a trader is not content with a profit of 30 or 40 on 10.[4] In Kabul can be had the products of Khurasan, Rum, 'Iraq and Chin (China); while it is Hindustan's own market.

(c. Products and climate of Kabul.)

In the country of Kabul, there are hot and cold districts close to one another. In one day, a man may go out of the town of Kabul to where snow never falls, or he may go, in two sidereal hours, to where it never thaws, unless when the heats are such that it cannot possibly lie.

Fruits of hot and cold climates are to be had in the districts near the town. Amongst those of the cold climate, there are had in the town the grape, pomegranate, apricot, apple, quince,

---

1 The original couplet is as follows:—

> *Bakhur dar arg-i Kabul mai, bagardan kasa pay dar pay,*
> *Kah ham koh ast, u ham darya, u ham shahr ast, u ham sahra'.*

What Talib's words may be inferred to conceal is the opinion that like Badi'u'z-zaman and like the meaning of his name, Kabul is the Wonder-of-the-world. (*Cf.* M. Garçin de Tassy's *Rhétorique* [p. 165], for *ces combinaisons énigmatiques*.)
2 All MSS. do not mention Kashghar.
3 Khita (Cathay) is Northern China; Chin (*infra*) is China; Rum is Turkey and particularly the provinces near Trebizond (Erskine).
4 300% to 400% (Erskine).

pear, peach, plum, *sinjid*, almond and walnut.[1] I had cuttings
of the *alu-balu*[2] brought there and planted; they grew and have
done well. Of fruits of the hot climate people bring into the
town;—from the Lamghanat, the orange, citron, *amluk* (*diospyrus
lotus*), and sugar-cane; this last I had had brought and planted
there;[3]—from Nijr-au (Nijr-water), they bring the *jil-ghuza*,[4]
and, from the hill-tracts, much honey. Bee-hives are in use; it
is only from towards Ghazni, that no honey comes.

The rhubarb[5] of the Kabul district is good, its quinces and plums
very good, so too its *badrang*;[6] it grows an excellent grape, known as
the water-grape.[7] Kabul wines are heady, those of the Khwaja
Khawand Sa'id hill-skirt being famous for their strength; at this
time however I can only repeat the praise of others about them:—[8]

> The flavour of the wine a drinker knows;
> What chance have sober men to know it?

Kabul is not fertile in grain, a four or five-fold return is
reckoned good there; nor are its melons first-rate, but they are
not altogether bad when grown from Khurasan seed.

It has a very pleasant climate; if the world has another so
pleasant, it is not known. Even in the heats, one cannot sleep

---

1 Persian *sinjid*, Brandis, *elægnus hortensis*; Erskine (Mems. p. 138) jujube, presumably the *zizyphus jujuba* of Speede, Supplement p. 86. Turki *yangaq*, walnut, has
several variants, of which the most marked is *yanghkaq*. For a good account of
Kabul fruits *see* Masson, ii, 230.

2 a kind of plum (?). It seems unlikely to be a cherry since Babur does not
mention cherries as good in his old dominions, and Firminger (p. 244) makes
against it as introduced from India. Steingass explains *alu-balu* by "sour-cherry, an
armarylla"; if sour, is it the Morello cherry?

3 The sugar-cane was seen in abundance in Lan-po (Lamghan) by a Chinese
pilgrim (Beale, p. 90); Babur's introduction of it may have been into his own
garden only in Ningnahar (f. 132b).

4 *i.e.* the seeds of *pinus Gerardiana*.

5 *rawashlar*. The green leaf-stalks (*chukri*) of *ribes rheum* are taken into Kabul in
mid-April from the Pamghan-hills; a week later they are followed by the
blanched and tended *rawash* (Masson, ii, 7). *See* Gul-badan's H.N. trs. p. 188,
Vigne, p. 100 and 107, Masson, ii, 230, Conolly, i, 213.

6 a large green fruit, shaped something like a citron; also a large sort of cucumber
(Erskine).

7 The *sahibi*, a grape praised by Babur amongst Samarkandi fruits, grows in Koh-
daman; another well-known grape of Kabul is the long stoneless *husaini*, brought by
Afghan traders into Hindustan in round, flat boxes of poplar wood (Vigne, p. 172).

8 An allusion, presumably, to the renouncement of wine made by Babur and
some of his followers in 933 AH. (1527 AD. f. 312). He may have had 'Umar
Khayyam's quatrain in mind, "Wine's power is known to wine-bibbers alone"
(Whinfield's 2nd ed. 1901, No. 164).

at night without a fur-coat.[1] Although the snow in most places lies deep in winter, the cold is not excessive; whereas in Samarkand and Tabriz, both, like Kabul, noted for their pleasant climate, the cold is extreme.

(d. Meadows of Kabul.)

There are good meadows on the four sides of Kabul. An excellent one, Sung-qurghan, is some 4 miles (2 *kuroh*) to the north-east; it has grass fit for horses and few mosquitos. To the north-west is the Chalak meadow, some 2 miles (1 *shar'i*) away, a large one but in it mosquitos greatly trouble the horses. On the west is the Durrin, in fact there are two, Tipa and Qush-nadir (var. nawar),—if two are counted here, there would be five in all. Each of these is about 2 miles from the town; both are small, have grass good for horses, and no mosquitos; Kabul has no others so good. On the east is the Siyah-sang meadow with Qutluq-qadam's tomb[2] between it and the Curriers'-gate; it is not worth much because, in the heats, it swarms with mosquitos. Kamari meadow adjoins it; counting this in, the meadows of Kabul would be six, but they are always spoken of as four.

(e. Mountain-passes into Kabul.)

The country of Kabul is a fastness hard for a foreign foe to make his way into.

The Hindu-kush mountains, which separate Kabul from Balkh, Qunduz and Badakhshan, are crossed by seven roads.[3] Three

---

1 *pustin*, usually of sheep-skin. For the wide range of temperature at Kabul in 24 hours, *see* Ency. Brtt. art. Afghanistan. The winters also vary much in severity (Burnes, p. 273).

2 Index *s.n.* As he fought at Kanwaha, he will have been buried after March 1527 AD.; this entry therefore will have been made later. The Curriers'-gate is the later Lahor-gate (Masson, ii, 259).

3 For lists of the Hindu-kush passes *see* Leech's Report VII; Yule's *Introductory Essay* to Wood's *Journey* 2nd ed.; PRGS 1879, Markham's art. p. 121.

The highest *cols* on the passes here enumerated by Babur are,—Khawak 11,640 ft.—Tul, height not known,—Parandi 15,984 ft.—Baj-gah (Toll-place) 12,000 ft.—Walian (Saints) 15,100 ft.—Chahar-dar (Four-doors) 18,900 ft. and Shibr-tu 9800 ft. In considering the labour of their ascent and descent, the general high level, north and south of them, should be borne in mind; *e.g.* Charikar (Char-yak-kar) stands 5200 ft. and Kabul itself at 5780 ft. above the sea.

of these lead out of Panjhir (Panj-sher), *viz.* Khawak, the upper-most, Tul, the next lower, and Bazarak.[1] Of the passes on them, the one on the Tul road is the best, but the road itself is rather the longest whence, seemingly, it is called Tul. Bazarak is the most direct; like Tul, it leads over into Sir-i-ab; as it passes through Parandi, local people call its main pass, the Parandi. Another road leads up through Parwan; it has seven minor passes, known as Haft-bacha (Seven-younglings), between Parwan and its main pass (Baj-gah). It is joined at its main pass by two roads from Andar-ab, which go on to Parwan by it. This is a road full of difficulties. Out of Ghur-bund, again, three roads lead over. The one next to Parwan, known as the Yangi-yul pass (New-road), goes through Wa(lian) to Khinjan; next above this is the Qibchaq road, crossing to where the water of Andar-ab meets the Surkh-ab (Qizil-su); this also is an excellent road; and the third leads over the Shibr-tu pass;[2] those crossing by this in the heats take their way by Bamian and Saighan, but those crossing by it in winter, go on by Ab-dara (Water-valley).[3] Shibr-tu excepted, all the Hindu-kush roads are closed for four or five months in winter.[4] After crossing Shibr-tu people go on through Ab-dara. In the heats, when the waters come down in flood, these roads have the same rule as in winter, because no road through a valley-bottom is passable when the waters are high. If any-one thinks to cross the Hindu-kush at that time, over the mountains instead of through a valley-bottom, his journey is hard indeed. The time to cross is during the three or four autumn months when the snow is less and the waters are low. Whether on the mountains or in the valley-bottoms, Kafir highwaymen are not few.

The road from Kabul into Khurasan passes through Qandahar; it is quite level, without a pass.

1 *i.e.* the hollow, long, and small-bazar roads respectively. Panjhir is explained by Hindus to be Panj-sher, the five lion-sons of Pandu (Masson, iii, 168).

2 Shibr is a Hazara district between the head of the Ghur-bund valley and Bamian. It does not seem to be correct to omit the *tu* from the name of the pass. Persian *tu*, turn, twist (syn. *pich*) occurs in other names of local passes; to read it here as a *turn* agrees with what is said of Shibr-tu pass as not crossing but turning the Hindu-kush (Cunningham). Lord uses the same wording about the Haji-ghat (var. -kak etc.) traverse of the same spur, which "turns the extremity of the Hindu-kush". *See* Cunningham's *Ancient Geography*, i, 25; Lord's *Ghur-bund* (JASB 1838 p. 528), Masson, iii, 169 and Leech's *Report* VII.

3 Perhaps through Jalmish into Saighan.

4 *i.e.* they are closed.

Four roads lead into Kabul from the Hindustan side; one by rather a low pass through the Khaibar mountains, another by way of Bangash, another by way of Naghr (var. Naghz),[1] and another through Farmul;[2] the passes being low also in the three last-named. These roads are all reached from three ferries over the Sind. Those who take the Nil-ab[3] ferry, come on through the Lamghanat.[4] In winter, however, people ford the Sind-water (at Haru) above its junction with the Kabul-water,[5] and ford this also. In most of my expeditions into Hindustan, I crossed those fords, but this last time (932 AH.—1525 AD.), when I came, defeated Sl. Ibrahim and conquered the country, I crossed by boat at Nil-ab. Except at the one place mentioned above, the Sind-water can be crossed only by boat. Those again, who cross at Din-kot[6] go on through Bangash. Those crossing at Chaupara, if they take the Farmul road, go on to Ghazni, or, if they go by the Dasht, go on to Qandahar.[7]

1 It was unknown in Mr. Erskine's day (Mems. p. 140). Several of the routes in Raverty's *Notes* (p. 92 etc.) allow it to be located as on the Iri-ab, near to or identical with Baghzan, 35 *kurohs* (70 m.) s.s.e. of Kabul.

2 Farmul, about the situation of which Mr. Erskine was in doubt, is now marked in maps, Urghun being its principal village.

3 15 miles below Atak (Erskine). Mr. Erskine notes that he found no warrant, previous to Abu'l-fazl's, for calling the Indus the Nil-ab, and that to find one would solve an ancient geographical difficulty. This difficulty, my husband suggests, was Alexander's supposition that the Indus was the Nile. In books grouping round the *Babur-nama*, the name Nil-ab is not applied to the Indus, but to the ferry-station on that river, said to owe its name to a spring of azure water on its eastern side. (*Cf.* Afzal Khan *Khattak*, R.'s *Notes* p. 447.)

I find the name Nil-ab applied to the Kabul-river:—1. to its Arghandi affluent (Cunningham, p. 17, Map); 2. through its boatman class, the Nil-abis of Lalpura, Jalalabad and Kunar (G. of I. 1907, art. Kabul); 3. inferentially to it as a tributary of the Indus (D'Herbélot); 4. to it near its confluence with the grey, silt-laden Indus, as blue by contrast (Sayyid Ghulam-i-muhammad, R.'s *Notes* p. 34). (For Nil-ab (Naulibis?) in Ghur-bund *see* Cunningham, p. 32 and Masson, iii, 169.)

4 By one of two routes perhaps,—either by the Khaibar–Ningnahar–Jagdalik road, or along the north bank of the Kabul-river, through Goshta to the crossing where, in 1879, the 10th Hussars met with disaster. See *S.A. War*, Map 2 and p. 63; Leech's *Reports* II and IV (Fords of the Indus); and R.'s *Notes* p. 44.

5 Haru, Leech's Harroon, apparently, 10 m. above Atak. The text might be read to mean that both rivers were forded near their confluence, but, finding no warrant for supposing the Kabul-river fordable below Jalalabad, I have guided the translation accordingly; this may be wrong and may conceal a change in the river.

6 known also as Dhan-kot and as Mu'azzam-nagar (*Ma'asiru'l-'umra* i, 249 and A.N. trs. H.B. index *s.n.* Dhan-kot). It was on the east bank of the Indus, probably near modern Kala-bagh, and was washed away not before 956 AH. (1549 AD. H. Beveridge).

7 Chaupara seems, from f. 148*b*, to be the Chapari of Survey Map 1889. Babur's *Dasht* is modern Daman.

(*f. Inhabitants of Kabul.*)

There are many differing tribes in the Kabul country; in its dales and plains are Turks and clansmen[1] and 'Arabs; in its town and in many villages, Sarts; out in the districts and also Fol. 131*b.* in villages are the Pashai, Paraji, Tajik, Birki and Afghan tribes. In the western mountains are the Hazara and Nikdiri tribes, some of whom speak the Mughuli tongue. In the north-eastern mountains are the places of the Kafirs, such as Kitur (Gawar?) and Gibrik. To the south are the places of the Afghan tribes.

Eleven or twelve tongues are spoken in Kabul,—'Arabi, Persian, Turki, Mughuli, Hindi, Afghani, Pashai, Paraji, Gibri, Birki and Lamghani. If there be another country with so many differing tribes and such a diversity of tongues, it is not known.

(*e. Sub-divisions of the Kabul country.*)

The [Kabul] country has fourteen *tumans.*[2]

Bajaur, Sawad and Hash-nagar may at one time have been dependencies of Kabul, but they now have no resemblance to cultivated countries (*wilayat*), some lying desolate because of the Afghans, others being now subject to them.

In the east of the country of Kabul is the Lamghanat, 5 *tumans* and 2 *buluks* of cultivated lands.[3] The largest of these is Ningnahar, sometimes written Nagarahar in the histories.[4] Its *darogha*'s residence is in Adinapur,[5] some 13 *yighach* east of Kabul by a very bad and tiresome road, going in three or four places over small hill-passes, and in three or four others, through Fol. 132.

---

1 *aimaq*, used usually of Mughuls, I think. It may be noted that Lieutenant Leech compiled a vocabulary of the tongue of the Mughul Aimaq in Qandahar and Harat (JASB [Journal of the Asiatic Society of Bengal] 1838, p. 785).

2 The *Ayin-i-akbari* account of Kabul both uses and supplements the *Babur-nama.*

3 *viz.* 'Ali-shang, Alangar and Mandrawar (the Lamghanat proper), Ningnahar (with its *buluk*, Kama), Kunar-with-Nur-gal, (and the two *buluks* of Nur-valley and Chaghan-sarai).

4 *See* Appendix E, *On Nagarahara.*

5 The name Adinapur is held to be descended from ancient Udyanapura (Garden-town); its ancestral form however was applied to Nagarahara, apparently, in the Baran-Surkh-rud *du-ab*, and not to Babur's *darogha*'s seat. The Surkh-rud's deltaic mouth was a land of gardens; when Masson visited Adinapur he went from Bala-bagh (High-garden); this appears to stand where Babur locates his Bagh-i-wafa, but he was shown a garden he took to be this one of Babur's, a mile higher up the Surkh-rud. A later ruler made the Char-bagh of maps. It may be mentioned that Bala-bagh has become in some maps Rozabad (Garden-town). *See* Masson, i, 182 and iii, 186; R.'s *Notes*; and Wilson's *Ariana Antiqua*, Masson's art.

narrows.[1] So long as there was no cultivation along it, the Khirilchi and other Afghan thieves used to make it their beat, but it has become safe[2] since I had it peopled at Qara-tu,[3] below Quruq-sai. The hot and cold climates are separated on this road by the pass of Badam-chashma (Almond-spring); on its Kabul side snow falls, none at Quruq-sai, towards the Lamghanat.[4] After descending this pass, another world comes into view, other trees, other plants (or grasses), other animals, and other manners and customs of men. Ningnahar is nine torrents (*tuquz-rud*).[5] It grows good crops of rice and corn, excellent and abundant oranges, citrons and pomegranates. In 914 AH. (1508–9 AD.) I laid out the Four-gardens, known as the Bagh-i-wafa (Garden-of-fidelity), on a rising-ground, facing south and having the Surkh-rud between it and Fort Adinapur.[6] There oranges, citrons and pomegranates grow in abundance. The year I defeated Pahar Khan and took Lahor and Dipalpur,[7] I had plantains (bananas) brought and planted there; they did very well. The year before I had had sugar-cane planted there; it also did well; some of it was sent to Bukhara and Badakhshan.[8] The garden lies high, has running-water close at hand, and a mild winter

Fol. 132b.   climate. In the middle of it, a one-mill stream flows constantly past the little hill on which are the four garden-plots. In the south-west part of it there is a reservoir, 10 by 10,[9] round which

1 One of these *tangi* is now a literary asset in Mr. Kipling's *My Lord the Elephant*. Babur's 13 y. represent some 82 miles; on f. 137b the Kabul-Ghazni road of 14 y. represents some 85; in each case the *yighach* works out at over six miles. Sayyid Ghulam-i-muhammad traces this route minutely (R.'s *Notes* pp. 57, 59).

2 Masson was shewn "Chaghatai castles", attributed to Babur (iii, 174).

3 Dark-turn, perhaps, as in Shibr-tu, Jal-tu, *etc.* (f. 130b and note to Shibr-tu).

4 f. 145 where the change is described in identical words, as seen south of the Jagdalik-pass. The Badam-chashma pass appears to be a traverse of the eastern rampart of the Tizin-valley.

5 Appendix E, *On Nagarahara*.

6 No record exists of the actual laying-out of the garden; the work may have been put in hand during the Mahmand expedition of 914 AH. (f. 216); the name given to it suggests a gathering there of loyalists when the stress was over of the bad Mughul rebellion of that year (f. 216b where the narrative breaks off abruptly in 914 AH. and is followed by a gap down to 925 AH.–1519 AD.).

7 No annals of 930 AH. are known to exist; from Safar 926 AH. to 932 AH. (Jan. 1520–Nov. 1525 AD.) there is a lacuna. Accounts of the expedition are given by Khafi Khan, i, 47 and Firishta, lith. ed. p. 202.

8 Presumably to his son, Humayun, then governor in Badakhshan; Bukhara also was under Babur's rule.

9 here, *qari*, yards. The dimensions 10 by 10, are those enjoined for places of ablution.

are orange-trees and a few pomegranates, the whole encircled by a trefoil-meadow. This is the best part of the garden, a most beautiful sight when the oranges take colour. Truly that garden is admirably situated!

The Safed-koh runs along the south of Ningnahar, dividing it from Bangash; no riding-road crosses it; nine torrents (*tuquz-rud*) issue from it.[1] It is called Safed-koh[2] because its snow never lessens; none falls in the lower parts of its valleys, a half-day's journey from the snow-line. Many places along it have an excellent climate; its waters are cold and need no ice.

The Surkh-rud flows along the south of Adinapur. The fort stands on a height having a straight fall to the river of some 130 ft. (40–50 *qari*) and isolated from the mountain behind it on the north; it is very strongly placed. That mountain runs between Ningnahar and Lamghan;[3] on its head snow falls when it snows in Kabul, so Lamghanis know when it has snowed in the town. Fol. 133.

In going from Kabul into the Lamghanat,[4]—if people come by Quruq-sai, one road goes on through the Diri-pass, crosses the Baran-water at Bulan, and so on into the Lamghanat,— another goes through Qara-tu, below Quruq-sai, crosses the Baran-water at Aulugh-nur (Great-rock?), and goes into Lamghan by the pass of Bad-i-pich.[5] If however people come by Nijr-au, they traverse Badr-au (Tag-au), and Qara-nakariq (?), and go on on through the pass of Bad-i-pich.

1 Presumably those of the *tuquz-rud*, *supra*. Cf. Appendix E, *On Nagarahara*.
2 White-mountain; Pushtu, Spin-ghur (or ghar).
3 *i.e.* the Lamghanat proper. The range is variously named; in (Persian) Siyah-koh (Black-mountain), which like Turki Qara-tagh may mean non-snowy; by Tajiks, Bagh-i-ataka (Foster-father's garden); by Afghans, Kanda-ghur, and by Lamghanis Koh-i-bulan,—Kanda and Bulan both being ferry-stations below it (Masson, iii, 189; also the Times Nov. 20th 1912 for a cognate illustration of diverse naming).
4 A comment made here by Mr. Erskine on changes of name is still appropriate, but some seeming changes may well be due to varied selection of land-marks. Of the three routes next described in the text, one crosses as for Mandrawar; the second, as for 'Ali-shang, a little below the outfall of the Tizin-water; the third may take off from the route, between Kabul and Tag-au, marked in Col. Tanner's map (PRGS 1881 p. 180). Cf. R's Route 11; and for Aulugh-nur, Appendix F, *On the name Nur.*
5 The name of this pass has several variants. Its second component, whatever its form, is usually taken to mean *pass*, but to read it here as pass would be redundant, since Babur writes "pass (*kutal*) of Bad-i-pich". Pich occurs as a place name both east (Pich) and west (Pichghan) of the *kutal*, but what would suit the bitter and even fatal winds of the pass would be to read the name as Whirling-wind (*bad-i-pich*). Another explanation suggests itself from finding a considerable number of pass-names such as Shibr-tu, Jal-tu, Qara-tu, in which *tu* is a synonym of *pich*, turn, twist; thus Bad-i-pich may be the local form of Bad-tu, Windy-turn.

Although Ningnahar is one of the five *tumans* of the Lamghan *tuman* the name Lamghanat applies strictly only to the three (mentioned below).

One of the three is the 'Ali-shang *tuman*, to the north of which are fastness-mountains, connecting with Hindu-kush and inhabited by Kafirs only. What of Kafiristan lies nearest to 'Ali-shang, is Mil out of which its torrent issues. The tomb of Lord Lam,[1] father of his Reverence the prophet Nuh (Noah), is in this *tuman*. In some histories he is called Lamak and Lamakan. Some people are observed often to change *kaf* for *ghain* (*k* for *gh*); it would seem to be on this account that the country is called Lamghan.

The second is Alangar. The part of Kafiristan nearest to it is Gawar (Kawar), out of which its torrent issues (the Gau or Kau). This torrent joins that of 'Ali-shang and flows with it into the Baran-water, below Mandrawar, which is the third *tuman* of the Lamghanat.

Fol. 133*b*.

Of the two *buluks* of Lamghan one is the Nur-valley.[2] This is a place (*yir*) without a second;[3] its fort is on a beak (*tumshuq*) of rock in the mouth of the valley, and has a torrent on each side; its rice is grown on steep terraces, and it can be traversed by one road only.[4] It has the orange, citron and other fruits of hot climates in abundance, a few dates even. Trees cover the banks of both the torrents below the fort; many are *amluk*, the fruit of which some Turks call *qara-yimish*;[5] here they are many, but none has been seen elsewhere. The valley grows grapes also, all trained on trees.[6] Its wines are those of Lamghan that have reputation. Two sorts of grapes are grown,

1 *See* Masson, iii, 197 and 289. Both in Pashai and Lamghani, *lam* means fort.
2 *See* Appendix F, *On the name Dara-i-nur*.
3 *ghair mukarrar*. Babur may allude to the remarkable change men have wrought in the valley-bottom (Appendix F, for Col. Tanner's account of the valley).
4 f. 154.
5 *diospyrus lotus*, the European date-plum, supposed to be one of the fruits eaten by the Lotophagi. It is purple, has bloom and is of the size of a pigeon's egg or a cherry. *See* Watts' *Economic Products of India*; Brandis' *Forest Trees*, Illustrations; and Speede's *Indian Hand-book*.
6 As in Lombardy, perhaps; in Luhugur vines are clipped into standards; in most other places in Afghanistan they are planted in deep trenches and allowed to run over the intervening ridges or over wooden framework. In the narrow Khulm-valley they are trained up poplars so as to secure them the maximum of sun. *See* Wood's *Report* VI p. 27; Bellew's *Afghanistan* p. 175 and *Mems.* p. 142 note.

the *arah-tashi* and the *suhan-tashi*;[1] the first are yellowish, the second, full-red of fine colour. The first make the more cheering wine, but it must be said that neither wine equals its reputation for cheer. High up in one of its glens, apes (*maimun*) are found, none below. Those people (*i.e.* Nuris) used to keep swine but they have given it up in our time.[2]

Another *tuman* of Lamghan is Kunar-with-Nur-gal. It lies somewhat out-of-the-way, remote from the Lamghanat, with its borders in amongst the Kafir lands; on these accounts its people give in tribute rather little of what they have. The Chaghan- Fol. 134. sarai water enters it from the north-east, passes on into the *buluk* of Kama, there joins the Baran-water and with that flows east.

Mir Sayyid 'Ali *Hamadani*,[3]—God's mercy on him!—coming here as he journeyed, died 2 miles (1 *shar'i*) above Kunar. His disciples carried his body to Khutlan. A shrine was erected at the honoured place of his death, of which I made the circuit when I came and took Chaghan-sarai in 924 AH.[4]

The orange, citron and coriander[5] abound in this *tuman*. Strong wines are brought down into it from Kafiristan.

A strange thing is told there, one seeming impossible, but one told to us again and again. All through the hill-country above Multa-kundi, *viz.* in Kunar, Nur-gal, Bajaur, Sawad and

> (*Author's note to Multa-kundi.*)   As Multa-kundi is known the lower part of the *tuman* of Kunar-with-Nur-gal; what is below (*i.e.* on the river) belongs to the valley of Nur and to Atar.[6]

---

1 Appendix G, *On the names of two Nuri wines.*

2 This practice Babur viewed with disgust, the hog being an impure animal according to Muhammadan Law (Erskine).

3 The *Khazinatu'l-asfiya* (ii, 293) explains how it came about that this saint, one honoured in Kashmir, was buried in Khutlan. He died in Hazara (Pakli) and there the Pakli Sultan wished to have him buried, but his disciples, for some unspecified reason, wished to bury him in Khutlan. In order to decide the matter they invited the Sultan to remove the bier with the corpse upon it. It could not be stirred from its place. When, however a single one of the disciples tried to move it, he alone was able to lift it, and to bear it away on his head. Hence the burial in Khutlan. The death occurred in 786 AH. (1384 AD.). A point of interest in this legend is that, like the one to follow, concerning dead women, it shews belief in the living activities of the dead.

4 The MSS. vary between 920 and 925 AH.—neither date seems correct. As the annals of 925 AH. begin in Muharram, with Babur to the east of Bajaur, we surmise that the Chaghan-sarai affair may have occurred on his way thither, and at the end of 924 AH.

5 *karanj, coriandrum sativum.*

6 some 20–24 m. north of Jalalabad. The name Multa-kundi may refer to the Ram-kundi range, or mean Lower district, or mean Below Kundi. *See* Biddulph's *Khowari Dialect s.n.* under; R.'s *Notes* p. 108 and *Dict. s.n. kund*; Masson, i, 209.

thereabouts, it is commonly said that when a woman dies and has been laid on a bier, she, if she has not been an ill-doer, gives the bearers such a shake when they lift the bier by its four sides, that against their will and hindrance, her corpse falls to the ground; but, if she has done ill, no movement occurs. This was heard not only from Kunaris but, again and again, in

Fol. 134b. Bajaur, Sawad and the whole hill-tract. Haidar-'ali *Bajauri*,—a sultan who governed Bajaur well,—when his mother died, did not weep, or betake himself to lamentation, or put on black, but said, "Go! lay her on the bier! if she move not, I will have her burned."[1] They laid her on the bier; the desired movement followed; when he heard that this was so, he put on black and betook himself to lamentation.

Another *buluk* is Chaghan-sarai,[2] a single village with little land, in the mouth of Kafiristan; its people, though Musalman, mix with the Kafirs and, consequently, follow their customs.[3] A great torrent (the Kunar) comes down to it from the north-east from behind Bajaur, and a smaller one, called Pich, comes down out of Kafiristan. Strong yellowish wines are had there, not in any way resembling those of the Nur-valley, however. The village has no grapes or vineyards of its own; its wines are all brought from up the Kafiristan-water and from Pich-i-kafiristani.

The Pich Kafirs came to help the villagers when I took the place. Wine is so commonly used there that every Kafir has his leathern wine-bag (*khig*) at his neck, and drinks wine instead of water.[4]

1 *i.e.* treat her corpse as that of an infidel (Erskine).
2 It would suit the position of this village if its name were found to link to the Turki verb *chiqmaq*, to go out, because it lies in the mouth of a defile (Dahanah-i-koh, Mountain-mouth) through which the road for Kafiristan goes out past the village. A not-infrequent explanation of the name to mean White-house, Aq-sarai, may well be questioned. *Chaghan*, white, is Mughuli and it would be less probable for a Mughuli than for a Turki name to establish itself. Another explanation may lie in the tribe name Chugani. The two forms *chaghan* and *chaghar* may well be due to the common local interchange in speech of *n* with *r*. (For Dahanah-i-koh *see* [some] maps and Raverty's Bajaur routes.)
3 Nimchas, presumably,—half-bred in custom, perhaps in blood—; and not improbably, converted Kafirs. It is useful to remember that Kafiristan was once bounded, west and south, by the Baran-water.
4 Kafir wine is mostly poor, thin and, even so, usually diluted with water. When kept two or three years, however, it becomes clear and sometimes strong. Sir G. S. Robertson never saw a Kafir drunk (*Kafirs of the Hindu-kush*, p. 591).

Kama, again, though not a separate district but dependent on Ningnahar, is also called a *buluk*.[1]

Nijr-au[2] is another *tuman*. It lies north of Kabul, in the Kohistan, with mountains behind it inhabited solely by Kafirs; it is a quite sequestered place. It grows grapes and fruits in abundance. Its people make much wine but, they boil it. They fatten many fowls in winter, are wine-bibbers, do not pray, have no scruples and are Kafir-like.[3]

In the Nijr-au mountains is an abundance of *archa, jilghuza, bilut* and *khanjak*.[4] The first-named three do not grow above Nigr-au but they grow lower, and are amongst the trees of Hindustan. *Jilghuza*-wood is all the lamp the people have; it burns like a candle and is very remarkable. The flying-squirrel[5] is found in these mountains, an animal larger than a bat and having a curtain (*parda*), like a bat's wing, between its arms and legs. People often brought one in; it is said to fly, downward from one tree to another, as far as a *giz* flies;[6] I myself have never seen one fly. Once we put one to a tree; it clambered up directly and got away, but, when people went after it, it spread its wings and came down, without hurt, as if it had flown. Another of the curiosities of the Nijr-au mountains is the *lukha* (var. *luja*) bird, called also *bu-qalamun* (chameleon) because, between head and tail, it has four or five changing colours, resplendent like a pigeon's throat.[7] It is about as large as the

1 Kama might have classed better under Ningnahar of which it was a dependency.
2 *i.e.* water-of-Nijr; so too, Badr-au and Tag-au. Nijr-au has seven-valleys (JASB 1838 p. 329 and Burnes' *Report X*). Sayyid Ghulam-i-muhammad mentions that Babur established a frontier-post between Nijr-au and Kafiristan which in his own day was still maintained. He was an envoy of Warren Hastings to Timur Shah *Sadozi* (R.'s *Notes* p. 36 and p. 142).
3 *Kafirwash*; they were Kafirs converted to Muhammadanism.
4 *Archa*, if not inclusive, meaning conifer, may represent *juniperus excelsa*, this being the common local conifer. The other trees of the list are *pinus Gerardiana* (Brandis, p. 690), *quercus bilut*, the holm-oak, and *pistacia mutica* or *khanjak*, a tree yielding mastic.
5 *ruba-i-parran, pteromys inornatus*, the large, red flying-squirrel (Blanford's *Fauna of British India, Mammalia*, p. 363).
6 The *giz* is a short-flight arrow used for shooting small birds etc. Descending flights of squirrels have been ascertained as 60 yards, one, a record, of 80 (Blanford).
7 Apparently *tetrogallus himalayensis*, the Himalayan snow-cock (Blanford, iv, 143). Burnes (*Cabool* p. 163) describes the *kabg-i-dari* as the *rara avis* of the Kabul Kohistan, somewhat less than a turkey, and of the *chikor* (partridge) species. It was procured for him first in Ghur-bund, but, when snow has fallen, it could be had nearer Kabul. Babur's *bu-qalamun* may have come into his vocabulary, either as a survival direct from Greek occupation of Kabul and Panj-ab, or through Arabic writings. PRGS 1879 p. 251, Kaye's art. and JASB 1838 p. 863, Hodgson's art.

kabg-i-dari and seems to be the *kabg-i-dari* of Hindustan.[1]
People tell this wonderful thing about it:—When the birds, at
Fol. 135b. the on-set of winter, descend to the hill-skirts, if they come
over a vineyard, they can fly no further and are taken.[2] There
is a kind of rat in Nijr-au, known as the musk-rat, which
smells of musk; I however have never seen it.[3]

Panjhir (Panj-sher) is another *tuman*; it lies close to Kafiristan,
along the Panjhir road, and is the thoroughfare of Kafir highwaymen who also, being so near, take tax of it. They have gone
through it, killing a mass of persons, and doing very evil deeds,
since I came this last time and conquered Hindustan (932 AH.-
1526 AD.).[4]

Another is the *tuman* of Ghur-bund. In those countries they
call a *kutal* (*koh*?) a *bund*;[5] they go towards Ghur by this pass
(*kutal*); apparently it is for this reason that they have called (the
tuman?) Ghur-bund. The Hazara hold the heads of its valleys.[6]
It has few villages and little revenue can be raised from it. There
are said to be mines of silver and lapis lazuli in its mountains.

Again, there are the villages on the skirts of the
(Hindu-kush) mountains,[7] with Mita-kacha and Parwan at

1 Bartavelle's *Greek-partridge, tetrao-* or *perdrix-rufus* [f. 279 and Mems. p. 320 n.].
2 A similar story is told of some fields near Whitby:—"These wild geese, which
in winter fly in great flocks to the lakes and rivers unfrozen in the southern parts,
to the great amazement of every-one, fall suddenly down upon the ground
when they are in flight over certain neighbouring fields thereabouts; a relation
I should not have made, if I had not received it from several credible men."
See *Notes to Marmion* p. xlvi (Erskine); Scott's *Poems*, Black's ed. 1880, vii, 104.
3 Are we to infer from this that the musk-rat (*Crocidura cærulea*, Lydekker, p. 626)
was not so common in Hindustan in the age of Babur as it has now become? He
was not a careless observer (Erskine).
4 Index *s.n. Babur-nama*, date of composition; also f. 131.
5 In the absence of examples of *bund* to mean *kutal*, and the presence "in those
countries" of many in which *bund* means *koh*, it looks as though a clerical error
had here written *kutal* for *koh*. But on the other hand, the wording of the next
passage shows just the confusion an author's unrevised draft might shew if a place
were, as this is, both a *tuman* and a *kutal* (*i.e.* a steady rise to a traverse). My
impression is that the name Ghur-bund applies to the embanking spur at the
head of the valley-*tuman*, across which roads lead to Ghuri and Ghur (PRGS
1879, Maps; Leech's Report VII; and Wood's VI).
6 So too when, because of them, Leech and Lord turned back, *re infectâ*.
7 It will be noticed that these villages are not classed in any *tuman*; they include places
"rich without parallel" in agricultural products, and level lands on which towns have
risen and fallen, one being Alexandria ad Caucasum. They cannot have been part of
the unremunerative Ghur-bund *tuman*; from their place of mention in Babur's list of
tumans, they may have been part of the Kabul *tuman* (f. 178), as was Koh-daman (Burnes'
Cabool p. 154; Haughton's *Charikar* p. 73; and Cunningham's *Ancient History*, i, 18).

their head, and Dur-nama[1] at their foot, 12 or 13 in all. They are fruit-bearing villages, and they grow cheering wines, those of Khwaja Khawand Sa'id being reputed the strongest roundabouts. The villages all lie on the foot-hills; some pay taxes but not all are taxable because they lie so far back in the mountains.

Between the foot-hills and the Baran-water are two detached stretches of level land, one known as *Kurrat-taziyan*,[2] the other as *Dasht-i-shaikh* (Shaikh's-plain). As the green grass of the millet[3] grows well there, they are the resort of Turks and (Mughul) clans (*aimaq*).   Fol. 136.

Tulips of many colours cover these foot-hills; I once counted them up; it came out at 32 or 33 different sorts. We named one the Rose-scented, because its perfume was a little like that of the red rose; it grows by itself on Shaikh's-plain, here and nowhere else. The Hundred-leaved tulip is another; this grows, also by itself, at the outlet of the Ghur-bund narrows, on the hill-skirt below Parwan. A low hill known as Khwaja-i-reg-rawan (Khwaja-of-the-running-sand), divides the afore-named two pieces of level land; it has, from top to foot, a strip of sand from which people say the sound of nagarets and tambours issues in the heats.[4]

Again, there are the villages depending on Kabul itself. South-west from the town are great snow mountains[5] where snow falls on snow, and where few may be the years when, falling, it does not light on last year's snow. It is fetched, 12 miles may-be, from these mountains, to cool the drinking water when ice-houses in Kabul are empty. Like the Bamian mountains,

1 Dur-namai, seen from afar (Masson, iii, 152) is not marked on the Survey Maps; Masson, Vigne and Haughton locate it. Babur's "head" and "foot" here indicate status and not location.

2 Mems. p. 146 and *Méms.* i, 297, Arabs' encampment and *Cellule des Arabes.* Perhaps the name may refer to uses of the level land and good pasture by horse *qafilas*, since *Kurra* is written with *tashdid* in the Haidarabad Codex, as in *kurra-taz*, a horse-breaker. Or the *taziyan* may be the fruit of a legend, commonly told, that the saint of the neighbouring Running-sands was an Arabian.

3 Presumably this is the grass of the millet, the growth before the ear, on which grazing is allowed (Elphinstone, i, 400; Burnes, p. 237).

4 Wood, p. 115; Masson, iii, 167; Burnes, p. 157 and JASB 1838 p. 324 with illustration; Vigne, pp. 219, 223; Lord, JASB 1838 p. 537; *Cathay and the way thither*, Hakluyt Society vol. I. p. xx, para. 49; *History of Musical Sands*, C. Carus-Wilson.

5 *West* might be more exact, since some of the group are a little north, others a little south of the latitude of Kabul.

these are fastnesses. Out of them issue the Harmand (Halmand), Sind, Dughaba of Qunduz, and Balkh-ab,[1] so that in a single day, a man might drink of the water of each of these four rivers.

It is on the skirt of one of these ranges (Pamghan) that most of the villages dependent on Kabul lie.[2] Masses of grapes ripen in their vineyards and they grow every sort of fruit in abundance. No-one of them equals Istalif or Astarghach; these must be the

Fol. 136b.   two which Aulugh Beg Mirza used to call his Khurasan and Samarkand. Pamghan is another of the best, not ranking in fruit and grapes with those two others, but beyond comparison with them in climate. The Pamghan mountains are a snowy range. Few villages match Istalif, with vineyards and fine orchards on both sides of its great torrent, with waters needing no ice, cold and, mostly, pure. Of its Great garden Aulugh Beg Mirza had taken forcible possession; I took it over, after paying its price to the owners. There is a pleasant halting-place outside it, under great planes, green, shady and beautiful. A one-mill stream, having trees on both banks, flows constantly through the middle of the garden; formerly its course was zig-zag and irregular; I had it made straight and orderly; so the place became very beautiful. Between the village and the valley-bottom, from 4 to 6 miles down the slope, is a spring, known as Khwaja Sih-yaran (Three-friends), round which three sorts of tree grow. A group of planes gives pleasant shade above it; holm-

Fol. 137.   oak (*quercus bilut*) grows in masses on the slope at its sides,—these two oaklands (*bilutistan*) excepted, no holm-oak grows in the mountains of western Kabul,—and the Judas-tree (*arghwan*)[3] is much cultivated in front of it, that is towards the level ground,—cultivated there and nowhere else. People say the three different sorts of tree were a gift made by three saints,[4] whence

1 Affluents and not true sources in some cases (Col. Holdich's *Gates of India, s.n.* Koh-i-baba; and PRGS 1879, maps pp. 80 and 160).

2 The Pamghan range. These are the villages every traveller celebrates. Masson's and Vigne's illustrations depict them well.

3 *Cercis siliquastrum*, the Judas-tree. Even in 1842 it was sparingly found near Kabul, adorning a few tombs, one Babur's own. It had been brought from Sih-yaran where, as also at Charikar, (Char-yak-kar) it was still abundant and still a gorgeous sight. It is there a tree, as at Kew, and not a bush, as in most English gardens (Masson, ii, 9; Elphinstone, i, 194; and for the tree near Harat, f. 191 n. to Safar).

4 Khwaja Maudud of Chisht, Khwaja Khawand Sa'id and the Khwaja of the Running-sands (Elph. MS. f. 104b, marginal note).

its name. I ordered that the spring should be enclosed in mortared stone-work, 10 by 10, and that a symmetrical, right-angled platform should be built on each of its sides, so as to overlook the whole field of Judas-trees. If, the world over, there is a place to match this when the *arghwans* are in full bloom, I do not know it. The yellow *arghwan* grows plentifully there also, the red and the yellow flowering at the same time.[1]

In order to bring water to a large round seat which I had built on the hillside and planted round with willows, I had a channel dug across the slope from a half-mill stream, constantly flowing in a valley to the south-west of Sih-yaran. It became a very good halting-place. I had a vineyard planted on the hill above the seat. The date of cutting this channel was found in *jui-khush* (kindly channel).[2]

Another of the *tumans* of Kabul is Luhugur (mod. Logar). Its one large village is Chirkh from which were his Reverence Maulana Ya'qub and Mulla-zada 'Usman.[3] Khwaja Ahmad and Khwaja Yunas were from Sajawand, another of its villages. Chirkh has many gardens, but there are none in any other village of Luhugur. Its people are Aughan-shal, a term common in Kabul, seeming to be a mispronouncement of Aughan-sha'ar.[4]

Again, there is the *wilayat*, or, as some say, *tuman* of Ghazni, said to have been[5] the capital of Sabuk-tigin, Sl. Mahmud and their descendants. Many write it Ghaznin. It is said also to have been the seat of government of Shihabu'd-din *Ghuri*,[6] styled Mu'izzu'd-din in the *Tabaqat-i-nasiri* and also some of the histories of Hind.

Ghazni is known also as Zabulistan; it belongs to the Third climate. Some hold that Qandahar is a part of it. It lies 14 *yighach* (south-) west of Kabul; those leaving it at dawn, may reach Kabul between the Two Prayers (*i.e.* in the afternoon);

Fol. 137*b*.

---

1 The yellow-flowered plant is not *cercis siliquastrum* but one called *mahaka* (?) in Persian, a shrubby plant with pea-like blossoms, common in the plains of Persia, Biluchistan and Kabul (Masson, iii, 9 and Vigne, p. 216).

2 The numerical value of these words gives 925 (Erskine). F. 246*b et seq.* for the expedition.

3 f. 178. I.O. MS. No. 724, *Haft-iqlim* f. 135 (Ethé, p. 402); Rieu, pp. 21*a*, 1058*b*.

4 of Afghan habit. The same term is applied (f. 139*b*) to the Zurmutis; it may be explained in both places by Babur's statement that Zurmutis grow corn, but do not cultivate gardens or orchards.

5 *aikan dur.* Sabuk-tigin, d. 387 AH.–997 AD., was the father of Sl. Mahmud *Ghaznawi*, d. 421 AH.–1030 AD.

6 d. 602 AH.–1206 AD.

whereas the 13 *yighach* between Adinapur and Kabul can never be done in one day, because of the difficulties of the road.

Ghazni has little cultivated land. Its torrent, a four-mill or five-mill stream may-be, makes the town habitable and fertilizes four or five villages; three or four others are cultivated from under-ground water-courses (*karez*). Ghazni grapes are better than those of Kabul; its melons are more abundant; its apples are very good, and are carried to Hindustan. Agriculture is very laborious in Ghazni because, whatever the quality of the soil, it must be newly top-dressed every year; it gives a better return, however, than Kabul. Ghazni grows madder; the entire crop goes to Hindustan and yields excellent profit to the growers. In the open-country of Ghazni dwell Hazara and Afghans. Compared with Kabul, it is always a cheap place. Its people hold to the Hanafi faith, are good, orthodox Musalmans, many keep a three months' fast,[1] and their wives and children live modestly secluded.

One of the eminent men of Ghazni was Mulla 'Abdu'r-rahman, a learned man and always a learner (*dars*), a most orthodox, pious and virtuous person; he left this world the same year as Nasir Mirza (921 AH.-1515 AD.). Sl. Mahmud's tomb is in the sub-urb called Rauza,[2] from which the best grapes come; there also are the tombs of his descendants, Sl. Mas'ud and Sl. Ibrahim. Ghazni has many blessed tombs. The year[3] I took Kabul and Ghazni, over-ran Kohat, the plain of Bannu and lands of the Afghans, and went on to Ghazni by way of Duki (Dugi) and Ab-istada, people told me there was a tomb, in a village of Ghazni, which moved when a benediction on the Prophet was pronounced over it. We went to see it. In the end I discovered that the movement was a trick, presumably of the servants at the tomb, who had put a sort of platform above it which moved when pushed, so that, to those on it, the tomb seemed to move, just as the shore does to those passing in a boat. I ordered the

Fol. 138. (margin)

Fol. 138b. (margin)

---

1 Some Musalmans fast through the months of Rajab, Sha'ban and Ramzan; Muhammadans fast only by day; the night is often given to feasting (Erskine).

2 The Garden; the tombs of more eminent Musalmans are generally in gardens (Erskine). *See* Vigne's illustrations, pp. 133, 266.

3 *i.e.* the year now in writing. The account of the expedition, Babur's first into Hindustan, begins on f. 145.

scaffold destroyed and a dome built over the tomb; also I forbad the servants, with threats, ever to bring about the movement again.

Ghazni is a very humble place; strange indeed it is that rulers in whose hands were Hindustan and Khurasanat,[1] should have chosen it for their capital. In the Sultan's (Mahmud's) time there may have been three or four dams in the country; one he made, some three *yighach* (18 m. ?) up the Ghazni-water to the north; it was about 40–50 *qari* (yards) high and some 300 long; through it the stored waters were let out as required.[2] It was destroyed by 'Alau'u'd-din *Jahan-soz Ghuri* when he conquered the country (550 AH.-1152 AD.), burned and ruined the tombs of several descendants of Sl. Mahmud, sacked and burned the town, in short, left undone no tittle of murder and rapine. Since that time, the Sultan's dam has lain in ruins, but, through God's favour, there is hope that it may become of use again, by means of the money which was sent, in Khwaja Kalan's hand, in the year Hindustan was conquered (932 AH.-1526 AD.).[3] The Sakhan-dam is another, 2 or 3 *yighach* (12–18 m.), may-be, on the east of the town; it has long been in ruins, indeed is past repair. There is a dam in working order at Sar-i-dih (Village-head).

Fol. 139.

In books it is written that there is in Ghazni a spring such that, if dirt and foul matter be thrown into it, a tempest gets up instantly, with a blizzard of rain and wind. It has been seen said also in one of the histories that Sabuk-tigin, when besieged by the Rai (Jai-pal) of Hind, ordered dirt and foulness to be thrown into the spring, by this aroused, in an instant, a tempest with blizzard of rain and snow, and, by this device, drove off his foe.[4] Though we made many enquiries, no intimation of the spring's existence was given us.

In these countries Ghazni and Khwarizm are noted for cold, in the same way that Sultania and Tabriz are in the two 'Iraqs and Azarbaijan.

---

1 *i.e.* the countries groupable as Khurasan.
2 For picture and account of the dam, *see* Vigne, pp. 138, 202.
3 f. 295*b*.
4 The legend is told in numerous books with varying location of the spring. One narrator, Zakariya *Qazwini*, reverses the parts, making Jai-pal employ the ruse; hence Leyden's note (Mems. p. 150; E. and D.'s *History of India* ii, 20, 182 and iv, 162; for historical information, R.'s *Notes* p. 320). The date of the events is shortly after 378 AH.-988 AD.

Zurmut is another *tuman*, some 12–13 *yighach* south of Kabul and 7–8 south-east of Ghazni.[1] Its *darogha*'s head-quarters are in Girdiz; there most houses are three or four storeys high. It does not want for strength, and gave Nasir Mirza trouble when it went into hostility to him. Its people are Aughan-shal; they grow corn but have neither vineyards nor orchards. The tomb of Shaikh Muhammad *Musalman* is at a spring, high on the skirt of a mountain, known as Barakistan, in the south of the *tuman*.

Farmul is another *tuman*,[2] a humble place, growing not bad apples which are carried into Hindustan. Of Farmul were the Shaikh-zadas, descendants of Shaikh Muhammad *Musalman*, who were so much in favour during the Afghan period in Hindustan.

Bangash is another *tuman*.[3] All round about it are Afghan highwaymen, such as the Khugiani, Khirilchi, Turi and Landar. Lying out-of-the-way, as it does, its people do not pay taxes willingly. There has been no time to bring it to obedience; greater tasks have fallen to me,—the conquests of Qandahar, Balkh, Badakhshan and Hindustan! But, God willing! when I get the chance, I most assuredly will take order with those Bangash thieves.

One of the *buluks* of Kabul is Ala-sai,[4] 4 to 6 miles (2–3 *shar'i*) east of Nijr-au. The direct road into it from Nijr-au leads, at a place called Kura, through the quite small pass which in that locality separates the hot and cold climates. Through this pass the birds migrate at the change of the seasons, and at those times many are taken by the people of Pichghan, one of the dependencies of Nijr-au, in the following manner:— From distance to distance near the mouth of the pass, they make hiding-places for the bird-catchers. They fasten one corner of a net five or six yards away, and weight the lower side to the

Fol. 139b.

Fol. 140.

---

1 R.'s *Notes s.n.* Zurmut.

2 The question of the origin of the Farmuli has been written of by several writers; perhaps they were Turks of Persia, Turks and Tajiks.

3 This completes the list of the 14 *tumans* of Kabul, *viz.* Ningnahar, 'Ali-shang, Alangar, Mandrawar, Kunar-with-Nur-gal, Nijr-au, Panjhir, Ghur-bund, Koh-daman (with Kohistan?), Luhugur (of the Kabul *tuman*), Ghazni, Zurmut, Farmul and Bangash.

4 Between Nijr-au and Tag-au (Masson, iii, 165). Mr. Erskine notes that Babur reckoned it in the hot climate but that the change of climate takes place further east, between 'Ali-shang and Auzbin (*i.e.* the valley next eastwards from Tag-au).

ground with stones. Along the other side of the net, for half its
width, they fasten a stick some 3 to 4 yards long. The hidden
bird-catcher holds this stick and by it, when the birds approach,
lifts up the net to its full height. The birds then go into the net
of themselves. Sometimes so many are taken by this contrivance
that there is not time to cut their throats.[1]

Though the Ala-sai pomegranates are not first-rate, they have
local reputation because none are better there-abouts; they are
carried into Hindustan. Grapes also do not grow badly, and the
wines of Ala-sai are better and stronger than those of Nijr-au.

Badr-au (Tag-au) is another *buluk*; it runs with Ala-sai,
grows no fruit, and for cultivators has corn-growing Kafirs.[2]

(f. Tribesmen of Kabul.)

Just as Turks and (Mughul) clans (*aimaq*) dwell in the open
country of Khurasan and Samarkand, so in Kabul do the
Hazara and Afghans. Of the Hazara, the most widely-scattered
are the Sultan-mas'udi Hazara, of Afghans, the Mahmand.

(g. Revenue of Kabul.)

The revenues of Kabul, whether from the cultivated lands
or from tolls (*tamgha*) or from dwellers in the open country,
amount to 8 *laks* of shahrukhis.[3]

Fol. 140*b*.

(h. The mountain-tracts of Kabul.)

The mountains to the eastward of the cultivated land of
Kabul are of two kinds as also are those to its westward.
Where the mountains of Andar-ab, Khwast,[4] and the Badakh-
shanat have conifers (*archa*), many springs and gentle slopes,
those of eastern Kabul have grass (*aut*), grass like a beautiful
floor, on hill, slope and dale. For the most part it is *buta-kah*
grass (*aut*), very suitable for horses. In the Andijan country
they talk of *buta-kah*, but why they do so was not known (to
me?); in Kabul it was heard-say to be because the grass comes

1 *bughuzlarigha fursat bulmas*; *i.e.* to kill them in the lawful manner, while
pronouncing the *Bi'smi'llah*.
2 This completes the *buluks* of Kabul *viz*. Badr-au (Tag-au), Nur-valley,
Chaghan-sarai, Kama and Ala-sai.
3 The *rupi* being equal to 2½ *shahrukhis*, the *shahrukhi* may be taken at 10*d*. thus
making the total revenue only £33,333 6*s*. 8*d*. See *Ayin-i-akbari* ii, 169 (Erskine).
4 *sic* in all B.N. MSS. Most maps print Khost. Muh. Salih says of Khwast, "Who
sees it, would call it a Hell" (Vambéry, p. 361).

up in tufts (*buta, buta*).[1] The alps of these mountains are like those
of Hisar, Khutlan, Farghana, Samarkand and Mughulistan,—
all these being alike in mountain and alp, though the alps
of Farghana and Mughulistan are beyond comparison with
the rest.

From all these the mountains of Nijr-au, the Lamghanat and
Sawad differ in having masses of cypresses,[2] holm-oak, olive and
mastic (*khanjak*); their grass also is different,—it is dense, it is
tall, it is good neither for horse nor sheep. Although these
mountains are not so high as those already described, indeed
they look to be low, none-the-less, they are strongholds; what
to the eye is even slope, really is hard rock on which it is
impossible to ride. Many of the beasts and birds of Hindustan

Fol. 141.   are found amongst them, such as the parrot, *mina*, peacock and
luja (*lukha*), the ape, *nil-gau* and hog-deer (*kuta-pai*);[3] some
found there are not found even in Hindustan.

The mountains to the west of Kabul are also all of one sort,
those of the Zindan-valley, the Suf-valley, Garzawan and Gharjistan (Gharchastan).[4] Their meadows are mostly in the dales;
they have not the same sweep of grass on slope and top as some
of those described have; nor have they masses of trees; they
have, however, grass suiting horses. On their flat tops, where all
the crops are grown, there is ground where a horse can gallop.
They have masses of *kiyik*.[5] Their valley-bottoms are strongholds, mostly precipitous and inaccessible from above. It is
remarkable that, whereas other mountains have their fastnesses
in their high places, these have theirs below.

Of one sort again are the mountains of Ghur, Karnud (var.
Kuzud) and Hazara; their meadows are in their dales; their
trees are few, not even the *archa* being there;[6] their grass is fit

1 Babur's statement about this fodder is not easy to translate; he must have seen
grass grow in tufts, and must have known the Persian word *buta* (bush). Perhaps
kah should be read to mean plant, not grass. Would Wood's *bootr* fit in, a small
furze bush, very plentiful near Bamian? (Wood's Report VI, p. 23; and for regional grasses, Aitchison's *Botany of the Afghan Delimitation Commission*, p. 122.)

2 *nazu*, perhaps *cupressus torulosa* (Brandis, p. 693).

3 f. 276.

4 A laborious geographical note of Mr. Erskine's is here regretfully left behind,
as now needless (Mems. p. 152).

5 Here, mainly wild-sheep and wild-goats, including *mar-khwar*.

6 Perhaps, no conifers; perhaps none of those of the contrasted hill-tract.

for horses and for the masses of sheep they keep. They differ from those last described in this, their strong places are not below.

The mountains (south-east of Kabul) of Khwaja Isma'il, Dasht, Dugi (Duki)[1] and Afghanistan are all alike; all low, scant of vegetation, short of water, treeless, ugly and good-for-nothing. Their people take after them, just as has been said, *Ting bulma-ghuncha tush bulmas.*[2] Likely enough the world has few mountains so useless and disgusting.

Fol. 141*b*.

(h. Fire-wood of Kabul.)

The snow-fall being so heavy in Kabul, it is fortunate that excellent fire-wood is had near by. Given one day to fetch it, wood can be had of the *khanjak* (mastic), *bilut* (holm-oak), *badamcha* (small-almond) and *qarqand.*[3] Of these *khanjak* wood is the best; it burns with flame and nice smell, makes plenty of hot ashes and does well even if sappy. Holm-oak is also first-rate fire-wood, blazing less than mastic but, like it, making a hot fire with plenty of hot ashes, and nice smell. It has the peculiarity in burning that when its leafy branches are set alight, they fire up with amazing sound, blazing and crackling from bottom to top. It is good fun to burn it. The wood of the small-almond is the most plentiful and commonly-used, but it does not make a lasting fire. The *qarqand* is quite a low shrub, thorny, and burning sappy or dry; it is the fuel of the Ghazni people.

(i. Fauna of Kabul.)

The cultivated lands of Kabul lie between mountains which are like great dams[4] to the flat valley-bottoms in which most villages and peopled places are. On these mountains *kiyik* and

---

1 While here *dasht* (plain) represents the eastern skirt of the Mehtar Sulaiman range, *duki* or *dugi* (desert) seems to stand for the hill tracts on the west of it, and not, as on f. 152, for the place there specified.

2 Mems. p. 152, "A narrow place is large to the narrow-minded"; *Méms.* i, 311, "Ce qui n'est pas trop large, ne reste pas vide." Literally, "So long as heights are not equal, there is no vis-a-vis," or, if *tang* be read for *ting*, "No dawn, no noon," *i.e.* no effect without a cause.

3 I have not lighted on this name in botanical books or explained by dictionaries. Perhaps it is a Cis-oxanian name for the *sax-aol* of Transoxania. As its uses are enumerated by some travellers, it might be *Haloxylon ammodendron, ta-ghaz etc.* and *sax-aol* (Aitchison, p. 102).

4 f. 135*b* note to Ghur-bund. *See also,* Additional Notes, p. 798.

ahu[1] are scarce. Across them, between its summer and winter quarters, the dun sheep,[2] the *arqarghalcha*, have their regular track,[3] to which braves go out with dogs and birds[4] to take them.

Fol. 142. Towards Khurd-kabul and the Surkh-rud there is wild-ass, but there are no white *kiyik* at all; Ghazni has both and in few other places are white *kiyik* found in such good condition.[5]

In the heats the fowling-grounds of Kabul are crowded. The birds take their way along the Baran-water. For why? It is because the river has mountains along it, east and west, and a great Hindu-kush pass in a line with it, by which the birds must cross since there is no other near.[6] They cannot cross when the north wind blows, or if there is even a little cloud on Hindu-kush; at such times they alight on the level lands of the Baran-water and are taken in great numbers by the local people. Towards the end of winter, dense flocks of mallards (*aurduq*) reach the banks of the Baran in very good condition. Follow these the cranes and herons,[7] great birds, in large flocks and countless numbers.

(*j. Bird-catching.*)

Along the Baran people take masses of cranes (*turna*) with the cord; masses of *auqar*, *qarqara* and *qutan* also.[8] This

1 I understand that wild-goats, wild-sheep and deer (*ahu*) were not localized, but that the dun-sheep migrated through. Antelope (*ahu*) was scarce in Elphinstone's time.

2 *qizil kiyik* which, taken with its alternative name, *arqarghalcha*, allows it to be the dun-sheep of Wood's *Journey* p. 241. From its second name it may be *Ovis amnon* (*Raos*), or *O. argali*.

3 *tusqawal*, var. *tutqawal*, *tusaqawal* and *tushqawal*, a word which has given trouble to scribes and translators. As a sporting-term it is equivalent to *shikar-i-nihilam*; in one or other of its forms I find it explained as *Weg-hüter*, *Fahnen-hüter*, *Zahl-meister*, *Schlucht*, *Gefahrlicher-weg* and *Schmaler-weg*. It recurs in the B.N. on f. 197b l. 5 and l. 6 and there might mean either a narrow road or a *Weg-hüter*. If its Turki root be *tus*, the act of stopping, all the above meanings can follow, but there may be two separate roots, the second, *tush*, the act of descent (JRAS 1900 p. 137, H. Beveridge's art. *On the word nihilam*).

4 *qushlik*, *aitlik*. Elphinstone writes (i, 191) of the excellent greyhounds and hawking birds of the region; here the bird may be the *charkh*, which works with the dogs, fastening on the head of the game (Von Schwarz, p. 117, for the same use of eagles).

5 An antelope resembling the usual one of Hindustan is common south of Ghazni (Vigne, p. 110); what is not found may be some classes of wild-sheep, frequent further north, at higher elevation, and in places more familiar to Babur.

6 The Parwan or Hindu-kush pass, concerning the winds of which *see* f. 128.

7 *turna u qarqara*; the second of which is the Hindi *bugla*, heron, *egret ardea gazet-ta*, the furnisher of the aigrette of commerce.

8 The *auqar* is *ardea cinerea*, the grey heron; the *qarqara* is *ardea gazetta*, the egret. *Qutan* is explained in the Elph. Codex (f. 110) by *khawasil*, goldfinch, but the context concerns large birds; Scully (Shaw's Voc.) has *qodan*, water-hen, which suits better.

method of bird-catching is unique. They twist a cord as long as the arrow's[1] flight, tie the arrow at one end and a *bildurga*[2] at the other, and wind it up, from the arrow-end, on a piece of wood, span-long and wrist-thick, right up to the *bildurga*. They then pull out the piece of wood, leaving just the hole it was in. The *bildurga* being held fast in the hand, the arrow is shot off[3] towards the coming flock. If the cord twist round a neck or wing, it brings the bird down. On the Baran everyone takes birds in this way; it is difficult; it must be done on rainy nights, because on such nights the birds do not alight, but fly continually and fly low till dawn, in fear of ravening beasts of prey. Through the night the flowing river is their road, its moving water showing through the dark; then it is, while they come and go, up and down the river, that the cord is shot. One night I shot it; it broke in drawing in; both bird and cord were brought in to me next day. By this device Baran people catch the many herons from which they take the turban-aigrettes sent from Kabul for sale in Khurasan.

Of bird-catchers there is also the band of slave-fowlers, two or three hundred households, whom some descendant of Timur Beg made migrate from near Multan to the Baran.[4] Bird-catching is their trade; they dig tanks, set decoy-birds[5] on them, put a net over the middle, and in this way take all sorts of birds. Not fowlers only catch birds, but every dweller on the Baran does it, whether by shooting the cord, setting the springe, or in various other ways.

(k. Fishing.)

The fish of the Baran migrate at the same seasons as birds. At those times many are netted, and many are taken on wattles

Fol. 142*b*.

Fol. 143.

---

1 *giz*, the short-flight arrow.

2 a small, round-headed nail with which a whip-handle is decorated (Vambéry). Such a stud would keep the cord from slipping through the fingers and would not check the arrow-release.

3 It has been understood (Mems. p. 158 and *Méms.* i, 313) that the arrow was flung by hand but if this were so, something heavier than the *giz* would carry the cord better, since it certainly would be difficult to direct a missile so light as an arrow without the added energy of the bow. The arrow itself will often have found its billet in the closely-flying flock; the cord would retrieve the bird. The verb used in the text is *aitmaq*, the one common to express the discharge of arrows *etc.*

4 For Timurids who may have immigrated the fowlers *see* Raverty's *Notes* p. 579 and his Appendix p. 22.

5 *milwah*; this has been read by all earlier translators, and also by the Persian annotator of the Elph. Codex, to mean *shakh*, bough. For decoy-ducks *see* Bellew's *Notes on Afghanistan* p. 404.

(*chigh*) fixed in the water. In autumn when the plant known
as *wild-ass-tail*[1] has come to maturity, flowered and seeded,
people take 10–20 loads (of seed?) and 20–30 of green branches
(*guk-shibak*) to some head of water, break it up small and cast
it in. Then going into the water, they can at once pick up
drugged fish. At some convenient place lower down, in a hole
below a fall, they will have fixed before-hand a wattle of
finger-thick willow-withes, making it firm by piling stones on
its sides. The water goes rushing and dashing through the wattle,
but leaves on it any fish that may have come floating down. This
way of catching fish is practised in Gul-bahar, Parwan and Istalif.

Fol. 143*b*.   Fish are had in winter in the Lamghanat by this curious
device:—People dig a pit to the depth of a house, in the bed of
a stream, below a fall, line it with stones like a cooking-place,
and build up stones round it above, leaving one opening only,
under water. Except by this one opening, the fish have no inlet
or outlet, but the water finds its way through the stones. This
makes a sort of fish-pond from which, when wanted in winter,
fish can be taken, 30–40 together. Except at the opening, left
where convenient, the sides of the fish-pond are made fast with
rice-straw, kept in place by stones. A piece of wicker-work is
pulled into the said opening by its edges, gathered together, and
into this a second piece, (a tube,) is inserted, fitting it at the
mouth but reaching half-way into it only.[2] The fish go through
the smaller piece into the larger one, out from which they cannot
get. The second narrows towards its inner mouth, its pointed
ends being drawn so close that the fish, once entered, cannot
Fol. 144.   turn, but must go on, one by one, into the larger piece. Out of
that they cannot return because of the pointed ends of the inner,
narrow mouth. The wicker-work fixed and the rice-straw making
the pond fast, whatever fish are inside can be taken out;[3] any also
which, trying to escape may have gone into the wicker-work,

1 *qulan quyirughi*. Amongst the many plants used to drug fish I have not found
this one mentioned. *Khar-zahra* and *khar-faq* approach it in verbal meaning; the
first describes colocynth, the second, wild rue. *See* Watts' *Economic Products of
India* iii, 366 and Bellew's *Notes* pp. 182, 471 and 478.

2 Much trouble would have been spared to himself and his translators, if Babur
had known a lobster-pot.

3 The fish, it is to be inferred, came down the fall into the pond.

are taken in it, because they have no way out. This method of catching fish we have seen nowhere else.[1]

HISTORICAL NARRATIVE RESUMED[2]

(*a. Departure of Muqim and allotment of lands.*)

A few days after the taking of Kabul, Muqim asked leave to set off for Qandahar. As he had come out of the town on terms and conditions, he was allowed to go to his father (Zu'n-nun) and his elder brother (Shah Beg), with all his various people, his goods and his valuables, safe and sound.

Directly he had gone, the Kabul-country was shared out to the Mirzas and the guest-begs.[3] To Jahangir Mirza was given Ghazni with its dependencies and appurtenances; to Nasir Mirza, the Ningnahar *tuman*, Mandrawar, Nur-valley, Kunar, Nur-gal (Rock-village?) and Chighan-sarai. To some of the begs who had been with us in the guerilla-times and had come to Kabul with us, were given villages, fief-fashion.[4] *Wilayat* itself was not given at all.[5] It was not only then that I looked with more favour on guest-begs and stranger-begs than I did on old servants and Andijanis; this I have always done whenever the Most High God has shown me His favour; yet it is remarkable that, spite of this, people have blamed me constantly as though I had favoured none but old servants and Andijanis. There is a proverb, (Turki) "What will a foe not say? what enters not into dream?" and (Persian) "A town-gate can be shut, a foe's mouth never."

Fol. 144*b*.

1 Burnes and Vigne describe a fall 20 miles from Kabul, at "Tangi Gharoi", [below where the Tag-au joins the Baran-water,] to which in their day, Kabulis went out for the amusement of catching fish as they try to leap up the fall. Were these migrants seeking upper waters or were they captives in a fish-pond?
2 Elph. MS. f. 111; W.-i-B. I.O. 215 f. 116*b* and 217 f. 97*b*; Mems. p. 155; *Méms.* i, 318.
3 *mihman-beglar*, an expression first used by Babur here, and due, presumably, to accessions from Khusrau Shah's following. A parallel case is given in Max Muller's *Science of Language* i, 348 ed. 1871, "Turkman tribes … call themselves, not subjects, but guests of the Uzbeg Khans."
4 *tiyul-dik* in all the Turki MSS. Ilminsky, de Courteille and Zenker, *yitul-dik*, Turki, a fief.
5 *Wilayat khud hech birilmadi*; W.-i-B. 215 f. 116*b*, *Wilayat dada na shuda* and 217 f. 97*b*, *Wilayat khud hech dada na shud*. By this I understand that he kept the lands of Kabul itself in his own hands. He mentions (f. 350) and Gul-badan mentions (H.N. f. 40*b*) his resolve so to keep Kabul. I think he kept not only the fort but all lands constituting the Kabul *tuman* (f. 135*b* and note).

(b. A levy in grain.)

Many clans and hordes had come from Samarkand, Hisar and Qunduz into the Kabul-country. Kabul is a small country; it is also of the sword, not of the pen;[1] to take in money from it for all these tribesmen was impossible. It therefore seemed advisable to take in grain, provision for the families of these clans so that their men could ride on forays with the army. Accordingly it was decided to levy 30,000 ass-loads[2] of grain on Kabul, Ghazni and their dependencies; we knew nothing at that time about the harvests and incomings; the impost was excessive, and under it the country suffered very grievously.

In those days I devised the Baburi script.[3]

(c. Foray on the Hazara.)

A large tribute in horses and sheep had been laid on the Sultan Mas'udi Hazaras;[4] word came a few days after collectors had gone to receive it, that the Hazaras were refractory and would not give their goods. As these same tribesmen had before that come down on the Ghazni and Girdiz roads, we got to horse, meaning to take them by surprise. Riding by the Maidan-road, we crossed the Nirkh-pass[5] by night and at the Morning-prayer fell upon them near Jal-tu (var. Cha-tu). The incursion was not what was wished.[6] We came back by the Tunnel-rock (Sang-i-surakh); Jahangir Mirza (there?) took leave for Ghazni. On our reaching Kabul, Yar-i-husain, son of Darya Khan, coming in from Bhira, waited on me.[7]

Fol. 145.

1 *Saifi dur, qalami aimas, i.e.* tax is taken by force, not paid on a written assessment.
2 *khar-war,* about 700 lbs Averdupois (Erskine). *Cf. Ayin-i-akbari* (Jarrett, ii, 394).
3 Nizamu'd-din Ahmad and Badayuni both mention this script and say that in it Babur transcribed a copy of the Qoran for presentation to Makka. Badayuni says it was unknown in his day, the reign of Akbar (*Tabaqat-i-akbari,* lith. ed. p. 193, and *Muntakhabu't-tawarikh* Bib. Ind. ed. iii, 273).
4 Babur's route, taken with one given by Raverty (*Notes* p. 691), allows these Hazaras, about whose location Mr. Erskine was uncertain, to be located between the Takht-pass (Arghandi-Maidan-Unai road), on their east, and the Sang-lakh mountains, on their west.
5 The Takht-pass, one on which from times immemorial, toll (*nirkh*) has been taken.
6 *khatir-khwah chapilmadi,* which perhaps implies mutual discontent, Babur's with his gains, the Hazaras' with their losses. As the second Persian translation omits the negative, the Memoirs does the same.
7 Bhira being in Shahpur, this Khan's *darya* will be the Jehlam.

(*d. Babur's first start for Hindustan.*)

When, a few days later, the army had been mustered, persons acquainted with the country were summoned and questioned about its every side and quarter. Some advised a march to the Plain (Dasht);[1] some approved of Bangash; some wished to go into Hindustan. The discussion found settlement in a move on Hindustan.

It was in the month of Sha'ban (910 AH.–Jan. 1505 AD.), the Sun being in Aquarius, that we rode out of Kabul for Hindustan. We took the road by Badam-chashma and Jagdalik and reached Adinapur in six marches. Till that time I had never seen a hot country or the Hindustan border-land. In Ningnahar[2] another world came to view,—other grasses, other trees, other animals, other birds, and other manners and customs of clan and horde. We were amazed, and truly there was ground for amaze.   Fol. 145*b*.

Nasir Mirza, who had gone earlier to his district, waited on me in Adinapur. We made some delay in Adinapur in order to let the men from behind join us, also a contingent from the clans which had come with us into Kabul and were wintering in the Lamghanat.[3] All having joined us, we marched to below Jui-shahi and dismounted at Qush-gumbaz.[4] There Nasir Mirza asked for leave to stay behind, saying he would follow in a few days after making some sort of provision for his dependants and followers. Marching on from Qush-gumbaz, when we dismounted at Hot-spring (Garm-chashma), a head-man of the Gagiani was brought in, a *Fajji*,[5] presumably with his caravan. We took him with us to point out the roads. Crossing Khaibar in a march or two, we dismounted at Jam.[6]

1 Babur uses Persian *dasht* and Hindi *duki*, plain and hill, for the tracts east and west of Mehtar Sulaiman. The first, *dasht*, stands for Daman (skirt) and Dara-i-jat, the second, *duki*, indefinitely for the broken lands west of the main range, but also, in one instance for the Duki [Dugi] district of Qandahar, as will be noted.
2 f. 132. The Jagdalik-pass for centuries has separated the districts of Kabul and Ningnahar. Forster (*Travels* ii, 68), making the journey the reverse way, was sensible of the climatic change some 3m. east of Gandamak. *Cf.* Wood's *Report* I. p. 6.
3 These are they whose families Nasir Mirza shepherded out of Kabul later (f. 154, f. 155).
4 Bird's-dome, opposite the mouth of the Kunar-water (*S.A. War*, Map p. 64).
5 This word is variously pointed and is uncertain. Mr. Erskine adopted "Pekhi", but, on the whole, it may be best to read, here and on f. 146, Ar. *fajj* or pers. *paj*, mountain or pass. To do so shews the guide to be one located in the Khaibar-pass, a *Fajji* or *Paji*.
6 mod. Jam-rud (Jam-torrent), presumably.

Tales had been told us about Gur-khattri;[1] it was said to be a holy place of the Jogis and Hindus who come from long distances to shave their heads and beards there. I rode out at once from Jam to visit Bigram,[2] saw its great tree,[3] and all the country round, but, much as we enquired about Gur-khattri, our guide, one Malik Bu-sa'id *Kamari*,[4] would say nothing

Fol. 146. about it. When we were almost back in camp, however, he told Khwaja Muhammad-amin that it was in Bigram and that he had said nothing about it because of its confined cells and narrow passages. The Khwaja, having there and then abused him, repeated to us what he had said, but we could not go back because the road was long and the day far spent.

(*e. Move against Kohat.*)

Whether to cross the water of Sind, or where else to go, was discussed in that camp.[5] Baqi *Chaghaniani* represented that it seemed we might go, without crossing the river and with one night's halt, to a place called Kohat where were many rich tribesmen; moreover he brought Kabulis forward who represented the matter just as he had done. We had never heard of the place, but, as he, my man in great authority, saw it good to go to Kohat and had brought forward support of his recommendation,—this being so! we broke up our plan of crossing the Sind-water into Hindustan, marched from Jam, forded the Bara-water, and dismounted not far from the pass (*daban*) through the Muhammad-mountain (*fajj*). At the time the Gagiani Afghans were located in Parashawar but, in dread of our army, had drawn off to the skirt-hills. One of their head-men, Khusrau *Gagiani*, coming into this camp, did me obeisance; we took him,

---

1 G. of I. xx, 125 and Cunningham's *Ancient History* i, 80. Babur saw the place in 925 AH. (f. 232b).

2 Cunningham, p. 29. Four ancient sites, not far removed from one another, bear this name, Bigram, *viz*. those near Hupian, Kabul, Jalalabad and Pashawar.

3 Cunningham, i, 79.

4 Perhaps a native of Kamari on the Indus, but *kamari* is a word of diverse application.

5 The annals of this campaign to the eastward shew that Babur was little of a free agent; that many acts of his own were merciful; that he sets down the barbarity of others as it was, according to his plan of writing (f. 86); and that he had with him undisciplined robbers of Khusrau Shah's former following. He cannot be taken as having power to command or control the acts of those, his guest-begs and their following, who dictated his movements in this disastrous journey, one worse than a defeat, says Haidar Mirza.

as well as the Fajji, with us, so that, between them, they might point out the roads. We left that camp at midnight, crossed Muhammad-fajj at day-rise[1] and by breakfast-time descended on Kohat. Much cattle and buffalo fell to our men; many Afghans were taken but I had them all collected and set them free. In the Kohat houses corn was found without limit. Our foragers raided as far as the Sind-river (*darya*), rejoining us after one night's halt. As what Baqi *Chaghaniani* had led us to expect did not come to hand, he grew rather ashamed of his scheme.

When our foragers were back and after two nights in Kohat, we took counsel together as to what would be our next good move, and we decided to over-run the Afghans of Bangash and the Bannu neighbourhood, then to go back to Kabul, either through Naghr (Baghzan?), or by the Farmul-road (Tochi-valley?).

In Kohat, Darya Khan's son, Yar-i-husain, who had waited on me in Kabul made petition, saying, "If royal orders were given me for the Dilazak,[2] the Yusuf-zai, and the Gagiani, these would not go far from my orders if I called up the Padshah's swords on the other side of the water of Sind."[3] The farman he petitioned for being given, he was allowed to go from Kohat.

(f. March to Thal.)

Marching out of Kohat, we took the Hangu-road for Bangash. Between Kohat and Hangu that road runs through a valley shut in on either hand by the mountains. When we entered this valley, the Afghans of Kohat and thereabouts who were gathered on both hill-skirts, raised their war-cry with great clamour. Our then guide, Malik Bu-sa'id *Kamari* was well-acquainted with the Afghan locations; he represented that further on there was a detached hill on our right, where, if the Afghans came down to it from the hill-skirt, we might surround and take them. God brought it right! The Afghans, on reaching the place, did come down. We ordered one party of braves to seize the neck of land

1 For the route here *see* Masson, i, 117 and Colquhoun's *With the Kuram Field-force* p. 48.
2 The Hai. MS. writes this Dilah-zak.
3 *i.e.* raised a force in Babur's name. He took advantage of this *farman* in 911 AH. to kill Baqi *Chaghaniani* (f. 159b-160).

between that hill and the mountains, others to move along
its sides, so that under attack made from all sides at once, the
Afghans might be made to reach their doom. Against the all-
round assault, they could not even fight; a hundred or two were
taken, some were brought in alive but of most, the heads only
were brought. We had been told that when Afghans are power-
less to resist, they go before their foe with grass between their
teeth, this being as much as to say, "I am your cow."[1] Here
Fol. 147b. we saw this custom; Afghans unable to make resistance, came
before us with grass between their teeth. Those our men had
brought in as prisoners were ordered to be beheaded and a
pillar of their heads was set up in our camp.[2]

Next day we marched forward and dismounted at Hangu,
where local Afghans had made a *sangur* on a hill. I first heard
the word *sangur* after coming to Kabul where people describe
fortifying themselves on a hill as making a *sangur*. Our men
went straight up, broke into it and cut off a hundred or two of
insolent Afghan heads. There also a pillar of heads was set up.

From Hangu we marched, with one night's halt, to Til (Thal),[3]
below Bangash; there also our men went out and raided the
Afghans near-by; some of them however turned back rather
lightly from a *sangur*.[4]

(g. Across country into Bannu.)

On leaving Til (Thal) we went, without a road, right down
a steep descent, on through out-of-the-way narrows, halted one
night, and next day came down into Bannu,[5] man, horse and
camel all worn out with fatigue and with most of the booty in
cattle left on the way. The frequented road must have been

1 Of the Yusuf-zai and Ranjit-singh, Masson says, (i, 141) "The miserable, hunted
wretches threw themselves on the ground, and placing a blade or tuft of grass in
their mouths, cried out, 'I am your cow.' This act and explanation, which would
have saved them from an orthodox Hindu, had no effect with the infuriated
Sikhs." This form of supplication is at least as old as the days of Firdausi (Erskine,
p. 159 n.). The *Bahar-i-'ajam* is quoted by Vullers as saying that in India, suppliants
take straw in the mouth to indicate that they are blanched and yellow from fear.
2 This barbarous custom has always prevailed amongst the Tartar conquerors of
Asia (Erskine). For examples under Timur *see* Raverty's *Notes* p. 137.
3 For a good description of the road from Kohat to Thal *see* Bellew's *Mission* p. 104.
4 F. 88b has the same phrase about the doubtful courage of one Sayyidi Qara.
5 Not to the mod. town of Bannu, [that having been begun only in 1848 AD.]
but wherever their wrong road brought them out into the Bannu amphitheatre.
The Survey Map of 1868, No. 15, shews the physical features of the wrong route.

a few miles to our right; the one we came by did not seem a
riding-road at all; it was understood to be called the Gosfan- Fol. 148.
dliyar (Sheep-road),—*liyar* being Afghani for a road,—because
sometimes shepherds and herdsmen take their flocks and herds
by it through those narrows. Most of our men regarded our
being brought down by that left-hand road as an ill-design of
Malik Bu-sa'id *Kamari*.[1]

(h. Bannu and the 'Isa-khail country.)

The Bannu lands lie, a dead level, immediately outside the
Bangash and Naghr hills, these being to their north. The Bangash
torrent (the Kuram) comes down into Bannu and fertilizes its
lands. South(-east) of them are Chaupara and the water of Sind;
to their east is Din-kot; (south-)west is the Plain (Dasht), known
also as Bazar and Taq.[2] The Bannu lands are cultivated by the
Kurani, Kiwi, Sur, 'Isa-khail and Nia-zai of the Afghan tribesmen.

After dismounting in Bannu, we heard that the tribesmen
in the Plain (Dasht) were for resisting and were entrenching
themselves on a hill to the north. A force headed by Jahangir
Mirza, went against what seemed to be the Kiwi *sangur*, took
it at once, made general slaughter, cut off and brought in many
heads. Much white cloth fell into (their) hands. In Bannu also
a pillar of heads was set up. After the *sangur* had been taken, the
Kiwi head-man, Shadi Khan, came to my presence, with grass
between his teeth, and did me obeisance. I pardoned all the
prisoners.

After we had over-run Kohat, it had been decided that
Bangash and Bannu should be over-run, and return to Kabul Fol. 148b.
made through Naghr or through Farmul. But when Bannu had
been over-run, persons knowing the country represented that
the Plain was close by, with its good roads and many people;
so it was settled to over-run the Plain and to return to Kabul
afterwards by way of Farmul.[3]

1 Perhaps he connived at recovery of cattle by those raided already.

2 Taq is the Tank of Maps; Bazar was s.w. of it. Tank for Taq looks to be a variant
due to nasal utterance (Vigne, p. 77, p. 203 and Map; and, as bearing on the nasal,
in loco, Appendix E).

3 If return had been made after over-running Bannu, it would have been made by
the Tochi-valley and so through Farmul; if after over-running the Plain, Babur's
details shew that the westward turn was meant to be by the Gumal-valley and one of

Marching next day, we dismounted at an 'Isa-khail village on that same water (the Kuram) but, as the villagers had gone into the Chaupara hills on hearing of us, we left it and dismounted on the skirt of Chaupara. Our foragers went from there into the hills, destroyed the 'Isa-khail *sangur* and came back with sheep, herds and cloth. That night the 'Isa-khail made an attack on us but, as good watch was kept all through these operations, they could do nothing. So cautious were we that at night our right and left, centre and van were just in the way they had dismounted, each according to its place in battle, each prepared for its own post, with men on foot all round the camp, at an arrow's distance from the tents. Every night the army was posted in this way and every night three or four of my household

made the rounds with torches, each in his turn. I for my part made the round once each night. Those not at their posts had their noses slit and were led round through the army. Jahangir Mirza was the right wing, with Baqi *Chaghaniani*, Sherim Taghai, Sayyid Husain Akbar, and other begs. Mirza Khan was the left wing, with 'Abdu'r-razzaq Mirza, Qasim Beg and other begs. In the centre there were no great begs, all were household-begs. Sayyid Qasim Lord-of-the-gate, was the van, with Baba Aughuli, Allah-birdi (var. Allah-quli Puran), and some other begs. The army was in six divisions, each of which had its day and night on guard.

Marching from that hill-skirt, our faces set west, we dismounted on a waterless plain (*qul*) between Bannu and the Plain. The soldiers got water here for themselves, their herds and so on, by digging down, from one to one-and-a-half yards, into the dry water-course, when water came. Not here only did this happen for all the rivers of Hindustan have the peculiarity that water is safe to be found by digging down from one to one-and-a-half yards in their beds. It is a wonderful provision of God that where, except for the great rivers, there are no running-waters,[1] water should be so placed within reach in dry water-courses.

---

two routes out of it, still to Farmul; but the extended march southward to near Dara-i-Ghazi Khan made the westward turn be taken through the valley opening at Sakhi-sawar.

1 This will mean, none of the artificial runlets familiar where Babur had lived before getting to know Hindustan.

We left that dry channel next morning. Some of our men, riding light, reached villages of the Plain in the afternoon, raided a few, and brought back flocks, cloth and horses bred for trade.[1] Pack-animals and camels and also the braves we had outdistanced, kept coming into camp all through that night till dawn and on till that morrow's noon. During our stay there, the foragers   Fol. 149b. brought in from villages in the Plain, masses of sheep and cattle, and, from Afghan traders met on the roads, white cloths, aromatic roots, sugars, *tipuchaqs*, and horses bred for trade. Hindi (var. Mindi) *Mughul* unhorsed Khwaja Khizr *Nuhani*, a well-known and respected Afghan merchant, cutting off and bringing in his head. Once when Sherim Taghai went in the rear of the foragers, an Afghan faced him on the road and struck off his index-finger.

(i. Return made for Kabul.)

Two roads were heard of as leading from where we were to Ghazni; one was the Tunnel-rock (Sang-i-surakh) road, passing Birk (Barak) and going on to Farmul; the other was one along the Gumal, which also comes out at Farmul but without touching Birk (Barak).[2] As during our stay in the Plain rain had fallen incessantly, the Gumal was so swollen that it would have been difficult to cross at the ford we came to; moreover persons well-acquainted with the roads, represented that going by the Gumal road, this torrent must be crossed several times, that this was always difficult when the waters were so high and that there was always uncertainty on the Gumal road. Nothing was settled then as to which of these two roads to take; I expected it to be settled next day when, after the drum of departure had sounded,   Fol. 150. we talked it over as we went.[3] It was the 'Id-i-fitr (March 7th 1505 AD.); while I was engaged in the ablutions due for the breaking of the fast, Jahangir Mirza and the begs discussed

1 *sauda-at*, perhaps, pack-ponies, perhaps, bred for sale and not for own use. Burnes observes that in 1837 Luhani merchants (for Luhani/Nuhani *see* p. 455 n. 3, p. 659 n. 1) carried precisely the same articles of trade as in Babur's day, 332 years earlier (*Report* IX p. 99).

2 Mr. Erskine thought it probable that the first of these routes went through Kaniguram, and the second through the Ghwaliri-pass and along the Gumal. *Birk*, fastness, would seem an appropriate name for Kaniguram, but, if Babur meant to go to Ghazni, he would be off the ordinary Gumal-Ghazni route in going through Farmul (Aurgun). Raverty's *Notes* give much useful detail about these routes, drawn from native sources. For Barak (Birk) *see Notes* pp. 88, 89; Vigne, p. 102.

3 From this it would seem that the alternative roads were approached by one in common.

the question of the roads. Some-one said that if we were to
turn the bill[1] of the Mehtar Sulaiman range, this lying between
the Plain and the Hill-country (*desht u duki*),[2] we should get
a level road though it might make the difference of a few marches.
For this they decided and moved off; before my ablutions were
finished the whole army had taken the road and most of it was
across the Gumal. Not a man of us had ever seen the road;
no-one knew whether it was long or short; we started off just
on a rumoured word!

The Prayer of the 'Id was made on the bank of the Gumal.
That year New-year's Day[3] fell close to the 'Id-i-fitr, there being
only a few days between; on their approximation I composed
the following (Turki) ode:—

> Glad is the Bairam-moon for him who sees both the face of the Moon and
> the Moon-face of his friend;
> Sad is the Bairam-moon for me, far away from thy face and from thee.[4]
> O Babur! dream of your luck when your Feast is the meeting, your New-year
> the face;
> For better than that could not be with a hundred New-years and Bairams.

After crossing the Gumal torrent, we took our way along the
skirt of the hills, our faces set south. A mile or two further on,
Fol. 150b. some death-devoted Afghans shewed themselves on the lower
edge of the hill-slope. Loose rein, off we went for them; most
of them fled but some made foolish stand on rocky-piles[5] of the
foot-hills. One took post on a single rock seeming to have
a precipice on the further side of it, so that he had not even a way
of escape. Sl. Quli *Chunaq* (One-eared), all in his mail as he was,
got up, slashed at, and took him. This was one of Sl. Quli's
deeds done under my own eyes, which led to his favour and
promotion.[6] At another pile of rock, when Qutluq-qadam
exchanged blows with an Afghan, they grappled and came down

---

1 *tumshuq*, a bird's bill, used here, as in Selsey-bill, for the naze (nose), or snout,
the last spur, of a range.

2 Here these words may be common nouns.

3 Nu-roz, the feast of the old Persian New-year (Erskine); it is the day on which
the Sun enters Aries.

4 In the [Turki] Elph. and Hai. MSS. and in some Persian ones, there is a space
left here as though to indicate a known omission.

5 *kamari*, sometimes a cattle-enclosure, which may serve as a *sangur*. The word may
stand in one place of its *Babur-nama* uses for Gum-rahi (R.'s *Notes s.n.* Gumrahan).

6 Index *s.n.*

together, a straight fall of 10 to 12 yards; in the end Qutluq-qadam cut off and brought in his man's head. Kupuk Beg got hand-on-collar with an Afghan at another hill; both rolled down to the bottom; that head also was brought in. All Afghans taken prisoner were set free.

Marching south through the Plain, and closely skirting Mehtar Sulaiman, we came, with three nights' halt, to a small township, called Bilah, on the Sind-water and dependent on Multan.[1] The villagers crossed the water, mostly taking to their boats, but some flung themselves in to cross. Some were seen standing on an island in front of Bilah. Most of our men, man and horse in mail, plunged in and crossed to the island; some were carried down, one being Qul-i-aruk (thin slave), one of my servants, another the head tent-pitcher, another Jahangir Mirza's servant, Qaitmas *Turkman*.[2] Cloth and things of the baggage (*partaldik nima*) fell to our men. The villagers all crossed by boat to the further side of the river; once there, some of them, trusting to the broad water, began to make play with their swords. Qul-i-bayazid, the taster, one of our men who had crossed to the island, stripped himself and his horse and, right in front of them, plunged by himself into the river. The water on that side of the island may have been twice or thrice as wide as on ours. He swum his horse straight for them till, an arrow's-flight away, he came to a shallow where his weight must have been up-borne, the water being as high as the saddle-flap. There he stayed for as long as milk takes to boil; no-one supported him from behind; he had not a chance of support. He made a dash at them; they shot a few arrows at him but, this not checking him, they took to flight. To swim such a river as the Sind, alone, bare on a bare-backed horse, no-one behind him, and to chase off a foe and occupy his ground, was a mightily bold deed! He having driven the enemy off, other soldiers went over who returned with cloth and droves of various sorts. Qul-i-bayazid had already his place in my favour and kindness on account of his good service, and of courage several times shewn; from the cook's office I had raised him to the royal taster's; this time, as

Fol. 151.

Fol. 151b.

---

1 Vigne, p. 241.
2 This name can be translated "He turns not back" or "He stops not".

will be told, I took up a position full of bounty, favour and promotion,—in truth he was worthy of honour and advancement.

Two other marches were made down the Sind-water. Our men, by perpetually galloping off on raids, had knocked up their horses; usually what they took, cattle mostly, was not worth the gallop; sometimes indeed in the Plain there had been sheep, sometimes one sort of cloth or other, but, the Plain left behind, nothing was had but cattle. A mere servant would bring in 3 or 400 head during our marches along the Sind-water, but every march many more would be left on the road than they brought in.

(*j. The westward march.*)

Having made three more marches[1] close along the Sind, we left it when we came opposite Pir Kanu's tomb.[2] Going to the tomb, we there dismounted. Some of our soldiers having injured Fol. 152. several of those in attendance on it, I had them cut to pieces. It is a tomb on the skirt of one of the Mehtar Sulaiman mountains and held in much honour in Hindustan.

Marching on from Pir Kanu, we dismounted in the (Pawat) pass; next again in the bed of a torrent in Duki.[3] After we left this camp there were brought in as many as 20 to 30 followers of a retainer of Shah Beg, Fazil *Kukuldash*, the darogha of Siwi. They had been sent to reconnoitre us but, as at that time, we were not on bad terms with Shah Beg, we let them go, with horse and arms. After one night's halt, we reached Chutiali, a village of Duki.

Although our men had constantly galloped off to raid, both before we reached the Sind-water and all along its bank, they had not left horses behind, because there had been plenty of green food and corn. When, however, we left the river and set our faces for Pir Kanu, not even green food was to be had; a little land under green crop might be found every two or three

1 *i.e.* five from Bilah.
2 Raverty gives the saint's name as Pir Kanun (Ar. *kanun*, listened to). It is the well-known Sakhi-sarwar, honoured by Hindus and Muhammadans. (G. of I., xxi, 390; R.'s *Notes* p. 11 and p. 12 and JASB 1855; Calcutta Review 1875, Macauliffe's art. *On the fair at Sakhi-sarwar*; Leech's *Report* VII, for the route; *Khazinatu 'l-asfiya* iv, 245.)
3 This seems to be the sub-district of Qandahar, Duki or Dugi.

marches, but of horse-corn, none. So, beyond the camps mentioned, there began the leaving of horses behind. After passing Chutiali, my own felt-tent[1] had to be left from want of baggage-beasts. One night at that time, it rained so much, that water stood knee-deep in my tent (*chadar*); I watched the night out till dawn, uncomfortably sitting on a pile of blankets.

(*k. Baqi Chaghaniani's treachery.*)

A few marches further on came Jahangir Mirza, saying, "I have a private word for you." When we were in private, he said, "Baqi *Chaghaniani* came and said to me, 'You make the Padshah cross the water of Sind with 7, 8, 10 persons, then make yourself Padshah.'" Said I, "What others are heard of as consulting with him?" Said he, "It was but a moment ago Baqi Beg spoke to me; I know no more." Said I, "Find out who the others are; likely enough Sayyid Husain Akbar and Sl. 'Ali the page are in it, as well as Khusrau Shah's begs and braves." Here the Mirza really behaved very well and like a blood-relation; what he now did was the counterpart of what I had done in Kahmard,[2] in this same ill-fated mannikin's other scheme of treachery.[3]

On dismounting after the next march, I made Jahangir Mirza lead a body of well-mounted men to raid the Aughans (Afghans) of that neighbourhood.

Many men's horses were now left behind in each camping-ground, the day coming when as many as 2 or 300 were left. Braves of the first rank went on foot; Sayyid Mahmud *Aughlaqchi*, one of the best of the household-braves, left his horses behind and walked. In this state as to horses we went all the rest of the way to Ghazni.

Three or four marches further on, Jahangir Mirza plundered some Afghans and brought in a few sheep.

(*l. The Ab-i-istada.*)

When, with a few more marches, we reached the Standing-water (*Ab-i-istada*) a wonderfully large sheet of water presented

1 *khar-gah*, a folding tent on lattice frame-work, perhaps a *khibitka*.
2 It may be more correct to write Kah-mard, as the Hai. MS. does and to understand in the name a reference to the grass(*kah*)-yielding capacity of the place.
3 f. 121.

itself to view; the level lands on its further side could not be seen at all; its water seemed to join the sky; the higher land and the mountains of that further side looked to hang between Heaven and Earth, as in a mirage. The waters there gathered are said to be those of the spring-rain floods of the Kattawaz-plain, the Zurmut-valley, and the Qara-bagh meadow of the Ghazni-torrent,—floods of the spring-rains, and the over-plus[1] of the summer-rise of streams.

When within two miles of the Ab-i-istada, we saw a wonderful thing,—something as red as the rose of the dawn kept shewing and vanishing between the sky and the water. It kept coming and going. When we got quite close we learned that what seemed the cause were flocks of geese,[2] not 10,000, not 20,000 in a flock, but geese innumerable which, when the mass of birds flapped their wings in flight, sometimes shewed red feathers, sometimes not. Not only was this bird there in countless numbers, but birds of every sort. Eggs lay in masses on the shore. When two Afghans, come there to collect eggs, saw us, Fol. 153b. they went into the water half a *kuroh* (a mile). Some of our men following, brought them back. As far as they went the water was of one depth, up to a horse's belly; it seemed not to lie in a hollow, the country being flat.

We dismounted at the torrent coming down to the Ab-i-istada from the plain of Kattawaz. The several other times we have passed it, we have found a dry channel with no water whatever,[3] but this time, there was so much water, from the spring-rains, that no ford could be found. The water was not very broad but very deep. Horses and camels were made to swim it; some of the baggage was hauled over with ropes. Having got across, we went on through Old Nani and Sar-i-dih to Ghazni where for a few days Jahangir Mirza was our host, setting food before us and offering his tribute.

1 This may mean, what irrigation has not used.
2 Mr. Erskine notes that the description would lead us to imagine a flock of flamingoes. Masson found the lake filled with red-legged, white fowl (i, 262); these and also what Babur saw, may have been the China-goose which has body and neck white, head and tail russet (Bellew's *Mission* p. 402). Broadfoot seems to have visited the lake when migrants were few, and through this to have been led to adverse comment on Babur's accuracy (p. 350).
3 The usual dryness of the bed may have resulted from the irrigation of much land some 12 miles from Ghazni.

(m. Return to Kabul.)

That year most waters came down in flood. No ford was found through the water of Dih-i-yaq'ub.[1] For this reason we went straight on to Kamari, through the Sajawand-pass. At Kamari I had a boat fashioned in a pool, brought and set on the Dih-i-yaq'ub-water in front of Kamari. In this all our people were put over.

We reached Kabul in the month of Zu'l-hijja (May 1505 AD.).[2] A few days earlier Sayyid Yusuf *Aughlaqchi* had gone to God's mercy through the pains of colic.

Fol. 154.

(n. Misconduct of Nasir Mirza.)

It has been mentioned that at Qush-gumbaz, Nasir Mirza asked leave to stay behind, saying that he would follow in a few days after taking something from his district for his retainers and followers.[3] But having left us, he sent a force against the people of Nur-valley, they having done something a little refractory. The difficulty of moving in that valley owing to the strong position of its fort and the rice-cultivation of its lands, has already been described.[4] The Mirza's commander, Fazli, in ground so impracticable and in that one-road tract, instead of safe-guarding his men, scattered them to forage. Out came the valesmen, drove the foragers off, made it impossible to the rest to keep their ground, killed some, captured a mass of others and of horses,—precisely what would happen to any army chancing to be under such a person as Fazli! Whether because of this affair, or whether from want of heart, the Mirza did not follow us at all; he stayed behind.

Moreover Ayub's sons, Yusuf and Bahlul (Begchik), more seditious, silly and arrogant persons than whom there may not exist,—to whom I had given, to Yusuf Alangar, to Bahlul 'Ali-shang, they like Nasir Mirza, were to have taken something from their districts and to have come on with him, but, he not coming,

Fol. 154b.

1 This is the Luhugur (Logar) water, knee-deep in winter at the ford but spreading in flood with the spring-rains. Babur, not being able to cross it for the direct roads into Kabul, kept on along its left bank, crossing it eventually at the Kamari of maps, s.e. of Kabul.
2 This disastrous expedition, full of privation and loss, had occupied some four months (T.R. p. 201).
3 f. 145b.   4 f. 133b and Appendix F.

neither did they. All that winter they were the companions of his cups and social pleasures. They also over-ran the Tarkalani Afghans in it.[1] With the on-coming heats, the Mirza made march off the families of the clans, outside-tribes and hordes who had wintered in Ningnahar and the Lamghanat, driving them like sheep before him, with all their goods, as far as the Baran-water.[2]

(*o. Affairs of Badakhshan.*)

While Nasir Mirza was in camp on the Baran-water, he heard that the Badakhshis were united against the Auzbegs and had killed some of them.

Here are the particulars:—When Shaibaq Khan had given Qunduz to Qambar Bi and gone himself to Khwarizm;[3] Qambar Bi, in order to conciliate the Badakhshis, sent them a son of Muhammad-i-makhdumi, Mahmud by name, but Mubarak Shah,—whose ancestors are heard of as begs of the Badakhshan Shahs,—having uplifted his own head, and cut off Mahmud's and those of some Auzbegs, made himself fast in the fort once known as Shaf-tiwar but re-named by him Qila'-i-zafar. Moreover, in Rustaq Muhammad *qurchi*, an armourer of Khusrau Shah, then occupying Khamalangan, slew Shaibaq Khan's *sadr* and some Auzbegs and made that place fast. Zubair of Ragh, again, whose forefathers also will have been begs of the Badakhshan Shahs, uprose in Ragh.[4] Jahangir *Turkman*, again, a servant of Khusrau Shah's Wali, collected some of the fugitive soldiers and tribesmen Wali had left behind, and with them withdrew into a fastness.[5]

Fol. 155.

Nasir Mirza, hearing these various items of news and spurred on by the instigation of a few silly, short-sighted persons to covet Badakhshan, marched along the Shibr-tu and Ab-dara road, driving like sheep before him the families of the men who had come into Kabul from the other side of the Amu.[6]

1 They were located in Mandrawar in 926 AH. (f. 251).
2 This was done, manifestly, with the design of drawing after the families their fighting men, then away with Babur.
3 f. 163. Shaibaq Khan besieged Chin Sufi, Sl. Husain Mirza's man in Khwarizm (T.R. p. 204; *Shaibani-nama*, Vambéry, Table of Contents and note 89).
4 Survey Map 1889, Sadda. The Ragh-water flows n.w. into the Oxus (Amu).
5 *birk*, a mountain stronghold; *cf.* f. 149*b* note to Birk (Barak).
6 They were thus driven on from the Baran-water (f. 154*b*).

(*p. Affairs of Khusrau Shah.*)

At the time Khusrau Shah and Ahmad-i-qasim were in flight from Ajar for Khurasan,[1] they meeting in with Badi'u'z-zaman Mirza and Zu'n-nun Beg, all went on together to the presence of Sl. Husain Mirza in Heri. All had long been foes of his; all had behaved unmannerly to him; what brands had they not set on his heart! Yet all now went to him in their distress, and all went through me. For it is not likely they would have seen him if I had not made Khusrau Shah helpless by parting him from his following, and if I had not taken Kabul from Zu'n'nun's son, Muqim. Badi'u'z-zaman Mirza himself was as dough in the hands of the rest; beyond their word he could not go. Sl. Husain Mirza took up a gracious attitude towards one and all, mentioned no-one's misdeeds, even made them gifts. Fol. 155b.

Shortly after their arrival Khusrau Shah asked for leave to go to his own country, saying, "If I go, I shall get it all into my hands." As he had reached Heri without equipment and without resources, they finessed a little about his leave. He became importunate. Muhammad Baranduq retorted roundly on him with, "When you had 30,000 men behind you and the whole country in your hands, what did you effect against the Auzbeg? What will you do now with your 500 men and the Auzbegs in possession?" He added a little good advice in a few sensible words, but all was in vain because the fated hour of Khusrau Shah's death was near. Leave was at last given because of his importunity; Khusrau Shah with his 3 or 400 followers, went straight into the borders of Dahanah. There as Nasir Mirza had just gone across, these two met.

Now the Badakhshi chiefs had invited only the Mirza; they had not invited Khusrau Shah. Try as the Mirza did to persuade Khusrau Shah to go into the hill-country,[2] the latter, quite understanding the whole time, would not consent to go, his own idea being that if he marched under the Mirza, he would get the country into his own hands. In the end, unable to agree, each of them, near Ishkimish, arrayed his following, put on mail, drew out to fight, and—departed. Nasir Mirza went on for Badakhshan; Khusrau Shah after collecting a disorderly rabble, good and bad Fol. 156.

1 f. 126b.   2 Hisar, presumably.

of some 1000 persons, went, with the intention of laying siege
to Qunduz, to Khwaja Char-taq, one or two *yighach* outside it.

(*q. Death of Khusrau Shah.*)

At the time Shaibaq Khan, after overcoming Sultan Ahmad
Tambal and Andijan, made a move on Hisar, his Honour
Khusrau Shah[1] flung away his country (Qunduz and Hisar)
without a blow struck, and saved himself. Thereupon Shaibaq
Khan went to Hisar in which were Sherim the brave and a few
good braves. *They* did not surrender Hisar, though their
honourable beg had flung *his* country away and gone off; they
made Hisar fast. The siege of Hisar Shaibaq Khan entrusted to
Hamza Sl. and Mahdi Sultan,[2] went to Qunduz, gave Qunduz to
his younger brother, Mahmud Sultan and betook himself without
delay to Khwarizm against Chin Sufi. But as, before he reached
Samarkand on his way to Khwarizm, he heard of the death in
Qunduz of his brother, Mahmud Sultan, he gave that place to
Qambar Bi of Marv.[3]

Qambar Bi was in Qunduz when Khusrau Shah went against
it; he at once sent off gallopers to summon Hamza Sl. and the
Fol. 156b. others Shaibaq Khan had left behind. Hamza Sl. came himself
as far as the *sarai* on the Amu bank where he put his sons and
begs in command of a force which went direct against Khusrau
Shah. There was neither fight nor flight for that fat, little man;
Hamza Sultan's men unhorsed him, killed his sister's son,
Ahmad-i-qasim, Sherim the brave and several good braves. Him
they took into Qunduz, there struck his head off and from there
sent it to Shaibaq Khan in Khwarizm.[4]

(*r. Conduct in Kabul of Khusrau Shah's retainers.*)

Just as Khusrau Shah had said they would do, his former
retainers and followers, no sooner than he marched against

---

1 Here "His Honour" translates Babur's clearly ironical honorific plural.
2 These two sultans, almost always mentioned in alliance, may be Timurids by
maternal descent (Index *s.nn.*). So far I have found no direct statement of their
parentage. My husband has shewn me what may be one indication of it, *viz.* that
two of the uncles of Shaibaq Khan (whose kinsmen the sultans seem to be),
Quj-kunji and Siunjak, were sons of a daughter of the Timurid Aulugh Beg
Samarkandi (H.S. ii, 318). *See* Vambéry's *Bukhara* p. 248 note.
3 For the deaths of Tambal and Mahmud, mentioned in the above summary of
Shaibaq Khan's actions, *see* the *Shaibani-nama*, Vambéry, p. 323.
4 H.S. ii, 323, for Khusrau Shah's character and death.

Qunduz, changed in their demeanour to me,[1] most of them marching off to near Khwaja-i-riwaj.[2] The greater number of the men in my service had been in his. The Mughuls behaved well, taking up a position of adherence to me.[3] On all this the news of Khusrau Shah's death fell like water on fire; it put his men out.

1 f. 124.
2 Khwaja-of-the-rhubarb, presumably a shrine near rhubarb-grounds (f. 129b).
3 *yakshi bardilar*, lit. went well, a common expression in the *Babur-nama*, of which the reverse statement is *yamanlik bila bardi* (f. 163). Some Persian MSS. make the Mughuls disloyal but this is not only in opposition to the Turki text, it is a redundant statement since if disloyal, they are included in Babur's previous statement, as being Khusrau Shah's retainers. What might call for comment in Mughuls would be loyalty to Babur.

(a. Death of Qutluq-nigar Khanim.)

In the month of Muharram my mother had fever. Blood was let without effect and a Khurasani doctor, known as Sayyid Tabib, in accordance with the Khurasan practice, gave her water-melon, but her time to die must have come, for on the Saturday after six days of illness, she went to God's mercy.

On Sunday I and Qasim Kukuldash conveyed her to the New-year's Garden on the mountain-skirt[2] where Aulugh Beg Mirza had built a house, and there, with the permission of his heirs,[3] we committed her to the earth. While we were mourning for her, people let me know about (the death of) my younger Khan *dada* Alacha Khan, and my grandmother Aisan-daulat Begim.[4] Close upon Khanim's Fortieth[5] arrived from Khurasan Shah Begim the mother of the Khans, together with my maternal-aunt Mihr-nigar Khanim, formerly of Sl. Ahmad Mirza's *haram*, and Muhammad Husain *Kurkan Dughlat*.[6] Lament broke out afresh; the bitterness of these partings was extreme. When the mourning-rites had been observed, food and victuals set out for the poor and destitute, the Qoran recited, and prayers offered for the departed souls, we steadied ourselves and all took heart again.

(b. A futile start for Qandahar.)

When set free from these momentous duties, we got an army to horse for Qandahar under the strong insistence of Baqi

---

Fol. 157.

1 Elph. MS. f. 121b: W.-i-B. I.O. 215 f. 126 and 217 f. 106b; Mems. p. 169.

2 *tagh-damanasi*, presumably the Koh-daman, and the garden will thus be the one of f. 136b.

3 If these heirs were descendants of Aulugh Beg M. one would be at hand in 'Abdu'r-razzaq, then a boy, and another, a daughter, was the wife of Muqim *Arghun*. As Mr. Erskine notes, Musalmans are most scrupulous not to bury their dead in ground gained by violence or wrong.

4 The news of Ahmad's death was belated; he died some 13 months earlier, in the end of 909 AH. and in Eastern Turkistan. Perhaps details now arrived.

5 *i.e.* the fortieth day of mourning, when alms are given.

6 Of those arriving, the first would find her step-daughter dead, the second her sister, the third, his late wife's sister (T.R. p. 196).

Chaghaniani. At the start I went to Qush-nadir (var. nawar) meadow where on dismounting I got fever. It was a strange sort of illness for whenever with much trouble I had been awakened, my eyes closed again in sleep. In four or five days I got quite well.

(c. An earthquake.)

At that time there was a great earthquake[1] such that most of the ramparts of forts and the walls of gardens fell down; houses were levelled to the ground in towns and villages and many persons lay dead beneath them. Every house fell in Paghman-village, and 70 to 80 strong heads-of-houses lay dead under their walls. Between Pagh-man and Beg-tut[2] a piece of ground, a good stone-throw[3] wide may-be, slid down as far as an arrow's-flight; where it had slid springs appeared. On the road between Istarghach and Maidan the ground was so broken up for 6 to 8 *yighach* (36–48 m.) that in some places it rose as high as an elephant, in others sank as deep; here and there people were sucked in. When the Earth quaked, dust rose from the tops of the mountains. Nuru'l-lah the *tambourchi*[4] had been playing before me; he had two instruments with him and at the moment of the quake had both in his hands; so out of his own control was he that the two knocked against each other. Jahangir Mirza was in the porch of an upper-room at a house built by Aulugh Beg Mirza in Tipa; when the Earth quaked, he let himself down and was not hurt, but the roof fell on some-one with him in that upper-room, presumably one of his own circle; that this person was not hurt in the least must have been solely through God's mercy. In Tipa most of the houses were levelled to the ground. The Earth quaked 33 times on the first day, and for a month afterwards used to quake two or three times in the 24 hours. The begs and soldiers having been

Fol. 157b.

---

1 This will be the earthquake felt in Agra on Safar 3rd 911 AH. (July 5th 1505 AD. Erskine's *History of India* i, 229 note). *Cf.* Elliot and Dowson, iv, 465 and v, 99.

2 Raverty's *Notes* p. 690.

3 *bir kitta tash atimi*; var. *bash atimi*. If *tash* be right, the reference will probably be to the throw of a catapult.

4 Here almost certainly, a drummer, because there were two tambours and because also Babur uses '*audi & ghachaki* for the other meanings of *tambourchi*, lutanist and guitarist. The word has found its way, as *tambourgi*, into Childe Harold's Pilgrimage (Canto ii, lxxii. H.B.).

ordered to repair the breaches made in the towers and ramparts of the fort (Kabul), everything was made good again in 20 days or a month by their industry and energy.

(*d. Campaign against Qalat-i-ghilzai.*)

Owing to my illness and to the earthquake, our plan of going to Qandahar had fallen somewhat into the background. The illness left behind and the fort repaired, it was taken up again. We were undecided at the time we dismounted below Shniz[1] whether to go to Qandahar, or to over-run the hills and plains. Jahangir Mirza and the begs having assembled, counsel was taken and the matter found settlement in a move on Qalat. On this move Jahangir Mirza and Baqi *Chaghaniani* insisted strongly.

At Tazi[2] there was word that Sher-i-'ali the page with Kichik Baqi *Diwana* and others had thoughts of desertion; all were arrested; Sher-i-'ali was put to death because he had given clear signs of disloyalty and misdoing both while in my service and not in mine, in this country and in that country.[3] The others were let go with loss of horse and arms.

On arriving at Qalat we attacked at once and from all sides, without our mail and without siege-appliances. As has been mentioned in this History, Kichik Khwaja, the elder brother of Khwaja Kalan, was a most daring brave; he had used his sword in my presence several times; he now clambered up the south-west tower of Qalat, was pricked in the eye with a spear when almost up, and died of the wound two or three days after the place was taken. Here that Kichik Baqi *Diwana* who had been arrested when about to desert with Sher-i-'ali the page, expiated his baseness by being killed with a stone when he went under the ramparts. One or two other men died also. Fighting of this sort went on till the Afternoon Prayer when, just as our men were worn-out with the struggle and labour, those in the fort asked for peace and made surrender. Qalat had been given by Zu'n-nun *Arghun* to Muqim, and in it now were Muqim's retainers, Farrukh *Arghun* and Qara *Bilut* (Afghan). When they came out with their swords and quivers hanging round

1 Kabul-Ghazni road (R.'s *Notes* index *s.n.*).
2 var. Yari. Tazi is on the Ghazni-Qalat-i-ghilzai road (R.'s *Notes*, Appendix p. 46).
3 *i.e.* in Kabul and in the Trans-Himalayan country.

their necks, we forgave their offences.[1] It was not my wish to reduce this high family[2] to great straits; for why? Because if we did so when such a foe as the Auzbeg was at our side, what would be said by those of far and near, who saw and heard?

As the move on Qalat had been made under the insistence of Jahangir Mirza and Baqi *Chaghaniani*, it was now made over to the Mirza's charge. He would not accept it; Baqi also could give no good answer in the matter. So, after such a storming and assaulting of Qalat, its capture was useless.

We went back to Kabul after over-running the Afghans of Sawa-sang and Ala-tagh on the south of Qalat.   Fol. 159.

The night we dismounted at Kabul I went into the fort; my tent and stable being in the Char-bagh, a Khirilchi thief going into the garden, fetched out and took away a bay horse of mine with its accoutrements, and my *khachar*.[3]

(e. Death of Baqi Chaghaniani.)

From the time Baqi *Chaghaniani* joined me on the Amu-bank, no man of mine had had more trust and authority.[4] If a word were said, if an act were done, that word was his word, that act, his act. Spite of this, he had not done me fitting service, nor had he shewn me due civility. Quite the contrary! he had done things bad and unmannerly. Mean he was, miserly and malicious, ill-tongued, envious and cross-natured. So miserly was he that although when he left Tirmiz, with his family and possessions, he may have owned 30 to 40,000 sheep, and although those masses of sheep used to pass in front of us at every camping-ground, he did not give a single one to our bare

1 These will be those against Babur's suzerainty done by their defence of Qalat for Muqim.

2 *tabaqa*, dynasty. By using this word Babur shews recognition of high birth. It is noticeable that he usually writes of an Arghun chief either simply as "Beg" or without a title. This does not appear to imply admission of equality, since he styles even his brothers and sisters Mirza and Begim; nor does it shew familiarity of intercourse, since none seems to have existed between him and Zu'n-nun or Muqim. That he did not admit equality is shewn on f. 208. The T.R. styles Zu'n-nun "Mirza", a title by which, as also by Shah, his descendants are found styled (A.-i-a. Blochmann, *s.n.*).

3 Turki *khachar* is a camel or mule used for carrying personal effects. The word has been read by some scribes as *khanjar*, dagger.

4 In 910 AH. he had induced Babur to come to Kabul instead of going into Khurasan (H.S. iii, 319); in the same year he dictated the march to Kohat, and the rest of that disastrous travel. His real name was not Baqi but Muhammad Baqir (H.S. iii, 311).

braves, tortured as they were by the pangs of hunger; at last in Kah-mard, he gave 50!

Spite of acknowledging me for his chief (*padshah*), he had nagarets beaten at his own Gate. He was sincere to none, had regard for none. What revenue there is from Kabul (town) comes from the *tamgha*;[1] the whole of this he had, together Fol. 159b. with the *darogha*-ship in Kabul and Panjhir, the Gadai (var. Kidi) Hazara, and *kushluk*[2] and control of the Gate.[3] With all this favour and finding, he was not in the least content; quite the reverse! What medley of mischief he planned has been told; we had taken not the smallest notice of any of it, nor had we cast it in his face. He was always asking for leave, affecting scruple at making the request. We used to acknowledge the scruple and excuse ourselves from giving the leave. This would put him down for a few days; then he would ask again. He went too far with his affected scruple and his takings of leave! Sick were we too of his conduct and his character. We gave the leave; he repented asking for it and began to agitate against it, but all in vain! He got written down and sent to me, "His Highness made compact not to call me to account till nine[4] misdeeds had issued from me." I answered with a reminder of eleven successive faults and sent this to him through Mulla Baba of Pashaghar. He submitted and was allowed to go towards Hindustan, taking his family and possessions. A few of his retainers escorted him through Khaibar and returned; he joined Baqi *Gagiani*'s caravan and crossed at Nil-ab.

Darya Khan's son, Yar-i-husain was then in Kacha-kot,[5] having drawn into his service, on the warrant of the *farman* taken from me in Kohat, a few Afghans of the Dilazak (var. Dilah-zak) and Yusuf-zai and also a few Jats and Gujurs.[6] With these he beat the roads, taking toll with might and main.

1 These transit or custom duties are so called because the dutiable articles are stamped with a *tamgha*, a wooden stamp.

2 Perhaps this word is an equivalent of Persian *goshi*, a tax on cattle and beasts of burden.

3 Baqi was one only and not the head of the Lords of the Gate.

4 The choice of the number nine, links on presumably to the mystic value attached to it e.g. Tarkhans had nine privileges; gifts were made by nines.

5 It is near Hasan-abdal (A. i-A. Jarrett, ii, 324).

6 For the *farman*, f. 146b; for Gujurs, G. of I.

Hearing about Baqi, he blocked the road, made the whole party prisoner, killed Baqi and took his wife.

We ourselves had let Baqi go without injuring him, but his own misdeeds rose up against him; his own acts defeated him.

> Leave thou to Fate the man who does thee wrong;
> For Fate is an avenging servitor.[1]

(f. Attack on the Turkman Hazaras.)

That winter we just sat in the Char-bagh till snow had fallen once or twice.

The Turkman Hazaras, since we came into Kabul, had done a variety of insolent things and had robbed on the roads. We thought therefore of over-running them, went into the town to Aulugh Beg Mirza's house at the Bustan-sarai, and thence rode out in the month of Sha'ban (Feb. 1506 AD.).

We raided a few Hazaras at Janglik, at the mouth of the Dara-i-khush (Happy-valley).[2] Some were in a cave near the valley-mouth, hiding perhaps. Shaikh Darwish Kukuldash went

> (*Author's note on Shaikh Darwish.*) He had been with me in the guerilla-times, was Master-armourer (*qur-begi*), drew a strong bow and shot a good shaft.

incautiously right (*auq*) up to the cave-mouth, was shot (*auqlab*) in the nipple by a Hazara inside and died there and then (*auq*).[3]

As most of the Turkman Hazaras seemed to be wintering inside the Dara-i-khush, we marched against them.

The valley is shut in,[4] by a mile-long gully stretching inwards from its mouth. The road engirdles the mountain, having a straight fall of some 50 to 60 yards below it and above it a precipice. Horsemen go along it in single-file. We passed the gully and went on through the day till between the Two Prayers (3 p.m.) without meeting a single person. Having spent the night somewhere, we found a fat camel[5] belonging to the Hazaras, had it killed, made part of its flesh into *kababs*[6] and

---

1 See Additional Notes, p. 798.
2 var. Khwesh. Its water flows into the Ghur-bund stream; it seems to be the Dara-i-Turkman of Stanford and the Survey Maps both of which mark Janglik. For Hazara turbulence, f. 135b and note.
3 The repetition of *auq* in this sentence can hardly be accidental.
4 *taur* [*dara*], which I take to be Turki, round, complete.
5 Three MSS. of the Turki text write *bir simizluq tiwah*; but the two Persian translations have *yak shuturluq farbih*, a *shuturluq* being a baggage-camel with little hair (Erskine).
6 *brochettes*, meat cut into large mouthfuls, spitted and roasted.

cooked part in a ewer (*aftab*). Such good camel-flesh had never been tasted; some could not tell it from mutton.

Next day we marched on for the Hazara winter-camp. At the first watch (9 a.m.) a man came from ahead, saying that the Hazaras had blocked a ford in front with branches, checked our men and were fighting. That winter the snow lay very deep; to move was difficult except on the road. The swampy meadows (*tuk-ab*) along the stream were all frozen; the stream could only be crossed from the road because of snow and ice. The Hazaras had cut many branches, put them at the exit from the water and were fighting in the valley-bottom with horse and foot or raining arrows down from either side.

Fol. 161.

Muhammad 'Ali *Mubashshir*[1] Beg one of our most daring braves, newly promoted to the rank of beg and well worthy of favour, went along the branch-blocked road without his mail, was shot in the belly and instantly surrendered his life. As we had gone forward in haste, most of us were not in mail. Shaft after shaft flew by and fell; with each one Yusuf's Ahmad said anxiously, "Bare[2] like this you go into it! I have seen two arrows go close to your head!" Said I, "Don't fear! Many as good arrows as these have flown past my head!" So much said, Qasim Beg, his men in full accoutrement,[3] found a ford on our right and crossed. Before their charge the Hazaras could make no stand; they fled, swiftly pursued and unhorsed one after the other by those just up with them.

In guerdon for this feat Bangash was given to Qasim Beg. Hatim the armourer having been not bad in the affair, was promoted to Shaikh Darwish's office of *qur-begi*. Baba Quli's Kipik (*sic*) also went well forward in it, so we entrusted Muh. 'Ali *Mubashshir*'s office to him.

Sl. Quli *Chunaq* (one-eared) started in pursuit of the Hazaras but there was no getting out of the hollow because of the snow.

Fol. 161b.

For my own part I just went with these braves.

Near the Hazara winter-camp we found many sheep and herds of horses. I myself collected as many as 4 to 500 sheep

---

1 Perhaps he was officially an announcer; the word means also bearer of good news.

2 *yilang*, without mail, as in the common phrase *yigit yilang*, a bare brave.

3 *aupchin*, of horse and man (f. 113b and note).

and from 20 to 25 horses. Sl. Quli *Chunaq* and two or three of
my personal servants were with me. I have ridden in a raid
twice;[1] this was the first time; the other was when, coming in
from Khurasan (912 AH.), we raided these same Turkman
Hazaras. Our foragers brought in masses of sheep and horses.
The Hazara wives and their little children had gone off up the
snowy slopes and stayed there; we were rather idle and it was
getting late in the day; so we turned back and dismounted in
their very dwellings. Deep indeed was the snow that winter!
Off the road it was up to a horse's *qaptal*,[2] so deep that the
night-watch was in the saddle all through till shoot of dawn.

Going out of the valley, we spent the next night just inside
the mouth, in the Hazara winter-quarters. Marching from there,
we dismounted at Janglik. At Janglik Yarak Taghai and other
late-comers were ordered to take the Hazaras who had killed
Shaikh Darwish and who, luckless and death-doomed, seemed
still to be in the cave. Yarak Taghai and his band by sending
smoke into the cave, took 70 to 80 Hazaras who mostly died by
the sword.

(*g. Collection of the Nijr-au tribute.*)

On the way back from the Hazara expedition we went to the
Ai-tughdi neighbourhood below Baran[3] in order to collect
the revenue of Nijr-au. Jahangir Mirza, come up from Ghazni,   Fol. 162.
waited on me there. At that time, on Ramzan 13th (Feb. 7th)
such sciatic-pain attacked me that for 40 days some-one had
to turn me over from one side to the other.

Of the (seven) valleys of the Nijr-water the Pichkan-valley,—
and of the villages in the Pichkan-valley Ghain,—and of Ghain
its head-man Husain *Ghaini* in particular, together with his elder
and younger brethren, were known and notorious for obstinacy
and daring. On this account a force was sent under Jahangir
Mirza, Qasim Beg going too, which went to Sar-i-tup (Hill-top),
stormed and took a *sangur* and made a few meet their doom.

1 Manifestly Babur means that he twice actually helped to collect the booty.
2 This is that part of a horse covered by the two side-pieces of a Turki saddle,
from which the side-arch springs on either side (Shaw).
3 *Baran-ning ayaghi*. Except the river I have found nothing called Baran; the
village marked Baian on the French Map would suit the position; it is n.e. of
Charyak-kar (f. 184*b* note).

Because of the sciatic pain, people made a sort of litter for me in which they carried me along the bank of the Baran and into the town to the Bustan-sarai. There I stayed for a few days; before that trouble was over a boil came out on my left cheek; this was lanced and for it I also took a purge. When relieved, I went out into the Char-bagh.

(h. Misconduct of Jahangir Mirza.)

At the time Jahangir Mirza waited on me, Ayub's sons Yusuf and Buhlul, who were in his service, had taken up a strifeful and seditious attitude towards me; so the Mirza was not found to be what he had been earlier. In a few days he marched out of Tipa in his mail,[1] hurried back to Ghazni, there took Nani, killed some of its people and plundered all. Fol. 162b. After that he marched off with whatever men he had, through the Hazaras,[2] his face set for Bamian. God knows that nothing had been done by me or my dependants to give him ground for anger or reproach! What was heard of later on as perhaps explaining his going off in the way he did, was this;—When Qasim Beg went with other begs, to give him honouring meeting as he came up from Ghazni, the Mirza threw a falcon off at a quail. Just as the falcon, getting close, put out its pounce to seize the quail, the quail dropped to the ground. Hereupon shouts and cries, "Taken! is it taken?" Said Qasim Beg, "Who looses the foe in his grip?" Their misunderstanding of this was their sole reason for going off, but they backed themselves on one or two other worse and weaker old cronish matters.[3] After doing in Ghazni what has been mentioned, they drew off through the Hazaras to the Mughul

1 i.e. prepared to fight.
2 For the Hazara (Turki, Ming) on the Mirza's road see Raverty's routes from Ghazni to the north. An account given by the *Tarikh-i-rashidi* (p. 196) of Jahangir's doings is confused; its parenthetical "(at the same time)" can hardly be correct. Jahangir left Ghazni now, (911 AH.), as Babur left Kabul in 912 AH. without knowledge of Husain's death (911 AH.). Babur had heard it (f. 183b) before Jahangir joined him (912 AH.); after their meeting they went on together to Heri. The petition of which the T.R. speaks as made by Jahangir to Babur, that he might go into Khurasan and help the Bai-qara Mirzas must have been made after the meeting of the two at Saf-hill (f. 184b).
3 The plurals *they* and *their* of the preceding sentence stand no doubt for the Mirza, Yusuf and Buhlul who all had such punishment due as would lead them to hear threat in Qasim's words now when all were within Babur's pounce.

clans.[1] These clans at that time had left Nasir Mirza but had not joined the Auzbeg, and were in Yai, Astar-ab and the summer-pastures thereabouts.

(i. Sl. Husain Mirza calls up help against Shaibaq Khan.)

Sl. Husain Mirza, having resolved to repel Shaibaq Khan, summoned all his sons; me too he summoned, sending to me Sayyid Afzal, son of Sayyid 'Ali *Khwab-bin* (Seer-of-dreams). It was right on several grounds for us to start for Khurasan. One ground was that when a great ruler, sitting, as Sl. Husain Mirza sat, in Timur Beg's place, had resolved to act against Fol. 163. such a foe as Shaibaq Khan and had called up many men and had summoned his sons and his begs, if there were some who went on foot it was for us to go if on our heads! if some took the bludgeon, we would take the stone! A second ground was that, since Jahangir Mirza had gone to such lengths and had behaved so badly,[2] we had either to dispel his resentment or to repel his attack.

(j. Chin Sufi's death.)

This year Shaibaq Khan took Khwarizm after besieging Chin Sufi in it for ten months. There had been a mass of fighting during the siege; many were the bold deeds done by the Khwarizmi braves; nothing soever did they leave undone. Again and again their shooting was such that their arrows pierced shield and cuirass, sometimes the two cuirasses.[3] For ten months they sustained that siege without hope in any quarter. A few bare braves then lost heart, entered into talk with the Auzbeg and were in the act of letting him up into the fort when Chin Sufi had the news and went to the spot. Just as he was beating and forcing down the Auzbegs, his own page, in a discharge of arrows, shot him from behind. No man was left to fight; the Auzbegs took Khwarizm. God's mercy on

1 These are the *aimaqs* from which the fighting-men went east with Babur in 910 AH. and the families in which Nasir shepherded across Hindu-kush (f. 154 and f. 155).

2 *yamanlik bila bardi*; cf. f. 156b and n. for its opposite, *yakhshi bardilar*; and T.R. p. 196.

3 One might be of mail, the other of wadded cloth.

Fol. 163b.

Chin Sufi, who never for one moment ceased to stake his life for his chief![1]

Shaibaq Khan entrusted Khwarizm to Kupuk (*sic*) Bi and went back to Samarkand.

(*k. Death of Sultan Husain Mirza.*)

Sl. Husain Mirza having led his army out against Shaibaq Khan as far as Baba Ilahi[2] went to God's mercy, in the month of Zu'l-hijja (Zu'l-hijja 11th 911 AH.—May 5th 1506 AD.).

SULTAN HUSAIN MIRZA AND HIS COURT[3]

(*a.*) *His birth and descent.*

He was born in Heri (Harat), in (Muharram) 842 (AH.—June–July, 1438 AD.) in Shahrukh Mirza's time[4] and was the son of Mansur Mirza, son of Bai-qara Mirza, son of 'Umar Shaikh Mirza, son of Amir Timur. Mansur Mirza and Bai-qara Mirza never reigned.

His mother was Firuza Begim, a (great-)grandchild (*nabira*) of Timur Beg; through her he became a grandchild of Miran-shah also.[5] He was of high birth on both sides, a ruler of royal

1 Chin Sufi was Husain *Bai-qara*'s man (T.R. p. 204). His arduous defence, faithfulness and abandonment recall the instance of a later time when also a long road stretched between the man and the help that failed him. But the Mirza was old, his military strength was, admittedly, sapped by ease; hence his elder Khartum, his neglect of his Gordon.

It should be noted that no mention of the page's fatal arrow is made by the *Shaibani-nama* (Vambéry, p. 442), or by the *Tarikh-i-rashidi* (p. 204). Chin Sufi's death was on the 21st of the Second Rabi 911 AH. (Aug. 22nd 1505 AD.).

2 This may be the "Baboulei" of the French Map of 1904, on the Heri-Kushk-Maruchaq road.

3 Elph. MS. f. 127; W.-i-B. I.O. 215 f. 132 and 217 f. 111b; Mems. p. 175; Méms. i, 364.

That Babur should have given his laborious account of the Court of Heri seems due both to loyalty to a great Timurid, seated in Timur Beg's place (f. 122b), and to his own interest, as a man-of-letters and connoisseur in excellence, in that ruler's galaxy of talent. His account here opening is not complete; its sources are various; they include the *Habibu's-siyar* and what he will have learned himself in Heri or from members of the Bai-qara family, knowledgeable women some of them, who were with him in Hindustan. The narrow scope of my notes shews that they attempt no more than to indicate further sources of information and to clear up a few obscurities.

4 Timur's youngest son, d. 850 AH. (1446 AD.). *Cf.* H.S. iii, 203. The use in this sentence of Amir and not Beg as Timur's title is, up to this point, unique in the *Babur-nama*; it may be a scribe's error.

5 Firuza's paternal line of descent was as follows:—Firuza, daughter of Sl. Husain Qanjut, son of Aka Begim, daughter of Timur. Her maternal descent was:—Firuza, d. of Qutluq-sultan Begim, d. of Miran-shah, s. of Timur. She died Muh. 24th 874 AH. (July 25th 1489 AD. H.S. iii, 218).

lineage.¹ Of the marriage (of Mansur with Firuza) were born two sons and two daughters, namely, Bai-qara Mirza and Sl. Husain Mirza, Aka Begim and another daughter, Badka Begim whom Ahmad Khan took.²

Bai-qara Mirza was older than Sl. Husain Mirza; he was his younger brother's retainer but used not to be present as head of the Court;³ except in Court, he used to share his brother's divan (*tushak*). He was given Balkh by his younger brother and was its Commandant for several years. He had three sons, Sl. Muhammad Mirza, Sl. Wais Mirza and Sl. Iskandar Mirza.⁴

Aka Begim was older than the Mirza; she was taken by Fol. 164. Sl. Ahmad Mirza,⁵ a grandson (*nabira*) of Miran-shah; by him she had a son (Muhammad Sultan Mirza), known as Kichik (Little) Mirza, who at first was in his maternal-uncle's service, but later on gave up soldiering to occupy himself with letters. He is said to have become very learned and also to have taste in verse.⁶ Here is a Persian quatrain of his:—

> For long on a life of devotion I plumed me,
> As one of the band of the abstinent ranged me;
> Where when Love came was devotion? denial?
> By the mercy of God it is I have proved me!

---

1 "No-one in the world had such parentage", writes Khwand-amir, after detailing the Timurid, Chingiz-khanid, and other noted strains meeting in Husain *Bai-qara* (H.S. iii, 204).

2 The Elph. MS. gives the Begim no name; Badi'u'l-jamal is correct (H.S. iii, 242). The curious "Badka" needs explanation. It seems probable that Babur left one of his blanks for later filling-in; the natural run of his sentence here is "Aka B. and Badi'u'l-jamal B." and not the detail, which follows in its due place, about the marriage with Ahmad.

3 *Diwan bashida hasir bulmas aidi*; the sense of which may be that Bai-qara did not sit where the premier retainer usually sat at the head of the Court (Pers. trs. *sar-i-diwan*).

4 From this Wais and Sl. Husain M.'s daughter Sultanim (f. 167*b*) were descended the Bai-qara Mirzas who gave Akbar so much trouble.

5 As this man might be mistaken for Babur's uncle (*q.v.*) of the same name, it may be well to set down his parentage. He was a s. of Mirza Sayyidi Ahmad, s. of Miran-shah, s. of Timur (H.S. iii, 217, 241). I have not found mention elsewhere of "Ahmad s. of Miran-shah"; the *sayyidi* in his style points to a sayyida mother. He was Governor of Heri for a time, for Sl. H.M.; 'Ali-sher has notices of him and of his son, Kichik Mirza (*Journal Asiatique* xvii, 293, M. Belin's art. where may be seen notices of many other men mentioned by Babur).

6 He collected and thus preserved 'Ali-sher's earlier poems (Rieu's Pers. Cat. p. 294). Mu'inu'd-din al Zamji writes respectfully of his being worthy of credence in some Egyptian matters with which he became acquainted in twice passing through that country on his Pilgrimage (*Journal Asiatique* xvi, 476, de Meynard's article).

This quatrain recalls one by the Mulla.[1] Kichik Mirza made
the circuit of the *ka'ba* towards the end of his life.

Badka (Badi'u'l-jamal) Begim also was older[2] than the Mirza.
She was given in the guerilla times to Ahmad Khan of Haji-
tarkhan;[3] by him she had two sons (Sl. Mahmud Khan and
Bahadur Sl.) who went to Heri and were in the Mirza's service.

(b.) *His appearance and habits.*

He was slant-eyed (*qiyik guzluq*) and lion-bodied, being
slender from the waist downwards. Even when old and white-
bearded, he wore silken garments of fine red and green. He
used to wear either the black lambskin cap (*burk*) or the
qalpaq,[4] but on a Feast-day would sometimes set up a little
three-fold turban, wound broad and badly,[5] stick a heron's
plume in it and so go to Prayers.

Fol. 164*b*.
When he first took Heri, he thought of reciting the names of
the Twelve Imams in the *khutba*,[6] but 'Ali-sher Beg and others
prevented it; thereafter all his important acts were done in
accordance with orthodox law. He could not perform the
Prayers on account of a trouble in the joints,[7] and he kept no
fasts. He was lively and pleasant, rather immoderate in temper,
and with words that matched his temper. He shewed great
respect for the law in several weighty matters; he once
surrendered to the Avengers of blood a son of his own who had

1 Kichik M.'s quatrain is a mere plagiarism of Jami's which I am indebted to my
husband for locating as in the *Diwan* I.O. MS. 47 p. 47; B.M. Add. 7774 p. 290;
and Add. 7775 p. 285. M. Belin interprets the verse as an expression of the rise
of the average good man to mystical rapture, not as his lapse from abstinence to
indulgence (l.c. xvii, 296 and notes).

2 Elph. MS. *younger* but Hai. MS. *older* in which it is supported by the "also"
(*ham*) of the sentence.

3 modern Astrakhan. Husain's guerilla wars were those through which he cut his way
to the throne of Heri. This begim was married first to Pir Budagh Sl. (H.S. iii, 242);
he dying, she was married by Ahmad, presumably by levirate custom (*yinkalik*; f. 12
and note). By Ahmad she had a daughter, styled Khan-zada Begim whose affairs find
comment on f. 206*b* and H.S. iii, 359. (The details of this note negative a suggestion
of mine that Badka was the Rabi'a-sultan of f. 168 (Gul-badan, App. *s. nn.*).)

4 This is a felt wide-awake worn by travellers in hot weather (Shaw); the Turkman
bonnet (Erskine).

5 Hai. MS. *yamanlik*, badly, but Elph. MS. *namayan*, whence Erskine's *showy*.

6 This was a proof that he was then a Shi'a (Erskine).

7 The word *perform* may be excused in speaking of Musalman prayers because
they involve ceremonial bendings and prostrations (Erskine).

killed a man, and had him taken to the Judgment-gate (*Daru'l-qaza*). He was abstinent for six or seven years after he took the throne; later on he degraded himself to drink. During the almost 40 years of his rule[1] in Khurasan, there may not have been one single day on which he did not drink after the Mid-day prayer; earlier than that however he did not drink. What happened with his sons, the soldiers and the town was that every-one pursued vice and pleasure to excess. Bold and daring he was! Time and again he got to work with his own sword, getting his own hand in wherever he arrayed to fight; no man of Timur Beg's line has been known to match him in the slashing of swords. He had a leaning to poetry and even put a *diwan* together, writing in Turki with Husaini for his pen-name.[2] Many couplets in his *diwan* are not bad; it is however in one and the same metre throughout. Great ruler though he was, both by the length of his reign (*yash*) and the breadth of his dominions, he yet, like little people kept fighting-rams, flew pigeons and fought cocks.

Fol. 165.

(c.) His wars and encounters.[3]

He swam the Gurgan-water[4] in his guerilla days and gave a party of Auzbegs a good beating.

Again,—with 60 men he fell on 3000 under Pay-master Muhammad 'Ali, sent ahead by Sl. Abu-sa'id Mirza, and gave them a downright good beating (868 AH.). This was his one fine, out-standing feat-of-arms.[5]

Again,—he fought and beat Sl. Mahmud Mirza near Astarabad (865 AH.).[6]

1 If Babur's 40 include rule in Heri only, it over-states, since Yadgar died in 875 AH. and Husain in 911 AH. while the intervening 36 years include the 5 or 6 temperate ones. If the 40 count from 861 AH. when Husain began to rule in Merv, it under-states. It is a round number, apparently.

2 Relying on the Ilminsky text, Dr. Rieu was led into the mistake of writing that Babur gave Husain the wrong pen-name, *i.e.* Husain, and not Husaini (Turk. Cat. p. 256).

3 Daulat-shah says that as he is not able to enumerate all Husain's feats-of-arms, he, Turkman fashion, offers a gift of Nine. The Nine differ from those of Babur's list in some dates; they are also records of victory only (Browne, p. 521; *Not. et Extr.* iv, 262, de Saçy's article).

4 Wolves'-water, a river and its town at the s.e. corner of the Caspian, the ancient boundary between Russia and Persia. The name varies a good deal in MSS.

5 The battle was at Tarshiz; Abu-sa'id was ruling in Heri; Daulat-shah (l.c. p. 523) gives 90 and 10,000 as the numbers of the opposed forces!

6 f. 26 and note; H.S. iii, 209; Daulat-shah p. 524.

Again,—this also in Astarabad, he fought and beat Sa'idliq Sa'id, son of Husain *Turkman* (873 AH.?).

Again,—after taking the throne (of Heri in Ramzan 873 AH.—March 1469 AD.), he fought and beat Yadgar-i-muhammad Mirza at Chanaran (874 AH.).[1]

Again,—coming swiftly[2] from the Murgh-ab bridge-head (Sar-i-pul), he fell suddenly on Yadgar-i-muhammad Mirza where he lay drunk in the Ravens'-garden (875 AH.), a victory which kept all Khurasan quiet.

Again,—he fought and beat Sl. Mahmud Mirza at Chikman-sarai in the neighbourhood of Andikhud and Shibrghan (876 AH.).[3]

Again,—he fell suddenly on Aba-bikr Mirza[4] after that Mirza, joined by the Black-sheep Turkmans, had come out of 'Iraq, beaten Aulugh Beg Mirza (*Kabuli*) in Takana and Khimar (var. Himar), taken Kabul, left it because of turmoil in 'Iraq, crossed Khaibar, gone on to Khush-ab and Multan, on again to Fol. 165b.	Siwi,[5] thence to Karman and, unable to stay there, had entered the Khurasan country (884 AH.).[6]

Again,—he defeated his son Badi'u'z-zaman Mirza at Pul-i-chiragh (902 AH.); he also defeated his sons Abu'l-muhsin Mirza and Kupuk (Round-shouldered) Mirza at Halwa-spring (904 AH.).[7]

Again,—he went to Qunduz, laid siege to it, could not take it, and retired; he laid siege to Hisar, could not take that either, and rose from before it (901 AH.); he went into Zu'n-nun's country, was given Bast by its *darogha*, did no more and retired (903 AH.).[8] A ruler so great and so brave, after resolving royally on these three movements, just retired with nothing done!

1 The loser was the last Shahrukhi ruler. Chanaran (variants) is near Abiward, Anwari's birth-place (H.S. iii, 218; D.S. p. 527).
2 f. 85. D.S. (p. 540) and the H.S. (iii, 223) dwell on Husain's speed through three continuous days and nights.
3 f. 26; H.S. iii, 227; D.S. p. 532.
4 Abu-sa'id's son by a Badakhshi Begim (T.R. p. 108); he became his father's Governor in Badakhshan and married Husain *Bai-qara*'s daughter Begim Sultan at a date after 873 AH. (f. 168 and note; H.S. iii, 196, 229, 234–37; D.S. p. 535).
5 f. 152.
6 Aba-bikr was defeated and put to death at the end of Rajab 884 AH.-Oct. 1479 AD. after flight before Husain across the Gurgan-water (H.S. iii, 196 and 237 but D.S. p. 539, Safar 885 AH.).
7 f. 41, Pul-i-chiragh; for Halwa-spring, H.S. iii, 283 and Rieu's Pers. Cat. p. 443.
8 f. 33 (p. 57) and f. 57b.

Again,—he fought his son Badi'u'z-zaman Mirza in the Nishin-meadow, who had come there with Zu'n-nun's son, Shah Beg (903 AH.). In that affair were these curious coincidences:— The Mirza's force will have been small, most of his men being in Astarabad; on the very day of the fight, one force rejoined him coming back from Astarabad, and Sl. Mas'ud Mirza arrived to join Sl. Husain Mirza after letting Bai-sunghar Mirza take Hisar, and Haidar Mirza came back from reconnoitring Badi'u'z-zaman Mirza at Sabzawar.

(d.) His countries.

His country was Khurasan, with Balkh to the east, Bistam and Damghan to the west, Khwarizm to the north, Qandahar and Sistan to the south. When he once had in his hands such a town as Heri, his only affair, by day and by night, was with comfort and pleasure; nor was there a man of his either who did not take his ease. It followed of course that, as he no longer tolerated the hardships and fatigue of conquest and soldiering, his retainers and his territories dwindled instead of increasing right down to the time of his departure.[1]

Fol. 166.

(e.) His children.

Fourteen sons and eleven daughters were born to him.[2] The oldest of all his children was Badi'u'z-zaman Mirza; (Bega Begim) a daughter of Sl. Sanjar of Marv, was his mother.

Shah-i-gharib Mirza was another; he had a stoop (bukuri); though ill to the eye, he was of good character; though weak of body, he was powerful of pen. He even put a diwan together, using Gharbati (Lowliness) for his pen-name and writing both Turki and Persian verse. Here is a couplet of his:—

> Seeing a peri-face as I passed, I became its fool;
> Not knowing what was its name, where was its home.

For a time he was his father's Governor in Heri. He died before his father, leaving no child.

---

1 In commenting thus Babur will have had in mind what he best knew, Husain's futile movements at Qunduz and Hisar.

2 qalib aidi; if qalib be taken as Turki, survived or remained, it would not apply here since many of Husain's children predeceased him; Ar. qalab would suit, meaning begotten, born.

There are discrepancies between Babur's details here and Khwand-amir's scattered through the Habibu's-siyar, concerning Husain's family.

Muzaffar-i-husain Mirza was another; he was his father's favourite son, but though this favourite, had neither accomplishments nor character. It was Sl. Husain Mirza's over-fondness for this son that led his other sons into rebellion. The mother of Shah-i-gharib Mirza and of Muzaffar-i-husain Mirza was Khadija Begim, a former mistress of Sl. Abu-sa'id Mirza by whom she had had a daughter also, known as Aq (Fair) Begim.

Fol. 166b.

Two other sons were Abu'l-muhsin Mirza and Kupuk (var. Kipik) Mirza whose name was Muhammad Muhsin Mirza; their mother was Latif-sultan Aghacha.

Abu-turab Mirza was another. From his early years he had an excellent reputation. When the news of his father's increased illness[1] reached him and other news of other kinds also, he fled with his younger brother Muhammad-i-husain Mirza into 'Iraq,[2] and there abandoned soldiering to lead the darwish-life; nothing further has been heard about him.[3] His son Sohrab was in my service when I took Hisar after having beaten the sultans led by Hamza Sl. and Mahdi Sl. (917 AH.— 1511 AD.); he was blind of one eye and of wretchedly bad aspect; his disposition matched even his ill-looks. Owing to some immoderate act (bi i'tidal), he could not stay with me, so went off. For some of his immoderate doings, Nijm Sani put him to death near Astarabad.[4]

Muhammad-i-husain Mirza was another. He must have been shut up (bund) with Shah Isma'il at some place in 'Iraq and have become his disciple;[5] he became a rank heretic later on and became this although his father and brethren, older and younger, were all orthodox. He died in Astarabad, still on the same wrong road, still with the same absurd opinions. A good deal is heard about his courage and heroism, but no deed of his

1 bi huzuri, which may mean aversion due to Khadija Begim's malevolence.
2 Some of the several goings into 'Iraq chronicled by Babur point to refuge taken with Timurids, descendants of Khalil and 'Umar, sons of Miran-shah (Lane-Poole's Muhammadan Dynasties, Table of the Timurids).
3 He died before his father (H.S. iii, 327).
4 He will have been killed previous to Ramzan 3rd 918 AH. (Nov. 12th, 1512 AD.), the date of the battle of Ghaj-dawan when Nijm Sani died.
5 The bund here may not imply that both were in prison, but that they were bound in close company, allowing Isma'il, a fervent Shi'a, to convert the Mirza.

stands out as worthy of record. He may have been poetically-disposed; here is a couplet of his:—

> Grimed with dust, from tracking what game dost thou come?
> Steeped in sweat, from whose heart of flame dost thou come?

Faridun-i-husain Mirza was another. He drew a very strong Fol. 167. bow and shot a first-rate shaft; people say his cross-bow (*kaman-i-guroha*) may have been 40 *batmans*.[1] He himself was very brave but he had no luck in war; he was beaten wherever he fought. He and his younger brother Ibn-i-husain Mirza were defeated at Rabat-i-duzd (var. Dudur) by Timur Sl. and 'Ubaid Sl. leading Shaibaq Khan's advance (913 AH.?), but he had done good things there.[2] In Damghan he and Muhammad-i-zaman Mirza[3] fell into the hands of Shaibaq Khan who, killing neither, let both go free. Faridun-i-husain Mirza went later on to Qalat[4] where Shah Muhammad *Diwana* had made himself fast; there when the Auzbegs took the place, he was captured and killed. The three sons last-named were by Mingli Bibi Aghacha, Sl. Husain Mirza's Auzbeg mistress.

Haidar Mirza was another; his mother Payanda-sultan Begim was a daughter of Sl. Abu-sa'id Mirza. Haidar Mirza was Governor of Balkh and Mashhad for some time during his father's life. For him his father, when besieging Hisar (901 AH.) took (Bega Begim) a daughter of Sl. Mahmud Mirza and Khan-zada Begim; this done, he rose from before Hisar. One daughter only[5] was born of that marriage; she was named Shad (Joy)

---

1 The *batman* is a Turkish weight of 13lbs (Meninsky) or 15lbs (Wollaston). The weight seems likely to refer to the strength demanded for rounding the bow (*kaman guroha-si*) i.e. as much strength as to lift 40 *batmans*. Rounding or bending might stand for stringing or drawing. The meaning can hardly be one of the weight of the cross-bow itself. Erskine read *gurdehieh* for *guroha* (p. 180) and translated by "double-stringed bow"; de Courteille (i, 373) read *guirdhiyeh, arrondi, circulaire*, in this following Ilminsky who may have followed Erskine. The Elph. and Hai. MSS. and the first W.-i-B. (I.O. 215 f. 113*b*) have *kaman guroha-si*; the second W.-i-B. omits the passage, in the MSS. I have seen.

2 *yakhshilar barib tur*; lit. good things went (on); *cf.* f. 156*b* and note.

3 Badi'u'z-zaman's son, drowned at Chausa in 946 AH. (1539 AD.) A.N. (H. Beveridge, i, 344).

4 Qalat-i-nadiri, in Khurasan, the birth-place of Nadir Shah (T.R. p. 209).

5 *bir gina qiz*, which on f. 86*b* can fitly be read to mean daughterling, *Töchterchen, fillette*, but here and i.a. f. 168, must have another meaning than diminutive and may be an equivalent of German *Stück* and mean *one only*. Gul-badan gives an account of Shad's manly pursuits (H.N. f. 25*b*).

Begim and given to 'Adil Sl.[1] when she came to Kabul later on.

Haidar Mirza departed from the world in his father's life-time.

Muhammad Ma'sum Mirza was another. He had Qandahar given to him and, as was fitting with this, a daughter of Aulugh Beg Mirza, (Bega Begim), was set aside for him; when she went to Heri (902 AH.), Sl. Husain Mirza made a splendid feast, setting up a great *char-taq* for it.[2] Though Qandahar was given to Muh. Ma'sum Mirza, he had neither power nor influence there, since, if black were done, or if white were done, the act was Shah Beg *Arghun's*. On this account the Mirza left Qandahar and went into Khurasan. He died before his father.

Farrukh-i-husain Mirza was another. Brief life was granted to him; he bade farewell to the world before his younger brother Ibrahim-i-husain Mirza.

1 He was the son of Mahdi Sl. (f. 320b) and the father of 'Aqil Sl. *Auzbeg* (A.N. index *s.n.*). Several matters suggest that these men were of the Shaban Auzbegs who intermarried with Husain *Bai-qara's* family and some of whom went to Babur in Hindustan. One such matter is that Kabul was the refuge of dispossessed Haratis, after the Auzbeg conquest; that there 'Aqil married Shad *Bai-qara* and that 'Adil went on to Babur. Moreover Khafi Khan makes a statement which (if correct) would allow 'Adil's father Mahdi to be a grandson of Husain *Bai-qara*; this statement is that when Babur defeated the Auzbegs in 916 AH. (1510 AD.), he freed from their captivity two sons (descendants) of his paternal uncle, named Mahdi Sl. and Sultan Mirza. [Leaving the authenticity of the statement aside for a moment, it will be observed that this incident is of the same date and place as another well-vouched for, namely that Babur then and there killed Mahdi Sl. *Auzbeg* and Hamza Sl. *Auzbeg* after defeating them.] What makes in favour of Khafi Khan's correctness is, not only that Babur's foe Mahdi is not known to have had a son 'Adil, but also that his "Sultan Mirza" is not a style so certainly suiting Hamza as it does a Shaban sultan, one whose father was a Shaban sultan, and whose mother was a Mirza's daughter. Moreover this point of identification is pressed by the correctness, according to oriental statement of relationship, of Khafi Khan's "paternal uncle" (of Babur), because this precisely suits Sl. Husain Mirza with whose family these Shaban sultans allied themselves. On the other hand it must be said that Khafi Khan's statement is not in the English text of the *Tarikh-i-rashidi*, the book on which he mostly relies at this period, nor is it in my husband's MS. [a copy from the Rampur Codex]; and to this must be added the verbal objection that a modicum of rhetoric allows a death to be described both in Turki and Persian, as a release from the captivity of a sinner's own acts (f. 160). Still Khafi Khan may be right; his statement may yet be found in some other MS. of the T.R. or some different source; it is one a scribe copying the T.R. might be led to omit by reason of its coincidences. The killing and the release may both be right; 'Adil's Mahdi may be the Shaban sultan inference makes him seem. This little *crux* presses home the need of much attention to the *lacunae* in the *Babur-nama*, since in them are lost some exits and some entries of Babur's *dramatis personae*, pertinently, mention of the death of Mahdi with Hamza in 916 AH., and possibly also that of 'Adil's Mahdi's release.

2 A *char-taq* may be a large tent rising into four domes or having four porches.

Ibrahim-i-husain Mirza was another. They say his disposition
was not bad; he died before his father from bibbing and bibbing
Heri wines.

Ibn-i-husain Mirza and Muh. Qasim Mirza were others;[1]
their story will follow. Papa Aghacha was the mother of the
five sons last-named.

Of all the Mirza's daughters, Sultanim Begim was the oldest.
She had no brother or sister of the full-blood. Her mother,
known as Chuli (Desert) Begim, was a daughter of one of the
Azaq begs. Sultanim Begim had great acquaintance with words
(*soz bilur aidi*); she was never at fault for a word. Her father
sent her out[2] to Sl. Wais Mirza, the middle son of his own elder
brother Bai-qara Mirza; she had a son and a daughter by him;
the daughter was sent out to Aisan-quli Sl. younger brother of
Yili-bars of the Shaban sultans;[3] the son is that Muhammad Sl.
Mirza to whom I have given the Qanauj district.[4] At that
same date Sultanim Begim, when on her way with her grandson Fol. 168.
from Kabul to Hindustan, went to God's mercy at Nil-ab. Her
various people turned back, taking her bones; her grandson
came on.[5]

Four daughters were by Payanda-sultan Begim. Aq Begim,
the oldest, was sent out to Muhammad Qasim *Arlat*, a grandson of
Bega Begim the younger sister of Babur Mirza;[6] there was one
daughter (*bir gina qiz*), known as Qara-guz (Dark-eyed) Begim,
whom Nasir Mirza (*Miran-shahi*) took. Kichik Begim was the
second; for her Sl. Mas'ud Mirza had great desire but, try as he
would, Payanda-sultan Begim, having an aversion for him, would
not give her to him;[7] she sent Kichik Begim out afterwards

1 H.S. iii, 367.

2 This phrase, common but not always selected, suggests unwillingness to leave the
paternal roof.

3 Abu'l-ghazi's *History of the Mughuls*, Desmaisons, p. 207.

4 The appointment was made in 933 AH. (1527 AD.) and seems to have been held
still in 934 AH. (ff. 329, 332).

5 This grandson may have been a child travelling with his father's household,
perhaps Aulugh Mirza, the oldest son of Muhammad Sultan Mirza (A.A. Blochmann,
p. 461). No mention is made here of Sultanim Begim's marriage with 'Abdu'l-baqi
Mirza (f. 175*b*).

6 Abu'l-qasim Babur *Shahrukhi* presumably.

7 The time may have been 902 AH. when Mas'ud took his sister Bega Begim to
Heri for her marriage with Haidar (H.S. iii, 260).

to Mulla Khwaja of the line of Sayyid Ata.[1] Her third and
fourth daughters Bega Begim and Agha Begim, she gave to
Babur Mirza and Murad Mirza the sons of her younger sister,
Rabi'a-sultan Begim.[2]

Two other daughters of the Mirza were by Mingli Bibi
Aghacha. They gave the elder one, Bairam-sultan Begim to
Sayyid 'Abdu'l-lah, one of the sayyids of Andikhud who was a
grandson of Bai-qara Mirza[3] through a daughter. A son of this
marriage, Sayyid Barka[4] was in my service when Samarkand
was taken (917 AH.–1511 AD.); he went to Aurganj later and there
made claim to rule; the Red-heads[5] killed him in Astarabad.
Mingli Bibi's second daughter was Fatima-sultan Begim; her
they gave to Yadgar(-i-farrukh) Mirza of Timur Beg's line.[6]

Three daughters[7] were by Papa Aghacha. Of these the
oldest, Sultan-nizhad Begim was made to go out to Iskandar
Mirza, youngest son of Sl. Husain Mirza's elder brother Bai-qara
Mirza. The second, (Sa'adat-bakht, known as) Begim Sultan,
Fol. 168b. was given to Sl. Mas'ud Mirza after his blinding.[8] By Sl. Mas'ud

1 Khwaja Ahmad *Yasawi*, known as Khwaja Ata, founder of the Yasawi religious
order.
2 Not finding mention of a daughter of Abu-sa'id named Rabi'a-sultan, I think
she may be the daughter styled Aq Begim who is No. 3 in Gul-badan's guest-list
for the Mystic Feast.
3 This man I take to be Husain's grandfather and not brother, both because
'Abdu'l-lah was of Husain's and his brother's generation, and also because of the
absence here of Babur's usual defining words "elder brother" (of Sl. Husain
Mirza). In this I have to differ from Dr. Rieu (Pers. Cat. p. 152).
4 So-named after his ancestor Sayyid Barka whose body was exhumed from
Andikhud for reburial in Samarkand, by Timur's wish and there laid in such a
position that Timur's body was at its feet (*Zafar-nama* ii, 719; H.S. iii, 82). (For
the above interesting detail I am indebted to my husband.)
5 *Qizil-bash*, Persians wearing red badges or caps to distinguish them as Persians.
6 Yadgar-i-farrukh *Miran-shahi* (H.S. iii, 327). He may have been one of those
Miran-shahis of 'Iraq from whom came Aka's and Sultanim's husbands, Ahmad
and 'Abdu'l-baqi (ff. 164, 175b).
7 This should be four (f. 169b). The H.S. (iii, 327) also names three only when
giving Papa Aghacha's daughters (the omission linking it with the B.N.), but
elsewhere (iii, 229) it gives an account of a fourth girl's marriage; this fourth is
needed to make up the total of 11 daughters. Babur's and Khwand-amir's details
of Papa Aghacha's quartette are defective; the following may be a more correct
list:—(1) Begim Sultan (a frequent title), married to Aba-bikr *Miran-shahi* (who
died 884 AH.) and seeming too old to be the one [No. 3] who married Mas'ud
(H.S. iii, 229); (2) Sultan-nizhad, married to Iskandar *Bai-qara*; (3) Sa'adat-bakht
also known as Begim Sultan, married to Mas'ud *Miran-shahi* (H.S. iii, 327);
(4) Manauwar-sultan, married to a son of Aulugh Beg *Kabuli* (H.S. iii, 327).
However, if four, the total of eleven (p. 261) is exceeded.
8 This "after" seems to contradict the statement (f. 58) that Mas'ud was made to
kneel as a son-in-law (*kuyadlik-ka yukundurub*) at a date previous to his blinding, but
the seeming contradiction may be explained by considering the following details;

Mirza she had one daughter and one son. The daughter was brought up by Apaq Begim of Sl. Husain Mirza's *haram*; from Heri she came to Kabul and was there given to Sayyid Mirza Apaq.[1] (Sa'adat-bakht) Begim Sultan after the Auzbeg killed her husband, set out for the *ka'ba* with her son.[2] News has just come (*circa* 934 AH.) that they have been heard of as in Makka and that the boy is becoming a bit of a great personage.[3] Papa Aghacha's third daughter was given to a sayyid of Andikhud, generally known as Sayyid Mirza.[4]

Another of the Mirza's daughters, 'Ayisha-sultan Begim was by a mistress, Zubaida Aghacha the grand-daughter of Husain-i-Shaikh Timur.[5] They gave her to Qasim Sl. of the Shaban sultans; she had by him a son, named Qasim-i-husain Sl. who came to serve me in Hindustan, was in the Holy Battle with Rana Sanga, and was given Badayun.[6] When Qasim Sl. died, (his widow) 'Ayisha-sultan Begim was taken by Buran Sl. one of his relations,[7] by whom she had a son, named 'Abdu'l-lah Sl. now serving me and though young, not doing badly.

(*f. His wives and concubines.*)

The wife he first took was Bega Sultan Begim, a daughter of Sl. Sanjar of Marv. She was the mother of Badi'u'z-zaman Mirza. She was very cross-tempered and made the Mirza endure

---

he left Heri hastily (f. 58), went to Khusrau Shah and was blinded by him,—all in the last two months of 903 AH. (1498 AD.), after the kneeling on Zu'l-qa'da 3rd, (June 23rd) in the Ravens'-garden. Here what Babur says is that the Begim was given (*birib*) after the blinding, the inference allowed being that though Mas'ud had kneeled before the blinding, she had remained in her father's house till his return after the blinding.

1 The first W.-i-B. writes "Apaq Begim" (I.O. 215 f. 136) which would allow Sayyid Mirza to be a kinsman of Apaq Begim, wife of Husain *Bai-qara*.

2 This brief summary conveys the impression that the Begim went on her pilgrimage shortly after Mas'ud's death (913 AH.?), but may be wrong:—After Mas'ud's murder, by one Bimash Mirza, *darogha* of Sarakhs, at Shaibaq Khan's order, she was married by Bimash M. (H.S. iii, 278). How long after this she went to Makka is not said; it was about 934 AH. when Babur heard of her as there.

3 This clause is in the Hai. MS. but not in the Elph. MS. (f. 131), or Kehr's (Ilminsky, p. 210), or in either Persian translation. The boy may have been 17 or 18.

4 This appears a mistake (f. 168 foot, and note on Papa's daughters).

5 f. 171*b*.

6 933 AH.—1527 AD. (f. 329).

7 Presumably this was a *yinkalik* marriage; it differs from some of those chronicled and also from a levirate marriage in not being made with a childless wife.

much wretchedness, until driven at last to despair, he set himself
Fol. 169.   free by divorcing her. What was he to do? Right was with him.[1]

> A bad wife in a good man's house
> Makes this world already his hell.[2]

God preserve every Musalman from this misfortune! Would
that not a single cross or ill-tempered wife were left in the world!

Chuli Begim was another; she was a daughter of the Azaq
begs and was the mother of Sultanim Begim.

Shahr-banu Begim was another; she was Sl. Abu-sa'id Mirza's
daughter, taken after Sl. Husain Mirza took the throne (873 AH.).
When the Mirza's other ladies got out of their litters and mounted
horses, at the battle of Chikman, Shahr-banu Begim, putting her
trust in her younger brother (Sl. Mahmud M.), did not leave her
litter, did not mount a horse;[3] people told the Mirza of this, so
he divorced her and took her younger sister Payanda-sultan
Begim. When the Auzbegs took Khurasan (913 AH.), Payanda-
sultan Begim went into 'Iraq, and in 'Iraq she died in great misery.

Khadija Begim was another.[4] She had been a mistress of
Sl. Abu-sa'id Mirza and by him had had a daughter, Aq Begim;
after his defeat (873 AH.–1468 AD.) she betook herself to Heri
where Sl. Husain Mirza took her, made her a great favourite,
and promoted her to the rank of Begim. Very dominant indeed
she became later on; she it was wrought Muh. Mumin Mirza's
death;[5] she in chief it was caused Sl. Husain Mirza's sons to
rebel against him. She took herself for a sensible woman but
was a silly chatterer, may also have been a heretic. Of her were
Fol. 169b.   born Shah-i-gharib Mirza and Muzaffar-i-husain Mirza.

Apaq Begim was another;[6] she had no children; that Papa
Aghacha the Mirza made such a favourite of was her foster-sister.

1 Khwand-amir says that Bega Begim was jealous, died of grief at her divorce, and
was buried in a College, of her own erection, in 893 AH. (1488 AD. H.S. iii, 245).
2 Gulistan Cap. II, Story 31 (Platts, p. 114).
3 i.e. did not get ready to ride off if her husband were beaten by her brother (f. 11
and note to Habiba).
4 Khadija Begi Agha (H.S. ii, 230 and iii, 327); she would be promoted probably
after Shah-i-gharib's birth.
5 He was a son of Badi'u'z-zaman.
6 It is singular that this honoured woman's parentage is not mentioned; if it be right
on f. 168b (q.v. with note) to read Sayyid Mirza of Apaq Begim, she may be a sayyida
of Andikhud.

Being childless, Apaq Begim brought up as her own the children of Papa Aghacha. She nursed the Mirza admirably when he was ill; none of his other wives could nurse as she did. The year I came into Hindustan (932 AH.)[1] she came into Kabul from Heri and I shewed her all the honour and respect I could. While I was besieging Chandiri (934 AH.) news came that in Kabul she had fulfilled God's will.[2]

One of the Mirza's mistresses was Latif-sultan Aghacha of the Char-shamba people;[3] she became the mother of Abu'l-muhsin Mirza and Kupuk (or Kipik) Mirza (i.e. Muhammad Muhsin).

Another mistress was Mingli Bibi Aghacha,[4] an Auzbeg and one of Shahr-banu Begim's various people. She became the mother of Abu-turab Mirza, Muhammad-i-husain Mirza, Faridun-i-husain Mirza and of two daughters.

Papa Aghacha, the foster-sister of Apaq Begim was another mistress. The Mirza saw her, looked on her with favour, took her and, as has been mentioned, she became the mother of five of his sons and four of his daughters.[5]

Begi Sultan Aghacha was another mistress; she had no child. There were also many concubines and mistresses held in little respect; those enumerated were the respected wives and mistresses of Sl. Husain Mirza.

Strange indeed it is that of the 14 sons born to a ruler so great as Sl. Husain Mirza, one governing too in such a town as Heri, three only were born in legal marriage.[6] In him, in his sons, and in his tribes and hordes vice and debauchery were extremely prevalent. What shews this point precisely is that of the many sons born to his dynasty not a sign or trace was left

Fol. 170.

1 As Babur left Kabul on Safar 1st (Nov. 17th 1525 AD.), the Begim must have arrived in Muharram 932 AH. (Oct. 18th to Nov. 17th).

2 f. 333. As Chandiri was besieged in Rabi'u'l-akhar 934 AH. this passage shews that, as a minimum estimate, what remains of Babur's composed narrative (i.e. down to f. 216b) was written after that date (Jan. 1528).

3 Char-shambalar. Mention of another inhabitant of this place with the odd name, Wednesday (Char-shamba), is made on f. 42b.

4 Mole-marked Lady; most MSS. style her Bi but H.S. iii, 327, writes Bibi; it varies also by calling her a Turk. She was a purchased slave of Shahr-banu's and was given to the Mirza by Shahr-banu at the time of her own marriage with him.

5 As noted already, f. 168b enumerates three only.

6 The three were almost certainly Badi'u'z-zaman, Haidar, son of a Timurid mother, and Muzaffar-i-husain, born after his mother had been legally married.

in seven or eight years, excepting only Muhammad-i-zaman
Mirza.[1]

(*g. His amirs.*)

There was Muhammad Baranduq *Barlas*, descending from
Chaku *Barlas* as follows,—Muhammad Baranduq, son of 'Ali, son
of Baranduq, son of Jahan-shah, son of Chaku *Barlas*.[2] He had
been a beg of Babur Mirza's presence; later on Sl. Abu-sa'id Mirza
favoured him, gave him Kabul conjointly with Jahangir *Barlas*,
and made him Aulugh Beg Mirza's guardian. After the death of
Sl. Abu-sa'id Mirza, Aulugh Beg Mirza formed designs against
the two Barlas; they got to know this, kept tight hold of him,
made the tribes and hordes march,[3] moved as for Qunduz, and
when up on Hindu-kush, courteously compelled Aulugh Beg
Mirza to start back for Kabul, they themselves going on to Sl.
Husain Mirza in Khurasan, who, in his turn, shewed them great
favour. Muhammad Baranduq was remarkably intelligent, a very
leaderlike man indeed! He was extravagantly fond of a hawk; so
much so, they say, that if a hawk of his had strayed or had died, he
would ask, taking the names of his sons on his lips, what it would
have mattered if such or such a son had died or had broken his
neck, rather than this or that bird had died or had strayed.

Muzaffar *Barlas* was another.[4] He had been with the Mirza in
the guerilla fighting and, for some cause unknown, had received
extreme favour. In such honour was he in those guerilla days
that the compact was for the Mirza to take four *dang* (sixths)
Fol. 170b. of any country conquered, and for him to take two *dang*.
A strange compact indeed! How could it be right to make
even a faithful servant a co-partner in rule? Not even a younger

---

1 Seven sons predeceased him:—Farrukh, Shah-i-gharib, Muh. Ma'sum, Haidar,
Ibrahim-i-husain, Muh. Husain and Abu-turab. So too five daughters:—Aq, Bega,
Agha, Kichik and Fatima-sultan Begims. So too four wives:—Bega-sultan and
Chuli Begims, Zubaida and Latif-sultan Aghachas (H.S. iii, 327).

2 Chaku, a Barlas, as was Timur, was one of Timur's noted men.

At this point some hand not the scribe's has entered on the margin of the Hai.
MS. the descendants of Muh. Baranduq down into Akbar's reign:—
Muh. Faridun, bin Muh. Quli Khan, bin Mirza 'Ali, bin Muh. Baranduq *Barlas*.
Of these Faridun and Muh. Quli are amirs of the *Ayin-i-akbari* list (Blochmann,
pp. 341, 342; H.S. iii, 233).

3 Enforced marches of Mughuls and other nomads are mentioned also on f. 154b
and f. 155.

4 H.S. iii, 228, 233, 235.

brother or a son obtains such a pact; how then should a beg?[1]
When the Mirza had possession of the throne, he repented the
compact, but his repentance was of no avail; that muddy-minded
mannikin, favoured so much already, made growing assumption
to rule. The Mirza acted without judgment; people say
Muzaffar *Barlas* was poisoned in the end.[2] God knows the
truth!

'Ali-sher *Nawa'i* was another, the Mirza's friend rather than
his beg. They had been learners together in childhood and even
then are said to have been close friends. It is not known for
what offence Sl. Abu-sa'id Mirza drove 'Ali-sher Beg from Heri;
he then went to Samarkand where he was protected and
supported by Ahmad Haji Beg during the several years of his
stay.[3] He was noted for refinement of manner; people fancied
this due to the pride of high fortune but it may not have been
so, it may have been innate, since it was equally noticeable also
in Samarkand.[4] 'Ali-sher Beg had no match. For as long as
verse has been written in the Turki tongue, no-one has written
so much or so well as he. He wrote six books of poems
(*masnawi*), five of them answering to the Quintet (*Khamsah*),[5]
the sixth, entitled the *Lisanu't-tair* (Tongue of the birds), was
in the same metre as the *Mantiqu't-tair* (Speech of the birds).[6]
He put together four *diwans* (collections) of odes, bearing the
names, *Curiosities of Childhood*, *Marvels of Youth*, *Wonders of
Manhood* and *Advantages of Age*.[7] There are good quatrains
of his also. Some others of his compositions rank below those   Fol. 171.
mentioned; amongst them is a collection of his letters, imitating
that of Maulana 'Abdu'r-rahman *Jami* and aiming at gathering
together every letter on any topic he had ever written to any
person. He wrote also the *Mizanu'l-auzan* (Measure of
measures) on prosody; it is very worthless; he has made
mistake in it about the metres of four out of twenty-four

1 *beg kishi*, beg-person.
2 Khwand-amir says he died a natural death (H.S. iii, 235).
3 f. 21. For a fuller account of Nawa'i, *J. Asiatique* xvii, 175, M. Belin's article.
4 *i.e.* when he was poor and a beg's dependant. He went back to Heri at
Sl. Husain M.'s request in 873 AH.
5 Nizami's (Rieu's Pers. Cat. s.n.).
6 Faridu'd-din-'attar's (Rieu l.c. and Ency. Br.).
7 *Ghara'ibu's-sighar, Nawadiru'sh-shahab, Bada'i'u'l-wasat* and *Fawa'idu'l-kibr*.

quatrains, while about other measures he has made mistake such as any-one who has given attention to prosody, will understand. He put a Persian *diwan* together also, Fani (transitory) being his pen-name for Persian verse.[1] Some couplets in it are not bad but for the most part it is flat and poor. In music also he composed good things (*nima*), some excellent airs and preludes (*nakhsh u peshrau*). No such patron and protector of men of parts and accomplishments is known, nor has one such been heard of as ever appearing. It was through his instruction and support that Master (Ustad) Qul-i-muhammad the lutanist, Shaikhi the flautist, and Husain the lutanist, famous performers all, rose to eminence and renown. It was through his effort and supervision that Master Bih-zad and Shah Muzaffar became so distinguished in painting. Few are heard of as having helped to lay the good foundation for future excellence he helped to lay. He had neither son nor daughter, wife or family; he let the world pass by, alone and unencumbered. At first he was Keeper of the Seal; in middle-life he became a beg and for a time was Commandant in Astarabad; later on he forsook soldiering. He took nothing from the Mirza, on the contrary, he each year
Fol. 171b. offered considerable gifts. When the Mirza was returning from the Astarabad campaign, 'Ali-sher Beg went out to give him meeting; they saw one another but before 'Ali-sher Beg should have risen to leave, his condition became such that he could not rise. He was lifted up and carried away; the doctors could not tell what was wrong; he went to God's mercy next day,[2] one of his own couplets suiting his case:—

> I was felled by a stroke out of their ken and mine;
> What, in such evils, can doctors avail?

Ahmad the son of Tawakkal *Barlas* was another;[3] for a time he held Qandahar.

Wali Beg was another; he was of Haji Saifu'd-din Beg's line,[4] and had been one of the Mirza's father's (Mansur's) great

---

1 Every Persian poet has a *takhallus* (pen-name) which he introduces into the last couplet of each ode (Erskine).
2 The death occurred in the First Jumada 906 AH. (Dec. 1500 AD.).
3 Nizamu'd-din Ahmad bin Tawakkal *Barlas* (H.S. iii, 229).
4 This may be that uncle of Timur who made the Haj (T.R. p. 48, quoting the *Zafar-nama*).

begs.[1] Short life was granted to him after the Mirza took the throne (973 AH.); he died directly afterwards. He was orthodox and made the Prayers, was rough (*turk*) and sincere.

Husain of Shaikh Timur was another; he had been favoured and raised to the rank of beg[2] by Babur Mirza.

Nuyan Beg was another. He was a Sayyid of Tirmiz on his father's side; on his mother's he was related both to Sl. Abu-sa'id Mirza and to Sl. Husain Mirza.[3] Sl. Abu-sa'id Mirza had favoured him; he was the beg honoured in Sl. Ahmad Mirza's presence and he met with very great favour when he went to Sl. Husain Mirza's. He was a bragging, easy-going, wine-bibbing, jolly person. Through being in his father's service,[4] Hasan of Ya'qub used to be called also Nuyan's Hasan.

Jahangir *Barlas* was another.[5] For a time he shared the Kabul command with Muhammad Baranduq *Barlas*, later on Fol. 172. went to Sl. Husain Mirza's presence and received very great favour. His movements and poses (*harakat u sakanat*) were graceful and charming; he was also a man of pleasant temper. As he knew the rules of hunting and hawking, in those matters the Mirza gave him chief charge. He was a favourite of Badi'u'z-zaman Mirza and, bearing that Mirza's friendliness in mind, used to praise him.

Mirza Ahmad of 'Ali *Farsi Barlas* was another. Though he wrote no verse, he knew what was poetry. He was a gay-hearted, elegant person, one by himself.

'Abdu'l-khaliq Beg was another. Firuz Shah, Shahrukh Mirza's

---

1 Some MSS. omit the word "father" here but to read it obviates the difficulty of calling Wali a great beg of Sl. Husain Mirza although he died when that mirza took the throne (973 AH.) and although no leading place is allotted to him in Babur's list of Heri begs. Here as in other parts of Babur's account of Heri, the texts vary much whether Turki or Persian, *e.g.* the Elph. MS. appears to call Wali a blockhead (*dunkuz dur*), the Hai. MS. writing *n:kuz dur*(?).

2 He had been Babur *Shahrukhi*'s *yasawal* (Court-attendant), had fought against Husain for Yadgar-i-muhammad and had given a grand-daughter to Husain (H.S. iii, 206, 228, 230–32; D.S. in *Not. et Ex.* de Saçy p. 265).

3 f. 29b.

4 *Sic*, Elph. MS. and both Pers. trss. but the Hai. MS. omits "father". To read it, however, suits the circumstance that Hasan of Ya'qub was not with Husain and in Harat but was connected with Mahmud *Miranshahi* and Tirmiz (f. 24). Nuyan is not a personal name but is a title; it implies good-birth; all uses of it I have seen are for members of the religious family of Tirmiz.

5 He was the son of Ibrahim *Barlas* and a Badakhshi begim (T.R. p. 108).

greatly favoured beg, was his grandfather;[1] hence people called
him Firuz Shah's 'Abdu'l-khaliq. He held Khwarizm for a time.

Ibrahim *Duldai* was another. He had good knowledge of
revenue matters and the conduct of public business; his work
was that of a second Muh. Baranduq.

Zu'n-nun *Arghun* was another.[2] He was a brave man, using
his sword well in Sl. Abu-sa'id Mirza's presence and later on
getting his hand into the work whatever the fight. As to his
courage there was no question at all, but he was a bit of a fool.
After he left our (*Miran-shahi*) Mirzas to go to Sl. Husain
Mirza, the Mirza gave him Ghur and the Nikdiris. He did

Fol. 172b. excellent work in those parts with 70 to 80 men, with so few
beating masses and masses of Hazaras and Nikdiris; he had
not his match for keeping those tribes in order. After a while
Zamin-dawar was given to him. His son Shah-i-shuja' *Arghun*
used to move about with him and even in childhood used to
chop away with his sword. The Mirza favoured Shah-i-shuja'
and, somewhat against Zu'n-nun Beg's wishes, joined him with
his father in the government of Qandahar. Later on this father
and son made dissension between that father and that son,[3] and
stirred up much commotion. After I had overcome Khusrau
Shah and parted his retainers from him, and after I had taken
Kabul from Zu'n-nun *Arghun*'s son Muqim, Zu'n-nun Beg and
Khusrau Shah both went, in their helplessness, to see Sl. Husain
Mirza. Zu'n-nun *Arghun* grew greater after the Mirza's death
when they gave him the districts of the Heri Koh-daman, such
as Auba (Ubeh) and Chachcharan.[4] He was made Lord of
Badi'u'z-zaman Mirza's Gate[5] and Muhammad Baranduq *Barlas*
Lord of Muzaffar-i-husain Mirza's, when the two Mirzas became

---

1 He will have been therefore a collateral of Daulat-shah whose relation to
Firuz-shah is thus expressed by Nawa'i:—*Mir Daulat-shah Firuz-shah Beg-ning
'amm-zada-si Amir 'Ala'u'd-daula Isfarayini-ning aughuli dur, i.e.* Mir Daulat-shah
was the son of Firuz-shah Beg's paternal uncle's son, Amir 'Ala'u'd-daula *Isfarayini*.
Thus, Firuz-shah and Isfarayini were first cousins; Daulat-shah and 'Abdu'l-khaliq's
father were second cousins; while Daulat-shah and Firuz-shah were first cousins,
once removed (Rieu's Pers. Cat. p. 534; Browne's D.S. English preface p. 14 and its
reference to the Pers. preface).

2 *Tarkhan-nama*, E. & D.'s *History of India* i, 303; H.S. iii, 227.

3 f. 41 and note.

4 Both places are in the valley of the Heri-rud.

5 Badi'u'z-zaman married a daughter of Zu'n-nun; she died in 911 AH. (E. & D. i,
305; H.S. iii, 324).

joint-rulers in Heri. Brave though he was, he was a little crazed and shallow-pated; if he had not been so, would he have accepted flattery as he did? would he have made himself so contemptible? Here are the details of the matter:—While he was so dominant and so trusted in Heri, a few shaikhs and mullas went to him and said, "The Spheres are holding commerce with us; you are to be styled *Hizabru'l-lah* (Lion of God); you will overcome the Auzbeg." Fully accepting this flattery, he put his *futa* (bathing-cloth) round his neck[1] and gave thanks. Then, after Shaibaq Khan, coming against the Mirzas, had beaten them one by one near Badghis, Zu'n-nun *Arghun* met him face to face near Qara-rabat and, relying on that promise, stood up against him with 100 to 150 men. A mass of Auzbegs came up, overcame them and hustled them off; he himself was taken and put to death.[2] He was orthodox and no neglecter of the Prayers, indeed made the extra ones. He was mad for chess; he played it according to his own fancy and, if others play with one hand, he played with both.[3] Avarice and stinginess ruled in his character.

Fol. 173.

Darwish-i-'ali Beg was another,[4] the younger full-brother of 'Ali-sher Beg. He had the Balkh Command for a time and there did good beg-like things, but he was a muddle-head and somewhat wanting in merit. He was dismissed from the Balkh Command because his muddle-headedness had hampered the Mirza in his first campaign against Qunduz and Hisar. He came to my presence when I went to Qunduz in 916 AH. (1510 AD.), brutalized and stupefied, far from capable begship and out-side peaceful home-life. Such favour as he had had, he appears to have had for 'Ali-sher Beg's sake.

Mughul Beg was another. He was Governor of Heri for a time, later on was given Astarabad, and from there fled to Ya'qub Beg in 'Iraq. He was of amorous disposition[5] and an incessant dicer.

---

1 This indicates, both amongst Musalmans and Hindus, obedience and submission. Several instances occur in Macculloch's *Bengali Household Stories*.

2 T.R. p. 205.

3 This is an idiom expressive of great keenness (Erskine).

4 H.S. iii, 250, *kitabdar*, librarian; so too Hai. MS. f. 174*b*.

5 *mutaiyam* (f. 7*b* and note). Mir Mughul Beg was put to death for treachery in 'Iraq (H.S. iii, 227, 248).

Sayyid Badr (Full-moon) was another, a very strong man,
Fol. 173b. graceful in his movements and singularly well-mannered. He
danced wonderfully well, doing one dance quite unique and
seeming to be his own invention.[1] His whole service was with
the Mirza whose comrade he was in wine and social pleasure.

Islim *Barlas* was another, a plain (*turk*) person who understood
hawking well and did some things to perfection. Drawing a bow
of 30 to 40 *batmans* strength,[2] he would make his shaft pass right
through the target (*takhta*). In the gallop from the head of the
qabaq-maidan,[3] he would loosen his bow, string it again, and
then hit the gourd (*qabaq*). He would tie his string-grip (*zih-gir*)
to the one end of a string from 1 to 1½ yards long, fasten the
other end to a tree, let his shaft fly, and shoot through the string-
grip while it revolved.[4] Many such remarkable feats he did. He
served the Mirza continuously and was at every social gathering.

Sl. Junaid *Barlas* was another;[5] in his latter days he went to
Sl. Ahmad Mirza's presence.[6] He is the father of the Sl. Junaid
Barlas on whom at the present time[7] the joint-government of
Jaunpur depends.[8]

Shaikh Abu-sa'id Khan *Dar-miyan* (In-between) was another.
It is not known whether he got the name of Dar-miyan because
he took a horse to the Mirza *in the middle* of a fight, or whether
because he put himself *in between* the Mirza and some-one
designing on his life.[9]

1 Babur speaks as an eye-witness (f. 187b). For a single combat of Sayyid Badr,
H.S. iii, 233.
2 f. 167 and note to *batman*.
3 A level field in which a gourd (*qabaq*) is set on a pole for an archer's mark to be
hit in passing at the gallop (f. 19 and note).
4 Or possibly during the gallop the archer turned in the saddle and shot backwards.
5 Junaid was the father of Nizamu'd-din 'Ali, Babur's Khalifa (Vice-gerent).
That Khalifa was of a religious house on his mother's side may be inferred from his
being styled both Sayyid and Khwaja neither of which titles could have come from
his Turki father. His mother may have been a sayyida of one of the religious families
of Marghinan (f. 18 and note), since Khalifa's son Muhibb-i-'ali writes his father's
name "Nizamu'd-din 'Ali *Marghilani*" (*Marghinani*) in the Preface of his *Book on
Sport* (Rieu's Pers. Cat. p. 485).
6 This northward migration would take the family into touch with Babur's in
Samarkand and Farghana.
7 He was left in charge of Jaunpur in Rabi' I, 933 AH. (Jan. 1527 AD.) but exchanged
for Chunar in Ramzan 935 AH. (June 1529 AD.); so that for the writing of this part
of the *Babur-nama* we have the major and minor limits of Jan. 1527 and June 1529.
8 *See* Additional Notes, p. 798.   9 H.S. iii, 227.

Bih-bud Beg was another. He had served in the pages' circle (*chuhra jirgasi*) during the guerilla times and gave such Fol. 174. satisfaction by his service that the Mirza did him the favour of putting his name on the stamp (*tamgha*) and the coin (*sikka*).[1]

Shaikhim Beg was another.[2] People used to call him Shaikhim *Suhaili* because Suhaili was his pen-name. He wrote all sorts of verse, bringing in terrifying words and mental images. Here is a couplet of his:—

In the anguish of my nights, the whirlpool of my sighs engulphs the firmament;
Like a dragon, the torrent of my tears swallows the quarters of the world.

Well-known it is that when he once recited that couplet in Maulana 'Abdu'r-rahman *Jami*'s presence, the honoured Mulla asked him whether he was reciting verse or frightening people. He put a *diwan* together; *masnawis* of his are also in existence.

Muhammad-i-wali Beg was another, the son of the Wali Beg already mentioned. Latterly he became one of the Mirza's great begs but, great beg though he was, he never neglected his service and used to recline (*yastanib*) day and night in the Gate. Through doing this, his free meals and open table were always set just outside the Gate. Quite certainly a man who was so constantly in waiting, *would* receive the favour he received! It is an evil noticeable today that effort must be made before the man, dubbed Beg because he has five or six of the bald and blind at his back, can be got into the Gate at all! Where this sort of service is, it must be to their own misfortune! Muhammad-i-wali Beg's public table and free meals were good; he kept his servants neat and well-dressed and with his own hands gave Fol. 174b. ample portion to the poor and destitute, but he was foul-mouthed and evil-spoken. He and also Darwish-i-'ali the librarian were in my service when I took Samarkand in 917 AH. (Oct. 1511 AD.); he was palsied then; his talk lacked salt; his former claim to favour was gone. His assiduous waiting appears to have been the cause of his promotion.

---

1 *See* Additional Notes, p. 798. *See also* Appendix H, *On the counter-mark Bih-bud on coins.*

2 Nizamu'd-din Amir Shaikh Ahmadu's-suhaili was surnamed Suhaili through a *fal* (augury) taken by his spiritual guide, Kamalu'd-din Husain *Gazur-gahi*; it was he induced Husain *Kashifi* to produce his *Anwar-i-suhaili* (Lights of Canopus) (f. 125 and note; Rieu's Pers. Cat. p. 756; and for a couplet of his, H.S. iii, 242 l. 10).

Baba 'Ali the Lord of the Gate was another. First, 'Ali-sher
Beg showed him favour; next, because of his courage, the Mirza
took him into service, made him Lord of the Gate, and promoted
him to be a beg. One of his sons is serving me now (*circa* 934 AH.),
that Yunas of 'Ali who is a beg, a confidant, and of my household.
He will often be mentioned.[1]

Badru'd-din (Full-moon of the Faith) was another. He had
been in the service of Sl. Abu-sa'id Mirza's Chief Justice Mirak
'Abdu'r-rahim; it is said he was very nimble and sure-footed,
a man who could leap over seven horses at once. He and Baba
'Ali were close companions.

Hasan of 'Ali *Jalair* was another. His original name was
Husain *Jalair* but he came to be called 'Ali's Hasan.[2] His father
'Ali *Jalair* must have been favoured and made a beg by Babur
Mirza; no man was greater later on when Yadgar-i-muhammad
M. took Heri. Hasan-i-'ali was Sl. Husain Mirza's *Qush-begi*.[3] He
made Tufaili (Uninvited-guest) his pen-name; wrote good odes
and was the Master of this art in his day. He wrote odes on
my name when he came to my presence at the time I took
Samarkand in 917 AH. (1511 AD.). Impudent (*bi bak*) and
prodigal he was, a keeper of catamites, a constant dicer and
draught-player.

Fol. 175.

Khwaja 'Abdu'l-lah *Marwarid* (Pearl)[4] was another; he was
at first Chief Justice but later on became one of the Mirza's
favourite household-begs. He was full of accomplishments; on
the dulcimer he had no equal, and he invented the shake on the
dulcimer; he wrote in several scripts, most beautifully in
the *ta'liq*; he composed admirable letters, wrote good verse,
with Bayani for his pen-name, and was a pleasant companion.
Compared with his other accomplishments, his verse ranks low,
but he knew what was poetry. Vicious and shameless, he became

---

1 Index *s.n.*

2 Did the change complete an analogy between 'Ali *Jalair* and his (perhaps) elder
son with 'Ali Khalifa and his elder son Hasan?

3 The Qush-begi is, in Central Asia, a high official who acts for an absent ruler
(Shaw); he does not appear to be the Falconer, for whom Babur's name is Qushchi
(f. 15 n.).

4 He received this sobriquet because when he returned from an embassy to the
Persian Gulf, he brought, from Bahrein, to his Timurid master a gift of royal
pearls (Sam Mirza). For an account of Marwarid *see* Rieu's Pers. Cat. p. 1094 and
(*re* portrait) p. 787.

the captive of a sinful disease through his vicious excesses, out-lived his hands and feet, tasted the agonies of varied torture for several years, and departed from the world under that affliction.[1]

Sayyid Muhammad-i-aurus was another; he was the son of that Aurus (Russian?) *Arghun* who, when Sl. Abu-sa'id Mirza took the throne, was his beg in chief authority. At that time there were excellent archer-braves; one of the most distinguished was Sayyid Muhammad-i-aurus. His bow strong, his shaft long, he must have been a bold (*yurak*) shot and a good one. He was Commandant in Andikhud for some time.

Mir (Qambar-i-)'ali the Master of the Horse was another. He it was who, by sending a man to Sl. Husain Mirza, brought him down on the defenceless Yadgar-i-muhammad Mirza.

Sayyid Hasan *Aughlaqchi* was another, a son of Sayyid *Aughlaqchi* and a younger brother of Sayyid Yusuf Beg.[2] He was the father of a capable and accomplished son, named Mirza Farrukh. He had come to my presence before I took Samar-kand in 917 AH. (1511 AD.). Though he had written little verse, he wrote fairly; he understood the astrolabe and astronomy well, was excellent company, his talk good too, but he was rather a bad drinker (*bad shrab*). He died in the fight at Ghaj-dawan.[3] Fol. 175*b*.

Tingri-birdi the storekeeper (*samanchi*) was another; he was a plain (*turk*), bold, sword-slashing brave. As has been said, he charged out of the Gate of Balkh on Khusrau Shah's great retainer Nazar Bahadur and overcame him (903 AH.).

There were a few Turkman braves also who were received with great favour when they came to the Mirza's presence. One of the first to come was 'Ali Khan *Bayandar*.[4] Asad Beg and Taham-tan (Strong-bodied) Beg were others, an elder and younger brother these; Badi'u'z-zaman Mirza took Taham-tan Beg's daughter and by her had Muhammad-i-zaman Mirza. Another was Ibrahim *Chaghatai*. Mir 'Umar Beg was another; later on he was in Badi'u'z-zaman Mirza's service; he was a

---

1 Sam Mirza specifies this affliction as *abla-i-farang*, thus making what may be one of the earliest Oriental references to *morbus gallicus* [as de Saçy here translates the name], the foreign or European pox, the "French disease of Shakespeare" (H.B.).

2 Index *s.n.*Yusuf.

3 Ramzan 3rd 918 AH.–Nov. 12th 1512.

4 *i.e.* of the White-sheep Turkmans.

brave, plain, excellent person. His son, Abu'l-fath by name, came from 'Iraq to my presence, a very soft, unsteady and feeble person; such a son from such a father!

Of those who came into Khurasan after Shah Isma'il took 'Iraq and Azarbaijan (*circa* 906 AH.—1500 AD.), one was 'Abdu'l-baqi Mirza of Timur Beg's line. He was a Miran-shahi[1] whose ancestors will have gone long before into those parts, put thought of sovereignty out of their heads, served those ruling there, and from them have received favour. That Timur 'Usman who was the great, trusted beg of Ya'qub Beg (*White-sheep Turkman*) and who had once even thought of sending against Khurasan the mass of men he had gathered to himself, must have been this 'Abdu'l-baqi Mirza's paternal-uncle. Sl. Husain Mirza took 'Abdu'l-baqi Mirza at once into favour, making him a son-in-law by giving him Sultanim Begim, the mother of Muhammad Sl. Mirza.[2] Another late-comer was Murad Beg *Bayandari*.

Fol. 176.

(h. His Chief Justices (sadur).)

One was Mir Sar-i-barahna (Bare-head);[3] he was from a village in Andijan and appears to have made claim to be a sayyid (*mutasayyid*). He was a very agreeable companion, pleasant of temper and speech. His were the judgment and rulings that carried weight amongst men of letters and poets of Khurasan. He wasted his time by composing, in imitation of the story of Amir Hamza,[4] a work which is one long, far-fetched lie, opposed to sense and nature.

Kamalu'd-din Husain *Gazur-gahi*[5] was another. Though not a Sufi, he was mystical.[6] Such mystics as he will have

1 His paternal line was, 'Abdu'l-baqi, son of 'Usman, son of Sayyidi Ahmad, son of Miran-shah. His mother's people were begs of the White-sheep (H.S. iii, 290).
2 Sultanim had married Wais (f. 167b) not later than 895 or 896 AH. (H.S. iii, 253); she married 'Abdu'l-baqi in 908 AH. (1502-3 AD.).
3 Sayyid Shamsu'd-din Muhammad, Mir Sayyid *Sar-i-barahna* owed his sobriquet of Bare-head to love-sick wanderings of his youth (H.S. iii, 328). The H.S. it is clear, recognizes him as a sayyid.
4 Rieu's Pers. Cat. p. 760; it is immensely long and "filled with tales that shock all probability" (Erskine).
5 f. 94 and note. Sl. Husain M. made him curator of Ansari's shrine, an officer represented, presumably, by Col. Yate's "Mir of Gazur-gah", and he became Chief Justice in 904 AH. (1498-99 AD.). *See* H.S. iii, 330 and 340; JASB 1887, art. *On the city of Harat* (C. E. Yate) p. 85.
6 *mutasauwif*, perhaps meaning not a professed Sufi.

gathered in 'Ali-sher Beg's presence and there have gone into their raptures and ecstasies. Kamalu'd-din will have been better-born than most of them; his promotion will have been due to his good birth, since he had no other merit to speak of.[1] A production of his exists, under the name *Majalisu'l-'ushshaq* (Assemblies of lovers), the authorship of which he ascribes (in its preface) to Sl. Husain Mirza.[2] It is mostly a lie and a taste-less lie. He has written such irreverent things in it that some of them cast doubt upon his orthodoxy; for example, he represents the Prophets,—Peace be on them,—and Saints as subject to earthly passion, and gives to each a minion and a mistress. Another and singularly absurd thing is that, although in his preface he says, "This is Sl. Husain Mirza's own written word and literary composition," he, never-the-less, enters, in the body of the book, "All by the sub-signed author", at the head of odes and verses well-known to be his own. It was his flattery gave Zu'n-nun *Arghun* the title Lion of God.

Fol. 176b.

(i. His wazirs.)

One was Majdu'd-din Muhammad, son of Khwaja Pir Ahmad of Khwaf, the one man (*yak-qalam*) of Shahrukh Mirza's Finance-office.[3] In Sl. Husain Mirza's Finance-office there was not at first proper order or method; waste and extravagance resulted; the peasant did not prosper, and the soldier was not satisfied. Once while Majdu'd-din Muhammad was still *par-wanchi*[4] and styled Mirak (Little Mir), it became a matter of importance to the Mirza to have some money; when he asked the Finance-officials for it, they said none had been collected and that there was none. Majdu'd-din Muhammad must have heard this and have smiled, for the Mirza asked him why he smiled; privacy was made and he told Mirza what was in his mind.

1 He was of high birth on both sides, of religious houses of Tabas and Nishapur (D.S. pp. 161, 163).

2 In agreement with its preface, Dr. Rieu entered the book as written by Sl. Husain Mirza; in his Addenda, however, he quotes Babur as the authority for its being by Gazur-gahi; Khwand-amir's authority can be added to Babur's (H.S. 340; Pers. Cat. pp. 351, 1085).

3 *Diwan*. The Wazir is a sort of Minister of Finance; the Diwan is the office of revenue receipts and issues (Erskine).

4 a secretary who writes out royal orders (H.S. iii, 244).

Said he, "If the honoured Mirza will pledge himself to strengthen
Fol. 177.   my hands by not opposing my orders, it shall so be before long
that the country shall prosper, the peasant be content, the soldier
well-off, and the Treasury full." The Mirza for his part gave
the pledge desired, put Majdu'd-din Muhammad in authority
throughout Khurasan, and entrusted all public business to him.
He in his turn by using all possible diligence and effort, before
long had made soldier and peasant grateful and content, filled
the Treasury to abundance, and made the districts habitable
and cultivated. He did all this however in face of opposition
from the begs and men high in place, all being led by 'Ali-sher
Beg, all out of temper with what Majdu'd-din Muhammad had
effected. By their effort and evil suggestion he was arrested
and dismissed.[1] In succession to him Nizamu'l-mulk of Khwaf
was made Diwan but in a short time they got him arrested also,
and him they got put to death.[2] They then brought Khwaja
Afzal out of 'Iraq and made him Diwan; he had just been
made a beg when I came to Kabul (910 AH.), and he also
impressed the Seal in Diwan.

Khwaja 'Ata[3] was another; although, unlike those already
mentioned, he was not in high office or Finance-minister (*diwan*),
nothing was settled without his concurrence the whole
Khura-sanat over. He was a pious, praying, upright (*mutadaiyin*)
person; he must have been diligent in business also.

1   Count von Noer's words about a cognate reform of later date suit this man's work,
it also was "a bar to the defraudment of the Crown, a stumbling-block in the path of
avaricious chiefs" (*Emperor Akbar* trs. i, 11). The opposition made by 'Ali-sher to
reform so clearly to Husain's gain and to Husain's begs' loss, stirs the question,
"What was the source of his own income?" Up to 873 AH. he was for some years
the dependant of Ahmad Haji Beg; he took nothing from the Mirza, but gave to
him; he must have spent much in benefactions. The question may have presented
itself to M. Belin for he observes, "'Ali-sher qui sans doute, à son retour de l'exil,
recouvra l'héritage de ses pères, et depuis occupa de hautes positions dans le gouvernement de son pays, avait acquis une grande fortune" (*J. Asiatique* xvii, 227). While
not contradicting M. Belin's view that vested property such as can be described as
"paternal inheritance", may have passed from father to son, even in those days of
fugitive prosperity and changing appointments, one cannot but infer, from
Nawa'i's opposition to Majdu'd-din, that he, like the rest, took a partial view of
the "rights" of the cultivator.
2   This was in 903 AH. after some 20 years of service (H.S. iii, 231; Ethé I.O. Cat. p. 252).
3   Amir Jamalu'd-din 'Ata'u'l-lah, known also as Jamalu'd-din Husain, wrote a
History of Muhammad (H.S. iii, 348-9; Rieu's Pers. Cat. p. 147 & (a correction)
p. 1081).

(*j. Others of the Court.*)

Those enumerated were Sl. Husain Mirza's retainers and followers.[1] His was a wonderful Age; in it Khurasan, and Heri above all, was full of learned and matchless men. What- Fol. 177*b*. ever the work a man took up, he aimed and aspired at bringing that work to perfection. One such man was Maulana 'Abdu'r-rahman *Jami*, who was unrivalled in his day for esoteric and exoteric knowledge. Famous indeed are his poems! The Mulla's dignity it is out of my power to describe; it has occurred to me merely to mention his honoured name and one atom of his excellence, as a benediction and good omen for this part of my humble book.

Shaikhu'l-islam Saifu'd-din Ahmad was another. He was of the line of that Mulla Sa'du'd-din (Mas'ud) *Taftazani*[2] whose descendants from his time downwards have given the Shaikhu'l-islam to Khurasan. He was a very learned man, admirably versed in the Arabian sciences[3] and the Traditions, most God-fearing and orthodox. Himself a Shafi'i,[4] he was tolerant of all the sects. People say he never once in 70 years omitted the Congregational Prayer. He was martyred when Shah Isma'il took Heri (916 AH.); there now remains no man of his honoured line.[5]

Maulana Shaikh Husain was another; he is mentioned here, although his first appearance and his promotion were under Sl. Abu-sa'id Mirza, because he was living still under Sl. Husain Fol. 178. Mirza. Being well-versed in the sciences of philosophy, logic and rhetoric, he was able to find much meaning in a few words and to bring it out opportunely in conversation. Being very intimate and influential with Sl. Abu-sa'id Mirza, he took part in all momentous affairs of the Mirza's dominions; there was

1 Amongst noticeable omissions from Babur's list of Heri celebrities are Mir Khwand Shah ("Mirkhond"), his grandson Khwand-amir, Husain *Kashifi* and Muinu'd-din al Zamji, author of a *History of Harat* which was finished in 897 AH.
2 Sa'du'd-din Mas'ud, son of 'Umar, was a native of Taft in Yazd, whence his cognomen (Bahar-i-'ajam); he died in 792 AH.—1390 AD. (H.S. iii, 59, 343; T.R. p. 236; Rieu's Pers. Cat. pp. 352, 453).
3 These are those connected with grammar and rhetoric (Erskine).
4 This is one of the four principal sects of Muhammadanism (Erskine).
5 T.R. p. 235, for Shah Isma'il's murders in Heri.

no better *muhtasib*;[1] this will have been why he was so much
trusted. Because he had been an intimate of that Mirza, the
incomparable man was treated with insult in Sl. Husain
Mirza's time.

Mulla-zada Mulla 'Usman was another. He was a native of
Chirkh, in the Luhugur *tuman* of the *tuman* of Kabul[2] and was
called the Born Mulla (*Mulla-zada*) because in Aulugh Beg
Mirza's time he used to give lessons when 14 years old. He went
to Heri on his way from Samarkand to make the circuit of the
ka'ba, was there stopped, and made to remain by Sl. Husain
Mirza. He was very learned, the most so of his time. People
say he was nearing the rank of Ijtihad[3] but he did not reach it.
It is said of him that he once asked, "How should a person
forget a thing heard?" A strong memory he must have had!

Mir Jamalu'd-din the Traditionalist[4] was another. He had no
equal in Khurasan for knowledge of the Muhammadan Traditions.
He was advanced in years and is still alive (934 to 937 AH.).

Mir Murtaz was another. He was well-versed in the sciences
Fol. 178b. of philosophy and metaphysics; he was called *murtaz* (ascetic)
because he fasted a great deal. He was madly fond of chess,
so much so that if he had met two players, he would hold one
by the skirt while he played his game out with the other, as
much as to say, "Don't go!"

Mir Mas'ud of Sherwan was another.[5]

Mir 'Abdu'l-ghafur of Lar was another. Disciple and pupil
both of Maulana 'Abdu'r-rahman *Jami*, he had read aloud most
of the Mulla's poems (*masnawi*) in his presence, and wrote
a plain exposition of the *Nafahat*.[6] He had good acquaintance

1 Superintendent of Police, who examines weights, measures and provisions, also
prevents gambling, drinking and so on.
2 f. 137.
3 The rank of Mujtahid, which is not bestowed by any individual or class of men
but which is the result of slow and imperceptible opinion, finally prevailing and
universally acknowledged, is one of the greatest peculiarities of the religion of Persia.
The Mujtahid is supposed to be elevated above human fears and human enjoyments,
and to have a certain degree of infallibility and inspiration. He is consulted with
reverence and awe. There is not always a Mujtahid necessarily existing. *See*
Kaempfer, *Amoenitates Exoticae* (Erskine).
4 *muhaddas*, one versed in the traditional sayings and actions of Muhammad.
5 H.S. iii, 340.
6 B.M. Or. 218 (Rieu's Pers. Cat. p. 350). The Commentary was made in order
to explain the *Nafahat* to Jami's son.

with the exoteric sciences, and in the esoteric ones also was very successful. He was a curiously casual and unceremonious person; no person styled Mulla by any-one soever was debarred from submitting a (Qoran) chapter to him for exposition; more-over whatever the place in which he heard there was a darwish, he had no rest till he had reached that darwish's presence. He was ill when I was in Khurasan (912 AH.); I went to enquire for him where he lay in the Mulla's College,[1] after I had made the circuit of the Mulla's tomb. He died a few days later, of that same illness.

Mir 'Ata'u'l-lah of Mashhad was another.[2] He knew the Arabian sciences well and also wrote a Persian treatise on rhyme. That treatise is well-done but it has the defect that he brings into it, as his examples, couplets of his own and, assuming them   Fol. 179. to be correct, prefixes to each, "As must be observed in the following couplet by your slave" (*banda*). Several rivals of his find deserved comment in this treatise. He wrote another on the curiosities of verse, entitled *Badai'u's-sanai*; a very well-written treatise. He may have swerved from the Faith.

Qazi Ikhtiyar was another. He was an excellent Qazi and wrote a treatise in Persian on Jurisprudence, an admirable treatise; he also, in order to give elucidation (*iqtibas*), made a collection of homonymous verses from the Qoran. He came with Muhammad-i-yusuf to see me at the time I met the Mirzas on the Murgh-ab (912 AH.). Talk turning on the Baburi script,[3] he asked me about it, letter by letter; I wrote it out, letter by letter; he went through it, letter by letter, and having learned its plan, wrote something in it there and then.

Mir Muhammad-i-yusuf was another; he was a pupil of the Shaikhu'l-islam[4] and afterwards was advanced to his place. In some assemblies he, in others, Qazi Ikhtiyar took the higher place. Towards the end of his life he was so infatuated

1 He was buried by the Mulla's side.
2 Amir Burhanu'd-din 'Ata'u'l-lah bin Mahmudu'l-husaini was born in Nishapur but known as Mashhadi because he retired to that holy spot after becoming blind.
3 f. 144*b* and note. Qazi Ikhtiyaru'd-din Hasan (H.S. iii, 347) appears to be the Khwaja Ikhtiyar of the *Ayin-i-akbari*, and, if so, will have taken professional interest in the script, since Abu'l-fazl describes him as a distinguished calligrapher in Sl. Husain M.'s presence (Blochmann, p. 101).
4 Saifu'd-din (Sword of the Faith) Ahmad, presumably.

with soldiering and military command, that except of those two
tasks, what could be learned from his conversation? what known
from his pen? Though he failed in both, those two ambitions
ended by giving to the winds his goods and his life, his house
and his home. He may have been a Shi'a.

(*k. The Poets.*)

Fol. 179*b*.　　The all-surpassing head of the poet-band was Maulana
'Abdu'r-rahman *Jami*. Others were Shaikhim Suhaili and Hasan
of 'Ali *Jalair*[1] whose names have been mentioned already as in
the circle of the Mirza's begs and household.

Asafi was another,[2] he taking Asafi for his pen-name because
he was a wazir's son. His verse does not want for grace or
sentiment, but has no merit through passion and ecstasy. He
himself made the claim, "I have never packed up (*bulmadi*) my
odes to make the oasis (*wadi*) of a collection."[3] This was
affectation, his younger brothers and his intimates having
collected his odes. He wrote little else but odes. He waited
on me when I went into Khurasan (912 AH.).

Bana'i was another; he was a native of Heri and took such
a pen-name (Bana'i) on account of his father Ustad Muhammad
Sabz-bana.[4] His odes have grace and ecstasy. One poem
(*masnawi*) of his on the topic of fruits, is in the *mutaqarib*
measure;[5] it is random and not worked up. Another short
poem is in the *khafif* measure, so also is a longer one finished
towards the end of his life. He will have known nothing of
music in his young days and 'Ali-sher Beg seems to have taunted
him about it, so one winter when the Mirza, taking 'Ali-sher Beg

1 A sister of his, Apaq Bega, the wife of 'Ali-sher's brother Darwish-i-'ali *kitabdar*,
is included as a poet in the *Biography of Ladies* (Sprenger's Cat. p. 11). Amongst
the 20 women named one is a wife of Shaibaq Khan, another a daughter of Hilali.
2 He was the son of Khw. Ni'amatu'l-lah, one of Sl. Abu-sa'id M.'s wazirs.
When dying *aet.* 70 (923 AH.), he made this chronogram on his own death, "With
70 steps he measured the road to eternity." The name Asaf, so frequent amongst
wazirs, is that of Solomon's wazir.
3 Other interpretations are open; *wadi*, taken as *river*, might refer to the going on
from one poem to another, the stream of verse; or it might be taken as *desert*, with
disparagement of collections.
4 Maulana Jamalu'd-din *Bana'i* was the son of a *sabz-bana*, an architect, a good
builder.
5 Steingass's Dictionary allows convenient reference for examples of metres.

with him, went to winter in Merv, Bana'i stayed behind in Heri
and so applied himself to study music that before the heats he
had composed several works. These he played and sang, airs
with variations, when the Mirza came back to Heri in the heats.   Fol. 180.
All amazed, 'Ali-sher Beg praised him. His musical compositions
are perfect; one was an air known as *Nuh-rang* (Nine modula-
tions), and having both the theme (*tukanash*) and the variation
(*yila*) on the note called *rast*(?). Bana'i was 'Ali-sher Beg's
rival; it will have been on this account he was so much ill-treated.
When at last he could bear it no longer, he went into Azarbaijan
and 'Iraq to the presence of Ya'qub Beg; he did not remain however in those parts after Ya'qub Beg's death (896 AH.–1491 AD.)
but went back to Heri, just the same with his jokes and retorts.
Here is one of them:—'Ali-sher at a chess-party in stretching
his leg touched Bana'i on the hinder-parts and said jestingly,
"It is the sad nuisance of Heri that a man can't stretch his leg
without its touching a poet's backside." "Nor draw it up again,"
retorted Bana'i.[1] In the end the upshot of his jesting was that
he had to leave Heri again; he went then to Samarkand.[2]
A great many good new things used to be made for 'Ali-sher
Beg, so whenever any-one produced a novelty, he called it
'Ali-sher's in order to give it credit and vogue.[3] Some things were
called after him in compliment *e.g.* because when he had ear-ache,
he wrapped his head up in one of the blue triangular kerchiefs
women tie over their heads in winter, that kerchief was called
'Ali-sher's comforter. Then again, Bana'i when he had decided
to leave Heri, ordered a quite new kind of pad for his ass and   Fol. 180*b*.
dubbed it 'Ali-sher's.

1 Other jokes made by *Bana'i* at the expense of Nawa'i are recorded in the various
sources.
2 Babur saw Bana'i in Samarkand at the end of 901 AH. (1496 AD. f. 38).
Here Dr. Leyden's translation ends; one other fragment which he translated will
be found under the year 925 AH. (Erskine). This statement allows attention to be
drawn to the inequality of the shares of the work done for the Memoirs of 1826 by
Leyden and by Erskine. It is just to Mr. Erskine, but a justice he did not claim,
to point out that Dr. Leyden's share is slight both in amount and in quality; his
essential contribution was the initial stimulus he gave to the great labours of his
collaborator.
3 So of Lope de Vega (b. 1562; d. 1635 AD.), "It became a common proverb to
praise a good thing by calling it *a Lope*, so that jewels, diamonds, pictures, *etc.* were
raised into esteem by calling them his" (Montalvan in Ticknor's *Spanish Literature*
ii, 270).

Maulana Saifi of Bukhara was another;[1] he was a Mulla complete[2] who in proof of his mulla-ship used to give a list of the books he had read. He put two *diwans* together, one being for the use of tradesmen (*harfa-kar*), and he also wrote many fables. That he wrote no *masnawi* is shewn by the following quatrain:—

> Though the *masnawi* be the orthodox verse,
>   I know the ode has Divine command;
> Five couplets that charm the heart
>   I know to outmatch the Two Quintets.[3]

A Persian prosody he wrote is at once brief and prolix, brief in the sense of omitting things that should be included, and prolix in the sense that plain and simple matters are detailed down to the diacritical points, down even to their Arabic points.[4] He is said to have been a great drinker, a bad drinker, and a mightily strong-fisted man.

'Abdu'l-lah the *masnawi*-writer was another.[5] He was from Jam and was the Mulla's sister's son. Hatifi was his pen-name. He wrote poems (*masnawi*) in emulation of the Two Quintets,[6] and called them *Haft-manzar* (Seven-faces) in imitation of the *Haft-paikar* (Seven-faces). In emulation of the *Sikandar-nama* he composed the *Timur-nama*. His most renowned *masnawi* is *Laila and Majnun*, but its reputation is greater than its charm.

Mir Husain the Enigmatist[7] was another. He seems to have had no equal in making riddles, to have given his whole time to it, and to have been a curiously humble, disconsolate (*na-murad*) and harmless (*bi-bad*) person.

Fol. 181.

Mir Muhammad *Badakhshi* of Ishkimish was another. As Ishkimish is not in Badakhshan, it is odd he should have made it

1 Maulana Saifi, known as 'Aruzi from his mastery in prosody (Rieu's Pers. Cat. p. 525).
2 Here pedantry will be implied in the mullahood.
3 *Khamsatin* (*infra* f. 180*b* and note).
4 This appears to mean that not only the sparse diacritical pointing common in writing Persian was dealt with but also the fuller Arabic.
5 He is best known by his pen-name Hatifi. The B.M. and I.O. have several of his books.
6 *Khamsatin*. Hatifi regarded himself as the successor of Nizami and Khusrau; this, taken with Babur's use of the word *Khamsatin* on f. 7 and here, and Saifi's just above, leads to the opinion that the *Khamsatin* of the *Babur-nama* are always those of Nizami and Khusrau, *the* Two Quintets (Rieu's Pers. Cat. p. 653).
7 Maulana Mir Kamalu'd-din Husain of Nishapur (Rieu l.c. index s.n.; Ethé's I.O. Cat. pp. 433 and 1134).

his pen-name. His verse does not rank with that of the poets previously mentioned,[1] and though he wrote a treatise on riddles, his riddles are not first-rate. He was a very pleasant companion; he waited on me in Samarkand (917 AH.).

Yusuf the metaphorist (badi')[2] was another. He was from the Farghana country; his odes are said not to be bad.

Ahi was another, a good ode-writer, latterly in Ibn-i-husain Mirza's service, and sahib-i-diwan.[3]

Muhammad Salih was another.[4] His odes are tasty but better-flavoured than correct. There is Turki verse of his also, not badly written. He went to Shaibaq Khan later on and found complete favour. He wrote a Turki poem (masnawi), named from Shaibaq Khan, in the raml masaddas majnun measure, that is to say the metre of the Subhat.[5] It is feeble and flat; Muhammad Salih's reader soon ceases to believe in him.[6] Here is one of his good couplets:—

> A fat man (Tambal) has gained the land of Farghana,
> Making Farghana the house of the fat-man (Tambal-khana).

Farghana is known also as Tambal-khana.[7] I do not know whether the above couplet is found in the masnawi mentioned.

---

1 One of his couplets on good and bad fortune is striking; "The fortune of men is like a sand-glass; one hour up, the next down." See D'Herbélot in his article (Erskine).

2 H.S. iii, 336; Rieu's Pers. Cat. p. 1089.

3 Ahi (sighing) was with Shah-i-gharib before Ibn-i-husain and to him dedicated his diwan. The words sahib-i-diwan seem likely to be used here with double meaning i.e. to express authorship and finance office. Though Babur has made frequent mention of authorship of a diwan and of office in the Diwan, he has not used these words hitherto in either sense; there may be a play of words here.

4 Muhammad Salih Mirza Khwarizmi, author of the Shaibani-nama which manifestly is the poem (masnawi) mentioned below. This has been published with a German translation by Professor Vambéry and has been edited with Russian notes by Mr. Platon Melioransky (Rieu's Turkish Cat. p. 74; H.S. iii, 301).

5 Jami's Subhatu'l-abrar (Rosary of the righteous).

6 The reference may be to things said by Muh. Salih the untruth of which was known to Babur through his own part in the events. A crying instance of mis-representation is Salih's assertion, in rhetorical phrase, that Babur took booty in jewels from Khusrau Shah; other instances concern the affairs of The Khans and of Babur in Transoxiana (f. 124b and index s.nn. Ahmad and Mahmud Chaghatai etc.; T.R. index s.nn.).

7 The name Fat-land (Tambal-khana) has its parallel in Fat-village (Simiz-kint) a name of Samarkand; in both cases the nick-name is accounted for by the fertility of irrigated lands. We have not been able to find the above-quoted couplet in the Shaibani-nama (Vambéry); needless to say, the pun is on the nick-name [tambal, fat] of Sl. Ahmad Tambal.

Muhammad *Salih* was a very wicked, tyrannical and heartless person.[1]

Maulana Shah Husain *Kami*[2] was another. There are not-bad verses of his; he wrote odes, and also seems to have put a *diwan* together.

Hilali (New-moon) was another; he is still alive.[3] Correct and graceful though his odes are, they make little impression. There is a *diwan* of his;[4] and there is also the poem (*masnawi*) in the Fol. 181*b*. *khafif* measure, entitled *Shah and Darwish* of which, fair though many couplets are, the basis and purport are hollow and bad. Ancient poets when writing of love and the lover, have represented the lover as a man and the beloved as a woman; but Hilali has made the lover a darwish, the beloved a king, with the result that the couplets containing the king's acts and words set him forth as shameless and abominable. It is an extreme effrontery in Hilali that for a poem's sake he should describe a young man and that young man a king, as resembling the shameless and immoral.[5] It is heard-said that Hilali had a very retentive memory, and that he had by heart 30 or 40,000 couplets, and the greater part of the Two Quintets,—all most useful for the minutiae of prosody and the art of verse.

Ahli[6] was another; he was of the common people ('*ami*), wrote verse not bad, even produced a *diwan*.

1 Muh. Salih does not show well in his book; he is sometimes coarse, gloats over spoil whether in human captives or goods, and, his good-birth not-forbidding, is a servile flatterer. Babur's word "heartless" is just; it must have had sharp prompting from Salih's rejoicing in the downfall of The Khans, Babur's uncles.
2 the Longer (H.S. iii, 349).
3 Maulana Badru'd-din (Full-moon of the Faith) whose pen-name was Hilali, was of Astarabad. It may be noted that two dates of his death are found, 936 and 939 AH. the first given by de Saçy, the second by Rieu, and that the second seems to be correct (*Not. et Extr.* p. 285; Pers. Cat. p. 656; Hammer's *Geschichte* p. 368).
4 B.M. Add. 7783.
5 Opinions differ as to the character of this work:—Babur's is uncompromising; von Hammer (p. 369) describes it as "*ein romantisches Gedicht, welches eine sentimentale Männerliebe behandelt*"; Sprenger (p. 427), as a mystical *masnawi* (poem); Rieu finds no spiritual symbolism in it and condemns it (Pers. Cat. p. 656 and, quoting the above passage of Babur, p. 1090); Ethé, who has translated it, takes it to be mystical and symbolic (I.O. Cat. p. 783).
6 Of four writers using the pen-name Ahli (Of-the-people), *viz.* those of Turan, Shiraz, Tarshiz (in Khurasan), and 'Iraq, the one noticed here seems to be he of Tarshiz. Ahli of Tarshiz was the son of a locally-known pious father and became a Superintendent of the Mint; Babur's '*ami* may refer to Ahli's first patrons, tanners and shoe-makers by writing for whom he earned his living (Sprenger, p. 319). Erskine read '*ummi*, meaning that Ahli could neither read nor write; de Courteille that he was *un homme du commun*.

(*l. Artists.*)

Of fine pen-men there were many; the one standing-out in *nakhsh ta'liq* was Sl.'Ali of Mashhad[1] who copied many books for the Mirza and for 'Ali-sher Beg, writing daily 30 couplets for the first, 20 for the second.

Of the painters, one was Bih-zad.[2] His work was very dainty but he did not draw beardless faces well; he used greatly to lengthen the double chin (*ghab-ghab*); bearded faces he drew admirably.

Shah Muzaffar was another; he painted dainty portraits, representing the hair very daintily.[3] Short life was granted him; he left the world when on his upward way to fame.

Fol. 182.

Of musicians, as has been said, no-one played the dulcimer so well as Khwaja 'Abdu'l-lah *Marwarid*.

Qul-i-muhammad the lutanist ('*audi*) was another; he also played the guitar (*ghichak*) beautifully and added three strings to it. For many and good preludes (*peshrau*) he had not his equal amongst composers or performers, but this is only true of his preludes.

Shaikhi the flautist (*nayi*) was another; it is said he played also the lute and the guitar, and that he had played the flute from his 12th or 13th year. He once produced a wonderful air on the flute, at one of Badi'u'z-zaman Mirza's assemblies; Qul-i-muhammad could not reproduce it on the guitar, so declared this a worthless instrument; Shaikhi *Nayi* at once took the guitar from Qul-i-muhammad's hands and played the air on it, well and in perfect tune. They say he was so expert in music that having once heard an air, he was able to say, "This or that is the tune of so-and-so's or so-and-so's flute."[4] He composed few works; one or two airs are heard of.

Shah Quli the guitar-player was another; he was of 'Iraq, came into Khurasan, practised playing, and succeeded. He composed many airs, preludes and works (*nakhsh, peshrau u aishlar*).

1 He was an occasional poet (H.S. iii, 350 and iv, 118; Rieu's Pers. Cat. p. 531; Ethé's I.O. Cat. p. 428).
2 Ustad Kamalu'd-din Bih-zad (well-born; H.S. iii, 350). Work of his is reproduced in Dr. Martin's *Painting and Painters of Persia* of 1913 AD.
3 This sentence is not in the Elph. MS.
4 Perhaps he could reproduce tunes heard and say where heard.

Husain the lutanist was another; he composed and played with taste; he would twist the strings of his lute into one and play on that. His fault was affectation about playing. He Fol. 182b. made a fuss once when Shaibaq Khan ordered him to play, and not only played badly but on a worthless instrument he had brought in place of his own. The Khan saw through him at once and ordered him to be well beaten on the neck, there and then. This was the one good action Shaibaq Khan did in the world; it was well-done truly! a worse chastisement is the due of such affected mannikins!

Ghulam-i-shadi (Slave of Festivity), the son of Shadi the reciter, was another of the musicians. Though he performed, he did it less well than those of the circle just described. There are excellent themes (sut) and beautiful airs (nakhsh) of his; no-one in his day composed such airs and themes. In the end Shaibaq Khan sent him to the Qazan Khan, Muhammad Amin; no further news has been heard of him.

Mir Azu was another composer, not a performer; he produced few works but those few were in good taste.

Bana'i was also a musical composer; there are excellent airs and themes of his.

An unrivalled man was the wrestler Muhammad Bu-sa'id; he was foremost amongst the wrestlers, wrote verse too, composed themes and airs, one excellent air of his being in char-gah (four-time),—and he was pleasant company. It is extraordinary that such accomplishments as his should be combined with wrestling.[1]

HISTORICAL NARRATIVE RESUMED

(a. Burial of Sl. Husain Mirza.)

At the time Sl. Husain Mirza took his departure from the world, there were present of the Mirzas only Badi'u'z-zaman Mirza and Muzaffar-i-husain Mirza. The latter had been his father's favourite son; his leading beg was Muhammad Baranduq Barlas; his mother Khadija Begim had been the Mirza's most

1 M. Belin quotes quatrains exchanged by 'Ali-sher and this man (J. Asiatique xvii, 199).

influential wife; and to him the Mirza's people had gathered.
For these reasons Badi'u'z-zaman Mirza had anxieties and
thought of not coming,[1] but Muzaffar-i-husain Mirza and
Muhammad Baranduq Beg themselves rode out, dispelled his
fears and brought him in.

Sl. Husain Mirza was carried into Heri and there buried in
his own College with royal rites and ceremonies.

(b. A dual succession.)

At this crisis Zu'n-nun Beg was also present. He, Muh.
Baranduq Beg, the late Mirza's begs and those of the two (young)
Mirzas having assembled, decided to make the two Mirzas
joint-rulers in Heri. Zu'n-nun Beg was to have control in
Badi'u'z-zaman Mirza's Gate, Muh. Baranduq Beg, in Muzaffar-
i-husain Mirza's. Shaikh 'Ali Taghai was to be *darogha* in Heri
for the first, Yusuf-i-'ali for the second. Theirs was a strange
plan! Partnership in rule is a thing unheard of; against it
stand Shaikh Sa'di's words in the Gulistan:—"Ten darwishes
sleep under a blanket (*gilim*); two kings find no room in
a clime" (*aqlim*).[2]

1 *i.e.* from his own camp to Baba Ilahi.
2 f. 121 has a fuller quotation. On the dual succession, *see* T.R. p. 196.

(a. Babur starts to join Sl. Husain Mirza.)

In the month of Muharram we set out by way of Ghur-
bund and Shibr-tu to oppose the Auzbeg.

As Jahangir Mirza had gone out of the country in some sort
of displeasure, we said, "There might come much mischief and
trouble if he drew the clans (aimaq) to himself;" and "What
trouble might come of it!" and, "First let's get the clans in
hand!" So said, we hurried forward, riding light and leaving
the baggage (auruq) at Ushtur-shahr in charge of Wali the
treasurer and Daulat-qadam of the scouts. That day we reached
Fort Zahaq; from there we crossed the pass of the Little-dome
(Gumbazak-kutal), trampled through Saighan, went over the
Dandan-shikan pass and dismounted in the meadow of Kahmard.
From Kahmard we sent Sayyid Afzal the Seer-of-dreams
(Khwab-bin) and Sl. Muhammad Duldai to Sl. Husain Mirza
with a letter giving the particulars of our start from Kabul.[2]

Jahangir Mirza must have lagged on the road, for when he
got opposite Bamian and went with 20 or 30 persons to visit it,
he saw near it the tents of our people left with the baggage.
Thinking we were there, he and his party hurried back to their
camp and, without an eye to anything, without regard for their
own people marching in the rear, made off for Yaka-aulang.[3]

(b. Action of Shaibaq Khan.)

When Shaibaq Khan had laid siege to Balkh, in which was
Sl. Qul-i-nachaq,[4] he sent two or three sultans with 3 or 4000
men to overrun Badakhshan. At the time Mubarak Shah and

---

1 Elph. MS. f. 144; W.-i-B. I.O. 215 f. 148b and 217 f. 125b; Mems. p. 199.
2 News of Husain's death in 911 AH. (f. 163b) did not reach Babur till 912 AH. (f. 184b).
3 Lone-meadow (f. 195b). Jahangir will have come over the 'Iraq-pass, Babur's
baggage-convoy, by Shibr-tu. Cf. T.R. p. 199 for Babur and Jahangir at this time.
4 Servant-of-the-mace; but perhaps, Qilinj-chaq, swords-man.

Zubair had again joined Nasir Mirza, spite of former resentments and bickerings, and they all were lying at Shakdan, below Kishm Fol. 184. and east of the Kishm-water. Moving through the night, one body of Auzbegs crossed that water at the top of the morning and advanced on the Mirza; he at once drew off to rising-ground, mustered his force, sounded trumpets, met and overcame them. Behind the Auzbegs was the Kishm-water in flood, many were drowned in it, a mass of them died by arrow and sword, more were made prisoner. Another body of Auzbegs, sent against Mubarak Shah and Zubair where they lay, higher up the water and nearer Kishm, made them retire to the rising-ground. Of this the Mirza heard; when he had beaten off his own assailants, he moved against theirs. So did the Kohistan begs, gathered with horse and foot, still higher up the river. Unable to make stand against this attack, the Auzbegs fled, but of this body also a mass died by sword, arrow, and water. In all some 1000 to 1500 may have died. This was Nasir Mirza's one good success; a man of his brought us news about it while we were in the dale of Kahmard.

(c. *Babur moves on into Khurasan.*)

While we were in Kahmard, our army fetched corn from Ghuri and Dahana. There too we had letters from Sayyid Fol. 184b. Afzal and Sl. Muhammad *Duldai* whom we had sent into Khurasan; their news was of Sl. Husain Mirza's death.

This news notwithstanding, we set forward for Khurasan; though there were other grounds for doing this, what decided us was anxious thought for the reputation of this (Timurid) dynasty. We went up the trough (*aichi*) of the Ajar-valley, on over Tup and Mandaghan, crossed the Balkh-water and came out on Saf-hill. Hearing there that Auzbegs were overrunning San and Char-yak,[1] we sent a force under Qasim Beg against them; he got up with them, beat them well, cut many heads off, and returned.

We lay a few days in the meadow of Saf-hill, waiting for news of Jahangir Mirza and the clans (*aimaq*) to whom persons

1 One of four, a fourth. Char-yak may be a component of the name of the well-known place, n. of Kabul, "Charikar"; but also the *Char* in it may be Hindustani and refer to the permits-to-pass after tolls paid, given to caravans halted there for taxation. Raverty writes it Chariakar.

had been sent. We hunted once, those hills being very full of wild sheep and goats (*kiyik*). All the clans came in and waited on me within a few days; it was to me they came; they had not gone to Jahangir Mirza though he had sent men often enough to them, once sending even 'Imadu'd-din Mas'ud. He himself was forced to come at last; he saw me at the foot of the valley when I came down off Saf-hill. Being anxious about Khurasan, we neither paid him attention nor took thought for the clans, but went right on through Garzawan, Almar, Qaisar, Chichik-tu, and Fakhru'd-din's-death (*aulum*) into the Bam-valley, one of the dependencies of Badghis.

Fol. 185.

The world being full of divisions,[1] things were being taken from country and people with the long arm; we ourselves began to take something, by laying an impost on the Turks and clans of those parts, in two or three months taking perhaps 300 *tumans* of *kipki*.[2]

(d. Coalition of the Khurasan Mirzas.)

A few days before our arrival (in Bam-valley?) some of the Khurasan light troops and of Zu'n-nun Beg's men had well beaten Auzbeg raiders in Pand-dih (Panj-dih?) and Maruchaq, killing a mass of men.[3]

Badi'u'z-zaman Mirza and Muzaffar-i-husain Mirza with Muhammad Baranduq *Barlas*, Zu'n-nun *Arghun* and his son Shah Beg resolved to move on Shaibaq Khan, then besieging Sl. Qul-i-nachaq (?) in Balkh. Accordingly they summoned all Sl. Husain Mirza's sons, and got out of Heri to effect their purpose. At Chihil-dukhtaran Abu'l-muhsin M. joined them from Marv; Ibn-i-husain M. followed, coming up from Tun and Qain. Kupuk (Kipik) M. was in Mashhad; often though they sent to him, he behaved unmanly, spoke senseless words, and did not come. Between him and Muzaffar Mirza, there was jealousy; when Muzaffar M. was made (joint-)ruler, he said, "How should *I* go to *his* presence?" Through this disgusting jealousy he did

---

1 Amongst the disruptions of the time was that of the Khanate of Qibchaq (Erskine).
2 The nearest approach to *kipki* we have found in Dictionaries is *kupaki*, which comes close to the Russian *copeck*. Erskine notes that the *casbeké* is an oval copper coin (Tavernier, p. 121); and that a *tuman* is a myriad (10,000). *Cf.* Manucci (Irvine), i, 78 and iv, 417 note; Chardin iv, 278.
3 Muharram 912 AH.–June 1506 AD. (H.S. iii, 353).

not come now, even at this crisis when all his brethren, older and younger, were assembling in concord, resolute against such a foe   Fol. 185*b*. as Shaibaq Khan. Kupuk M. laid his own absence to rivalry, but everybody else laid it to his cowardice. One word! In this world acts such as his outlive the man; if a man have any share of intelligence, why try to be ill-spoken of after death? if he be ambitious, why not try so to act that, he gone, men will praise him? In the honourable mention of their names, wise men find a second life!

Envoys from the Mirzas came to me also, Muh. Baranduq *Barlas* himself following them. As for me, what was to hinder my going? It was for that very purpose I had travelled one or two hundred *yighach* (500–600 miles)! I at once started with Muh. Baranduq Beg for Murgh-ab[1] where the Mirzas were lying.

(*e. Babur meets the Mirzas.*)

The meeting with the Mirzas was on Monday the 8th of the latter Jumada (Oct. 26th 1506 AH.). Abu'l-muhsin Mirza came out a mile to meet me; we approached one another; on my side, I dismounted, on his side, he; we advanced, saw one another and remounted. Near the camp Muzaffar Mirza and Ibn-i-husain Mirza met us; they, being younger than Abu'l-muhsin Mirza ought to have come out further than he to meet me.[2] Their dilatoriness may not have been due to pride, but to heaviness after   Fol. 186. wine; their negligence may have been no slight on me, but due to their own social pleasures. On this Muzaffar Mirza laid stress;[3] we two saw one another without dismounting, so did Ibn-i-husain Mirza and I. We rode on together and, in an amazing crowd and press, dismounted at Badi'u'z-zaman Mirza's Gate. Such was the throng that some were lifted off the ground for three or four steps together, while others, wishing for some reason to get out, were carried, willy-nilly, four or five steps the other way.

---

1 I take Murgh-ab here to be the fortified place at the crossing of the river by the main n.e. road; Babur when in Dara-i-bam was on a tributary of the Murgh-ab. Khwand-amir records that the information of his approach was hailed in the Mirzas' camp as good news (H.S. iii, 354).

2 Babur gives the Mirzas precedence by age, ignoring Muzaffar's position as joint-ruler.

3 *mubalgha qildi*; perhaps he laid stress on their excuse; perhaps did more than was ceremonially incumbent on him.

We reached Badi'u'z-zaman Mirza's Audience-tent. It had been agreed that I, on entering, should bend the knee (*yukunghai*) once, that the Mirza should rise and advance to the edge of the estrade,[1] and that we should see one another there. I went in, bent the knee once, and was going right forward; the Mirza rose rather languidly and advanced rather slowly; Qasim Beg, as he was my well-wisher and held my reputation as his own, gave my girdle a tug; I understood, moved more slowly, and so the meeting was on the appointed spot.

Four divans (*tushuk*) had been placed in the tent. Always in the Mirza's tents one side was like a gate-way[2] and at the edge of this gate-way he always sat. A divan was set there now on which he

Fol. 186b.

and Muzaffar Mirza sat together. Abu'l-muhsin, Mirza and I sat on another, set in the right-hand place of honour (*tur*). On another, to Badi'u'z-zaman Mirza's left, sat Ibn-i-husain Mirza with Qasim Sl. *Auzbeg*, a son-in-law of the late Mirza and father of Qasim-i-husain Sultan. To my right and below my divan was one on which sat Jahangir Mirza and 'Abdu'r-razzaq Mirza. To the left of Qasim Sl. and Ibn-i-husain Mirza, but a good deal lower, were Muh. Baranduq Beg, Zu'n-nun Beg and Qasim Beg.

Although this was not a social gathering, cooked viands were brought in, drinkables[3] were set with the food, and near them gold and silver cups. Our forefathers through a long space of time, had respected the Chingiz-tura (ordinance), doing nothing opposed to it, whether in assembly or Court, in sittings-down

1 '*irq*, to which estrade answers in its sense of a carpet on which stands a raised seat.
2 Perhaps it was a recess, resembling a gate-way (W.-i-B. I.O. 215 f. 151 and 217 f. 127b). The impression conveyed by Babur's words here to the artist who in B.M. Or. 3714, has depicted the scene, is that there was a vestibule opening into the tent by a door and that the Mirza sat near that door. It must be said however that the illustration does not closely follow the text, in some known details.
3 *shira*, fruit-syrups, sherbets. Babur's word for wine is *chaghir* and this reception being public, wine could hardly have been offered in Sunni Heri. Babur's strictures can apply to the vessels of precious metal he mentions, these being forbidden to Musalmans; from his reference to the Tura it would appear to repeat the same injunctions. Babur broke up such vessels before the battle of Kanwaha (f. 312). Shah-i-jahan did the same; when sent by his father Jahangir to reconquer the Deccan (1030 AH.–1621 AD.) he asked permission to follow the example of his ancestor Babur, renounced wine, poured his stock into the Chambal, broke up his cups and gave the fragments to the poor ('*Amal-i-salih*,; Hughes' *Dict. of Islam* quoting the *Hidayah* and *Mishkat, s.nn.* Drinkables, Drinking-vessels, and Gold; Lane's *Modern Egyptians* p. 125 n.).

or risings-up. Though it has not Divine authority so that a man obeys it of necessity, still good rules of conduct must be obeyed by whom-soever they are left; just in the same way that, if a forefather have done ill, his ill must be changed for good.

After the meal I rode from the Mirza's camp some 2 miles to our own dismounting-place. _{Fol. 187.}

(f. Babur claims due respect.)

At my second visit Badi'u'z-zaman Mirza shewed me less respect than at my first. I therefore had it said to Muh. Baranduq Beg and to Zu'n-nun Beg that, small though my age was (*aet.* 24), my place of honour was large; that I had seated myself twice on the throne of our forefathers in Samarkand by blow straight-dealt; and that to be laggard in shewing me respect was unreasonable, since it was for this (Timurid) dynasty's sake I had thus fought and striven with that alien foe. This said, and as it was reasonable, they admitted their mistake at once and shewed the respect claimed.

(g. Babur's temperance.)

There was a wine-party (*chaghir-majlisi*) once when I went after the Mid-day Prayer to Badi'u'z-zaman Mirza's presence. At that time I drank no wine. The party was altogether elegant; every sort of relish to wine (*gazak*) was set out on the napery, with brochettes of fowl and goose, and all sorts of viands. The Mirza's entertainments were much renowned; truly was this one free from the pang of thirst (*bi ghall*), reposeful and tranquil. I was at two or three of his wine-parties while we were on the bank of the Murgh-ab; once it was known I did not drink, no pressure to do so was put on me.

I went to one wine-party of Muzaffar Mirza's. Husain of 'Ali *Jalair* and Mir Badr were both there, they being in his service. When Mir Badr had had enough (*kaifiyat*), he danced, _{Fol. 187b.} and danced well what seemed to be his own invention.

(h. Comments on the Mirzas.)

Three months it took the Mirzas to get out of Heri, agree amongst themselves, collect troops, and reach Murgh-ab.

Meantime Sl. Qul-i-nachaq (?), reduced to extremity, had surrendered Balkh to the Auzbeg but that Auzbeg, hearing of our alliance against him, had hurried back to Samarkand. The Mirzas were good enough as company and in social matters, in conversation and parties, but they were strangers to war, strategy, equipment, bold fight and encounter.

(i. Winter plans.)

While we were on the Murgh-ab, news came that Haq-nazir *Chapa* (var. Hian) was over-running the neighbourhood of Chichik-tu with 4 or 500 men. All the Mirzas there present, do what they would, could not manage to send a light troop against those raiders! It is 10 *yighach* (50–55 m.) from Murgh-ab to Chichik-tu. I asked the work; they, with a thought for their own reputation, would not give it to me.

The year being almost at an end when Shaibaq Khan retired, the Mirzas decided to winter where it was convenient and to reassemble next summer in order to repel their foe.

They pressed me to winter in Khurasan, but this not one of my well-wishers saw it good for me to do because, while Kabul and Ghazni were full of a turbulent and ill-conducted medley of Fol. 188. people and hordes, Turks, Mughuls, clans and nomads (*aimaq u ahsham*), Afghans and Hazara, the roads between us and that not yet desirably subjected country of Kabul were, one, the mountain-road, a month's journey even without delay through snow or other cause,—the other, the low-country road, a journey of 40 or 50 days.

Consequently we excused ourselves to the Mirzas, but they would accept no excuse and, for all our pleas, only urged the more. In the end Badi'u'z-zaman Mirza, Abu'l-muhsin Mirza and Muzaffar Mirza themselves rode to my tent and urged me to stay the winter. It was impossible to refuse men of such ruling position, come in person to press us to stay on. Besides this, the whole habitable world has not such a town as Heri had become under Sl. Husain Mirza, whose orders and efforts had increased its splendour and beauty as ten to one, rather, as twenty to one. As I greatly wished to stay, I consented to do so.

Abu'l-muhsin M. went to Marv, his own district; Ibn-i-husain M. went to his, Tun and Qain; Badi'u'z-zaman M. and Muzaffar M. set off for Heri; I followed them a few days later, taking the road by Chihil-dukhtaran and Tash-rabat.[1]

(*j. Babur visits the Begims in Heri.*)

All the Begims, *i.e.* my paternal-aunt Payanda-sultan Begim, Khadija Begim, Apaq Begim, and my other paternal-aunt Begims, daughters of Sl. Abu-sa'id Mirza,[2] were gathered together, at the time I went to see them, in Sl. Husain Mirza's College at his **Fol. 188b.** Mausoleum. Having bent the knee with (*yukunub bila*) Payanda-sultan Begim first of all, I had an interview with her; next, not bending the knee,[3] I had an interview with Apaq Begim; next, having bent the knee with Khadija Begim, I had an interview with her. After sitting there for some time during recitation of the Qoran,[4] we went to the South College where Khadija Begim's tents had been set up and where food was placed before us. After partaking of this, we went to Payanda-sultan Begim's tents and there spent the night.

The New-year's Garden was given us first for a camping-ground; there our camp was arranged; and there I spent the night of the day following my visit to the Begims, but as I did not find it a convenient place, 'Ali-sher Beg's residence was

1 This may be the Rabat-i-sanghi of some maps, on a near road between the "Forty-daughters" and Harat; or Babur may have gone out of his direct way to visit Rabat-i-sang-bast, a renowned halting place at the Carfax of the Heri-Tus and Nishapur-Mashhad roads, built by one Arslan *Jazala* who lies buried near, and rebuilt with great magnificence by 'Ali-sher *Nawa'i* (Daulat-shah, Browne, p. 176). 2 The wording here is confusing to those lacking family details. The paternal-aunt begims can be Payanda-sultan (named), Khadija-sultan, Apaq-sultan, and Fakhr-jahan Begims, all daughters of Abu-sa'id. The Apaq Begim named above (also on f. 168*b q.v.*) does not now seem to me to be Abu-sa'id's daughter (Gul-badan, trs. Bio. App.). 3 *yukunmai.* Unless all copies I have seen reproduce a primary clerical mistake of Babur's, the change of salutation indicated by there being no kneeling with Apaq Begim, points to a *nuance* of etiquette. Of the verb *yukunmak* it may be noted that it both describes the ceremonious attitude of intercourse, *i.e.* kneeling and sitting back on both heels (Shaw), and also the kneeling on meeting. From Babur's phrase *Begim bila yukunub* [having kneeled with], it appears that each of those meeting made the genuflection; I have not found the phrase used of other meetings; it is not the one used when a junior or a man of less degree meets a senior or superior in rank (*e.g.* Khusrau and Babur f. 123, or Babur and Badi'u'z-zaman f. 186). 4 Musalmans employ a set of readers who succeed one another in reading (reciting) the Qoran at the tombs of their men of eminence. This reading is sometimes continued day and night. The readers are paid by the rent of lands or other funds assigned for the purpose (Erskine).

assigned to me, where I was as long as I stayed in Heri, every few days shewing myself in Badi'u'z-zaman Mirza's presence in the World-adorning Garden.

(k. The Mirzas entertain Babur in Heri.)

A few days after Muzaffar Mirza had settled down in the White-garden, he invited me to his quarters; Khadija Begim was also there, and with me went Jahangir Mirza. When we had eaten a meal in the Begim's presence,[1] Muzaffar Mirza took me to where there was a wine-party, in the Tarab-khana (Joy-house) built by Babur Mirza, a sweet little abode, a smallish, two-storeyed house in the middle of a smallish garden. Great pains have been taken with its upper storey; this has a retreat (*hujra*) in each of its four corners, the space between each two retreats being like a *shah-nishin*;[2] in between these retreats and

Fol. 189.   *shah-nishins* is one large room on all sides of which are pictures which, although Babur Mirza built the house, were commanded by Abu-sa'id Mirza and depict his own wars and encounters.

Two divans had been set in the north *shah-nishin*, facing each other, and with their sides turned to the north. On one Muzaffar Mirza and I sat, on the other Sl. Mas'ud Mirza[3] and Jahangir Mirza. We being guests, Muzaffar Mirza gave me place above himself. The social cups were filled, the cup-bearers ordered to carry them to the guests; the guests drank down the mere wine as if it were water-of-life; when it mounted to their heads, the party waxed warm.

They thought to make me also drink and to draw me into their own circle. Though up till then I had not committed the sin of wine-drinking[4] and known the cheering sensation of comfortable drunkenness, I was inclined to drink wine and my heart was drawn to cross that stream (*wada*). I had had no inclination for wine in my childhood; I knew nothing of its cheer and pleasure. If, as sometimes, my father pressed wine

---

1 A suspicion that Khadija put poison in Jahangir's wine may refer to this occasion (T.R. p. 199).

2 These are *jharokha-i-darsan*, windows or balconies from which a ruler shews himself to the people.

3 Mas'ud was then blind.

4 Babur first drank wine not earlier than 917 AH. (f. 49 and note), therefore when nearing 30.

on me, I excused myself; I did not commit the sin. After he Fol. 189b. died, Khwaja Qazi's right guidance kept me guiltless; as at that time I abstained from forbidden viands, what room was there for the sin of wine? Later on when, with the young man's lusts and at the prompting of sensual passion, desire for wine arose, there was no-one to press it on me, no-one indeed aware of my leaning towards it; so that, inclined for it though my heart was, it was difficult of myself to do such a thing, one thitherto undone. It crossed my mind now, when the Mirzas were so pressing and when too we were in a town so refined as Heri, "Where should I drink if not here? here where all the chattels and utensils of luxury and comfort are gathered and in use." So saying to myself, I resolved to drink wine; I determined to cross that stream; but it occurred to me that as I had not taken wine in Badi'u'z-zaman Mirza's house or from his hand, who was to me as an elder brother, things might find way into his mind if I took wine in his younger brother's house and from his hand. Having so said to myself, I mentioned my doubt and difficulty. Said they, "Both the excuse and the obstacle are reasonable," pressed me no more to drink then but settled that when I was in company with both Mirzas, I should drink under the insistence of both.

Amongst the musicians present at this party were Hafiz Haji, Fol. 190. Jalalu'd-din Mahmud the flautist, and Ghulam *shadi*'s younger brother, Ghulam *bacha* the Jews'-harpist. Hafiz Haji sang well, as Heri people sing, quietly, delicately, and in tune. With Jahangir Mirza was a Samarkandi singer Mir Jan whose singing was always loud, harsh and out-of-tune. The Mirza, having had enough, ordered him to sing; he did so, loudly, harshly and without taste. Khurasanis have quite refined manners; if, under this singing, one did stop his ears, the face of another put question, not one could stop the singer, out of consideration for the Mirza.

After the Evening Prayer we left the Tarab-khana for a new house in Muzaffar Mirza's winter-quarters. There Yusuf-i-'ali danced in the drunken time, and being, as he was, a master in music, danced well. The party waxed very warm there. Muzaffar Mirza gave me a sword-belt, a lambskin surtout, and a grey *tipuchaq* (horse). Janak recited in Turki. Two slaves of the Mirza's, known as Big-moon and Little-moon, did offensive, drunken tricks in the drunken time. The party was warm till night when those assembled scattered, I, however, staying the night in that house.

Qasim Beg getting to hear that I had been pressed to drink wine, sent some-one to Zu'n-nun Beg with advice for him and for Muzaffar Mirza, given in very plain words; the result

Fol. 190b. was that the Mirzas entirely ceased to press wine upon me.

Badi'u'z-zaman Mirza, hearing that Muzaffar M. had entertained me, asked me to a party arranged in the Maqauwi-khana of the World-adorning Garden. He asked also some of my close circle[1] and some of our braves. Those about me could never drink (openly) on my own account; if they ever did drink, they did it perhaps once in 40 days, with doorstrap fast and under a hundred fears. Such as these were now invited; here too they drank with a hundred precautions, sometimes calling off my attention, sometimes making a screen of their hands, notwithstanding that I had given them permission to follow common custom, because this party was given by one standing to me as a father or elder brother. People brought in weeping-willows ...[2]

At this party they set a roast goose before me but as I was no carver or disjointer of birds, I left it alone. "Do you not like it?" inquired the Mirza. Said I, "I am a poor carver." On this he at once disjointed the bird and set it again before

Fol. 191. me. In such matters he had no match. At the end of the party he gave me an enamelled waist-dagger, a *char-qab*,[3] and a *tipuchaq*.

(l. Babur sees the sights of Heri.)

Every day of the time I was in Heri I rode out to see a new sight; my guide in these excursions was Yusuf-i-'ali Kukuldash; wherever we dismounted, he set food before me. Except Sl.

---

1 *aichkilar*, French, *intérieur*.
2 The obscure passage following here is discussed in Appendix I, *On the weeping-willows* of f. 190b.
3 Here this may well be a gold-embroidered garment.

Husain Mirza's Almshouse, not one famous spot, maybe, was left unseen in those 40 days.

I saw the Gazur-gah,[1] 'Ali-sher's Baghcha (Little-garden), the Paper-mortars,[2] Takht-astana (Royal-residence), Pul-i-gah, Kahad-stan,[3] Nazar-gah-garden, Ni'matabad (Pleasure-place), Gazur-gah Avenue, Sl. Ahmad Mirza's Hazirat,[4] Takht-i-safar,[5] Takht-i-nawa'i, Takht-i-barkar, Takht-i-Haji Beg, Takht-i-Baha'-u'd-din 'Umar, Takht-i-Shaikh Zainu'd-din, Maulana 'Abdu'r-rahman *Jami*'s honoured shrine and tomb,[6] Namaz-gah-i-mukhtar,[7] the Fish-pond,[8] Saq-i-sulaiman,[9] Buluri (Crystal) which originally may have been Abu'l-walid,[10] Imam Fakhr,[11] Avenue-garden, Mirza's Colleges and tomb, Guhar-shad Begim's College, tomb,[12] and Congregational Mosque, the Ravens'-garden,

1 This, the tomb of Khwaja 'Abdu'l-lah *Ansari* (d. 481 AH.) stands some 2m. north of Heri. Babur mentions one of its numerous attendants of his day, Kamalu'd-din Husain *Gazur-gahi*. Mohan Lall describes it as he saw it in 1831; says the original name of the locality was Kar-zar-gah, place-of-battle; and, as perhaps his most interesting detail, mentions that Jalalu'd-din *Rumi*'s *Masnawi* was recited every morning near the tomb and that people fainted during the invocation (*Travels in the Panj-ab* etc. p. 252). Colonel Yate has described the tomb as he saw it some 50 years later (JASB 1887); and explains the name Gazur-gah (lit. bleaching-place) by the following words of an inscription there found; "His tomb (Ansari's) is a washing-place (*gazur-gah*) wherein the cloud of the Divine forgiveness washes white the black records of men" (p. 88 and p. 102).

2 *juaz-i-kaghazlar* (f. 47*b* and note).

3 The *Habibu's-siyar* and Hai. MS. write this name with medial "round *ha*"; this allows it to be Kahad-stan, a running-place, race-course. Khwand-amir and Daulat-shah call it a meadow (*aulang*); the latter speaks of a feast as held there; it was Shaibani's head-quarters when he took Harat.

4 *var.* Khatira; either an enclosure (*quruq*?) or a fine and lofty building.

5 This may have been a usual halting-place on a journey (*safar*) north. It was built by Husain *Bai-qara*, overlooked hills and fields covered with *arghwan* (f. 137*b*) and seems once to have been a Paradise (Mohan Lall, p. 256).

6 Jami's tomb was in the 'Id-gah of Heri (H.S. ii, 337), which appears to be the Musalla (Praying-place) demolished by Amir 'Abdu'r-rahman in the 19th century. Col. Yate was shewn a tomb in the Musalla said to be Jami's and agreeing in the age, 81, given on it, with Jami's at death, but he found a *crux* in the inscription (pp. 99, 106).

7 This may be the Musalla (Yate, p. 98).

8 This place is located by the H.S. at 5 *farsakh* from Heri (de Meynard at 25 *kilomètres*). It appears to be rather an abyss or fissure than a pond, a crack from the sides of which water trickles into a small basin in which dwells a mysterious fish, the beholding of which allows the attainment of desires. The story recalls Wordsworth's undying fish of Bow-scale Tarn. (*Cf.* H.S. Bomb. ed. ii, *Khatmat* p. 20 and de Meynard, *Journal Asiatique* xvi, 480 and note.)

9 This is on maps to the north of Heri.

10 d. 232 AH. (847 AD.). *See* Yate, p. 93.

11 Imam Fakhru'd-din *Razi* (de Meynard, *Journal Asiatique* xvi, 481).

12 d. 861 AH.–1457 AD. Guhar-shad was the wife of Timur's son Shahrukh. *See* Mohan Lall, p. 257 and Yate, p. 98.

New-garden, Zubaida-garden,[1] Sl. Abu-sa'id Mirza's White-
Fol. 191b. house outside the 'Iraq-gate, Puran,[2] the Archer's-seat, Chargh
(hawk)-meadow, Amir Wahid,[3] Malan-bridge,[4] Khwaja-taq,[5]
White-garden, Tarab-khana, Bagh-i-jahan-ara, Kushk,[6]
Maqauwi-khana, Lily-house, Twelve-towers, the great tank to
the north of Jahan-ara and the four dwellings on its four sides,
the five Fort-gates, viz. the Malik, 'Iraq, Firuzabad, Khush[7] and
Qibchaq Gates, Char-su, Shaikhu'l-islam's College, Maliks'
Congregational Mosque, Town-garden, Badi'u'z-zaman Mirza's
College on the bank of the Anjil-canal, 'Ali-sher Beg's dwellings
where we resided and which people call Unsiya (Ease), his
tomb and mosque which they call Qudsiya (Holy), his College
and Almshouse which they call Khalasiya and Akhlasiya (Freedom
and Sincerity), his Hot-bath and Hospital which they call
Safa'iya and Shafa'iya. All these I visited in that space of time.

(*m. Babur engages Ma'suma-sultan in marriage.*)

It must have been before those throneless times[8] that Habiba-
sultan Begim, the mother of Sl. Ahmad Mirza's youngest
daughter Ma'suma-sultan Begim, brought her daughter into
Heri. One day when I was visiting my Aka, Ma'suma-sultan
Begim came there with her mother and at once felt arise in her a
great inclination towards me. Private messengers having been
sent, my Aka and my Yinka, as I used to call Payanda-sultan
Fol. 192. Begim and Habiba-sultan Begim, settled between them that
the latter should bring her daughter after me to Kabul.[9]

1 This Marigold-garden may be named after Harunu'r-rashid's wife Zubaida.
2 This will be the place n. of Heri from which Maulana Jalalu'd-din *Purani*
(d. 862 AH.) took his cognomen, as also Shaikh Jamalu'd-din Abu-sa'id *Puran* (f. 206)
who was visited there by Sl. Husain Mirza, ill-treated by Shaibani (f. 206), left
Heri for Qandahar, and there died, through the fall of a roof, in 921 AH. (H.S. iii,
345; *Khazinatu'l-asfiya* ii, 321).
3 His tomb is dated 35 or 37 AH. (656 or 658 AD.; Yate, p. 94).
4 Malan was a name of the Heri-rud (*Journal Asiatique* xvi, 476, 511; Mohan Lall,
p. 279; Ferrier, p. 261; *etc.*).
5 Yate, p. 94.
6 The position of this building between the Khush and Qibchaq Gates (de
Meynard, l.c. p. 475) is the probable explanation of the variant, noted just below,
of Kushk for Khush as the name of the Gate. The *Tarikh-i-rashidi* (p. 429),
mentions this kiosk in its list of the noted ones of the world.
7 var. Kushk (de Meynard, l.c. p. 472).
8 The reference here is, presumably, to Babur's own losses of Samarkand and Andijan.
9 Aka or Aga is used of elder relations; a *yinka* or *yinga* is the wife of an uncle or
elder brother; here it represents the widow of Babur's uncle Ahmad *Miran-shahi*.
From it is formed the word *yinkalik*, levirate.

(n. Babur leaves Khurasan.)

Very pressingly had Muh. Baranduq Beg and Zu'n-nun *Arghun* said, "Winter here!" but they had given me no winter-quarters nor had they made any winter-arrangements for me. Winter came on; snow fell on the mountains between us and Kabul; anxiety grew about Kabul; no winter-quarters were offered, no arrangements made! As we could not speak out, of necessity we left Heri!

On the pretext of finding winter-quarters, we got out of the town on the 7th day of the month of Sha'ban (Dec. 24th 1506 AD.), and went to near Badghis. Such were our slowness and our tarryings that the Ramzan-moon was seen a few marches only beyond the Langar of Mir Ghiyas.[1] Of our braves who were absent on various affairs, some joined us, some followed us into Kabul 20 days or a month later, some stayed in Heri and took service with the Mirzas. One of these last was Sayyidim 'Ali the gate-ward, who became Badi'u'z-zaman Mirza's retainer. To no servant of Khusrau Shah had I shewn so much favour as to him; he had been given Ghazni when Jahangir Mirza abandoned it, and in it when he came away with the army, had left his younger brother Dost-i-anju (?) Shaikh. There were in truth no better men amongst Khusrau Shah's retainers than this man Sayyidim 'Ali the gate-ward and Muhibb-i-'ali the armourer. Sayyidim was of excellent nature and manners, a bold swordsman, a singularly competent and methodical man. His house was never without company and assembly; he was greatly generous, had wit and charm, a variety of talk and story, and was a sweet-natured, good-humoured, ingenious, fun-loving person. His fault was that he practised vice and pederasty. He may have swerved from the Faith; may also have been a hypocrite in his dealings; some of what seemed double-dealing people attributed to his jokes, but, still, there must have been a something![2] When Badi'u'z-zaman Mirza had let Shaibaq Khan take Heri and had gone to Shah Beg (*Arghun*), he had Sayyidim 'Ali thrown into the Harmand because of his double-dealing words

Fol. 192*b*.

---

1 The almshouse or convent was founded here in Timur's reign (de Meynard, l.c. p. 500).
2 *i.e.* No smoke without fire.

spoken between the Mirza and Shah Beg. Muhibb-i-'ali's story will come into the narrative of events hereafter to be written.

(o. A perilous mountain-journey.)

From the Langar of Mir Ghiyas we had ourselves guided past the border-villages of Gharjistan to Chach-charan.[1] From the almshouse to Gharjistan was an unbroken sheet of snow; it was deeper further on; near Chach-charan itself it was above the horses' knees. Chach-charan depended on Zu'n-nun *Arghun*; his retainer Mir Jan-airdi was in it now; from him we took, on payment, the whole of Zu'n-nun Beg's store of provisions. A march or two further on, the snow was very deep, being above the stirrup, indeed in many places the horses' feet did not touch the ground. Moreover it snowed incessantly and, after leaving Chiragh-dan, not only was there very deep snow but the road was unknown.

We had consulted at the Langar of Mir Ghiyas which road to take for return to Kabul; most of us agreed in saying, "It is winter, the mountain-road is difficult and dangerous; the Qandahar road, though a little longer, is safe and easy." Qasim Beg said, "That road is long; you will go by this one." As he made much dispute, we took the mountain-road.

Our guide was a Pashai named Pir Sultan (Old sultan?). Whether it was through old age, whether from want of heart, whether because of the deep snow, he lost the road and could not guide us. As we were on this route under the insistence of Qasim Beg, he and his sons, for his name's sake, dismounted, trampled the snow down, found the road again and took the lead. One day the snow was so deep and the way so uncertain that we could not go on; there being no help for it, back we turned, dismounted where there was fuel, picked out 60 or 70 good men and sent them down the valley in our tracks to fetch any one soever of the Hazara, wintering in the valley-bottom, who might shew us the road. That place could not be left till our men returned three or four days later. They brought no guide; once more we sent Sultan *Pashai* ahead and, putting our

Fol. 193.

Fol. 193b.

---

1 This name may be due to the splashing of water. A Langar which may be that of Mir Ghiyas, is shewn in maps in the Bam valley; from it into the Heri-rud valley Babur's route may well have been the track from that Langar which, passing the villages on the southern border of Gharjistan, goes to Ahangaran.

trust in God, again took the road by which we had come back from where it was lost. Much misery and hardship were endured in those few days, more than at any time of my life. In that stress I composed the following opening couplet:—

> Is there one cruel turn of Fortune's wheel unseen of me?
> Is there a pang, a grief my wounded heart has missed?

We went on for nearly a week, trampling down the snow and not getting forward more than two or three miles a day. I was one of the snow-stampers, with 10 or 15 of my household, Qasim Beg, his sons Tingri-birdi and Qambar-i-'ali and two or three of their retainers. These mentioned used to go forward for 7 or 8 yards, stamping the snow down and at each step sinking to the waist or the breast. After a few steps the leading man would stand still, exhausted by the labour, and another would go forward. By the time 10, 15, 20, men on foot had stamped the snow down, it became so that a horse might be led over it. A horse would be led, would sink to the stirrups, could do no more than 10 or 12 steps, and would be drawn aside to let another go on. After we, 10, 15, 20, men had stamped down the snow and had led horses forward in this fashion, very serviceable braves and men of renowned name would enter the beaten track, hanging their heads. It was not a time to urge or compel! the man with will and hardihood for such tasks does them by his own request! Stamping the snow down in this way, we got out of that afflicting place (*anjukan yir*) in three or four days to a cave known as the Khawal-i-quti (Blessed-cave), below the Zirrin-pass. Fol. 194.

That night the snow fell in such an amazing blizzard of cutting wind that every man feared for his life. The storm had become extremely violent by the time we reached the *khawal*, as people in those parts call a mountain-cave (*ghar*) or hollow (*khawak*). We dismounted at its mouth. Deep snow! a one-man road! and even on that stamped-down and trampled road, pitfalls for horses! the days at their shortest! The first arrivals reached the cave by daylight; others kept coming in from the Evening Prayer till the Bed-time one; later than that people dismounted wherever they happened to be; dawn shot with many still in the saddle.

The cave seeming to be rather small, I took a shovel and shovelled out a place near its mouth, the size of a sitting-mat *(takiya-namad)*, digging it out breast-high but even then not reaching the ground. This made me a little shelter from the wind when I sat right down in it. I did not go into the cave though people kept saying, "Come inside," because this was in my mind, "Some of my men in snow and storm, I in the comfort of a warm house! the whole horde *(aulus)* outside in misery and pain, I inside sleeping at ease! That would be far from a man's act, quite another matter than comradeship! Whatever hardship and wretchedness there is, I will face; what strong men stand, I will stand; for, as the Persian proverb says, to die with friends is a nuptial." Till the Bed-time Prayer I sat through that blizzard of snow and wind in the dug-out, the snow-fall being such that my head, back, and ears were overlaid four hands thick. The cold of that night affected my ears. At the Bed-time Prayer some-one, looking more carefully at the cave, shouted out, "It is a very roomy cave with place for every-body." On hearing this I shook off my roofing of snow and, asking the braves near to come also, went inside. There was room for 50 or 60! People brought out their rations, cold meat, parched grain, whatever they had. From such cold and tumult to a place so warm, cosy and quiet![1]

Next day the snow and wind having ceased, we made an early start and we got to the pass by again stamping down a road in the snow. The proper road seems to make a détour up the flank of the mountain and to go over higher up, by what is understood to be called the Zirrin-pass. Instead of taking that road, we went straight up the valley-bottom *(qul)*.[2] It was night before we reached the further side of the (Bakkak-)pass; we spent the night there in the mouth of the valley, a night of

Fol. 194*b*.

Fol. 195.

1 This escape ought to have been included in the list of Babur's transportations from risk to safety given in my note to f. 96.

2 The right and wrong roads are shewn by the Indian Survey and French Military maps. The right road turns off from the wrong one, at Daulat-yar, to the right, and mounts diagonally along the south rampart of the Heri-rud valley, to the Zirrin-pass, which lies above the Bakkak-pass and carries the regular road for Yaka-aulang. It must be said, however, that we are not told whether Yaka-aulang was Qasim Beg's objective; the direct road for Kabul from the Heri-rud valley is not over the Zirrin-pass but goes from Daulat-yar by "Aq-zarat", and the south-ern flank of Koh-i-baba (babar) to the Unai-pass (Holdich's *Gates of India* p. 262).

mighty cold, got through with great distress and suffering.
Many a man had his hands and feet frost-bitten; that night's
cold took both Kipa's feet, both Siunduk *Turkman*'s hands,
both Ahi's feet. Early next morning we moved down the
valley; putting our trust in God, we went straight down, by bad
slopes and sudden falls, knowing and seeing it could not be the
right way. It was the Evening Prayer when we got out of that
valley. No long-memoried old man knew that any-one had
been heard of as crossing that pass with the snow so deep, or
indeed that it had ever entered the heart of man to cross it at
that time of year. Though for a few days we had suffered greatly
through the depth of the snow, yet its depth, in the end, enabled
us to reach our destination. For why? How otherwise should
we have traversed those pathless slopes and sudden falls?   Fol. 195*b*.

All ill, all good in the count, is gain if looked at aright!

The Yaka-aulang people at once heard of our arrival and
our dismounting; followed, warm houses, fat sheep, grass and
horse-corn, water without stint, ample wood and dried dung for
fires! To escape from such snow and cold to such a village, to such
warm dwellings, was comfort those will understand who have
had our trials, relief known to those who have felt our hardships.
We tarried one day in Yaka-aulang, happy-of-heart and easy-
of-mind; marched 2 *yighach* (10–12 m.) next day and dismounted. The day following was the Ramzan Feast;[1] we went
on through Bamian, crossed by Shibr-tu and dismounted
before reaching Janglik.

(*p. Second raid on the Turkman Hazaras.*)

The Turkman Hazaras with their wives and little children
must have made their winter-quarters just upon our road;[2] they
had no word about us; when we got in amongst their cattle-
pens and tents (*alachuq*) two or three groups of these went to
ruin and plunder, the people themselves drawing off with their
little children and abandoning houses and goods. News was   Fol. 196.
brought from ahead that, at a place where there were narrows,

1 *circa* Feb. 14th 1507, Babur's 24th birthday.
2 The Hazaras appear to have been wintering outside their own valley, on the
Ghur-bund road, in wait for travellers [*cf.* T.R. p. 197]. They have been perennial
highwaymen on the only pass to the north not closed entirely in winter.

a body of Hazaras was shooting arrows, holding up part of the
army, and letting no-one pass. We, hurrying on, arrived to
find no narrows at all; a few Hazaras were shooting from
a naze, standing in a body on the hill[1] like very good soldiers.[2]

> They saw the blackness of the foe;
>   Stood idle-handed and amazed;
> I arriving, went swift that way,
>   Pressed on with shout, "Move on! move on!"
> I wanted to hurry my men on,
>   To make them stand up to the foe.
> With a "Hurry up!" to my men,
>   I went on to the front.
> Not a man gave ear to my words.
>   I had no armour nor horse-mail nor arms,
> I had but my arrows and quiver.
>   I went, the rest, maybe all of them, stood,
> Stood still as if slain by the foe!
>   Your servant you take that you may have use
> Of his arms, of his life, the whole time;
>   Not that the servant stand still
> While the beg makes advance to the front;
>   Not that the servant take rest
> While his beg is making the rounds.
>   From no such a servant will come
> Speed, or use in your Gate, or zest for your food.
>   At last I charged forward myself,

Fol. 196b.

> Herding the foe up the hill;
>   Seeing me go, my men also moved,
> Leaving their terrors behind.
>   With me they swift spread over the slope,
> Moving on without heed to the shaft;
>   Sometimes on foot, mounted sometimes,
> Boldly we ever moved on,
>   Still from the hill poured the shafts.
> Our strength seen, the foe took to flight.
>   We got out on the hill; we drove the Hazaras,
> Drove them like deer by valley and ridge;
>   We shot those wretches like deer;
> We shared out the booty in goods and in sheep;
>   The Turkman Hazaras' kinsfolk we took;
> We made captive their people of sorts (qara);
>   We laid hands on their men of renown;
> Their wives and their children we took.

1 The Ghur-bund valley is open in this part; the Hazaras may have been posted
on the naze near the narrows leading into the Janglik and their own side valleys.
2 Although the verses following here in the text are with the Turki Codices, doubt
cannot but be felt as to their authenticity. They do not fit verbally to the sentence they
follow; they are a unique departure from Babur's plain prose narrative and nothing in
the small Hazara affair shews cause for such departure; they differ from his usual topics
in their bombast and comment on his men (cf. f. 194 for comment on shirking begs).
They appear in the 2nd Persian translation (217 f. 134) in Turki followed by a prose
Persian rendering (khalasa). They are not with the 1st Pers. trs. (215 f. 159), the text of

I myself collected a few of the Hazaras' sheep, gave them into Yarak Taghai's charge, and went to the front. By ridge and valley, driving horses and sheep before us, we went to Timur Beg's Langar and there dismounted. Fourteen or fifteen Hazara thieves had fallen into our hands; I had thought of having them put to death when we next dismounted, with various torture, as a warning to all highwaymen and robbers, but Qasim Beg came across them on the road and, with mis-timed compassion, set them free.   Fol. 197.

> To do good to the bad is one and the same
>   As the doing of ill to the good;
> On brackish soil no spikenard grows,
>   Waste no seed of toil upon it.[1]

Out of compassion the rest of the prisoners were released also.

(*j. Disloyalty in Kabul.*)

News came while we were raiding the Turkman Hazaras, that Muhammad Husain Mirza *Dughlat* and Sl. Sanjar *Barlas* had drawn over to themselves the Mughuls left in Kabul, declared Mirza Khan (Wais) supreme (*padshah*), laid siege to the fort and spread a report that Badi'u'z-zaman Mirza and Muzaffar Mirza had sent me, a prisoner, to Fort Ikhtiyaru'd-din, now known as Ala-qurghan.

In command of the Kabul-fort there had been left Mulla Baba of Pashaghar, Khalifa, Muhibb-i-'ali the armourer, Ahmad-i-yusuf and Ahmad-i-qasim. They did well, made the fort fast, strengthened it, and kept watch.

(*k. Babur's advance to Kabul.*)

From Timur Beg's Langar we sent Qasim Beg's servant, Muh. of Andijan, a *Tuqbai*, to the Kabul begs, with written details of our arrival and of the following arrangements:—"When we

---

which runs on with a plain prose account suiting the size of the affair, as follows:—"The braves, seeing their (the Hazaras) good soldiering, had stopped surprised; wishing to hurry them I went swiftly past them, shouting 'Move on! move on!' They paid me no attention. When, in order to help, I myself attacked, dismounting and going up the hill, they shewed courage and emulation in following. Getting to the top of the pass, we drove that band off, killing many, capturing others, making their families prisoner and plundering their goods." This is followed by "I myself collected" *etc.* as in the Turki text after the verse. It will be seen that the above extract is not a translation of the verse; no translator or even summariser would be likely to omit so much of his original. It is just a suitably plain account of a trivial matter.

1 *Gulistan* Cap. I. Story 4.

are out of the Ghur-bund narrows,[1] we will fall on them suddenly; let our signal to you be the fire we will light directly we have passed Minar-hill; do you in reply light one in the citadel, on the old Kushk (kiosk)," now the Treasury, "so that we may be sure you know of our coming. We will come up from our side; you come out from yours; neglect nothing your hands can find to do!" This having been put into writing, Muhammad *Andijani* was sent off.

Fol. 197*b*.

Riding next dawn from the Langar, we dismounted over against Ushtur-shahr. Early next morning we passed the Ghur-bund narrows, dismounted at Bridge-head, there watered and rested our horses, and at the Mid-day Prayer set forward again. Till we reached the *tutqawal*,[2] there was no snow, beyond that, the further we went the deeper the snow. The cold between Zamma-yakhshi and Minar was such as we had rarely felt in our lives.

We sent on Ahmad the messenger (*yasawal*) and Qara Ahmad *yurunchi*[3] to say to the begs, "Here we are at the time promised; be ready! be bold!" After crossing Minar-hill[4] and dismounting on its skirt, helpless with cold, we lit fires to warm ourselves. It was not time to light the signal-fire; we just lit these because we were helpless in that mighty cold. Near shoot of dawn we rode on from Minar-hill; between it and Kabul the snow was up to the horses' knees and had hardened, so off the road to move was difficult. Riding single-file the whole way, we got to Kabul in good time undiscovered.[5] Before we were at Bibi Mah-rui (Lady Moon-face), the blaze of fire on the citadel let us know that the begs were looking out.

Fol. 198.

(*l. Attack made on the rebels.*)

On reaching Sayyid Qasim's bridge, Sherim Taghai and the men of the right were sent towards Mulla Baba's bridge, while

1 Babur seems to have left the Ghur-bund valley, perhaps pursuing the Hazaras towards Janglik, and to have come "by ridge and valley" back into it for Ushtur-shahr. I have not located Timur Beg's Langar. As has been noted already, the Ghur-bund narrows are at the lower end of the valley; they have been surmised to be the fissured rampart of an ancient lake.

2 Here this may represent a guard- or toll-house.

3 As *yurun* is a patch, the bearer of the sobriquet might be Black Ahmad the repairing-tailor.

4 *Second Afghan War*, Map of Kabul and its environs.

5 I understand that the arrival undiscovered was a result of riding in single-file and thus shewing no black mass.

we of the left and centre took the Baba Luli road. Where Khalifa's
garden now is, there was then a smallish garden made by Aulugh
Beg Mirza for a Langar (almshouse); none of its trees or shrubs
were left but its enclosing wall was there. In this garden Mirza
Khan was seated, Muh. Husain Mirza being in Aulugh Beg
Mirza's great Bagh-i-bihisht. I had gone as far along the lane
of Mulla Baba's garden as the burial-ground when four men met
us who had hurried forward into Mirza Khan's quarters, been
beaten, and forced to turn back. One of the four was Sayyid
Qasim Lord of the Gate, another was Qasim Beg's son
Qambar-i-'ali, another was Sher-quli the scout, another was Sl.
Ahmad *Mughul* one of Sher-quli's band. These four, without a
"God forbid!" (*tahashi*) had gone right into Mirza Khan's quarters; thereupon he, hearing an uproar, had mounted and got
away. Abu'l-hasan the armourer's younger brother even, Muh.
Husain by name, had taken service with Mirza Khan; he had
slashed at Sher-quli, one of those four, thrown him down, and   Fol. 198*b*.
was just striking his head off, when Sher-quli freed himself. Those
four, tasters of the sword, tasters of the arrow, wounded one
and all, came pelting back on us to the place mentioned.

Our horsemen, jammed in the narrow lane, were standing
still, unable to move forward or back. Said I to the braves
near, "Get off and force a road." Off got Nasir's Dost, Khwaja
Muhammad 'Ali the librarian, Baba Sher-zad (Tiger-whelp),
Shah Mahmud and others, pushed forward and at once cleared
the way. The enemy took to flight.

We had looked for the begs to come out from the Fort but
they could not come in time for the work; they only dropped
in, by ones and twos, after we had made the enemy scurry off.
Ahmad-i-yusuf had come from them before I went into the
Char-bagh where Mirza Khan had been; he went in with me,
but we both turned back when we saw the Mirza had gone off.
Coming in at the garden-gate was Dost of Sar-i-pul, a foot-soldier
I had promoted for his boldness to be Kotwal and had left in
Kabul; he made straight for me, sword in hand. I had my
cuirass on but had not fastened the *gharicha*[1] nor had I put on   Fol. 199.

---

1 or *gharbicha*, which Mr. Erskine explains to be the four plates of mail, made
to cover the back, front and sides; the *jiba* would thus be the wadded under-coat to
which they are attached.

my helm. Whether he did not recognize me because of change
wrought by cold and snow, or whether because of the flurry of
the fight, though I shouted "Hai Dost! hai Dost!" and though
Ahmad-i-yusuf also shouted, he, without a "God forbid!" brought
down his sword on my unprotected arm. Only by God's grace
can it have been that not a hairbreadth of harm was done to me.

> If a sword shook the Earth from her place,
> Not a vein would it cut till God wills.

It was through the virtue of a prayer I had repeated that the
Great God averted this danger and turned this evil aside. That
prayer was as follows:—

> "O my God! Thou art my Creator; except Thee there is no God. On
> Thee do I repose my trust; Thou art the Lord of the mighty throne. What
> God wills comes to pass; and what he does not will comes not to pass;
> and there is no power or strength but through the high and exalted God;
> and, of a truth, in all things God is almighty; and verily He comprehends
> all things by his knowledge, and has taken account of everything. O my
> Creator! as I sincerely trust in Thee, do Thou seize by the forelock all evil
> proceeding from within myself, and all evil coming from without, and all
> evil proceeding from every man who can be the occasion of evil, and
> all such evil as can proceed from any living thing, and remove them far
> from me; since, of a truth, Thou art the Lord of the exalted throne!"[1]

On leaving that garden we went to Muh. Husain Mirza's
quarters in the Bagh-i-bihisht, but he had fled and gone off to
hide himself. Seven or eight men stood in a breach of the
garden-wall; I spurred at them; they could not stand; they
fled; I got up with them and cut at one with my sword; he
rolled over in such a way that I fancied his head was off, passed
on and went away; it seems he was Mirza Khan's foster-brother,
Tulik Kukuldash and that my sword fell on his shoulder.

At the gate of Muh. Husain Mirza's quarters, a Mughul
I recognized for one of my own servants, drew his bow and aimed
at my face from a place on the roof as near me as a gate-ward
stands to a Gate. People on all sides shouted, "Hai! hai! it is
the Padshah." He changed his aim, shot off his arrow and ran
away. The affair was beyond the shooting of arrows! His Mirza,
his leaders, had run away or been taken; why was he shooting?

Fol. 199b.

1 This prayer is composed of extracts from the Qoran (*Méms*. i, 454 note); it is
reproduced as it stands in Mr. Erskine's wording (p. 216).

There they brought Sl. Sanjar *Barlas*, led in by a rope round his neck; he even, to whom I had given the Ningnahar *tuman*, had had his part in the mutiny! Greatly agitated, he kept crying out, "Hai! what fault is in me?" Said I, "Can there be one clearer than that you are higher than the purpose and counsels of this crew?"[1] But as he was the sister's son of my Khan *dada*'s mother, Shah Begim, I gave the order, "Do not lead him with such dishonour; it is not death."

On leaving that place, I sent Ahmad-i-qasim *Kohbur*, one of the begs of the Fort, with a few braves, in pursuit of Mirza Khan.   Fol. 200.

(*m. Babur's dealings with disloyal women.*)

When I left the Bagh-i-bihisht, I went to visit Shah Begim and (Mihr-nigar) Khanim who had settled themselves in tents by the side of the garden.

As townspeople and black-bludgeoners had raised a riot, and were putting hands out to pillage property and to catch persons in corners and outside places, I sent men, to beat the rabble off, and had it herded right away.[2]

Shah Begim and Khanim were seated in one tent. I dismounted at the usual distance, approached with my former deference and courtesy, and had an interview with them. They were extremely agitated, upset, and ashamed; could neither excuse themselves reasonably[3] nor make the enquiries of affection. I had not expected this (disloyalty) of them; it was not as though that party, evil as was the position it had taken up, consisted of persons who would not give ear to the words of Shah Begim and Khanim; Mirza Khan was the begim's grandson, in her presence night and day; if she had not fallen in with the affair, she could have kept him with her.

---

1 Babur's reference may well be to Sanjar's birth as well as to his being the holder of Ningnahar. Sanjar's father had been thought worthy to mate with one of the six Badakhshi begims whose line traced back to Alexander (T.R. p. 107); and his father was a Barlas, seemingly of high family.

2 It may be inferred that what was done was for the protection of the two women.

3 Not a bad case could have been made out for now putting a Timurid in Babur's place in Kabul; *viz.* that he was believed captive in Heri and that Mirza Khan was an effective *locum tenens* against the Arghuns. Haidar sets down what in his eyes pleaded excuse for his father Muh. Husain (T.R. p. 198).

Twice over when fickle Fortune and discordant Fate had
Fol. 200b. parted me from throne and country, retainer and following, I, and
my mother with me, had taken refuge with them and had had no
kindness soever from them. At that time my younger brother
(*i.e.* cousin) Mirza Khan and his mother Sultan-nigar Khanim
held valuable cultivated districts; yet my mother and I,—to
leave all question of a district aside,—were not made possessors
of a single village or a few yoke of plough-oxen.[1] Was my
mother not Yunas Khan's daughter? was I not his grandson?

In my days of plenty I have given from my hand what matched
the blood-relationship and the position of whatsoever member
of that (Chaghatai) dynasty chanced down upon me. For
example, when the honoured Shah Begim came to me, I gave
her Pamghan, one of the best places in Kabul, and failed in no
sort of filial duty and service towards her. Again, when Sl. Sa'id
Khan, Khan in Kashghar, came [914 AH.] with five or six naked
followers on foot, I looked upon him as an honoured guest and
gave him Mandrawar of the Lamghan *tumans*. Beyond this also,
when Shah Isma'il had killed Shaibaq Khan in Marv and
I crossed over to Qunduz (916 AH.—1511 AD.), the Andijanis,
some driving their (Auzbeg) *daroghas* out, some making their
places fast, turned their eyes to me and sent me a man; at that
time I trusted those old family servants to that same Sl. Sa'id
Khan, gave him a force, made him Khan and sped him forth.
Again, down to the present time (*circa* 934 AH.) I have not
looked upon any member of that family who has come to me,
in any other light than as a blood-relation. For example, there
Fol. 201. are now in my service Chin-timur Sultan; Aisan-timur Sultan,
Tukhta-bugha Sultan, and Baba Sultan;[2] on one and all of
these I have looked with more favour than on blood-relations
of my own.

I do not write this in order to make complaint; I have
written the plain truth. I do not set these matters down in order to
make known my own deserts; I have set down exactly what
has happened. In this History I have held firmly to it that the
truth should be reached in every matter, and that every

---

1 *qush*, not even a little plough-land being given.
2 They were sons of Sl. Ahmad Khan *Chaghatai*.

act should be recorded precisely as it occurred. From this it follows of necessity that I have set down of good and bad whatever is known, concerning father and elder brother, kinsman and stranger; of them all I have set down carefully the known virtues and defects. Let the reader accept my excuse; let the reader pass on from the place of severity!

(*n. Letters of victory.*)

Rising from that place and going to the Char-bagh where Mirza Khan had been, we sent letters of victory to all the countries, clans, and retainers. This done, I rode to the citadel.

(*o. Arrest of rebel leaders.*)

Muhammad Husain Mirza in his terror having run away into Khanim's bedding-room and got himself fastened up in a bundle of bedding, we appointed Mirim *Diwan* with other begs of the fort, to take control in those dwellings, capture, and bring him in. Mirim *Diwan* said some plain rough words at Khanim's Fol. 201*b*. gate, by some means or other found the Mirza, and brought him before me in the citadel. I rose at once to receive the Mirza with my usual deference, not even shewing too harsh a face. If I had had that Muh. Husain M. cut in pieces, there was the ground for it that he had had part in base and shameful action, started and spurred on mutiny and treason. Death he deserved with one after another of varied pain and torture, but because there had come to be various connexion between us, his very sons and daughters being by my own mother's sister Khub-nigar Khanim, I kept this just claim in mind, let him go free, and permitted him to set out towards Khurasan. The cowardly ingrate then forgot altogether the good I did him by the gift of his life; he blamed and slandered me to Shaibaq Khan. Little time passed, however, before the Khan gave him his deserts by death.

> Leave thou to Fate the man who does thee wrong,
> For Fate is an avenging servitor.[1]

---

1 f. 160.

Ahmad-i-qasim *Kohbur* and the party of braves sent in pursuit of Mirza Khan, overtook him in the low hills of Qargha-yilaq, not able even to run away, without heart or force to stir a finger! They took him, and brought him to where I sat in the north-east porch of the old Court-house. Said I to him, "Come! let's have a look at one another" (*kurushaling*), but twice before he could bend the knee and come forward, he fell down through agitation. When we had looked at one another, I placed him by my side to give him heart, and I drank first of the sherbet brought in, in order to remove his fears.[1]

As those who had joined him, soldiers, peasants, Mughuls and Chaghatais,[2] were in suspense, we simply ordered him to remain for a few days in his elder sister's house; but a few days later he was allowed to set out for Khurasan[3] because those mentioned above were somewhat uncertain and it did not seem well for him to stay in Kabul.

(p. Excursion to Koh-daman.)

After letting those two go, we made an excursion to Baran, Chash-tupa, and the skirt of Gul-i-bahar.[4] More beautiful in

1 Haidar's opinion of Babur at this crisis is of the more account that his own father was one of the rebels let go to the mercy of the "avenging servitor". When he writes of Babur, as being, at a time so provoking, gay, generous, affectionate, simple and gentle, he sets before us insight and temper in tune with Kipling's "If ..."

2 Babur's distinction, made here and elsewhere, between Chaghatai and Mughul touches the old topic of the right or wrong of the term "Mughul dynasty". What he, as also Haidar, allows said is that if Babur were to describe his mother in tribal terms, he would say she was half-Chaghatai, half-Mughul; and that if he so described himself, he would say he was half-Timurid-Turk, half-Chaghatai. He might have called the dynasty he founded in India Turki, might have called it Timuriya; he would never have called it Mughul, after his maternal grandmother.

Haidar, with imperfect classification, divides Chingiz Khan's "Mughul horde" into Mughuls and Chaghatais and of this Chaghatai offtake says that none remained in 953 AH. (1547 AD.) except the rulers, *i.e.* sons of Sl. Ahmad Khan (T.R. 148). Manifestly there was a body of Chaghatais with Babur and there appear to have been many near his day in the Heri region,—'Ali-sher *Nawa'i* the best known.

Babur supplies directions for naming his dynasty when, as several times, he claims to rule in Hindustan where the "Turk" had ruled (f. 233*b*, f. 224*b*, f. 225). To call his dynasty Mughul seems to blot out the centuries, something as we should do by calling the English Teutons. If there is to be such blotting-out, Abu'l-ghazi would allow us, by his tables of Turk descent, to go further, to the primal source of all the tribes concerned, to Turk, son of Japhet. This traditional descent is another argument against "Mughul dynasty."

3 They went to Qandahar and there suffered great privation.

4 Baran seems likely to be the Baian of some maps. Gul-i-bahar is higher up on the Panjhir road. Chash-tupa will have been near-by; its name might mean *Hill of the heap of winnowed-corn.*

Spring than any part even of Kabul are the open-lands of Baran, the plain of Chash-tupa, and the skirt of Gul-i-bahar. Many sorts of tulip bloom there; when I had them counted once, it came out at 34 different kinds as [has been said].[1] This couplet has been written in praise of these places,—

> Kabul in Spring is an Eden of verdure and blossom;
> Matchless in Kabul the Spring of Gul-i-bahar and Baran.

On this excursion I finished the ode,—

> My heart, like the bud of the red, red rose,
>   Lies fold within fold aflame;
> Would the breath of even a myriad Springs
>   Blow my heart's bud to a rose?

Fol. 202b.

In truth, few places are quite equal to these for spring-excursions, for hawking (*qush salmaq*) or bird-shooting (*qush atmaq*), as has been briefly mentioned in the praise and description of the Kabul and Ghazni country.

(*q. Nasir Mirza expelled from Badakhshan.*)

This year the begs of Badakhshan *i.e.* Muhammad the armourer, Mubarak Shah, Zubair and Jahangir, grew angry and mutinous because of the misconduct of Nasir Mirza and some of those he cherished. Coming to an agreement together, they drew out an army of horse and foot, arrayed it on the level lands by the Kukcha-water, and moved towards Yaftal and Ragh, to near Khamchan, by way of the lower hills. The Mirza and his inexperienced begs, in their thoughtless and unobservant fashion, came out to fight them just in those lower hills. The battle-field was uneven ground; the Badakhshis had a dense mass of men on foot who stood firm under repeated charges by the Mirza's horse, and returned such attack that the horsemen fled, unable to keep their ground. Having beaten the Mirza, the Badakhshis plundered his dependants and connexions.

Beaten and stripped bare, he and his close circle took the road through Ishkimish and Narin to Kila-gahi, from there followed the Qizil-su up, got out on the Ab-dara road, crossed at Shibr-tu, and so came to Kabul, he with 70 or 80 followers, worn-out, naked and famished.

1 f. 136.

That was a marvellous sign of the Divine might! Two or three years earlier the Mirza had left the Kabul country like a foe, driving tribes and hordes like sheep before him, reached Badakhshan and made fast its forts and valley-strongholds. With what fancy in his mind had he marched out?[1] Now he was back, hanging the head of shame for those earlier misdeeds, humbled and distraught about that breach with me!

My face shewed him no sort of displeasure; I made kind enquiry about himself, and brought him out of his confusion.

1 Answer; Visions of his father's sway.

(*a. Raid on the Ghilji Afghans.*)

We had ridden out of Kabul with the intention of over-running the Ghilji;[2] when we dismounted at Sar-i-dih news was brought that a mass of Mahmands (Afghans) was lying in Masht and Sih-kana one *yighach* (*circa* 5 m.) away from us.[3] Our begs and braves agreed in saying, "The Mahmands must be over-run", but I said, "Would it be right to turn aside and raid our own peasants instead of doing what we set out to do? It cannot be."

Riding at night from Sar-i-dih, we crossed the plain of Kattawaz in the dark, a quite black night, one level stretch of land, no mountain or rising-ground in sight, no known road or track, not a man able to lead us! In the end I took the lead. I had been in those parts several times before; drawing inferences from those times, I took the Pole-star on my right shoulder-blade[4] and, with some anxiety, moved on. God brought it right! We went straight to the Qiaq-tu and the Aulaba-tu torrent, that is to say, straight for Khwaja Isma'il *Siriti* where the Ghiljis were lying, the road to which crosses the torrent named. Dismounting near the torrent, we let ourselves and our horses sleep a little, took breath, and bestirred ourselves at shoot of dawn. The Sun was up before we got out of those low hills and valley-bottoms to the plain on which the Ghilji lay with a good *yighach*[5] of

Fol. 203*b*.

---

1 Elph. MS. f. 161; W.-i-B. I.O. 215 f. 164 and 217 f. 139*b*; Mems. p. 220.
2 The narrative indicates the location of the tribe, the modern Ghilzai or Ghilzi.
3 Sih-kana lies s.e. of Shorkach, and near Kharbin. Sar-i-dih is about 25 or 30 miles s. of Ghazni (Erskine). A name suiting the pastoral wealth of the tribe *viz.* Mesh-khail, Sheep-tribe, is shewn on maps somewhat s. from Kharbin. *Cf.* Steingass *s.n.* Masht.
4 *yaghrun*, whence *yaghrunchi*, a diviner by help of the shoulder-blades of sheep. The defacer of the Elphinstone Codex has changed *yaghrun* to *yan*, side, thus making Babur turn his side and not his half-back to the north, altering his direction, and missing what looks like a jesting reference to his own divination of the road. The Pole Star was seen, presumably, before the night became quite black.
5 From the subsequent details of distance done, this must have been one of those good *yighach* of perhaps 5–6 miles, that are estimated by the ease of travel on level lands.

road between them and us; once out on the plain we could see their blackness, either their own or from the smoke of their fires.

Whether bitten by their own whim,[1] or whether wanting to hurry, the whole army streamed off at the gallop (*chapqun quidilar*); off galloped I after them and, by shooting an arrow now at a man, now at a horse, checked them after a *kuroh* or two (3 m.?). It is very difficult indeed to check 5 or 6000 braves galloping loose-rein! God brought it right! They were checked! When we had gone about one *shar'i* (2 m.) further, always with the Afghan blackness in sight, the raid[2] was allowed. Masses of sheep fell to us, more than in any other raid.

After we had dismounted and made the spoils turn back,[3] one body of Afghans after another came down into the plain, provoking a fight. Some of the begs and of the household went against one body and killed every man; Nasir Mirza did the same with another, and a pillar of Afghan heads was set up. An arrow pierced the foot of that foot-soldier Dost the Kotwal who has been mentioned already;[4] when we reached Kabul, he died.

Marching from Khwaja Isma'il, we dismounted once more at Aulaba-tu. Some of the begs and of my own household were ordered to go forward and carefully separate off the Fifth (*Khums*) of the enemy's spoils. By way of favour, we did not take the Fifth from Qasim Beg and some others.[5] From what

Fol. 204.

1 I am uncertain about the form of the word translated by "whim". The Elph. and Hai. Codices read *khud d:lma* (altered in the first to *y:lma*); Ilminsky (p. 257) reads *khud l:ma* (de C. ii, 2 and note); Erskine has been misled by the Persian translation (215 f. 164b and 217 f. 139b). Whether *khud-dilma* should be read, with the sense of "out of their own hearts" (spontaneously), or whether *khud-yalma*, own pace (Turki, *yalma*, pace) the contrast made by Babur appears to be between an unpremeditated gallop and one premeditated for haste. Persian *dalama*, tarantula, also suggests itself.

2 *chapqun*, which is the word translated by gallop throughout the previous passage. The Turki verb *chapmaq* is one of those words-of-all-work for which it is difficult to find a single English equivalent. The verb *quimaq* is another; in its two occurrences here the first may be a metaphor from the pouring of molten metal; the second expresses that permission to gallop off for the raid without which to raid was forbidden. The root-notion of *quimaq* seems to be letting-go, that of *chapmaq*, rapid motion.

3 *i.e.* on the raiders' own road for Kabul. 4 f. 198b.

5 The Fifth taken was manifestly at the ruler's disposition. In at least two places when dependants send gifts to Babur the word [*tassaduq*] used might be rendered as "gifts for the poor". Does this mean that the *padshah* in receiving this stands in the place of the Imam of the Qoran injunction which orders one-fifth of spoil to be given to the Imam for the poor, orphans, and travellers,—four-fifths being reserved for the troops? (Qoran, Sale's ed. 1825, i, 212 and Hidayat, Book ix).

was written down,[1] the Fifth came out at 16,000, that is to say, this 16,000 was the fifth of 80,000 sheep; no question however but that with those lost and those not asked for, a *lak* (100,000) of sheep had been taken.

(b. A hunting-circle.)

Next day when we had ridden from that camp, a hunting-circle was formed on the plain of Kattawaz where deer (*kiyik*)[2] and wild-ass are always plentiful and always fat. Masses went into the ring; masses were killed. During the hunt I galloped after a wild-ass, on getting near shot one arrow, shot another, but did not bring it down, it only running more slowly for the two wounds. Spurring forwards and getting into position[3] quite close to it, I chopped at the nape of its neck behind the ears, and cut through the wind-pipe; it stopped, turned over and died. My sword cut well! The wild-ass was surprisingly fat. Its rib may have been a little under one yard in length. Sherim Taghai and other observers of *kiyik* in Mughulistan said with surprise, "Even in Mughulistan we have seen few *kiyik* so fat!" I shot another wild-ass; most of the wild-asses and deer brought down in that hunt were fat, but not one of them was so fat as the one I first killed.

Turning back from that raid, we went to Kabul and there dismounted.

(c. Shaibaq Khan moves against Khurasan.)

Shaibaq Khan had got an army to horse at the end of last year, meaning to go from Samarkand against Khurasan, his Fol. 204b. march out being somewhat hastened by the coming to him of a servant of that vile traitor to his salt, Shah Mansur the Pay-master, then in Andikhud. When the Khan was approaching Andikhud, that vile wretch said, "I have sent a man to the Auzbeg," relied on this, adorned himself, stuck up an aigrette on his head, and went out, bearing gift and tribute. On this the leaderless[4] Auzbegs poured down on him from all sides, and

---

1 This may be the sum of the separate items of sheep entered in account-books by the commissaries.

2 Here this comprehensive word will stand for deer, these being plentiful in the region.

3 Three Turki MSS. write *sighinib*, but the Elph. MS. has had this changed to *yitib*, having reached.

4 *bash-siz*, lit. without head, doubtless a pun on Auz-beg (own beg, leaderless). B.M. Or. 3714 shows an artist's conception of this *tart-part*.

turned upside down (*tart-part*) the blockhead, his offering and his people of all sorts.

(*d. Irresolution of the Khurasan Mirzas.*)

Badi'u'z-zaman Mirza, Muzaffar Mirza, Muh. Baranduq *Barlas* and Zu'n-nun *Arghun* were all lying with their army in Baba Khaki,[1] not decided to fight, not settled to make (Heri) fort fast, there they sat, confounded, vague, uncertain what to do. Muhammad Baranduq *Barlas* was a knowledgeable man; he kept saying, "You let Muzaffar Mirza and me make the fort fast; let Badi'u'z-zaman Mirza and Zu'n-nun Beg go into the mountains near Heri and gather in Sl. 'Ali *Arghun* from Sistan and Zamin-dawar, Shah Beg and Muqim from Qandahar with all their armies, and let them collect also what there is of Nikdiri and Hazara force; this done, let them make a swift and telling move. The enemy would find it difficult to go into the mountains, and could not come against the (Heri) fort because he would be afraid of the army outside." He said well, his plan was practical.

Fol. 205.

Brave though Zu'n-nun *Arghun* was, he was mean, a lover-of-goods, far from businesslike or judicious, rather shallow-pated, and a bit of a fool. As has been mentioned,[2] when that elder and that younger brother became joint-rulers in Heri, he had chief authority in Badi'u'z-zaman Mirza's presence. He was not willing now for Muh. Baranduq Beg to remain inside Heri town; being the lover-of-goods he was, he wanted to be there himself. But he could not make this seem one and the same thing![3] Is there a better sign of his shallow-pate and craze than that he degraded himself and became contemptible by accepting the lies and flattery of rogues and sycophants? Here are the particulars[4]:—While he was so dominant and trusted in Heri, certain Shaikhs and Mullas went to him and said, "The Spheres are holding commerce with us; you are styled *Hizabru'l-lah* (Lion of God); you will overcome the Auzbeg." Believing

---

1 Baba Khaki is a fine valley, some 13 *yighach* e. of Heri (f. 13) where the Heri sultans reside in the heats (*J. Asiatique* xvi, 501, de Meynard's article; H.S. iii, 356).
2 f. 172*b*.
3 *aukhshata almadi.* This is one of many passages which Ilminsky indicates he has made good by help of the Memoirs (p. 261; *Mémoires* ii, 6).
4 They are given also on f. 172.

these words, he put his bathing-cloth round his neck and gave thanks. It was through this he did not accept Muhammad Baranduq Beg's sensible counsel, did not strengthen the works (*aish*) of the fort, get ready fighting equipment, set scout or rearward to warn of the foe's approach, or plan out such method of array that, should the foe appear, his men would fight with ready heart.

(*e. Shaibaq Khan takes Heri.*)

Shaibaq Khan passed through Murgh-ab to near Sir-kai[1] in the month of Muharram (913 AH. May–June 1507 AD.). When the Mirzas heard of it, they were altogether upset, could not act, collect troops, array those they had. Dreamers, they moved through a dream![2] Zu'n-nun *Arghun*, made glorious by that flattery, went out to Qara-rabat, with 100 to 150 men, to face 40,000 to 50,000 Auzbegs: a mass of these coming up, hustled his off, took him, killed him and cut off his head.[3]

Fol. 205*b*.

In Fort Ikhtiyaru'd-din, it is known as Ala-qurghan,[4] were the Mirzas' mothers, elder and younger sisters, wives and treasure. The Mirzas reached the town at night, let their horses rest till midnight, slept, and at dawn flung forth again. They could not think about strengthening the fort; in the respite and crack of time there was, they just ran away,[5] leaving mother, sister, wife and little child to Auzbeg captivity.

What there was of Sl. Husain Mirza's *haram*, Payanda-sultan Begim and Khadija Begim at the head of it, was inside Ala-qurghan; there too were the *harams* of Badi'u'z-zaman

---

1 This may be Sirakhs or Sirakhsh (Erskine).

2 *Tushliq tushdin yurdi binurlar.* At least two meanings can be given to these words. Circumstances seem to exclude the one in which the Memoirs (p. 222) and *Mémoires* (ii, 7) have taken them here, *viz.* "each man went off to shift for himself", and "chacun s'en alla de son côté et s'enfuit comme il put", because Zu'n-nun did not go off, and the Mirzas broke up after his defeat. I therefore suggest another reading, one prompted by the Mirzas' vague fancies and dreams of what they might do, but did not.

3 The encounter was between "Belaq-i-maral and Rabat-i-'ali-sher, near Badghis" (Raverty's *Notes* p. 580). For particulars of the taking of Heri *see* H.S. iii, 353.

4 One may be the book-name, the second the name in common use, and due to the colour of the buildings. But Babur may be making an ironical jest, and nickname the fort by a word referring to the defilement (*ala*) of Auzbeg possession. (*Cf.* H.S. iii, 359.)

5 Mr. Erskine notes that Badi'u'z-zaman took refuge with Shah Isma'il *Safawi* who gave him Tabriz. When the Turkish Emperor Salim took Tabriz in 920 AH. (1514 AD.), he was taken prisoner and carried to Constantinople, where he died in 923 AH. (1517 AD.).

Mirza[1] and Muzaffar Mirza with their little children, treasure, and households (*biyutat*). What was desirable for making the fort fast had not been done; even braves to reinforce it had not arrived. 'Ashiq-i-muhammad *Arghun*, the younger brother of Mazid Beg, had fled from the army on foot and gone into it; in it was also Amir 'Umar Beg's son 'Ali Khan (*Turkman*); Shaikh 'Abdu'l-lah the taster was there; Mirza Beg *Kai-khusraui* was there; and Mirak *Gur* (or *Kur*) the Diwan was there.

Fol. 206.

When Shaibaq Khan arrived two or three days later, the Shaikhu'l-islam and notables went out to him with the keys of the outer-fort. That same 'Ashiq-i-muhammad held Ala-qurghan for 16 or 17 days; then a mine, run from the horse-market outside, was fired and brought a tower down; the garrison lost heart, could hold out no longer, so let the fort be taken.

(*f. Shaibaq Khan in Heri.*)

Shaibaq Khan, after taking Heri,[2] behaved badly not only to the wives and children of its rulers but to every person soever. For the sake of this five-days' fleeting world, he earned himself a bad name. His first improper act and deed in Heri was that, for the sake of this rotten world (*chirk dunya*), he caused Khadija Begim various miseries, through letting the vile wretch Pay-master Shah Mansur get hold of her to loot. Then he let 'Abdu'l-wahhab *Mughul* take to loot a person so saintly and so revered as Shaikh Puran, and each one of Shaikh Puran's children be taken by a separate person. He let the band of poets be seized by Mulla Bana'i, a matter about which this verse is well-known in Khurasan:—

> Except 'Abdu'l-lah the stupid fool (*kir-khar*),
> Not a poet to-day sees the colour of gold;
> From the poets' band Bana'i would get gold,
> All he will get is *kir-khar*.[3]

Fol. 206*b*.

---

1 In the fort were his wife Kabuli Begim, d. of Aulugh Beg M. *Kabuli* and Ruqaiya Agha, known as the Nightingale. A young daughter of the Mirza, named the Rose-bud (Chuchak), had died just before the siege. After the surrender of the fort, Kabuli Begim was married by Mirza Kukuldash (perhaps 'Ashiq-i-muhammad *Arghun*); Ruqaiya by Timur Sl. *Auzbeg* (H.S. iii, 359).

2 The *Khutba* was first read for Shaibaq Khan in Heri on Friday Muharram 15th 913 AH. (May 27th 1507 AD.).

3 There is a Persian phrase used when a man engages in an unprofitable undertaking *Kir-i-khar gerift*, i.e. *Asini nervum deprehendet* (Erskine). The H.S. does not

Directly he had possession of Heri, Shaibaq Khan married and took Muzaffar Mirza's wife, Khan-zada Khanim, without regard to the running-out of the legal term.[1] His own illiteracy not forbidding, he instructed in the exposition of the Qoran, Qazi Ikhtiyar and Muhammad Mir Yusuf, two of the celebrated and highly-skilled mullas of Heri; he took a pen and corrected the hand-writing of Mulla Sl. 'Ali of Mashhad and the drawing of Bih-zad; and every few days, when he had composed some tasteless couplet, he would have it read from the pulpit, hung in the Char-su [Square], and for it accept the offerings of the towns-people![2] Spite of his early-rising, his not neglecting the Five Prayers, and his fair knowledge of the art of reciting the Qoran, there issued from him many an act and deed as absurd, as impudent, and as heathenish as those just named.

(g. Death of two Mirzas.)

Ten or fifteen days after he had possession of Heri, Shaibaq Khan came from Kahd-stan[3] to Pul-i-salar. From that place he sent Timur Sl. and 'Ubaid Sl. with the army there present, against Abu'l-muhsin Mirza and Kupuk (Kipik) Mirza then seated carelessly in Mashhad. The two Mirzas had thought at one time of making Qalat[4] fast; at another, this after they had had news of the approach of the Auzbeg, they were for moving on Shaibaq Khan himself, by forced marches and along a different

---

mention Bana'i as fleecing the poets but has much to say about one Maulana 'Abdu'r-rahim a Turkistani favoured by Shaibani, whose victim Khwand-amir was, amongst many others. Not infrequently where Babur and Khwand-amir state the same fact, they accompany it by varied details, as here (H.S. iii, 358, 360).

1 'adat. Muhammadan Law fixes a term after widowhood or divorce within which re-marriage is unlawful. Light is thrown upon this re-marriage by H.S. iii, 359. The passage, a somewhat rhetorical one, gives the following details:—"On coming into Heri on Muharram 11th, Shaibani at once set about gathering in the property of the Timurids. He had the wives and daughters of the former rulers brought before him. The great lady Khan-zada Begim (f. 164) who was daughter of Ahmad Khan, niece of Sl. Husain Mirza, and wife of Muzaffar Mirza, shewed herself pleased in his presence. Desiring to marry him, she said Muzaffar M. had divorced her two years before. Trustworthy persons gave evidence to the same effect, so she was united to Shaibani in accordance with the glorious Law. Mihr-angez Begim, Muzaffar M.'s daughter, was married to 'Ubaidu'llah Sl. (Auzbeg); the rest of the chaste ladies having been sent back into the city, Shaibani resumed his search for property." Manifestly Babur did not believe in the divorce Khwand-amir thus records.

2 A sarcasm this on the acceptance of literary honour from the illiterate.

3 f. 191 and note; Pul-i-salar may be an irrigation-dam.

4 Qalat-i-nadiri, the birth-place of Nadir Shah, n. of Mashhad and standing on very strong ground (Erskine).

road,[1]—which might have turned out an amazingly good idea! But while they sit still there in Mashhad with nothing decided, the Sultans arrive by forced marches. The Mirzas for their part array and go out; Abu'l-muhsin Mirza is quickly overcome and routed; Kupuk Mirza charges his brother's assailants with somewhat few men; him too they carry off; both brothers are dismounted and seated in one place; after an embrace (*quchush*), they kiss farewell; Abu'l-muhsin shews some want of courage; in Kupuk Mirza it all makes no change at all. The heads of both are sent to Shaibaq Khan in Pul-i-salar.

(*h. Babur marches for Qandahar.*)

In those days Shah Beg and his younger brother Muhammad Muqim, being afraid of Shaibaq Khan, sent one envoy after another to me with dutiful letters ('*arz-dasht*), giving sign of amity and good-wishes. Muqim, in a letter of his own, explicitly invited me. For us to look on at the Auzbeg over-running the whole country, was not seemly; and as by letters and envoys, Shah Beg and Muqim had given me invitation, there remained little doubt they would wait upon me.[2] When all begs and counsellors had been consulted, the matter was left at this:— We were to get an army to horse, join the Arghun begs and decide in accord and agreement with them, whether to move into Khurasan or elsewhere as might seem good.

(*i. In Ghazni and Qalat-i-ghilzai.*)

Habiba-sultan Begim, my aunt (*yinka*) as I used to call her, met us in Ghazni, having come from Heri, according to arrangement, in order to bring her daughter Mas'uma-sultan Begim. With the honoured Begim came Khusrau Kukuldash, Sl. Quli *Chunaq* (One-eared) and Gadai *Balal* who had returned to me

---

1 This is likely to be the road passing through the Carfax of Rabat-i-sangbast, described by Daulat-shah (Browne, p. 176).

2 This will mean that the Arghuns would acknowledge his suzerainty; Haidar Mirza however says that Shah Beg had higher views (T.R. p. 202). There had been earlier negotiations between Zu'n-nun with Badi'u'z-zaman and Babur which may have led to the abandonment of Babur's expedition in 911 AD. (f. 158; H.S. iii, 323; Raverty's account (*Notes* p. 581–2) of Babur's dealings with the Arghun chiefs needs revision).

after flight from Heri, first to Ibn-i-husain Mirza then to Abu'l-muhsin Mirza,[1] with neither of whom they could remain.

In Qalat the army came upon a mass of Hindustan traders, come there to traffic and, as it seemed, unable to go on. The general opinion about them was that people who, at a time of such hostilities, are coming into an enemy's country[2] must be plundered. With this however I did not agree; said I, "What is the traders' offence? If we, looking to God's pleasure, leave such scrapings of gain aside, the Most High God will apportion our reward. It is now just as it was a short time back when we rode out to raid the Ghilji; many of you then were of one mind to raid the Mahmand Afghans, their sheep and goods, their wives and families, just because they were within five miles of you! Then as now I did not agree with you. On the very next day the Most High God apportioned you more sheep belonging to Afghan enemies, than had ever before fallen to the share of the army." Something by way of *peshkash* (offering) was taken from each trader when we dismounted on the other side of Qalat.

(*j. Further march south.*)

Beyond Qalat two Mirzas joined us, fleeing from Qandahar. One was Mirza Khan (Wais) who had been allowed to go into Khurasan after his defeat at Kabul. The other was 'Abdu'r- Fol. 208. razzaq Mirza who had stayed on in Khurasan when I left. With them came and waited on me the mother of Jahangir Mirza's son Pir-i-muhammad, a grandson of Pahar Mirza.[3]

(*k. Behaviour of the Arghun chiefs.*)

When we sent persons and letters to Shah Beg and Muqim, saying, "Here we are at your word; a stranger-foe like the

1 They will have gone first to Tun or Qain, thence to Mashhad, and seem likely to have joined the Begim after cross-cutting to avoid Heri.

2 *yaghi wilayati-gha kiladurghan.* There may have been an accumulation of caravans on their way to Herat, checked in Qalat by news of the Auzbeg conquest.

3 Jahangir's son, thus brought by his mother, will have been an infant; his father had gone back last year with Babur by the mountain road and had been left, sick and travelling in a litter, with the baggage when Babur hurried on to Kabul at the news of the mutiny against him (f. 197); he must have died shortly afterwards, seemingly between the departure of the two rebels from Kabul (f. 201b–202) and the march out for Qandahar. Doubtless his widow now brought her child to claim his uncle Babur's protection.

Auzbeg has taken Khurasan; come! let us settle, in concert and amity, what will be for the general good," they returned a rude and ill-mannered answer, going back from the dutiful letters they had written and from the invitations they had given. One of their incivilities was that Shah Beg stamped his letter to me in the middle of its reverse, where begs seal if writing to begs, where indeed a great beg seals if writing to one of the lower circle.[1] But for such ill-manners and his rude answers, his affair would never have gone so far as it did, for, as they say,—

A strife-stirring word will accomplish the downfall of an ancient line.

By these their headstrong acts they gave to the winds house, family, and the hoards of 30 to 40 years.

One day while we were near Shahr-i-safa[2] a false alarm being given in the very heart of the camp, the whole army was made to arm and mount. At the time I was occupied with a bath

Fol. 208b. and purification; the begs were much flurried; I mounted when I was ready; as the alarm was false, it died away after a time.

March by march we moved on to Guzar.[3] There we tried again to discuss with the Arghuns but, paying no attention to us, they maintained the same obstinate and perverse attitude. Certain well-wishers who knew the local land and water, represented to me, that the head of the torrents (*rudlar*) which come down to Qandahar, being towards Baba Hasan Abdal and Khalishak,[4] a move ought to be made in that direction, in order

1 Persians pay great attention in their correspondence not only to the style but to the kind of paper on which a letter is written, the place of signature, the place of the seal, and the situation of the address. Chardin gives some curious information on the subject (Erskine). Babur marks the distinction of rank he drew between the Arghun chiefs and himself when he calls their letter to him, '*arz-dasht*, his to them *khatt*. His claim to suzerainty over those chiefs is shewn by Haidar Mirza to be based on his accession to Timurid headship through the downfall of the Bai-qaras, who had been the acknowledged suzerains of the Arghuns now repudiating Babur's claim. *Cf.* Erskine's *History of India* i, cap. 3.

2 on the main road, some 40 miles east of Qandahar.

3 var. Kur or Kawar. If the word mean *ford*, this might well be the one across the Tarnak carrying the road to Qara. Here Babur seems to have left the main road along the Tarnak, by which the British approach was made in 1880 AD., for one crossing west into the valley of the Argand-ab.

4 Baba Hasan *Abdal* is the Baba Wali of maps. The same saint has given his name here, and also to his shrine east of Atak where he is known as Baba Wali of Qandahar. The torrents mentioned are irrigation off-takes from the Argand-ab, which river flows between Baba Wali and Khalishak. Shah Beg's force was south of the torrents (*cf.* Murghan-koh on S.A.W. map).

to cut off (*yiqmaq*) all those torrents.[1] Leaving the matter there, we next day made our men put on their mail, arrayed in right and left, and marched for Qandahar.

(l. Battle of Qandahar.)

Shah Beg and Muqim had seated themselves under an awning which was set in front of the naze of the Qandahar-hill where I am now having a rock-residence cut out.[2] Muqim's men pushed forward amongst the trees to rather near us. Tufan *Arghun* had fled to us when we were near Shahr-i-safa; he now betook himself alone close up to the Arghun array to where one named 'Ashiqu'l-lah was advancing rather fast leading 7 or 8 men. Alone, Tufan *Arghun* faced him, slashed swords with him, unhorsed him, cut off his head and brought it to me as we were passing Sang-i-lakhshak;[3] an omen we accepted! Not thinking it well to fight where we were, amongst suburbs and trees, we went on along the skirt of the hill. Just as we had settled on ground for the camp, in a meadow on the Qandahar side of the   Fol. 209. torrent,[4] opposite Khalishak, and were dismounting, Sher Quli the scout hurried up and represented that the enemy was arrayed to fight and on the move towards us.

As on our march from Qalat the army had suffered much from hunger and thirst, most of the soldiers on getting near Khalishak scattered up and down for sheep and cattle, grain

1 The narrative and plans of *Second Afghan War* (Murray 1908) illustrate Babur's movements and show most of the places he names. The end of the 280-mile march, from Kabul to within sight of Qandahar, will have stirred in the General of 1507 what it stirred in the General of 1880. Lord Roberts speaking in May 1913 in Glasgow on the rapid progress of the movement for National Service thus spoke:— "A memory comes over me which turns misgiving into hope and apprehension into confidence. It is the memory of the morning when, accompanied by two of Scotland's most famous regiments, the Seaforths and the Gordons, at the end of a long and arduous march, *I saw in the distance the walls and minarets of Qandahar, and knew that the end of a great resolve and a great task was near.*"

2 *min tash* '*imarat qazdurghan tumshughi-ning alida*; 215 f. 168b, '*imarati kah az sang yak para farmuda budim*; 217 f. 143b, *jay kah man* '*imarati sakhtam*; Mems. p. 226, where I have built a palace; *Méms.* ii, 15, *l'endroit même où j'ai bâti un palais.* All the above translations lose the sense of *qazdurghan*, am causing to dig out, to quarry stone. Perhaps for coolness' sake the dwelling was cut out in the living rock. That the place is south-west of the main *ariqs*, near Murghan-koh or on it, Babur's narrative allows. *Cf.* Appendix J.

3 *sic*, Hai. MS. There are two Lakhshas, Little Lakhsha, a mile west of Qandahar, and Great Lakhsha, about a mile s.w. of Old Qandahar, 5 or 6 m. from the modern one (Erskine).

4 This will be the main irrigation channel taken off from the Argand-ab.

and eatables. Without looking to collect them, we galloped off. Our force may have been 2000 in all, but perhaps not over 1000 were in the battle because those mentioned as scattering up and down could not rejoin in time to fight.

Though our men were few I had them organized and posted on a first-rate plan and method; I had never arrayed them before by such a good one. For my immediate command (*khasa tabin*) I had selected braves from whose hands comes work[1] and had inscribed them by tens and fifties, each ten and each fifty under a leader who knew the post in the right or left of the centre for his ten or his fifty, knew the work of each in the battle, and was there on the observant watch; so that, after mounting, the right and left, right and left hands, right and left sides, charged right and left without the trouble of arraying them or the need of a *tawachi*.[2]

Fol. 209b.

> (*Author's note on his terminology.*)   Although *baranghar, aung qul, aung yan* and *aung* (right wing, right hand, right side and right) all have the same meaning, I have applied them in different senses in order to vary terms and mark distinctions. As, in the battle-array, the (Ar.) *maimana* and *maisara* i.e. what people call (Turki) *baranghar* and *jawanghar* (r. and l. wings) are not included in the (Ar.) *qalb*, i.e. what people call (T.) *ghul* (centre), so it is in arraying the centre itself. Taking the array of the centre only, its (Ar.) *yamin* and *yasar* (r. and l.) are called (by me) *aung qul* and *sul qul* (r. and l. hands). Again,—the (Ar.) *khasa tabin* (royal troop) in the centre has its *yamin* and *yasar* which are called (by me) *aung yan* and *sul yan* (r. and l. sides, T. *yan*). Again,—in the *khasa tabin* there is the (T.) *bui* (*ning*) *tikini* (close circle); its *yamin* and *yasar* are called *sung* and *sul*. In the Turki tongue they call one single thing a *bui*,[3] but that is not the *bui* meant here; what is meant here is close (*yaqin*).

The right wing (*baranghar*) was Mirza Khan (Wais), Sherim Taghai, Yarak Taghai with his elder and younger brethren, Chilma *Mughul*, Ayub Beg, Muhammad Beg, Ibrahim Beg, 'Ali Sayyid *Mughul* with his Mughuls, Sl. Quli *chuhra*, Khuda-bakhsh and Abu'l-hasan with his elder and younger brethren.

The left (*jawanghar*) was 'Abdu'r-razzaq Mirza, Qasim Beg, Tingri-birdi, Qambar-i-'ali, Ahmad *Ailchi-bugha*, Ghuri *Barlas*, Sayyid Husain Akbar, and Mir Shah *Quchin*.

---

1 *tamam ailikidin—aish-kilur yikitlar*, an idiomatic phrase used of 'Ali-dost (f. 14*b* and n.), not easy to express by a single English adjective.

2 The *tawachi* was a sort of adjutant who attended to the order of the troops and carried orders from the general (Erskine). The difficult passage following gives the Turki terms Babur selected to represent Arabic military ones.

3 Ar. *ahad* (*Ayin-i-akbari*, Blochmann, index *s.n.*). The word *bui* recurs in the text on f. 210.

The advance (*airawal*) was Nasir Mirza, Sayyid Qasim Lord of the Gate, Muhibb-i-'ali the armourer, Papa Aughuli (Papa's son?), Allah-wairan *Turkman*, Sher Quli *Mughul* the scout with his elder and younger brethren, and Muhammad 'Ali.

In the centre (*ghul*), on my right hand, were Qasim Kukuldash, Khusrau Kukuldash, Sl. Muhammad *Duldai*, Shah Mahmud the secretary, Qul-i-bayazid the taster, and Kamal the sherbet-server; on my left were Khwaja Muhammad 'Ali, Nasir's Dost, Nasir's Mirim, Baba Sher-zad, Khan-quli, Wali the treasurer, Qutluq-qadam the scout, Maqsud the water-bearer (*su-chi*), and Baba Shaikh. Those in the centre were all of my household; there were no great begs; not one of those enumerated had reached the rank of beg. Those inscribed in this *bui*[1] were Sher Beg, Hatim the Armoury-master, Kupuk, Quli Baba, Abu'l-hasan the armourer;—of the Mughuls, Aurus (Russian) 'Ali Sayyid,[2] Darwish-i-'ali Sayyid, Khush-kildi, Chilma, Dost-kildi, Chilma *Taghchi*, Damachi, Mindi;—of the Turkmans, Mansur, Rustam-i-'ali with his elder and younger brother, and Shah Nazir and Siunduk. Fol. 210.

The enemy was in two divisions, one under Shah Shuja' *Arghun*, known as Shah Beg and hereafter to be written of simply as Shah Beg, the other under his younger brother Muqim.

Some estimated the dark mass of Arghuns[3] at 6 or 7000 men; no question whatever but that Shah Beg's own men in mail were 4 or 5000. He faced our right, Muqim with a force smaller may-be than his brother's, faced our left. Muqim made a mightily strong attack on our left, that is on Qasim Beg from whom two or three persons came before fighting began, to ask for reinforcement; we however could not detach a man because in front of us also the enemy was very strong. We made our onset without any delay; the enemy fell suddenly on our van, turned it back and rammed it on our centre. When we, after a discharge of arrows, advanced, they, who also had been Fol. 210*b*.

---

1 *i.e.* the *bui tikini* of f. 209*b*, the *khasa tabin*, close circle.

2 As Mughuls seem unlikely to be descendants of Muhammad, perhaps the title Sayyid in some Mughul names here, may be a translation of a Mughul one meaning Chief.

3 *Arghun-ning qarasi*, a frequent phrase.

shooting for a time, seemed likely to make a stand (*tukhtaghan-dik*). Some-one, shouting to his men, came forward towards me, dismounted and was for adjusting his arrow, but he could do nothing because we moved on without stay. He remounted and rode off; it may have been Shah Beg himself. During the fight Piri Beg *Turkman* and 4 or 5 of his brethren turned their faces from the foe and, turban in hand,[1] came over to us.

> (*Author's note on Piri Beg.*) This Piri Beg was one of those Turkmans who came [into Heri] with the Turkman Begs led by 'Abdu'l-baqi Mirza and Murad Beg, after Shah Isma'il vanquished the Bayandar sultans and seized the 'Iraq countries.[2]

Our right was the first to overcome the foe; it made him hurry off. Its extreme point had gone pricking (*sanjilib*)[3] as far as where I have now laid out a garden. Our left extended as far as the great tree-tangled[4] irrigation-channels, a good way below Baba Hasan Abdal. Muqim was opposite it, its numbers very small compared with his. God brought it right! Between it and Muqim were three or four of the tree-tangled water-channels going on to Qandahar;[5] it held the crossing-place and allowed no passage; small body though it was, it made splendid stand and kept its ground. Halwachi Tarkhan[6] slashed away in the water with Tingri-birdi and Qambar-i-'ali. Qambar-i-'ali was wounded; an arrow stuck in Qasim Beg's forehead; another struck Ghuri *Barlas* above the eyebrow and came out above his cheek.[7]

Fol. 211.

We meantime, after putting our adversary to flight, had crossed those same channels towards the naze of Murghan-koh (Birds'-hill). Some-one on a grey *tipuchaq* was going backwards and forwards irresolutely along the hill-skirt, while we

1 in sign of submission.
2 f. 175b. It was in 908 AH. [1502 AD.].
3 This word seems to be from *sanjmaq*, to prick or stab; and here to have the military sense of *prick*, *viz.* riding forth. The Second Pers. trs. (217 f. 144b) translates it by *ghauta khurda raft*, went tasting a plunge under water (215 f. 170; Muh. *Shirazi's* lith. ed. p. 133). Erskine (p. 228), as his Persian source dictates, makes the men sink into the soft ground; de Courteille varies much (ii, 21).
4 Ar. *akhmail*, so translated under the known presence of trees; it may also imply soft ground (Lane p. 813 col. b) but soft ground does not suit the purpose of *ariqs* (channels), the carrying on of water to the town.
5 The S.A.W. map is useful here.
6 That he had a following may be inferred.
7 Hai. MS. *qachar*; Ilminsky, p. 268; and both Pers. trss. *rukhsar* or *rukhsara* (f. 25 and note to *qachar*).

were getting across; I likened him to Shah Beg; seemingly it was he.

Our men having beaten their opponents, all went off to pursue and unhorse them. Remained with me eleven to count, 'Abdu'l-lah the librarian being one. Muqim was still keeping his ground and fighting. Without a glance at the fewness of our men, we had the nagarets sounded and, putting our trust in God, moved with face set for Muqim.

> (Turki)   For few or for many God is full strength;
>   No man has might in His Court.
> (Arabic)   How often, God willing it, a small force has vanquished a large one!

Learning from the nagarets that we were approaching, Muqim forgot his fixed plan and took the road of flight. God brought it right!

After putting our foe to flight, we moved for Qandahar and dismounted in Farrukh-zad Beg's Char-bagh, of which at this time not a trace remains!

(*m. Babur enters Qandahar.*)   Fol. 211*b*.

Shah Beg and Muqim could not get into Qandahar when they took to flight; Shah Beg went towards Shal and Mastung (Quetta), Muqim towards Zamin-dawar. They left no-one able to make the fort fast. Ahmad 'Ali Tarkhan was in it together with other elder and younger brethren of Quli Beg *Arghun* whose attachment and good-feeling for me were known. After parley they asked protection for the families of their elder and younger brethren; their request was granted and all mentioned were encompassed with favour. They then opened the Mashur-gate of the town; with leaderless men in mind, no other was opened. At that gate were posted Sherim Taghai and Yarim Beg. I went in with a few of the household, charged the leaderless men and had two or three put to death by way of example.[1]

(*n. The spoils of Qandahar.*)

I got to Muqim's treasury first, that being in the outer-fort; 'Abdu'r-razzaq Mirza must have been quicker than I, for he was

---

1 So in the Turki MSS. and the first Pers. trs. (215 f. 170*b*). The second Pers. trs. (217 f. 145*b*) has a gloss of *atqu u tika*; this consequently Erskine follows (p. 229) and adds a note explaining the punishment. Ilminsky has the gloss also (p. 269), thus indicating Persian and English influence.

just dismounting there when I arrived; I gave him a few things from it. I put Dost-i-nasir Beg, Qul-i-bayazid the taster and, of pay-masters, Muhammad *bakhshi* in charge of it, then passed on into the citadel and posted Khwaja Muhammad 'Ali, Shah Mahmud and, of the pay-masters, Taghai Shah *bakhshi* in charge of Shah Beg's treasury.

Nasir's Mirim and Maqsud the sherbet-server were sent to keep the house of Zu'n-nun's *Diwan* Mir Jan for Nasir Mirza; for Mirza Khan was kept Shaikh Abu-sa'id *Tarkhani's*; for 'Abdu'r-razzaq Mirza ... ... 's.[1]

Such masses of white money had never been seen in those countries; no-one indeed was to be heard of who had seen so much. That night, when we ourselves stayed in the citadel, Shah Beg's slave Sambhal was captured and brought in. Though he was then Shah Beg's intimate, he had not yet received his later favour.[2] I had him given into some-one's charge but as good watch was not kept, he was allowed to escape. Next day I went back to my camp in Farrukh-zad Beg's Char-bagh.

I gave the Qandahar country to Nasir Mirza. After the treasure had been got into order, loaded up and started off, he took the loads of white *tankas* off a string of camels (*i.e.* 7 beasts) at the citadel-treasury, and kept them. I did not demand them back; I just gave them to him.

On leaving Qandahar, we dismounted in the Qush-khana meadow. After setting the army forward, I had gone for an excursion, so I got into camp rather late. It was another camp! not to be recognized! Excellent *tipuchaqs*, strings and strings of he-camels, she-camels, and mules, bearing saddle-bags (*khur-zin*) of silken stuffs and cloth,—tents of scarlet (cloth) and velvet, all sorts of awnings, every kind of work-shop, ass-load after ass-load of chests! The goods of the elder and younger (Arghun) brethren had been kept in separate treasuries; out of each had come chest upon chest, bale upon bale of stuffs and

1 No MS. gives the missing name.
2 The later favour mentioned was due to Sambhal's laborious release of his master from Auzbeg captivity in 917 AH. (1511 AD.) of which Erskine quotes a full account from the *Tarikh-i-sind* (History of India i, 345).

clothes-in-wear (*artmaq artmaq*), sack upon sack of white *tankas*. In *autagh* and *chadar* (lattice-tent and pole-tent) was much spoil for every man soever; many sheep also had been taken but sheep were less cared about!

I made over to Qasim Beg Muqim's retainers in Qalat,   Fol. 212b. under Quj *Arghun* and Taju'd-din Mahmud, with their goods and effects. Qasim Beg was a knowing person; he saw it unadvisable for us to stay long near Qandahar, so, by talking and talking, worrying and worrying, he got us to march off. As has been said, I had bestowed Qandahar on Nasir Mirza; he was given leave to go there; we started for Kabul.

There had been no chance of portioning out the spoils while we were near Qandahar; it was done at Qara-bagh where we delayed two or three days. To count the coins being difficult, they were apportioned by weighing them in scales. Begs of all ranks, retainers and household (*tabin*) loaded up ass-load after ass-load of sacks full of white *tankas*, and took them away for their own subsistence and the pay of their soldiers.

We went back to Kabul with masses of goods and treasure, great honour and reputation.

(o. Babur's marriage with Ma'suma-sultan.)

After this return to Kabul I concluded alliance ('*aqd qildim*) with Sl. Ahmad Mirza's daughter Ma'suma-sultan Begim whom I had asked in marriage at Khurasan, and had had brought from there.

(p. Shaibaq Khan before Qandahar.)

A few days later a servant of Nasir Mirza brought the news that Shaibaq Khan had come and laid siege to Qandahar. That Muqim had fled to Zamin-dawar has been said already; from there he went on and saw Shaibaq Khan. From Shah Beg also one person after another had gone to Shaibaq Khan. At the   Fol. 213. instigation and petition of these two, the Khan came swiftly down on Qandahar by the mountain road,[1] thinking to find me there. This was the very thing that experienced person

---

1 Presumably he went by Sabzar, Daulatabad, and Washir.

Qasim Beg had in his mind when he worried us into marching off from near Qandahar.

> (Persian)   What a mirror shews to the young man,
>   A baked brick shews to the old one!

Shaibaq Khan arriving, besieged Nasir Mirza in Qandahar.

(q. Alarm in Kabul.)

When this news came, the begs were summoned for counsel.
The matters for discussion were these:—Strangers and ancient
foes, such as are Shaibaq Khan and the Auzbegs, are in possession of all the countries once held by Timur Beg's descendants;
even where Turks and Chaghatais[1] survive in corners and
border-lands, they have all joined the Auzbeg, willingly or
with aversion; one remains, I myself, in Kabul, the foe mightily
strong, I very weak, with no means of making terms, no strength
to oppose; that, in the presence of such power and potency, we
had to think of some place for ourselves and, at this crisis and
in the crack of time there was, to put a wider space between
us and the strong foeman; that choice lay between Badakhshan
and Hindustan and that decision must now be made.

Qasim Beg and Sherim Taghai were agreed for Badakhshan;

> (Author's note on Badakhshan.)   Those holding their heads up in
> Badakhshan at this crisis were, of Badakhshis, Mubarak Shah and Zubair,
> Jahangir *Turkman* and Muhammad the armourer. They had driven Nasir
> Mirza out but had not joined the Auzbeg.

Fol. 213b.   I and several household-begs preferred going towards Hindustan
and were for making a start to Lamghan.[2]

(r. Movements of some Mirzas.)

After taking Qandahar, I had bestowed Qalat and the Turnuk
(Tarnak) country on 'Abdu'r-razzaq Mirza and had left him in
Qalat, but with the Auzbeg besieging Qandahar, he could not
stay in Qalat, so left it and came to Kabul. He arriving just as
we were marching out, was there left in charge.[3]

There being in Badakhshan no ruler or ruler's son, Mirza Khan
inclined to go in that direction, both because of his relationship

---

1 f. 202 and note to *Chaghatai*.
2 This will be for the Ningnahar *tuman* of Lamghan.
3 He was thus dangerously raised in his father's place of rule.

to Shah Begim[1] and with her approval. He was allowed to go and the honoured Begim herself started off with him. My honoured maternal-aunt Mihr-nigar Khanim also wished to go to Badakh-shan, notwithstanding that it was more seemly for her to be with me, a blood-relation; but whatever objection was made, she was not to be dissuaded; she also betook[2] herself to Badakhshan.

(*s. Babur's second start for Hindustan.*)

Under our plan of going to Hindustan, we marched out of Kabul in the month of the first Jumada (September 1507 AD.), taking the road through Little Kabul and going down by Surkh-rabat to Quruq-sai.

The Afghans belonging between Kabul and Lamghan (Ning-nahar) are thieves and abettors of thieves even in quiet times; for just such a happening as this they had prayed in vain. Said they, "He has abandoned Kabul", and multiplied their misdeeds by ten, changing their very merits for faults. To such lengths did things go that on the morning we marched from Jagdalik, the Afghans located between it and Lamghan, such as the Khizr-khail, Shimu-khail, Khirilchi and Khugiani, thought of blocking the pass, arrayed on the mountain to the north, and advancing with sound of tambour and flourish of sword, began to shew themselves off. On our mounting I ordered our men to move along the mountain-side, each man from where he had dismounted;[3] off they set at the gallop up every ridge and every valley of the saddle.[4] The Afghans stood awhile, but could not let even one arrow fly,[5] and betook themselves to flight. While I was on the mountain during the pursuit, I shot one in the hand as he was running back below me. That arrow-stricken man and a few others were brought in; some were put to death by impalement, as an example.

Fol. 214.

---

1 ff. 10*b*, 11*b*. Haidar M. writes, "Shah Begim laid claim to Badakhshan, saying, 'It has been our hereditary kingdom for 3000 years; though I, being a woman, cannot myself attain sovereignty, yet my grandson Mirza Khan can hold it'" (T.R. p. 203).
2 *tibradilar.* The agitation of mind connoted, with movement, by this verb may well have been, here, doubt of Babur's power to protect.
3 *tushluq tushdin taghgha yurukailar. Cf.* 205*b* for the same phrase, with supposedly different meaning.
4 *qangshar* lit. ridge of the nose.
5 *bir auq ham quia-almadilar* (f. 203*b* note to *chapqun*).

We dismounted over against the Adinapur-fort in the Ning-nahar *tuman*.

(t. A raid for winter stores.)

Up till then we had taken no thought where to camp, where to go, where to stay; we had just marched up and down, camping in fresh places, while waiting for news.[1] It was late in the autumn; most lowlanders had carried in their rice. People knowing the local land and water represented that the Mil Kafirs up the water of the 'Alishang *tuman* grow great quantities of rice, so that we might be able to collect winter supplies from them for the army. Accordingly we rode out of the Ningnahar dale (*julga*), crossed (the Baran-water) at Sai-kal, and went swiftly as far as the Pur-amin (easeful) valley.

Fol. 214b. There the soldiers took a mass of rice. The rice-fields were all at the bottom of the hills. The people fled but some Kafirs went to their death. A few of our braves had been sent to a look-out (*sar-kub*) on a naze of the Pur-amin valley; when they were returning to us, the Kafirs rushed from the hill above, shooting at them. They overtook Qasim Beg's son-in-law Puran, chopped at him with an axe, and were just taking him when some of the braves went back, brought strength to bear, drove them off and got Puran away. After one night spent in the Kafirs' rice-fields, we returned to camp with a mass of provisions collected.

(u. Marriage of Muqim's daughter.)

While we were near Mandrawar in those days, an alliance was concluded between Muqim's daughter Mah-chuchuk, now married to Shah Hasan *Arghun*, and Qasim Kukuldash.[2]

---

1 This will have been news both of Shaibaq Khan and of Mirza Khan. The Pers. trss. vary here (215 f. 173 and 217 f. 148).

2 Mah-chuchuk can hardly have been married against her will to Qasim. Her mother regarded the alliance as a family indignity; appealed to Shah Beg and compassed a rescue from Kabul while Babur and Qasim were north of the Oxus [*circa* 916 AH.]. Mah-chuchuk quitted Kabul after much hesitation, due partly to reluctance to leave her husband and her infant of 18 months, [Nahid Begim,] partly to dread less family honour might require her death (Erskine's *History*, i, 348 and Gul-badan's *Humayun-nama*).

(*v. Abandonment of the Hindustan project.*)

As it was not found desirable to go on into Hindustan, I sent Mulla Baba of Pashaghar back to Kabul with a few braves. Meantime I marched from near Mandrawar to Atar and Shiwa and lay there for a few days. From Atar I visited Kunar and Nur-gal; from Kunar I went back to camp on a raft; it was the first time I had sat on one; it pleased me much, and the raft came into common use thereafter.

(*w. Shaibaq Khan retires from Qandahar.*)

In those same days Mulla Baba of Farkat came from Nasir Mirza with news in detail that Shaibaq Khan, after taking the outer-fort of Qandahar, had not been able to take the citadel but had retired; also that the Mirza, on various accounts, had left Qandahar and gone to Ghazni.

Shaibaq Khan's arrival before Qandahar, within a few days of our own departure, had taken the garrison by surprise, and they had not been able to make fast the outer-fort. He ran mines several times round about the citadel and made several assaults. The place was about to be lost. At that anxious time Khwaja Muh. Amin, Khwaja Dost Khawand, Muh. 'Ali, a foot-soldier, and Shami (Syrian?) let themselves down from the walls and got away. Just as those in the citadel were about to surrender in despair, Shaibaq Khan interposed words of peace and uprose from before the place. Why he rose was this:—It appears that before he went there, he had sent his *haram* to Nirah-tu,[1] and that in Nirah-tu some-one lifted up his head and got command in the fort; the Khan therefore made a sort of peace and retired from Qandahar.

Fol. 215.

(*x. Babur returns to Kabul.*)

Mid-winter though it was we went back to Kabul by the Bad-i-pich road. I ordered the date of that transit and that crossing of the pass to be cut on a stone above Bad-i-pich;[2] Hafiz Mirak wrote the inscription, Ustad Shah Muhammad did the cutting, not well though, through haste.

1 Erskine gives the fort the alternative name "Kaliun", locates it in the Badghis district east of Heri, and quotes from Abu'l-ghazi in describing its strong position (*History* i, 282). H.S. Tirah-tu.

2 f. 133 and note. Abu'l-fazl mentions that the inscription was to be seen in his time.

I bestowed Ghazni on Nasir Mirza and gave 'Abdu'r-razzaq Mirza the Ningnahar *tuman* with Mandrawar, Nur-valley, Kunar and Nur-gal.[1]

(y. *Babur styles himself Padshah.*)

Up to that date people had styled Timur Beg's descendants *Mirza*, even when they were ruling; now I ordered that people should style me *Padshah*.[2]

(z. *Birth of Babur's first son.*)

At the end of this year, on Tuesday the 4th day of the month of Zu'l-qa'da (March 6th 1508 AD.), the Sun being in Pisces (*Hut*), Humayun was born in the citadel of Kabul. The date of his birth was found by the poet Maulana Masnadi in the words *Sultan Humayun Khan*,[3] and a minor poet of Kabul found it in *Shah-i-firus-qadr* (Shah of victorious might). A few days later he received the name Humayun; when he was five or six days old, I went out to the Char-bagh where was had the feast of his nativity. All the begs, small and great, brought gifts; such a mass of white *tankas* was heaped up as had never been seen before. It was a first-rate feast!

Fol. 215b. *(in margin at line beginning "Zu'l-qa'da")*

1 This fief ranks in value next to the Kabul *tuman*.

2 Various gleanings suggest motives for Babur's assertion of supremacy at this particular time. He was the only Timurid ruler and man of achievement; he filled Husain *Bai-qara*'s place of Timurid headship; his actions through a long period show that he aimed at filling Timur Beg's. There were those who did not admit his suzerainty,—Timurids who had rebelled, Mughuls who had helped them, and who would also have helped Sa'id Khan *Chaghatai*, if he had not refused to be treacherous to a benefactor; there were also the Arghuns, Chingiz-khanids of high pretensions. In old times the Mughul Khaqans were *padshah* (supreme); Padshah is recorded in history as the style of at least Satuq-bughra Khan Padshah Ghazi; no Timurid had been lifted by his style above all Mirzas. When however Timurids had the upper hand, Babur's Timurid grandfather Abu-sa'id asserted his *de facto* supremacy over Babur's Chaghatai grandfather Yunas (T.R. p. 83). For Babur to re-assert that supremacy by assuming the Khaqan's style was highly opportune at this moment. To be Babur Supreme was to declare over-lordship above Chaghatai and Mughul, as well as over all Mirzas. It was done when his sky had cleared; Mirza Khan's rebellion was scotched; the Arghuns were defeated; he was the stronger for their lost possessions; his Auzbeg foe had removed to a less ominous distance; and Kabul was once more his own.

Gul-badan writes as if the birth of his first-born son Humayun were a part of the uplift in her father's style, but his narrative does not support her in this, since the order of events forbids.

3 The "Khan" in Humayun's title may be drawn from his mother's family, since it does not come from Babur. To whose family Mahim belonged we have not been able to discover. It is one of the remarkable omissions of Babur, Gul-badan and Abu'l-fazl that they do not give her father's name. The topic of her family is discussed in my Biographical Appendix to Gul-badan's *Humayun-nama* and will be taken up again, here, in a final Translator's Note (p. 711) on Babur's family.

THIS spring a body of Mahmand Afghans was over-run near Muqur.[2]

(a. A Mughul rebellion.)

A few days after our return from that raid, Quj Beg, Faqir-i-'ali, Karim-dad and Baba *chuhra* were thinking about deserting, but their design becoming known, people were sent who took them below Astarghach. As good-for-nothing words of theirs had been reported to me, even during Jahangir M.'s life-time,[3] I ordered that they should be put to death at the top of the *bazar*. They had been taken to the place; the ropes had been fixed; and they were about to be hanged when Qasim Beg sent Khalifa to me with an urgent entreaty that I would pardon their offences. To please him I gave them their lives, but I ordered them kept in custody.

What there was of Khusrau Shah's retainers from Hisar and Qunduz, together with the head-men of the Mughuls, Chilma, 'Ali Sayyid,[4] Sakma (?), Sher-quli and Aiku-salam (?), and also Khusrau Shah's favourite Chaghatai retainers under Sl. 'Ali *chuhra* and Khudabakhsh, with also 2 or 3000 serviceable Turkman braves led by Siunduk and Shah Nazar,[5] the whole of these, after consultation, took up a bad position towards me. They were all seated in front of Khwaja Riwaj, from the Sung-qurghan meadow to the Chalak; 'Abdu'r-razzaq Mirza, come in from Ning-nahar, being in Dih-i-afghan.[6]

Fol. 216.

---

1 Elph. MS. f. 172b; W.-i-B. I.O. 215 f. 174b and 217 f. 148b; Mems. p. 234.

2 on the head-waters of the Tarnak (R.'s *Notes* App. p. 34).

3 Babur has made no direct mention of his half-brother's death (f. 208 and n. to Mirza).

4 This may be Darwesh-i-'ali of f. 210; the Sayyid in his title may merely mean chief, since he was a Mughul. (However, later consideration has cast doubts on this identification. A.B.)

5 Several of these mutineers had fought for Babur at Qandahar.

6 It may be useful to recapitulate this Mirza's position:—In the previous year he had been left in charge of Kabul when Babur went eastward in dread of Shaibani,

Earlier on Muhibb-i-'ali the armourer had told Khalifa and
Mulla Baba once or twice of their assemblies, and both had
given me a hint, but the thing seeming incredible, it had had no
attention. One night, towards the Bed-time Prayer, when I was
sitting in the Audience-hall of the Char-bagh, Musa Khwaja,
coming swiftly up with another man, said in my ear, "The
Mughuls are really rebelling! We do not know for certain
whether they have got 'Abdu'r-razzaq M. to join them. They
have not settled to rise to-night." I feigned disregard and a
little later went towards the *harams* which at the time were in
the Yurunchqa-garden[1] and the Bagh-i-khilwat, but after page,
servitor and messenger (*yasawal*) had turned back on getting

Fol. 216b. near them, I went with the chief-slave towards the town, and
on along the ditch. I had gone as far as the Iron-gate when
Khwaja Muh.'Ali[2] met me, he coming by the *bazar* road from
the opposite direction. He joined me ... ... of the porch of
the Hot-bath (*hammam*) ... ...[3]

---

and, so left, occupied his hereditary place. He cannot have hoped to hold Kabul
if the Auzbeg attacked it; for its safety and his own he may have relied, and Babur
also in appointing him, upon influence his Arghun connections could use. For
these, one was Muqim his brother-in-law, had accepted Shaibani's suzerainty after
being defeated in Qandahar by Babur. It suited them better no doubt to have the
younger Mirza rather than Babur in Kabul; the latter's return thither will have
disappointed them and the Mirza; they, as will be instanced later, stood ready to
invade his lands when he moved East; they seem likely to have promoted the
present Mughul uprising. In the battle which put this down, the Mirza was
captured; Babur pardoned him; but he having rebelled again, was then put to death.
1 Bagh-i-yurunchqa may be an equivalent of Bagh-i-safar, and the place be
one of waiting "up to" (*unchqa*) the journey (*yur*). *Yurunchqa* also means *clover*
(De Courteille).
2 He seems to have been a brother or uncle of Humayun's mother Mahim
(Index; A.N. trs. i, 492 and note).
3 In all MSS. the text breaks off abruptly here, as it does on f. 118b as though
through loss of pages, and a blank of narrative follows. Before the later gap of
f. 251b however the last sentence is complete.

From several references made in the *Babur-nama* and from
a passage in Gul-badan's *Humayun-nama* (f. 15), it is inferrible
that Babur was composing the annals of 914 AH. not long
before his last illness and death.[1]

Before the diary of 925 AH. (1519 AD.) takes up the broken
thread of his autobiography, there is a *lacuna* of narrative
extending over nearly eleven years. The break was not intended,
several references in the *Babur-nama* shewing Babur's purpose
to describe events of the unchronicled years.[2] Mr. Erskine, in
the Leyden and Erskine *Memoirs*, carried Babur's biography
through the major *lacunæ*, but without first-hand help from the
best sources, the *Habibu's-siyar* and *Tarikh-i-rashidi*. He had not
the help of the first even in his *History of India*. M. de Courteille
working as a translator only, made no attempt to fill the gaps.

Babur's biography has yet to be completed; much time is
demanded by the task, not only in order to exhaust known
sources and seek others further afield, but to weigh and balance
the contradictory statements of writers deep-sundered in
sympathy and outlook. To strike such a balance is essential when
dealing with the events of 914 to 920 AH. because in those years
Babur had part in an embittered conflict between Sunni and
Shi'a. What I offer below, as a stop-gap, is a mere summary of
events, mainly based on material not used by Mr. Erskine, with
a few comments prompted by acquaintance with Baburiana.

USEFUL SOURCES

Compared with what Babur could have told of this most
interesting period of his life, the yield of the sources is scant,

---

1 Index *s.n. Babur-nama*, date of composition and gaps.
2 *ibid.*

a natural sequel from the fact that no one of them had his biography for its main theme, still less had his own action in crises of enforced ambiguity.

Of all known sources the best are Khwand-amir's *Habibu's-siyar* and Haidar Mirza *Dughlat's Tarikh-i-rashidi*. The first was finished nominally in 930 AH. (1524–5 AD.), seven years therefore before Babur's death, but it received much addition of matter concerning Babur after its author went to Hindustan in 934 AH. (f. 339). Its fourth part, a life of Shah Isma'il *Safawi* is especially valuable for the years of this *lacuna*. Haidar's book was finished under Humayun in 953 AH. (1547 AD.), when its author had reigned five years in Kashmir. It is the most valuable of all the sources for those interested in Babur himself, both because of Haidar's excellence as a biographer, and through his close acquaintance with Babur's family. From his eleventh to his thirteenth year he lived under Babur's protection, followed this by 19 years service under Sa'id Khan, the cousin of both, in Kashghar, and after that Khan's death, went to Babur's sons Kamran and Humayun in Hindustan.

A work issuing from a Sunni Auzbeg centre, Fazl bin Ruzbahan *Isfahani's Suluku'l-muluk*, has a Preface of special value, as shewing one view of what it writes of as the spread of heresy in Mawara'u'n-nahr through Babur's invasions. The book itself is a Treatise on Musalman Law, and was prepared by order of 'Ubaidu'l-lah Khan *Auzbeg* for his help in fulfilling a vow he had made, before attacking Babur in 918 AH., at the shrine of Khwaja Ahmad *Yasawi* [in Hazrat Turkistan], that, if he were victorious, he would conform exactly with the divine Law and uphold it in Mawara'u'n-nahr (Rieu's Pers. Cat. ii, 448).

The *Tarikh-i Haji Muhammad 'Arif Qandahari* appears, from the frequent use Firishta made of it, to be a useful source, both because its author was a native of Qandahar, a place much occupying Babur's activities, and because he was a servant of Bairam Khan-i-khanan, whose assassination under Akbar he witnessed.[1] Unfortunately, though his life of Akbar survives

---

1 Jumada I, 14th 968 AH.—Jan. 31st 1561 AD. Concerning the book *see* Elliot and Dowson's *History of India* vi, 572 and JRAS 1901 p. 76, H. Beveridge's art. *On Persian MSS. in Indian Libraries.*

no copy is now known of the section of his General History which deals with Babur's.

An early source is Yahya *Kazwini*'s *Lubbu't-tawarikh*, written in 948 AH. (1541 AD.), but brief only in the Babur period. It issued from a Shi'a source, being commanded by Shah Isma'il *Safawi*'s son Bahram.

Another work issuing also from a *Safawi* centre is Mir Sikandar's *Tarikh-i-'alam-arai*, a history of Shah 'Abbas I, with an introduction treating of his predecessors which was completed in 1025 AH. (1616 AD.). Its interest lies in its outlook on Babur's dealings with Shah Isma'il.

A later source, brief only, is Firishta's *Tarikh-i-firishta*, finished under Jahangir in the first quarter of the 17th century.

Mr. Erskine makes frequent reference to Kh(w)afi Khan's *Tarikh*, a secondary authority however, written under Aurangzib, mainly based on Firishta's work, and merely summarizing Babur's period. References to detached incidents of the period are found in Shaikh 'Abdu'l-qadir's *Tarikh-i-badayuni* and Mir Ma'sum's *Tarikh-i-sind*.

EVENTS OF THE UNCHRONICLED YEARS
914 AH.—MAY 2ND 1508 TO APRIL 21ST 1509 AD.

The mutiny, of which an account begins in the text, was crushed by the victory of 500 loyalists over 3000 rebels, one factor of success being Babur's defeat in single combat of five champions of his adversaries.[1] The disturbance was not of long duration; Kabul was tranquil in Sha'ban (November) when Sl. Sa'id Khan *Chaghatai*, then 21, arrived there seeking his cousin's protection, after defeat by his brother Mansur at Almatu, escape from death, commanded by Shaibani, in Farghana, a winter journey through Qara-tigin to Mirza Khan in Qila'-i-zafar, refusal of an offer to put him in that feeble Mirza's place, and so on to Kabul, where he came a destitute fugitive and

---

1 The T.R. gives the names of two only of the champions but Firishta, writing much later gives all five; we surmise that he found his five in the book of which copies are not now known, the *Tarikh-i Muh. 'Arif Qandahari*. Firishta's five are 'Ali *shab-kur* (night-blind), 'Ali *Sistani*, Nazar Bahadur *Auzbeg*, Ya'qub *tez-jang* (swift in fight), and Auzbeg Bahadur. Haidar's two names vary in the MSS. of the T.R. but represent the first two of Firishta's list.

enjoyed a freedom from care never known by him before
(f. 200*b*; T.R. p. 226). The year was fatal to his family and
to Haidar's; in it Shaibani murdered Sl. Mahmud Khan and his
six sons, Muhammad Husain Mirza and other Dughlat sultans.

915 AH.—APRIL 21ST 1509 TO APRIL 11TH 1510 AD.

In this year hostilities began between Shah Isma'il *Safawi*
and Muh. Shaibani Khan *Auzbeg*, news of which must have
excited keen interest in Kabul.

In it occurred also what was in itself a minor matter of
a child's safety, but became of historical importance, namely,
the beginning of personal acquaintance between Babur and
his sympathetic biographer Haidar Mirza *Dughlat*. Haidar, like
Sa'id, came a fugitive to the protection of a kinsman; he was
then eleven, had been saved by servants from the death commanded by Shaibani, conveyed to Mirza Khan in Badakhshan,
thence sent for by Babur to the greater security of Kabul (f. 11;
Index *s.n.*; T.R. p. 227).

916 AH.—APRIL 11TH 1510 TO MARCH 31ST 1510 AD.

a. News of the battle of Merv.

Over half of this year passed quietly in Kabul; Ramzan
(December) brought from Mirza Khan (Wais) the stirring news
that Isma'il had defeated Shaibani near Merv.[1] "It is not
known," wrote the Mirza, "whether Shahi Beg Khan has been
killed or not. All the Auzbegs have crossed the Amu. Amir Aurus,
who was in Qunduz, has fled. About 20,000 Mughuls, who left
the Auzbeg at Merv, have come to Qunduz. I have come there."
He then invited Babur to join him and with him to try for the
recovery of their ancestral territories (T.R. p. 237).

[1] There are curious differences of statement about the date of Shaibani's death,
possibly through confusion between this and the day on which preliminary
fighting began near Merv. Haidar's way of expressing the date carries weight by
its precision, he giving *roz-i-shakk* of Ramzan, *i.e.* a day of which there was doubt
whether it was the last of Sha'ban or the first of Ramzan (Lane, *yauma'u'l-shakk*).
As the sources support Friday for the day of the week and on a Friday in the year
915 AH. fell the 29th of Sha'ban, the date of Shaibani's death seems to be Friday
Sha'ban 29th 915 AH. (Friday December 2nd 1510 AD.).

b. Babur's campaign in Transoxiana begun.

The Mirza's letter was brought over passes blocked by snow; Babur, with all possible speed, took the one winter-route through Ab-dara, kept the Ramzan Feast in Bamian, and reached Qunduz in Shawwal (Jan. 1511 AD.). Haidar's detail about the Feast seems likely to have been recorded because he had read Babur's own remark, made in Ramzan 933 AH. (June 1527) that up to that date, when he kept it in Sikri, he had not since his eleventh year kept it twice in the same place (f. 330).

c. Mughul affairs.

Outside Qunduz lay the Mughuls mentioned by Mirza Khan as come from Merv and so mentioned, presumably, as a possible reinforcement. They had been servants of Babur's uncles Mahmud and Ahmad, and when Shaibani defeated those Khans at Archian in 908 AH., had been compelled by him to migrate into Khurasan to places remote from Mughulistan. Many of them had served in Kashghar; none had served a Timurid Mirza. Set free by Shaibani's death, they had come east, a Khan-less 20,000 of armed and fully equipped men and they were there, as Haidar says, in their strength while of Chaghatais there were not more than 5000. They now, and with them the Mughuls from Kabul, used the opportunity offering for return to a more congenial location and leadership, by the presence in Qunduz of a legitimate Khaqan and the clearance in Andijan, a threshold of Mughulistan, of its Auzbeg governors (f. 200b). The chiefs of both bodies of Mughuls, Sherim Taghai at the head of one, Ayub *Begchik* of the other, proffered the Mughul Khanship to Sa'id with offer to set Babur aside, perhaps to kill him. It is improbable that in making their offer they contemplated locating themselves in the confined country of Kabul; what they seem to have wished was what Babur gave, Sa'id for their Khaqan and permission to go north with him.

Sa'id, in words worth reading, rejected their offer to injure Babur, doing so on the grounds of right and gratitude, but, the two men agreeing that it was now expedient for them to part, asked to be sent to act for Babur where their friendship could be maintained for their common welfare. The matter was settled by Babur's sending him into Andijan in response to an urgent petition for help there just arrived from Haidar's uncle. He "was made Khan" and started forth in the following year, on Safar 14th 917 AH. (May 13th 1511 AD.); with him went most of the Mughuls but not all, since even of those from Merv, Ayub *Begchik* and others are found mentioned on several later occasions as being with Babur.

Babur's phrase "I made him Khan" (f. 200*b*) recalls his earlier mention of what seems to be the same appointment (f. 10*b*), made by Abu-sa'id of Yunas as Khan of the Mughuls; in each case the meaning seems to be that the Timurid Mirza made the Chaghatai Khan Khaqan of the Mughuls.

d. First attempt on Hisar.

After spending a short time in Qunduz, Babur moved for Hisar in which were the Auzbeg sultans Mahdi and Hamza. They came out into Wakhsh to meet him but, owing to an imbroglio, there was no encounter and each side retired (T.R. p. 238).

e. Intercourse between Babur and Isma'il Safawi.

While Babur was now in Qunduz his sister Khan-zada arrived there, safe-returned under escort of the Shah's troops, after the death in the battle of Merv of her successive husbands Shaibani and Sayyid Hadi, and with her came an envoy from Isma'il proffering friendship, civilities calculated to arouse a hope of Persian help in Babur. To acknowledge his courtesies, Babur sent Mirza Khan with thanks and gifts; Haidar says that the Mirza also conveyed protestations of good faith and a request for military assistance. He was well received and his request for help was granted; that it was granted under hard conditions then stated later occurrences shew.

917 AH.—MARCH 31ST 1511 TO MARCH 19TH 1512 AD.

a. Second attempt on Hisar.

In this year Babur moved again on Hisar. He took post, where once his forebear Timur had wrought out success against great odds, at the Pul-i-sangin (Stone-bridge) on the Surkh-ab, and lay there a month awaiting reinforcement. The Auzbeg sultans faced him on the other side of the river, they too, presumably, awaiting reinforcement. They moved when they felt themselves strong enough to attack, whether by addition to their own numbers, whether by learning that Babur had not largely increased his own. Concerning the second alternative it is open to surmise that he hoped for larger reinforcement than he obtained; he appears to have left Qunduz before the return of Mirza Khan from his embassy to Isma'il, to have expected Persian reinforcement with the Mirza, and at Pul-i-sangin, where the Mirza joined him in time to fight, to have been strengthened by the Mirza's own following, and few, if any, foreign auxiliaries. These surmises are supported by what Khwand-amir relates of the conditions [specified later] on which the Shah's main contingent was despatched and by his shewing that it did not start until after the Shah had had news of the battle at Pul-i-sangin.

At the end of the month of waiting, the Auzbegs one morning swam the Surkh-ab below the bridge; in the afternoon of the same day, Babur retired to better ground amongst the mountain fastnesses of a local Ab-dara. In the desperate encounter which followed the Auzbegs were utterly routed with great loss in men; they were pursued to Darband-i-ahanin (Iron-gate) on the Hisar border, on their way to join a great force assembled at Qarshi under Kuchum Khan, Shaibani's successor as Auzbeg Khaqan. The battle is admirably described by Haidar, who was then a boy of 12 with keen eye watching his own first fight, and that fight with foes who had made him the last male survivor of his line. In the evening of the victory Mahdi, Hamza and Hamza's son Mamak were brought before Babur who, says Haidar, did to them what they had done to the Mughul Khaqans and Chaghatai Sultans, that is, he retaliated in blood for the blood of many kinsmen.

b. Persian reinforcement.

After the battle Babur went to near Hisar, was there joined by many local tribesmen, and, some time later, by a large body of Isma'il's troops under Ahmad Beg *Safawi*, 'Ali Khan *Istilju* and Shahrukh Sl. *Afshar*, Isma'il's seal-keeper. The following particulars, given by Khwand-amir, about the despatch of this contingent help to fix the order of occurrences, and throw light on the price paid by Babur for his auxiliaries. He announced his victory over Mahdi and Hamza to the Shah, and at the same time promised that if he reconquered the rest of Trans-oxiana by the Shah's help, he would read his name in the *khutba*, stamp it on coins together with those of the Twelve Imams, and work to destroy the power of the Auzbegs. These undertakings look like a response to a demand; such conditions cannot have been proffered; their acceptance must have been compelled. Khwand-amir says that when Isma'il fully under-stood the purport of Babur's letter, [by which would seem to be meant, when he knew that his conditions of help were accepted,] he despatched the troops under the three Commanders named above.

The Persian chiefs advised a move direct on Bukhara and Samarkand; and with this Babur's councillors concurred, they saying, according to Haidar, that Bukhara was then empty of troops and full of fools. 'Ubaid Khan had thrown himself into Qarshi; it was settled not to attack him but to pass on and encamp a stage beyond the town. This was done; then scout followed scout, bringing news that he had come out of Qarshi and was hurrying to Bukhara, his own fief. Instant and swift pursuit followed him up the 100 miles of caravan-road, into Bukhara, and on beyond, sweeping him and his garrison, plundered as they fled, into the open land of Turkistan. Many sultans had collected in Samarkand, some no doubt being, like Timur its governor, fugitives escaped from Pul-i-sangin. Dismayed by Babur's second success, they scattered into Turkistan, thus leaving him an open road.

c. Samarkand re-occupied and relations with Isma'il Safawi.

He must now have hoped to be able to dispense with his dangerous colleagues, for he dismissed them when he reached Bukhara, with gifts and thanks for their services. It is Haidar, himself present, who fixes Bukhara as the place of the dismissal (T.R. p. 246).

From Bukhara Babur went to Samarkand. It was mid-Rajab 917 AH. (October 1511 AD.), some ten months after leaving Kabul, and after 9 years of absence, that he re-entered the town, itself gay with decoration for his welcome, amidst the acclaim of its people.[1]

Eight months were to prove his impotence to keep it against the forces ranged against him,—Auzbeg strength in arms compacted by Sunni zeal, Sunni hatred of a Shi'a's suzerainty intensified by dread lest that potent Shi'a should resolve to perpetuate his dominance. Both as a Sunni and as one who had not owned a suzerain, the position was unpleasant for Babur. That his alliance with Isma'il was dangerous he will have known, as also that his risks grew as Transoxiana was over-spread by news of Isma'il's fanatical barbarism to pious and learned Sunnis, notably in Heri. He manifested desire for release both now and later,—now when he not only dismissed his Persian helpers but so behaved to the Shah's envoy Muhammad Jan,—he was Najm Sani's Lord of the Gate,—that the envoy felt neglect and made report of Babur as arrogant, in opposition, and unwilling to fulfil his compact,—later when he eagerly attempted success unaided against 'Ubaid Khan, and was then worsted. It illustrates the Shah's view of his suzerain relation to Babur that on hearing Muhammad Jan's report, h e ordered Najm Sani to bring the offender to order.

Meantime the Shah's conditions seem to have been carried out in Samarkand and Babur's subservience clearly shewn.[2] Of this there are the indications,—that Babur had promised and was a man of his word; that Sunni irritation against him waxed and did not wane as it might have done without food to nourish it; that Babur knew himself impotent against the Auzbegs unless he had foreign aid, expected attack, knew it was preparing; that he would hear of Muhammad Jan's report and of Najm Sani's commission against himself. Honesty, policy and necessity

1 If my reading be correct of the Turki passage concerning wines drunk by Babur which I have noted on f. 49 (*in loco* p. 83 n. 1), it was during this occupation of Kabul that Babur first broke the Law against stimulants.
2 Mr. R. S. Poole found a coin which he took to be one struck in obedience to Babur's compact with the Shah (B.M. Cat. of the coins of Persian Shahs 1887, pp. xxiv *et seq.*; T.R. p. 246 n.).

combined to enforce the fulfilment of his agreement. What were the precise terms of that agreement beyond the two as to the *khutba* and the coins, it needs close study of the wording of the sources to decide, lest metaphor be taken for fact. Great passions,—ambition, religious fervour, sectarian bigotry and fear confronted him. His problem was greater than that of Henry of Navarre and of Napoleon in Egypt; they had but to seem what secured their acceptance; he had to put on a guise that brought him hate.

Khan-zada was not the only member of Babur's family who now rejoined him after marriage with an Auzbeg. His half-sister Yadgar-sultan had fallen to the share of Hamza Sultan's son 'Abdu'l-latif in 908 AH. when Shaibani defeated the Khans near Akhsi. Now that her half-brother had defeated her husband's family, she returned to her own people (f. 9).

918 AH.—MARCH 19TH 1512 TO MARCH 9TH 1513 AD.

a. Return of the Auzbegs.

Emboldened by the departure of the Persian troops, the Auzbegs, in the spring of the year, came out of Turkistan, their main attack being directed on Tashkint, then held for Babur.[1] 'Ubaid Khan moved for Bukhara. He had prefaced his march by vowing that, if successful, he would thenceforth strictly observe Musalman Law. The vow was made in Hazrat Turkistan at the shrine of Khwaja Ahmad *Yasawi*, a saint revered in Central Asia through many centuries; he had died about 1120 AD.; Timur had made pilgrimage to his tomb, in 1397 AD., and then had founded the mosque still dominating the town, still the pilgrim's land-mark.[2] 'Ubaid's vow, like Babur's of 933 AH., was one of return to obedience. Both men took oath in the Ghazi's mood, Babur's set against the Hindu whom he saw as a heathen, 'Ubaid's set against Babur whom he saw as a heretic.

1 It was held by Ahmad-i-qasim *Kohbur* and is referred to on f. 234b, as one occasion of those in which Dost Beg distinguished himself.
2 Schuyler's *Turkistan* has a good account and picture of the mosque. 'Ubaid's vow is referred to in my earlier mention of the *Suluku'l-muluk*. It may be noted here that this MS. supports the spelling *Babur* by making the second syllable rhyme to *pur*, as against the form *Babar*.

b. Babur's defeat at Kul-i-malik.

In Safar (April–May) 'Ubaid moved swiftly down and attacked the Bukhara neighbourhood. Babur went from Samarkand to meet him. Several details of what followed, not given by Haidar and, in one particular, contradicting him, are given by Khwand-amir. The statement in which the two historians contradict one another is Haidar's that 'Ubaid had 3000 men only, Babur 40,000. Several considerations give to Khwand-amir's opposed statement that Babur's force was small, the semblance of being nearer the fact. Haidar, it may be said, did not go out on this campaign; he was ill in Samarkand and continued ill there for some time; Khwand-amir's details have the well-informed air of things learned at first-hand, perhaps from some-one in Hindustan after 934 AH.

Matters which make against Babur's having a large effective force at Kul-i-malik, and favour Khwand-amir's statement about the affair are these:—'Ubaid must have formed some estimate of what he had to meet, and he brought 3000 men. Where could Babur have obtained 40,000 men worth reckoning in a fight? In several times of crisis his own immediate and ever-faithful troop is put at 500; as his cause was now unpopular, local accretions may have been few. Some Mughuls from Merv and from Kabul were near Samarkand (T.R. pp. 263, 265); most were with Sa'id in Andijan; but however many Mughuls may have been in his neighbourhood, none could be counted on as resolute for his success. If too, he had had more than a small effective force, would he not have tried to hold Samarkand with the remnant of defeat until Persian help arrived? All things considered, there is ground for accepting Khwand-amir's statement that Babur met 'Ubaid with a small force.

Following his account therefore:—Babur in his excess of daring, marched to put the Auzbeg down with a small force only, against the advice of the prudent, of whom Muhammad Mazid Tarkhan was one, who all said it was wrong to go out unprepared and without reinforcement. Paying them no attention, Babur marched for Bukhara, was rendered still more daring by news had when he neared it, that the enemy had retired some stages, and followed him up almost to his camp. 'Ubaid was in great force; many Auzbegs perished but, in the end, they were victors and Babur was compelled to take refuge in Bukhara. The encounter took place near Kul-i-malik (King's-lake) in Safar 918 AH. (April–May 1512 AD.).

c. Babur leaves Samarkand.

It was not possible to maintain a footing in Samarkand; Babur therefore collected his family and train[1] and betook himself to Hisar. There went with him on this expedition Mahim and her children Humayun, Mihr-jahan and Barbul,—the motherless Ma'suma,—Gul-rukh with her son Kamran (Gul-badan f. 7). I have not found any account of his route; Haidar gives no details about the journey; he did not travel with Babur, being still invalided in Samarkand. Perhaps the absence of information is a sign that the Auzbegs had not yet appeared on the direct road for Hisar. A local tradition however would make Babur go round through Farghana. He certainly might have gone into Farghana hoping to co-operate with Sa'id Khan; Tashkint was still holding out under Ahmad-i-qasim *Kohbur* and it is clear that all activity in Babur's force had not been quenched because during the Tashkint siege, Dost Beg broke through the enemy's ranks and made his way into the town. Sairam held out longer than Tashkint. Of any such move by Babur into Andijan the only hint received is given by what may be a mere legend.[2]

1 *auruq*. Babur refers to this exodus on f. 12b when writing of Daulat-sultan Khanim.

2 It is one recorded with some variation, in Niyaz Muhammad *Khukandi's Tarikh-i-shahrukhi* (Kazan, 1885) and Nalivkine's *Khanate of Khokand* (p. 63). It says that when Babur in 918 AH. (1512 AD.) left Samarkand after defeat by the Auzbegs, one of his wives, Sayyida Afaq who accompanied him in his flight, gave birth to a son in the desert which lies between Khujand and Kand-i-badam; that Babur, not daring to tarry and the infant being too young to make the impending journey, left it under some bushes with his own girdle round it in which were things of price; that the child was found by local people and in allusion to the valuables amongst which it lay, called Altun bishik (golden cradle); that it received other names and was best known in later life as Khudayan Sultan. He is said to have spent most of his life in Akhsi; to have had a son Tingri-yar; and to have died in 952 AH. (1545 AD.). His grandson Yar-i-muhammad is said to have gone to India to relations who were descendants of Babur (JASB 1905 p. 137 H. Beveridge's art. *The Emperor Babur*). What is against the truth of this tradition is that Gul-badan mentions no such wife as Sayyida Afaq. Mahim however seems to have belonged to a religious family, might therefore be styled Sayyida, and, as Babur mentions (f. 220), had several children who did not live (a child left as this infant was, might if not heard of, be supposed dead). There is this opening allowed for considering the tradition.

d. Babur in Hisar.

After experiencing such gains and such losses, Babur was still under 30 years of age.

The Auzbegs, after his departure, re-occupied Bukhara and Samarkand without harm done to the towns-people, and a few weeks later, in Jumada I (July–August) followed him to Hisar. Meantime he with Mirza Khan's help, had so closed the streets of the town by massive earth-works that the sultans were convinced its defenders were ready to spend the last drop of their blood in holding it, and therefore retired without attack.[1] Some sources give as their reason for retirement that Babur had been reinforced from Balkh; Bairam Beg, it is true, had sent a force but one of 300 men only; so few cannot have alarmed except as the harbinger of more. Greater precision as to dates would shew whether they can have heard of Najm Sani's army advancing by way of Balkh.

e. Qarshi and Ghaj-davan.

Meantime Najm Sani, having with him some 11,000 men, had started on his corrective mission against Babur. When he reached the Khurasan frontier, he heard of the defeat at Kul-i-malik and the flight to Hisar, gathered other troops from Harat and elsewhere, and advanced to Balkh. He stayed there for 20 days with Bairam Beg, perhaps occupied, in part, by communications with the Shah and Babur. From the latter repeated request for help is said to have come; help was given, some sources say without the Shah's permission. A rendezvous was fixed, Najm Sani marched to Tirmiz, there crossed the Amu and in Rajab (Sep.–Oct.) encamped near the Darband-i-ahanin. On Babur's approach through the Chak-chaq pass, he paid him the civility of going several miles out from his camp to give him honouring reception.

Advancing thence for Bukhara, the combined armies took Khuzar and moved on to Qarshi. This town Babur wished to pass by, as it had been passed by on his previous march for Bukhara; each time perhaps he wished to spare its people,

---

1 Babur refers to this on f. 265.

formerly his subjects, whom he desired to rule again, and who are reputed to have been mostly his fellow Turks. Najm Sani refused to pass on; he said Qarshi must be taken because it was 'Ubaidu'l-lah Khan's nest; in it was 'Ubaid's uncle Shaikhim Mirza; it was captured; the Auzbeg garrison was put to the sword and, spite of Babur's earnest entreaties, all the towns-people, 15,000 persons it is said, down to the "suckling and decrepit", were massacred. Amongst the victims was Bana'i who happened to be within it. This action roused the utmost anger against Najm Sani; it disgusted Babur, not only through its merciless slaughter but because it made clear the disregard in which he was held by his magnificent fellow-general.

From murdered Qarshi Najm Sani advanced for Bukhara. On getting within a few miles of it, he heard that an Auzbeg force was approaching under Timur and Abu-sa'id, presumably from Samarkand therefore. He sent Bairam Beg to attack them; they drew off to the north and threw themselves into Ghaj-davan, the combined armies following them. This move placed Najm Sani across the Zar-afshan, on the border of the desert with which the Auzbegs were familiar, and with 'Ubaid on his flank in Bukhara.

As to what followed the sources vary; they are brief; they differ less in statement of the same occurrence than in their choice of details to record; as Mr. Erskine observes their varying stories are not incompatible. Their widest difference is a state-ment of time but the two periods named, one a few days, the other four months, may not be meant to apply to the same event. Four months the siege is said to have lasted; this could not have been said if it had been a few days only. The siege seems to have been of some duration.

At first there were minor engagements, ending with varying success; provisions and provender became scarce; Najm Sani's officers urged retirement, so too did Babur. He would listen to none of them. At length 'Ubaid Khan rode out from Bukhara at the head of excellent troops; he joined the Ghaj-davan garrison and the united Auzbegs posted themselves in the suburbs where walled lanes and gardens narrowed the field and lessened Najm Sani's advantage in numbers. On Tuesday

Ramzan 3rd (Nov. 12th)[1] a battle was fought in which his army was routed and he himself slain.

f. Babur and Yar-i-ahmad Najm Sani.

Some writers say that Najm Sani's men did not fight well; it must be remembered that they may have been weakened by privation and that they had wished to retire. Of Babur it is said that he, who was the reserve, did not fight at all; it is difficult to see good cause why, under all the circumstances, he should risk the loss of his men. It seems likely that Haidar's strong language about this defeat would suit Babur's temper also. "The victorious breezes of Islam overturned the banners of the schismatics. ... Most of them perished on the field; the rents made by the sword at Qarshi were sewn up at Ghaj-davan by the arrow-stitches of vengeance. Najm Sani and all the Turkman amirs were sent to hell."

The belief that Babur had failed Najm Sani persisted at the Persian Court, for his inaction was made a reproach to his son Humayun in 951 AH. (1544 AD.), when Humayun was a refugee with Isma'il's son Tahmasp. Badayuni tells a story which, with great inaccuracy of name and place, represents the view taken at that time. The part of the anecdote pertinent here is that Babur on the eve of the battle at Ghaj-davan, shot an arrow into the Auzbeg camp which carried the following couplet, expressive of his ill-will to the Shah and perhaps also of his rejection of the Shi'a guise he himself had worn.

> I made the Shah's Najm road-stuff for the Auzbegs;
> If fault has been mine, I have now cleansed the road.[2]

g. The Mughuls attack Babur.

On his second return to Hisar Babur was subjected to great danger by a sudden attack made upon him by the Mughuls where he lay at night in his camp outside the town. Firishta says, but without particulars of their offence, that Babur had reproached

---

1 The *Lubbu't-tawarikh* would fix Ramzan 7th.
2 Mr. Erskine's quotation of the Persian original of the couplet differs from that which I have translated (*History of India* ii, 326; *Tarikh-i-badayuni* Bib. Ind. ed. f. 444). Perhaps in the latter a pun is made on Najm as the leader's name and as meaning *fortune*; if so it points the more directly at the Shah. The second line is quoted by Badayuni on his f. 362 also.

them for their misconduct; the absence of detail connecting the affair with the defeat just sustained, leads to the supposition that their misdeeds were a part of the tyranny over the country-people punished later by 'Ubaidu'l-lah Khan. Roused from his sleep by the noise of his guards' resistance to the Mughul attack, Babur escaped with difficulty and without a single attendant[1] into the fort. The conspirators plundered his camp and withdrew to Qara-tigin. He was in no position to oppose them, left a few men in Hisar and went to Mirza Khan in Qunduz.

After he left, Hisar endured a desolating famine, a phenomenal snowfall and the ravages of the Mughuls. 'Ubaid Khan avenged Babur on the horde; hearing of their excesses, he encamped outside the position they had taken up in Wakhsh defended by river, hills and snow, waited till a road thawed, then fell upon them and avenged the year's misery they had inflicted on the Hisaris. Haidar says of them that it was their villainy lost Hisar to Babur and gained it for the Auzbeg.[2]

These Mughuls had for chiefs men who when Sa'id went to Andijan, elected to stay with Babur. One of the three named by Haidar was Ayub *Begchik*. He repented his disloyalty; when he lay dying some two years later (920 AH.) in Yangi-hisar, he told Sa'id Khan who visited him, that what was "lacerating his bowels and killing him with remorse", was his faithlessness to Babur in Hisar, the oath he had broken at the instigation of those "hogs and bears", the Mughul chiefs (T.R. p. 315).

In this year but before the Mughul treachery to Babur, Haidar left him, starting in Rajab (Sep.–Oct.) to Sa'id in Andijan and thus making a beginning of his 19 years spell of service.

919 AH.—MARCH 9TH 1513 TO FEB. 26TH 1514 AD.

Babur may have spent this year in Khishm (H.S. iii, 372). During two or three months of it, he had one of the Shah's

---

1 Some translators make Babur go "naked" into the fort but, on his own authority (f. 106b), it seems safer to understand what others say, that he went stripped of attendance, because it was always his habit even in times of peace to lie down in his tunic; much more would he have done so at such a crisis of his affairs as this of his flight to Hisar.

2 Haidar gives a graphic account of the misconduct of the horde and of their punishment (T.R. p. 261–3).

retainers in his service, Khwaja Kamalu'd-din Mahmud, who had fled from Ghaj-davan to Balkh, heard there that the Balkhis favoured an Auzbeg chief whose coming was announced, and therefore went to Babur. In Jumada II (August), hearing that the Auzbeg sultan had left Balkh, he returned there but was not admitted because the Balkhis feared reprisals for their welcome to the Auzbeg, a fear which may indicate that he had taken some considerable reinforcement to Babur. He went on into Khurasan and was there killed; Balkh was recaptured for the Shah by Deo Sultan, a removal from Auzbeg possession which helps to explain how Babur came to be there in 923 AH.

920 AH.—FEB. 26TH 1514 TO FEB. 15TH 1515 AD.

Haidar writes of Babur as though he were in Qunduz this year (T.R. p. 263), says that he suffered the greatest misery and want, bore it with his accustomed courtesy and patience but, at last, despairing of success in recovering Hisar, went back to Kabul. Now it seems to be that he made the stay in Khwast to which he refers later (f. 241b) and during which his daughter Gul-rang was born, as Gul-badan's chronicle allows known.

It was at the end of the year, after the privation of winter therefore, that he reached Kabul. When he re-occupied Samarkand in 917 AH., he had given Kabul to his half-brother Nasir Mirza; the Mirza received him now with warm welcome and protestations of devotion and respect, spoke of having guarded Kabul for him and asked permission to return to his own old fief Ghazni. His behaviour made a deep impression on Babur; it would be felt as a humane touch on the sore of failure.

921 AH.—FEB. 15TH 1515 TO FEB. 5TH 1516 AD.

a. Rebellion of chiefs in Ghazni.

Nasir Mirza died shortly after (dar haman ayyam) his return to Ghazni. Disputes then arose amongst the various commanders who were in Ghazni; Sherim Taghai was one of them and the main strength of the tumult was given by the Mughuls. Many others were however involved in it, even such an old servant as Baba of Pashaghar taking part (f. 235; T.R. p. 356). Haidar did not know precisely the cause of the dispute, or shew why it should have turned against Babur, since he attributes it to possession taken by Satan of the brains of the chiefs and a consequent access of vain-glory and wickedness. Possibly some question of succession to Nasir arose. Dost Beg distinguished himself in the regular battle which ensued; Qasim Beg's son Qambar-i-'ali hurried down from Qunduz and also did his good part to win it for Babur. Many of the rioters were killed, others fled to Kashghar. Sherim Taghai was one of the latter; as Sa'id Khan gave him no welcome, he could not stay there; he fell back on the much injured Babur who, says Haidar, showed him his usual benevolence, turned his eyes from his offences and looked only at his past services until he died shortly afterwards (T.R. p. 357).[1]

922 AH.—FEB. 5TH 1516 TO JAN. 24TH 1517 AD.

This year may have been spent in and near Kabul in the quiet promoted by the dispersion of the Mughuls.

In this year was born Babur's son Muhammad known as 'Askari from his being born in camp. He was the son of Gulrukh Begchik and full-brother of Kamran.

923 AH.—JAN. 24TH 1517 TO JAN. 13TH 1518 AD.

a. Babur visits Balkh.

Khwand-amir is the authority for the little that is known of Babur's action in this year (H.S. iii, 367 et seq.). It is connected with the doings of Badi'u'z-zaman Bai-qara's son Muhammad-i-zaman. This Mirza had had great wanderings, during a part of which Khwand-amir was with him. In 920 AH. he was in Shah Isma'il's service and in Balkh, but was not able to keep it. Babur invited him to Kabul,—the date of invitation will have been later therefore than Babur's return there at the end of 920 AH. The Mirza was on his way but was dissuaded from going into Kabul by Mahdi Khwaja and went instead into

---

1 One of the mutineers named as in this affair (T.R. p. 257) was Sl. Quli *chunaq*, a circumstance attracting attention by its bearing on the cause of the *lacunae* in the *Babur-nama*, inasmuch as Babur, writing at the end of his life, expresses (f. 65) his intention to tell of this man's future misdeeds. These misdeeds may have been also at Hisar and in the attack there made on Babur; they are known from Haidar to have been done at Ghazni; both times fall within this present gap. Hence it is clear that Babur meant to write of the events falling in the gap of 914 AH. onwards.

Ghurjistan. Babur was angered by his non-arrival and pursued him in order to punish him but did not succeed in reaching Ghurjistan and went back to Kabul by way of Firuz-koh and Ghur. The Mirza was captured eventually and sent to Kabul. Babur treated him with kindness, after a few months gave him his daughter Ma'suma in marriage, and sent him to Balkh. He appears to have been still in Balkh when Khwand-amir was writing of the above occurrences in 929 AH. The marriage took place either at the end of 923 or beginning of 924 AH. The Mirza was then 21, Ma'suma 9; she almost certainly did not then go to Balkh. At some time in 923 AH. Babur is said by Khwand-amir to have visited that town.[1]

b. Attempt on Qandahar.

In this year Babur marched for Qandahar but the move ended peacefully, because a way was opened for gifts and terms by an illness which befell him when he was near the town.

The *Tarikh-i-sind* gives what purports to be Shah Beg's explanation of Babur's repeated attempts on Qandahar. He said these had been made and would be made because Babur had not forgiven Muqim for taking Kabul 14 years earlier from the Timurid 'Abdu'r-razzaq; that this had brought him to Qandahar in 913 AH., this had made him then take away Mah-chuchak, Muqim's daughter; that there were now (923 AH.) many unemployed Mirzas in Kabul for whom posts could not be found in regions where the Persians and Auzbegs were dominant; that an outlet for their ambitions and for Babur's own would be sought against the weaker opponent he himself was.

Babur's decision to attack in this year is said to have been taken while Shah Beg was still a prisoner of Shah Isma'il in the Harat country; he must have been released meantime by the admirable patience of his slave Sambhal.

924 AH.——JAN. 13TH 1518 TO JAN. 3RD 1519 AD.

In this year Shah Beg's son Shah Hasan came to Babur after quarrel with his father. He stayed some two years, and during

---

1 In 925 AH. (ff. 227 and 238) mention is made of courtesies exchanged between Babur and Muhammad-i-zaman in Balkh. The Mirza was with Babur later on in Hindustan.

that time was married to Khalifa's daughter Gul-barg (Rose-leaf). His return to Qandahar will have taken place shortly before Babur's campaign of 926 AH. against it, a renewed effort which resulted in possession on Shawwal 13th 928 AH. (Sep. 6th 1522 AD.).[1]

In this year began the campaign in the north-east territories of Kabul, an account of which is carried on in the diary of 925 AH. It would seem that in the present year Chaghan-sarai was captured, and also the fortress at the head of the valley of Baba-qara, belonging to Haidar-i-'ali *Bajauri* (f. 216b).[2]

1 Mir Ma'sum's *Tarikh-i-sind* is the chief authority for Babur's action after 913 AH. against Shah Beg in Qandahar; its translation, made in 1846 by Major Malet, shews some manifestly wrong dates; they appear also in the B.M. MS. of the work.
2 f. 216b and note to "Monday".

(a. Babur takes the fort of Bajaur.)

(*Jan. 3rd*) On Monday[2] the first day of the month of Muharram, there was a violent earthquake in the lower part of the dale (*julga*) of Chandawal,[3] which lasted nearly half an astronomical hour.

(*Jan. 4th*) Marching at dawn from that camp with the intention of attacking the fort of Bajaur,[4] we dismounted near it and sent a trusty man of the Dilazak[5] Afghans to advise its

---

1 Elph. MS. f. 173*b*; W.-i-B. I.O. 215 f. 178 and 217 f. 149; Mems. p. 246. The whole of the Hijra year is included in 1519 AD. (Erskine). What follows here and completes the Kabul section of the *Babur-nama* is a diary of a little over 13 months' length, supplemented by matter of later entry. The product has the character of a draft, awaiting revision to harmonize it in style and, partly, in topic with the composed narrative that breaks off under 914 AH.; for the diary, written some 11 years earlier than that composed narrative, varies, as it would be expected *a priori* to vary, in style and topic from the terse, lucid and idiomatic output of Babur's literary maturity. A good many obscure words and phrases in it, several new from Babur's pen, have opposed difficulty to scribes and translators. Interesting as such *minutiae* are to a close observer of Turki and of Babur's diction, comment on all would be tedious; a few will be found noted, as also will such details as fix the date of entry for supplementary matter.

2 Here Mr. Erskine notes that Dr. Leyden's translation begins again; it broke off on f. 180*b*, and finally ends on f. 223*b*.

3 This name is often found transliterated as Chandul or [mod.] Jandul but the Hai. MS. supports Raverty's opinion that Chandawal is correct.

The year 925 AH. opens with Babur far from Kabul and east of the Khahr (fort) he is about to attack. Afghan and other sources allow surmise of his route to that position; he may have come down into the Chandawal-valley, first, from taking Chaghan-sarai (f. 134 and n.), and, secondly, from taking the Gibri stronghold of Haidar-i-'ali *Bajauri* which stood at the head of the Baba Qara-valley. The latter surmise is supported by the romantic tales of Afghan chroniclers which at this date bring into history Babur's Afghan wife, Bibi Mubaraka (f. 220*b* and note; Mems. p. 250 n.; and Appendix K, *An Afghan legend*). (It must be observed here that R.'s *Notes* (pp. 117, 128) confuse the two sieges, *viz.* of the Gibri fort in 924 AH. and of the Khahr of Bajaur in 925 AH.)

4 Raverty lays stress on the circumstance that the fort Babur now attacks has never been known as Bajaur, but always simply as Khahr, the fort (the Arabic name for the place being, he says, plain *Shahr*); just as the main stream is called simply Rud (the torrent). The name Khahr is still used, as modern maps shew. There are indeed two neighbouring places known simply as Khahr (Fort), *i.e.* one at the mouth of the "Mahmand-valley" of modern campaigns, the other near the Malakand (Fincastle's map).

5 This word the Hai. MS. writes, *passim*, Dilah-zak.

sultan [1] and people to take up a position of service (*qulluq*) and
surrender the fort. Not accepting this counsel, that stupid and
ill-fated band sent back a wild answer, where-upon the army
was ordered to make ready mantelets, ladders and other
appliances for taking a fort. For this purpose a day's (*Jan. 5th*)
halt was made on that same ground.

(*Jan. 6th*) On Thursday the 4th of Muharram, orders were
given that the army should put on mail, arm and get to horse;[2]
that the left wing should move swiftly to the upper side of the
fort, cross the water at the water-entry,[3] and dismount on the
north side of the fort; that the centre, not taking the way
across the water, should dismount in the rough, up-and-down
land to the north-west of the fort; and that the right should
dismount to the west of the lower gate. While the begs of the
left under Dost Beg were dismounting, after crossing the water,
a hundred to a hundred and fifty men on foot came out of the
fort, shooting arrows. The begs, shooting in their turn,
advanced till they had forced those men back to the foot of the
ramparts, Mulla 'Abdu'l-maluk of Khwast, like a madman,[4]
going up right under them on his horse. There and then the fort
would have been taken if the ladders and mantelets had been
ready, and if it had not been so late in the day. Mulla Tirik-
i-'ali[5] and a servant of Tingri-birdi crossed swords with the
enemy; each overcame his man, cut off and brought in his
head; for this each was promised a reward.

As the Bajauris had never before seen matchlocks (*tufang*)
they at first took no care about them, indeed they made fun
when they heard the report and answered it by unseemly

Fol. 217.

---

1 Either Haidar-i-'ali himself or his nephew, the latter more probably, since no
name is mentioned.

2 Looking at the position assigned by maps to Khahr, in the *du-ab* of the
Charmanga-water and the Rud of Bajaur, it may be that Babur's left moved
along the east bank of the first-named stream and crossed it into the *du-ab*, while
his centre went direct to its post, along the west side of the fort.

3 *su-kirishi*; to interpret which needs local knowledge; it might mean where water
entered the fort, or where water disembogued from narrows, or, perhaps, where
water is entered for a ford.

4 *diwanawar*, perhaps a jest on a sobriquet earned before this exploit, perhaps the
cause of the man's later sobriquet *diwana* (f. 245b).

5 Text, t:r:k, read by Erskine and de Courteille as Turk; it might however be
a Turki component in Jan-i-'ali or Muhibb-i-'ali. (*Cf.* Zenker *s.n. tirik*.)

gestures. On that day[1] Ustad 'Ali-quli shot at and brought
down five men with his matchlock; Wali the Treasurer, for
his part, brought down two; other matchlockmen were also
very active in firing and did well, shooting through shield,
through cuirass, through *kusaru*,[2] and bringing down one man
after another. Perhaps 7, 8, or 10 Bajauris had fallen to the
matchlock-fire (*zarb*) before night. After that it so became
that not a head could be put out because of the fire. The order   Fol. 217*b*.
was given, "It is night; let the army retire, and at dawn, if the
appliances are ready, let them swarm up into the fort."

(*Jan. 7th*) At the first dawn of light (*farz waqt*) on Friday
the 5th of Muharram, orders were given that, when the battle-
nagarets had sounded, the army should advance, each man from
his place to his appointed post (*yirlik yirdin*) and should swarm
up. The left and centre advanced from their ground with
mantelets in place all along their lines, fixed their ladders, and
swarmed up them. The whole left hand of the centre, under
Khalifa, Shah Hasan *Arghun* and Yusuf's Ahmad, was ordered
to reinforce the left wing. Dost Beg's men went forward to the
foot of the north-eastern tower of the fort, and busied themselves
in undermining and bringing it down. Ustad 'Ali-quli was
there also; he shot very well on that day with his matchlock, and
he twice fired off the *firingi*.[3] Wali the Treasurer also brought
down a man with his matchlock. Malik 'Ali *qutni*[4] was first
up a ladder of all the men from the left hand of the centre,

1 *aushul guni*, which contrasts with the frequent *aushbu guni* (this same day,
today) of manifestly diary entries; it may indicate that the full account of the siege
is a later supplement.

2 This puzzling word might mean cow-horn (*kau-saru*) and stand for the common
horn trumpet. Erskine and de Courteille have read it as *gau-sar*, the first explaining
it as *cow-head*, surmised to be a protection for matchlockmen when loading; the
second, as *justaucorps de cuir*. That the word is baffling is shewn by its omission in
I.O. 215 (f. 178*b*), in 217 (f. 149*b*) and in Muh. *Shirazi*'s lith. ed. (p. 137).

3 or *farangi*. Much has been written concerning the early use of gun-powder in the
East. There is, however, no well-authenticated fact to prove the existence of anything
like artillery there, till it was introduced from Europe. Babur here, and in other places
(f. 266*b*) calls his larger ordnance Firingi, a proof that they were then regarded as owing
their origin to Europe. The Turks, in consequence of their constant intercourse with
the nations of the West, have always excelled all the other Orientals in the use of
artillery; and, when heavy cannon were first used in India, Europeans or Turks were
engaged to serve them (Erskine). It is owing no doubt to the preceding gap in his
writings that we are deprived of Babur's account of his own introduction to fire-arms.
See E. & D.'s *History of India*, vi, Appendix *On the early use of gun-powder in India*.

4 var. *qutbi*, *quchini*.

and there was busy with fight and blow. At the post of the centre, Muh. 'Ali *Jang-jang*[1] and his younger brother Nau-roz got up, each by a different ladder, and made lance and sword to touch. Baba the waiting man (*yasawal*), getting up by another ladder, occupied himself in breaking down the fort-wall with his

Fol. 218.
axe. Most of our braves went well forward, shooting off dense flights of arrows and not letting the enemy put out a head; others made themselves desperately busy in breaching and pulling down the fort, caring naught for the enemy's fight and blow, giving no eye to his arrows and stones. By breakfast-time Dost Beg's men had undermined and breached the north-eastern tower, got in and put the foe to flight. The men of the centre got in up the ladders by the same time, but those (*aul*) others were first (*awwal*?) in.[2] By the favour and pleasure of the High God, this strong and mighty fort was taken in two or three astronomical hours! Matching the fort were the utter struggle and effort of our braves; distinguish themselves they did, and won the name and fame of heroes.

As the Bajauris were rebels and at enmity with the people of Islam, and as, by reason of the heathenish and hostile customs prevailing in their midst, the very name of Islam was rooted out from their tribe, they were put to general massacre and their wives and children were made captive. At a guess more than 3000 men went to their death; as the fight did not reach to the eastern side of the fort, a few got away there.

The fort taken, we entered and inspected it. On the walls, in houses, streets and alleys, the dead lay, in what numbers! Comers and goers to and fro were passing over the bodies.

Fol. 218b.
Returning from our inspection, we sat down in the Bajaur sultan's residence. The country of Bajaur we bestowed on Khwaja Kalan,[3] assigning a large number of braves to reinforce him. At the Evening Prayer we went back to camp.

1 This sobriquet might mean "ever a fighter", or an "argle-bargler", or a brass shilling (Zenker), or (if written *jing-jing*) that the man was visaged like the bearded reeding (Scully in Shaw's Vocabulary). The *Tabaqat-i-akbari* includes a Mirak Khan *Jang-jang* in its list of Akbar's Commanders.

2 *ghul-din (awwal) aul qurghan-gha chiqti*. I suggest to supply *awwal*, first, on the warrant of Babur's later statement (f. 234b) that Dost was first in.

3 He was a son of Maulana Muh. *Sadr*, one of the chief men of 'Umar-shaikh M.'s Court; he had six brothers, all of whom spent their lives in Babur's service, to whom, if we may believe Abu'l-fazl, they were distantly related (Erskine).

(*b. Movements in Bajaur.*)

(*Jan. 8th*) Marching at dawn (Muh. 6th), we dismounted by the spring[1] of Baba Qara in the dale of Bajaur. At Khwaja Kalan's request the prisoners remaining were pardoned their offences, reunited to their wives and children, and given leave to go, but several sultans and of the most stubborn were made to reach their doom of death. Some heads of sultans and of others were sent to Kabul with the news of success; some also to Badakhshan, Qunduz and Balkh with the letters-of-victory.

Shah Mansur *Yusuf-zai*,—he was with us as an envoy from his tribe,—[2] was an eye-witness of the victory and general massacre. We allowed him to leave after putting a coat (*tun*) on him and after writing orders with threats to the Yusuf-zai.

(*Jan. 11th*) With mind easy about the important affairs of the Bajaur fort, we marched, on Tuesday the 9th of Muharram, one *kuroh* (2 m.) down the dale of Bajaur and ordered that a tower of heads should be set up on the rising-ground.

(*Jan. 12th*) On Wednesday the 10th of Muharram, we rode out to visit the Bajaur fort. There was a wine-party in Khwaja Kalan's house,[3] several goat-skins of wine having been brought

1 Babur now returns towards the east, down the Rud. The *chashma* by which he encamped, would seem to be near the mouth of the valley of Baba Qara, one 30 miles long; it may have been, anglicé, a spring [not that of the main stream of the long valley], but the word may be used as it seems to be of the water supplying the Bagh-i-safa (f. 224), *i.e.* to denote the first considerable gathering-place of small head-waters. It will be observed a few lines further on that this same valley seems to be meant by "Khwaja Khizr".

2 He will have joined Babur previous to Muharram 925 AH.

3 This statement, the first we have, that Babur has broken Musalman Law against stimulants (f. 49 and n.), is followed by many others more explicit, jotting down where and what and sometimes why he drank, in a way which arrests attention and asks some other explanation than that it is an unabashed record of conviviality such conceivably as a non-Musalman might write. Babur is now 37 years old; he had obeyed the Law till past early manhood; he wished to return to obedience at 40; he frequently mentions his lapses by a word which can be translated as "commitment of sin" (*irtqab*); one gathers that he did not at any time disobey with easy conscience. Does it explain his singular record,—one made in what amongst ourselves would be regarded as a private diary,—that his sins were created by Law? Had he a balance of reparation in his thoughts?

Detaching into their separate class as excesses, all his instances of confessed drunkenness, there remains much in his record which, seen from a non-Musalman point of view, is venial; *e.g.* his *subuhi* appears to be the "morning" of the Scot, the *Morgen-trank* of the Teuton; his afternoon cup, in the open air usually, may have been no worse than the sober glass of beer or local wine of modern Continental Europe. Many of these legal sins of his record were interludes in the day's long ride, stirrup-cups some of them, all in a period of strenuous physical activity. Many of his

down by Kafirs neighbouring on Bajaur. All wine and fruit
had in Bajaur comes from adjacent parts of Kafiristan.

(*Jan. 13th*) We spent the night there and after inspecting the
towers and ramparts of the fort early in the morning (Muh. 11th),
I mounted and went back to camp.

(*Jan. 14th*) Marching at dawn (Muh. 12th), we dismounted on
the bank of the Khwaja Khizr torrent.[1]

(*Jan. 15th*) Marching thence, we dismounted (Muh. 13th) on
the bank of the Chandawal torrent. Here all those inscribed in
the Bajaur reinforcement, were ordered to leave.

(*Jan. 16th*) On Sunday the 14th of Muharram, a standard was
bestowed on Khwaja Kalan and leave given him for Bajaur. A
few days after I had let him go, the following little verse having
come into my head, it was written down and sent to him:—[2]

> Not such the pact and bargain betwixt my friend and me,
> At length the tooth of parting, unpacted grief for me!
> Against caprice of Fortune, what weapons (*chara*) arm the man?
> At length by force of arms (*ba jaur*) my friend is snatched from me!

(*Jan. 19th*) On Wednesday the 17th of Muharram, Sl. 'Ala'u'd-
din of Sawad, the rival (*mu'ariz*) of Sl. Wais of Sawad,[3] came
and waited on me.

---

records are collective and are phrased impersonally; they mention that there was
drinking, drunkenness even, but they give details sometimes such as only a sober
observer could include.

Babur names a few men as drunkards, a few as entirely obedient; most of his men
seem not to have obeyed the Law and may have been "temperate drinkers"; they
effected work, Babur amongst them, which habitual drunkards could not have compassed. Spite of all he writes of his worst excesses, it must be just to remember his
Musalman conscience, and also the distorting power of a fictitious sin. Though he
broke the law binding all men against excess, and this on several confessed occasions,
his rule may have been no worse than that of the ordinarily temperate Western. It
cannot but lighten judgment that his recorded lapses from Law were often
prompted by the bounty and splendour of Nature; were committed amidst the
falling petals of fruit-blossom, the flaming fire of autumn leaves, where the eye
rested on the *arghwan* or the orange grove, the coloured harvest of corn or vine.

1 As Mr. Erskine observes, there seems to be no valley except that of Baba Qara,
between the Khahr and the Chandawal-valley; "Khwaja Khizr" and "Baba Qara"
may be one and the same valley.

2 Time and ingenuity would be needed to bring over into English all the quips of
this verse. The most obvious pun is, of course, that on Bajaur as the compelling
cause (*ba jaur*) of the parting; others may be meant on *guzid* and *gazid*, on *sazid*
and *chara*. The verse would provide the holiday amusement of extracting from it
two justifiable translations.

3 *See* Additional Notes, p. 798. His possessions extended from the river of Sawad
to Baramula; he was expelled from them by the Yusuf-zai (Erskine).

(*Jan. 20th*) On Thursday the 18th of the month, we hunted the hill between Bajaur and Chandawal.[1] There the *bughu-maral*[2] have become quite black, except for the tail which is of another colour; lower down, in Hindustan, they seem to become black all over.[3] Today a *sariq-qush*[4] was taken; that was black all over, its very eyes being black! Today an eagle (*burkut*)[5] took a deer (*kiyik*).

Corn being somewhat scarce in the army, we went into the Kahraj-valley, and took some.

Fol. 219b.

(*Jan. 21st*) On Friday (Muh. 19th) we marched for Sawad, with the intention of attacking the Yusuf-zai Afghans, and dismounted in between[6] the water of Panj-kura and the united waters of Chandawal and Bajaur. Shah Mansur *Yusuf-zai* had brought a few well-flavoured and quite intoxicating confections (*kamali*); making one of them into three, I ate one portion, Gadai Taghai another, 'Abdu'l-lah the librarian another. It produced remarkable intoxication; so much so that at the Evening Prayer when the begs gathered for counsel, I was not able to go out. A strange thing it was! If in these days[7] I ate the whole of such a confection, I doubt if it would produce half as much intoxication.

(*c. An impost laid on Kahraj.*)

(*Jan. 22nd*) Marching from that ground, (Muh. 20th), we dismounted over against Kahraj, at the mouth of the valleys of Kahraj and Peshgram.[8] Snow fell ankle-deep while we were on that ground; it would seem to be rare for snow to fall there-abouts, for people were much surprised. In agreement with

---

1 This will be the naze of the n.e. rampart of the Baba Qara valley.

2 f. 4 and note; f. 276. Babur seems to use the name for several varieties of deer.

3 There is here, perhaps, a jesting allusion to the darkening of complexion amongst the inhabitants of countries from west to east, from Highlands to Indian plains.

4 In Dr. E. D. Ross' *Polyglot list of birds* the *sarigh*(*sariq*)-*qush* is said to frequent fields of ripening grain; this suggests to translate its name as Thief-bird.

5 *Aquila chrysaetus*, the hunting eagle.

6 This *araligh* might be identified with the "Miankalai" of maps (since Soghd, lying between two arms of the Zar-afshan is known also as Miankal), but Raverty explains the Bajaur Miankalai to mean Village of the holy men (*mian*).

7 After 933 AH. presumably, when final work on the B.N. was in progress.

8 Mr. Erskine notes that Pesh-gram lies north of Mahyar (on the Chandawal-water), and that he has not found Kahraj (or Kohraj). Judging from Babur's next movements, the two valleys he names may be those in succession east of Chandawal.

Sl. Wais of Sawad there was laid on the Kahraj people an
impost of 4000 ass-loads of rice for the use of the army, and he
himself was sent to collect it. Never before had those rude
mountaineers borne such a burden; they could not give (all)
the grain and were brought to ruin.

(cc. Raid on Panj-kura.)

(*Jan. 25th*) On Tuesday the 23rd of Muharram an army was
Fol. 220. sent under Hindu Beg to raid Panj-kura. Panj-kura lies more
than half-way up the mountain;[1] to reach its villages a person
must go for nearly a *kuroh* (2 m.) through a pass. The people
had fled and got away; our men brought a few beasts of sorts,
and masses of corn from their houses.

(*Jan. 26th*) Next day (Muh. 24th) Quj Beg was put at the
head of a force and sent out to raid.

(*Jan. 27th*) On Thursday the 25th of the month, we dismounted
at the village of Mandish, in the trough of the Kahraj-valley, for
the purpose of getting corn for the army.

(d. Mahim's adoption of Dil-dar's unborn child.)

(*Jan. 28th*) Several children born of Humayun's mother had
not lived. Hind-al was not yet born.[2] While we were in those
parts, came a letter from Mahim in which she wrote, "Whether
it be a boy, whether it be a girl, is my luck and chance; give
it to me; I will declare it my child and will take charge of it."
On Friday the 26th of the month, we being still on that ground,
Yusuf-i-'ali the stirrup-holder was sent off to Kabul with letters[3]
bestowing Hind-al, not yet born, on Mahim.

1 There is hardly any level ground in the cleft of the Panj-kura (R.'s *Notes* p. 193);
the villages are perched high on the sides of the valley. The pass leading to them
may be Katgola (Fincastle's Map).
2 This account of Hind-al's adoption is sufficiently confused to explain why a note,
made apparently by Humayun, should have been appended to it (Appendix L, *On
Hind-al's adoption*). The confusion reminds the reader that he has before him a sort
of memorandum only, diary jottings, apt to be allusive and abbreviated. The
expected child was Dil-dar's; Mahim, using her right as principal wife, asked for it
to be given to her. That the babe in question is here called Hind-al shews that at least
part of this account of his adoption was added after the birth and naming (f. 227).
3 One would be, no doubt, for Dil-dar's own information. She then had no son
but had two daughters, Gul-rang and Gul-chihra. News of Hind-al's birth
reached Babur in Bhira, some six weeks later (f. 227).

(dd. Construction of a stone platform.)

While we were still on that same ground in the Mandish-country, I had a platform made with stones (*tash bila*) on a height in the middle of the valley, so large that it held the tents of the advance-camp. All the household and soldiers carried the stones for it, one by one like ants.

(e. Babur's marriage with his Afghan wife, Bibi Mubaraka.)

In order to conciliate the Yusuf-zai horde, I had asked for a daughter of one of my well-wishers, Malik Sulaiman Shah's son Malik Shah Mansur, at the time he came to me as envoy   Fol. 220*b*. from the Yusuf-zai Afghans.[1]

While we were on this ground news came that his daughter[2] was on her way with the Yusuf-zai tribute. At the Evening Prayer there was a wine-party to which Sl. 'Ala'u'd-din (of Sawad) was invited and at which he was given a seat and special dress of honour (*khilcat-i-khasa*).

(*Jan. 30th*) On Sunday the 28th, we marched from that valley. Shah Mansur's younger brother Taus (Handsome) Khan brought the above-mentioned daughter of his brother to our ground after we had dismounted.

(f. Repopulation of the fort of Bajaur.)

For the convenience of having the Bi-sut people in Bajaur-fort,[3] Yusuf'i-'ali the taster was sent from this camp to get them on the march and take them to that fort. Also, written orders were despatched to Kabul that the army there left should join us.

(*Feb. 4th*) On Friday the 3rd of the month of Safar, we dismounted at the confluence of the waters of Bajaur and Panj-kura.

(*Feb. 6th*) On Sunday the 5th of the month, we went from that ground to Bajaur where there was a drinking-party in Khwaja Kalan's house.

---

1 f. 218*b*.

2 Bibi Mubaraka, the Afghani Aghacha of Gul-badan. An attractive picture of her is drawn by the *Tawarikh-i-hafi-i-rahmat-khani*. As this gives not only one of Babur's romantic adventures but historical matter, I append it in my husband's translation [(A.Q.R. April 1901)] as Appendix K, *An Afghan Legend*.

3 *Bi-sut aili-ning Bajaur-qurghani-da manasabati-bar jihati*; a characteristic phrase.

(*g. Expedition against the Afghan clans.*)

(*Feb. 8th*) On Tuesday the 7th of the month the begs and the Dilazak Afghan headmen were summoned, and, after consultation, matters were left at this:—"The year is at its end,[1] only a few days of the Fish are left; the plainsmen have carried in all their corn; if we went now into Sawad, the army would dwindle through getting no corn. The thing to do is to march along the Ambahar and Pani-mani road, cross the Sawad-water above Hash-nagar, and surprise the Yusuf-zai and Muhammadi Afghans who are located in the plain over against the Yusuf-zai *sangur* of Mahura. Another year, coming earlier in the harvest-time, the Afghans of this place must be our first thought." So the matter was left.

Fol. 221.

(*Feb. 9th*) Next day, Wednesday, we bestowed horses and robes on Sl. Wais and Sl. 'Ala'u'u-din of Sawad, gave them leave to go, marched off ourselves and dismounted over against Bajaur.

(*Feb. 10th*) We marched next day, leaving Shah Mansur's daughter in Bajaur-fort until the return of the army. We dismounted after passing Khwaja Khizr, and from that camp leave was given to Khwaja Kalan; and the heavy baggage, the worn-out horses and superfluous effects of the army were started off into Lamghan by the Kunar road.

(*Feb. 11th*) Next morning Khwaja Mir-i-miran was put in charge of the camel baggage-train and started off by the Qurgha-tu and Darwaza road, through the Qara-kupa-pass. Riding light for the raid, we ourselves crossed the Ambahar-pass, and yet another great pass, and dismounted at Pani-mali nearer[2] the Afternoon Prayer. Aughan-birdi was sent forward with a few others to learn[3] how things were.

(*Feb. 12th*) The distance between us and the Afghans being short, we did not make an early start. Aughan-birdi came back at breakfast-time.[4] He had got the better of an Afghan

1 Perhaps the end of the early spring-harvest and the spring harvesting-year. It is not the end of the campaigning year, manifestly; and it is at the beginning of both the solar and lunar years.

2 Perhaps, more than half-way between the Mid-day and Afternoon Prayers. So too in the annals of Feb. 12th.

3 *til alghali* (Pers. *zaban-giri*), a new phrase in the B.N.

4 *chasht*, which, being half-way between sunrise and the meridian, is a variable hour.

and had cut his head off, but had dropped it on the road. He Fol. 221b.
brought no news so sure as the heart asks (*kunkul-tiladik*).
Mid-day come, we marched on, crossed the Sawad-water, and
dismounted nearer[1] the Afternoon Prayer. At the Bed-time
Prayer, we remounted and rode swiftly on.

(*Feb. 13th*) Rustam *Turkman* had been sent scouting; when
the Sun was spear-high he brought word that the Afghans had
heard about us and were shifting about, one body of them
making off by the mountain-road. On this we moved the faster,
sending raiders on ahead who killed a few, cut off their heads
and brought a band of prisoners, some cattle and flocks. The
Dilazak Afghans also cut off and brought in a few heads.
Turning back, we dismounted near Katlang and from there
sent a guide to meet the baggage-train under Khwaja Mir-i-
miran and bring it to join us in Maqam.[2]

(*Feb. 14th*) Marching on next day, we dismounted between
Katlang and Maqam. A man of Shah Mansur's arrived.
Khusrau Kukuldash and Ahmadi the secretary were sent with
a few more to meet the baggage-train.

(*Feb. 15th*) On Wednesday the 14th of the month, the
baggage-train rejoined us while we were dismounting at Maqam.

It will have been within the previous 30 or 40 years that
a heretic qalandar named Shahbaz perverted a body of Yusuf-
zai and another of Dilazak. His tomb was on a free and
dominating height of the lower hill at the bill (*tumshuq*) of the Fol. 222.
Maqam mountain. Thought I, "What is there to recommend
the tomb of a heretic qalandar for a place in air so free?" and
ordered the tomb destroyed and levelled with the ground. The
place was so charming and open that we elected to sit there
some time and to eat a confection (*ma'jun*).

(*h. Babur crosses the Indus for the first time.*)

We had turned off from Bajaur with Bhira in our thoughts.[3]
Ever since we came into Kabul it had been in my mind to
move on Hindustan, but this had not been done for a variety of

1 *See* n. 2, f. 221.
2 Perhaps Maqam is the Mardan of maps.
3 Bhira, on the Jehlam, is now in the Shahpur district of the Panj-ab.

reasons. Nothing to count had fallen into the soldiers' hands during the three or four months we had been leading this army. Now that Bhira, the borderland of Hindustan, was so near, I thought a something might fall into our men's hands if, riding light, we went suddenly into it. To this thought I clung, but some of my well-wishers, after we had raided the Afghans and dismounted at Maqam, set the matter in this way before me:—"If we are to go into Hindustan, it should be on a proper basis; one part of the army stayed behind in Kabul; a body of effective braves was left behind in Bajaur; a good part of this army has gone into Lamghan because its horses were worn-out; and the horses of those who have come this far, are so poor that they have not a day's hard riding in them." Reasonable as these considerations were, yet, having made the start, we paid no attention to them but set off next day for the ford through the water of Sind.[1] Mir Muhammad the raftsman and his elder and younger brethren were sent with a few braves to examine the Sind-river (*darya*), above and below the ford.

Fol. 222b.

(*Feb. 16th*) After starting off the camp for the river, I went to hunt rhinoceros on the Sawati side which place people call also Karg-khana (Rhino-home).[2] A few were discovered but the jungle was dense and they did not come out of it. When one with a calf came into the open and betook itself to flight, many arrows were shot at it and it rushed into the near jungle; the jungle was fired but that same rhino was not had. Another calf was killed as it lay, scorched by the fire, writhing and palpitating. Each person took a share of the spoil. After leaving Sawati, we wandered about a good deal; it was the Bed-time Prayer when we got to camp.

Those sent to examine the ford came back after doing it.

(*Feb. 17th*) Next day, Thursday the 16th,[3] the horses and baggage-camels crossed through the ford and the camp-bazar

---

1 This will be the ford on the direct road from Mardan for the eastward (Elphinstone's *Caubul* ii, 416).

2 The position of Sawati is represented by the Suabi of the G. of I. map (1909 AD.). Writing in about 1813 AD. Mr. Erskine notes as worthy of record that the rhinoceros was at that date no longer found west of the Indus.

3 Elph. MS. *ghura*, the 1st, but this is corrected to 16th by a marginal note. The Hai. MS. here, as in some other places, has the context for a number, but omits the figures. So does also the Elph. MS. in a good many places.

and foot-soldiers were put over on rafts. Some Nil-abis came and saw me at the ford-head (*guzar-bashi*), bringing a horse in mail and 300 *shahrukhis* as an offering. At the Mid-day Prayer of this same day, when every-one had crossed the river, we marched on; we went on until one watch of the night had passed (*circa* 9 p.m.) when we dismounted near the water of Kacha-kot.[1]

(*Feb. 18th*) Marching on next day, we crossed the Kacha-kot-water; noon returning, went through the Sangdaki-pass and dismounted. While Sayyid Qasim Lord of the Gate was   Fol. 223. in charge of the rear (*chaghdawal*) he overcame a few Gujurs who had got up with the rear march, cut off and brought in 4 or 5 of their heads.

(*Feb. 19th*) Marching thence at dawn and crossing the Suhan-water, we dismounted at the Mid-day Prayer. Those behind kept coming in till midnight; the march had been mightily long, and, as many horses were weak and out-of-condition, a great number were left on the road.

(*i. The Salt-range.*)

Fourteen miles (7 *kos*) north of Bhira lies the mountain-range written of in the *Zafar-nama* and other books as the Koh-i-jud.[2] I had not known why it was called this; I now knew. On it dwell two tribes, descendants from one parent-source, one is called Jud, the other Janjuha. These two from of old have been the rulers and lawful commanders of the peoples and hordes (*aulus*) of the range and of the country between Bhira and Nil-ab. Their rule is friendly and brotherly however; they cannot take what their hearts might desire; the portion ancient custom has fixed is given and taken, no less and no more. The agreement is to give one *shahrukhi*[3] for each yoke of oxen and seven for headship in a household; there is also service in the army. The Jud and Janjuha both are divided into several

1 This is the Harru. Mr. Erskine observes that Babur appears to have turned sharp south after crossing it, since he ascended a pass so soon after leaving the Indus and reached the Suhan so soon.

2 *i.e.* the Salt-range.

3 Mr. Erskine notes that (in his day) a *shahrukhi* may be taken at a shilling or eleven pence sterling.

clans. The Koh-i-jud runs for 14 miles along the Bhira country, taking off from those Kashmir mountains that are one with Fol. 223*b*. Hindu-kush, and it draws out to the south-west as far as the foot of Din-kot on the Sind-river.[1] On one half of it are the Jud, the Janjuha on the other. People call it Koh-i-jud through connecting it with the Jud tribe.[2] The principal headman gets the title of Rai; others, his younger brothers and sons, are styled Malik. The Janjuha headmen are maternal uncles of Langar Khan. The ruler of the people and horde near the Suhan-water was named Malik Hast. The name originally was Asad but as Hindustanis sometimes drop a vowel *e.g.* they say *khabr* for *khabar* (news), they had said Asd for Asad, and this went on to Hast.

Langar Khan was sent off to Malik Hast at once when we dismounted. He galloped off, made Malik Hast hopeful of our favour and kindness, and at the Bed-time Prayer, returned with him. Malik Hast brought an offering of a horse in mail and waited on me. He may have been 22 or 23 years old.[3]

The various flocks and herds belonging to the country-people were close round our camp. As it was always in my heart to possess Hindustan, and as these several countries, Bhira, Khush-ab, Chin-ab and Chiniut[4] had once been held by the Turk, I pictured them as my own and was resolved to get them into my hands, whether peacefully or by force. For these reasons it being imperative to treat these hillmen well, this following Fol. 224. order was given:—"Do no hurt or harm to the flocks and herds of these people, nor even to their cotton-ends and broken needles!"

1 It is somewhat difficult not to forget that a man who, like Babur, records so many observations of geographical position, had no guidance from Surveys, Gazetteers and Books of Travel. Most of his records are those of personal observation.

2 In this sentence Mr. Erskine read a reference to the Musalman Ararat, the Koh-i-jud on the left bank of the Tigris. What I have set down translates the Turki words but, taking account of Babur's eye for the double use of a word, and Erskine's careful work, done too in India, the Turki may imply reference to the Ararat-like summit of Sakeswar.

3 Here Dr. Leyden's version finally ends (Erskine).

4 Bhira, as has been noted, is on the Jehlam; Khush-ab is 40 m. lower down the same river; Chiniut (Chini-wat?) is 50 miles south of Bhira; Chin-ab (China-water?) seems the name of a tract only and not of a residential centre; it will be in the Bar of Kipling's border-thief. Concerning Chiniut *see* D. G. Barkley's letter, JRAS 1899 p. 132.

(*j. The Kalda-kahar lake.*)

(*Feb. 20th*) Marching thence next day, we dismounted at the Mid-day Prayer amongst fields of densely-growing corn in Kalda-kahar.

Kalda-kahar is some 20 miles north of Bhira, a level land shut in [1] amongst the Jud mountains. In the middle of it is a lake some six miles round, the in-gatherings of rain from all sides. On the north of this lake lies an excellent meadow; on the hill-skirt to the west of it there is a spring [2] having its source in the heights overlooking the lake. The place being suitable I have made a garden there, called the Bagh-i-safa, [3] as will be told later; it is a very charming place with good air.

(*Feb. 21st*) We rode from Kalda-kahar at dawn next day. When we reached the top of the Hamtatu-pass a few local people waited on me, bringing a humble gift. They were joined with 'Abdu'r-rahim the chief-scribe (*shaghawal*) and sent with him to speak the Bhira people fair and say, "The possession of this country by a Turk has come down from of old; beware not to bring ruin on its people by giving way to fear and anxiety; our eye is on this land and on this people; raid and rapine shall not be."

We dismounted near the foot of the pass at breakfast-time, and thence sent seven or eight men ahead, under Qurban of Chirkh and 'Abdu'l-maluk of Khwast. Of those sent one Mir Muhammad (a servant?) of Mahdi Khwaja [4] brought in a man. A few Afghan headmen, who had come meantime with offerings and done obeisance, were joined with Langar Khan to go and speak the Bhira people fair.   Fol. 224*b*

After crossing the pass and getting out of the jungle, we arrayed in right and left and centre, and moved forward for Bhira. As

1 *taur yiri waqi' bulub tur.* As on f. 160 of the valley of Khwesh, I have taken *taur* to be Turki, complete, shut in.

2 *chashma* (f. 218*b* and note).

3 The promised description is not found; there follows a mere mention only of the garden [f. 369]. This entry can be taken therefore as shewing an intention to write what is still wanting from Safar 926 AH. to Safar 932 AH.

4 Mir Muh. may have been a kinsman or follower of Mahdi Khwaja. The entry on the scene, unannounced by introduction as to parentage, of the Khwaja who played a part later in Babur's family affairs is due, no doubt, to the last gap of annals. He is mentioned in the Translator's Note, *s.a.* 923 AH. (*See* Gul-badan's H.N. Bio-graphical Appendix *s.n.*)

we got near it there came in, of the servants of Daulat Khan
Yusuf-khail's son 'Ali Khan, Siktu's son Diwa *Hindu*; with them
came several of the notables of Bhira who brought a horse and
camel as an offering and did me obeisance. At the Mid-day
Prayer we dismounted on the east of Bhira, on the bank of the
Bahat (Jehlam), in a sown-field, without hurt or harm being
allowed to touch the people of Bhira.

(*k. History of Bhira.*)

   Timur Beg had gone into Hindustan; from the time he went
out again these several countries *viz*. Bhira, Khush-ab, Chin-ab
and Chiniut, had been held by his descendants and the
dependants and adherents of those descendants. After the death
of Sl. Mas'ud Mirza and his son 'Ali *Asghar* Mirza, the sons of
Mir 'Ali Beg

> (*Author's note on Sl. Mas'ud Mirza.*)   He was the son of Suyurghatmish
> Mirza, son of Shahrukh Mirza, (son of Timur), and was known as
> Sl. Mas'ud *Kabuli* because the government and administration of Kabul
> and Zabul were then dependent on him (deposed 843 AH.–1440 AD.)

Fol. 225.   *viz*. Baba-i-kabuli, Darya Khan and Apaq Khan, known later as
Ghazi Khan, all of whom Sl. Mas'ud M. had cherished, through
their dominant position, got possession of Kabul, Zabul and the
afore-named countries and *parganas* of Hindustan. In Sl. Abu-
sa'id Mirza's time, Kabul and Zabul went from their hands, the
Hindustan countries remaining. In 910 AH. (1504 AD.) the year

> (*Author's note to 910 AH.*)   That year, with the wish to enter Hindustan,
> Khaibar had been crossed and Parashawur (*sic*) had been reached, when
> Baqi *Chaghaniani* insisted on a move against Lower Bangash *i.e.* Kohat, a
> mass of Afghans were raided and scraped clean (*qirib*), the Bannu plain
> was raided and plundered, and return was made through Duki (Dugi).

I first came into Kabul, the government of Bhira, Khush-ab and
Chin-ab depended on Sayyid 'Ali Khan, son of Ghazi Khan and
grandson of Mir 'Ali Beg, who read the *khutba* for Sikandar son
of Buhlul (*Ludi Afghan*) and was subject to him. When I led that
army out (910 AH.) Sayyid 'Ali Khan left Bhira in terror, crossed
the Bahat-water, and seated himself in Sher-kot, one of the
villages of Bhira. A few years later the Afghans became suspicious
about him on my account; he, giving way to his own fears and
anxieties, made these countries over to the then governor
Fol. 225b. in Lahur, Daulat Khan, son of Tatar Khan *Yusuf-khail*, who

gave them to his own eldest son 'Ali Khan, and in 'Ali Khan's possession they now were.

> (*Author's note on Daulat Khan Yusuf-khail.*)   This Tatar Khan, the father of Daulat Khan, was one of six or seven *sardars* who, sallying out and becoming dominant in Hindustan, made Buhlul Padshah. He held the country north of the Satluj (*sic*) and Sahrind,[1] the revenues of which exceeded 3 *krurs*.[2] On Tatar Khan's death, Sl. Sikandar (*Ludi*), as over-lord, took those countries from Tatar Khan's sons and gave Lahur only to Daulat Khan. That happened a year or two before I came into the country of Kabul (910 AH.).

(*l. Babur's journey resumed.*)

(*Feb. 22nd*) Next morning foragers were sent to several convenient places; on the same day I visited Bhira; and on the same day Sangur Khan *Janjuha* came, made offering of a horse, and did me obeisance.

(*Feb. 23rd*) On Wednesday the 22nd of the month, the headmen and *chauderis*[3] of Bhira were summoned, a sum of 400,000 *shahrukhis*[4] was agreed on as the price of peace (*mal-i-aman*), and collectors were appointed. We also made an excursion, going in a boat and there eating a confection.

(*Feb. 24th*) Haidar the standard-bearer had been sent to the Biluchis located in Bhira and Khush-ab; on Thursday morning they made an offering of an almond-coloured *tipuchaq* [horse], and did obeisance. As it was represented to me that some of the soldiery were behaving without sense and were laying-hands on Bhira people, persons were sent who caused some of those senseless people to meet their death-doom, of others slit the noses and so led them round the camp.

Fol. 226.

(*Feb. 25th*) On Friday came a dutiful letter from the Khush-abis; on this Shah Shuja' *Arghun*'s son Shah Hasan was appointed to go to Khush-ab.

---

1 or Sihrind, mod. Sirhind or Sar-i-hind (Head of Hind). It may be noted here, for what it may be found worth, that Kh(w)afi Khan [i, 402] calls Sar-i-hind the old name, says that the place was once held by the Ghazni dynasty and was its Indian frontier, and that Shah-jahan changed it to Sahrind. The W.-i-B. I.O. 217 f. 155 writes Shahrind.

2 Three krores or crores of dams, at 40 to the rupee, would make this 750,000 rupees, or about £75,000 sterling (Erskine); a statement from the ancient history of the rupi!

3 This Hindustani word in some districts signifies the head man of a trade, in others a landholder (Erskine).

4 In Mr. Erskine's time this sum was reckoned to be nearly £20,000.

(*Feb. 26th*) On Saturday the 25th of the month,[1] Shah Hasan was started for Khush-ab.

(*Feb. 27th*) On Sunday so much rain fell[2] that water covered all the plain. A small brackish stream[3] flowing between Bhira and the gardens in which the army lay, had become like a great river before the Mid-day Prayer; while at the ford near Bhira there was no footing for more than an arrow's flight; people crossing had to swim. In the afternoon I rode out to watch the water coming down (*kirkan su*); the rain and storm were such that on the way back there was some fear about getting in to camp. I crossed that same water (*kirkan su*) with my horse swimming. The army-people were much alarmed; most of them abandoned tents and heavy baggage, shouldered armour, horse-mail and arms, made their horses swim and crossed bareback. Most streams flooded the plain.

(*Feb. 28th*) Next day boats were brought from the river (Jehlam), and in these most of the army brought their tents and baggage over. Towards mid-day, Quj Beg's men went 2 miles up the water and there found a ford by which the rest crossed.

Fol. 226b. (*March 1st*) After a night spent in Bhira-fort, Jahan-nama they call it, we marched early on the Tuesday morning out of the worry of the rain-flood to the higher ground north of Bhira.

As there was some delay about the moneys asked for and agreed to (*taqabbul*), the country was divided into four districts and the begs were ordered to try to make an end of the matter. Khalifa was appointed to one district, Quj Beg to another, Nasir's Dost to another, Sayyid Qasim and Muhibb-i-'ali to another. Picturing as our own the countries once occupied by the Turk, there was to be no over-running or plundering.

(*m. Envoys sent to the court in Dihli.*)

(*March 3rd*) People were always saying, "It could do no harm to send an envoy, for peace's sake, to countries that once depended

1 Here originally neither the Elph. MS. nor the Hai. MS. had a date; it has been added to the former.

2 This rain is too early for the s. w. monsoon; it was probably a severe fall of spring rain, which prevails at this season or rather earlier, and extends over all the west of Asia (Erskine).

3 *az ghina shor su*. Streams rising in the Salt-range become brackish on reaching its skirts (G. of I.).

on the Turk." Accordingly on Thursday the 1st of Rabi'u'l-awwal, Mulla Murshid was appointed to go to Sl. Ibrahim who through the death of his father Sl. Iskandar had attained to rule in Hindustan some 5 or 6 months earlier(?). I sent him a goshawk (*qarchigha*) and asked for the countries which from of old had depended on the Turk. Mulla Murshid was given charge of writings (*khattlar*) for Daulat Khan (*Yusuf-khail*) and writings for Sl. Ibrahim; matters were sent also by word-of-mouth; and he was given leave to go. Far from sense and wisdom, shut off from judgment and counsel must people in Hindustan be, the Afghans above all; for they could not move and make stand like a foe, nor did they know ways and rules of friendliness. Fol. 227. Daulat Khan kept my man several days in Lahur without seeing him himself or speeding him on to Sl. Ibrahim; and he came back to Kabul a few months later without bringing a reply.

(*n. Birth of Hind-al.*)

(*March 4th*) On Friday the 2nd of the month, the foot-soldiers Shaibak and Darwesh-i-'ali,—he is now a matchlockman,— bringing dutiful letters from Kabul, brought news also of Hind-al's birth. As the news came during the expedition into Hindustan, I took it as an omen, and gave the name Hind-al (Taking of Hind). Dutiful letters came also from Muhammad-i-zaman M. in Balkh, by the hand of Qambar Beg.

(*March 5th*) Next morning when the Court rose, we rode out for an excursion, entered a boat and there drank '*araq*.[1] The people of the party were Khwaja Dost-khawand, Khusrau, Mirim, Mirza Quli, Muhammadi, Ahmadi, Gadai, Na'man, Langar Khan, Rauh-dam,[2] Qasim-i-'ali the opium-eater (*tariyaki*), Yusuf-i-'ali and Tingri-quli. Towards the head of the boat there was a *talar*[3] on the flat top of which I sat with a few people, a few others sitting below. There was a sitting-place also at the tail of the boat; there Muhammadi, Gadai and Na'man sat. '*Araq* was drunk till the Other Prayer when, disgusted by its bad flavour, by consent of those at the head of the boat, *ma'jun* was preferred.

1 Here this will be the fermented juice of rice or of the date-palm.
2 *Rauh* is sometimes the name of a musical note.
3 a platform, with or without a chamber above it, and supported on four posts.

Fol. 227b. Those at the other end, knowing nothing about our *ma'jun* drank '*araq* right through. At the Bed-time Prayer we rode from the boat and got into camp late. Thinking I had been drinking '*araq* Muhammadi and Gadai had said to one another, "Let's do befitting service," lifted a pitcher of '*araq* up to one another in turn on their horses, and came in saying with wonderful joviality and heartiness and speaking together, "Through this dark night have we come carrying this pitcher in turns!" Later on when they knew that the party was (now) meant to be otherwise and the hilarity to differ, that is to say, that [there would be that] of the *ma'jun* band and that of the drinkers, they were much disturbed because never does a *ma'jun* party go well with a drinking-party. Said I, "Don't upset the party! Let those who wish to drink '*araq*, drink '*araq*; let those who wish to eat *ma'jun*, eat *ma'jun*. Let no-one on either side make talk or allusion to the other." Some drank '*araq*, some ate *ma'jun*, and for a time the party went on quite politely. Baba Jan the *qabuz*-player had not been of our party (in the boat); we invited him when we reached the tents. He asked to drink '*araq*. We invited Tardi Muhammad *Qibchaq* also and made him a comrade of the drinkers. A *ma'jun* party never goes well with an '*araq* or a wine-party; the drinkers began to make wild talk and chatter from all sides, mostly in allusion to *ma'jun* and *ma'junis*. Baba Jan even, when drunk, said many wild things. The drinkers soon made Tardi Khan mad-drunk, by giving him one full bowl after another. Try as we did

Fol. 228. to keep things straight, nothing went well; there was much disgusting uproar; the party became intolerable and was broken up.

(*March 7th*) On Monday the 5th of the month, the country of Bhira was given to Hindu Beg.

(*March 8th*) On Tuesday the Chin-ab country was bestowed on Husain *Aikrak*(?) and leave was given to him and the Chin-ab people to set out. At this time Sayyid 'Ali Khan's son Minuchihr Khan, having let us know (his intention), came and waited on me. He had started from Hindustan by the upper road, had met in with Tatar Khan *Kakar*,[1] Tatar Khan had not let him pass on, but had kept him, made him a son-in-law by giving him his own daughter, and had detained him for some time.

---

1 so-written in the MSS. *Cf.* Raverty's *Notes* and G. of I.

(*o. The Kakars.*)

In amongst the mountains of Nil-ab and Bhira which connect with those of Kashmir, there are, besides the Jud and Janjuha tribes, many Jats, Gujurs, and others akin to them, seated in villages everywhere on every rising-ground. These are governed by headmen of the Kakar tribes, a headship like that over the Jud and Janjuha. At this time (925 AH.) the headmen of the people of those hill-skirts were Tatar *Kakar* and Hati *Kakar*, two descendants of one forefather; being paternal-uncles' sons.[1] Torrent-beds and ravines are their strongholds. Tatar's place, named Parhala,[2] is a good deal below the snow-mountains; Hati's country connects with the mountains and also he had made Babu Khan's fief Kalanjar,[3] look towards himself. Tatar *Kakar* had seen Daulat Khan (*Yusuf-khail*) and looked to him with complete obedience. Hati had not seen Daulat Khan; his attitude towards him was bad and turbulent. At the word of the Hindustan begs and in agreement with them, Tatar had so posted himself as to blockade Hati from a distance. Just when we were in Bhira, Hati moved on pretext of hunting, fell un-expectedly on Tatar, killed him, and took his country, his wives and his having (*bulghani*).[4]

Fol. 228*b*.

(*p. Babur's journey resumed.*)

Having ridden out at the Mid-day Prayer for an excursion, we got on a boat and '*araq* was drunk. The people of the party were Dost Beg, Mirza Quli, Ahmadi, Gadai, Muhammad 'Ali *Jang-jang*, 'Asas,[5] and Aughan-birdi *Mughul*. The musicians were Rauh-dam, Baba Jan, Qasim-i-'ali, Yusuf-i-'ali, Tingri-quli, Abu'l-qasim, Ramzan *Luli*. We drank in the boat till the Bed-time Prayer; then getting off it, full of drink, we mounted, took torches in our hands, and went to camp from the river's bank,

1 Anglicé, cousins on the father's side.
2 The G. of I. describes it.
3 Elph. MS. f. 183*b*, *mansub*; Hai. MS. and 2nd W.-i-B. *bisut*.
4 The 1st Pers. trs. (I.O. 215 f. 188*b*) and Kehr's MS. [Ilminsky p. 293] attribute Hati's last-recorded acts to Babur himself. The two mistaken sources err together elsewhere. M. de Courteille corrects the defect (ii, 67).
5 night-guard. He is the old servant to whom Babur sent a giant *ashrafi* of the spoils of India (Gul-badan's H.N. *s.n.*).

leaning over from our horses on this side, leaning over from that, at one loose-rein gallop! Very drunk I must have been for, when they told me next day that we had galloped loose-rein into camp, carrying torches, I could not recall it in the very least. After reaching my quarters, I vomited a good deal.

(*March 11th*) On Friday we rode out on an excursion, crossed the water (Jehlam) by boat and went about amongst the orchards (*baghat*) of blossoming trees and the lands of the sugar-cultivation. We saw the wheel with buckets, had water drawn, and asked

Fol. 229.   particulars about getting it out; indeed we made them draw it again and again. During this excursion a confection was preferred. In returning we went on board a boat. A confection (*ma'jun*) was given also to Minuchihr Khan, such a one that, to keep him standing, two people had to give him their arms. For a time the boat remained at anchor in mid-stream; we then went down-stream; after a while had it drawn up-stream again, slept in it that night and went back to camp near dawn.

(*March 12th*) On Saturday the 10th of the first Rabi', the Sun entered the Ram. Today we rode out before mid-day and got into a boat where 'araq was drunk. The people of the party were Khwaja Dost-khawand, Dost Beg, Mirim, Mirza Quli, Muhammadi, Ahmadi, Yunas-i-'ali, Muh. 'Ali *Jang-jang*, Gadai Taghai, Mir Khurd (and?) 'Asas. The musicians were Rauh-dam, Baba Jan, Qasim, Yusuf-i-'ali, Tingri-quli and Ramzan. We got into a branch-water (*shakh-i-ab*), for some time went down-stream, landed a good deal below Bhira and on its opposite bank, and went late into camp.

This same day Shah Hasan returned from Khush-ab whither he had been sent as envoy to demand the countries which from of old had depended on the Turk; he had settled peaceably with them and had in his hands a part of the money assessed on them.

The heats were near at hand. To reinforce Hindu Beg (in Bhira) were appointed Shah Muhammad Keeper of the Seal and his younger brother Dost Beg Keeper of the Seal, together with several suitable braves; an accepted (*yarasha*) stipend

Fol. 229b.   was fixed and settled in accordance with each man's position. Khush-ab was bestowed, with a standard, on Langar Khan, the prime cause and mover of this expedition; we settled also that he was to help Hindu Beg. We appointed also to help Hindu Beg, the Turk and local soldiery of Bhira, increasing the allowances and pay of both. Amongst them was the afore-named Minuchihr Khan whose name has been mentioned; there was also Nazar-i-'ali *Turk*, one of Minuchihr Khan's relations; there were also Sangar Khan *Janjuha* and Malik Hast *Janjuha*.

(pp. Return for Kabul.)

(*March 13th*) Having settled the country in every way making for hope of peace, we marched for Kabul from Bhira on Sunday the 11th of the first Rabi'. We dismounted in Kaldah-kahar. That day too it rained amazingly; people with rain-cloaks[1] were in the same case as those who had none! The rear of the camp kept coming in till the Bed-time Prayer.

(q. Action taken against Hati Kakar.)

(*March 14th*) People acquainted with the honour and glory (*ab u tab*) of this land and government, especially the Janjuhas, old foes of these Kakars, represented, "Hati is the bad man round-about; he it is robs on the roads; he it is brings men to ruin; he ought either to be driven out from these parts, or to be severely punished." Agreeing with this, we left Khwaja Mir-i-miran and Nasir's Mirim next day with the camp, parting from them at big breakfast,[2] and moved on Hati *Kakar*. As has been said, he had killed Tatar a few days earlier, and having taken possession of Parhala, was in it now. Dismounting at the Other Fol. 230. Prayer, we gave the horses corn; at the Bed-time Prayer we rode on again, our guide being a Gujur servant of Malik Hast, named Sar-u-pa. We rode the night through and dismounted at dawn, when Beg Muhammad *Mughul* was sent back to the

---

1 The *kiping* or *kipik* is a kind of mantle covered with wool (Erskine); the root of the word is *kip*, dry.

2 *aulugh chasht*, a term suggesting that Babur knew the *chota haziri*, little breakfast, of Anglo-India. It may be inferred, from several passages, that the big breakfast was taken after 9 a.m. and before 12 p.m. Just below men are said to put on their mail at *chasht* in the same way as, *passim*, things other than prayer are said to be done at this or that Prayer; this, I think, always implies that they are done after the Prayer mentioned; a thing done shortly before a Prayer is done "close to" or "near" or when done over half-way to the following Prayer, the act is said to be done "nearer" to the second (as was noted on f. 221).

camp, and we remounted when it was growing light. At break-fast-time (9 a.m.) we put our mail on and moved forward faster. The blackness of Parhala shewed itself from 2 miles off; the gallop was then allowed (*chapqun quiuldi*); the right went east of Parhala, Quj Beg, who was also of the right, following as its reserve; the men of the left and centre went straight for the fort, Dost Beg being their rear-reserve.

Parhala stands amongst ravines. It has two roads; one, by which we came, leads to it from the south-east, goes along the top of ravines and on either hand has hollows worn out by the torrents. A mile from Parhala this road, in four or five places before it reaches the Gate, becomes a one-man road with a ravine falling from its either side; there for more than an arrow's flight men must ride in single file. The other road comes from the north-west; it gets up to Parhala by the trough of a valley and it also is a one-man road. There is no other road on any side. Parhala though without breast-work or battlement, has no assailable place, its sides shooting perpendicu-

larly down for 7, 8, 10 yards.

When the van of our left, having passed the narrow place, went in a body to the Gate, Hati, with whom were 30 to 40 men in armour, their horses in mail, and a mass of foot-soldiers, forced his assailants to retire. Dost Beg led his reserve forward, made a strong attack, dismounted a number of Hati's men, and beat him. All the country-round, Hati was celebrated for his daring, but try as he did, he could effect nothing; he took to flight; he could not make a stand in those narrow places; he could not make the fort fast when he got back into it. His assailants went in just behind him and ran on through the ravine and narrows of the north-west side of the fort, but he rode light and made his flight good. Here again, Dost Beg did very well and recompense was added to renown.[1]

Meantime I had gone into the fort and dismounted at Tatar *Kakar*'s dwelling. Several men had joined in the attack for whom to stay with me had been arranged; amongst them were Amin-i-muhammad Tarkhan *Arghun* and Qaracha.[2] For this

[1] *Juldu Dost Beg-ning ati-gha buldi.*
[2] The disarray of these names in the MSS. reveals confusion in their source. Similar verbal disarray occurs in the latter part of f. 229.

fault they were sent to meet the camp, without *sar-u-pa*, into the wilds and open country with Sar-u-pa[1] for their guide, the Gujur mentioned already.

(*March 16th*) Next day we went out by the north-west ravine and dismounted in a sown field. A few serviceable braves under Wali the treasurer were sent out to meet the camp.[2]

(*March 17th*) Marching on Thursday the 15th, we dismounted at Andaraba on the Suhan, a fort said to have depended from of old on ancestors of Malik Hast. Hati *Kakar* had killed Malik Hast's father and destroyed the fort; there it now lay in ruins. Fol. 231.

At the Bed-time Prayer of this same day, those left at Kalda-kahar with the camp rejoined us.

(r. Submissions to Babur.)

It must have been after Hati overcame Tatar that he started his kinsman Parbat to me with tribute and an accoutred horse. Parbat did not light upon us but, meeting in with the camp we had left behind, came on in the company of the train. With it came also Langar Khan up from Bhira on matters of business. His affairs were put right and he, together with several local people, was allowed to leave.

(*March 18th*) Marching on and crossing the Suhan-water, we dismounted on the rising-ground. Here Hati's kinsman (Parbat) was robed in an honorary dress (*khil'at*), given letters of encouragement for Hati, and despatched with a servant of Muhammad 'Ali *Jang-jang*. Nil-ab and the Qarluq (Himalayan?) Hazara had been given to Humayun (*aet.* 12); some of his servants under Baba Dost and Halahil came now for their darogha-ship.[3] Sangur Khan Qarluq and Mirza-i-malui Qarluq came leading 30 or 40 men of the Qarluq elders, made offering of a horse in mail, and waited on me. Came also the army of the Dilah-zak Afghans.

(*March 19th*) Marching early next morning, we dismounted after riding 2 miles, went to view the camp from a height and ordered that the camp-camels should be counted; it came out at 570. Fol. 231b.

1 Manifestly a pun is made on the guide's name and on the *cap-à-pié* robe of honour the offenders did not receive.
2 *aurdu-ning aldi-gha*, a novel phrase.
3 I understand that the servants had come to do their equivalent for "kissing hands" on an appointment *viz.* to kneel.

We had heard of the qualities of the sambhal plant;[1] we saw it on this ground; along this hill-skirt it grows sparsely, a plant here, a plant there; it grows abundantly and to a large size further along the skirt-hills of Hindustan. It will be described when an account is given of the animals and plants of Hindustan.[2]

(*March 20th*) Marching from that camp at beat of drum (*i.e.* one hour before day), we dismounted at breakfast-time (9 a.m.) below the Sangdaki-pass, at mid-day marched on, crossed the pass, crossed the torrent, and dismounted on the rising-ground.

(*March 21st*) Marching thence at midnight, we made an excursion to the ford[3] we had crossed when on our way to Bhira. A great raft of grain had stuck in the mud of that same ford and, do what its owners would, could not be made to move. The corn was seized and shared out to those with us. Timely indeed was that corn!

Near noon we were a little below the meeting of the waters of Kabul and Sind, rather above old Nil-ab; we dismounted there between two waters.[4] From Nil-ab six boats were brought, and were apportioned to the right, left and centre, who busied themselves energetically in crossing the river (Indus). We got there on a Monday; they kept on crossing the water through the night preceding Tuesday (*March 22nd*), through Tuesday and up to Wednesday (*March 23rd*) and on Thursday (*24th*) also a few crossed.

Fol. 232.

Hati's kinsman Parbat, he who from Andaraba was sent to Hati with a servant of Muh. 'Ali *Jang-jang*, came to the bank of the river with Hati's offering of an accoutred horse. Nil-abis also came, brought an accoutred horse and did obeisance.

(*s. Various postings.*)

Muhammad 'Ali *Jang-jang* had wished to stay in Bhira but Bhira being bestowed on Hindu Beg, he was given the countries

1 spikenard. Speede's *Indian Handbook on Gardening* identifies *sambhal* with *Valeriana jatmansi* (Sir W. Jones & Roxburgh); "it is the real spikenard of the ancients, highly esteemed alike as a perfume and as a stimulant medicine; native practitioners esteeming it valuable in hysteria and epilepsy." Babur's word *dirakht* is somewhat large for the plant.
2 It is not given, however.   3 *i.e.* through the Indus.
4 Perhaps this *aiki-su-arasi* (*miyan-du-ab*) was the angle made by the Indus itself below Atak; perhaps one made by the Indus and an affluent.

between it and the Sind-river, such as the Qarluq Hazara, Hati, Ghiyas-wal and Kib (Kitib):—

> Where one is who submits like a *ra'iyat*, so treat him;
> But him who submits not, strike, strip, crush and force to obey.[1]

He also received a special head-wear in black velvet, a special Qilmaq corselet, and a standard. When Hati's kinsman was given leave to go he took for Hati a sword and head-to-foot (*bash-ayaq*) with a royal letter of encouragement.

(*March 24th*) On Thursday at sunrise we marched from the river's bank. That day confection was eaten. While under its influence[2] wonderful fields of flowers were enjoyed. In some places sheets of yellow flowers bloomed in plots; in others sheets of red (*arghwani*) flowers in plots, in some red and yellow bloomed together. We sat on a mound near the camp to enjoy the sight. There were flowers on all sides of the mound, yellow here, red there, as if arranged regularly to form a sextuple. On two sides there were fewer flowers but as far as the eye reached, flowers were in bloom. In spring near Parashawar the fields of flowers are very beautiful indeed.

Fol. 232b.

(*March 25th*) We marched from that ground at dawn. At one place on the road a tiger came out from the river's bank and roared. On hearing it, the horses, willy-nilly, flung off in terror, carrying their riders in all directions, and dashing into ravines and hollows. The tiger went again into the jungle. To bring it out, we ordered a buffalo brought and put on the edge of the jungle. The tiger again came out roaring. Arrows were shot at it from all sides;[3] I shot with the rest. Khalwi (var. Khalwa) a foot-soldier, pricked it with a spear; it bit the spear and broke off the spear-head. After tasting of those arrows, it went into the bushes (*buta*) and stayed there. Baba the waiting-man [*yasawal*] went with drawn sword close up to it; it sprang; he chopped at its head; 'Ali *Sistani*[4] chopped at its loins; it plunged into the river and was killed right in the water. It was got out and ordered to be skinned.

1 *See* Additional Notes, p. 798.
2 *ma'juni nakliki*, presumably under the tranquillity induced by the drug.
3 *massadus*, the six sides of the world, *i.e.* all sides.
4 This is the name of one of the five champions defeated by Babur in single combat in 914 AH. (Translator's Note *s.a.* 914 AH.).

(*March 26th*) Marching on next day, we reached Bigram and went to see Gur-khattri. This is a smallish abode, after the fashion of a hermitage (*sauma'at*), rather confined and dark. After entering at the door and going down a few steps, one must lie full length to get beyond. There is no getting in without a lamp. All round near the building there is let lie an enormous quantity of hair of the head and beard which men have shaved off there. There are a great many retreats (*hujra*) near Gur-khattri like those of a rest-house or a college. In the year we came into Kabul (910 AH.) and over-ran Kohat, Bannu and the plain, we made an excursion to Bigram, saw its great tree and were consumed with regret at not seeing Gur-khattri, but it does not seem a place to regret not-seeing.[1]

Fol. 233.

On this same day an excellent hawk of mine went astray out of Shaikhim the head-falconer's charge; it had taken many cranes and storks and had moulted (*tulab*) two or three times. So many things did it take that it made a fowler of a person so little keen as I!

At this place were bestowed 100 misqals of silver, clothing (*tunluq*), three bullocks and one buffalo, out of the offerings of Hindustan, on each of six persons, the chiefs of the Dilazak Afghans under Malik Bu Khan and Malik Musa; to others, in their degree, were given money, pieces of cloth, a bullock and a buffalo.

(*March 27th*) When we dismounted at 'Ali-masjid, a Dilazak Afghan of the Yaq'ub-khail, named Ma'ruf, brought an offering of 10 sheep, two ass-loads of rice and eight large cheeses.

(*March 28th*) Marching on from 'Ali-masjid, we dismounted at Yada-bir; from Yada-bir Jui-shahi was reached by the Mid-day Prayer and we there dismounted. Today Dost Beg was attacked by burning fever.

(*March 29th*) Marching from Jui-shahi at dawn, we ate our mid-day meal in the Bagh-i-wafa. At the Mid-day Prayer we betook ourselves out of the garden, close to the Evening Prayer forded the Siyah-ab at Gandamak, satisfied our horses' hunger in a field of green corn, and rode on in a *gari* or two (24–48 min.).

1 f. 145*b*.

After crossing the Surkh-ab, we dismounted at Kark and took a sleep.

(*March 30th*) Riding before shoot of day from Kark, I went with 5 or 6 others by the road taking off for Qara-tu in order to enjoy the sight of a garden there made. Khalifa and Shah Hasan Beg and the rest went by the other road to await me at Quruq-sai.

When we reached Qara-tu, Shah Beg *Arghun*'s commissary (*tawachi*) Qizil (Rufus) brought word that Shah Beg had taken Kahan, plundered it and retired.

An order had been given that no-one soever should take news of us ahead. We reached Kabul at the Mid-day Prayer, no person in it knowing about us till we got to Qutluq-qadam's bridge. As Humayun and Kamran heard about us only after that, there was not time to put them on horseback; they made their pages carry them, came, and did obeisance between the gates of the town and the citadel.[1] At the Other Prayer there waited on me Qasim Beg, the town Qazi, the retainers left in Kabul and the notables of the place.

(*April 2nd*) At the Other Prayer of Friday the 1st of the second Rabi' there was a wine-party at which a special head-to-foot (*bash-ayaq*) was bestowed on Shah Hasan.

(*April 3rd*) At dawn on Saturday we went on board a boat and took our morning.[2] Nur Beg, then not obedient (*ta'ib*), played the lute at this gathering. At the Mid-day Prayer we left the boat to visit the garden made between Kul-kina[3] and the mountain (Shah-i-kabul). At the Evening Prayer we went to the Violet-garden where there was drinking again. From Kul-kina I got in by the rampart and went into the citadel.

(*u. Dost Beg's death.*)

(*April 6th*) On the night of Tuesday the 5th of the month,[4] Dost Beg, who on the road had had fever, went to God's mercy.

1 Humayun was 12, Kamran younger; one surmises that Babur would have walked under the same circumstances.

2 *sabuhi*, the morning-draught. In 1623 AD. Pietro della Vallé took a *sabuhi* with Mr. Thomas Rastel, the head of the merchants of Surat, which was of hot spiced wine and sipped in the mornings to comfort the stomach (Hakluyt ed. p. 20).

3 f. 128 and note.

4 Anglicé, in the night preceding Tuesday.

Sad and grieved enough we were! His bier and corpse were
carried to Ghazni where they laid him in front of the gate of the
Sultan's garden (*rauza*).

Dost Beg had been a very good brave (*yikit*) and he was still
rising in rank as a beg. Before he was made a beg, he did
excellent things several times as one of the household. One
time was at Rabat-i-zauraq,[1] one *yighach* from Andijan when Sl.
Ahmad *Tambal* attacked me at night (908 AH.). I, with 10 to 15
men, by making a stand, had forced his gallopers back; when we
reached his centre, he made a stand with as many as 100 men;
there were then three men with me, *i.e.* there were four
counting myself. Nasir's Dost (*i.e.* Dost Beg) was one of the
three; another was Mirza Quli *Kukuldash*; Karim-dad *Turkman*
was the other. I was just in my *jiba*;[2] Tambal and another were
standing like gate-wards in front of his array; I came face to face
with Tambal, shot an arrow striking his helm; shot another
aiming at the attachment of his shield; they shot one through
my leg (*butum*); Tambal chopped at my head. It was wonderful!
The (under)-cap of my helm was on my head; not a thread of it
was cut, but on the head itself was a very bad wound. Of other
help came none; no-one was left with me; of necessity I brought
myself to gallop back. Dost Beg had been a little in my rear;
(Tambal) on leaving me alone, chopped at him.[3]

Fol. 234*b*.   Again, when we were getting out of Akhsi [908 AH.],[4] Dost
Beg chopped away at Baqi *Hiz*[5] who, although people called
him *Hiz*, was a mighty master of the sword. Dost Beg was one
of the eight left with me after we were out of Akhsi; he was
the third they unhorsed.

Again, after he had become a beg, when Siunjuk Khan
(*Auzbeg*), arriving with the (Auzbeg) sultans before Tashkint,
besieged Ahmad-i-qasim [*Kohbur*] in it [918 AH.],[6] Dost Beg

---

1 f. 106*b*.

2 This would be the under-corselet to which the four plates of mail were attached
when mail was worn. Babur in this adventure wore no mail, not even his helm; on
his head was the under-cap of the metal helm.

3 The earlier account helps to make this one clearer (f. 106*b*).

4 f. 112 *et seq*.

5 Catamite, mistakenly read as *khiz* on f. 112*b* (*Mémoires* ii, 82).

6 He was acting for Babur (Translator's Note *s.a.*; H.S. iii, 318; T.R. pp. 260, 270).

passed through them and entered the town. During the siege he risked his honoured life splendidly, but Ahmad-i-qasim, without a word to this honoured man,[1] flung out of the town and got away. Dost Beg for his own part got the better of the Khan and sultans and made his way well out of Tashkint.

Later on when Sherim Taghai, Mazid and their adherents were in rebellion,[2] he came swiftly up from Ghazni with two or three hundred men, met three or four hundred effective braves sent out by those same Mughuls to meet him, unhorsed a mass of them near Sherukan (?), cut off and brought in a number of heads.

Again, his men were first over the ramparts at the fort of Bajaur (925 AH.). At Parhala, again, he advanced, beat Hati, put him to flight, and won Parhala.

After Dost Beg's death, I bestowed his district on his younger brother Nasir's Mirim.[3]

(v. Various incidents.)

(*April 9th*) On Friday the 8th of the second Rabi', the walled-town was left for the Char-bagh.

(*April 13th*) On Tuesday the 12th there arrived in Kabul the honoured Sultanim Begim, Sl. Husain Mirza's eldest daughter, the mother of Muhammad Sultan Mirza. During those throneless times,[4] she had settled down in Khwarizm where Yili-pars Fol. 235. Sultan's younger brother Aisan-quli Sl. took her daughter. The Bagh-i-khilwat was assigned her for her seat. When she had settled down and I went to see her in that garden, out of respect and courtesy to her, she being as my honoured elder sister, I bent the knee. She also bent the knee. We both advancing, saw one another mid-way. We always observed the same ceremony afterwards.

(*April 18th*) On Sunday the 17th, that traitor to his salt, Baba Shaikh[5] was released from his long imprisonment, forgiven his offences and given an honorary dress.

---

1 "Honoured," in this sentence, represents Babur's honorific plural.
2 in 921 AH. (Translator's Note *s.a.*; T.R. p. 356).
3 *i.e.* Mir Muhammad son of Nasir.
4 *i.e.* after the dethronement of the Bai-qara family by Shaibani.
5 He had been one of rebels of 921 AH. (Translator's Note *s.a.*; T.R. p. 356).

(w. Visit to the Koh-daman.)

(April 20th) On Tuesday the 19th of the month, we rode out at the return of noon for Khwaja Sih-yaran. This day I was fasting. All astonished, Yunas-i-'ali and the rest said, "A Tuesday! a journey! and a fast! This is amazing!" At Bih-zadi we dismounted at the Qazi's house. In the evening when a stir was made for a social gathering, the Qazi set this before me, "In my house such things never are; it is for the honoured Padshah to command!" For his heart's content, drink was left out, though all the material for a party was ready.

(April 21st) On Wednesday we went to Khwaja Sih-yaran.

(April 22nd) On Thursday the 22nd of the month, we had a large round seat made in the garden under construction on the mountain-naze.[1]

(April 23rd) On Friday we got on a raft from the bridge. On our coming opposite the fowlers' houses, they brought a *dang* (or *ding*)[2] they had caught. I had never seen one before; it is an odd-looking bird. It will come into the account of the birds of Hindustan.[3]

Fol. 235b.

(April 24th) On Saturday the 23rd of the month cuttings were planted, partly of plane, partly of *tal*,[4] above the round seat. At the Mid-day Prayer there was a wine-party at the place.

(April 25th) At dawn we took our morning on the new seat. At noon we mounted and started for Kabul, reached Khwaja Hasan quite drunk and slept awhile, rode on and by midnight got to the Char-bagh. At Khwaja Hasan, 'Abdu'l-lah, in his drunkenness, threw himself into water just as he was in his *tun aufraghi*.[5] He was frozen with cold and could not go on with us when we mounted after a little of the night had passed. He stayed on Qutluq Khwaja's estate that night. Next day, awakened to his past intemperance, he came on repentant. Said I, "At once! will this sort of repentance answer or not? Would to God you would repent now at once in such a way that you

---

1 f. 137.
2 This is the Adjutant-bird, Pir-i-dang and Hargila (Bone-swallower) of Hindustan, a migrant through Kabul. The fowlers who brought it would be the Multanis of f. 142b.
3 f. 280.
4 *Memoirs*, p. 267, sycamore; *Mémoires* ii, 84, *saules*; f. 137.
5 Perhaps with his long coat out-spread.

would drink nowhere except at my parties!" He agreed to this and kept the rule for a few months, but could not keep it longer.

(x. *Hindu Beg abandons Bhira*.)

(*April 26th*) On Monday the 25th came Hindu Beg. There having been hope of peace, he had been left in those countries with somewhat scant support. No sooner was our back turned than a mass of Hindustanis and Afghans gathered, disregarded us and, not listening to our words, moved against Hindu Beg in Bhira. The local peoples also went over to the Afghans. Hindu Beg could make no stand in Bhira, came to Khush-ab, came through the Din-kot country, came to Nil-ab, came on to Kabul. Fol. 236. Siktu's son Diwa *Hindu* and another Hindu had been brought prisoner from Bhira. Each now giving a considerable ransom, they were released. Horses and head-to-foot dresses having been given them, leave to go was granted.

(*April 30th*) On Friday the 29th of the month, burning fever appeared in my body. I got myself let blood. I had fever with sometimes two, sometimes three days between the attacks. In no attack did it cease till there had been sweat after sweat. After 10 or 12 days of illness, Mulla Khwajaka gave me narcissus mixed with wine; I drank it once or twice; even that did no good.

(*May 15th*) On Sunday the 15th of the first Jumada[1] Khwaja Muhammad 'Ali came from Khwast, bringing a saddled horse as an offering and also *tasadduq* money.[2] Muh. Sharif the astrologer and the Mir-zadas of Khwast came with him and waited on me.

(*May 16th*) Next day, Monday, Mulla Kabir came from Kashghar; he had gone round by Kashghar on his way from Andijan to Kabul.

(*May 23rd*) On Monday the 23rd of the month, Malik Shah Mansur *Yusuf-zai* arrived from Sawad with 6 or 7 Yusuf-zai chiefs, and did obeisance.

---

1 The fortnight's gap of record, here ended, will be due to illness.

2 f. 203*b* and n. to *Khams*, the Fifth. *Tasadduq* occurs also on f. 238 denoting money sent to Babur. Was it sent to him as Padshah, as the Qoran commands the *Khams* to be sent to the Imam, for the poor, the traveller and the orphan?

(*May 31st*) On Monday the 1st of the second Jumada, the chiefs of the Yusuf-zai Afghans led by Malik Shah Mansur were dressed in robes of honour (*khil'at*). To Malik Shah Mansur was given a long silk coat and an under-coat (?*jiba*) with its buttons; to one of the other chiefs was given a coat with silk sleeves, and to six others silk coats. To all leave to go was granted. Agreement was made with them that they were not

Fol. 236b. to reckon as in the country of Sawad what was above Abuha (?), that they should make all the peasants belonging to it go out from amongst themselves, and also that the Afghan cultivators of Bajaur and Sawad should cast into the revenue 6000 ass-loads of rice.

(*June 2nd*) On Wednesday the 3rd, I drank *jul-ab*.[1]

(*June 5th*) On Saturday the 6th, I drank a working-draught (*daru-i-kar*).

(*June 7th*) On Monday the 8th, arrived the wedding-gift for the marriage of Qasim Beg's youngest son Hamza with Khalifa's eldest daughter. It was of 1000 *shahrukhi*; they offered also a saddled horse.

(*June 8th*) On Tuesday Shah Beg's Shah Hasan asked for permission to go away for a wine-party. He carried off to his house Khwaja Muh. 'Ali and some of the household-begs. In my presence were Yunas-i-'ali and Gadai Taghai. I was still abstaining from wine. Said I, "Not at all in this way is it (*hech andaq bulmai dur*) that I will sit sober and the party drink wine, I stay sane, full of water, and that set (*bulak*) of people get drunk; come you and drink in my presence! I will amuse myself a little by watching what intercourse between the sober and the drunk is like."[2] The party was held in a smallish tent in which I sometimes sat, in the Plane-tree garden south-east of the Picture-hall. Later on Ghiyas the house-buffoon (*kidi*) arrived; several times for fun he was ordered kept out, but at last he made a great disturbance and his buffooneries found him a way in. We invited Tardi Muhammad *Qibchaq* also and

---

1 Rose-water, sherbet, a purgative; English, jalap, julep.
2 Mr. Erskine understood Babur to say that he never had sat sober while others drank; but this does not agree with the account of Harat entertainments [912 AH.], or with the tenses of the passage here. My impression is that he said in effect "Every-one here shall not be deprived of their wine".

Mulla *kitab-dar* (librarian). The following quatrain, written impromptu, was sent to Shah Hasan and those gathered in his house:—

Fol. 237.

> In your beautiful flower-bed of banqueting friends,
>   Our fashion it is not to be;
> If there be ease (*huzur*) in that gathering of yours,
> Thank God! there is here no un-ease [*bi huzur*].[1]

It was sent by Ibrahim *chuhra*. Between the two Prayers (*i.e.* afternoon) the party broke up drunk.

I used to go about in a litter while I was ill. The wine-mixture was drunk on several of the earlier days, then, as it did no good I left it off, but I drank it again at the end of my convalescence, at a party had under an apple-tree on the south-west side of the Talar-garden.

(*June 11th*) On Friday the 12th came Ahmad Beg and Sl. Muhammad *Duldai* who had been left to help in Bajaur.

(*June 16th*) On Wednesday the 17th of the month, Tingri-birdi and other braves gave a party in Haidar *Taqi's* garden; I also went and there drank. We rose from it at the Bed-time Prayer when a move was made to the great tent where again there was drinking.

(*June 23rd*) On Thursday the 25th of the month, Mulla Mahmud was appointed to read extracts from the Qoran[2] in my presence.

(*June 28th*) On Tuesday the last day of the month, Abu'l-muslim Kukuldash arrived as envoy from Shah Shuja' *Arghun* bringing a *tipuchaq*. After bargain made about swimming the reservoir in the Plane-tree garden, Yusuf-i-'ali the stirrup-holder swam round it today 100 times and received a gift of a head-to-foot (dress), a saddled horse and some money.

(*July 6th*) On Wednesday the 8th of Rajab, I went to Shah Hasan's house and drank there; most of the household and of the begs were present.

Fol. 237*b*

(*July 9th*) On Saturday the 11th, there was drinking on the terrace-roof of the pigeon-house between the Afternoon and Evening Prayers. Rather late a few horsemen were observed,

1 This verse, a difficult one to translate, may refer to the unease removed from his attendants by Babur's permission to drink; the pun in it might also refer to *well* and *not well*.

2 Presumably to aid his recovery. *See* Additional Notes, p. 798.

going from Dih-i-afghan towards the town. It was made out
to be Darwish-i-muhammad *Sarban*, on his way to me as the
envoy of Mirza Khan (Wais). We shouted to him from the roof,
"Drop the envoy's forms and ceremonies! Come! come without
formality!" He came and sat down in the company. He was
then obedient and did not drink. Drinking went on till the end
of the evening. Next day he came into the Court Session with
due form and ceremony, and presented Mirza Khan's gifts.

(*y. Various incidents.*)

Last year[1] with 100 efforts, much promise and threats, we had got
the clans to march into Kabul from the other side (of Hindu-kush).
Kabul is a confined country, not easily giving summer and winter
quarters to the various flocks and herds of the Turks and (Mughul?)
clans. If the dwellers in the wilds follow their own hearts, they do
not wish for Kabul! They now waited (*khidmat qilib*) on Qasim
Beg and made him their mediator with me for permission to
re-cross to that other side. He tried very hard, so in the end, they
were allowed to cross over to the Qunduz and Baghlan side.

Hafiz the news-writer's elder brother had come from Samarkand; when I now gave him leave to return, I sent my *Diwan*
by him to Pulad Sultan.[2] On the back of it I wrote the following

Fol. 238. verse:—

> O breeze! if thou enter that cypress' chamber (*harim*)
> Remind her of me, my heart reft by absence;
> She yearns not for Babur; he fosters a hope
> That her heart of steel God one day may melt.[3]

(*July 15th*) On Friday the 17th of the month, Shaikh Mazid
Kukuldash waited on me from Muhammad-i-zaman Mirza,
bringing *tasadduq* tribute and a horse.[4] Today Shah Beg's
envoy Abu'l-muslim Kukuldash was robed in an honorary dress

---

1 *autkan yil*, perhaps in the last and unchronicled year; perhaps in earlier ones.
There are several references in the B.N. to the enforced migrations and emigrations
of tribes into Kabul.

2 Pulad (Steel) was a son of Kuchum, the then Khaqan of the Auzbegs, and
Mihr-banu who may be Babur's half-sister. [Index *s.n.*]

3 This may be written for Mihr-banu, Pulad's mother and Babur's half-sister (?)
and a jest made on her heart as Pulad's and as steel to her brother. She had not left
husband and son when Babur got the upper hand, as his half-sister Yadgar-sultan
did and other wives of capture *e.g.* Haidar's sister *Habiba*. Babur's rhymes in this
verse are not of his later standard, *ai subah, kunkulika, kunkuli-ka.*

4 *Tasadduq* sent to Babur would seem an acknowledgment of his suzerainty in
Balkh.

and given leave to go. Today also leave was given for their
own districts of Khwast and Andar-ab to Khwaja Muhammad
'Ali and Tingri-birdi.

(*July 21st*) On Thursday the 23rd came Muh. 'Ali *Jang-jang*
who had been left in charge of the countries near Kacha-kot
and the Qarluq. With him came one of Hati's people and
Mirza-i-malu-i-qarluq's son Shah Hasan. Today Mulla 'Ali-jan
waited on me, returned from fetching his wife from Samarkand.

(*z. The 'Abdu'r-rahman Afghans and Rustam-maidan.*)

(*July 27th*) The 'Abdu'r-rahman Afghans on the Girdiz border
were satisfactory neither in their tribute nor their behaviour;
they were hurtful also to the caravans which came and went.
On Wednesday the 29th of Rajab we rode out to over-run them.
We dismounted and ate food near Tang-i-waghchan,[1] and rode
on again at the Mid-day Prayer. In the night we lost the road
and got much bewildered in the ups and downs of the land to
the south-east of Patakh-i-ab-i-shakna.[2] After a time we lit on   Fol. 238*b.*
a road and by it crossed the Chashma-i-tura[3] pass.

(*July 28th*) At the first prayer (*farz-waqt*) we got out from
the valley-bottom adjacent[4] to the level land, and the raid was
allowed. One detachment galloped towards the Kar-mash[5]
mountain, south-east of Girdiz, the left-hand of the centre led
by Khusrau, Mirza Quli and Sayyid 'Ali in their rear. Most of
the army galloped up the dale to the east of Girdiz, having in
their rear men under Sayyid Qasim Lord of the Gate, Mir Shah
Quchin, Qayyam (Aurdu-shah Beg?), Hindu Beg, Qutluq-qadam
and Husain [Hasan?]. Most of the army having gone up the
dale, I followed at some distance. The dalesmen must have
been a good way up; those who went after them wore their
horses out and nothing to make up for this fell into their hands.

Some Afghans on foot, some 40 or 50 of them, having appeared
on the plain, the rear-reserve went towards them. A courier
was sent to me and I hastened on at once. Before I got up

1 This is the Girdiz-pass [Raverty's *Notes*, Route 101].
2 Raverty (p. 677) suggests that Patakh stands for *batqaq*, a quagmire (f. 16 and n.).
3 the dark, or cloudy spring.
4 *yaqish-liq qul*, an unusual phrase.
5 var. Karman, Kurmah, Karmas. M. de C. read Kir-mas, the impenetrable. The
forms would give Garm-as, hot embers.

with them, Husain Hasan, all alone, foolishly and thoughtlessly, put his horse at those Afghans, got in amongst them and began to lay on with his sword. They shot his horse, thus made him fall, slashed at him as he was getting up, flung him down, knifed him from all sides and cut him to pieces, while the other braves looked on, standing still and reaching him no helping hand! On hearing news of it, I hurried still faster forward, and sent some of the household and braves galloping loose-rein ahead

Fol. 239. under Gadai Taghai, Payanda-i-muhammad *Qiplan*, Abu'l-hasan the armourer and Mumin Ataka. Mumin Ataka was the first of them to bring an Afghan down; he speared one, cut off his head and brought it in. Abu'l-hasan the armourer, without mail as he was, went admirably forward, stopped in front of the Afghans, laid his horse at them, chopped at one, got him down, cut off and brought in his head. Known though both were for bravelike deeds done earlier, their action in this affair added to their fame. Every one of those 40 or 50 Afghans, falling to the arrow, falling to the sword, was cut in pieces. After making a clean sweep of them, we dismounted in a field of growing corn and ordered a tower of their heads to be set up. As we went along the road I said, with anger and scorn, to the begs who had been with Husain, "You! what men! there you stood on quite flat ground, and looked on while a few Afghans on foot overcame such a brave in the way they did! Your rank and station must be taken from you; you must lose *pargana* and country; your beards must be shaved off and you must be exhibited in towns; for there shall be punishment assuredly for

Fol. 239b. him who looks on while such a brave is beaten by such a foe on dead-level land, and reaches out no hand to help!" The troop which went to Kar-mash brought back sheep and other spoil. One of them was Baba Qashqa[1] *Mughul*; an Afghan had made at him with a sword; he had stood still to adjust an arrow, shot it off and brought his man down.

(*July 29th*) Next day at dawn we marched for Kabul. Paymaster Muhammad, 'Abdu'l-'aziz Master of the Horse, and Mir Khurd the taster were ordered to stop at Chashma-tura, and get pheasants from the people there.

---

1 *balafré*; marked on the face; of a horse, starred. For Baba Qashqa's family group, *see* Additional Notes, pp. 798–9.

As I had never been along the Rustam-maidan road,[1] I went with a few men to see it. Rustam-plain (*maidan*) lies amongst mountains and towards their head is not a very charming place. The dale spreads rather broad between its two ranges. To the south, on the skirt of the rising-ground is a smallish spring, having very large poplars near it. There are many trees also, but not so large, at the source on the way out of Rustam-maidan for Girdiz. This is a narrower dale, but still there is a plot of green meadow below the smaller trees mentioned, and the little dale is charming. From the summit of the range, looking south, the Karmash and Bangash mountains are seen at one's feet; and beyond the Karmash show pile upon pile of the rain-clouds of Hindustan. Towards those other lands where no rain falls, not a cloud is seen.   Fol. 240.

We reached Huni at the Mid-day Prayer and there dismounted.

(*July 30th*) Dismounting next day at Muhammad Agha's village,[2] we perpetrated (*irtqab*) a *ma'jun*. There we had a drug thrown into water for the fish; a few were taken.[3]

(*July 31st*) On Sunday the 3rd of Sha'ban, we reached Kabul.

(*August 2nd*) On Tuesday the 5th of the month, Darwish-i-muhammad *Fazli* and Khusrau's servants were summoned and, after enquiry made into what short-comings of theirs there may have been when Husain was overcome, they were deprived of place and rank. At the Mid-day Prayer there was a wine-party under a plane-tree, at which an honorary dress was given to Baba Qashqa *Mughul*.

(*August 5th*) On Friday the 8th Kipa returned from the presence of Mirza Khan.

(*aa. Excursion to the Koh-daman.*)

(*August 11th*) On Thursday at the Other Prayer, I mounted for an excursion to the Koh-daman, Baran and Khwaja Sih-yaran.[4] At the Bed-time Prayer, we dismounted at Mama Khatun.[5]

1 Raverty's *Notes* (p. 457) give a full account of this valley; in it are the head-waters of the Tochi and the Zurmut stream; and in it R. locates Rustam's ancient Zabul.
2 It is on the Kabul side of the Girdiz-pass and stands on the Luhugur-water (Logar).
3 f. 143.
4 At this point of the text there occurs in the Elph. MS. (f. 195b) a note, manifestly copied from one marginal in an archetype, which states that what follows is copied from Babur's own MS. The note (and others) can be seen in JRAS 1905 p. 754 *et seq.*
5 Masson, iii, 145.

(*August 12th*) Next day we dismounted at Istalif; a confection was eaten on that day.

(*August 13th*) On Saturday there was a wine-party at Istalif.

(*August 14th*) Riding at dawn from Istalif, we crossed the space between it and the Sinjid-valley. Near Khwaja Sih-yaran a great snake was killed as thick, it may be, as the fore-arm and as long as a *qulach*.[1] From its inside came out a slenderer snake, that seemed to have been just swallowed, every part of it being Fol. 240*b*. whole; it may have been a little shorter than the larger one. From inside this slenderer snake came out a little mouse; it too was whole, broken nowhere.[2]

On reaching Khwaja Sih-yaran there was a wine-party. To-day orders were written and despatched by Kich-kina the night-watch (*tunqtar*) to the begs on that side (*i.e.* north of Hindu-kush), giving them a rendezvous and saying, "An army is being got to horse, take thought, and come to the rendezvous fixed."

(*August 15th*) We rode out at dawn and ate a confection. At the infall of the Parwan-water many fish were taken in the local way of casting a fish-drug into the water.[3] Mir Shah Beg set food and water (*ash u ab*) before us; we then rode on to Gul-bahar. At a wine-party held after the Evening Prayer, Darwish-i-muhammad (*Sarban*) was present. Though a young man and a soldier, he had not yet committed the sin (*irtqab*) of wine, but was in obedience (*ta'ib*). Qutluq Khwaja *Kukuldash* had long before abandoned soldiering to become a darwish; moreover he was very old, his very beard was quite white; nevertheless he took his share of wine at these parties. Said I to Darwish-i-muhammad, "Qutluq Khwaja's beard shames you! He, a darwish and an old man, always drinks wine; you, a soldier, a young man, your beard quite black, never drink! What does it mean?" My custom being not to press wine on a non-drinker, with so much said, it all passed off as a joke; he was not pressed to drink.

---

1 A *qulach* is from finger-tip to finger-tip of the outstretched arms (Zenker p. 720 and *Méms.* ii, 98).
2 Neither *interne* is said to have died!   3 f. 143.

(*August 16th*) At dawn we made our morning (*subahi subuhi qilduk*).

(*August 17th*) Riding on Wednesday from Gul-i-bahar, we dismounted in Abun-village[1] ate food, remounted, went to a summer-house in the orchards (*baghat-i-kham*) and there dismounted. There was a wine-party after the Mid-day Prayer. Fol. 241.

(*August 18th*) Riding on next day, we made the circuit of Khwaja Khawand Sa'id's tomb, went to China-fort and there got on a raft. Just where the Panjhir-water comes in, the raft struck the naze of a hill and began to sink. Rauh-dam, Tingri-quli and Mir Muhammad the raftsman were thrown into the water by the shock; Rauh-dam and Tingri-quli were got on the raft again; a China cup and a spoon and a tambour went into the water. Lower down, the raft struck again opposite the Sang-i-barida (the cut-stone), either on a branch in mid-stream or on a stake stuck in as a stop-water (*qaqghan qazuq*). Right over on his back went Shah Beg's Shah Hasan, clutching at Mirza Quli Kukuldash and making him fall too. Darwish-i-muhammad *Sarban* was also thrown into the water. Mirza Quli went over in his own fashion! Just when he fell, he was cutting a melon which he had in his hand; as he went over, he stuck his knife into the mat of the raft. He swam in his *tun aufraghi*[2] and got out of the water without coming on the raft again. Leaving it that night, we slept at raftsmen's houses. Darwish-i-muhammad *Sarban* presented me with a seven-coloured cup exactly like the one lost in the water.

(*August 19th*) On Friday we rode away from the river's bank and dismounted below Aindiki on the skirt of Koh-i-bacha where, with our own hands, we gathered plenty of tooth-picks.[3] Fol. 241b. Passing on, food was eaten at the houses of the Khwaja Khizr people. We rode on and at the Mid-day Prayer dismounted in a village of Qutluq Khwaja's fief in Lamghan where he made ready a hasty meal (*ma haziri*); after partaking of this, we mounted and went to Kabul.

---

1 or Atun's-village, one granted to Babur's mother's old governess (f. 96); Gul-badan's guest-list has also an Atun Mama.

2 f. 235b and note.

3 *miswak*; *On les tire principalement de l'arbuste épineux appelé capparis-sodata* (de C. ii, 101 n.).

(*bb. Various incidents.*)

(*August 22nd*) On Monday the 25th, a special honorary dress and a saddled horse were bestowed on Darwish-i-muhammad *Sarban* and he was made to kneel as a retainer (*naukar*).

(*August 24th*) For 4 or 5 months I had not had my head shaved; on Wednesday the 27th, I had it done. Today there was a wine-party.

(*August 26th*) On Friday the 29th, Mir Khurd was made to kneel as Hind-al's guardian.[1] He made an offering of 1000 *shahrukhis* (*circa* £50).

(*August 31st*) On Wednesday the 5th of Ramzan, a dutiful letter was brought by Tulik Kukuldash's servant Barlas Juki(?). Auzbeg raiders had gone into those parts (Badakhshan); Tulik had gone out, fought and beaten them. Barlas Juki brought one live Auzbeg and one head.

(*Sep. 2nd*) In the night of Saturday the 8th, we broke our fast[2] in Qasim Beg's house; he led out a saddled horse for me.

(*Sep. 3rd*) On Sunday night the fast was broken in Khalifa's house; he offered me a saddled horse.

(*Sep. 4th*) Next day came Khwaja Muh. 'Ali and Jan-i-nasir who had been summoned from their districts for the good of the army.[3]

(*Sep. 7th*) On Wednesday the 12th, Kamran's maternal uncle Sl. 'Ali Mirza arrived.[4] As has been mentioned,[5] he had gone to Kashghar in the year I came from Khwast into Kabul.

Fol. 242.

(*cc. A Yusuf-zai campaign.*)

(*Sep. 8th*) We rode out on Thursday the 13th of the month of Ramzan, resolved and determined to check and ward off the

1 Gul-badan's H.N. Index s.n.
2 This being Ramzan, Babur did not break his fast till sun-set. In like manner, during Ramzan they eat in the morning before sun-rise (Erskine).
3 A result, doubtless, of the order mentioned on f. 240*b*.
4 Babur's wife Gul-rukh appears to have been his sister or niece; he was a Beg-chik. *Cf.* Gul-badan's H.N. trs. p. 233, p. 234; T.R. p. 264–5.
5 This remark bears on the question of whether we now have all Babur wrote of Autobiography. It refers to a date falling within the previous gap, because the man went to Kashghar while Babur was ruling in Samarkand (T.R. p. 265). The last time Babur came from Khwast to Kabul was probably in 920 AH.; if later, it was still in the gap. But an alternative explanation is that looking over and annotating the diary section, Babur made this reference to what he fully meant to write but died before being able to do so.

Yusuf-zai, and we dismounted in the meadow on the Dih-i-yaq'ub side of Kabul. When we were mounting, the equerry Baba Jan led forward a rather good-for-nothing horse; in my anger I struck him in the face a blow which dislocated my fist below the ring-finger.[1] The pain was not much at the time, but was rather bad when we reached our encampment-ground. For some time I suffered a good deal and could not write. It got well at last.

To this same assembly-ground were brought letters and presents (*bilak*) from my maternal-aunt Daulat-sultan Khanim[2] in Kashghar, by her foster-brother Qutluq-muhammad. On the same day Bu Khan and Musa, chiefs of the Dilazak, came, bringing tribute, and did obeisance.

(*Sep. 11th*) On Sunday the 16th Quj Beg came.

(*Sep. 14th*) Marching on Wednesday the 19th we passed through But-khak and, as usual, dismounted on the But-khak water.[3]

As Quj Beg's districts, Bamian, Kah-mard and Ghuri, are close to the Auzbeg, he was excused from going with this army and given leave to return to them from this ground. I bestowed on him a turban twisted for myself, and also a head-to-foot (*bash-ayaq*).

(*Sep. 16th*) On Friday the 21st, we dismounted at Badam-   Fol. 242b.
chashma.

(*Sep. 17th*) Next day we dismounted on the Barik-ab, I reaching the camp after a visit to Qara-tu. On this ground honey was obtained from a tree.

(*Sep. 20th*) We went on march by march till Wednesday the 26th, and dismounted in the Bagh-i-wafa.

(*Sep. 21st*) Thursday we just stayed in the garden.

(*Sep. 22nd*) On Friday we marched out and dismounted beyond Sultanpur. Today Shah Mir Husain came from his country. Today came also Dilazak chiefs under Bu Khan and

---

1 Anglicé, the right thumb, on which the archer's ring (*zih-gir*) is worn.

2 a daughter of Yunas Khan, Haidar's account of whom is worth seeing.

3 *i.e.* the water of Luhugur (Logar). Tradition says that But-khak (Idol-dust) was so named because there Sl. Mahmud of Ghazni had idols, brought by him out of Hindustan, pounded to dust. Raverty says the place is probably the site of an ancient temple (*vahara*).

Musa. My plan had been to put down the Yusuf-zai in Sawad, but these chiefs set forth to me that there was a large horde (*aulus*) in Hash-naghar and that much corn was to be had there. They were very urgent for us to go to Hash-naghar. After consultation the matter was left in this way:—As it is said there is much corn in Hash-naghar, the Afghans there shall be over-run; the forts of Hash-naghar and Parashawar shall be put into order; part of the corn shall be stored in them and they be left in charge of Shah Mir Husain and a body of braves. To suit Shah Mir Husain's convenience in this, he was given 15 days leave, with a rendezvous named for him to come to after going to his country and preparing his equipment.

(*Sep. 23rd*) Marching on next day, we reached Jui-shahi and there dismounted. On this ground Tingri-birdi and Sl. Muhammad *Duldai* overtook us. Today came also Hamza from Qunduz.[1]

(*Sep. 25th*) On Sunday the last day of the month (Ramzan), we marched from Jui-shahi and dismounted at Qiriq-ariq (forty-conduits), I going by raft, with a special few. The new moon of the Feast was seen at that station.[2] People had brought a few beast-loads of wine from Nur-valley;[3] after the Evening Prayer there was a wine-party, those present being Muhibb-i-'ali the armourer, Khwaja Muh. 'Ali the librarian, Shah Beg's Shah Hasan, Sl. Muh. *Duldai* and Darwish-i-muh. *Sarban*, then obedient (*ta'ib*). From my childhood up it had been my rule not to press wine on a non-drinker; Darwish-i-muhammad was at every party and no pressure was put on him (by me), but Khwaja Muh. 'Ali left him no choice; he pressed him and pressed him till he made him drink.

(*Sep. 26th*) On Monday we marched with the dawn of the Feast-day,[4] eating a confection on the road to dispel crop-sickness. While under its composing influence (*naklik*), we were brought a colocynth-apple (*hunzal*). Darwish-i-muhammad had never

1 Qasim Beg's son, come, no doubt, in obedience to the order of f. 240*b*.
2 The 'Id-i-fitr is the festival at the conclusion of the feast of Ramzan, celebrated on seeing the new moon of Shawwal (Erskine).
3 f. 133*b* and Appendix G, *On the names of tow Dara-i-Nur wines.*
4 *i.e.* of the new moon of Shawwal. The new moon having been seen the evening before, which to Musalmans was Monday evening, they had celebrated the 'Id-i-fitr on Monday eve (Erskine).

seen one; said I, "It is a melon of Hindustan," sliced it and gave him a piece. He bit into it at once; it was night before the bitter taste went out of his mouth. At Garm-chashma we dismounted on rising-ground where cold meat was being set out for us when Langar Khan arrived to wait on me after being for a time at his own place (Koh-i-jud). He brought an offering of a horse and a few confections. Passing on, we dismounted at Yada-bir, at the Other Prayer got on a raft there, went for as much as two miles on it, then left it.

(*Sep. 27th*) Riding on next morning, we dismounted below the Khaibar-pass. Today arrived Sl. Bayazid, come up by the Fol. 243*b*. Bara-road after hearing of us; he set forth that the Afridi Afghans were seated in Bara with their goods and families and that they had grown a mass of corn which was still standing (lit. on foot). Our plan being for the Yusuf-zai Afghans of Hash-naghar, we paid him no attention. At the Mid-day Prayer there was a wine-party in Khwaja Muhammad 'Ali's tent. During the party details about our coming in this direction were written and sent off by the hand of a sultan of Tirah to Khwaja Kalan in Bajaur. I wrote this couplet on the margin of the letter (*farman*):—

> Say sweetly o breeze, to that beautiful fawn,
> Thou hast given my head to the hills and the wild.[1]

(*Sep. 28th*) Marching on at dawn across the pass, we got through the Khaibar-narrows and dismounted at 'Ali-masjid. At the Mid-day Prayer we rode on, leaving the baggage behind, reached the Kabul-water at the second watch (midnight) and there slept awhile.

(*Sep. 29th*) A ford[2] was found at daylight; we had forded the water (*su-din kichildi*), when news came from our scout that the Afghans had heard of us and were in flight. We went on, passed through the Sawad-water and dismounted amongst the Afghan corn-fields. Not a half, not a fourth indeed of the promised corn was had. The plan of fitting-up Hash-naghar, made under the hope of getting corn here, came to nothing. Fol. 244.

---

1 Diwan of Hafiz lith. ed. p. 22. The couplet seems to be another message to a woman (f. 238); here it might be to Bibi Mubaraka, still under Khwaja Kalan's charge in Bajaur (f. 221).

2 Here and under date Sep. 30th the wording allows a ford.

The Dilazak Afghans, who had urged it on us, were ashamed. We next dismounted after fording the water of Sawad to its Kabul side.

(*Sep. 30th*) Marching next morning from the Sawad-water, we crossed the Kabul-water and dismounted. The Begs admitted to counsel were summoned and a consultation having been had, the matter was left at this:—that the Afridi Afghans spoken of by Sl. Bayazid should be over-run, Purshawur-fort be fitted up on the strength of their goods and corn, and some-one left there in charge.

At this station Hindu Beg *Quchin* and the Mir-zadas of Khwast overtook us. Today *ma'jun* was eaten, the party being Darwesh-i-muhammad *Sarban*, Muhammad Kukuldash, Gadai Taghai and 'Asas; later on we invited Shah Hasan also. After food had been placed before us, we went on a raft, at the Other Prayer. We called Langar Khan *Nia-zai* on also. At the Evening Prayer we got off the raft and went to camp.

(*Oct. 1st*) Marching at dawn, in accordance with the arrangement made on the Kabul-water, we passed Jam and dismounted at the outfall of the 'Ali-masjid water.[1]

(dd. Badakhshan affairs.)

Sl. 'Ali (Taghai's servant?) Abu'l-hashim overtaking us, said, "On the night of 'Arafa,[2] I was in Jui-shahi with a person from Badakhshan; he told me that Sl. Sa'id Khan had come with designs on Badakhshan, so I came on from Jui-shahi along the Jam-rud, to give the news to the Padshah." On this the begs were summoned and advice was taken. In consequence of this news, it seemed inadvisable to victual the fort (Purshawur), and we started back intending to go to Badakhshan.[3] Langar Khan was appointed to help Muh. 'Ali *Jang-jang*; he was given an honorary dress and allowed to go.

Fol. 244b.

1 This may be what Masson writes of (i, 149) "We reached a spot where the water supplying the rivulet (of 'Ali-masjid) gushes in a large volume from the rocks to the left. I slaked my thirst in the living spring and drank to repletion of the delightfully cool and transparent water."

2 Mr. Erskine here notes, "This appears to be a mistake or oversight of Babur. The eve of 'Arafa (9th of Zu'l-hijja) "was not till the evening of Dec. 2nd 1519. He probably meant to say the 'Id-i-fitr which had occurred only five days before, on Sep. 26th."

3 This was an affair of frontiers (T.R. p. 354).

That night a wine-party was held in Khwaja Muh. 'Ali's tent. We marched on next day, crossed Khaibar and dismounted below the pass.

(*ee. The Khizr-khail Afghans.*)

(*Oct. 3rd*) Many improper things the Khizr-khail had done! When the army went to and fro, they used to shoot at the laggards and at those dismounted apart, in order to get their horses. It seemed lawful therefore and right to punish them. With this plan we marched from below the pass at daybreak, ate our mid-day meal in Dih-i-ghulaman (Basaul),[1] and after feeding our horses, rode on again at the Mid-day Prayer.

Muh. Husain the armourer was made to gallop off to Kabul with orders to keep prisoner all Khizr-khailis there, and to submit to me an account of their possessions; also, to write a detailed account of whatever news there was from Badakhshan and to send a man off with it quickly from Kabul to me.

That night we moved on till the second watch (midnight), got a little beyond Sultanpur, there slept awhile, then rode on again. The Khizr-khail were understood to have their seat from Bahar (Vihara?) and Mich-gram to Kara-su (*sic*). Arriving before dawn, (*Oct. 4th*) the raid was allowed. Most of the goods of the Khizr-khailis and their small children fell into the army's hands; a few tribesmen, being near the mountains, drew off to them and were left. Fol. 245.

(*Oct. 5th*) We dismounted next day at Qilaghu where pheasants were taken on our ground. Today the baggage came up from the rear and was unloaded here. Owing to this punitive raid, the Waziri Afghans who never had given in their tribute well, brought 300 sheep.

(*Oct. 9th*) I had written nothing since my hand was dislocated; here I wrote a little, on Sunday the 14th of the month.[2]

(*Oct. 10th*) Next day came Afghan chiefs leading the Khirilchi [and] Samu-khail. The Dilazak Afghans entreated pardon for them; we gave it and set the captured free, fixed their tribute at 4000 sheep, gave coats (*tun*) to their chiefs, appointed and sent out collectors.

1 Manucci gives an account of the place (Irvine iv, 439 and ii, 447).
2 Sep. 8th to Oct. 9th.

(*Oct. 13th*) These matters settled, we marched on Thursday the 13th, and dismounted at Bahar (Vihara?) and Mich-gram.

(*Oct. 14th*) Next day I went to the Bagh-i-wafa. Those were the days of the garden's beauty; its lawns were one sheet of trefoil; its pomegranate-trees yellowed to autumn splendour,[1] their fruit full red; fruit on the orange-trees green and glad (*khurram*), countless oranges but not yet as yellow as our hearts desired! The pomegranates were excellent, not equal, however, to the best ones of Wilayat.[2] The one excellent and blessed content we have had from the Bagh-i-wafa was had at this time.

Fol. 245*b*. We were there three or four days; during the time the whole camp had pomegranates in abundance.

(*Oct. 17th*) We marched from the garden on Monday. I stayed in it till the first watch (9 a.m.) and gave away oranges; I bestowed the fruit of two trees on Shah Hasan; to several begs I gave the fruit of one tree each; to some gave one tree for two persons. As we were thinking of visiting Lamghan in the winter, I ordered that they should reserve (*qurughlailar*) at least 20 of the trees growing round the reservoir. That day we dismounted at Gandamak.

(*Oct. 18th*) Next day we dismounted at Jagdalik. Near the Evening Prayer there was a wine-party at which most of the household were present. After a time Qasim Beg's sister's son Gadai *bihjat*[3] used very disturbing words and, being drunk, slid down on the cushion by my side, so Gadai Taghai picked him up and carried him out from the party.

(*Oct. 19th*) Marching next day from that ground, I made an excursion up the valley-bottom of the Barik-ab towards Quruq-sai. A few poplar trees were in the utmost autumn beauty. On dismounting, seasonable[4] food was set out. The vintage

---

1 *khush rang-i khizan*. Sometimes Babur's praise of autumn allows the word *khizan* to mean the harvest-crops themselves, sometimes the autumnal colouring.
2 This I have taken to mean the Kabul *tuman*. The Hai. MS. writes *wilayatlar* (plural) thus suggesting that *aul* (those) may be omitted, and those countries (Transoxiana) be meant; but the second Pers. trs. (I.O. 217 f. 169) supports *wilayat*, Kabul.
3 joyous, happy.
4 *y:lk:ran*. This word has proved a difficulty to all translators. I suggest that it stands for *ailikaran*, what came to hand (*ailik see* de C.'s Dict.); also that it contains puns referring to the sheep taken from the road (*yulkaran*) and to the wine of the year's yield (*yilkaran*). The way-side meal was of what came to hand, mutton and wine, probably local.

was the cause! wine was drunk! A sheep was ordered brought from the road and made into *kababs* (*brochettes*). We amused ourselves by setting fire to branches of holm-oak.[1]

Mulla 'Abdu'l-malik *diwana*[2] having begged to take the news of our coming into Kabul, was sent ahead. To this place came Hasan Nabira from Mirza Khan's presence; he must have come after letting me know [his intention of coming].[3] There was drinking till the Sun's decline; we then rode off. People in our party had become very drunk, Sayyid Qasim so much so, that two of his servants mounted him and got him into camp with difficulty. Muh. Baqir's Dost was so drunk that people, headed by Amin-i-muhammad Tarkhan and Masti *chuhra*, could not get him on his horse; even when they poured water on his head, nothing was effected. At that moment a body of Afghans appeared. Amin-i-muhammad, who had had enough himself, had this idea, "Rather than leave him here, as he is, to be taken, let us cut his head off and carry it with us." At last after 100 efforts, they mounted him and brought him with them. We reached Kabul at midnight.

Fol. 246.

(*ff. Incidents in Kabul.*)

In Court next morning Quli Beg waited on me. He had been to Sl. Sa'id Khan's presence in Kashghar as my envoy. To him as envoy to me had been added Bishka Mirza *Itarchi*[4] who brought me gifts of the goods of that country.

(*Oct. 25th*) On Wednesday the 1st of Zu'l-qa'da, I went by myself to Qabil's tomb[5] and there took my morning. The people of the party came later by ones and twos. When the Sun waxed hot, we went to the Violet-garden and drank there, by the side of the reservoir. Mid-day coming on, we slept. At the Mid-day Prayer we drank again. At this mid-day party I gave wine to Tingri-quli Beg and to Mahndi (?) to whom at any earlier party, wine had not been given. At the Bed-time Prayer, I went to the Hot-bath where I stayed the night.

Fol. 246b.

---

1 f. 141b.   2 f. 217 and n.

3 I think Babur means that the customary announcement of an envoy or guest must have reached Kabul in his absence.

4 He is in the T. R. list of the tribe (p. 307); to it belonged Sl. Ahmad *Tambal* (*ib.* p. 316).

5 *Qabil-ning kuri-ning qashi-ka*, lit. to the presence of the tomb of Qabil, *i.e.* Cain the eponymous hero of Kabul. The Elph. MS. has been altered to "Qabil Beg"!

(*Oct. 26th*) On Thursday honorary dresses were bestowed on the Hindustani traders, headed by Yahya *Nuhani*, and they were allowed to go.

(*Oct. 28th*) On Saturday the 4th, a dress and gifts were bestowed on Bishka Mirza, who had come from Kashghar, and he was given leave to go.

(*Oct. 29th*) On Sunday there was a party in the little Picture-hall over the (Char-bagh) gate; small retreat though it is, 16 persons were present.

(*gg. Excursion to the Koh-daman.*)

(*Oct. 30th*) Today we went to Istalif to see the harvest (*khizan*). Today was done the sin (? *irtikab qilib aidi*) of *ma'jun*. Much rain fell; most of the begs and the household came into my tent, outside the Bagh-i-kalan.

(*Oct. 31st*) Next day there was a wine-party in the same garden, lasting till night.

(*November 1st*) At dawn we took our morning (*subahi subuhi qilduk*) and got drunk, took a sleep, and at the Mid-day Prayer rode from Istalif. On the road a confection was eaten. We reached Bih-zadi at the Other Prayer. The harvest-crops were very beautiful; while we were viewing them those disposed for wine began to agitate about it. The harvest-colour was extremely beautiful; wine was drunk, though *ma'jun* had been eaten, sitting under autumnal trees. The party lasted till the Bed-time Prayer. Khalifa's Mulla Mahmud arriving, we had him summoned to join the party. 'Abdu'l-lah was very drunk indeed; a word affecting Khalifa (*tarfidin*) being said, 'Abdu'l-lah forgot Mulla Mahmud and recited this line:—

Fol. 247.

> Regard whom thou wilt, he suffers from the same wound.[1]

Mulla Mahmud was sober; he blamed 'Abdu'l-lah for repeating that line in jest; 'Abdu'l-lah came to his senses, was troubled in mind, and after this talked and chatted very sweetly.

Our excursion to view the harvest was over; we dismounted, close to the Evening Prayer, in the Char-bagh.

(*Nov. 12th*) On Friday the 16th, after eating a confection

---

1 Mr. Erskine surmised that the line was from some religious poem of mystical meaning and that its profane application gave offence. *See* Additional Notes, p. 799.

with a few special people in the Violet-garden, we went on a boat. Humayun and Kamran were with us later; Humayun made a very good shot at a duck.

(*hh. A Bohemian episode.*)

(*Nov. 14th*) On Saturday the 18th, I rode out of the Char-bagh at midnight, sent night-watch and groom back, crossed Mulla Baba's bridge, got out by the Diurin-narrows, round by the bazars and *karez* of Qush-nadur (var.), along the back of the Bear-house (*khirs-khana*), and near sunrise reached Tardi Beg *Khak-sar's*[1] *karez*. He ran out quickly on hearing of me. His shortness (*qalashlighi*) was known; I had taken 100 *shahrukhis* (£5) with me; I gave him these and told him to get wine and other things ready as I had a fancy for a private and unrestrained party. He went for wine towards Bih-zadi;[2] I sent my horse by his slave to the valley-bottom and sat down on the slope behind the *karez*. At the first watch (9 a.m.) Tardi Beg brought a pitcher of wine which we drank by turns. After him came Muhammad-i-qasim *Barlas* and Shah-zada who had got to know of his fetching the wine, and had followed him, their minds quite empty of any thought about me. We invited them to the party. Said Tardi Beg, "Hul-hul Aniga wishes to drink wine with you." Said I, "For my part, I never saw a woman drink wine; invite her." We also invited Shahi a qalandar, and one of the *karez*-men who played the rebeck. There was drinking till the Evening Prayer on the rising-ground behind the *karez*; we then went into Tardi Beg's house and drank by lamp-light almost till the Bed-time Prayer. The party was quite free and unpretending. I lay down, the others went to another house and drank there till beat of drum (midnight). Hul-hul Aniga came in and made me much disturbance; I got rid of her at last by flinging myself down as if drunk. It was in my mind to put people off their guard, and ride off alone to Astar-ghach, but it did not come off because they got to know. In the end, I rode

Fol. 247*b*.

1 His sobriquet *khaksar*, one who sits in the dust, suits the excavator of a *karez*. Babur's route can be followed in Masson's (iii, 110), apparently to the very *karez*.
2 In Masson's time this place was celebrated for vinegar. To reach it and return must have occupied several hours.

away at beat of drum, after letting Tardi Beg and Shah-zada know. We three mounted and made for Astar-ghach.

(*Nov. 15th*) We reached Khwaja Hasan below Istalif by the first prayer (*farz waqt*); dismounted for a while, ate a confection, and went to view the harvest. When the Sun was up, we dismounted at a garden in Istalif and ate grapes. We slept at Khwaja Shahab, a dependency of Astar-ghach. Ata, the Master of the Horse, must have had a house somewhere near, for before we were awake he had brought food and a pitcher of wine. The vintage was very fine. After drinking a few cups, we rode on. We next dismounted in a garden beautiful with autumn; there a party was held at which Khwaja Muhammad Amin joined us. Drinking went on till the Bed-time Prayer. During that day and night 'Abdu'l-lah, 'Asas, Nur Beg and Yusuf-i-'ali all arrived from Kabul.

(*Nov. 16th*) After food at dawn, we rode out and visited the Bagh-i-padshahi below Astar-ghach. One young apple-tree in it had turned an admirable autumn-colour; on each branch were left 5 or 6 leaves in regular array; it was such that no painter trying to depict it could have equalled. After riding from Astar-ghach we ate at Khwaja Hasan, and reached Bih-zadi at the Evening Prayer. There we drank in the house of Khwaja Muh. Amin's servant Imam-i-muhammad.

(*Nov. 17th*) Next day, Tuesday, we went into the Char-bagh of Kabul.

(*Nov. 18th*) On Thursday the 23rd, having marched (*kuchub*), the fort was entered.

(*Nov. 19th*) On Friday Muhammad 'Ali (son of ?) Haidar the stirrup-holder brought, as an offering, a *tuigun*[1] he had caught.

(*Nov. 20th*) On Saturday the 25th, there was a party in the Plane-tree garden from which I rose and mounted at the Bed-time Prayer. Sayyid Qasim being in shame at past occurrences,[2] we dismounted at his house and drank a few cups.

(*Nov. 24th*) On Thursday the 1st of Zu'l-hijja, Taju'd-din Mahmud, come from Qandahar, waited on me.

Fol. 248.

Fol. 248b.

---

1 Kunos, *aq tuigun*, white falcon; '*Amal-i-salih* (I.O. MS. No. 857, f. 45b), *taus tuighun*.
2 f. 246.

(*Dec. 12th*) On Monday the 19th, Muh. 'Ali *Jang-jang* came from Nil-ab.

(*Dec. 13th*) On Tuesday the ... of the month, Sangar Khan *Janjuha*, come from Bhira, waited on me.

(*Dec. 16th*) On Friday the 23rd, I finished (copying?) the odes and couplets selected according to their measure from 'Ali-sher Beg's four Diwans.[1]

(*Dec. 20th*) On Tuesday the 27th there was a social-gathering in the citadel, at which it was ordered that if any-one went out from it drunk, that person should not be invited to a party again.

(*Dec. 23rd*) On Friday the 30th of Zu'l-hijja it was ridden out with the intention of making an excursion to Lamghan.

---

1 Nawa'i himself arranged them according to the periods of his life (Rieu's Pers Cat. p. 294).

(*a. Excursion to the Koh-daman and Kohistan.*)

(*Dec. 23rd*) On Saturday Muharram 1st Khwaja Sih-yaran was reached. A wine-party was had on the bank of the conduit, where this comes out on the hill.[2]

(*Dec. 24th*) Riding on next morning (2nd), we visited the moving sands (*reg-i-rawan*). A party was held in Sayyid Qasim's *Bulbul*'s house.[3]

(*Dec. 25th*) Riding on from there, we ate a confection (*ma'jun*), went further and dismounted at Bilkir (?).

(*Dec. 26th*) At dawn (4th) we made our morning [*subahi subuhi qilduk*], although there might be drinking at night. We rode on at the Mid-day Prayer, dismounted at Dur-nama[4] and there had a wine party.

(*Dec. 27th*) We took our morning early. Haq-dad, the headman of Dur-nama made me an offering (*pesh-kash*) of his garden.

(*Dec. 28th*) Riding thence on Thursday (6th), we dismounted at the villages of the Tajiks in Nijr-au.

(*Dec. 29th*) On Friday (7th) we hunted the hill between Forty-ploughs (*Chihil-qulba*) and the water of Baran; many deer fell. I had not shot an arrow since my hand was hurt; now, with an easy[5] bow, I shot a deer in the shoulder, the arrow going in to half up the feather. Returning from hunting, we went on at the Other Prayer in Nijr-au.

Fol. 249.

---

1 Elph. MS. f. 202*b*; W.–i–B. I.O. 215 f. 175 (misplaced) and 217 f. 172; Mems. p. 281.
2 *pushta austida*; the Jui-khwush of f. 137.
3 The Hai. MS. omits a passage here; the Elph. MS. reads *Qasim Bulbuli ning awi*, thus making "nightingale" a sobriquet of Qasim's own. Erskine (p. 281) has "Bulbuli-hall"; Ilminsky's words translate as, the house of Sayyid Qasim's nightingale (p. 321).
4 or Dur-nama'i, seen from afar.
5 *narm-dik*, the opposite of a *qatiq yai*, a stiff bow. Some MSS. write *lazim-dik* which might be read to mean such a bow as his disablement allowed to be used.

(*Dec. 30th*) Next day (Saturday 8th) the tribute of the Nijr-au people was fixed at 60 gold misqals.[1]

(*Jan. 1st*) On Monday (10th) we rode on intending to visit Lamghan.[2] I had expected Humayun to go with us, but as he inclined to stay behind, leave was given him from Kura-pass. We went on and dismounted in Badr-au (Tag-au).

(*b. Excursions in Lamghan.*)

(*Jan...*) Riding on, we dismounted at Aulugh-nur.[3] The fishermen there took fish at one draught[4] from the water of Baran. At the Other Prayer (afternoon) there was drinking on the raft; and there was drinking in a tent after we left the raft at the Evening Prayer.

Haidar the standard-bearer had been sent from Dawar[5] to the Kafirs; several Kafir headmen came now to the foot of Bad-i-pich (pass), brought a few goat-skins of wine, and did obeisance. In descending that pass a surprising number of ...[6] was seen.

(*Jan...*) Next day getting on a raft, we ate a confection, got off below Bulan and went to camp. There were two rafts.

(*Jan. 5th*) Marching on Friday (14th), we dismounted below Mandrawar on the hill-skirt. There was a late wine-party.

(*Jan. 6th*) On Saturday (15th), we passed through the Daruta narrows by raft, got off a little above Jahan-nama'i (Jalalabad) and went to the Bagh-i-wafa in front of Adinapur. When we were leaving the raft the governor of Ningnahar Qayyam Aurdu Shah came and did obeisance. Langar Khan *Nia-zai*,—he had

Fol. 249*b*.

1 Mr. Erskine, writing early in the 19th century, notes that this seems an easy tribute, about 400 *rupis i.e.* £40.
2 This is one of the three routes into Lamghan of f. 133.
3 f. 251*b* and Appendix F, *On the name Dara-i-nur*.
4 This passage will be the basis of the account on f. 143*b* of the winter-supply of fish in Lamghan.
5 This word or name is puzzling. Avoiding extreme detail as to variants, I suggest that it is Daur-bin for Dur-nama'i if a place-name; or, if not, *dur-bin*, foresight (in either case the preposition requires to be supplied), and it may refer to foreseen need of and curiosity about Kafir wines.
6 *chiurtika* or *chiur-i-tika*, whether *sauterelle* as M. de Courteille understood, or *janwar-i-ranga* and *chikur*, partridge as the 1st Persian trs. and as Mr. Erskine (explaining *chur-i-tika*) thought, must be left open. Two points arise however, (1) the time is January, the place the deadly Bad-i-pich pass; would these suit locusts? (2) If Babur's account of a splendid bird (f. 135) were based on this experience, this would be one of several occurrences in which what is entered in the Description of Kabul of 910 AH. is found as an experience in the diary of 925–6 AH.

been in Nil-ab for a time,—waited upon me on the road. We
dismounted in the Bagh-i-wafa; its oranges had yellowed
beautifully; its spring-bloom was well-advanced, and it was very
charming. We stayed in it five or six days.

As it was my wish and inclination (*ju dagh-dagha*) to return
to obedience (*ta'ib*) in my 40th year, I was drinking to excess
now that less than a year was left.

(*Jan. 7th*) On Sunday the 16th, having made my morning
(*subuhi*) and became sober. Mulla Yarak played an air he had
composed in five-time and in the five-line measure (*makhammas*),
while I chose to eat a confection (*ma'jun*). He had composed
an excellent air. I had not occupied myself with such things
for some time; a wish to compose came over me now, so
I composed an air in four-time, as will be mentioned in time.[1]

(*Jan. 10th*) On Wednesday (19th) it was said for fun, while
we were making our morning (*subuhi*), "Let whoever speaks
like a Sart (*i.e.* in Persian) drink a cup." Through this many
drank. At *sunnat-waqt*[2] again, when we were sitting under the
willows in the middle of the meadow, it was said, "Let whoever
speaks like a Turk, drink a cup!" Through this also numbers
drank. After the sun got up, we drank under the orange-trees
on the reservoir-bank.

(*Jan. 11th*) Next day (20th) we got on a raft from Daruta;
got off again below Jui-shahi and went to Atar.

(*Jan…*) We rode from there to visit Nur-valley, went as
far as Susan (lily)-village, then turned back and dismounted
in Amla.

Fol. 250.   (*Jan. 14th*) As Khwaja Kalan had brought Bajaur into good
order, and as he was a friend of mine, I had sent for him and
had made Bajaur over to Shah Mir Husain's charge. On
Saturday the 22nd of the month (Muharram), Shah Mir Husain
was given leave to go. That day in Amla we drank.

(*Jan. 15th*) It rained (*yamghur yaghdurub*) next day (23rd).

1 Hai. MS. *mahali-da mazkur bulghusidur*, but W.-i-B. I.O. 215 f. 176 for *mahalida*,
in its place, has *dar majlis* [in the collection], which may point to an intended
collection of Babur's musical compositions. Either reading indicates intention to
write what we now have not.

2 Perhaps an equivalent for *farz-waqt*, the time of the first obligatory prayer. Much
seems to happen before the sun got up high!

When we reached Kula-gram in Kunar [1] where Malik-quli's house is, we dismounted at his middle son's house, overlooking an orange-orchard. We did not go into the orchard because of the rain but just drank where we were. The rain was very heavy. I taught Mulla 'Ali Khan a talisman I knew; he wrote it on four pieces of paper and hung them on four sides; as he did it, the rain stopped and the air began to clear.

(*Jan. 16th*) At dawn (24th) we got on a raft; on another several braves went. People in Bajaur, Sawad, Kunar and thereabouts make a beer (*bir buza*) [2] the ferment of which is a thing they call *kim*. [3] This *kim* they make of the roots of herbs and several simples, shaped like a loaf, dried and kept by them. Some sorts of beer are surprisingly exhilarating, but bitter and distasteful. We had thought of drinking beer but, because of its bitter taste, preferred a confection. 'Asas, Hasan *Aikirik*, [4] and Masti, on the other raft, were ordered to drink some; they did so and became quite drunk. Hasan *Aikirik* set up a disgusting disturbance; 'Asas, very drunk, did such _{Fol. 250b.} unpleasant things that we were most uncomfortable (*ba tang*). I thought of having them put off on the far side of the water, but some of the others begged them off.

I had sent for Khwaja Kalan at this time and had bestowed Bajaur on Shah Mir Husain. For why? Khwaja Kalan was a friend; his stay in Bajaur had been long; moreover the Bajaur appointment appeared an easy one.

At the ford of the Kunar-water Shah Mir Husain met me on his way to Bajaur. I sent for him and said a few trenchant words, gave him some special armour, and let him go.

Opposite Nur-gal (Rock-village) an old man begged from those on the rafts; every-one gave him something, coat (*tun*), turban, bathing-cloth and so on, so he took a good deal away.

At a bad place in mid-stream the raft struck with a great shock; there was much alarm; it did not sink but Mir Muhammad the raftsman was thrown into the water. We were near Atar that night.

---

1 Koh-i-nur, Rocky-mountains (?). *See* Appendix F, *On the name Dara-i-nur.*
2 Steingass gives *buza* as made of rice, millet, or barley.
3 Is this connected with Arabic *kimiya'*, alchemy, chemistry?
4 Turki, a whirlpool; but perhaps the name of an office from *aigar*, a saddle.

(*Jan. 17th*) On Tuesday (25th) we reached Mandrawar.[1] Qutluq-qadam and his father had arranged a party inside the fort; though the place had no charm, a few cups were drunk there to please them. We went to camp at the Other Prayer.

(*Jan. 18th*) On Wednesday (26th) an excursion was made to Kind-kir[2] spring. Kind-kir is a dependent village of the Mandrawar *tuman*, the one and only village of the Lamghanat where dates are grown. It lies rather high on the mountain-skirt, its date lands on its east side. At one edge of the date lands is the spring, in a place aside (*yan yir*). Six or seven yards below the spring-head people have heaped up stones to make a shelter[3] for bathing and by so-doing have raised the water in the reservoir high enough for it to pour over the heads of the bathers. The water is very soft; it is felt a little cold in wintry days but is pleasant if one stays in it.

(*Jan. 19th*) On Thursday (27th) Sher Khan *Tarkalani* got us to dismount at his house and there gave us a feast (*ziyafat*). Having ridden on at the Mid-day Prayer, fish were taken out of the fish-ponds of which particulars have been given.[4]

(*Jan. 20th*) On Friday (28th) we dismounted near Khwaja Mir-i-miran's village. A party was held there at the Evening Prayer.

(*Jan. 21st*) On Saturday (29th) we hunted the hill between 'Ali-shang and Alangar. One hunting-circle having been made on the 'Ali-shang side, another on the Alangar, the deer were driven down off the hill and many were killed. Returning from hunting, we dismounted in a garden belonging to the Maliks of Alangar and there had a party.

Half of one of my front-teeth had broken off, the other half remaining; this half broke off today while I was eating food.

(*Jan. 22nd*) At dawn (Safar 1st) we rode out and had a fishing-net cast, at mid-day went into 'Ali-shang and drank in a garden.

1 The river on which the rafts were used was the Kunar, from Chitral.
2 An uncertain name. I have an impression that these waters are medicinal, but I cannot trace where I found the information. The visit paid to them, and the arrangement made for bathing set them apart. The name of the place may convey this speciality.
3 *panahi*, the word used for the hiding-places of bird-catchers on f. 140.
4 This will be the basis of the details about fishing given on f. 143 and f. 143b. The statement that particulars have been given allows the inference that the diary was annotated after the *Description of Kabul*, in which the particulars are, was written.

(*Jan. 23rd*) Next day (Safar 2nd) Hamza Khan, Malik of 'Ali-shang was made over to the avengers-of-blood[1] for his evil deeds in shedding innocent blood, and retaliation was made.

(*Jan. 24th*) On Tuesday, after reading a chapter of the Qoran Fol. 251*b*. (*wird*), we turned for Kabul by the Yan-bulagh road. At the Other Prayer, we passed the [Baran]-water from Aulugh-nur (Great-rock); reached Qara-tu by the Evening Prayer, there gave our horses corn and had a hasty meal prepared, rode on again as soon as they had finished their barley.[2]

1 *qanliqlar*. This right of private revenge which forms part of the law of most rude nations, exists in a mitigated form under the Muhammadan law. The criminal is condemned by the judge, but is delivered up to the relations of the person murdered, to be ransomed or put to death as they think fit (Erskine).

2 Here the text breaks off and a *lacuna* separates the diary of 11 months length which ends the Kabul section of the *Babur-nama* writings, from the annals of 932 AH. which begin the Hindustan section. There seems no reason why the diary should have been discontinued.

Babur's diary breaks off here for five years and ten months.[1] His activities during the unrecorded period may well have left no time in which to keep one up, for in it he went thrice to Qandahar, thrice into India, once to Badakhshan, once to Balkh; twice at least he punished refractory tribesmen; he received embassies from Hindustan, and must have had much to oversee in muster and equipment for his numerous expeditions. Over and above this, he produced the *Mubin*, a Turki poem of 2000 lines.

That the gap in his autobiography is not intentional several passages in his writings show; he meant to fill it; there is no evidence that he ever did so; the reasonable explanation of his failure is that he died before he had reached this part of his book.

The events of these unrecorded years are less interesting than those of the preceding gap, inasmuch as their drama of human passion is simpler; it is one mainly of cross-currents of ambition, nothing in it matching the maelstrom of sectarian hate, tribal antipathy, and racial struggle which engulphed Babur's fortunes beyond the Oxus.

None-the-less the period has its distinctive mark, the biographical one set by his personality as his long-sustained effort works out towards rule in Hindustan. He becomes felt; his surroundings bend to his purpose; his composite following accepts his goal; he gains the southern key of Kabul and Hindustan and presses the Arghuns out from his rear; in the Panj-ab he becomes a power; the Rajput Rana of Chitor proffers him alliance against Ibrahim; and his intervention is sought in those warrings of the Afghans which were the matrix of his own success.

1 Jan. 24th 1520 to Nov. 17th 1525 AD. (Safar 926 to Safar 1st 932 AH.).

a. Dramatis personae.

The following men played principal parts in the events of the unchronicled years:—

Babur in Kabul, Badakhshan and Balkh,[1] his earlier following purged of Mughul rebellion, and augmented by the various Mirzas-in-exile in whose need of employment Shah Beg saw Babur's need of wider territory.[2]

Sultan Ibrahim *Ludi* who had succeeded after his father Sikandar's death (Sunday Zu'l-qa'da 7th 923 AH.—Nov. 21st 1517 AD.),[3] was now embroiled in civil war, and hated for his tyranny and cruelty.

Shah Isma'il *Safawi*, ruling down to Rajab 19th 930 AH. (May 24th 1524 AD.) and then succeeded by his son Tahmasp *aet.* 10.

Kuchum (Kuchkunji) Khan, Khaqan of the Auzbegs, Shaibani's successor, now in possession of Transoxiana.

Sultan Sa'id Khan *Chaghatai*, with head-quarters in Kashghar, a ruler amongst the Mughuls but not their Khaqan, the supreme Khanship being his elder brother Mansur's.

Shah Shuja' Beg *Arghun*, who, during the period, at various times held Qandahar, Shal, Mastung, Siwistan, and part of Sind. He died in 930 AH. (1524 AD.) and was succeeded by his son Hasan who read the *khutba* for Babur.

Khan Mirza *Miranshahi*, who held Badakhshan from Babur, with head-quarters in Qunduz; he died in 927 AH. (1520 AD.) and was succeeded in his appointment by Humayun *aet.* 13.

1 Nominally Balkh seems to have been a Safawi possession; but it is made to seem closely dependent on Babur by his receipt from Muhammad-i-zaman in it of *tasadduq* (money for alms), and by his action connected with it (*q.v.*).

2 *Tarikh-i-sind*, Malet's trs. p. 77 and *in loco*, p. 365.

3 A chronogram given by Badayuni decides the vexed question of the date of Sikandar *Ludi*'s death—*Jannatu'l-firdus nazla* = 923 (Bib. Ind. ed. i, 322, Ranking trs. p. 425 n. 6). Erskine supported 924 AH. (i, 407), partly relying on an entry in Babur's diary (f. 226b) *s.d.* Rabi'u'l-awwal 1st 925 AH. (March 3rd 1519 AD.) which states that on that day Mulla Murshid was sent to Ibrahim whose father *Sikandar had died five or six months before.*

Against this is the circumstance that the entry about Mulla Murshid is, perhaps entirely, certainly partly, of later entry than what precedes and what follows it in the diary. This can be seen on examination; it is a passage such as the diary section shews in other places, added to the daily record and giving this the character of a draft waiting for revision and rewriting (fol. 216b n.).

(To save difficulty to those who may refer to the L. & E. *Memoirs* on the point, I mention that the whole passage about Mulla Murshid is displaced in that book and that the date March 3rd is omitted.)

Muhammad-i-zaman *Bai-qara* who held Balkh perhaps direct from Babur, perhaps from Isma'il through Babur.

'Ala'u'd-din 'Alam Khan *Ludi*, brother of the late Sultan Sikandar *Ludi* and now desiring to supersede his nephew Ibrahim.

Daulat Khan *Yusuf-khail* (as Babur uniformly describes him), or *Ludi* (as other writers do), holding Lahor for Ibrahim *Ludi* at the beginning of the period.

SOURCES FOR THE EVENTS OF THIS GAP

A complete history of the events the *Babur-nama* leaves unrecorded has yet to be written. The best existing one, whether Oriental or European, is Erskine's *History of India*, but this does not exhaust the sources—notably not using the *Habibu's-siyar*—and could be revised here and there with advantage.

Most of the sources enumerated as useful for filling the previous gap are so here; to them must be added, for the affairs of Qandahar, Khwand-amir's *Habibu's-siyar*. This Mir Ma'sum's *Tarikh-i-sind* supplements usefully, but its brevity and its discrepant dates make it demand adjustment; in some details it is expanded by Sayyid Jamal's *Tarkhan-* or *Arghun-nama*.

For the affairs of Hindustan the main sources are enumerated in Elliot and Dowson's *History of India* and in Nassau Lees' *Materials for the history of India*. Doubtless all will be exhausted for the coming *Cambridge History of India*.

EVENTS OF THE UNCHRONICLED YEARS
926 AH.—DEC. 23RD 1519 TO DEC. 12TH 1520 AD.

The question of which were Babur's "Five expeditions" into Hindustan has been often discussed; it is useful therefore to establish the dates of those known as made. I have entered one as made in this year for the following reasons;—it broke short because Shah Beg made incursion into Babur's territories, and that incursion was followed by a siege of Qandahar which several matters mentioned below show to have taken place in 926 AH.

a. Expedition into Hindustan.

The march out from Kabul may have been as soon as muster and equipment allowed after the return from Lamghan chronicled in the diary. It was made through Bajaur where refractory tribesmen were brought to order. The Indus will have been forded at the usual place where, until the last one of 932 AH. (1525 AD.), all expeditions crossed on the outward march. Bhira was traversed in which were Babur's own Commanders, and advance was made, beyond lands yet occupied, to Sialkot, 72 miles north of Lahor and in the Rechna *du-ab*. It was occupied without resistance; and a further move made to what the MSS. call Sayyidpur; this attempted defence, was taken by assault and put to the sword. No place named Sayyidpur is given in the Gazetteer of India, but the *Ayin-i-akbari* mentions a Sidhpur which from its neighbourhood to Sialkot may be what Babur took.

Nothing indicates an intention in Babur to join battle with Ibrahim at this time; Lahor may have been his objective, after he had made a demonstration in force to strengthen his footing in Bhira. Whatever he may have planned to do beyond Sidhpur (?) was frustrated by the news which took him back to Kabul and thence to Qandahar, that an incursion into his territory had been made by Shah Beg.

b. Shah Shuja' Beg's position.

Shah Beg was now holding Qandahar, Shal, Mustang and Siwistan.[1] He knew that he held Qandahar by uncertain tenure, in face of its desirability for Babur and his own lesser power. His ground was further weakened by its usefulness for operations on Harat and the presence with Babur of Bai-qara refugees, ready to seize a chance, if offered by Isma'il's waning fortunes, for recovery of their former seat. Knowing his weakness, he for several years had been pushing his way out into Sind by way of the Bolan-pass.

His relations with Babur were ostensibly good; he had sent him envoys twice last year, the first time to announce a success

---

1 Shal (the local name of English Quetta) was taken by Zu'n-nun in 884 AH. (1479 AD.); Siwistan Shah Beg took, in second capture, about 917 AH. (1511 AD.), from a colony of Barlas Turks under Pir Wali *Barlas*.

at Kahan had in the end of 924 AH. (Nov. 1519 AD.). His son Hasan however, with whom he was unreconciled, had been for more than a year in Babur's company,—a matter not unlikely to stir under-currents of unfriendliness on either side.

His relations with Shah Isma'il were deferential, in appearance even vassal-like, as is shewn by Khwand-amir's account of his appeal for intervention against Babur to the Shah's officers in Harat. Whether he read the *khutba* for any suzerain is doubtful; his son Hasan, it may be said, read it later on for Babur.

c. The impelling cause of this siege of Qandahar.

Precisely what Shah Beg did to bring Babur back from the Panj-ab and down upon Qandahar is not found mentioned by any source. It seems likely to have been an affair of subordinates instigated by or for him. Its immediate agents may have been the Nikdiri (Nukdiri) and Hazara tribes Babur punished on his way south. Their location was the western border-land; they may have descended on the Great North Road or have raided for food in that famine year. It seems certain that Shah Beg made no serious attempt on Kabul; he was too much occupied in Sind to allow him to do so. Some unused source may throw light on the matter incidentally; the offence may have been small in itself and yet sufficient to determine Babur to remove risk from his rear.[1]

d. Qandahar.

The Qandahar of Babur's sieges was difficult of capture; he had not taken it in 913 AH. (f. 208b) by siege or assault, but by default after one day's fight in the open. The strength of its position can be judged from the following account of its ruins as they were seen in 1879 AD., the military details of which supplement Bellew's description quoted in Appendix J.

The fortifications are of great extent with a treble line of bastioned walls and a high citadel in the centre. The place is in complete ruin and its locality now useful only as a grazing ground. ... "The town is in three parts, each on a separate

1 Was the attack made in reprisal for Shah Beg's further aggression on the Barlas lands and Babur's hereditary subjects? Had these appealed to the head of their tribe?

eminence, and capable of mutual defence. The mountain had been covered with towers united by curtains, and the one on the culminating point may be called impregnable. It commanded the citadel which stood lower down on the second eminence, and this in turn commanded the town which was on a table-land elevated above the plain. The triple walls surrounding the city were at a considerable distance from it. After exploring the citadel and ruins, we mounted by the gorge to the summit of the hill with the impregnable fort. In this gorge are the ruins of two tanks, some 80 feet square, all destroyed, with the pillars fallen; the work is *pukka* in brick and *chunam* (cement) and each tank had been domed in; they would have held about 400,000 gallons each." (Le Messurier's *Kandahar in 1879 AD.* pp. 223, 245.)

e. Babur's sieges of Qandahar.

The term of five years is found associated with Babur's sieges of Qandahar, sometimes suggesting a single attempt of five years' duration. This it is easy to show incorrect; its root may be Mir Ma'sum's erroneous chronology.

The day on which the keys of Qandahar were made over to Babur is known, from the famous inscription which commemorates the event (Appendix J), as Shawwal 13th 928 AH. Working backwards from this, it is known that in 927 AH. terms of surrender were made and that Babur went back to Kabul; he is besieging it in 926 AH.—the year under description; his annals of 925 AH. are complete and contain no siege; the year 924 AH. appears to have had no siege, Shah Beg was on the Indus and his son was for at least part of it with Babur; 923 AH. was a year of intended siege, frustrated by Babur's own illness; of any siege in 922 AH. there is as yet no record known. So that it is certain there was no unremitted beleaguerment through five years.

f. The siege of 926 AH. (1520 AD.).

When Babur sat down to lay regular siege to Qandahar, with mining and battering of the walls,[1] famine was desolating the

---

1 Le Messurier writes (*l.c.* p. 224) that at Old Qandahar "many stone balls lay about, some with a diameter of 18 inches, others of 4 or 5, chiselled out of limestone.

country round. The garrison was reduced to great distress; "pestilence," ever an ally of Qandahar, broke out within the walls, spread to Babur's camp, and in the month of Tir (June) led him to return to Kabul.

In the succeeding months of respite, Shah Beg pushed on in Sind and his former slave, now commander, Mehtar Sambhal revictualled the town.

927 AH.—DEC. 12TH 1520 TO DEC. 1ST 1521 AD.

a. The manuscript sources.

Two accounts of the sieges of Qandahar in this and next year are available, one in Khwand-amir's *Habibu's-siyar,* the other in Ma'sum *Bhakkari's Tarikh-i-sind.* As they have important differences, it is necessary to consider the opportunities of their authors for information.

Khwand-amir finished his history in 1524–29 AD. His account of these affairs of Qandahar is contemporary; he was in close touch with several of the actors in them and may have been in Harat through their course; one of his patrons, Amir Ghiyasu'd-din, was put to death in this year in Harat because of suspicion that he was an ally of Babur; his nephew, another Ghiyasu'd-din was in Qandahar, the bearer next year of its keys to Babur; moreover he was with Babur himself a few years later in Hindustan.

Mir Ma'sum wrote in 1600 AD. 70 to 75 years after Khwand-amir. Of these sieges he tells what may have been traditional and mentions no manuscript authorities. Blochmann's biography of him (*Ayin-i-akbari* p. 514) shews his ample opportunity of learning orally what had happened in the Arghun invasion of Sind, but does not mention the opportunity for hearing traditions about Qandahar which his term of office there allowed him. During that term it was that he added an inscription, commemorative of Akbar's dominion, to Babur's own at Chihil-zina, which records the date of the capture of Qandahar (928 AH.—1522 AD.).

These were said to have been used in sieges in the times of the Arabs and propelled from a machine called *manjanic* a sort of balista or catapult." Meantime perhaps they served Babur!

b. The Habibu's-siyar account (lith. ed. iii, part 4, p. 97).

Khwand-amir's contemporary narrative allows Ma'sum's to dovetail into it as to some matters, but contradicts it in the important ones of date, and mode of surrender by Shah Beg to Babur. It states that Babur was resolved in 926 AH. (1520 AD.) to uproot Shah Shuja' Beg from Qandahar, led an army against the place, and "opened the Gates of war". It gives no account of the siege of 926 AH. but passes on to the occurrences of 927 AH. (1521 AD.) when Shah Beg, unable to meet Babur in the field, shut himself up in the town and strengthened the defences. Babur put his utmost pressure on the besieged, "often riding his piebald horse close to the moat and urging his men to fiery onset." The garrison resisted manfully, breaching the "life-fortresses" of the Kabulis with sword, arrow, spear and death-dealing stone, but Babur's heroes were most often victorious, and drove their assailants back through the Gates.

c. Death of Khan Mirza reported to Babur.

Meantime, continues Khwand-amir, Khan Mirza had died in Badakhshan; the news was brought to Babur and caused him great grief; he appointed Humayun to succeed the Mirza while he himself prosecuted the siege of Qandahar and the conquest of the Garm-sir.[1]

d. Negotiations with Babur.

The Governor of Harat at this time was Shah Isma'il's son Tahmasp, between six and seven years old. His guardian Amir Khan took chief part in the diplomatic intervention with Babur, but associated with him was Amir Ghiyasu'd-din—the patron of Khwand-amir already mentioned—until put to death as an ally of Babur. The discussion had with Babur reveals a complexity of motives demanding attention. Nominally undertaken though intervention was on behalf of Shah Beg, and certainly so at his request, the Persian officers seem to have been less anxious on

1 "Just then came a letter from Badakhshan saying, 'Mirza Khan is dead; Mirza Sulaiman (his son) is young; the Auzbegs are near; take thought for this kingdom lest (which God forbid) Badakhshan should be lost.' Mirza Sulaiman's mother had brought him to Kabul" (Gul-badan's H. N. f. 8).

his account than for their own position in Khurasan, their master's position at the time being weakened by ill-success against the Sultan of Rum. To Babur, Shah Beg is written of as though he were an insubordinate vassal whom Babur was reducing to order for the Shah, but when Amir Khan heard that Shah Beg was hard pressed, he was much distressed because he feared a victorious Babur might move on Khurasan. Nothing indicates however that Babur had Khurasan in his thoughts; Hindustan was his objective, and Qandahar a help on the way; but as Amir Khan had this fear about him, a probable ground for it is provided by the presence with Babur of Bai-qara exiles whose ambition it must have been to recover their former seat. Whether for Harat, Kabul, or Hindustan, Qandahar was strength. Another matter not fitting the avowed purpose of the diplomatic intervention is the death of Ghiyasu'd-din because an ally of Babur; this makes Amir Khan seem to count Babur as Isma'il's enemy.

Shah Beg's requests for intervention began in 926 AH. (1520 AD.), as also did the remonstrance of the Persian officers with Babur; his couriers followed one another with entreaty that the Amirs would contrive for Babur to retire, with promise of obeisance and of yearly tribute. The Amirs set forth to Babur that though Shah Shuja' Beg had offended and had been deserving of wrath and chastisement, yet, as he was penitent and had promised loyalty and tribute, it was now proper for Babur to raise the siege (of 926 AH.) and go back to Kabul. To this Babur answered that Shah Beg's promise was a vain thing, on which no reliance could be placed; please God!, said he, he himself would take Qandahar and send Shah Beg a prisoner to Harat; and that he should be ready then to give the keys of the town and the possession of the Garm-sir to any-one appointed to receive them.

This correspondence suits an assumption that Babur acted for Shah Isma'il, a diplomatic assumption merely, the verbal veil, on one side, for anxiety lest Babur or those with him should attack Harat,—on the other, for Babur's resolve to hold Qandahar himself.

Amir Khan was not satisfied with Babur's answer, but had his attention distracted by another matter, presumably 'Ubaidu'l-lah Khan's attack on Harat in the spring of the year (March–April

1521 AD.). Negotiations appear to have been resumed later, since Khwand-amir claims it as their result that Babur left Qandahar this year.

e. The Tarikh-i-sind account.

Mir Ma'sum is very brief; he says that in this year (his 922 AH.), Babur went down to Qandahar before the year's tribute in grain had been collected, destroyed the standing crops, encompassed the town, and reduced it to extremity; that Shah Beg, wearied under reiterated attack and pre-occupied by operations in Sind, proposed terms, and that these were made with stipulation for the town to be his during one year more and then to be given over to Babur. These terms settled, Babur went to Kabul, Shah Beg to Siwi.

The Arghun families were removed to Shal and Siwi, so that the year's delay may have been an accommodation allowed for this purpose.

f. Concerning dates.

There is much discrepancy between the dates of the two historians. Khwand-amir's agree with the few fixed ones of the period and with the course of events; several of Ma'sum's, on the contrary, are *seriatim* five (lunar) years earlier. For instance, events Khwand-amir places under 927 AH. Ma'sum places under 922 AH. Again, while Ma'sum correctly gives 913 AH. (1507 AD.) as the year of Babur's first capture of Qandahar, he sets up a discrepant series later, from the success Shah Beg had at Kahan; this he allots to 921 AH. (1515 AD.) whereas Babur received news of it (f. 233b) in the beginning of 925 AH. (1519 AD.). Again, Ma'sum makes Shah Hasan go to Babur in 921 AH. and stay two years; but Hasan spent the whole of 925 AH. with Babur and is not mentioned as having left before the second month of 926 AH. Again, Ma'sum makes Shah Beg surrender the keys of Qandahar in 923 AH. (1517 AD.), but 928 AH. (1522 AD.) is shewn by Khwand-amir's dates and narrative, and is inscribed at Chihil-zina.[1]

---

1 *infra* and Appendix J.

928 AH.—DEC. 1ST 1521 TO NOV. 20TH 1522 AD.

a. Babur visits Badakhshan.

Either early in this year or late in the previous one, Babur and Mahim went to visit Humayun in his government, probably to Faizabad, and stayed with him what Gul-badan calls a few days.

b. Expedition to Qandahar.

This year saw the end of the duel for possession of Qandahar. Khwand-amir's account of its surrender differs widely from Ma'sum's. It claims that Babur's retirement in 927 AH. was due to the remonstrances from Harat, and that Shah Beg, worn out by the siege, relied on the arrangement the Amirs had made with Babur and went to Siwi, leaving one 'Abdu'l-baqi in charge of the place. This man, says Khwand-amir, drew the line of obliteration over his duty to his master, sent to Babur, brought him down to Qandahar, and gave him the keys of the town— by the hand of Khwand-amir's nephew Ghiyasu'd-din, specifies the *Tarkhan-nama*. In this year messengers had come and gone between Babur and Harat; two men employed by Amir Khan are mentioned by name; of them the last had not returned to Harat when a courier of Babur's, bringing a tributary gift, announced there that the town was in his master's hands. Khwand-amir thus fixes the year 928 AH. as that in which the town passed into Babur's hands; this date is confirmed by the one inscribed in the monument of victory at Chihil-zina which Babur ordered excavated on the naze of the limestone ridge behind the town. The date there given is Shawwal 13th 928 AH. (Sep. 6th 1522 AD.).

Ma'sum's account, dated 923 AH. (1517 AD.), is of the briefest:— Shah Beg fulfilled his promise, much to Babur's approval, by sending him the keys of the town and royal residence.

Although Khwand-amir's account has good claim to be accepted, it must be admitted that several circumstances can be taken to show that Shah Beg had abandoned Qandahar, *e.g.* the removal of the families after Babur's retirement last year, and his own absence in a remote part of Sind this year.

c. The year of Shah Beg's death.

Of several variant years assigned for the death of Shah Beg in the sources, two only need consideration.[1] There is consensus of opinion about the month and close agreement about the day, Sha'ban 22nd or 23rd. Ma'sum gives a chronogram, *Shahr-Sha'ban*, (month of Sha'ban) which yields 928, but he does not mention where he obtained it, nor does anything in his narrative shew what has fixed the day of the month.

Two objections to 928 are patent: (1) the doubt engendered by Ma'sum's earlier ante-dating; (2) that if 928 be right, Shah Beg was already dead over two months when Qandahar was surrendered. This he might have been according to Khwand-amir's narrative, but if he died on Sha'ban 22nd 928 (July 26th 1522), there was time for the news to have reached Qandahar, and to have gone on to Harat before the surrender. Shah Beg's death at that time could not have failed to be associated in Khwand-amir's narrative with the fate of Qandahar; it might have pleaded some excuse with him for 'Abdu'l-baqi, who might even have had orders from Shah Hasan to make the town over to Babur whose suzerainty he had acknowledged at once on succession by reading the *khutba* in his name. Khwand-amir however does not mention what would have been a salient point in the events of the siege; his silence cannot but weigh against the 928 AH.

The year 930 AH. is given by Nizamu'd-din Ahmad's *Tabaqat-i-akbari* (lith. ed. p. 637), and this year has been adopted by Erskine, Beale, and Ney Elias, perhaps by others. Some light on the matter may be obtained incidentally as the sources are examined for a complete history of India, perhaps coming from the affairs of Multan, which was attacked by Shah Hasan after communication with Babur.

d. Babur's literary work in 928 AH. and earlier.

1. The *Mubin*. This year, as is known from a chronogram within the work, Babur wrote the Turki poem of 2000 lines to which Abu'l-fazl and Badayuni give the name *Mubin* (The

---

1 E. & D.'s *History of India*, i. 312.

Exposition), but of which the true title is said by the *Nafa'isu'l-ma'asir* to be *Dar fiqa mubaiyan* (The Law expounded). Sprenger found it called also *Fiqa-i-baburi* (Babur's Law). It is a versified and highly orthodox treatise on Muhammadan Law, written for the instruction of Kamran. A Commentary on it, called also *Mubin*, was written by Shaikh Zain. Babur quotes from it (f. 351b) when writing of linear measures. Berézine found and published a large portion of it as part of his *Chrestomathie Turque* (Kazan 1857); the same fragment may be what was published by Ilminsky. Teufel remarks that the MS. used by Berézine may have descended direct from one sent by Babur to a distinguished legist of Transoxiana, because the last words of Berézine's imprint are Babur's *Begleitschreiben* (*envoi*); he adds the expectation that the legist's name might be learned. Perhaps this recipient was the Khwaja Kalan, grandson of Khwaja Yahya, a Samarkandi to whom Babur sent a copy of his Memoirs on March 7th 1520 (935 AH. f. 363).[1]

2. The *Babur-nama* diary of 925–6 AH. (1519–20 AD.). This is almost contemporary with the *Mubin* and is the earliest part of the *Babur-nama* writings now known. It was written about a decade earlier than the narrative of 899 to 914 AH. (1494 to 1507 AD.), carries later annotations, and has now the character of a draft awaiting revision.

3. A *Diwan* (Collection of poems). By dovetailing a few fragments of information, it becomes clear that by 925 AH. (1519 AD.) Babur had made a Collection of poetical compositions distinct from the Rampur *Diwan*; it is what he sent to Pulad Sultan in 925 AH. (f. 238). Its date excludes the greater part of the Rampur one. It may have contained those verses to which my husband drew attention in the Asiatic Quarterly Review of 1911, as quoted in the *Abushqa*; and it may have contained, in agreement with its earlier date, the verses Babur quotes as written in his earlier years. None of the quatrains found in the *Abushqa* and there attributed to "Babur Mirza",

---

1 For accounts of the *Mubin*, *Akbar-nama* Bib. Ind. ed. i. 118, trs. H. Beveridge i. 278 note, Badayuni *ib*. i, 343, trs. Ranking p. 450, Sprenger ZDMG. 1862, Teufel *ib*. 1883. The *Akbar-nama* account appears in Turki in the "Fragments" associated with Kehr's transcript of the B.N. (JRAS. 1908, p. 76, A. S. B.'s art. *Babur-nama*. Babur mentions the *Mubin* (f. 252b, f. 351b).

are in the Rampur *Diwan*; nor are several of those early ones of the *Babur-nama*. So that the Diwan sent to Pulad Sultan may be the source from which the *Abushqa* drew its examples.

On first examining these verses, doubt arose as to whether they were really by Babur *Miranshahi*; or whether they were by "Babur Mirza" *Shahrukhi*. Fortunately my husband lighted on one of them quoted in the *Sanglakh* and there attributed to Babur Padshah. The *Abushqa* quatrains are used as examples in de Courteille's *Dictionary*, but without an author's name; they can be traced there through my husband's articles.[1]

929 AH.—NOV. 20TH 1522 TO NOV. 10TH 1523 AD.

a. Affairs of Hindustan.

The centre of interest in Babur's affairs now moves from Qandahar to a Hindustan torn by faction, of which faction one result was an appeal made at this time to Babur by Daulat Khan *Ludi* (*Yusuf-khail*) and 'Alau'd-din 'Alam Khan *Ludi* for help against Ibrahim.[2]

The following details are taken mostly from Ahmad Yadgar's *Tarikh-i-salatin-i-afaghana*:[3]—Daulat Khan had been summoned to Ibrahim's presence; he had been afraid to go and had sent his son Dilawar in his place; his disobedience angering Ibrahim, Dilawar had a bad reception and was shewn a ghastly exhibit of disobedient commanders. Fearing a like fate for himself, he made escape and hastened to report matters to his father in Lahor. His information strengthening Daulat Khan's previous apprehensions, decided the latter to proffer allegiance to Babur and to ask his help against Ibrahim. Apparently 'Alam Khan's interests were a part of this request. Accordingly Dilawar (or Apaq) Khan went to Kabul, charged with his father's message, and with intent to make known to Babur Ibrahim's

---

1 JRAS. 1901, *Persian MSS. in Indian Libraries* (description of the Rampur *Diwan*); AQR. 1911, *Babur's Diwan* (*i.e.* the Rampur *Diwan*); and *Some verses of the Emperor Babur* (the *Abushqa* quotations).

For Dr. E. D. Ross' Reproduction and account of the Rampur *Diwan*, JASB, 1910.

2 "After him (Ibrahim) was Babur King of Dihli, who owed his place to the Pathans," writes the Afghan poet Khush-hal *Khattak* (Afghan Poets of the XVII century, C. E. Biddulph, p. 58).

3 The translation only has been available (E. & D.'s H. of I., vol. 1).

evil disposition, his cruelty and tyranny, with their fruit of discontent amongst his Commanders and soldiery.

b. Reception of Dilawar Khan in Kabul.

Wedding festivities were in progress[1] when Dilawar Khan reached Kabul. He presented himself, at the Char-bagh may be inferred, and had word taken to Babur that an Afghan was at his Gate with a petition. When admitted, he demeaned himself as a suppliant and proceeded to set forth the distress of Hindustan. Babur asked why he, whose family had so long eaten the salt of the Ludis, had so suddenly deserted them for himself. Dilawar answered that his family through 40 years had upheld the Ludi throne, but that Ibrahim maltreated Sikandar's amirs, had killed 25 of them without cause, some by hanging, some burned alive, and that there was no hope of safety in him. Therefore, he said, he had been sent by many amirs to Babur whom they were ready to obey and for whose coming they were on the anxious watch.

c. Babur asks a sign.

At the dawn of the day following the feast, Babur prayed in the garden for a sign of victory in Hindustan, asking that it should be a gift to himself of mango or betel, fruits of that land. It so happened that Daulat Khan had sent him, as a present, half-ripened mangoes preserved in honey; when these were set before him, he accepted them as the sign, and from that time forth, says the chronicler, made preparation for a move on Hindustan.

d. 'Alam Khan.

Although 'Alam Khan seems to have had some amount of support for his attempt against his nephew, events show he had none valid for his purpose. That he had not Daulat Khan's, later occurrences make clear. Moreover he seems not to have been a man to win adherence or to be accepted as a trustworthy and sensible leader.[2] Dates are uncertain in the absence of

1 The marriage is said to have been Kamran's (E. & D.'s trs.).
2 Erskine calculated that 'Alam Khan was now well over 70 years of age (H. of I. i, 421 n.).

Babur's narrative, but it may have been in this year that 'Alam Khan went in person to Kabul and there was promised help against Ibrahim.

e. Birth of Gul-badan.

Either in this year or the next was born Dil-dar's third daughter Gul-badan, the later author of an *Humayun-nama* written at her nephew Akbar's command in order to provide information for the *Akbar-nama*.

930 AH.—NOV. 10TH 1523 TO OCT. 29TH 1524 AD.

a. Babur's fourth expedition to Hindustan.

This expedition differs from all earlier ones by its co-operation with Afghan malcontents against Ibrahim *Ludi*, and by having for its declared purpose direct attack on him through reinforcement of 'Alam Khan.

Exactly when the start from Kabul was made is not found stated; the route taken after fording the Indus, was by the sub-montane road through the Kakar country; the Jihlam and Chin-ab were crossed and a move was made to within 10 miles of Lahor.

Lahor was Daulat Khan's head-quarters but he was not in it now; he had fled for refuge to a colony of Biluchis, perhaps towards Multan, on the approach against him of an army of Ibrahim's under Bihar Khan *Ludi*. A battle ensued between Babur and Bihar Khan; the latter was defeated with great slaughter; Babur's troops followed his fugitive men into Lahor, plundered the town and burned some of the *bazars*.

Four days were spent near Lahor, then move south was made to Dibalpur which was stormed, plundered and put to the sword. The date of this capture is known from an incidental remark of Babur about chronograms (f. 325), to be mid-Rabi'u'l-awwal 930 AH. (*circa* Jan. 22nd 1524 AD.).[1] From Dibalpur a start was made for Sihrind but before this could be reached news arrived which dictated return to Lahor.

1 A. N. trs. H. Beveridge, i, 239.

b. The cause of return.

Daulat Khan's action is the obvious cause of the retirement. He and his sons had not joined Babur until the latter was at Dibalpur; he was not restored to his former place in charge of the important Lahor, but was given Jalandhar and Sultanpur, a town of his own foundation. This angered him extremely but he seems to have concealed his feelings for the time and to have given Babur counsel as if he were content. His son Dilawar, however, represented to Babur that his father's advice was treacherous; it concerned a move to Multan, from which place Daulat Khan may have come up to Dibalpur and connected with which at this time, something is recorded of co-operation by Babur and Shah Hasan *Arghun*. But the incident is not yet found clearly described by a source. Dilawar Khan told Babur that his father's object was to divide and thus weaken the invading force, and as this would have been the result of taking Daulat Khan's advice, Babur arrested him and Apaq on suspicion of treacherous intent. They were soon released, and Sultanpur was given them, but they fled to the hills, there to await a chance to swoop on the Panj-ab. Daulat Khan's hostility and his non-fulfilment of his engagement with Babur placing danger in the rear of an eastward advance, the Panj-ab was garrisoned by Babur's own followers and he himself went back to Kabul.

It is evident from what followed that Daulat Khan commanded much strength in the Panj-ab; evident also that something counselled delay in the attack on Ibrahim, perhaps closer cohesion in favour of 'Alam Khan, certainly removal of the menace of Daulat Khan in the rear; there may have been news already of the approach of the Auzbegs on Balkh which took Babur next year across Hindu-kush.

c. The Panj-ab garrison.

The expedition had extended Babur's command considerably, notably by obtaining possession of Lahor. He now posted in it Mir 'Abdu'l-'aziz his Master of the Horse; in Dibalpur he posted, with 'Alam Khan, Baba Qashqa *Mughul*; in Sialkot, Khusrau Kukuldash, in Kalanur, Muhammad 'Ali *Tajik*.

d. Two deaths.

This year, on Rajab 19th (May 23rd) died Isma'il *Safawi* at the age of 38, broken by defeat from Sultan Salim of Rum.[1] He was succeeded by his son Tahmasp, a child of ten.

This year may be that of the death of Shah Shuja' *Arghun*,[2] on Sha'ban 22nd (July 18th), the last grief of his burden being the death of his foster-brother Fazil concerning which, as well as Shah Beg's own death, Mir Ma'sum's account is worthy of full reproduction. Shah Beg was succeeded in Sind by his son Hasan, who read the *khutba* for Babur and drew closer links with Babur's circle by marrying, either this year or the next, Khalifa's daughter Gul-barg, with whom betrothal had been made during Hasan's visit to Babur in Kabul. Moreover Khalifa's son Muhibb-i-'ali married Nahid the daughter of Qasim Kukuldash and Mah-chuchuk *Arghun* (f. 214b). These alliances were made, says Ma'sum, to strengthen Hasan's position at Babur's Court.

e. A garden detail.

In this year and presumably on his return from the Panj-ab, Babur, as he himself chronicles (f. 132), had plantains (bananas) brought from Hindustan for the Bagh-i-wafa at Adinapur.

931 AH.——OCT. 29TH 1524 TO OCT. 18TH 1525 AD.

a. Daulat Khan.

Daulat Khan's power in the Panj-ab is shewn by what he effected after dispossessed of Lahor. On Babur's return to Kabul, he came down from the hills with a small body of his immediate followers, seized his son Dilawar, took Sultanpur, gathered a large force and defeated 'Alam Khan in Dibalpur. He detached 5000 men against Sialkot but Babur's begs of Lahor attacked and overcame them. Ibrahim sent an army to reconquer the Panj-ab;

---

1 The following old English reference to Isma'il's appearance may be quoted as found in a corner somewhat out-of-the-way from Oriental matters. In his essay on beauty Lord Bacon writes when arguing against the theory that beauty is usually not associated with highmindedness, "But this holds not always; for Augustus Cæsar, Titus Vespasianus, Philip le Bel of France, Edward the Fourth of England, Alcibiades of Athens, Isma'il the Sophy (Safawi) of Persia, were all high and great spirits, and yet the most beautiful men of their times."

2 *Cf. s.a.* 928 AH. for discussion of the year of death.

Daulat Khan, profiting by its dissensions and discontents, won over a part to himself and saw the rest break up.

b. 'Alam Khan.

From his reverse at Dibalpur, 'Alam Khan fled straight to Kabul. The further help he asked was promised under the condition that while he should take Ibrahim's place on the throne of Dihli, Babur in full suzerainty should hold Lahor and all to the west of it. This arranged, 'Alam Khan was furnished with a body of troops, given a royal letter to the Lahor begs ordering them to assist him, and started off, Babur promising to follow swiftly.

'Alam Khan's subsequent proceedings are told by Babur in the annals of 932 AH. (1525 AD.) at the time he received details about them (f. 255b).

c. Babur called to Balkh.

All we have yet found about this affair is what Babur says in explanation of his failure to follow 'Alam Khan as promised (f. 256), namely, that he had to go to Balkh because all the Auzbeg Sultans and Khans had laid siege to it. Light on the affair may come from some Persian or Auzbeg chronicle; Babur's arrival raised the siege; and risk must have been removed, for Babur returned to Kabul in time to set out for his fifth and last expedition to Hindustan on the first day of the second month of next year (932 AH.—1525 AD.). A considerable body of troops was in Badakhshan with Humayun; their non-arrival next year delaying his father's progress, brought blame on himself.

THE MEMOIRS OF BABUR

SECTION III. HINDUSTAN

932 AH.—OCT. 18TH 1525 TO OCT. 8TH 1526 AD.[1]

(a. Fifth expedition into Hindustan.)

(*Nov. 17th*) On Friday the 1st of the month of Safar at the date 932, the Sun being in the Sign of the Archer, we set out for Hindustan, crossed the small rise of Yak-langa, and dismounted in the meadow to the west of the water of Dih-i-ya'qub.[2] 'Abdu'l-maluk the armourer came into this camp; he had gone seven or eight months earlier as my envoy to Sultan Sa'id Khan (in Kashghar), and now brought one of the Khan's men, styled Yangi Beg (new beg) Kukuldash who conveyed letters, and

Haidarabad MS. Fol. 251*b*.

1 Elph. MS. f. 205*b*; W.-i-B. I.O. 215 f. 199*b* omits the year's events on the ground that Shaikh Zain has translated them; I.O. 217 f. 174; Mems. p. 290; Kehr's Codex p. 1084.

A considerable amount of reliable textual material for revising the Hindustan section of the English translation of the *Babur-nama* is wanting through loss of pages from the Elphinstone Codex; in one instance no less than an equivalent of 36 folios of the Haidarabad Codex are missing (f. 356 *et seq.*), but to set against this loss there is the valuable *per contra* that Kehr's manuscript throughout the section becomes of substantial value, losing its Persified character and approximating closely to the true text of the Elphinstone and Haidarabad Codices. Collateral help in revision is given by the works specified (*in loco* p. 428) as serving to fill the gap existing in Babur's narrative previous to 932 AH. and this notably by those described by Elliot and Dowson. Of these last, special help in supplementary details is given for 932 AH. and part of 933 AH. by Shaikh Zain [*Khawafi*]'s *Tabaqat-i-baburi*, which is a highly rhetorical paraphrase of Babur's narrative, requiring familiarity with ornate Persian to understand. For all my references to it, I am indebted to my husband. It may be mentioned as an interesting circumstance that the B.M. possesses in Or. 1999 a copy of this work which was transcribed in 998 AH. by one of Khwand-amir's grandsons and, judging from its date, presumably for Abu'l-fazl's use in the *Akbar-nama*.

Like part of the Kabul section, the Hindustan one is in diary-form, but it is still more heavily surcharged with matter entered at a date later than the diary. It departs from the style of the preceding diary by an occasional lapse into courtly phrase and by exchange of some Turki words for Arabic and Persian ones, doubtless found current in Hind, *e.g. fauj, dira, manzil, khail-khana.*

2 This is the Logar affluent of the Baran-water (Kabul-river). Masson describes this haltingplace (iii, 174).

small presents, and verbal messages[1] from the Khanims and the Khan.[2]

(*Nov. 18th to 21st*) After staying two days in that camp for the convenience of the army,[3] we marched on, halted one night,[4] and next dismounted at Badam-chashma. There we ate a confection (*ma'jun*).

(*Nov. 22nd*) On Wednesday (Safar 6th), when we had dismounted at Barik-ab, the younger brethren of Nur Beg—he himself remaining in Hindustan—brought gold *ashrafis* and *tankas*[5] to the value of 20,000 *shahrukhis*, sent from the Lahor revenues by Khwaja Husain. The greater part of these moneys was despatched by Mulla Ahmad, one of the chief men of Balkh, for the benefit of Balkh.[6]

(*Nov. 24th*) On Friday the 8th of the month (Safar), after dismounting at Gandamak, I had a violent discharge;[7] by God's mercy, it passed off easily.

Fol. 252.

1 *muhaqqar saughat u bilak* or *tilak*. A small verbal point arises about *bilak* (or *tilak*). *Bilak* is said by Quatremère to mean a gift (N. et E. xiv, 119 n.) but here *muhaqqar saughat* expresses gift. Another meaning can be assigned to *bilak* here, [one had also by *tilak*,] *viz.* that of word-of-mouth news or communication, sometimes supplementing written communication, possibly secret instructions, possibly small domestic details. In *bilak*, a gift, the root may be *bil*, the act of knowing, in *tilak* it is *til*, the act of speaking [whence *til*, the tongue, and *til tutmak*, to get news]. In the sentence noted, either word would suit for a verbal communication. Returning to *bilak* as a gift, it may express the *nuance* of English *token*, the maker-known of friendship, affection and so-on. This differentiates *bilak* from *saughat*, used in its frequent sense of ceremonial and diplomatic presents of value and importance.

2 With Sa'id at this time were two Khanims Sultan-nigar and Daulat-sultan who were Babur's maternal-aunts. Erskine suggested Khub-nigar, but she had died in 907 AH. (f. 96).

3 Humayun's non-arrival would be the main cause of delay. Apparently he should have joined before the Kabul force left that town.

4 The halt would be at But-khak, the last station before the Adinapur road takes to the hills.

5 Discussing the value of coins mentioned by Babur, Erskine says in his *History of India* (vol. i, Appendix E.) which was published in 1854 AD. that he had come to think his estimates of the value of the coins was set too low in the *Memoirs* (published in 1826 AD.). This sum of 20,000 *shahrukhis* he put at £1000. *Cf.* E. Thomas' *Pathan Kings of Dihli* and *Resources of the Mughal Empire*.

6 One of Masson's interesting details seems to fit the next stage of Babur's march (iii, 179). It is that after leaving But-khak, the road passes what in the thirties of the 19th Century, was locally known as Babur Padshah's Stone-heap (cairn) and believed piled in obedience to Babur's order that each man in his army should drop a stone on it in passing. No time for raising such a monument could be fitter than that of the fifth expedition into Hindustan when a climax of opportunity allowed hope of success.

7 *rezandalik*. This Erskine translates, both here and on ff. 253, 254, by *defluxion*, but de Courteille by *rhume de cerveau*. Shaikh Zain supports de Courteille by writing, not *rezandalik*, but *nuzla*, catarrh. De Courteille, in illustration of his

(*Nov. 25th*) On Saturday we dismounted in the Bagh-i-wafa. We delayed there a few days, waiting for Humayun and the army from that side.[1] More than once in this history the bounds and extent, charm and delight of that garden have been described; it is most beautifully placed; who sees it with the buyer's eye will know the sort of place it is. During the short time we were there, most people drank on drinking-days[2] and took their morning; on non-drinking days there were parties for *ma'jun*.

I wrote harsh letters to Humayun, lecturing him severely because of his long delay beyond the time fixed for him to join me.[3]

(*Dec. 3rd*) On Sunday the 17th of Safar, after the morning had been taken, Humayun arrived. I spoke very severely to him at once. Khwaja Kalan also arrived to-day, coming up from Ghazni. We marched in the evening of that same Sunday, and dismounted in a new garden between Sultanpur and Khwaja Rustam.

(*Dec. 6th*) Marching on Wednesday (Safar 20th), we got on a raft, and, drinking as we went reached Qush-gumbaz,[4] there landed and joined the camp.

---

reading of the word, quotes Burnes' account of an affection common in the Panj-ab and there called *nuzla*, which is a running at the nostrils, that wastes the brain and stamina of the body and ends fatally (*Travels in Bukhara* ed. 1839, ii, 41).

1 Tramontana, north of Hindu-kush.

2 Shaikh Zain says that the drinking days were Saturday, Sunday, Tuesday and Wednesday.

3 The Elph. Codex (f. 208*b*) contains the following note of Humayun's about his delay; it has been expunged from the text but is still fairly legible:—"The time fixed was after 'Ashura (10th Muharram, a voluntary fast); although we arrived after the next-following 10th ('*ashur, i.e.* of Safar), the delay had been necessary. The purpose of the letters (Babur's) was to get information; (in reply) it was represented that the equipment of the army of Badakhshan caused delay. If this slave (Humayun), trusting to his [father's] kindness, caused further delay, he has been sorry."

Babur's march from the Bagh-i-wafa was delayed about a week; Humayun started late from Badakhshan; his force may have needed some stay in Kabul for completion of equipment; his personal share of blame for which he counted on his father's forgiveness, is likely to have been connected with his mother's presence in Kabul.

Humayun's note is quoted in Turki by one MS. of the Persian text (B.M.W.-i-B. 16,623 f. 128); and from certain indications in Muhammad *Shirazi*'s lithograph (p. 163), appears to be in his archetype the Udaipur Codex; but it is not with all MSS. of the Persian text *e.g.* not with I.O. 217 and 218. A portion of it is in Kehr's MS. (p. 1086).

4 Bird's-dome [f. 145*b*, n.] or The pair (*qush*) of domes.

(*Dec. 7th*) Starting off the camp at dawn, we ourselves went on
a raft, and there ate confection (*ma'jun*). Our encamping-ground
was always Qiriq-ariq, but not a sign or trace of the camp could
Fol. 252*b*. be seen when we got opposite it, nor any appearance of our
horses. Thought I, "Garm-chashma (Hot-spring) is close by;
they may have dismounted there." So saying, we went on from
Qiriq-ariq. By the time we reached Garm-chashma, the very
day was late;[1] we did not stop there, but going on in its lateness
(*kichisi*), had the raft tied up somewhere, and slept awhile.

(*Dec. 8th*) At day-break we landed at Yada-bir where, as the
day wore on, the army-folks began to come in. The camp must
have been at Qiriq-ariq, but out of our sight.

There were several verse-makers on the raft, such as Shaikh
Abu'l-wajd,[2] Shaikh Zain, Mulla 'Ali-jan, Tardi Beg *Khaksar*
and others. In this company was quoted the following couplet
of Muhammad Salih:——[3]

> (Persian)   With thee, arch coquette, for a sweetheart, what can man do?
>   With another than thou where thou art, what can man do?

Said I, "Compose on these lines";[4] whereupon those given to
versifying, did so. As jokes were always being made at the expense
of Mulla 'Ali-jan, this couplet came off-hand into my head:——

> (Persian)   With one all bewildered as thou, what can man do?
>   .   .   .   .   .   .   , what can man do?[5]

---

1 *gun khud kich bulub aidi*; a little joke perhaps at the lateness both of the day
and the army.

2 Shaikh Zain's maternal-uncle.

3 Shaikh Zain's useful detail that this man's pen-name was Sharaf distinguishes
him from Muhammad Salih the author of the *Shaibani-nama*.

4 *gosha*, angle (*cf. gosha-i-kar*, limits of work). Parodies were to be made, having
the same metre, rhyme, and refrain as the model couplet.

5 I am unable to attach sense to Babur's second line; what is wanted is an illustration of two incompatible things. Babur's reflections [*infra*] condemned his verse.
Shaikh Zain describes the whole episode of the verse-making on the raft, and
goes on with, "He (Babur) excised this choice couplet from the pages of his Acts
(*Waqi'at*) with the knife of censure, and scratched it out from the tablets of his noble
heart with the finger-nails of repentance. I shall now give an account of this spiritual
matter" (*i.e.* the repentance), "by presenting the recantations of his Solomon-like
Majesty in his very own words, which are weightier than any from the lips of Aesop."
Shaikh Zain next quotes the Turki passage here translated in *b. Mention of the Mubin*.

(*b. Mention of the Mubin.*[1])

From time to time before it,[2] whatever came into my head, of good or bad, grave or jest, used to be strung into verse and written down, however empty and harsh the verse might be, but while I was composing the *Mubin*, this thought pierced through my dull wits and made way into my troubled heart, "A pity it will be if the tongue which has treasure of utterances so lofty as these are, waste itself again on low words; sad will it be if again vile imaginings find way into the mind that has made exposition of these sublime realities."[3] Since that time I had refrained from satirical and jesting verse; I was repentant (*ta'ib*); but these matters were totally out of mind and remembrance when I made that couplet (on Mulla 'Ali-jan).[4] A few days later in Bigram when I had fever and discharge, followed by cough, and I began to spit blood each time I coughed, I knew whence my reproof came; I knew what act of mine had brought this affliction on me.

Fol. 253.

"Whoever shall violate his oath, will violate it to the hurt of his own soul; but whoever shall perform that which he hath covenanted with God, to that man surely will He give great reward" (*Qoran* cap. 48 v. 10).

> (*Turki*) What is it I do with thee, ah! my tongue?
> My entrails bleed as a reckoning for thee.
> Good once[5] as thy words were, has followed this verse
> Jesting, empty,[6] obscene, has followed a lie.
> If thou say, "Burn will I not!" by keeping this vow
> Thou turnest thy rein from this field of strife.[7]

1 The *Mubin* is mentioned again and quoted on f. 351*b*. In both places its name escaped the notice of Erskine and de Courteille, who here took it for *min*, I, and on f. 351*b* omitted it, matters of which the obvious cause is that both translators were less familiar with the poem than it is now easy to be. There is amplest textual warrant for reading *Mubin* in both the places indicated above; its reinstatement gives to the English and French translations what they have needed, namely, the clinch of a definite stimulus and date of repentance, which was the influence of the Mubin in 928 AH. (1521–2 AD.). The whole passage about the peccant verse and its fruit of contrition should be read with others that express the same regret for broken law and may all have been added to the diary at the same time, probably in 935 AH. (1529 AD.). They will be found grouped in the Index *s.n.* Babur.
2 *mundin burun*, by which I understand, as the grammatical construction will warrant, *before writing the Mubin*. To read the words as referring to the peccant verse, is to take the clinch off the whole passage.
3 *i.e.* of the *Qoran* on which the *Mubin* is based.
4 Dropping down-stream, with wine and good company, he entirely forgot his good resolutions.
5 This appears to refer to the good thoughts embodied in the *Mubin*.
6 This appears to contrast with the "sublime realities" of the *Qoran*.
7 In view of the interest of the passage, and because this verse is not in the Rampur *Diwan*, as are many contained in the Hindustan section, the Turki original is

"O Lord! we have dealt unjustly with our own souls; if Thou forgive us not, and be not merciful unto us, we shall surely be of those that perish"[1] (*Qoran* cap. 7 v. 22).

Taking anew the place of the penitent pleading for pardon, I gave my mind rest[2] from such empty thinking and such unlawful occupation. I broke my pen. Made by that Court, such reproof of sinful slaves is for their felicity; happy are the highest and the slave when such reproof brings warning and its profitable fruit.

(*c. Narrative resumed.*)

(*Dec. 8th continued*) Marching on that evening, we dismounted at 'Ali-masjid. The ground here being very confined, I always used to dismount on a rise overlooking the camp in the valley-bottom.[3] The camp-fires made a wonderful illumination there at night; assuredly it was because of this that there had always been drinking there, and was so now.

Fol. 253*b*.

(*Dec. 9th and 10th*) To-day I rode out before dawn; I preferred a confection (*ma'jun*)[4] and also kept this day a fast. We dismounted near Bigram (Peshawar); and next morning, the camp remaining on that same ground, rode to Karg-awi.[5] We crossed the Siyah-ab in front of Bigram, and formed our hunting-circle looking down-stream. After a little, a person brought

---

quoted. My translation differs from those of Mr. Erskine and M. de Courteille; all three are tentative of a somewhat difficult verse.

> *Ni qila min sining bila ai til?*
> *Jihating din mining aichim qan dur.*
> *Nicha yakhshi disang bu hazl aila shi'r*
> *Biri-si fahash u biri yalghan dur.*
> *Gar disang kuima min, bu jazm bila*
> *Jalau'ingni bu 'arsa din yan dur.*

1 The Qoran puts these sayings into the mouths of Adam and Eve.

2 Hai. MS. *tindurub*; Ilminsky, p. 327, *yandurub*; W.-i-B. I.O. 217, f. 175, *sard sakhta*.

3 Of 'Ali-masjid the *Second Afghan War* (official account) has a picture which might be taken from Babur's camp.

4 Shaikh Zain's list of the drinking-days (f. 252 note) explains why sometimes Babur says he preferred *ma'jun*. In the instances I have noticed, he does this on a drinking-day; the preference will be therefore for a confection over wine. December 9th was a Saturday and drinking-day; on it he mentions the preference; Tuesday Nov. 21st was a drinking day, and he states that he ate *ma'jun*.

5 Presumably the *karg-khana* of f. 222*b*, rhinoceros-home in both places. A similar name applies to a tract in the Rawalpindi District,—Babur-khana, Tiger-home, which is linked to the tradition of Buddha's self-sacrifice to appease the hunger of seven tiger-cubs. [In this Babur-khana is the town Kacha-kot from which Babur always names the river Haru.]

word that there was a rhino in a bit of jungle near Bigram, and
that people had been stationed near-about it. We betook ourselves, loose rein, to the place, formed a ring round the jungle,
made a noise, and brought the rhino out, when it took its way
across the plain. Humayun and those come with him from that
side (Tramontana), who had never seen one before, were much
entertained. It was pursued for two miles; many arrows were
shot at it; it was brought down without having made a good set
at man or horse. Two others were killed. I had often wondered
how a rhino and an elephant would behave if brought face
to face; this time one came out right in front of some elephants
the mahauts were bringing along; it did not face them when the   Fol. 254.
mahauts drove them towards it, but got off in another direction.

(*d. Preparations for ferrying the Indus.*[1])

On the day we were in Bigram, several of the begs and
household were appointed, with pay-masters and diwans, six
or seven being put in command, to take charge of the boats at the
Nil-ab crossing, to make a list of all who were with the army,
name by name, and to count them up.

That evening I had fever and discharge[2] which led on to
cough and every time I coughed, I spat blood. Anxiety was
great but, by God's mercy, it passed off in two or three days.

(*Dec. 11th*) It rained when we left Bigram; we dismounted
on the Kabul-water.

(*e. News from Lahor.*)

News came that Daulat Khan[3] and (Apaq) Ghazi Khan,
having collected an army of from 20 to 30,000, had taken
Kilanur, and intended to move on Lahor. At once Mumin-i-'ali
the commissary was sent galloping off to say, "We are advancing
march by march;[4] do not fight till we arrive."

1 This is the first time on an outward march that Babur has crossed the Indus by
boat; hitherto he has used the ford above Attock, once however specifying that men
on foot were put over on rafts.
2 f. 253.
3 In my Translator's Note (p. 428), attention was drawn to the circumstance that
Babur always writes Daulat Khan *Yusuf-khail*, and not Daulat Khan *Ludi*. In doing
this, he uses the family- or clan-name instead of the tribal one, Ludi.
4 *i.e.* day by day.

(*Dec. 14th*) With two night-halts on the way, we reached the water of Sind (Indus), and there dismounted on Thursday the 28th (of Safar).

(*f. Ferrying the Indus.*)

(*Dec. 16th*) On Saturday the 1st of the first Rabi', we crossed the Sind-water, crossed the water of Kacha-kot (Haru), and dismounted on the bank of the river.[1] The begs, pay-masters and diwans who had been put in charge of the boats, reported that the number of those come with the army, great and small, good and bad, retainer and non-retainer, was written down as 12,000.

(*g. The eastward march.*)

The rainfall had been somewhat scant in the plains, but seemed to have been good in the cultivated lands along the hill-skirts; for these reasons we took the road for Sialkot along the skirt-hills. Opposite Hati *Kakar's* country[2] we came upon a torrent[3] the waters of which were standing in pools. Those pools were all frozen over. The ice was not very thick, as thick as the hand may-be. Such ice is unusual in Hindustan; not a sign or trace of any was seen in the years we were (*aiduk*) in the country.[4]

We had made five marches from the Sind-water; after the sixth (*Dec. 22nd*—Rabi' I. 7th) we dismounted on a torrent in the camping-ground (*yurt*) of the Bugials[5] below Balnath Jogi's hill which connects with the Hill of Jud.

Fol. 254b.

1 *darya*, which Babur's precise use of words *e.g.* of *darya*, *rud*, and *su*, allows to apply here to the Indus only.
2 Presumably this was near Parhala, which stands, where the Suhan river quits the hills, at the eastern entrance of a wild and rocky gorge a mile in length. It will have been up this gorge that Babur approached Parhala in 925 AH. (Rawalpindi Gazetteer p. 11).
3 *i.e.* here, bed of a mountain-stream.
4 The Elphinstone Codex here preserves the following note, the authorship of which is attested by the scribe's remark that it is copied from the handwriting of Humayun Padshah:—As my honoured father writes, we did not know until we occupied Hindustan (932 AH.), but afterwards did know, that ice does form here and there if there come a colder year. This was markedly so in the year I conquered Gujrat (942 AH.–1535 AD.) when it was so cold for two or three days between Bhulpur and Gualiar that the waters were frozen over a hand's thickness.
5 This is a Kakar (Gakkhar) clan, known also as Baragowah, of which the location in Jahangir Padshah's time was from Rohtas to Hatya, *i.e.* about where Babur encamped (*Memoirs of Jahangir*, Rogers and Beveridge, p. 97; E. and D. vi, 309; Provincial Gazetteers of Rawalpindi and Jihlam, p. 64 and p. 97 respectively).

(*Dec. 23rd*) In order to let people get provisions, we stayed the next day in that camp. '*Araq* was drunk on that day. Mulla Muh. *Parghari* told many stories; never had he been so talkative. Mulla Shams himself was very riotous; once he began, he did not finish till night.

The slaves and servants, good and bad, who had gone out after provisions, went further than this [1] and heedlessly scattered over jungle and plain, hill and broken ground. Owing to this, a few were overcome; Kichkina *tunqitar* died there.

(*Dec. 24th*) Marching on, we crossed the Bihat-water at a ford below Jilam (Jihlam) and there dismounted. Wali *Qisil* (Rufus) came there to see me. He was the Sialkot reserve, and held the parganas of Bimruki and Akriada. Thinking about Sialkot, Fol. 255. I took towards him the position of censure and reproach. He excused himself, saying "I had come to my *pargana* before Khusrau Kukuldash left Sialkot; he did not even send me word." After listening to his excuse, I said, "Since thou hast paid no attention to Sialkot, why didst thou not join the begs in Lahor?" He was convicted, but as work was at hand, I did not trouble about his fault.

(*h. Scouts sent with orders to Lahor.*)

(*Dec. 25th*) Sayyid Tufan and Sayyid Lachin were sent galloping off, each with a pair-horse,[2] to say in Lahor, "Do not join battle; meet us at Sialkot or Parsrur" (mod. Pasrur). It was in everyone's mouth that Ghazi Khan had collected 30 to 40,000 men, that Daulat Khan, old as he was, had girt two swords to his waist, and that they were resolved to fight. Thought I, "The proverb says that ten friends are better than nine; do you not make a mistake: when the Lahor begs have joined you, fight there and then!"

(*Dec. 26th and 27th*) After starting off the two men to the begs, we moved forward, halted one night, and next dismounted on the bank of the Chin-ab (Chan-ab).

---

1 *andin autub*, a reference perhaps to going out beyond the corn-lands, perhaps to attempt for more than provisions.
2 *qush-at*, a led horse to ride in change.

As Buhlulpur was *khalsa*,[1] we left the road to visit it. Its fort is situated above a deep ravine, on the bank of the Chin-ab. It pleased us much. We thought of bringing Sialkot to it. Please God! the chance coming, it shall be done straightway! Fol. 255b. From Buhlulpur we went to camp by boat. There was a party; some drinking '*araq*, some beer. After leaving the boat at the Bed-time Prayer, there was more drinking in the *khirgah* (tent). For the good of the horses, we gave them a day's breathing on the bank of this water.

(i. Jats and Gujurs.[2])

(*Dec. 29th*) On Friday the 14th of the first Rabi' we dismounted at Sialkot. If one go into Hindustan the Jats and Gujurs always pour down in countless hordes from hill and plain for loot in bullock and buffalo. These ill-omened peoples are just senseless oppressors! Formerly their doings did not concern us much because the country was an enemy's, but they began the same senseless work after we had taken it. When we reached Sialkot, they fell in tumult on poor and needy folks who were coming out of the town to our camp, and stripped them bare. I had the silly thieves sought for, and ordered two or three of them cut to pieces.

From Sialkot Nur Beg's brother Shaham also was made to gallop off to the begs in Lahor to say, "Make sure where the enemy is; find out from some well-informed person where he may be met, and send us word."

A trader, coming into this camp, represented that 'Alam Khan had let Sl. Ibrahim defeat him.

---

1 According to Shaikh Zain it was in this year that Babur made Buhlulpur a royal domain (B.M. Add. 26,202 f. 16), but this does not agree with Babur's explanation that he visited the place because it was *khalsa*. Its name suggests that it had belonged to Buhlul *Ludi*; Babur may have taken it in 930 AH. when he captured Sialkot. It never received the population of Sialkot, as Babur had planned it should do because pond-water was drunk in the latter town and was a source of disease. The words in which Babur describes its situation are those he uses of Akhsi (f. 4b); not improbably a resemblance inclined his liking towards Buhlulpur. (It may be noted that this Buhlulpur is mentioned in the *Ayin-i-akbari* and marked on large maps, but is not found in the G. of I. 1907.)

2 Erskine's note (*Memoirs* p. 294) is as follows: "The Jets or Jats are the Muhammadan peasantry of the Panj-ab, the bank of the Indus, Siwistan *etc.* and must not be confounded with the Jāts, a powerful Hindu tribe to the west of the Jamna, about Agra *etc.* and which occupies a subordinate position in the country of the Rajputs."

(j. 'Alam Khan's action and failure.[1])

Here are the particulars:—'Alam Khan, after taking leave of me (in Kabul, 931 AH.), went off in that heat by double marches, regardless of those with him.[2] As at the time I gave him leave to go, all the Auzbeg khans and sultans had laid siege to Balkh, Fol. 256. I rode for Balkh as soon as I had given him his leave. On his reaching Lahor, he insisted to the begs, "You reinforce me; the Padshah said so; march along with me; let us get (Apaq) Ghazi Khan to join us; let us move on Dihli and Agra." Said they, "Trusting to what, will you join Ghazi Khan? Moreover the royal orders to us were, 'If at any time Ghazi Khan has sent his younger brother Haji Khan with his son to Court, join him; or do so, if he has sent them, by way of pledge, to Lahor; if he has done neither, do not join him.' You yourself only yesterday fought him and let him beat you! Trusting to what, will you join him now? Besides all this, it is not for your advantage to join him!" Having said what-not of this sort, they refused 'Alam Khan. He did not fall in with their views, but sent his son Sher Khan to speak with Daulat Khan and with Ghazi Khan, and afterwards all saw one another.

'Alam Khan took with him Dilawar Khan, who had come into Lahor two or three months earlier after his escape from prison; he took also Mahmud Khan (son of) Khan-i-jahan,[3] to

---

1 The following section contains a later addition to the diary summarizing the action of 'Alam Khan before and after Babur heard of the defeat from the trader he mentions. It refutes an opinion found here and there in European writings that Babur used and threw over 'Alam Khan. It and Babur's further narrative shew that 'Alam Khan had little valid backing in Hindustan, that he contributed nothing to Babur's success, and that no abstention by Babur from attack on Ibrahim would have set 'Alam Khan on the throne of Dihli. It and other records, Babur's and those of Afghan chroniclers, allow it to be said that if 'Alam Khan had been strong enough to accomplish his share of the compact that he should take and should rule Dihli, Babur would have kept to his share, namely, would have maintained supremacy in the Panj-ab. He advanced against Ibrahim only when 'Alam Khan had totally failed in arms and in securing adherence.

2 This objurgation on over-rapid marching looks like the echo of complaint made to Babur by men of his own whom he had given to 'Alam Khan in Kabul.

3 Mahmud himself may have inherited his father's title Khan-i-jahan but a little further on he is specifically mentioned as the son of Khan-i-jahan, presumably because his father had been a more notable man than he was. Of his tribe it may be noted that the Haidarabad MS. uniformly writes Nuhani and not Luhani as is usual in European writings, and that it does so even when, as on f. 149b, the word is applied to a trader. Concerning the tribe, family, or caste *vide* G. of I. *s.n.* Lohanas and Crooke *l.c. s.n.* Pathan, para. 21.

whom a *pargana* in the Lahor district had been given. They
seem to have left matters at this:—Daulat Khan with Ghazi
Khan was to take all the begs posted in Hindustan to himself,
indeed he was to take everything on that side;[1] while 'Alam
Fol. 256b.   Khan was to take Dilawar Khan and Haji Khan and, reinforced
by them, was to capture Dihli and Agra. Isma'il *Jilwani* and
other amirs came and saw 'Alam Khan; all then betook
themselves, march by march, straight for Dihli. Near Indri
came also Sulaiman Shaikh-zada.[2] Their total touched 30 to
40,000 men.

They laid siege to Dihli but could neither take it by assault
nor do hurt to the garrison.[3] When Sl. Ibrahim heard of their
assembly, he got an army to horse against them; when they
heard of his approach, they rose from before the place and
moved to meet him. They had left matters at this:—"If we
attack by day-light, the Afghans will not desert (to us), for the
sake of their reputations with one another; but if we attack at
night when one man cannot see another, each man will obey
his own orders." Twice over they started at fall of day from
a distance of 12 miles (6 *kurohs*), and, unable to bring matters to a
point, neither advanced nor retired; but just sat on horseback
for two or three watches. On a third occasion they delivered
an attack when one watch of night remained—their purpose
seeming to be the burning of tents and huts! They went; they
set fire from every end; they made a disturbance. Jalal Khan
Jig-hat[4] came with other amirs and saw 'Alam Khan.

Sl. Ibrahim did not bestir himself till shoot of dawn from
where he was with a few of his own family[5] within his own
enclosure (*saracha*). Meantime 'Alam Khan's people were busy
Fol. 257.   with plunder and booty. Seeing the smallness of their number,
Sl. Ibrahim's people moved out against them in rather small

1   *i.e.* west of Dihli territory, the Panj-ab.
2   He was of the Farmul family of which Babur says (f. 139b) that it was in high
favour in Hindustan under the Afghans and of which the author of the *Waqi'at-i-
mushtaqi* says that it held half the lands of Dihli in *jagir* (E. and D. iv, 547).
3   Presumably he could not cut off supplies.
4   The only word similar to this that I have found is one "Jaghat" said to mean
serpent and to be the name of a Hindu sub-caste of Nats (Crooke, iv, 72 & 73).
The word here might be a nick-name. Babur writes it as two words.
5   *khasa-khail*, presumably members of the Sahu-khail (family) of the Ludi tribe of
the Afghan race.

force with one elephant. 'Alam Khan's party, not able to make
stand against the elephant, ran away. He in his flight crossed
over into the Mian–du–ab and crossed back again when he
reached the Panipat neighbourhood. In Indri he contrived on
some pretext to get 4 *laks* from Mian Sulaiman.[1] He was
deserted by Isma'il *Jilwani*, by Biban[2] and by his own oldest
son Jalal, who all withdrew into the Mian–du–ab; and he had
been deserted just before the fighting, by part of his troops,
namely, by Darya Khan (*Nuhani*)'s son Saif Khan, by Khan–i–
jahan (*Nuhani*)'s son Mahmud Khan, and by Shaikh Jamal
Farmuli. When he was passing through Sihrind with Dilawar
Khan, he heard of our advance and of our capture of Milwat
(Malot).[3] On this Dilawar Khan—who always had been my
well-wisher and on my account had dragged out three or four
months in prison,—left 'Alam Khan and the rest and went to
his family in Sultanpur. He waited on me three or four days
after we took Milwat. 'Alam Khan and Haji Khan crossed
the Shatlut (*sic*)-water and went into Ginguta,[4] one of the strongholds in the range that lies between the valley and the plain.[5]
There our Afghan and Hazara[6] troops besieged them, and had   Fol. 257*b*.
almost taken that strong fort when night came on. Those
inside were thinking of escape but could not get out because of
the press of horses in the Gate. There must have been elephants
also; when these were urged forward, they trod down and killed
many horses. 'Alam Khan, unable to escape mounted, got out
on foot in the darkness. After a *lak* of difficulties, he joined
Ghazi Khan, who had not gone into Milwat but had fled into the

1 Erskine suggested that this man was a rich banker, but he might well be the
Farmuli Shaikh-zada of f. 256*b*, in view of the exchange Afghan historians make
of the Farmuli title Shaikh for Mian (*Tarikh-i-sher-shahi*, E. & D. iv, 347 and
Tarikh-i-daudi ib. 457).

2 This Biban, as Babur always calls him without title, is Malik Biban *Jilwani*. He
was associated with Shaikh Bayazid *Farmuli* or, as Afghan writers style him, Mian
Bayazid *Farmuli*. (Another of his name was Mian Biban, son of Mian Ata
Sahu-khail (E. & D. iv, 347).)

3 This name occurs so frequently in and about the Panj-ab as to suggest that it
means a fort (Ar. *maluzat?*). This one in the Siwaliks was founded by Tatar Khan
Yusuf-khail (*Ludi*) in the time of Buhlul *Ludi* (E. and D. iv, 415).

4 In the Beth Jalandhar *du-ab*.

5 *i.e.* on the Siwaliks, here locally known as Katar Dhar.

6 Presumably they were from the Hazara district east of the Indus. The *Tabaqat-
i-akbari* mentions that this detachment was acting under Khalifa apart from Babur
and marching through the skirt-hills (lith. ed. p. 182).

hills. Not being received with even a little friendliness by Ghazi Khan; needs must! he came and waited on me at the foot of the dale [1] near Pehlur.

(*k. Diary resumed.*)

A person came to Sialkot from the Lahor begs to say they would arrive early next morning to wait on me.

(*Dec. 30th*) Marching early next day (Rabi' I. 15th), we dismounted at Parsrur. There Muh. 'Ali *Jang-jang*, Khwaja Husain and several braves waited on me. As the enemy's camp seemed to be on the Lahor side of the Ravi, we sent men out under Bujka for news. Near the third watch of the night they brought word that the enemy, on hearing of us, had fled, no man looking to another.

(*Dec. 31st*) Getting early to horse and leaving baggage and train in the charge of Shah Mir Husain and Jan Beg, we bestirred ourselves. We reached Kalanur in the afternoon, and there dismounted. Muhammad Sl. Mirza and 'Adil Sl. [2] came to wait on me there, together with some of the begs.

Fol. 258.

(*Jan. 1st 1526 AD.*) We marched early from Kalanur. On the road people gave us almost certain news of Ghazi Khan and other fugitives. Accordingly we sent, flying after those fliers, the commanders Muhammadi, Ahmadi, Qutluq-qadam, Treasurer Wali and most of those begs who, in Kabul, had recently bent the knee for their begship. So far it was settled:—That it would be good indeed if they could overtake and capture the fugitives; and that, if they were not able to do this, they were to keep careful watch round Milwat (Malot), so as to prevent those inside from getting out and away. Ghazi Khan was the object of this watch.

(*l. Capture of Milwat.*)

(*Jan. 2nd and 3rd*) After starting those begs ahead, we crossed the Biah-water (Beas) opposite Kanwahin[3] and dismounted. From there we marched to the foot of the valley of Fort Milwat, making two night-halts on the way. The begs who

1 *dun*, f. 260 and note.
2 These were both refugees from Harat.
3 Sarkar of Batala, in the Bari *du-ab* (A.-i-A. Jarrett, p. 110).

had arrived before us, and also those of Hindustan were ordered to dismount in such a way as to besiege the place closely.

A grandson of Daulat Khan, son of his eldest son 'Ali Khan, Isma'il Khan by name, came out of Milwat to see me; he took back promise mingled with threat, kindness with menace.

(*Jan. 5th*) On Friday (Rabi' I. 21st) I moved camp forward to within a mile of the fort, went myself to examine the place, posted right, left and centre, then returned to camp.

Daulat Khan sent to represent to me that Ghazi Khan had   Fol. 258b. fled into the hills, and that, if his own faults were pardoned, he would take service with me and surrender Milwat. Khwaja Mir-i-miran was sent to chase fear from his heart and to escort him out; he came, and with him his son 'Ali Khan. I had ordered that the two swords he had girt to his waist to fight me with, should be hung from his neck. Was such a rustic blockhead possible! With things as they were, he still made pretensions! When he was brought a little forward, I ordered the swords to be removed from his neck. At the time of our seeing one another he hesitated to kneel; I ordered them to pull his leg and make him do so. I had him seated quite in front, and ordered a person well acquainted with Hindustani to interpret my words to him, one after another. Said I, "Thus speak:—I called thee Father. I shewed thee more honour and respect than thou couldst have asked. Thee and thy sons I saved from door-to-door life amongst the Baluchis.[1] Thy family and thy *haram* I freed from Ibrahim's prison-house.[2] Three *krors* I gave thee on Tatar Khan's lands.[3] What ill sayest thou I have done thee, that thus thou shouldst hang a sword on thy either side,[4] lead an army out, fall on lands of ours,[5] and stir strife and trouble?" Dumbfounded, the old man

---

1 Babur's phrasing suggests beggary.

2 This might refer to the time when Ibrahim's commander Bihar (Bahadur) Khan *Nuhani* took Lahor (Translator's Note *in loco* p. 441).

3 They were his father's. Erskine estimated the 3 *krors* at £75,000.

4 *shiqq*, what hangs on either side, perhaps a satirical reference to the ass' burden.

5 As illustrating Babur's claim to rule as a Timurid in Hindustan, it may be noted that in 814 AH. (1411 AD.), Khizr Khan who is allowed by the date to have been a Sayyid ruler in Dihli, sent an embassy to Shahrukh Mirza the then Timurid ruler of Samarkand to acknowledge his suzerainty (*Matla'u's-sa'dain*, Quatremère, N. et Ex. xiv, 196).

Fol. 259. stuttered a few words, but he gave no answer, nor indeed could answer be given to words so silencing. He was ordered to remain with Khwaja Mir-i-miran.

(*Jan. 6th*) On Saturday the 22nd of the first Rabi', I went myself to safeguard the exit of the families and *harams*[1] from the fort, dismounting on a rise opposite the Gate. To me there came 'Ali Khan and made offering of a few *ashrafis*. People began to bring out the families just before the Other Prayer. Though Ghazi Khan was reported to have got away, there were who said they had seen him in the fort. For this reason several of the household and braves[2] were posted at the Gate, in order to prevent his escape by a ruse, for to get away was his full intention.[3] Moreover if jewels and other valuables were being taken away by stealth, they were to be confiscated. I spent that night in a tent pitched on the rise in front of the Gate.

(*Jan. 7th*) Early next morning, Muhammadi, Ahmadi, Sl. Junaid, 'Abdu'l-'aziz, Muhammad 'Ali *Jang-jang* and Qutluq-
Fol. 259b. qadam were ordered to enter the fort and take possession of all effects. As there was much disturbance at the Gate, I shot off a few arrows by way of chastisement. Humayun's story-teller (*qissa-khwan*) was struck by the arrow of his destiny and at once surrendered his life.

(*Jan. 7th and 8th*) After spending two nights[4] on the rise, I inspected the fort. I went into Ghazi Khan's book-room;[5] some of the precious things found in it, I gave to Humayun, some sent to Kamran (in Qandahar). There were many books of learned contents,[6] but not so many valuable ones as had at first appeared. I passed that night in the fort; next morning I went back to camp.

(*Jan. 9th*) It had been in our minds that Ghazi Khan was in the fort, but he, a man devoid of nice sense of honour, had

---

1 Firishta says that Babur mounted for the purpose of preserving the honour of the Afghans and by so doing enabled the families in the fort to get out of it safely (lith. ed. p. 204).

2 *chuhra*; they will have been of the Corps of braves (*yigit*; Appendix H. section *c*.).

3 *kim kulli gharz aul aidi*; Pers. trs. *ka gharz-i-kulli-i-au bud*.

4 Persicé, the eves of Sunday and Monday; Anglicé, Saturday and Sunday nights.

5 Ghazi Khan was learned and a poet (Firishta ii, 42).

6 *mullayana khud*, perhaps books of learned topic but not in choice copies.

escaped to the hills, abandoning father, brethren and sisters in Milwat.

> See that man without honour who never
> The face of good luck shall behold;
> Bodily ease he chose for himself,
> In hardship he left wife and child (*Gulistan* cap. i, story 17).

(*Jan. 10th*) Leaving that camp on Wednesday, we moved towards the hills to which Ghazi Khan had fled. When we dismounted in the valley–bottom two miles from the camp in the mouth of Milwat,[1] Dilawar Khan came and waited on me. Daulat Khan, 'Ali Khan and Isma'il Khan, with other chiefs, were given into Kitta Beg's charge who was to convey them to the Bhira fort of Milwat (Malot),[2] and there keep guard over them. In agreement with Dilawar Khan, blood–ransom was fixed for some who had been made over each to one man; some gave security, some were kept prisoner. Daulat Khan died when Kitta Beg reached Sultanpur with the prisoners.[3]

Fol. 260.

Milwat was given into the charge of Muh. 'Ali *Jang-jang* who, pledging his own life for it, left his elder brother Arghun and a party of braves in it. A body of from 200 to 250 Afghans were told off to reinforce him.

Khwaja Kalan had loaded several camels with Ghazni wines. A party was held in his quarters overlooking the fort and the whole camp, some drinking '*araq*, some wine. It was a varied party.

(*m. Jaswan-valley.*)
Marching on, we crossed a low hill of the grazing-grounds (*argha-dal-liq*) of Milwat and went into the *dun*, as Hindustanis

---

1 f. 257. It stands in 31° 50′ N. and 76° E. (G. of I.).

2 This is on the Salt-range, in 32° 42′ N. and 72° 50′ E. (*Ayin-i-akbari* trs. Jarrett, i, 325; Provincial Gazetteer, Jihlam District).

3 He died therefore in the town he himself built. Kitta Beg probably escorted the Afghan families from Milwat also; Dilawar Khan's own seems to have been there already (f. 257).

The *Babur-nama* makes no mention of Daulat Khan's relations with Nanak, the founder of the Sikh religion, nor does it mention Nanak himself. A tradition exists that Nanak, when on his travels, made exposition of his doctrines to an attentive Babur and that he was partly instrumental in bringing Babur against the Afghans. He was 12 years older than Babur and survived him nine. (*Cf. Dabistan* lith. ed. p. 270; and, for Jahangir Padshah's notice of Daulat Khan, *Tusuk-i-jahangiri*, Rogers and Beveridge, p. 87).

are understood to call a dale (*julga*).[1] In this dale is a running-water[2] of Hindustan; along its sides are many villages; and it is said to be the pargana of the Jaswal, that is to say, of Dilawar Khan's maternal uncles. It lies there shut-in, with meadows along its torrent, rice cultivated here and there, a three or four mill-stream flowing in its trough, its width from two to four miles, six even in places, villages on the skirts of its hills—hillocks they are rather—where there are no villages, peacocks, monkeys, and many fowls which, except that they are mostly of one colour, are exactly like house-fowls.

As no reliable news was had of Ghazi Khan, we arranged for Tardika to go with Birim Deo *Malinhas* and capture him wherever he might be found.

In the hills of this dale stand thoroughly strong forts; one on the north-east, named Kutila, has sides 70 to 80 yards (*qari*) of straight fall, the side where the great gate is being perhaps 7 or 8 yards.[3] The width of the place where the draw-bridge is made, may be 10 to 12 yards. Across this they have made a bridge of two tall trees[4] by which horses and herds are taken over. This was one of the local forts Ghazi Khan had strengthened; his man will have been in it now. Our raiders (*chapqunchi*) assaulted it and had almost taken it when night came on. The garrison abandoned this difficult place and went off. Near this dale is also the stronghold of Ginguta; it is girt

1 I translate *dun* by *dale* because, as its equivalent, Babur uses *julga* by which he describes a more pastoral valley than one he calls a *dara*.

2 *bir aqar-su.* Babur's earlier uses of this term connect it with the swift flow of water in irrigation channels; this may be so here but also the term may make distinction between the rapid mountain-stream and the slow movement of rivers across plains.

3 There are two readings of this sentence; Erskine's implies that the neck of land connecting the fort-rock with its adjacent hill measures 7–8 *qari* (yards) from side to side; de Courteille's that where the great gate was, the perpendicular fall surrounding the fort shallowed to 7–8 yards. The Turki might be read, I think, to mean whichever alternative was the fact. Erskine's reading best bears out Babur's account of the strength of the fort, since it allows of a cleft between the hill and the fort some 140–160 feet deep, as against the 21–24 of de Courteille's. Erskine may have been in possession of information [in 1826] by which he guided his translation (p. 300), "At its chief gate, for the space of 7 or 8 *gez* (*qari*), there is a place that admits of a draw-bridge being thrown across; it may be 10 or 12 *gez* wide." If de Courteille's reading be correct in taking 7–8 *qari* only to be the depth of the cleft, that cleft may be artificial.

4 *yighach*, which also means wood.

round by precipices as Kutila is, but is not so strong as Kutila. As has been mentioned 'Alam Khan went into it.[1]   Fol. 261.

(n. Babur advances against Ibrahim.)

After despatching the light troop against Ghazi Khan, I put my foot in the stirrup of resolution, set my hand on the rein of trust in God, and moved forward against Sultan Ibrahim, son of Sultan Sikandar, son of Buhlul *Ludi Afghan*, in possession of whose throne at that time were the Dihli capital and the dominions of Hindustan, whose standing-army was called a *lak* (100,000), whose elephants and whose begs' elephants were about 1000.

At the end of our first stage, I bestowed Dibalpur on Baqi *shaghawal*[2] and sent him to help Balkh;[3] sent also gifts, taken in the success of Milwat, for (my) younger children and various train in Kabul.

When we had made one or two marches down the (Jaswan) *dun*, Shah 'Imad *Shirazi* arrived from Araish Khan and Mulla Muhammad *Mazhab*,[4] bringing letters that conveyed their good wishes for the complete success of our campaign and indicated their effort and endeavour towards this. In response, we sent, by a foot-man, royal letters expressing our favour. We then marched on.

---

1 f. 257.

2 chief scribe (f. 13 n. to 'Abdu'l-wahhab). Shaw's Vocabulary explains the word as meaning also a "high official of Central Asian sovereigns, who is supreme over all *qazis* and *mullas*".

3 Babur's persistent interest in Balkh attracts attention, especially at this time so shortly before he does not include it as part of his own territories (f. 270).

Since I wrote of Balkh *s.a.* 923 AH. (1517 AD.), I have obtained the following particulars about it in that year; they are summarized from the *Habibu's-siyar* (lith. ed. iii, 371). In 923 AH. Khwand-amir was in retirement at Pasht in Ghurjistan where also was Muhammad-i-zaman Mirza. The two went in company to Balkh where the Mirza besieged Babur's man Ibrahim *chapuk* (Slash-face), and treacherously murdered one Aurdu-shah, an envoy sent out to parley with him. Information of what was happening was sent to Babur in Kabul. Babur reached Balkh when it had been besieged a month. His presence caused the Mirza to retire and led him to go into the Dara-i-gaz (Tamarind-valley). Babur, placing in Balkh Faqir-i-'ali, one of those just come up with him, followed the Mirza but turned back at Aq-gumbaz (White-dome) which lies between Chach-charan in the Heri-rud valley and the Ghurjistan border, going no further because the Ghurjistanis favoured the Mirza. Babur went back to Kabul by the Firuz-koh, Yaka-aulang (*cf.* f. 195) and Ghur; the Mirza was followed up by others, captured and conveyed to Kabul.

4 Both were amirs of Hind. I understand the cognomen Mazhab to imply that its bearer occupied himself with the Muhammadan Faith in its exposition by divines of Islam (*Hughes' Dictionary of Islam*).

(*o. 'Alam Khan takes refuge with Babur.*)

The light troop we had sent out from Milwat (Malot), took Hurur, Kahlur and all the hill-forts of the neighbourhood— places to which because of their strength, no-one seemed to have gone for a long time—and came back to me after plundering a little. Came also 'Alam Khan, on foot, ruined, stripped bare. We sent some of the begs to give him honourable meeting, sent horses too, and he waited (*malazamat qildi*) in that neighbourhood.[1]

Fol. 261*b.*

Raiders of ours went into the hills and valleys round-about, but after a few nights' absence, came back without anything to count. Shah Mir Husain, Jan Beg and a few of the braves asked leave and went off for a raid.

(*p. Incidents of the march for Pani-pat.*)

While we were in the (Jaswan) *dun*, dutiful letters had come more than once from Isma'il *Jilwani* and Biban; we replied to them from this place by royal letters such as their hearts desired. After we got out of the dale to Rupar, it rained very much and became so cold that a mass of starved and naked Hindustanis died.

When we had left Rupar and were dismounted at Karal,[2] opposite Sihrind, a Hindustani coming said, "I am Sl. Ibrahim's envoy," and though he had no letter or credentials, asked for an envoy from us. We responded at once by sending one or two Sawadi night-guards (*tunqitar*).[3] These humble persons Ibrahim put in prison; they made their escape and came back to us on the very day we beat him.

After having halted one night on the way, we dismounted on the bank of the torrent[4] of Banur and Sanur. Great rivers

---

1 These incidents are included in the summary of 'Alam Khan's affairs in section *i* (f. 255*b*). It will be observed that Babur's wording implies the "waiting" by one of lower rank on a superior.

2 Elph. MS. Karnal, obviously a clerical error.

3 Shaikh Sulaiman Effendi (Kunos) describes a *tunqitar* as the guardian in war of a prince's tent; a night-guard; and as one who repeats a prayer aloud while a prince is mounting.

4 *rud*, which, inappropriate for the lower course of the Ghaggar, may be due to Babur's visit to its upper course described immediately below. As has been noted, however, he uses the word *rud* to describe the empty bed of a mountain-stream as well as the swift water sometimes filling that bed. The account, here-following, of his visit to the upper course of the Ghaggar is somewhat difficult to translate.

apart, one running water there is in Hindustan, is this;[1] they call it the water of Kakar (Ghaggar). Chitr also is on its bank. We rode up it for an excursion. The rising-place (*zih*) of the water of this torrent (*rud*) is 3 or 4 *kurohs* (6–8 m.) above Chitr. Going up the (Kakar) torrent, we came to where a 4 or 5 mill-stream issues from a broad (side-)valley (*dara*), up which there are very pleasant places, healthy and convenient. I ordered a Char-bagh to be made at the mouth of the broad valley of this (tributary) water, which falls into the (Kakar-) torrent after flowing for one or two *kurohs* through level ground. From its infall to the springs of the Kakar the distance may be 3 to 4 *kurohs* (6–8 m.). When it comes down in flood during the rains and joins the Kakar, they go together to Samana and Sanam.[2]

Fol. 262.

In this camp we heard that Sl. Ibrahim had been on our side of Dihli and had moved on from that station, also that Hamid Khan *khasa-khail*,[3] the military-collector (*shiqdar*) of Hisar-firuza, had left that place with its army and with the army of its neighbourhood, and had advanced 10 or 15 *kurohs* (20–30 m.). Kitta Beg was sent for news to Ibrahim's camp, and Mumin Ataka to the Hisar-firuza camp.

(q. Humayun moves against Hamid Khan.)

(*Feb. 25th*) Marching from Ambala, we dismounted by the side of a lake. There Mumin Ataka and Kitta Beg rejoined us, both on the same day, Sunday the 13th of the first Jumada.

We appointed Humayun to act against Hamid Khan, and joined the whole of the right (wing) to him, that is to say, Khwaja Kalan, Sl. Muhammad *Duldai*, Treasurer Wali, and also some of the begs whose posts were in Hindustan, namely, Khusrau, Hindu Beg, 'Abdu'l-'aziz and Muhammad 'Ali *Jang-jang*, with also, from the household and braves of the centre, Shah Mansur *Barlas*, Kitta Beg and Muhibb-i 'ali.

Fol. 262b.

1 *Hindustanda daryalardin bashqa, bir aqar-su kim bar* (*dur*, is added by the Elph. MS.), *bu dur*. Perhaps the meaning is that the one (chief?) irrigation stream, apart from great rivers, is the Ghaggar. The bed of the Ghaggar is undefined and the water is consumed for irrigation (G. of I. xx, 33).

2 in Patiala. Maps show what may be Babur's strong millstream joining the Ghaggar.

3 Presumably he was of Ibrahim's own family, the Sahu-khail. His defeat was opportune because he was on his way to join the main army.

Biban waited on me in this camp. These Afghans remain very rustic and tactless! This person asked to sit although Dilawar Khan, his superior in following and in rank, did not sit, and although the sons of 'Alam Khan, who are of royal birth, did not sit. Little ear was lent to his unreason!

(*Feb. 26th*) At dawn on Monday the 14th Humayun moved out against Hamid Khan. After advancing for some distance, he sent between 100 and 150 braves scouting ahead, who went close up to the enemy and at once got to grips. But when after a few encounters, the dark mass of Humayun's troops shewed in the rear, the enemy ran right away. Humayun's men unhorsed from 100 to 200, struck the heads off one half and brought the other half in, together with 7 or 8 elephants.

(*March 2nd*) On Friday the 18th of the month, Beg Mirak *Mughul* brought news of Humayun's victory to the camp. He (Humayun?) was there and then given a special head-to-foot and a special horse from the royal stable, besides promise of guerdon (*juldu*).

(*March 5th*) On Monday the 25th of the month, Humayun arrived to wait on me, bringing with him as many as 100 prisoners and 7 or 8 elephants. Ustad 'Ali-quli and the matchlockmen were ordered to shoot all the prisoners, by way of example. This had been Humayun's first affair, his first experience of battle; it was an excellent omen!

Our men who had gone in pursuit of the fugitives, took Hisar-firuza at once on arrival, plundered it, and returned to us. It was given in guerdon to Humayun, with all its dependencies and appurtenances, with it also a *kror* of money.

We marched from that camp to Shahabad. After we had despatched a news-gatherer (*til-tutar kishi*) to Sl. Ibrahim's camp, we stayed a few days on that ground. Rahmat the foot-man was sent with the letters of victory to Kabul.

(*r. News of Ibrahim.*)

(*March 13th*) On Monday the 28th of the first Jumada,[1] we being in that same camp, the Sun entered the Sign of the Ram.

Fol. 263.

---

1 At this place the Elphinstone Codex has preserved, interpolated in its text, a note of Humayun's on his first use of the razor. Part of it is written as by Babur:—

News had come again and again from Ibrahim's camp, "He is coming, marching two miles" or "four miles", "stopping in each camp two days," or "three days". We for our part advanced from Shahabad and after halting on two nights, reached the bank of the Jun-river (Jumna) and encamped opposite Sarsawa. From that ground Khwaja Kalan's servant Haidar-quli was sent to get news (*til tuta*).

Having crossed the Jun-river at a ford, I visited Sarsawa. That day also we ate *ma'jun*. Sarsawa[1] has a source (*chashma*) from which a smallish stream issues, not a bad place! Tardi Beg *khaksar* praising it, I said, "Let it be thine!" so just because he praised it, Sarsawa was given to him! Fol. 263b.

I had a platform fixed in a boat and used to go for excursions on the river, sometimes too made the marches down it. Two marches along its bank had been made when, of those sent to gather news, Haidar-quli brought word that Ibrahim had sent Daud Khan (*Ludi*) and Hatim Khan (*Ludi*) across the river into the Mian-du-ab (Tween-waters) with 5 or 6000 men, and that these lay encamped some 6 or 7 miles from his own.

(*s. A successful encounter.*)

(*April 1st*) On Sunday the 18th of the second Jumada, we sent, to ride light against this force, Chin-timur Sultan,[2]

"Today in this same camp the razor or scissors was applied to Humayun's face." Part is signed by Humayun:—"As the honoured dead, earlier in these Acts (*waqi'at*) mentions the first application of the razor to his own face (f. 120), so in imitation of him I mention this. I was then at the age of 18; now I am at the age of 48, I who am the sub-signed Muhammad Humayun." A scribe's note attests that this is "copied from the hand-writing of that honoured one". As Humayun's 48th (lunar) birthday occurred a month before he left Kabul, to attempt the re-conquest of Hindustan, in November 1554 AD. (in the last month of 961 AH.), he was still 48 (lunar) years old on the day he re-entered Dihli on July 23rd 1555 AD. (Ramzan 1st 962 AH.), so that this "shaving passage" will have been entered within those dates. That he should study his Father's book at that time is natural; his grandson Jahangir did the same when going to Kabul; so doubtless would do its author's more remote descendants, the sons of Shah-jahan who reconquered Transoxiana.

(Concerning the "shaving passage" *vide* the notes on the Elphinstone Codex in JRAS. 1900 p. 443, 451; 1902 p. 653; 1905 p. 754; and 1907 p. 131.)

1 This ancient town of the Saharanpur district is associated with a saint revered by Hindus and Muhammadans. Cf. W. Crooke's *Popular Religion of Northern India* p. 133. Its *chashma* may be inferred (from Babur's uses of the word) as a water-head, a pool, a gathering place of springs.

2 He was the eighth son of Babur's maternal-uncle Sl. Ahmad Khan *Chaghatai* and had fled to Babur, other brothers following him, from the service of their eldest brother Mansur, Khaqan of the Mughuls (*Tarikh-i-rashidi* trs. p. 161).

Mahdi Khwaja, Muhammad Sl. Mirza, 'Adil Sultan, and the whole of the left, namely, Sl. Junaid, Shah Mir Husain, Qutluq-qadam, and with them also sent Yunas-i-ali and Ahmadi and 'Abdu'l-lah and Kitta Beg (of the centre). They crossed from our side of the water at the Mid-day Prayer, and between the Afternoon and the Evening Prayers bestirred themselves from the other bank. Biban having crossed the water on pretext of this movement, ran away.

(*April 2nd*) At day-break they came upon the enemy;[1] he made as if coming out in a sort of array, but our men closed with his at once, overcame them, hustled them off, pursued and unhorsed them till they were opposite Ibrahim's own camp. Hatim Khan was one of those unhorsed, who was Daud Khan (*Ludi*)'s elder brother and one of his commanders. Our men brought him in when they waited on me. They brought also Fol. 264. 60–70 prisoners and 6 or 7 elephants. Most of the prisoners, by way of warning, were made to reach their death-doom.

(*t. Preparations for battle.*)

While we were marching on in array of right, left and centre, the army was numbered;[2] it did not count up to what had been estimated.

At our next camp it was ordered that every man in the army should collect carts, each one according to his circumstances. Seven hundred carts (*araba*) were brought[3] in. The order given

---

1 *farz-waqti*, when there is light enough to distinguish one object from another.

2 *dim kuruldi*. Here the L. & E. *Memoirs* inserts an explanatory passage in Persian about the *dim*. It will have been in one of the *Waqi'at-i-baburi MSS*. Erskine used; it is in Muh. *Shirazi*'s lithograph copy of the Udaipur Codex (p. 173). It is not in the Turki text or in all the MSS. of the Persian translation. Manifestly, it was entered at a time when Babur's term *dim kuruldi* requires explanation in Hindustan. The writer of it himself does not make details clear; he says only, "It is manifest that people declare (the number) after counting the mounted army in the way agreed upon amongst them, with a whip or a bow held in the hand." This explanation suggests that in the march-past the troops were measured off as so many bow- or whip-lengths.

3 These *araba* may have been the baggage-carts of the army and also carts procured on the spot. Erskine omits (*Memoirs* p. 304) the words which show how many carts were collected and from whom. Doubtless it would be through not having these circumstances in his mind that he took the *araba* for gun-carriages. His incomplete translation, again, led Stanley Lane-Poole to write an interesting note in his *Babur* (p. 161) to support Erskine against de Courteille (with whose rendering mine agrees) by quoting the circumstance that Humayun had 700 guns at Qanauj in 1540 AD. It must be said in opposition to his support of Erskine's "gun-carriages" that there is no textual or circumstantial warrant for supposing Babur to have had guns, even if

to Ustad 'Ali-quli was that these carts should be joined together in Ottoman[1] fashion, but using ropes of raw hide instead of chains, and that between every two carts 5 or 6 mantelets should be fixed, behind which the matchlockmen were to stand to fire. To allow of collecting all appliances, we delayed 5 or 6 days in that camp. When everything was ready, all the begs with such braves as had had experience in military affairs were summoned to a General Council where opinion found decision at this:— Pani-pat[2] is there with its crowded houses and suburbs. It would be on one side of us; our other sides must be protected by carts and mantelets behind which our foot and matchlockmen would stand. With so much settled we marched forward, halted one night on the way, and reached Pani-pat on Thursday the last day (29th) of the second Jumada (April 12th).

(u. The opposed forces.)

On our right was the town of Pani-pat with its suburbs; in front of us were the carts and mantelets we had prepared; on our left and elsewhere were ditch and branch. At distances of an arrow's flight sally-places were left for from 100 to 200 horsemen.   Fol. 264b.

Some in the army were very anxious and full of fear. Nothing recommends anxiety and fear. For why? Because what God has fixed in eternity cannot be changed. But though this is so, it was no reproach to be afraid and anxious. For why? Because those thus anxious and afraid were there with a two or three months' journey between them and their homes; our affair was

---

made in parts, in such number as to demand 700 gun-carriages for their transport. What guns Babur had at Pani-pat will have been brought from his Kabul base; if he had acquired any, say from Lahor, he would hardly omit to mention such an important reinforcement of his armament; if he had brought many guns on carts from Kabul, he must have met with transit-difficulties harassing enough to chronicle, while he was making that long journey from Kabul to Pani-pat, over passes, through skirt-hills and many fords. The elephants he had in Bigram may have been his transport for what guns he had; he does not mention his number at Pani-pat; he makes his victory a bow-man's success; he can be read as indicating that he had two guns only.

1 These Ottoman (text, *Rumi*, Roman) defences Ustad 'Ali-quli may have seen at the battle of Chaldiran fought some 40 leagues from Tabriz between Sl. Salim *Rumi* and Shah Isma'il *Safawi* on Rajab 1st 920 AH. (Aug. 22nd 1514 AD.). Of this battle Khwand-amir gives a long account, dwelling on the effective use made in it of chained carts and palisades (*Habibu's-siyar* iii, part 4, p. 78; *Akbar-nama* trs. i, 241).

2 Is this the village of the Pani Afghans?

with a foreign tribe and people; none knew their tongue, nor did they know ours:—

> A wandering band, with mind a wander;
> In the grip of a tribe, a tribe unfamiliar.[1]

People estimated the army opposing us at 100,000 men; Ibrahim's elephants and those of his amirs were said to be about 1000. In his hands was the treasure of two forebears.[2] In Hindustan, when work such as this has to be done, it is customary to pay out money to hired retainers who are known as *b:d-hindi*.[3] If it had occurred to Ibrahim to do this, he might have had another *lak* or two of troops. God brought it right! Ibrahim could neither content his braves, nor share out his treasure. How should he content his braves when he was ruled by avarice and had a craving insatiable to pile coin on coin? He was an unproved brave;[4] he provided nothing for his military operations, he perfected nothing, nor stand, nor move, nor fight.

Fol. 265.

In the interval at Pani-pat during which the army was preparing defence on our every side with cart, ditch and branch, Darwish-i-muhammad *Sarban* had once said to me, "With such precautions taken, how is it possible for him to come?" Said I, "Are you likening him to the Auzbeg khans and sultans?

1 *Pareshan jam'i u jam'i pareshan;*
  Giriftar qaumi u qaumi 'aja'ib.
These two lines do not translate easily without the context of their original place of occurrence. I have not found their source.
2 *i.e.* of his father and grandfather, Sikandar and Buhlul.
3 As to the form of this word the authoritative MSS. of the Turki text agree and with them also numerous good ones of the Persian translation. I have made careful examination of the word because it is replaced or explained here and there in MSS. by *s:hb:ndi*, the origin of which is said to be obscure. The sense of *b:d-hindi* and of *s:hb:ndi* is the same, *i.e.* irregular levy. The word as Babur wrote it must have been understood by earlier Indian scribes of both the Turki and Persian texts of the *Babur-nama*. Some light on its correctness may be thought given by Hobson Jobson (Crooke's ed. p. 136) *s.n.* Byde or Bede Horse, where the word Byde is said to be an equivalent of *pindari*, *luti*, and *qazzaq*, raider, plunderer, so that Babur's word *b:d-hindi* may mean *qazzaq* of Hind. Wherever I have referred to the word in many MSS. it is pointed to read *b:d*, and not *p:d*, thus affording no warrant for understanding *pad*, foot, foot-man, infantry, and also negativing the spelling *bid*, *i.e.* with a long vowel as in *Byde*.
  It may be noted here that Muh. *Shirazi* (p. 174) substituted *s:hb:ndi* for Babur's word and that this led our friend the late William Irvine to attribute mistake to de Courteille who follows the Turki text (*Army of the Mughuls* p. 166 and *Mémoires* ii, 163).
4 *bi tajarba yigit aidi* of which the sense may be that Babur ranked Ibrahim, as a soldier, with a brave who has not yet proved himself deserving of the rank of beg. It cannot mean that he was a youth (*yigit*) without experience of battle.

In what of movement under arms or of planned operations is he to be compared with them?" God brought it right! Things fell out just as I said!

> (*Author's note on the Auzbeg chiefs.*)   When I reached Hisar in the year I left Samarkand (918 AH.–1512 AD.), and all the Auzbeg khans and sultans gathered and came against us, we brought the families and the goods of the Mughuls and soldiers into the Hisar suburbs and fortified these by closing the lanes. As those khans and sultans were experienced in equipment, in planned operations, and in resolute resistance, they saw from our fortification of Hisar that we were determined on life or death within it, saw they could not count on taking it by assault and, therefore, retired at once from near Nundak of Chaghanian.

(*v. Preliminary encounters.*)

During the 7 or 8 days we lay in Pani-pat, our men used to go, a few together, close up to Ibrahim's camp, rain arrows down on his massed troops, cut off and bring in heads. Still he made no move; nor did his troops sally out. At length, we acted on the advice of several Hindustani well-wishers and sent out 4 or 5000 men to deliver a night-attack on his camp, the leaders of it being Mahdi Khwaja, Muhammad Sl. Mirza, 'Adil Sultan, Khusrau, Shah Mir Husain, Sl. Junaid *Barlas*, 'Abdu'l-'aziz the Master of the Horse, Muh. 'Ali *Jang-jang*, Qutluq-qadam, Treasurer Wali, Khalifa's Muhibb-i-'ali, Pay-master Muhammad, Jan Beg and Qara-quzi. It being dark, they were not able to act together well, and, having scattered, could effect nothing on arrival. They stayed near Ibrahim's camp till dawn, when the nagarets sounded and troops of his came out in array with elephants. Though our men did not do their work, they got off safe and sound; not a man of them was killed, though they were in touch with such a mass of foes. One arrow pierced Muh. 'Ali *Jang-jang*'s leg; though the wound was not mortal, he was good-for-nothing on the day of battle.

On hearing of this affair, I sent off Humayun and his troops to go 2 or 3 miles to meet them, and followed him myself with the rest of the army in battle-array. The party of the night-attack joined him and came back with him. The enemy making no further advance, we returned to camp and dismounted. That night a false alarm fell on the camp; for some 20 minutes (one *gari*) there were uproar and call-to-arms; the disturbance died down after a time.

Fol. 265*b*.

Fol. 266.

(*w. Battle of Pani-pat.*[1])

(*April 20th*) On Friday the 8th of Rajab,[2] news came, when it was light enough to distinguish one thing from another (*farz-waqti*) that the enemy was advancing in fighting-array. We at once put on mail,[3] armed and mounted.[4] Our right was Humayun, Khwaja Kalan, Sultan Muhammad *Duldai*, Hindu Beg, Treasurer Wali and Pir-quli *Sistani*; our left was Muhammad Sl. Mirza, Mahdi Khwaja, 'Adil Sultan, Shah Mir Husain, Sl. Junaid *Barlas*, Qutluq-qadam, Jan Beg, Pay-master Muhammad, and Shah Husain (of) Yaragi *Mughul Ghanchi* (?).[5] The right hand of the centre[6] was Chin-timur Sultan, Sulaiman Mirza,[7] Muhammadi Kukuldash, Shah Mansur *Barlas*, Yunas-i-'ali, Darwish-i-muhammad *Sarban* and 'Abdu'l-lah the librarian. The left of the centre was Khalifa, Khwaja Mir-i-miran, Secretary Ahmadi, Tardi Beg (brother) of Quj Beg, Khalifa's Muhibb-i-'ali and Mirza Beg Tarkhan. The advance was Khusrau Kukuldash and Muh. 'Ali *Jang-jang*. 'Abdu'l-'aziz

1 Well-known are the three decisive historical battles fought near the town of Pani-pat, *viz.* those of Babur and Ibrahim in 1526, of Akbar and Himu in 1556, and of Ahmad *Abdali* with the Mahratta Confederacy in 1761. The following lesser particulars about the battle-field are not so frequently mentioned:—(*i*) that the scene of Babur's victory was long held to be haunted, Badayuni himself, passing it at dawn some 62 years later, heard with dismay the din of conflict and the shouts of the combatants; (*ii*) that Babur built a (perhaps commemorative) mosque one mile to the n.e. of the town; (*iii*) that one of the unaccomplished desires of Sher Shah *Sur*, the conqueror of Babur's son Humayun, was to raise two monuments on the battle-field of Pani-pat, one to Ibrahim, the other to those Chaghatai sultans whose martyrdom he himself had brought about; (*iv*) that in 1910 AD. the British Government placed a monument to mark the scene of Shah *Abdali's* victory of 1761 AD. This monument would appear, from Sayyid Ghulam-i-'ali's *Nigar-nama-i-hind*, to stand close to the scene of Babur's victory also, since the Mahrattas were entrenched as he was outside the town of Pani-pat. (*Cf.* E. & D. viii, 401.)
2 This important date is omitted from the L. & E. *Memoirs.*
3 This wording will cover armour of man and horse.
4 *atlanduk*, Pers. trs. *suwar shudim*. Some later oriental writers locate Babur's battle at two or more miles from the town of Pani-pat, and Babur's word *atlanduk* might imply that his cavalry rode forth and arrayed outside his defences, but his narrative allows of his delivering attack, through the wide sally-ports, after arraying behind the carts and mantelets which checked his adversary's swift advance. The Mahrattas, who may have occupied the same ground as Babur, fortified themselves more strongly than he did, as having powerful artillery against them. Ahmad Shah *Abdali's* defence against them was an ordinary ditch and *abbattis*, [Babur's ditch and branch,] mostly of *dhak* trees (*Butea frondosa*), a local product Babur also is likely to have used.
5 The preceding three words seem to distinguish this Shah Husain from several others of his name and may imply that he was the son of *Yaragi Mughul Ghanchi* (Index and I.O. 217 f. 184*b* I. 7).
6 For Babur's terms *vide* f. 209*b*.
7 This is Mirza Khan's son, *i.e.* Wais *Miran-shahi's.*

the Master of the Horse was posted as the reserve. For the turning-party (*tulghuma*) at the point of the right wing,[1] we fixed on Red Wali and Malik Qasim (brother) of Baba *Qashqa*, with their Mughuls; for the turning-party at the point of the left wing, we arrayed Qara-quzi, Abu'l-muhammad the lance-player, Shaikh Jamal *Barin's* Shaikh 'Ali, Mahndi(?) and Tingri-birdi *Bashaghi*(?) *Mughul*; these two parties, directly the enemy got near, were to turn his rear, one from the right, the other from the left.

Fol. 266b.

When the dark mass of the enemy first came in sight, he seemed to incline towards our right;'Abdu'l-'aziz, who was the right-reserve, was sent therefore to reinforce the right. From the time that Sl. Ibrahim's blackness first appeared, he moved swiftly, straight for us, without a check, until he saw the dark mass of our men, when his pulled up and, observing our formation and array,[2] made as if asking, "To stand or not? To advance or not?" They could not stand; nor could they make their former swift advance.

Our orders were for the turning-parties to wheel from right and left to the enemy's rear, to discharge arrows and to engage in the fight; and for the right and left (wings) to advance and join battle with him. The turning-parties wheeled round and began to rain arrows down. Mahdi Khwaja was the first of the left to engage; he was faced by a troop having an elephant with it; his men's flights of arrows forced it to retire. To reinforce the left I sent Secretary Ahmadi and also Quj Beg's Tardi Beg and Khalifa's Muhibb-i-'ali. On the right also there was some stubborn fighting. Orders were given for Muhammadi Kukuldash, Shah Mansur *Barlas*, Yunas-i-'ali and 'Abdu'l-lah to engage those facing them in front of the centre. From that same position Ustad 'Ali-quli made good discharge of *firingi* shots;[3]

---

1 A dispute for this right-hand post of honour is recorded on f. 100b, as also in accounts of Culloden.

2 *tartib u yasal*, which may include, as Erskine took it to do, the carts and mantelets; of these however, Ibrahim can hardly have failed to hear before he rode out of camp.

3 f. 217b and note; Irvine's *Army of the Indian Mughuls* p. 133. Here Erskine notes (*Mems.* p. 306) "The size of these artillery at this time is very uncertain. The word *firingi* is now (1826 AD.) used in the Deccan for a swivel. At the present day, *zarb-zan* in common usage is a small species of swivel. Both words in Babur's time

Mustafa the commissary for his part made excellent discharge of *zarb-zan* shots from the left hand of the centre. Our right, left, centre and turning-parties having surrounded the enemy, rained arrows down on him and fought ungrudgingly. He made one or two small charges on our right and left but under our men's arrows, fell back on his own centre. His right and left hands (*qul*) were massed in such a crowd that they could neither move forward against us nor force a way for flight.

When the incitement to battle had come, the Sun was spear-high; till mid-day fighting had been in full force; noon passed, the foe was crushed in defeat, our friends rejoicing and gay. By God's mercy and kindness, this difficult affair was made easy for us! In one half-day, that armed mass was laid upon the earth. Five or six thousand men were killed in one place close to Ibrahim. Our estimate of the other dead, lying all over the field, was 15 to 16,000, but it came to be known, later in Agra from the statements of Hindustanis, that 40 or 50,000 may have died in that battle.[1]

The foe defeated, pursuit and unhorsing of fugitives began. Our men brought in amirs of all ranks and the chiefs they captured; *mahauts* made offering of herd after herd of elephants.

Ibrahim was thought to have fled; therefore, while pursuing the enemy, we told off Qismatai Mirza, Baba *chuhra* and Bujka of the *khasa-tabin*[2] to lead swift pursuit to Agra and try to take him. We passed through his camp, looked into his own enclosure (*saracha*) and quarters, and dismounted on the bank of standing-water (*qara-su*).

---

appear to have been used for field-cannon." (For an account of guns, intermediate in date between Babur and Erskine, *see* the *Ayin-i-akbari, Cf.* f. 264 n. on the carts (*araba*).)

1 Although the authority of the *Tarikh-i-salatin-i-afaghana* is not weighty its reproduction of Afghan opinion is worth consideration. It says that astrologers fore-told Ibrahim's defeat; that his men, though greatly outnumbering Babur's, were out-of-heart through his ill-treatment of them, and his amirs in displeasure against him, but that never-the-less, the conflict at Pani-pat was more desperate than had ever been seen. It states that Ibrahim fell where his tomb now is (*i.e.* in *circa* 1002 AH.–1594 AD.); that Babur went to the spot and, prompted by his tender heart, lifted up the head of his dead adversary, and said, "Honour to your courage!", ordered brocade and sweetmeats made ready, enjoined Dilawar Khan and Khalifa to bathe the corpse and to bury it where it lay (E. & D. v, 2). Naturally, part of the reverence shewn to the dead would be the burial together of head and trunk.
2 f. 209*b* and App. H. section *c*. Baba *chuhra* would be one of the corps of braves.

It was the Afternoon Prayer when Khalifa's younger brother-in-law Tahir Tibri[1] who had found Ibrahim's body in a heap of dead, brought in his head.

(*x. Detachments sent to occupy Dihli and Agra.*)

On that very same day we appointed Humayun Mirza[2] to ride fast and light to Agra with Khwaja Kalan, Muhammadi, Shah Mansur *Barlas*, Yunas-i-'ali, 'Abdu'l-lah and Treasurer Wali, to get the place into their hands and to mount guard over the treasure. We fixed on Mahdi Khwaja, with Muhammad Sl. Mirza, 'Adil Sultan, Sl. Junaid *Barlas* and Qutluq-qadam to leave their baggage, make sudden incursion on Dihli, and keep watch on the treasuries.[3]

(*April 21st*) We marched on next day and when we had gone 2 miles, dismounted, for the sake of the horses, on the bank of the Jun (Jumna).

(*April 24th*) On Tuesday (Rajab 12th), after we had halted on two nights and had made the circuit of Shaikh Nizamu'd-din *Auliya*'s tomb[4] we dismounted on the bank of the Jun over against Dihli.[5] That same night, being Wednesday-eve, we made an excursion into the fort of Dihli and there spent the night.

(*April 25th*) Next day (Wednesday Rajab 13th) I made the circuit of Khwaja Qutbu'd-din's[6] tomb and visited the tombs and residences of Sl. Ghiyasu'd-din *Balban*[7] and Sl. 'Alau'u'd-din

1 He was a brother of Muhibb-i-'ali's mother.
2 To give Humayun the title Mirza may be a scribe's lapse, but might also be a *nuance* of Babur's, made to shew, with other *minutiae*, that Humayun was in chief command. The other minute matters are that instead of Humayun's name being the first of a simple series of commanders' names with the enclitic accusative appended to the last one (here Wali), as is usual, Humayun's name has its own enclitic *ni*; and, again, the phrase is "*Humayun with*" such and such begs, a turn of expression differentiating him from the rest. The same unusual variations occur again, just below, perhaps with the same intention of shewing chief command, there of Mahdi Khwaja.
3 A small matter of wording attracts attention in the preceding two sentences. Babur, who does not always avoid verbal repetition, here constructs two sentences which, except for the place-names Dihli and Agra, convey information of precisely the same action in entirely different words.
4 d. 1325 AD. The places Babur visited near Dihli are described in the *Reports of the Indian Archaeological Survey*, in Sayyid Ahmad's *Asar Sanadid* pp. 74–85, in Keene's *Hand-book to Dihli* and Murray's *Hand-book to Bengal etc.* The last two quote much from the writings of Cunningham and Fergusson.
5 and on the same side of the river.
6 d. 1235 AD. He was a native of Aush [Ush] in Farghana.
7 d. 1286 AD. He was a Slave ruler of Dihli.

Fol. 268. *Khilji*,[1] his Minar, and the Hauz-shamsi, Hauz-i-khas and the tombs and gardens of Sl. Buhlul and Sl. Sikandar (*Ludi*). Having done this, we dismounted at the camp, went on a boat, and there '*araq* was drunk.

We bestowed the Military Collectorate (*shiqdarlighi*) of Dihli on Red Wali, made Dost Diwan in the Dihli district, sealed the treasuries, and made them over to their charge.

(*April 26th*) On Thursday we dismounted on the bank of the Jun, over against Tughluqabad.[2]

(*y. The khutba read for Babur in Dihli.*)

(*April 27th*) On Friday (Rajab 15th) while we remained on the same ground, Maulana Mahmud and Shaikh Zain went with a few others into Dihli for the Congregational Prayer, read the *khutba* in my name, distributed a portion of money to the poor and needy,[3] and returned to camp.

(*April 28th*) Leaving that ground on Saturday (Rajab 16th), we advanced march by march for Agra. I made an excursion to Tughluqabad and rejoined the camp.

(*May 4th*) On Friday (Rajab 22nd), we dismounted at the mansion (*manzil*) of Sulaiman *Farmuli* in a suburb of Agra, but as the place was far from the fort, moved on the following day to Jalal Khan *Jig:hat*'s house.

On Humayun's arrival at Agra, ahead of us, the garrison had made excuses and false pretexts (about surrender). He and his noticing the want of discipline there was, said, "The long hand may be laid on the Treasury"! and so sat down to watch the roads out of Agra till we should come.

1 'Alau'u'd-din Muh. Shah *Khilji Turk* d. 1316 AD. It is curious that Babur should specify visiting his Minar (*minari*, Pers. trs. I.O. 217 f. 185b, *minar-i-au*) and not mention the Qutb Minar. Possibly he confused the two. The 'Alai Minar remains unfinished; the Qutb is judged by Cunningham to have been founded by Qutbu'd-din Aibak *Turk*, *circa* 1200 AD. and to have been completed by Sl. Shamsu'd-din Altamsh (Ailtimish?) *Turk*, *circa* 1220 AD. Of the two tanks Babur visited, the Royal-tank (*hauz-i-khaz*) was made by 'Alau'u'd-din in 1293 AD.

2 The familiar Turki word Tughluq would reinforce much else met with in Dihli to strengthen Babur's opinion that, as a Turk, he had a right to rule there. Many, if not all, of the Slave dynasty were Turks; these were followed by the Khilji Turks, these again by the Tughluqs. Moreover the Panj-ab he had himself taken, and lands on both sides of the Indus further south had been ruled by Ghaznawid Turks. His latest conquests were "where the Turk had ruled" (f. 226b) long, wide, and with interludes only of non-Turki sway.

3 Perhaps this charity was the *Khams* (Fifth) due from a victor.

(z. The great diamond.)

In Sultan Ibrahim's defeat the Raja of Gualiar Bikramajit the Hindu had gone to hell.[1]

> *(Author's note on Bikramajit.)*   The ancestors of Bikramajit had ruled in Gualiar for more than a hundred years.[2] Sikandar (*Ludi*) had sat down in Agra for several years in order to take the fort; later on, in Ibrahim's time, 'Azim Humayun *Sarwani*[3] had completely invested it for some while; following this, it was taken on terms under which Shamsabad was given in exchange for it.[4]

Bikramajit's children and family were in Agra at the time of Ibrahim's defeat. When Humayun reached Agra, they must have been planning to flee, but his postings of men (to watch the roads) prevented this and guard was kept over them. Humayun himself did not let them go (*barghali quimas*). They made him a voluntary offering of a mass of jewels and valuables amongst which was the famous diamond which 'Alau'u'd–din must have brought.[5] Its reputation is that every appraiser has estimated its value at two and a half days' food for the whole world. Apparently it weighs 8 *misqals*.[6] Humayun offered it to me when I arrived at Agra; I just gave it him back.

(aa. Ibrahim's mother and entourage.)

Amongst men of mark who were in the fort, there were Malik Dad *Karani*, Milli *Surduk* and Firuz Khan *Miwati*. They, being convicted of false dealing, were ordered out for capital punishment. Several persons interceded for Malik Dad *Karani* and four or five days passed in comings and goings before the

1 Bikramajit was a Tunur Rajput. Babur's unhesitating statement of the Hindu's destination at death may be called a fruit of conviction, rather than of what modern opinion calls intolerance.

2 120 years (Cunningham's *Report of the Archaeological Survey* ii, 330 *et seq.*).

3 The *Tarikh-i-sher-shahi* tells a good deal about the man who bore this title, and also about others who found themselves now in difficulty between Ibrahim's tyranny and Babur's advance (E. & D. iv, 301).

4 Gualiar was taken from Bikramajit in 1518 AD.

5 *i.e.* from the Deccan of which 'Alau'u'd–din is said to have been the first Muhammadan invader. An account of this diamond, identified as the Koh-i-nur, is given in *Hobson Jobson* but its full history is not told by Yule or by Streeter's *Great Diamonds of the World*, neither mentioning the presentation of the diamond by Humayun to Tahmasp of which Abu'l-fazl writes, dwelling on its overplus of payment for all that Humayun in exile received from his Persian host (*Akbarnama* trs. i, 349 and note; *Asiatic Quarterly Review*, April 1899 H. Beveridge's art. *Babur's diamond; was it the Koh-i-nur?*).

6 320 *ratis* (Erskine). The *rati* is 2.171 Troy grains, or in picturesque primitive equivalents, is 8 grains of rice, or 64 mustard seeds, or 512 poppy-seeds,— uncertain weights which Akbar fixed in cat's-eye stones.

matter was arranged. We then shewed to them (all?) kindness and favour in agreement with the petition made for them, and we restored them all their goods.[1] A *pargana* worth 7 *laks*[2] was bestowed on Ibrahim's mother; *parganas* were given also to these begs of his.[3] She was sent out of the fort with her old servants and given encamping-ground (*yurt*) two miles below Fol. 269. Agra.

(*May 10th*) I entered Agra at the Afternoon Prayer of Thursday (Rajab 28th) and dismounted at the mansion (*manzil*) of Sl. Ibrahim.

EXPEDITIONS OF TRAMONTANE MUHAMMADANS INTO HIND

(*a. Babur's five attempts on Hindustan.*)

From the date 910 at which the country of Kabul was conquered, down to now (932 AH.) (my) desire for Hindustan had been constant, but owing sometimes to the feeble counsels of begs, sometimes to the non-accompaniment of elder and younger brethren,[4] a move on Hindustan had not been practicable and its territories had remained unsubdued. At length no such obstacles were left; no beg, great or small (*beg begat*) of lower birth,[5] could speak an opposing word. In 925 AH. (1519 AD.) we led an army out and, after taking Bajaur by storm in 2–3 *gari* (44–66 minutes), and making a general massacre of its people, went on into Bhira. Bhira we neither over-ran nor plundered; we imposed a ransom on its people, taking from them in money and goods to the value

1 Babur's plurals allow the supposition that the three men's lives were spared. Malik Dad served him thenceforth.
2 Erskine estimated these as *dams* and worth about £1750, but this may be an underestimate (*H. of I.* i, App. E.).
3 "These begs of his" (or hers) may be the three written of above.
4 These will include cousins and his half-brothers Jahangir and Nasir as opposing before he took action in 925 AH. (1519 AD.). The time between 910 AH. and 925 AH. at which he would most desire Hindustan is after 920 AH. in which year he returned defeated from Transoxiana.
5 *kichik karim*, which here seems to make contrast between the ruling birth of members of his own family and the lower birth of even great begs still with him. Where the phrase occurs on f. 295, Erskine renders it by "down to the dregs", and de Courteille (ii, 235) by "*de toutes les bouches*" but neither translation appears to me to suit Babur's uses of the term, inasmuch as both seem to go too low (*cf.* f. 270b).

of 4 *laks* of *shahrukhis* and having shared this out to the army
and auxiliaries, returned to Kabul. From then till now we
laboriously held tight[1] to Hindustan, five times leading an army
into it.[2] The fifth time, God the Most High, by his own mercy
and favour, made such a foe as Sl. Ibrahim the vanquished and
loser, such a realm as Hindustan our conquest and possession.

(b. Three invaders from Tramontana.)

From the time of the revered Prophet down till now[3] three
men from that side[4] have conquered and ruled Hindustan. Sl.
Mahmud *Ghazi*[5] was the first, who and whose descendants sat
long on the seat of government in Hindustan. Sl. Shihabu'd-din   Fol. 269b.
of Ghur was the second,[6] whose slaves and dependants royally
shepherded[7] this realm for many years. I am the third.

But my task was not like the task of those other rulers. For
why? Because Sl. Mahmud, when he conquered Hindustan, had
the throne of Khurasan subject to his rule, vassal and obedient to
him were the sultans of Khwarizm and the Marches (*Daru'l-marz*),
and under his hand was the ruler of Samarkand. Though his
army may not have numbered 2 *laks*, what question is there that
it[8] was one. Then again, rajas were his opponents; all Hindustan
was not under one supreme head (*padshah*), but each raja
ruled independently in his own country. Sl. Shihabu'd-din
again,—though he himself had no rule in Khurasan, his elder
brother Ghiyasu'd-din had it. The *Tabaqat-i-nasiri*[9] brings it forward

1 *aiurushub*, Pers. trs. *chaspida*, stuck to.
2 The first expedition is fixed by the preceding passage as in 925 AH. which was
indeed the first time a passage of the Indus is recorded. Three others are found
recorded, those of 926, 930 and 932 AH. Perhaps the fifth was not led by Babur in
person, and may be that of his troops accompanying 'Alam Khan in 931 AH. But
he may count into the set of five, the one made in 910 AH. which he himself meant
to cross the Indus. Various opinions are found expressed by European writers as
to the dates of the five.
3 Muhammad died 632 AD. (11 AH.).
4 Tramontana, n. of Hindu-kush. For particulars about the dynasties mentioned
by Babur *see* Stanley Lane-Poole's *Muhammadan Dynasties*.
5 Mahmud of Ghazni, a Turk by race, d. 1030 AD. (421 AH.).
6 known as Muh. *Ghuri*, d. 1206 AD. (602 AH.).
7 *surubturlar*, lit. drove them like sheep (*cf.* f. 154b).
8 *khud*, itself, not Babur's only Hibernianism.
9 "This is an excellent history of the Musalman world down to the time of Sl. Nasir
of Dihli A.D. 1252. It was written by Abu 'Umar Minhaj al Jurjani. See Stewart's
catalogue of Tipoo's Library, p. 7" (Erskine). It has been translated by Raverty.

that he once led into Hindustan an army of 120,000 men and horse in mail.[1] His opponents also were rais and rajas; one man did not hold all Hindustan.

That time we came to Bhira, we had at most some 1500 to 2000 men. We had made no previous move on Hindustan with an army equal to that which came the fifth time, when we beat Sl. Ibrahim and conquered the realm of Hindustan, the total written down for which, taking one retainer with another, and Fol. 270. with traders and servants, was 12,000. Dependent on me were the countries of Badakhshan, Qunduz, Kabul and Qandahar, but no reckonable profit came from them, rather it was necessary to reinforce them fully because several lie close to an enemy. Then again, all Mawara'u'n-nahr was in the power of the Auzbeg khans and sultans, an ancient foe whose armies counted up to 100,000. Moreover Hindustan, from Bhira to Bihar, was in the power of the Afghans and in it Sl. Ibrahim was supreme. In proportion to his territory his army ought to have been 5 *laks*, but at that time the Eastern amirs were in hostility to him. His army was estimated at 100,000 and people said his elephants and those of his amirs were 1000.

Under such conditions, in this strength, and having in my rear 100,000 old enemies such as are the Auzbegs, we put trust in God and faced the ruler of such a dense army and of domains so wide. As our trust was in Him, the most high God did not make our labour and hardships vain, but defeated that powerful foe and conquered that broad realm. Not as due to strength and effort of our own do we look upon this good fortune, but as had solely through God's pleasure and kindness. We know that this happiness was not the fruit of our own ambition and resolve, but that it was purely from His mercy and favour.

DESCRIPTION OF HINDUSTAN

(*a. Hindustan.*)

The country of Hindustan is extensive, full of men, and full Fol. 270b. of produce. On the east, south, and even on the west, it ends at its great enclosing ocean (*muhit darya-si-gha*). On the north

---

1 *bargustwan-war*, Erskine, cataphract horse.

it has mountains which connect with those of Hindu-kush, Kafiristan and Kashmir. North-west of it lie Kabul, Ghazni and Qandahar. Dihli is held (*airimish*) to be the capital of the whole of Hindustan. From the death of Shihabu'd-din *Ghuri* (d. 602 AH.—1206 AD.) to the latter part of the reign of Sl. Firuz Shah (*Tughluq Turk* d. 790 AH.—1388 AD.), the greater part of Hindustan must have been under the rule of the sultans of Dihli.

(b. Rulers contemporary with Babur's conquest.)

At the date of my conquest of Hindustan it was governed by five Musalman rulers (*padshah*)[1] and two Pagans (*kafir*). These were the respected and independent rulers, but there were also, in the hills and jungles, many rais and rajas, held in little esteem (*kichik karim*).

First, there were the Afghans who had possession of Dihli, the capital, and held the country from Bhira to Bihar. Junpur, before their time, had been in possession of Sl. Husain *Sharqi* (Eastern)[2] whose dynasty Hindustanis call Purabi (Eastern). His ancestors will have been cup-bearers in the presence of Sl. Firuz Shah and those (Tughluq) sultans; they became supreme in Junpur after his death.[3] At that time Dihli was in the hands of Sl. 'Alau'd-din ('Alam Khan) of the Sayyid dynasty to whose ancestor Timur Beg had given it when, after having captured it, he went away.[4] Sl. Buhlul *Ludi* and his son (Sikandar) got possession of the capital Junpur and the capital Dihli, and brought both under one government (881 AH.—1476 AD.).

Secondly, there was Sl. Muhammad Muzaffer in Gujrat; he departed from the world a few days before the defeat of Sl. Ibrahim. He was skilled in the Law, a ruler (*padshah*) seeking Fol. 271. after knowledge, and a constant copyist of the Holy Book. His dynasty people call Tank.[5] His ancestors also will have been

1 The numerous instances of the word *padshah* in this part of the *Babur-nama* imply no such distinction as attaches to the title Emperor by which it is frequently translated.

2 d. 1500 AD. (905 AH.).

3 d. 1388 AD. (790 AH.).

4 The ancestor mentioned appears to be Nasrat Shah, a grandson of Firuz Shah *Tughluq* (S. L.-Poole p. 300 and Beale, 298).

5 His family belonged to the Rajput sept of Tank, and had become Muhammadan in the person of Sadharan the first ruler of Gujrat (Crooke's *Tribes and Castes*; *Mirat-i-sikandari*, Bayley p. 67 and n.).

wine-servers to Sl. Firuz Shah and those (Tughluq) sultans; they became possessed of Gujrat after his death.

Thirdly, there were the Bahmanis of the Dakkan (Deccan, *i.e.* South), but at the present time no independent authority is left them; their great begs have laid hands on the whole country, and must be asked for whatever is needed.[1]

Fourthly, there was Sl. Mahmud in the country of Malwa, which people call also Mandau.[2] His dynasty they call Khilij (*Turk*). Rana Sanga had defeated Sl. Mahmud and taken possession of most of his country. This dynasty also has become feeble. Sl. Mahmud's ancestors also must have been cherished by Sl. Firuz Shah; they became possessed of the Malwa country after his death.[3]

Fifthly, there was Nasrat Shah[4] in the country of Bengal. His father (Husain Shah), a sayyid styled 'Alau'u'd-din, had ruled in Bengal and Nasrat Shah attained to rule by inheritance. A surprising custom in Bengal is that hereditary succession is rare. The royal office is permanent and there are permanent offices of amirs, wazirs and mansab-dars (officials). It is the office that Bengalis regard with respect. Attached to each office is a body of obedient, subordinate retainers and servants. If the royal heart demand that a person should be dismissed and another be appointed to sit in his place, the whole body of subordinates attached to that office become the (new) office-holder's. There is indeed this peculiarity of the royal office itself that any person who kills the ruler (*padshah*) and seats himself on the throne, becomes ruler himself; amirs, wazirs, soldiers and peasants submit to him at once, obey him, and recognize him for the rightful ruler his predecessor in office had been.[5] Bengalis say, "We are faithful to the throne; we loyally

Fol. 271*b*.

---

1 S. L.-Poole p. 316-7.

2 Mandau (Mandu) was the capital of Malwa.

3 Stanley Lane-Poole shews (p. 311) a dynasty of three Ghuris interposed between the death of Firuz Shah in 790 AH. and the accession in 839 AH. of the first Khilji ruler of Malwa Mahmud Shah.

4 He reigned from 1518 to 1532 AD. (925 to 939 AH. S.L.-P. p. 308) and had to wife a daughter of Ibrahim *Ludi* (*Riyazu's-salatin*). His dynasty was known as the Husain-shahi, after his father.

5 "Strange as this custom may seem, a similar one prevailed down to a very late period in Malabar. There was a jubilee every 12 years in the Samorin's country, and any-one who succeeded in forcing his way through the Samorin's guards and slew

obey whoever occupies it." As for instance, before the reign of
Nasrat Shah's father 'Alau'u'd-din, an Abyssinian (*Habshi*,
named Muzaffar Shah) had killed his sovereign (Mahmud
Shah *Ilyas*), mounted the throne and ruled for some time.
'Alau'u'd-din killed that Abyssinian, seated himself on the throne
and became ruler. When he died, his son (Nasrat) became
ruler by inheritance. Another Bengali custom is to regard it
as a disgraceful fault in a new ruler if he expend and consume
the treasure of his predecessors. On coming to rule he must
gather treasure of his own. To amass treasure Bengalis regard
as a glorious distinction. Another custom in Bengal is that
from ancient times *parganas* have been assigned to meet the
charges of the treasury, stables, and all royal expenditure and
to defray these charges no impost is laid on other lands.

These five, mentioned above, were the great Musalman rulers,
honoured in Hindustan, many-legioned, and broad-landed. Of
the Pagans the greater both in territory and army, is the Raja
of Bijanagar.[1]

The second is Rana Sanga who in these latter days had
grown great by his own valour and sword. His original country
was Chitur; in the downfall from power of the Mandau sultans,
he became possessed of many of their dependencies such as
Rantanbur, Sarangpur, Bhilsan and Chandiri. Chandiri I stormed
in 934 AH. (1528 AD.)[2] and, by God's pleasure, took it in a few
hours; in it was Rana Sanga's great and trusted man Midni

Fol. 272.

---

him, reigned in his stead. 'A jubilee is proclaimed throughout his dominions at the
end of 12 years, and a tent is pitched for him in a spacious plain, and a great feast
is celebrated for 10 or 12 days with mirth and jollity, guns firing night and day, so,
at the end of the feast, any four of the guests that have a mind to gain a throne by
a desperate action in fighting their way through 30 or 40,000 of his guards, and kill
the Samorin in his tent, he that kills him, succeeds him in his empire.' See Hamilton's
New Account of the East Indies vol. i. p. 309. The attempt was made in 1695, and
again a very few years ago, but without success" (Erskine p. 311).

The custom Babur writes of—it is one dealt with at length in Frazer's *Golden
Bough*—would appear from Blochmann's *Geography and History of Bengal* (JASB
1873 p. 286) to have been practised by the Habshi rulers of Bengal of whom he
quotes Faria y Souza as saying, "They observe no rule of inheritance from father to
son, but even slaves sometimes obtain it by killing their master, and whoever holds
it three days, they look upon as established by divine providence. Thus it fell out
that in 40 years space they had 13 kings successively."

1 No doubt this represents Vijayanagar in the Deccan.
2 This date places the composition of the *Description of Hindustan* in agreement
with Shaikh Zain's statement that it was in writing in 935 AH.

Rao with four or five thousand Pagans; we made general massacre of the Pagans in it and, as will be narrated, converted what for many years had been a mansion of hostility, into a mansion of Islam.

There are very many rais and rajas on all sides and quarters of Hindustan, some obedient to Islam, some, because of their remoteness or because their places are fastnesses, not subject to Musalman rule.

(c. Of Hindustan.)

Hindustan is of the first climate, the second climate, and the third climate; of the fourth climate it has none. It is a wonderful country. Compared with our countries it is a different world; its mountains, rivers, jungles and deserts, its towns, its cultivated lands, its animals and plants, its peoples and their tongues, its rains, and its winds, are all different. In some respects the hot–country (*garm-sil*) that depends on Kabul, is like Hindustan, but in others, it is different. Once the water of Sind is crossed, everything is in the Hindustan way (*tariq*) Fol. 272b. land, water, tree, rock, people and horde, opinion and custom.

(d. Of the northern mountains.)

After crossing the Sind-river (eastwards), there are countries, in the northern mountains mentioned above, appertaining to Kashmir and once included in it, although most of them, as for example, Pakli and Shahmang (?), do not now obey it. Beyond Kashmir there are countless peoples and hordes, *parganas* and cultivated lands, in the mountains. As far as Bengal, as far indeed as the shore of the great ocean, the peoples are without break. About this procession of men no-one has been able to give authentic information in reply to our enquiries and investigations. So far people have been saying that they call these hill-men *Kas*.[1] It has struck me that as a Hindustani pronounces *shin* as *sin* (*i.e. sh* as *s*), and as Kashmir is the one respectable town in these mountains, no other indeed being heard of, Hindustanis might pronounce it Kasmir.[2] These

1 Are they the Khas of Nepal and Sikkim? (G. of I.).
2 Here Erskine notes that the Persian (trs.) adds, "*mir* signifying a hill, and *kas* being the name of the natives of the hill-country." This may not support the name *kas* as correct but may be merely an explanation of Babur's meaning. It is not in I.O. 217 f. 189 or in Muh. *Shirazi*'s lithographed *Waqi'at-i-baburi* p. 190.

people trade in musk-bags, *b:hri-qutas*,[1] saffron, lead and copper.

Hindis call these mountains Sawalak-parbat. In the Hindi tongue *sawai-lak* means one lak and a quarter, that is, 125,000, and *parbat* means a hill, which makes 125,000 hills.[2] The snow on these mountains never lessens; it is seen white from many districts of Hind, as, for example, Lahor, Sihrind and Sambal. The range, which in Kabul is known as Hindu-kush, comes from Kabul eastwards into Hindustan, with slight inclination to the south. The Hindustanat[3] are to the south of it. Tibet lies to the north of it and of that unknown horde called Kas.

Fol. 273.

(*e. Of rivers.*)

Many rivers rise in these mountains and flow through Hindustan. Six rise north of Sihrind, namely Sind, Bahat (Jilam), Chan-ab [*sic*], Rawi, Biah, and Sutluj;[4] all meet near Multan, flow westwards under the name of Sind, pass through the Tatta country and fall into the 'Uman(-sea).

Besides these six there are others, such as Jun (Jumna), Gang (Ganges), Rahap (Rapti?), Gui, Gagar (Ghaggar), Siru, Gandak, and many more; all unite with the Gang-darya, flow east under its name, pass through the Bengal country, and are poured into the great ocean. They all rise in the Sawalak-parbat.

Many rivers rise in the Hindustan hills, as, for instance, Chambal, Banas, Bitwi, and Sun (Son). There is no snow whatever on these mountains. Their waters also join the Gang-darya.

(*f. Of the Aravalli.*)

Another Hindustan range runs north and south. It begins in the Dihli country at a small rocky hill on which is Firuz Shah's residence, called Jahan-nama,[5] and, going on from there, appears near Dihli in detached, very low, scattered here and there, rocky

---

1 Either yak or the tassels of the yak. *See* Appendix M.
2 My husband tells me that Babur's authority for this interpretation of Sawalak may be the *Zafar-nama* (Bib. Ind. ed. ii, 149).
3 *i.e.* the countries of Hindustan.
4 so pointed, carefully, in the Hai. MS. Mr. Erskine notes of these rivers that they are the Indus, Hydaspes, Ascesines, Hydraotes, Hesudrus and Hyphasis.
5 *Ayin-i-akbari*, Jarrett 279.

little hills.[1] Beyond Miwat, it enters the Biana country. The hills of Sikri, Bari and Dulpur are also part of this same including (*tuta*)range. The hills of Gualiar—they write it Galiur—although they do not connect with it, are off-sets of this range; so are the hills of Rantanbur, Chitur, Chandiri, and Mandau. They are cut off from it in some places by 7 to 8 *kurohs* (14 to 16 m.). These hills are very low, rough, rocky and jungly. No snow whatever falls on them. They are the makers, in Hindustan, of several rivers.

(g. Irrigation.)

The greater part of the Hindustan country is situated on level land. Many though its towns and cultivated lands are, it nowhere has running waters.[2] Rivers and, in some places, standing-waters are its "running-waters" (*aqar-sular*). Even where, as for some towns, it is practicable to convey water by digging channels (*ariq*), this is not done. For not doing it there may be several reasons, one being that water is not at all a necessity in cultivating crops and orchards. Autumn crops grow by the downpour of the rains themselves; and strange it is that spring crops grow even when no rain falls. To young trees water is made to flow by means of buckets or a wheel. They are given water constantly during two or three years; after which they need no more. Some vegetables are watered constantly.

In Lahor, Dibalpur and those parts, people water by means of a wheel. They make two circles of ropes long enough to suit the depth of the well, fix strips of wood between them, and on these fasten pitchers. The ropes with the wood and attached
pitchers are put over the well-wheel. At one end of the wheel-axle a second wheel is fixed, and close (*qash*) to it another on an upright axle. This last wheel the bullock turns; its teeth catch in the teeth of the second, and thus the wheel with the pitchers is turned. A trough is set where the water empties from the pitchers and from this the water is conveyed everywhere.

---

1 *parcha parcha, kichikrak kichikrak, anda munda, tashliq taqghina.* The Gazetteer of India (1907 i, 1) puts into scientific words, what Babur here describes, the ruin of a great former range.
2 Here *aqar-sular* might safely be replaced by "irrigation channels".

In Agra, Chandwar, Biana and those parts, again, people water with a bucket; this is a laborious and filthy way. At the well-edge they set up a fork of wood, having a roller adjusted between the forks, tie a rope to a large bucket, put the rope over the roller, and tie its other end to the bullock. One person must drive the bullock, another empty the bucket. Every time the bullock turns after having drawn the bucket out of the well, that rope lies on the bullock-track, in pollution of urine and dung, before it descends again into the well. To some crops needing water, men and women carry it by repeated efforts in pitchers.[1]

(*h. Other particulars about Hindustan.*)

The towns and country of Hindustan are greatly wanting in charm. Its towns and lands are all of one sort; there are no walls to the orchards (*baghat*), and most places are on the dead level plain. Under the monsoon-rains the banks of some of its rivers and torrents are worn into deep channels, difficult and troublesome to pass through anywhere. In many parts of the plains thorny jungle grows, behind the good defence of which the people of the *pargana* become stubbornly rebellious and pay no taxes. Fol. 274b.

Except for the rivers and here and there standing-waters, there is little "running-water". So much so is this that towns and countries subsist on the water of wells or on such as collects in tanks during the rains.

In Hindustan hamlets and villages, towns indeed, are depopulated and set up in a moment! If the people of a large town, one inhabited for years even, flee from it, they do it in such a way that not a sign or trace of them remains in a day or a day and a half.[2] On the other hand, if they fix their eyes on

1 The verb here is *tashmaq*; it also expresses to carry like ants (f. 220), presumably from each person's carrying a pitcher or a stone at a time, and repeatedly.

2 "This" notes Erskine (p. 315) "is the *wulsa* or *walsa*, so well described by Colonel Wilks in his Historical Sketches vol. i. p. 309, note 'On the approach of an hostile army, the unfortunate inhabitants of India bury under ground their most cumbrous effects, and each individual, man, woman, and child above six years of age (the infant children being carried by their mothers), with a load of grain proportioned to their strength, issue from their beloved homes, and take the direction of a country (if such can be found,) exempt from the miseries of war; sometimes of a strong fortress, but more generally of the most unfrequented hills and woods, where they prolong a miserable existence until the departure of the enemy, and if this should be

a place in which to settle, they need not dig water-courses or construct dams because their crops are all rain-grown,[1] and as the population of Hindustan is unlimited, it swarms in. They make a tank or dig a well; they need not build houses or set up walls— khas-grass (*Andropogon muricatum*) abounds, wood is unlimited, huts are made, and straightway there is a village or a town!

(*i. Fauna of Hindustan:—Mammals.*)

The elephant, which Hindustanis call *hat(h)i*, is one of the wild animals peculiar to Hindustan. It inhabits the (western?) borders of the Kalpi country, and becomes more numerous in its wild state the further east one goes (in Kalpi?). From this tract it is that captured elephants are brought; in Karrah and Manikpur elephant-catching is the work of 30 or 40 villages.[2] People answer (*jawab birurlar*) for them direct to the exchequer.[3] The elephant is an immense animal and very sagacious. If people speak to it, it understands; if they command anything from it, it does it. Its value is according to its size; it is sold by measure (*qarilab*); the larger it is, the higher its price. People

Fol. 275.

---

protracted beyond the time for which they have provided food, a large portion necessarily dies of hunger.' See the note itself. The Historical Sketches should be read by every-one who desires to have an accurate idea of the South of India. It is to be regretted that we do not possess the history of any other part of India, written with the same knowledge or research."

"The word *wulsa* or *walsa* is Dravidian. Telugu has *valasa*, 'emigration, flight, or removing from home for fear of a hostile army.' Kanarese has *valasĕ*, *ŏlasĕ*, and *ŏlisĕ*, 'flight, a removing from home for fear of a hostile army.' Tamil has *valasei*, 'flying for fear, removing hastily.' The word is an interesting one. I feel pretty sure it is not Aryan, but Dravidian; and yet it stands alone in Dravidian, with nothing that I can find in the way of a root or affinities to explain its etymology. Possibly it may be a borrowed word in Dravidian. Malayalam has no corresponding word. Can it have been borrowed from Kolarian or other primitive Indian speech?" (Letter to H. Beveridge from Mr. F. E. Pargiter, 8th August, 1914.)

Wulsa seems to be a derivative from Sanscrit *ulvan*, and to answer to Persian *wairani* and Turki *buzughlughi*. *See* Additional Notes, p. 799.

1 *lalmi*, which in Afghani (Pushtu) signifies grown without irrigation.

2 "The improvement of Hindustan since Babur's time must be prodigious. The wild elephant is now confined to the forests under Hemala, and to the Ghats of Malabar. A wild elephant near Karrah, Manikpur, or Kalpi, is a thing, at the present day (1826 AD.), totally unknown. May not their familiar existence in these countries down to Babur's days, be considered rather hostile to the accounts given of the superabundant population of Hindustan in remote times?" (Erskine).

3 *diwan*. I.O. 217 f. 190*b*, *dar diwan fil jawab miguind*; Mems. p. 316. They account to the government for the elephants they take; *Méms*. ii, 188, *Les habitants payent l'impôt avec le produit de leur chasse*. Though de Courteille's reading probably states the fact, Erskine's includes de C.'s and more, inasmuch as it covers all captures and these might reach to a surplusage over the imposts.

rumour that it is heard of in some islands as 10 *qari*[1] high, but in this tract it[2] is not seen above 4 or 5. It eats and drinks entirely with its trunk; if it lose the trunk, it cannot live. It has two great teeth (tusks) in its upper jaw, one on each side of its trunk; by setting these against walls and trees, it brings them down; with these it fights and does whatever hard tasks fall to it. People call these ivory ('*aj*, var. *ghaj*); they are highly valued by Hindustanis. The elephant has no hair.[3] It is much relied on by Hindustanis, accompanying every troop of their armies. It has some useful qualities:—it crosses great rivers with ease, carrying a mass of baggage, and three or four have gone dragging without trouble the cart of the mortar (*qazan*) it takes four or five hundred men to haul.[4] But its stomach is large; one elephant eats the corn (*bughuz*) of two strings (*qitar*) of camels.[5]

The rhinoceros is another. This also is a large animal, equal *Fol. 275b.* in bulk to perhaps three buffaloes. The opinion current in those countries (Tramontana) that it can lift an elephant on its horn, seems mistaken. It has a single horn on its nose, more than nine inches (*qarish*) long; one of two *qarish* is not seen.[6] Out of one large horn were made a drinking-vessel[7] and a dice-box, leaving over [the thickness of] 3 or 4 hands.[8] The rhinoceros'

1 Pers. trs. *gaz* = 24 inches. *Il est bon de rappeler que le mot turk qari, que la version persane rend par gaz, désigne proprement l'espace compris entre le haut de l'épaule jusqu'au bout des doigts* (de Courteille, ii, 189 note). The *qari* like one of its equivalents, the ell (Zenker), is a variable measure; it seems to approach more nearly to a yard than to a *gaz* of 24 inches. *See Memoirs of Jahangir* (R. & B. pp. 18, 141 and notes) for the heights of elephants, and for discussion of some measures.

2 *khud*, itself.

3 *i.e.* pelt; as Erskine notes, its skin is scattered with small hairs. Details such as this one stir the question, for whom was Babur writing? Not for Hindustan where what he writes is patent; hardly for Kabul; perhaps for Transoxania.

4 Shaikh Zain's wording shows this reference to be to a special piece of artillery, perhaps that of f. 302.

5 A string of camels contains from five to seven, or, in poetry, even more (Vullers, ii, 728, *sermone poetico series decem camelorum*). The item of food compared is corn only (*bughuz*) and takes no account therefore of the elephant's green food.

6 The Ency. Br. states that the horn seldom exceeds a foot in length; there is one in the B.M. measuring 18 inches.

7 *ab-khwura kishti*, water-drinker's boat, in which name *kishti* may be used with reference to shape as boat is in *sauce-boat*. Erskine notes that rhinoceros-horn is supposed to sweat on approach of poison.

8 *ailik*, Pers. trs. *angusht*, finger, each seemingly representing about one inch, a hand's thickness, a finger's breadth.

hide is very thick; an arrow shot from a stiff bow, drawn with full strength right up to the arm-pit, if it pierce at all, might penetrate 4 inches (*ailik*, hands). From the sides (*qash*) of its fore and hind legs,[1] folds hang which from a distance look like housings thrown over it. It resembles the horse more than it does any other animal.[2] As the horse has a small stomach (appetite?), so has the rhinoceros; as in the horse a piece of bone (pastern?) grows in place of small bones (T. *ashuq*, Fr. *osselets* (Zenker), knuckles), so one grows in the rhinoceros; as in the horse's hand (*ailik*, Pers. *dast*) there is *kumuk* (or *gumuk*, a *tibia*, or marrow), so there is in the rhinoceros.[3] It is more ferocious than the elephant and cannot be made obedient and submissive. There are masses of it in the Parashawar and Hashnagar jungles, so too between the Sind-river and the jungles of the Bhira country. Masses there are also on the banks of the Saru-river in Hindustan. Some were killed in the Parashawar and Hashnagar jungles in our moves on Hindustan. It strikes powerfully with its horn; men and horses enough have been horned in those hunts. In one of them the horse of a *chuhra* (brave) named Maqsud was tossed a spear's-length, for which reason the man was nick-named the rhino's aim (*maqsud-i-karg*).

Fol. 276.

The wild-buffalo[4] is another. It is much larger than the (domestic) buffalo and its horns do not turn back in the same way.[5] It is a mightily destructive and ferocious animal.

The *nila-gau* (blue-bull)[6] is another. It may stand as high as a horse but is somewhat lighter in build. The male is bluish-gray, hence, seemingly, people call it *nila-gau*. It has two rather small horns. On its throat is a tuft of hair, nine inches long; (in this) it resembles the yak.[7] Its hoof is cleft (*airi*)

1 lit. hand (*qul*) and leg (*but*).

2 The anatomical details by which Babur supports this statement are difficult to translate, but his grouping of the two animals is in agreement with the modern classification of them as two of the three *Ungulata vera*, the third being the tapir (Fauna of British India:—Mammals, Blanford 467 and, illustration, 468).

3 De Courteille (ii, 190) reads *kumuk*, osseuse; Erskine reads *gumuk*, marrow.

4 *Bos bubalus*.

5 "so as to grow into the flesh" (Erskine, p. 317).

6 *sic* in text. It may be noted that the name *nil-gai*, common in general European writings, is that of the cow; *nil-gau*, that of the bull (Blanford).

7 *b:h:ri qutas*; *see* Appendix M.

like the hoof of cattle. The doe is of the colour of the *bughu-maral*;[1] she, for her part, has no horns and is plumper than the male.

The hog-deer (*kotah-paicha*) is another.[2] It may be of the size of the white deer (*aq kiyik*). It has short legs, hence its name, little-legged. Its horns are like a *bughu*'s but smaller; like the *bughu* it casts them every year. Being rather a poor runner, it does not leave the jungle.

Another is a deer (*kiyik*) after the fashion of the male deer (*airkaki huna*) of the *jiran*.[3] Its back is black, its belly white, its horns longer than the *huna*'s, but more crooked. A Hindustani Fol. 276b. calls it *kalahara*,[4] a word which may have been originally *kala-haran*, black-buck, and which has been softened in pronunciation to *kalahara*. The doe is light-coloured. By means of this *kalahara* people catch deer; they fasten a noose (*halqa*) on its horns, hang a stone as large as a ball[5] on one of its feet, so as to keep it from getting far away after it has brought about the capture of a deer, and set it opposite wild deer when these are seen. As these (*kalahara*) deer are singularly combative, advance to fight is made at once. The two deer strike with their horns and push one another backwards and forwards, during which the wild one's horns become entangled in the net that is fast to the tame one's. If the wild one would run away, the tame one does not go; it is impeded also by the stone on its foot. People take many deer in this way; after capture they tame them and use them in their turn to take others;[6] they also set them to fight at home; the deer fight very well.

There is a smaller deer (*kiyik*) on the Hindustan hill-skirts, as large may-be as the one year's lamb of the *arqarghalcha* (*Ovis poli*).

1 The doe is brown (Blanford, p. 518). The word *bughu* (stag) is used alone just below and seems likely to represent the bull of the Asiatic wapiti (f. 4 n. on *bughu-maral*.)

2 *Axis porcinus* (Jerdon, *Cervus porcinus*).

3 *Saiga tartarica* (Shaw). Turki *huna* is used, like English deer, for male, female, and both. Here it seems defined by *airkaki* to mean stag or buck.

4 *Antelope cervicapra*, black-buck, so called from the dark hue of its back (Yule's H.J. *s.n.* Black-buck).

5 *tuyuq*, underlined in the Elph. MS. by *kura*, cannon-ball; Erskine, foot-ball, de Courteille, *pierre plus grosse que la cheville* (*tuyaq*).

6 This mode of catching antelopes is described in the *Ayin-i-akbari*, and is noted by Erskine as common in his day.

The *gini*–cow[1] is another, a very small one, perhaps as large as the *quchqar* (ram) of those countries (Tramontana). Its flesh is very tender and savoury.

The monkey (*maimun*) is another—a Hindustani calls it *bandar*. Of this too there are many kinds, one being what people take to those countries. The jugglers (*luli*) teach them tricks. This kind is in the mountains of Nur-dara, in the skirt-hills of Safid-koh neighbouring on Khaibar, and from there downwards all through Hindustan. It is not found higher up. Its hair is yellow, its face white, its tail not very long.—Another kind, not found in Bajaur, Sawad and those parts, is much larger than the one taken to those countries (Tramontana). Its tail is very long, its hair whitish, its face quite black. It is in the mountains and jungles of Hindustan.[2]—Yet another kind is distinguished (*bula dur*), quite black in hair, face and limbs.[3]

The *nawal* (*nul*)[4] is another. It may be somewhat smaller than the *kish*. It climbs trees. Some call it the *mush-i-khurma* (palm-rat). It is thought lucky.

A mouse (T. *sichqan*) people call *galahri* (squirrel) is another. It is just always in trees, running up and down with amazing alertness and speed.[5]

Fol. 277.

1 H. *gaina*. It is 3 feet high (Yule's H.J. *s.n.* Gynee). *Cf.* A. A. Blochmann, p. 149. The ram with which it is compared may be that of *Ovis ammon* (Vigné's *Kashmir etc.* ii, 278).

2 Here the Pers. trs. adds:—They call this kind of monkey *langur* (baboon, I.O. 217 f. 192).

3 Here the Pers. trs. adds what Erskine mistakenly attributes to Babur:—People bring it from several islands.—They bring yet another kind from several islands, yellowish-grey in colour like a *pustin tin* (leather coat of?; Erskine, skin of the fig, *tin*). Its head is broader and its body much larger than those of other monkeys. It is very fierce and destructive. It is singular *quod penis ejus semper sit erectus, et nunquam non ad coitum idoneus* [Erskine].

4 This name is explained on the margin of the Elph. MS. as "*rasu*, which is the weasel of Tartary" (Erskine). *Rasu* is an Indian name for the squirrel *Sciurus indicus*. The *kish*, with which Babur's *nul* is compared, is explained by de C. as *belette*, weasel, and by Steingass as a fur-bearing animal; the fur-bearing weasel is (*Mustelidae*) *putorius ermina*, the ermine-weasel (Blanford, p. 165), which thus seems to be Babur's *kish*. The alternative name Babur gives for his *nul*, i.e. *mush-i-khurma*, is, in India, that of *Sciurus palmarum*, the palm-squirrel (G. of I. i, 227); this then, it seems that Babur's *nul* is. (Erskine took *nul* here to be the mongoose (*Herpestes mungus*) (p. 318); and Blanford, perhaps partly on Erskine's warrant, gives *mush-i-khurma* as a name of the lesser *mungus* of Bengal. I gather that the name *nawal* is not exclusively confined even now to the *mungus*.)

5 If this be a tree-mouse and not a squirrel, it may be *Vandeleuria oleracea* (G. of I. i, 228).

(*j. Fauna of Hindustan:—Birds.*) [1]

The peacock (Ar. *taus*) is one. It is a beautifully coloured and splendid animal. Its form (*andam*) is not equal to its colouring and beauty. Its body may be as large as the crane's (*turna*) but it is not so tall. On the head of both cock and hen are 20 to 30 feathers rising some 2 or 3 inches high. The hen has neither colour nor beauty. The head of the cock has an iridescent collar (*tauq susani*); its neck is of a beautiful blue; Fol. 277b. below the neck, its back is painted in yellow, parrot-green, blue and violet colours. The flowers [2] on its back are much the smaller; below the back as far as the tail-tips are [larger] flowers painted in the same colours. The tail of some peacocks grows to the length of a man's extended arms. [3] It has a small tail under its flowered feathers, like the tail of other birds; this ordinary tail and its primaries [4] are red. It is in Bajaur and Sawad and below them; it is not in Kunur and the Lamghanat or any place above them. Its flight is feebler than the pheasant's (*qirghawal*); it cannot do more than make one or two short flights. [5] On account of its feeble flight, it frequents the hills or jungles, which is curious, since jackals abound in the jungles it frequents. What damage might these jackals not do to birds that trail from jungle to jungle, tails as long as a man's stretch (*qulach*)! Hindustanis call the peacock *mor*. Its flesh is lawful food, according to the doctrine of Imam Abu Hanifa; it is like that of the partridge and not unsavoury, but is eaten with instinctive aversion, in the way camel-flesh is.

The parrot (H. *tuti*) is another. This also is in Bajaur and countries lower down. It comes into Ningnahar and the

---

1 The notes to this section are restricted to what serves to identify the birds Babur mentions, though temptation is great to add something to this from the mass of interesting circumstance scattered in the many writings of observers and lovers of birds. I have thought it useful to indicate to what language a bird's name belongs.

2 Persian, *gul*; English, eyes.

3 *qulach* (Zenker, p. 720); Pers. trs. (217 f. 192b) *yak qad-i-adm*; de Courteille, *brasse* (fathom). These three are expressions of the measure from finger-tip to finger-tip of a man's extended arms, which should be his height, a fathom (6 feet).

4 *qanat*, of which here "primaries" appears to be the correct rendering, since Jerdon says (ii, 506) of the bird that its "wings are striated black and white, primaries and tail deep chestnut".

5 The *qirghawal*, which is of the pheasant species, when pursued, will take several flights immediately after each other, though none long; peacocks, it seems, soon get tired and take to running (Erskine).

Lamghanat in the heats when mulberries ripen; it is not there at other times. It is of many, many kinds. One sort is that which people carry into those (Tramontane) countries. They Fol. 278. make it speak words.—Another sort is smaller; this also they make speak words. They call it the jungle-parrot. It is numerous in Bajaur, Sawad and that neighbourhood, so much so that 5 or 6000 fly in one flock (*khail*). Between it and the one first-named the difference is in bulk; in colouring they are just one and the same.—Another sort is still smaller than the jungle-parrot. Its head is quite red, the top of its wings (*i.e.* the primaries) is red also; the tip of its tail for two hands'-thickness is lustrous.[1] The head of some parrots of this kind is iridescent (*susani*). It does not become a talker. People call it the Kashmir parrot.—Another sort is rather smaller than the jungle-parrot; its beak is black; round its neck is a wide black collar; its primaries are red. It is an excellent learner of words.—We used to think that whatever a parrot or a *sharak* (*mina*) might say of words people had taught it, it could not speak of any matter out of its own head. At this juncture[2] one of my immediate servants Abu'l-qasim *Jalair*, reported a singular thing to me. A parrot of this sort whose cage must have been covered up, said, "Uncover my face; I am stifling." And another time when palki bearers sat down to take breath, this parrot, presumably on hearing wayfarers pass by, said, "Men are going past, are you not going on?" Let credit rest with the narrator,[3] but never-the-less, so long as a person has not heard with his own ears, he may not believe!—Another kind is of a beautiful Fol. 278b. full red; it has other colours also, but, as nothing is distinctly remembered about them, no description is made. It is a very beautiful bird, both in colour and form. People are understood to make this also speak words.[4] Its defect is a most unpleasant, sharp voice, like the drawing of broken china on a copper plate.[5]

---

1 Ar. *barraq*, as on f. 278b last line where the Elph. MS. has *barraq*, marked with the *tashdid*.

2 This was, presumably, just when Babur was writing the passage.

3 This sentence is in Arabic.

4 A Persian note, partially expunged from the text of the Elph. MS. is to the effect that 4 or 5 other kinds of parrot are heard of which the revered author did not see.

5 Erskine suggests that this may be the *loory* (*Loriculus vernalis*, Indian loriquet).

The (P.) *sharak*[1] is another. It is numerous in the Lamghanat and abounds lower down, all over Hindustan. Like the parrot, it is of many kinds.—The kind that is numerous in the Lamghanat has a black head; its primaries (*qanat*) are spotted, its body rather larger and thicker[2] than that of the (T.) *chughur-chuq*.[3] People teach it to speak words.—Another kind they call *p:ndawali*;[4] they bring it from Bengal; it is black all over and of much greater bulk than the *sharak* (here, house-*mina*). Its bill and foot are yellow and on each ear are yellow wattles which hang down and have a bad appearance.[5] It learns to speak well and clearly.—Another kind of *sharak* is slenderer than the last and is red round the eyes. It does not learn to speak. People call it the wood-*sharak*.[6] Again, at the time when (934 AH.) I had made a bridge over Gang (Ganges), crossed it, and put my adversaries to flight, a kind of *sharak* was seen, in the neighbourhood of Laknau and Aud (Oude), for the first time, which had a white breast, piebald head, and black back. This kind does not learn to speak.[7]

1 The birds Babur classes under the name *sharak* seem to include what Oates and Blanford (whom I follow as they give the results of earlier workers) class under *Sturnus*, *Eulabes* and *Calornis*, starling, grackle and mina, and tree-stare (*Fauna of British India*, Oates, vols. i and ii, Blanford, vols. iii and iv).

2 Turki, *qaba*; Ilminsky, p. 361, *tang* (*tund?*).

3 E. D. Ross's *Polyglot List of Birds*, p. 314, *Chighir-chiq*, Northern swallow; Elph. MS. f. 230*b* interlined *jil* (Steingass lark). The description of the bird allows it to be *Sturnus humii*, the Himalayan starling (Oates, i, 520).

4 Elph. and Hai. MSS. (Sans. and Bengali) *p:ndui*; two good MSS. of the Pers. trs. (I.O. 217 and 218) *p:ndawali*; Ilminsky (p. 361) *mina*; Erskine (*Mems.* p. 319) *pindaweli*, but without his customary translation of an Indian name. The three forms shewn above can all mean "having protuberance or lump" (*pinda*) and refer to the bird's wattle. But the word of the presumably well-informed scribes of I.O. 217 and 218 can refer to the bird's sagacity in speech and be *pandawali*, possessed of wisdom. With the same spelling, the word can translate into the epithet *religiosa*, given to the wattled *mina* by Linnæus. This epithet Mr. Leonard Wray informs me has been explained to him as due to the frequenting of temples by the birds; and that in Malaya they are found living in cotes near Chinese temples.—An alternative name (one also connecting with *religiosa*) allowed by the form of the word is *binda-wali*. H. *binda* is a mark on the forehead, made as a preparative to devotion by Hindus, or in Sans. and Bengali, is the spot of paint made on an elephant's trunk; the meaning would thus be "having a mark". Cf. Jerdon and Oates *s.n. Eulabes religiosa*.

5 *Eulabes intermedia*, the Indian grackle or hill-mina. Here the Pers. trs. adds that people call it *mina*.

6 *Calornis chalybeius*, the glossy starling or tree-stare, which never descends to the ground.

7 *Sturnopastor contra*, the pied mina.

The *luja*[1] is another. This bird they call (Ar.) *bu-qalamun* (chameleon) because, between head and tail, it has five or six changing colours, resplendent (*barraq*) like a pigeon's throat.

Fol. 279. It is about as large as the *kabg-i-dari*[2] and seems to be the *kabg-i-dari* of Hindustan. As the *kabg-i-dari* moves (*yurur*) on the heads (*kulah*) of mountains, so does this. It is in the Nijr-au mountains of the countries of Kabul, and in the mountains lower down but it is not found higher up. People tell this wonderful thing about it:—When the birds, at the onset of winter, descend to the hill-skirts, if they come over a vineyard, they can fly no further and are taken. God knows the truth! The flesh of this bird is very savoury.

The partridge (*durraj*)[3] is another. This is not peculiar to Hindustan but is also in the *Garm-sir* countries;[4] as however some kinds are only in Hindustan, particulars of them are given here. The *durraj* (*Francolinus vulgaris*) may be of the same bulk as the *kiklik*;[5] the cock's back is the colour of the hen-pheasant (*qirghawal-ning mada-si*); its throat and breast are black, with quite white spots.[6] A red line comes down on both sides of both eyes.[7] It is named from its cry[8] which is something like *Shir daram shakrak*.[9] It pronounces *shir* short; *daram shakrak* it says distinctly. Astarabad partridges are said to cry *Bat mini tutilar* (Quick! they have caught me). The partridge of Arabia and those parts is understood to cry, *Bi'l*

---

1 Part of the following passage about the *luja* (var. *lukha, lucha*) is *verbatim* with part of that on f. 135; both were written about 934–5 AH. as is shewn by Shaikh Zain and by inference from references in the text. *See* Appendix N.

2 Lit. mountain-partridge. There is ground for understanding that one of the birds known in the region as *monals* is meant. *See* Appendix N.

3 Sans. *chakora*; Ar. *durraj*; P. *kabg*; T. *kiklik*.

4 Here, probably, southern Afghanistan.

5 *Caccabis chukur* (Scully, Shaw's Vocabulary) or *C. pallescens* (Hume, quoted under No. 126 E. D. Ross' *Polyglot List*).

6 "In some parts of the country (*i.e.* India before 1841 AD.), tippets used to be made of the beautiful black, white-spotted feathers of the lower plumage (of the *durraj*), and were in much request, but they are rarely procurable now" (*Bengal Sporting Magazine* for 1841, quoted by Jerdon, ii, 561).

7 A broad collar of red passes round the whole neck (Jerdon, ii, 558).

8 Ar. *durraj* means one who repeats what he hears, a tell-tale.

9 Various translations have been made of this passage, "I have milk and sugar" (Erskine), "*J'ai du lait, un peu de sucre*" (de Courteille), but with short *sh:r*, it might be read in more than one way ignoring milk and sugar. *See* Jerdon, ii, 558 and Hobson Jobson *s.n.* Black-partridge.

shakar tadawm al ni'am (with sugar pleasure endures)! The hen-bird has the colour of the young pheasant. These birds are found below Nijr-au.—Another kind is called *kanjal*. Its bulk may be that of the one already described. Its voice is very like that of the *kiklik* but much shriller. There is little difference in colour between the cock and hen. It is found in Parashawar, Hashnagar and countries lower down, but not higher up. Fol. 279b.

The *p(h)ul-paikar*[1] is another. Its size may be that of the *kabg-i-dari*; its shape is that of the house-cock, its colour that of the hen. From forehead (*tumagh*) to throat it is of a beautiful colour, quite red. It is in the Hindustan mountains.

The wild-fowl (*sahrai-taugh*)[2] is another. It flies like a pheasant, and is not of all colours as house-fowl are. It is in the mountains of Bajaur and lower down, but not higher up.

The *chilsi* (or *jilsi*)[3] is another. In bulk it equals the *p(h)ul-paikar* but the latter has the finer colouring. It is in the mountains of Bajaur.

The *sham*[4] is another. It is about as large as a house-fowl; its colour is unique (*ghair mukarrar*).[5] It also is in the mountains of Bajaur.

The quail (P.*budana*) is another. It is not peculiar to Hindustan but four or five kinds are so.—One is that which goes to our countries (Tramontana), larger and more spreading than the (Hindustan) quail.[6]—Another kind[7] is smaller than the one first named. Its primaries and tail are reddish. It flies in flocks like the *chir* (*Phasianus Wallichii*).—Another kind is smaller than that which goes to our countries and is darker on throat

1 Flower-faced, *Trapogon melanocephala*, the horned (*sing*) -monal. It is described by Jahangir (*Memoirs*, R. and B., ii, 220) under the names [H. and P.] *phul-paikar* and Kashmiri, *sonlu*.

2 *Gallus sonneratii*, the grey jungle-fowl.

3 Perhaps *Bambusicola fytchii*, the western bambu-partridge. For *chil* see E. D. Ross, *l.c.* No. 127.

4 Jahangir (*l.c.*) describes, under the Kashmiri name *put*, what may be this bird. It seems to be *Gallus ferrugineus*, the red jungle-fowl (Blanford, iv, 75).

5 Jahangir helps to identify the bird by mentioning its elongated tail-feathers,— seasonal only.

6 The migrant quail will be *Coturnix communis*, the grey quail, 8 inches long; what it is compared with seems likely to be the bush-quail, which is non-migrant and shorter.

7 Perhaps *Perdicula argunda*, the rock bush-quail, which flies in small coveys.

and breast.[1]—Another kind goes in small numbers to Kabul; it is very small, perhaps a little larger than the yellow wag-tail (*qarcha*);[2] they call it *quratu* in Kabul.

The Indian bustard (P. *kharchal*)[3] is another. It is about as large as the (T.) *tughdaq* (*Otis tarda*, the great bustard), and seems to be the *tughdaq* of Hindustan.[4] Its flesh is delicious; of some birds the leg is good, of others, the wing; of the bustard all the meat is delicious and excellent.

The florican (P. *charz*)[5] is another. It is rather less than the *tughdiri* (*houbara*);[6] the cock's back is like the *tughdiri*'s, and its breast is black. The hen is of one colour. The flesh of the florican is very delicate. As the *kharchal* (Indian buzzard) resembles the *tughdaq* (great buzzard) so the *tharz* (florican) resembles the *tughdiri*.

The Hindustan sand-grouse (T. *baghri-qara*)[7] is another. It is smaller and slenderer than the *baghri-qara* [*Pterocles arenarius*] of those countries (Tramontana). The blackness of its breast is less deep, its cry also is sharper.

Of the birds that frequent water and the banks of rivers, one is the *ding*,[8] an animal of great bulk, each wing measuring a *qulach* (fathom). It has no plumage (*tuqi*) on head or neck; a thing like a bag hangs from its neck; its back is black; its breast is white. It goes sometimes to Kabul; one year people brought one they had caught. It became very tame; if meat

1 Perhaps *Coturnix coromandelica*, the black-breasted or rain quail, 7 inches long.

2 Perhaps *Motacilla citreola*, a yellow wag-tail which summers in Central Asia (Oates, ii, 298). If so, its Kabul name may refer to its flashing colour. *Cf.* E. D. Ross, *l.c.* No. 301; de Courteille's *Dictionary* which gives *qarcha*, wag-tail, and Zenker's which fixes the colour.

3 *Eupodotis edwardsii*; Turki, *tughdar* or *tughdiri*.

4 Erskine noting (Mems. p. 321), that the bustard is common in the Dakkan where it is bigger than a turkey, says it is called *tughdar* and suggests that this is a corruption of *tughdaq*. The uses of both words are shewn by Babur, here, and in the next following, account of the *charz*. *Cf.* G. of I. i, 260 and E. D. Ross *l.c.* Nos. 36, 40.

5 *Sypheotis bengalensis* and *S. aurita*, which are both smaller than *Otis houbara* (*tughdiri*). In Hindustan *S. aurita* is known as *likh* which name is the nearest approach I have found to Babur's [*luja*] *lukha*.

6 Jerdon mentions (ii, 615) that this bird is common in Afghanistan and there called *dugdaor* (*tughdar, tughdiri*).

7 *Cf.* Appendix B, since I wrote which, further information has made it fairly safe to say that the Hindustan *baghri-qara* is *Pterocles exustus*, the common sand-grouse and that the one of f. 49b is *Pterocles arenarius*, the larger or black-bellied sand-grouse. *P. exustus* is said by Yule (H. J. *s.n.* Rock-pigeon) to have been miscalled rock-pigeon by Anglo-Indians, perhaps because its flight resembles the pigeon's. This accounts for Erskine's rendering (p. 321) *baghri-qara* here by rock-pigeon.

8 *Leptoptilus dubius*, Hind. *hargila*. Hindustanis call it *pir-i-ding* (Erskine) and *peda dhauk* (Blanford), both names referring, perhaps, to its pouch. It is the adjutant of Anglo-India. *Cf.* f. 235.

were thrown to it, it never failed to catch it in its bill. Once it swallowed a six-nailed shoe, another time a whole fowl, wings and feathers, all right down.   Fol. 280b.

The *saras* (*Grus antigone*) is another. Turks in Hindustan call it *tiwa-turna* (camel-crane). It may be smaller than the *ding* but its neck is rather longer. Its head is quite red.[1] People keep this bird at their houses; it becomes very tame.

The *manek*[2] is another. In stature it approaches the *saras*, but its bulk is less. It resembles the *lag-lag* (*Ciconia alba*, the white stork) but is much larger; its bill is larger and is black. Its head is iridescent, its neck white, its wings partly-coloured; the tips and border-feathers and under parts of the wings are white, their middle black.

Another stork (*lag-lag*) has a white neck and all other parts black. It goes to those countries (Tramontana). It is rather smaller than the *lag-lag* (*Ciconia alba*). A Hindustani calls it *bak-ding* (one colour?).

Another stork in colour and shape is exactly like the storks that go to those countries. Its bill is blacker and its bulk much less than the *lag-lag*'s (*Ciconia alba*).[3]

Another bird resembles the grey heron (*auqar*) and the *lag-lag*; but its bill is longer than the heron's and its body smaller than the white stork's (*lag-lag*).

Another is the large *buzak*[4] (black ibis). In bulk it may equal the buzzard (Turki, *sar*). The back of its wings is white. It has a loud cry.

The white *buzak*[5] is another. Its head and bill are black.

---

1 only when young (Blanford, ii, 188).

2 Elph. MS. *mank:sa* or *mankia*; Hai. MS. *m:nk*. Haughton's *Bengali Dictionary* gives two forms of the name *manek-jur* and *manak-yoi*. It is *Dissura episcopus*, the white-necked stork (Blanford iv, 370, who gives *manik-jor* amongst its Indian names). Jerdon classes it (ii, 737) as *Ciconia leucocephala*. It is the beef-steak bird of Anglo-India.

3 *Ciconia nigra* (Blanford, iv, 369).

4 Under the Hindustani form, *buza*, of Persian *buzak* the birds Babur mentions as *buzak* can be identified. The large one is *Inocotis papillosus*, *buza*, *kala buza*, black curlew, king-curlew. The bird it equals in size is a buzzard, Turki *sar* (not Persian *sar*, starling). The king-curlew has a large white patch on the inner lesser and marginal coverts of its wings (Blanford, iv, 303). This agrees with Babur's statement about the wings of the large *buzak*. Its length is 27 inches, while the starling's is 9½ inches.

5 *Ibis melanocephala*, the white ibis, Pers. *safed buzak*, Bengali *sabut buza*. It is 30 inches long.

Fol. 281. It is much larger than the one that goes to those countries,[1] but smaller than the Hindustan *buzak*.[2]

The *gharm-pai*[3] (spotted-billed duck) is another. It is larger than the *suna burchin*[4] (mallard). The drake and duck are of one colour. It is in Hashnagar at all seasons, sometimes it goes into the Lamghanat. Its flesh is very savoury.

The *shah-murgh* (*Sarcidiornis melanonotus*, comb duck or *nukta*) is another. It may be a little smaller than a goose. It has a swelling on its bill; its back is black; its flesh is excellent eating.

The *zummaj* is another. It is about as large as the *burgut* (*Aquila chrysaetus*, the golden eagle).

Another is the buzzard (T. *sar*); its tail and back are red.

The (T.) *ala-qargha* of Hindustan is another (*Corvus cornix*, the pied crow). This is slenderer and smaller than the *ala-qargha* of those countries (Tramontana). Its neck is partly white.

Another Hindustan bird resembles the crow (T. *qargha*, *C. splendens*) and the magpie (Ar. *'aqqa*). In the Lamghanat people call it the jungle-bird (P. *murgh-i-jangal*).[5] Its head and breast are black; its wings and tail reddish; its eye quite red. Having a feeble flight, it does not come out of the jungle, whence its name.

The great bat (P. *shapara*)[6] is another. People call it (Hindi) *chumgadur*. It is about as large as the owl (T. *yapalaq*, *Otus brachyotus*), and has a head like a puppy's. When it is thinking of lodging for the night on a tree, it takes hold of a branch, turns head-downwards, and so remains. It has much singularity.

The magpie (Ar. *'aqqa*) is another. People call it (H.?) *mata* (*Dendrocitta rufa*, the Indian tree-pie). It may be somewhat

---

1 Perhaps, *Plegadis falcinellus*, the glossy ibis, which in most parts of India is a winter visitor. Its length is 25 inches.

2 Erskine suggests that this is *Platalea leucorodia*, the *chamach-buza*, spoon-bill. It is 33 inches long.

3 *Anas poecilorhyncha*. The Hai. MS. writes *gharm-pai*, and this is the Indian name given by Blanford (iv, 437).

4 *Anas boschas*. Dr. Ross notes (No. 147), from the *Sanglakh*, that *suna* is the drake, *burchin*, the duck and that it is common in China to call a certain variety of bird by the combined sex-names. Something like this is shewn by the uses of *bugha* and *maral*.

5 *Centropus rufipennis*, the common coucal (Yule's H.J. *s.n.* Crow-pheasant); H. *makokha*, *Cuculus castaneus* (Buchanan, quoted by Forbes).

6 *Pteropus edwardsii*, the flying-fox. The inclusion of the bat here amongst birds, may be a clerical accident, since on f. 135 a flying-fox is not written of as a bird.

less than the 'aqqa (*Pica rustica*), which moreover is pied black and white, while the *mata* is pied brown and black.[1]

Another is a small bird, perhaps of the size of the (T.) *sandulach*.[2] Fol. 281b. It is of a beautiful red with a little black on its wings.

The *karcha*[3] is another; it is after the fashion of a swallow (T. *qarlughach*), but much larger and quite black.

The *kuil*[4] (*Eudynamys orientalis*, the koel) is another. It may be as large as the crow (P. *zag*) but is much slenderer. It has a kind of song and is understood to be the bulbul of Hindustan. Its honour with Hindustanis is as great as is the bulbul's. It always stays in closely-wooded gardens.

Another bird is after the fashion of the (Ar.) *shiqarrak* (*Cissa chinensis*, the green-magpie). It clings to trees, is perhaps as large as the green-magpie, and is parrot-green (*Gecinus striolatus*, the little green-woodpecker?).

(*k. Fauna of Hindustan:—Aquatic animals.*)

One is the water-tiger (P. *shir-abi*, *Crocodilus palustris*).[5] This is in the standing-waters. It is like a lizard (T. *gilas*).[6] People say it carries off men and even buffaloes.

1 Babur here uses what is both the Kabul and Andijan name for the magpie, Ar. 'aqqa (Oates, i, 31 and Scully's Voc.), instead of T. *saghizghan* or P. *dam-sicha* (tail-wagger).

2 The Pers. trs. writes *sandulach mamula*, *mamula* being Arabic for wag-tail. De Courteille's Dictionary describes the *sandulach* as small and having a long tail, the cock-bird green, the hen, yellow. The wag-tail suiting this in colouring is *Motacilla borealis* (Oates, ii, 294; syn. *Budytes viridis*, the green wag-tail); this, as a migrant, serves to compare with the Indian "little bird", which seems likely to be a red-start.

3 This word may represent Scully's *kirich* and be the Turki name for a swift, perhaps *Cypselus affinis*.

4 This name is taken from its cry during the breeding season (Yule's H.J. *s.n.* Koel).

5 Babur's distinction between the three crocodiles he mentions seems to be that of names he heard, *shir-abi*, *siyah-sar*, and *gharial*.

6 In this passage my husband finds the explanation of two somewhat vague statements of later date, one made by Abu'l-fazl (A. A. Blochmann, p. 65) that Akbar called the *kilas* (cherry) the *shah-alu* (king-plum), the other by Jahangir that this change was made because *kilas* means lizard (*Jahangir's Memoirs*, R. & B. i, 116). What Akbar did is shewn by Babur; it was to reject the *Persian* name *kilas*, cherry, because it closely resembled *Turki gilas*, lizard. There is a lizard *Stellio Lehmanni* of Transoxiana with which Babur may well have compared the crocodile's appearance (Schuyler's *Turkistan*, i, 383). Akbar in Hindustan may have had *Varanus salvator* (6 ft. long) in mind, if indeed he had not the great lizard, *al lagarto*, the alligator itself in his thought. The name *kilas* evidently was banished only from the Court circle, since it is still current in Kashmir (Blochmann *l.c.* p. 616); and Speede (p. 201) gives *keeras*, cherry, as used in India.

The (P.) *siyah-sar* (black-head) is another. This also is like a lizard. It is in all rivers of Hindustan. One that was taken and brought in was about 4–5 *qari* (*cir.* 13 feet) long and as thick perhaps as a sheep. It is said to grow still larger. Its snout is over half a yard long. It has rows of small teeth in its upper and lower jaws. It comes out of the water and sinks into the mud (*bata*).

The (Sans.) *g[h]arial* (*Gavialus gangeticus*) is another.[1] It is said to grow large; many in the army saw it in the Saru (Gogra) river. It is said to take people; while we were on that river's banks (934–935 AH.), it took one or two slave-women (*daduk*), and it took three or four camp-followers between Ghazipur and Banaras. In that neighbourhood I saw one but from a distance only and not quite clearly.

The water-hog (P. *khuk-abi*, *Platanista gangetica*, the porpoise) is another. This also is in all Hindustan rivers. It comes up suddenly out of the water; its head appears and disappears; it dives again and stays below, shewing its tail. Its snout is as long as the *siyah-sar*'s and it has the same rows of small teeth. Its head and the rest of its body are fish-like. When at play in the water, it looks like a water-carrier's bag (*mashak*). Water-hogs, playing in the Saru, leap right out of the water; like fish, they never leave it.

Again there is the *kalah* (or *galah*)-fish [*baligh*].[2] Two bones

Fol. 282.

---

1 This name as now used, is that of the purely fish-eating crocodile. [In the Turki text Babur's account of the *gharial* follows that of the porpoise; but it is grouped here with those of the two other crocodiles.]

2 As the Hai. MS. and also I.O. 216 f. 137 (Pers. trs.) write *kalah* (*galah*)-fish, this may be a large cray-fish. One called by a name approximating to *galah*-fish is found in Malayan waters, *viz.* the *galah*-prawn (*hudang*) (*cf.* Bengali *gula-chingri*, *gula*-prawn, Haughton). *Galah* and *gula* may express lament made when the fish is caught (Haughton pp. 931, 933, 952); or if *kalah* be read, this may express scolding. Two good MSS. of the *Waqi'at-i-baburi* (Pers. trs.) write *kaka*; and their word cannot but have weight. Erskine reproduces *kaka* but offers no explanation of it, a failure betokening difficulty in his obtaining one. My husband suggests that *kaka* may represent a stuttering sound, doing so on the analogy of Vullers' explanation of the word,—*Vir ridiculus et facetus qui simul balbutiat*; and also he inclines to take the fish to be a crab (*kakra*). Possibly *kaka* is a popular or vulgar name for a cray-fish or a crab. Whether the sound is lament, scolding, or stuttering the fisherman knows! Shaikh Zain enlarges Babur's notice of this fish; he says the bones are prolonged (*bar awarda*) from the ears, that these it agitates at time of capture, making a noise like the word *kaka* by which it is known, that it is two *wajab* (18 in.) long, its flesh surprisingly tasty, and that it is very active, leaping a *gaz* (*cir.* a yard) out of the water when the fisherman's net is set to take it. For information about the Malayan fish, I am indebted to Mr. Cecil Wray.

each about 3 inches (*ailik*) long, come out in a line with its ears; these it shakes when taken, producing an extraordinary noise, whence, seemingly, people have called it *kalah* [or *galah*].

The flesh of Hindustan fishes is very savoury; they have no odour (*aid*) or tiresomeness.[1] They are surprisingly active. On one occasion when people coming, had flung a net across a stream, leaving its two edges half a yard above the water, most fish passed by leaping a yard above it. In many rivers are little fish which fling themselves a yard or more out of the water if there be harsh noise or sound of feet.   Fol. 282*b*.

The frogs of Hindustan, though otherwise like those others (Tramontane), run 6 or 7 yards on the face of the water.[2]

(*l. Vegetable products of Hindustan: Fruits.*)

The mango (P. *anbah*) is one of the fruits peculiar to Hindustan. Hindustanis pronounce the *b* in its name as though no vowel followed it (*i.e.* Sans. *anb*);[3] this being awkward to utter, some people call the fruit [P.] *naghzak*[4] as Khwaja Khusrau does:—

> Naghzak-i ma [var. *khwash*] naghz-kun-i bustan,
> Naghztarin mewa [var. *na'mat*]-i-Hindustan.[5]

Mangoes when good, are very good, but, many as are eaten, few are first-rate. They are usually plucked unripe and ripened in the house. Unripe, they make excellent condiments (*qatiq*), are good also preserved in syrup.[6] Taking it altogether, the mango is the best fruit of Hindustan. Some so praise it as to give it preference over all fruits except the musk-melon (T. *qawun*), but

1 T. *qiyunlighi*, presumably referring to spines or difficult bones; T. *qin*, however, means a scabbard [Shaw].

2 One of the common frogs is a small one which, when alarmed, jumps along the surface of the water (G. of I. i, 273).

3 *Anb* and *anbah* (pronounced *amb* and *ambah*) are now less commonly used names than *am*. It is an interesting comment on Babur's words that Abu'l-fazl spells *anb*, letter by letter, and says that the *b* is quiescent (*Ayin* 28; for the origin of the word mango, *vide* Yule's H.J. *s.n.*).

4 A corresponding diminutive would be fairling.

5 The variants, entered in parenthesis, are found in the Bib. Ind. ed. of the *Ayin-i-akbari* p. 75 and in a (bazar) copy of the *Quranu's-sa'dain* in my husband's possession. As Amir Khusrau was a poet of Hindustan, either *khwash* (*khwesh*) [our own] or *ma* [our] would suit his meaning. The couplet is, literally:—

> Our fairling, [*i.e.* mango] beauty-maker of the garden,
> Fairest fruit of Hindustan.

6 Daulat Khan *Yusuf-khail Ludi* in 929 AH. sent Babur a gift of mangoes preserved in honey (*in loco* p. 440).

such praise outmatches it. It resembles the *kardi* peach.[1] It ripens in the rains. It is eaten in two ways: one is to squeeze it to a pulp, make a hole in it, and suck out the juice,—the other, to peel and eat it like the *kardi* peach. Its tree grows very large[2] and has a leaf somewhat resembling the peach-tree's. The trunk is ill-looking and ill-shaped, but in Bengal and Gujrat is heard of as growing handsome (*khub*).[3]

Fol. 283.

The plantain (Sans. *kela*, *Musa sapientum*) is another.[4] An 'Arab calls it *mauz*.[5] Its tree is not very tall, indeed is not to be called a tree, since it is something between a grass and a tree. Its leaf is a little like that of the *aman-qara*[6] but grows about 2 yards (*qari*) long and nearly one broad. Out of the middle of its leaves rises, heart-like, a bud which resembles a sheep's heart. As each leaf (petal) of this bud expands, there grows at its base a row of 6 or 7 flowers which become the plantains. These flowers become visible with the lengthening of the heart-like shoot and the opening of the petals of the bud. The tree is understood to flower once only.[7] The fruit has two pleasant qualities, one that it peels easily, the other that it has neither stone nor fibre.[8] It is rather longer and thinner than the egg-plant (P. *badanjan*; *Solanum melongena*). It is not very sweet; the Bengal plantain (*i.e. chini-champa*) is, however, said to be very

1 I have learned nothing more definite about the word *kardi* than that it is the name of a superior kind of peach (*Ghiyasu'l-lughat*).

2 The preceding sentence is out of place in the Turki text; it may therefore be a marginal note, perhaps not made by Babur.

3 This sentence suggests that Babur, writing in Agra or Fathpur did not there see fine mango-trees.

4 *See* Yule's H.J. on the plantain, the banana of the West.

5 This word is a descendant of Sanscrit *mocha*, and parent of *musa* the botanical name of the fruit (Yule).

6 Shaikh Effendi (Kunos), Zenker and de Courteille say of this only that it is the name of a tree. Shaw gives a name that approaches it, *arman*, a grass, a weed; Scully explains this as *Artemisia vulgaris*, wormwood, but Roxburgh gives no *Artemisia* having a leaf resembling the plantain's. Scully has *aramadan*, unexplained, which, like *aman-qara*, may refer to comfort in shade. Babur's comparison will be with something known in Transoxiana. Maize has general resemblance with the plantain. So too have the names of the plants, since *mocha* and *mauz* stand for the plantain and (Hindi) *muka'i* for maize. These incidental resemblances bear, however lightly, on the question considered in the Ency. Br. (art. maize) whether maize was early in Asia or not; some writers hold that it was; if Babur's *aman-qara* were maize, maize will have been familiar in Transoxiana in his day.

7 Abu'l-fazl mentions that the plantain-tree bears no second crop unless cut down to the stump.

8 Babur was fortunate not to have met with a seed-bearing plantain.

sweet. The plantain is a very good-looking tree, its broad, broad, leaves of beautiful green having an excellent appearance.

The *anbli* (H. *imli*, *Tamarindus indica*, the tamarind) is another. By this name (*anbli*) people call the *khurma-i-hind* (Indian date-tree).[1] It has finely-cut leaves (leaflets), precisely like those of the (T.) *buia*,[2] except that they are not so finely-cut. It is a very good-looking tree, giving dense shade. It grows wild in masses too.

The (Beng.) *mahuwa* (*Bassia latifolia*) is another.[3] People call it also (P.) *gul-chikan* (or *chigan*, distilling-flower). This also is a very large tree. Most of the wood in the houses of Hindu- Fol. 283*b*. stanis is from it. Spirit ('*araq*) is distilled from its flowers,[4] not only so, but they are dried and eaten like raisins, and from them thus dried, spirit is also extracted. The dried flowers taste just like *kishmish*;[5] they have an ill-flavour. The flowers are not bad in their natural state;[6] they are eatable. The *mahuwa* grows wild also. Its fruit is tasteless, has rather a large seed with a thin husk, and from this seed, again,[7] oil is extracted.

The mimusops (Sans. *khirni*, *Mimusops kauki*) is another. Its tree, though not very large, is not small. The fruit is yellow and

1 The ripe "dates" are called P. *tamar-i Hind*, whence our tamarind, and *Tamarindus Indica*.

2 *Sophora alopecuroides*, a leguminous plant (Scully).

3 Abu'l-fazl gives *galaunda* as the name of the "fruit" [*mewa*],—Forbes, as that of the fallen flower. *Cf*. Brandis p. 426 and Yule's H.J. *s.n*. Mohwa.

4 Babur seems to say that spirit is extracted from both the fresh and the dried flowers. The fresh ones are favourite food with deer and jackals; they have a sweet spirituous taste. Erskine notes that the spirit made from them was well-known in Bombay by the name of Moura, or of Parsi-brandy, and that the farm of it was a considerable article of revenue (p. 325 n.). Roxburgh describes it as strong and intoxicating (p. 411).

5 This is the name of a green, stoneless grape which when dried, results in a raisin resembling the sultanas of Europe (*Jahangir's Memoirs* and Yule's H.J. *s.n*.; Griffiths' *Journal of Travel* pp. 359, 388).

6 *Aul*, lit. the *aul* of the flower. The Persian translation renders *aul* by *bu* which may allow both words to be understood in their (root) sense of *being*, *i.e*. natural state. De Courteille translates by *quand la fleur est fraiche* (ii, 210); Erskine took *bu* to mean smell (*Memoirs* p. 325), but the *aul* it translates, does not seem to have this meaning. For reading *aul* as "the natural state", there is circumstantial support in the flower's being eaten raw (Roxburgh). The annotator of the Elphinstone MS. [whose defacement of that Codex has been often mentioned], has added points and *tashdid* to the *aul-i* (*i.e*. its *aul*), so as to produce *auwali* (first, f. 235). Against this there are the obvious objections that the Persian translation does not reproduce, and that its *bu* does not render *auwali*; also that *aul-i* is a noun with its enclitic genitive *ya* (*i*).

7 This word seems to be meant to draw attention to the various merits of the *mahuwa* tree.

thinner than the red jujube (T. *chikda*, *Elæagnus angustifolia*). It has just the grape's flavour, but a rather bad after-taste; it is not bad, however, and is eatable. The husk of its stone is thin.

The (Sans.) *jaman* (*Eugenia jambolana*)[1] is another. Its leaf, except for being thicker and greener, is quite like the willow's (T. *tal*). The tree does not want for beauty. Its fruit is like a black grape, is sourish, and not very good.

The (H.) *kamrak* (Beng. *kamrunga*, *Averrhoa carambola*) is another. Its fruit is five-sided, about as large as the '*ain-alu*[2] and some 3 inches long. It has no stone. It ripens to yellow; gathered unripe, it is very bitter; gathered ripe, its bitterness has become sub-acid, not bad, not wanting in pleasantness.[3]

The jack-fruit (H. *kadhil*, B. *kanthal*, *Artocarpus integrifolia*) is another.[4] This is a fruit of singular form and flavour; it looks like a sheep's stomach stuffed and made into a haggis (*gipa*);[5] and it is sickeningly-sweet. Inside it are filbert-like stones[6] which, on the whole, resemble dates, but are round, not long, and have softer substance; these are eaten. The jack-fruit is very adhesive; for this reason people are said to oil mouth and hands before eating of it. It is heard of also as growing, not only on the branches of its tree, but on trunk and root too.[7] One would say that the tree was all hung round with haggises.[8]

The monkey-jack (H. *badhal*, B. *burhul*, *Artocarpus lacoocha*) is another. The fruit may be of the size of a quince (var. apple).

Fol. 284.

1 Erskine notes that this is not to be confounded with E. *jambu*, the rose-apple (*Memoirs* p. 325 n.). *Cf.* Yule's H.J. *s.n. Jambu*.

2 var. *ghat-alu*, *ghab-alu*, *ghain-alu*, *shaft-alu*. Scully enters '*ain-alu* (true-plum?) unexplained. The *kamrak* fruit is 3 in. long (Brandis) and of the size of a lemon (Firminger); dimensions which make Babur's 4 *ailik* (hand's-thickness) a slight excess only, and which thus allow *ailik*, with its Persion translation, *angusht*, to be approximately an inch.

3 Speede, giving the fruit its Sanscrit name *kamarunga*, says it is acid, rather pleasant, something like an insipid apple; also that its pretty pink blossoms grow on the trunk and main branches (i, 211).

4 *Cf.* Yule's H.J. *s.n.* jack-fruit. In a Calcutta nurseryman's catalogue of 1914 AD. three kinds of jack-tree are offered for sale, *viz.* "Crispy or Khaja, Soft or Neo, Rose-scented" (Seth, Feronia Nursery).

5 The *gipa* is a sheep's stomach stuffed with rice, minced meat, and spices, and boiled as a pudding. The resemblance of the jack, as it hangs on the tree, to the haggis, is wonderfully complete (Erskine).

6 These when roasted have the taste of chestnuts.

7 Firminger (p. 186) describes an ingenious method of training.

8 For a note of Humayun's on the jack-fruit *see* Appendix O.

Its smell is not bad.¹ Unripe it is a singularly tasteless and empty² thing; when ripe, it is not so bad. It ripens soft, can be pulled to pieces and eaten anywhere, tastes very much like a rotten quince, and has an excellent little austere flavour.

The lote-fruit (Sans. *ber*, *Zizyphus jujuba*) is another. Its Persian name is understood to be *kanar*.³ It is of several kinds: of one the fruit is larger than the plum (*alucha*);⁴ another is shaped like the Husaini grape. Most of them are not very good; we saw one in Bandir (Gualiar) that was really good. The lote-tree sheds its leaves under the Signs *Saur* and *Jauza* (Bull and Twins), burgeons under *Saratan* and *Asad* (Crab and Lion) which are the true rainy-season,—then becoming fresh and green, and it ripens its fruit under *Dalu* and *Haut* (Bucket *i.e.* Aquarius, and Fish).

The (Sans.) *karaunda* (*Carissa carandas*, the corinda) is another. It grows in bushes after the fashion of the (T.) *chika* of our country,⁵ but the *chika* grows on mountains, the *karaunda* on the plains. In flavour it is like the rhubarb itself,⁶ but is sweeter and less juicy. Fol. 284*b*.

The (Sans.) *paniyala* (*Flacourtia cataphracta*)⁷ is another. It is larger than the plum (*alucha*) and like the red-apple unripe.⁸ It is a little austere and is good. The tree is taller than the pomegranate's; its leaf is like that of the almond-tree but smaller.

The (H.) *gular* (*Ficus glomerata*, the clustered fig)⁹ is another. The fruit grows out of the tree-trunk, resembles the fig (P. *anjir*), but is singularly tasteless.

1 *aid-i-yaman aimas*. It is somewhat curious that Babur makes no comment on the odour of the jack itself.
2 *bush*, English bosh (Shaw). The Persian translation inserts no more about this fruit.
3 Steingass applies this name also to the plantain (banana).
4 Erskine notes that "this is the bullace-plum, small, not more than twice as large as the sloe and not so high-flavoured; it is generally yellow, sometimes red." Like Babur, Brandis enumerates several varieties and mentions the seasonal changes of the tree (p. 170).
5 This will be Kabul, probably, because Transoxiana is written of by Babur usually, if not invariably, as "that country", and because he mentions the *chikda* (*i.e. chika*?), under its Persian name *sinjid*, in his *Description of Kabul* (f. 129*b*).
6 P. *mar manjan*, which I take to refer to the *riwajlar* of Kabul. (*Cf.* f. 129*b*, where, however, (note 5) are *corrigenda* of Masson's *rawash* for *riwaj*, and his third to second volume.) Kehr's Codex contains an extra passage about the *karaun da*, *viz.* that from it is made a tasty fritter-like dish, resembling a rhubarb-fritter (Ilminsky, p. 369).
7 People call it (P.) *palasa* also (Elph. MS. f. 236, marginal note).
8 Perhaps the red-apple of Kabul, where two sorts are common, both rosy, one very much so, but much inferior to the other (Griffith's *Journal of Travel* p. 388).
9 Its downy fruit grows in bundles from the trunk and large branches (Roxburgh).

The (Sans.) *amla* (*Phyllanthus emblica*, the myrobalan-tree) is another. This also is a five-sided fruit.[1] It looks like the un-blown cotton-pod. It is an astringent and ill-flavoured thing, but confiture made of it is not bad. It is a wholesome fruit. Its tree is of excellent form and has very minute leaves.

The (H.) *chirunji* (*Buchanania latifolia*)[2] is another. This tree had been understood to grow in the hills, but I knew later about it, because there were three or four clumps of it in our gardens. It is much like the *mahuwa*. Its kernel is not bad, a thing between the walnut and the almond, not bad! rather smaller than the pistachio and round; people put it in custards (P. *paluda*) and sweetmeats (Ar. *halwa*).

The date-palm (P. *khurma*, *Phœnix dactylifera*) is another. This is not peculiar to Hindustan, but is here described because it is not in those countries (Tramontana). It grows in Lamghan also.[3] Its branches (*i.e.* leaves) grow from just one place at its top; its leaves (*i.e.* leaflets) grow on both sides of the branches (midribs) from neck (*buin*) to tip; its trunk is rough and ill-coloured; its fruit is like a bunch of grapes, but much larger.

People say that the date-palm amongst vegetables resembles an animal in two respects: one is that, as, if an animal's head be cut off, its life is taken, so it is with the date-palm, if its head is cut off, it dries off; the other is that, as the offspring of animals is not produced without the male, so too with the date-palm, it gives no good fruit unless a branch of the male-tree be brought into touch with the female-tree. The truth of this last matter is not known (to me). The above-mentioned head of the date-palm is called its cheese. The tree so grows that where its leaves come out is cheese-white, the leaves becoming green as they lengthen. This white part, the so-called cheese, is tolerable eating, not bad, much like the walnut. People make a wound in the cheese, and into this wound insert a leaf(let), in such a way that all liquid flowing from the wound runs down it.[4] The tip of the leaflet is set over the mouth of a pot suspended to the tree

1 The reference by "also" (*ham*) will be to the *kamrak* (f. 283*b*), but both Roxburgh and Brandis say the *amla* is six striated.
2 The Sanscrit and Bengali name for the chirunji-tree is *piyala* (Roxburgh p. 363).
3 *Cf.* f. 250*b*.
4 The leaflet is rigid enough to serve as a runlet, but soon wears out; for this reason, the usual practice is to use one of split bamboo.

in such a way that it collects whatever liquor is yielded by the
wound. This liquor is rather pleasant if drunk at once; if drunk
after two or three days, people say it is quite exhilarating
(*kaifiyat*). Once when I had gone to visit Bari,[1] and made an   Fol. 285*b*.
excursion to the villages on the bank of the Chambal-river, we
met in with people collecting this date-liquor in the valley-bottom.
A good deal was drunk; no hilarity was felt; much must be
drunk, seemingly, to produce a little cheer.

The coco-nut palm (P. *nargil*, *Cocos nucifera*) is another. An
'Arab gives it Arabic form[2] and says *narjil*; Hindustan people
say *nalir*, seemingly by popular error.[3] Its fruit is the Hindi-
nut from which black spoons (*qara qashuq*) are made and the
larger ones of which serve for guitar-bodies. The coco-palm has
general resemblance to the date-palm, but has more, and more
glistening leaves. Like the walnut, the coco-nut has a green
outer husk; but its husk is of fibre on fibre. All ropes for ships
and boats and also cord for sewing boat-seams are heard of as
made from these husks. The nut, when stripped of its husk, near
one end shews a triangle of hollows, two of which are solid, the
third a nothing (*bush*), easily pierced. Before the kernel forms,
there is fluid inside; people pierce the soft hollow and drink
this; it tastes like date-palm cheese in solution, and is not bad.

The (Sans.) *tar* (*Borassus flabelliformis*, the Palmyra-palm) is
another. Its branches (*i.e.* leaves) also are quite at its top. Just as   Fol. 286.
with the date-palm, people hang a pot on it, take its juice and
drink it. They call this liquor *tari*;[4] it is said to be more exhilarating than date liquor. For about a yard along its branches
(*i.e.* leaf-stems)[5] there are no leaves; above this, at the tip of
the branch (stem), 30 or 40 open out like the spread fingers of the
hand, all from one place. These leaves approach a yard in length.

1 This is a famous hunting-ground between Biana and Dhulpur, Rajputana,
visited in 933 AH. (f. 330*b*). Babur's great-great-grandson Shah-jahan built a
hunting-lodge there (G. of I.).
2 Hai. MS. *mu'arrab*, but the Elph. MS. *maghrib*, [occidentalizing]. The Hai.
MS. when writing of the orange (*infra*) also has *maghrib*. A distinction of locality
may be drawn by *maghrib*.
3 Babur's "Hindustan people" (*ail*) are those neither Turks nor Afghans.
4 This name, with its usual form *tadi* (toddy), is used for the fermented sap of the
date, coco, and *mhar* palms also (*cf.* Yule's H.J. *s.n.* toddy).
5 Babur writes of the long leaf-stalk as a branch (*shakh*); he also seems to have
taken each spike of the fan-leaf to represent a separate leaf. [For two omissions
from my trs. *see* Appendix O.]

People often write Hindi characters on them after the fashion of account rolls (*daftar yusunluq*).

The natives of Hindustan when not wearing their ear-rings, put into the large ear-ring holes, slips of the palm-leaf bought in the bazars, ready for the purpose. The trunk of this tree is handsomer and more stately than that of the date.

The orange (Ar. *naranj*, *Citrus aurantium*) and orange-like fruits are others of Hindustan.[1] Oranges grow well in the Lamghanat, Bajaur and Sawad. The Lamghanat one is smallish, has a navel,[2] is very agreeable, fragile and juicy. It is not at all like the orange of Khurasan and those parts, being so fragile that many spoil before reaching Kabul from the Lamghanat which may be 13–14 *yighach* (65–70 miles), while the Astarabad orange, by reason of its thick skin and scant juice, carries with less damage from there to Samarkand, some 270–280 *yighach*.[3] The Bajaur orange is about as large as a quince, very juicy and more acid than other oranges. Khwaja Kalan once said to me, "We counted the oranges gathered from a single tree of this sort in Bajaur and it mounted up to 7000." It had been always in my mind that the word *naranj* was an Arabic form;[4] it would seem to be really so, since every-one in Bajaur and Sawad says (P.) *narang*.[5]

Fol. 286b.

1 Most of the fruits Babur describes as orange-like are named in the following classified list, taken from Watts' *Economic Products of India*:—"**Citrus aurantium,** *narangi*, *sangtara*, *amrit-phal*; **C. decumana,** *pumelo*, shaddock, forbidden-fruit, *sada-phal*; **C. medica** proper, *turunj*, *limu*; **C. medica limonum,** *jambhira*, *karna-nebu*." Under *C. aurantium* Brandis enters both the sweet and the Seville oranges (*narangi*); this Babur appears to do also.

2 *kindiklik*, explained in the Elph. Codex by *nafwar* (f. 238). This detail is omitted by the Persian translation. Firminger's description (p. 221) of Aurangabad oranges suggests that they also are navel-oranges. At the present time one of the best oranges had in England is the navel one of California.

3 Useful addition is made to earlier notes on the variability of the *yighach*, a variability depending on time taken to cover the ground, by the following passage from Henderson and Hume's *Lahor to Yarkand* (p. 120), which shews that even in the last century the *farsang* (the P. word used in the Persian translation of the *Babur-nama* for T. *yighach*) was computed by time. "All the way from Kargallik (Qarghaliq) to Yarkand, there were tall wooden mile-posts along the roads, at intervals of about 5 miles, or rather one hour's journey, apart. On a board at the top of each post, or *farsang* as it is called, the distances were very legibly written in Turki."

4 *ma'rib*, Elph. MS. *magharrib*; (*cf.* f. 285b note).

5 *i.e. narang* (Sans. *naranga*) has been changed to *naranj* in the 'Arab mouth. What is probably one of Humayun's notes preserved by the Elph. Codex (f. 238), appears to say—it is mutilated—that *narang* has been corrupted into *naranj*.

The lime (B. *limu*, C. *acida*) is another. It is very plentiful, about the size of a hen's egg, and of the same shape. If a person poisoned drink the water in which its fibres have been boiled, danger is averted.[1]

The citron (P. *turunj*,[2] C. *medica*) is another of the fruits resembling the orange. Bajauris and Sawadis call it *balang* and hence give the name *balang-marabba* to its marmalade (*marabba*) confiture. In Hindustan people call the *turunj bijaura*.[3] There are two kinds of *turunj*: one is sweet, flavourless and nauseating, of no use for eating but with peel that may be good for marmalade; it has the same sickening sweetness as the Lamghanat *turunj*; the other, that of Hindustan and Bajaur, is acid, quite deliciously acid, and makes excellent sherbet, well-flavoured, and wholesome drinking. Its size may be that of the Khusrawi melon; it has a thick skin, wrinkled and uneven, with one end thinner and beaked. It is of a deeper yellow than the orange (*naranj*). Its tree has no trunk, is rather low, grows in bushes, and has a larger leaf than the orange. Fol. 287.

The *sangtara*[4] is another fruit resembling the orange (*naranj*).

1 The Elph. Codex has a note—mutilated in early binding—which is attested by its scribe as copied from Humayun's hand-writing, and is to the effect that once on his way from the Hot-bath, he saw people who had taken poison and restored them by giving lime-juice.

Erskine here notes that the same antidotal quality is ascribed to the citron by Virgil:—

> Media fert tristes succos. tardumque saporem
> Felicis mali, quo non praesentius ullum,
> Pocula si quando saevae infecere novercae,
> Miscueruntque herbas et non innoxia verba,
> Auxilium venit, ac membris agit atra venena.
>
> Georgics II. v. 126.

Vide Heyne's note i, 438.

2 P. *turunj*, wrinkled, puckered; Sans. *vijapura* and H. *bijaura* (*Ayin* 28), seed-filled.

3 Babur may have confused this with H. *bijaura*; so too appears to have done the writer (Humayun?) of a [now mutilated] note in the Elph. Codex (f. 238), which seems to say that the fruit or its name went from Bajaur to Hindustan. Is the country of Bajaur so-named from its indigenous orange (*vijapura*, whence *bijaura*)? The name occurs also north of Kangra.

4 Of this name variants are numerous, *santra*, *santhara*, *samtara*, etc. Watts classes it as a C. *aurantium*; Erskine makes it the common sweet orange; Firminger, quoting Ross (p. 221) writes that, as grown in the Nagpur gardens it is one of the finest Indian oranges, with rind thin, smooth and close. The Emperor Muhammad Shah is said to have altered its name to *rang-tara* because of its fine colour (*rang*) (Forbes). Speede (ii, 109) gives both names. As to the meaning and origin of the name *santara* or *santra*, so suggestive of Cintra, the Portuguese home of a similar orange, it may be said that it looks like a hill-name used in N.E. India, for there is a village in the

It is like the citron (*turunj*) in colour and form, but has both ends of its skin level;[1] also it is not rough and is somewhat the smaller fruit. Its tree is large, as large as the apricot (*auruq*), with a leaf like the orange's. It is a deliciously acid fruit, making a very pleasant and wholesome sherbet. Like the lime it is a powerful stomachic, but not weakening like the orange (*naranj*).

The large lime which they call (H.) *gal-gal*[2] in Hindustan is another fruit resembling the orange. It has the shape of a goose's egg, but unlike that egg, does not taper to the ends. Its skin is smooth like the *sangtara*'s; it is remarkably juicy.

The (H.) *janbiri* lime[3] is another orange-like fruit. It is orange-shaped and, though yellow, not orange-yellow. It smells like the citron (*turunj*); it too is deliciously acid.

The (Sans.) *sada-fal* (*phal*)[4] is another orange-like fruit. This is pear-shaped, colours like the quince, ripens sweet, but not to the sickly-sweetness of the orange (*naranj*).

The *amrd-fal* (sic. Hai. MS.—Sans. *amrit-phal*)[5] is another orange-like fruit.

The lemon (H. *karna*, C. *limonum*) is another fruit resembling the orange (*naranj*); it may be as large as the *gal-gal* and is also acid.

The (Sans.) *amal-bid*[6] is another fruit resembling the orange.

Bhutan Hills, (Western Duars) known from its orange groves as Santra-bari, Abode of the orange. To this (mentioned already as my husband's suggestion in Mr. Crooke's ed. of Yule's H.J.) support is given by the item "Suntura, famous Nipal variety", entered in Seth's Nursery-list of 1914 (Feronia Nurseries, Calcutta). Light on the question of origin could be thrown, no doubt, by those acquainted with the dialects of the hill-tract concerned.

1 This refers, presumably, to the absence of the beak characteristic of all citrons.
2 melter, from the Sans. root *gal*, which provides the names of several lemons by reason of their solvent quality, specified by Babur (*infra*) of the *amal-bid*. Erskine notes that in his day the *gal-gal* was known as *kilmek* (*galmak?*).
3 Sans. *jambira*, H. *jambir*, classed by Abu'l-fazl as one of the somewhat sour fruits and by Watts as *Citrus medica limonum*.
4 Watts, *C. decumana*, the shaddock or pumelo; Firminger (p. 223) has *C. decumana pyriformis* suiting Babur's "pear-shaped". What Babur compared it with will be the Transoxanian pear and quince (*P. amrud* and *bihi*) and not the Indian guava and Bengal quince (*P. amrud* and *H. bael*).
5 The Turki text writes *amrd*. Watts classes the *amrit-phal* as a *C. aurantium*. This supports Erskine's suggestion that it is the mandarin-orange. Humayun describes it in a note which is written pell-mell in the text of the Elph. Codex and contains also descriptions of the *kamila* and *santara* oranges; it can be seen translated in Appendix O.
6 So spelled in the Turki text and also in two good MSS. of the Pers. trs. I.O. 217 and 218, but by Abu'l-fazl *amal-bit*. Both P. *bid* and P. *bit* mean willow and cane (ratan), so that *amal-bid* (*bit*) can mean acid-willow and acid-cane. But as

After three years (in Hindustan), it was first seen to-day.[1] They
say a needle melts away if put inside it,[2] either from its acidity   Fol. 287b.
or some other property. It is as acid, perhaps, as the citron and
lemon (*turunj* and *limu*).[3]

(*m. Vegetable products of Hindustan:—Flowers.*)

In Hindustan there is great variety of flowers. One is the (D.)
jasun (*Hibiscus rosa sinensis*), which some Hindustanis call
(Hindi) *gazhal*.[4] *It is not a grass (*giyah*); its tree (is in stems
like the bush of the red-rose; it) is rather taller than the bush
of the red-rose.[5] *The flower of the *jasun* is fuller in colour than
that of the pomegranate, and may be of the size of the red-rose,
but, the red-rose, when its bud has grown, opens simply, whereas,
when the *jasun*-bud opens, a stem on which other petals grow,
is seen like a heart amongst its expanded petals. Though the two
are parts of the one flower, yet the outcome of the lengthening
and thinning of that stem-like heart of the first-opened petals
gives the semblance of two flowers.[6] It is not a common matter.
The beautifully coloured flowers look very well on the tree, but

---

Babur is writing of a fruit like an orange, the cane that bears an acid fruit,
Calamus rotang, can be left aside in favour of *Citrus medica acidissima*. Of this fruit
the solvent property Babur mentions, as well as the commonly-known service in
cleansing metal, link it, by these uses, with the willow and suggest a ground for
understanding, as Erskine did, that *amal-bid* meant acid-willow; for willow-wood
is used to rub rust off metal.

1 This statement shows that Babur was writing the *Description of Hindustan* in
935 AH. (1528–9 AD.), which is the date given for it by Shaikh Zain.

2 This story of the needle is believed in India of all the citron kind, which are hence
called *sui-gal* (needle-melter) in the Dakhin (Erskine). Cf. Forbes, p. 489 *s.n. sui-gal.*

3 Erskine here quotes information from Abu'l-fazl (*Ayin* 28) about Akbar's
encouragement of the cultivation of fruits.

4 Hindustani (Urdu) *garhal*. Many varieties of Hibiscus (syn. Althea) grow in
India; some thrive in Surrey gardens; the *jasun* by name and colour can be taken
as what is known in Malayan, Tamil, etc., as the shoe-flower, from its use in darkening
leather (Yule's H.J.).

5 I surmise that what I have placed between asterisks here belongs to the next-
following plant, the oleander. For though the branches of the *jasun* grow vertically,
the bush is a dense mass upon one stout trunk, or stout short stem. The words placed
in parenthesis above are not with the Haidarabad but are with the Elphinstone Codex.
There would seem to have been a scribe's skip from one "rose" to the other. As has
been shewn repeatedly, this part of the Babur-nama has been much annotated;
in the Elph. Codex, where only most of the notes are preserved, some are entered by
the scribe pell-mell into Babur's text. The present instance may be a case of a
marginal note, added to the text in a wrong place.

6 The peduncle supporting the plume of medial petals is clearly seen only when the
flower opens first. The plumed Hibiscus is found in florists' catalogues described
as "double".

they do not last long; they fade in just one day. The *jasun* blossoms very well through the four months of the rains; it seems indeed to flower all through the year; with this profusion, however, it gives no perfume.

The (H.) *kanir* (*Nerium odorum*, the oleander)[1] is another. It grows both red and white. Like the peach-flower, it is five petalled. It is like the peach-bloom (in colour?), but opens 14 or 15 flowers from one place, so that seen from a distance, they look like one great flower. The oleander-bush is taller than the rose-bush. The red oleander has a sort of scent, faint and agreeable. (Like the *jasun*,) it also blooms well and profusely in the rains, and it also is had through most of the year.

Fol. 288.

The (H.) (*kiura*) (*Pandanus odoratissimus*, the screw-pine) is another.[2] It has a very agreeable perfume.[3] Musk has the defect of being dry; this may be called moist musk—a very agreeable perfume. The tree's singular appearance notwithstanding, it has flowers perhaps 1½ to 2 *qarish* (13½ to 18 inches) long. It has long leaves having the character of the reed (P.) *gharau*[4] and having spines. Of these leaves, while pressed together bud-like, the outer ones are the greener and more spiny; the inner ones are soft and white. In amongst these inner leaves grow things like what belongs to the middle of a flower, and from these things comes the excellent perfume. When the tree first comes up not yet shewing any trunk, it is like the bush (*buta*) of the male-reed,[5] but with wider and more spiny leaves. What serves it for a trunk is very shapeless, its roots remaining shewn.

1 This Anglo-Indians call also rose-bay. A Persian name appears to be *zahr-giyah*, poison-grass, which makes it the more probable that the doubtful passage in the previous description of the *jasun* belongs to the rod-like oleander, known as the poison-grass. The oleander is common in river-beds over much country known to Babur, outside India.

2 Roxburgh gives a full and interesting account of this tree.

3 Here the Elph. Codex, only, has the (seeming) note, "An 'Arab calls it *kazi*" (or *kawi*). This fills out Steingass' part-explanation of *kawi*, "the blossom of the fragrant palm-tree, *armat*" (p. 1010), and of *armat*, "a kind of date-tree with a fragrant blossom" (p. 39), by making *armat* and *kawi* seem to be the *Pandanus* and its flower.

4 *Calamus scriptorius* (Vullers ii, 607. H.B.). Abu'l-fazl compares the leaves to *jawari*, the great millet (Forbes); Blochmann (A. A. p. 83) translates *jawari* by *maize* (*juwara*, Forbes).

5 T. *airkak-qumush*, a name Scully enters unexplained. Under *qumush* (reed) he enters *Arundo madagascarensis*; Babur's comparison will be with some Transoxanian *Arundo* or *Calamus*, presumably.

The (P.) *yasman* (jasmine) is another; the white they call (B.) *champa*.[1] It is larger and more strongly scented than our *yasman*-flower.

(n. Seasons of the year.)

Again:—whereas there are four seasons in those countries,[2] there are three in Hindustan, namely, four months are summer; four are the rains; four are winter. The beginning of their months is from the welcome of the crescent-moons.[3] Every three years they add a month to the year; if one had been added to the rainy season, the next is added, three years later, to the winter months, the next, in the same way, to the hot months. This is their mode of intercalation.[4] (*Chait, Baisakh, Jeth* and *Asarh*) are the hot months, corresponding with the Fish, (Ram, Bull and Twins; *Sawan, Bhadon, Ku,ar* and *Katik*) are the rainy months, corresponding with the Crab, (Lion, Virgin and Balance; *Aghan, Pus, Magh* and *Phalgun*) are the cold months, corresponding with the Scorpion, (Archer, Capricorn, and Bucket or Aquarius). Fol. 288*b*.

The people of Hind, having thus divided the year into three seasons of four months each, divide each of those seasons by taking from each, the two months of the force of the heat, rain,[5] and cold. Of the hot months the last two, *i.e. Jeth* and *Asarh* are the force of the heat; of the rainy months, the first two, *i.e. Sawan* and *Bhadon* are the force of the rains; of the cold season, the middle two, *i.e. Pus* and *Magh* are the force of the cold. By this classification there are six seasons in Hindustan.

1 *Champa* seems to have been Babur's word (Elph. and Hai. MSS.), but is the (B.) name for *Michelia champaka*; the Pers. translation corrects it by (B.) *chambeli*, (*yasman*, jasmine).

2 Here, "outside India" will be meant, where Hindu rules do not prevail.

3 *Hind ailari-ning ibtida-si hilal ailar-ning istiqbal-din dur.* The use here of *istiqbal*, welcome, attracts attention; does it allude to the universal welcome of lighter nights? or is it reminiscent of Muhammadan welcome to the Moon's crescent in Shawwal?

4 For an exact statement of the intercalary months *vide* Cunningham's *Indian Eras*, p. 91. In my next sentence (*supra*) the parenthesis-marks indicate blanks left on the page of the Hai. MS. as though waiting for information. These and other similar blanks make for the opinion that the Hai. Codex is a direct copy of Babur's draft manuscript.

5 The sextuple division (*ritu*) of the year is referred to on f. 284, where the Signs Crab and Lion are called the season of the true Rains.

(o. Days of the week.)

To the days also they have given names:—[1] (*Sanichar* is Saturday; *Rabi-bar* is Sunday; *Som-war* is Monday; *Mangal-war* is Tuesday; *Budh-bar* is Wednesday; *Brihaspat-bar* is Thursday; *Shukr-bar* is Friday).

(p. Divisions of time.)

As in our countries what is known by the (Turki) term *kicha-gunduz* (a day-and-night, nycthemeron) is divided into 24 parts, each called an hour (Ar. *sa'at*), and the hour is divided into 60 parts, each called a minute (Ar. *daqiqa*), so that a day-and-night

Fol. 289.

> *(Author's note on the daqiqa.)*   The *daqiqa* is about as long as six repetitions of the *Fatiha* with the *Bismillah*, so that a day-and-night is as long as 8640 repetitions of the *Fatiha* with the *Bismillah*.

consists of 1440 minutes,—so the people of Hind divide the night-and-day into 60 parts, each called a (S.) *g'hari*.[2] They also divide the night into four and the day into four, calling each part a (S.) *pahr* (watch) which in Persian is a *pas*. A watch and watchman (*pas u pasban*) had been heard about (by us) in those countries (Transoxania), but without these particulars. Agreeing with the division into watches, a body of *g'harialis*[3] is chosen and appointed in all considerable towns of Hindustan. They cast a broad brass (plate-) thing,[4] perhaps as large as a tray (*tabaq*) and about two hands'-thickness; this they call a *g'harial* and hang up in a high place (*bir buland yir-da*). Also they have a vessel perforated at the bottom like an hour-cup[5] and filling

1 Babur appears not to have entered either the Hindi or the Persian names of the week:—the Hai. MS. has a blank space; the Elph. MS. had the Persian names only, and Hindi ones have been written in above these; Kehr has the Persian ones only; Ilminsky has added the Hindi ones. (The spelling of the Hindi names, in my translation, is copied from Forbes' Dictionary.)

2 The Hai. MS. writes *gari* and *garial*. The word now stands for the hour of 60 minutes.

3 *i.e.* gong-men. The name is applied also to an alligator *Lacertus gangeticus* (Forbes).

4 There is some confusion in the text here, the Hai. MS. reading *birinj-din tishi* (?) *nima quiubturlar*—the Elph. MS. (f. 240*b*) *biring-din bir yassi nima quiubturlar*. The Persian translation, being based on the text of the Elphinstone Codex reads *az biring yak chiz pahni rekhta and*. The word *tishi* of the Hai. MS. may represent *tasht* plate or *yassi*, broad; against the latter however there is the sentence that follows and gives the size.

5 Here again the wording of the Hai. MS. is not clear; the sense however is obvious. Concerning the clepsydra *vide* A. A. Jarrett, ii, 15 and notes; Smith's *Dictionary of Antiquities*; Yule's H.J. *s.n.* Ghurry.

in one *g'hari* (*i.e.* 24 minutes). The *g'harialis* put this into water and wait till it fills. For example, they will put the perforated Fol. 289*b*. cup into water at day-birth; when it fills the first time, they strike the gong once with their mallets; when a second time, twice, and so on till the end of the watch. They announce the end of a watch by several rapid blows of their mallets. After these they pause; then strike once more, if the first day-watch has ended, twice if the second, three times if the third, and four times if the fourth. After the fourth day-watch, when the night-watches begin, these are gone through in the same way. It used to be the rule to beat the sign of a watch only when the watch ended; so that sleepers chancing to wake in the night and hear the sound of a third or fourth *g'hari*, would not know whether it was of the second or third night-watch. I therefore ordered that at night or on a cloudy day the sign of the watch should be struck after that of the *g'hari*, for example, that after striking the third *g'hari* of the first night-watch, the *g'harialis* were to pause and then strike the sign of the watch, in order to make it known that this third *g'hari* was of the first night-watch,—and that after striking four *g'haris* of the third night-watch, they should pause and then strike the sign of the third watch, in order to make it known that this fourth *g'hari* was of the third night-watch. It did very well; anyone happening to wake in the night and hear the gong, would know what *g'hari* of what watch of night it was.

Again, they divide the *g'hari* into 60 parts, each part being called a *pal*;[1] by this each night-and-day will consist of 3500 *pals*. Fol. 290.

> (*Author's note on the pal.*)   They say the length of a *pal* is the shutting and opening of the eyelids 60 times, which in a night-and-day would be 216,000 shuttings and openings of the eyes. Experiment shews that a *pal* is about equal to 8 repetitions of the *Qul-huwa-allah*[2] and *Bismillah*; this would be 28,000 repetitions in a night-and-day.

(*q. Measures.*)

The people of Hind have also well-arranged measures:—[3] 8 *ratis* = 1 *masha*; 4 *masha* = 1 *tank* = 32 *ratis*; 5 *masha* = 1 *misqal* = 40 *ratis*; 12 *masha* = 1 *tula* = 96 *ratis*; 14 *tula* = 1 *ser.*

---

1 The table is:—60 *bipals* = 1 *pal*; 60 *pals* = 1 *g'hari* (24 m.); 60 *g'hari* or 8 *pahr* = one *din-rat* (nycthemeron).

2 Qoran, cap. CXII, which is a declaration of God's unity.

3 The (S.) *rati* = 8 rice-grains (Eng. 8 barley-corns); the (S.) *masha* is a kidney-bean; the (P.) *tank* is about 2 oz.; the (Ar.) *misqal* is equal to 40 *ratis*; the (S.) *tula* is about 145 oz.; the (S.) *ser* is of various values (Wilson's *Glossary* and Yule's H.J.).

This is everywhere fixed:—40 *ser* = 1 *manban*; 12 *manban* = 1 *mani*; 100 *mani* they call a *minasa*.[1]

Pearls and jewels they weigh by the *tank*.

(*r. Modes of reckoning*.)

The people of Hind have also an excellent mode of reckoning: 100,000 they call a *lak*; 100 *laks*, a *krur*; 100 *krurs*, an *arb*; 100 *arbs*, 1 *karb*; 100 *karbs*, 1 *nil*; 100 *nils*, 1 *padam*; 100 *padams*, 1 *sang*. The fixing of such high reckonings as these is proof of the great amount of wealth in Hindustan.

(*s. Hindu inhabitants of Hindustan*.)

Most of the inhabitants of Hindustan are pagans; they call a pagan a Hindu. Most Hindus believe in the transmigration of souls. All artisans, wage-earners, and officials are Hindus. In our countries dwellers in the wilds (*i.e.* nomads) get tribal names; here the settled people of the cultivated lands and villages get tribal names.[2] Again:—every artisan there is follows the trade that has come down to him from forefather to forefather.

Fol. 290b.

(*t. Defects of Hindustan*.)

Hindustan is a country of few charms. Its people have no good looks; of social intercourse, paying and receiving visits there is none; of genius and capacity none; of manners none; in handicraft and work there is no form or symmetry, method or quality; there are no good horses, no good dogs, no grapes, musk-melons or first-rate fruits, no ice or cold water, no good bread or cooked food in the *bazars*, no Hot-baths, no Colleges, no candles, torches or candlesticks.

In place of candle and torch they have a great dirty gang they call lamp-men (*diwati*), who in the left hand hold a smallish wooden tripod to one corner of which a thing like the top of

---

1 There being 40 Bengal *sers* to the *man*, Babur's word *manban* seems to be another name for the *man* or *maund*. I have not found *manban* or *minasa*. At first sight *manban* might be taken, in the Hai. MS. for (T.) *batman*, a weight of 13 or 15 lbs., but this does not suit. *Cf.* f. 167 note to *batman* and f. 173b. For Babur's table of measures the Pers. trs. has 40 *sers* = 1 *man*; 12 *mans* = 1 *mani*; 100 *mani* they call *minasa* (217, f. 201b, l. 8).

2 Presumably these are caste-names.

a candlestick is fixed, having a wick in it about as thick as the thumb. In the right hand they hold a gourd, through a narrow slit made in which, oil is let trickle in a thin thread when the wick needs it. Great people keep a hundred or two of these lamp-men. This is the Hindustan substitute for lamps and candlesticks! If their rulers and begs have work at night needing candles, these dirty lamp-men bring these lamps, go close up and there stand. Fol. 291.

Except their large rivers and their standing-waters which flow in ravines or hollows (there are no waters). There are no running-waters in their gardens or residences (*'imaratlar*).[1] These residences have no charm, air (*hawa*), regularity or symmetry.

Peasants and people of low standing go about naked. They tie on a thing called *lunguta*,[2] a decency-clout which hangs two spans below the navel. From the tie of this pendant decency-clout, another clout is passed between the thighs and made fast behind. Women also tie on a cloth (*lung*), one-half of which goes round the waist, the other is thrown over the head.

(*u. Advantages of Hindustan.*)

Pleasant things of Hindustan are that it is a large country and has masses of gold and silver. Its air in the Rains is very fine. Sometimes it rains 10, 15 or 20 times a day; torrents pour down all at once and rivers flow where no water had been. While it rains and through the Rains, the air is remarkably fine, not to be surpassed for healthiness and charm. The fault is that the air becomes very soft and damp. A bow of those (Transoxanian) countries after going through the Rains in Hindustan, may not be drawn even; it is ruined; not only the bow, everything is Fol. 291b. affected, armour, book, cloth, and utensils all; a house even does

---

1 The words in parenthesis appear to be omitted from the text; to add them brings Babur's remark into agreement with others on what he several times makes note of, *viz.* the absence not only of irrigation-channels but of those which convey "running-waters" to houses and gardens. Such he writes of in Farghana; such are a well-known charm *e.g.* in Madeira, where the swift current of clear water flowing through the streets, turns into private precincts by side-runlets.

2 The Hai. MS. writes *lunguta-dik*, like a lunguta, which better agrees with Babur's usual phrasing. *Lung* is Persian for a cloth passed between the loins, is an equivalent of S. *dhoti*. Babur's use of it (*infra*) for the woman's (P.) *chaddar* or (S.) *sari* does not suit the Dictionary definition of its meaning.

not last long. Not only in the Rains but also in the cold and
the hot seasons, the airs are excellent; at these times, however,
the north-west wind constantly gets up laden with dust and earth.
It gets up in great strength every year in the heats, under the
Bull and Twins when the Rains are near; so strong and carrying
so much dust and earth that there is no seeing one another.
People call this wind Darkener of the Sky (H. *andhi*). The
weather is hot under the Bull and Twins, but not intolerably so,
not so hot as in Balkh and Qandahar and not for half so long.

Another good thing in Hindustan is that it has unnumbered
and endless workmen of every kind. There is a fixed caste (*jam'i*)
for every sort of work and for every thing, which has done that
work or that thing from father to son till now. Mulla Sharaf,
writing in the *Zafar-nama* about the building of Timur Beg's
Stone Mosque, lays stress on the fact that on it 200 stone-cutters
worked, from Azarbaijan, Fars, Hindustan and other countries.
But 680 men worked daily on my buildings in Agra and of Agra
stone-cutters only; while 1491 stone-cutters worked daily on my
buildings in Agra, Sikri, Biana, Dulpur, Gualiar and Kuil. In
Fol. 292.   the same way there are numberless artisans and workmen of
every sort in Hindustan.

(*v. Revenues of Hindustan.*)

The revenue of the countries now held by me (935 AH.–
1528 AD.) from Bhira to Bihar is 52 *krurs*,[1] as will be known in
detail from the following summary.[2] Eight or nine *krurs* of this

1 When Erskine published the Memoirs in 1826 AD. he estimated this sum at 1½
millions Sterling, but when he published his *History of India* in 1845, he had made
further research into the problem of Indian money values, and judged then that
Babur's revenue was £4,212,000.
2 Erskine here notes that the promised details had not been preserved, but in
1854 AD. he had found them in a "paraphrase of part of Babur", manifestly in
Shaikh Zain's work. He entered and discussed them and some matters of money-
values in Appendices D. and E. of his *History of India*, vol. I. Ilminsky found
them in Kehr's Codex (C. ii, 230). The scribe of the Elph. MS. has entered the
revenues of three *sarkars* only, with his usual quotation marks indicating something
extraneous or doubtful. The Hai. MS. has them in contents precisely as I have
entered them above, but with a scattered mode of setting down. They are in Persian,
presumably as they were rendered to Babur by some Indian official. This official
statement will have been with Babur's own papers; it will have been copied by
Shaikh Zain into his own paraphrase. It differs slightly in Erskine's and again, in
de Courteille's versions. I regret that I am incompetent to throw any light upon the

are from parganas of rais and rajas who, as obedient from of old, receive allowance and maintenance.

REVENUES OF HINDUSTAN FROM WHAT HAS SO FAR
COME UNDER THE VICTORIOUS STANDARDS

Sarkars.	Krurs.	Laks.	Tankas.	
Trans-sutluj:—Bhira, Lahur, Sialkut, Dibalpur, etc.	3	33	15,989	
Sihrind	1	29	31,985	
Hisar-firuza	1	30	75,174	
The capital Dihli and Mian-du-ab	3	69	50,254	
Miwat, not included in Sikandar's time	1	69	81,000	
Biana	1	44	14,930	Fol. 292b.
Agra		29	76,919	
Mian-wilayat (Midlands)	2	91	19	
Gualiar	2	23	57,450	
Kalpi and Sehonda (Seondha)	4	28	55,950	
Qanauj	1	36	63,358	
Sambhal	1	38	44,000	
Laknur and Baksar	1	39	82,433	
Khairabad		12	65,000	
Aud (Oude) and Bahraj (Baraich)	1	17	1,369	Fol. 293.
Junpur	4	0	88,333	
Karra and Manikpur	1	63	27,282	
Bihar	4	5	60,000	
Sarwar	1	55	17,506½	
Saran	1	10	18,373	
Champaran	1	90	86,060	
Kandla		43	30,300	
Tirhut from Raja Rup-narain's tribute, silver		2	55,000	
black (i.e. copper)		27	50,000	
Rantanbhur from Buli, Chatsu, and Malarna		20	00,000	
Nagur	—	—	—	
Raja Bikramajit in Rantanbhur	—	—	—	
Kalanjari	—	—	—	
Raja Bir-sang-deo (or, Sang only)	—	—	—	
Raja Bikam-deo	—	—	—	
Raja Bikam-chand	—	—	—	

¹ So far as particulars and details about the land and people of the country of Hindustan have become definitely known, they have been narrated and described; whatever matters worthy of record may come to view hereafter, I shall write down.

question of its values and that I must leave some uncertain names to those more expert than myself. *Cf.* Erskine's Appendices *l.c.* and Thomas' *Revenue resources of the Mughal Empire*. For a few comments *see* App. P.
1 Here the Turki text resumes in the Hai. MS.

HISTORICAL NARRATIVE RESUMED

(*a. Distribution of treasure in Agra.*)[1]

(*May 12th*) On Saturday the 29th[2] of Rajab the examination and distribution of the treasure were begun. To Humayun were given 70 laks from the Treasury, and, over and above this, a treasure house was bestowed on him just as it was, without ascertaining and writing down its contents. To some begs 10 laks were given, 8, 7, or 6 to others.[3] Suitable money-gifts were bestowed from the Treasury on the whole army, to every tribe there was, Afghan, Hazara, 'Arab, Biluch *etc.* to each according to its position. Every trader and student, indeed every man who had come with the army, took ample portion and share of bounteous gift and largess. To those not with the army went a mass of treasure in gift and largess, as for instance, 17 laks to Kamran, 15 laks to Muhammad-i-zaman Mirza, while to 'Askari, Hindal and indeed to the whole various train of relations and younger children[4] went masses of red and white (gold and silver), of plenishing, jewels and slaves.[5] Many gifts went to the begs and soldiery on that side (Tramontana). Valuable gifts (*saughat*) were sent for the various relations in Samarkand, Khurasan, Kashghar and 'Iraq. To holy men belonging to Samarkand and Khurasan went offerings vowed to God (*nuzur*); so too to

Fol. 294.

1 Elph. MS. f. 243*b*; W. i. B. I.O. 215 has not the events of this year (as to which omission *vide* note at the beginning of 932 AH. f. 251*b*) and 217 f. 203; Mems. p. 334; Ilminsky's imprint p. 380; *Méms.* ii, 232.

2 This should be 30th if Saturday was the day of the week (Gladwin, Cunningham and Babur's narrative of f. 269). Saturday appears likely to be right; Babur entered Agra on Thursday 28th; Friday would be used for the Congregational Prayer and preliminaries inevitable before the distribution of the treasure. The last day of Babur's narrative 932 AH. is Thursday Rajab 28th; he would not be likely to mistake between Friday, the day of his first Congregational prayer in Agra, and Saturday. It must be kept in mind that the *Description of Hindustan* is an interpolation here, and that it was written in 935 AH., three years later than the incidents here recorded. The date Rajab 29th may not be Babur's own entry; or if it be, may have been made after the interpolation of the dividing mass of the *Description* and made wrongly.

3 Erskine estimated these sums as "probably £56,700 to Humayun; and the smaller ones as £8,100, £6,480, £5,670 and £4,860 respectively; very large sums for the age" (*History of India*, i. 440 n. and App. E.)

4 These will be his daughters. Gul-badan gives precise details of the gifts to the family circle (*Humayun-nama* f. 10).

5 Some of these slaves were Sl. Ibrahim's dancing-girls (Gul-badan, *ib.*).

Makka and Madina. We gave one *shahrukhi* for every soul in the country of Kabul and the valley-side[1] of Varsak, man and woman, bond and free, of age or non-age.[2]

(b. Disaffection to Babur.)

On our first coming to Agra, there was remarkable dislike and hostility between its people and mine, the peasantry and soldiers running away in fear of our men. Delhi and Agra excepted, not a fortified town but strengthened its defences and neither was in obedience nor submitted. Qasim Sambhali was in Sambhal; Nizam Khan was in Biana; in Miwat was Hasan Khan Miwati himself, impious mannikin! who was the sole leader of the trouble and mischief.[3] Muhammad *Zaitun* was in Dulpur; Tatar Khan *Sarang-khani*[4] was in Gualiar; Husain Khan *Nuhani* was in Rapri; Qutb Khan was in Itawa (Etawa); 'Alam Khan (*Kalpi*) was in Kalpi. Qanauj and the other side of Gang (Ganges) was all held by Afghans in independent hostility,[5] such as Nasir Khan *Nuhani*, Ma'ruf *Farmuli* and a crowd of other amirs. These had been in rebellion for three or four years before Ibrahim's death and when I defeated him, were holding Qanauj and the whole country beyond it. At the present time they were lying two or three marches on our side of Qanauj and had made Bihar Khan the son of Darya Khan *Nuhani* their *padshah*, under the style Sultan Muhammad. Fol. 294*b*. Marghub the slave was in Mahawin (*Muttra?*); he remained there, thus close, for some time but came no nearer.

1 Ar. *sada*. Perhaps it was a station of a hundred men. Varsak is in Badakhshan, on the water flowing to Taliqan from the Khwaja Muhammad range. Erskine read (p. 335) *sada Varsak* as *sadur rashk*, incentive to emulation; de C. (ii, 233) translates *sada* conjecturally by *circonscription*. Shaikh Zain has Varsak and to the recipients of the gifts adds the "Khwastis, people noted for their piety" (A.N. trs. H.B. i, 248 n.). The gift to Varsak may well have been made in gratitude for hospitality received by Babur in the time of adversity after his loss of Samarkand and before his return to Kabul in 920 AH.

2 *circa* 10d. or 11d. Babur left himself stripped so bare by his far-flung largess that he was nick-named Qalandar (Firishta).

3 Badayuni says of him (Bib. Ind. ed. i, 340) that he was *kafir kalima-gu*, a pagan making the Muhammadan Confession of Faith, and that he had heard of him, in Akbar's time from Bairam Khan-i-khanan, as kingly in appearance and poetic in temperament. He was killed fighting for Rana Sanga at Kanwaha.

4 This is his family name.

5 *i.e.* not acting with Hasan *Miwati*.

(c. Discontent in Babur's army.)

It was the hot-season when we came to Agra. All the inhabitants (*khalaiq*) had run away in terror. Neither grain for ourselves nor corn for our horses was to be had. The villages, out of hostility and hatred to us had taken to thieving and highway-robbery; there was no moving on the roads. There had been no chance since the treasure was distributed to send men in strength into the parganas and elsewhere. Moreover the year was a very hot one; violent pestilential winds struck people down in heaps together; masses began to die off.

On these accounts the greater part of the begs and best braves became unwilling to stay in Hindustan, indeed set their faces for leaving it. It is no reproach to old and experienced begs if they speak of such matters; even if they do so, this man (Babur) has enough sense and reason to get at what is honest or what is mutinous in their representations, to distinguish between loss and gain. But as this man had seen his task whole, for himself, when he resolved on it, what taste was there in their reiterating that things should be done differently? What recommends the expression of distasteful opinions by men of little standing

Fol. 295. (*kichik karim*)? Here is a curious thing:—This last time of our riding out from Kabul, a few men of little standing had just been made begs; what I looked for from them was that if I went through fire and water and came out again, they would have gone in with me unhesitatingly, and with me have come out, that wherever I went, there at my side would they be,—not that they would speak against my fixed purpose, not that they would turn back from any task or great affair on which, all counselling, all consenting, we had resolved, so long as that counsel was not abandoned. Badly as these new begs behaved, Secretary Ahmadi and Treasurer Wali behaved still worse. Khwaja Kalan had done well in the march out from Kabul, in Ibrahim's defeat and until Agra was occupied; he had spoken bold words and shewn ambitious views. But a few days after the capture of Agra, all his views changed,—the one zealous for departure at any price was Khwaja Kalan.[1]

---

1 Gul-badan says that the Khwaja several times asked leave on the ground that his constitution was not fitted for the climate of Hindustan; that His Majesty was not at all, at all, willing for him to go, but gave way at length to his importunity.

(d. Babur calls a council.)

When I knew of this unsteadiness amongst (my) people, I summoned all the begs and took counsel. Said I, "There is no supremacy and grip on the world without means and resources; without lands and retainers sovereignty and command (*padshahliq u amirliq*) are impossible. By the labours of several years, by encountering hardship, by long travel, by flinging myself and the army into battle, and by deadly slaughter, we, through God's grace, beat these masses of enemies in order that we might take their broad lands. And now what force compels us, what necessity has arisen that we should, without cause, abandon countries taken at such risk of life? Was it for us to remain in Kabul, the sport of harsh poverty? Henceforth, let no well-wisher of mine speak of such things! But let not those turn back from going who, weak in strong persistence, have set their faces to depart!" By these words, which recalled just and reasonable views to their minds, I made them, willy-nilly, quit their fears.

Fol. 295*b*.

(e. Khwaja Kalan decides to leave Hindustan.)

As Khwaja Kalan had no heart to stay in Hindustan, matters were settled in this way:—As he had many retainers, he was to convoy the gifts, and, as there were few men in Kabul and Ghazni, was to keep these places guarded and victualled. I bestowed on him Ghazni, Girdiz and the Sultan Mas'udi Hazara, gave also the Hindustan *pargana* of G'huram,[1] worth 3 or 4 *laks*. It was settled for Khwaja Mir-i-miran also to go to Kabul; the gifts were put into his immediate charge, under the custody of Mulla Hasan the banker (*sarraf*) and Tuka[2] *Hindu*.

Loathing Hindustan, Khwaja Kalan, when on his way, had the following couplet inscribed on the wall of his residence (*'imarati*) in Dihli:—

Fol. 296.

> If safe and sound I cross the Sind,
> Blacken my face ere I wish for Hind!

It was ill-mannered in him to compose and write up this partly-jesting verse while I still stayed in Hind. If his departure

---

1 in Patiala, about 25 miles s.w. of Ambala.
2 Shaikh Zain, Gul-badan and Erskine write Nau-kar. It was now that Khwaja Kalan conveyed money for the repair of the great dam at Ghazni (f. 139).

caused me one vexation, such a jest doubled it.[1] I composed
the following off-hand verse, wrote it down and sent it to him:—

> Give a hundred thanks, Babur, that the generous Pardoner
> Has given thee Sind and Hind and many a kingdom.
> If thou (i.e. the Khwaja) have not the strength for their heats,
> If thou say, "Let me see the cold side (yuz)," Ghazni is there.[2]

(f. Accretions to Babur's force.)

At this juncture, Mulla Apaq was sent into Kul with royal
letters of favour for the soldiers and quiver-wearers (tarkash-
band) of that neighbourhood. Shaikh Guran (G'huran)[3] came

> (Author's note on Mulla Apaq.) Formerly he had been in a very low position
> indeed, but two or three years before this time, had gathered his elder and
> younger brethren into a compact body and had brought them in (to me),
> together with the Auruq-zai and other Afghans of the banks of the Sind.

trustfully and loyally to do obeisance, bringing with him from 2
to 3000 soldiers and quiver-wearers from Between-two-
waters (Mian-du-ab).

Yunas-i-'ali when on his way from Dihli to Agra[4] had lost
his way a little and got separated from Humayun; he then met
in with 'Ali Khan Farmuli's sons and train,[5] had a small affair
with them, took them prisoners and brought them in. Taking
advantage of this, one of the sons thus captured was sent to his
Fol. 296b. father in company with Daulat-qadam Turk's son Mirza Mughul
who conveyed royal letters of favour to 'Ali Khan. At this
time of break-up, 'Ali Khan had gone to Miwat; he came to

1 The friends did not meet again; that their friendship weathered this storm is
shewn by Babur's letter of f. 359. The Abushqa says the couplet was inscribed on
a marble tablet near the Hauz-i-khas at the time the Khwaja was in Dihli after
bidding Babur farewell in Agra.
2 This quatrain is in the Rampur Diwan. The Abushqa quotes the following as
Khwaja Kalan's reply, but without mentioning where the original was found.
Cf. de Courteille, Dict. s.n. taskari. An English version is given in my husband's
article Some verses by the Emperor Babur (A.Q.R. January, 1911).

> You shew your gaiety and your wit,
> In each word there lie acres of charm.
> Were not all things of Hind upside-down,
> How could you in the heat be so pleasant on cold?

It is an old remark of travellers that everything in India is the opposite of what
one sees elsewhere. Timur is said to have remarked it and to have told his soldiers
not to be afraid of the elephants of India, "For," said he, "their trunks are empty
sleeves, and they carry their tails in front; in Hindustan everything is reversed"
(H. Beveridge ibid.). Cf. App. Q.
3 Badayuni i, 337 speaks of him as unrivalled in music.
4 f. 267b.
5 auruq, which here no doubt represents the women of the family.

me when Mirza *Mughul* returned, was promoted, and given valid (?) *parganas*[1] worth 25 laks.

(g. Action against the rebels of the East.)

Sl. Ibrahim had appointed several amirs under Mustafa *Farmuli* and Firuz Khan *Sarang-khani*, to act against the rebel amirs of the East (*Purab*). Mustafa had fought them and thoroughly drubbed them, giving them more than one good beating. He dying before Ibrahim's defeat, his younger brother Shaikh Bayazid—Ibrahim being occupied with a momentous matter[2]—had led and watched over his elder brother's men. He now came to serve me, together with Firuz Khan, Mahmud Khan *Nuhani* and Qazi Jia. I shewed them greater kindness and favour than was their claim; giving to Firuz Khan 1 *krur*, 46 *laks* and 5000 *tankas* from Junpur, to Shaikh Bayazid 1 *krur*, 48 *laks* and 50,000 *tankas* from Aud (Oude), to Mahmud Khan 90 *laks* and 35,000 *tankas* from Ghazipur, and to Qazi Jia 20 *laks*.[3]

(h. Gifts made to various officers.)

It was a few days after the 'Id of Shawwal[4] that a large party was held in the pillared-porch of the domed building standing in the middle of Sl. Ibrahim's private apartments. At this party there were bestowed on Humayun a *char-qab*,[5] a sword-belt,[6] a *tipuchaq* horse with saddle mounted in gold; on Chin-timur Sultan, Mahdi Khwaja and Muhammad Sl. Mirza *char-qabs*, sword-belts and dagger-belts; and to the begs and braves, to each according to his rank, were given sword-belts, dagger-belts, and dresses of honour, in all to the number specified below:—

Fol. 297.

1 'ain parganalar.
2 Babur's advance, presumably.
3 The full amounts here given are not in all MSS., some scribes contenting themselves with the largest item of each gift (*Memoirs* p. 337).
4 The 'Id of Shawwal, it will be remembered, is celebrated at the conclusion of the Ramzan fast, on seeing the first new moon of Shawwal. In AH. 932 it must have fallen about July 11th 1526 (Erskine).
5 A square shawl, or napkin, of cloth of gold, bestowed as a mark of rank and distinction (*Memoirs* p. 338 n.); *une tunique enrichie de broderies* (*Mémoires*, ii, 240 n.).
6 *kamar-shamshir*. This Steingass explains as sword-belt, Erskine by "sword with a belt". The summary following shews that many weapons were given and not belts alone. There is a good deal of variation in the MSS. The Hai. MS. has not a complete list. The most all the lists show is that gifts were many.

> 2 items (*ra's*) of *tipuchaq* horses with saddles.
> 16 items (*qabza*) of poinards, set with jewels, etc.
> 8 items (*qabza*) of purpet over-garments.
> 2 items (*tob*) of jewelled sword-belts.
> — items (*qabza*) of broad daggers (*jamd'har*) set with jewels.
> 25 items of jewelled hangers (*khanjar*).
> — items of gold-hilted Hindi knives (*kard*).
> 51 pieces of purpet.

On the day of this party it rained amazingly, rain falling thirteen times. As outside places had been assigned to a good many people, they were drowned out (*gharaq*).

(*i. Of various forts and postings.*)

Samana (in Patiala) had been given to Muhammadi Kukuldash and it had been arranged for him to make swift descent on Sambal (Sambhal), but Sambal was now bestowed on Humayun, in addition to his guerdon of Hisar-firuza, and in his service was Hindu Beg. To suit this, therefore, Hindu Beg was sent to make the incursion in Muhammadi's place, and with him Kitta Beg, Baba *Qashqa's* (brother) Malik Qasim and his elder and younger brethren, Mulla Apaq and Shaikh Guran (G'huran) with the quiver-wearers from Between-two-waters (*Mian-du-ab*).

Fol. 297b. Three or four times a person had come from Qasim *Sambali*, saying, "The renegade Biban is besieging Sambal and has brought it to extremity; come quickly." Biban, with the array and the preparation (*hayat*) with which he had deserted us,[1] had gone skirting the hills and gathering up Afghan and Hindustani deserters, until, finding Sambal at this juncture ill-garrisoned, he laid siege to it. Hindu Beg and Kitta Beg and the rest of those appointed to make the incursion, got to the Ahar-passage[2] and from there sent ahead Baba *Qashqa's* Malik Qasim with his elder and younger brethren, while they themselves were getting over the water. Malik Qasim crossed, advanced swiftly with from 100 to 150 men—his own and his brethren's—and reached Sambal by the Mid-day Prayer. Biban for his part came out of his camp in array. Malik Qasim and his troop moved rapidly forward, got the fort in their rear, and came to grips. Biban could make no stand; he fled. Malik Qasim cut off the heads of part of his force, took many horses,

---

1 f. 263b.
2 over the Ganges, a little above Anup-shahr in the Buland-shahr district.

a few elephants and a mass of booty. Next day when the other begs arrived, Qasim *Sambali* came out and saw them, but not liking to surrender the fort, made them false pretences. One day Shaikh Guran (G'huran) and Hindu Beg having talked the matter over with them, got Qasim *Sambali* out to the presence of the begs, and took men of ours into the fort. They brought Qasim's wife and dependants safely out, and sent Qasim (to Court).[1]

Qalandar the foot-man was sent to Nizam Khan in Biana with royal letters of promise and threat; with these was sent Fol. 298. also the following little off-hand (Persian) verse:—[2]

> Strive not with the Turk, o Mir of Biana!
> His skill and his courage are obvious.
> If thou come not soon, nor give ear to counsel,—
> What need to detail (*bayan*) what is obvious?

Biana being one of the famous forts of Hindustan, the senseless mannikin, relying on its strength, demanded what not even its strength could enforce. Not giving him a good answer, we ordered siege apparatus to be looked to.

Baba Quli Beg was sent with royal letters of promise and threat to Muhammad *Zaitun* (in Dulpur); Muhammad *Zaitun* also made false excuses.

While we were still in Kabul, Rana Sanga had sent an envoy to testify to his good wishes and to propose this plan: "If the honoured Padshah will come to near Dihli from that side, I from this will move on Agra." But I beat Ibrahim, I took Dihli and Agra, and up to now that Pagan has given no sign soever of moving. After a while he went and laid siege to Kandar[3] a fort in which was Makan's son, Hasan by name. This Hasan-of-Makan had sent a person to me several times, but had not shewn himself. We had not been able to detach Fol. 298b. reinforcement for him because, as the forts round-about—Atawa (Etawa), Dulpur, Gualiar and Biana—had not yet surrendered, and the Eastern Afghans were seated with their army in obstinate rebellion two or three marches on the Agra side of Qanuj, my mind was not quite free from the whirl and strain of things

1 A seeming omission in the text is made good in my translation by Shaikh Zain's help, who says Qasim was sent to Court.
2 This quatrain is in the Rampur *Diwan*. It appears to pun on Biana and *bi(y)an*.
3 Kandar is in Rajputana; Abu'l-fazl writes Kuhan-dar, old habitation.

close at hand. Makan's Hasan therefore, becoming helpless, had surrendered Kandar two or three months ago.

Husain Khan (*Nuhani*) became afraid in Rapri, and he abandoning it, it was given to Muhammad 'Ali *Jang-jang*.

To Qutb Khan in Etawa royal letters of promise and threat had been sent several times, but as he neither came and saw me, nor abandoned Etawa and got away, it was given to Mahdi Khwaja and he was sent against it with a strong reinforcement of begs and household troops under the command of Muhammad Sl. Mirza, Sl. Muhammad *Duldai*, Muhammad 'Ali *Jang-jang* and 'Abdu'l-'aziz the Master of the Horse. Qanuj was given to Sl. Muhammad *Duldai*; he was also (as mentioned) appointed against Etawa; so too were Firuz Khan, Mahmud Khan, Shaikh Bayazid and Qazi Jia, highly favoured commanders to whom Eastern *parganas* had been given.

Fol. 299. Muhammad *Zaitun*, who was seated in Dulpur, deceived us and did not come. We gave Dulpur to Sl. Junaid *Barlas* and reinforced him by appointing 'Adil Sultan, Muhammadi Kukuldash, Shah Mansur *Barlas*, Qutluq-qadam, Treasurer Wali, Jan Beg, 'Abdu'l-lah, Pir-quli, and Shah Hasan *Yaragi* (or *Baragi*), who were to attack Dulpur, take it, make it over to Sl. Junaid *Barlas* and advance on Biana.

(*j. Plan of operations adopted.*)

These armies appointed, we summoned the Turk amirs[1] and the Hindustan amirs, and tossed the following matters in amongst them:—The various rebel amirs of the East, that is to say, those under Nasir Khan *Nuhani* and Ma'ruf *Farmuli*, have crossed Gang (Ganges) with 40 to 50,000 men, taken Qanuj, and now lie some three miles on our side of the river. The Pagan Rana Sanga has captured Kandar and is in a hostile and mischievous attitude. The end of the Rains is near. It seems expedient to move either against the rebels or the Pagan, since the task of the forts near-by is easy; when the great foes are got rid of, what road will remain open for the rest? Rana Sanga is thought not to be the equal of the rebels.

---

1 This is the first time Babur's begs are called amirs in his book; it may be by a scribe's slip.

To this all replied unanimously, "Rana Sanga is the most distant, and it is not known that he will come nearer; the enemy who is closest at hand must first be got rid of. We are for riding against the rebels." Humayun then represented, Fol. 299b. "What need is there for the Padshah to ride out? This service I will do." This came as a pleasure to every-one; the Turk and Hind amirs gladly accepted his views; he was appointed for the East. A Kabuli of Ahmad-i-qasim's was sent galloping off to tell the armies that had been despatched against Dulpur to join Humayun at Chandwar;[1] also those sent against Etawa under Mahdi Khwaja and Muhammad Sl. M. were ordered to join him.

(*August 21st*) Humayun set out on Thursday the 13th of Zu'l-qa'da, dismounted at a little village called Jilisir (Jalesar) some 3 *kurohs* from Agra, there stayed one night, then moved forward march by march.

(*k. Khwaja Kalan's departure.*)

(*August 28th*) On Thursday the 20th of this same month, Khwaja Kalan started for Kabul.

(*l. Of gardens and pleasaunces.*)

One of the great defects of Hindustan being its lack of running-waters,[2] it kept coming to my mind that waters should be made to flow by means of wheels erected wherever I might settle down, also that grounds should be laid out in an orderly and symmetrical way. With this object in view, we crossed the Jun-water to look at garden-grounds a few days after entering Agra. Those grounds were so bad and unattractive that we traversed them with a hundred disgusts and repulsions. So ugly and displeasing were they, that the idea of making a Fol. 300. Char-bagh in them passed from my mind, but needs must! as there was no other land near Agra, that same ground was taken in hand a few days later.

The beginning was made with the large well from which water comes for the Hot-bath, and also with the piece of ground where

1 Chandwar is on the Jumna, between Agra and Etawah.
2 Here *aqar-sular* will stand for the waters which flow—sometimes in marble channels—to nourish plants and charm the eye, such for example as beautify the Taj-mahal pleasaunce.

the tamarind-trees and the octagonal tank now are. After that came the large tank with its enclosure; after that the tank and *talar*[1] in front of the outer (?) residence;[2] after that the private-house (*khilwat-khana*) with its garden and various dwellings; after that the Hot-bath. Then in that charmless and disorderly Hind, plots of garden[3] were seen laid out with order and symmetry, with suitable borders and parterres in every corner, and in every border rose and narcissus in perfect arrangement.

(*m. Construction of a chambered-well.*)

Three things oppressed us in Hindustan, its heat, its violent winds, its dust. Against all three the Bath is a protection, for in it, what is known of dust and wind? and in the heats it is so chilly that one is almost cold. The bath-room in which the heated tank is, is altogether of stone, the whole, except for the *izara* (dado?) of white stone, being, pavement and roofing, of red Biana stone.

Khalifa also and Shaikh Zain, Yunas-i-'ali and whoever got
Fol. 300b. land on that other bank of the river laid out regular and orderly gardens with tanks, made running-waters also by setting up wheels like those in Dipalpur and Lahor. The people of Hind who had never seen grounds planned so symmetrically and thus laid out, called the side of the Jun where (our) residences were, Kabul.

In an empty space inside the fort, which was between Ibrahim's residence and the ramparts, I ordered a large chambered-well (*wain*) to be made, measuring 10 by 10,[4] a large

1 The *talar* is raised on pillars and open in front; it serves often for an Audience-hall (Erskine).

2 *tash 'imarat*, which may refer to the extra-mural location of the house, or contrast it with the inner *khilwat-khana*, the women's quarters, of the next sentence. The point is noted as one concerning the use of the word *tash*. I have found no instance in which it is certain that Babur uses *tash*, a stone or rock, as an adjective. On f. 301 he writes *tashdin 'imarat*, house-of-stone, which the Persian text renders by '*imarat-i-sangin*. Wherever *tash* can be translated as meaning outer, this accords with Babur's usual diction.

3 *baghcha*. That Babur was the admitted pioneer of orderly gardens in India is shewn by the 30th *Ayin*, On Perfumes:—"After the foot-prints of Firdaus-makani (Babur) had added to the glory of Hindustan, embellishment by avenues and landscape-gardening was seen, while heart-expanding buildings and the sound of falling-waters widened the eyes of beholders."

4 Perhaps *gaz*, each somewhat less than 36 inches.

well with a flight of steps, which in Hindustan is called a *wain*.[1]
This well was begun before the Char-bagh;[2] they were busy
digging it in the true Rains (*'ain bishkal*, Sawan and Bhadon); it
fell in several times and buried the hired workmen; it was
finished after the Holy Battle with Rana Sanga, as is stated in
the inscription on the stone that bears the chronogram of its
completion. It is a complete *wain*, having a three-storeyed house
in it. The lowest storey consists of three rooms, each of which
opens on the descending steps, at intervals of three steps from
one another. When the water is at its lowest, it is one step below
the bottom chamber; when it rises in the Rains, it sometimes
goes into the top storey. In the middle storey an inner chamber
has been excavated which connects with the domed building in
which the bullock turns the well-wheel. The top storey is a   Fol. 301.
single room, reached from two sides by 5 or 6 steps which lead
down to it from the enclosure overlooked from the well-head.
Facing the right-hand way down, is the stone inscribed with the
date of completion. At the side of this well is another the bottom
of which may be at half the depth of the first, and into which
water comes from that first one when the bullock turns the
wheel in the domed building afore-mentioned. This second well
also is fitted with a wheel, by means of which water is carried
along the ramparts to the high-garden. A stone building (*tashdin
'imarat*) stands at the mouth of the well and there is an outer (?)
mosque[3] outside (*tashqari*) the enclosure in which the well is.
The mosque is not well done; it is in the Hindustani fashion.

(*n. Humayun's campaign.*)

At the time Humayun got to horse, the rebel amirs under
Nasir Khan *Nuhani* and Ma'ruf *Farmuli* were assembled at
Jajmau.[4] Arrived within 20 to 30 miles of them, he sent out

1 The more familiar Indian name is *baoli*. Such wells attracted Peter Mundy's
attention; Yule gives an account of their names and plan (Mundy's *Travels in Asia*,
Hakluyt Society, ed. R. C. Temple, and Yule's *Hobson Jobson s.n.* Bowly). Babur's
account of his great *wain* is not easy to translate; his interpreters vary from one
another; probably no one of them has felt assured of translating correctly.

2 *i.e.* the one across the river.

3 *tash masjid*; this, unless some adjectival affix (*e.g. din*) has been omitted by the
scribe, I incline to read as meaning extra, supplementary, or outer, not as "mosque-
of-stone".

4 or Jajmawa, the old name for the sub-district of Kanhpur (Cawnpur).

Mumin Ataka for news; it became a raid for loot; Mumin
Ataka was not able to bring even the least useful information.
The rebels heard about him however, made no stay but fled and
got away. After Mumin Ataka, Qusm-nai (?) was sent for news,
with Baba Chuhra[1] and Bujka; they brought it of the breaking-
up and flight of the rebels. Humayun advancing, took Jajmau
Fol. 301b. and passed on. Near Dilmau[2] Fath Khan *Sarwani* came and saw
him, and was sent to me with Mahdi Khwaja and Muhammad
Sl. Mirza.

(o. News of the Auzbegs.)

This year 'Ubaidu'l-lah Khan (*Auzbeg*) led an army out of
Bukhara against Marv. In the citadel of Marv were perhaps
10 to 15 peasants whom he overcame and killed; then having
taken the revenues of Marv in 40 or 50 days,[3] he went on to
Sarakhs. In Sarakhs were some 30 to 40 Red-heads (*Qizil-bash*)
who did not surrender, but shut the Gate; the peasantry however
scattered them and opened the Gate to the Auzbeg who entering,
killed the Red-heads. Sarakhs taken, he went against Tus and
Mashhad. The inhabitants of Mashhad being helpless, let him
in. Tus he besieged for 8 months, took possession of on terms,
did not keep those terms, but killed every man of name and
made their women captive.

(p. Affairs of Gujrat.)

In this year Bahadur Khan,—he who now rules in Gujrat in
the place of his father Sl. Muzaffar *Gujrati*—having gone to
Sl. Ibrahim after quarrel with his father, had been received
without honour. He had sent dutiful letters to me while I was
near Pani-pat; I had replied by royal letters of favour and
kindness summoning him to me. He had thought of coming,
but changing his mind, drew off from Ibrahim's army towards
Gujrat. Meantime his father Sl. Muzaffar had died (Friday
Jumada II. 932 AH.—March 16th 1526 AD.); his elder brother
Sikandar Shah who was Sl. Muzaffar's eldest son, had become

1 *i.e.* of the Corps of Braves.
2 Dilmau is on the left bank of the Ganges, s.e. from Bareilly (Erskine).
3 *Marv-ning bundi-ni baghlab*, which Erskine renders by "Having settled the
revenue of Merv", and de Courteille by, "*Après avoir occupé Merv.*" Were the
year's revenues compressed into a 40 to 50 days collection?

ruler in their father's place and, owing to his evil disposition, Fol. 302. had been strangled by his slave 'Imadu'l-mulk, acting with others (Sha'ban 14th—May 25th). Bahadur Khan, while he was on his road for Gujrat, was invited and escorted to sit in his father's place under the style Bahadur Shah (Ramzan 26th—July 6th). He for his part did well; he retaliated by death on 'Imadu'l-mulk for his treachery to his salt, and killed some of his father's begs.[1] People point at him as a dread-naught (*bi bak*) youth and a shedder of much blood.

1 *i.e.* those who had part in his brother's murder. *Cf.* Nizamu'd-din Ahmad's *Tabaqat-i-akbari* and the *Mirat-i-sikandari* (trs. *History of Gujrat* E. C. Bayley).

(a. Announcement of the birth of a son.)

In Muharram Beg Wais brought the news of Faruq's birth; though a foot-man had brought it already, he came this month for the gift to the messenger of good tidings.[2] The birth must have been on Friday eve, Shawwal 23rd (932 AH.–August 2nd 1526 AD.); the name given was Faruq.

(b. Casting of a mortar.)

(October 22nd – Muharram 15th) Ustad 'Ali-quli had been ordered to cast a large mortar for use against Biana and other forts which had not yet submitted. When all the furnaces and materials were ready, he sent a person to me and, on Monday the 15th of the month, we went to see the mortar cast. Round the mortar-mould he had had eight furnaces made in which were the molten materials. From below each furnace a channel went direct to the mould. When he opened the furnace-holes on our arrival, the molten metal poured like water through all these channels into the mould. After awhile and before the mould was full, the flow stopped from one furnace after another. Ustad 'Ali-quli must have made some miscalculation either as to the furnaces or the materials. In his great distress, he was for throwing himself into the mould of molten metal, but we comforted him, put a robe of honour on him, and so brought him out of his shame. The mould was left a day or two to cool; when it was opened, Ustad 'Ali-quli with great delight sent to say, "The stone-chamber (*tash-awi*) is without defect; to cast the powder-compartment (*daru-khana*) is easy." He got

Fol. 302b.

1 Elph. MS. f. 252; W.-i-B. I.O. 215 f. 199b and 217 f. 208b; Mems. p. 343.
2 *siunchi* (Zenker). Faruq was Mahim's son; he died in 934 AH. before his father had seen him.

the stone-chamber out and told off a body of men to accoutre[1] it, while he busied himself with casting the powder-compartment.

(*c. Varia.*)

Mahdi Khwaja arrived bringing Fath Khan *Sarwani* from Humayun's presence, they having parted from him in Dilmau. I looked with favour on Fath Khan, gave him the *parganas* that had been his father 'Azam-humayun's, and other lands also, one *pargana* given being worth a *krur* and 60 *laks*.[2]

In Hindustan they give permanent titles [*muqarrari khitablar*] to highly-favoured amirs, one such being 'Azam-humayun (August Might), one Khan-i-jahan (Khan-of-the-world), another Khan-i-khanan (Khan-of-khans). Fath Khan's father's title was 'Azam-humayun but I set this aside because on account of Humayun it was not seemly for any person to bear it, and I gave Fath Khan *Sarwani* the title of Khan-i-jahan.

Fol. 303.

(*November 14th*) On Wednesday the 8th of Safar[3] awnings were set up (in the Char-bagh) at the edge of the large tank beyond the tamarind-trees, and an entertainment was prepared there. We invited Fath Khan *Sarwani* to a wine-party, gave him wine, bestowed on him a turban and head-to-foot of my own wearing, uplifted his head with kindness and favour[4] and allowed him to go to his own districts. It was arranged for his son Mahmud to remain always in waiting.

(*d. Various military matters.*)

(*November 30th*) On Wednesday the 24th of Muharram[5] Muhammad 'Ali (son of Mihtar) Haidar the stirrup-holder was

---

1 *salah*. It is clear from the "*tash-awi*" (Pers. trs. *khana-i-sang*) of this mortar (*qazan*) that stones were its missiles. Erskine notes that from Babur's account cannon would seem sometimes to have been made in parts and clamped together, and that they were frequently formed of iron bars strongly compacted into a circular shape. The accoutrement (*salah*) presumably was the addition of fittings.

2 About £40,000 sterling (Erskine).

3 The MSS. write Safar but it seems probable that Muharram should be substituted for this; one ground for not accepting Safar being that it breaks the consecutive order of dates, another that Safar allows what seems a long time for the journey from near Dilmau to Agra. All MSS. I have seen give the 8th as the day of the month but Erskine has 20th. In this part of Babur's writings dates are sparse; it is a narrative and not a diary.

4 This phrase, foreign to Babur's diction, smacks of a Court-Persian milieu.

5 Here the Elph. MS. has Safar Muharram (f. 253), as has also I.O. 215 f. 200*b*, but it seems unsafe to take this as an *al Safarani* extension of Muharram because Muh.-Safar 24th was not a Wednesday. As in the passage noted just above, it seems likely that Muharram is right.

sent (to Humayun) with this injunction, "As—thanks be to God!—the rebels have fled, do you, as soon as this messenger arrives, appoint a few suitable begs to Junpur, and come quickly to us yourself, for Rana Sanga the Pagan is conveniently close; let us think first of him!"

After (Humayun's) army had gone to the East, we appointed, to make a plundering excursion into the Biana neighbourhood, Tardi Beg (brother) of Quj Beg with his elder brother Sher-afgan, Muhammad Khalil the master-gelder (*akhta-begi*) with his brethren and the gelders (*akhtachilar*),[1] Rustam *Turkman* with his brethren, and also, of the Hindustani people, Daud *Sarwani*. If they, by promise and persuasion, could make the Biana garrison look towards us, they were to do so; if not, they were to weaken the enemy by raid and plunder.

Fol. 303b.

In the fort of Tahangar[2] was 'Alam Khan the elder brother of that same Nizam Khan of Biana. People of his had come again and again to set forth his obedience and well-wishing; he now took it on himself to say, "If the Padshah appoint an army, it will be my part by promise and persuasion to bring in the quiver-weavers of Biana and to effect the capture of that fort." This being so, the following orders were given to the braves of Tardi Beg's expedition, "As 'Alam Khan, a local man, has taken it on himself to serve and submit in this manner, act you with him and in the way he approves in this matter of Biana." Swordsmen though some Hindustanis may be, most of them are ignorant and unskilled in military move and stand (*yurush u turush*), in soldierly counsel and procedure. When our expedition joined 'Alam Khan, he paid no attention to what any-one else said, did not consider whether his action was good or bad, but went close up to Biana, taking our men with him. Our expedition numbered from 250 to 300 Turks with somewhat over 2000 Hindustanis and local people, while Nizam Khan of Biana's Afghans and *sipahis*[3] were an army of over 4000 horse and of foot-men themselves again, more than 10,000. Nizam Khan

Fol. 304.

1 Cf. f. 15b note to Qambar-i-'ali. The title *Akhta-begi* is to be found translated by "Master of the Horse", but this would not suit both uses of *akhta* in the above sentence. Cf. Shaw's Vocabulary.
2 *i.e.* Tahangarh in Karauli, Rajputana.
3 Perhaps *sipahi* represents Hindustani foot-soldiers.

looked his opponents over, sallied suddenly out and, his massed horse charging down, put our expeditionary force to flight. His men unhorsed his elder brother 'Alam Khan, took 5 or 6 others prisoner and contrived to capture part of the baggage. As we had already made encouraging promises to Nizam Khan, we now, spite of this last impropriety, pardoned all earlier and this later fault, and sent him royal letters. As he heard of Rana Sanga's rapid advance, he had no resource but to call on Sayyid Rafi'[1] for mediation, surrender the fort to our men, and come in with Sayyid Rafi', when he was exalted to the felicity of an interview.[2] I bestowed on him a pargana in Mian-du-ab worth 20 *laks*.[3] Dost, Lord-of-the-gate was sent for a time to Biana, but a few days later it was bestowed on Madhi Khwaja with a fixed allowance of 70 *laks*,[4] and he was given leave to go there.

Tatar Khan *Sarang-khani*, who was in Gualiar, had been sending constantly to assure us of his obedience and good-wishes. After the pagan took Kandar and was close to Biana, Dharmankat, one of the Gualiar rajas, and another pagan styled Khan-i-jahan, went into the Gualiar neighbourhood and, coveting the fort, began to stir trouble and tumult. Tatar Khan, thus placed in difficulty, was for surrendering Gualiar (to us). Most of our begs, household and best braves being away with (Humayun's) army or on various raids, we joined to Rahim-dad Fol. 304*b*. a few Bhira men and Lahoris with Hastachi[5] *tunqitar* and his brethren. We assigned *parganas* in Gualiar itself to all those mentioned above. Mulla Apaq and Shaikh Guran (G'huran) went also with them, they to return after Rahim-dad was established in Gualiar. By the time they were near Gualiar however, Tatar Khan's views had changed, and he did not invite them into the fort. Meantime Shaikh Muhammad *Ghaus* (Helper), a darwish-like man, not only very learned but with a large following of students and disciples, sent from inside the fort to say to Rahim-dad, "Get yourselves into the fort somehow, for

1 Rafi'u-d-din *Safawi*, a native of Ij near the Persian Gulf, teacher of Abu'l-fazl's father and buried near Agra (*Ayin-i-akbari*).
2 This phrase, again, departs from Babur's simplicity of statement.
3 About £5000 (Erskine).
4 About £17,500 (Erskine).
5 Hai. MS. and 215 f. 201*b*, Hasti; Elph. MS. f. 254, and Ilminsky, p. 394, Aimishchi; *Memoirs*, p. 346, Imshiji, so too *Mémoires*, ii, 257.

the views of this person (Tatar Khan) have changed, and he has evil in his mind." Hearing this, Rahim-dad sent to say to Tatar Khan, "There is danger from the Pagan to those outside; let me bring a few men into the fort and let the rest stay outside." Under insistence, Tatar Khan agreed to this, and Rahim-dad went in with rather few men. Said he, "Let our people stay near this Gate," posted them near the Hati-pul (Elephant-gate) and through that Gate during that same night brought in the whole of his troop. Next day, Tatar Khan, reduced to helplessness, willy-nilly, made over the fort, and set out to come and wait on me in Agra. A subsistence allowance of 20 *laks* was assigned to him on Bianwan *pargana*.[1]

Muhammad *Zaitun* also took the only course open to him by surrendering Dulpur and coming to wait on me. A *pargana* worth a few *laks* was bestowed on him. Dulpur was made a royal domain (*khalsa*) with Abu'l-fath *Turkman*[2] as its military-collector (*shiqdar*).

In the Hisar-firuza neighbourhood Hamid Khan *Sarang-khani* with a body of his own Afghans and of the Pani Afghans he had collected—from 3 to 4000 in all—was in a hostile and troublesome attitude. On Wednesday the 15th Safar (Nov. 21st) we appointed against him Chin-timur Sl. (*Chaghatai*) with the commanders Secretary Ahmadi, Abu'l-fath *Turkman*, Malik Dad *Kararani*[3] and Mujahid Khan of Multan. These going, fell suddenly on him from a distance, beat his Afghans well, killed a mass of them and sent in many heads.

(e. Embassy from Persia.)

In the last days of Safar, Khwajagi Asad who had been sent to Shah-zada Tahmasp[4] in 'Iraq, returned with a Turkman named Sulaiman who amongst other gifts brought two Circassian girls (*qizlar*).

---

1 About £5000 (Erskine). Bianwan lies in the *subah* of Agra.
2 *Cf*. f. 175*b* for Babur's estimate of his service.
3 *Cf*. f. 268*b* for Babur's clemency to him.
4 Firishta (Briggs ii, 53) mentions that Asad had gone to Tahmasp from Kabul to congratulate him on his accession. Shah Isma'il had died in 930 AH. (1524 AD.); the title Shah-zada is a misnomer therefore in 933 AH.—one possibly prompted by Tahmasp's youth. *See* Additional Notes, pp. 799–800.

(*f. Attempt to poison Babur.*)

(*Dec. 21st*) On Friday the 16th of the first Rabi' a strange event occurred which was detailed in a letter written to Kabul. That letter is inserted here just as it was written, without addition or taking-away, and is as follows:—[1]

"The details of the momentous event of Friday the 16th of the first Rabi' in the date 933 [Dec. 21st 1526 AD.] are as follows:—The ill-omened old woman[2] Ibrahim's mother heard Fol. 305*b*. that I ate things from the hands of Hindustanis—the thing being that three or four months earlier, as I had not seen Hindustani dishes, I had ordered Ibrahim's cooks to be brought and out of 50 or 60 had kept four. Of this she heard, sent to Atawa (Etawa) for Ahmad the *chashnigir*—in Hindustan they call a taster (*bakawal*) a *chashnigir*—and, having got him,[3] gave a *tula* of poison, wrapped in a square of paper,—as has been mentioned a *tula* is rather more than 2 *misqals*[4]—into the hand of a slave-woman who was to give it to him. That poison Ahmad gave to the Hindustani cooks in our kitchen, promising them four *parganas* if they would get it somehow into the food. Following the first slave-woman that ill-omened old woman sent a second to see if the first did or did not give the poison she had received to Ahmad. Well was it that Ahmad put the poison not into the cooking-pot but on a dish! He did not put it into the pot because I had strictly ordered the tasters to compel any Hindustanis who were present while food was cooking in the pots, to taste that food.[5] Our graceless tasters were neglectful when the food (*ash*) was being dished up. Thin slices of bread were put on a porcelain dish; on these less than half of the paper packet of poison was sprinkled, and over this buttered

1 The letter is likely to have been written to Mahim and to have been brought back to India by her in 935 AH. (f. 380*b*). Some MSS. of the Pers. trs. reproduce it in Turki and follow this by a Persian version; others omit the Turki.

2 Turki, *bua*. Hindi *bawa* means sister or paternal-aunt but this would not suit from Babur's mouth, the more clearly not that his epithet for the offender is *bad-bakht*. Gul-badan (H.N. f. 19) calls her "ill-omened demon".

3 She may have been still in the place assigned to her near Agra when Babur occupied it (f. 269).

4 f. 290. Erskine notes that the *tula* is about equal in weight to the silver *rupi*.

5 It appears from the kitchen-arrangements detailed by Abu'l-fazl, that before food was dished up, it was tasted from the pot by a cook and a subordinate taster, and next by the Head-taster.

Fol. 306. fritters were laid. It would have been bad if the poison had been strewn on the fritters or thrown into the pot. In his confusion, the man threw the larger half into the fire-place."

"On Friday, late after the Afternoon Prayer, when the cooked meats were set out, I ate a good deal of a dish of hare and also much fried carrot, took a few mouthfuls of the poisoned Hindustani food without noticing any unpleasant flavour, took also a mouthful or two of dried-meat (*qaq*). Then I felt sick. As some dried meat eaten on the previous day had had an unpleasant taste, I thought my nausea due to the dried-meat. Again and again my heart rose; after retching two or three times I was near vomiting on the table-cloth. At last I saw it would not do, got up, went retching every moment of the way to the water-closet (*ab-khana*) and on reaching it vomited much. Never had I vomited after food, used not to do so indeed while drinking. I became suspicious; I had the cooks put in ward and ordered some of the vomit given to a dog and the dog to be watched. It was somewhat out-of-sorts near the first watch of the next day; its belly was swollen and however much people threw stones at it and turned it over, it did not get up. In that state it remained till mid-day; it then got up; it did not die.

Fol. 306b. One or two of the braves who also had eaten of that dish, vomited a good deal next day; one was in a very bad state. In the end all escaped. (*Persian*) 'An evil arrived but happily passed on!' God gave me new-birth! I am coming from that other world; I am born today of my mother; I was sick; I live; through God, I know today the worth of life!"[1]

"I ordered Pay-master Sl. Muhammad to watch the cook; when he was taken for torture (*qin*), he related the above particulars one after another."

"Monday being Court-day, I ordered the grandees and notables, amirs and wazirs to be present and that those two men and two women should be brought and questioned. They there related the particulars of the affair. That taster I had cut in pieces, that cook skinned alive; one of those women I had thrown

---

1 The Turki sentences which here follow the well-known Persian proverb, *Rasida bud balai wali ba khair guzasht*, are entered as verse in some MSS.; they may be a prose quotation.

under an elephant, the other shot with a match-lock. The old woman (*bua*) I had kept under guard; she will meet her doom, the captive of her own act."[1]

"On Saturday I drank a bowl of milk, on Sunday '*araq* in which stamped-clay was dissolved.[2] On Monday I drank milk in which were dissolved stamped-clay and the best theriac,[3] a strong purge. As on the first day, Saturday, something very dark like parched bile was voided."

"Thanks be to God! no harm has been done. Till now I had not known so well how sweet a thing life can seem! As the line has it, 'He who has been near to death knows the worth of life.' Spite of myself, I am all upset whenever the dreadful occurrence comes back to my mind. It must have been God's favour gave me life anew; with what words can I thank him?" Fol. 307.

"Although the terror of the occurrence was too great for words, I have written all that happened, with detail and circumstance, because I said to myself, 'Don't let their hearts be kept in anxiety!' Thanks be to God! there may be other days yet to see! All has passed off well and for good; have no fear or anxiety in your minds."

"This was written on Tuesday the 20th of the first Rabi', I being then in the Char-bagh."

When we were free from the anxiety of these occurrences, the above letter was written and sent to Kabul.

(*g. Dealings with Ibrahim's family.*)

As this great crime had raised its head through that ill-omened old woman (*bua-i-bad-bakht*), she was given over to Yunas-i-'ali and Khwajagi Asad who after taking her money and goods, slaves and slave-women (*daduk*), made her over for careful watch to 'Abdu'r-rahim *shaghawal*. Her grandson, Ibrahim's son had been cared for with much respect and delicacy, but as the attempt on my life had been made, clearly, by that family, it

1 She, after being put under contribution by two of Babur's officers (f. 307) was started off for Kabul, but, perhaps dreading her reception there, threw herself into the Indus in crossing and was drowned. (*Cf.* A.N. trs. H. Beveridge *Errata* and *addenda* p. xi for the authorities.)
2 *gil makhtum*, Lemnian earth, *terra sigillata*, each piece of which was impressed, when taken from the quarry, with a guarantee-stamp (*Cf.* Ency. Br. *s.n.* Lemnos).
3 *tiriaq-i-faruq*, an antidote.

did not seem advisable to keep him in Agra; he was joined therefore to Mulla Sarsan—who had come from Kamran on important business—and was started off with the Mulla to Kamran on Thursday Rabi' I. 29th (Jan. 3rd 1527 AD.).[1]

(*h. Humayun's campaign.*)

Fol. 307b.

Humayun, acting against the Eastern rebels[2] took Juna-pur (*sic*), went swiftly against Nasir Khan (*Nuhani*) in Ghazi-pur and found that he had gone across the Gang-river, presumably on news* of Humayun's approach. From Ghazi-pur Humayun went against Kharid[3] but the Afghans of the place had crossed the Saru-water (Gogra) presumably on the news* of his coming. Kharid was plundered and the army turned back.

Humayun, in accordance with my arrangements, left Shah Mir Husain and Sl. Junaid with a body of effective braves in Juna-pur, posted Qazi Jia with them, and placed Shaikh Bayazid [*Farmuli*] in Aude (Oude). These important matters settled, he crossed Gang from near Karrah-Manikpur and took the Kalpi road. When he came opposite Kalpi, in which was Jalal Khan *Jik-hat's* (son) 'Alam Khan who had sent me dutiful letters but had not waited on me himself, he sent some-one to chase fear from 'Alam Khan's heart and so brought him along (to Agra).

Humayun arrived and waited on me in the Garden of Eight-paradises[4] on Sunday the 3rd of the 2nd Rabi' (Jan. 6th 1527 AD.). On the same day Khwaja Dost-i-khawand arrived from Kabul.

(*i. Rana Sanga's approach.*)[5]

Meantime Mahdi Khwaja's people began to come in, treading on one another's heels and saying, "The Rana's advance is

1 Kamran was in Qandahar. Erskine observes here that Babur's omission to give the name of Ibrahim's son, is noteworthy; the son may however have been a child and his name not known to or recalled by Babur when writing some years later.
2 f. 299b.
3 The *Ayin-i-akbari* locates this in the *sarkar* of Jun-pur, a location suiting the context. The second Persian translation ('Abdu'r-rahim's) has here a scribe's skip from one "news" to another (both asterisked in my text); hence Erskine has an omission.
4 This is the Char-bagh of f. 300, known later as the Ram (Aram)-bagh (Garden-of-rest).
5 Presumably he was coming up from Marwar.

certain. Hasan Khan *Miwati* is heard of also as likely to join him. They must be thought about above all else. It would favour our fortune, if a troop came ahead of the army to reinforce Biana."

Fol. 308.

Deciding to get to horse, we sent on, to ride light to Biana, the commanders Muhammad Sl. Mirza, Yunas-i-'ali, Shah Mansur *Barlas*, Kitta Beg, Qismati[1] and Bujka.

In the fight with Ibrahim, Hasan Khan *Miwati*'s son Nahar Khan had fallen into our hands; we had kept him as a hostage and, ostensibly on his account, his father had been making comings-and-goings with us, constantly asking for him. It now occurred to several people that if Hasan Khan were conciliated by sending him his son, he would thereby be the more favourably disposed and his waiting on me might be the better brought about. Accordingly Nahar Khan was dressed in a robe of honour; promises were made to him for his father, and he was given leave to go. That hypocritical mannikin [Hasan Khan] must have waited just till his son had leave from me to go, for on hearing of this and while his son as yet had not joined him, he came out of Alur (Alwar) and at once joined Rana Sanga in Toda(bhim). It must have been ill-judged to let his son go just then.

Meantime much rain was falling; parties were frequent; even Humayun was present at them and, abhorrent though it was to him, sinned[2] every few days.

(*j. Tramontane affairs.*)

One of the strange events in these days of respite[3] was this:— When Humayun was coming from Fort Victory (Qila'-i-zafar) to join the Hindustan army, (Muh. 932 AH.–Oct. 1525 AD.) Mulla Baba of Pashaghar (*Chaghatai*) and his younger brother Baba Shaikh deserted on the way, and went to Kitin-qara Sl. (*Auzbeg*), into whose hands Balkh had fallen through the

Fol. 308*b*.

---

1 This name varies; the Hai. MS. in most cases writes Qismati, but on f. 267*b*, Qismatai; the Elph. MS. on f. 220 has Q:s:mnai; De Courteille writes Qismi.
2 *artkab qildi*, perhaps drank wine, perhaps ate opium-confections to the use of which he became addicted later on (Gulbadan's *Humayun-nama* f. 30*b* and 73*b*).
3 *fursatlar, i.e.* between the occupation of Agra and the campaign against Rana Sanga.

enfeeblement of its garrison.[1] This hollow mannikin and his younger brother having taken the labours of this side (Cis-Balkh?) on their own necks, come into the neighbourhood of Aibak, Khurram and Sar-bagh.[2]

Shah Sikandar—his footing in Ghuri lost through the surrender of Balkh—is about to make over that fort to the Auzbeg, when Mulla Baba and Baba Shaikh, coming with a few Auzbegs, take possession of it. Mir Hamah, as his fort is close by, has no help for it; he is for submitting to the Auzbeg, but a few days later Mulla Baba and Baba Shaikh come with a few Auzbegs to Mir Hamah's fort, purposing to make the Mir and his troop march out and to take them towards Balkh. Mir Hamah makes Baba Shaikh dismount inside the fort, and gives the rest felt huts (*autaq*) here and there. He slashes at Baba Shaikh, puts him and some others in bonds, and sends a man galloping off to Tingri-birdi (*Quchin*, in Qunduz). Tingri-birdi sends off Yar-i-'ali and 'Abdu'l-latif with a few effective braves, but before they reach Mir Hamah's fort, Mulla Baba has arrived there with his Auzbegs; he had thought of a hand-to-hand fight (*aurush-murush*), but he can do nothing. Mir Hamah and his men joined Tingri-birdi's and came to Qunduz. Baba Shaikh's wound must have been severe; they cut his head off and Mir Hamah brought it (to Agra) in these same days of respite. I uplifted his head with favour and kindness, distinguishing him amongst his fellows and equals. When Baqi *shaghawal* went [to Balkh][3] I promised him a *ser* of gold for the head of each of the ill-conditioned old couple; one *ser* of gold was now given to Mir Hamah for Baba Shaikh's head, over and above the favours referred to above.[4]

Fol. 309.

(*k. Action of part of the Biana reinforcement.*)

Qismati who had ridden light for Biana, brought back several heads he had cut off; when he and Bujka had gone with a few

---

1 Apparently the siege Babur broke up in 931 AH. had been renewed by the Auzbegs (f. 255*b* and Trs. Note *s.a.* 931 AH. section *c*).

2 These places are on the Khulm-river between Khulm and Kahmard. The present tense of this and the following sentences is Babur's.

3 f. 261.

4 Erskine here notes that if the *ser* Babur mentions be one of 14 *tulas*, the value is about £27; if of of 24 *tulas*, about £45.

braves to get news, they had beaten two of the Pagan's scouting-parties and had made 70 to 80 prisoners. Qismati brought news that Hasan Khan *Miwati* really had joined Rana Sanga.

(l. Trial-test of the large mortar of f. 302.)

(Feb. 10th) On Sunday the 8th of the month (Jumada I.), I went to see Ustad 'Ali-quli discharge stones from that large mortar of his in casting which the stone-chamber was without defect and which he had completed afterwards by casting the powder-compartment. It was discharged at the Afternoon Prayer; the throw of the stone was 1600 paces. A gift was made to the Master of a sword-belt, robe of honour, and *tipuchaq* (horse).

(m. Babur leaves Agra against Rana Sanga.)

(Feb. 11th) On Monday the 9th of the first Jumada, we got out of the suburbs of Agra, on our journey *(safar)* for the Holy War, and dismounted in the open country, where we remained three or four days to collect our army and be its rallying-point.[1] As little confidence was placed in Hindustani people, the Hindustan amirs were inscribed for expeditions to this or to that side:—'Alam Khan *(Tahangari)* was sent hastily to Gualiar to reinforce Rahim-dad; Makan, Qasim Beg *Sanbali (Sambhali)*, Hamid with his elder and younger brethren and Muhammad *Zaitun* were inscribed to go swiftly to Sanbal.

Fol. 309b.

(n. Defeat of the advance-force.)

Into this same camp came the news that owing to Rana Sanga's swift advance with all his army,[2] our scouts were able neither to get into the fort (Biana) themselves nor to send news into it. The Biana garrison made a rather incautious sally too far out; the enemy fell on them in some force and put them to

---

1 T. *chapduq*. Cf. the two Persian translations 215 f. 205b and 217 f. 215; also Ilminsky, p. 401.

2 *bulghan chiriki*. The Rana's forces are thus stated by Tod (*Rajastan; Annals of Marwar* Cap. ix):—"Eighty thousand horse, 7 Rajas of the highest rank, 9 Raos, and 104 chieftains bearing the titles of Rawul and Rawut, with 500 war-elephants, followed him into the field." Babur's army, all told, was 12,000 when he crossed the Indus from Kabul; it will have had accretions from his own officers in the Panj-ab and some also from other quarters, and will have had losses at Panipat; his reliable kernel of fighting-strength cannot but have been numerically insignificant, compared with the Rajput host. Tod says that almost all the princes of Rajastan followed the Rana at Kanwa.

rout.[1] There Sangur Khan *Janjuha* became a martyr. Kitta Beg
had galloped into the pell-mell without his cuirass; he got
one pagan afoot (*yayaglatib*) and was overcoming him, when
the pagan snatched a sword from one of Kitta Beg's own
servants and slashed the Beg across the shoulder. Kitta Beg
suffered great pain; he could not come into the Holy-battle
with Rana Sanga, was long in recovering and always remained
blemished.

Whether because they were themselves afraid, or whether to
frighten others is not known but Qismati, Shah Mansur *Barlas*
and all from Biana praised and lauded the fierceness and valour
of the pagan army.

Qasim Master-of-the-horse was sent from the starting-ground
(*safar qilghan yurt*) with his spadesmen, to dig many wells
where the army was next to dismount in the Madhakur *pargana*.

(*Feb. 16th*) Marching out of Agra on Saturday the 14th of
the first Jumada, dismount was made where the wells had been
dug. We marched on next day. It crossed my mind that the
well-watered ground for a large camp was at Sikri.[2] It being
possible that the Pagan was encamped there and in possession
of the water, we arrayed precisely, in right, left and centre. As
Qismati and Darwish-i-muhammad *Sarban* in their comings and
goings had seen and got to know all sides of Biana, they were
sent ahead to look for camping-ground on the bank of the Sikri-
lake (*kul*). When we reached the (Madhakur) camp, persons
were sent galloping off to tell Mahdi Khwaja and the Biana
garrison to join me without delay. Humayun's servant Beg
Mirak *Mughul* was sent out with a few braves to get news of
the Pagan. They started that night, and next morning brought
word that he was heard of as having arrived and dismounted at
a place one *kuroh* (2 miles) on our side (*ailkarak*) of Basawar.[3]
On this same day Mahdi Khwaja and Muhammad Sl. Mirza
rejoined us with the troops that had ridden light to Biana.

Fol. 310.

---

1 *durbatur.* This is the first use of the word in the *Babur-nama*; the defacer of
the Elph. Codex has altered it to *auratur.*

2 Shaikh Zain records [Abu'l-fazl also, perhaps quoting from him] that Babur, by
varying diacritical points, changed the name Sikri to Shukri (meaning "thanks"
in Persian) in sign of gratitude for his victory over the Rana. The place became
the Fathpur-sikri of Akbar.

3 Erskine locates this as 10 to 12 miles n.w. of Biana.

(*o. Discomfiture of a reconnoitring party.*)

The begs were appointed in turns for scouting-duty. When it was 'Abdu'l-'aziz's turn, he went out of Sikri, looking neither before nor behind, right out along the road to Kanwa which is 5 *kuroh* (10 m.) away. The Rana must have been marching forward; he heard of our men's moving out in their reinless (*jalau-siz*) way, and made 4 or 5000 of his own fall suddenly on them. With 'Abdu'l-'aziz and Mulla Apaq may have been 1000 to 1500 men; they took no stock of their opponents but just got to grips; they were hurried off at once, many of them being made prisoner.

On news of this, we despatched Khalifa's Muhibb-i-'ali with Khalifa's retainers. Mulla Husain and some others *aubruq-subruq*[1]* were sent to support them,[2] and Muhammad 'Ali *Jang-jang* also. Presumably it was before the arrival of this first, Muhibb-i-'ali's, reinforcement that the Pagan had hurried off 'Abdu'l-'aziz and his men, taken his standard, martyred Mulla Ni'mat, Mulla Daud and the younger brother of Mulla Apaq, with several more. Directly the reinforcement arrived the pagans overcame Tahir-tibri, the maternal uncle of Khalifa's Muhibb-i-'ali, who had not got up with the hurrying reinforcement [?].[3] Meantime Muhibb-i-'ali even had been thrown down,

Fol. 310b.

1 This phrase has not occurred in the B.N. before; presumably it expresses what has not yet been expressed; this Erskine's rendering, "each according to the speed of his horse," does also. The first Persian translation, which in this portion is by Muhammad-quli *Mughul Hisari*, translates by *az dambal yak digar* (I.O. 215, f. 205b); the second, 'Abdu'r-rahim's, merely reproduces the phrase; De Courteille (ii, 272) appears to render it by (amirs) *que je ne nomme pas*. If my reading of Tahir-tibri's failure be correct (*infra*), Erskine's translation suits the context.

2 The passage cut off by my asterisks has this outside interest that it forms the introduction to the so-called "Fragments", that is, to certain Turki matter not included in the standard *Babur-nama*, but preserved with the Kehr – Ilminsky – de Courteille text. As is well-known in Baburiana, opinion has varied as to the genesis of this matter; there is now no doubt that it is a translation into Turki from the (*Persian*) *Akbar-nama*, prefaced by the above-asterisked passage of the *Babur-nama* and continuous (with slight omissions) from Bib. Ind. ed. i, 106 to 120 (trs. H. Beveridge i, 260 to 282). It covers the time from before the battle of Kanwa to the end of Abu'l-fazl's description of Babur's death, attainments and Court; it has been made to seem Babur's own, down to his death-bed, by changing the third person of A.F.'s narrative into the autobiographical first person. (*Cf.* Ilminsky, p. 403 l. 4 and p. 494; *Mémoires* ii, 272 and 443 to 464; JRAS. 1908, p. 76.)

A minute point in the history of the B.N. manuscripts may be placed on record here; *viz.* that the variants from the true *Babur-nama* text which occur in the Kehr – Ilminsky one, occur also in the corrupt Turki text of I.O. No. 214 (JRAS 1900, p. 455).

3 *chapar kumak yitmas*, perhaps implying that the speed of his horses was not equal to that of Muhibb-i-'ali's. Translators vary as to the meaning of the phrase.

but Baltu getting in from the rear, brought him out. The enemy pursued for over a *kuroh* (2 m.), stopped however at the sight of the black mass of Muh. 'Ali *Jang-jang*'s troops.

Foot upon foot news came that the foe had come near and nearer. We put on our armour and our horses' mail, took our arms and, ordering the carts to be dragged after us, rode out at the gallop. We advanced one *kuroh*. The foe must have turned aside.

(*p. Babur fortifies his camp.*)

For the sake of water, we dismounted with a large lake (*kul*) on one side of us. Our front was defended by carts chained together, the space between each two, across which the chains stretched, being 7 or 8 *qari* (*circa* yards). Mustafa *Rumi* had

Fol. 311.

had the carts made in the Rumi way, excellent carts, very strong and suitable.[1] As Ustad 'Ali-quli was jealous of him, Mustafa was posted to the right, in front of Humayun. Where the carts did not reach to, Khurasani and Hindustani spadesmen and miners were made to dig a ditch.

Owing to the Pagan's rapid advance, to the fighting-work in Biana and to the praise and laud of the pagans made by Shah Mansur, Qismati and the rest from Biana, people in the army shewed sign of want of heart. On the top of all this came the defeat of 'Abdu'l-'aziz. In order to hearten our men, and give a look of strength to the army, the camp was defended and shut in where there were no carts, by stretching ropes of raw hide on wooden tripods, set 7 or 8 *qari* apart. Time had drawn out to 20 or 25 days before these appliances and materials were fully ready.[2]

(*q. A reinforcement from Kabul.*)

Just at this time there arrived from Kabul Qasim-i-husain Sl. (*Auzbeg Shaiban*) who is the son of a daughter of Sl. Husain M. (*Bai-qara*), and with him Ahmad-i-yusuf (*Aughlaqchi*), Qawwam-i-aurdu Shah and also several single friends of mine,

---

1 Erskine and de Courteille both give Mustafa the commendation the Turki and Persian texts give to the carts.

2 According to Tod's *Rajastan*, negotiations went on during the interval, having for their object the fixing of a frontier between the Rana and Babur. They were conducted by a "traitor" Salah'd-din *Tuar* the chief of Raisin, who moreover is said to have deserted to Babur during the battle.

counting up in all to 500 men. Muhammad Sharif, the astrologer of ill-augury, came with them too, so did Baba Dost the water-bearer (*suchi*) who, having gone to Kabul for wine, had there Fol. 311*b*. loaded three strings of camels with acceptable Ghazni wines.

At a time such as this, when, as has been mentioned, the army was anxious and afraid by reason of past occurrences and vicissitudes, wild words and opinions, this Muhammad Sharif, the ill-augurer, though he had not a helpful word to say to me, kept insisting to all he met, "Mars is in the west in these days;[1] who comes into the fight from this (east) side will be defeated." Timid people who questioned the ill-augurer, became the more shattered in heart. We gave no ear to his wild words, made no change in our operations, but got ready in earnest for the fight.

(*Feb. 24th*) On Sunday the 22nd (of Jumada I.) Shaikh Jamal was sent to collect all available quiver-wearers from between the two waters (Ganges and Jumna) and from Dihli, so that with this force he might over-run and plunder the Miwat villages, leaving nothing undone which could awaken the enemy's anxiety for that side. Mulla Tirik-i-'ali, then on his way from Kabul, was ordered to join Shaikh Jamal and to neglect nothing of ruin and plunder in Miwat; orders to the same purport were given also to Maghfur the Diwan. They went; they over-ran and raided a few villages in lonely corners (*bujqaq*); they took some prisoners; but their passage through did not arouse much anxiety!

(*r. Babur renounces wine.*)

On Monday the 23rd of the first Jumada (Feb. 25th), when Fol. 312. I went out riding, I reflected, as I rode, that the wish to cease from sin had been always in my mind, and that my forbidden acts had set lasting stain upon my heart. Said I, "Oh! my soul!"

> (*Persian*) "How long wilt thou draw savour from sin?
> Repentance is not without savour, taste it!"[2]

---

1 *Cf.* f. 89 for Babur's disastrous obedience to astrological warning.
2 For the reading of this second line, given by the good MSS. *viz. Tauba ham bi maza nist, bachash*, Ilminsky (p. 405) has *Tauba ham bi maza, mast bakhis*, which de Courteille [II, 276] renders by, "*O ivrogne insensé! que ne goûtes-tu aussi à la pénitence?*" The Persian couplet seems likely to be a quotation and may yet be found elsewhere. It is not in the Rampur Diwan which contains the Turki verses following it (E. D. Ross p. 21).

(*Turki*) Through years how many has sin defiled thee?
How much of peace has transgression given thee?
How much hast thou been thy passions' slave?
How much of thy life flung away?

With the Ghazi's resolve since now thou hast marched,
Thou hast looked thine own death in the face!
Who resolves to hold stubbornly fast to the death,
Thou knowest what change he attains,

That far he removes him from all things forbidden,
That from all his offences he cleanses himself.
With my own gain before me, I vowed to obey,
In this my transgression,[1] the drinking of wine.[2]

The flagons and cups of silver and gold, the vessels of feasting,
I had them all brought;
I had them all broken up[3] then and there.
Thus eased I my heart by renouncement of wine.

The fragments of the gold and silver vessels were shared out
to deserving persons and to darwishes. The first to agree in
renouncing wine was 'Asas;[4] he had already agreed also about
leaving his beard untrimmed.[5] That night and next day some
Fol. 312*b.* 300 begs and persons of the household, soldiers and not soldiers,
renounced wine. What wine we had with us was poured on the
ground; what Baba Dost had brought was ordered salted to
make vinegar. At the place where the wine was poured upon
the ground, a well was ordered to be dug, built up with stone
and having an almshouse beside it. It was already finished in
Muharram 935 (AH.—Sep. 1528 AD.) at the time I went to
Sikri from Dulpur on my way back from visiting Gualiar.

1 *kichmaklik*, to pass over (to exceed?), to ford or go through a river, whence to
transgress. The same metaphor of crossing a stream occurs, in connection with
drinking, on f. 189*b*.
2 This line shews that Babur's renouncement was of wine only; he continued to
eat confections (*ma'jun*).
3 *Cf*. f. 186*b*. Babur would announce his renunciation in Diwan; there too the
forbidden vessels of precious metals would be broken. His few words leave it to his
readers to picture the memorable scene.
4 This night-guard ('*asas*) cannot be the one concerning whom Gul-badan records
that he was the victim of a little joke made at his expense by Babur (H. N. Index *s.n.*).
He seems likely to be the Haji Muh. '*asas* whom Abu'l-fazl mentions in connection
with Kamran in 953 AH. (1547 AD.). He may be the '*asas* who took charge of Babur's
tomb at Agra (*cf*. Gul-badan's H. N. *s.n.* Muh. 'Ali '*asas taghai*, and *Akbar-nama* trs. i, 502).
5 *saqali qirqmaqta u quimaqta*. Erskine here notes that "a vow to leave the beard
untrimmed was made sometimes by persons who set out against the infidels.
They did not trim the beard till they returned victorious. Some vows of similar
nature may be found in Scripture", *e.g.* II Samuel, cap. 19 v. 24.

(*s. Remission of a due.*)

I had vowed already that, if I gained the victory over Sanga the pagan, I would remit the *tamgha*[1] to all Musalmans. Of this vow Darwish-i-muhammad *Sarban* and Shaikh Zain reminded me at the time I renounced wine. Said I, "You do well to remind me."

The tamgha was remitted to all Musalmans of the dominions I held.[2] I sent for the clerks (*munshilar*), and ordered them to write for their news-letters (*akhbar*) the *farman* concerning the two important acts that had been done. Shaikh Zain wrote the *farman* with his own elegance (*inshasi bila*) and his fine letter (*insha*) was sent to all my dominions. It is as follows:——[3]

FARMAN ANNOUNCING BABUR'S RENUNCIATION OF WINE[4]

[5] *Let us praise the Long-suffering One who loveth the penitent and who loveth the cleansers of themselves; and let thanks be rendered to the Gracious One who absolveth His debtors, and forgiveth those who seek forgiveness. Blessings be upon Muhammad the Crown of Creatures, on the Holy family, on the pure Companions,* and on the mirrors of the glorious congregation, to wit, the Masters of Wisdom who are treasure-houses of the pearls of purity and who bear the impress of the sparkling jewels of this purport:—that the nature of man is prone to evil, and that the abandonment of sinful appetites is only feasible by Divine aid   Fol. 313.

1 The *tamgha* was not really abolished until Jahangir's time—if then (H. Beveridge). *See* Thomas' *Revenue Resources of the Mughal Empire*.

2 There is this to notice here:—Babur's narrative has made the remission of the *tamgha* contingent on his success, but the *farman* which announced that remission is dated some three weeks before his victory over Rana Sanga (Jumada II, 13th—March 16th). Manifestly Babur's remission was absolute and made at the date given by Shaikh Zain as that of the *farman*. The *farman* seems to have been despatched as soon as it was ready, but may have been inserted in Babur's narrative at a later date, together with the preceding paragraph which I have asterisked.

3 "There is a lacuna in the Turki copy" (*i.e.* the Elphinstone Codex) "from this place to the beginning of the year 935. Till then I therefore follow only Mr. Metcalfe's and my own Persian copies" (Erskine).

4 I am indebted to my husband for this revised version of the *farman*. He is indebted to M. de Courteille for help generally, and specially for the references to the Qoran (*q.v. infra*).

5 The passages in italics are Arabic in the original, and where traced to the Qoran, are in Sale's words.

and the help that cometh from on high. "*Every soul is prone unto evil*,"[1] (and again) "*This is the bounty of God; He will give the same unto whom He pleaseth; and God is endued with great bounty*."[2]

Our motive for these remarks and for repeating these statements is that, by reason of human frailty, of the customs of kings and of the great, all of us, from the Shah to the sipahi, in the heyday of our youth, have transgressed and done what we ought not to have done. After some days of sorrow and repentance, we abandoned evil practices one by one, and the gates of retrogression became closed. But the renunciation of wine, the greatest and most indispensable of renunciations, remained under a veil in the chamber of deeds *pledged to appear in due season*, and did not show its countenance until the glorious hour when we had put on the garb of the holy warrior and had encamped with the army of Islam over against the infidels in order to slay them. On this occasion I received a secret inspiration and heard an infallible voice say "*Is not the time yet come unto those who believe, that their hearts should humbly submit to the admonition of God, and that truth which hath been revealed?*"[3] Thereupon we set ourselves to extirpate the things of wickedness, and we earnestly knocked at the gates of repentance. The Guide of Help assisted us, according to the saying "*Whoever knocks and re-knocks, to him it will be opened*", and an order was given that with the Holy War there should begin the still greater war which has to be waged against sensuality. In short, we declared with sincerity that *we would subjugate our passions*, and I engraved on the tablet of my heart "*I turn unto Thee with repentance, and I am the first of true believers*".[4] And I made public the resolution to abstain from wine, which had been hidden in the treasury of my breast. The victorious servants, in accordance with the illustrious order, dashed upon the earth of contempt and destruction the flagons and the cups, and the other utensils in gold and silver, which in their number and their brilliance were like the stars of the firmament. They dashed them in pieces, as, God willing! soon

Fol. 313*b*.

1 *Qoran*, Surah XII, v. 53. 2 *Surah* LVII, v. 21.
3 *Surah* LVII, v. 15. 4 *Surah* VII, v. 140.

will be dashed the gods of the idolaters,—and they distributed the fragments among the poor and needy. By the blessing of this acceptable repentance, many of the courtiers, by virtue of the saying that *men follow the religion of their kings*, embraced abstinence at the same assemblage, and entirely renounced the use of wine, and up till now crowds of our subjects hourly attain this auspicious happiness. I hope that in accordance with the saying "*He who incites to good deeds has the same reward as he who does them*" the benefit of this action will react on the royal fortune and increase it day by day by victories.

After carrying out this design an universal decree was issued that in the imperial dominions—May God protect them from every danger and calamity—no-one shall partake of strong drink, or engage in its manufacture, nor sell it, nor buy it or possess it, nor convey it or fetch it. "*Beware of touching it.*" "*Perchance this will give you prosperity.*"[1]

Fol. 314.

In thanks for these great victories,[2] and as a thank-offering for God's acceptance of repentance and sorrow, the ocean of the royal munificence became commoved, and those waves of kindness, which are the cause of the civilization of the world and of the glory of the sons of Adam, were displayed,—and throughout all the territories the tax (*tamgha*) on Musalmans was abolished,—though its yield was more than the dreams of avarice, and though it had been established and maintained by former rulers,—for it is a practice outside of the edicts of the Prince of Apostles (Muhammad). So a decree was passed that in no city, town, road, ferry, pass, or port, should the tax be levied or exacted. No alteration whatsoever of this order is to be permitted. "*Whoever after hearing it makes any change therein, the sin of such change will be upon him.*"[3]

The proper course (*sabil*) for all who shelter under the shade of the royal benevolence, whether they be Turk, Tajik, 'Arab, Hindi, or Farsi (Persian), peasants or soldiers, of every nation or tribe

1 *Surah* II, v. 185.
2 These may be self-conquests as has been understood by Erskine (p. 356) and de Courteille (ii. 281) but as the Divine "acceptance" would seem to Babur vouched for by his military success, "victories" may stand for his success at Kanwa.
3 *Surah* II, 177 where, in Sale's translation, the change referred to is the special one of altering a legacy.

of the sons of Adam, is to strengthen themselves by the tenets of religion, and to be full of hope and prayer for the dynasty which is linked with eternity, and to adhere to these ordinances, and not in any way to transgress them. It behoves all to act according to this *farman*; they are to accept it as authentic when it comes attested by the Sign-Manual.

Written by order of the Exalted one,—May his excellence endure for ever! on the 24th of Jumada I. 933 (February 26th 1527).

(t. Alarm in Babur's camp.)

Fol. 314b.   In these days, as has been mentioned, (our people) great and small, had been made very anxious and timid by past occurrences. No manly word or brave counsel was heard from any one soever. What bold speech was there from the wazirs who are to speak out (*diguchi*), or from the amirs who will devour the land (*wilayat-yighuchi*)?[1] None had advice to give, none a bold plan of his own to expound. Khalifa (however) did well in this campaign, neglecting nothing of control and supervision, painstaking and diligence.

At length after I had made enquiry concerning people's want of heart and had seen their slackness for myself, a plan occurred to me; I summoned all the begs and braves and said to them, "Begs and braves!

(Persian)	Who comes into the world will die; What lasts and lives will be God.
(Turki)	He who hath entered the assembly of life, Drinketh at last of the cup of death.
	He who hath come to the inn of life, Passeth at last from Earth's house of woe.

---

1 The words *diguchi* and *yiguchi* are translated in the second *Waqi'at-i-baburi* by *sukhan-gui* and [*wilayat*]-*khwar*. This ignores in them the future element supplied by their component *gu* which would allow them to apply to conditions dependent on Babur's success. The Hai. MS. and Ilminsky read *tiguchi*, supporter- or helper-to-be, in place of the *yiguchi*, eater-to-be I have inferred from the *khwar* of the Pers. translation; hence de Courteille writes "*amirs auxquels incombait l'obligation de raffermir le gouvernement*". But Erskine, using the Pers. text alone, and thus having *khwar* before him, translates by, "amirs who enjoyed the wealth of kingdoms." The two Turki words make a depreciatory "jingle", but the first one, *diguchi*, may imply serious reference to the duty, declared by Muhammad to be incumbent upon a wazir, of reminding his sovereign "when he forgetteth his duty". Both may be taken as alluding to dignities to be attained by success in the encounter from which wazirs and amirs were shrinking.

"Better than life with a bad name, is death with a good one.

> (*Persian*) Well is it with me, if I die with good name!
> A good name must I have, since the body is death's.[1]

"God the Most High has allotted to us such happiness and has created for us such good-fortune that we die as martyrs, we kill as avengers of His cause. Therefore must each of you take oath ~~Fol. 315.~~ upon His Holy Word that he will not think of turning his face from this foe, or withdraw from this deadly encounter so long as life is not rent from his body." All those present, beg and retainer, great and small, took the Holy Book joyfully into their hands and made vow and compact to this purport. The plan was perfect; it worked admirably for those near and afar, for seers and hearers, for friend and foe.

(*u. Babur's perilous position.*)

In those same days trouble and disturbance arose on every side:—Husain Khan *Nuhani* went and took Rapri; Qutb Khan's man took Chandwar;[2] a mannikin called Rustam Khan who had collected quiver-wearers from Between-the-two-waters (Ganges and Jamna), took Kul (Koel) and made Kichik 'Ali prisoner; Khwaja Zahid abandoned Sambal and went off; Sl. Muhammad *Duldai* came from Qanuj to me; the Gualiar pagans laid siege to that fort; 'Alam Khan when sent to reinforce it, did not go to Gualiar but to his own district. Every day bad news came from every side. Desertion of many Hindustanis set in; Haibat Khan *Karg-andaz*[3] deserted and went to Sambal; Hasan Khan of Bari deserted and joined the Pagan. We gave attention to none of them but went straight on with our own affair.

(*v. Babur advances to fight.*)

The apparatus and appliances, the carts and wheeled tripods being ready, we arrayed in right, left and centre, and marched forward on New Year's Day,[4] Tuesday, the 9th of the second ~~Fol. 315b.~~ Jumada (March 13th), having the carts[5] and wheeled tripods

---

1 Firdausi's *Shah-nama* [Erskine]. *See* Additional Notes, p. 800.
2 Also Chand-wal; it is 25 m. east of Agra and on the Jamna [*Tabaqat-i-nasiri*, Raverty, p. 742 n.9].
3 Probably, Overthrower of the rhinoceros, but if *Gurg-andaz* be read, of the wolf.
4 According to the Persian calendar this is the day the Sun enters Aries.
5 The practical purpose of this order of march is shewn in the account of the battle of Panipat, and in the Letter of Victory, f. 319.

moving in front of us, with Ustad 'Ali-quli and all the matchlock-men ranged behind them in order that these men, being on foot, should not be left behind the array but should advance with it.

When the various divisions, right, left and centre, had gone each to its place, I galloped from one to another to give encouragement to begs, braves, and *sipahis*. After each man had had assigned to him his post and usual work with his company, we advanced, marshalled on the plan determined, for as much as one *kuroh* (2 m.)[1] and then dismounted.

The Pagan's men, for their part, were on the alert; they came from their side, one company after another.

The camp was laid out and strongly protected by ditch and carts. As we did not intend to fight that day, we sent a few unmailed braves ahead, who were to get to grips with the enemy and thus take an omen. They made a few pagans prisoner, cut off and brought in their heads. Malik Qasim also cut off and brought in a few heads; he did well. By these successes the hearts of our men became very strong.

When we marched on next day, I had it in my mind to fight, but Khalifa and other well-wishers represented that the camping-ground previously decided on was near and that it would favour our fortunes if we had a ditch and defences made there and went there direct. Khalifa accordingly rode off to get Fol. 316. the ditch dug; he settled its position with the spades-men, appointed overseers of the work and returned to us.

(w. The battle of Kanwa.)[2]

On Saturday the 13th of the second Jumada (March 17th, 1527 AD.) we had the carts dragged in front of us (as before), made a *kuroh* (2 m.) of road, arrayed in right, left and centre, and dismounted on the ground selected.

---

1 *kurohcha*, perhaps a short *kuroh*, but I have not found Babur using *cha* as a diminutive in such a case as *kurohcha*.

2 or Kanua, in the Biana district and three marches from Biana-town. "It had been determined on by Rana Sangram Singh (*i.e.* Sanga) for the northern limit of his dominions, and he had here built a small palace." Tod thus describes Babur's foe, "Sanga Rana was of the middle stature, and of great muscular strength, fair in complexion, with unusually large eyes which appear to be peculiar to his descendants. He exhibited at his death but the fragments of a warrior: one eye was lost in the broil with his brother, an arm in action with the Lodi kings of Dehli, and he was a cripple owing to a limb being broken by a cannon-ball in another; while he counted 80 wounds from the sword or the lance on various parts of his body" (Tod's *Rajastan*, cap. Annals of Mewar).

A few tents had been set up; a few were in setting up when news of the appearance of the enemy was brought. Mounting instantly, I ordered every man to his post and that our array should be protected with the carts.[1]

* As the following Letter-of-victory (*Fath-nama*) which is what Shaikh Zain had indited, makes known particulars about the army of Islam, the great host of the pagans with the position of their arrayed ranks, and the encounters had between them and the army of Islam, it is inserted here without addition or deduction.[2]

SHAIKH ZAIN'S LETTER-OF-VICTORY

(a. Introduction.)

Praise be to God the Faithful Promiser, the Helper of His servants, the Supporter of His armies, the Scatterer of hostile hosts, the One alone without whom there is nothing.

Fol. 316b.

1 Here M. de C. has the following note (ii, 273 n.); it supplements my own of f. 264 [n. 3]. "*Le mot araba, que j'ai traduit par chariot est pris par M. Leyden*" (this should be Erskine) "*dans le sens de 'gun', ce que je ne crois pas exact; tout au plus signifierait-il affût*" (gun-carriage). "*Il me parait impossible d'admettre que Baber eût à sa disposition une artillerie attelée aussi considérable. Ces araba pouvaient servir en partie à transporter des pièces de campagne, mais ils avaient aussi une autre destination, comme on le voit par la suite du récit.*" It does not appear to me that Erskine *translates* the word *araba* by the word *gun*, but that the *arabas* (all of which he took to be gun-carriages) being there, he supposed the guns. This was not correct as the various passages about carts as defences show.

2 It is characteristic of Babur that he reproduces Shaikh Zain's *Fath-nama*, not because of its eloquence but because of its useful details. Erskine and de Courteille have the following notes concerning Shaikh Zain's *farman*:—"Nothing can form a more striking contrast to the simple, manly and intelligent style of Baber himself, than the pompous, laboured periods of his secretary. Yet I have never read this Firman to any native of India who did not bestow unlimited admiration on the official bombast of Zeineddin, while I have met with none but Turks who paid due praise to the calm simplicity of Baber" [Mems. p. 359]."*Comme la précédente (farman), cette pièce est rédigée en langue persane et offre un modèle des plus accomplis du style en usage dans les chancelleries orientales. La traduction d'un semblable morceau d'éloquence est de la plus grande difficulté, si on veut être clair, tout en restant fidèle à l'original.*"

Like the Renunciation *farman*, the Letter-of-victory with its preceding sentence which I have asterisked, was probably inserted into Babur's narrative somewhat later than the battle of Kanwa. Hence Babur's pluperfect-tense "had indited". I am indebted to my husband for help in revising the difficult *Fath-nama*; he has done it with consideration of the variants between the earlier English and the French translations. No doubt it could be dealt with more searchingly still by one well-versed in the Qoran and the Traditions, and thus able to explain others of its allusions. The italics denote Arabic passages in the original; many of these are from the Qoran, and in tracing them M. de Courteille's notes have been most useful to us.

O Thou the Exalter of the pillars of Islam, Helper of thy faithful minister, Overthrower of the pedestals of idols, Overcomer of rebellious foes, Exterminator to the uttermost of the followers of darkness!

Lauds be to God the Lord of the worlds, and may the blessing of God be upon the best of His creatures Muhammad, Lord of ghazis and champions of the Faith, and upon his companions, the pointers of the way, until the Day of Judgment.

The successive gifts of the Almighty are the cause of frequent praises and thanksgivings, and the number of these praises and thanksgivings is, in its turn, the cause of the constant succession of God's mercies. For every mercy a thanksgiving is due, and every thanksgiving is followed by a mercy. To render full thanks is beyond men's power; the mightiest are helpless to discharge their obligations. Above all, adequate thanks cannot be rendered for a benefit than which none is greater in the world and nothing is more blessed, in the world to come, to wit, victory over most powerful infidels and dominion over wealthiest heretics, "*these are the unbelievers, the wicked.*"[1] In the eyes of the judicious, no blessing can be greater than this. Thanks be to God! that this great blessing and mighty boon, which from the cradle until now has been the real object of this right-thinking mind (Babur's), has now manifested itself by the graciousness of the King of the worlds; the Opener who dispenses his treasures without awaiting solicitation, hath opened them with a master-key before our victorious Nawab (Babur),[2] so that the names of our[3] conquering heroes have been emblazoned in the records of glorious *ghazis*. By the help of our victorious soldiers the

Fol. 317.   standards of Islam have been raised to the highest pinnacles. The account of this auspicious fortune is as follows:—

1 Qoran, cap. 80, last sentence.

2 Shaikh Zain, in his version of the *Babur-nama*, styles Babur Nawab where there can be no doubt of the application of the title, *viz.* in describing Shah Tahmasp's gifts to him (mentioned by Babur on f. 305). He uses the title also in the *farman* of renunciation (f. 313*b*), but it does not appear in my text, "royal" (fortune) standing for it (*in loco* p. 555, l. 10).

3 The possessive pronoun occurs several times in the Letter-of-victory. As there is no semblance of putting forward that letter as being Babur's, the pronoun seems to imply "on our side".

(b. Rana Sanga and his forces.)

When the flashing-swords of our Islam-guarded soldiers had illuminated the land of Hindustan with rays of victory and conquest, as has been recorded in former letters-of-victory,[1] the Divine favour caused our standards to be upreared in the territories of Dihli, Agra, Jun-pur, Kharid,[2] Bihar, *etc.*, when many chiefs, both pagans and Muhammadans submitted to our generals and shewed sincere obedience to our fortunate Nawab. But Rana Sanga the pagan who in earlier times breathed submissive to the Nawab,[3] now *was puffed up with pride and became of the number of unbelievers.*[4] Satan-like he threw back his head and collected an army of accursed heretics, thus gathering a rabble-rout of whom some wore the accursed torque (*tauq*), the *zinar*,[5] on the neck, some had in the skirt the calamitous thorn of apostasy.[6] Previous to the rising in Hindustan of the Sun of dominion and the emergence there of the light of the Shahanshah's Khalifate [*i.e.* Babur's] the authority of that execrated pagan (Sanga)—*at the Judgment Day he shall have no friend,*[7] was such that not one of all the exalted sovereigns of this wide realm, such as the Sultan of Dihli, the Sultan of Gujrat and the Sultan of Mandu, could cope with this evil-dispositioned one, without the help of other pagans; one and all they cajoled him and temporized with him; and he had this authority although the rajas and rais of high degree, who obeyed him in this battle, and the governors and commanders

Fol. 317b.

---

1 The *Babur-nama* includes no other than Shaikh Zain's about Kanwa. Those here alluded to will be the announcements of success at Milwat, Panipat, Dibalpur and perhaps elsewhere in Hindustan.

2 In Jun-pur (*Ayin-i-akbari*); Elliot & Dowson note (iv, 283–4) that it appears to have included, near Sikandarpur, the country on both sides of the Gogra, and thence on that river's left bank down to the Ganges.

3 That the word Nawab here refers to Babur and not to his lieutenants, is shewn by his mention (f. 298) of Sanga's messages to himself.

4 Qoran, cap. 2, v. 32. The passage quoted is part of a description of Satan, hence mention of Satan in Shaikh Zain's next sentence.

5 The brahminical thread.

6 *khar-i-mihnat-i-irtidad dar daman*. This Erskine renders by "who fixed thorns from the pangs of apostasy in the hem of their garments" (p. 360). Several good MSS. have *khar*, thorn, but Ilminsky has Ar. *khimar*, cymar, instead (p. 411). De Courteille renders the passage by "*portent au pan de leurs habits la marque douloureuse de l'apostasie*" (ii, 290). To read *khimar*, cymar (scarf), would serve, as a scarf is part of some Hindu costumes.

7 Qoran, cap. 69, v. 35.

who were amongst his followers in this conflict, had not obeyed him in any earlier fight or, out of regard to their own dignity, been friendly with him. Infidel standards dominated some 200 towns in the territories of Islam; in them mosques and shrines fell into ruin; from them the wives and children of the Faithful were carried away captive. So greatly had his forces grown that, according to the Hindu calculation by which one *lak* of revenue should yield 100 horsemen, and one *krur* of revenue, 10,000 horsemen, the territories subject to the Pagan (Sanga) yielding 10 *krurs*, should yield him 100,000 horse. Many noted pagans who hitherto had not helped him in battle, now swelled his ranks out of hostility to the people of Islam. Ten powerful chiefs, each the leader of a pagan host, uprose in rebellion, as smoke rises, and linked themselves, as though enchained, to that perverse one (Sanga); and this infidel decade who, unlike the blessed ten,[1] uplifted misery-freighted standards which *denounce unto them excruciating punishment*,[2] had many dependants, and troops, and wide-extended lands. As, for instance, Salahu'd-din[3] had territory yielding 30,000 horse, Rawal Udai Singh of Bagar had 12,000, Medini Rai had 12,000, Hasan Khan of Miwat had 12,000, Bar-mal of Idr had 4000, Narpat Hara had 7000, Satrvi of Kach (Cutch) had 6000, Dharm-deo had 4000, Bir-sing-deo had 4000, and Mahmud Khan, son of Sl. Sikandar, to whom, though he possessed neither district nor *pargana*, 10,000 horse had gathered in hope of his attaining supremacy. Thus, according to the calculation of Hind, 201,000 was the total of those sundered from salvation. In brief, that haughty pagan, inwardly blind, and hardened of

---

1 M. Defrémery, when reviewing the French translation of the B.N. (*Journal des Savans* 1873), points out (p. 18) that it makes no mention of the "blessed ten". Erskine mentions them but without explanation. They are the '*asharah mubash-sharah*, the decade of followers of Muhammad who "received good tidings", and whose certain entry into Paradise he foretold.

2 Qoran, cap. 3, v. 20. M. Defrémery reads Shaikh Zain to mean that these words of the Qoran were on the infidel standards, but it would be simpler to read Shaikh Zain as meaning that the infidel insignia on the standards "denounce punishment" on their users.

3 He seems to have been a Rajput convert to Muhammadanism who changed his Hindi name Silhadi for what Babur writes. His son married Sanga's daughter; his fiefs were Raisin and Sarangpur; he deserted to Babur in the battle of Kanwa. (*Cf.* Erskine's *History of India* i, 471 note; *Mirat-i-sikandari*, Bayley's trs. *s.n.*; *Akbar-nama*, H.B.'s trs. i, 261; Tod's *Rajastan* cap. Mewar.)

heart, having joined with other pagans, dark-fated and doomed to perdition, advanced to contend with the followers of Islam and to destroy the foundations of the law of the Prince of Men (Muhammad), on whom be God's blessing! The protagonists of the royal forces fell, like divine destiny, on that one-eyed Dajjal[1] who, to understanding men, shewed the truth of the saying, *When Fate arrives, the eye becomes blind*, and, setting before their eyes the scripture which saith, *Whosoever striveth to promote the true religion, striveth for the good of his own soul*,[2] they acted on the precept to which obedience is due, *Fight against infidels and hypocrites*.

Fol. 318*b*.

(*c. Military movements.*)

(*March 17th, 1527*) On Saturday the 13th day of the second Jumada of the date 933, a day blessed by the words, *God hath blessed your Saturday*, the army of Islam was encamped near the village of Kanwa, a dependency of Biana, hard by a hill which was 2 *kurohs* (4 m.) from the enemies of the Faith. When those accursed infidel foes of Muhammad's religion heard the reverberation of the armies of Islam, they arrayed their ill-starred forces and moved forward with one heart, relying on their mountain-like, demon-shaped elephants, as had relied the Lords of the Elephant[3] who went to overthrow the sanctuary (*ka'ba*) of Islam.

1 "Dejal or al Masih al Dajjal, the false or lying Messiah, is the Muhammadan Anti-christ. He is to be one-eyed, and marked on the forehead with the letters K.FR. signifying Kafer, or Infidel. He is to appear in the latter days riding on an ass, and will be followed by 70,000 Jews of Ispahan, and will continue on the Earth 40 days, of which one will be equal to a year, another to a month, another to a week, and the rest will be common days. He is to lay waste all places, but will not enter Mekka or Medina, which are to be guarded by angels. He is finally to be slain at the gate of Lud by Jesus, for whom the Musalmans profess great veneration, calling him the breath or spirit of God.—*See* Sale's *Introductory Discourse to the Koran*" [Erskine].
2 Qoran, cap. 29, v. 5.
3 "This alludes to the defeat of [an Abyssinian Christian] Abraha the prince of Yemen who [in the year of Muhammad's birth] marched his army and some elephants to destroy the *ka'ba* of Makka. 'The Meccans,' says Sale, 'at the appearance of so considerable a host, retired to the neighbouring mountains, being unable to defend their city or temple. But God himself undertook the defence of both. For when Abraha drew near to Mecca, and would have entered it, the elephant on which he rode, which was a very large one and named Mahmud, refused to advance any nigher to the town, but knelt down whenever they endeavoured to force him that way, though he would rise and march briskly enough if they turned him towards any other quarter; and while matters were in this posture, on a sudden a large flock of birds, like swallows, came flying from the sea-coast, every-one of which carried three stones,

> "Having these elephants, the wretched Hindus
> Became proud, like the Lords of the Elephant;
> Yet were they odious and vile as is the evening of death,
> Blacker[1] than night, outnumbering the stars,
> All such as fire is[2] but their heads upraised
> In hate, as rises its smoke in the azure sky,
> Ant-like they come from right and from left,
> Thousands and thousands of horse and foot."

Fol. 319. They advanced towards the victorious encampment, intending to give battle. The holy warriors of Islam, trees in the garden of valour, moved forward in ranks straight as serried pines and, like pines uplift their crests to heaven, uplifting their helmet-crests which shone even as shine the hearts of those *that strive in the way of the Lord*; their array was like Alexander's iron-wall,[3] and, as is the way of the Prophet's Law, straight and firm and strong, *as though they were a well-compacted building*;[4] and they became fortunate and successful in accordance with the saying, *They are directed by their Lord, and they shall prosper.*[5]

> In that array no rent was frayed by timid souls;
> Firm was it as the Shahanshah's resolve, strong as the Faith;
> Their standards brushed against the sky;
> *Verily we have granted thee certain victory.*[6]

Obeying the cautions of prudence, we imitated the *ghazis* of Rum by posting matchlockmen (*tufanchian*) and cannoneers (*ra'd-andazan*) along the line of carts which were chained to one another in front of us; in fact, Islam's army was so arrayed and so steadfast that primal Intelligence[7] and the firmament (*'aql-i-pir u charkh-i-asir*) applauded the marshalling thereof. To effect this arrangement and organization, Nizamu'd-din 'Ali Khalifa, the pillar of the Imperial fortune, exerted himself

---

one in each foot and one in its bill; and these stones they threw down upon the heads of Abraha's men, certainly killing every one they struck.' The rest were swept away by a flood or perished by a plague, Abraha alone reaching Senaa, where he also died" [Erskine]. The above is taken from Sale's note to the 105 chapter of the Qoran, entitled "the Elephant".

1 Presumably black by reason of their dark large mass.
2 Presumably, devouring as fire.
3 This is 50 m. long and blocked the narrow pass of the Caspian Iron-gates. It ends south of the Russian town of Dar-band, on the west shore of the Caspian. Erskine states that it was erected to repress the invasions of Yajuj and Mujuj (Gog and Magog).
4 Qoran, cap. lxi, v. 4.
5 Qoran, cap. ii, v. 4. Erskine appears to quote another verse.
6 Qoran, cap. xlviii, v. 1.
7 *Khirad*, Intelligence or the first Intelligence, was supposed to be the guardian of the empyreal heaven (Erskine).

strenuously; his efforts were in accord with Destiny, and were approved by his sovereign's luminous judgment.

(d. Commanders of the centre.)

His Majesty's post was in the centre. In the right-hand of the centre were stationed the illustrious and most upright **Fol. 319b.** brother, the beloved friend of Destiny, the favoured of Him whose aid is entreated (*i.e.* God), Chin-timur Sultan,[1]—the illustrious son, accepted in the sight of the revered Allah, Sulaiman Shah,[2]—the reservoir of sanctity, the way-shower, Khwaja Kamalu'd-din (Perfect-in-the Faith) Dost-i-khawand,— the trusted of the sultanate, the abider near the sublime threshold, the close companion, the cream of associates, Kamalu'd-din Yunas-i-'ali,—the pillar of royal retainers, the perfect in friendship, Jalalu'd-din (Glory-of-the-Faith) Shah Mansur *Barlas*,—the pillar of royal retainers, most excellent of servants, Nizamu'd-din (Upholder-of-the-Faith) Darwish-i-muhammad *Sarban*,—the pillars of royal retainers, the sincere in fidelity, Shihabu'd-din (Meteor-of-the-Faith) 'Abdu'l-lah the librarian and Nizamu'd-din Dost Lord-of-the-Gate.

In the left-hand of the centre took each his post, the reservoir of sovereignty, ally of the Khalifate, object of royal favour, Sultan 'Ala'u'd-din 'Alam Khan son of Sl. Bahlul *Ludi*,—the intimate of illustrious Majesty, the high priest (*dastur*) of *sadrs* amongst men, the refuge of all people, the pillar of Islam, Shaikh Zain of Khawaf,[3]—the pillar of the nobility, Kamalu'd-din Muhibb-i-'ali, son of the intimate counsellor named above (*i.e.* Khalifa),—the pillar of royal retainers, Nizamu'd-din Tardi Beg brother of Quj (son of) Ahmad, whom God hath taken into His mercy,—Shir- **Fol. 320.** afgan son of the above-named Quj Beg deceased,—the pillar of great ones, the mighty khan, Araish Khan,[4]—the wazir, greatest

---

1 Chin-timur *Chingiz-khanid Chaghatai* is called Babur's brother because a (maternal-) cousin of Babur's own generation, their last common ancestor being Yunas Khan.

2 Sulaiman *Timurid Miran-shahi* is called Babur's son because his father was of Babur's generation, their last common ancestor being Sl. Abu-sa'id Mirza. He was 13 years old and, through Shah Begim, hereditary shah of Badakhshan.

3 The Shaikh was able, it would appear, to see himself as others saw him, since the above description of him is his own. It is confirmed by Abu'l-fazl and Badayuni's accounts of his attainments.

4 The honourable post given to this amir of Hind is likely to be due to his loyalty to Babur.

of wazirs amongst men, Khwaja Kamalu'd-din Husain,—and a number of other attendants at Court (*diwanian*).

(*e. Commanders of the right wing.*)

In the right wing was the exalted son, honourable and fortunate, the befriended of Destiny, the Star of the Sign of sovereignty and success, Sun of the sphere of the Khalifate, lauded of slave and free, Muhammad Humayun Bahadur. On that exalted prince's right hand there were, one whose rank approximates to royalty and who is distinguished by the favour of the royal giver of gifts, Qasim-i-husain Sultan,—the pillar of the nobility Nizamu'd-din Ahmad-i-yusuf *Aughlaqchi*,[1]—the trusted of royalty, most excellent of servants, Jalalu'd-din Hindu Beg *quchin*,[2]—the trusted of royalty, perfect in loyalty, Jalalu'd-din Khusrau Kukuldash,—the trusted of royalty, Qawam (var. Qiyam) Beg *Aurdu-shah*,—the pillar of royal retainers, of perfect sincerity, Wali *Qara-quzi* the treasurer,[3]—the pillar of royal retainers, Nizamu'd-din Pir-quli of Sistan,—the pillar of wazirs, Khwaja Kamalu'd-din *pahlawan* (champion) of Badakhshan,— the pillar of royal retainers, 'Abdu'l-shakur,—the pillar of the nobility, most excellent of servants, the envoy from 'Iraq Sulaiman Aqa,—and Husain Aqa the envoy from Sistan. On the victory-crowned left of the fortunate son already named there were, the sayyid of lofty birth, of the family of Murtiza ('Ali), Mir Hama,—the pillar of royal retainers, the perfect in sincerity, Shamsu'd-din Muhammadi Kukuldash and Nizamu'd-din Khwajagi Asad *jan-dar*.[4] In the right wing

Fol. 320b.

1 Ahmad Beg, a nephew of Yusuf of the same agnomen (Index *s.nn.*).

2 I have not discovered the name of this old servant or the meaning of his seeming-sobriquet, Hindu. As a *quchin* he will have been a Mughul or Turk. The circumstance of his service with a son of Mahmud *Miran-shahi* (down to 905 AH.) makes it possible that he drew his name in his youth from the tract s.e. of Mahmud's Hisar territory which has been known as Little Hind. This is however conjecture merely. Another suggestion is that as *hindu* can mean *black*, it may stand for the common *qara* of the Turks *e.g.* Qara Barlas, Black Barlas.

3 I am uncertain whether Qara-quzi is the name of a place, or the jesting sobriquet of more than one meaning it can be.

4 Soul-full, animated; var. Hai. MS. *khan-dar*. No agnomen is used for Asad by Babur. The *Akbar-nama* varies to *jamadar*, wardrobe-keeper, cup-holder (*Bib. Ind.* ed. i, 107), and Firishta to *sar-jamadar*, head wardrobe-keeper (lith. ed. p. 209 top). It would be surprising to find such an official sent as envoy to 'Iraq, as Asad was both before and after he fought at Kanwa.

there were, of the amirs of Hind,—the pillar of the State, the Khan-of-Khans, Dilawar Khan,[1]—the pillar of the nobility, Malik Dad *Kararani*,—and the pillar of the nobility, the Shaikh-of-shaikhs, Shaikh Guran, each standing in his appointed place.

(f. Commanders of the left wing.)

In the left wing of the armies of Islam there extended their ranks,—the lord of lofty lineage, the refuge of those in authority, the ornament of the family of *Ta Ha* and *Ya Sin*,[2] the model for the descendants of the prince of ambassadors (Muhammad), Sayyid Mahdi Khwaja,—the exalted and fortunate brother, the well-regarded of his Majesty, Muhammad Sl. Mirza,[3]— the personage approximating to royalty, the descended of monarchs, 'Adil Sultan son of Mahdi Sultan,[4]—the trusted in the State, perfect in attachment, 'Abdu'l-'aziz Master of the Horse,—the trusted in the State, the pure in friendship, Shamsu'd-din Muhammad 'Ali *Jang-jang*,[5]—the pillar of royal retainers, Jalalu'd-din Qutluq-qadam *qarawal* (scout),—the pillar of royal retainers, the perfect in sincerity, Jalalu'd-din Shah Husain *yaragi Mughul Ghanchi*(?),[6]—and Nizamu'd-din Jan-i-muhammad *Beg Ataka*.

Of amirs of Hind there were in this division, the scions of sultans, Kamal Khan and Jalal Khan sons of the Sl. 'Ala'u'd-din above-mentioned,—the most excellent officer 'Ali Khan Shaikh-zada of Farmul,—and the pillar of the nobility, Nizam Khan of Biana.

Fol. 321.

1 son of Daulat Khan *Yusuf-khail Ludi*.
2 These are the titles of the 20th and 36th chapters of the Qoran; Sale offers conjectural explanations of them. The "family" is Muhammad's.
3 a Bai-qara Timurid of Babur's generation, their last common ancestor being Timur himself.
4 an Auzbeg who married a daughter of Sl. Husain M. *Bai-qara*.
5 It has been pointed out to me that there is a Chinese title of nobility *Yun-wang*, and that it may be behind the words *jang-jang*. Though this appears to me improbable, looking to the record of Babur's officer, to the prevalence of sobriquets amongst his people, and to what would be the sporadic appearance of a Chinese title or even class-name borne by a single man amongst them, I add the suggestion to my note on the meaning of the words (p. 370 n. 1). The title *Jun-wang* occurs in Dr. Denison Ross' *Three MSS. from Kashghar*, p. 5, v. 5 and translator's preface, p. 14.
6 *Cf.* f. 266 and f. 299. *Yaragi* may be the name of his office, (*from yaraq*) and mean provisioner of arms or food or other military requirements.

(g. The flanking parties.)

For the flank-movement (*tulghama*) of the right wing there were posted two of the most trusted of the household retainers, Tardika[1] and Malik Qasim the brother of Baba Qashqa, with a body of Mughuls; for the flank-movement of the left wing were the two trusted chiefs Mumin Ataka and Rustam *Turkman*, leading a body of special troops.

(h. The Chief of the Staff.)

The pillar of royal retainers, the perfect in loyalty, the cream of privy-counsellors, Nizamu'd-din Sultan Muhammad *Bakhshi*, after posting the *ghazis* of Islam, came to receive the royal commands. He despatched adjutants (*tawachi*) and messengers (*yasawal*) in various directions to convey imperative orders concerning the marshalling of the troops to the great sultans and amirs. And when the Commanders had taken up their positions, an imperative order was given that none should quit his post or, uncommanded, stretch forth his arm to fight.

(i. The battle.)

One watch[2] of the afore-mentioned day had elapsed when the opposing forces approached each other and the battle began. As Light opposes Darkness, so did the centres of the two armies oppose one another. Fighting began on the right and left wings, such fighting as shook the Earth and filled highest Heaven with clangour.

Fol. 321b.

The left wing of the ill-fated pagans advanced against the right wing of the Faith-garbed troops of Islam and charged down on Khusrau Kukuldash and Baba Qashqa's brother Malik Qasim. The most glorious and most upright brother Chin-timur Sultan, obeying orders, went to reinforce them and, engaging in the conflict with bold attack, bore the pagans back almost to the rear of their centre. Guerdon was made for the brother's glorious fame.[3] The marvel of the Age, Mustafa of Rum, had his post in the centre (of the right wing) where was the exalted son, upright and fortunate, the object of the favourable regard of

---

1 or, Tardi *yakka*, the champion, Gr. *monomachus* (A.N. trs. i, 107 n.).

2 var. 1 watch and 2 *g'haris*; the time will have been between 9 and 10 a.m.

3 *juldu ba nam al 'aziz-i-baradar shud*, a phrase not easy to translate.

Creative Majesty (*i.e.* God), the one *distinguished by the particular grace of the mighty Sovereign who commands to do and not to do* (*i.e.* Babur), Muhammad Humayun Bahadur. This Mustafa of Rum had the carts (*arabaha*)[1] brought forward and broke the ranks of pagans with matchlock and culverin dark like their hearts (?).[2] In the thick of the fight, the most glorious brother Qasim-i-husain Sultan and the pillars of royal retainers, Nizamu'd-din Ahmad-i-yusuf and Qawam Beg, obeying orders, hastened to their help. And since band after band of pagan troops followed each other to help their men, so we, in our turn, sent the trusted in the State, the glory of the Faith, Hindu Beg, and, after him, the pillars of the nobility, Muhammadi Kukuldash and Khwajagi Asad *jan-dar*, and, after them, the trusted in the State, the trustworthy in the resplendent Court, the most confided-in of nobles, the elect of confidential servants, Yunas-i-'ali, together with the pillar of the nobility, the perfect in friendship, Shah Mansur *Barlas* and the pillar of the grandees, the pure in fidelity, 'Abdu'l-lah the librarian, and after these, the pillar of the nobles, Dost the Lord-of-the-Gate, and Muhammad Khalil the master-gelder (*akhta-begi*).[3]

Fol. 322.

The pagan right wing made repeated and desperate attack on the left wing of the army of Islam, falling furiously on the holy warriors, possessors of salvation, but each time was made to turn back or, smitten with the arrows of victory, was *made to descend into Hell, the house of perdition; they shall be thrown to burn therein, and an unhappy dwelling shall it be.*[4] Then the trusty amongst the nobles, Mumin Ataka and Rustam *Turkman* betook themselves to the rear[5] of the host of darkened pagans; and to help them were sent the Commanders Khwaja Mahmud and 'Ali Ataka, servants of him who amongst the royal retainers is near the throne, the trusted of the Sultanate, Nizamu'd-din 'Ali Khalifa.

1 *viz.* those chained together as a defence and probably also those conveying the culverins.

2 The comparison may be between the darkening smoke of the fire-arms and the heresy darkening pagan hearts.

3 There appears to be a distinction of title between the *akhta-begi* and the *mirakhwur* (master of the horse).

4 Qoran, cap. 14, v. 33.

5 These two men were in one of the flanking-parties.

Our high-born brother[1] Muhammad Sl. Mirza, and the representative of royal dignity, 'Adil Sultan, and the trusted in the State, the strengthener of the Faith, 'Abdu'l-'aziz, the Master of the Horse, and the glory of the Faith, Qutluq-qadam *qarawal*, and the meteor of the Faith, Muhammad 'Ali *Jang-jang*, and the pillar of royal retainers, Shah Husain *yaragi Mughul Ghanchi*(?) stretched out the arm to fight and stood firm. To support them we sent the *Dastur*, the highest of wazirs, Khwaja

Fol. 322b. Kamalu'd-din Husain with a body of *diwanis*.[2] Every holy warrior was eager to show his zeal, entering the fight with desperate joy as if approving the verse, *Say, Do you expect any other should befall us than one of the two most excellent things, victory or martyrdom?*[3] and, with display of life-devotion, uplifted the standard of life-sacrifice.

As the conflict and battle lasted long, an imperative order was issued that the special royal corps (*tabinan-i-khasa-i-padshahi*) who, heroes of one hue,[4] were standing, like tigers enchained, behind the carts,[5] should go out on the right and the left of the centre,[6] leaving the matchlockmen's post in-between, and join battle on both sides. As the True Dawn emerges from its cleft in the horizon, so they emerged from behind the carts; they poured a ruddy crepuscule of the blood of those ill-fated pagans on the nadir of the Heavens, that battle-field; they made fall from the firmament of existence many heads of the headstrong, as stars fall from the firmament of heaven. The marvel of the Age, Ustad 'Ali-quli, who with his own appurtenances stood in front of the centre, did deeds of valour, discharging against the iron-mantled forts of the infidels[7] stones of such size that were (one) put into a scale of the Balance in which actions are weighed, that *scale shall be heavy with good works and he*

---

1 This phrase "our brother" would support the view that Shaikh Zain wrote as for Babur, if there were not, on the other hand, mention of Babur as His Majesty, and the precious royal soul.

2 *diwanian* here may mean those associated with the wazir in his duties: and not those attending at Court.

3 Qoran, cap. 14, v. 52.

4 *hizabran-i-besha yakrangi*, literally, forest-tigers (or, lions) of one hue.

5 There may be reference here to the chains used to connect the carts into a defence.

6 The braves of the *khasa tabin* were part of Babur's own centre.

7 perhaps the cataphract elephants; perhaps the men in mail.

(*i.e.* its owner) *shall lead a pleasing life*;[1] and were such stones discharged against a hill, broad of base and high of summit, it would *become like carded wool*.[2] Such stones Ustad 'Ali-quli discharged at the iron-clad fortress of the pagan ranks and by this discharge of stones, and abundance of culverins and matchlocks (?)[3] destroyed many of the builded bodies of the Fol. 323. pagans. The matchlockmen of the royal centre, in obedience to orders, going from behind the carts into the midst of the battle, each one of them made many a pagan taste of the poison of death. The foot-soldiers, going into a most dangerous place, made their names to be blazoned amongst those of the forest-tigers (*i.e.* heroes) of valour and the champions in the field of manly deeds. Just at this time came an order from his Majesty the Khaqan that the carts of the centre should be advanced; and the gracious royal soul (*i.e.* Babur) moved towards the pagan soldiers, Victory and Fortune on his right, Prestige and Conquest on his left. On witnessing this event, the victorious troops followed from all sides; the whole surging ocean of the army rose in mighty waves; the courage of all the crocodiles[4] of that ocean was manifested by the strength of their deeds; an obscuring cloud of dust o'erspread the sky (?). The dust that gathered over the battle-field was traversed by the lightning-flashes of the sword; the Sun's face was shorn of light as is a mirror's back; the striker and the struck, the victor and the vanquished were commingled, all distinction between them lost. The Wizard of Time produced such a night that its only planets were arrows,[5] its only constellations of fixed stars were the steadfast squadrons.

> Upon that day of battle sank and rose
> Blood to the Fish and dust-clouds to the Moon,
> While through the horse-hoofs on that spacious plain,   Fol. 323*b*.
> One Earth flew up to make another Heaven.[6]

1 Qoran, cap. 101, v. 54.
2 Qoran, cap. 101, v. 4.
3 *ba andakhtan-i-sang u zarb-zan tufak bisyari*. As Babur does not in any place mention metal missiles, it seems safest to translate *sang* by its plain meaning of *stone*.
4 Also, metaphorically, swords.
5 *tir*. My husband thinks there is a play upon the two meanings of this word, arrow and the planet Mercury; so too in the next sentence, that there may be allusion in the *kuakib sawabit* to the constellation Pegasus, opposed to Babur's squadrons of horse.
6 The Fish mentioned in this verse is the one pictured by Muhammadan cosmogony as supporting the Earth. The violence of the fray is illustrated by supposing that of

At the moment when the holy warriors were heedlessly flinging away their lives, they heard a secret voice say, *Be not dismayed, neither be grieved, for, if ye believe, ye shall be exalted above the unbelievers,*[1] and from the infallible Informer heard the joyful words, *Assistance is from God, and a speedy victory! And do thou bear glad tidings to true believers.*[2] Then they fought with such delight that the plaudits of the saints of the Holy Assembly reached them and the angels from near the Throne, fluttered round their heads like moths. Between the first and second Prayers, there was such blaze of combat that the flames thereof raised standards above the heavens, and the right and left of the army of Islam rolled back the left and right of the doomed infidels in one mass upon their centre.

When signs were manifest of the victory of the Strivers and of the up-rearing of the standards of Islam, those accursed infidels and wicked unbelievers remained for one hour confounded. At length, their hearts abandoning life, they fell upon the right and left of our centre. Their attack on the left was the more vigorous and there they approached furthest, but the holy warriors, their minds set on the reward, planted shoots (*nihal*) of arrows in the field of the breast of each one of them, and, such being their gloomy fate, overthrew them. In this state of affairs, the breezes of victory and fortune blew over the meadow of our happy Nawab, and brought the good news, *Verily we have granted thee a manifest victory.*[3] And Victory the beautiful woman (*shahid*) whose world-adornment of waving tresses was embellished by *God will aid you with a mighty aid,*[4] bestowed on us the good fortune that had been hidden behind a veil, and made it a reality. The absurd (*batil*) Hindus, knowing their position perilous, *dispersed like carded wool before the wind*, and *like moths scattered abroad.*[4a] Many fell dead on the field of battle; others, desisting from fighting, fled to the desert of exile and

Fol. 324.

Earth's seven climes, one rose to Heaven in dust, thus giving Heaven eight. The verse is from Firdausi's *Shah-nama*, [Turner-Macan's ed. i, 222]. The translation of it is Warner's, [ii, 15 and n.]. I am indebted for the information given in this note to my husband's long search in the *Shah-nama*.

1 Qoran, cap. 3, v. 133.
2 Qoran, cap. 61, v. 13.
3 Qoran, cap. 48, v. I.
4 Qoran, cap. 48, v. 3.

became the food of crows and kites. Mounds were made of the bodies of the slain, pillars of their heads.

(j. Hindu chiefs killed in the battle.)

Hasan Khan of Miwat was enrolled in the list of the dead by the force of a matchlock (*zarb-i-tufak*); most of those headstrong chiefs of tribes were slain likewise, and ended their days by arrow and matchlock (*tir u tufak*). Of their number was Rawal Udi Singh of Bagar,[1] ruler (*wali*) of the Dungarpur country, who had 12,000 horse, Rai Chandraban *Chuhan* who had 4000 horse, Bhupat Rao son of that Salahu'd-din already mentioned, who was lord of Chandiri and had 6000 horse, Manik-chand *Chuhan* and Dilpat Rao who had each 4000 horse, Kanku (or Gangu) and Karm Singh and Dankusi (?)[2] who had each 3000 horse, and a number of others, each one of whom was leader of a great   Fol. 324*b*. command, a splendid and magnificent chieftain. All these trod the road to Hell, removing from this house of clay to the pit of perdition. The enemy's country (*daru'l-harb*) was full, as Hell is full, of wounded who had died on the road. The lowest pit was gorged with miscreants who had surrendered their souls to the lord of Hell. In whatever direction one from the army of Islam hastened, he found everywhere a self-willed one dead; whatever march the illustrious camp made in the wake of the fugitives, it found no foot-space without its prostrate foe.

> All the Hindus slain, abject (*khwar*, var. *zar*) and mean,
> By matchlock-stones, like the Elephants' lords,[3]
> Many hills of their bodies were seen,
> And from each hill a fount of running blood.
> Dreading the arrows of (our) splendid ranks,
> Passed[4] they in flight to each waste and hill.

4a [see p. 572] *farash*. De Courteille, reading *firash*, translates this metaphor by *comme un lit lorsqu'il est défait*. He refers to Qoran, cap. 101, v. 3. A better metaphor for the breaking up of an army than that of moths scattering, one allowed by the word *farash*, but possibly not by Muhammad, is *vanished like bubbles on wine*.

1 Bagar is an old name for Dungarpur and Banswara [G. of I. vi, 408 s.n. Banswara].
2 *sic*, Hai. MS. and may be so read in I.O. 217 f.220*b*; Erskine writes Bikersi (p. 367) and notes the variant Nagersi; Ilminsky (p. 421) N:krsi; de Courteille (ii, 307) Niguersi.
3 *Cf.* f. 318*b*, and note, where it is seen that the stones which killed the lords of the Elephants were so small as to be carried in the bill of a bird like a swallow. Were such stones used in matchlocks in Babur's day?
4 *guzaran*, var. *gurazan*, caused to flee and hogs (Erskine notes the double-meaning).

They turn their backs. The command of God is to be performed. Now praise be to God, All-hearing and All-wise, for victory is from God alone, the Mighty, the Wise.[1] Written Jumada II. 25th 933 (AH.—March 29th 1527 AD.).[2]

MINOR SEQUELS OF VICTORY

(a. Babur assumes the title of Ghazi.)

After this success *Ghazi* (Victor in a Holy-war) was written amongst the royal titles.

---

1 This passage, entered in some MSS. as if verse, is made up of Qoran, cap. 17, v. 49, cap. 33, v. 38, and cap. 3, v. 122.

2 As the day of battle was Jumada II. 13th (March 16th), the *Fath-nama* was ready and dated twelve days after that battle. It was started for Kabul on Rajab 9th (April 11th). Something may be said here appropriately about the surmise contained in Dr. Ilminsky's Preface and M. de Courteille's note to *Mémoires* ii, 443 and 450, to the effect that Babur wrote a plain account of the battle of Kanwa and for this in his narrative substituted Shaikh Zain's *Fath-nama*, and that the plain account has been preserved in Kehr's *Babur-nama* volume [whence Ilminsky reproduced it, it was translated by M. de Courteille and became known as a "Fragment" of Baburiana]. Almost certainly both scholars would have judged adversely of their suggestion by the light of to-day's easier research. The following considerations making against its value, may be set down:—

(1) There is no sign that Babur ever wrote a plain account of the battle or any account of it. There is against his doing so his statement that he inserts Shaikh Zain's *Fath-nama* because it gives particulars. If he had written any account, it would be found preceding the *Fath-nama*, as his account of his renunciation of wine precedes Shaikh Zain's *Farman* announcing the act.

(2) Moreover, the "Fragment" cannot be described as a plain account such as would harmonize with Babur's style; it is in truth highly rhetorical, though less so as Shaikh Zain's.

(3) The "Fragment" begins with a quotation from the *Babur-nama* (f.310b and n.), skips a good deal of Babur's matter preliminary to the battle, and passes on with what there can be no doubt is a translation in inferior Turki of the *Akbar-nama* account.

(4) The whole of the extra matter is seen to be continuous and not fragmentary, if it is collated with the chapter in which Abu'l-fazl describes the battle, its sequel of events, the death, character, attainments, and Court of Babur. Down to the death, it is changed to the first person so as to make Babur seem to write it. The probable concocter of it is Jahangir.

(5) If the Fragment were Babur's composition, where was it when 'Abdu-r-rahim translated the *Babur-nama* in 998 AH.—1590 AD.; where too did Abu'l-fazl find it to reproduce in the *Akbar-nama*?

(6) The source of Abu'l-fazl's information seems without doubt to be Babur's own narrative and Shaikh Zain's *Fath-nama*. There are many significant resemblances between the two rhetoricians' metaphors and details selected.

(7) A good deal might be said of the dissimilarities between Babur's diction and that of the "Fragment". But this is needless in face of the larger and more circumstantial objections already mentioned.

(For a fuller account of the "Fragment" *see* JRAS. Jan. 1906 pp. 81, 85 and 1908 p. 75 ff.)

Below the titles (*tughra*)[1] entered on the *Fath-nama*, I wrote the following quatrain:—[2]

> For Islam's sake, I wandered in the wilds,
> Prepared for war with pagans and Hindus,
> Resolved myself to meet the martyr's death.
> Thanks be to God! a *ghazi* I became.

Fol. 325.

(b. Chronograms of the victory.)

Shaikh Zain had found (*tapib aidi*) the words *Fath-i-padshah-i-islam*[3] (Victory of the Padshah of the Faith) to be a chronogram of the victory. Mir Gesu, one of the people come from Kabul, had also found these same words to be a chronogram, had composed them in a quatrain and sent this to me. It was a coincidence that Shaikh Zain and Mir Gesu should bring forward precisely the same words in the quatrains they composed to embellish their discoveries.[4] Once before when Shaikh Zain found the date of the victory at Dibalpur in the words *Wasat-i-shahr Rabi'u'l-awwal*[5] (Middle of the month Rabi' I.), Mir Gesu had found it in the very same words.

HISTORICAL NARRATIVE RESUMED

(a. After the victory.)

The foes beaten, we hurried them off, dismounting one after another. The Pagan's encirclement[6] may have been 2 *kurohs*

---

1 *Tughra* means an imperial signature also, but would Babur sign Shaikh Zain's *Fath-i-nama*? His autograph verse at the end of the *Rampur Diwan* has his signature following it. He is likely to have signed this verse. *Cf.* App. Q. [Erskine notes that titles were written on the back of despatches, an unlikely place for the quatrain, one surmises.]

2 This is in the *Rampur diwan* (E.D.R. Plate 17). Dr. E. Denison Ross points out (p. 17 n.) that in the 2nd line the Hai. Codex varies from the *Diwan*. The MS. is wrong; it contains many inaccuracies in the latter part of the Hindustan section, perhaps due to a change of scribe.

3 These words by *abjad* yield 933. From Babur's use of the pluperfect tense, I think it may be inferred that (my) Sections *a* and *b* are an attachment to the *Fath-nama*, entered with it at a somewhat later date.

4 My translation of this puzzling sentence is tentative only.

5 This statement shews that the Dibalpur affair occurred in one of the B.N. gaps, and in 930 AH. The words make 330 by *abjad*. It may be noted here that on f.312b and notes there are remarks concerning whether Babur's remission of the *tamgha* was contingent on his winning at Kanwa. If the remission had been delayed until his victory was won, it would have found fitting mention with the other sequels of victory chronicled above; as it is not with these sequels, it may be accepted as an absolute remission, proclaimed before the fight. The point was a little uncertain owing to the seemingly somewhat deferred insertion in Babur's narrative of Shaikh Zain's *Farman*.

6 *da'ira*, presumably a defended circle. As the word *aurdu* [bracketed in the text] shows, Babur used it both for his own and for Sanga's camps.

from our camp (*aurdu*); when we reached his camp (*aurdu*), we sent Muhammadi, 'Abdu'l-'aziz, 'Ali Khan and some others in pursuit of him. There was a little slackness;[1] I ought to have gone myself, and not have left the matter to what I expected from other people. When I had gone as much as a *kuroh* (2 m.) beyond the Pagan's camp, I turned back because it was late in the day; I came to our camp at the Bed-time Prayer.

With what ill-omened words Muhammad Sharif the astrologer had fretted me! Yet he came at once to congratulate me! I emptied my inwards[2] in abuse of him, but, spite of his being heathenish, ill-omened of speech, extremely self-satisfied, and a most disagreeable person, I bestowed a *lak* upon him because there had been deserving service from him in former times, and, Fol. 325*b*. after saying he was not to stay in my dominions, I gave him leave to go.

(*b. Suppression of a rebellion.*)

(*March 17th*) We remained next day (*Jumada II. 14th*) on that same ground. Muhammad 'Ali *Jang-jang* and Shaikh Guran and 'Abdu'l-malik[3] the armourer were sent off with a dense (*qalin*) army against Ilias Khan who, having rebelled in Between-the-two-waters (Ganges and Jumna), had taken Kul (Koel) and made Kichik 'Ali prisoner.[4] He could not fight when they came up; his force scattered in all directions; he himself was taken a few days later and brought into Agra where I had him flayed alive.

(*c. A trophy of victory.*)

An order was given to set up a pillar of pagan heads on the infant-hill (*koh-bacha*) between which and our camp the battle had been fought.

1 Hence the Rana escaped. He died in this year, not without suspicion of poison. *See* Additional Notes, p. 800.

2 *aichimni khali qildim*, a seeming equivalent for English, "I poured out my spleen."

3 var. *maluk* as *e.g.* in I.O. 217 f.225*b*, and also elsewhere in the *Babur-nama*.

4 On f. 315 the acts attributed to Ilias Khan are said to have been done by a "mannikin called Rustam Khan". Neither name appears elsewhere in the B.N.; the hero's name seems a sarcasm on the small man.

(*d. Biana visited.*)

(*March 20th*) Marching on from that ground, and after halting on two nights, we reached Biana (*Sunday, Jumada II. 17th*). Countless numbers of the bodies of pagans and apostates[1] who had fallen in their flight, lay on the road as far as Biana, indeed as far as Alur and Miwat.[2]

(*e. Discussion of plans.*)

On our return to camp, I summoned the Turk amirs and the amirs of Hind to a consultation about moving into the Pagan (Sanga)'s country; the plan was given up because of the little water and much heat on the road.

(*f. Miwat.*)

Near Dihli lies the Miwat country which yields revenue of 3 or 4 *krurs*.[3] Hasan Khan *Miwati*[4] and his ancestors one after another had ruled it with absolute sway for a hundred years or two. They must have made[5] imperfect submission to the Dihli Sultans; the Sultans of Hind,[6] whether because their own dominions were wide, or because their opportunity was narrow, or because of the Miwat hill-country,[7] did not turn in the Miwat direction, did not establish order in it, but just   Fol. 326.

1 Babur so-calls both Hasan and his followers, presumably because they followed their race sympathies, as of Rajput origin, and fought against co-religionists. Though Hasan's subjects, Meos, were nominally Muhammadans, it appears that they practised some Hindu customs. For an account of Miwat, see *Gazetteer of Ulwur* (Alwar, Alur) by Major P.W. Powlett.

2 Alwar being in Miwat, Babur may mean that bodies were found beyond that town in the main portion of the Miwat country which lies north of Alwar towards Dihli.

3 Major Powlett speaking (p. 9) of the revenue Miwat paid to Babur, quotes Thomas as saying that the coins stated in Babur's Revenue Accounts, *viz.* 169,81,000 *tankas* were probably Sikandarl *tankas*, or Rs. 8,490,50.

4 This word appears to have been restricted in its use to the Khan-zadas of the ruling house in Miwat, and was not used for their subjects, the Meos (Powlett *l.c.* Cap. I.). The uses of "Miwati" and "Meo" suggest something analogous with those of "Chaghatai" and "Mughul" in Babur's time. The resemblance includes mutual dislike and distrust (Powlett *l.c.*).

5 *qilurlar aikan dur.* This presumptive past tense is frequently used by the cautious Babur. I quote it here and in a few places near-following because it supports Shaw's statement that in it the use of *aikan* (*ikan*) reduces the positive affirmation of the perfect to presumption or rumour. With this statement all grammarians are not agreed; it is fully supported by the *Babur-nama*.

6 Contrast here is suggested between Sultans of Dihli & Hind; is it between the greater Turks with whom Babur classes himself immediately below as a conqueror of Hind, and the Ludi Sultans of Dihli?

7 The strength of the Tijara hills towards Dihli is historical (Powlett *l.c.* p. 132).

put up with this amount of (imperfect) submission. For our own part, we did after the fashion of earlier Sultans; having conquered Hind, we shewed favour to Hasan Khan, but that thankless and heathenish apostate disregarded our kindness and benefits, was not grateful for favour and promotion, but became the mover of all disturbance and the cause of all misdoing.

When, as has been mentioned, we abandoned the plan (against Rana Sanga), we moved to subdue Miwat. Having made 4 night-halts on the way, we dismounted on the bank of the Manas-ni[1] 6 *kurohs* (12 m.) from Alur, the present seat of government in Miwat. Hasan Khan and his forefathers must have had their seat[2] in Tijara, but when I turned towards Hindustan, beat Pahar (or Bihar) Khan and took Lahor and Dibalpur (930 AH.-1524 AD.), he bethought himself betimes and busied himself for a residence ('*imarat*) in Fort Alur (Alwar).

His trusted man, Karm-chand by name, who had come from him to me in Agra when his son (Nahar *i.e.* Tiger) was with me there,[3] came now from that son's presence in Alur and asked Fol. 326b. for peace. 'Abdu'r-rahim *shaghawal* went with him to Alur, conveying letters of royal favour, and returned bringing Nahar Khan who was restored to favour and received *parganas* worth several *laks* for his support.

(*g. Rewards to officers.*)

Thinking, "What good work Khusrau did in the battle!" I named him for Alur and gave him 50 *laks* for his support, but unluckily for himself, he put on airs and did not accept this. Later on it [*khwud*, itself] came to be known that Chin-timur must have done[4] that work; guerdon was made him for his renown (?);[5] Tijara-town, the seat of government

---

1 This is one of the names of the principal river which flows eastwards to the south of Alwar town; other names are Barah and Ruparel. Powlett notes that it appears in Thorn's Map of the battle of Laswarree (1803 AD.), which he reproduces on p. 146. But it is still current in Gurgaon, with also a variant Manas-le, man-killer (*G. of Gurgaon* 1910 AD. ivA, p.6).

2 *aulturular aikan dur*, the presumptive past tense.

3 f. 308.

4 *qilghan aikan dur*, the presumptive past tense.

5 *Sultan atigha juldu bulub*; Pers. trs. *Juldu ba nam-i Sultan shud*. The *juldu* guerdon seems to be apart from the fief and allowance.

in Miwat, was bestowed on him together with an allowance of 50 *laks* for his support.

Alur and an allowance of 15 *laks* was bestowed on Tardika (or, Tardi *yakka*) who in the flanking-party of the right-hand (*qul*) had done better than the rest. The contents of the Alur treasury were bestowed on Humayun.

(h. Alwar visited.)

(*April 3rd*) Marching from that camp on Wednesday the 1st of the month of Rajab, we came to within 2 *kurohs* (4 m.) of Alur. I went to see the fort, there spent the night, and next day went back to camp.

(i. Leave given to various followers.)

When the oath before-mentioned[1] was given to great and small before the Holy-battle with Rana Sanga, it had been mentioned[2] that there would be nothing to hinder leave after this victory, and that leave would be given to anyone wishing to go away (from Hindustan). Most of Humayun's men were from Badakhshan or elsewhere on that side (of Hindu-kush); they had never before been of an army led out for even a month or two; there had been weakness amongst them before the fight; on these accounts and also because Kabul was empty of troops, it was now decided to give Humayun leave for Kabul. Fol. 327.

(*April 11th*) Leaving the matter at this, we marched from Alur on Thursday the 9th of Rajab, did 4 or 5 *kurohs* (8–10 m.) and dismounted on the bank of the Manas-water.

Mahdi Khwaja also had many discomforts; he too was given leave for Kabul. The military-collectorate of Biana [he held] was bestowed on Dost Lord-of-the-gate, and, as previously Etawa had been named for Mahdi Khwaja,[3] Mahdi Khwaja's son Ja'far Khwaja was sent there in his father's place when (later) Qutb Khan abandoned it and went off.[4]

---

1 f. 315.
2 Babur does not record this detail (f.315).
3 f. 298b and f. 328b. Ja'far is mentioned as Mahdi's son by Gul-badan and in the *Habibu's-siyar* iii, 311, 312.
4 f. 328b.

(*j. Despatch of the Letter-of-victory.*)

Because of the leave given to Humayun, two or three days were spent on this ground. From it Mumin-i-'ali the messenger (*tawachi*) was sent off for Kabul with the *Fath-nama*.

(*k. Excursions and return to Agra.*)

Praise had been heard of the Firuzpur-spring and of the great lake of Kutila.¹ Leaving the camp on that same ground, I rode out on Sunday (*Rajab 12th–April 14th*) both to visit Fol. 327b. these places and to set Humayun on his way. After visiting Firuzpur and its spring on that same day, *ma'jun* was eaten. In the valley where the spring rises, oleanders (*kanir*) were in bloom; the place is not without charm but is over-praised. I ordered a reservoir of hewn stone, 10 by 10² to be made where the water widened, spent the night in that valley, next day rode on and visited the Kutila lake. It is surrounded by mountain-skirts. The Manas-ni is heard-say to go into it.³ It is a very large lake, from its one side the other side is not well seen. In the middle of it is rising ground. At its sides are many small boats, by going off in which the villagers living near it are said to escape from any tumult or disturbance. Even on our arrival a few people went in them to the middle of the lake.

On our way back from the lake, we dismounted in Humayun's camp. There we rested and ate food, and after having put robes of honour on him and his begs, bade him farewell at the Bed-time Prayer, and rode on. We slept for a little at some place on the road, at shoot of day passed through the *pargana* of Khari, again slept a little, and at length got to our camp

1 The town of Firuzpur is commonly known as Firuzpur-jhirka (Firuzpur of the spring), from a small perennial stream which issues from a number of fissures in the rocks bordering the road through a pass in the Miwat hills which leads from the town *via* Tijara to Rewari (G. *of Gurgaon*, p.249). In Abu'l-fazl's day there was a Hindu shrine of Mahadeo near the spring, which is still a place of annual pilgrimage. The Kutila lake is called Kotla-*jhil* in the G. *of G.* (p. 7). It extends now 3 m. by 2½ m. varying in size with the season; in Abu'l-fazl's day it was 4 *kos* (8 m.) round. It lies partly in the district of Nuh, partly in Gurgaon, where the two tracts join at the foot of the Alwar hills.

2 This is the frequently mentioned size for reservoirs; the measure here is probably the *qari*, *cir.* a yard.

3 Babur does not state it as a fact known to himself that the Manas-ni falls into the Kutila lake; it did so formerly, but now does not, tradition assigning a cause for the change (G. *of G.* p.6). He uses the hear-say tense, *kirar aimish*.

which had dismounted at Toda-(bhim).[1] After leaving Toda, we dismounted at Sunkar; there Hasan Khan *Miwati*'s son Nahar Khan escaped from 'Abdu'r-rahim's charge.   Fol. 328.

Going on from that place, we halted one night, then dismounted at a spring situated on the bill of a mountain between Busawar and Chausa[2] (or Jusa); there awnings were set up and we committed the sin of *ma'jun*. When the army had passed by this spring, Tardi Beg *khaksar* had praised it; he (or we) had come and seen it from on horse-back (*sar-asbgi*) and passed on. It is a perfect spring. In Hindustan where there are never running-waters,[3] people seek out the springs themselves. The rare springs that are found, come oozing drop by drop (*ab-zih*) out of the ground, not bubbling up like springs of those lands.[4] From this spring comes about a half-mill-water. It bubbles up on the hill-skirt; meadows lie round it; it is very beautiful. I ordered an octagonal reservoir of hewn stone made above[5] it. While we were at the border of the spring, under the soothing influence of *ma'jun*, Tardi Beg, contending for its surpassing beauty, said again and again, (*Persian*) "Since I am celebrating the beauty of the place,[6] a name ought to be settled for it". 'Abdu'l-lah said, "It must be called the Royal-spring approved of by Tardi Beg." This saying caused much joke and laughter.

Dost Lord-of-the-gate coming up from Biana, waited on me at this spring-head. Leaving this place, we visited Biana again,   Fol. 328*b*. went on to Sikri, dismounted there at the side of a garden which had been ordered made, stayed two days supervising the garden, and on Thursday the 23rd of Rajab (*April 25th*), reached Agra.

(*l. Chandwar and Rapri regained.*)

During recent disturbances, the enemy, as has been mentioned,[7] had possessed themselves of Chandwar[8] and Rapri. Against

1 Khari and Toda were in Akbar's *sarkar* of Rantambhor.
2 Bhosawar is in Bhurtpur, and Chausa (or Jusa) may be the Chausath of the *Ayin-i-akbari*, ii, 183.
3 As has been noted frequently, this phrase stands for artificial water-courses.
4 Certainly Trans-Hindu-kush lands; presumably also those of Trans-Indus, Kabul in chief.
5 *austi*; perhaps the reservoir was so built as to contain the bubbling spring.
6 *Chun ja'i khwush karda am.*
7 f. 315.
8 var. Janwar (Jarrett). It is 25 m. east of Agra on the Muttra—Etawa road (*G. of I.*).

those places we now sent Muhammad 'Ali *Jang-jang*; Quj Beg's (brother) Tardi Beg, 'Abdu'l-malik the armourer, and Hasan Khan with his Darya-khanis. When they were near Chandwar, Qutb Khan's people in it got out and away. Our men laid hands on it, and passed on to Rapri. Here Husain Khan *Nuhani's* people came to the lane-end[1] thinking to fight a little, could not stand the attack of our men, and took to flight. Husain Khan himself with a few followers went into the Jun-river (Jumna) on an elephant and was drowned. Qutb Khan, for his part, abandoned Etawa on hearing these news, fled with a few and got away. Etawa having been named for Mahdi Khwaja, his son Ja'far Khwaja was sent there in his place.[2]

(m. Apportionment of fiefs.)

When Rana Sanga sallied out against us, most Hindustanis and Afghans, as has been mentioned,[3] turned round against us and took possession of their *parganas* and districts.[4]

Fol. 329.
Sl. Muhammad *Duldai* who had abandoned Qanuj and come to me, would not agree to go there again, whether from fear or for his reputation's sake; he therefore exchanged the 30 *laks* of Qanuj for the 15 of Sihrind, and Qanuj was bestowed with an allowance of 30 *laks* on Muhammad Sl. Mirza. Badaun[5] was given to Qasim-i-husain Sultan and he was sent against Biban who had laid siege to Luknur[6] during the disturbance with Rana Sanga, together with Muhammad Sl. Mirza, and, of Turk amirs, Baba Qashqa's Malik Qasim with his elder and younger brethren and his Mughuls, and Abu'l-muhammad the lance-player, and Mu'yad with his father's Darya-khanis and those of Husain Khan *Darya-khani* and the retainers of Sl. Muhammad *Duldai*, and again, of amirs of Hind, 'Ali Khan *Farmuli* and Malik Dad *Kararani* and Shaikh Muhammad of Shaikh *Bhakhari* (?) and Tatar Khan Khan-i-jahan.

1 *kucha-band*, perhaps a barricade at the limit of a suburban lane.
2 This has been mentioned already (f. 327).
3 f. 315.
4 *i.e.* those professedly held for Babur.
5 Or, according to local pronunciation, Badayun.
6 This is the old name of Shahabad in Rampur (G. *of I.* xxii, 197). The *A.-i-A.* locates it in Sambal. *Cf.* E. and D.'s *History of India*, iv, 384 n. and v. 215 n.

At the time this army was crossing the Gang-river (Ganges), Biban, hearing about it, fled, abandoning his baggage. Our army followed him to Khairabad,[1] stayed there a few days and then turned back.

(*n. Appointments and dispersion for the Rains.*)

After the treasure had been shared out, Rana Sanga's great affair intervened before districts and *parganas* were apportioned. During the respite now from Holy-war against the Pagan (Sanga), this apportionment was made. As the Rains were near, it was settled for every-one to go to his *pargana*, get equipment ready, and be present when the Rains were over.   Fol. 329*b*.

(*o. Misconduct of Humayun.*)

Meantime news came that Humayun had gone into Dihli, there opened several treasure-houses and, without permission, taken possession of their contents. I had never looked for such a thing from him; it grieved me very much; I wrote and sent off to him very severe reproaches.[2]

(*p. An embassy to 'Iraq.*)

Khwajagi Asad who had already gone as envoy to 'Iraq and returned with Sulaiman *Turkman*,[3] was again joined with him and on the 15th of Sha'ban (*May 17th*) sent with befitting gifts to Shah-zada Tahmasp.

(*q. Tardi Beg khaksar resigns service.*)

I had brought Tardi Beg out from the darwish-life and made a soldier of him; for how many years had he served me! Now his desire for the darwish-life was overmastering and he asked for leave. It was given and he was sent as an envoy to Kamran conveying 3 *laks* from the Treasury for him.[4]

---

1 Perhaps the one in Sitapur.
2 As the Elphinstone Codex which is the treasure-house of Humayun's notes, has a long *lacuna* into which this episode falls, it is not known if the culprit entered in his copy of the *Babur-nama* a marginal excuse for his misconduct (*cf.* f. 252 and n.); such excuse was likely to be that he knew he would be forgiven by his clement father.
3 f.305.
4 Kamran would be in Qandahar. Erskine notes that the sum sent to him would be about £750, but that if the coins were rupis, it would be £30,000.

(r. Lines addressed to deserting friends.)

A little fragment[1] had been composed suiting the state of those who had gone away during the past year; I now addressed it to Mulla 'Ali Khan and sent it to him by Tardi Beg. It is as follows:——[2]

> Ah you who have gone from this country of Hind,
> Aware for yourselves of its woe and its pain,
> With longing desire for Kabul's fine air,
> You went hot-foot forth out of Hind.
> The pleasure you looked for you will have found there
> With sociable ease and charm and delight;
> As for us, God be thanked! we still are alive,
> In spite of much pain and unending distress;
> Pleasures of sense and bodily toil
> Have been passed-by by you, passed-by too by us.

(s. Of the Ramzan Feast.)

Ramzan was spent this year with ablution and *tarawih*[3] in the Garden-of-eight-paradises. Since my 11th year I had not kept the Ramzan Feast for two successive years in the same place; last year I had kept it in Agra; this year, saying, "Don't break the rule!" I went on the last day of the month to keep it in Sikri. Tents were set up on a stone platform made on the n.e. side of the Garden-of-victory which is now being laid out at Sikri, and in them the Feast was held.[4]

(t. Playing cards.)

The night we left Agra Mir 'Ali the armourer was sent to Shah Hasan (*Arghun*) in Tatta to take him playing-cards [*ganjifa*] he much liked and had asked for.[5]

---

1 *qita'*, for account of which form of poem *see* Blochmann's translations of Saifi's and Jami's *Prosody*, p.86.

2 *Rampur Diwan* (E. D. Ross' ed. p.16 and Plate 14a). I am uncertain as to the meaning of ll.4 and 10. I am not sure that what in most MSS. ends line 4, *viz. aul dam*, should not be read as *aulum*, death; this is allowed by Plate 14a where for space the word is divided and may be *aulum*. To read *aulum* and that the deserters fled from the death in Hind they were anxious about, has an answering phrase in "we still are alive". Ll. 9 and 10 perhaps mean that in the things named all have done alike. [Ilminsky reads *khair nafsi* for the elsewhere *hazz-nafsi*.]

3 These are 20 attitudes (*rak'ah*) assumed in prayer during Ramzan after the Bed-time Prayer. The ablution (*ghusl*) is the bathing of the whole body for ceremonial purification.

4 This Feast is the 'Id-i-fitr, held at the breaking of the Ramzan Fast on the 1st of Shawwal.

5 Erskine notes that this is the earliest mention of playing-cards he can recall in oriental literature.

(*u. Illness and a tour.*)

(*August 3rd*) On Sunday the 5th of Zu'l-qaʻda I fell ill; the illness lasted 17 days.

(*August 24th*) On Friday the 24th of the same month we set out to visit Dulpur. That night I slept at a place half-way; Fol. 330*b*. reached Sikandar's dam[1] at dawn, and dismounted there.

At the end of the hill below the dam the rock is of building-stone. I had Ustad Shah Muhammad the stone-cutter brought and gave him an order that if a house could be cut all in one piece in that rock, it was to be done, but that if the rock were too low for a residence ('*imarat*), it was to be levelled and have a reservoir, all in one piece, cut out of it.

From Dulpur we went on to visit Bari. Next morning (*August 26th*) I rode out from Bari through the hills between it and the Chambal-river in order to view the river. This done I went back to Bari. In these hills we saw the ebony-tree, the fruit of which people call *tindu*. It is said that there are white ebony-trees also and that most ebony-trees in these hills are of this kind.[2] On leaving Bari we went to Sikri; we reached Agra on the 29th of the same month (*August 28th*).

(*v. Doubts about Shaikh Bayazid Farmuli.*)

As in these days people were telling wild news about Shaikh Bayazid, Sl. Quli *Turk* was sent to him to give him tryst[3] in 20 days.

(*w. Religious and metrical exercises.*)

(*August 28th*) On Friday the 2nd of Zu'l-hijja I began what one is made to read 41 times.[4]

In these same days I cut up [*taqtiʻ*] the following couplet of mine into 504 measures:[5]—

---

1 f. 339*b*.
2 The two varieties mentioned by Babur seem to be *Diospyrus melanoxylon*, the wood of which is called *tindu abnus* in Hindustani, and *D. tomentosa*, Hindi, *tindu* (Brandis *s.nn.*). Bari is 19 m. west of Dulpur.
3 *miʻad*, perhaps the time at which the Shaikh was to appear before Babur.
4 The Pers. trs. makes the more definite statement that what had to be read was a Section of the Qoran (*wird*). This was done with remedial aim for the illness.
5 As this statement needs comment, and as it is linked to matters mentioned in the *Rampur Diwan*, it seems better to remit remarks upon it to Appendix Q, *Some matters concerning the Rampur Diwan*.

> "Shall I tell of her eye or her brow, her fire or her speech?
> Shall I tell of her stature or cheek, of her hair or her waist?"

On this account a treatise[1] was arranged.

(*x. Return of illness.*)

On this day (*i.e.* 2nd Zu'l-hijja) I fell ill again; the illness lasted nine days.

(*y. Start for Sambal.*)

(*Sep. 24th*) On Thursday the 29th of Zu'l-hijja we rode out for an excursion to Kul and Sambal.

1 *risala. See* Appendix Q.

(a. Visit to Kul (Aligarh) and Sambal.)

(*Sep. 27th*) On Saturday the 1st of Muharram we dismounted in Kul (Koel). Humayun had left Darwish(-i-'ali) and Yusuf-i-'ali[2] in Sambal; they crossed one river,[3] fought Qutb *Sirwani*[4] and a party of rajas, beat them well and killed a mass of men. They sent a few heads and an elephant into Kul while we were there. After we had gone about Kul for two days, we dismounted at Shaikh Guran's house by his invitation, where he entertained us hospitably and laid an offering before us.

(*Sep. 30th—Muh. 4th*) Riding on from that place, we dismounted at Autruli (Atrauli).[5]

(*Oct. 1st—Muh. 5th*) On Wednesday we crossed the river Gang (Ganges) and spent the night in villages of Sambal.

(*Oct. 2nd—Muh. 6th*) On Thursday we dismounted in Sambal. After going about in it for two days, we left on Saturday.

(*Oct. 5th—Muh. 9th*) On Sunday we dismounted in Sikandara[6]

---

1 Elph. MS. *lacuna*; I.O. 215 *lacuna* and 217 f.229; Mems. p.373. This year's narrative resumes the diary form.

2 There is some uncertainty about these names and also as to which adversary crossed the river. The sentence which, I think, shews, by its plural verb, that Humayun left two men and, by its co-ordinate participles, that it was they crossed the river, is as follows:—(Darwish and Yusuf, understood) *Qutb Sirwani-ni u bir para rajalar-ni bir darya autub aurushub yakshi basib turlar. Autub, aurushub* and *basib* are grammatically referable to the same subject, [whatever was the fact about the crossing].

3 *bir darya*; W.-i-B. 217 f.229, *yak darya*, one river, but many MSS. *har darya*, every river. If it did not seem pretty certain that the rebels were not in the Miyan-du-ab one would surmise the river to be "one river" of the two enclosing the tract "between the waters", and that one to be the Ganges. It may be one near Sambhal, east of the Ganges.

4 var. Shirwani. The place giving the cognomen may be Sarwan, a *thakurat* of the Malwa Agency (*G. of I.*). Qutb of Sirwan may be the Qutb Khan of earlier mention without the cognomen.

5 n.w. of Aligarh (Kul). It may be noted here, where instances begin to be frequent, that my translation "we marched" is an evasion of the Turki impersonal "it was marched". Most rarely does Babur write "we marched", never, "I marched."

6 in the Aligarh (Kul) district; it is the Sikandara Rao of the *A.-i-A.* and the *G. of I.*

at the house of Rao *Sirwani* who set food before us and served us. When we rode out at dawn, I made some pretext to leave the rest, and galloped on alone to within a *kuroh* of Agra where they overtook me. At the Mid-day Prayer we dismounted in Agra.

(*b. Illness of Babur.*)

(*Oct. 12th*) On Sunday the 16th of Muharram I had fever and ague. This returned again and again during the next 25 or 26 days. I drank operative medicine and at last relief came. I suffered much from thirst and want of sleep.

ol. 331b.　　While I was ill, I composed a quatrain or two; here is one of them:—[1]

> Fever grows strong in my body by day,
> Sleep quits my eyes as night comes on;
> Like to my pain and my patience the pair,
> For while that goes waxing, this wanes.

(*c. Arrival of kinswomen.*)

(*Nov. 23rd*) On Saturday the 28th of Safar there arrived two of the paternal-aunt begims, Fakhr-i-jahan Begim and Khadija-sultan Begim.[2] I went to above Sikandarabad to wait on them.[3]

(*d. Concerning a mortar.*)

(*Nov. 24th—Safar 29th*) On Sunday Ustad 'Ali-quli discharged a stone from a large mortar; the stone went far but the mortar broke in pieces, one of which, knocking down a party of men, killed eight.

(*e. Visit to Sikri.*)

(*Dec. 1st*) On Monday the 7th of the first Rabi' I rode out to visit Sikri. The octagonal platform ordered made in the middle of the lake was ready; we went over by boat, had an awning set up on it and elected for *ma'jun.*

---

1 *Rampur Diwan* (E.D. Ross' ed., p. 19, Plate 16b). This *Diwan* contains other quatrains which, judging from their contents, may well be those Babur speaks of as also composed in Sambal. *See* Appendix Q, *Some matters concerning the Rampur Diwan.*

2 These are aunts of Babur, daughters of Sl. Abu-sa'id *Miran-shahi.*

3 Sikandarabad is in the Buland-shahr district of the United Provinces.

(*f. Holy-war against Chandiri.*)

(*Dec. 9th*) After returning from Sikri we started on Monday night the 14th of the first Rabi',[1] with the intention of making Holy-war against Chandiri, did as much as 3 *kurohs* (6 m.) and dismounted in Jalisir.[2] After staying there two days for people to equip and array, we marched on Thursday (*Dec. 12th—Rabi' I. 17th*) and dismounted at Anwar. I left Anwar by boat, and disembarked beyond Chandwar.[3]

(*Dec. 23rd*) Advancing march by march, we dismounted at the Kanar-passage[4] on Monday the 28th.

(*Dec. 26th*) On Thursday the 2nd of the latter Rabi' I crossed the river; there was 4 or 5 days delay on one bank or the other before the army got across. On those days we went more than once on board a boat and ate *ma'jun*. The junction of the river Chambal is between one and two *kurohs* (2–4 m.) above the Kanar-passage; on Friday I went into a boat on the Chambal, passed the junction and so to camp.

Fol. 332.

(*g. Troops sent against Shaikh Bayazid Farmuli.*)

Though there had been no clear proof of Shaikh Bayazid's hostility, yet his misconduct and action made it certain that he had hostile intentions. On account of this Muhammad 'Ali *Jang-jang* was detached from the army and sent to bring together from Qanuj Muhammad Sl. Mirza and the sultans and amirs of that neighbourhood, such as Qasim-i-husain Sultan, Bi-khub (or, Ni-khub) Sultan, Malik Qasim, Kuki, Abu'l-muhammad the lancer, and Minuchihr Khan with his elder and younger brethren and Darya-khanis, so that they might move against the hostile Afghans. They were to invite Shaikh Bayazid to go with them; if he came frankly, they were to take him along; if not, were to drive him off. Muhammad 'Ali

1 It is not clear whether Babur returned from Sikri on the day he started for Jalisir; no question of distance would prevent him from making the two journeys on the Monday.

2 As this was the rendezvous for the army, it would be convenient if it lay between Agra and Anwar; as it was 6 m. from Agra, the only mapped place having approximately the name Jalisir, *viz.* Jalesar, in Etah, seems too far away.

3 Anwar would be suitably the Unwara of the *Indian Atlas*, which is on the first important southward dip of the Jumna below Agra. Chandwar is 25 m. east of Agra, on the Muttra-Etawah road (G. *of* I.); Jarrett notes that Tiefenthaler identifies it with Firuzabad (*A.-i-A.* ii, 183 n.).

4 In the district of Kalpi. The name does not appear in maps I have seen.

asking for a few elephants, ten were given him. After he had leave to set off, Baba Chuhra (the Brave) was sent to and ordered to join him.

(h. Incidents of the journey to Chandiri.)

From Kanar one *kuroh* (2 m.) was done by boat.

(*Jan. 1st 1528 AD.*) On Wednesday the 8th of the latter Rabi' we dismounted within a *kuroh* of Kalpi. Baba Sl. came to wait on me in this camp; he is a son of Khalil Sl. who is a younger brother of the full-blood of Sl. Sa'id Khan. Last

ol. 332b. year he fled from his elder brother[1] but, repenting himself, went back from the Andar-ab border; when he neared Kashghar, The Khan (Sa'id) sent Haidar M. to meet him and take him back.

(*Jan. 2nd—Rabi' II. 9th*) Next day we dismounted at 'Alam Khan's house in Kalpi where he set Hindustani food before us and made an offering.

(*Jan. 6th*) On Monday the 13th of the month we marched from Kalpi.

(*Jan. 10th—Rabi' II. 17th*) On Friday we dismounted at Irij.[2]

(*Jan. 11th*) On Saturday we dismounted at Bandir.[3]

(*Jan. 12th*) On Sunday the 19th of the month Chin-timur Sl. was put at the head of 6 or 7000 men and sent ahead against Chandiri. With him went the begs Baqi *ming-bashi* (head of a thousand), Quj Beg's (brother) Tardi Beg, 'Ashiq the taster, Mulla Apaq, Muhsin[4] *Duldai* and, of the Hindustani begs, Shaikh Guran.

(*Jan 17th*) On Friday the 24th of the month we dismounted near Kachwa. After encouraging its people, it was bestowed on the son of Badru'd-din.[5]

Kachwa[6] is a shut-in place, having lowish hills all round it.

---

1 *agha*, Anglicé, uncle. He was Sa'id Khan of Kashghar. Haidar M. says Baba Sl. was a spoiled child and died without mending his ways.

2 From Kalpi Babur will have taken the road to the s.w. near which now runs the Cawnpur (Kanhpur) branch of the Indian Midland Railway, and he must have crossed the Betwa to reach Irij (Irich, *Indian Atlas*, Sheet 69 N.W.).

3 Leaving Irij, Babur will have recrossed the Betwa and have left its valley to go west to Bandir (Bhander) on the Pahuj (*Indian Atlas*, Sheet 69 S.W.).

4 beneficent, or Muhassan, comely.

5 The one man of this name mentioned in the *B.N.* is an amir of Sl. Husain *Bai-qara*.

6 It seems safe to take Kachwa [Kajwa] as the Kajwarra of Ibn Batuta, and the Kadwaha (Kadwaia) of the *Indian Atlas*, Sheet 52 N.E. and of Luard's *Gazetteer*

A dam has been thrown across between hills on the south-east of it, and thus a large lake made, perhaps 5 or 6 *kurohs* (10–12 m.) round. This lake encloses Kachwa on three sides; on the north-west a space of ground is kept dry;[1] here, therefore is its Gate. On the lake are a great many very small boats, able to hold 3 or 4 persons; in these the inhabitants go out on the lake, if they have to flee. There are two other lakes before Kachwa is reached, smaller than its own and, like that, made by throwing a dam across between hills.

Fol. 333.

---

of Gwalior (i, 247), which is situated in 24° 58′ N. and 77° 57′ E. Each of the three names is of a place standing on a lake; Ibn Batuta's lake was a league (4 m.) long, Babur's about 11 miles round; Luard mentions no lake, but the *Indian Atlas* marks one quite close to Kadwaha of such form as to seem to have a tongue of land jutting into it from the north-west, and thus suiting Babur's description of the site of Kachwa. Again,—Ibn Batuta writes of Kajwarra as having, round its lake, idol-temples; Luard says of Kadwaha that it has four idol-temples standing and nine in ruins; there may be hinted something special about Babur's Kachwa by his remark that he encouraged its people, and this speciality may be interaction between Muhammadanism and Hinduism serving here for the purpose of identification. For Ibn Batuta writes of the people of Kajwarra that they were *jogis*, yellowed by asceticism, wearing their hair long and matted, and having Muhammadan followers who desired to learn their (occult ?) secrets. If the same interaction existed in Babur's day, the Muhammadan following of the Hindu ascetics may well have been the special circumstance which led him to promise protection to those Hindus, even when he was out for Holy-war. It has to be remembered of Chandiri, the nearest powerful neighbour of Kadwaha, that though Babur's capture makes a vivid picture of Hinduism in it, it had been under Muhammadan rulers down to a relatively short time before his conquest. The *jogis* of Kachwa could point to long-standing relations of tolerance by the Chandiri Governors; this, with their Muhammadan following, explains the encouragement Babur gave them, and helps to identify Kachwa with Kajarra. It may be observed that Babur was familiar with the interaction of the two creeds, witness his "apostates", mostly Muhammadans following Hindu customs, witness too, for the persistent fact, the reports of District-officers under the British *Raj*. Again,—a further circumstance helping to identify Kajwarra, Kachwa and Kadwaha is that these are names of the last important station the traveller and the soldier, as well perhaps as the modern wayfarer, stays in before reaching Chandiri. The importance of Kajwarra is shewn by Ibn Batuta, and of Kadwaha by its being a *mahall* in Akbar's *sarkar* of Bayawan of the *suba* of Agra. Again,—Kadwaha is the place nearest to Chandiri about which Babur's difficulties as to intermediate road and jungle would arise. That intermediate road takes off the main one a little south of Kadwaha and runs through what looks like a narrow valley and broken country down to Bhamor, Bhuranpur and Chandiri. Again,—no bar to identification of the three names is placed by their differences of form, in consideration of the vicissitudes they have weathered in tongue, script, and transliteration. There is some ground, I believe, for surmising that their common source is *kajur*, the date-fruit. [I am indebted to my husband for the help derived from Ibn Batuta, traced by him in Sanguinetti's trs. iv, 33, and S. Lee's trs. p. 162.]

(Two places similar in name to Kachwa, and situated on Babur's route *viz*. Kocha near Jhansi, and Kuchoowa north of Kadwaha (Sheet 69 S.W.) are unsuitable for his "Kachwa", the first because too near Bandir to suit his itinerary, the second because too far from the turn off the main-road mentioned above, because it has no lake, and has not the help in identification detailed above of Kadwaha.)

1 *quruqtur* which could mean also *reserved* (from the water ?).

(*Jan. 18th*) We waited a day in Kachwa in order to appoint active overseers and a mass of spadesmen to level the road and cut jungle down, so that the carts and mortar[1] might pass along it easily. Between Kachwa and Chandiri the country is jungly.

(*Jan. 19th—Rabi' II. 26th*) After leaving Kachwa we halted one night, passed the Burhanpur-water (Bhuranpur)[2] and dismounted within 3 *kurohs* (6 m.) of Chandiri.

(*i. Chandiri and its capture.*)

The citadel of Chandiri stands on a hill; below it are the town (*shahr*) and outer-fort (*tash-qurghan*), and below these is the level road along which carts pass.[3] When we left Burhanpur (*Jan. 10th*) we marched for a *kuroh* below Chandiri for the convenience of the carts.[4]

(*Jan. 21st*) After one night's halt we dismounted beside Bahjat Khan's tank[5] on the top of its dam, on Tuesday the 28th of the month.

(*Jan. 22nd—Rabi' II. 29th*) Riding out at dawn, we assigned post after post (*buljar, buljar*),[6] round the walled town (*qurghan*)

---

1 *qazan*. There seems to have been one only; how few Babur had is shewn again on f. 337.

2 *Indian Atlas*, Sheet 52 N. E. near a tributary of the Betwa, the Or, which appears to be Babur's Burhanpur-water.

3 The bed of the Betwa opposite Chandiri is 1050 ft. above the sea; the walled-town (*qurghan*) of Chandiri is on a table-land 250 ft. higher, and its citadel is 230 ft. higher again (Cunningham's *Archeological Survey Report*, 1871 AD. ii, 404).

4 The plan of Chandiri illustrating Cunningham's Report (*see* last note) allows surmise about the road taken by Babur, surmise which could become knowledge if the names of tanks he gives were still known. The courtesy of the Government of India allows me to reproduce that plan [Appendix R, *Chandiri* and *Gwaliawar*].

5 He is said to have been Governor of Chandiri in 1513 AD.

6 Here and in similar passages the word *m:ljar* or *m:lchar* is found in MSS. where the meaning is that of T. *buljar*. It is not in any dictionary I have seen; Mr. Irvine found it "obscure" and surmised it to mean "approach by trenches", but this does not suit its uses in the *Babur-nama* of a military post, and a rendezvous. This surmise, containing, as it does, a notion of protection, links *m:ljar* in sense with Ar. *malja'*. The word needs expert consideration, in order to decide whether it is to be received into dictionaries, or to be rejected because explicable as the outcome of unfamiliarity in Persian scribes with T. *buljar* or, *more Persico* with narrowed vowels, *buljăr*. Shaw in his Vocabulary enters *buljaq* (*buljar*?), "a station for troops, a rendezvous, see *malja*'," thus indicating, it would seem, that he was aware of difficulty about *m:ljar* and *buljaq* (*buljar*?). There appears no doubt of the existence of a Turki word *buljar* with the meanings Shaw gives to *buljaq*; it could well be formed from the root *bul*, being, whence follows, being in a place, posted. *Malja* has the meaning of a standing-place, as well as those of a refuge and an asylum; both meanings seem combined in the *m:ljar* of f.336b, where for matchlockmen a *m:ljar* was ordered "raised". (*Cf.* Irvine's *Army of the Indian Moghuls* p. 278.)

to centre, right, and left. Ustad 'Ali-quli chose, for his stone-discharge, ground that had no fall;[1] overseers and spadesmen were told off to raise a place (*m:ljar*) for the mortar to rest on, and the whole army was ordered to get ready appliances for taking a fort, mantelets, ladders[2] and ... -mantelets (*tura*).[3]

Formerly Chandiri will have belonged to the Sultans of Mandau (Mandu). When Sl. Nasiru'd-din passed away,[4] one of his sons Sl. Mahmud who is now holding Mandu, took possession of it and its neighbouring parts, and another son called Muhammad Shah laid hands on Chandiri and put it under Sl. Sikandar (*Ludi*)'s protection, who, in his turn, took Muhammad Shah's side and sent him large forces. Muhammad Shah survived Sl. Sikandar and died in Sl. Ibrahim's time, leaving a very young son called Ahmad Shah whom Sl. Ibrahim drove out and replaced by a man of his own. At the time Rana Sanga led out an army against Sl. Ibrahim and Ibrahim's begs turned against him at Dulpur, Chandiri fell into the Rana's hands and by him was given to Medini [Mindni] Rao[5] the greatly-trusted pagan who was now in it with 4 or 5000 other pagans.

As it was understood there was friendship between Medini

Fol. 333*b*.

1 *yaghda*; Pers. trs. *sar-ashib*. Babur's remark seems to show that for effect his mortar needed to be higher than its object. Presumably it stood on the table-land north of the citadel.

2 *shatu*. It may be noted that this word, common in accounts of Babur's sieges, may explain one our friend the late Mr. William Irvine left undecided (*l.c.* p.278), *viz. shatur*. On p. 281 he states that *narduban* is the name of a scaling-ladder and that Babur mentions scaling-ladders more than once. Babur mentions them however always as *shatu*. Perhaps *shatur* which, as Mr. Irvine says, seems to be made of the trunks of trees and to be a siege appliance, is really *shatu u* ... (ladder and ...) as in the passage under note and on f.216*b*, some other name of an appliance following.

3 The word here preceding *tura* has puzzled scribes and translators. I have seen the following variants in MSS.;—*nukri* or *tukri*, b: *kri* or *y: kri*, *bukri* or *yukri*, *bukrai* or *yukrai*, in each of which the *k* may stand for *g*. Various suggestions might be made as to what the word is, but all involve reading the Persian enclitic *i* (forming the adjective) instead of Turki *lik*. Two roots, *tig* and *yug*, afford plausible explanations of the unknown word; appliances suiting the case and able to bear names formed from one or other of these roots are *wheeled mantelet*, and *head-strike* (P. *sar-kob*). That the word is difficult is shewn not only by the variants I have quoted, but by Erskine's reading *naukari tura*, "to serve the *turas*," a requisite not specified earlier by Babur, and by de Courteille's paraphrase, *tout ce qui est nécessaire aux touras*.

4 Sl. Nasiru'd-din was the Khilji ruler of Malwa from 906 to 916 AH. (1500–1510 AD.).

5 He was a Rajput who had been prime minister of Sl. Mahmud II. *Khilji* (son of Nasiru'd-din) and had rebelled. Babur (like some other writers) spells his name Mindni, perhaps as he heard it spoken.

Rao and Araish Khan, the latter was sent with Shaikh Guran to speak to Medini Rao with favour and kindness, and promise Shamsabad[1] in exchange for Chandiri. One or two of his trusted men got out (?).[2] No adjustment of matters was reached, it is not known whether because Medini Rao did not trust what was said, or whether because he was buoyed up by delusion about the strength of the fort.

(*Jan. 28th*) At dawn on Tuesday the 6th of the first Jumada we marched from Bahjat Khan's tank intending to assault Chandiri. We dismounted at the side of the middle-tank near the fort.

(*j. Bad news.*)

On this same morning after reaching that ground, Khalifa brought a letter or two of which the purport was that the troops appointed for the East[3] had fought without consideration, been beaten, abandoned Laknau, and gone to Qanuj. Seeing that Khalifa was much perturbed and alarmed by these news, I said,[4] (*Persian*) "There is no ground for perturbation or alarm; nothing comes to pass but what is predestined of God. As this task (Chandiri) is ahead of us, not a breath must be drawn about what has been told us. Tomorrow we will assault the fort; that done, we shall see what comes."

(*k. Siege of Chandiri, resumed.*)

The enemy must have strengthened just the citadel, and have posted men by twos and threes in the outer-fort for prudence' sake. That night our men went up from all round; those few in the outer-fort did not fight; they fled into the citadel.

---

1 Presumably the one in the United Provinces. For Shamsabad in Gualiar *see* Luard *l.c.* i, 286.

2 *chiqti*; Pers. trs. *bar amad* and, also in some MSS. *nami bar amad*; Mems. p. 376, "averse to conciliation"; *Méms,* ii, 329, "*s'élevèrent contre cette proposition.*" So far I have not found Babur using the verb *chiqmaq* metaphorically. It is his frequent verb to express "getting away", "going out of a fort". It would be a short step in metaphor to understand here that Medini's men "got out of it", *i.e.* what Babur offered. They may have left the fort also; if so, it would be through dissent.

3 f. 332.

4 I.O.217, f.231, inserts here what seems a gloss, "*Ta in ja Farsi farmuda*" (*gufta*, said). As Babur enters his speech in Persian, it is manifest that he used Persian to conceal the bad news.

(*Jan. 29th*) At dawn on Wednesday the 7th of the first Jumada, we ordered our men to arm, go to their posts, provoke to fight, and attack each from his place when I rode out with drum and standard.

I myself, dismissing drum and standard till the fighting should grow hot, went to amuse myself by watching Ustad 'Ali-quli's stone-discharge.[1] Nothing was effected by it because his ground had no fall (*yaghda*) and because the fort-walls, being entirely of stone, were extremely strong.   Fol. 334b.

That the citadel of Chandiri stands on a hill has been said already. Down one side of this hill runs a double-walled road (*du-tahi*) to water.[2] This is the one place for attack; it had been assigned as the post of the right and left hands and royal corps of the centre.[3] Hurled though assault was from every side, the greatest force was here brought to bear. Our braves did not turn back, however much the pagans threw down stones and flung flaming fire upon them. At length Shahim the centurion[4] got up where the *du-tahi* wall touches the wall of the outer fort; braves swarmed up in two or three places; the pagans in the *du-tahi* began to run away; the *du-tahi* was taken.

Not even as much as this did the pagans fight in the citadel; when a number of our men swarmed up, they fled in haste.[5] In a little while they came out again, quite naked, and renewed the fight; they put many of our men to flight; they made them fly (*auchurdilar*) over the ramparts; some they cut down and killed. Why they had gone so suddenly off the walls seems to have been that they had taken the resolve of those who give up a place as lost; they put all their ladies and beauties (*suratilar*) to death, then, looking themselves to die, came naked out to fight. Our men attacking, each one from his post, drove   Fol. 335. them from the walls whereupon 2 or 300 of them entered Medini Rao's house and there almost all killed one another in this way:—one having taken stand with a sword, the rest

1 *The Illustrated London News* of July 10th, 1915 (on which day this note is written), has an àpropos picture of an ancient fortress-gun, with its stone-ammunition, taken by the Allies in a Dardanelles fort.
2 The *du-tahi* is the *ab-duzd*, water-thief, of f. 67. Its position can be surmised from Cunningham's Plan [Appendix R].
3 For Babur's use of hand (*qul*) as a military term *see* f. 209b.
4 His full designation would be Shah Muhammad *yuz-begi*.
5 This will be flight from the ramparts to other places in the fort.

eagerly stretched out the neck for his blow.[1] Thus went the greater number to hell.

By God's grace this renowned fort was captured in 2 or 3 *garis*[2] (*cir.* an hour), without drum and standard,[3] with no hard fighting done. A pillar of pagan-heads was ordered set up on a hill north-west of Chandiri. A chronogram of this victory having been found in the words *Fath-i-daru'l-harb*[4] (Conquest of a hostile seat), I thus composed them:—

> Was for awhile the station Chandiri
> Pagan-full, the seat of hostile force;
> By fighting, I vanquished its fort,
> The date was *Fath-i-daru' l-harb.*

(*l.   Further description of Chandiri.*)

Chandiri is situated (in) rather good country,[5] having much running-water round about it. Its citadel is on a hill and inside it

1 Babur's account of the siege of Chandiri is incomplete, inasmuch as it says nothing of the general massacre of pagans he has mentioned on f. 272. Khwafi Khan records the massacre, saying, that after the fort was surrendered, as was done on condition of safety for the garrison, from 3 to 4000 pagans were put to death by Babur's troops on account of hostility shewn during the evacuation of the fort. The time assigned to the massacre is previous to the *juhar* of 1000 women and children and the self-slaughter of men in Medini Rao's house, in which he himself died. It is not easy to fit the two accounts in; this might be done, however, by supposing that a folio of Babur's MS. was lost, as others seem lost at the end of the narrative of this year's events (*q.v.*). The lost folio would tell of the surrender, one clearly affecting the mass of Rajput followers and not the chiefs who stood for victory or death and who may have made sacrifice to honour after hearing of the surrender. Babur's narrative in this part certainly reads less consecutive than is usual with him; something preceding his account of the *juhar* would improve it, and would serve another purpose also, since mention of the surrender would fix a term ending the now too short time of under one hour he assigns as the duration of the fighting. If a surrender had been mentioned, it would be clear that his "2 or 3 *garis*" included the attacking and taking of the *du-tahi* and down to the retreat of the Rajputs from the walls. On this Babur's narrative of the unavailing sacrifice of the chiefs would follow in due order. Khwafi Khan is more circumstantial than Firishta who says nothing of surrender or massacre, but states that 6000 men were killed fighting. Khwafi Khan's authorities may throw light on the matter, which so far does not hang well together in any narrative, Babur's, Firishta's, or Khwafi Khan's. One would like to know what led such a large body of Rajputs to surrender so quickly; had they been all through in favour of accepting terms ? One wonders, again, why from 3 to 4000 Rajputs did not put up a better resistance to massacre. Perhaps their assailants were Turks, stubborn fighters down to 1915 AD.

2 For suggestion about the brevity of this period, *see* last note.

3 Clearly, without Babur's taking part in the fighting.

4 These words by *abjad* make 934. The Hai. MS. mistakenly writes *Bud Chandiri* in the first line of the quatrain instead of *Bud chandi*. Khwafi Khan quotes the quatrain with slight variants.

5 *Chandiri tauri wilayat (da ?) waqi' bulub tur*, which seems to need *da*, in, because the fort, and not the country, is described. Or there may be an omission *e.g.* of a second sentence about the walled-town (fort).

has a tank cut out of the solid rock. There is another large tank[1] at the end of the *du-tahi* by assaulting which the fort was taken. All houses in Chandiri, whether of high or low, are built of stone, those of chiefs being laboriously carved;[2] those of the lower classes are also of stone but are not carved. They are covered in   Fol. 335b. with stone-slabs instead of with earthen tiles. In front of the fort are three large tanks made by former governors who threw dams across and made tanks round about it; their ground lies high.[3] It has a small river (*daryacha*), Betwa[4] by name, which may be some 3 *kurohs* (6 m.) from Chandiri itself; its water is noted in Hindustan as excellent and pleasant drinking. It is a perfect little river (*darya-ghina*). In its bed lie piece after piece of sloping rock (*qialar*)[5] fit for making houses.[6] Chandiri is 90 *kurohs* (180 m.) by road to the south of Agra. In Chandiri the altitude of the Pole-star (?) is 25 degrees.[7]

(*m. Enforced change of campaign.*)

(*Jan. 30th—Jumada I. 8th*) At dawn on Thursday we went round the fort and dismounted beside Mallu Khan's tank.[8]

---

1 This is the "Kirat-sagar" of Cunningham's Plan of Chandiri; it is mentioned under this name by Luard (*l.c.* i, 210). "Kirat" represents Kirti or Kirit Singh who ruled in Gualiar from 1455 to 1479 AD., there also making a tank (Luard, *l.c.* i, 232).

2 For illustrative photographs *see* Luard, *l.c.* vol.i, part iv.

3 I have taken this sentence to apply to the location of the tanks, but with some doubt; they are on the table-land.

4 Babur appears to have written Betwi, this form being in MSS. I have read the name to be that of the river Betwa which is at a considerable distance from the fort. But some writers dispraise its waters where Babur praises.

5 T. *qia* means a slope or slant; here it may describe tilted *strata*, such as would provide slabs for roofing and split easily for building purposes. (*See* next note.)

6 '*imarat qilmaq munasib*. This has been read to mean that the *qialar* provide good sites (Mems. & *Méms.*), but position, distance from the protection of the fort, and the merit of local stone for building incline me to read the words quoted above as referring to the convenient lie of the stone for building purposes. (*See* preceding note.)

7 *Chandiri-da judai (jady)-ning irtiqa'i yigirma-bish darja dur*, Erskine, p. 378, Chanderi is situated in the 25th degree of N. latitude; de Courteille, ii, 334, *La hauteur du Capricorne à Tchanderi est de 25 degrées*. The latitude of Chandiri, it may be noted, is 24° 43'. It does not appear to me indisputable that what Babur says here is a statement of latitude. The word *judai* (or *jady*) means both Pole-star and the Sign Capricorn. M. de Courteille translates the quoted sentence as I have done, but with Capricorn for Pole-star. My acquaintance with such expressions in French does not allow me to know whether his words are a statement of latitude. It occurs to me against this being so, that Babur uses other words when he gives the latitude of Samarkand (f. 44b); and also that he has shewn attention to the Pole-star as a guide on a journey (f. 203, where he uses the more common word *Qutb*). Perhaps he notes its lower altitude when he is far south, in the way he noted the first rise of Canopus to his view (f. 125).

8 Mallu Khan was a noble of Malwa, who became ruler of Malwa in 1532 or 1533 AD. [?], under the style of Qadir Shah.

We had come to Chandiri meaning, after taking it, to move against Raising, Bhilsan, and Sarangpur, pagan lands dependent on the pagan Salahu'd-din, and, these taken, to move on Rana Sanga in Chitur. But as that bad news had come, the begs were summoned, matters were discussed, and decision made that the proper course was first to see to the rebellion of those malignants. Chandiri was given to the Ahmad Shah already mentioned, a grandson of Sl. Nasiru'd-din; 50 *laks* from it were made *khalsa*;[1] Mulla Apaq was entrusted with its military-collectorate, and left to reinforce Ahmad Shah with from 2 to 3000 Turks and Hindustanis.

Fol. 336. (*Feb. 2nd*) This work finished, we marched from Mallu Khan's tank on Sunday the 11th of the first Jumada, with the intention of return (north), and dismounted on the bank of the Burhanpur-water.

(*Feb. 9th*) On Sunday again, Yakka Khwaja and Ja'far Khwaja were sent from Bandir to fetch boats from Kalpi to the Kanar-passage.

(*Feb. 22nd*) On Saturday the 24th of the month we dismounted at the Kanar-passage, and ordered the army to begin to cross.

(*n. News of the rebels.*)

News came in these days that the expeditionary force[2] had abandoned Qanuj also and come to Rapri, and that a strong body of the enemy had assaulted and taken Shamsabad although Abu'l-muhammad the lancer must have strengthened it.[3] There was delay of 3 or 4 days on one side or other of the river before the army got across. Once over, we moved march by march towards Qanuj, sending scouting braves (*qazaq yigitlar*) ahead to get news of our opponents. Two or three marches from Qanuj, news was brought that Ma'ruf's son had fled on seeing the dark mass of the news-gatherers, and got away. Biban, Bayazid and Ma'ruf, on hearing news of us, crossed Gang (Ganges) and seated themselves on its eastern bank opposite Qanuj, thinking to prevent our passage.

1 *i.e.* paid direct to the royal treasury.
2 This is the one concerning which bad news reached Babur just before Chandiri was taken.
3 This presumably is the place offered to Medini Rao (f. 333*b*), and Bikramajit (f. 343).

(o. *A bridge made over the Ganges.*)

(*Feb. 27th*) On Thursday the 6th of the latter Jumada we passed Qanuj and dismounted on the western bank of Gang. Some of the braves went up and down the river and took boats by force,[1] bringing in 30 or 40, large or small. Mir Muhammad the raftsman was sent to find a place convenient for making a bridge and to collect requisites for making it. He came back approving of a place about a *kuroh* (2 m.) below the camp. Energetic overseers were told off for the work. Ustad 'Ali-quli placed the mortar for his stone-discharge near where the bridge was to be and shewed himself active in discharging it. Mustafa *Rumi* had the culverin-carts crossed over to an island below the place for the bridge, and from that island began a culverin-discharge. Excellent matchlock fire was made from a post[2] raised above the bridge. Malik Qasim *Mughul* and a very few men went across the river once or twice and fought excellently (*yakhshilar aurushtilar*). With equal boldness Baba Sl. and Darwish Sl. also crossed, but went with the insufficient number of from 10 to 15 men; they went after the Evening Prayer and came back without fighting, with nothing done; they were much blamed for this crossing of theirs. At last Malik Qasim, grown bold, attacked the enemy's camp and, by shooting arrows into it, drew him out (?);[3] he came with a mass of men and an elephant, fell on Malik Qasim and hurried him off. Malik Qasim got into a boat, but before it could put off, the elephant came up and swamped it. In that encounter Malik Qasim died.

In the days before the bridge was finished Ustad 'Ali-quli did good things in stone-discharge (*yakhshilar tash aiti*), on the first day discharging 8 stones, on the second 16, and going on equally well for 3 or 4 days. These stones he discharged from the Ghazi-mortar which is so-called because it was used in the battle with Rana Sanga the pagan. There had been another and larger mortar which burst after discharging one stone.[4] The match-lockmen made a mass (*qalin*) of discharges, bringing down many

Fol. 336b.

Fol. 337.

---

1 Obviously for the bridge.

2 *m:ljar* (*see* f. 333 n.). Here the word would mean befittingly a protected standing-place, a refuge, such as matchlockmen used (f. 217).

3 *sighirurdi*, a vowel-variant, perhaps, of *sughururdi*.

4 f. 331b. This passage shews that Babur's mortars were few.

men and horses; they shot also slave-workmen running scared away (?) and men and horses passing-by.[1]

(*March 11th*) On Wednesday the 19th of the latter Jumada the bridge being almost finished, we marched to its head. The Afghans must have ridiculed the bridge-making as being far from completion.[2]

(*March 12th*) The bridge being ready on Thursday, a small body of foot-soldiers and Lahoris went over. Fighting as small followed.

(*p. Encounter with the Afghans.*)

(*March 13th*) On Friday the royal corps, and the right and left hands of the centre crossed on foot. The whole body of Afghans, armed, mounted, and having elephants with them, attacked us. They hurried off our men of the left hand, but our centre itself (*i.e.* the royal corps) and the right hand stood firm, fought, and forced the enemy to retire. Two men from these divisions had galloped ahead of the rest; one was dismounted and taken; the horse of the other was struck again and again, had had enough,[3] turned round and when amongst our men, fell down. On that day 7 or 8 heads were brought in; many of the enemy had arrow or matchlock wounds. Fighting went on till the Other Prayer. That night all who had gone across were made to return; if (more) had gone over on that Saturday's eve,[4] most of the enemy would probably have fallen into our hands, but this was in my mind:—Last year we marched out of Sikri to fight Rana Sanga on Tuesday, New-year's-day, and crushed that rebel on Saturday; this year we had marched to crush these rebels on Wednesday, New-year's-day,[5] and it would be one of singular things, if we beat them on Sunday. So thinking, we did not make the rest of

Fol. 337b.

1 *nufur qul-lar-din ham karka bila rah rawa kishi u at aitilar*, a difficult sentence.

2 *Afghanlar kupruk baghlamaq-ni istib'ad qilib tamaskhur qilurlar aikandur*. The ridicule will have been at slow progress, not at the bridge-making itself, since pontoon-bridges were common (Irvine's *Army of the Indian Moghuls*).

3 *tuilab*; Pers. trs. *uftan u khezan*, limping, or falling and rising, a translation raising doubt, because such a mode of progression could hardly have allowed escape from pursuers.

4 Anglicé, on Friday night.

5 According to the Persian calendar, New-year's-day is that on which the Sun enters Aries.

the army cross. The enemy did not come to fight on Saturday, but stood arrayed a long way off.

(*Sunday March 15th—Jumada II. 23rd*) On this day the carts were taken over, and at this same dawn the army was ordered to cross. At beat of drum news came from our scouts that the enemy had fled. Chin-timur Sl. was ordered to lead his army in pursuit and the following leaders also were made pursuers who should move with the Sultan and not go beyond his word:—Muhammad 'Ali *Jang-jang*, Husamu'd-din 'Ali (son) of Khalifa, Muhibb-i-'ali (son) of Khalifa, Kuki (son) of Baba Qashqa, Dost-i-muhammad (son) of Baba Qashqa, Baqi of Fol. 338. Tashkint, and Red Wali. I crossed at the Sunnat Prayer. The camels were ordered to be taken over at a passage seen lower down. That Sunday we dismounted on the bank of standing-water within a *kuroh* of Bangarmawu.[1] Those appointed to pursue the Afghans were not doing it well; they had dismounted in Bangarmawu and were scurrying off at the Mid-day Prayer of this same Sunday.

(*March 16th—Jumada II. 24th*) At dawn we dismounted on the bank of a lake belonging to Bangarmawu.

(q. Arrival of a Chaghatai cousin.)

On this same day (*March 16th*) Tukhta-bugha Sl. a son of my mother's brother (*dada*) the Younger Khan (*Ahmad Chaghatai*) came and waited on me.

(*March 21st*) On Saturday the 29th of the latter Jumada I visited Laknau, crossed the Gui-water[2] and dismounted. This day I bathed in the Gui-water. Whether it was from water getting into my ear, or whether it was from the effect of the climate, is not known, but my right ear was obstructed and for a few days there was much pain.[3]

(r. The campaign continued.)

One or two marches from Aud (Oudh) some-one came from Chin-timur Sl. to say, "The enemy is seated on the far side of

---

1 so-spelled in the Hai. MS.; by de Courteille Banguermadu; the two forms may represent the same one of the Arabic script.
2 or Gui, from the context clearly the Gumti. Jarrett gives Godi as a name of the Gumti; Gui and Godi may be the same word in the Arabic script.
3 Some MSS. read that there was not much pain.

the river Sird[a?];[1] let His Majesty send help." We detached a reinforcement of 1000 braves under Qaracha.

Fol. 338b.

(*March 28th*) On Saturday the 7th of Rajab we dismounted 2 or 3 *kurohs* from Aud above the junction of the Gagar (Gogra) and Sird[a]. Till today Shaikh Bayazid will have been on the other side of the Sird[a] opposite Aud, sending letters to the Sultan and discussing with him, but the Sultan getting to know his deceitfulness, sent word to Qaracha at the Mid-day Prayer and made ready to cross the river. On Qaracha's joining him, they crossed at once to where were some 50 horsemen with 3 or 4 elephants. These men could make no stand; they fled; a few having been dismounted, the heads cut off were sent in.

Following the Sultan there crossed over Bi-khub (var. Ni-khub) Sl. and Tardi Beg (the brother) of Quj Beg, and Baba Chuhra (the Brave), and Baqi *shaghawal*. Those who had crossed first and gone on, pursued Shaikh Bayazid till the Evening Prayer, but he flung himself into the jungle and escaped. Chin-timur dismounted late on the bank of standing-water, rode on at midnight after the rebel, went as much as 40 *kurohs* (80 m.), and came to where Shaikh Bayazid's family and relations (*nisba?*) had been; they however must have fled. He sent gallopers off in all directions from that place; Baqi *shaghawal* and a few braves drove the enemy like sheep before them, overtook the family and brought in some Afghan prisoners.

We stayed a few days on that ground (near Aud) in order to settle the affairs of Aud. People praised the land lying along the Sird[a] 7 or 8 *kurohs* (14–16 m.) above Aud, saying it was hunting-ground. Mir Muhammad the raftsman was sent out and returned after looking at the crossings over the Gagar-water (Gogra) and the Sird[a]-water (Chauka?).

Fol. 339.

(*April 2nd*) On Thursday the 12th of the month I rode out intending to hunt.[2]

---

1 I take this to be the Kali-Sarda-Chauka affluent of the Gogra and not its Sarju or Saru one. To so take it seems warranted by the context; there could be no need for the fords on the Sarju to be examined, and its position is not suitable.
2 Unfortunately no record of the hunting-expedition survives.

Here, in all known texts of the *Babur-nama* there is a break of the narrative between April 2nd and Sep. 18th 1528 AD.—— Jumada II. 12th 934 AH. and Muharram 3rd 935 AH., which, whether intentional or accidental, is unexplained by Babur's personal circumstances. It is likely to be due to a loss of pages from Babur's autograph manuscript, happening at some time preceding the making of either of the Persian translations of his writings and of the Elphinstone and Haidarabad transcripts. Though such a loss might have occurred easily during the storm chronicled on f. 376*b*, it seems likely that Babur would then have become aware of it and have made it good. A more probable explanation of the loss is the danger run by Humayun's library during his exile from rule in Hindustan, at which same time may well have occurred the seeming loss of the record of 936 and 937 AH.

a. Transactions of the period of the lacuna.

Mr. Erskine notes (*Mems.* p. 381 n.) that he found the gap in all MSS. he saw and that historians of Hindustan throw no light upon the transactions of the period. Much can be gleaned however as to Babur's occupations during the 5½ months of the *lacuna* from his chronicle of 935 AH. which makes several references to occurrences of "last year" and also allows several inferences to be drawn. From this source it becomes known that the Afghan campaign the record of which is broken by the gap, was carried on and that in its course Babur was at Jun-pur (f. 365), Chausa (f. 365*b*) and Baksara (f. 366–366*b*) and between Ghazipur and Banaras (p. 502); that he swam the Ganges (f. 366*b*), bestowed Sarun on a Farmuli Shaikh-zada (f. 374*b* and f. 377), negotiated with Rana Sanga's son Bikramajit (f. 342*b*), ordered a Char-bagh laid out (f. 340), and was ill for 40 days (f. 346*b*). It may be inferred too that he visited Dulpur (f. 353*b*), recalled 'Askari (f. 339), sent Khwaja Dost-i-khawand on family affairs to Kabul (f. 345*b*), and was much pre-occupied by the disturbed state of Kabul (*see* his letters to Humayun and Khwaja Kalan written in 935 AH.).[1]

It is not easy to follow the dates of events in 935 AH. because in many instances only the day of the week or a "next day" is entered. I am far from sure that one passage at least now found *s.a.* 935 AH. does not belong to 934 AH. It is not in the Hai. Codex (where its place would have been on f. 363*b*), and, so far as I can see, does not fit with the dates of 935 AH. It will be considered with least trouble with its context and my notes (*q.v.* f. 363*b* and ff. 366–366*b*).

b. Remarks on the lacuna.

One interesting biographical topic is likely to have found mention in the missing record, *viz.* the family difficulties which led to 'Askari's supersession by Kamran in the government of Multan (f. 359).

Another is the light an account of the second illness of 934 AH. might have thrown on a considerable part of the Collection of verses already written in Hindustan and now known to us as the *Rampur Diwan*. The *Babur-nama* allows the dates of much of its contents to be known, but there remain poems which seem prompted by the self-examination of some illness not found in the *B.N.* It contains the metrical version of Khwaja 'Ubaidu'l-lah's *Walidiyyah* of which Babur writes on f. 346 and it is dated Monday Rabi' II. 15th 935 AH. (Dec. 29th 1528 AD.). I surmise that the reflective verses following the *Walidiyyah* belong to the 40 days' illness of 934 AH. *i.e.* were composed in the period of the *lacuna*. The Collection, as it is in the "Rampur Diwan", went to a friend who was probably Khwaja Kalan; it may have been the only such collection made by Babur. No other copy of it has so far been found. It has the character of an individual gift with verses specially addressed to its recipient. Any light upon it which may have vanished with pages of 934 AH. is an appreciable loss.

1 One historian, Ahmad-i-yadgar states in his *Tarikh-i-salatin-i-afaghana* that Babur went to Lahor immediately after his capture of Chandiri, and on his return journey to Agra suppressed in the Panj-ab a rising of the Mundahar (or, Mandhar) Rajputs. His date is discredited by Babur's existing narrative of 934 AH. as also by the absence in 935 AH. of allusion to either episode. My husband who has considered the matter, advises me that the Lahor visit may have been made in 936 or early in 937 AH. [These are a period of which the record is lost or, less probably, was not written.]

(a. Arrivals at Court.)

(Sep. 18th) On Friday the 3rd[2] of Muharram, 'Askari whom I had summoned for the good of Multan[3] before I moved out for Chandiri, waited on me in the private-house.[4]

(Sep. 19th) Next day waited on me the historian Khwand-amir, Maulana Shihab[5] the enigmatist, and Mir Ibrahim the harper a relation of Yunas-i-'ali, who had all come out of Heri long before, wishing to wait on me.[6]

(b. Babur starts for Gualiar.)[7]

(Sep. 20th) With the intention of visiting Gualiar which in books they write Galiur,[8] I crossed the Jun at the Other

---

1 Elph. MS. f. 262; I. O. 215 f. 207b and 217 f. 234b; *Mems.* p. 382. Here the Elphinstone MS. recommences after a *lacuna* extending from Hai. MS. f. 312b.

2 *See* Appendix S:—*Concerning the dating of* 935 AH.

3 Askari was now about 12 years old. He was succeeded in Multan by his elder brother Kamran, transferred from Qandahar [Index; JRAS. 1908 p. 829 para. (1)]. This transfer, it is safe to say, was due to Babur's resolve to keep Kabul in his own hands, a resolve which his letters to Humayun (f. 348), to Kamran (f. 359), and to Khwaja Kalan (f. 359) attest, as well as do the movements of his family at this time. What would make the stronger government of Kamran seem now more "for the good of Multan" than that of the child 'Askari are the Biluchi incursions, mentioned somewhat later (f. 355b) as having then occurred more than once.

4 This will be his own house in the Garden-of-eight-paradises, the Char-bagh begun in 932 AH. (August 1526 AD.).

5 To this name Khwand-amir adds Ahmadu'l-haqiri, perhaps a pen-name; he also quotes verses of Shihab's (*Habibu's-siyar* lith. ed. iii, 350).

6 Khwand-amir's account of his going into Hindustan is that he left his "dear home" (Herat) for Qandahar in mid-Shawwal 933 AH. (mid-July 1527 AD.); that on Jumada I. 10th 934 AH. (Feb. 1st 1528 AD.) he set out from Qandahar on the hazardous journey into Hindustan; and that owing to the distance, heat, setting-in of the Rains, and breadth of rapid rivers, he was seven months on the way. He mentions no fellow-travellers, but he gives as the day of his arrival in Agra the one on which Babur says he presented himself at Court. (For an account of annoyances and misfortunes to which he was subjected under Auzbeg rule in Herat *see Journal des Savans*, July 1843, pp. 389, 393, Quatremère's art.)

7 Concerning Gualiar *see* Cunningham's *Archeological Survey Reports* vol. ii; Louis Rousselet's *L'Inde des Rajas*; Lepel Griffin's *Famous Monuments of Central India*, especially for its photographs; *Gazetteer of India*; Luard's *Gazetteer of Gwalior*, text and photographs; *Travels of Peter Mundy*, Hakluyt Society ed. R. C. Temple, ii, 61, especially for its picture of the fort and note (p. 62) enumerating early writers on Gualiar. Of Persian books there is Jalal *Hisari's Tarikh-i-Gwaliawar* (B.M. Add. 16,859) and Hiraman's (B.M.Add. 16,709) unacknowledged version of it, which is of the B.M. MSS. the more legible.

8 Perhaps this stands for Gwaliawar, the form seeming to be used by Jalal *Hisari*, and having good traditional support (Cunningham p. 373 and Luard p. 228).

Prayer of Sunday the 5th of the month, went into the fort of
Agra to bid farewell to Fakhr-i-jahan Begim and Khadija-
sultan Begim who were to start for Kabul in a few days, and
got to horse. Muhammad-i-zaman Mirza asked for leave and
stayed behind in Agra. That night we did 3 or 4 *kurohs* (6–8 m.)
of the road, dismounted near a large lake (*kul*) and there slept.

(*Sep. 21st*) We got through the Prayer somewhat before
time (*Muh. 6th*) and rode on, nooned[1] on the bank of the
Gamb[h]ir-water,[2] and went on shortly after the Mid-day Prayer.
On the way we ate[3] powders mixed with the flour of parched
Fol. 339*b.* grain,[4] Mulla Rafi' having prepared them for raising the spirits.
They were found very distasteful and unsavoury. Near the Other
Prayer we dismounted a *kuroh* (2 m.) west of Dulpur, at a place
where a garden and house had been ordered made.[5]

(*c. Work in Dulpur (Dhulpur).*)

That place is at the end of a beaked hill,[6] its beak being of
solid red building-stone ('*imarat-tash*). I had ordered the (beak
of the) hill cut down (dressed down?) to the ground-level and
that if there remained a sufficient height, a house was to be cut
out in it, if not, it was to be levelled and a tank (*hauz*) cut out
in its top. As it was not found high enough for a house, Ustad
Shah Muhammad the stone-cutter was ordered to level it and
cut out an octagonal, roofed tank. North of this tank the
ground is thick with trees, mangoes, *jaman* (*Eugenia jambolana*),
all sorts of trees; amongst them I had ordered a well made,
10 by 10; it was almost ready; its water goes to the afore-named
tank. To the north of this tank Sl. Sikandar's dam is flung across
(the valley); on it houses have been built, and above it the waters
of the Rains gather into a great lake. On the east of this lake
is a garden; I ordered a seat and four-pillared platform (*talar*)

1 *tushlanib, i.e.* they took rest and food together at mid-day.
2 This seems to be the conjoined Gambhir and Banganga which is crossed by the
Agra-Dhulpur road (*G. of I.* Atlas, Sheet 34).
3 *aichtuq*, the plural of which shews that more than one partook of the powders
(*safuf*).
4 T. *talqan*, Hindi *sattu* (Shaw). M. de Courteille's variant translation may be due to
his reading for *talqan, talghaq, flot, agitation* (his Dict. *s.n.*) and *yil*, wind, for *bila*, with.
5 in 933 AH. f. 330*b.*
6 "Each beaked promontory" (Lycidas). Our name "Selsey-bill" is an English
instance of Babur's (not infrequent) *tumshuq*, beak, bill of a bird.

to be cut out in the solid rock on that same side, and a mosque Fol. 340.
built on the western one.

(*Sept. 22nd and 23rd—Muh. 7th and 8th*) On account of these
various works, we stayed in Dulpur on Tuesday and Wednesday.

(d. Journey to Gualiar resumed.)

(*Sep. 24th*) On Thursday we rode on, crossed the Chambal-
river and made the Mid-day Prayer on its bank, between the
two Prayers (the Mid-day and the Afternoon) bestirred ourselves to leave that place, passed the Kawari and dismounted.
The Kawari-water being high through rain, we crossed it by
boat, making the horses swim over.

(*Sep. 25th*) Next day, Friday which was 'Ashur (*Muh. 10th*),
we rode on, took our nooning at a village on the road, and at
the Bed-time Prayer dismounted a *kuroh* north of Gualiar, in a
Char-bagh ordered made last year.[1]

(*Sep. 26th*) Riding on next day after the Mid-day Prayer, we
visited the low hills to the north of Gualiar, and the Praying-
place, went into the fort[2] through the Gate called Hati-pul
which joins Man-sing's buildings ('*imarat*),[3] and dismounted, close
to the Other Prayer, at those ('*imaratlar*)[4] of Raja Bikramajit
in which Rahim-dad[5] had settled himself.

1 No order about this Char-bagh is in existing annals of 934 AH. Such order is
likely to have been given after Babur's return from his operations against
the Afghans, in his account of which the annals of 934 AH. break off.

2 The fort-hill at the northern end is 300 ft. high, at the southern end, 274 ft.; its
length from north to south is 1¾ m.; its breadth varies from 600 ft. opposite the main
entrance (Hati-pul) to 2800 ft. in the middle opposite the great temple (Sas-bhao).
Cf. Cunningham p. 330 and Appendix R, *in loco*, for his Plan of Gualiar.

3 This Arabic plural may have been prompted by the greatness and distinction of
Man-sing's constructions.

4 A translation point concerning the (Arabic) word '*imarat* is that the words
"palace", "*palais*", and "residence" used for it respectively by Erskine, de Courteille, and, previous to the Hindustan Section, by myself, are too limited in meaning
to serve for Babur's uses of it in Hindustan; and this (1) because he uses it throughout
his writings for buildings under palatial rank (*e.g.* those of high and low in Chandiri);
(2) because he uses it in Hindustan for non-residential buildings (*e.g.* for the Badalgarh
outwork, f. 341*b*, and a Hindu temple *ib.*); and (3) because he uses it for the word
"building" in the term building-stone, f. 335*b* and f. 339*b*. *Building* is the comprehensive word under which all his uses of it group. For labouring this point a truism
pleads my excuse, namely, that a man's vocabulary being characteristic of himself, for
a translator to increase or diminish it is to intrude on his personality, and this the
more when an autobiography is concerned. Hence my search here (as elsewhere) for
an English grouping word is part of an endeavour to restrict the vocabulary of my
translation to the limits of my author's.

5 Jalal *Hisari* describes "Khwaja Rahim-dad" as a paternal-nephew of Mahdi
Khwaja. Neither man has been introduced by Babur, as it is his rule to introduce

To-night I elected to take opium because of ear-ache; another reason was the shining of the moon.[1]

(*e. Visit to the Rajas' palaces.*)

(*Sep. 27th*) Opium sickness gave me much discomfort next day (*Muh. 12th*); I vomited a good deal. Sickness notwithstanding, I visited the buildings ('*imaratlar*) of Man-sing and Bikramajit thoroughly. They are wonderful buildings, entirely of hewn stone, in heavy and unsymmetrical blocks however.[2] Of all the Rajas' buildings Man-sing's is the best and loftiest.[3] It is more elaborately worked on its eastern face than on the others. This face may be 40 to 50 *qari* (yards) high,[4] and is entirely of hewn stone, whitened with plaster.[5] In parts it is four storeys high; the lower two are very dark; we went through them with

Fol. 340b.

---

when he first mentions a person of importance, by particulars of family, *etc.* Both men became disloyal in 935 AH. (1529 AD.) as will be found referred to by Babur. Jalal *Hisari* supplements Babur's brief account of their misconduct and Shaikh Muhammad *Ghaus'* mediation in 936 AH. For knowledge of his contribution I am indebted to my husband's perusal of the *Tarikh-i-Gwaliawar*.

1 Erskine notes that Indians and Persians regard moonshine as cold but this only faintly expresses the wide-spread fear of moon-stroke expressed in the Psalm (121 v.6), "The Sun shall not smite thee by day, nor the Moon by night."

2 *Agarcha luk baluk u bi siyaq.* Ilminsky [p. 441] has *baluk baluk* but without textual warrant and perhaps following Erskine, as he says, speaking generally, that he has done in case of need (Ilminsky's Preface). Both Erskine and de Courteille, working, it must be remembered, without the help of detailed modern descriptions and pictures, took the above words to say that the buildings were scattered and without symmetry, but they are not scattered and certainly Man-sing's has symmetry. I surmise that the words quoted above do not refer to the buildings themselves but to the stones of which they are made. T. *luk* means heavy, and T. *baluk* [? block] means a thing divided off, here a block of stone. Such blocks might be *bi siyaq*, *i.e.* irregular in size. To take the words in this way does not contradict known circumstances, and is verbally correct.

3 The Rajas' buildings Babur could compare were Raja Karna (or Kirti)'s [who ruled from 1454 to 1479 AD.], Raja Man-sing's [1486 to 1516 AD.], and Raja Bikramajit's [1516 to 1526 AD. when he was killed at Panipat].

4 The height of the eastern face is 100 ft. and of the western 60 ft. The total length from north to south of the outside wall is 300 ft.; the breadth of the residence from east to west 160 ft. The 300 ft. of length appears to be that of the residence and service-courtyard (Cunningham p. 347 and Plate lxxxvii).

5 *kaj bila aqaritib.* There can be little doubt that a white pediment would show up the coloured tiles of the upper part of the palace-walls more than would pale red sandstone. These tiles were so profuse as to name the building Chit Mandir (Painted Mandir). Guided by Babur's statement, Cunningham sought for and found plaster in crevices of carved work; from which one surmises that the white coating approved itself to successors of Man-sing. [It may be noted that the word Mandir is in the same case for a translator as is '*imarat* (f. 339b n.) since it requires a grouping word to cover its uses for temple, palace, and less exalted buildings.]

candles.[1] On one (or, every) side of this building are five cupolas[2] having between each two of them a smaller one, square after the fashion of Hindustan. On the larger ones are fastened sheets of gilded copper. On the outside of the walls is painted-tile work, the semblance of plantain-trees being shewn all round with green tiles. In a bastion of the eastern front is the Hati-pul,[3] *hati* being what these people call an elephant, *pul*, a gate. A sculptured image of an elephant with two drivers (*fil-ban*)[4] stands at the out-going (*chiqish*) of this Gate; it is exactly like an elephant; from it the gate is called Hati-pul. A window in the Fol. 341. lowest storey where the building has four, looks towards this elephant and gives a near view of it.[5] The cupolas which have been mentioned above are themselves the topmost stage (*murtaba*) of the building;[6] the sitting-rooms are on the second storey (*tabaqat*), in a hollow even;[7] they are rather airless places although Hindustani pains have been taken with them.[8] The buildings of Man-sing's son Bikramajit are in a central position (*aurta da*) on the north side of the fort.[9] The son's buildings do not match the father's. He has made a great dome, very dark but growing lighter if one stays awhile in it.[10] Under it is a smaller building

1 The lower two storeys are not only backed by solid ground but, except near the Hati-pul, have the rise of ground in front of them which led Babur to say they were "even in a pit" (*chuqur*).

2 MSS. vary between *har* and *bir*, every and one, in this sentence. It may be right to read *bir*, and apply it only to the eastern façade as that on which there were most cupolas. There are fewer on the south side, which still stands (Luard's photo. No. 37).

3 The ground rises steeply from this Gate to an inner one, called Hawa-pul from the rush of air (*hawa*) through it.

4 Cunningham says the riders were the Raja and a driver. Perhaps they were a mahout and his mate. The statue stood to the left on exit (*chiqish*).

5 This window will have been close to the Gate where no mound interferes with outlook.

6 Rooms opening on inner and open courts appear to form the third storey of the residence.

7 T. *chuqur*, hollow, pit. This storey is dark and unventilated, a condition due to small windows, absence of through draught, and the adjacent mound. Cunningham comments on its disadvantages.

8 *Agarcha Hindustani takalluflar qilib turlar wali bi hawalik-raq yirlar dur.* Perhaps amongst the pains taken were those demanded for *punkhas*. I regret that Erskine's translation of this passage, so superior to my own in literary merit, does not suit the Turki original. He worked from the Persian translation, and not only so, but with a less rigid rule of translation than binds me when working on Babur's *ipsissima verba* (Mems. p. 384; Cunningham p. 349; Luard p. 226).

9 The words *aurta da* make apt contrast between the outside position of Man-sing's buildings which helped to form the fort-wall, and Bikramajit's which were further in except perhaps one wall of his courtyard (*see* Cunningham's Plate lxxxiii).

10 Cunningham (p. 350) says this was originally a *bara-duri*, a twelve-doored open hall, and must have been light. His "originally" points to the view that the hall

into which no light comes from any side. When Rahim-dad settled
down in Bikramajit's buildings, he made a rather small hall
[*kichikraq talarghina*] on the top of this dome.[1] From Bikramajit's buildings a road has been made to his father's, a road
such that nothing is seen of it from outside and nothing known
of it inside, a quite enclosed road.[2]

Fol. 341b.
After visiting these buildings, we rode to a college Rahim-dad
had made by the side of a large tank, there enjoyed a flower-
garden[3] he had laid out, and went late to where the camp was
in the Charbagh.

(f. Rahim-dad's flower-garden.)

Rahim-dad has planted a great numbers of flowers in his garden
(*baghcha*), many being beautiful red oleanders. In these places
the oleander-flower is peach,[4] those of Gualiar are beautiful,
deep red. I took some of them to Agra and had them planted
in gardens there. On the south of the garden is a large lake[5]
where the waters of the Rains gather; on the west of it is
a lofty idol-house,[6] side by side with which Sl. Shihabu'd-din
Ailtmish (Altamsh) made a Friday mosque; this is a very lofty
building ('*imarat*), the highest in the fort; it is seen, with the fort,
from the Dulpur-hill (*cir.* 30 m. away). People say the stone for
it was cut out and brought from the large lake above-mentioned.
Rahim-dad has made a wooden (*yighach*) *talar* in his garden, and

---

had been altered before Babur saw it but as it was only about 10 years old at that time,
it was in its first form, presumably. Perhaps Babur saw it in a bad light. The
dimensions Cunningham gives of it suggest that the high dome must have been
frequently ill-lighted.

1 The word *talar*, having various applications, is not easy to match with a single
English word, nor can one be sure in all cases what it means, a platform, a hall, or
etc. To find an equivalent for its diminutive *talar-ghina* is still more difficult.
Rahim-dad's *talar*-ette will have stood on the flat centre of the dome, raised on four
pillars or perhaps with its roof only so-raised; one is sure there would be a roof as
protection against sun or moon. It may be noted that the dome is not visible outside
from below, but is hidden by the continuation upwards of walls which form a mean-
looking parallelogram of masonry.

2 T. *tur yul*. Concerning this hidden road *see* Cunningham p. 350 and Plate lxxxvii.

3 *baghcha*. The context shews that the garden was for flowers.

4 *shaft-alu* i.e. the rosy colour of peach-flowers, perhaps lip-red (Steingass).
Babur's contrast seems to be between those red oleanders of Hindustan that are rosy-
red, and the deep red ones he found in Gualiar.

5 *kul*, any large sheet of water, natural or artificial (Babur). This one will be the
Suraj-kund (Sun-tank).

6 This is the Teli Mandir, or Telingana Mandir (Luard). *Cf.* Cunningham, p. 356
and Luard p. 227 for accounts of it; and *G. of I. s.n.* Teliagarhi for Teli Rajas.

porches at the gates, which, after the Hindustani fashion, are somewhat low and shapeless.

(g. *The Urwah-valley.*)

(*Sep. 28th*) Next day (*Muh. 13th*) at the Mid-day Prayer we rode out to visit places in Gualiar we had not yet seen. We saw the '*imarat* called Badalgar[1] which is part of Man-sing's fort (*qila'*), went through the Hati-pul and across the fort to a place called Urwa (Urwah), which is a valley-bottom (*qul*) on its western side. Though Urwa is outside the fort-wall running along the top of the hill, it has two stages (*murtaba*) of high wall at its mouth. The higher of these walls is some 30 or 40 *qari* (yards) high; this is the longer one; at each end it joins   Fol. 342. the wall of the fort. The second wall curves in and joins the middle part of the first; it is the lower and shorter of the two. This curve of wall will have been made for a water-thief;[2] within it is a stepped well (*wa'in*) in which water is reached by 10 or 15 steps. Above the Gate leading from the valley to this walled-well the name of Sl. Shihabu'd-din Ailtmish (Altamsh) is inscribed, with the date 630 (AH.—1233 AD.). Below this outer wall and outside the fort there is a large lake which seems to dwindle (at times) till no lake remains; from it water goes to the water-thief. There are two other lakes inside Urwa the water of which those who live in the fort prefer to all other.

Three sides of Urwa are solid rock, not the red rock of Biana but one paler in colour. On these sides people have cut out idol-statues, large and small, one large statue on the south side being perhaps 20 *qari* (yds.) high.[3] These idols are shewn quite

---

1 This is a large outwork reached from the Gate of the same name. Babur may have gone there specially to see the Gujari Mandir said by Cunningham to have been built by Man-sing's Gujar wife Mriga-nayana (fawn-eyed). *Cf.* Cunningham p. 351 and, for other work done by the same Queen, in the s.e. corner of the fort, p. 344; Luard p. 226. In this place "construction" would serve to translate '*imarat* (f. 340 n.).

2 *ab-duzd*, a word conveying the notion of a stealthy taking of the water. The walls at the mouth of Urwa were built by Altamsh for the protection of its water for the fort. The date Babur mentions (a few lines further) is presumably that of their erection.

3 Cunningham, who gives 57 ft. as the height of this statue, says Babur estimated it at 20 *gaz*, or 40 ft., but this is not so. Babur's word is not *gaz* a measure of 24 fingers—breadth, but *qari*, the length from the tip of the shoulder to the fingers-ends; it is about 33 inches, not less, I understand. Thus stated in *qaris* Babur's estimate of the height comes very near Cunningham's, being a good 55 ft. to 57 ft. (I may note that I have usually translated *qari* by "yard", as the yard is its nearest English equivalent. The Pers. trs. of the B.N. translates by *gaz*, possibly a larger *gaz* than that of 24 fingers-breadth *i.e.* inches.)

Fol. 342b. naked without covering for the privities. Along the sides of the two Urwa lakes 20 or 30 wells have been dug, with water from which useful vegetables (*sabzi karliklar*), flowers and trees are grown. Urwa is not a bad place; it is shut in (T. *tur*); the idols are its defect; I, for my part, ordered them destroyed.[1]

Going out of Urwa into the fort again, we enjoyed the window[2] of the Sultani-pul which must have been closed through the pagan time till now, went to Rahim-dad's flower-garden at the Evening Prayer, there dismounted and there slept.

(h. A son of Rana Sanga negotiates with Babur.)

(*Sep. 29th*) On Tuesday the 14th of the month came people from Rana Sanga's second son, Bikramajit by name, who with his mother Padmawati was in the fort of Rantanbur. Before I rode out for Gualiar,[3] others had come from his great and trusted Hindu, Asuk by name, to indicate Bikramajit's submission and obeisance and ask a subsistence-allowance of 70 *laks* for him; it had been settled at that time that *parganas* to the amount he asked should be bestowed on him, his men were given leave to go, with tryst for Gualiar which we were about to visit. They came into Gualiar somewhat after the trysting-day. The Hindu Asuk[4] is said to be a near relation of Bikramajit's mother Padmawati; he, for his part, set these particulars forth father-

Fol. 343. like and son-like;[5] they, for theirs, concurring with him, agreed to wish me well and serve me. At the time when Sl. Mahmud (*Khilji*) was beaten by Rana Sanga and fell into pagan captivity

---

1 The statues were not broken up by Babur's agents; they were mutilated; their heads were restored with coloured plaster by the Jains (Cunningham p. 365; Luard p. 228).

2 *rozan* [or, *auz:n*] ... *tafarruj qilib*. Neither Cunningham nor Luard mentions this window, perhaps because Erskine does not; nor is this name of a Gate found. It might be that of the Dhonda-paur (Cunningham, p. 339). The 1st Pers. trs. [I.O. 215 f. 210] omits the word *rozan* (or, *auz:n*); the 2nd (I.O. 217 f. 236b) renders it by *ja'i*, place. Manifestly the Gate was opened by Babur, but, presumably, not precisely at the time of his visit. I am inclined to understand that *rozan* ... *tafarruj karda* means enjoying the window formerly used by Muhammadan rulers. If *auz:n* be the right reading, its sense is obscure.

3 This will have occurred in the latter half of 934 AH. of which no record is now known.

4 He is mentioned under the name Asuk Mal *Rajput*, as a servant of Rana Sanga by the *Mirat-i-sikandari*, lith. ed. p. 161. In Bayley's Translation p. 273 he is called Awasuk, manifestly by clerical error, the sentence being *az janib-i-au Asuk Mal Rajput dar an (qila') buda* ...

5 *ata-lik, aughul-lik, i.e.* he spoke to the son as a father, to the mother as a son.

(925 AH.—1519 AD.) he possessed a famous crown-cap (*taj-kula*) and golden belt, accepting which Sanga let him go free. That crown-cap and golden belt must have become Bikramajit's; his elder brother Ratan-si, now Rana of Chitur in his father's place, had asked for them but Bikramajit had not given them up,[1] and now made the men he sent to me, speak to me about them, and ask for Biana in place of Rantanbur. We led them away from the Biana question and promised Shamsabad in exchange for Rantanbur. To-day (*Muh. 14th*) they were given a nine days' tryst for Biana, were dressed in robes of honour, and allowed to go.

(i. Hindu temples visited.)

We rode from the flower-garden to visit the idol-houses of Gualiar. Some are two, and some are three storeys high, each storey rather low, in the ancient fashion. On their stone plinths (*izara*) are sculptured images. Some idol-houses, College-fashion, have a portico, large high cupolas[2] and *madrasa*-like cells, each topped by a slender stone cupola.[3] In the lower cells are idols carved in the rock.

Fol. 343b.

After enjoying the sight of these buildings ('*imaratlar*) we left the fort by the south Gate,[4] made an excursion to the south, and went (north) to the Char-bagh Rahim-dad had made over-against the Hati-pul.[5] He had prepared a feast of cooked-meat (*ash*) for us and, after setting excellent food before us, made offering of a mass of goods and coin worth 4 *laks*. From his Char-bagh I rode to my own.

(j. Excursion to a waterfall.)

(*Sep. 30th*) On Wednesday the 15th of the month I went to see a waterfall 6 *kurohs* (12 m.) to the south-east of Gualiar. Less

1 The *Mirat-i-sikandari* (lith. ed. p. 234, Bayley's trs. p. 372) confirms Babur's statement that the precious things were at Bikramajit's disposition. Perhaps they had been in his mother's charge during her husband's life. They were given later to Bahadur Shah of Gujrat.

2 The Teli Mandir has not a cupola but a waggon-roof of South Indian style, whence it may be that it has the southern name Telingana, suggested by Col. Luard.

3 See Luard's Photo. No. 139 and P. Mundy's sketch of the fort p. 62.

4 This will be the Ghargaraj-gate which looks south though it is not at the south end of the fort-hill where there is only a postern approached by a flight of stone steps (Cunningham p. 332).

5 The garden will have been on the lower ground at the foot of the ramp and not near the Hati-pul itself where the scarp is precipitous.

than that must have been ridden;[1] close to the Mid-day Prayer
we reached a fall where sufficient water for one mill was coming
down a slope (*qia*) an *arghamchi*[2] high. Below the fall there
is a large lake; above it the water comes flowing through solid
rock; there is solid rock also below the fall. A lake forms
wherever the water falls. On the banks of the water lie piece
after piece of rock as if for seats, but the water is said not
always to be there. We sat down above the fall and ate *ma'jun*,
went up-stream to visit its source (*badayat*), returned, got out on
higher ground, and stayed while musicians played and reciters

repeated things (*nima aitilar*). The Ebony-tree which Hindis
call *tindu*, was pointed out to those who had not seen it before.
We went down the hill and, between the Evening and Bed-time
Prayers, rode away, slept at a place reached near the second
watch (midnight), and with the on-coming of the first watch of
day (6 a.m. *Muh. 16th—Oct. 1st*) reached the Char-bagh and
dismounted.

(k. Salahu'd-din's birth-place.)[3]

(*Oct. 2nd*) On Friday the 17th of the month, I visited the
garden of lemons and pumeloes (*sada-fal*) in a valley-bottom
amongst the hills above a village called Sukhjana (?)[4] which is
Salahu'd-din's birth-place. Returning to the Char-bagh, I dismounted there in the first watch.[5]

(l. Incidents of the march from Gualiar.)

(*Oct. 4th*) On Sunday the 19th of the month, we rode before
dawn from the Char-bagh, crossed the Kawari-water and took our
nooning (*tushlanduk*). After the Mid-day Prayer we rode on,
at sunset passed the Chambal-water, between the Evening and
Bed-time Prayers entered Dulpur-fort, there, by lamp-light,

1 *Mundin kichikraq atlanilghan aikandur.* This may imply that the distance
mentioned to Babur was found by him an over-estimate. Perhaps the fall was on the
Murar-river.

2 Rope (Shaw); *corde qui sert à attacher le bagage sur les chameaux* (de Courteille);
a thread of 20 cubits long for weaving (Steingass); I have the impression that an
arghamchi is a horse's tether.

3 For information about this opponent of Babur in the battle of Kanwa, *see* the
Asiatic Review, Nov. 1915, H. Beveridge's art. *Silhadi, and the Mirat-i-sikandari.*

4 Colonel Luard has suggested to us that the Babur-nama word Sukhjana may stand
for Salwai or Sukhalhari, the names of two villages near Gualiar.

5 Presumably of night, 6–9 p.m., of Saturday Muh. 18th—Oct. 2nd.

visited a Hot-bath which Abu'l-fath had made, rode on, and dismounted at the dam-head where the new Char-bagh is in making.

(Oct. 5th) Having stayed the night there, at dawn (Monday 20th) I visited what places had been ordered made.[1] The face (yuz) of the roofed-tank, ordered cut in the solid rock, was not being got up quite straight; more stone-cutters were sent for who were to make the tank-bottom level, pour in water, and, by help of the water, to get the sides to one height. They got the face up straight just before the Other Prayer, were then ordered to fill the tank with water, by help of the water made the sides Fol. 344b. match, then busied themselves to smooth them. I ordered a water-chamber (ab-khana) made at a place where it would be cut in the solid rock; inside it was to be a small tank also cut in the solid rock.

(Here the record of 6 days is wanting.)[2]

(Oct. 12th?) To-day, Monday (27th?), there was a ma'jun party. (Oct. 13th) On Tuesday I was still in that same place. (Oct. 14th) On the night of Wednesday,[3] after opening the mouth and eating something[4] we rode for Sikri. Near the second watch (midnight), we dismounted somewhere and slept; I myself could not sleep on account of pain in my ear, whether caused by cold, as is likely, I do not know. At the top of the dawn, we bestirred ourselves from that place, and in the first watch dismounted at

1 f. 330b and f. 339b.
2 Between the last explicit date in the text, viz. Sunday, Muh. 19th, and the one next following, viz. Saturday, Safar 3rd, the diary of six days is wanting. The gap seems to be between the unfinished account of doings in Dhulpur and the incomplete one of those of the Monday of the party. For one of the intermediate days Babur had made an appointment, when in Gualiar (f. 343), with the envoys of Bikramajit, the trysting-day being Muh. 23rd (i.e. 9 days after Muh. 14th). Babur is likely to have gone to Biana as planned; that envoys met him there may be surmised from the circumstance that when negotiations with Bikramajit were renewed in Agra (f. 345), two sets of envoys were present, a "former" one and a "later" one, and this although all envoys had been dismissed from Gualiar. The "former" ones will have been those who went to Biana, were not given leave there, but were brought on to Agra; the "later" ones may have come to Agra direct from Ranthambhor. It suits all round to take it that pages have been lost on which was the record of the end of the Dhulpur visit, of the journey to the, as yet unseen, fort of Biana, of tryst kept by the envoys, of other doings in Biana where, judging from the time taken to reach Sikri, it may be that the ma'jun party was held.
3 Anglicé, Tuesday after 6 p.m.
4 aghaz aichib nima yib, which words seem to imply the breaking of a fast.

the garden now in making at Sikri. The garden-wall and well-buildings were not getting on to my satisfaction; the overseers therefore were threatened and punished. We rode on from Sikri between the Other and Evening Prayers, passed through Madhakur, dismounted somewhere and slept.

(*Oct. 15th*) Riding on (*Thursday 30th*), we got into Agra during the first watch (6–9 a.m.). In the fort I saw the honoured Khadija-sultan Begim who had stayed behind for several reasons when Fakhr-i-jahan Begim started for Kabul. Crossing Jun (Jumna), I went to the Garden-of-eight paradises.[1]

(*m. Arrival of kinswomen.*)

(*Oct. 17th*) On Saturday the 3rd of Safar, between the Other and Evening Prayers, I went to see three of the great-aunt begims,[2] Gauhar-shad Begim, Badi'u'l-jamal Begim, and Aq Begim, with also, of lesser begims,[3] Sl. Mas'ud Mirza's daughter Khan-zada Begim, and Sultan-bakht Begim's daughter, and my *yinka chicha*'s grand-daughter, that is to say, Zainab-sultan Begim.[4] They had come past Tuta and dismounted at a small standing-water (*darya qaraghi* or *qaraghina*) on the edge of the suburbs. I came back direct by boat.

Fol. 345.

(*n. Despatch of an envoy to receive charge of Ranthambhor.*)

(*Oct. 19th*) On Monday the 5th of the month of Safar, Hamusi son of Diwa, an old Hindu servant from Bhira, was joined with Bikramajit's former[5] and later envoys in order that pact and agreement for the surrender of Ranthanbur and for the conditions of Bikramajit's service might be made in their own (hindu) way and custom. Before our man returned, he was to see, and learn, and make sure of matters; this done, if that

---

1 Doubtless the garden owes its name to the eight heavens or paradises mentioned in the Quran (Hughes' *Dictionary of Islam s.n.* Paradise). Babur appears to have reached Agra on the 1st of Safar; the 2nd may well have been spent on the home affairs of a returned traveller.

2 The great, or elder trio were daughters of Sl. Abu-sa'id Mirza, Babur's paternal-aunts therefore, of his dutiful attendance on whom, Gul-badan writes.

3 "Lesser," *i.e.* younger in age, lower in rank as not being the daughters of a sovereign Mirza, and held in less honour because of a younger generation.

4 Gul-badan mentions the arrival in Hindustan of a khanim of this name, who was a daughter of Sl. Mahmud Khan *Chaghatai*, Babur's maternal-uncle; to this maternal relationship the word *chicha* (mother) may refer. *Yinka*, uncle's or elder brother's wife, has occurred before (ff. 192, 207), *chicha* not till now.

5 *Cf.* f. 344*b* and n. 5 concerning the surmised movements of this set of envoys.

person (*i.e.* Bikramajit) stood fast to his spoken word, I, for my part, promised that, God bringing it aright, I would set him in his father's place as Rana of Chitur.[1]

(*Here the record of 3 days is wanting.*)

(*o. A levy on stipendiaries.*)

(*Oct. 22nd*) By this time the treasure of Iskandar and Ibrahim in Dihli and Agra was at an end. Royal orders were given therefore, on Thursday the 8th of Safar, that each stipendiary (*wajhdar*) should drop into the Diwan, 30 in every 100 of his allowance, to be used for war-material and appliances, for equipment, for powder, and for the pay of gunners and matchlockmen.

(*p. Royal letters sent into Khurasan.*)

(*Oct. 24th*) On Saturday the 10th of the month, Pay-master Sl. Muhammad's foot-man Shah Qasim who once before had taken letters of encouragement to kinsfolk in Khurasan,[2] was sent to Heri with other letters to the purport that, through God's grace, our hearts were at ease in Hindustan about the rebels and Fol. 345*b*. pagans of east and west; and that, God bringing it aright, we should use every means and assuredly in the coming spring should touch the goal of our desire.[3] On the margin of a royal letter sent to Ahmad *Afshar* (*Turk*) a summons to Faridun the *qabuz*-player was written with my own hand.

(*Here the record of 11 days is wanting.*)

---

1 This promise was first proffered in Gualiar (f. 343).

2 These may be Bai-qara kinsfolk or Miran-shahis married to them. No record of Shah Qasim's earlier mission is preserved; presumably he was sent in 934 AH. and the record will have been lost with much more of that year's. Khwand-amir may well have had to do with this second mission, since he could inform Babur of the discomfort caused in Heri by the near leaguer of 'Ubaidu'l-lah *Auzbeg*.

3 *Albatta auzumizni har nu' qilib tigurkumiz dur.* The following versions of this sentence attest its difficulty:—*Waqi'at-i-baburi*, 1st trs. I.O. 215 f. 212, *albatta khudra ba har nu'i ka bashad dar an khub khwahim rasanad*; and 2nd trs. I.O. 217 f. 238*b*, *albatta dar har nu' karda khudra mi rasanim*; *Memoirs* p. 388, "I would make an effort and return in person to Kabul"; *Mémoires* ii, 356, *je ferais tous mes efforts pour pousser en avant*. I surmise, as Payanda-i-hasan seems to have done (1st Pers. trs. *supra*), that the passage alludes to Babur's aims in Hindustan which he expects to touch in the coming spring. What seems likely to be implied is what Erskine says and more, *viz.* return to Kabul, renewal of conflict with the Auzbeg and release of Khurasan kin through success. As is said by Babur immediately after this, Tahmasp of Persia had defeated 'Ubaidu'l-lah *Auzbeg* before Babur's letter was written.

In today's forenoon (*Tuesday 20th?*) I made a beginning of eating quicksilver.[1]

(*q. News from Kabul and Khurasan.*)[2]

(*Nov. 4th*) On Wednesday the 21st of the month (*Safar*) a Hindustani foot-man (*piada*) brought dutiful letters ('*arz-dashtlar*) from Kamran and Khwaja Dost-i-khawand. The Khwaja had reached Kabul on the 10th of Zu'l-hijja[3] and will have been anxious to go on[4] to Humayun's presence, but there comes to him a man from Kamran, saying, "Let the honoured Khwaja come (to see me); let him deliver whatever royal orders there may be; let him go on to Humayun when matters have been talked over."[5] Kamran will have gone into Kabul on the 17th of Zu'l-hijja (*Sep. 2nd*), will have talked with the Khwaja and, on the 28th of the same month, will have let him go on for Fort Victory (*Qila'-i-zafar*).

There was this excellent news in the dutiful letters received:— that Shah-zada Tahmasp, resolute to put down the Auzbeg,[6] had overcome and killed Rinish (var. Zinish) *Auzbeg* in Damghan and made a general massacre of his people; that 'Ubaid Khan, getting sure news about the *Qizil-bash* (Red-head) had risen from round Heri, gone to Merv, called up to him there all the sultans of Samarkand and those parts, and that all the sultans of Ma wara'u'n-nahr had gone to help him.[7]

Fol. 346. This same foot-man brought the further news that Humayun was said to have had a son by the daughter of Yadgar Taghai,

---

1 *Simab yimakni bunyad qildim,* a statement which would be less abrupt if it followed a record of illness. Such a record may have been made and lost.
2 The preliminaries to this now somewhat obscure section will have been lost in the gap of 934 AH. They will have given Babur's instructions to Khwaja Dost-i-khawand and have thrown light on the unsatisfactory state of Kabul, concerning which a good deal comes out later, particularly in Babur's letter to its Governor Khwaja Kalan. It may be right to suppose that Kamran wanted Kabul and that he expected the Khwaja to bring him an answer to his request for it, whether made by himself or for him, through some-one, his mother perhaps, whom Babur now sent for to Hindustan.
3 934 AH.—August 26th 1528 AD.
4 The useful verb *tibramak* which connotes agitation of mind with physical move-ment, will here indicate anxiety on the Khwaja's part to fulfil his mission to Humayun.
5 Kamran's messenger seems to repeat his master's words, using the courteous imperative of the 3rd person plural.
6 Though Babur not infrequently writes of *e.g.* Bengalis and Auzbegs and Turks in the singular, the Bengali, the Auzbeg, the Turk, he seems here to mean 'Ubaidu'l-lah, the then dominant Auzbeg, although Kuchum was Khaqan.
7 This muster preceded defeat near Jam of which Babur heard some 19 days later.

and that Kamran was said to be marrying in Kabul, taking the daughter of his mother's brother Sl. 'Ali Mirza (*Begchik*).[1]

(r. Honours for an artificer.)[2]

On this same day Sayyid Dakni of Shiraz the diviner (*ghaiba-gar?*) was made to wear a dress of honour, given presents, and ordered to finish the arched (?) well (*khwaraliq-chah*) as he best knew how.

(s. The Walidiyyah-risala (Parental-tract).)

(*Nov. 6th*) On Friday the 23rd of the month[3] such heat[4] appeared in my body that with difficulty I got through the Congregational Prayer in the Mosque, and with much trouble through the Mid-day Prayer, in the book-room, after due time, and little by little. Thereafter[5] having had fever, I trembled less on Sunday (*Nov. 28th*). During the night of Tuesday[6] the 27th of the month Safar, it occurred to me to versify (*nazm qilmaq*)

---

1 Humayun's wife was Bega Begim, the later Haji Begim; Kamran's bride was her cousin perhaps named Mah-afruz (Gul-badan's *Humayun-nama* f. 64b). The hear-say tense used by the messenger allows the inference that he was not accredited to give the news but merely repeated the rumour of Kabul. The accredited bearer-of-good-tidings came later (f. 346b).

2 There are three enigmatic words in this section. The first is the Sayyid's cognomen; was he *dakni*, rather dark of hue, or *zakni*, one who knows, or *rukni*, one who props, erects scaffolding, *etc.*? The second mentions his occupation; was he a *ghaiba-gar*, diviner (Erskine, water-finder), *jībar-gar* a cuirass-maker, or a *jibār-gar* cistern-maker, which last suits with well-making? The third describes the kind of well he had in hand, perhaps the stone one of f. 353b; had it scaffolding, or was it for drinking-water only (*khwaraliq*); had it an arch, or was it chambered (*khwazaliq*)? If Babur's orders for the work had been preserved,—they may be lost from f. 344b, trouble would have been saved to scribes and translators, as an example of whose uncertainty it may be mentioned that from the third word (*khwaraliq?*) Erskine extracted "jets d'eau and artificial water-works", and de Courteille "*taillé dans le roc vif*".

3 All Babur's datings in Safar are inconsistent with his of Muharram, if a Muharram of 30 days [as given by Gladwin and others].

4 *hararat*. This Erskine renders by "so violent an illness" (p. 388), de Courteille by "*une inflammation d'entrailles*" (ii, 357), both swayed perhaps by the earlier mention, on Muh. 10th, of Babur's medicinal quick-silver, a drug long in use in India for internal affections (Erskine). Some such ailment may have been recorded and the record lost (f. 345b and n. 8), but the heat, fever, and trembling in the illness of Safar 23rd, taken with the reference to last's year's attack of fever, all point to climatic fever.

5 *aindini* (or, *andini*). Consistently with the readings quoted in the preceding note, E. and de C. date the onset of the fever as Sunday and translate *aindini* to mean "two days after". It cannot be necessary however to specify the interval between Friday and Sunday; the text is not explicit; it seems safe to surmise only that the cold fit was less severe on Sunday; the fever had ceased on the following Thursday.

6 Anglicé, Monday after 6 p.m.

the *Walidiyyah-risala* of his Reverence Khwaja 'Ubaidu'l-lah.[1]
I laid it to heart that if I, going to the soul of his Reverence[2] for
protection, were freed from this disease, it would be a sign that
my poem was accepted, just as the author of the *Qasidatu'l-
burda*[3] was freed from the affliction of paralysis when his poem
Fol. 346b. had been accepted. To this end I began to versify the tract,
using the metre[4] of Maulana 'Abdu'r-rahman *Jami's Subhatu'l-
abrar* (Rosary of the Righteous). Thirteen couplets were made
in that same night. I tasked myself not to make fewer than 10
a day; in the end one day had been omitted. While last year
every time such illness had happened, it had persisted at least
a month or 40 days,[5] this year, by God's grace and his Reverence's
favour, I was free, except for a little depression (*afsurda*), on
Thursday the 29th of the month (*Nov. 12th*). The end of versifying
the contents of the tract was reached on Saturday the 8th of the
first Rabi' (*Nov. 20th*). One day 52 couplets had been made.[6]

(t. Troops warned for service.)

(*Nov. 11th*) On Wednesday the 28th of the month royal
orders were sent on all sides for the armies, saying, "God

1 The *Rashahat-i-'ainu'l-hayat* (Tricklings from the fountain of life) contains an
interesting and almost contemporary account of the Khwaja and of his *Walidiyyah-
risala*. A summary of what in it concerns the Khwaja can be read in the JRAS.
Jan. 1916, H. Beveridge's art. The tract, so far as we have searched, is now known
in European literature only through Babur's metrical translation of it; and this, again,
is known only through the *Rampur Diwan*. [It may be noted here, though the topic
belongs to the beginning of the *Babur-nama* (f. 2), that the *Rashahat* contains particulars
about Ahrari's interventions for peace between Babur's father 'Umar Shaikh and those
with whom he quarrelled.]
2 "Here unfortunately, Mr. Elphinstone's Turki copy finally ends" (Erskine), that is
to say, the Elphinstone Codex belonging to the Faculty of Advocates of Edinburgh.
3 This work, Al-busiri's famous poem in praise of the Prophet, has its most recent
notice in M. René Basset's article of the *Encyclopædia of Islam* (Leyden and London).
4 Babur's technical terms to describe the metre he used are, *ramal musaddas
makhbun 'aruz* and *zarb gah abtar gah makhbun muhzuf wazn.*
5 *autkan yil* (u) *har mahal mundaq 'arizat kim buldi*, from which it seems correct
to omit the *u* (and), thus allowing the reference to be to last year's illnesses only;
because no record, of any date, survives of illness lasting even one full month, and
no other year has a *lacuna* of sufficient length unless one goes improbably far back: for
these attacks seem to be of Indian climatic fever. One in last year (934 AH.) lasting
25–26 days (f. 331) might be called a month's illness; another or others may have
happened in the second half of the year and their record be lost, as several have been
lost, to the detriment of connected narrative.
6 Mr. Erskine's rendering (*Memoirs* p. 388) of the above section shows something
of what is gained by acquaintance which he had not, with the *Rashahat-i-'ainu'l-hayat*
and with Babur's versified *Walidiyyah-risala*.

bringing it about, at an early opportunity my army will be got to horse. Let all come soon, equipped for service."

(*Here the record of 9 days is wanting.*)[1]

(*u. Messengers from Humayun.*)

(*Nov. 21st*) On Sunday the 9th of the first Rabi', Beg Muhammad *ta'alluqchi*[2] came, who had been sent last year (934 AH.) at the end of Muharram to take a dress of honour and a horse to Humayun.[3]

(*Nov. 22nd*) On Monday the 10th of the month there came from Humayun's presence Wais *Laghari*'s (son) Beg-gina (Little Beg) and Bian Shaikh, one of Humayun's servants who had come as the messenger of the good tidings of the birth of Humayun's son whose name he gave as Al-aman. Shaikh Abu'l-wajd found *Shăh sa'adatmand*[4] to be the date of his birth.

Fol. 347.

(*v. Rapid travel.*)

Bian Shaikh set out long after Beg-gina. He parted from Humayun on Friday the 9th of Safar (*Oct. 23rd*) at a place below Kishm called Du-shamba (Monday); he came into Agra on Monday the 10th of the first Rabi' (*Nov. 23rd*). He came very quickly! Another time he actually came from Qila'-i-zafar to Qandahar in 11 days.[5]

---

1 This gap, like some others in the diary of 935 AH. can be attributed safely to loss of pages, because preliminaries are now wanting to several matters which Babur records shortly after it. Such are (1) the specification of the three articles sent to Nasrat Shah, (2) the motive for the feast of f. 351*b*, (3) the announcement of the approach of the surprising group of envoys, who appear without introduction at that entertainment, in a manner opposed to Babur's custom of writing, (4) an account of their arrival and reception.

2 Land-holder (*see Hobson-Jobson s.n.* talookdar).

3 The long detention of this messenger is mentioned in Babur's letter to Humayun (f. 349).

4 These words, if short *a* be read in Shăh, make 934 by *abjad*. The child died in infancy; no son of Humayun's had survived childhood before Akbar was born, some 14 years later. Concerning Abu'l-wajd *Farighi, see Habibu's-siyar,* lith. ed. ii, 347; *Muntakhabu't-tawarikh,* Bib. Ind. ed. i, 3.

5 I am indebted to Mr. A. E. Hinks, Secretary of the Royal Geographical Society, for the following approximate estimate of the distances travelled by Bian Shaikh:— (*a*) From Kishm to Kabul 240m.—from Kabul to Peshawar 175m.—from Peshawar to Agra (railroad distance) 759 m.—total 1174m.; daily average *cir.* 38 miles; (*b*) Qila'-i-zafar to Kabul 264 m.—Kabul to Qandahar 316 m.—total 580 m.; daily average *cir.* 53 miles. The second journey was made probably in 913 AH. and to inform Babur of the death of the Shah of Badakhshan (f. 213*b*).

(w. News of Tahmasp's victory over the Auzbegs.)

Bian Shaikh brought news about Shah-zada Tahmasp's advancing out of 'Iraq and defeating the Auzbeg.[1] Here are his particulars:—Shah-zada Tahmasp, having come out of 'Iraq with 40,000 men arrayed in Rumi fashion of matchlock and cart,[2] advances with great speed, takes Bastam, slaughters Rinish (var. Zinish) *Auzbeg* and his men in Damghan, and from there passes right swiftly on.[3] Kipik Bi's son Qambar-i-'ali Beg is beaten by one of the *Qizil-bash* (Red-head)'s men, and with his few followers goes to 'Ubaid Khan's presence. 'Ubaid Khan finds it undesirable to stay near Heri, hurriedly sends off gallopers to all the sultans of Balkh, Hisar, Samarkand, and Tashkend (Tashkint) and goes himself to Merv. Siunjuk Sl.'s younger son Baraq Sl. from Tashkint, Kuchum Khan, with (his sons) Abu-sa'id Sl. and Pulad Sl., and Jani Beg Sl. with his sons, from Fol. 347*b*. Samarkand and Mian-kal, Mahdi Sl.'s and Hamza Sl.'s sons from Hisar, Kitin-qara Sl. from Balkh, all these sultans assemble right swiftly in Merv. To them their informers (*til-chi*) take news that Shah-zada, after saying, "'Ubaid Khan is seated near Heri with few men only," had been advancing swiftly with his 40,000 men, but that when he heard of this assembly (*i.e.* in Merv), he made a ditch in the meadow of Radagan[4] and seated

---

1 On Muh. 10th 935 AH.—Sep. 26th 1528 AD. For accounts of the campaign *see* Rieu's Suppl. Persian Cat. under *Histories of Tahmasp* (Churchill Collection); the *Habibu's-siyar* and the *'Alam-arai-'abbasi*, the last a highly rhetorical work. Babur's accounts are merely repetitions of news given to him; he is not responsible for mistakes he records, such as those of f. 354. [It must be mentioned that Mr. Erskine has gone wrong in his description of the battle, the starting-point of error being his reversal of two events, the encampment of Tahmasp at Radagan and his passage through Mashhad. A century ago less help, through maps and travel, was available than now.]

2 *tufak u araba*, the method of array Babur adopted from the Rumi-Persian model.

3 Tahmasp's main objective, aimed at earlier than the Auzbeg muster in Merv, was Herat, near which 'Ubaid Khan had been for 7 months. He did not take the shortest route for Mashhad, *viz*. the Damghan-Sabzawar-Nishapur road, but went from Damghan for Mashhad by way of Kalpush ('*Alam-arai* lith. ed. p. 45) and Radagan. Two military advantages are obvious on this route; (1) it approaches Mashhad by the descending road of the Kechef-valley, thus avoiding the climb into that valley by a pass beyond Nishapur on the alternative route; and (2) it passes through the fertile lands of Radagan. [For Kalpush and the route *see* Fr. military map, Sheets Astarabad and Merv, n.e. of Bastam.]

4 7 m. from Kushan and 86 m. from Mashhad. As Lord Curzon reports (*Persia*, ii, 120) that his interlocutors on the spot were not able to explain the word "Radkan," it may be useful to note here that the town seems to borrow its name from the ancient tower standing near it, the *Mil-i-radagan*, or, as Réclus gives it, *Tour de méimandan*, both names meaning, Tower of the bounteous (or, beneficent, highly-distinguished,

himself there.[1] Here-upon the Auzbegs, with entire disregard of their opponents,[2] left their counsels at this:—"Let all of us sultans and khans seat ourselves in Mashhad;[3] let a few of us be told off with 20,000 men to go close to the Qizil-bash camp[4] and not let them put head out; let us order magicians[5] to work their magic directly Scorpio appears;[6] by this stratagem the enemy will be enfeebled, and we shall overcome." So said, they march from Merv. Shah-zada gets out of Mashhad.[7] He confronts them near Jam-and-Khirgird.[8] There defeat befalls the Auzbeg side.[9] A mass of sultans are overcome and slaughtered.

In one letter it (khud) was written,"It is not known for certain Fol. 348. that any sultan except Kuchum Khan has escaped; not a man who went with the army has come back up to now." The

---

etc.). (Cf. Vullers Dict. s.n. rad; Réclus' L'Asie Antérieure p. 219; and O'Donovan's Merv Oasis.) Perhaps light on the distinguished people (radagan) is given by the Dabistan's notice of an ancient sect, the Radiyan, seeming to be fire-worshippers whose chief was Rad-guna, an eminently brave hero of the latter part of Jamshid's reign (800 BC. ?). Of the town Radagan Daulat Shah makes frequent mention. A second town so-called and having a tower lies north of Ispahan.

1 In these days of trench-warfare it would give a wrong impression to say that Tahmasp entrenched himself; he did what Babur did before his battles at Panipat and Kanwa (q.v.).

2 The Auzbegs will have omitted from their purview of affairs that Tahmasp's men were veterans.

3 The holy city had been captured by 'Ubaid Khan in 933 AH. (1525 AD.), but nothing in Bian Shaikh's narrative indicates that they were now there in force.

4 Presumably the one in the Radagan-meadow.

5 using the yada-tash to ensure victory.

6 If then, as now, Scorpio's appearance were expected in Oct.–Nov., the Auzbegs had greatly over-estimated their power to check Tahmasp's movements; but it seems fairly clear that they expected Scorpio to follow Virgo in Sept.–Oct. according to the ancient view of the Zodiacal Signs which allotted two houses to the large Scorpio and, if it admitted Libra at all, placed it between Scorpio's claws (Virgil's Georgics i, 32 and Ovid's Metamorphoses, ii, 195.—H.B.).

7 It would appear that the Auzbegs, after hearing that Tahmasp was encamped at Radagan, expected to interpose themselves in his way at Mashhad and to get their 20,000 to Radagan before he broke camp. Tahmasp's swiftness spoiled their plan; he will have stayed at Radagan a short time only, perhaps till he had further news of the Auzbegs, perhaps also for commissariat purposes and to rest his force. He visited the shrine of Imam Reza, and had reached Jam in time to confront his adversaries as they came down to it from Zawarabad (Pilgrims'-town).

8 or, Khirjard, as many MSS. have it. It seems to be a hamlet or suburb of Jam. The 'Alam-arai (lith. ed. p. 40) writes Khusrau-jard-i-Jam (the Khusrau-throne of Jam), perhaps rhetorically. The hamlet is Maulana 'Abdu'r-rahman Jami's birthplace (Daulat Shah's Tazkirat, E. G. Browne's ed. p. 483). Jam now appears on maps as Turbat-i-Shaikh Jami, the tomb (turbat) being that of the saintly ancestor of Akbar's mother Hamida-banu.

9 The 'Alam-arai (lith. ed. p. 31) says, but in grandiose language, that 'Ubaid Khan placed at the foot of his standard 40 of the most eminent men of Transoxania who prayed for his success, but that as his cause was not good, their supplications were turned backwards, and that all were slain where they had prayed.

sultans who were in Hisar abandoned it. Ibrahim *Jani*'s son Chalma, whose real name is Isma'il, must be in the fort.[1]

(x. Letters written by Babur.)

(Nov. 27th and 28th) This same Bian Shaikh was sent quite quickly back with letters for Humayun and Kamran. These and other writings being ready by Friday the 14th of the month *(Nov. 27th)* were entrusted to him, his leave was given, and on Saturday the 15th he got well out of Agra.

COPY OF A LETTER TO HUMAYUN[2]

"The first matter, after saying, 'Salutation' to Humayun whom I am longing to see, is this:—

Exact particulars of the state of affairs on that side and on this[3] have been made known by the letters and dutiful representations brought on Monday the 10th of the first Rabi' by Beg-gina and Bian Shaikh.

> *(Turki)*   Thank God! a son is born to thee!
> A son to thee, to me a heart-enslaver *(dil-bandi)*.

May the Most High ever allot to thee and to me tidings as joyful! So may it be, O Lord of the two worlds!"

"Thou sayest thou hast called him Al-aman; God bless and prosper this! Thou writest it so thyself *(i.e. Al-aman)*, but hast

---

1 Here the 1st Pers. trs. (I.O. 215 f. 214) mentions that it was Chalma who wrote and despatched the exact particulars of the defeat of the Auzbegs. This information explains the presumption Babur expresses. It shows that Chalma was in Hisar where he may have written his letter to give news to Humayun. At the time Bian Shaikh left, the Mirza was near Kishm; if he had been the enterprising man he was not, one would surmise that he had moved to seize the chance of the sultans' abandonment of Hisar, without waiting for his father's urgency (f. 348*b*). Whether he had done so and was the cause of the sultans' flight, is not known from any chronicle yet come to our hands. Chalma's father Ibrahim *Jani* died fighting for Babur against Shaibaq Khan in 906 AH. (f. 90*b*).

As the sense of the name-of-office Chalma is still in doubt, I suggest that it may be an equivalent of *aftabachi*, bearer of the water-bottle on journeys. *T. chalma* can mean a water-vessel carried on the saddle-bow; one Chalma on record was a *safarchi*; if, in this word, *safar* be read to mean journey, an approach is made to *aftabachi* (fol. 15*b* and note; Blochmann's A.-i-A. p. 378 and n. 3).

2 The copies of Babur's Turki letter to Humayun and the later one to Khwaja Kalan (f. 359) are in some MSS. of the Persian text translated only (I.O. 215 f. 214); in others appear in Turki only (I.O. 217 f. 240); in others appear in Turki and Persian (B.M. Add. 26,000 and I.O. 2989); while in Muh. Shirazi's lith. ed. they are omitted altogether (p. 228).

3 Trans- and Cis-Hindukush. Payanda-hasan (in one of his useful glosses to the 1st Pers. trs.) amplifies here by "Khurasan, Ma wara'u'n-nahr and Kabul".

over-looked that common people mostly say *alama* or *ailaman*.[1] Fol. 348b.
Besides that, this *Al* is rare in names.[2] May God bless and
prosper him in name and person; may He grant us to keep
Al-aman (peace) for many years and many decades of years![3]
May He now order our affairs by His own mercy and favour;
not in many decades comes such a chance as this!"[4]

"Again:—On Tuesday the 11th of the month (*Nov. 23rd*) came
the false rumour that the Balkhis had invited and were fetching
Qurban[5] into Balkh."

"Again:—Kamran and the Kabul begs have orders to join
thee; this done, move on Hisar, Samarkand, Heri or to whatever side favours fortune. Mayst thou, by God's grace, crush
foes and take lands to the joy of friends and the down-casting
of adversaries! Thank God! now is your time to risk life and
slash swords.[6] Neglect not the work chance has brought; slothful
life in retirement befits not sovereign rule:—

> (*Persian*)   He grips the world who hastens;
>   Empire yokes not with delay;
>   All else, confronting marriage, stops,
>   Save only sovereignty.[7]

If through God's grace, the Balkh and Hisar countries be won
and held, put men of thine in Hisar, Kamran's men in Balkh.
Should Samarkand also be won, there make thy seat. Hisar, Fol. 349.
God willing, I shall make a crown-domain. Should Kamran
regard Balkh as small, represent the matter to me; please God!
I will make its defects good at once out of those other countries."

"Again:—As thou knowest, the rule has always been that

1 The words Babur gives as mispronunciations are somewhat uncertain in sense;
manifestly both are of ill-omen:—Al-aman itself [of which the *alama* of the Hai. MS.
and Ilminsky may be an abbreviation,] is the cry of the vanquished, "Quarter! mercy!";
Ailaman and also *alaman* can represent a Turkman raider.

2 Presumably amongst Timurids.

3 Perhaps Babur here makes a placatory little joke.

4 *i.e.* that offered by Tahmasp's rout of the Auzbegs at Jam.

5 He was an adherent of Babur. *Cf.* f. 353.

6 The plural "your" will include Humayun and Kamran. Neither had yet shewn
himself the heritor of his father's personal dash and valour; they had lacked the stress
which shaped his heroism.

7 My husband has traced these lines to Nizami's *Khusrau* and *Shirin*. [They occur
on f. 256b in his MS. of 317 folios.] Babur may have quoted from memory, since his
version varies. The lines need their context to be understood; they are part of
Shirin's address to Khusrau when she refuses to marry him because at the time he is
fighting for his sovereign position; and they say, in effect, that while all other work
stops for marriage (*kadkhudai*), kingly rule does not.

when thou hadst six parts, Kamran had five; this having been constant, make no change."

"Again:—Live well with thy younger brother. Elders must bear the burden![1] I have the hope that thou, for thy part, wilt keep on good terms with him; he, who has grown up an active and excellent youth, should not fail, for his part, in loyal duty to thee."[2]

Fol. 349*b*. "Again:—Words from thee are somewhat few; no person has come from thee for two or three years past; the man I sent to thee (Beg Muhammad *ta'alluqchi*) came back in something over a year; is this not so?"

"Again:—As for the 'retirement', 'retirement', spoken of in thy letters,—retirement is a fault for sovereignty; as the honoured (Sa'di) says:—[3]

> (*Persian*) If thy foot be fettered, choose to be resigned;
> If thou ride alone, take thou thine own head.

No bondage equals that of sovereignty; retirement matches not with rule."

"Again:—Thou hast written me a letter, as I ordered thee to do; but why not have read it over? If thou hadst thought of reading it, thou couldst not have done it, and, unable thyself to read it, wouldst certainly have made alteration in it. Though by taking trouble it can be read, it is very puzzling, and who ever saw an enigma in prose?[4] Thy spelling, though not bad, is not quite correct; thou writest *iltafāt* with *ṭā* (*iltafāṭ*) and *qūlinj* with *yā* (*qīlinj?*).[5] Although thy letter can be read if every sort

1 *Aulughlar kutarimlik kirak*; 2nd Pers. trs. *buzurgan bardasht mi baid kardand.* This dictum may be a quotation. I have translated it to agree with Babur's reference to the ages of the brothers, but *aulughlar* expresses greatness of position as well as seniority in age, and the dictum may be taken as a Turki version of "*Noblesse oblige*", and may also mean "The great must be magnanimous". (*Cf.* de C.'s Dict. *s.n. kutarimlik.*) [It may be said of the verb *bardashtan* used in the Pers. trs., that Abu'l-fazl, perhaps translating *kutarimlik* reported to him, puts it into Babur's mouth when, after praying to take Humayun's illness upon himself, he cried with conviction, "I have borne it away" (A.N. trs. H.B. i, 276).]

2 If Babur had foreseen that his hard-won rule in Hindustan was to be given to the winds of one son's frivolities and the other's disloyalty, his words of scant content with what the Hindustan of his desires had brought him, would have expressed a yet keener pain (*Rampur Diwan* E.D.R.'s ed. p. 15 l.5 fr. ft.).

3 *Bostan*, cap. *Advice of Noshirwan to Hurmuz* (H.B.).

4 A little joke at the expense of the mystifying letter.

5 For *ya*, Mr. Erskine writes *be*. What the mistake was is an open question; I have guessed an exchange of *ī* for *ū*, because such an exchange is not infrequent amongst Turki long vowels.

of pains be taken, yet it cannot be quite understood because of that obscure wording of thine. Thy remissness in letter-writing seems to be due to the thing which makes thee obscure, that is to say, to elaboration. In future write without elaboration; use plain, clear words. So will thy trouble and thy reader's be less."

"Again:—Thou art now to go on a great business;[1] take counsel with prudent and experienced begs, and act as they say. If thou seek to pleasure me, give up sitting alone and avoiding society. Summon thy younger brother and the begs twice daily to thy presence, not leaving their coming to choice; be the business what it may, take counsel and settle every word and act in agreement with those well-wishers."

"Again:—Khwaja Kalan has long had with me the house-friend's intimacy; have thou as much and even more with him.   Fol. 350. If, God willing, the work becomes less in those parts, so that thou wilt not need Kamran, let him leave disciplined men in Balkh and come to my presence."

"Again:—Seeing that there have been such victories, and such conquests, since Kabul has been held, I take it to be well-omened; I have made it a crown-domain; let no one of you covet it."

"Again:—Thou hast done well (*yakhshi qilib sin*); thou hast won the heart of Sl. Wais;[2] get him to thy presence; act by his counsel, for he knows business."

"Until there is a good muster of the army, do not move out."

"Bian Shaikh is well-apprised of word-of-mouth matters, and will inform thee of them. These things said, I salute thee and am longing to see thee."—

The above was written on Thursday the 13th of the first Rabi' (*Nov. 26th*). To the same purport and with my own hand, I wrote also to Kamran and Khwaja Kalan, and sent off the letters (by Bian Shaikh).

(*Here the record fails from Rabi' 15th to 19th.*)

(*y. Plans of campaign.*)

(*Dec. 2nd*) On Wednesday the 19th of the month (*Rabi' I.*) the mirzas, sultans, Turk and Hind amirs were summoned for

---

1 That of reconquering Timurid lands.
2 of *Kulab*; he was the father of Haram Begim, one of Gul-badan's personages.

counsel, and left the matter at this:—That this year the army must move in some direction; that 'Askari should go in advance towards the East, be joined by the sultans and amirs from beyond Gang (Ganges), and march in whatever direction favoured fortune. These particulars having been written down, Ghiasu'd-din the

Fol. 350b. armourer was given rendezvous for 16 days,[1] and sent galloping off, on Saturday the 22nd of the month, to the amirs of the East headed by Sl. Junaid *Barlas*. His word-of-mouth message was, that 'Askari was being sent on before the fighting apparatus, culverin, cart and matchlock, was ready; that it was the royal order for the sultans and amirs of the far side of Gang to muster in 'Askari's presence, and, after consultation with well-wishers on that side, to move in whatever direction, God willing! might favour fortune; that if there should be work needing me, please God! I would get to horse as soon as the person gone with the (16 days) tryst (*mi'ad*) had returned; that explicit representation should be made as to whether the Bengali (Nasrat Shah) were friendly and single-minded; that, if nothing needed my presence in those parts, I should not make stay, but should move elsewhere at once;[2] and that after consulting with well-wishers, they were to take 'Askari with them, and, God willing! settle matters on that side.

(*Here the record of 5 days is wanting.*)

(*z.* '*Askari receives the insignia and rank of a royal commander.*)

(*Dec. 12th*) On Saturday the 29th of the first Rabi', 'Askari was made to put on a jewelled dagger and belt, and a royal dress of honour, was presented with flag, horse-tail standard,

Fol. 351. drum, a set (6–8) of *tipuchaq* (horses), 10 elephants, a string of camels, one of mules, royal plenishing, and royal utensils. Moreover he was ordered to take his seat at the head of a *Diwan*. On his mulla and two guardians were bestowed jackets having buttons;[3] on his other servants, three sets of nine coats.

---

1 *aun alti gunluk m:ljar bila*, as on f. 354b, and with exchange of T. *m:ljar* for P. *mi'ad*, f. 355b.

2 Probably into Rajput lands, notably into those of Salahu'd-din.

3 *tukhmaliq chakmanlar*; as *tukhma* means both button and gold-embroidery, it may be right, especially of Hindustan articles, to translate sometimes in the second sense.

(aa. Babur visits one of his officers.)

(Dec. 13th) On Sunday the last day of the month (*Rabi' I. 30th*)[1] I went to Sl. Muhammad *Bakhshi's* house. After spreading a carpet, he brought gifts. His offering in money and goods was more than 2 *laks*.[2] When food and offering had been set out, we went into another room where sitting, we ate *ma'jun*. We came away at the 3rd watch (midnight?), crossed the water, and went to the private house.

(bb. The Agra-Kabul road measured.)

(Dec. 17th) On Thursday the 4th of the latter Rabi', it was settled that Chiqmaq Beg with Shahi *tamghachi's*[3] clerkship, should measure the road between Agra and Kabul. At every 9th *kuroh* (*cir.* 18 m.), a tower was to be erected 12 *qaris* high[4] and having a *char-dara*[5] on the top; at every 18th *kuroh* (*cir.* 36 m.),[6] 6 post-horses were to be kept fastened; and arrangement was to be made for the payment of post-masters and grooms, and for horse-corn. The order was, "If the place where the horses are fastened up,[7] be near a crown-domain, let those there provide for the matters mentioned; if not, let the cost be charged on the beg

1 These statements of date are consistent with Babur's earlier explicit entries and with Erskine's equivalents of the Christian Era, but at variance with Gladwin's and with Wustenfeldt's calculation that Rabi' II. 1st was Dec. 13th. Yet Gladwin (*Revenue Accounts*, ed. 1790 AD. p. 22) gives Rabi' I. 30 days. Without in the smallest degree questioning the two European calculations, I follow Babur, because in his day there may have been allowed variation which finds no entry in methodical calendars. Erskine followed Babur's statements; he is likely nevertheless to have seen Gladwin's book.
2 Erskine estimated this at £500, but later cast doubts on such estimates as being too low (*History of India*, vol. i, App. D.).
3 The bearer of the stamp (*tamgha*) who by impressing it gave quittance for the payment of tolls and other dues.
4 Either 24 ft. or 36 ft. according to whether the short or long *qari* be meant (*infra*). These towers would provide resting-place, and some protection against ill-doers. They recall the two *mil-i-radagan* of Persia (f. 347 *n.* 9), the purpose of which is uncertain. Babur's towers were not "*kos minars*", nor is it said that he ordered each *kuroh* to be marked on the road. Some of the *kos minars* on the "old Mughal roads" were over 30 ft. high; a considerable number are entered and depicted in the *Annual Progress Report* of the Archæological Survey for 1914 (Northern Circle, p. 45 and Plates 44, 45). Some at least have a *lower* chamber.
5 Four-doored, open-on-all-sides. We have not found the word with this meaning in Dictionaries. It may translate H. *chaukandi*.
6 Erskine makes 9 *kos* (*kurohs*) to be 13–14 miles, perhaps on the basis of the smaller *gaz* of 24 inches.
7 *alti yam-ati baghlaghailar* which, says one of Erskine's manuscripts, is called a *dak-choki*.

in whose *pargana* the post-house may be." Chiqmaq Beg got out of Agra with Shahi on that same day.

Fol. 351b.

> (*Author's note on the kuroh.*) These *kurohs* were established in relation to the *mil*, in the way mentioned in the *Mubin*:—[1]

> > (*Turki*) Four thousand paces (*qadam*) are one *mil*;
> > > Know that Hind people call this a *kuroh*;
> > > The pace (*qadam*) they say is a *qari* and a half (36 in.);
> > > > Know that each *qari* (24 in.) is six hand-breadths (*tutam*)
> > > That each *tutam* is four fingers (*ailik*),
> > > > Each *ailik*, six barley-corns. Know this knowledge.[2]

> The measuring-cord (*tanab*)[3] was fixed at 40 *qari*, each being the one-and-a-half *qari* mentioned above, that is to say, each is 9 hand-breadths.

(*cc. A feast.*)

(*Dec. 18th*) On Saturday the 6th of the month (Rabi' II.) there was a feast[4] at which were present Qizil-bash (Red-head), and Auzbeg, and Hindu envoys.[5] The Qizil-bash envoys sat

1 Neither Erskine (*Mems.* p. 394), nor de Courteille (*Méms.* ii, 370) recognized the word *Mubin* here, although each mentions the poem later (p. 431 and ii, 461), deriving his information about it from the *Akbar-nama*, Erskine direct, de Courteille by way of the Turki translation of the same *Akbar-nama* passage, which Ilminsky found in Kehr's volume and which is one of the much discussed "Fragments", at first taken to be extra writings of Babur's. Ilminsky (p. 455) prints the word clearly, as one who knows it; he may have seen that part of the poem itself which is included in Berésine's *Chrestomathie Turque* (p. 226 to p. 272), under the title *Fragment d'un poème inconnu de Babour*, and have observed that Babur himself shews his title to be *Mubin*, in the lines of his colophon (p. 271),

> Chu bian qildim anda shar'iyat,
> Ni 'ajab gar Mubin didim at?

(Since in it I have made exposition of Laws, what wonder if I named it *Mubin* (exposition)?) Cf. *Translator's Note*, p. 437. [Berésine says (Ch. T.) that he prints half of his "*unique manuscrit*" of the poem.]

2 The passage Babur quotes comes from the *Mubin* section on *tayammum masa'la* (purification with sand), where he tells his son sand may be used, *Su yuraq bulsa sindin air bir mil* (if from thee water be one *mil* distant), and then interjects the above explanation of what the *mil* is. Two lines of his original are not with the *Babur-nama*.

3 The *tanab* was thus 120ft. long. Cf. A.-i-A. Jarrett i, 414; Wilson's *Glossary of Indian Terms* and Gladwin's *Revenue Accounts*, p. 14.

4 Babur's customary method of writing allows the inference that he recorded, in due place, the coming and reception of the somewhat surprising group of guests now mentioned as at this entertainment. That preliminary record will have been lost in one or more of the small gaps in his diary of 935 AH. The envoys from the Samarkand Auzbegs and from the Persian Court may have come in acknowledgment of the *Fath-nama* which announced victory over Rana Sanga; the guests from Farghana will have accepted the invitation sent, says Gul-badan, "in all directions," after Babur's defeat of Sl. Ibrahim *Ludi*, to urge hereditary servants and Timurid and Chingiz-khanid kinsfolk to come and see prosperity with him now when "the Most High has bestowed sovereignty" (f. 293a; Gul-badan's H.N. f. 11).

5 Hindu here will represent Rajput. D'Herbélot's explanation of the name Qizil-bash (Red-head) comes in usefully here:—"KEZEL BASCH or KIZIL BASCH. Mot Turc qui signifie *Tête rouge*. Les Turcs appellent les Persans de ce nom, depuis qu'Ismaël Sofi, fondateur de la Dynastie des princes qui regnent aujourd'hui en Perse,

under an awning placed some 70–80 qaris[1] on my right, of the begs Yunas-i-'ali being ordered to sit with them. On my left the Auzbeg envoys sat in the same way, of the begs 'Abdu'l-lah being ordered to sit with them. I sat on the north side of a newly-erected octagonal pavilion (talar) covered in with khas.[2] Five or six qaris on my right sat Tukhta-bugha Sl. and 'Askari, with Khwaja 'Abdu'sh-shahid and Khwaja Kalan, descendants of his Reverence the Khwaja,[3] and Khwaja Chishti (var. Husaini), and Khalifa, together with the hafizes and mullas dependent on the Khwajas who had come from Samarkand. Five or six qaris on my left sat Muhammad-i-zaman M. and Tang-atmish Sl.[4]   Fol. 352. and Sayyid Rafi', Sayyid Rumi, Shaikh Abu'l-fath, Shaikh Jamali, Shaikh Shihabu'd-din 'Arab and Sayyid Dakkani.[5] Before food all the sultans, khans, grandees, and amirs brought gifts[6] of red, of white, of black,[7] of cloth and various other goods. They poured the red and white on a carpet I had ordered spread, and side by side with the gold and silver piled plenishing, white cotton piece-cloth and purses (badra) of money. While the gifts were being brought and before food, fierce camels and fierce elephants[8] were set to fight on an island opposite,[9] so too a few rams; thereafter wrestlers grappled. After the

---

commanda à ses soldats de porter un bonnet rouge autour duquel il y a une écharpe ou Turban à douze plis, en mémoire et à l'honneur des 12 Imams, successeurs d'Ali, desquels il prétendoit descendre. Ce bonnet s'appelle en Persan, Taj, et fut institué l'an 907ᵉ de l'Hég." Tahmasp himself uses the name Qizil-bash; Babur does so too. Other explanations of it are found (Steingass), but the one quoted above suits its use without contempt. (Cf. f. 354 n. 3).

1 cir. 140–150ft. or more if the 36in. qari be the unit.

2 Andropogon muricatus, the scented grass of which the roots are fitted into window spaces and moistened to mitigate dry, hot winds. Cf. Hobson-Jobson s.n. Cuscuss.

3 A nephew and a grandson of Ahrari's second son Yahya (f. 37b) who had stood staunch to Babur till murdered in 906 AH.–1500 AD. (80b). They are likely to be those to whom went a copy of the Mubin under cover of a letter addressed to lawyers of Ma wara'u'n-nahr (f. 351b n. 1). The Khwajas were in Agra three weeks after Babur finished his metrical version of their ancestor's Walidiyyah-risala; whether their coming (which must have been announced some time before their arrival), had part in directing his attention to the tract can only be surmised (f. 346).

4 He was an Auzbeg (f. 371) and from his association here with a Bai-qara, and, later with Qasim-i-husain who was half Bai-qara, half Auzbeg, seems likely to be of the latter's family.

5 See Additional Notes, p. 800.

6 sachaq kiurdi (kilturdi?) No record survives to tell the motive for this feast; perhaps the gifts made to Babur were congratulatory on the birth of a grandson, the marriage of a son, and on the generally-prosperous state of his affairs.

7 Gold, silver and copper coins.   8 Made so by bhang or other exciting drug.

9 aral, presumably one left by the winter-fall of the Jumna; or, a peninsula.

chief of the food had been set out, Khwaja 'Abdu'sh-shahid
and Khwaja Kalan were made to put on surtouts (*jabbah*) of fine
muslin,[1] spotted with gold-embroidery, and suitable dresses of
honour, and those headed by Mulla Farrukh and *Hafiz*[2] had
jackets put on them. On Kuchum Khan's envoy[3] and on Hasan
Chalabi's younger brother[4] were bestowed silken head-wear
(*bashliq*) and gold-embroidered surtouts of fine muslin, with
suitable dresses of honour. Gold-embroidered jackets and silk
coats were presented to the envoys of Abu-sa'id Sl. (*Auzbeg*),
of Mihr-ban Khanim and her son Pulad Sl., and of Shah Hasan

Fol. 352b.　(*Arghun*). The two Khwajas and the two chief envoys, that is
to say Kuchum Khan's retainer and Hasan *Chalabi*'s younger
brother, were presented with a silver stone's weight of gold and
a gold stone's weight of silver.

> (*Author's note on the Turki stone-weight.*)　The gold stone (*tash*) is 500 *misqals*,
> that is to say, one Kabul *sir*; the silver stone is 250 *misqals*, that is to say, half
> a Kabul *sir*.[5]

To Khwaja Mir Sultan and his sons, to Hafiz of Tashkint,
to Mulla Farrukh at the head of the Khwajas' servants, and
also to other envoys, silver and gold were given with a quiver.[6]
Yadgar-i-nasir[7] was presented with a dagger and belt. On Mir

---

1　Scribes and translators have been puzzled here. My guess at the Turki clause is
aurang airalik kish jabbah. In reading *muslin*, I follow Erskine who worked in India and
could take local opinion; moreover gifts made in Agra probably would be Indian.

2　For one Hafiz of Samarkand *see* f. 237b.

3　Kuchum was Khaqan of the Auzbegs and had his seat in Samarkand. One of
his sons, Abu-sa'id, mentioned below, had sent envoys. With Abu-sa'id is named
Mihr-ban who was one of Kuchum's wives; Pulad was their son. Mihr-ban was,
I think, a half-sister of Babur, a daughter of 'Umar Shaikh and Umid of Andijan
(f. 9), and a full-sister of Nasir. No doubt she had been captured on one of the
occasions when Babur lost her to the Auzbegs. In 925 AH.–1519 AD. (f. 237b) when he
sent his earlier *Diwan* to Pulad Sl. (*Translator's Note*, p. 438) he wrote a verse on its
back which looks to be addressed to his half-sister through her son.

4　Tahmasp's envoy; the title Chalabi shews high birth.

5　This statement seems to imply that the weight made of silver and the weight made
of gold were of the same size and that the differing specific gravity of the two
metals,—that of silver being *cir.* 10 and that of gold *cir.* 20—gave their equivalents the
proportion Babur states. Persian Dictionaries give *sang* (*tash*), a weight, but without
further information. We have not found mention of the *tash* as a recognized Turki
weight; perhaps the word *tash* stands for an ingot of unworked metal of standard size.
(*Cf. inter alios libros*, A.-i-A. Blochmann p. 36, Codrington's *Musalman Numismatics*
p. 117, concerning the *misqal, dinar, etc.*)

6　*tarkash bila*. These words are clear in the Hai. MS. but uncertain in some others.
E. and de C. have no equivalent of them. Perhaps the coins were given by the
quiverful; that a quiver of arrows was given is not expressed.

7　Babur's half-nephew; he seems from his name Keepsake-of-nasir to have been
posthumous.

Muhammad the raftsman who was deserving of reward for the excellent bridge he had made over the river Gang (Ganges),[1] a dagger was bestowed, so too on the matchlockmen Champion [*pahlawan*] Haji Muhammad and Champion Buhlul and on Wali the cheeta-keeper (*parschi*); one was given to Ustad 'Ali's son also. Gold and silver were presented to Sayyid Daud *Garm-siri*. Jackets having buttons,[2] and silk dresses of honour were presented to the servants of my daughter Ma'suma[3] and my son Hind-al. Again:—presents of jackets and silk dresses of honour, of gold and silver, of plenishing and various goods were given to those from Andijan, and to those who had come from Sukh and Hushiar, the places whither we had gone landless and homeless.[4] Gifts of the same kind were given to the servants of Qurban and Shaikhi and the peasants of Kahmard.[5]

Fol. 353.

After food had been sent out, Hindustani players were ordered to come and show their tricks. Lulis came.[6] Hindustani performers shew several feats not shewn by (Tramontane) ones. One is this:—They arrange seven rings, one on the forehead, two on the knees, two of the remaining four on fingers, two on toes, and in an instant set them turning rapidly. Another is this:—Imitating the port of the peacock, they place one hand on the ground, raise up the other and both legs, and then in an instant make rings on the uplifted hand and feet revolve rapidly. Another is this:—In those (Tramontane) countries two people grip one another and turn two somersaults, but Hindustani *lulis*, clinging together, go turning over three or four times. Another is this:—a *luli* sets the end of a 12 or 14 foot pole on his middle and holds it upright while another climbs up it and does his tricks up there. Another is this:—A small *luli* gets up on a big one's head, and stands there upright while the big one moves

Fol. 353*b*.

---

1 934 AH.—1528 AD. (f. 336*b*).

2 Or, gold-embroidered.

3 Wife of Muhammad-i-zaman Mirza.

4 These Highlanders of Asfara will have come by invitation sent after the victory at Panipat; their welcome shows remembrance of and gratitude for kindness received a quarter of a century earlier. Perhaps villagers from Dikh-kat will have come too, who had seen the Padshah run barefoot on their hills.

5 Here gratitude is shewn for protection given in 910 AH.—1504 AD. to the families of Babur and his men when on the way to Kabul. Qurban and Shaikhi were perhaps in Fort Ajar (f. 122*b*, f. 126*b*).

6 Perhaps these acrobats were gipsies.

quickly from side to side shewing his tricks, the little one shewing
his on the big one's head, quite upright and without tottering.
Many dancing-girls came also and danced.

A mass of red, white, and black was scattered (*sachildi*) on
which followed amazing noise and pushing. Between the
Evening and Bed-time Prayers I made five or six special people
sit in my presence for over one watch. At the second watch of
the day (9 a.m., *Sunday, Rabi' II. 7th*) having sat in a boat, I went
to the Eight-Paradises.

(*dd.* '*Askari starts eastwards.*)

(*Dec. 20th*) On Monday (*8th*) 'Askari who had got (his army)
out (of Agra) for the expedition, came to the Hot-bath, took
leave of me and marched for the East.

(*ee. A visit to Dhulpur.*)

(*Dec. 21st*) On Tuesday (*Rabi' II. 9th*) I went to see the
buildings for a reservoir and well at Dulpur.[1] I rode from the
(Agra) garden at one watch (*pahr*) and one *gari* (9.22 a.m.), and
I entered the Dulpur garden when 5 *garis* of the 1st night-watch
(*pas*)[2] had gone (7.40 p.m.).[3]

(*Dec. 23rd*) On Thursday the 11th day of the month the
stone-well (*sangin-chah*), the 26 rock-spouts (*tash-tar-nau*) and
rock-pillars (*tash-situn*), and the water-courses (*ariqlar*) cut on
the solid slope (*yak para qia*) were all ready.[4] At the 3rd watch
(*pahr*) of this same day preparation for drawing water from the
well was made. On account of a smell (*aid*) in the water,
it was ordered, for prudence' sake, that they should turn the
well-wheel without rest for 15 days-and-nights, and so draw off
the water. Gifts were made to the stone-cutters, and labourers,
and the whole body of workmen in the way customary for
master-workmen and wage-earners of Agra.

Fol. 354.

1 This may be the one with which Sayyid Dakni was concerned (f. 346).
2 Babur obviously made the distinction between *pahr* and *pas* that he uses the first
for day-watches, the second for those of the night.
3 Anglicé, Tuesday, Dec. 21st; by Muhammadan plan, Wednesday 22nd. Dhulpur
is 34 m. s. of Agra; the journey of 10 hrs. 20 m. would include the nooning and the
time taken in crossing rivers.
4 The well was to fill a cistern; the 26 spouts with their 26 supports were to take
water into (26?) conduits. Perhaps *tash* means that they were hewn in the solid rock;
perhaps that they were on the outer side of the reservoir. They will not have been
built of hewn stone, or the word would have been *sangin* or *tashdin*.

(*Dec. 24th*) We rode from Dulpur while one *gari* of the 1st watch (*pahr*) of Friday remained (*cir.* 8.40 a.m.), and we crossed the river (Jumna) before the Sun had set.

(*Here the record of 3 days is wanting.*)[1]

(*ff. A Persian account of the battle of Jam.*)

(*Dec. 28th*) On Tuesday the 16th of the month (*Rabi' II.*) came one of Div Sl.'s[2] servants, a man who had been in the fight between the Qizil-bash and Auzbeg, and who thus described it:—The battle between the Auzbegs and Turkmans[3] took place on 'Ashur-day (*Muh. 10th*) near Jam-and-Khirgird.[4] They fought from the first dawn till the Mid-day Prayer. The Auzbegs were 300,000; the Turkmans may have been (as is said?) 40 to 50,000; he said that he himself estimated their dark mass at 100,000; on the other hand, the Auzbegs said they themselves were 100,000. The Qizil-bash leader (*adam*) fought after arraying cart, culverin and matchlockmen in the Rumi fashion, and after protecting himself.[5] Shah-zada[6] and Juha Sl. stood behind the carts with 20,000 good braves. The rest of the begs were posted right and left beyond the carts. Fol. 354*b*. These the Auzbeg beat at once on coming up, dismounted and

1 One occupation of these now blank days is indicated by the date of the "*Rampur Diwan*", Thursday Rabi' II. 15th (Dec. 27th).

2 The demon (or, athlete) sultan of Rumelia (*Rumlu*); once Tahmasp's guardian (*Tazkirat-i-Tahmasp*, Bib. Ind. ed. Phillott, p. 2). Some writers say he was put to death by Tahmasp (*æt.* 12) in 933 AH.; if this were so, it is strange to find a servant described as his in 935 AH. (An account of the battle is given in the *Sharaf-nama*, written in 1005 AH. by Sharaf Khan who was reared in Tahmasp's house. The book has been edited by Veliaminof-Zernof and translated into French by Charmoy; *cf.* Trs. vol. ii, part i, p. 555.—H. Beveridge.)

3 This name, used by one who was with the Shah's troops, attracts attention; it may show the composition of the Persian army; it may differentiate between the troops and their "Qizil-bash leader".

4 Several writers give Saru-qamsh (Charmoy, *roseau jaune*) as the name of the village where the battle was fought; Sharaf Khan gives 'Umarabad and mentions that after the fight Tahmasp spent some time in the meadow of Saru-qamsh.

5 The number of Tahmasp's guns being a matter of interest, reference should be made to Babur's accounts of his own battles in which he arrayed in Rumi (Ottoman) fashion; it will then be seen that the number of carts does not imply the number of guns.

6 This cannot but represent Tahmasp who was on the battle-field (*see* his own story *infra*). He was 14 years old; perhaps he was called Shah-zada, and not Shah, on account of his youth, or because under guardianship (?). Readers of the Persian histories of his reign may know the reason. Babur hitherto has always called the boy Shah-zada; after the victory at Jam, he styles him Shah. Juha Sl. (*Taklu*) who was with him on the field, was Governor of Ispahan.

overcame many, making all scurry off. He then wheeled to the
(Qizil-bash) rear and took loot in camel and baggage. At length
those behind the carts loosed the chains and came out. Here
also the fight was hard. Thrice they flung the Auzbeg back; by
God's grace they beat him. Nine sultans, with Kuchum Khan,
'Ubaid Khan and Abu-sa'id Sl. at their head, were captured;
one, Abu-sa'id Sl. is said to be alive; eight others have gone to
death.[1] 'Ubaid Khan's body was found, but not his head. Of
Auzbegs 50,000, and of Turkmans 20,000 were slain.[2]

(Here matter seems to have been lost.)[3]

(gg. Plan of campaign.)

(Dec. 30th) On this same day (Thursday *Rabi' II. 18th*) came
Ghiasu'd-din the armourer[4] who had gone to Juna-pur (Junpur)
with tryst of 16 days,[5] but, as Sl. Junaid and the rest had led

1 If this Persian account of the battle be in its right place in Babur's diary, it is
singular that the narrator should be so ill-informed at a date allowing facts to be
known; the three sultans he names as killed escaped to die, Kuchum in 937 AH.—
1530 AD., Abu-sa'id in 940 AH.—1533 AD., 'Ubaid in 946 AH.—1539 AD. (Lane-
Poole's *Muhammadan Dynasties*). It would be natural for Babur to comment on the
mistake, since envoys from two of the sultans reported killed, were in Agra. There
had been time for the facts to be known: the battle was fought on Sep. 26th; the
news of it was in Agra on Nov. 23rd; envoys from both adversaries were at Babur's
entertainment on Dec. 19th. From this absence of comment and for the reasons
indicated in note 3 (*infra*), it appears that matter has been lost from the text.
2 Tahmasp's account of the battle is as follows (*T.-i-T.* p. 11):—"I marched against
the Auzbegs. The battle took place outside Jam. At the first onset, Auzbeg
prevailed over Qizil-bash. Ya'qub Sl. fled and Sl. Walama *Taklu* and other officers
of the right wing were defeated and put to flight. Putting my trust in God, I prayed
and advanced some paces.... One of my body-guard getting up with 'Ubaid struck
him with a sword, passed on, and occupied himself with another. Qulij Bahadur and
other Auzbegs carried off the wounded 'Ubaid; Kuchkunji (Kuchum) Khan and
Jani Khan Beg, when they became aware of this state of affairs, fled to Merv. Men
who had fled from our army rejoined us that day. That night I spent on the barren
plain (*sahra*). I did not know what had happened to 'Ubaid. I thought perhaps they
were devising some stratagem against me." The '*A.-'A.* says that 'Ubaid's assailant, on
seeing his low stature and contemptible appearance, left him for a more worthy foe.
3 Not only does some comment from Babur seem needed on an account of deaths he
knew had not occurred, but loss of matter may be traced by working backward from
his next explicit date (*Friday 19th*), to do which shows fairly well that the "same
day" will be not Tuesday the 16th but Thursday the 18th. Ghiasu'd-din's reception
was on the day preceding Friday 19th, so that part of Thursday's record (as shewn
by "on this same day"), the whole of Wednesday's, and (to suit an expected comment
by Babur on the discrepant story of the Auzbeg deaths) part of Tuesday's are missing.
The gap may well have contained mention of Hasan *Chalabi*'s coming (f. 357), or
explain why he had not been at the feast with his younger brother.
4 *qurchi*, perhaps body-guard, life-guardsman.
5 As on f. 350*b* (*q.v.* p. 628 n. 1) *aun alti gunluk büljar* (or, *m:ljar*) *bila*.

out their army for Kharid,[1] he (Ghiasu'd-din) was not able to be back at the time fixed.[2] Sl. Junaid said, by word-of-mouth, "Thank God! through His grace, no work worth the Padshah's attention has shewn itself in these parts; if the honoured Mirza ('Askari) come, and if the sultans, khans and amirs here-abouts be ordered to move in his steps, there is hope that everything in these parts will be arranged with ease." Though such was Sl. Fol. 355. Junaid's answer, yet, as people were saying that Mulla Muhammad Mazhab, who had been sent as envoy to Bengal after the Holy-battle with Sanga the Pagan,[3] would arrive today or tomorrow, his news also was awaited.

(*Dec. 31st*) On Friday the 19th of the month I had eaten *ma'jun* and was sitting with a special few in the private house, when Mulla Mazhab who had arrived late, that is to say, in the night of Saturday,[4] came and waited on me. By asking one particular after another, we got to know that the attitude of the Bengali[5] was understood to be loyal and single-minded.

(*Jan. 2nd*) On Sunday (*Rabi' II. 21st*), I summoned the Turk and Hind amirs to the private house, when counsel was taken and the following matters were brought forward:—As the Bengali (Nasrat Shah) has sent us an envoy[6] and is said to be loyal and single-minded, to go to Bengal itself would be improper; if the move be not on Bengal, no other place on that side has treasure helpful for the army; several places to the west are both rich and near,

> (*Turki*) Abounding wealth, a pagan people, a short road;
> Far though the East lie, this is near.

At length the matter found settlement at this:—As our westward road is short, it will be all one if we delay a few days, so that our minds may be at ease about the East. Again Ghiasu'd-din Fol. 355b. the armourer was made to gallop off, with tryst of 20 days,[7] to

---

1 A sub-division of the Ballia district of the United Provinces, on the right bank of the Ghogra.

2 *i.e.* in 16 days; he was 24 or 25 days away.

3 The envoy had been long in returning; Kanwa was fought in March, 1527; it is now the end of 1528 AD.

4 Rabi' II. 20th—January 1st 1529 AD.; Anglicé, Friday, after 6 p.m.

5 This "Bengali" is territorial only; Nasrat Shah was a Sayyid's son (f. 271).

6 Isma'il Mita (f. 357) who will have come with Mulla Mazhab.

7 *mi'ad, cf.* f. 350b and f. 354b. Ghiasu'd-din may have been a body-guard.

convey written orders to the eastern amirs for all the sultans, khans, and amirs who had assembled in 'Askari's presence, to move against those rebels.[1] The orders delivered, he was to return by the trysted day with what ever news there might be.

(hh. Baluchi incursions.)

In these days Muhammadi Kukuldash made dutiful representation that again Baluchis had come and overrun several places. Chin-timur Sl. was appointed for the business; he was to gather to his presence the amirs from beyond Sihrind and Samana and with them, equipped for 6 months, to proceed against the Baluchis; namely, such amirs as 'Adil Sultan, Sl. Muh. *Duldai*, Khusrau Kukuldash, Muhammad 'Ali *Jang-jang*, 'Abdu'l-'aziz the Master-of-the-horse, Sayyid 'Ali, Wali Qizil, Qaracha, Halahil, 'Ashiq the House-steward, Shaikh 'Ali, Kitta (*Beg Kuhbur*), Gujur Khan, Hasan 'Ali *Siwadi*. These were to present themselves at the Sultan's call and muster and not to transgress his word by road or in halt.[2] The messenger[3] appointed to carry these orders was 'Abdu'l-ghaffar; he was to deliver them first to Chin-timur Sl., then to go on and shew them to the afore-named begs who were to present themselves with their troops at whatever place the Sultan gave rendezvous (*buljar*); 'Abdu'l-ghaffar himself was to remain with the army and was to make dutiful representation of slackness or carelessness if shewn by any person soever; this done, we should remove the offender from the circle of the approved (*muwajjah-jirgasi*) and from his country or *pargana*. These orders having been entrusted to 'Abdu'l-ghaffar, words-of-mouth were made known to him and he was given leave to go.

Fol. 356.

(The last explicit date is a week back.)

1 Ludi Afghans and their friends, including Biban and Bayazid.

2 *yulluq turalik*; *Memoirs*, p. 398, "should act in every respect in perfect conformity to his commands"; *Mémoires* ii, 379, "*chacun suivant son rang et sa dignité.*"

3 *tawachi*. Babur's uses of this word support Erskine in saying that "the *tawachi* is an officer who corresponds very nearly to the Turkish *chawush*, or special messenger" (Zenker, p. 346, col. iii) "but he was also often employed to act as a commissary for providing men and stores, as a commissioner in superintending important affairs, as an aide-de-camp in carrying orders, *etc.*"

(ii. News of the loss of Bihar reaches Dhulpur.)

(*Jan. 9th*) On the eve of Sunday the 28th of the month (*Rabi' II.*) we crossed the Jun (Jumna) at the 6th *gari* of the 3rd watch (2.15 a.m.) and started for the Lotus-garden of Dulpur. The 3rd watch was near[1] (Sunday mid-day) when we reached it. Places were assigned on the border of the garden, where begs and the household might build or make camping-grounds for themselves.

(*Jan. 13th*) On Thursday the 3rd of the first Jumada, a place was fixed in the s.e. of the garden for a Hot-bath; the ground was to be levelled; I ordered a plinth (?) (*kursi*) erected on the levelled ground, and a Bath to be arranged, in one room of which was to be a reservoir 10 × 10.

On this same day Khalifa sent from Agra dutiful letters of Qazi Jia and Bir-sing Deo, saying it had been heard said that Iskandar's son Mahmud (*Ludi*) had taken Bihar (town). This news decided for getting the army to horse.

(*Jan. 14th*) On Friday (*Jumada I. 4th*), we rode out from the Lotus-garden at the 6th *gari* (8.15 a.m.); at the Evening Prayer we reached Agra. We met Muhammad-i-zaman Mirza on the road who would have gone to Dulpur, Chin-timur also who must have been coming into Agra.[2]

(*Jan. 15th*) On Saturday (*5th*) the counselling begs having been summoned, it was settled to ride eastwards on Thursday the 10th of the month (*Jan. 21st*).

(*jj. News of Badakhshan.*)

On this same Saturday letters came from Kabul with news Fol. 356*b*. that Humayun, having mustered the army on that side (Tramontana), and joined Sl. Wais to himself, had set out with 40,000 men for Samarkand;[3] on this Sl. Wais' younger brother

---

1 *yawushub aidi*, which I translate in accordance with other uses of the verb, as meaning approach, but is taken by some other workers to mean "near its end".

2 Though it is not explicitly said, Chin-timur may have been met with on the road; as the "also" (*ham*) suggests.

3 To the above news the *Akbar-nama* adds the important item reported by Humayun, that there was talk of peace. Babur replied that, if the time for negotiation were not past, Humayun was to make peace until such time as the affairs of Hindustan were cleared off. This is followed in the A.N. by a seeming quotation from Babur's letter, saying in effect that he was about to leave Hindustan, and that his followers in Kabul and Tramontana must prepare for the expedition against Samarkand which would be made on his own arrival. None of the above matter is now with the *Babur-nama*;

Shah-quli goes and enters Hisar, Tarsun Muhammad leaves
Tirmiz, takes Qabadian and asks for help; Humayun sends
Tulik Kukuldash and Mir Khwurd[1] with many of his men and
what Mughuls there were, then follows himself.[2]

(*Here 4 days record is wanting.*)

(*kk. Babur starts for the East.*)

Fol. 357. (*Jan. 20th*) On Thursday the 10th of the first Jumada, I set
out for the East after the 3rd *gari* (*cir.* 7.10 a.m.), crossed Jun
by boat a little above Jalisar, and went to the Gold-scattering-
garden.[3] It was ordered that the standard (*tugh*), drum, stable
and all the army-folk should remain on the other side of the
water, opposite to the garden, and that persons coming for an
interview[4] should cross by boat.

(*ll. Arrivals.*)

(*Jan. 22nd*) On Saturday (*12th*) Isma'il Mita, the Bengal
envoy brought the Bengali's offering (Nasrat Shah's), and waited
on me in Hindustan fashion, advancing to within an arrow's
flight, making his reverence, and retiring. They then put on him
the due dress of honour (*khi'lat*) which people call****,[5] and

---

either it was there once, was used by Abu'l-fazl and lost before the Persian trss. were
made; or Abu'l-fazl used Babur's original, or copied, letter itself. That desire for
peace prevailed is shewn by several matters:—Tahmasp, the victor, asked and obtained
the hand of an Auzbeg in marriage; Auzbeg envoys came to Agra, and with them Turk
Khwajas having a mission likely to have been towards peace (f. 357*b*); Babur's wish
for peace is shewn above and on f. 359 in a summarized letter to Humayun. (*Cf.* Abu'l-
ghazi's *Shajarat-i-Turk* [*Histoire des Mongols*, Desmaisons' trs. p. 216]; *Akbar-nama*,
H.B.'s trs. i, 270.)

A here-useful slip of reference is made by the translator of the *Akbar-nama* (*l.c.* n. 3)
to the Fragment (*Mémoires* ii, 456) instead of to the *Babur-nama* translation (*Mémoires*
ii, 381). The utility of the slip lies in its accompanying comment that de C.'s translation
is in closer agreement with the *Akbar-nama* than with Babur's words. Thus the
Akbar-nama passage is brought into comparison with what it is now safe to regard as
its off-shoot, through Turki and French, in the Fragment. When the above comment
on their resemblance was made, we were less assured than now as to the genesis of
the Fragment.

1 Hind-al's guardian (G. B.'s *Humayun-nama* trs. p. 106, n. 1).

2 Nothing more about Humayun's expedition is found in the B.N.; he left
Badakhshan a few months later and arrived in Agra, after his mother (f. 380*b*), at a date
in August of which the record is wanting.

3 under 6 m. from Agra. Gul-badan (f. 16) records a visit to the garden, during
which her father said he was weary of sovereignty. *Cf.* f. 331*b*, p. 589 n. 2.

4 *kurnish kilkan kishilar.*

5 MSS. vary or are indecisive as to the omitted word. I am unable to fill the gap.
Erskine has "*Sir Mawineh* (or hair-twist)" (p. 399), De Courteille, *Sir-mouïneh* (ii, 382).
Muina means ermine, sable and other fine fur (*Shamsu'l-lughat*, p. 274, col. 1).

brought him before me. He knelt thrice in our fashion, advanced, handed Nasrat Shah's letter, set before me the offering he had brought, and retired.

(*Jan. 24th*) On Monday (*14th*) the honoured Khwaja 'Abdu'l-haqq having arrived, I crossed the water by boat, went to his tents and waited on him.[1]

(*Jan. 25th*) On Tuesday (*15th*) Hasan *Chalabi* arrived and waited on me.[2]

(*mm. Incidents of the eastward march.*)

On account of our aims (*chapduq*) for the army,[3] some days were spent in the Char-bagh.

(*Jan. 27th*) On Thursday the 17th of the month, that ground was left after the 3rd *gari* (7.10 a.m.), I going by boat. It was dismounted 7 *kurohs* (14 m.) from Agra, at the village of Anwar.[4]

(*Jan. 30th*) On Sunday (*Jumada I. 20th*), the Auzbeg envoys were given their leave. To Kuchum Khan's envoy Amin Mirza were presented a dagger with belt, cloth of gold,[5] and 70,000 *tankas*.[6] Abu-sa'id's servant Mulla Taghai and the servants of Mihr-ban Khanim and her son Pulad Sl. were made to put on dresses of honour with gold-embroidered jackets, and were presented also with money in accordance with their station. Fol. 357*b*.

(*Jan. 31st?*) Next morning[7] (*Monday 21st?*) leave was given to Khwaja 'Abdu'l-haqq for stay in Agra and to Khwaja Yahya's

1 His brother Hazrat Makhdumi Nura (Khwaja Khawand Mahmud) is much celebrated by Haidar Mirza, and Babur describes his own visit in the words he uses of the visit of an inferior to himself. *Cf. Tarikh-i-rashidi* trs. pp. 395, 478; *Akbar-nama* trs., i, 356, 360.
2 No record survives of the arrival of this envoy or of why he was later in coming than his brother who was at Babur's entertainment. *Cf.* f. 361*b*.
3 Presumably this refers to the appliances mentioned on f. 350*b*.
4 f. 332, n.3.
5 *zarbaft m:l:k.* Amongst gold stuffs imported into Hindustan, Abu'l-fazl mentions *milak* which may be Babur's cloth. It came from Turkistan (A.-i-A. Blochmann, p. 92 and n.).
6 A *tang* is a small silver coin of the value of about a penny (Erskine).
7 *tanglasi*, lit. at its dawning. It is not always clear whether *tanglasi* means, Anglicé, next dawn or day, which here would be Monday, or whether it stands for the dawn (daylight) of the Muhammadan day which had begun at 6 p.m. on the previous evening, here Sunday. When Babur records, *e.g.* a late audience, *tanglasi*, following, will stand for the daylight of the day of audience. The point is of some importance as bearing on discrepancies of days, as these are stated in MSS., with European calendars; it is conspicuously so in Babur's diary sections.

grandson Khwaja Kalan for Samarkand, who had come by way of a mission from Auzbeg khans and sultans.[1]

In congratulation on the birth of Humayun's son and Kamran's marriage, Mulla Tabrizi and Mirza Beg Taghai[2] were sent with gifts (sachaq) to each Mirza of 10,000 shahrukhis, a coat I had worn, and a belt with clasps. Through Mulla Bihishti were sent to Hind-al an inlaid dagger with belt, an inlaid ink-stand, a stool worked in mother-o'pearl, a tunic and a girdle,[3] together with the alphabet of the Baburi script and fragments (qita'lar) written in that script. To Humayun were sent the translation (tarjuma) and verses made in Hindustan.[4] To Hind-al and Khwaja Kalan also the translation and verses were sent. They were sent too to Kamran, through Mirza Beg Taghai, together with head-lines (sar-khat) in the Baburi script.[5]

(Feb. 1st) On Tuesday, after writing letters to be taken by those going to Kabul, the buildings in hand at Agra and Dulpur were recalled to mind, and entrusted to the charge of Mulla Qasim, Ustad Shah Muhammad the stone-cutter, Mirak, MirGhias, Mir Sang-tarash (stone-cutter) and Shah Baba the spadesman. Their leave was then given them.

(Feb. 2nd) The first watch (6 a.m.) was near[6] when we rode out from Anwar (Wednesday, Jumada I. 23rd); in the end,[7] we dismounted, at the Mid-day Prayer, in the village of Abapur, one kuroh (2 m.) from Chandawar.[8]

(Feb. 3rd) On the eve of Thursday (24th)[9] 'Abdu'l-maluk the armourer[10] was joined with Hasan Chalabi and sent as envoy

Fol. 358.

---

1 risalat tariqi bila; their special mission may have been to work for peace (f. 359b, n. 1).
2 He may well be Kamran's father-in-law Sl. 'Ali Mirza Taghai Begchik.
3 nimcha u takband. The tak-band is a silk or woollen girdle fastening with a "hook and eye" (Steingass), perhaps with a buckle.
4 This description is that of the contents of the "Rampur Diwan"; the tarjuma being the Walidiyyah-risala (f. 361 and n.). What is said here shows that four copies went to Kabul or further north. Cf. Appendix Q.
5 Sar-khat may mean "copies" set for Kamran to imitate.
6 bir pahr yawushub aidi; I.O. 215 f. 221, qarib yak pas roz bud.
7 akhar, a word which may reveal a bad start and uncertainty as to when and where to halt.
8 This, and not Chandawar (f. 331b), appears the correct form. Neither this place nor Abapur is mentioned in the G. of I.'s Index or shewn in the I.S. Map of 1900 (cf. f. 331b n. 3). Chandawar lies s.w. of Firuzabad, and near a village called Sufipur.
9 Anglicé, Wednesday after 6 p.m.
10 or life-guardsman, body-guard.

to the Shah;[1] and Chapuq[2] was joined with the Auzbeg envoys and sent to the Auzbeg khans and sultans.

We moved from Abapur while 4 *garis* of the night remained (4.30 a.m.). After passing Chandawar at the top of the dawn, I got into a boat. I landed in front of Rapri and at the Bed-time Prayer got to the camp which was at Fathpur.[3]

(*Feb. 4th and 5th*) Having stayed one day (*Friday*) at Fathpur, we got to horse on Saturday (*26th*) after making ablution (*wazu*) at dawn. We went through the Morning Prayer in assembly near Rapri, Maulana Mahmud of Farab being the leader (*imam*). At sun-rise I got into a boat below the great crook[4] of Rapri.

Today I put together a line-marker (*mistar*) of eleven lines[5] in order to write the mixed hands of the translation.[6] Today

1 This higher title for Tahmasp, which first appears here in the B.N., may be an early slip in the Turki text, since it occurs in many MSS. and also because "Shah-zada" reappears on f. 359.

2 Slash-face, *balafré*; perhaps Ibrahim *Begchik* (Index *s.n.*), but it is long since he was mentioned by Babur, at least by name. He may however have come, at this time of reunion in Agra, with Mirza Beg Taghai (his uncle or brother?), father-in-law of Kamran.

3 The army will have kept to the main road connecting the larger towns mentioned and avoiding the ravine district of the Jumna. What the boat-journey will have been between high banks and round remarkable bends can be learned from the G. of I. and Neave's *District Gazetteer of Mainpuri*. Rapri is on the road from Firuzabad to the ferry for Bateswar, where a large fair is held annually. (It is misplaced further east in the I.S. Map of 1900.) There are two Fathpurs, n.e. of Rapri.

4 *aulugh tughaining tubi*. Here it suits to take the Turki word *tughai* to mean bend of a river, and as referring to the one shaped (on the map) like a soda-water bottle, its neck close to Rapri. Babur avoided it by taking boat below its mouth.—In neither Persian translation has *tughai* been read to mean a bend of a river; the first has *az payan nuia Rapri*, perhaps referring to the important ford (*payan*); the second has *az zir bulandi kalan Rapri*, perhaps referring to a height at the meeting of the bank of the ravine down which the road to the ford comes, with the high bank of the river. Three examples of *tughai* or *tuqai* [a synonym given by Dictionaries], can be seen in Abu'l-ghazi's *Shajrat-i-Turk*, Fraehn's imprint, pp. 106, 107, 119 (Desmaisons' trs. pp. 204, 205, 230). In each instance Desmaisons renders it by *coude*, elbow, but one of the examples may need reconsideration, since the word has the further meanings of wood, dense forest by the side of a river (Vambéry), prairie (Zenker), and reedy plain (Shaw).

5 Blochmann describes the apparatus for marking lines to guide writing (A.-i-A. trs. p. 52 n. 5):—On a card of the size of the page to be written on, two vertical lines are drawn within an inch of the edges; along these lines small holes are pierced at regular intervals, and through these a string is laced backwards and forwards, care being taken that the horizontal strings are parallel. Over the lines of string the pages are placed and pressed down; the strings then mark the paper sufficiently to guide the writing.

6 *tarkib (ning) khati bila tarjuma bitir auchun*. The *Rampur Diwan* may supply the explanation of the uncertain words *tarkib khati*. The "translation" (*tarjuma*), mentioned in the passage quoted above, is the *Walidiyyah-risala*, the first item of the *Diwan*, in which it is entered on crowded pages, specially insufficient for the larger hand of the chapter-headings. The number of lines per page is 13; Babur now

the words of the honoured man-of-God admonished my heart.[1]

Fol. 358b.

(*Feb. 6th*) Opposite Jakin,[2] one of the Rapri *parganas*, we had the boats drawn to the bank and just spent the night in them. We had them moved on from that place before the dawn (*Sunday 27th*), after having gone through the Morning Prayer. When I was again on board, Pay-master Sl. Muhammad came, bringing a servant of Khwaja Kalan, Shamsu'd-din Muhammad, from whose letters and information particulars about the affairs of Kabul became known.[3] Mahdi Khwaja also came when I was in the boat.[4] At the Mid-day Prayer I landed in a garden opposite Etawa, there bathed (*ghusl*) in the Jun, and fulfilled the duty of prayer. Moving nearer towards Etawa, we sat down in that same garden under trees on a height over-looking the river, and there set the braves to amuse us.[5] Food ordered by Mahdi Khwaja, was set before us. At the Evening Prayer we crossed the river; at the bed-time one we reached camp.

There was a two or three days' delay on that ground both to collect the army, and to write letters in answer to those brought by Shamsu'd-din Muhammad.

(*nn. Letters various.*)

(*Feb. 9th*) On Wednesday the last day (*30th*) of the 1st Jumada, we marched from Etawa, and after doing 8 *kurohs* (16 m.), dismounted at Muri-and-Adusa.[6]

---

fashions a line-marker for 11. He has already despatched 4 copies of the translation (f. 357b); he will have judged them unsatisfactory; hence to give space for the mixture of hands (*tarkib khati*), *i.e.* the smaller hand of the poem and the larger of the headings, he makes an 11 line marker.

1 Perhaps Ahrari's in the *Walidiyyah-risala*, perhaps those of Muhammad. A quatrain in the *Rampur Diwan* connects with this admonishment [Plate xiva, 2nd quatrain].

2 Jakhan (*G. of Mainpuri*). The *G. of Etawa* (Drake-Brockman) p. 213, gives this as some 18 m. n. w. of Etawa and as lying amongst the ravines of the Jumna.

3 f. 359b allows some of the particulars to be known.

4 Mahdi may have come to invite Babur to the luncheon he served shortly afterwards. The Hai. MS. gives him the honorific plural; either a second caller was with him or an early scribe has made a slip, since Babur never so-honours Mahdi. This small point touches the larger one of how Babur regarded him, and this in connection with the singular story Nizamu'd-din Ahmad tells in his *Tabaqat-i-akbari* about Khalifa's wish to supplant Humayun by Mahdi Khwaja.

5 *yigitlarni shokhluqgha salduq*, perhaps set them to make fun. *Cf.* f. 366, *yigitlar bir para shokhluq qildilar*. Muh. *Shirazi* (p. 232 *foot*) makes the startling addition of *dar ab* (*andakhtim*), *i.e.* he says that the royal party flung the braves into the river.

6 The *Gazetteer of Etawa* (Drake-Brockman) p. 186, *s.n.* Baburpur, writes of two village sites [which from their position are Muri-and-Adusa], as known by the name

Several remaining letters for Kabul were written on this same ground. One to Humayun was to this purport:—If the work have not yet been done satisfactorily, stop the raiders and thieves thyself; do not let them embroil the peace now descending amongst the peoples.[1] Again, there was this:—I have made Kabul a crown-domain, let no son of mine covet it. Again:—that I had summoned Hind-al.

Kamran, for his part, was written to about taking the best of care in intercourse with the Shah-zada,[2] about my bestowal on himself of Multan, making Kabul a crown-domain, and the coming of my family and train.[3]

As my letter to Khwaja Kalan makes several particulars known, it is copied in here without alteration:—[4]

[COPY OF A LETTER TO KHWAJA KALAN]

"After saying 'Salutation to Khwaja Kalan', the first matter is that Shamsu'd-din Muhammad has reached Etawa, and that the particulars about Kabul are known."

"Boundless and infinite is my desire to go to those parts.[5] Matters are coming to some sort of settlement in Hindustan; there is hope, through the Most High, that the work here will soon be arranged. This work brought to order, God willing! my start will be made at once."

"How should a person forget the pleasant things of those countries, especially one who has repented and vowed to sin no more? How should he banish from his mind the permitted flavours of melons and grapes? Taking this opportunity,[6]

Sarai Baburpur from having been Babur's halting-place. They are 24 m. to the s.e. of Etawa, on the old road for Kalpi. Near the name Baburpur in the Gazetteer Map there is Muhuri (Muri?); there is little or no doubt that Sarai Baburpur represents the camping-ground Muri-and-Adusa.

1 This connects with Kitin-qara's complaints of the frontier-begs (f. 361), and with the talk of peace (f. 356b).

2 This injunction may connect with the desired peace; it will have been prompted by at least a doubt in Babur's mind as to Kamran's behaviour perhaps e.g. in manifested dislike for a Shia'. Concerning the style Shah-zada see f. 358, p. 643, n. 1.

3 Kamran's mother Gul-rukh Begchik will have been of the party who will have tried in Kabul to forward her son's interests.

4 f. 348, p. 624, n. 2.

5 Kabul and Tramontana.

6 Presumably that of Shamsu'd-din Muhammad's mission. One of Babur's couplets expresses longing for the fruits, and also for the "running waters", of lands other than Hindustan, with conceits recalling those of his English contemporaries in verse, as indeed do several others of his short poems (Rampur Diwan Plate xvii A.).

a melon was brought to me; to cut and eat it affected me strangely; I was all tears!"

"The unsettled state[1] of Kabul had already been written of
Fol. 359b. to me. After thinking matters over, my choice fell on this:—
How should a country hold together and be strong (*marbut u mazbut*), if it have seven or eight Governors? Under this aspect of the affair, I have summoned my elder sister (Khanzada) and my wives to Hindustan, have made Kabul and its neighbouring countries a crown-domain, and have written in this sense to both Humayun and Kamran. Let a capable person take those letters to the Mirzas. As you may know already, I had written earlier to them with the same purport. About the safeguarding and prosperity of the country, there will now be no excuse, and not a word to say. Henceforth, if the town-wall[2] be not solid or subjects not thriving, if provisions be not in store or the Treasury not full, it will all be laid on the back of the inefficiency of the Pillar-of-the State."[3]

"The things that must be done are specified below; for some of them orders have gone already, one of these being, 'Let treasure accumulate.' The things which must be done are these:— First, the repair of the fort; again:—the provision of stores; again:—the daily allowance and lodging[4] of envoys going backwards and forwards;[5] again:—let money, taken legally from revenue,[6] be spent for building the Congregational Mosque; again:—the repairs of the Karwan-sara (Caravan-sarai) and the Hot-baths; again:—the completion of the unfinished building
Fol. 360. made of burnt-brick which Ustad Hasan 'Ali was constructing in the citadel. Let this work be ordered after taking counsel with Ustad Sl. Muhammad; if a design exist, drawn earlier by Ustad

---

1 Hai. MS. *na marbutlighi*; so too the 2nd Pers. trs. but the 1st writes *wairani u karabi* which suits the matter of defence.

2 *qurghan*, walled-town; from the *mazbut* following, the defences are meant.

3 *viz.* Governor Khwaja Kalan, on whose want of dominance his sovereign makes good-natured reflection.

4 '*alufa u qunal*; *cf.* 364b.

5 Following *ailchi* (envoys) there is in the Hai. MS. and in I.O. 217 a doubtful word, *bumla*, *yumla*; I.O. 215 (which contains a Persian trs. of the letter) is obscure, Ilminsky changes the wording slightly; Erskine has a free translation. Perhaps it is *yaumi*, daily, misplaced (*see* above).

6 Perhaps, endow the Mosque so as to leave no right of property in its revenues to their donor, here Babur. *Cf.* Hughes' *Dict. of Islam* s.nn. *shari'*, *masjid* and *waqf*.

Hasan 'Ali, let Ustad Sl. Muhammad finish the building precisely according to it; if not, let him do so, after making a gracious and harmonious design, and in such a way that its floor shall be level with that of the Audience-hall; again:—the Khwurd-Kabul dam which is to hold up the But-khak-water at its exit from the Khwurd-Kabul narrows; again:—the repair of the Ghazni dam;[1] again:—the Avenue-garden in which water is short and for which a one-mill stream must be diverted;[2] again:—I had water brought from Tutum-dara to rising ground south-west of Khwaja Basta, there made a reservoir and planted young trees. The place got the name of Belvedere,[3] because it faces the ford and gives a first-rate view. The best of young trees must be planted there, lawns arranged, and borders set with sweet-herbs and with flowers of beautiful colour and scent; again:—Sayyid Qasim has been named to reinforce thee; again:—do not neglect the condition of matchlockmen and of Ustad Muhammad Amin the armourer;[4] again:—directly this letter arrives, thou must get my elder sister (Khan-zada Begim) and my wives right out of Kabul, and escort them to Nil-ab. However averse they may still be, they most certainly must start within a week of the arrival of   Fol. 360b. this letter. For why? Both because the armies which have gone from Hindustan to escort them are suffering hardship in a cramped place (tar yirda), and also because they[5] are ruining the country."

"Again:—I made it clear in a letter written to 'Abdu'l-lah ('asas), that there had been very great confusion in my mind (dúghdugha), to counterbalance being in the oasis (wadi) of penitence. This quatrain was somewhat dissuading (mani'):—[6]

---

1 f. 139. Khwaja Kalan himself had taken from Hindustan the money for repairing this dam.

2 sapqun alip; the 2nd Pers. trs. as if from satqun alip, kharida, purchasing.

3 nazar-gah, perhaps, theatre, as showing the play enacted at the ford. Cf. ff. 137, 330. Tutun-dara will be Masson's Tutam-dara. Erskine locates Tutun-dara some 8 kos (16 m.) n.w. of Hupian (Upian). Masson shews that it was a charming place (Journeys in Biluchistan, Afghanistan and the Panj-ab, vol. iii, cap. vi and vii).

4 jibachi. Babur's injunction seems to refer to the maintaining of the corps and the manufacture of armour rather than to care for the individual men involved.

5 Either the armies in Nil-ab, or the women in the Kabul-country (f. 375).

6 Perhaps what Babur means is, that both what he had said to 'Abdu'l-lah and what the quatrain expresses, are dissuasive from repentance. Erskine writes (Mems. p. 403) but without textual warrant, "I had resolution enough to persevere"; de Courteille (Mems. ii, 390), "Voici un quatrain qui exprime au juste les difficultés de ma position."

> Through renouncement of wine bewildered am I;
> How to work know I not, so distracted am I;
> While others repent and make vow to abstain,
> I have vowed to abstain, and repentant am I.

A witticism of Banai's came back to my mind:—One day when he had been joking in 'Ali-sher Beg's presence, who must have been wearing a jacket with buttons,[1] 'Ali-sher Beg said, 'Thou makest charming jokes; but for the buttons, I would give thee the jacket; they are the hindrance (*mani'*).' Said Banai, 'What hindrance are buttons? It is button-holes (*madagi*) that hinder.'[2] Let responsibility for this story lie on the teller! hold me excused for it; for God's sake do not be offended by it.[3] Again:—that quatrain was made before last year, and in truth the longing and craving for a wine-party has been infinite and endless for two years past, so much so that sometimes the craving for wine brought me to the verge of tears. Thank God! this year that trouble has passed from my mind, perhaps by virtue of the blessing and sustainment of versifying the translation.[4] Do thou also renounce wine! If had with equal associates and boon-companions, wine and company are pleasant things; but with whom canst thou now associate? with whom drink wine? If thy boon-companions are Sher-i-ahmad and Haidar-quli, it should not be hard for thee to forswear wine. So much said, I salute thee and long to see thee."[5]

Fol. 361.

The above letter was written on Thursday the 1st of the latter Jumada (*Feb. 10th*). It affected me greatly to write concerning

---

1 The surface retort seems connected with the jacket, perhaps with a request for the gift of it.

2 Clearly what recalled this joke of Banai's long-silent, caustic tongue was that its point lay ostensibly in a baffled wish—in 'Ali-sher's professed desire to be generous and a professed impediment, which linked in thought with Babur's desire for wine, baffled by his abjuration. So much Banai's smart verbal retort shows, but beneath this is the *double-entendre* which cuts at the Beg as miserly and as physically impotent, a defect which gave point to another jeer at his expense, one chronicled by Sam Mirza and translated in Hammer-Purgstall's *Geschichte von schönen Redekünste Persiens*, art. CLV. (*Cf.* f. 179–80.)—The word *madagi* is used metaphorically for a button-hole; like *na-mardi*, it carries secondary meanings, miserliness, impotence, *etc.* (*Cf.* Wollaston's *English-Persian Dictionary s.n.* button-hole, where only we have found *madagi* with this sense.)

3 The 1st Pers. trs. expresses "all these jokes", thus including with the double-meanings of *madagi*, the jests of the quatrain.

4 The 1st Pers. trs. fills out Babur's allusive phrase here with "of the *Walidiyyah*". His wording allows the inference that what he versified was a prose Turki translation of a probably Arabic original.

5 Erskine comments here on the non-translation into Persian of Babur's letters. Many MSS., however, contain a translation (f. 348, p. 624, n. 2 and E.'s n. f. 377*b*).

those matters, with their mingling of counsel. The letters were entrusted to Shamsu'd-din Muhammad on Friday night,[1] he was apprised of word-of-mouth messages and given leave to go.

(*oo. Complaints from Balkh.*)

(*Feb. 11th*) On Friday (*Jumada II. 2nd*) we did 8 *kurohs* (16 m.) and dismounted at Jumandna.[2] Today a servant of Kitin-qara Sl. arrived whom the Sultan had sent to his retainer and envoy Kamalu'd-din *Qiaq*,[3] with things written concerning the behaviour of the begs of the (Balkh) border, their intercourse with himself, and complaints of theft and raid. Leave to go was given to *Qiaq*, and orders were issued to the begs of the border to put an end to raiding and thieving, to behave well and to maintain intercourse with Balkh. These orders were entrusted to Kitin-qara Sl.'s servant and he was dismissed from this ground.

A letter, accepting excuse for the belated arrival of Hasan *Chalabi*,[4] was sent to the Shah today by one Shah-quli who had come to me from Hasan *Chalabi* and reported the details of the battle (of Jam).[5] Shah-quli was given his leave on this same day, the 2nd of the month.

Fol. 361*b*.

(*pp. Incidents of the eastward march resumed.*)

(*Feb. 12th*) On Saturday (*3rd*) we did 8 *kurohs* (16 m.) and dismounted in the Kakura and Chachawali[6] *parganas* of Kalpi.

(*Feb. 13th*) On Sunday the 4th of the month, we did 9 *kurohs* (18 m.) and dismounted in Dirapur[7] a *pargana* of Kalpi. Here I shaved my head,[8] which I had not done for the past two months, and bathed in the Singar-water (Sengar).

---

1 Anglicé, Thursday after 6 p.m.

2 What would suit measurement on maps and also Babur's route is "Jumoheen" which is marked where the Sarai Baburpur-Atsu-Phaphand road turns south, east of Phaphand (I.S. Map of 1900, Sheet 68).

3 var. *Qabaq, Qatak, Qanak*, to each of which a meaning might be attached. Babur had written to Humayun about the frontier affair, as one touching the desired peace (f. 359).

4 This will refer to the late arrival in Agra of the envoy named, who was not with his younger brother at the feast of f. 351*b* (f. 357, p. 641, n. 2).—As to Tahmasp's style, *see* f. 354, f. 358.

5 Shah-quli may be the ill-informed narrator of f. 354.

6 Both are marked on the southward road from Jumoheen (Jumandna?) for Auraiya.

7 The old Kalpi *pargana* having been sub-divided, Dirapur is now in the district of Cawnpore (Kanhpur).

8 That this operation was not hair-cutting but head-shaving is shewn by the verbs T. *qirmaq* and its Pers. trs. *tarash kardan*. To shave the head frequently is common in Central Asia.

(*Feb. 14th*) On Monday (*5th*) we did 14 *kurohs* (28 m.), and dismounted in Chaparkada[1] one of the *parganas* of Kalpi.

(*Feb. 15th*) At the dawn of Tuesday (*6th*), a Hindustani servant of Qaracha's arrived who had taken a command (*farman*) from Mahim to Qaracha from which it was understood that she was on the road. She had summoned escort from people in Lahor, Bhira and those parts in the fashion I formerly wrote orders (*parwanas*) with my own hand. Her command had been written in Kabul on the 7th of the 1st Jumada (*Jan. 17th*).[2]

(*Feb. 16th*) On Wednesday (*7th*) we did 7 *kurohs* (14 m.), and dismounted in the Adampur *pargana*.[3] Today I mounted before dawn, took the road[4] alone, reached the Jun (Jumna), and went on along its bank. When I came opposite to Adampur, I had awnings set up on an island (*aral*) near the camp and seated there, ate *ma'jun*.

Today we set Sadiq to wrestle with Kalal who had come to Agra with a challenge.[5] In Agra he had asked respite for 20 days on the plea of fatigue from his journey; as now 40–50 days had passed since the end of his respite, he was obliged to wrestle. Sadiq did very well, throwing him easily. Sadiq was given 10,000 *tankas*, a saddled horse, a head-to-foot, and a jacket with buttons; while Kalal, to save him from despair, was given 3000 *tankas*, spite of his fall.

Fol. 362.

1 This will be Chaparghatta on the Dirapur-Bhognipur-Chaparghatta-Musanagar road, the affixes *kada* and *ghatta* both meaning house, temple, *etc.*

2 Mahim, and with her the child Gul-badan, came in advance of the main body of women. Babur seems to refer again to her assumption of royal style by calling her Wali, Governor (f. 369 and n.). It is unusual that no march or halt is recorded on this day.

3 or, Arampur. We have not succeeded in finding this place; it seems to have been on the west bank of the Jumna, since twice Babur when on the east bank, writes of coming opposite to it (*supra* and f. 379). If no move was made on Tuesday, Jumada II. 6th (*cf.* last note), the distance entered as done on Wednesday would locate the halting-place somewhere near the Akbarpur of later name, which stands on a road and at a ferry. But if the army did a stage on Tuesday, of which Babur omits mention, Wednesday's march might well bring him opposite to Hamirpur and to the "Rampur"-ferry. The verbal approximation of Arampur and "Rampur" arrests attention.—Local encroachment by the river, which is recorded in the District Gazetteers, may have something to do with the disappearance from these most useful books and from maps, of *pargana* Adampur (or, Arampur).

4 *tushlab*. It suits best here, since solitude is the speciality of the excursion, to read *tushmak* as meaning to take the road, Fr. *cheminer*.

5 *da'wi bila*; Mems. p. 404, challenge; Méms. ii, 391, *il avait fait des façons*, a truth probably, but one inferred only.

The carts and mortar were ordered landed from the boats, and we spent 3 or 4 days on this same ground while the road was made ready, the ground levelled and the landing effected.

(*Feb. 21st*) On Monday the 12th of the month (*Jumada II.*), we did 12 *kurohs* (24 m.) and dismounted at Kurarah.[1] Today I travelled by litter.

(*Feb. 22nd–25th*) After marching 12 *kurohs* (24 m.) from Kurarah (*13th*), we dismounted in Kuria[2] a *pargana* of Karrah. From Kuria we marched 8 *kurohs* (16 m.) and dismounted (*14th*) in Fathpur–Aswa.[3] After 8 *kurohs* (16 m.) done from Fathpur, we dismounted (*15th*) at Sarai Munda.[4] ... Today at the Bed-time Prayer (*Friday 16th, after dark*), Sl. Jalalu'd-din (*Sharqi*)[5] came with his two young sons to wait on me.

(*Feb. 26th*) Next day, Saturday the 17th of the month, we did 8 *kurohs* (16 m.), and dismounted at Dugdugi a Karrah *pargana* on the bank of the Gang.[6]

(*Feb. 27th*) On Sunday (*18th*) came to this ground Muhammad Sl. M., Ni-khub (or, Bi-khub) Sl. and Tardika (or, Tardi *yakka*, champion).   Fol. 362b.

(*Feb. 28th*) On Monday (*19th*) 'Askari also waited on me. They all came from the other side of Gang (Ganges). 'Askari and his various forces were ordered to march along the other bank of the river keeping opposite the army on this side, and wherever our camp might be, to dismount just opposite it.

(*qq. News of the Afghans.*)

While we were in these parts news came again and again that Sl. Mahmud (*Ludi*) had collected 10,000 Afghans; that he had

---

1 This will be more to the south than Kura Khas, the headquarters of the large district; perhaps it is "Koora Khera" (? Kura-khiraj) which suits the route (I.S. Map, Sheet 88).

2 Perhaps Kunda Kanak, known also as "Kuria, Koria, Kura and Kunra Kanak" (*D. G. of Fathpur*).

3 Haswa or Hanswa. The conjoint name represents two villages some 6 m. apart, and is today that of their railway-station.

4 almost due east of Fathpur, on the old King's Highway (*Badshahi Sar-rah*).

5 His ancestors had ruled in Junpur from 1394 to 1476 AD., his father Husain Shah having been conquered by Sl. Sikandar *Ludi* at the latter date. He was one of three rivals for supremacy in the East (*Sharq*), the others being Jalalu'd-din *Nuhani* and Mahmud *Ludi*,—Afghans all three. Cf. Erskine's *History of India*, *Babur*, i, 501.

6 This name appears on the I.S. Map, Sheet 88, but too far north to suit Babur's distances, and also off the Sarai Munda-Kusar-Karrah road. The position of Naubasta suits better.

detached Shaikh Bayazid and Biban with a mass of men towards Sarwar [Gorakhpur]; that he himself with Fath Khan *Sarwani* was on his way along the river for Chunar; that Sher Khan *Sur* whom I had favoured last year with the gift of several *parganas* and had left in charge of this neighbourhood,[1] had joined these Afghans who thereupon had made him and a few other amirs cross the water; that Sl. Jalalu'd-din's man in Benares had not been able to hold that place, had fled, and got away; what he was understood to have said being, that he had left soldiers (*sipahilar*) in Benares-fort and gone along the river to fight Sl. Mahmud.[2]

(rr. Incidents of the march resumed.)

(*March 1st*) Marching from Dugdugi (*Tuesday, Jumada II. 20th*) the army did 6 *kurohs* (12 m.) and dismounted at Kusar,[3] 3 or 4 *kurohs* from Karrah. I went by boat. We stayed here 3 or 4 days because of hospitality offered by Sl. Jalalu'd-din.

Fol. 363.

(*March 4th*) On Friday (*23rd*), I dismounted at Sl. Jalalu'd-din's house inside Karrah-fort where, host-like, he served me a portion of cooked meat and other viands.[4] After the meal, he and his sons were dressed in unlined coats (*yaktai jamah*) and short tunics (*nimcha*).[5] At his request his elder son was given the style Sl. Mahmud.[6] On leaving Karrah, I rode about one *kuroh* (2 m.) and dismounted on the bank of Gang.

Here letters were written and leave was given to Shahrak Beg who had come from Mahim to our first camp on Gang (*i.e.* Dugdugi). As Khwaja Yahya's grandson Khwaja Kalan

1 Sher Khan was associated with Dudu Bibi in the charge of her son's affairs. Babur's favours to him, his son Humayun's future conqueror, will have been done during the Eastern campaign in 934 AH., of which so much record is missing. *Cf. Tarikh-i-sher-shahi*, E. & D.'s *History of India*, iv, 301 *et seq.* for particulars of Sher Khan (Farid Khan *Sur Afghan*).

2 In writing "Sl. Mahmud", Babur is reporting his informant's style, he himself calling Mahmud "Khan" only (f. 363 and f. 363*b*).

3 This will be the more northerly of two Kusars marked as in Karrah; even so, it is a very long 6 *kurohs* (12 m.) from the Dugdugi of the I.S. Map (*cf.* n. *supra*).

4 *bir para ash u ta'am*, words which suggest one of those complete meals served, each item on its separate small dish, and all dishes fitting like mosaic into one tray. T. *ash* is cooked meat (f. 2 n. 1 and f. 343*b*); Ar. *ta'am* will be sweets, fruit, bread, perhaps rice also.

5 The *yaktai*, one-fold coat, contrasts with the *du-tahi*, two-fold (A.-i-A. Bib. Ind. ed., p. 101, and Blochmann's trs. p. 88).

6 This acknowledgement of right to the style Sultan recognized also supremacy of the Sharqi claim to rule over that of the Nuhani and Ludi competitors.

had been asking for the records I was writing,[1] I sent him by Shahrak a copy I had had made.

(*March 5th*) On Saturday move was made at dawn (*24th*), I going by boat direct, and after 4 *kurohs* done (8 m.), halt was made at Koh.[2] Our ground, being so near, was reached quite early. After awhile, we seated ourselves inside[3] a boat where we ate *ma'jun*. We invited the honoured Khwaja 'Abdu'sh-shahid[4] who was said to be in Nur Beg's quarters (*awi*), invited also Mulla Mahmud (*Farabi?*), bringing him from Mulla 'Ali Khan's. After staying for some time on that spot, we crossed the river, and on the other side, set wrestlers to wrestle. In opposition to the rule of gripping the strongest first, Dost-i-yasin-khair was told not to grapple with Champion Sadiq, but with others; he did so very well with eight.

Fol. 363*b*.

(*ss. News of the Afghan enemy.*)

At the Afternoon Prayer, Sl. Muhammad the Pay-master came by boat from the other side of the river, bringing news that the army of Sl. Iskandar's son Mahmud Khan whom rebels style

1 *mindin biti turgan waqai'*. This passage Teufel used to support his view that Babur's title for his book was *Waqai'*, and not *Babur-nama* which, indeed, Teufel describes as the *Kazaner Ausgabe adoptirte Titel*. *Babur-nama*, however, is the title [or perhaps, merely scribe's name] associated both with Kehr's text and with the Haidarabad Codex.—I have found no indication of the selection by Babur of any title; he makes no mention of the matter and where he uses the word *waqai'* or its congeners, it can be read as a common noun. In his colophon to the *Rampur Diwan*, it is a parallel of *ash'ar*, poems. Judging from what is found in the *Mubin*, it may be right to infer that, if he had lived to complete his book—now broken off *s.a.* 914 AH. (f. 216*b*)—he would have been explicit as to its title, perhaps also as to his grounds for choosing it. Such grounds would have found fitting mention in a preface to the now abrupt opening of the *Babur-nama* (f. 1*b*), and if the *Malfuzat-i-timuri* be Timur's authentic autobiography, this book might have been named as an ancestral example influencing Babur to write his own. Nothing against the authenticity of the *Malfuzat* can be inferred from the circumstance that Babur does not name it, because the preface in which such mention would be in harmony with *e.g.* his *Walidiyyah* preface, was never written. It might accredit the *Malfuzat* to collate passages having common topics, as they appear in the *Babur-nama, Malfuzat-i-timuri* and *Zafar-nama* (*cf.* E. & D.'s H. of I. iv, 559 for a discussion by Dr. Sachau and Prof. Dowson on the *Malfuzat*). (*Cf.* Z.D.M. xxxvii, p. 184, Teufel's art. *Babur und Abu'l-fazl*; Smirnow's Cat. of *Manuscrits Turcs*, p. 142).

2 Koh-khiraj, Revenue-paying Koh (H. G. Nevill's *D.G. of Allahabad*, p. 261).

3 *kima aichida*, which suggests a boat with a cabin, a *bajra* (*Hobson-Jobson s.n.* budgerow).

4 He had stayed behind his kinsman Khwaja Kalan. Both, as Babur has said, were descendants of Khwaja 'Ubaidu'l-lah *Ahrari*. Khwaja Kalan was a grandson of Ahrari's second son Yahya; Khwaja 'Abdu'sh-shahid was the son of his fifth, Khwaja 'Abdu'l-lah (Khwajagan-khwaja). 'Abdu'sh-shahid returned to India under Akbar, received a fief, maintained 2000 poor persons, left after 20 years, and died in Samarkand in 982 AH.—1574–5 AD. (A.-i-A., Blochmann's trs. and notes, pp. 423, 539).

Sl. Mahmud,[1] had broken up. The same news was brought in by a spy who had gone out at the Mid-day Prayer from where we were; and a dutiful letter, agreeing with what the spy had reported, came from Taj Khan *Sarang-khani* between the Afternoon and Evening Prayers. Sl. Muhammad gave the following particulars:—that the rebels on reaching Chunar seemed to have laid siege to it and to have done a little fighting, but had risen in disorderly fashion when they heard of our approach; that Afghans who had crossed the river for Benares, had turned back in like disorder; that two of their boats had sunk in crossing and a body of their men been drowned.

(tt. Incidents of the eastward march resumed.)

(*March 6th*) After marching at Sunday's dawn (*25th*) and doing 6 *kurohs* (12 m.), Sir-auliya,[2] a *pargana* of Piag[*3] was reached. I went direct by boat.

Aisan-timur Sl. and Tukhta-bugha Sl. had dismounted halfway, and were waiting to see me.[4] I, for my part, invited them into the boat. Tukhta-bugha Sl. must have wrought magic, for a bitter wind rose and rain began to fall. It became quite windy (?)[5] on which account I ate *ma'jun*, although I had done so on the previous day. Having come to the encamping-ground …[6]

1 f. 363.

2 Not found on maps; OOjani or Ujahni about suits the measured distance.

3 Prayag, Ilahabad, Allahabad. Between the asterisk in my text (*supra*) and the one following "ford" before the foliation mark f. 364, the Hai. MS. has a lacuna which, as being preceded and followed by broken sentences, can hardly be due to a scribe's skip, but may result from the loss of a folio. What I have entered above between the asterisks is translated from the Kehr-Ilminsky text; it is in the two Persian translations also. Close scrutiny of it suggests that down to the end of the swimming episode it is not in order and that the account of the swim across the Ganges may be a survival of the now missing record of 934 AH. (f. 339). It is singular that the Pers. trss. make no mention of Piag or of Sir-auliya; their omission arouses speculation, as to in which text, the Turki or Persian, it was first tried to fill what remains a gap in the Hai. Codex. A second seeming sign of disorder is the incomplete sentence *yurtgha kilib*, which is noted below. A third is the crowd of incidents now standing under "Tuesday". A fourth, and an important matter, is that on grounds noted at the end of the swimming passage (p. 655 n. 3) it is doubtful whether that passage is in its right place.—It may be that some-one, at an early date after Babur's death, tried to fill the *lacuna* discovered in his manuscript, with help from loose folios or parts of them. *Cf.* f. 377b, p. 680 n. 2.

4 The Chaghatai sultans will have been with 'Askari east of the Ganges.

5 *tur hawalik*; *Mems.* p. 406, violence of the wind; *Méms.* ii, 398, *une température très agréable*.

6 *yurtgha kilib*, an incomplete sentence.

(*March 7th?*) Next day (*Monday 26th?*) we remained on the same ground.

(*March 8th?*) On Tuesday (*27th?*) we marched on.

Opposite the camp was what may be an island,[1] large and verdant. I went over by boat to visit it, returning to the boat during the 1st watch (6–9 a.m.). While I rode carelessly along the ravine (*jar*) of the river, my horse got to where it was fissured and had begun to give way. I leapt off at once and flung myself on the bank; even the horse did not go down; probably, however, if I had stayed on its back, it and I would have gone down together.

On this same day, I swam the Gang-river (Ganges), counting every stroke;[2] I crossed with 33, then, without resting, swam back. I had swum the other rivers, Gang had remained to do.[3]

We reached the meeting of the waters of Gang and Jun at the Evening Prayer, had the boat drawn to the Piag side, and got to camp at 1 watch, 4 *garis* (10.30 p.m.).

(*March 9th*) On Wednesday (*Jumada II. 28th*) from the 1st watch onwards, the army began to cross the river Jun; there were 420 boats.[4]

(*March 11th*) On Friday, the 1st of the month of Rajab, I crossed the river.

(*March 14th*) On Monday, the 4th of the month, the march

---

1 *aral bar aikandur*, phrasing implying uncertainty; there may have been an island, or such a peninsula as a narrow-mouthed bend of a river forms, or a spit or bluff projecting into the river. The word *aral* represents *Aiki-su-arasi, Miyan-du-ab, Entre-eaux*, Twixt-two-streams, Mesopotamia.

2 *qul*; Pers. trss. *dast andakhtan* and *dast*. Presumably the 33 strokes carried the swimmer across the deep channel, or the Ganges was crossed higher than Piag.

3 The above account of Babur's first swim across the Ganges which is entered under date Jumada II. 27th, 935 AH. (March 8th, 1529 AD.), appears misplaced, since he mentions under date Rajab 25th, 935 AH. (April 4th, 1529 AD. f. 366*b*), that he had swum the Ganges at Baksara (Buxar) a year before, *i.e.* on or close to Rajab 25th, 934 AH. (April 15th, 1528 AD.). Nothing in his writings shews that he was near Piag (Allahabad) in 934 AH.; nothing indisputably connects the swimming episode with the "Tuesday" below which it now stands; there is no help given by dates. One supposes Babur would take his first chance to swim the Ganges; this was offered at Qanauj (f. 336), but nothing in the short record of that time touches the topic. The next chance would be after he was in Aud, when, by an unascertained route, perhaps down the Ghogra, he made his way to Baksara where he says (f. 366*b*) he swam the river. Taking into consideration the various testimony noted, there seems warrant for supposing that this swimming passage is a survival of the missing record of 934 AH. (f. 339). *Cf.* f. 377*b*, p. 680 and n. 2 for another surmised survival of 934 AH.

4 "Friday" here stands for Anglicé, Thursday after 6 p.m.; this, only, suiting Babur's next explicit date Sha'ban 1st, Saturday.

for Bihar began along the bank of Jun. After 5 *kurohs* (10 m.) done, halt was made at Lawain.[1] I went by boat. The people of the army were crossing the Jun up to today. They were ordered to put the culverin-carts[2] which had been landed at Adampur, into boats again and to bring them on by water from Piag.

On this ground we set wrestlers to wrestle. Dost-i-yasin-khair gripped the boatman Champion of Lahor; the contest was stubborn; it was with great difficulty that Dost gave the throw. A head-to-foot was bestowed on each.

(*March 15th and 16th*) People said that ahead of us was a swampy, muddy, evil river called Tus.[3] In order to examine the ford[*4] and repair the road, we waited two days (*Tuesday Ramzan 5th and Wednesday 6th*) on this ground. For the horses and camels a ford was found higher up, but people said laden carts could not get through it because of its uneven, stony bottom.

Fol. 364. They were just ordered to get them through.

(*March 17th*) On Thursday (*7th*) we marched on. I myself went by boat down to where the Tus meets the Gang (Ganges), there landed, thence rode up the Tus, and, at the Other Prayer,

---

1 The march, beginning on the Jumna, is now along the united rivers.

2 *zarb-zanlik arabalar*. Here the carts are those carrying the guns.

3 From the particulars Babur gives about the Tus (Tons) and Karma-naśa, it would seem that he had not passed them last year, an inference supported by what is known of his route in that year:—He came from Gualiar to the Kanar-passage (f. 336), there crossed the Jumna and went direct to Qanauj (f. 336), above Qanauj bridged the Ganges, went on to Bangarmau (f. 338), crossed the Gumti and went to near the junction of the Ghogra and Sarda (f. 338b). The next indication of his route is that he is at Baksara, but whether he reached it by water down the Ghogra, as his meeting with Muh. Ma'ruf *Farmuli* suggests (f. 377), or by land, nothing shews. From Baksara (f. 366) he went up-stream to Chausa (f. 365b), on perhaps to Sayyidpur, 2 m. from the mouth of the Gumti, and there left the Ganges for Junpur (f. 365). I have found nothing about his return route to Agra; it seems improbable that he would go so far south as to near Piag; a more northerly and direct road to Fathpur and Sarai Baburpur may have been taken.—Concerning Babur's acts in 934 AH. the following item, (met with since I was working on 934 AH.), continues his statement (f. 338b) that he spent a few days near Aud (Ajodhya) to settle its affairs. The *D. G. of Fyzabad* (H. E. Nevill) p. 173 says "In 1528 AD. Babur came to Ajodhya (Aud) and halted a week. He destroyed the ancient temple" (marking the birth-place of Rama) "and on its site built a mosque, still known as Babur's Mosque ... It has two inscriptions, one on the outside, one on the pulpit; both are in Persian; and bear the date 935 AH." This date may be that of the completion of the building.—(*Corrigendum:*—On f. 338 n. 1, I have too narrowly restricted the use of the name Sarju. Babur used it to describe what the maps of Arrowsmith and Johnson shew, and not only what the *Gazetteer of India* map of the United Provinces does. It applies to the Sarda (f. 338) as Babur uses it when writing of the fords.)

4 Here the lacuna of the Hai. Codex ends.

reached where the army had encamped after crossing the ford.
Today 6 *kurohs* (12 m.) were done.

(*March 18th*) Next day (*Friday 8th*), we stayed on that ground.

(*March 19th*) On Saturday (*9th*), we marched 12 *kurohs* and
got to the bank of Gang again at Nuliba.[1]

(*March 20th*) Marching on (*Sunday 10th*), we did 6 *kurohs* of
road, and dismounted at Kintit.[2]

(*March 21st*) Marching on (*Monday 11th*), we dismounted at
Nanapur.[3] Taj Khan *Sarang-khani* came from Chunar to this
ground with his two young sons, and waited on me.

In these days a dutiful letter came from Pay-master Sl.
Muhammad, saying that my family and train were understood to
be really on their way from Kabul.[4]

(*March 23rd*) On Wednesday (*13th*) we marched from that
ground. I visited the fort of Chunar, and dismounted about
one *kuroh* beyond it.

During the days we were marching from Piag, painful boils
had come out on my body. While we were on this ground, an
Ottoman Turk (Rumi) used a remedy which had been recently
discovered in Rum. He boiled pepper in a pipkin; I held the
sores in the steam and, after steaming ceased, laved them with
the hot water. The treatment lasted 2 sidereal hours.

While we were on this ground, a person said he had seen
tiger and rhinoceros on an *aral*[5] by the side of the camp.

(*March 24th?*) In the morning (*14th?*), we made the hunting-
circle[6] on that *aral*, elephants also being brought. Neither tiger
nor rhino appeared; one wild buffalo came out at the end of
the line. A bitter wind rising and the whirling dust being
very troublesome, I went back to the boat and in it to the camp
which was 2 *kurohs* (4 m.) above Banaras.

Fol. 364b.

1 Perhaps, where there is now the railway station of "Nulibai" (I.S. Map). The
direct road on which the army moved, avoids the windings of the river.
2 This has been read as T. *kint*, P. *dih*, Eng. village and Fr. *village*.
3 "Nankunpur" lying to the north of Puhari railway-station suits the distance
measured on maps.
4 These will be the women-travellers.
5 Perhaps jungle tracts lying in the curves of the river.
6 *jirga*, which here stands for the beaters' incurving line, witness the exit of the
buffalo at the end. *Cf.* f. 367b for a *jirga* of boats.

(uu. News of the Afghans.)

(March 25th(?) and 26th) Having heard there were many elephants in the Chunar jungles, I had left (Thursday's) ground thinking to hunt them, but Taj Khan bringing the news *(Friday 15th(?))* that Mahmud Khan *(Ludi)* was near the Son-water, I summoned the begs and took counsel as to whether to fall upon him suddenly. In the end it was settled to march on continuously, fast[1] and far.

(March 27th) Marching on *(Sunday 17th)*, we did 9 *kurohs* (18 m.), and dismounted at the Bilwah-ferry.[2]

(March 28th) On Monday night[3] the 18th of the month, Tahir was started for Agra from this camp (Bilwah-ferry), taking money-drafts for the customary gifts of allowance and lodging[4] to those on their way from Kabul.

Before dawn next morning (Monday) I went on by boat. When we came to where the Gui-water (Gumti) which is the water of Junpur, meets the Gang-water (Ganges), I went a little way up it and back. Narrower[5] though it is, it has no ford; the army-folk crossed it (last year) by boat, by raft, or by swimming their horses.

To look at our ground of a year ago,[6] from which we had started for Junpur,[7] I went to about a *kuroh* lower than the mouth of the Junpur-water (Gumti). A favourable wind getting up behind, our larger boat was tied to a smaller Bengali one which, spreading its sail, made very quick going. Two *garis* of day remained (5.15 p.m.) when we had reached that ground (Sayyidpur?), we went on without waiting there, and by the Bed-time Prayer had got to camp, which was a *kuroh* above Madan-Benares,[8] long before the boats following us. Mughul Beg had been ordered to

Fol. 365.

---

1 *auzun auzagh*, many miles and many hours?

2 Bulloa? (I.S. Map).

3 Anglicé, Sunday after 6 p.m.

4 *'alufa u qunal* (f. 359b).

5 than the Ganges perhaps; or narrowish compared with other rivers, *e.g.* Ganges, Ghogra, and Jun.

6 *yil-turgi yurt*, by which is meant, I think, close to the same day a year back, and not an indefinite reference to some time in the past year.

7 Maps make the starting-place likely to be Sayyidpur.

8 re-named Zamania, after Akbar's officer 'Ali-quli Khan Khan-i-zaman, and now the head-quarters of the Zamania *pargana* of Ghazipur. Madan-Benares was in Akbar's *sarkar* of Ghazipur. (It was not identified by E. or by de C.) *Cf. D. G. of Ghazipur.*

measure all marches from Chunar on the direct road, Lutfi Beg to measure the river's bank whenever I went by boat. The direct road today was said to be 11 *kurohs* (22 m.), the distance along the river, 18 (36 m.).

(*March 29th*) Next day (*Tuesday 19th*), we stayed on that ground.

(*March 30th*) On Wednesday (*20th*), we dismounted a *kuroh* (2 m.) below Ghazipur, I going by boat.

(*March 31st*) On Thursday (*21st*) Mahmud Khan *Nuhani*[1] waited on me on that ground. On this same day dutiful letters[2] came from Bihar Khan *Bihari*'s son Jalal Khan (*Nuhani*),[3] from Nasir Khan (*Nuhani*)'s son Farid Khan,[4] from Sher Khan *Sur*, from 'Alaul Khan *Sur* also, and from other Afghan amirs. Today came also a dutiful letter from 'Abdu'l-'aziz *Master-of-the-horse*, which had been written in Lahor on the 20th of the latter Jumada (*Feb. 29th*), the very day on which Qaracha's Hindustani servant whom we had started off from near Kalpi,[5] reached Lahor. 'Abdu'l-'aziz wrote that he had gone with the others assigned to meet my family at Nil-ab, had met them there on the 9th of the latter Jumada (*Feb. 18th*), had accompanied them to Chin-ab (Chan-ab), left them there, and come ahead to Lahor where he was writing his letter.

Fol. 365b.

(*April 1st*) We moved on, I going by boat, on Friday (*Rajab 22nd*). I landed opposite Chausa to look at the ground of a year ago[6] where the Sun had been eclipsed and a fast kept.[7] After I got back to the boat, Muhammad-i-zaman Mirza, coming up behind by boat, overtook me; at his suggestion *ma'jun* was eaten.

The army had dismounted on the bank of the Karma-nasa-river, about the water of which Hindus are understood to be extremely scrupulous. They do not cross it, but go past its

1 In the earlier part of the Hai. Codex this Afghan tribal-name is written Nuhani, but in this latter portion a different scribe occasionally writes it Luhani.
2 '*arza-dasht*, *i.e.* phrased as from one of lower station to a superior.
3 His letter may have announced his and his mother Dudu Bibi's approach (f. 368–9).
4 Nasir Khan had been an amir of Sl. Sikandar *Ludi*. Sher Khan *Sur* married his widow "Guhar Kusain", bringing him a large dowry (A.N. trs. p. 327; and *Tarikh-i-sher-shahi*, E. & D.'s *History of India* iv, 346).
5 He started from Chaparghatta (f. 361b, p. 650 n. 1).
6 *yil-turgi yurt*.
7 "This must have been the Eclipse of the 10th of May 1528 AD.; a fast is enjoined on the day of an eclipse" (Erskine).

mouth by boat along the Gang (Ganges). They firmly believe
that, if its water touch a person, the merit of his works is destroyed;
with this belief its name accords.[1] I went some way up it by
Fol. 366. boat, turned back, went over to the north bank of Gang, and tied
up. There the braves made a little fun, some wrestling. Muhsin
the cup-bearer challenged, saying, "I will grapple with four or
five." The first he gripped, he threw; the second, who was
Shadman (Joyous), threw him, to Muhsin's shame and vexation.
The (professional) wrestlers came also and set to.

(*April 2nd*) Next morning, Saturday (*23rd*) we moved, close
to the 1st watch (6 a.m.), in order to get people off to look at the
ford through the Karma-naśa-water. I rode up it for not less
than a *kuroh* (2 m.), but the ford being still far on,[2] took boat and
went to the camp below Chausa.

Today I used the pepper remedy again; it must have been
somewhat hotter than before, for it blistered (*qapardi*) my body,
giving me much pain.

(*April 3rd*) We waited a day for a road to be managed across
a smallish, swampy rivulet heard to be ahead.[3]

(*April 4th*) On the eve of Monday (*25th*),[4] letters were written
and sent off in answer to those brought by the Hindustani foot-
man of 'Abdu'l-'aziz.

The boat I got into at Monday's dawn, had to be towed because
of the wind. On reaching the ground opposite Baksara (Buxar)
Fol. 366b. where the army had been seated many days last year,[5] we went
over to look at it. Between 40 and 50 landing-steps had been
then made on the bank; of them the upper two only were left,
the river having destroyed the rest. *Ma'jun* was eaten after
return to the boat. We tied up at an *aral*[6] above the camp, set
the champions to wrestle, and went on at the Bed-time Prayer.
A year ago (*yil-tur*), an excursion had been made to look at the
ground on which the camp now was, I passing through Gang

1 Karma-naśa means loss of the merit acquired by good works.
2 The I.S. Map marks a main road leading to the mouth of the Karma-naśa and no
other leading to the river for a considerable distance up-stream.
3 Perhaps "Thora-nadee" (I.S. Map).
4 Anglicé, Sunday after 6 p.m.
5 *autkan yil*.
6 Perhaps the *du-aba* between the Ganges and "Thora-nadee".

swimming (? *dastak bila*),[1] some coming mounted on horses, some on camels. That day I had eaten opium.

(*vv. Incidents of the military operations.*)

(*April 5th*) At Tuesday's dawn (*26th*), we sent out for news not under 200 effective braves led by Karim-birdi and Haidar the stirrup-holder's son Muhammad 'Ali and Baba Shaikh.

While we were on this ground, the Bengal envoy was commanded to set forth these three articles:—[2]

(*April 6th*) On Wednesday (*27th*) Yunas-i-'ali who had been sent to gather Muhammad-i-zaman Mirza's objections to Bihar, brought back rather a weak answer.

Dutiful letters from the (Farmuli) Shaikh-zadas of Bihar gave news that the enemy had abandoned the place and gone off.

(*April 7th*) On Thursday (*28th*) as many as 2000 men of the Turk and Hind amirs and quiver-wearers were joined to Muhammad 'Ali *Jang-jang*'s son Tardi-muhammad, and he was given leave to go, taking letters of royal encouragement to people in Bihar. He was joined also by Khwaja Murshid '*Iraqi* who had been made Diwan of Bihar.

Fol. 367.

(*April 8th* (?)) Muhammad-i-zaman M. who had consented to go to Bihar, made representation of several matters through

1 *yil-tur ... Gang-sui-din min dastak bila autub, ba'zi at, ba'zi tiwah minib, kilib, sair qililib aidi.* Some uncertainty as to the meaning of the phrase *dastak bila autub* is caused by finding that while here de Courteille agrees with Erskine in taking it to mean swimming, he varies later (f. 373*b*) to *appuyés sur une pièce de bois.* Taking the Persian translations of three passages about crossing water into consideration (p. 655 after f. 363*b*, f. 366*b* (here), f. 373*b*), and also the circumstances that E. and de C. are once in agreement and that Erskine worked with the help of Oriental *munshis*, I incline to think that *dastak bila* does express swimming.—The question of its precise meaning bears on one concerning Babur's first swim across the Ganges (p. 655, n. 3).—Perhaps I should say, however, that if the sentence quoted at the head of this note stood alone, without the extraneous circumstances supporting the reading of *dastak bila* to mean swimming, I should incline to read it as stating that Babur went on foot through the water, feeling his footing with a pole (*dastak*), and that his followers rode through the ford after him. Nothing in the quoted passage suggests that the horses and camels swam. But whether the Ganges was fordable at Baksara in Babur's time, is beyond surmise.

2 *fasl soz*, which, manifestly, were to be laid before the envoy's master. The articles are nowhere specified; one is summarized merely on f. 365. The incomplete sentence of the Turki text (*supra*) needs their specification at this place, and an explicit statement of them would have made clearer the political relations of Babur with Nasrat Shah.—A folio may have been lost from Babur's manuscript; it might have specified the articles, and also have said something leading to the next topic of the diary, now needing preliminaries, *viz.* that of the Mirza's discontent with his new appointment, a matter not mentioned earlier.

Shaikh Zain and Yunas-i-'ali. He asked for reinforcement; for this several braves were inscribed and several others were made his own retainers.

(*April 9th*)[1] On Saturday the 1st of the month of Sha'ban, we left that ground where we had been for 3 or 4 days. I rode to visit Bhujpur and Bihiya,[2] thence went to camp.

Muhammad 'Ali and the others, who had been sent out for news, after beating a body of pagans as they went along, reached the place where Sl. Mahmud (*Ludi*) had been with perhaps 2000 men. He had heard of our reconnaissance, had broken up, killed two elephants of his, and marched off. He seemed to have left braves and an elephant[3] scout-fashion; they made no stand when our men came up but took to flight. Ours unhorsed a few of his, cut one head off, brought in a few good men alive.

(*ww. Incidents of the eastward march resumed.*)

(*April 10th*) We moved on next day (*Sunday 2nd*), I going by boat. From our today's ground Muhammad-i-zaman M. crossed (his army) over the river (Son), leaving none behind. We spent 2 or 3 days on this ground in order to put his work through and
Fol. 367b. get him off.

(*April 13th*) On Wednesday the 4th[4] of the month, Muhammad-i-zaman M. was presented with a royal head-to-foot, a sword and belt, a *tipuchaq* horse and an umbrella.[5] He also was made to kneel (*yukunduruldi*) for the Bihar country. Of the Bihar revenues one *krur* and 25 *laks* were reserved for the Royal Treasury; its Diwani was entrusted to Murshid 'Iraqi.

(*April 14th*) I left that ground by boat on Thursday (*6th*). I had already ordered the boats to wait, and on getting up with them, I had them fastened together abreast in line.[6] Though all

---

1 This suits Babur's series, but Gladwin and Wustenfeld have 10th.

2 The first is near, the second on the direct road from Buxar for Arrah.

3 The Hai. MS. makes an elephant be posted as the sole scout; others post a *sardar*, or post braves; none post man and beast.

4 This should be 5th; perhaps the statement is confused through the gifts being given late, Anglicé, on Tuesday 4th, Islamicé on Wednesday night.

5 The Mirza's Timurid birth and a desire in Babur to give high status to a representative he will have wished to leave in Bihar when he himself went to his western dominions, sufficiently explain the bestowal of this sign of sovereignty.

6 *jirga*. This instance of its use shews that Babur had in mind not a completed circle, but a line, or in sporting parlance, not a hunting-circle but a beaters'-line. [*Cf.* f. 251, f. 364b and *infra* of the crocodile.] The word is used also for a governing-circle, a tribal-council.

were not collected there, those there were greatly exceeded the breadth of the river. They could not move on, however, so-arranged, because the water was here shallow, there deep, here swift, there still. A crocodile (*gharial*) shewing itself, a terrified fish leaped so high as to fall into a boat; it was caught and brought to me.

When we were nearing our ground, we gave the boats names:—— a large[1] one, formerly the Baburi,[2] which had been built in Agra before the Holy-battle with Sanga, was named Asaish (Repose).[3] Another, which Araish Khan had built and presented to me this year before our army got to horse, one in which I had had a platform set up on our way to this ground, was named Araish (Ornament). Another, a good-sized one presented to me by Jalalu'd-din *Sharqi*, was named the Gunjaish (Capacious); in it I had ordered a second platform set up, on the top of the one already in it. To a little skiff, having a *chaukandi*,[4] one used for every task (*har aish*) and duty, was given the name Farmaish (Commissioned).

(*April 15th*) Next day, Friday (*7th*), no move was made. Muhammad-i-zaman M. who, his preparations for Bihar complete, had dismounted one or two *kurohs* from the camp, came today to take leave of me.[5]

(xx. News of the army of Bengal.)

Two spies, returned from the Bengal army, said that Bengalis[6] under Makhdum-i-'alam were posted in 24 places on the Gandak and there raising defences; that they had hindered the Afghans from carrying out their intention to get their families across the

---

1 *aulugh* (*kima*). Does *aulugh* (*auluq, uluq*) connect with the "bulky Oolak or baggage-boat of Bengal"? (*Hobson-Jobson s.n.* Woolock, oolock).

2 De Courteille's reading of Ilminsky's "Baburi" (p. 476) as Bairi, old servant, hardly suits the age of the boat.

3 Babur anticipated the custom followed *e.g.* by the White Star and Cunard lines, when he gave his boats names having the same terminal syllable; his is *aish*; on it he makes the quip of the *har aish* of the Farmaish.

4 As Vullers makes Ar. *ghurfat* a synonym of *chaukandi*, the Farmaish seems likely to have had a cabin, open at the sides. De Courteille understood it to have a rounded stern. [*Cf.* E. & D's *History of India* v, 347, 503 n.; and Gul-badan's H.N. trs. p. 98, n. 2.]

5 *mindin rukhsat aldi*; phrasing which bespeaks admitted equality, that of Timurid birth.

6 *i.e.* subjects of the Afghan ruler of Bengal; many will have been Biharis and Purbiyas. Makhdum-i-'alam was Nasrat Shah's Governor in Hajipur.

river (Ganges?), and had joined them to themselves.[1] This news making fighting probable, we detained Muhammad-i-zaman Mirza, and sent Shah Iskandar to Bihar with 3 or 400 men.

(*yy. Incidents of the eastward march resumed.*)

(*April 16th*) On Saturday (*8th*) a person came in from Dudu and her son Jalal Khan (son) of Bihar Khan[2] whom the Bengali (Nasrat Shah) must have held as if eye-bewitched.[3] After letting me know they were coming,[4] they had done some straight fighting to get away from the Bengalis, had crossed the river,[5] reached Bihar, and were said now to be on their way to me.

This command was given today for the Bengal envoy Isma'il Mita:—Concerning those three articles, about which letters have already been written and despatched, let him write that an answer is long in coming, and that if the honoured (Nasrat Shah) be loyal and of single-mind towards us, it ought to come soon.

(*April 17th*) In the night of Sunday (*9th*)[6] a man came in from Tardi-muhammad *Jang-jang* to say that when, on Wednesday the 5th of the month Sha'ban, his scouts reached Bihar from this side, the Shiqdar of the place went off by a gate on the other side.

On Sunday morning we marched on and dismounted in the *pargana* of Ari (Arrah).[7]

(*zz. News and negotiations.*)

To this ground came the news that the Kharid[8] army, with 100–150 boats, was said to be on the far side of the Saru near the

1 This might imply that the Afghans had been prevented from joining Mahmud Khan *Ludi* near the Son.

2 Sl. Muhammad Shah *Nuhani Afghan*, the former ruler of Bihar, dead within a year. He had trained Farid Khan *Sur* in the management of government affairs; had given him, for gallant encounter with a tiger, the title Sher Khan by which, or its higher form Sher Shah, history knows him, and had made him his young son's "deputy", an office Sher Khan held after the father's death in conjunction with the boy's mother Dudu Bibi (*Tarikh-i-sher-shahi*, E. & D.'s *History of India* iv, 325 *et seq.*).

3 *guz baghi yusunluq*; by which I understand they were held fast from departure, as *e.g.* a mouse by the fascination of a snake.

4 f. 365 mentions a letter which may have announced their intention.

5 Ganges; they thus evaded the restriction made good on other Afghans.

6 Anglicé, Saturday 8th after 6 p.m.

7 The *D. G. of Shahabad* (pp. 20 and 127) mentions that "it is said Babur marched to Arrah after his victory over Mahmud *Ludi*", and that "local tradition still points to a place near the Judge's Court as that on which he pitched his camp".

8 Kharid which is now a *pargana* of the Ballia district, lay formerly on both sides of the Ghogra. When the army of Kharid opposed Babur's progress, it acted for Nasrat Shah, but this Babur diplomatically ignored in assuming that there was peace between

meeting of Saru and Gang (Ghogra and Ganges). As a sort of peace existed between us and the Bengali (Nasrat Shah *Afghan*), and as, for the sake of a benediction, peace was our first endeavour whenever such work was toward as we were now on, we kept to our rule, notwithstanding his unmannerly conduct in setting himself on our road;[1] we associated Mulla Mazhab with his envoy Isma'il Mita, spoke once more about those three articles (*fasl soz*), and decided to let the envoy go. Fol. 369.

(*April 18th*) On Monday (*10th*) when the Bengal envoy came to wait on me, he was let know that he had his leave, and what follows was mentioned:[2]—"We shall be going to this side and that side, in pursuit of our foe, but no hurt or harm will be done to any dependency of yours. As one of those three articles said,[3] when you have told the army of Kharid to rise off our road and to go back to Kharid, let a few Turks be joined with it to reassure these Kharid people and to escort them to their own place.[4] If they quit not the ferry-head, if they cease not their unbecoming words, they must regard as their own act any ill that befalls them, must count any misfortune they confront as the fruit of their own words."

(*April 20th*) On Wednesday (*12th*) the usual dress of honour was put on the Bengal envoy, gifts were bestowed on him and his leave to go was given.

(*April 21st*) On Thursday (*13th*) Shaikh Jamali was sent with royal letters of encouragement to Dudu and her son Jalal Khan.

Today a servant of Mahim's came, who will have parted from the Wali (?)[5] on the other side of the Bagh-i-safa.

Bengal and himself.—At this time Nasrat Shah held the riverain on the left bank of the Ghogra but had lost Kharid of the right bank, which had been taken from him by Junaid *Barlas*. A record of his occupation still survives in Kharid-town, an inscription dated by his deputy as for 1529 AD. (*District Gazetteer of Ballia* (H. R. Nevill), and *D.G. of Saran* (L. L. S. O'Malley), Historical Chapters).

1 Babur's opinion of Nasrat Shah's hostility is more clearly shewn here than in the verbal message of f. 369.

2 This will be an unceremonious summary of a word-of-mouth message.

3 *Cf.* f. 366b, p. 661 n. 2.

4 This shews that Babur did not recognize the Saran riverain down to the Ganges as belonging to Kharid. His offered escort of Turks would safe-guard the Kharidis if they returned to the right bank of the Ghogra which was in Turk possession.

5 The Hai. MS. has *wali*, clearly written; which, as a word representing Mahim would suit the sentence best, may make playful reference to her royal commands (f. 361b), by styling her the Governor (*wali*). Erskine read the word as a place-name Dipali, which I have not found; De Courteille omits Ilminsky's *w:ras* (p. 478). The MSS. vary and are uncertain.

(*April 23rd*) On Saturday (*15th*) an envoy from 'Iraq, Murad Qajar[1] the life-guardsman, was seen.

(*April 24th*) On Sunday (*16th*) Mulla Mazhab received his usual keepsakes (*yadgarlar*) and was given leave to go.

Fol. 369b.

(*April 25th*) On Monday (*17th*) Khalifa was sent, with several begs, to see where the river (Ganges) could be crossed.

(*April 27th*) On Wednesday, (*19th*) Khalifa again was sent out, to look at the ground between the two rivers (Ganges and Ghogra).

On this same day I rode southward in the Ari (Arrah) *pargana* to visit the sheets of lotus[2] near Ari. During the excursion Shaikh Guran brought me fresh-set lotus-seeds, first-rate little things just like pistachios. The flower, that is to say, the *nilufar* (lotus), Hindustanis call *kuwul-kikri* (lotus-pistachio), and its seed *dudah* (soot).

As people said, "The Son is near," we went to refresh ourselves on it. Masses of trees could be seen down-stream; "Munir is there," said they, "where the tomb is of Shaikh Yahya the father of Shaikh Sharafu'd-din *Muniri*."[3] It being so close, I crossed the Son, went 2 or 3 *kurohs* down it, traversed the Munir orchards, made the circuit of the tomb, returned to the Son-bank, made ablution, went through the Mid-day Prayer before time, and made for camp. Some of our horses, being fat,[4] had fallen behind; some were worn out; a few people were left to gather them together, water them, rest them, and bring them on without pressure; but for this many would have been ruined.

When we turned back from Munir, I ordered that some-one should count a horse's steps between the Son-bank and the camp. They amounted to 23,100, which is 46,200 paces, which is 11½

Fol. 370.

---

1 This is the "Kadjar" of Réclus' *L'Asie antérieure* and is the name of the Turkman tribe to which the present ruling house of Persia belongs. "Turkman" might be taken as applied to Shah Tahmasp by Div Sultan's servant on f. 354.

2 *Nelumbium speciosum*, a water-bean of great beauty.

3 Shaikh Yahya had been the head of the Chishti Order. His son (d. 782 AH.— 1380–1 AD.) was the author of works named by Abu'l-fazl as read aloud to Akbar, a discursive detail which pleads in my excuse that those who know Babur well cannot but see in his grandson's character and success the fruition of his mental characteristics and of his labours in Hindustan. (For Sharafu'd-din *Muniri*, *cf. Khazinatu'l-asfiya* ii, 390–92; and *Ayin-i-akbari s.n.*)

4 Kostenko's *Turkistan Region* describes a regimen for horses which Babur will have seen in practice in his native land, one which prevented the defect that hindered his at Munir from accomplishing more than some 30 miles before mid-day.

kurohs (23 m.).[1] It is about half a *kuroh* from Munir to the Son; the return journey from Munir to the camp was therefore 12 *kurohs* (24 m.). In addition to this were some 15–16 *kurohs* done in visiting this and that place; so that the whole excursion was one of some 30 *kurohs* (60 m.). Six *garis* of the 1st night-watch had passed [8.15 p.m.] when we reached the camp.

(*April 28th*) At the dawn of Thursday (*Sha'ban 19th*) Sl. Junaid *Barlas* came in with the Junpur braves from Junpur. I let him know my blame and displeasure on account of his delay; I did not see him. Qazi Jia I sent for and saw.

(*aaa. Plan of the approaching battle with the Bengal army.*)

On the same day the Turk and Hind amirs were summoned for a consultation about crossing Gang (Ganges), and matters found settlement at this:[2]—that Ustad 'Ali-quli should collect mortar, *firingi*,[3] and culverin[4] to the point of rising ground between the rivers Saru and Gang, and, having many matchlockmen with him, should incite to battle from that place;[5] that

1 The distance from Munir to the bank of the Ganges will have been considerably longer in Babur's day than now because of the change of the river's course through its desertion of the Burh-ganga channel (*cf.* next note).

2 In trying to locate the site of Babur's coming battle with the forces of Nasrat Shah, it should be kept in mind that previous to the 18th century, and therefore, presumably, in his day, the Ganges flowed in the "Burh-ganga" (Old Ganges) channel which now is closely followed by the western boundary of the Ballia *pargana* of Du-aba; that the Ganges and Ghogra will have met where this old channel entered the bed of the latter river; and also, as is seen from Babur's narrative, that above the confluence the Ghogra will have been confined to a narrowed channel. When the Ganges flowed in the Burh-ganga channel, the now Ballia *pargana* of Du-aba was a sub-division of Bihiya and continuous with Shahabad. From it in Bihiya Babur crossed the Ganges into Kharid, doing this at a place his narrative locates as some 2 miles from the confluence. *Cf. D. G. of Ballia*, pp. 9, 192–3, 206, 213. It may be observed that the former northward extension of Bihiya to the Burh-ganga channel explains Babur's estimate (f. 370) of the distance from Munir to his camp on the Ganges; his 12*k.* (24 m.) may then have been correct; it is now too high.

3 De Courteille, *pierrier*, which may be a balista. Babur's writings give no indication of other than stone-ammunition for any projectile-engine or fire-arm. *Cf.* R.W.F. Payne-Gallwey's *Projectile-throwing engines of the ancients*.

4 Sir R.W.F. Payne-Gallwey writes in *The Cross-bow* (p. 40 and p. 41) what may apply to Babur's *zarb-zan* (culverin?) and *tufang* (matchlock), when he describes the larger culverin as a heavy hand-gun of from 16–18lb., as used by the foot-soldier and requiring the assistance of an attendant to work it; also when he says that it became the portable arquebus which was in extensive use in Europe by the Swiss in 1476 AD.; and that between 1510 and 1520 the arquebus described was superseded by what is still seen amongst remote tribes in India, a matchlock arquebus.

5 The two positions Babur selected for his guns would seem to have been opposite two ferry-heads, those, presumably, which were blocked against his pursuit of Biban and Bayazid.'Ali-quli's emplacement will have been on the high bank of old alluvium of south-eastern Kharid, overlooking the narrowed channel demanded by Babur's

Mustafa, he also having many matchlockmen, should get his
material and implements ready on the Bihar side of Gang, a little
below the meeting of the waters and opposite to where on an
island the Bengalis had an elephant and a mass of boats tied
up, and that he should engage battle from this place;[1] that
Muhammad-i-zaman Mirza and the others inscribed for the work
should take post behind Mustafa as his reserve; that both for
Ustad 'Ali-quli and Mustafa shelters (*muljar*) for the culverin-
firers should be raised by a mass of spadesmen and coolies (*kahar*)

Fol. 370b. under appointed overseers; that as soon as these shelters were
ready, 'Askari and the sultans inscribed for the work should cross
quickly at the Haldi-passage[2] and come down on the enemy;
that meantime, as Sl. Junaid and Qazi Jia had given information
about a crossing-place[3] 8 *kurohs* (16 m.) higher up,[4] Zard-rui(Pale-
face?) should go with a few raftsmen and some of the people of
the Sultan, Mahmud Khan *Nuhani* and Qazi Jia to look at that
crossing; and that, if crossing there were, they should go over at
once, because it was rumoured that the Bengalis were planning
to post men at the Haldi-passage.

A dutiful letter from Mahmud Khan the Military-collector
(*shiqdar*) of Sikandarpur now came, saying that he had collected
as many as 50 boats at the Haldi-passage and had given wages
to the boatmen, but that these were much alarmed at the rumoured
approach of the Bengalis.

(*April 30th*) As time pressed[5] for crossing the Saru, I did not
wait for the return of those who had gone to look at the passage,

---

narrative, one pent in presumably by *kankar* reefs such as there are in the region. As
illustrating what the channel might have been, the varying breadth of the Ghogra
along the 'Azamgarh District may be quoted, *viz*. from 10 miles to 2/5 m., the latter
being where, as in Kharid, there is old alluvium with *kankar* reefs preserving the
banks. *Cf.* Reid's *Report of Settlement Operations in 'Azamgarh, Sikandarpur, and
Bhadaon.*—Firishta gives Badru as the name of one ferry (lith. ed. i. 210).

1 Mustafa, like 'Ali-quli, was to take the offensive by gun-fire directed on the opposite
bank. Judging from maps and also from the course taken by the Ganges through the
Burh-ganga channel and from Babur's narrative, there seems to have been a narrow
reach of the Ghogra just below the confluence, as well as above.

2 This ferry, bearing the common name Haldi (turmeric), is located by the course
of events as at no great distance above the enemy's encampment above the confluence.
It cannot be the one of Sikandarpur West.

3 *guzr*, which here may mean a casual ford through water low just before the Rains.
As it was not found, it will have been temporary.

4 *i.e.* above Babur's positions.

5 *sarwar* (or *dar*) *waqt*.

but on Saturday (*21st*) summoned the begs for consultation and said,"As it has been reported that there are (no?) crossing-places (fords?) along the whole of the ground from Chatur-muk in Sikandarpur to Baraich and Aud,[1] let us, while seated here, assign the large force to cross at the Haldi-passage by boat and from there Fol. 371. to come down on the enemy; let Ustad 'Ali-quli and Mustafa engage battle with gun (*top*), matchlock, culverin and *firingi*, and by this draw the enemy out before 'Askari comes up.[2] Let us after crossing the river (Ganges) and assigning reinforcement to Ustad 'Ali-quli, take our stand ready for whatever comes; if 'Askari's troops get near, let us fling attack from where we are, cross over and assault; let Muhammad-i-zaman Mirza and those appointed to act with him, engage battle from near Mustafa on the other side of Gang."

The matter having been left at this, the force for the north of the Gang was formed into four divisions to start under 'Askari's command for the Haldi-passage. One division was of 'Askari and his retainers; another was Sl. Jalalu'd-din *Sharqi*; another was of the Auzbeg sultans Qasim-i-husain Sultan, Bi-khub Sultan and Tang-aitmish Sultan, together with Mahmud Khan *Nuhani* of Ghazipur, Baba Qashqa's Kuki, Tulmish *Auzbeg*, Qurban of Chirkh, and the Darya-khanis led by Hasan Khan; another was of Musa Sl. (*Farmuli*) and Sl. Junaid with what-not of the Junpur army, some 20,000 men. Officers were appointed to oversee the getting of the force to horse that very night, that is to say, the Fol. 371*b*. night of Sunday.[3]

(*May 1st*) The army began to cross Gang at the dawn of Sunday (*Sha'ban 22nd*); I went over by boat at the 1st watch (6 a.m.). Zard-rui and his party came in at mid-day; the ford itself they had not found but they brought news of boats and of having met on the road the army getting near them.[4]

---

1 The preceding sentence is imperfect and varies in the MSS. The 1st Pers. trs., the wording of which is often explanatory, says that there were *no* passages, which, as there were many ferries, will mean fords. The Haldi-guzr where 'Askari was to cross, will have been far below the lowest Babur mentions, *viz*. Chatur-muk (Chaupara).
2 This passage presupposes that guns in Kharid could hit the hostile camp in Saran. If the river narrowed here as it does further north, the Ghazi mortar, which seems to have been the only one Babur had with him, would have carried across, since it threw a stone 1600 paces (*qadam*, f. 309). *Cf*. Reid's *Report* quoted above.
3 Anglicé, Saturday after 6 p.m.
4 *yaqin bulghan fauj*, var. *ta'in bulghan fauj*, the army appointed (to cross). The boats will be those collected at the Haldi-ferry, and the army 'Askari's.

(*May 3rd*) On Tuesday (*Sha'ban 24th*) we marched from where the river had been crossed, went on for nearly one *kuroh* (2 m.) and dismounted on the fighting-ground at the confluence.[1] I myself went to enjoy Ustad 'Ali-quli's firing of culverin and *firingi*; he hit two boats today with *firingi*-stones, broke them and sank them. Mustafa did the same from his side. I had the large mortar[2] taken to the fighting-ground, left Mulla Ghulam to superintend the making of its position, appointed a body of *vasawals*[3] and active braves to help him, went to an island facing the camp and there ate *ma'jun*.

Whilst still under the influence of the confection[4] I had the boat taken to near the tents and there slept. A strange thing happened in the night, a noise and disturbance arising about the 3rd watch (midnight) and the pages and others snatching up pieces of wood from the boat, and shouting "Strike! strike!"

Fol. 372.

What was said to have led to the disturbance was that a night-guard who was in the Farmaish along-side the Asaish in which I was sleeping,[5] opening his eyes from slumber, sees a man with his hand on the Asaish as if meaning to climb into her. They fall on him;[6] he dives, comes up again, cuts at the night-guard's head, wounding it a little, then runs off at once towards the river.[7] Once before, on the night we returned from Munir, one or two night-guards had chased several Hindustanis from near the boats, and had brought in two swords and a dagger of theirs. The Most High had me in His Keeping!

> (*Persian*) Were the sword of the world to leap forth,
>   It would cut not a vein till God will.[8]

1 *i.e.* near 'Ali-quli's emplacement.   2 *Cf.* f. 302, f. 309, f. 337 and n. 4.

3 "The *yasawal* is an officer who carries the commands of the prince, and sees them enforced" (Erskine). Here he will have been the superintendent of coolies moving earth.

4 *ma'jun-nak* which, in these days of Babur's return to obedience, it may be right to translate in harmony with his psychical outlook of self-reproach, by *ma'jun*-polluted. Though he had long ceased to drink wine, he still sought cheer and comfort, in his laborious days, from inspiriting and forbidden confections.

5 Probably owing to the less precise phrasing of his Persian archetype, Erskine here has reversed the statement, made in the Turki, that Babur slept in the Asaish (not the Farmaish).

6 *austida tashlar.* An earlier reading of this, *viz.* that stones were thrown on the intruder is negatived by Babur's mention of wood as the weapon used.

7 *su sari* which, as the boats were between an island and the river's bank, seems likely to mean that the man went off towards the main stream. *Mems.* p. 415, "made his escape in the river"; *Méms.* ii, 418, *dans la direction du large.*

8 This couplet is quoted by Jahangir also (*Tuzuk*, trs. Rogers & Beveridge, i, 348).

(*May 4th*) At the dawn of Wednesday (*25th*), I went in the boat Gunjaish to near the stone-firing ground (*tash-atar-yir*) and there posted each soever to his work.

(*bbb. Details of the engagement.*)

Aughan-birdi *Mughul*, leading not less than 1000 men, had been sent to get, in some way or other, across the river (Saru) one, two, three *kurohs* (2, 4, 6 m.) higher up. A mass of foot-soldiers, crossing from opposite 'Askari's camp,[1] landed from 20–30 boats on his road, presumably thinking to show their superiority, but Aughan-birdi and his men charged them, put them to flight, took a few and cut their heads off, shot many with arrows, and got possession of 7 or 8 boats. Today also Bengalis crossed in a few boats to Muhammad-i-zaman Mirza's side, there landed and Fol. 372*b*. provoked to fight. When attacked they fled, and three boat-loads of them were drowned. One boat was captured and brought to me. In this affair Baba the Brave went forward and exerted himself excellently.

Orders were given that in the darkness of night the boats Aughan-birdi had captured should be drawn[2] up-stream, and that in them there should cross Muhammad Sl. Mirza, Yakka Khwaja, Yunas-i-'ali, Aughan-birdi and those previously assigned to go with them.

Today came a man from 'Askari to say that he had crossed the [Saru]-water, leaving none behind, and that he would come down on the enemy at next day's dawn, that is to say, on Thursday's. Here-upon those already ordered to cross over were told to join 'Askari and to advance upon the enemy with him.

At the Mid-day Prayer a person came from Usta, saying "The stone is ready; what is the order?" The order was, "Fire this stone off; keep the next till I come." Going at the Other Prayer in a very small Bengali skiff to where shelter (*muljar*) had been raised, I saw Usta fire off one large stone and several

1 This, taken with the positions of other crossing-parties, serves to locate 'Askari's "Haldi-passage" at no great distance above 'Ali-quli's emplacement at the confluence, and above the main Bengal force.

2 perhaps, towed from the land. I have not found Babur using any word which clearly means to row, unless indeed a later *rawan* does so. The force meant to cross in the boats taken up under cover of night was part of Babur's own, no doubt.

small *firingi* ones. Bengalis have a reputation for fire-working;[1] we tested it now; they do not fire counting to hit a particular spot, but fire at random.

At this same Other Prayer orders were given to draw a few boats up-stream along the enemy's front. A few were got past without a "God forbid!"[2] from those who, all unprotected, drew

Fol. 373. them up. Aisan-timur Sl. and Tukhta-bugha Sl. were ordered to stay at the place those boats reached, and to keep watch over them. I got back to camp in the 1st night-watch of Thursday.[3]

Near midnight came news from (Aughan-birdi's) boats which were being drawn up-stream, "The force appointed had gone somewhat ahead; we were following, drawing the boats, when the Bengalis got to know where we were drawing them and attacked. A stone hit a boatman in the leg and broke it, we could not pass on."

(*May 5th*) At dawn on Thursday (*Sha'ban 26th*) came the news from those at the shelter, "All the boats have come from above.[4] The enemy's horse has ridden to meet our approaching army." On this, I got our men mounted quickly and rode out to above those boats[5] that had been drawn up in the night. A galloper was sent off with an order for Muhammad Sl. M. and those appointed to cross with him, to do it at once and join 'Askari. The order for Aisan-timur Sl. and Tukhta-bugha Sl. who were above these boats,[6] was that they should busy themselves to cross. Baba Sl. was not at his post.[7]

---

1 *atish-bazi* lit. fire-playing, if a purely Persian compound; if *atish* be Turki, it means discharge, shooting. The word "fire-working" is used above under the nearest to contemporary guidance known to me, *viz.* that of the list of persons who suffered in the Patna massacre "during the troubles of October 1763 AD.", in which list are the names of four Lieutenants fire-workers (*Calcutta Review*, Oct. 1884, and Jan. 1885, art. *The Patna Massacre*, H. Beveridge).

2 *bi tahashi*, without protest or demur.

3 Anglicé, Wednesday after 6 p.m.

4 Perhaps those which had failed to pass in the darkness; perhaps those from Haldi-guzr, which had been used by 'Askari's troops. There appear to be obvious reasons for their keeping abreast on the river with the troops in Saran, in order to convey reinforcements or to provide retreat.

5 *kimalar austida*, which may mean that he came, on the high bank, to where the boats lay below.

6 as in the previous note, *kimalar austida*. These will have been the few drawn up-stream along the enemy's front.

7 The reproach conveyed by Babur's statement is borne out by the strictures of Haidar Mirza *Dughlat* on Baba Sultan's neglect of duty (*Tarikh-i-rashidi* trs. cap. lxxvii).

Aisan-timur Sl. at once crosses, in one boat with 30–40 of his retainers who hold their horses by the mane at the boat-side. A second boat follows. The Bengalis see them crossing and start off a mass of foot-soldiers for them. To meet these go 7 or 8 of Aisan-timur Sl.'s retainers, keeping together, shooting off arrows, drawing those foot-soldiers towards the Sultan who meantime is getting his men mounted; meantime also the second boat is moving (*rawan*). When his 30–35 horsemen charge those foot-soldiers, they put them well to flight. Aisan-timur did distinguished work, first in crossing before the rest, swift, steady, and without a "God forbid!", secondly in his excellent advance, with so few men, on such a mass of foot, and by putting these to flight. Tukhta-bugha Sl. also crossed. Then boats followed one after another. Lahoris and Hindustanis began to cross from their usual posts[1] by swimming or on bundles of reeds.[2] Seeing how matters were going, the Bengalis of the boats opposite the shelter (Mustafa's), set their faces for flight down-stream.

Darwish-i-muhammad *Sarban*, Dost Lord-of-the-gate, Nur Beg and several braves also went across the river. I made a man gallop off to the Sultans to say, "Gather well together those who cross, go close to the opposing army, take it in the flank, and get to grips." Accordingly the Sultans collected those who crossed, formed up into 3 or 4 divisions, and started for the foe. As they draw near, the enemy-commander, without breaking his array, flings his foot-soldiers to the front and so comes on. Kuki comes up with a troop from 'Askari's force and gets to grips on his side; the Sultans get to grips on theirs; they get the upper hand, unhorse man after man, and make the enemy scurry off. Kuki's men bring down a Pagan of repute named Basant Rao and cut off his head; 10 or 15 of his people fall on Kuki's, and are instantly cut to pieces. Tukhta-bugha Sl. gallops along the enemy's front and gets his sword well in. Mughul 'Abdu'l-

Fol. 373b.

Fol. 374.

1 *yusunluq tushi*, Pers. trss. *tarf khud*, *i.e.* their place in the array, a frequent phrase.
2 *dastak bila dosta-i-qamish bila. Cf.* f. 363b and f. 366b, for passages and notes connected with swimming and *dastak*. Erskine twice translates *dastak bila* by swimming; but here de Courteille changes from his earlier *à la nage* (f. 366b) to *appuyés sur une pièce de bois*. Perhaps the swift current was crossed by swimming with the support of a bundle of reeds, perhaps on rafts made of such bundles (*cf. Illustrated London News*, Sep. 16th, 1916, for a picture of Indian soldiers so crossing on rafts).

wahhab and his younger brother gets theirs in well too. Mughul though he did not know how to swim, had crossed the river in his mail holding to his horse's mane.

I sent for my own boats which were behind;[1] the Farmaish coming up first, I went over in it to visit the Bengalis' encamping-grounds. I then went into the Gunjaish. "Is there a crossing-place higher up?" I asked. Mir Muhammad the raftsman represented that the Saru was better to cross higher up;[2] accordingly the army-folk[3] were ordered to cross at the higher place he named.

While those led by Muhammad Sl. Mirza were crossing the river,[4] the boat in which Yakka Khwaja was, sank and he went to God's mercy. His retainers and lands were bestowed on his younger brother Qasim Khwaja.

Fol. 374b.

The Sultans arrived while I was making ablution for the Mid-day Prayer; I praised and thanked them and led them to expect guerdon and kindness. 'Askari also came; this was the first affair he had seen; one well-omened for him!

As the camp had not yet crossed the river, I took my rest in the boat Gunjaish, near an island.

(ccc. Various incidents of the days following the battle.)

(May 6th) During the day of Friday (Sha'ban 27th) we landed at a village named Kundih[5] in the Nirhun pargana of Kharid on the north side of the Saru.[6]

(May 8th) On Sunday (29th) Kuki was sent to Hajipur for news.

1 Perhaps they were in the Burh-ganga channel, out of gun-fire.
2 If the Ghogra flowed at this point in a narrow channel, it would be the swifter, and less easy to cross than where in an open bed.
3 chirik-aili, a frequent compound, but one of which the use is better defined in the latter than the earlier part of Babur's writings to represent what then answered to an Army Service Corps. This corps now crosses into Saran and joins the fighting force.
4 This appears to refer to the crossing effected before the fight.
5 or Kundbah. I have not succeeded in finding this name in the Nirhun pargana; it may have been at the southern end, near the "Domaigarh" of maps. In it was Tir-muhani, perhaps a village (f. 377, f. 381).
6 This passage justifies Erskine's surmise (Memoirs, p. 411, n. 4) that the Kharid-country lay on both banks of the Ghogra. His further surmise that, on the east bank of the Ghogra, it extended to the Ganges would be correct also, since the Ganges flowed, in Babur's day, through the Burh-ganga (Old Ganges) channel along the southern edge of the present Kharid, and thus joined the Ghogra higher than it now does.

Shah Muhammad (son) of Ma'ruf to whom in last year's campaign (934 AH.) I had shown great favour and had given the Saran-country, had done well on several occasions, twice fighting and overcoming his father Ma'ruf.[1] At the time when Sl. Mahmud *Ludi* perfidiously took possession of Bihar and was opposed by Shaikh Bayazid and Biban, Shah Muhammad had no help for it, he had to join them; but even then, when people were saying wild words about him, he had written dutifully to me. When 'Askari crossed at the Haldi-passage, Shah Fol. 375. Muhammad had come at once with a troop, seen him and with him gone against the Bengalis. He now came to this ground and waited on me.

During these days news came repeatedly that Biban and Shaikh Bayazid were meaning to cross the Saru-river.

In these days of respite came the surprising news from Sanbal (Sambhal) where 'Ali-i-yusuf had stayed in order to bring the place into some sort of order, that he and a physician who was by way of being a friend of his, had gone to God's mercy on one and the same day. 'Abdu'l-lah (*kitabdar*) was ordered to go and maintain order in Sanbal.

(*May 13th*) On Friday the 5th of the month Ramzan, 'Abdu'l-lah was given leave for Sanbal.[2]

(ddd. News from the westward.)

In these same days came a dutiful letter from Chin-timur Sl. saying that on account of the journey of the family from Kabul, several of the begs who had been appointed to reinforce him, had not been able to join him;[3] also that he had gone out with Muhammadi and other begs and braves, not less than 100 *kurohs*

---

1 Bayazid and Ma'ruf *Farmuli* were brothers. Bayazid had taken service with Babur in 932 AH. (1526 AD.), left him in 934 AH. (end of 1527 AD.) and opposed him near Qanuj. Ma'ruf, long a rebel against Ibrahim *Ludi*, had never joined Babur; two of his sons did so; of the two, Muhammad and Musa, the latter may be the one mentioned as at Qanuj, "Ma'ruf's son" (f. 336).—For an interesting sketch of Maruf's character and for the location in Hindustan of the Farmuli clan, *see* the *Waqi'at-i-mushtaqi*, E. & D.'s *History of India*, iv, 584.—In connection with Qanuj, the discursive remark may be allowable, that Babur's halt during the construction of the bridge of boats across the Ganges in 934 AH. is still commemorated by the name Badshah-nagar of a village between Bangarmau and Nanamau (Elliot's *Onau*, p. 45).
2 On f. 381 'Abdu'l-lah's starting-place is mentioned as Tir-muhani.
3 The failure to join would be one of the evils predicted by the dilatory start of the ladies from Kabul (f. 360b).

(200 m.), attacked the Baluchis and given them a good beating.[1] Orders were sent through 'Abdu'l-lah (*kitabdar*) for the Sultan that he and Sl. Muhammad *Duldai*, Muhammadi, and some of the begs and braves of that country-side should assemble in Agra and there remain ready to move to wherever an enemy appeared.

(*eee. Settlement with the Nuhani Afghans.*)

Fol. 375b.

(*May 16th*) On Monday the 8th of the month, Darya Khan's grandson Jalal Khan to whom Shaikh Jamali had gone, came in with his chief amirs and waited on me.[2] Yahya *Nuhani* also came, who had already sent his younger brother in sign of submission and had received a royal letter accepting his service. Not to make vain the hope with which some 7 or 8000 *Nuhani* Afghans had come in to me, I bestowed 50 *laks* from Bihar on Mahmud Khan *Nuhani*, after reserving one *krur* for Government uses (*khalsa*), and gave the remainder of the Bihar revenues in trust for the above-mentioned Jalal Khan who for his part agreed to pay one *krur* of tribute. Mulla Ghulam *yasawal* was sent to collect this tribute.[3] Muhammad-i-zaman Mirza received the Junapur-country.[4]

(*fff. Peace made with Nasrat Shah.*)

(*May 19th*) On the eve of Thursday (*11th*) that retainer of Khalifa's, Ghulam-i-'ali by name, who in company with a retainer of the Shah-zada of Mungir named Abu'l-fath,[5] had gone earlier than Isma'il Mita, to convey those three articles (*fasl soz*), now returned, again in company with Abu'l-fath, bringing letters for Khalifa written by the Shah-zada and by Husain Khan *Laskar*(?) *Wazir*, who, in these letters, gave assent to those three conditions, took upon themselves to act for Nasrat Shah and interjected a word for peace. As the object of this campaign was to put

1 The order for these operations is given on f. 355b.
2 f. 369. The former Nuhani chiefs are now restored to Bihar as tributaries of Babur.
3 Erskine estimated the *krur* at about £25,000, and the 50 *laks* at about £12,500.
4 The Mirza thus supersedes Junaid *Barlas* in Junpur.—The form Junapur used above and elsewhere by Babur and his Persian translators, supports the *Gazetteer of India* xlv, 74 as to the origin of the name Junpur.
5 a son of Nasrat Shah. No record of this earlier legation is with the *Babur-nama* manuscripts; probably it has been lost. The only article found specified is the one asking for the removal of the Kharid army from a ferry-head Babur wished to use; Nasrat Shah's assent to this is an anti-climax to Babur's victory on the Ghogra.

down the rebel Afghans of whom some had taken their heads and gone off, some had come in submissive and accepting my service, and the remaining few were in the hands of the Bengali Fol. 376. (Nasrat Shah) who had taken them in charge, and as, moreover, the Rains were near, we in our turn wrote and despatched words for peace on the conditions mentioned.

(*ggg. Submissions and guerdon.*)

(*May 21st*) On Saturday (*13th*) Isma'il *Jalwani*, 'Alaul Khan *Nuhani*, Auliya Khan *Ashraqi*(?) and 5 and 6 amirs came in and waited on me.

Today guerdon was bestowed on Aisan-timur Sl. and Tukhta-bugha Sl., of swords and daggers with belts, cuirasses, dresses of honour, and *tipuchaq* horses; also they were made to kneel, Aisan-timur Sl. for the grant of 36 *laks* from the Narnul *pargana*, Tukhta-bugha Sl. for 30 *laks* from that of Shamsabad.

(*hhh. Pursuit of Bayazid and Biban.*)

(*May 23rd*) On Monday the 15th of the month (*Ramzan*), we marched from our ground belonging to Kundbah (or Kundih) on the Saru-river, with easy mind about Bihar and Bengal, and resolute to crush the traitors Biban and Shaikh Bayazid.

(*May 25th*) On Wednesday (*17th*) after making two night-halts by the way, we dismounted at a passage across the Saru, called Chaupara-Chaturmuk of Sikandarpur.[1] From today people were busy in crossing the river.

As news began to come again and again that the traitors, after crossing Saru and Gogar,[2] were going toward Luknu,[3] the

1 Chaupara is at the Saran end of the ferry, at the Sikandarpur one is Chatur-muk (Four-faces, an epithet of Brahma and Vishnu).

2 It may be inferred from the earlier use of the phrase Gogar (or Gagar) and Saru (Siru or Sird), on f. 338–8*b*, that whereas the rebels were, earlier, for crossing Saru only, *i.e.* the Ghogra below its confluence with the Sarda, they had now changed for crossing above the confluence and further north. Such a change is explicable by desire to avoid encounter with Babur's following, here perhaps the army of Aud, and the same desire is manifested by their abandonment of a fort captured (f. 377*b*) some days before the rumour reached Babur of their crossing Saru and Gogar.—Since translating the passage on f. 338, I have been led, by enforced attention to the movement of the confluence of Ghogra with Ganges (Saru with Gang) to see that translation, eased in obedience to distances shewn in maps, may be wrong and that Babur's statement that he dismounted 2–3 *kurohs* (4–6 m.) above Aud at the confluence of Gogar with Saru, may have some geographical interest and indicate movement of the two affluents such *e.g.* as is indicated of the Ganges and Ghogra by tradition and by the name Burh-ganga (*cf.* f. 370, p. 667, n. 2).

3 or L:knur, perhaps Liknu or Liknur. The capricious variation in the MSS.

following leaders were appointed to bar (their) crossing:[1]—The
Turk and Hind amirs Sultan Jalalu'd-din *Sharqi*,'Ali Khan *Farmuli*;
Tardika (or, Tardi *yakka*), Nizam Khan of Biana, together with
Tulmish *Auzbeg*, Qurban of Chirk and Darya Khan (of Bhira's

Fol. 376b. son) Hasan Khan. They were given leave to go on the night
of Thursday.[2]

(*iii. Damage done to the Babur-nama writings.*)

That same night when 1 watch (*pas*), 5 *garis* had passed (*cir.*
10.55 p.m.) and the *tarawih*-prayers were over,[3] such a storm
burst, in the inside of a moment, from the up-piled clouds of
the Rainy-season, and such a stiff gale rose, that few tents were
left standing. I was in the Audience-tent, about to write (*kitabat
qila dur aidim*); before I could collect papers and sections,[4] the
tent came down, with its porch, right on my head. The *tungluq*
went to pieces.[5] God preserved me! no harm befell me!
Sections and book[6] were drenched under water and gathered
together with much difficulty. We laid them in the folds of a
woollen throne-carpet,[7] put this on the throne and on it piled
blankets. The storm quieted down in about 2 *garis* (45 m.); the

---

between L:knu and L:knur makes the movements of the rebels difficult to follow.
Comment on these variants, tending to identify the places behind the words, is
grouped in Appendix T, *On L:knu (Lakhnau) and L:knur (Lakhnar)*.

1 Taking *guzr* in the sense it has had hitherto in the *Babur-nama* of ferry or ford,
the detachment may have been intended to block the river-crossings of "Saru and
Gogar". If so, however, the time for this was past, the rebels having taken a fort west
of those rivers on Ramzan 13th. Nothing further is heard of the detachment.—
That news of the rebel-crossing of the rivers did not reach Babur before the 18th
and news of their capture of L:knu or L:knur before the 19th may indicate that
they had crossed a good deal to the north of the confluence, and that the fort
taken was one more remote than Lakhnau (Oude). Cf. Appendix T.

2 Anglicé, Wednesday after 6 p.m.

3 These are recited late in the night during Ramzan.

4 *kaghaz u ajza'*, perhaps writing-paper and the various sections of the *Babur-nama*
writings, *viz.* biographical notices, descriptions of places, detached lengths of diary,
farmans of Shaikh Zain. The *lacunae* of 934 AH., 935 AH., and perhaps earlier ones
also may be attributed reasonably to this storm. It is easy to understand the loss of
e.g. the conclusion of the Farghana section, and the diary one of 934 AH., if they lay
partly under water. The accident would be better realized in its disastrous results to
the writings, if one knew whether Babur wrote in a bound or unbound volume.
From the minor losses of 935 AH., one guesses that the current diary at least had
not reached the stage of binding.

5 The *tungluq* is a flap in a tent-roof, allowing light and air to enter, or smoke to
come out.

6 *ajza' u kitab. See* last note but one. The *kitab* (book) might well be Babur's
composed narrative on which he was now working, as far as it had then gone
towards its untimely end (Hai. MS. f. 216b).

7 *saqarlat kut-zilucha*, where *saqarlat* will mean warm and woollen.

bedding-tent was set up, a lamp lighted, and, after much trouble, a fire kindled. We, without sleep, were busy till shoot of day drying folios and sections.

(*jjj. Pursuit of Biban and Bayazid resumed.*)

(*May 26th*) I crossed the water on Thursday morning (*Raman 18th*).

(*May 27th*) On Friday (*19th*) I rode out to visit Sikandarpur and Kharid.[1] Today came matters written by 'Abdu'l-lah (*kitabdar*) and Baqi about the taking of Luknur.[2]

(*May 28th*) On Saturday (*20th*) Kuki was sent ahead, with a troop, to join Baqi.[3]

(*May 29th*) That nothing falling to be done before my arrival might be neglected, leave to join Baqi was given on Sunday (*21st*) to Sl. Junaid *Barlas*, Khalifa's (son) Hasan, Mulla Apaq's retainers, and the elder and younger brethren of Mumin Ataka. Fol. 377.

Today at the Other Prayer a special dress of honour and a *tipuchaq* horse were bestowed on Shah Muhammad (son) of Ma'ruf *Farmuli*, and leave to go was given. As had been done last year (934 AH.), an allowance from Saran and Kundla[4] was bestowed on him for the maintenance of quiver-wearers. Today too an allowance of 72 *laks*[5] from Sarwar and a *tipuchaq* horse were bestowed on Isma'il *Jalwani*, and his leave was given. It was settled that a son of each of them should be always in waiting in Agra.

About the boats Gunjaish and Araish and two others it was settled with Bengalis that they should take them to Ghazipur by way of Tir-muhani.[6] The boats Asaish and Farmaish were ordered taken up the Saru with the camp.

(*May 30th*) On Monday (*Ramzan 22nd*) we marched from the Chaupara–Chaturmuk passage along the Saru towards Oude, with mind at ease about Bihar and Sarwar,[7] and after

---

1 Kharid-town is some 4 m. s.e. of the town of Sikandarpur.
2 or L:knu. *Cf.* Appendix T. It is now 14 days since 'Abdu'l-lah *kitabdar* had left Tir-muhani (f. 375) for Sambhal; as he was in haste, there had been time for him to go beyond Aud (where Baqi was) and yet get the news to Babur on the 19th.
3 In a way not usual with him, Babur seems to apply three epithets to this follower, *viz. ming-begi, shaghawal, Tashkindi.*
4 or Kandla; *cf.* Revenue list f. 293; is it now Saran Khas?
5 £18,000 (Erskine). For the total yield of Kundla (or Kandla) and Sarwar, *see* Revenue list (f. 293).
6 f. 375, p. 675 n. 2 and f. 381, p. 687 n. 3.
7 A little earlier Babur has recorded his ease of mind about Bihar and Bengal, the fruit doubtless of his victory over Mahmud *Ludi* and Nasrat Shah; he now does the

ol. 377b.   doing as much as 10 *kurohs* (20 m.) dismounted on the Saru in
a village called Kilirah (?) dependent on Fathpur.[1]

(*kkk. A surmised survival of the record of 934 AH.*[2])

* After spending several days pleasantly in that place where
there are gardens, running-waters, well-designed buildings, trees,
particularly mango-trees, and various birds of coloured plumage,
I ordered the march to be towards Ghazipur.

Isma'il Khan *Jalwani* and 'Alaul Khan *Nuhani* had it represented to me that they would come to Agra after seeing their
native land (*watn*). On this the command was, "I will give an
order in a month."*[3]

same about Bihar and Sarwar, no doubt because he has replaced in Bihar, as his tributaries, the Nuhani chiefs and has settled other Afghans, Jalwanis and Farmulis in a
Sarwar cleared of the Jalwani (?) rebel Biban and the Farmuli opponents Bayazid
and Ma'ruf. The Farmuli Shaikh-zadas, it may be recalled, belonged by descent to
Babur's Kabul district of Farmul.—The *Waqi'at-i-mushtaqi* (E. & D.'s *H. of I.* iv, 548)
details the position of the clan under Sikandar *Ludi.*

1 The MSS. write Fathpur but Nathpur suits the context, a *pargana* mentioned in
the *Ayin-i-akbari* and now in the 'Azamgarh district. There seems to be no Fathpur
within Babur's limit of distance. The *D. G. of 'Azamgarh* mentions two now insignificant Fathpurs, one as having a school, the other a market. The name G:l:r:h
(K:l:r:h) I have not found.

2 The passage contained in this section seems to be a survival of the lost record
of 934 AH. (f. 339). I have found it only in the *Memoirs* p. 420, and in Mr. Erskine's
own Codex of the *Waqi'at-i-baburi* (now B.M. Add. 26,200), f. 371 where however
several circumstances isolate it from the context. It may be a Persian translation of
an authentic Turki fragment, found, perhaps with other such fragments, in the
Royal Library. Its wording disassociates it from the 'Abdu'r-rahim text. The Codex
(No. 26,200) breaks off at the foot of a page (*supra*, Fathpur) with a completed
sentence. The supposedly-misplaced passage is entered on the next folio as a sort
of ending of the Babur-nama writings; in a rough script, inferior to that of the
Codex, and is followed by *Tam, tam* (Finis), and an incomplete date 98–, in words.
Beneath this a line is drawn, on which is subtended the triangle frequent with
scribes; within this is what seems to be a completion of the date to 980 AH. and a
pious wish, scrawled in an even rougher hand than the rest.—Not only in diction
and in script but in contents also the passage is a misfit where it now stands; it can
hardly describe a village on the Saru; Babur in 935 AH. did not march for Ghazipur
but may have done so in 934 AH. (p. 656, n. 3); Isma'il *Jalwani* had had leave given
already in 935 AH. (f. 377) under other conditions, ones bespeaking more trust and
tried allegiance.—Possibly the place described as having fine buildings, gardens *etc.*
is Aud (Ajodhya) where Babur spent some days in 934 AH. (*cf.* f. 363b, p. 655 n. 3).

3 "Here my Persian manuscript closes" (This is B.M. Add. 26,200). "The two
additional fragments are given from Mr. Metcalfe's manuscript alone" (now B.M.
Add. 26,202) "and unluckily, it is extremely incorrect" (Erskine). This note will have
been written perhaps a decade before 1826, in which year the *Memoirs of Babur* was
published, after long delay. Mr. Erskine's own Codex (No. 26,200) was made good
at a later date, perhaps when he was working on his History of India (pub. 1854),
by a well-written supplement which carries the diary to its usual end *s.a.* 936 AH.
and also gives Persian translations of Babur's letters to Humayun and Khwaja Kalan.

(*lll. The westward march resumed.*)

(*May 31st*) Those who marched early (*Tuesday, Ramzan 23rd*), having lost their way, went to the great lake of Fathpur (?).[1] People were sent galloping off to fetch back such as were near and Kichik Khwaja was ordered to spend the night on the lake-shore and to bring the rest on next morning to join the camp. We marched at dawn; I got into the Asaish half-way and had it towed to our ground higher up.

(*mmm. Details of the capture of a fort by Biban and Bayazid.*)

On the way up, Khalifa brought Shah Muhammad *diwana*'s son who had come from Baqi bringing this reliable news about Luknur:[2]—They (*i.e.* Biban and Bayazid) hurled their assault on Saturday the 13th of the month Ramzan (*May 21st*) but could do nothing by fighting; while the fighting was going on, a collection of wood-chips, hay, and thorns in the fort took fire, so that inside the walls it became as hot as an oven (*tanurdik tafsan*); the garrison could not move round the rampart; the fort was lost. When the enemy heard, two or three days later, of our return (westwards), he fled towards Dalmau.[3]

Today after doing as much as 10 *kurohs* (20 m.), we dismounted beside a village called Jalisir,[4] on the Saru-bank, in the Sagri *pargana*.

(*June 1st*) We stayed on the same ground through Wednesday (*24th*), in order to rest our cattle.

(*nnn. Dispositions against Biban and Bayazid.*)

Some said they had heard that Biban and Bayazid had crossed Gang, and thought of withdrawing themselves to their kinsfolk   Fol. 378.

1 Here, as earlier, Nathpur suits the context better than Fathpur. In the Nathpur *pargana*, at a distance from Chaupara approximately suiting Babur's statement of distance, is the lake "Tal Ratoi", formerly larger and deeper than now. There is a second further west and now larger than Tal Ratoi; through this the Ghogra once flowed, and through it has tried within the last half-century to break back. These changes in Tal Ratoi and in the course of the Ghogra dictate caution in attempting to locate places which were on it in Babur's day *e.g.* K:l:r:h (*supra*).

2 Appendix T.

3 This name has the following variants in the Hai. MS. and in Kehr's:—Dalm-u-uu-ur-ud-ut. The place was in Akbar's *sarkar* of Manikpur and is now in the Rai Bareilly district.

4 Perhaps Chaksar, which was in Akbar's *sarkar* of Junpur, and is now in the 'Azamgarh district.

(*nisbahsilar*) by way of ... ...[1] Here-upon the begs were summoned for a consultation and it was settled that Muhammad-i-zaman Mirza and Sl. Junaid *Barlas* who in place of Junpur had been given Chunar with several *parganas*, Mahmud Khan *Nuhani*, Qazi Jia, and Taj Khan *Sarang-khani* should block the enemy's road at Chunar.[2]

(*June 2nd*) Marching early in the morning of Thursday (*25th*), we left the Saru-river, did 11 *kurohs* (22 m.), crossed the Parsaru (Sarju) and dismounted on its bank.

Here the begs were summoned, discussion was had, and the leaders named below were appointed to go detached from the army, in rapid pursuit of Biban and Bayazid towards Dalmut (Dalmau):—Aisan-timur Sl., Muhammad Sl. M., Tukhta-bugha Sl., Qasim-i-husain Sl., Bi-khub (Ni-khub) Sl., Muzaffar-i-husain Sl., Qasim Khwaja, Ja'far Khwaja, Zahid Khwaja, Jani Beg, 'Askari's retainer Kichik Khwaja, and, of Hind amirs, 'Alam Khan of Kalpi, Malik-dad *Kararani*, and Rao (Rawui) *Sarwani*.

(*ooo. The march continued.*)

When I went at night to make ablution in the Parsaru, people were catching a mass of fish that had gathered round a lamp on the surface of the water. I like others took fish in my hands.[3]

---

1 Hai. MS. *J:nara khund tawabi si bila* (perhaps *tawabi'si* but not so written). The obscurity of these words is indicated by their variation in the manuscripts. Most scribes have them as Chunar and Junpur, guided presumably by the despatch of a force to Chunar on receipt of the news, but another force was sent to Dalmau at the same time. The rebels were defeated s.w. of Dalmau and thence went to Mahuba; it is not certain that they had crossed the Ganges at Dalmau; there are difficulties in supposing the fort they captured and abandoned was Lakhnau (Oude); they might have gone south to near Kalpi and Adampur, which are at no great distance from where they were defeated by Baqi *shaghawal*, if Lakhnur (now Shahabad in Rampur) were the fort. (*Cf.* Appendix T.)—To take up the interpretation of the words quoted above, at another point, that of the kinsfolk or fellow-Afghans the rebels planned to join:—these kinsfolk may have been, of Bayazid, the Farmulis in Sarwar, and of Biban, the Jalwanis of the same place. The two may have trusted to relationship for harbourage during the Rains, disloyal though they were to their kinsmen's accepted suzerain. Therefore if they were once across Ganges and Jumna, as they were in Mahuba, they may have thought of working eastwards south of the Ganges and of getting north into Sarwar through territory belonging to the Chunar and Junpur governments. This however is not expressed by the words quoted above; perhaps Babur's record was hastily and incompletely written.—Another reading may be Chunar and Jaund (in Akbar's *sarkar* of Rohtas).

2 *yulini tushqailar.* It may be observed concerning the despatch of Muhammad-i-zaman M. and of Junaid *Barlas* that they went to their new appointments Junpur and Chunar respectively; that their doing so was an orderly part of the winding-up of Babur's Eastern operations; that they remained as part of the Eastern garrison, on duty apart from that of blocking the road of Biban and Bayazid.

3 This mode of fishing is still practised in India (Erskine).

(*June 3rd*) On Friday (*26th*) we dismounted on a very slender stream, the head-water of a branch of the Parsaru. In order not to be disturbed by the comings and goings of the army-folk, Fol. 378*b*. I had it dammed higher up and had a place, 10 by 10, made for ablution. The night of the 27th[1] was spent on this ground.

(*June 4th*) At the dawn of the same day (*Saturday 27th*) we left that water, crossed the Tus and dismounted on its bank.[2]

(*June 5th*) On Sunday (*28th*) we dismounted on the bank of the same water.

(*June 6th*) On Monday the 29th of the month (*Ramzan*), our station was on the bank of the same Tus-water. Though tonight the sky was not quite clear, a few people saw the Moon, and so testifying to the Qazi, fixed the end of the month (*Ramzan*).

(*June 7th*) On Tuesday (*Shawwal 1st*) we made the Prayer of the Festival, at dawn rode on, did 10 *kurohs* (20 m.), and dismounted on the bank of the Gui (Gumti), a *kuroh* (2 m.) from Maing.[3] The sin of *ma'jun* was committed (*irtikab qilildi*) near the Mid-day Prayer; I had sent this little couplet of invitation to Shaikh Zain, Mulla Shihab and Khwand-amir:—

> (*Turki*) Shaikh and Mulla Shihab and Khwand-amir,
> Come all three, or two, or one.

Darwish-i-muhammad (*Sarban*), Yunas-i-'ali and 'Abdu'l-lah ('*asas*)[4] were also there. At the Other Prayer the wrestlers set to.

(*June 8th*) On Wednesday (*2nd*) we stayed on the same ground. Near breakfast-time *ma'jun* was eaten. Today Malik Sharq came in who had been to get Taj Khan out of Chunar.[5] When the wrestlers set to today, the Champion of Aud who had come earlier, grappled with and threw a Hindustani wrestler who had Fol. 379. come in the interval.

Today Yahya *Nuhani* was granted an allowance of 15 *laks*

1 Islamicé, Saturday night; Anglicé, Friday after 6 p.m.

2 This Tus, "Tousin, or Tons, is a branch from the Ghogra coming off above Faizabad and joining the Sarju or Parsaru below 'Azamgarh" (Erskine).

3 Kehr's MS. p. 1132, Mang (or Mank); Hai. MS. Taik; I.O. 218 f. 328 Ba:k; I.O. 217 f. 236*b*, Biak. Maing in the Sultanpur district seems suitably located (*D. G. of Sultanpur*, p. 162).

4 This will be the night-guard ('*asas*); the librarian (*kitabdar*) is in Sambhal. I.O. 218 f. 325 inserts *kitabdar* after 'Abdu'l-lah's name where he is recorded as sent to Sambhal (f. 375).

5 He will have announced to Taj Khan the transfer of the fort to Junaid *Barlas*.

from Parsarur,[1] made to put on a dress of honour, and given his leave.

(*June 9th*) Next day (*Thursday 3rd*) we did 11 *kurohs* (22 m.), crossed the Gui-water (Gumti), and dismounted on its bank.

(*ppp. Concerning the pursuit of Biban and Bayazid.*)

News came in about the sultans and begs of the advance that they had reached Dalmud (Dalmau), but were said not yet to have crossed the water (Ganges). Angered by this (delay), I sent orders, "Cross the water at once; follow the track of the rebels; cross Jun (Jumna) also; join 'Alam Khan to yourselves; be energetic and get to grips with the adversary."

(*qqq. The march continued.*)

(*June 10th*) After leaving this water (*Gumti, Friday 4th*) we made two night-halts and reached Dalmud (Dalmau), where most of the army-folk crossed Gang, there and then, by a ford. While the camp was being got over, *ma'jun* was eaten on an island (*aral*) below the ford.

(*June 13th*) After crossing, we waited one day (*Monday 7th*) for all the army-folk to get across. Today Baqi *Tashkindi* came in with the army of Aud (Ajodhya) and waited on me.

(*June 14th*) Leaving the Gang-water (Ganges, *Tuesday 8th*), we made one night-halt, then dismounted (*June 15th–Shawwal 9th*) beside Kurarah (Kura Khas) on the Arind-water. The distance from Dalmud (Dalmau) to Kurarah came out at 22 *kurohs* (44 m.).[2]

(*June 16th*) On Thursday (*10th*) we marched early from that ground and dismounted opposite the Adampur *pargana*.[3]

To enable us to cross (Jun) in pursuit of our adversaries, a few Fol. 379b. raftsmen had been sent forward to collect at Kalpi what boats were to be had; some boats arrived the night we dismounted, moreover a ford was found through the Jun-river.

As the encamping-place was full of dust, we settled ourselves

1 £3750. Parsarur was in Akbar's *subah* of Lahor; G. of I. xx, 23, Pasrur.
2 The estimate may have been made by measurement (ff. 351–351b) or by counting a horse's steps (f. 370). Here the Hai. MS. and Kehr's have D:lmud, but I.O. 218 f. 328b (D:lmuu).
3 As on f. 361b, so here, Babur's wording tends to locate Adampur on the right (west) bank of the Jumna.

on an island and there stayed the several days we were on that ground.

(rrr. Concerning Biban and Bayazid.)

Not getting reliable news about the enemy, we sent Baqi *shaghawal* with a few braves of the interior[1] to get information about him.

(*June 17th*) Next day (*Friday 11th*) at the Other Prayer, one of Baqi Beg's retainers came in. Baqi had beaten scouts of Biban and Bayazid, killed one of their good men, Mubarak Khan *Jalwani*, and some others, sent in several heads, and one man alive.

(*June 18th*) At dawn (*Saturday 12th*) Paymaster Shah Husain came in, told the story of the beating of the scouts, and gave various news.

Tonight, that is to say, the night of Sunday the 13th of the month,[2] the river Jun came down in flood, so that by the dawn, the whole of the island on which I was settled, was under water. I moved to another an arrow's-flight down-stream, there had a tent set up and settled down.

(*June 20th*) On Monday (*14th*) Jalal *Tashkindi* came from the begs and sultans of the advance. Shaikh Bayazid and Biban, on hearing of their expedition, had fled to the *pargana* of Mahuba.[3]   Fol. 380.

As the Rains had set in and as after 5 or 6 months of active service, horses and cattle in the army were worn out, the sultans and begs of the expedition were ordered to remain where they were till they received fresh supplies from Agra and those parts. At the Other Prayer of the same day, leave was given to Baqi and the army of Aud (Ajodhya). Also an allowance of 30 *laks*[4] from Amroha was assigned to Musa (son) of Ma'ruf *Farmuli*, who had waited on me at the time the returning army was crossing the Saru-water,[5] a special head-to-foot and saddled horse were bestowed on him, and he was given his leave.

---

1 Hai. MS. *auta*, presumably for *aurta*; Kehr's p. 1133, Aud-daghi, which, as Baqi led the Aud army, is *ben trovato*; both Persian translations, *miangani*, central, inner, *i.e. aurta*, perhaps household troops of the Centre.
2 Anglicé, Saturday 12th after 6 p.m.
3 In Akbar's *sarkar* of Kalanjar, now in the Hamirpur district.
4 £7500 (Erskine). Amroha is in the Moradabad district.
5 At the Chaupara-Chaturmuk ferry (f. 376).—*Corrigendum*:—In the Index of the *Babur-nama Facsimile*, Musa *Farmuli* and Musa Sl. are erroneously entered as if one man.

(sss. Babur returns to Agra.)

(*June 21st*) With an easy mind about these parts, we set out for
Agra, raid-fashion,[1] when 3 *pas* 1 *gari* of Tuesday night were
past.[2] In the morning (*Tuesday 15th*) we did 16 *kurohs* (32 m.),
near mid-day made our nooning in the *pargana* of Baladar, one
of the dependencies of Kalpi, there gave our horses barley, at the
Evening Prayer rode on, did 13 *kurohs* (26 m.) in the night, at
the 3rd night-watch (*mid-night, Shawwal 15–16th*) dismounted
at Bahadur Khan *Sarwani's* tomb at Sugandpur, a *pargana* of
Kalpi, slept a little, went through the Morning Prayer and hurried
on. After doing 16 *kurohs* (32 m.), we reached Etawa at the fall
of day, where Mahdi Khwaja came out to meet us.[3] Riding
Fol. 380b. on after the 1st night-watch (9 p.m.), we slept a little on the way,
did 16 *kurohs* (32 m.), took our nooning at Fathpur of Rapri, rode
on soon after the Mid-day Prayer (*Thursday Shawwal 17th*),
did 17 *kurohs* (34 m.), and in the 2nd night-watch[4] dismounted
in the Garden-of-eight-paradises at Agra.

(*June 24th*) At the dawn of Friday (*18th*) Pay-master Sl.
Muhammad came with several more to wait on me. Towards the
Mid-day Prayer, having crossed Jun, I waited on Khwaja 'Abdu'l-
haqq, went into the Fort and saw the begims my paternal-aunts.

(ttt. Indian-grown fruits.)

A Balkhi melon-grower had been set to raise melons; he now
brought a few first-rate small ones; on one or two bush-vines
(*buta-tak*) I had had planted in the Garden-of-eight-paradises
very good grapes had grown; Shaikh Guran sent me a basket
of grapes which too were not bad. To have grapes and melons
grown in this way in Hindustan filled my measure of content.

(uuu. Arrival of Mahim Begim.)

(*June 26th*) Mahim arrived while yet two watches of Sunday
night (*Shawwal 20th*)[5] remained. By a singular agreement

---

1 *i.e.* riding light and fast. The distance done between Adampur and Agra was
some 157 miles, the time was from 12 a.m. on Tuesday morning to about 9 p.m. of
Thursday. This exploit serves to show that three years of continuous activity in the
plains of Hindustan had not destroyed Babur's capacity for sustained effort, spite of
several attacks of (malarial?) fever.

2 Anglicé, Tuesday 12.25 a.m.   3 He was governor of Etawa.

4 Islamicé, Friday, Shawwal 18th, Anglicé, Thursday, June 24th, soon after 9 p.m.

5 Anglicé, she arrived at mid-night of Saturday.—Gul-badan writes of Mahim's
arrival as unexpected and of Babur's hurrying off on foot to meet her (*Humayun-
nama* f. 14, trs. p. 100).

of things they had left Kabul on the very day, the 10th of the
1st Jumada (*Jan. 21st 1529*) on which I rode out to the army.[1]

(*Here the record of 11 days is wanting.*)

(*July 7th*) On Thursday the 1st of Zu'l-qaʻda the offerings
made by Humayun and Mahim were set out while I sat in the
large Hall of Audience.

Today also wages were given to 150 porters (*kahar*) and they
were started off under a servant of Faghfur *Diwan* to fetch
melons, grapes, and other fruits from Kabul.   Fol. 381.

(*vvv. Concerning Sambhal.*)

(*July 9th*) On Saturday the 3rd of the month, Hindu Beg who
had come as escort from Kabul and must have been sent to
Sambhal on account of the death of ʻAli-i-yusuf, came and
waited on me.[2] Khalifa's (son) Husamu'd-din came also today
from Alwar and waited on me.

(*July 10th*) On Sunday morning (*4th*) came ʻAbdu'l-lah
(*kitabdar*), who from Tir-muhani[3] had been sent to Sambhal on
account of the death of ʻAli-i-yusuf.

(*Here the record of 7 days is wanting.*)

(*www. Sedition in Lahor.*)

People from Kabul were saying that Shaikh Sharaf of Qara-
bagh, either incited by ʻAbdu'l-ʻaziz or out of liking for him,
had written an attestation which attributed to me oppression
I had not done, and outrage that had not happened; that he

1 Mahim's journey from Kabul to Agra had occupied over 5 months.
2 Hindu Beg *quchin* had been made Humayun's retainer in 932 AH. (f. 297), and had
taken possession of Sambhal for him. Hence, as it seems, he was ordered, while
escorting the ladies from Kabul, to go to Sambhal. He seems to have gone before
waiting on Babur, probably not coming into Agra till now.—It may be noted here
that in 933 AH. he transformed a Hindu temple into a Mosque in Sambhal; it was
done by Babur's orders and is commemorated by an inscription still existing on the
Mosque, one seeming not to be of his own composition, judging by its praise of
himself. (JASB. *Proceedings*, May 1873, p. 98, Blochmann's art. where the inscription
is given and translated; and *Archæological Survey Reports*, xii, p. 24–27, with Plates
showing the Mosque).
3 *Cf.* f. 375, f. 377, with notes concerning ʻAbdu'l-lah and Tir-muhani. I have not
found the name Tir-muhani on maps; its position can be inferred from Babur's statement (f. 375) that he had sent ʻAbdu'l-lah to Sambhal, he being then at Kunba or
Kunia in the Nurhun *pargana*.—The name Tir-muhani occurs also in Gorakhpur.—
It was at Tir-muhani (Three-mouths) that Khwand-amir completed the *Habibu's-
siyar* (lith. ed. i, 83; Rieu's *Pers. Cat.* p. 1079). If the name imply three water-
mouths, they might be those of Ganges, Ghogra and Daha.

had extorted the signatures of the Prayer-leaders (*imamlar*) of Lahor to this accusation, and had sent copies of it to the various towns; that 'Abdu'l-'aziz himself had failed to give ear to several royal orders, had spoken unseemly words, and done acts which ought to have been left undone. On account of these matters Qambar-i-'ali *Arghun* was started off on Sunday the 11th of the month (*Zu'l-qa'da*), to arrest Shaikh Sharaf, the Lahor *imams* with their associates, and 'Abdu'l-'aziz, and to bring them all to Court.

(*xxx. Varia.*)

(*July 22nd*) On Thursday the 15th of the month Chin-timur Sl. came in from Tijara and waited on me. Today Champion Sadiq and the great champion-wrestler of Aud wrestled. Sadiq gave a half-throw;[1] he was much vexed.

(*July 28th*) On Monday the 19th of the month (*Zu'l-qa'da*) the Qizil-bash envoy Murad the life-guardsman was made to put on an inlaid dagger with belt, and a befitting dress of honour, was presented with 2 *laks* of *tankas* and given leave to go.

(*Here the record of 15 days is wanting.*)

(*yyy. Sedition in Gualiar.*)

(*August 11th*) Sayyid Mashhadi who had come from Gualiar in these days, represented that Rahim-dad was stirring up sedition.[2] On account of this, Khalifa's servant Shah Muhammad the seal-bearer was sent to convey to Rahim-dad matters written with commingling of good counsel. He went; and in a few days came back bringing Rahim-dad's son, but, though the son came, Rahim-dad himself had no thought of coming. On Wednesday the 5th of *Zu'l-hijja*, Nur Beg was sent to Gualiar

---

1 *nim-kara*. E. and de C. however reverse the *rôles*.

2 The *Tarikh-i-gualiari* (B.M. Add. 16,709, p. 18) supplements the fragmentary accounts which, above and s.a. 936 AH., are all that the *Babur-nama* now preserves concerning Khwaja Rahim-dad's misconduct. It has several mistakes but the gist of its information is useful. It mentions that the Khwaja and his paternal-uncle Mahdi Khwaja had displeased Babur; that Rahim-dad resolved to take refuge with the ruler of Malwa (Mahmud *Khilji*) and to make over Gualiar to a Rajput landholder of that country; that upon this Shaikh Muhammad *Ghaus* went to Agra and interceded with Babur and obtained his forgiveness for Rahim-dad. Gualiar was given back to Rahim-dad but after a time he was superseded by Abu'l-fath [Shaikh Guran]. For particulars about Mahdi Khwaja and a singular story told about him by Nizamu'd-din Ahmad in the *Tabaqat-i-akbari*, *vide* Gul-badan's *Humayun-nama*, Appendix B, and *Translator's Note* p. 702, Section *f*.

to allay Rahim-dad's fears, came back in a few days, and laid requests from Rahim-dad before us. Orders in accordance with those requests had been written and were on the point of despatch when one of Rahim-dad's servants arriving, represented that he had come to effect the escape of the son and that Rahim-dad himself had no thought of coming in. I was for riding out at once to Gualiar, but Khalifa set it forth to me, "Let me write one more letter commingled with good counsel; he may even yet come peacefully." On this mission Khusrau's (son?) Shihabu'd-din was despatched.

(*August 12th*) On Thursday the 6th of the month mentioned (*Zu'l-hijja*) Mahdi Khwaja came in from Etawa.[1]

Fol. 382.

(*August 16th*) On the Festival-day[2] (*Monday 10th*) Hindu Beg was presented with a special head-to-foot, an inlaid dagger with belt; also a *pargana* worth 7 *laks*[3] and a head-to-foot (dress) was bestowed on Hasan-i-'ali, well-known among the Turkmans[4] for a Chaghatai.[5]

1 He may have come about the misconduct of his nephew Rahim-dad.
2 The 'Idu'l-kabir, the Great Festival of 10th Zu'l-hijja.
3 About £1750 (Erskine).
4 Perhaps he was from the tract in Persia still called Chaghatai Mountains. One Ibrahim *Chaghatai* is mentioned by Babur (f. 175*b*) with Turkman begs who joined Husain *Bai-qara*. This Hasan-i-'ali *Chaghatai* may have come in like manner, with Murad the Turkman envoy from 'Iraq (f. 369 and n. 1).
5 Several incidents recorded by Gul-badan (writing half a century later) as following Mahim's arrival in Agra, will belong to the record of 935 AH. because they preceded Humayun's arrival from Badakhshan. Their omission from Babur's diary is explicable by its minor *lacunæ*. Such are:—(1) a visit to Dhulpur and Sikri the interest of which lies in its showing that Bibi Mubarika had accompanied Mahim Begim to Agra from Kabul, and that there was in Sikri a quiet retreat, a *chaukandi*, where Babur "used to write his book";—(2) the arrival of the main caravan of ladies from Kabul, which led Babur to go four miles out, to Naugram, in order to give honouring reception to his sister Khan-zada Begim;—(3) an excursion to the Gold-scattering garden (*Bagh-i-zar-afshan*), where seated among his own people, Babur said he was "bowed down by ruling and reigning", longed to retire to that garden with a single attendant, and wished to make over his sovereignty to Humayun;—(4) the death of Dil-dar's son Alwar (var. Anwar) whose birth may be assigned to the gap preceding 932 AH. because not chronicled later by Babur, as is Faruq's. As a distraction from the sorrow for this loss, a journey was "pleasantly made by water" to Dhulpur.

(*a. Rahim-dad's affairs.*)

(*Sep. 7th*) On Wednesday the 3rd of Muharram, Shaikh Muhammad *Ghaus*[1] came in from Gualiar with Khusrau's (son) Shihabu'd-din to plead for Rahim-dad. As Shaikh Muhammad *Ghaus* was a pious and excellent person, Rahim-dad's faults were forgiven for his sake. Shaikh Guran and Nur Beg were sent off for Gualiar, so that the place having been made over to their charge …[2]

1 *Cf.* f. 381*b* n. 2. For his earlier help to Rahim-dad *see* f. 304*b*. For Biographies of him *see* Blochmann's A.-i-A. trs. p. 446, and Badayuni's *Muntakhabu-'t-tawarikh* (Ranking's and Lowe's trss.).

2 Beyond this broken passage, one presumably at the foot of a page in Babur's own manuscript, nothing of his diary is now known to survive. What is missing seems likely to have been written and lost. It is known from a remark of Gul-badan's (H.N. p. 103) that he "used to write his book" after Mahim's arrival in Agra, the place coming into her anecdote being Sikri.

It is difficult to find material for filling the *lacuna* of some
15 months, which occurs in Babur's diary after the broken
passage of Muharram 3rd 936 AH. (Sept. 7th 1529 AD.) and down
to the date of his death on Jumada I. 6th 937 AH. (Dec. 26th
1530 AD.). The known original sources are few, their historical
matter scant, their contents mainly biographical. Gleanings
may yet be made, however, in unexpected places, such gleanings
as are provided by Ahmad-i-yadgar's interpolation of Timurid
history amongst his lives of Afghan Sultans.

The earliest original source which helps to fill the gap of
936 AH. is Haidar Mirza's *Tarikh-i-rashidi*, finished as to its
Second Part which contains Babur's biography, in 948 AH.
(1541 AD.), 12 years therefore after the year of the gap 936 AH.
It gives valuable information about the affairs of Badakhshan,
based on its author's personal experience at 30 years of age, and
was Abu'l-fazl's authority for the *Akbar-nama*.

The next in date of the original sources is Gul-badan Begim's
Humayun-nama, a chronicle of family affairs, which she wrote in
obedience to her nephew Akbar's command, given in about
995 AH. (1587 AD.), some 57 years after her Father's death, that
whatever any person knew of his father (Humayun) and grandfather (Babur) should be written down for Abu'l-fazl's use. It
embodies family memories and traditions, and presumably gives
the recollections of several ladies of the royal circle.[1]

1 Jauhar's *Humayun-nama* and Bayazid *Biyat's* work of the same title were written
under the same royal command as the Begim's. They contribute nothing towards
filling the gap of 936 AH.; their authors, being Humayun's servants, write about him.
It may be observed that criticism of these books, as recording trivialities, is disarmed
if they were commanded because they would obey an order to set down whatever
was known, selection amongst their contents resting with Abu'l-fazl. Even more
completely must they be excluded from a verdict on the literary standard of their
day.—Abu'l-fazl must have had a source of Baburiana which has not found its way
into European libraries. A man likely to have contributed his recollections, directly
or transmitted, is Khwaja Muqim *Harawi*. The date of Muqim's death is conjectural
only, but he lived long enough to impress the worth of historical writing on his
son Nizamu'-d-din Ahmad. (*Cf.* E. and D.'s H. of I. art. *Tabaqat-i-akbari* v, 177 and
187; T.-i-A. lith. ed. p. 193; and for Bayazid *Biyat's* work, JASB. 1898, p. 296.)

The *Akbar-nama* derives much of its narrative for 936–937 AH. from Haidar Mirza and Gul-badan Begim, but its accounts of Babur's self-surrender and of his dying address to his chiefs presuppose the help of information from a contemporary witness. It is noticeable that the *Akbar-nama* records no public events as occurring in Hindustan during 936–937 AH., nothing of the sequel of rebellion by Rahim-dad[1] and 'Abdu'l-'aziz, nothing of the untiring Biban and Bayazid. That something could have been told is shown by what Ahmad-i-yadgar has preserved (*vide post*); but 50 years had passed since Babur's death and, manifestly, interest in filling the *lacunæ* in his diary was then less keen than it is over 300 years later. What in the *Akbar-nama* concerns Babur is likely to have been written somewhat early in the *cir.* 15 years of its author's labours on it,[2] but, even so, the elder women of the royal circle had had rest after the miseries Humayun had wrought, the forgiveness of family affection would veil his past, and certainly has provided Abu'l-fazl with an over-mellowed estimate of him, one ill-assorting with what is justified by his Babur-nama record.

The contribution made towards filling the gap of 936–937 AH. in the body of Nizamu-'d-din Ahmad's *Tabaqat-i-akbari* is limited to a curious and doubtfully acceptable anecdote about a plan for the supersession of Humayun as Padshah, and about the part played by Khwaja Muqim *Harawi* in its abandonment. A further contribution is made, however, in Book VII which contains the history of the Muhammadan Kings of Kashmir, namely, that Babur despatched an expedition into that country. As no such expedition is recorded or referred to in surviving Babur-nama writings, it is likely to have been sent in 936 AH. during Babur's tour to and from Lahor. If it were made with the aim of extending Timurid authority in the Himalayan borderlands, a hint of similar policy elsewhere may be given by the ceremonious visit of the Raja of Kahlur to Babur,

---

1 Ibn Batuta (Lee's trs. p. 133) mentions that after his appointment to Gualiar, Rahim-dad fell from favour … but was restored later, on the representation of Muhammad Ghaus; held Gualiar again for a short time, (he went to Bahadur Shah in Gujrat) and was succeeded by Abu'l-fath (*i.e.* Shaikh Guran) who held it till Babur's death.

2 Its translation and explanatory noting have filled two decades of hard-working years. *Tanti labores auctoris et traductoris!*

mentioned by Ahmad-i-yadgar (*vide post*).[1] The T.-i-A. was written within the term of Abu'l-fazl's work on the *Akbar-nama*, being begun later, and ended about 9 years earlier, in 1002 AH.—1593 AD. It appears to have been Abu'-l-fazl's authority for his account of the campaign carried on in Kashmir by Babur's chiefs (*Ayin-i-akbari* vol. ii, part i, Jarrett's trs. p. 389).

An important contribution, seeming to be authentic, is found interpolated in Ahmad-i-yadgar's *Tarikh-i-salatin-i-afaghana*, one which outlines a journey made by Babur to Lahor in 936 AH. and gives circumstantial details of a punitive expedition sent by him from Sihrind at the complaint of the Qazi of Samana against a certain Mundahir Rajput. The whole contribution dovetails into matters found elsewhere. Its precision of detail bespeaks a closely-contemporary written source.[2] As its fullest passage concerns the Samana Qazi's affair, its basis of record may have been found in Samana. Some considerations about the date of Ahmad-i-yadgar's own book and what Niamatu'l-lah says of Haibat Khan of Samana, his own generous helper in the *Tarikh-i-Khan-i-jahan Ludi*, point towards Haibat Khan as providing the details of the Qazi's wrongs and avenging. The indication is strengthened by the circumstance that what precedes and what follows the account of the punitive expedition is outlined only.[3] Ahmad-i-yadgar interpolates an account of Humayun also, which is a frank plagiarism from the *Tabaqat-i-akbari*. He tells too a story purporting to explain why Babur "selected" Humayun to succeed him, one parallel with Nizamu'd-din Ahmad's about what led Khalifa to abandon his plan of setting the Mirza aside. Its sole value lies in its testimony to a belief, held by its first narrator whoever he was, that choice was exercised in the matter by Babur. Reasons for thinking Nizamu'd-din's story, as it stands, highly improbable, will be found later in this note.

1 I am indebted to my husband for acquaintance with Nizamu'-d-din Ahmad's record about Babur and Kashmir.
2 In view of the vicissitudes to which under Humayun the royal library was subjected, it would be difficult to assert that this source was not the missing continuation of Babur's diary.
3 E. and D.'s H. of I. art. *Tarikh-i Khan-i-jahan Ludi* v, 67. For Ahmad-i-yadgar's book and its special features *vide l.c.* v, 2, 24, with notes; Rieu's *Persian Catalogue* iii, 922a; JASB. 1916, H. Beveridge's art. *Note on the Tarikh-i-salatin-i-afaghana*.

Muhammad Qasim Hindu Shah *Firishta*'s *Tarikh-i-firishta* contains an interesting account of Babur but contributes towards filling the gap in the events of 936–937 AH. little that is not in the earlier sources. In M. Jules Mohl's opinion it was under revision as late as 1623 AD. (1032–3 AH.).

a. *Humayun and Badakhshan.*

An occurrence which had important results, was the arrival of Humayun in Agra, unsummoned by his Father, from the outpost station of Badakhshan. It will have occurred early in 936 AH. (autumn 1529 AD.), because he was in Kabul in the first ten days of the last month of 935 AH. (*vide post*). Curiously enough his half-sister Gul-badan does not mention his coming, whether through avoidance of the topic or from inadvertence; the omission may be due however to the loss of a folio from the only known MS. of her book (that now owned by the British Museum), and this is the more likely that Abu'l-fazl writes, at some length, about the arrival and its motive, what the Begim might have provided, this especially by his attribution of filial affection as Humayun's reason for coming to Agra.

Haidar Mirza is the authority for the Akbar-nama account of Humayun's departure from Qila'-i-zafar and its political and military sequel. He explains the departure by saying that when Babur had subdued Hindustan, his sons Humayun and Kamran were grown-up; and that wishing to have one of them at hand in case of his own death, he summoned Humayun, leaving Kamran in Qandahar. No doubt these were the contemporary impressions conveyed to Haidar, and strengthened by the accomplished fact before he wrote some 12 years later; nevertheless there are two clear indications that there was no royal order for Humayun to leave Qila'-i-zafar, *viz.* that no-one had been appointed to relieve him even when he reached Agra, and that Abu'l-fazl mentions no summons but attributes the Mirza's departure from his post to an overwhelming desire to see his Father. What appears probable is that Mahim wrote to her son urging his coming to Agra, and that this was represented as Babur's wish. However little weight may be due to the rumour, preserved in anecdotes recorded long after 935 AH., that any-one, Babur or Khalifa, inclined against Humayun's succession, that rumour she would set herself to falsify by reconciliation.[1]

When the Mirza's intention to leave Qila'-i-zafar became known there, the chiefs represented that they should not be able to withstand the Auzbeg on their frontier without him (his troops implied).[2] With this he agreed, said that still he must go, and that he would send a Mirza in his place as soon as possible. He then rode, in one day, to Kabul, an item of rapid travel preserved by Abu'l-fazl.

Humayun's departure caused such anxiety in Qila'-i-zafar that some (if not all) of the Badakhshi chiefs hurried off an invitation to Sa'id Khan *Chaghatai*, the then ruler in Kashghar in whose service Haidar Mirza was, to come at once and occupy the fort. They said that Faqir-i-'ali who had been left in charge, was not strong enough to cope with the Auzbeg, begged Sa'id to come, and strengthened their petition by reminding him of his hereditary right to Badakhshan, derived from Shah Begim *Badakhshi*. Their urgency convincing the Khan that risk threatened the country, he started from Kashghar in Muharram 936 AH. (Sept.–Oct. 1529 AD.). On reaching Sarigh-chupan which by the annexation of Aba-bakr Mirza *Dughlat* was now his own most western territory[3] but which formerly was one of the upper districts of Badakhshan, he waited while Haidar went on towards Qila'-i-zafar only to learn on his road, that Hind-al (*æt.* 10) had been sent from Kabul by Humayun and had entered the fort 12 days before.

The Kashgharis were thus placed in the difficulty that the fort was occupied by Babur's representative, and that the snows would prevent their return home across the mountains till winter was past. Winter-quarters were needed and asked for by Haidar, certain districts being specified in which to await the re-opening of the Pamir routes. He failed in his request, "They did not trust us," he writes, "indeed suspected us of deceit." His own account of Sa'id's earlier invasion of Badakhshan (925 AH.— 1519 AD.) during Khan Mirza's rule, serves to explain Badakhshi

1 Humayun's last recorded act in Hindustan was that of 933 AH. (f. 329b) when he took unauthorized possession of treasure in Dihli.

2 *Tarikh-i-rashidi* trs. p. 387.

3 T.-i-R. trs. p. 353 *et seq.* and Mr. Ney Elias' notes.

distrust of Kashgharis. Failing in his negotiations, he scoured and pillaged the country round the fort, and when a few days later the Khan arrived, his men took what Haidar's had left.

Sa'id Khan is recorded to have besieged the fort for three months, but nothing serious seems to have been attempted since no mention of fighting is made, none of assault or sally, and towards the end of the winter he was waited on by those who had invited his presence, with apology for not having admitted him into the fort, which they said they would have done but for the arrival of Hind-al Mirza. To this the Khan replied that for him to oppose Babur Padshah was impossible; he reminded the chiefs that he was there by request, that it would be as hurtful for the Padshah as for himself to have the Auzbeg in Badakhshan and, finally, he gave it as his opinion that, as matters stood, every man should go home. His view of the general duty may include that of Badakhshi auxiliaries such as Sultan Wais of Kul-ab who had reinforced the garrison. So saying, he himself set out for Kashghar, and at the beginning of Spring reached Yarkand.

b. Humayun's further action.

Humayun will have reached Kabul before Zu'l-hijja 10th 935 AH. (Aug. 26th 1529 AD.) because it is on record that he met Kamran on the Kabul 'Id-gah, and both will have been there to keep the 'Idu'l-kabir, the Great Festival of Gifts, which is held on that day. Kamran had come from Qandahar, whether to keep the Feast, or because he had heard of Humayun's intended movement from Badakhshan, or because changes were foreseen and he coveted Kabul, as the *Babur-nama* and later records allow to be inferred. He asked Humayun, says Abu'l-fazl, why he was there and was told of his brother's impending journey to Agra under overwhelming desire to see their Father.[1] Presumably the two Mirzas discussed the position in which Badakhshan had been left; in the end Hind-al was sent to Qila'-i-zafar, notwithstanding that he was under orders for Hindustan.

Humayun may have stayed some weeks in Kabul, how many those familiar with the seasons and the routes between Yarkand

---

[1] Abu'l-fazl's record of Humayun's sayings and minor doings at this early date in his career, can hardly be anything more accurate than family-tradition.

and Qila'-i-zafar, might be able to surmise if the date of Hind-al's start northward for which Humayun is likely to have waited, were found by dovetailing the Muharram of Sa'id's start, the approximate length of his journey to Sarigh-chupan, and Haidar's reception of news that Hind-al had been 12 days in the fort.

Humayun's arrival in Agra is said by Abu'l-fazl to have been cheering to the royal family in their sadness for the death of Alwar (end of 935 AH.) and to have given pleasure to his Father. But the time is all too near the date of Babur's letter (f. 348) to Humayun, that of a dissatisfied parent, to allow the supposition that his desertion of his post would fail to displease.

That it was a desertion and not an act of obedience seems clear from the circumstance that the post had yet to be filled. Khalifa is said to have been asked to take it and to have refused;[1] Humayun to have been sounded as to return and to have expressed unwillingness. Babur then did what was an honourable sequel to his acceptance in 926 AH. of the charge of the fatherless child Sulaiman, by sending him, now about 16, to take charge where his father Khan Mirza had ruled, and by still keeping him under his own protection.

Sulaiman's start from Agra will not have been delayed, and (accepting Ahmad-i-yadgar's record,) Babur himself will have gone as far as Lahor either with him or shortly after him, an expedition supporting Sulaiman, and menacing Sa'id in his winter leaguer round Qila'-i-zafar. Meantime Humayun was ordered to his fief of Sambhal.

After Sulaiman's appointment Babur wrote to Sa'id a letter of which Haidar gives the gist:—It expresses surprise at Sa'id's doings in Badakhshan, says that Hind-al has been recalled and Sulaiman sent, that if Sa'id regard hereditary right, he will

1 The statement that Khalifa was asked to go so far from where he was of the first importance as an administrator, leads to consideration of why it was done. So little is known explicitly of Babur's intentions about his territories after his death that it is possible only to put that little together and read between its lines. It may be that he was now planning an immediate retirement to Kabul and an apportionment during life of his dominions, such as Abu-sa'id had made of his own. If so, it would be desirable to have Badakhshan held in strength such as Khalifa's family could command, and especially desirable because as Barlas Turks, that family would be one with Babur in desire to regain Transoxiana. Such a political motive would worthily explain the offer of the appointment.

leave "Sulaiman Shah Mirza"[1] in possession, who is as a son to them both,[2] that this would be well, that otherwise he (Babur) will make over responsibility to the heir (Sulaiman);[3] and, "The rest you know."[4]

c. Babur visits Lahor.

If Ahmad-i-yadgar's account of a journey made by Babur to Lahor and the Panj-ab be accepted, the *lacuna* of 936 AH. is appropriately filled. He places the expedition in the 3rd year of Babur's rule in Hindustan, which, counting from the first reading of the *khutba* for Babur in Dihli (f. 268), began on Rajab 15th 935 AH. (March 26th 1529 AD.). But as Babur's diary-record for 935 AH. is complete down to end of the year, (minor *lacunæ* excepted), the time of his leaving Agra for Lahor is relegated to 936 AH. He must have left early in the year, (1) to allow time, before the occurrence of the known events preceding his own death, for the long expedition Ahmad-i-yadgar calls one of a year, and (2) because an early start after Humayun's arrival and Sulaiman's departure would suit the position of affairs and the dates mentioned or implied by Haidar's and by Ahmad-i-yadgar's narratives.

Two reasons of policy are discernible, in the known events of the time, to recommend a journey in force towards the North-west; first, the sedition of 'Abdu'l-'aziz in Lahor (f. 381), and secondly, the invasion of Badakhshan by Sa'id Khan with its resulting need of supporting Sulaiman by a menace of armed intervention.[5]

1 The "Shah" of this style is derived from Sulaiman's Badakhshi descent through Shah Begim; the "Mirza" from his Miran-shahi descent through his father Wais Khan Mirza. The title Khan Mirza or Mirza Khan, presumably according to the outlook of the speaker, was similarly derived from forebears, as would be also Shah Begim's; (her personal name is not mentioned in the sources).

2 Sa'id, on the father's, and Babur, on the mother's side, were of the same generation in descent from Yunas Khan; Sulaiman was of a younger one, hence his pseudo-filial relation to the men of the elder one.

3 Sa'id was Shah Begim's grandson through her son Ahmad, Sulaiman her great-grandson through her daughter Sultan-Nigar, but Sulaiman could claim also as the heir of his father who was nominated to rule by Shah Begim; moreover, he could claim by right of conquest on the father's side, through Abu-sa'id the conqueror, his son Mahmud long the ruler, and so through Mahmud's son Wais Khan Mirza.

4 The menace conveyed by these words would be made the more forceful by Babur's move to Lahor, narrated by Ahmad-i-yadgar. Some ill-result to Sa'id of independent rule by Sulaiman seems foreshadowed; was it that if Babur's restraining hand were withdrawn, the Badakhshis would try to regain their lost districts and would have help in so-doing from Babur?

5 It is open to conjecture that if affairs in Hindustan had allowed it, Babur would now have returned to Kabul. Ahmad-i-yadgar makes the expedition to be one for

In Sihrind the Raja of Kahlur, a place which may be one of the Simla hill-states, waited on Babur, made offering of 7 falcons and 3 *mans*[1] of gold, and was confirmed in his fief.[2]

In Lahor Kamran is said to have received his Father, in a garden of his own creation, and to have introduced the local chiefs as though he were the Governor of Lahor some writers describe him as then being. The best sources, however, leave him still posted in Qandahar. He had been appointed to Multan (f. 359) when 'Askari was summoned to Agra (f. 339), but whether he actually went there is not assured; some months later (Zu'l-hijja 10th 935 AH.) he is described by Abu'l-fazl as coming to Kabul from Qandahar. He took both Multan[3] and Lahor by force from his (half-)brother Humayun in 938 AH. (1531 AD.) the year after their Father's death. That he should wait upon his Father in Lahor would be natural, Hind-al did so, coming from Kabul. Hind-al will have come to Lahor after making over charge of Qila'-i-zafar to Sulaiman, and he went back at the end of the cold season, going perhaps just before his Father started from Lahor on his return journey, the gifts he received before leaving being 2 elephants, 4 horses, belts and jewelled daggers.[4]

Babur is said to have left Lahor on Rajab 4th (936 AH.)—March 4th, 1530 AD.). From Ahmad-i-yadgar's outline of Babur's doings in Lahor, he, or his original, must be taken as ill-informed

---

pleasure only, and describes Babur as hunting and sight-seeing for a year in Lahor, the Panj-ab and near Dihli. This appears a mere flourish of words, in view of the purposes the expedition served, and of the difficulties which had arisen in Lahor itself and with Sa'id Khan. Part of the work effected may have been the despatch of an expedition to Kashmir.

1 This appears a large amount.

2 The precision with which the Raja's gifts are stated, points to a closely-contemporary and written source. A second such indication occurs later where gifts made to Hind-al are mentioned.

3 An account of the events in Multan after its occupation by Shah Hasan *Arghun* is found in the latter part of the *Tabaqat-i-akbari* and in Erskine's H. of I. i, 393 *et seq. See* Additional Notes, p. 800. It may be noted here that several instances of confusion amongst Babur's sons occur in the extracts made by Sir H. Elliot and Professor Dowson in their *History of India* from the less authoritative sources [*e.g.* v, 35 Kamran for Humayun, 'Askari said to be in Kabul (pp. 36 and 37); Hind-al for Humayun *etc.*] and that these errors have slipped into several of the District Gazetteers of the United Provinces.

4 As was said of the offering made by the Raja of Kahlur, the precision of statement as to what was given to Hind-al, bespeaks a closely-contemporary written source. So too does the mention (text, *infra*) of the day on which Babur began his return journey from Lahor.

or indifferent about them. His interest becomes greater when he writes of Samana.

d. Punishment of the Mundahirs.

When Babur, on his return journey, reached Sihrind, he received a complaint from the Qazi of Samana against one Mohan *Mundahir* (or *Mundhar*)[1] *Rajput* who had attacked his estates, burning and plundering, and killed his son. Here-upon 'Ali-quli of Hamadan[2] was sent with 3000 horse to avenge the Qazi's wrongs, and reached Mohan's village, in the Kaithal *pargana*, early in the morning when the cold was such that the archers "could not pull their bows."[3] A marriage had been celebrated over-night; the villagers, issuing from warm houses, shot such flights of arrows that the royal troops could make no stand; many were killed and nothing was effected; they retired into the jungle, lit fires, warmed themselves (?), renewed the attack and were again repulsed. On hearing of their failure, Babur sent off, perhaps again from Sihrind, Tarsam Bahadur and Naurang Beg with 6000 horse and many elephants. This force reached the village at night and when marriage festivities were in progress. Towards morning it was formed into three divisions,[4] one of which was ordered to go to the west of the village and show itself. This having been done, the villagers advanced towards it, in the pride of their recent success. The royal troops, as ordered beforehand, turned their backs and fled, the Mundahirs pursuing them some two miles. Meantime Tarsam Bahadur had attacked and fired the village, killing many of its inhabitants. The pursuers on the west saw the flames of their burning homes, ran back and were intercepted on their way. About 1000 men, women and children were made prisoner; there

---

1 *Cf.* G. of I. xvi, 55; Ibbetson's *Report on Karnal*.
2 It is noticeable that no one of the three royal officers named as sent against Mohan *Mundahir*, is recognizable as mentioned in the *Babur-nama*. They may all have had local commands, and not have served further east. Perhaps this, their first appearance, points to the origin of the information as independent of Babur, but he might have been found to name them, if his diary were complete for 936 AH.
3 The E. and D. translation writes twice as though the inability to "pull" the bows were due to feebleness in the men, but an appropriate reading would refer the difficulty to the hardening of sinews in the composite Turkish bows, which prevented the archers from bending the bows for stringing.
4 One infers that fires were burned all night in the bivouac.

was also great slaughter, and a pillar of heads was raised. Mohan was captured and later on was buried to the waist and shot to death with arrows.[1] News of the affair was sent to the Padshah.[2]

As after being in Sihrind, Babur is said to have spent two months hunting near Dihli, it may be that he followed up the punitive expedition sent into the Kaithal *pargana* of the Karnal District, by hunting in Nardak, a favourite ground of the Timurids, which lies in that district.

Thus the gap of 936 AH. with also perhaps a month of 937 AH. is filled by the "year's" travel west of Dihli. The record is a mere outline and in it are periods of months without mention of where Babur was or what affairs of government were brought before him. At some time, on his return journey presumably, he will have despatched to Kashmir the expedition referred to in the opening section of this appendix. Something further may yet be gleaned from local chronicles, from unwritten tradition, or from the witness of place-names commemorating his visit.

e. Babur's self-surrender to save Humayun.

The few months, perhaps 4 to 5, between Babur's return to Agra from his expedition towards the North-west, and the time of his death are filled by Gul-badan and Abu'l-fazl with matters concerning family interests only.

The first such matter these authors mention is an illness of Humayun during which Babur devoted his own life to save his son's.[3] Of this the particulars are, briefly:—That Humayun, while still in Sambhal, had had a violent attack of fever; that he was brought by water to Agra, his mother meeting him in

---

1 At this point the A.S.B. copy (No. 137) of the *Tarikh-i-salatin-i-afaghana* has a remark which may have been a marginal note originally, and which cannot be supposed made by Ahmad-i-yadgar himself because this would allot him too long a spell of life. It may show however that the interpolations about the two Timurids were not inserted in his book by him. Its purport is that the Mundahir village destroyed by Babur's troops in 936 AH.—1530 AD. was still in ruins at the time it was written 160 (lunar) years later (*i.e.* in 1096 AH.—1684–85 AD.). The better Codex (No. 3887) of the Imperial Library of Calcutta has the same passage.—Both that remark and its context show acquaintance with Samana and Kaithal.—The writings now grouped under the title *Tarikh-i-salatin-i-afaghana* present difficulties both as to date and contents (*cf.* Rieu's *Persian Catalogue s.n.*).

2 Presumably in Tihrind.

3 *Cf.* G. B.'s H. N. trs. and the *Akbar-nama* Bib. Ind. ed. and trs., Index *s.nn.*; Hughes' *Dictionary of Islam s.n.* Intercession.

Muttra; and that when the disease baffled medical skill, Babur resolved to practise the rite believed then and now in the East to be valid, of intercession and devotion of a suppliant's most valued possession in exchange for a sick man's life. Rejecting counsel to offer the Koh-i-nur for pious uses, he resolved to supplicate for the acceptance of his life. He made intercession through a saint his daughter names, and moved thrice round Humayun's bed, praying, in effect, "O God! if a life may be exchanged for a life, I, who am Babur, give my life and my being for Humayun." During the rite fever surged over him, and, convinced that his prayer and offering had prevailed, he cried out, "I have borne it away! I have borne it away!"[1] Gul-badan says that he himself fell ill on that very day, while Humayun poured water on his head, came out and gave audience; and that they carried her Father within on account of his illness, where he kept his bed for 2 or 3 months.

There can be no doubt as to Babur's faith in the rite he had practised, or as to his belief that his offering of life was accepted; moreover actual facts would sustain his faith and belief. On-lookers also must have believed his prayer and offering to have prevailed, since Humayun went back to Sambhal,[2] while Babur fell ill at once and died in a few weeks.[3]

f. A plan to set Babur's sons aside from the succession.

Reading the *Akbar-nama* alone, there would seem to be no question about whether Babur ever intended to give Hindustan, at any rate, to Humayun, but, by piecing together various con-tributory matters, an opposite opinion is reached, *viz.* that not Khalifa only whom Abu'l-fazl names perhaps on Nizamu'd-din Ahmad's warrant, but Babur also, with some considerable number of chiefs, wished another ruler for Hindustan. The starting-point of this opinion is a story in the *Tabaqat-i-akbari* and,

---

1 A closer translation would be, "I have taken up the burden." The verb is *bardashtan* (*cf.* f. 349, p. 626 n. 1).

2 *See* Erskine's *History of India* ii, 9.

3 At this point attention is asked to the value of the Ahmad-i-yadgar interpolation which allows Babur a year of active life before Humayun's illness and his own which followed. With no chronicle known of 936 AH. Babur had been supposed ill all through the year, a supposition which destroys the worth of his self-sacrifice. Moreover several inferences have been drawn from the supposed year of illness which are disproved by the activities recorded in that interpolation.

with less detail, in the *Akbar-nama*, of which the gist is that Khalifa planned to supersede Humayun and his three brothers in their Father's succession.[1]

The story, in brief, is as follows:—At the time of Babur's death Nizamu'd-din Ahmad's father Khwaja Muhammad Muqim *Harawi* was in the service of the Office of Works.[2] Amir Nizamu'd-din 'Ali Khalifa, the Chief of the Administration, had dread and suspicion about Humayun and did not favour his succession as Padshah. Nor did he favour that of Babur's other sons. He promised "Babur Padshah's son-in-law (*damad*)" Mahdi Khwaja who was a generous young man, very friendly to himself, that he would make him Padshah. This promise becoming known, others made their *salam* to the Khwaja who put on airs and accepted the position. One day when Khalifa, accompanied by Muqim, went to see Mahdi Khwaja in his tent, no-one else being present, Babur, in the pangs of his disease, sent for him[3] when he had been seated a few minutes only. When Khalifa had gone out, Mahdi Khwaja remained standing in such a way that Muqim could not follow but, the Khwaja unaware, waited respectfully behind him. The Khwaja, who was noted for the wildness of youth, said, stroking his beard, "Please God! first, I will flay thee!" turned round and saw Muqim, took him by the ear, repeated a proverb of menace, "The red tongue gives the green head to the wind," and let him go. Muqim hurried to Khalifa, repeated the Khwaja's threat against him, and remonstrated about the plan to set all Babur's sons aside in favour of a stranger-house.[4] Here-upon Khalifa sent for Humayun,[5] and despatched an officer with orders to the Khwaja to retire to his house, who found him about to dine and hurried him off without ceremony. Khalifa also issued a proclamation for-bidding intercourse with him, excluded him from Court, and when Babur died, supported Humayun.

1 E. and D.'s *History of India* v, 187; G. B.'s *Humayun-nama* trs. p. 28.
2 *dar khidmat-i-diwani-i-buyutat*; perhaps he was a Barrack-officer. His appoint-ment explains his attendance on Khalifa.
3 Khalifa prescribed for the sick Babur.
4 *khanwada-i-biganah*, perhaps, foreign dynasty.
5 From Sambhal; Gul-badan, by an anachronism made some 60 years later, writes Kalanjar, to which place Humayun moved 5 months after his accession.

As Nizamu'd-din Ahmad was not born till 20 years after Babur died, the story will have been old before he could appreciate it, and it was some 60 years old when it found way into the *Tabaqat-i-akbari* and, with less detail, into the *Akbar-nama*.

Taken as it stands, it is incredible, because it represents Khalifa, and him alone, planning to subject the four sons of Babur to the suzerainty of Mahdi Khwaja who was not a Timurid, who, so far as well-known sources show, was not of a ruling dynasty or personally illustrious,[1] and who had been associated, so lately as the autumn of 1529 AD., with his nephew Rahim-dad in seditious action which had so angered Babur that, whatever the punishment actually ordered, rumour had it both men were to die.[2] In two particulars the only Mahdi Khwaja then of Babur's following, does not suit the story; he was not a young man in 1530 AD.,[3] and was not a *damad* of Babur, if that word be taken in its usual sense of son-in-law, but he was a *yazna*, husband of a Padshah's sister, in his case, of Khan-zada Begim.[4] Some writers style him Sayyid Mahdi Khwaja, a double title which may indicate descent on both sides from religious houses; one is suggested to be that of Tirmiz by the circumstance that in his and Khan-zada Begim's mausoleum was buried a Tirmiz sayyid

1 I am indebted to my husband's perusal of Sayyid Ahmad Khan's *Asar-i-sanadid* (Dihli ed. 1854 p. 37, and Lakhnau ed. 1895 pp. 40, 41) for information that, perhaps in 935 AH., Mahdi Khwaja set up a tall slab of white marble near Amir Khusrau's tomb in Dihli, which bears an inscription in praise of the poet, composed by that Shihabu'd-din the Enigmatist who reached Agra with Khwand-amir in Muharram 935 AH. (f. 339). The inscription gives two chronograms of Khusrau's death (725 AH.), mentions that Mahdi Khwaja was the creator of the memorial, and gives its date in the words, "The beautiful effort of Mahdi Khwaja."—The Dihli ed. of the *Asar-i-sanadid* depicts the slab with its inscription; the Lakhnau ed. depicts the tomb, may show the slab *in situ*, and contains interesting matter by Sayyid Ahmad Khan. The slab is mentioned without particulars in Murray's *Hand-book to Bengal*, p. 329.
2 Lee's *Ibn Batuta* p. 133 and Hiraman's *Tarikh-i-gualiari*. Cf. G. B.'s *Humayun-nama* trs. (1902 AD.), Appendix B.—*Mahdi Khwaja*.
3 In an anonymous *Life of Shah Isma'il Safawi*, Mahdi Khwaja [who may be a son of the Musa Khwaja mentioned by Babur on f. 216] is described as being, in what will be 916–7 AH., Babur's *Diwan-begi* and as sent towards Bukhara with 10,000 men. This was 20 years before the story calls him a young man. Even if the word *jawan* (young man) be read, as T. *yigit* is frequently to be read, in the sense of "efficient fighting man", Mahdi was over-age. Other details of the story, besides the word *jawan*, bespeak a younger man.
4 G. B.'s H. N. trs. p. 126; *Habibu's-siyar*, B.M. Add. 16,679 f. 370, l. 16, lith. ed. Sec. III. iii, 372 (where a clerical error makes Babur give Mahdi *two* of his full-sisters in marriage).—Another *yazna* of Babur was Khalifa's brother Junaid *Barlas*, the husband of Shahr-banu, a half-sister of Babur.

of later date, Shah Abu'l-ma'ali. But though he were of Tirmiz, it is doubtful if that religious house would be described by the word *khanwada* which so frequently denotes a ruling dynasty.

His name may have found its way into Nizamu'd-din Ahmad's story as a gloss mistakenly amplifying the word *damad*, taken in its less usual sense of brother-in-law. To Babur's contemporaries the expression "Babur Padshah's *damad*" (son-in-law) would be explicit, because for some 11 years before he lay on his death-bed, he had one son-in-law only, *viz.* Muhammad-i-zaman Mirza *Bai-qara*,[1] the husband of Ma'suma Sultan Begim. If that Mirza's name were where Mahdi Khwaja's is entered, the story of an exclusion of Babur's sons from rule might have a core of truth.

It is incredible however that Khalifa, with or without Babur's concurrence, made the plan attributed to him of placing any man not a Timurid in the position of Padshah over all Babur's territory. I suggest that the plan concerned Hindustan only and was one considered in connection with Babur's intended return to Kabul, when he must have left that difficult country, hardly yet a possession, in charge of some man giving promise of power to hold it. Such a man Humayun was not. My suggestion rests on the following considerations:—

(1) Babur's outlook was not that of those in Agra in 1587 AD. who gave Abu'l-fazl his Baburiana material, because at that date Dihli had become the pivot of Timurid power, so that not to hold Hindustan would imply not to be Padshah. Babur's outlook on his smaller Hindustan was different; his position in it was precarious, Kabul, not Dihli, was his chosen centre, and from Kabul his eyes looked northwards as well as to the East. If he had lost the Hindustan which was approximately the modern United Provinces, he might still have held what lay west of it to the Indus, as well as Qandahar.

(2) For several years before his death he had wished to return to Kabul. Ample evidence of this wish is given by his diary, his letters, and some poems in his second *Diwan* (that found in the Rampur MS.). As he told his sons more than once, he kept Kabul

1 Babur, shortly before his death, married Gul-rang to Aisan-timur and Gul-chihra to Tukhta-bugha *Chaghatai*. *Cf. post*, Section *h*, *Babur's wives and children*; and G. B.'s H. N. trs. Biographical Appendix *s.nn.* Dil-dar Begim and Salima Sultan Begim *Miran-shahi*.

for himself.[1] If, instead of dying in Agra, he had returned to Kabul, had pushed his way on from Badakhshan, whether as far as Samarkand or less, had given Humayun a seat in those parts,— action foreshadowed by the records—a reasonable interpretation of the story that Humayun and his brothers were not to govern Hindustan, is that he had considered with Khalifa the apportionment of his territories according to the example of his ancestors Chingiz Khan, Timur and Abu-sa'id; that by his plan of apportionment Humayun was not to have Hindustan but something Tramontane; Kamran had already Qandahar; Sulaiman, if Humayun had moved beyond the out-post of Badakhshan, would have replaced him there; and Hindustan would have gone to "Babur Padshah's *damad*".

(3) Muhammad-i-zaman had much to recommend him for Hindustan:—Timurid-born, grandson and heir of Sl. Husain Mirza, husband of Ma'suma who was a Timurid by double descent,[2] protected by Babur after the Bai-qara *débâcle* in Herat, a landless man leading such other exiles as Muhammad Sultan Mirza,[3] 'Adil Sultan, and Qasim-i-husain Sultan, half-Timurids all, who with their Khurasani following, had been Babur's guests in Kabul, had pressed on its poor resources, and thus had helped in 932 AH. (1525 AD.) to drive him across the Indus. This Bai-qara group needed a location; Muhammad-i-zaman's future had to be cared for and with his, Ma'suma's.

(4) It is significant of intention to give Muhammad-i-zaman ruling status that in April 1529 AD. (Sha'ban 935 AH.) Babur bestowed on him royal insignia, including the umbrella-symbol of sovereignty.[4] This was done after the Mirza had raised

1 *Cf.* G. B.'s H. N. trs. p. 147.
2 She is the only adult daughter of a Timurid mother named as being such by Babur or Gul-badan, but various considerations incline to the opinion that Dil-dar Begim also was a Timurid, hence her three daughters, all named from the Rose, were so too. *Cf.* references of penultimate note.
3 It attaches interest to the Mirza that he can be taken reasonably as once the owner of the Elphinstone Codex (*cf.* JRAS. 1907, pp. 136 and 137).
4 Death did not threaten when this gift was made; life in Kabul was planned for.—Here attention is asked again to the value of Ahmad-i-yadgar's Baburiana for removing the impression set on many writers by the blank year 936 AH. that it was one of illness, instead of being one of travel, hunting and sight-seeing. The details of the activities of that year have the further value that they enhance the worth of Babur's sacrifice of life.—Haidar Mirza also fixes the date of the beginning of illness as 937 AH.

objections, unspecified now in the *Babur-nama* against Bihar; they were overcome, the insignia were given and, though for military reasons he was withheld from taking up that appointment, the recognition of his royal rank had been made. His next appointment was to Junpur, the capital of the fallen Sharqi dynasty. No other chief is mentioned by Babur as receiving the insignia of royalty.

(5) It appears to have been within a Padshah's competence to select his successor; and it may be inferred that choice was made between Humayun and another from the wording of more than one writer that Khalifa "supported" Humayun, and from the word "selected" used in Ahmad-i-yadgar's anecdote.[1] Much more would there be freedom of choice in a division of territory such as there is a good deal to suggest was the basis of Nizamu'd-din Ahmad's story. Whatever the extent of power proposed for the *damad*, whether, as it is difficult to believe, the Padshah's whole supremacy, or whether the limited sovereignty of Hindustan, it must have been known to Babur as well as to Khalifa. Whatever their earlier plan however, it was changed by the sequel of Humayun's illness which led to his becoming Padshah. The *damad* was dropped, on grounds it is safe to believe more impressive than his threat to flay Khalifa or than the remonstrance of that high official's subordinate Muqim of Herat.

Humayun's arrival and continued stay in Hindustan modified earlier dispositions which included his remaining in Badakhshan. His actions may explain why Babur, when in 936 AH. he went as far as Lahor, did not go on to Kabul. Nothing in the sources excludes the surmise that Mahim knew of the bestowal of royal insignia on the Bai-qara Mirza, that she summoned her son to Agra and there kept him, that she would do this the more resolutely if the *damad* of the plan she must have heard of, were that Bai-qara, and that but for Humayun's presence in Agra and its attendant difficulties, Babur would have gone to Kabul, leaving his *damad* in charge of Hindustan.

Babur, however, turned back from Lahor for Agra, and there

---

[1] The author, or embroiderer, of that anonymous story did not know the *Babur-nama* well, or he would not have described Babur as a wine-drinker after 933 AH. The anecdote is parallel with Nizamu'd-din Ahmad's, the one explaining why the Mirza was selected, the other why the *damad* was dropped.

he made the self-surrender which, resulting in Humayun's "selection" as Padshah, became a turning point in history.

Humayun's recovery and Babur's immediate illness will have made the son's life seem Divinely preserved, the father's as a debt to be paid. Babur's impressive personal experience will have dignified Humayun as one whom God willed should live. Such distinction would dictate the bestowal on him of all that fatherly generosity had yet to give. The imminence of death defeating all plans made for life, Humayun was nominated to supreme power as Padshah.

g. Babur's death.

Amongst other family matters mentioned by Gul-badan as occurring shortly before her Father's death, was his arrangement of marriages for Gul-rang with Aisan-timur and for Gul-chihra with Tukhta-bugha *Chaghatai*. She also writes of his anxiety to see Hind-al who had been sent for from Kabul but did not arrive till the day after the death.

When no remedies availed, Humayun was summoned from Sambhal. He reached Agra four days before the death; on the morrow Babur gathered his chiefs together for the last of many times, addressed them, nominated Humayun his successor and bespoke their allegiance for him. Abu'l-fazl thus summarizes his words, "Lofty counsels and weighty mandates were imparted. Advice was given (to Humayun) to be munificent and just, to acquire God's favour, to cherish and protect subjects, to accept apologies from such as had failed in duty, and to pardon transgressors. And, he (Babur) exclaimed, the cream of my testamentary dispositions is this, 'Do naught against your brothers, even though they may deserve it.' In truth," continues the historian, "it was through obedience to this mandate that his Majesty Jannat-ashiyani suffered so many injuries from his brothers without avenging himself." Gul-badan's account of her Father's last address is simple:—"He spoke in this wise, 'For years it has been in my heart to make over the throne to Humayun and to retire to the Gold-scattering Garden. By the Divine grace I have obtained in health of body everything but the fulfilment of this wish. Now that illness has laid me low,

I charge you all to acknowledge Humayun in my stead. Fail not in loyalty towards him. Be of one heart and mind towards him. I hope to God that he, for his part, will bear himself well towards men. Moreover, Humayun, I commit you and your brothers and all my kinsfolk and your people and my people to God's keeping, and entrust them all to you.'"

It was on Monday Jumada I. 5th 937 AH. (Dec. 26th 1530 AD.) that Babur made answer to his summons with the *Adsum* of the Musalman, "Lord! I am here for Thee."

"Black fell the day for children and kinsfolk and all," writes his daughter;

> "Alas! that time and the changeful heaven should exist without thee;
> Alas! and Alas! that time should remain and thou shouldst be gone;"

mourns Khwaja Kalan in the funeral ode from which Badayuni quoted these lines.[1]

The body was laid in the Garden-of-rest (*Aram-bagh*) which is opposite to where the Taj-i-mahall now stands. Khwaja Muhammad 'Ali '*asas*[2] was made the guardian of the tomb, and many well-voiced readers and reciters were appointed to conduct the five daily Prayers and to offer supplication for the soul of the dead. The revenues of Sikri and 5 *laks* from Biana were set aside for the endowment of the tomb, and Mahim Begim, during the two and a half years of her remaining life, sent twice daily from her own estate, an allowance of food towards the support of its attendants.

In accordance with the directions of his will, Babur's body was to be conveyed to Kabul and there to be laid in the garden of his choice, in a grave open to the sky, with no building over it, no need of a door-keeper.

Precisely when it was removed from Agra we have not found stated. It is known from Gul-badan that Kamran visited his Father's tomb in Agra in 1539 AD. (946 AH.) after the battle of Chausa; and it is known from Jauhar that the body had been brought to Kabul before 1544 AD. (952 AH.), at which date Humayun, in Kabul, spoke with displeasure of Kamran's incivility to "Bega Begim", the "Bibi" who had conveyed their

1 *Bib. Ind.* i, 341; Ranking's trs. p. 448.
2 The night-guard; perhaps Mahim Begim's brother (G. B.'s H. N. trs. pp. 27–8).

Father's body to that place.[1] That the widow who performed this duty was the Afghan Lady, Bibi Mubarika[2] is made probable by Gul-badan's details of the movements of the royal ladies. Babur's family left Agra under Hind-al's escort, after the defeat at Chausa (June 7th, 1539 AD.); whoever took charge of the body on its journey to Kabul must have returned at some later date to fetch it. It would be in harmony with Sher Shah's generous character if he safe-guarded her in her task.

The terraced garden Babur chose for his burial-place lies on the slope of the hill Shah-i-Kabul, the Sher-darwaza of European writers.[3] It has been described as perhaps the most beautiful of the Kabul gardens, and as looking towards an unsurpassable view over the Char-dih plain towards the snows of Paghman and the barren, rocky hills which have been the hunting-grounds of rulers in Kabul. Several of Babur's descendants coming to Kabul from Agra have visited and embellished his burial-garden. Shah-i-jahan built the beautiful mosque which stands near the grave; Jahangir seems to have been, if not the author, at least the prompter of the well-cut inscription adorning the upright slab of white marble of Maidan, which now stands at the grave-head. The tomb-stone itself is a low grave-covering, not less simple than those of relations and kin whose remains have been placed near Babur's. In the thirties of the last century [the later Sir] Alexander Burnes visited and admirably described the garden and the tomb. With him was Munshi Mohan Lal who added to his own account of the beauties of the spot, copies of the inscriptions on the monumental slab and on the portal of the Mosque.[4] As is shown by the descriptions these two visitors give, and by Daniel's drawings of the garden and the tomb, there were in their time two upright slabs, one behind the other, near the head of the grave. Mr. H. H. Hayden who visited the garden in the first decade of the present century, shows in his photograph of the grave, one upright stone only, the place of

---

1 G. B.'s H. N. trs. f. 34*b*, p. 138; Jauhar's *Memoirs of Humayun*, Stewart's trs. p. 82.
2 *Cf.* G. B.'s H. N. trs. p. 216, Bio. App. *s.n.* Bega Begam.
3 f. 128, p. 200 n. 3. *Cf.* Appendix V.—*Babur's Gardens in and near Kabul.*
4 *Cf.* H. H. Hayden's *Notes on some monuments in Afghanistan*, [*Memoirs of the Asiatic Society of Bengal* ii, 344]; and *Journal asiatique* 1888, M. J. Darmesteter's art. *Inscriptions de Caboul.*

one of the former two having been taken by a white-washed lamp holder (*chiraghdan*).

The purport of the verses inscribed on the standing-slab is as follows:—

> A ruler from whose brow shone the Light of God was that[1] Back-bone of the Faith (*zahiru'd-din*) Muhammad Babur Padshah. Together with majesty, dominion, fortune, rectitude, the open-hand and the firm Faith, he had share in prosperity, abundance and the triumph of victorious arms. He won the material world and became a moving light; for his every conquest he looked, as for Light, towards the world of souls. When Paradise became his dwelling and Ruzwan[2] asked me the date, I gave him for answer, "Paradise is forever Babur Padshah's abode."

h. Babur's wives and children.[3]

Babur himself mentions several of his wives by name, but Gul-badan is the authority for complete lists of them and their children.

1. 'Ayisha Sultan Begim, daughter of Sl. Ahmad Mirza *Miran-shahi* was betrothed, when Babur was *cir.* 5 years old, in 894 AH. (1488–89 AD.), bore Fakhru'n-nisa' in 906 AH. [who died in about one month], left Babur before 909 AH. (1503 AD.).

2. Zainab Sl. Begim, daughter of Sl. Mahmud Mirza *Miran-shahi*, was married in 910 AH. (1504–5 AD.), died childless two or three years later.

3. Mahim Begim, whose parentage is not found stated, was married in 912 AH. (1506 AD.), bore Bar-bud, Mihr-jan, Aisan-daulat, Faruq [who all died in infancy], and Humayun.

4. Ma'suma Sl. Begim, daughter of Sl. Ahmad Mirza *Miran-shahi*, was married in 913 AH. (1507 AD.), bore Ma'suma and died at her birth, presumably early in the *lacuna* of 914–925 AH. (1508–19 AD.).

---

1 *an*, a demonstrative suggesting that it refers to an original inscription on the second, but now absent, upright slab, which presumably would bear Babur's name.
2 Ruzwan is the door-keeper of Paradise.
3 Particulars of the women mentioned by Babur, Haidar, Gul-badan and other writers of their time, can be seen in my Biographical Appendix to the Begim's *Humayun-nama*. As the Appendix was published in 1902, variants from it occurring in this work are corrections superseding earlier and less-informed statements.

5. Gul-rukh Begim, whose parentage is not found stated, was perhaps a Begchik Mughul, was married between 914 AH. and 925 AH. (1508–19 AD.), probably early in the period, bore Shah-rukh, Ahmad [who both died young], Gul'izar [who also may have died young], Kamran and 'Askari.

6. Dil-dar Begim, whose parentage is not found stated, was married in the same period as Gul-rukh, bore Gul-rang, Gul-chihra, Hind-al, Gul-badan and Alwar, [who died in childhood].

7. The Afghan Lady (Afghani Aghacha), Bibi Mubarika *Yusuf-zai*, was married in 925 AH. (1519 AD.), and died childless.

The two Circassian slaves Gul-nar Aghacha and Nar-gul Aghacha of whom Tahmasp made gift to Babur in 933 AH. (f.305), became recognized ladies of the royal household. They are mentioned several times by Gul-badan as taking part in festivities and in family conferences under Humayun. Gul-nar is said by Abu'l-fazl to have been one of Gul-badan's pilgrim band in 983 AH. (1575 AD.).

The above list contains the names of three wives whose parentage is not given or is vaguely given by the well-known sources,—namely, Mahim, Gul-rukh and Dil-dar. What would sufficiently explain the absence of mention by Babur of the parentage of Gul-rukh and Dil-dar is that his record of the years within which the two Begims were married is not now with the *Babur-nama*. Presumably it has been lost, whether in diary or narrative form, in the *lacuna* of 914–25 AH. (1508–19 AD.). Gul-rukh appears to have belonged to the family of Begchik Mughuls described by Haidar Mirza;[1] her brothers are styled Mirza; she was of good but not royal birth. Dil-dar's case is less simple. Nothing in her daughter Gul-badan's book suggests that she and her children were other than of the highest rank; numerous details and shades of expression show their ease of equality with royal personages. It is consistent with Gul-badan's method of enumerating her father's wives that she should not state her own mother's descent; she states it of none of her "mothers". There is this interest in trying to trace Dil-dar's parentage, that she may have been the third daughter of Sl. Mahmud Mirza and Pasha Begim, and a daughter of hers may have been the mother of

1 *Tarikh-i-rashidi* trs. Ney Elias and Ross p. 308.

Salima Sultan Begim who was given in marriage by Humayun to Bairam Khan, later was married by Akbar, and was a woman of charm and literary accomplishments. Later historians, Abu'l-fazl amongst their number, say that Salima's mother was a daughter of Babur's wife Saliha Sultan Begim, and vary that daughter's name as Gul-rang-rukh-barg or -'izar (the last form being an equivalent of *chihra*, face). As there cannot have been a wife with her daughter growing up in Babur's household, who does not appear in some way in Gul-badan's chronicle, and as Salima's descent from Babur need not be questioned, the knot is most readily loosened by surmising that "Saliha" is the real name of Gul-badan's "Dil-dar". Instances of double names are frequent, *e.g.* Mahim, Mah-chicham, Qara-guz, Aq, (My Moon, My Moon sister, Black-eyed, Fair). "Heart-holding" (Dil-dar) sounds like a home-name of affection. It is the *Ma'asir-i-rahimi* which gives Saliha as the name of Babur's wife, Pasha's third daughter. Its author may be wrong, writing so late as he did (1025 AH.–1616 AD.), or may have been unaware that Saliha was (if she were) known as Dil-dar. It would not war against seeming facts to take Pasha's third daughter to be Babur's wife Dil-dar, and Dil-dar's daughter Gul-chihra to be Salima's mother. Gul-chihra was born in about 1516 AD., married to Tukhta-bugha in 1530 AD., widowed in *cir.* 1533 AD., might have remarried with Nuru'd-din *Chaqaniani* (Sayyid Amir), and in 945 AH. might have borne him Salima; she was married in 1547 AD. (954 AH.) to 'Abbas Sultan *Auzbeg*.[1] Two matters, neither having much weight, make against taking Dil-dar to be a *Miran-shahi*; the first being that the anonymous annotator who added to the archetype of Kehr's Codex what is entered in Appendix L.-*On Mahim's adoption of Hind-al*, styles her Dil-dar Aghacha; he, however, may have known no more than others knew of her descent; the second, that Mahim forcibly took Dil-dar's child Hind-al to rear; she was the older wife and the mother of the heir, but could she have taken the upper hand over a Miran-shahi? A circumstance complicating the question of Salima's maternal descent is, that historians searching the *Babur-nama* or its Persian translation the *Waqi'at-i-baburi* for information about the three daughters of Mahmud *Miran-shahi*

1 Bio. App. *s.n.* Gul-chihra.

and Pasha *Baharlu Turkman*, would find an incomplete record, one in which the husbands of the first and second daughters are mentioned and nothing is said about the third who was Babur's wife and the grandmother of Salima. Babur himself appears to have left the record as it is, meaning to fill it in later; presumably he waited for the names of the elder two sisters to complete his details of the three. In the Haidarabad Codex, which there is good ground for supposing a copy of his original manuscript, about three lines are left blank (f. 27) as if awaiting information; in most manuscripts, however, this indication of intention is destroyed by running the defective passage on to join the next sentence. Some chance remark of a less well-known writer, may clear up the obscurity and show that Saliha was Dil-dar.

Mahim's case seems one having a different cause for silence about her parentage. When she was married in Herat, shortly after the death of Sl. Husain Mirza, Babur had neither wife nor child. What Abu'l-fazl tells about her is vague; her father's name is not told; she is said to have belonged to a noble Khurasan family, to have been related (*nisbat-i-khwesh*) to Sl. Husain Mirza and to have traced her descent to Shaikh Ahmad of Jam. If her birth had been high, even though not royal, it is strange that it is not stated by Babur when he records the birth of her son Humayun, incidentally by Gul-badan, or more precisely by Abu'l-fazl. Her brothers belonged to Khost, and to judge from a considerable number of small records, seem to have been quiet, unwarlike Khwajas. Her marriage took place in a year of which a full record survives; it is one in the composed narrative, not in the diary. In the following year, this also being one included in the composed narrative, Babur writes of his meeting with Ma'suma *Miran-shahi* in Herat, of their mutual attraction, and of their marriage. If the marriage with Humayun's mother had been an equal alliance, it would agree with Babur's custom to mention its occurrence, and to give particulars about Mahim's descent.[1]

---

1 The story of the later uprisings against Mahim's son Humayun by his brothers, by Muhammad-i-zaman *Bai-qara* and others of the same royal blood, and this in spite of Humayun's being his father's nominated successor, stirs surmise as to whether the rebels were not tempted by more than his defects of character to disregard his claim to supremacy; perhaps pride of higher maternal descent, this particularly amongst the Bai-qara group, may have deepened a disregard created by antagonisms of temperament.

i. Mr. William Erskine's estimate of Babur.

"Zahiru'd-din Muhammad Babur was undoubtedly one of the most illustrious men of his age, and one of the most eminent and accomplished princes that ever adorned an Asiatic throne. He is represented as having been above the middle size, of great vigour of body, fond of all field and warlike sports, an excellent swordsman, and a skilful archer. As a proof of his bodily strength, it is mentioned, that he used to leap from one pinnacle to another of the pinnacled ramparts used in the East, in his double-soled boots; and that he even frequently took a man under each arm and went leaping along the rampart from one of the pointed pinnacles to another. Having been early trained to the conduct of business, and tutored in the school of adversity, the powers of his mind received full development. He ascended the throne at the age of twelve, and before he had attained his twentieth year, had shared every variety of fortune; he had not only been the ruler of subject provinces but had been in thraldom to his own ambitious nobles, and obliged to conceal every senti-ment of his heart; he had been alternately hailed and obeyed as a conqueror and deliverer by rich and extensive kingdoms, and forced to lurk in the deserts and mountains of Farghana as a houseless wanderer. Down to the last dregs of life, we perceive in him strong feelings of affection for his early friends and early enjoyments. * * * He had been taught betimes, by the voice of events that cannot lie, that he was a man dependent on the kindness and fidelity of other men; and, in his dangers and escapes with his followers, had learned that he was only one of an association. * * * The native benevolence and gaiety of his disposition seems ever to overflow on all around him; * * * of his companions in arms he speaks with the frank gaiety of a soldier. * * * Ambitious he was and fond of conquest and glory in all its shapes; the enterprise in which he was for a season engaged, seems to have absorbed his whole soul, and all his faculties were exerted to bring it to a fortunate issue. His elastic mind was not broken by discomfiture, and few who have achieved such glorious conquests, have suffered more numerous or more decisive defeats. His personal courage was conspicuous during his whole life. Upon the whole, if we review with impartiality the history of Asia, we find few princes entitled to rank higher than Babur in genius and accomplishments. * * * In activity of mind, in the gay equanimity and unbroken spirit with which he bore the extremes of good and bad fortune, in the possession of the manly and social virtues, in his love of letters and his success in the cultivation of them, we shall probably find no other Asiatic prince who can justly be placed beside him."

THE END.

APPENDICES

A.—THE SITE AND DISAPPEARANCE
OF OLD AKHSI.

SOME modern writers, amongst whom are Dr. Schuyler, General Nalivkine and Mr. Pumpelly, have inferred from the Babur-nama account of Akhsi, (in its translations?) that the landslip through which Babur's father died and the disappearance of old Akhsi were brought about by erosion. Seen by the light of modern information, this erosion theory does not seem to cover the whole ground and some other cause seems necessary in explanation of both events.

For convenience of reference, the Babur-nama passages required, are quoted here, with their translations.

> Hai. MS. f. 4b. *Saihun darya-si qurghani astidin aqar. Qurghani baland jar austida waqi' bulub tur. Khandaqi-ning aurunigha 'umiqjarlar dur. 'Umar Shaikh M. kim muni pay-takht qildi, bir iki martaba tashraq-din yana jarlar saldi.*
>
> Of this the translations are as follows:—
>
> (a) Pers. trans. (I.O. 217, f. 3b): *Darya-i Saihun az payha qila'-i o mirezad u qila'-i o bar jar balandi waqi' shuda ba jay khandaq jarha-i 'umiq uftada. 'U. Sh. M. kah anra pay-takht sakhta, yak du martaba az birun ham baz jarha andakht.*
>
> (b) Erskine (p. 5, translating from the Persian): "The river Saihun flows under the walls of the castle. The castle is situated on a high precipice, and the steep ravines around serve instead of a moat. When U. Sh. M. made it his capital he, in one or two instances, scarped the ravines outside the fort."
>
> (c) De Courteille (i, 8, translating from Ilminsky's imprint, p. 6): "Le Seihoun coule au pied de la fortresse qui se dresse sur le sommet d'un ravin, dont les profondeurs lui tiennent lieu d'un fossé. 'U. Sh. M. à l'époque où il en avait fait son capitale, avait augmenté à une ou deux réprises, les escarpements qui la ceignent naturellement."

Concerning 'Umar Shaikh's death, the words needed are (f. 6b);—

> *Mazkur bulub aidi kim Akhsi qurghani buland jar austida waqi' bulub tur. 'Imaratlar jar yaqasida airdi. ... Mirza jardin kabutar u kabutar-khana bila auchub shunqar*

buldi;—"It has been mentioned that the walled-town of Akhsi is situated above ravine(s). The royal dwellings are along a ravine. The Mirza, having flown with his pigeons and their house from the ravine, became a falcon (*i.e.* died)."

A few particulars about Akhsi will shew that, in the translations just quoted, certain small changes of wording are dictated by what, amongst other writers, Kostenko and von Schwarz have written about the oases of Turkistan.

The name Akhsi, as used by Ibn Haukal, Yaqut and Babur, describes an oasis township, *i.e.* a walled-town with its adjacent cultivated lands. In Yaqut's time Akhsi had a second circumvallation, presumably less for defence than for the protection of crops against wild animals. The oasis was created by the Kasan-water,[1] upon the riverain loess of the right and higher bank of the Saihun (Sir), on level ground west of the junction of the Narin and the Qara-darya, west too of spurs from the northern hills which now abut upon the river. Yaqut locates it in the 12th century, at one *farsakh* (*circa* 4 m.) north of the river.[2] Depending as it did solely on the Kasan-water, nothing dictated its location close to the Sir, along which there is now, and there seems to have been in the 12th century, a strip of waste land. Babur says of Akhsi what Kostenko says (i, 321) of modern Tashkint, that it stood above ravines (*jarlar*). These were natural or artificial channels of the Kasan-water.[3]

To turn now to the translations;—Mr. Erskine imaged Akhsi as a castle, high on a precipice in process of erosion by the Sir. But Babur's word, *qurghan* means the walled-town; his for a castle is *ark*, citadel; and his *jar*, a cleft, is not rendered by "precipice." Again;—it is no more necessary to understand

1 Until the Yangi-ariq was taken off the Sir, late in the last century, for Namangan, the oasis land of Farghana was fertilized, not from the river but by its intercepted tributaries.

2 Ujfalvy's translation of Yaqut (ii, 179) reads one *farsakh* from the mountains instead of "north of the river."

3 Kostenko describes a division of Tashkint, one in which is Ravine-lane (*jar-kucha*), as divided by a deep ravine; of another he says that it is cut by deep ravines (Babur's *'umiq jarlar*).

that the Sir flowed close to the walls than it is to understand, when one says the Thames flows past below Richmond, that it washes the houses on the hill.

The key to the difficulties in the Turki passage is provided by a special use of the word *jar* for not only natural ravines but artificial water-cuts for irrigation. This use of it makes clear that what 'Umar Shaikh did at Akhsi was not to make escarpments but to cut new water-channels. Presumably he joined those "further out" on the deltaic fan, on the east and west of the town, so as to secure a continuous defensive cleft round the town[1] or it may be, in order to bring it more water.

Concerning the historic pigeon-house (f. 6b), it can be said safely that it did not fall into the Sir; it fell from a *jar*, and in this part of its course, the river flows in a broad bed, with a low left bank. Moreover the Mirza's residence was in the walled-town (f. 110b) and there his son stayed 9 years after the accident. The slip did not affect the safety of the residence therefore; it may have been local to the birds' house. It will have been due to some ordinary circumstance since no cause for it is mentioned by Babur, Haidar or Abu'l-fazl. If it had marked the crisis of the Sir's approach, Akhsi could hardly have been described, 25 years later, as a strong fort.

Something is known of Akhsi, in the 10th, the 12th, the 15th and the 19th centuries, which testifies to sæcular decadence. Ibn Haukal and Yaqut give the township an extent of 3 *farsakh* (12 miles), which may mean from one side to an opposite one. Yaqut's description of it mentions four gates, each opening into well-watered lands extending a whole *farsakh*, in other words it had a ring of garden-suburb four miles wide.

Two meanings have been given to Babur's words indicating the status of the oasis in the 15th century. They are,

1 Babur writes as though Akhsi had one Gate only (f. 112b). It is unlikely that the town had come down to having a single exit; the Gate by which he got out of Akhsi was the one of military importance because served by a draw-bridge, presumably over the ravine-moat, and perhaps not close to that bridge.

mahallati qurghan-din bir shar'i yuraqraq tushub tur. They
have been understood as saying that the suburbs were two
miles from their *urbs*. This may be right but I hesitate to
accept it without pointing out that the words may mean, "Its
suburbs extend two miles farther than the walled-town."
Whichever verbal reading is correct, reveals a decayed oasis.

In the 19th century, Nalivkine and Ujfalvy describe the
place then bearing the name Akhsi, as a small village, a
mere winter-station, at some distance from the river's bank,
that bank then protected from denudation by a sand-bank.

Three distinctly-marked stages of decadence in the oasis
township are thus indicated by Yaqut, Babur and the two
modern travellers.

It is necessary to say something further about the position of
the suburbs in the 15th century. Babur quotes as especially
suitable to Akhsi, the proverbial questions, "Where is the
village?"[1] (qy. Akhsi-kint.) "Where are the trees?" and these
might be asked by some-one in the suburbs unable to see Akhsi
or *vice versa*. But granting that there were no suburbs within
two miles of the town, why had the whole inner circle, two
miles of Yaqut's four, gone out of cultivation? Erosion would
have affected only land between the river and the town.

Again;—if the Sir only were working in the 15th century
to destroy a town standing on the Kasan-water, how is it that
this stream does not yet reach the Sir?

Various ingatherings of information create the impression
that failure of Kasan-water has been the dominant factor in
the loss of the Akhsi township. Such failure might be due to
the general desiccation of Central Asia and also to increase of
cultivation in the Kasan-valley itself. There may have been
erosion, and social and military change may have had its part,
but for the loss of the oasis lands and for, as a sequel, the decay
of the town, desiccation seems a sufficient cause.

1 For mention of upper villages *see* f. 110 and note 1.

The Kasan-water still supports an oasis on its riverain slope, the large Auzbeg town of Tupa-qurghan (Town-of-the-hill), from the modern castle of which a superb view is had up the Kasan-valley, now thickly studded with villages.[1]

B.—THE BIRDS, *QIL QUYIRUGH* AND *BAGHRI QARA*.

DESCRIBING a small bird (*qush-qina*), abundant in the Qarshi district (f. 49*b*), Babur names it the *qil-quyirugh*, horse-tail, and says it resembles the *baghri qara*.

Later on he writes (f. 280) that the *baghri qara* of India is smaller and more slender than "those" *i.e.* of Transoxiana (f. 49*b*), the blackness of its breast less deep, and its cry less piercing.

We have had difficulty in identifying the birds but at length conclude that the *baghri qara* of Transoxiana is *Pterocles arenarius*, Pallas's black-bellied sand-grouse and that the Indian one is a smaller sand-grouse, perhaps a *Syrrhaptes*. As the *qil quyirugh* resembles the other two, it may be a yet smaller *Syrrhaptes*.

Muh. Salih, writing of sport Shaibaq Khan had in Qarshi (*Shaibani-nama*, Vambéry, p. 192) mentions the "Little bird (*murghak*) of Qarshi," as on all sides making lament. The Sang-lakh[2] gives its Persian name as *khar-pala*, ass-hair, says it

1 *Cf.* f. 114 for distances which would be useful in locating Akhsi if Babur's *yighach* were not variable; Ritter, vii, 3 and 733; Réclus, vi, index *s.n.* Farghana; Ujfalvy ii, 168, his quotation from Yaqut and his authorities; Nalivkine's *Histoire du Khanat de Kokand*, p. 14 and p. 53; Schuyler, i, 324; Kostenko, Tables of Contents for cognate general information and i, 320, for Tashkint; von Schwarz, index under related names, and especially p. 345 and plates; Pumpelly, p. 18 and p. 115.

2 This Turki-Persian Dictionary was compiled by Mirza Mahdi Khan, Nadir Shah's secretary and historian, whose life of his master Sir William Jones translated into French (Rieu's Turki Cat. p. 264*b*).

flies in large flocks and resembles the *baghri qara*. Of the latter he writes as abundant in the open country and as making noise (*baghir*).

The Sang-lakh (f. 119) gives the earliest and most informing account we have found of the *baghri qara*. Its says the bird is larger than a pigeon, marked with various colours, yellow especially, black-breasted and a dweller in the stony and water-less desert. These details are followed by a quotation from 'Ali-sher *Nawa'i*, in which he likens his own heart to that of the bird of the desert, presumably referring to the gloom of the bird's plumage. Three synonyms are then given; Ar. *qita*, one due to its cry (Meninsky); Pers. *sang-shikan*, stone-eating, (Steingass, *sang-khwara*, stone-eating); and Turki *baghir-tilaq* which refers, I think, to its cry.

Morier (Haji Baba) in his *Second journey through Persia* (Lond. 1818, p. 181), mentions that a bird he calls the black-breasted partridge, (*i.e. Francolinus vulgaris*) is known in Turkish as *bokara kara* and in Persian as *siyah-sina*, both names, (he says), meaning black-breast; that it has a horse-shoe of black feathers round the forepart of the trunk, more strongly marked in the female than in the male; that they fly in flocks of which he saw immense numbers near Tabriz (p. 283), have a soft note, inhabit the plains, and, once settled, do not run. Cock and hen alike have a small spur,—a characteristic, it may be said, identifying rather with *Francolinus vulgaris* than with *Pterocles arenarius*. Against this identification, however, is Mr. Blandford's statement that *siyah-sina* (Morier's *bokara kara*) is *Pterocles arenarius* (Report of the Persian Boundary Com-mission, ii, 271).

In Afghanistan and Bikanir, the sand-grouse is called *tuturak* and *boora kurra* (Jerdon, ii, 498). Scully explains *baghitaq* as *Pterocles arenarius*.

Perhaps I may mention something making me doubt whether it is correct to translate *baghri qara* by *black-liver* and *gorge-noir* or other names in which the same meaning is expressed. To translate thus, is to understand a Turki noun and adjective in

Persian construction, and to make exception to the rule, amply exemplified in lists of birds, that Turki names of birds are commonly in Turki construction, *e.g. qara bash* (black-head), *aq-bash* (white-head), *sarigh-sunduk* (yellow-headed wagtail). *Baghir* may refer to the cry of the bird. We learn from Mr. Ogilvie Grant that the Mongol name for the sand-grouse *njupterjun*, is derived from its cry in flight, *truck, truck*, and its Arabic name *qita* is said by Meninsky to be derived from its cry *kaetha, kaetha.* Though the dissimilarity of the two cries is against taking the *njupterjun* and the *qita* to be of one class of sand-grouse, the significance of the derivation of the names remains, and shows that there are examples in support of thinking that when a sand-grouse is known as *baghri qara*, it may be so known because of its cry (*baghir*).

The word *qara* finds suggestive interpretation in a B. N. phrase (f. 72*b*) *Tambal-ning qara-si*, Tambal's blackness, *i.e.* the dark mass of his moving men, seen at a distance. It is used also for an indefinite number, *e.g.* "family, servants, retainers, followers, *qara*," and I think it may imply a massed flock.

Babur's words (f. 280) *baghri-ning qara-si ham kam dur*, [its belly (lit. liver) also is less black], do not necessarily contradict the view that the word *baghri* in the bird's name means crying. The root *bagh* has many and pliable derivatives; I suspect both Babur (here) and Muh. Salih (l. c.) of ringing changes on words.

We are indebted for kind reply to our questions to Mr. Douglas Carruthers, Mr. Ogilvie Grant and to our friend, Mr. R. S. Whiteway.

C.—ON THE *GOSHA-GIR*.

I AM indebted to my husband's examination of two Persian MSS. on archery for an explanation of the word *gosha-gir*, in its technical sense in archery. The works consulted are the Cyclopædia of Archery (*Kulliyatu'r-rami* I. O. 2771) and the Archer's Guide (*Hidayatu'r-rami* I. O. 2768).

It should be premised that in archery, the word *gosha* describes, in the arrow, the notch by which it grips and can be carried on the string, and, in the bow, both the tip (horn) and the notch near the tip in which the string catches. It is explained by Vullers as *cornu et crena arcûs cui immititur nervus*.

Two passages in the Cyclopædia of Archery (f. 9 and f. 36*b*) shew *gosha* as the bow-tip. One says that to bend the bow, two men must grasp the two *gosha*; the other reports a tradition that the Archangel Gabriel brought a bow having its two *gosha* (tips) made of ruby. The same book directs that the *gosha* be made of seasoned ivory, the Archer's Guide prescribing seasoned mulberry wood.

The C. of A. (f. 125*b*) says that a bowman should never be without two things, his arrows and his *gosha-gir*. The *gosha-gir* may be called an item of the repairing kit; it is an implement (f. 53) for making good a warped bow-tip and for holding the string into a displaced notch. It is known also as the *chapras*, brooch or buckle, and the *kardang*; and is said to bear these names because it fastens in the string. Its shape is that of the upper part of the Ar. letter *jim*, two converging lines of which the lower curves slightly outward. It serves to make good a warped bow, without the use of fire and it should be kept upon the bow-tip till this has reverted to its original state. Until the warp has been straightened by the *gosha-gir*, the bow must be kept from the action of fire because it, (composite of sinew and glutinous substance,) is of the nature of wax.

The same implement can be used to straighten the middle of the bow, the *kaman khana*. It is then called *kar-dang*. It can be used there on condition that there are not two *daur* (curves) in the bow. If there are two the bow cannot be repaired without fire. The *halal daur* is said to be characteristic of the Turkish bow. There are three *daur*. I am indebted to Mr. Inigo Simon for the suggestions that *daur* in this connection means *warp* and that the three twists (*daur*) may be those of one horn (*gosha*), of the whole bow warped in one curve, and of the two horns warped in opposite directions.

Of repair to the *kaman-khana* it is said further that if no *kardang* be available, its work can be done by means of a stick and string, and if the damage be slight only, the bow and the string can be tightly tied together till the bow comes straight. "And the cure is with God!"

Both manuscripts named contain much technical information. Some parts of this are included in my husband's article, *Oriental Crossbows* (A.Q.R. 1911, p. 1). Sir Ralph Payne-Gallwey's interesting book on the Cross-bow allows insight into the fine handicraft of Turkish bow-making.

D.—ON THE RESCUE PASSAGE.

I HAVE omitted from my translation an account of Babur's rescue from expected death, although it is with the Haidarabad Codex, because closer acquaintance with its details has led both my husband and myself to judge it spurious. We had welcomed it because, being with the true Babur-nama text, it accredited the same account found in the Kehr–Ilminsky text, and also because, however inefficiently, it did something towards filling the gap found elsewhere within 908 AH.

It is in the Haidarabad MS. (f. 118*b*), in Kehr's MS. (p. 385), in Ilminsky's imprint (p. 144), in *Les Mémoires de Babour* (i, 255) and with the St. P. University Codex, which is a copy of Kehr's.

On the other hand, it is not with the Elphinstone Codex (f. 89*b*); that it was not with the archetype of that codex the scribe's note shews (f. 90); it is with neither of the *Waqi'at-i-baburi* (Pers. translations) nor with Leyden and Erskine's *Memoirs* (p. 122).[1]

Before giving our grounds for rejecting what has been offered to fill the gap of 908 AH. a few words must be said about the lacuna itself. Nothing indicates that Babur left it and, since both in the Elphinstone Codex and its archetype, the sentence preceding it lacks the terminal verb, it seems due merely to loss of pages. That the loss, if any, was of early date is clear,— the Elph. MS. itself being copied not later than 1567 AD. (JRAS. 1907, p. 137).

Two known circumstances, both of earlier date than that of the Elphinstone Codex, might have led to the loss,—the first is the storm which in 935 AH. scattered Babur's papers (f. 376*b*), the second, the vicissitudes to which Humayun's library was exposed in his exile.[2] Of the two the first seems the more probable cause.

The rupture of a story at a point so critical as that of Babur's danger in Karnan would tempt to its completion; so too would wish to make good the composed part of the Babur-nama. Humayun annotated the archetype of the Elphinstone Codex a good deal but he cannot have written the Rescue passage if only because he was in a position to avoid some of its inaccuracies.

CONTEXT AND TRANSLATION OF THE RESCUE PASSAGE.

To facilitate reference, I quote the last words preceding the gap purported to be filled by the Rescue passage, from several texts;—

1 The *Padshah-nama* whose author, 'Abdu'l-hamid, the biographer of Shah-jahan, died in 1065 AH. (1655 AD.) mentions the existence of lacunæ in a copy of the Babur-nama, in the Imperial Library and allowed by his wording to be Babur's autograph MS. (i, 42 and ii, 703).
2 *Akbar-nama*, Bib. Ind. ed. i, 305; H.B. i, 571.

(*a*) Elphinstone MS. f. 89*b*,—*Quptum. Bagh gosha-si-gha bardim. Auzum bila andesha qildim. Didim kim kishi agar yuz u agar ming yashasa, akhir hech* ...

(*b*) The Hai. MS. (f. 118*b*) varies from the Elphinstone by omitting the word *hech* and adding *aulmak kirak*, he must die.

(*c*) Payanda-hasan's *Waqi'at-i-baburi* (I. O. 215, f. 96*b*),— *Barkhwastam u dar gosha-i bagh raftam. Ba khud andesha karda, guftam kah agar kase sad sal ya hazar sal 'umr dashta bashad, akhir hech ast.* (It will be seen that this text has the *hech* of the Elph. MS.)

(*d*) 'Abdu'r-rahim's *Waqi'at-i-baburi* (I. O. 217, f. 79),— *Barkhwastam u ba gosha-i-bagh raftam. Ba khud andeshidam u guftam kah agar kase sad sal u agar hazar sal 'umr bayabad akhir* ...

(*e*) Muh. Shirazi's lith. ed. (p. 75) finishes the sentence with *akhir khud bayad murd*, at last one must die,—varying as it frequently does, from both of the *Waqi'at*.

(*f*) Kehr's MS. (p. 383-454), Ilminsky, p. 144.—*Qupub bagh-ning bir burji-gha barib, khatirim-gha kilturdim kim agar adam yuz yil u agar ming yil tirik bulsa, akhir aulmak din auzka chara yuq tur.* (I rose. Having gone to a tower of the garden, I brought it to my mind that if a person be alive 100 years or a thousand years, at last he has no help other than to die.)

The Rescue passage is introduced by a Persian couplet, identified by my husband as from Nizami's *Khusrau u Shirin*, which is as follows;—

> If you stay a hundred years, and if one year,
> Forth you must go from this heart-delighting palace.

I steadied myself for death (*qarar birdim*). In that garden a stream came flowing;[1] I made ablution; I recited the prayer of two inclinations (*ra'kat*); having raised my head for silent prayer, I was making earnest petition when my eyes closed in sleep.[2] I am seeing[3] that Khwaja Yaq'ub, the son of

---

1 Hai. MS. f. 118*b*; *aushal baghda su aqib kila dur aidi. Babur-nama, su aqib*, water flowed and *aushal* is rare, but in the R.P. occurs 7 times.

2 *guzum awiqi-gha barib tur.* B.N. f. 117*b*, *guzum awiqu-gha bardi*.

3 *kura dur min*, B.N. f. 83, *tush kurdum* and *tush kurar min*.

Khwaja Yahya and grandson of His Highness Khwaja 'Ubaidu'l-lah, came facing me, mounted on a piebald horse, with a large company of piebald horsemen (sic).[1] He said: "Lay sorrow aside! Khwaja *Ahrar* (i.e. 'Ubaidu'l-lah) has sent me to you; he said, 'We, having asked help for him (i.e. Babur), will seat him on the royal throne;[2] wherever difficulty befalls him, let him look towards us (lit. bring us to sight) and call us to mind; there will we be present.' Now, in this hour, victory and success are on your side; lift up your head! awake!"

At that time I awoke happy, when Yusuf and those with him[3] were giving one another advice. "We will make a pretext to deceive; to seize and bind[4] is necessary." Hearing these words, I said, "Your words are of this sort, but I will see which of you will come to my presence to take me." I was saying this when outside the garden wall[5] came the noise of approaching horsemen. Yusuf *darogha* said, "If we had taken you to Tambal our affairs would have gone forward. Now he has sent again many persons to seize you." He was certain that this noise might be the footfall of the horses of those sent by Tambal. On hearing those words anxiety grew upon me; what to do I did not know. At this time those horsemen, not happening to find the garden gate, broke down the wall where it was old (and) came in. I saw (*kursam*, lit. might see) that Qutluq Muh. *Barlas* and Baba-i *Parghari*, my life-devoted servants, having arrived [with], it may be, ten, fifteen, twenty persons, were approaching. Having flung themselves from their horses,[6] bent the knee from afar and showed respect, they fell at my feet. In that state (*hal*) such ecstasy (*hal*) came over me that you might say (*goya*) God gave me life from a new source (*bash*). I said, "Seize and bind that Yusuf *darogha* and these here (*turghan*) hireling mannikins." These same mannikins had taken to flight. They (i.e. the rescuers), having taken them, one by one, here and there, brought them bound. I said, "Where do you come from? How did you get news?" Qutluq Muh. *Barlas* said: "When, having fled from Akhsi, we were separated from you in the flight, we went to Andijan when the Khans also came to Andijan. I saw a vision that Khwaja 'Ubaidu'l-lah said, 'Babur *padshah*[7] is in a village called Karnan; go and bring him, since the royal seat (*masnad*) has become his possession (*ta'alluq*).' I having seen this vision and become happy, represented (the matter) to the Elder Khan (and) the Younger Khan. I said to the Khans, 'I have five or six younger brothers (and) sons; do you add a few soldiers. I will go through the Karnan side and bring news.' The Khans said, 'It occurs to our minds also that (he) may have gone that same road (?).' They appointed ten persons; they said, 'Having gone in that direction (*sari*) and made very sure, bring news. Would to God you might get true news!' We were saying this when Baba-i *Parghari* said, 'I too will go and seek.' He also having agreed with two young men, (his) younger brothers, we rode out. It is three days

---

1 *ablaq suwar bilan*; P. *suwar* for T. *atliq* or *atliq kishi*; *bilan* for B.N. *bila*, and an odd use of piebald (*ablaq*).

2 *masnad*, B.N. *takht*, throne. *Masnad* betrays Hindustan.

3 *Hamra'ilari* (sic) *bir bir ga* (sic) *maslahat qila durlar. Maslahat* for B.N. *kingash* or *kingaish; hamrah*, companion, for *mining bila bar*, etc.

4 *baghlamaq* and f. 119b *baghlaghanlar*; B.N. *almak* or *tutmaq* to seize or take prisoner.

5 *diwar* for *tam*.

6 f. 119, *at-tin auzlar-ni tashlab*; B.N. *tushmak*, dismount. *Tashlamaq* is not used in the sense of dismount by B.

7 *padshah* so used is an anachronism (f. 215); Babur Mirza would be correct.

to-day that we are on the road. Thank God! we have found you." They said (*didilar*, for *dib*). They spoke (*aitilar*), "Make a move! Ride off! Take these bound ones with you! To stay here is not well; Tambal has had news of your coming here; go, in whatever way, and join yourself to the Khans!" At that time we having ridden out, moved towards Andijan. It was two days that we had eaten no food; the evening prayer had come when we found a sheep, went on, dismounted, killed, and roasted. Of that same roast we ate as much as a feast. After that we rode on, hurried forward, made a five days' journey in a day and two nights, came and entered Andijan. I saluted my uncle the Elder Khan (and) my uncle the Younger Khan, and made recital of past days. With the Khans I spent four months. My servants, who had gone looking in every place, gathered themselves together; there were more than 300 persons. It came to my mind (*kim*), "How long must I wander, a vagabond (*sar-gardan*),[1] in this Farghana country? I will make search (*talab*) on every side (*dib*)." Having said, I rode out in the month of Muharram to seek Khurasan, and I went out from the country of Farghana.[2]

REASONS AGAINST THE REJECTION OF THE RESCUE PASSAGE.

Two circumstances have weight against rejecting the passage, its presence with the Haidarabad Codex and its acceptance by Dr. Ilminsky and M. de Courteille.

That it is with the Codex is a matter needing consideration and this the more that it is the only extra matter there found. Not being with the Persian translations, it cannot be of early date. It seems likely to owe its place of honour to distinguished authorship and may well be one of the four portions (*juzwe*) mentioned by Jahangir in the Tuzuk-i-jahangiri,[3] as added by himself to his ancestor's book. If so, it may be mentioned, it will have been with Babur's autograph MS. [now not to be found], from which the Haidarabad Codex shews signs of being a direct copy.[4]

[The incongruity of the Rescue passage with the true text has

1 *zahiran*; B.N. *yaqin*.
2 Ilminsky's imprint stops at *dib*; he may have taken *kim-dib* for signs of quotation merely. (This I did earlier, JRAS 1902, p. 749.)
3 Aligarh ed. p. 52; Rogers' trs. i, 109.
4 *Cf.* f. 63*b*, n. 3.

been indicated by foot-notes to the translation of it already given. What condemns it on historic and other grounds will follow.]

On linguistic grounds it is a strong argument in its favour that Dr. Ilminsky and M. de Courteille should have accepted it but the argument loses weight when some of the circumstances of their work are taken into account.

In the first place, it is not strictly accurate to regard Dr. Ilminsky as accepting it unquestioned, because it is covered by his depreciatory remarks, made in his preface, on Kehr's text. He, like M. de Courteille, worked with a single Turki MS. and neither of the two ever saw a complete true text. When their source (the Kehr-Ilminsky) was able to be collated with the Elph. and Hai. MSS. much and singular divergence was discovered.

I venture to suggest what appears to me to explain M. de Courteille's acceptance of the Rescue passage. Down to its insertion, the Kehr-Ilminsky text is so continuously and so curiously corrupt that it seems necessary to regard it as being a re-translation into Turki from one of the Persian translations of the *Babur-nama*. There being these textual defects in it, it would create on the mind of a reader initiated through it, only, in the book, an incorrect impression of Babur's style and vocabulary, and such a reader would feel no transition when passing on from it to the Rescue passage.

In opposition to this explanation, it might be said that a wrong standard set up by the corrupt text, would or could be changed by the excellence of later parts of the Kehr-Ilminsky one. In words, this is sound, no doubt, and such reflex crit-icism is now easy, but more than the one defective MS. was wanted even to suggest the need of such reflex criticism. The *Babur-nama* is lengthy, ponderous to poise and grasp, and work on it is still tentative, even with the literary gains since the Seventies.

Few of the grounds which weigh with us for the rejection of the Rescue passage were known to Dr. Ilminsky or M. de Courteille;—the two good Codices bring each its own and varied help; Teufel's critique on the "Fragments," though made without acquaintance with those adjuncts as they stand in Kehr's own volume, is of much collateral value; several useful oriental histories seem not to have been available for M. de Courteille's use. I may add, for my own part, that I have the great advantage of my husband's companionship and the guidance of his wide acquaintance with related oriental books. In truth, looking at the drawbacks now removed, an earlier acceptance of the passage appears as natural as does today's rejection.

GROUNDS FOR REJECTING THE RESCUE PASSAGE.

The grounds for rejecting the passage need here little more than recapitulation from my husband's article in the JASB. 1910, p. 221, and are as follows;—

i. The passage is in neither of the *Waqi'at-i-baburi*.

ii. The dreams detailed are too à propos and marvellous for credence.

iii. Khwaja Yahya is not known to have had a son, named Ya'qub.

iv. The *Babur-nama* does not contain the names assigned to the rescuers.

v. The Khans were not in Andijan and Babur did not go there.

vi. He did not set out for Khurasan after spending 4 months with The Khans but after Ahmad's death (end of 909 AH.), while Mahmud was still in Eastern Turkistan and after about a year's stay in Sukh.

vii. The followers who gathered to him were not "more than 300" but between 2 and 300.

viii. The "3 days," and the "day and two nights," and the "5 days" journey was one of some 70 miles, and one recorded as made in far less time.

ix. The passage is singularly inadequate to fill a gap of 14 to 16 months, during which events of the first importance occurred to Babur and to the Chaghatai dynasty.

x. Khwaja *Ahrari's* promises did nothing to fulfil Babur's wishes for 908 AH. while those of Ya'qub for immediate victory were closely followed by defeat and exile. Babur knew the facts; the passage cannot be his. It looks as though the writer saw Babur in Karnan across Timurid success in Hindustan.

xi. The style and wording of the passage are not in harmony with those of the true text.

Other reasons for rejection are marked change in choice of the details chosen for commemoration, *e.g.* when Babur mentions prayer, he does so simply; when he tells a dream, it seems a real one. The passage leaves the impression that the writer did not think in Turki, composed in it with difficulty, and looked at life from another view-point than Babur's.

On these various grounds, we have come to the conclusion that it is no part of the *Babur-nama*.

[APPENDICES TO THE KABUL SECTION]

E.—NAGARAHAR AND NING-NAHAR.

THOSE who consult books and maps about the riverain tract between the Safed-koh (Spin-ghur) and (Anglicé) the Kabul-river find its name in several forms, the most common being Nangrahar and Nangnahar (with variant vowels). It would be useful to establish a European book-name for the district. As European opinion differs about the origin and meaning of the names now in use, and as a good deal of interesting circumstance gathers round the small problem of a correct form (there may be two), I offer about the matter what has come into the restricted field of my own work, premising that I do this merely as one who drops a casual pebble on the cairn of observation already long rising for scholarly examination.

a. The origin and meaning of the names.

I have met with three opinions about the origin and meaning of the names found now and earlier. To each one of them obvious objection can be made. They are:—

1. That all forms now in use are corruptions of the Sanscrit word Nagarahara, the name of the Town-of-towns which in the *du-ab* of the Baran-su and Surkh-rud left the ruins Masson describes in Wilson's *Ariana Antiqua*. But if this is so, why is the Town-of-towns multiplied into the nine of Na-nagrahar (Nangrahar)?[1]

2. That the names found represent Sanscrit *nawa vihara*, nine monasteries, an opinion the Gazetteer of India of 1907 has

---

[1] Another but less obvious objection will be mentioned later.

adopted from Bellew. But why precisely nine monasteries? Nine appears an understatement.

3. That Nang (Ning or Nung) -nahar verbally means nine streams, (Babur's Tuquz-rud,) an interpretation of long standing (Section *b infra*). But whence *nang, ning, nung*, for nine? Such forms are not in Persian, Turki or Pushtu dictionaries, and, as Sir G. A. Grierson assures me, do not come into the Linguistic Survey.

b. On nang, ning, nung for nine.

Spite of their absence from the natural homes of words, however, the above sounds have been heard and recorded as symbols of the number nine by careful men through a long space of time.

The following instances of the use of "Nangnahar" show this, and also show that behind the variant forms there may be not a single word but two of distinct origin and sense.

1. In Chinese annals two names appear as those of the district and town (I am not able to allocate their application with certainty). The first is Na-kie-lo-ho-lo, the second Nang-g-lo-ho-lo and these, I understand to represent Nagarahara and Nang-nahar, due allowance being made for Chinese idiosyncrasy.[1]

2. Some 900 years later (1527–30 AD.) Babur also gives two names, Nagarahar (as the book-name of his *tuman*) and Ning-nahar.[2] He says the first is found in several histories (B.N. f. 131*b*); the second will have been what he heard and also presumably what appeared in revenue accounts; of it he says, "it is nine torrents" (*tuquz-rud*).

3. Some 300 years after Babur, Elphinstone gives two

1 Julien notes (*Voyages des pélerins Bouddhistes*, ii, 96), "Dans les annales des Song on trouve Nang-go-lo-ho, qui répond exactement à l'orthographe indienne Nangarahara, que fournit l'inscription découverte par le capitaine Kittoe" (JASB. 1848). The reference is to the Ghoswara inscription, of which Professor Kielhorn has also written (*Indian Antiquary*, 1888), but with departure from Nangarahara to Nagarahara.

2 The scribe of the Haidarabad Codex appears to have been somewhat uncertain as to the spelling of the name. What is found in histories is plain, N:g:r:har. The other name name; on first appearance (fol. 131*b*) and also on fols. 144 and 154*b*, there is a vagrant dot below the word, which if it were above would make Ning-nahar. In all other cases the word reads N:g:nahar. Nahar is a constant component, as is also the letter *g* (or *k*).

names for the district, neither of them being Babur's book-name, "Nangrahaur[1] or Nungnahaur, from the nine streams which issue from the Safed-koh, *nung* in Pushtoo signifying *nine*, and *nahaura*, a stream" (*Caubul*, i, 160).

4. In 1881 Colonel H. S. Tanner had heard, in Nur-valley on the north side of the Kabul-water, that the name of the opposite district was Ning-nahar and its meaning Nine-streams. He did not get a list of the nine and all he heard named do not flow from Safed-koh.

5. In 1884 Colonel H. G. McGregor gives two names with their explanation, "Ningrahar and Nungnihar; the former is a corruption of the latter word[2] which in the Afghan language signifies nine rivers or rivulets." He names nine, but of them six only issue from Safed-koh.

6. I have come across the following instances in which the number nine is represented by other words than *na* (*ni* or *nu*); *viz.* the *nenhan* of the Chitrali Kafir and the *noun* of the Panjabi, recorded by Leech,—the *nyon* of the Khowari and the *huncha* of the Boorishki, recorded by Colonel Biddulph.

The above instances allow opinion that in the region concerned and through a long period of time, nine has been expressed by *nang* (*ning* or *nung*) and other nasal or high palatal sounds, side by side with *na* (*ni* or *nu*). The whole matter may be one of nasal utterance,[3] but since a large number of tribesmen express nine by a word containing a nasal sound, should that word not find place in lists of recognized symbols of sounds?

c. Are there two names of distinct origin?

1. Certainly it makes a well-connected story of decay in the Sanscrit word Nagarahara to suppose that tribesmen, prone by their organism to nasal utterance, pronounced that word

1 Some writers express the view that the medial *r* in this word indicates descent from Nagarahara, and that the medial *n* of Elphinstone's second form is a corruption of it. Though this might be, it is true also that in local speech *r* and *n* often interchange, *e.g.* Chighar- and Chighan-sarai, Suhar and Suhan (in Nur-valley).

2 This asserts *n* to be the correct consonant, and connects with the interchange of *n* and *r* already noted.

3 Since writing the above I have seen Laidlaw's almost identical suggestion of a nasal interpolated in Nagarahara (JASB. 1848, art. on Kittoe). The change is of course found elsewhere; is not Tank for Taq an instance?

Nangrahar, and by force of their numbers made this corruption current,—that this was recognized as the name of the town while the Town-of-towns was great or in men's memory, and that when through the decay of the town its name became a meaningless husk, the wrong meaning of the Nine-streams should enter into possession.

But as another and better one can be put together, this fair-seeming story may be baseless. Its substitute has the advantage of explaining the double sequence of names shown in Section *b*.

The second story makes all the variant names represent one or other of two distinct originals. It leaves Nagrahar to represent Nagarahara, the dead town; it makes the nine torrents of Safed-koh the primeval sponsors of Ning-nahar, the name of the riverain tract. Both names, it makes contemporary in the relatively brief interlude of the life of the town. For the fertilizing streams will have been the dominant factors of settlement and of revenue from the earliest times of population and government. They arrest the eye where they and their ribbons of cultivation space the riverain waste; they are obvious units for grouping into a sub-government. Their name has a counterpart in adjacent Panj-ab; the two may have been given by one dominant power, how long ago, in what tongue matters not. The riverain tract, by virtue of its place on a highway of transit, must have been inhabited long before the town Nagarahara was built, and must have been known by a name. What better one than Nine-streams can be thought of?

2. Bellew is quoted by the Gazetteer of India (ed. 1907) as saying, in his argument in favour of *nawa vihara*, that no nine streams are found to stand sponsor, but modern maps shew nine outflows from Safed-koh to the Kabul-river between the Surkh-rud and Daka, while if affluents to the former stream be reckoned, more than nine issue from the range.[1]

Against Bellew's view that there are not nine streams, is the long persistence of the number nine in the popular name (Sect. *b*).

1 These affluents I omit from main consideration as sponsors because they are less obvious units of taxable land than the direct affluents of the Kabul-river, but they remain a reserve force of argument and may or may not have counted in Babur's nine.

It is also against his view that he supposes there were nine monasteries, because each of the nine must have had its fertilizing water.

Babur says there were nine; there must have been nine of significance; he knew his *tuman* not only by frequent transit but by his revenue accounts. A supporting point in those accounts is likely to have been that the individual names of the villages on the nine streams would appear, with each its payment of revenue.

3. In this also is some weight of circumstance against taking Nagarahara to be the parent of Ning-nahar:—An earlier name of the town is said to be Udyanapura, Garden town.[1] Of this Babur's Adinapur is held to be a corruption; the same meaning of garden has survived on approximately the same ground in Bala-bagh and Rozabad.

Nagarahara is seen, therefore, to be a parenthetical name between others which are all derived from gardens. It may shew the promotion of a "Garden-town" to a "Chief-town". If it did this, there was relapse of name when the Chief-town lost status. Was it ever applied beyond the delta? If it were, would it, when dead in the delta, persist along the riverain tract? If it were not, *cadit quæstio*; the suggestion of two names distinct in origin, is upheld.

Certainly the riverain tract would fall naturally under the government of any town flourishing in the delta, the richest and most populous part of the region. But for this very reason it must have had a name older than parenthetical Nagarahara. That inevitable name would be appropriately Ning-nahar (or Na-nahar) Nine-streams; and for a period Nagarahara would be the Chief-town of the district of Na-nahar (Nine-streams).[2]

d. Babur's statements about the name.

What the cautious Babur says of his *tuman* of Ning-nahar has weight:—

1. That some histories write it Nagarahar (Haidarabad Codex, f. 131*b*);

1 Cunningham, i, 42. My topic does not reach across the Kabul-river to the greater Udyanapura of Beal's *Buddhist Records* (p. 119) nor raise the question of the extent of that place.
2 The strong form Ning-nahar is due to euphonic impulse.

2. That Ning-nahar is nine torrents, *i.e.* mountain streams, *tuquz-rud*;

3. That (the) nine torrents issue from Safed-koh (f. 132 *b*).

Of his first statement can be said, that he will have seen the book-name in histories he read, but will have heard Ning-nahar, probably also have seen it in current letters and accounts.

Of his second,—that it bears and may be meant to bear two senses, (*a*) that the *tuman* consisted of nine torrents,—their lands implied; just as he says "Asfara is four *buluks*" (sub-divisions f. 3*b*)—(*b*) that *tuquz rud* translates *ning-nahar*.

Of his third,—that in English its sense varies as it is read with or without the definite article Turki rarely writes, but that either sense helps out his first and second, to mean that verbally and by its constituent units Ning-nahar is nine-torrents; as verbally and by its constituents Panj-ab is five-waters.

e. Last words.

Detailed work on the Kabul section of the *Babur-nama* has stamped two impressions so deeply on me, that they claim mention, not as novel or as special to myself, but as set by the work.

The first is of extreme risk in swift decision on any problem of words arising in North Afghanistan, because of its local concourse of tongues, the varied utterance of its unlettered tribes resident or nomad, and the frequent translation of proper names in obedience to their verbal meanings. Names lie there too in *strata*, relics of successive occupation—Greek, Turki, Hindi, Pushtu and tribes *galore*.

The second is that the region is an exceptionally fruitful field for first-hand observation of speech, the movent ocean of the uttered word, free of the desiccated symbolism of alphabets and books.

The following books, amongst others, have prompted the above note:—

Ghoswara Inscription, Kittoe, JASB., 1848, and Kielhorn, *Indian Antiquary*, 1888, p. 311.

H. Sastri's *Ramacarita*, Introduction, p. 7 (ASB. Memoirs).

Cunningham's *Ancient India*, vol. i.

Beal's *Buddhist Records*, i, xxxiv, and cii, 91.

Leech's Vocabularies, JASB., 1838.

The writings of Masson (*Travels* and *Ariana Antiqua*), Wood, Vigne, etc.

Raverty's *Tabaqat-i-nasiri*.

Jarrett's *Ayin-i-akbari*.

P.R.G.S. for maps, 1879; Macnair on the Kafirs, 1884; Tanner's *On the Chugani and neighbouring tribes of Kafiristan*, 1881.

Simpson's *Nagarahara*, JASB., xiii.

Biddulph's *Dialects of the Hindu-kush*, JRAS.

Gazette of India, 1907, art. Jalalabad.

Bellew's *Races of Afghanistan*.

F.—ON THE NAME DARA-I-NUR.

SOME European writers have understood the name Dara-i-nur to mean Valley of light, but natural features and also the artificial one mentioned by Colonel H. G. Tanner (*infra*), make it better to read the component *nur*, not as Persian *nur*, light, but as Pushtu *nur*, rock. Hence it translates as Valley of Rocks, or Rock-valley. The region in which the valley lies is rocky and boulder-strewn; its own waters flow to the Kabul-river east of the water of Chitral. It shews other names composed with *nur*, in which *nur* suits if it means rock, but is inexplicable if it means light, *e.g.* Nur-lam (Nur-fort), the master-fort in the mouth of Nur-valley, standing high on a rock between two streams, as Babur and Tanner have both described it from eye-witness,— Nur-gal (village), a little to the north-west of the valley,— Aulugh-nur (great rock), at a crossing mentioned by Babur, higher up the Baran-water,—and Koh-i-nur (Rocky-mountains), which there is ground for taking as the correct form of the familiar "Kunar" of some European writers (Raverty's *Notes*, p. 106). The dominant feature in these places dictates reading *nur* as rock; so too the work done in Nur-valley with boulders, of which Colonel H. G. Tanner's interesting account is subjoined (P.R.G.S. 1881, p. 284).

"Some 10 miles from the source of the main stream of the Nur-valley the Dameneh stream enters, but the waters of the two never meet; they flow side by side about three-quarters of a mile apart for about 12 miles and empty themselves into the Kunar river by different mouths, each torrent hugging closely the foot of the hills at its own side of the valley. Now, except in countries where terracing has been practised continuously for thousands of years, such unnatural topography as exists in the valley of Nur is next to impossible. The forces which were sufficient to scoop out the valley in the first instance, would have kept a water-way at the lowest part, into which would have poured the drainage of the surrounding mountains; but in the Nur-valley long-continued terracing has gradually raised the centre of the valley high above the edges. The population has increased to its maximum limit and every available inch of ground is required for cultivation; the people, by means of terrace-walls built of ponderous boulders in the bed of the original single stream, have little by little pushed the waters out of their true course, until they run, where now found, in deep rocky cuttings at the foot of the hills on either side" (p. 280).

"I should like to go on and say a good deal more about boulders; and while I am about it I may as well mention one that lies back from a hamlet in Shulut, which is so big that a house is built in a fault or crack running across its face. Another pebble lies athwart the village and covers the whole of the houses from that side."

G.—ON THE NAMES OF TWO DARA-I-NUR WINES.

FROM the two names, Arat-tashi and Suhan (Suhar) -tashi, which Babur gives as those of two wines of the Dara-i-nur, it can be inferred that he read *nur* to mean rock. For if in them Turki *tash*, rock, be replaced by Pushtu *nur*, rock, two place-names emerge, Arat (-nuri) and Suhan (-nuri), known in the Nur-valley.

These may be villages where the wines were grown, but it would be quite exceptional for Babur to say that wines are called from their villages, or indeed by any name. He says here not where they grow but what they are called.

I surmise that he is repeating a joke, perhaps his own, perhaps a standing local one, made on the quality of the wines. For whether with *tash* or with *nur* (rock), the names can be translated as Rock-saw and Rock-file, and may refer to the rough and acid quality of the wines, rasping and setting the teeth on edge as does iron on stone.

The villages themselves may owe their names to a serrated edge or splintered pinnacle of weathered granite, in which local people, known as good craftsmen, have seen resemblance to tools of their trade.

H.—ON THE COUNTERMARK BIH BUD ON COINS.

AS coins of Sl. Husain Mirza *Bai-qara* and other rulers do actually bear the words *Bih bud*, Babur's statement that the name of Bihbud Beg was on the Mirza's coins acquires a numismatic interest which may make serviceable the following particulars concerning the passage and the beg.[1]

a. *The Turki passage* (Elph. MS. f. 135*b*; Haidarabad Codex f. 173*b*; Ilminsky p. 217).

For ease of reference the Turki, Persian and English version are subjoined:—

(1) *Yana Bihbud Beg aidi. Burunlar chuhra-jirga-si-da khidmat qilur aidi. Mirza-ning qazaqliqlarida khidmati baqib Bihbud Beg-ka bu 'inayatni qilib aidi kim tamgha u sikka-da aning ati aidi.*

(2) The Persian translation of 'Abdu'r-rahim (Muh. Shirazi's lith. ed. p. 110):—

Digar Bihbud Beg bud. Auwalha dar jirga-i-chuhraha khidmat mikard. Chun dar qazaqiha Mirzara khidmat karda bud u anra mulahaza namuda, ainra 'inayat karda bud kah dar tamghanat sikka[2] nam-i-au bud.

(3) A literal English translation of the Turki:—

Another was Bihbud Beg. He served formerly in the *chuhra-jirga-si* (corps of braves). Looking to his service in the Mirza's guerilla-times, the favour had been done to Bihbud Beg that his name was on the stamp and coin.[3]

b. *Of Bihbud Beg.*

We have found little so far to add to what Babur tells of Bihbud Beg and what he tells we have not found elsewhere. The likely sources of his information are Daulat Shah and Khwand-amir who have written at length of Husain *Bai-qara*. Considerable search in the books of both men has failed to discover mention of signal service or public honour connected with the beg. Babur may have heard what he tells in Harat in 912 AH. (1506 AD.) when he would see Husain's coins

1 Some discussion about these coins has already appeared in JRAS. 1913 and 1914 from Dr. Codrington, Mr. M. Longworth Dames and my husband.
2 This variant from the Turki may be significant. Should *tamghanat(-i-)sikka* be read and does this describe countermarking?
3 It will be observed that Babur does not explicitly say that Husain put the beg's name on the coin.

presumably; but later opportunity to see them must have been frequent during his campaigns and visits north of Hindu-kush, notably in Balkh.

The sole mention we have found of Bihbud Beg in the *Habibu's-siyar* is that he was one of Husain's commanders at the battle of Chikman-sarai which was fought with Sl. Mahmud Mirza *Miranshahi* in Muharram 876 AH. (June–July 1471 AD.).[1] His place in the list shews him to have had importance. "Amir Nizamu'd-din 'Ali-sher's brother Darwesh-i-'ali the librarian (*q.v.* Hai. Codex Index), and Amir Bihbud, and Muh. 'Ali *ataka*, and Bakhshika, and Shah Wali *Qipchaq*, and Dost-i-muhammad *chuhra*, and Amir Qul-i-'ali, and" (another).

The total of our information about the man is therefore:—

(1) That when Husain[2] from 861 to 873 AH. (1457 to 1469 AD.) was fighting his way up to the throne of Harat, Bihbud served him well in the corps of braves, (as many others will have done).

(2) That he was a beg and one of Husain's commanders in 876 AH. (1471 AD.).

(3) That Babur includes him amongst Husain's begs and says of him what has been quoted, doing this *circa* 934 AH. (1528 AD.), some 56 years after Khwand-amir's mention of him *s.a.* 876 AH. (1471 AD.).

c. Of the term chuhra-jirga-si used by Babur.

Of this term Babur supplies an explicit explanation which I have not found in European writings. His own book amply exemplifies his explanation, as do also Khwand-amir's and Haidar's.

He gives the explanation (f. 15*b*) when describing a retainer of his father's who afterwards became one of his own begs. It is as follows:—

"'Ali-darwesh of Khurasan served in the Khurasan *chuhra-jirga-si*, one of two special corps (*khasa tabin*) of serviceable braves (*yarar yigitlar*) formed by Sl. Abu-sa'id Mirza when

1 *Habibu's-siyar* lith. ed. iii, 228; *Haidarabad* Codex text and trs. f. 26*b* and f. 169; Browne's Daulat Shah p. 533.
2 Husain born 842 AH. (1438 AD.); d. 911 AH. (1506 AD.).

he first began to arrange the government of Khurasan and Samarkand and, presumably, called by him the Khurasan corps and the Samarkand corps."

This shews the circle to have consisted of fighting-men, such serviceable braves as are frequently mentioned by Babur; and his words "*yarar yigit*" make it safe to say that if instead of using a Persian phrase, he had used a Turki one, *yigit*, brave would have replaced *chuhra*, "young soldier" (Erskine). A considerable number of men on active service are styled *chuhra*, one at least is styled *yigit*, in the same way as others are styled *beg*.[1]

Three military circles are mentioned in the *Babur-nama*, consisting respectively of braves, household begs (under Babur's own command), and great begs. Some men are mentioned who never rose from the rank of brave (*yigit*), some who became household-begs, some who went through the three grades.

Of the corps of braves Babur conveys the information that Abu-sa'id founded it at a date which will have lain between 1451 and 1457 AD.; that 'Umar Shaikh's man 'Ali-darwesh belonged to it; and that Husain's man Bihbud did so also. Both men, 'Ali-darwesh and Bihbud, when in its circle, would appropriately be styled *chuhra* as men of the beg-circle were styled beg; the Dost-i-muhammad *chuhra* who was a commander, (he will have had a brave's command,) at Chikman-sarai (*see* list *supra*) will also have been of this circle. Instances of the use by Babur of the name *khasa-tabin* and its equivalent *bui-tikini* are shewn on f. 209 and f. 210. A considerable number of Babur's fighting men, the braves he so frequently mentions as sent on service, are styled *chuhra* and inferentially belong to the same circle.[2]

---

1 Cf. f. 7b note to braves (*yigitlar*). There may be instances, in the earlier Farghana section where I have translated *chuhra* wrongly by *page*. My attention had not then been fixed on the passage about the coins, nor had I the same familiarity with the Kabul section. For a household page to be clearly recognizable as such from the context, is rare—other uses of the word are translated as their context dictates.

2 They can be traced through my Index and in some cases their careers followed. Since I translated *chuhra-jirga-si* on f. 15 by cadet-corps, I have found in the Kabul section instances of long service in the corps which make the word cadet, as it is used in English, too young a name.

d. Of Bih bud on Husain Bai-qara's coins.

So far it does not seem safe to accept Babur's statement literally. He may tell a half-truth and obscure the rest by his brevity.

Nothing in the sources shows ground for signal and public honour to Bihbud Beg, but a good deal would allow surmise that jesting allusion to his name might decide for *Bih bud* as a coin mark when choice had to be made of one, in the flush of success, in an assembly of the begs, and, amongst those begs, lovers of word-play and enigma.

The personal name is found written Bihbud, as one word and with medial *h*; the mark is *Bih bud* with the terminal *h* in the *Bih*. There have been discussions moreover as to whether to read on the coins *Bih bud*, it was good, or *Bih buvad*, let it be, or become, good (valid for currency?).

The question presents itself; would the beg's name have appeared on the coins, if it had not coincided in form with a suitable coin-mark?

Against literal acceptance of Babur's statement there is also doubt of a thing at once so *ben trovato* and so unsupported by evidence.

Another doubt arises from finding *Bih bud* on coins of other rulers, one of Iskandar Khan's being of a later date,[1] others, of Timur, Shahrukh and Abu-sa'id, with nothing to shew who counterstruck it on them.

On some of Husain's coins the sentence *Bih bud* appears as part of the legend and not as a counterstrike. This is a good basis for finding a half-truth in Babur's statement. It does not allow of a whole-truth in his statement because, as it is written, it is a coin-mark, not a name.

An interesting matter as bearing on Husain's use of *Bih bud* is that in 865 AH. (1461 AD.) he had an incomparable horse named Bihbud, one he gave in return for a falcon on making peace with Mustapha Khan.[2]

1 This Mr. M. Longworth Dames pointed out in JRAS. 1913.
2 *Habibu's-siyar* lith. ed. iii, 219; Ferté trs. p. 28. For the information about Husain's coins given in this appendix I am indebted to Dr. Codrington and Mr. M. Longworth Dames.

e. Of Babur's vassal-coinage.

The following historical details narrow the field of numismatic observation on coins believed struck by Babur as a vassal of Isma'il *Safawi*. They are offered because not readily accessible.

The length of Babur's second term of rule in Transoxiana was not the three solar years of the B.M. Coin Catalogues but did not exceed eight months. He entered Samarkand in the middle of Rajab 917 AH. (*c.* Oct. 1st, 1511 AD.). He returned to it defeated and fled at once, after the battle of Kul-i-malik which was fought in Safar 918 AH. (mid-April to mid-May 1512 AD.). Previous to the entry he was in the field, without a fixed base; after his flight he was landless till at the end both of 920 AH. and of 1514 AD. he had returned to Kabul.

He would not find a full Treasury in Samarkand because the Auzbegs evacuated the fort at their own time; eight months would not give him large tribute in kind. He failed in Transoxiana because he was the ally of a Shi'a; would coins bearing the Shi'a legend have passed current from a Samarkand mint? These various circumstances suggest that he could not have struck many coins of any kind in Samarkand.

The coins classed in the B.M. Catalogues as of Babur's vassalage, offer a point of difficulty to readers of his own writings, inasmuch as neither the "Sultan Muhammad" of No. 652 (gold), nor the "Sultan Babur Bahadur" of the silver coins enables confident acceptance of them as names he himself would use.

I.—ON THE WEEPING-WILLOWS OF f. 190*b*.

THE passage omitted from f. 190*b*, which seems to describe something decorative done with weeping willows, (*bed-i-mawallah*) has been difficult to all translators. This may be due to inaccurate pointing in Babur's original MS. or may be what a traveller seeing other willows at another feast could explain.

The first Persian translation omits the passage (I.O. 215 f. 154*b*); the second varies from the Turki, notably by changing *sach* and *saj* to *shakh* throughout (I.O. 217 f. 150*b*). The English and French translations differ much (*Memoirs* p. 206, *Mémoires* i, 414), the latter taking the *mawallah* to be *mula*, a hut, against which much is clear in the various MSS.

Three Turki sources[1] agree in reading as follows:—

Mawallahlar-ni (or *muwallah* Hai. MS.) *kilturdilar. Bilman sachlari-ning ya 'amli sachlari-ning aralarigha k:msan-ni* (Ilminsky, *kaman*) *shakh-ning* (Hai. MS. *sakh*) *auzunlughi bila ainjiga ainjiga kisib, quiub turlar.*

The English and French translations differ from the Turki and from one another:—

(*Memoirs*, p. 206) They brought in branching willow-trees. I do not know if they were in the natural state of the tree, or if the branches were formed artificially, but they had small twigs cut the length of the ears of a bow and inserted between them.

(*Mémoires* i, 434) On façonna des huttes (*mouleh*). Ils les établissent en taillant des baguettes minces, de la longeur du bout recourbé de l'arc, qu'on place entre des branches naturelles ou façonnées artificiellement, je l'ignore.

The construction of the sentence appears to be thus:—*Mawallahlar-ni kilturdilar*, they brought weeping-willows; *k:msan-ni quiubturlar*, they had put *k:msan-ni*; *ainjiga ainjiga kisib*, cut very fine (or slender); *shakh* (or *sakh*)-*ning auzunlughi*, of the length of a *shakh*, bow, or *sakh* …; *bilman sachlari-ning ya'amli sachlari-ning aralarigha*, to (or at) the spaces of the *sachlar* whether their (*i.e.* the willows') own or artificial *sachlar*.

These translations clearly indicate felt difficulty. Mr. Erskine does not seem to have understood that the trees were *Salix babylonica*. The crux of the passage is the word *k:msan-ni*, which tells what was placed in the spaces. It has been read as *kaman*, bow, by all but the scribes of the two good Turki MSS. and as in a phrase *horn of a bow*. This however is not allowed by the Turki, for the reason that *k:msan-ni* is not in the genitive but in the accusative case. (I may say that Babur does not use *ni* for *ning*; he keeps strictly to the prime uses of each enclitic,

1 Elphinstone MS. f. 150*b*; Haidarabad MS. f. 190*b*; Ilminsky, imprint p. 241.

ni accusative, *ning* genitive.) Moreover, if *k:msan-ni* be taken as a genitive, the verbs *quiub-turlar* and *kisib* have no object, no other accusative appearing in the sentence than *k:msan-ni*.

A weighty reason against changing *sach* into *shakh* is that Dr. Ilminsky has not done so. He must have attached meaning to *sach* since he uses it throughout the passage. He was nearer the region wherein the original willows were seen at a feast. Unfortunately nothing shows how he interpreted the word.

Sachmaq is a tassel; is it also a catkin and were there decorations, *kimsan-ni* (things *kimsa*, or flowers Ar. *kim*, or something shining, *kimcha*, gold brocade) hung in between the catkins?

Ilminsky writes *mu'lah* (with *hamza*) and this de Courteille translates by hut. The Hai. MS. writes *muwallah* (marking the *zamma*).

In favour of reading *mawallah* (*mulah*) as a tree and that tree *Salix babylonica* the weeping-willow, there are annotations in the Second Persian translation and, perhaps following it, in the Elphinstone MS. of *nam-i-dirakht*, name of a tree, *didan-i-bed*, sight of the willow, *bed-i-mawallah*, mournful-willow. Standing alone *mawallah* means weeping-willow, in this use answering to *majnun* the name Panj-abis give the tree, from Leila's lover the distracted *i.e.* Majnun (Brandis).

The whole question may be solved by a chance remark from a traveller witnessing similar festive decoration at another feast in that conservative region.

J.—ON BABUR'S EXCAVATED CHAMBER AT QANDAHAR (f. 208*b*).

SINCE making my note (f. 208*b*) on the wording of the passage in which Babur mentions excavation done by him at Qandahar, I have learned that he must be speaking of the vaulted chamber containing the celebrated inscriptions about which much has been written.[1]

The primary inscription, the one commemorating Babur's final possession of Qandahar, gives the chamber the character of a Temple of Victory and speaks of it as *Rawaq-i-jahan namai*, World-shewing-portal,[2] doubtless because of its conspicuous position and its extensive view, probably also in allusion to its declaration of victory. Mir Ma'sum writes of it as a Pesh-taq, frontal arch, which, coupled with Mohan Lall's word arch (*taq*) suggests that the chamber was entered through an arch pierced in a parallelogram smoothed on the rock and having resemblance to the *pesh-taq* of buildings, a suggestion seeming the more probable that some inscriptions are on the "wings" of the arch. But by neither of the above-mentioned names do Mohan Lall and later travellers call the chamber or write of the place; all describe it by its approach of forty steps, Chihil-zina.[3]

The excavation has been chipped out of the white-veined limestone of the bare ridge on and below which stood Old Qandahar. It does not appear from the descriptions to have been on the summit of the ridge; Bellew says that the forty steps start half-way up the height. I have found no estimate of the height of the ridge, or statement that the steps end at the chamber. The ridge however seems to have been of noticeably dominating height. It rises steeply to the north and there ends in the naze of which Babur writes. The foot of the steps is guarded by two towers. Mohan Lall, unaccustomed to mountains, found their ascent steep and dizzy. The excavated chamber of the inscriptions, which Bellew describes as "bow-shaped and dome-roofed", he estimated as 12 feet at the highest point,

1 Muh. Ma'sum *Bhakkari's Tarikh-i-sind* 1600, Malet's Trs. 1855, p. 89; Mohan Lall's *Journal* 1834, p. 279 and *Travels* 1846, p. 311; Bellew's *Political Mission to Afghanistan* 1857, p. 232; *Journal Asiatique* 1890, Darmesteter's *La grande inscription de Qandahar*, JRAS. 1898, Beames' *Geography of the Qandahar inscription*. Murray's *Hand-book of the Panjab etc.* 1883 has an account which as to the Inscriptions shares in the inaccuracies of its sources (Bellew & Lumsden).

2 The plan of Qandahar given in the official account of the Second Afghan War, makes Chihil-zina appear on the wrong side of the ridge, n.w. instead of n.e.

3 destroyed in 1714 AD. It lay 3 m. west of the present Qandahar (not its immediate successor). It must be observed that Darmesteter's insufficient help in plans and maps led him to identify Chihil-zina with Chihil-dukhtaran (Forty-daughters).

12 feet deep and 8 feet wide. Two sculptured beasts guard the entrance; Bellew calls them leopards but tigers would better symbolize the watch and ward of the Tiger Babur. In truth the whole work, weary steps of approach, tiger guardians, commemorative chamber, laboriously incised words, are admirably symbolic of his long-sustained resolve and action, taken always with Hindustan as the goal.

There are several inscriptions of varying date, within and without the chamber. Mohan Lall saw and copied them; Darmesteter worked on a copy; the two English observers Lumsden and Bellew made no attempt at correct interpretation. In the versions all give there are inaccuracies, arising from obvious causes, especially from want of historical *data*. The last word has not been said; revision awaits photography and the leisured expert. A part of the needed revision has been done by Beames, who deals with the geography of what Mir Ma'sum himself added under Akbar after he had gone as Governor to Qandahar in 1007 AH. (1598 AD.). This commemorates not Babur's but Akbar's century of cities.

It is the primary inscription only which concerns this Appendix. This is one in relief in the dome of the chamber, recording in florid Persian that Abu'l-ghazi Babur took possession of Qandahar on Shawwal 13th 928 AH. (Sep. 1st 1522 AD.), that in the same year he commanded the construction of this *Rawaq-i-jahan-namai*, and that the work had been completed by his son Kamran at the time he made over charge of Qandahar to his brother 'Askari in 9 . . (mutilated). After this the gravure changes in character.

In the above, Babur's title Abu'l-ghazi fixes the date of the inscription as later than the battle of Kanwaha (f. 324b), because it was assumed in consequence of this victory over a Hindu, in March 1527 (Jumada II 933 AH.).

The mutilated date 9 . . is given by Mohan Lall as 952 AH. but this does not suit several circumstances, *e.g.* it puts completion too far beyond the time mentioned as consumed by the work, nine years,—and it was not that at which Kamran made over charge to 'Askari, but followed the expulsion of both full-brothers from Qandahar by their half-brother Humayun.

The mutilated date 9 . . is given by Darmesteter as 933 AH. but this again does not fit the historical circumstance that Kamran was in Qandahar after that date and till 937 AH. This date (937 AH.) we suggest as fitting to replace the lost figures, (1) because in that year and after his father's death, Kamran gave the town to 'Askari and went himself to Hindustan, and (2) because work begun in 928 AH. and recorded as occupying 70–80 men for nine years would be complete in 937 AH.[1] The inscription would be one of the last items of the work.

The following matters are added here because indirectly connected with what has been said and because not readily accessible.

a. Birth of Kamran.

Kamran's birth falling in a year of one of the Babur-nama gaps, is nowhere mentioned. It can be closely inferred as 914 or 915 AH. from the circumstances that he was younger than Humayun born late in 913 AH., that it is not mentioned in the fragment of the annals of 914 AH., and that he was one of the children enumerated by Gul-badan as going with her father to Samarkand in 916 AH. (Probably the children did not start with their father in the depth of winter across the mountains.) Possibly the joyful name Kamran is linked to the happy issue of the Mughul rebellion of 914 AH. Kamran would thus be about 18 when left in charge of Kabul and Qandahar by Babur in 932 AH. before the start for the fifth expedition to Hindustan.

A letter from Babur to Kamran in Qandahar is with Kehr's Latin version of the Babur-nama, in Latin and entered on the lining of the cover. It is shewn by its main topic viz. the despatch of Ibrahim Ludi's son to Kamran's charge, to date somewhere close to Jan. 3rd 1527 (Rabi'u'l-awwal 29th 933 AH.) because on that day Babur writes of the despatch (Hai. Codex f. 307 foot).

Presumably the letter was with Kamran's own copy of the Babur-nama. That copy may have reached Humayun's hands

1 Tarikh-i-rashidi trs. p. 387; Akbar-nama trs. i, 290.

(JRAS 1908 p. 828 *et seq.*). The next known indication of the letter is given in St. Petersburg by Dr. Kehr. He will have seen it or a copy of it with the B.N. Codex he copied (one of unequal correctness), and he, no doubt, copied it in its place on the fly-leaf or board of his own transcript, but if so, it has disappeared.

Fuller particulars of it and of other items accompanying it are given in JRAS 1908 p. 828 *et seq.*

K.—AN AFGHAN LEGEND.

MY husband's article in the Asiatic Quarterly Review of April 1901 begins with an account of the two MSS. from which it is drawn, *viz.* I.O. 581 in Pushtu, I.O. 582 in Persian. Both are mainly occupied with an account of the Yusuf-zai. The second opens by telling of the power of the tribe in Afghanistan and of the kindness of Malik Shah Sulaiman, one of their chiefs, to Aulugh Beg Mirza *Kabuli*, (Babur's paternal uncle,) when he was young and in trouble, presumably as a boy ruler.

It relates that one day a wise man of the tribe, Shaikh 'Usman saw Sulaiman sitting with the young Mirza on his knee and warned him that the boy had the eyes of Yazid and would destroy him and his family as Yazid had destroyed that of the Prophet. Sulaiman paid him no attention and gave the Mirza his daughter in marriage. Subsequently the Mirza having invited the Yusuf-zai to Kabul, treacherously killed Sulaiman and 700 of his followers. They were killed at the place called Siyah-sang near Kabul; it is still known, writes the chronicler in about 1770 AD. (1184 AH.), as the Grave of the Martyrs. Their tombs are revered and that of Shaikh 'Usman in particular.

Shah Sulaiman was the eldest of the seven sons of Malik Taju'd–din; the second was Sultan Shah, the father of Malik Ahmad. Before Sulaiman was killed he made three requests of Aulugh Beg; one of them was that his nephew Ahmad's life might be spared. This was granted.

Aulugh Beg died (after ruling from 865 to 907 AH.), and Babur defeated his son-in-law and successor M. Muqim (*Arghun*, 910 AH.). Meantime the Yusuf-zai had migrated to Pashawar but later on took Sawad from Sl. Wais (Hai. Codex ff. 219, 220b, 221).

When Babur came to rule in Kabul, he at first professed friendship for the Yusuf-zai but became prejudiced against them through their enemies the Dilazak[1] who gave force to their charges by a promised subsidy of 70,000 *shahrukhi*. Babur therefore determined, says the Yusuf-zai chronicler, to kill Malik[2] Ahmad and so wrote him a friendly invitation to Kabul. Ahmad agreed to go, and set out with four brothers who were famous musicians. Meanwhile the Dilazak had persuaded Babur to put Ahmad to death at once, for they said Ahmad was so clever and eloquent that if allowed to speak, he would induce the Padshah to pardon him.

On Ahmad's arrival in Kabul, he is said to have learned that Babur's real object was his death. His companions wanted to tie their turbans together and let him down over the wall of the fort, but he rejected their proposal as too dangerous for him and them, and resolved to await his fate. He told his companions however, except one of the musicians, to go into hiding in the town.

Next morning there was a great assembly and Babur sat on the dais-throne. Ahmad made his reverence on entering but Babur's only acknowledgment was to make bow and arrow ready to shoot him. When Ahmad saw that Babur's intention was to shoot him down without allowing him to speak, he unbuttoned his jerkin and stood still before the Padshah. Babur, astonished, relaxed the tension of his bow and asked Ahmad what he meant. Ahmad's only reply was to tell the Padshah not to question him but to do what he intended. Babur again asked his meaning and again got the same reply.

1 Hai. Codex.
2 It is needless to say that a good deal in this story may be merely fear and supposition accepted as occurrence.

Babur put the same question a third time, adding that he could not dispose of the matter without knowing more. Then Ahmad opened the mouth of praise, expatiated on Babur's excellencies and said that in this great assemblage many of his subjects were looking on to see the shooting; that his jerkin being very thick, the arrow might not pierce it; the shot might fail and the spectators blame the Padshah for missing his mark; for these reasons he had thought it best to bare his breast. Babur was so pleased by this reply that he resolved to pardon Ahmad at once, and laid down his bow.

Said he to Ahmad, "What sort of man is Buhlul *Ludi*?" "A giver of horses," said Ahmad.

"And of what sort his son Sikandar?" "A giver of robes."

"And of what sort is Babur?" "He," said Ahmad, "is a giver of heads."

"Then," rejoined Babur, "I give you yours."

The Padshah now became quite friendly with Ahmad, came down from his throne, took him by the hand and led him into another room where they drank together. Three times did Babur have his cup filled, and after drinking a portion, give the rest to Ahmad. At length the wine mounted to Babur's head; he grew merry and began to dance. Meantime Ahmad's musician played and Ahmad who knew Persian well, poured out an eloquent harangue. When Babur had danced for some time, he held out his hands to Ahmad for a reward (*bakhshish*), saying, "I am your performer." Three times did he open his hands, and thrice did Ahmad, with a profound reverence, drop a gold coin into them. Babur took the coins, each time placing his hand on his head. He then took off his robe and gave it to Ahmad; Ahmad took off his own coat, gave it to Adu the musician, and put on what the Padshah had given.

Ahmad returned safe to his tribe. He declined a second invitation to Kabul, and sent in his stead his brother Shah Mansur. Mansur received speedy dismissal as Babur was displeased at Ahmad's not coming. On his return to his tribe Mansur advised them to retire to the mountains and make a strong *sangur*. This they did; as foretold, Babur came into their country with a large army. He devastated their lands but could make no impression on their fort. In order the better to judge of its character, he, as was his wont, disguised himself as a Qalandar, and went with friends one dark night to the Mahura hill where the stronghold was, a day's journey from the Padshah's camp at Diarun.

It was the 'Id-i-qurban and there was a great assembly and feasting at Shah Mansur's house, at the back of the Mahura-mountain, still known as Shah Mansur's throne. Babur went in his disguise to the back of the house and stood among the crowd in the courtyard. He asked servants as they went to and fro about Shah Mansur's family and whether he had a daughter. They gave him straightforward answers.

At the time Musammat Bibi Mubaraka, Shah Mansur's daughter was sitting with other women in a tent. Her eye fell on the qalandars and she sent a servant to Babur with some cooked meat folded between two loaves. Babur asked who had sent it; the servant said it was Shah Mansur's daughter Bibi Mubaraka. "Where is she?" "That is she, sitting in front of you in the tent." Babur Padshah became entranced with her beauty and asked the woman-servant, what was her disposition and her age and whether she was betrothed. The servant replied by extolling her mistress, saying that her virtue equalled her beauty, that she was pious and brimful of rectitude and placidity; also that she was not betrothed. Babur then left with his friends, and behind the house hid between two stones the food that had been sent to him.

He returned to camp in perplexity as to what to do; he saw he could not take the fort; he was ashamed to return to Kabul with nothing effected; moreover he was in the fetters of love. He therefore wrote in friendly fashion to Malik Ahmad and asked for the daughter of Shah Mansur, son of Shah Sulaiman. Great objection was made and earlier misfortunes accruing to Yusuf-zai chiefs who had given daughters to Aulugh Beg and Sl. Wais (Khan Mirza?) were quoted. They even said they had no daughter to give. Babur replied with a "beautiful" royal letter, told of his visit disguised to Shah Mansur's house, of his seeing Bibi Mubaraka and as token of the truth of his story, asked them to search for the food he had hidden. They searched and found. Ahmad and Mansur were still averse, but the tribesmen urged that as before they had always made sacrifice for the tribe so should they do now, for by giving the daughter in marriage, they would save the tribe from Babur's anger. The Maliks then said that it should be done "for the good of the tribe".

When their consent was made known to Babur, the drums of joy were beaten and preparations were made for the marriage; presents were sent to the bride, a sword of his also, and the two Maliks started out to escort her. They are said to have come from Thana by M'amura (?), crossed the river at Chakdara, taken a narrow road between two hills and past Talash-village to the back of Tiri (?) where the Padshah's escort met them. The Maliks returned, spent one night at Chakdara and next morning reached their homes at the Mahura *sangur*.

Meanwhile Runa the nurse who had control of Malik Mansur's household, with two other nurses and many male and female servants, went on with Bibi Mubaraka to the royal camp. The bride was set down with all honour at a large tent in the middle of the camp.

That night and on the following day the wives of the officers came to visit her but she paid them no attention. So, they said to one another as they were returning to their tents, "Her beauty is beyond question, but she has shewn us no kindness, and has not spoken to us; we do not know what mystery there is about her."

Now Bibi Mubaraka had charged her servants to let her know when the Padshah was approaching in order that she might receive him according to Malik Ahmad's instructions. They said to her, "That was the pomp just now of the Padshah's going to prayers at the general mosque." That same day after the Mid-day Prayer, the Padshah went towards her tent. Her servants informed her, she immediately left her divan and advancing, lighted up the carpet by her presence, and stood respectfully with folded hands. When the Padshah entered, she bowed herself before him. But her face remained entirely covered. At length the Padshah seated himself on the divan and said to her, "Come Afghaniya, be seated." Again she bowed before him, and stood as before. A second time he said, "Afghaniya, be seated." Again she prostrated herself before him and came a little nearer, but still stood. Then the Padshah pulled the veil from her face and beheld incomparable beauty. He was entranced, he said again, "O, Afghaniya, sit down." Then she bowed herself again, and said, "I have a petition to make. If an order be given, I will make it." The Padshah said kindly, "Speak." Whereupon she with both hands took up her dress and said, "Think that the whole Yusuf-zai tribe is enfolded in my skirt, and pardon their offences for my sake." Said the Padshah, "I forgive the Yusuf-zai all their offences in thy presence, and cast them all into thy skirt. Hereafter I shall have no ill-feeling to the Yusuf-zai." Again she bowed before him; the Padshah took her hand and led her to the divan.

When the Afternoon Prayer time came and the Padshah rose from the divan to go to prayers, Bibi Mubaraka jumped up and fetched him his shoes.[1] He put them on and said very pleasantly, "I am extremely pleased with you and your tribe and I have pardoned them all for your sake." Then he said with a smile, "We know it was Malik Ahmad taught you all these ways." He then went to prayers and the Bibi remained to say hers in the tent.

After some days the camp moved from Diarun and proceeded by Bajaur and Tanki to Kabul.[2] ...

Bibi Mubaraka, the Blessed Lady, is often mentioned by Gul-badan; she had no children; and lived an honoured life, as her chronicler says, until the beginning of Akbar's reign, when she died. Her brother Mir Jamal rose to honour under Babur, Humayun and Akbar.

1 Always left beyond the carpet on which a reception is held.
2 This is not in agreement with Babur's movements.

L.—ON MAHIM'S ADOPTION OF HIND-AL.

THE passage quoted below about Mahim's adoption of the
unborn Hind-al we have found so far only in Kehr's transcript
of the *Babur-nama* (*i.e.* the St. Petersburg Foreign Office Codex).
Ilminsky reproduced it (Kasan imprint p. 281) and de Courteille
translated it (ii, 45), both with endeavour at emendation. It is
interpolated in Kehr's MS. at the wrong place, thus indicating
that it was once marginal or apart from the text.

I incline to suppose the whole a note made by Humayun,
although part of it might be an explanation made by Babur, at
a later date, of an over-brief passage in his diary. Of such
passages there are several instances. What is strongly against its
being Babur's where otherwise it might be his, is that Mahim,
as he always calls her simply, is there written of as Hazrat
Walida, Royal Mother and with the honorific plural. That
plural Babur uses for his own mother (dead 14 years before
925 AH.) and never for Mahim. The note is as follows:—

"The explanation is this:—As up to that time those of one
birth (*tuqqan*, womb) with him (Humayun), that is to say a son
Bar-bul, who was younger than he but older than the rest, and
three daughters, Mihr-jan and two others, died in childhood,
he had a great wish for one of the same birth with him.[1] I had
said 'What it would have been if there had been one of the
same birth with him!' (Humayun). Said the Royal Mother,
'If Dil-dar Aghacha bear a son, how is it if I take him and rear
him?' 'It is very good' said I."

So far doubtfully *might* be Babur's but it may be Humayun's
written as a note for Babur. What follows appears to be by
some-one who knew the details of Mahim's household talk and
was in Kabul when Dil-dar's child was taken from her.

"Seemingly women have the custom of taking omens in the
following way:—When they have said, 'Is it to be a boy? is it

---

1 *i.e.* Humayun wished for a full-brother or sister, another child in the house
with him. The above names of his brother and sister are given elsewhere only by
Gul-badan (f. 6*b*).

to be a girl?' they write 'Ali or Hasan on one of two pieces of paper and Fatima on the other, put each paper into a ball of clay and throw both into a bowl of water. Whichever opens first is taken as an omen; if the man's, they say a man-child will be born; if the woman's, a girl will be born. They took the omen; it came out a man."

"On this glad tidings we at once sent letters off.[1] A few days later God's mercy bestowed a son. Three days before the news[2] and three days after the birth, they[3] took the child from its mother, (she) willy-nilly, brought it to our house[4] and took it in their charge. When we sent the news of the birth, Bhira was being taken. They named him Hind-al for a good omen and benediction."[5]

The whole may be Humayun's, and prompted by a wish to remove an obscurity his father had left and by sentiment stirred through reminiscence of a cherished childhood.

Whether Humayun wrote the whole or not, how is it that the passage appears only in the Russian group of Baburiana?

An apparent answer to this lies in the following little mosaic of circumstances:—The St. Petersburg group of Baburiana[6] is linked to Kamran's own copy of the *Babur-nama* by having with it a letter of Babur to Kamran and also what *may be* a note indicating its passage into Humayun's hands (JRAS 1908 p. 830). If it did so pass, a note by Humayun may have become associated with it, in one of several obvious ways. This would be at a date earlier than that of the Elphinstone MS. and would explain why it is found in Russia and not in Indian MSS.[7]

1 The "we" might be Mahim and Humayun, to Babur in camp.
2 Perhaps before announcing the birth anywhere.
3 Presumably this plural is honorific for the Honoured Mother Mahim.
4 Mahim's and Humayun's quarters.
5 Gul-badan's *Humayun-nama*, f. 8.
6 JRAS. A. S. Beveridge's Notes on *Babur-nama* MSS. 1900, [1902,] 1905, 1906, [1907,] 1908 (Kehr's transcript, p. 76, and Latin translation with new letter of Babur p. 828).
7 In all such matters of the *Babur-nama* Codices, it has to be remembered that their number has been small.

[APPENDICES TO THE HINDUSTAN SECTION]

M.—ON THE TERM *BAHRI QUTAS*.

THAT the term *bahri qutas* is interpreted by Meninski, Erskine, and de Courteille in senses so widely differing as *equus maritimus*, mountain–cow, and *bœuf vert de mer* is due, no doubt, to their writing when the *qutas*, the yak, was less well known than it now is.

The word *qutas* represents both the yak itself and its neck-tassel and tail. Hence Meninski explains it by *nodus fimbriatus ex cauda seu crinibus equi maritimi*. His "sea-horse" appears to render *bahri qutas*, and is explicable by the circumstance that the same purposes are served by horse-tails and by yak-tails and tassels, namely, with both, standards are fashioned, horse-equipage is ornamented or perhaps furnished with fly-flappers, and the ordinary hand–fly–flappers are made, *i.e.* the *chowries* of Anglo-India.

Erskine's "mountain-cow" (*Memoirs* p. 317) may well be due to his *munshi*'s giving the yak an alternative name, *viz. Kosh-gau* (Vigne) or *Khash-gau* (Ney Elias), which appears to mean mountain-cow (cattle, oxen).[1]

De Courteille's *Dictionary* p.422, explains *qutas* (*qutas*) as *bœuf marin* (*bahri qutas*) and his *Mémoires* ii, 191, renders Babur's *bahri qutas* by *bœuf vert de mer* (f. 276, p. 490 and n. 8).

The term *bahri qutas* could be interpreted with more confidence if one knew where the seemingly Arabic-Turki compound originated.[2] Babur uses it in Hindustan where the neck-tassel

---

1 Vigne's *Travels in Kashmir* ii, 277–8; *Tarikh-i-rashidi* trs., p. 302 and n. and p. 466 and note.

2 It is not likely to be one heard current in Hindustan, any more than is Babur's Ar. *bu-qalamun* as a name of a bird; both seem to be "book-words" and may be traced or known as he uses them in some ancient dictionary or book of travels originating outside Hindustan.

and the tail of the domestic yak are articles of commerce, and where, as also probably in Kabul, he will have known of the same class of yak as a saddle-animal and as a beast of burden into Kashmir and other border-lands of sufficient altitude to allow its survival. A part of its wide Central Asian habitat abutting on Kashmir is Little Tibet, through which flows the upper Indus and in which tame yak are largely bred, Skardo being a place specially mentioned by travellers as having them plentifully. This suggests that the term *bahri qutas* is due to the great river (*bahr*) and that those of which Babur wrote in Hindustan were from Little Tibet and its great river. But *bahri* may apply to another region where also the domestic yak abounds, that of the great lakes, inland seas such as Pangong, whence the yak comes and goes between *e.g.* Yarkand and the Hindustan border.

The second suggestion, *viz.* that "*bahri qutas*" refers to the habitat of the domestic yak in lake and marsh lands of high altitude (the wild yak also but, as Tibetan, it is less likely to be concerned here) has support in Dozy's account of the *bahri* falcon, a bird mentioned also by Abu'l-fazl amongst sporting birds (*Ayin-i-akbari*, Blochmann's trs. p. 295):—"*Bahri, espèce de faucon le meilleur pour les oiseaux de marais. Ce renseignement explique peut-être l'origine du mot. Marguerite en donne la même etymologie que Tashmend et le Père Guagix. Selon lui ce faucon aurait été appelé ainsi parce qu'il vient de l'autre côté de la mer, mais peut-être dériva-t-il de bahri dans le sens de marais, flaque, étang.*"

Dr. E. Denison Ross' *Polyglot List of Birds* (*Memoirs of the Asiatic Society of Bengal* ii, 289) gives to the Qara Qirghawal (Black pheasant) the synonym "Sea-pheasant", this being the literal translation of its Chinese name, and quotes from the Manchu-Chinese "Mirror" the remark that this is a black pheasant but called "sea-pheasant" to distinguish it from other black ones.

It may be observed that Babur writes of the yak once only and then of the *bahri qutas* so that there is no warrant from him for taking the term to apply to the wild yak. His cousin and contemporary Haidar Mirza, however, mentions the wild yak twice and simply as the wild *qutas*.

The following are random gleanings about "*bahri*" and the yak:—

(1) An instance of the use of the Persian equivalent *darya'i* of *bahri*, sea-borne or over-sea, is found in the *Akbar-nama* (Bib. Ind. ed. ii, 216) where the African elephant is described as *fil-i-darya'i*.

(2) In Egypt the word *bahri* has acquired the sense of northern, presumably referring to what lies or is borne across its northern sea, the Mediterranean.

(3) Vigne (*Travels in Kashmir* ii, 277–8) warns against confounding the *quch-qar i.e.* the gigantic *moufflon*, Pallas' *Ovis ammon*, with the *Kosh-gau*, the cow of the Kaucasus, *i.e.* the yak. He says, "Kaucasus (*hodie* Hindu-kush) was originally from Kosh, and Kosh is applied occasionally as a prefix, *e.g. Kosh-gau*, the yak or ox of the mountain or Kaucasus." He wrote from Skardo in Little Tibet and on the upper Indus. He gives the name of the female yak as *yak-mo* and of the half-breeds with common cows as *bzch*, which class he says is common and of "all colours".

(4) Mr. Ney Elias' notes (*Tarikh-i-rashidi* trs. pp. 302 and 466) on the *qutas* are of great interest. He gives the following synonymous names for the wild yak, *Bos Poëphagus*, *Khash-gau*, the Tibetan yak or Dong.

(5) Hume and Henderson (*Lahor to Yarkand* p. 59) write of the numerous black yak-hair tents seen round the Pangong Lake, of fine saddle yaks, and of the tame ones as being some white or brown but mostly black.

(6) Olufsen's *Through the Unknown Pamirs* (p. 118) speaks of the large numbers of *Bos grunniens* (yak) domesticated by the Kirghiz in the Pamirs.

(7) Cf. Gazetteer of India *s.n.* yak.

(8) Shaikh Zain applies the word *bahri* to the porpoise, when paraphrasing the *Babur-nama* f. 281*b*.

N.—NOTES ON A FEW BIRDS.

IN attempting to identify some of the birds of Babur's lists difficulty arises from the variety of names provided by the different tongues of the region concerned, and also in some cases by the application of one name to differing birds. The following random gleanings enlarge and, in part, revise some earlier notes and translations of Mr. Erskine's and my own. They are offered as material for the use of those better acquainted with bird-lore and with Himalayan dialects.

a. Concerning the lukha, luja, lucha, kuja (f. 135 and f. 278*b*).
The nearest word I have found to *lukha* and its similars is *likkh*, a florican (Jerdon, ii, 615), but the florican has not the chameleon colours of the *lukha* (var.). As Babur when writing in Hindustan, uses such "book-words" as Ar. *bahri* (*qutas*) and Ar. *bu-qalamun* (chameleon), it would not be strange if his name for the "*lukha*" bird represented Ar. *awja*, very beautiful, or connected with Ar. *loh*, shining splendour.

The form *kuja* is found in Ilminsky's imprint p. 361 (*Mémoires* ii, 198, *koudjeh*).

What is confusing to translators is that (as it now seems to me) Babur appears to use the name *kabg-i-dari* in both passages (f. 135 and f. 278*b*) to represent two birds; (1) he compares the *lukha* as to size with the *kabg-i-dari* of the Kabul region, and (2) for size and colour with that of Hindustan. But the bird of the Western Himalayas known by the name *kabg-i-dari* is the Himalayan snow-cock, *Tetraogallus himalayensis*, Turki, *aular* and in the Kabul region, *chiurtika* (f. 249, Jerdon, ii, 549–50); while the *kabg-i-dari* (syn. *chikor*) of Hindustan, whether of hill or plain, is one or more of much smaller birds.

The snow-cock being 28 inches in length, the *lukha* bird must be of this size. Such birds as to size and plumage of changing colour are the *Lophophori* and *Trapagons*, varieties of which are found in places suiting Babur's account of the *lukha*.

It may be noted that the Himalayan snow-cock is still called *kabg-i-dari* in Afghanistan (Jerdon, ii, 550) and in Kashmir (Vigne's *Travels in Kashmir* ii, 18). As its range is up to 18,000 feet, its Persian name describes it correctly whether read as "of the mountains" (*dari*), or as "royal" (*dari*) through its splendour.

I add here the following notes of Mr. Erskine's, which I have not quoted already where they occur (cf. f. 135 and f. 278*b*):—

On f. 135, "*lokheh*" is said to mean *hill-chikor*.

On f. 278*b*, to "*lujeh*", "The Persian has *lukheh*."

,, to "*kepki durri*", "The *kepki deri*, or *durri* is much larger than the common *kepk* of Persia and is peculiar to Khorasan. It is said to be a beautiful bird. The common *kepk* of Persia and Khorasan is the *hill-chikor* of India."

,, to "higher up", "The *lujeh* may be the *chikor* of the plains which Hunter calls bartavelle or Greek partridge."

The following corrections are needed about my own notes:— (1) on f. 135 (p. 213) n. 7 is wrongly referred; it belongs to the first word, *viz. kabg-i-dari*, of p. 214; (2) on f. 279 (p. 496) n. 2 should refer to the second *kabg-i-dari*.

b. Birds called munal (var. monal and moonaul).

Yule writing in *Hobson Jobson* (p. 580) of the "*moonaul*" which he identifies as *Lophophorus Impeyanus*, queries whether, on grounds he gives, the word *moonaul* is connected etymologically with Sanscrit *muni*, an "eremite". In continuation of his topic, I give here the names of other birds called *munal*, which I have noticed in various ornithological works while turning their pages for other information.

Besides *L. Impeyanus* and *Trapagon Ceriornis satyra* which Yule mentions as called "*moonaul*", there are *L. refulgens*, *munal* and *Ghur* (mountain)-*munal*; *Trapagon Ceriornis satyra*, called *munal* in Nipal; *T. C. melanocephalus*, called *sing* (horned)-*munal* in the N.W. Himalayas; *T. himalayensis*, the *jer*- or *cher-munal* of the same region, known also as *chikor*; and *Lerwa nevicola*, the snow-partridge known in Garhwal as *Quoir*- or *Qur-munal*. Do all these birds behave in such a way as to suggest that *munal* may imply the individual isolation related by Jerdon of *L. Impeyanus*, "In the autumnal and winter months numbers are generally collected in the same quarter of the forest, though often so widely scattered that each bird appears to be alone"? My own search amongst vocabularies of hill-dialects for the meaning of the word has been unsuccessful, spite of the long range *munals* in the Himalayas.

c. Concerning the word chiurtika, chourtka.

Jerdon's entry (ii, 549, 554) of the name *chourtka* as a synonym of *Tetraogallus himalayensis* enables me to fill a gap I have left on f. 249 (p. 491 and n. 6),[1] with the name Himalayan snow-cock, and to allow Babur's statement to be that he, in January 1520 AD. when coming down from the *Bad-i-pich* pass, saw many snow-cocks. The *Memoirs* (p. 282) has "*chikors*", which in India is a synonym for *kabg-i-dari*; the *Mémoires* (ii, 122) has *sauterelles*, but this meaning of *chiurtika* does not suit wintry January. That month would suit for the descent from higher altitudes of snow-cocks. Griffith, a botanist who travelled in Afghanistan *cir.* 1838 AD., saw myriads of *cicadæ* between Qilat-i-ghilzai and Ghazni, but the month was July.

d. On the qutan (f. 142, p. 224; *Memoirs*, p. 153; *Mémoires* ii, 313).

Mr. Erskine for *qutan* enters *khawasil* [gold-finch] which he will have seen interlined in the Elphinstone Codex (f. 109*b*) in explanation of *qutan*.

Shaikh Effendi (Kunos' ed., p. 139) explains *qutan* to be the gold-finch, *Steiglitz*.

Ilminsky's *qutan* (p. 175) is translated by M. de Courteille as *pélicane* and certainly some copies of the 2nd Persian translation [Muh. *Shirazi*'s p. 90] have *hawasil*, pelican.

The pelican would class better than the small finch with the

1 My note 6 on p. 421 shows my earlier difficulties, due to not knowing (when writing it) that *kabg-i-dari* represents the snow-cock in the Western Himalayas.

herons and egrets of Babur's trio; it also would appear a more likely bird to be caught "with the cord".

That Babur's *qutan* (*hawasil*) migrated in great numbers is however against supposing it to be *Pelicanus onocrotatus* which is seen in India during the winter, because it appears there in moderate numbers only, and Blanford with other ornithologists states that no western pelican migrates largely into India.

Perhaps the *qutan* was Linnæus' *Pelicanus carbo* of which one synonym is *Carbo comoranus*, the cormorant, a bird seen in India in large numbers of both the large and small varieties. As cormorants are not known to breed in that country, they will have migrated in the masses Babur mentions.

A translation matter falls to mention here:—After saying that the *auqar* (grey heron), *qarqara* (egret), and *qutan* (cormorant) are taken with the cord, Babur says that this method of bird-catching is unique (*bu nuh qush tutmaq ghair muqarrar dur*) and describes it. The Persian text omits to translate the *tutmaq* (by *P. giriftan*); hence Erskine (*Mems*. p. 153) writes, "The last mentioned fowl" (*i.e.* the *qutan*) "is rare," notwithstanding Babur's statement that all three of the birds he names are caught in masses. De Courteille (p. 313) writes, as though only of the *qutan*, "*ces derniers toutefois ne se prennent qu'accidentelment*," perhaps led to do so by knowledge of the circumstance that *Pelicanus onocrotatus* is rare in India.

O.—NOTES BY HUMAYUN ON SOME HINDUSTAN FRUITS.

THE following notes, which may be accepted as made by Humayun and in the margin of the archetype of the Elphinstone Codex, are composed in Turki which differs in diction from his father's but is far closer to that classic model than is that of the producer [Jahangir?] of the "Fragments". Various circumstances make the notes difficult to decipher *verbatim* and, unfortunately, when writing in Jan. 1917, I am unable to collate with its original in the Advocates Library, the copy I made of them in 1910.

a. On the kadhil, jack-fruit, Artocarpus integrifolia (f. 283*b*, p. 506; Elphinstone MS. f. 235*b*).[1]

The contents of the note are that the strange-looking pumpkin (*qarʿ*, which is also Ibn Batuta's word for the fruit), yields excellent white juice, that the best fruit grows from the roots of the tree,[2] that many such grow in Bengal, and that in Bengal and Dihli there grows a *kadhil*-tree covered with hairs (*Artocarpus hirsuta?*).

b. On the amrit-phal, mandarin-orange, Citrus aurantium (f.287, p. 512; Elphinstone Codex, f.238*b*, l. 12).

The interest of this note lies in its reference to Babur.

A Persian version of it is entered, without indication of what it is or of who was its translator, in one of the volumes of Mr. Erskine's manuscript remains, now in the British Museum (Add. 26,605, p. 88). Presumably it was made by his Turkish *munshi* for his note in the Memoirs (p. 329).

Various difficulties oppose the translation of the Turki note; it is written into the text of the Elphinstone Codex in two instalments, neither of them in place, the first being interpolated in the account of the *amil-bid* fruit, the second in that of the *jasun* flower; and there are verbal difficulties also. The Persian translation is not literal and in some particulars Mr. Erskine's rendering of this differs from what the Turki appears to state.

The note is, tentatively, as follows:[3]—"His honoured Majesty Firdaus-makan[4]—may God make his proof clear!—did not

---

1 By over-sight mention of this note was omitted from my article on the Elphinstone Codex (JRAS. 1907, p. 131).

2 Speede's *Indian Hand-book* (i, 212) published in 1841 AD. thus writes, "It is a curious circumstance that the finest and most esteemed fruit are produced from the roots below the surface of the ground, and are betrayed by the cracking of the earth above them, and the effluvia issuing from the fissure; a high price is given by rich natives for fruit so produced."

3 In the margin of the Elphinstone Codex opposite the beginning of the note are the words, "This is a marginal note of Humayun Padshah's."

4 Every Emperor of Hindustan has an epithet given him after his death to distinguish him, and prevent the necessity of repeating his name too familiarly. Thus *Firdaus-makan* (dweller-in-paradise) is Babur's; Humayun's is *Jannat-ashi-yani*, he whose nest is in Heaven; Muhammad Shah's *Firdaus-aramgah*, he whose place of rest is Paradise; *etc.* (Erskine).

favour the *amrit-phal*;[1] as he considered it insipid,[2] he likened it to the mild-flavoured[3] orange and did not make choice of it. So much was the mild-flavoured orange despised that if any person had disgusted (him) by insipid flattery (?) he used to say, 'He is like orange-juice.'"[4]

"The *amrit-phal* is one of the very good fruits. Though its juice is not relishing (? *chuchuq*), it is extremely pleasant-drinking. Later on, in my own time, its real merit became known. Its tartness may be that of the orange (*naranj*) and *lemu*."[5]

The above passage is followed, in the text of the Elphinstone Codex, by Babur's account of the *jasun* flower, and into this a further instalment of Humayun's notes is interpolated, having opposite its first line the marginal remark, "This extra note, seemingly made by Humayun Padshah, the scribe has mistakenly written into the text." Whether its first sentence refer to the *amrit-phal* or to the *amil-bid* must be left for decision to those well acquainted with the orange-tribe. It is obscure in my copy and abbreviated in its Persian translation; summarized it may state that when the fruit is unripe, its acidity is harmful to the digestion, but that it is very good when ripe.—The note then continues as below:—

c. The kamila, H. kaunla, the orange.[6]

"There are in Bengal two other fruits of the acid kind. Though the *amrit-phal* be not agreeable, they have resemblance to it(?)."

1 Here Mr. Erskine notes, "Literally, *nectar-fruit*, probably the mandarin orange, by the natives called *naringi*. The name *amrat*, or pear, in India is applied to the guava or *Psidium pyriferum*—(*Spondias mangifera*, Hort. Ben.—D. Wallich)." ... Mr. E. notes also that the note on the *amrit-phal* "is not found in either of the Persian translations".
2 *chuchuman*, Pers. trs. *shirini bi maza*, perhaps flat, sweet without relish. Babur does not use the word, nor have I traced it in a dictionary.
3 *chuchuk*, savoury, nice-tasting, not acid (Shaw).
4 *chuchuk naranj andaq* (?) *mat'un aidi kim har kim-ni shirin-karlighi bi maza qilkandi, naranj-su'i dik tur dirlar aidi.*
5 The *lemu* may be *Citrus limona*, which has abundant juice of a mild acid flavour.
6 The *kamila* and *samtara* are the real oranges (*kaunla* and *sangtara*), which are now (*cir.* 1816 AD.) common all over India. Dr. Hunter conjectures that the *sangtara* may take its name from Cintra, in Portugal. This early mention of it by Babur and Humayun may be considered as subversive of that supposition. (This description of the *samtara*, vague as it is, applies closer to the *Citrus decumana* or *pampelmus*, than to any other.—D. Wallich.)—Erskine.

"One is the *kamila* which may be as large as an orange (*naranj*); some took it to be a large *narangi* (orange) but it is much pleasanter eating than the *narangi* and is understood not to have the skin of that (fruit)."

d. The samtara.[1]

The other is the *samtara* which is larger than the orange (*naranj*) but is not tart; unlike the *amrit-phal* it is not of poor flavour (*kam maza*) or little relish (*chuchuk*). In short a better fruit is not seen. It is good to see, good to eat, good to digest. One does not forget it. If it be there, no other fruit is chosen. Its peel may be taken off by the hand. However much of the fruit be eaten, the heart craves for it again. Its juice does not soil the hand at all. Its skin separates easily from its flesh. It may be taken during and after food. In Bengal the *samtara* is rare (*gharib*) (or excellent, '*aziz*). It is understood to grow in one village Sanargam (Sonargaon) and even there in a special quarter. There seems to be no fruit so entirely good as the *samtara* amongst fruits of its class or, rather, amongst fruits of all kinds."

P.—REMARKS ON BABUR'S REVENUE
LIST (fol. 292).

a. Concerning the date of the List.

The Revenue List is the last item of Babur's account of Hindustan and, with that account, is found *s.a.* 932 AH., manifestly

---

1 Humayun writes of this fruit as though it were not the *sang-tara* described by his father on f. 287 (p. 511 and note).

too early, (1) because it includes districts and their revenues which did not come under Babur's authority until subdued in his Eastern campaigns of 934 and 935 AH., (2) because Babur's statement is that the "countries" of the List "are *now* in my possession" (*in loco* p. 520).

The List appears to be one of revenues realized in 936 or 937 AH. and not one of assessment or estimated revenue, (1) because Babur's wording states as a fact that the revenue was 52 *krurs*; (2) because the Persian heading of the (Persian) List is translatable as "Revenue (*jama*')[1] of Hindustan from what has so far come under the victorious standards".

b. The entry of the List into European Literature.

Readers of the L. and E. *Memoirs of Babur* are aware that it does not contain the Revenue List (p.334). The omission is due to the absence of the List from the Elphinstone Codex and from the 'Abdu'r-rahim Persian translation. Since the *Memoirs of Babur* was published in 1826 AD., the List has come from the *Babur-nama* into European literature by three channels.

Of the three the one used earliest is Shaikh Zain's *Tabaqat-i-baburi* which is a Persian paraphrase of part of Babur's Hindustan section. This work provided Mr. Erskine with what he placed in his *History of India* (London 1854, i, 540, Appendix D), but his manuscript, now B.M. Add. 26,202, is not the best copy of Shaikh Zain's book, being of far less importance than B.M. Or. 1999, [as to which more will be said.][2]

The second channel is Dr. Ilminsky's imprint of the Turki text (Kasan 1857, p. 379), which is translated by the *Mémoires de Baber* (Paris 1871, ii, 230).

The third channel is the Haidarabad Codex, in the English translation of which [*in loco*] the List is on p. 521.

Shaikh Zain may have used Babur's autograph manuscript for his paraphrase and with it the Revenue List. His own autograph manuscript was copied in 998 AH. (1589–90 AD.) by

---

1 M. de Courteille translated *jama*' in a general sense by *totalité* instead of in its Indian technical one of revenue (as here) or of assessment. Hence Professor Dowson's "totality" (iv, 262 n.).

2 The B.M. has a third copy, Or. 5879, which my husband estimates as of little importance.

Khwand-amir's grandson 'Abdu'l-lah who may be the scribe "Mir 'Abdu'l-lah" of the *Ayin-i-akbari* (Blochmann's trs. p. 109). 'Abdu'l-lah's transcript (from which a portion is now absent,) after having been in Sir Henry Elliot's possession, has become B.M. Or. 1999. It is noticed briefly by Professor Dowson (*l.c.* iv, 288), but he cannot have observed that the "old, worm-eaten" little volume contains Babur's Revenue List, since he does not refer to it.

c. *Agreement and variation in copies of the List.*

The figures in the two copies (Or. 1999 and Add. 26,202) of the *Tabaqat-i-baburi* are in close agreement. They differ, however, from those in the Haidarabad Codex, not only in a negligible unit and a ten of *tankas* but in having 20,000 more *tankas* from Oudh and Baraich and 30 *laks* of *tankas* more from Trans-sutlej.

The figures in the two copies of the *Babur-nama*, *viz.* the Haidarabad Codex and the Kehr–Ilminsky imprint are not in agreement throughout, but are identical in opposition to the variants (20,000 *t.* and 30 *l.*) mentioned above. As the two are independent, being collateral descendants of Babur's original papers, the authority of the Haidarabad Codex in the matter of the List is still further enhanced.

d. *Varia.*

(1) The place-names of the List are all traceable, whatever their varied forms. About the entry L:knu [or L:knur] and B:ks:r [or M:ks:r] a difficulty has been created by its variation in manuscripts, not only in the List but where the first name occurs *s.a.* 934 and 935 AH. In the Haidarabad List and in that of Or. 1999 L:knur is clearly written and may represent (approximately) modern Shahabad in Rampur. Erskine and de Courteille, however, have taken it to be Lakhnau in Oudh. [The distinction of Lakhnaur from Lakhnau in the historical narrative is discussed in Appendix T.]

(2) It may be noted, as of interest, that the name Sarwar is an abbreviation of Sarjupar which means "other side of Sarju" (Saru, Goghra; E. and D.'s H. of I. i, 56, n.4).

(3) Rup-narain (Deo or Dev) is mentioned in Ajodhya Prasad's short history of Tirhut and Darbhanga, the *Gulzar-i-Bihar* (Calcutta 1869, Cap. v, 88) as the 9th of the Brahman rulers of Tirhut and as having reigned for 25 years, from 917 to 942 *Fasli*(?). If the years were Hijri, 917–42 AH. would be 1511–1535.[1]

(4) Concerning the *tanka* the following modern description is quoted from Mr. R. Shaw's *High Tartary* (London 1871, p. 464) "The *tanga*" (or *tanka*) "is a nominal coin, being composed of 25 little copper cash, with holes pierced in them and called *dahcheen*. These are strung together and the quantity of them required to make up the value of one of these silver ingots" ("*kooroos* or *yamboo*, value nearly £17") "weighs a considerable amount. I once sent to get change for a *kooroos*, and my servants were obliged to charter a donkey to bring it home."

(5) The following interesting feature of Shaikh Zain's *Tabaqat-i-baburi* has been mentioned to me by my husband:— Its author occasionally reproduces Babur's Turki words instead of paraphrasing them in Persian, and does this for the noticeable passage in which Babur records his dissatisfied view of Hindustan (f. 290*b*, *in loco* p. 518), prefacing his quotation with the remark that it is best and will be nearest to accuracy not to attempt translation but to reproduce the Padshah's own words. The main interest of the matter lies in the motive for reproducing the *ipsissima verba*. Was that motive deferential? Did the revelation of feeling and opinion made in the quoted passage clothe it with privacy so that Shaikh Zain reserved its perusal from the larger public of Hindustan who might read Persian but not Turki? Some such motive would explain the insertion untranslated of Babur's letters to Humayun and to Khwaja Kalan which are left in Turki by 'Abdu'r-rahim Mirza.[2]

---

1 Sir G. A. Grierson, writing in the *Indian Antiquary* (July 1885, p. 187), makes certain changes in Ajodhya Prasad's list of the Brahman rulers of Tirhut, on grounds he states.

2 The passage Shaikh Zain quotes is found in Or. 1999, f. 65*b*, Add. 26,202, f. 66*b*, Or. 5879, f. 79*b*.

Q.—CONCERNING THE "RAMPUR DIWAN"

PENDING the wide research work necessary to interpret those of Babur's Hindustan poems which the Rampur manuscript preserves, the following comments, some tentative and open to correction, may carry further in making the poems publicly known, what Dr. E. Denison Ross has effected by publishing his Facsimile of the manuscript.[1] It is legitimate to associate comment on the poems with the *Babur-nama* because many of them are in it with their context of narrative; most, if not all, connect with it; some without it, would be dull and vapid.

a. An authorized English title.

The contents of the Rampur MS. are precisely what Babur describes sending to four persons some three weeks after the date attached to the manuscript,[2] *viz.* "the Translation and what-not of poems made on coming to Hindustan";[3] and a similar description may be meant in the curiously phrased first clause of the colophon, but without mention of the Translation (of the *Walidiyyah-risala*).[4] Hence, if the poems, including the Translation, became known as the *Hindustan Poems* or *Poems made in Hindustan*, such title would be justified by their author's words. Babur does not call the Hindustan poems a *diwan* even when, as in the above quotation, he speaks of them apart from his versified translation of the Tract. In what has come down to us of his autobiography, he applies the name *Diwan* to poems of his own once only, this in 925 AH. (f. 237*b*) when he records sending "my *diwan*" to Pulad Sl. *Auzbeg*.

1 *Cf.* JASB. 1910, Extra Number.

2 Monday, Rabi' II. 15th 935 AH.—Dec. 27th 1528 AD. At this date Babur had just returned from Dhulpur to Agra (f. 354, p. 635, where in note 1 for Thursday read Monday).

3 Owing to a scribe's "skip" from one *yibarildi* (was sent) to another at the end of the next sentence, the passage is not in the Hai. MS. It is not well given in my translation (f. 357*b*, p. 642); what stands above is a closer rendering of the full Turki, *Humayungha tarjuma* [*u?*] *ni-kim Hindustangha kilkani aitqan ash'arni yibarildi* (Ilminsky p. 462, l. 4 fr. ft., where however there appears a slight clerical error).

4 Hesitation about accepting the colophon as unquestionably applying to the whole contents of the manuscript is due to its position of close association with one section only of the three in the manuscript (*cf. post* p. lx).

b. The contents of the Rampur MS.

There are three separate items of composition in the manuscript, marked as distinct from one another by having each its ornamented frontispiece, each its scribe's sign (*mim*) of Finis, each its division from its neighbour by a space without entry. The first and second sections bear also the official sign [*sahh*] that the copy has been inspected and found correct.

(1) The first section consists of Babur's metrical translation of Khwaja 'Ubaidu'l-lah *Ahrari's Parental Tract* (*Walidiyyah-risala*), his prologue in which are his reasons for versifying the Tract and his epilogue which gives thanks for accomplishing the task. It ends with the date 935 (Hai. MS. f. 346). Below this are *mim* and *sahh*, the latter twice; they are in the scribe's handwriting, and thus make against supposing that Babur wrote down this copy of the Tract or its archetype from which the official *sahh* will have been copied. Moreover, spite of bearing two vouchers of being a correct copy, the Translation is emended, in a larger script which may be that of the writer of the marginal quatrain on the last page of the [Rampur] MS. and there attested by Shah-i-jahan as Babur's autograph entry. His also may have been the now expunged writing on the half-page left empty of text at the end of the Tract. Expunged though it be, fragments of words are visible.[1]

(2) The second section has in its frontispiece an inscription illegible (to me) in the Facsimile. It opens with a *masnawi* of 41 couplets which is followed by a *ghazel* and numerous poems in several measures, down to a triad of rhymed couplets (*matla'?*), the whole answering to descriptions of a *Diwan* without formal arrangement. After the last couplet are *mim* and *sahh* in the scribe's hand-writing, and a blank quarter-page. Mistakes in this section have been left uncorrected, which supports the view that its *sahh* avouches the accuracy of its archetype and not its own.[2]

1 Plate XI, and p. 15 (mid-page) of the Facsimile booklet.—The Facsimile does not show the whole of the marginal quatrain, obviously because for the last page of the manuscript a larger photographic plate was needed than for the rest.
2 The second section ends on Plate XVII, and p. 21 of the Facsimile booklet.

(3) The third section shows no inscription on its frontispiece. It opens with the *masnawi* of eight couplets, found also in the *Babur-nama* (f. 312), one of earlier date than many of the poems in the second section. It is followed by three *ruba'i* which complete the collection of poems made in Hindustan. A prose passage comes next, describing the composition and trans-position-in-metre of a couplet of 16 feet, with examples in three measures, the last of which ends in l.4 of the photograph.— While fixing the date of this metrical game, Babur incidentally allows that of his *Treatise on Prosody* to be inferred from the following allusive words:—"When going to Sambhal (f. 330b) in the year (933 AH.) after the conquest of Hindustan (932 AH.), two years after writing the '*Aruz*, I composed a couplet of 16 feet."— From this the date of the Treatise is seen to be 931 AH., some two years later than that of the *Mubin*. The above metrical exercise was done about the same time as another concerning which a Treatise was written, *viz.* that mentioned on f. 330b, when a couplet was transposed into 504 measures (Section *f*, p. 780).—The Facsimile, it will be noticed, shows something unusual in the last line of the prose passage on Plate XVIII B, where the scattering of the words suggests that the scribe was trying to copy page *per* page.

The colophon (which begins on l. 5 of the photograph) is curiously worded, as though the frequent fate of last pages had befallen its archetype, that of being mutilated and difficult for a scribe to make good; it suggests too that the archetype was verse.[1] Its first clause, even if read as *Hind-stan janibi 'azimat qilghani* (i.e. not *qilghali*, as it can be read), has an indirectness unlike Babur's corresponding "after coming to Hindustan" (f. 357b), and is not definite; (2) *bu airdi* (these were) is not the complement suiting *aul durur* (those are); (3) Babur does not use the form *durur* in prose; (4) the undue space after *durur* suggests connection with verse; (5) there is no final verb such as prose needs. The meaning, however, may be as follows:—The poems made after resolving on (the)

1 Needless to say that whatever the history of the manuscript, its value as preserving poems of which no other copy is known publicly, is untouched. This value would be great without the marginal entries on the last page; it finds confirmation in the identity of many of the shorter poems with counterparts in the *Babur-nama*.

Hindustan parts (*janibi*?) were these I have written down (*tahrir qildim*), and past events are those I have narrated (*taqrir*) in the way that (*ni-chuk kim*) (has been) written in these folios (*auraq*) and recorded in those sections (*ajza'*).—From this it would appear that sections of the *Babur-nama* (f. 376*b*, p. 678) accompanied the Hindustan poems to the recipient of the message conveyed by the colophon.

Close under the colophon stands *Harara-hu Babur* and the date Monday, Rabi' II. 15th 935 (Monday, December 27th 1528 AD.), the whole presumably brought over from the archetype. To the question whether a signature in the above form would be copied by a scribe, the Elphinstone Codex gives an affirmative answer by providing several examples of notes, made by Humayun in its archetype, so-signed and brought over either into its margin or interpolated in its text. Some others of Humayun's notes are not so-signed, the scribe merely saying they are Humayun Padshah's.—It makes against taking the above entry of Babur's name to be an autograph signature, (1) that it is enclosed in an ornamented border, as indeed is the case wherever it occurs throughout the manuscript; (2) that it is followed by the scribe's *mim*. [See end of following section.]

c. The marginal entries shown in the photograph.

The marginal note written length-wise by the side of the text is signed by Shah-i-jahan and attests that the *ruba'i* and the signature to which it makes reference are in Babur's autograph hand-writing. His note translates as follows:—This quatrain and blessed name are in the actual hand-writing of that Majesty (*an hazrat*) *Firdaus-makani* Babur Padshah *Ghazi*—May God make his proof clear!—Signed (*Harara-hu*), Shah-i-jahan son of Jahangir Padshah son of Akbar Padshah son of Humayun Padshah son of Babur Padshah.[1]

---

1 Another autograph of Shah-i-jahan's is included in the translation volume (p. xiii) of Gul-badan Begam's *Humayun-nama*. It surprises one who works habitually on historical writings more nearly contemporary with Babur, in which he is spoken of as *Firdaus-makani* or as *Giti-sitani Firdaus-makani* and not by the name used during his life, to find Shah-i-jahan giving him the two styles (*cf. Jahangir's Memoirs* trs. ii, 5). Those familiar with the writings of Shah-i-jahan's biographers will know whether this is usual at that date. There would seem no doubt as to the identity of *an Hazrat*.—The words *an hazrat* by which Shah-i-jahan refers to Babur are used also in the epitaph placed by Jahangir at Babur's tomb (Trs. Note p. 710–711).

The second marginal entry is the curiously placed *ruba'i*, which is now the only one on the page, and now has no signature attaching to it. It has the character of a personal message to the recipient of one of more books having identical contents. That these two entries are there while the text seems so clearly to be written by a scribe, is open to the explanation that when (as said about the colophon, p. 775) the rectangle of text was made good from a mutilated archetype, the original margin was placed round the *rifacimento*? This superposition would explain the entries and seal-like circles, discernible against a strong light, on the reverse of the margin only, through the *rifacimento* page. The upper edge of the rectangle shows sign that the margin has been adjusted to it [so far as one can judge from a photograph]. Nothing on the face of the margin hints that the text itself is autograph; the words of the colophon, *tahrir qildim* (*i.e.* I have written down) cannot hold good against the cumulative testimony that a scribe copied the whole manuscript.—The position of the last syllable [*ni*] of the *ruba'i* shows that the signature below the colophon was on the margin before the diagonal couplet of the *ruba'i* was written,—therefore when the margin was fitted, as it looks to have been fitted, to the *rifacimento*. If this be the order of the two entries [*i.e.* the small-hand signature and the diagonal couplet], Shah-i-jahan's "blessed name" may represent the small-hand signature which certainly shows minute differences from the writing of the text of the MS. in the name Babur (*q.v. passim* in the Rampur MS.).

d. The Baburi-khatt (Babur's script).

So early as 910 AH. the year of his conquest of Kabul, Babur devised what was probably a variety of *nakhsh*, and called it the *Baburi-khatt* (f. 144*b*), a name used later by Haidar Mirza, Nizamu'd-din Ahmad and 'Abdu'l-qadir *Badayuni*. He writes of it again (f. 179) *s.a.* 911 AH. when describing an interview had in 912 AH. with one of the Harat Qazis, at which the script was discussed, its specialities (*mufradat*) exhibited to, and read by the Qazi who there and then wrote in it.[1] In what remains to us

---

1 The Qazi's rapid acquirement of the *mufradat* of the script allows the inference that few letters only and those of a well-known script were varied.—*Mufradat* was translated by Erskine, de Courteille and myself (f. 357*b*) as alphabet but reconsideration

of the *Babur-nama* it is not mentioned again till 935 AH. (fol. 357*b*) but at some intermediate date Babur made in it a copy of the Qoran which he sent to Makka.[1] In 935 AH. (f. 357*b*) it is mentioned in significant association with the despatch to each of four persons of a copy of the Translation (of the *Walidiyyah-risala*) and the Hindustan poems, the significance of the association being that the simultaneous despatch with these copies of specimens of the *Baburi-khatt* points to its use in the manuscripts, and at least in Hind-al's case, to help given for reading novel forms in their text. The above are the only instances now found in the *Babur-nama* of mention of the script.

The little we have met with—we have made no search—about the character of the script comes from the *Abushqa, s.n. sighnaq*, in the following entry:—

Sighnaq ber nu'ah khatt der Chaghataida khatt Baburi u ghairi kibi ki Babur Mirza ash'ar'nda kilur bait

> *Khublar khatti nasib'ng bulmasa Babur ni tang?*
> *Baburi khatti aimas dur khatt sighnaqi mu dur?*[2]

The old Osmanli-Turkish prose part of this appears to mean:— "*Sighnaq* is a sort of hand-writing, in Chaghatai the *Baburi-khatt* and others resembling it, as appears in Babur Mirza's poems. Couplet":—

Without knowing the context of the couplet I make no attempt to translate it because its words *khatt* or *khat* and

---

by the light of more recent information about the *Baburi-khatt* leads me to think this is wrong because "alphabet" includes every letter.—On f. 357*b* three items of the *Baburi-khatt* are specified as despatched with the Hindustan poems, *viz. mufradat, qita'lar* and *sar-i-khatt*. Of these the first went to Hind-al, the third to Kamran, and no recipient is named for the second; all translators have sent the *qita'lar* to Hind-al but I now think this wrong and that a name has been omitted, probably Humayun's.

1 f. 144*b*, p. 228, n. 3. Another interesting matter missing from the *Babur-nama* by the gap between 914 and 925 AH. is the despatch of an embassy to Czar Vassili III. in Moscow, mentioned in Schuyler's *Turkistan* ii, 394, Appendix IV, Grigorief's *Russian Policy in Central Asia*. The mission went after "Sultan Babur" had established himself in Kabul; as Babur does not write of it before his narrative breaks off abruptly in 914 AH. it will have gone after that date.

2 I quote from the Véliaminof-Zernov edition (p. 287) from which de Courteille's plan of work involved extract only; he translates the couplet, giving to *khatt* the double-meanings of script and down of youth (*Dictionnaire Turque s.n. sighnaqi*). The *Sanglakh* (p. 252) *s.n. sighnaq* has the following as Babur's:—

> *Chu balai khatti nasib'ng bulmasa Babur ni tang?*
> *Bare khatt almansur khatt sighnaqi mu dur?*

sighnaq lend themselves to the kind of pun (*iham*) "which consists in the employment of a word or phrase having more than one appropriate meaning, whereby the reader is often left in doubt as to the real significance of the passage."[1] The rest of the *ruba'i* may be given [together with the six other quotations of Babur's verse now known only through the *Abushqa*], in early *Tazkiratu 'sh-shu'ara* of date earlier than 967 AH.

The root of the word *sighnaq* will be *siq*, pressed together, crowded, included, *etc.*; taking with this notion of compression, the explanations *feine Schrift* of Shaikh Effendi (Kunos) and Vambéry's *petite écriture*, the Sighnaqi and Baburi Scripts are allowed to have been what that of the Rampur MS. is, a small, compact, elegant hand-writing.—A town in the Caucasus named Sighnakh, "*située à peu près à 800 mètres d'altitude, commença par être une forteresse et un lieu de refuge, car telle est la signification de son nom tartare.*"[2] *Sighnaqi* is given by de Courteille (Dict. p. 368) as meaning a place of refuge or shelter.

The *Baburi-khatt* will be only one of the several hands Babur is reputed to have practised; its description matches it with other niceties he took pleasure in, fine distinctions of eye and ear in measure and music.

e. Is the Rampur MS. an example of the Baburi-khatt?

Though only those well-acquainted with Oriental manuscripts dating before 910 AH. (1504 AD.) can judge whether novelties appear in the script of the Rampur MS. and this particularly in its head-lines, there are certain grounds for thinking that though the manuscript be not Babur's autograph, it may be in his script and the work of a specially trained scribe.

I set these grounds down because although the signs of a scribe's work on the manuscript seem clear, it is "locally" held to be Babur's autograph. Has a tradition of its being in the *Baburi-khatt* glided into its being in the *khatt-i-Babur*? Several circumstances suggest that it may be written in the *Baburi-khatt*:—
(1) the script is specially associated with the four transcripts

---

of the Hindustan poems (f. 357b), for though many letters must have gone to his sons, some indeed are mentioned in the *Babur-nama*, it is only with the poems that specimens of it are recorded as sent; (2) another matter shows his personal interest in the arrangement of manuscripts, namely, that as he himself about a month after the four books had gone off, made a new ruler, particularly on account of the head-lines of the Translation, it may be inferred that he had made or had adopted the one he superseded, and that his plan of arranging the poems was the model for copyists; the Rampur MS. bearing, in the Translation section, corrections which may be his own, bears also a date earlier than that at which the four gifts started; it has its head-lines ill-arranged and has throughout 13 lines to the page; his new ruler had 11; (3) perhaps the words *tahrir qildim* used in the colophon of the Rampur MS. should be read with their full connotation of careful and elegant writing, or, put modestly, as saying, "I wrote down in my best manner," which for poems is likely to be in the *Baburi-khatt*.[1]

Perhaps an example of Babur's script exists in the colophon, if not in the whole of the *Mubin* manuscript once owned by Berézine, by him used for his *Chréstomathie Turque*, and described by him as "unique". If this be the actual manuscript Babur sent into Ma wara'u'n-nahr (presumably to Khwaja Ahrari's family), its colophon which is a personal message addressed to the recipients, is likely to be autograph.

f. Metrical amusements.

(1) Of two instances of metrical amusements belonging to the end of 933 AH. and seeming to have been the distractions of illness, one is a simple transposition "in the fashion of the circles" (*dawa'ir*) into three measures (Rampur MS. Facsimile, Plate XVIII and p. 22); the other is difficult because of the high number of 504 into which Babur says (f. 330b) he cut up the following couplet:—

> *Guz u qash u soz u tilini mu di?*
> *Qad u khadd u saj u bilini mu di?*

[1] On this same *tahrir qildim* may perhaps rest the opinion that the Rampur MS. is autograph.

All manuscripts agree in having 504, and Babur wrote a tract (*risala*) upon the transpositions.[1] None of the modern treatises on Oriental Prosody allows a number so high to be practicable, but Maulana Saifi of Bukhara, of Babur's own time (f. 180*b*) makes 504 seem even moderate, since after giving much detail about *ruba'i* measures, he observes, "Some say there are 10,000" (*Aruz-i-Saifi*, Ranking's trs. p. 122). Presumably similar possibilities were open for the couplet in question. It looks like one made for the game, asks two foolish questions and gives no reply, lends itself to poetic licence, and, if permutation of words have part in such a game, allows much without change of sense. Was Babur's cessation of effort at 504 capricious or enforced by the exhaustion of possible changes? Is the arithmetical statement $9 \times 8 \times 7 = 504$ the formula of the practicable permutations?

(2) To improvise verse having a given rhyme and topic must have demanded quick wits and much practice. Babur gives at least one example of it (f. 252*b*) but Jahangir gives a fuller and more interesting one, not only because a *ruba'i* of Babur's was the model but from the circumstances of the game:[2]—It was in 1024 AH. (1615 AD.) that a letter reached him from Ma wara'u'n-nahr written by Khwaja Hashim *Naqsh-bandi* [who by the story is shown to have been of Ahrari's line], and recounting the long devotion of his family to Jahangir's ancestors. He sent gifts and enclosed in his letter a copy of one of Babur's quatrains which he said Hazrat Firdaus-makani had written for Hazrat Khwajagi (Ahrari's eldest son; f. 36*b*, p. 62 n. 2). Jahangir quotes a final hemistich only, "*Khwajagira manda'im, Khwajagira banda'im,*" and thereafter made an impromptu verse upon the one sent to him.

A curious thing is that the line he quotes is not part of the quatrain he answered, but belongs to another not appropriate for a message between *darwesh* and *padshah*, though likely to have been sent by Babur to Khwajagi. I will quote both because

---

1 I have found no further mention of the tract; it may be noted however that whereas Babur calls his *Treatise on Prosody* (written in 931 AH.) the '*Aruz*, Abu'l-fazl writes of a *Mufassal*, a suitable name for 504 details of transposition.

2 *Tuzuk-i-jahangir* lith.ed. p. 149; and *Memoirs of Jahangir* trs. i, 304. [In both books the passage requires amending.]

the matter will come up again for who works on the Hindustan poems.[1]

> (1) The quatrain from the *Hindustan Poems* is:—
> *Dar hawa'i nafs gumrah 'umr zai' karda'im [kanda'im?]*;
> *Pesh ahl-i-allah az af'al-i-khud sharmanda'im;*
> *Yak nazr ba mukhlasan-i-khasta-dil farma ki ma*
> *Khwajagira manda'im u Khwajagira banda'im.*
>
> (2) That from the *Akbar-nama* is:—
> *Darweshanra agarcha nah az khweshanim,*
> *Lek az dil u jan mu'taqid eshanim;*
> *Dur ast magu'i shahi az darweshi,*
> *Shahim wali banda-i-darweshanim.*

The greater suitability of the second is seen from Jahangir's answering impromptu for which by sense and rhyme it sets the model; the meaning, however, of the fourth line in each may be identical, namely, "I remain the ruler but am the servant of the *darwesh*." Jahangir's impromptu is as follows:—

> *Ai anki mara mihr-i-tu besh az besh ast,*
> *Az daulat yad-i-budat ai darwesh ast;*
> *Chandanki 'z muzhdahat dilam shad shavad*
> *Shadim az anki latif az hadd besh ast.*

He then called on those who had a turn for verse to "speak one" *i.e.* to improvise on his own; it was done as follows:—

> *Darim agarcha shaghal-i-shahi dar pesh,*
> *Har lahza kunim yad-i-darweshan besh;*
> *Gar shad shavad 'z ma dil-i-yak darwesh,*
> *Anra shumarim hasil-i-shahi khwesh.*

R.—CHANDIRI AND GUALIAR.

THE courtesy of the Government of India enables me to reproduce from the *Archæological Survey Reports* of 1871, Sir Alexander Cunningham's plans of Chandiri and Gualiar, which illustrate Babur's narrative on f. 333, p. 592, and f. 340, p. 607.

1 Rampur MS. Facsimile Plate XIV and p. 16, verse 3; *Akbar-nama* trs. i, 279, and lith. ed. p. 91.

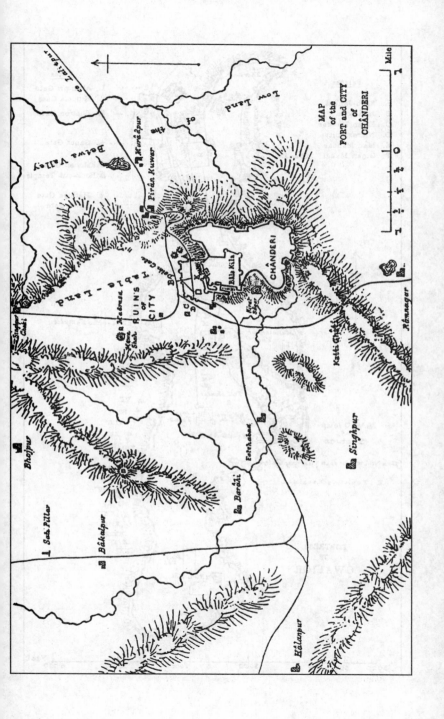

MAP
of the
FORT and CITY
of CHÂNDERI

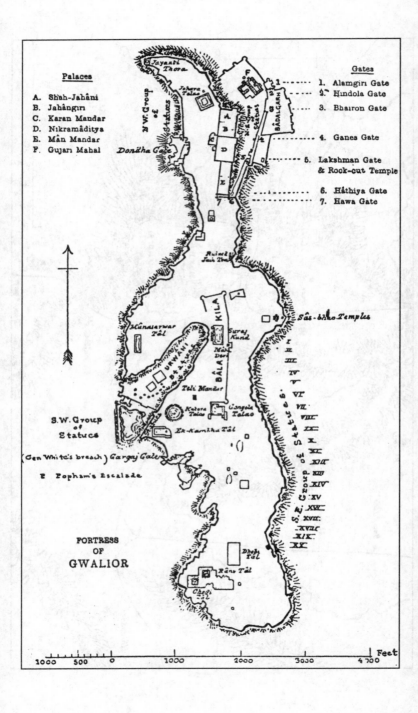

Palaces

A. Shah-Jahâni
B. Jahângiri
C. Karan Mandar
D. Nikramâditya
E. Mân Mandar
F. Gujari Mahal

Gates

1. Alamgiri Gate
2. Hindola Gate
3. Bhairon Gate
4. Ganes Gate
5. Lakshman Gate & Rook-cut Temple
6. Hâthiya Gate
7. Hawa Gate

Jayanti Thora

Johara Talao

BÂDALGARH

N.W. Group of Statues

Donâha Gate

Ruined Jain Tal

KILA

Sâs-bâhu Temples

Múnasarwar Tâl

URWAHI

BÂLA

Suraj Kund

Nûr Dera

Teli Mandar

Katora Talao

Gangola Talao

Ek-Kamkha Tâl

S.W. Group of Statues

(Gen White's breach) Gargaj Gate

E Popham's Escalade

S.E. Group of Statues

I
II
III
IV
V
VI
VII
VIII
IX
X
XI
XII
XIII
XIV
XV
XVI
XVII
XVIII
XIX
XX

FORTRESS OF GWALIOR

Dhobi Tâl

Râni Tâl

Chedi

Feet

1000   500   0   1000   2000   3000   4000

S.—CONCERNING THE BABUR-NAMA DATING OF 935 AH.

THE dating of the diary of 935 AH. (f. 339 *et seq.*) is several times in opposition to what may be distinguished as the "book-rule" that the 12 lunar months of the Hijra year alternate in length between 30 and 29 days (intercalary years excepted), and that Muharram starts the alternation with 30 days. An early book stating the rule is Gladwin's *Bengal Revenue Accounts*; a recent one, Ranking's ed. of Platts' *Persian Grammar*.

As to what day of the week was the initial day of some of the months in 935 AH. Babur's days differ from Wüstenfeld's who gives the full list of twelve, and from Cunningham's single one of Muharram 1st.

It seems worth while to draw attention to the flexibility, within limits, of Babur's dating, [not with the object of adversely criticizing a rigid and convenient rule for common use, but as supplementary to that rule from a somewhat special source], because he was careful and observant, his dating was contemporary, his record, as being *de die in diem*, provides a check of consecutive narrative on his dates, which, moreover, are all held together by the external fixtures of Feasts and by the marked recurrence of Fridays observed. Few such writings as the Baburnama diaries appear to be available for showing variation within a year's limit.

In 935 AH. Babur enters few full dates, *i.e.* days of the week and month. Often he gives only the day of the week, the safest, however, in a diary. He is precise in saying at what time of the night or the day an action was done; this is useful not only as helping to get over difficulties caused by minor losses of text, but in the more general matter of the transference of a Hijra night-and-day which begins after sunset, to its Julian equivalent, of a day-and-night which begins at 12 a.m. This sometimes difficult transference affords a probable explanation of a good number of the discrepant dates found in Oriental-Occidental books.

Two matters of difference between the Babur-nama dating and that of some European calendars are as follows:—

a. Discrepancy as to the day of the week on which Muh. 935 AH. began.

This discrepancy is not a trivial matter when a year's diary is concerned. The record of Muh. 1st and 2nd is missing from the *Babur-nama*; Friday the 3rd day of Muharram is the first day specified; the 1st was a Wednesday therefore. Erskine accepted this day; Cunningham and Wüstenfeld give Tuesday. On three grounds Wednesday seems right—at any rate at that period and place:—(1) The second Friday in Muharram was 'Ashur, the 10th (f. 340); (2) Wednesday is in serial order if reckoning be made from the last surviving date of 934 AH. with due allowance of an intercalary day to Zu'l-hijja (Gladwin), *i.e.* from Thursday Rajab 12th (April 2nd 1528 AD. f. 339, p.602); (3) Wednesday is supported by the daily record of far into the year.

b. Variation in the length of the months of 935 AH.

There is singular variation between the *Babur-nama* and Wüstenfeld's *Tables*, both as to the day of the week on which months began, and as to the length of some months. This variation is shown in the following table, where asterisks mark agreement as to the days of the week, and the capital letters, quoted from W.'s *Tables*, denote A, Sunday; B, Tuesday, *etc.* (the bracketed names being of my entry).

	Babur-nama.			*Wüstenfeld.*
	Days.		Days.	
Muharram	29	Wednesday	30	C (Tuesday).
Safar	30	Thursday *	29	E (Thursday).*
Rabi' I.	30	Saturday	30	F (Friday).
,, II.	29	Monday	29	A (Sunday).
Jumada I.	30	Tuesday	30	B (Monday).
,, II.	29	Thursday	29	D (Wednesday).
Rajab	29	Friday	30	E (Thursday).
Sha'ban	30	Saturday *	29	G (Saturday).*
Ramzan	29	Monday	30	A (Sunday).
Shawwal	30	Tuesday *	29	C (Tuesday).*
Zu'l-qa'da	29	Thursday	30	D (Wednesday).
Zu'l-hijja	30	Friday *	29	T (Friday).*

The table shows that notwithstanding the discrepancy discussed in section *a*, of Babur's making 935 AH. begin on a Wednesday, and Wüstenfeld on a Tuesday, the two authorities agree as to the initial week-day of four months out of twelve, *viz*. Safar, Sha'ban, Shawwal and Zu'l-hijja.

Again:—In eight of the months the *Babur-nama* reverses the "book-rule" of alternative Muharram 30 days, Safar 29 days *et seq*. by giving Muharram 29, Safar 30. (This is seen readily by following the initial days of the week.) Again:—these eight months are in pairs having respectively 29 and 30 days, and the year's total is 364.—Four months follow the fixed rule, *i.e.* as though the year had begun Muh. 30 days, Safar 29 days— namely, the two months of Rabi' and the two of Jumada.— Ramzan to which under "book-rule" 30 days are due, had 29 days, because, as Babur records, the Moon was seen on the 29th.—In the other three instances of the reversed 30 and 29, one thing is common, *viz*. Muharram, Rajab, Zu'l-qa'da (as also Zu'l-hijja) are "honoured" months.—It would be interesting if some expert in this Musalman matter would give the reasons dictating the changes from rule noted above as occurring in 935 AH.

c. Varia.

(1) On f. 367 Saturday is entered as the 1st day of Sha'ban and Wednesday as the 4th, but on f. 368*b* stands Wednesday 5th, as suits the serial dating. If the mistake be not a mere slip, it may be due to confusion of hours, the ceremony chronicled being accomplished on the eve of the 5th, Anglicé, after sunset on the 4th.

(2) A fragment only survives of the record of Zu'l-hijja 935 AH. It contains a date, Thursday 7th, and mentions a Feast which will be that of the *'Idu'l-kabir* on the 10th (Sunday). Working on from this to the first-mentioned day of 936 AH. *viz*. Tuesday, Muharram 3rd, the month (which is the second of a pair having 29 and 30 days) is seen to have 30 days and so to fit on to 936 AH. The series is Sunday 10th, 17th, 24th (Sat. 30th) Sunday 1st, Tuesday 3rd.

Two clerical errors of mine in dates connecting with this Appendix are corrected here:—(1) On p. 614 n. 5, for Oct. 2nd read Oct. 3rd; (2) on p. 619 penultimate line of the text, for Nov. 28th read Nov. 8th.

T.—ON L:KNU (LAKHNAU) AND L:KNUR (LAKHNUR, NOW SHAHABAD IN RAMPUR).

ONE or other of the above-mentioned names occurs eight times in the *Babur-nama* (*s.a.* 932, 934, 935 AH.), some instances being shown by their context to represent Lakhnau in Oudh, others inferentially and by the verbal agreement of the Haidarabad Codex and Kehr's Codex to stand for Lakhnur (now Shahabad in Rampur). It is necessary to reconsider the identification of those not decided by their context, both because there is so much variation in the copies of the 'Abdu'r-rahim Persian translation that they give no verbal help, and because Mr. Erskine and M. de Courteille are in agreement about them and took the whole eight to represent Lakhnau. This they did on different grounds, but in each case their agreement has behind it a defective textual basis.—Mr. Erskine, as is well known, translated the 'Abdu'r-rahim Persian text without access to the original Turki but, if he had had the Elphinstone Codex when translating, it would have given him no help because all the eight instances occur on folios not preserved by that codex. His only sources were not-first-rate Persian MSS. in which he found casual variation from terminal *nu* to *nur*, which latter form may have been read by him as *nuu* (whence perhaps the old Anglo-Indian transliteration he uses, Luknow)—M. de Courteille's position is different; his uniform *Lakhnau* obeyed the same uniformity in his source the Kasan Imprint, and would appear to him the more assured for the concurrence of the *Memoirs*. His textual basis, however, for these words is Dr. Ilminsky's and not Kehr's. No doubt the uniform *Lakhnu* of the Kasan Imprint is the result of Dr. Ilminsky's uncertainty as to the accuracy of his single Turki archetype [Kehr's MS.], and also of his acceptance of Mr. Erskine's uniform *Luknow*.[1]—Since the Haidarabad Codex became available and its collation with Kehr's Codex has been made, a better basis for distinguishing between the L:knu and L:knur of the Persian MSS. has been obtained.[2] The results of the collation are entered in the following table, together with what is found in the Kasan Imprint and the *Memoirs*. [N.B. The two sets of bracketed instances refer each to one place; the asterisks show where Ilminsky varies from Kehr.]

		Hai. MS.	Kehr's MS.	Kasan Imprint.	Memoirs.
1.	{f. 278b	L:knur	L:knu	L:knu, p. 361	Luknow.
2.	{f. 338	L:knu	,,	,, p. 437	,,
3.	f. 292b	L:knur	L:knur	,, p. 379*	not entered.
4.	f. 329	L:knur	L:knur	,, p. 362*	Luknow.
5.	f. 334	L:knu	L:knu	,, p. 432*	,,
6.	{f. 376	L:knu	L:knur	,, p. 486*	,,
7.	{f. 376b	L:knur	,,	,, p. 487*	,,
8.	{f. 377b	L:knu	,,	,, p. 488*	,,

The following notes give some grounds for accepting the names as the two Turki codices agree in giving them:—

The first and second instances of the above table, those of the Hai. Codex f. 278b and f. 338, are shown by their context to represent Lakhnau.

The third (f. 292b) is an item of Babur's Revenue List. The Turki codices are supported by B.M. Or. 1999, which is a direct copy of Shaikh Zain's autograph *Tabaqat-i-baburi*, all three having L:knur. Kehr's MS. and Or. 1999 are descendants of the second degree from the original List; that the Hai. Codex is a direct copy is suggested by its pseudo-tabular arrangement

1 Dr. Ilminsky says of the Leyden & Erskine *Memoirs of Babur* that it was a constant and indispensable help.

2 My examination of Kehr's Codex has been made practicable by the courtesy of the Russian Foreign Office in lending it for my use, under the charge of the Librarian of the India Office, Dr. F. W. Thomas.—It should be observed that in this Codex the Hindustan Section contains the purely Turki text found in the Haidarabad Codex (*cf.* JRAS. 1908, p. 78).

of the various items.—An important consideration supporting
L:knur, is that the List is in Persian and may reasonably be
accepted as the one furnished officially for the Padshah's
information when he was writing his account of Hindustan
(cf. Appendix P, p. 769). This official character disassociates it
from any such doubtful spelling by the foreign Padshah as cannot
but suggest itself when the variants of *e.g.* Dalmau and Bangarmau are considered. L:knur is what three persons copying
independently read in the official List, and so set down that
careful scribes *i.e.* Kehr and 'Abdu'l-lah (App. P) again wrote
L:knur.[1]—Another circumstance favouring L:knur (Lakhnur) is
that the place assigned to it in the List is its geographical one
between Sambhal and Khairabad.—Something for [or perhaps
against] accepting Lakhnur as the *sarkar* of the List may be
known in local records or traditions. It had been an important
place, and later on it paid a large revenue to Akbar [as part of
Sambhal].—It appears to have been worth the attention of
Biban *Jalwani* (f. 329).—Another place is associated with L:knur
in the Revenue List, the forms of which are open to a considerable number of interpretations besides that of Baksar shown
in loco on p. 521. Only those well acquainted with the United
Provinces or their bye-gone history can offer useful suggestion
about it. Maps show a "Madkar" 6m. south of old Lakhnur;
there are in the United Provinces two Baksars and as many
other Lakhnurs (none however being so suitable as what is now
Shahabad). Perhaps in the archives of some old families there
may be help found to interpret the entry *L:knur u B:ks:r* (var.),
a conjecture the less improbable that the *Gazetteer of the
Province of Oude* (ii, 58) mentions a *farman* of Babur Padshah's
dated 1527 AD. and upholding a grant to Shaikh Qazi of Bilgram.

The fourth instance (f.329) is fairly confirmed as Lakhnur
by its context, *viz.* an officer received the district of Badayun
from the Padshah and was sent against Biban who had laid
siege to L:knur on which Badayun bordered.—At the time
Lakhnau may have been held from Babur by Shaikh Bayazid

1 It may indicate that the List was not copied by Babur but lay loose with his
papers, that it is not with the Elphinstone Codex, and is not with the 'Abdu'r-rahim
Persian translation made from a manuscript of that same annotated line.

Farmuli in conjunction with Aud. Its estates are recorded as still in Farmuli possession, that of the widow of "Kala Pahar" *Farmuli*.—(*See infra*.)

The fifth instance (f. 334) connects with Aud (Oudh) because royal troops abandoning the place L:knu were those who had been sent against Shaikh Bayazid in Aud.

The remaining three instances (f. 376, f. 376*b*, f. 377*b*) appear to concern one place, to which Biban and Bayazid were rumoured to intend going, which they captured and abandoned. As the table of variants shows, Kehr's MS. reads Lakhnur in all three places, the Hai. MS. once only, varying from itself as it does in Nos. 1 and 2.—A circumstance supporting *Lakhnur* is that one of the messengers sent to Babur with details of the capture was the son of Shah Muh. *Diwana* whose record associates him rather with Badakhshan, and with Humayun and Sambhal [perhaps with Lakhnur itself] than with Babur's own army.— Supplementing my notes on these three instances, much could be said in favour of reading Lakhnur, about time and distance done by the messengers and by 'Abdu'l-lah *kitabdar*, on his way to Sambhal and passing near Lakhnur; much too about the various rumours and Babur's immediate counter-action. But to go into it fully would need lengthy treatment which the historical unimportance of the little problem appears not to demand.—Against taking the place to be Lakhnau there are the considerations (*a*) that Lakhnur was the safer harbourage for the Rains and less near the westward march of the royal troops returning from the battle of the Goghra; (*b*) that the fort of Lakhnau was the renowned old Machchi-bawan (cf. *Gazetteer of the Province of Oude*, 3 vols., 1877, ii, 366).—So far as I have been able to fit dates and transactions together, there seems no reason why the two Afghans should not have gone to Lakhnur, have crossed the Ganges near it, dropped down south [perhaps even intending to recross at Dalmau] with the intention of getting back to the Farmulis and Jalwanis perhaps in Sarwar, perhaps elsewhere to Bayazid's brother Ma'ruf.

U.—THE INSCRIPTIONS ON BABUR'S MOSQUE IN AJODHYA (OUDH).

THANKS to the kind response made by the Deputy-Commissioner of Fyzabad to my husband's enquiry about two inscriptions mentioned by several Gazetteers as still existing on "Babur's Mosque" in Oudh, I am able to quote copies of both.[1]

a. The inscription inside the Mosque is as follows:—

١. بفرموده شاه بابر که عدلش * بنایست تا کاخ گردون ملاقی

٢. بنا کرد این مهبط قدسیان * امیر سعادت نشان میر باقی

٣. بود خیر باقی چو سال بنایش * عیان شد که گفتم بود خیر باقی

1. *Ba farmuda-i-Shah Babur ki 'adilash*
   Bana'ist ta kakh-i-gardun mulaqi,
2. *Bana kard in muhbit-i-qudsiyan*
   Amir-i-sa'adat-nishan Mir Baqi
3. *Bavad khair baqi! chu sal-i-bana'ish*
   'Iyan shud ki guftam,—Buvad khair baqi (935).

The translation and explanation of the above, manifestly made by a Musalman and as such having special value, are as follows:—[2]

1. By the command of the Emperor Babur whose justice is an edifice reaching up to the very height of the heavens,

2. The good-hearted Mir Baqi built this alighting-place of angels;[3]

3. *Bavad khair baqi!* (May this goodness last for ever!)[4]

---

1 *Cf. in loco* p. 656, n. 3.
2 A few slight changes in the turn of expressions have been made for clearness sake.
3 Index *s.n.* Baqi Beg *Tashkindi.* Perhaps a better epithet for *sa'adat-nishan* than "good-hearted" would be one implying his good fortune in being designated to build a mosque on the site of the ancient Hindu temple.
4 There is a play here on Baqi's name; perhaps a good wish is expressed for his prosperity together with one for the long permanence of the sacred building *khair* (*khairat*).

The year of building it was made clear likewise when I said, *Buvad khair baqi* (= 935).[1]

The explanation of this is:—

1st couplet:—The poet begins by praising the Emperor Babur under whose orders the mosque was erected. As justice is the (chief) virtue of kings, he naturally compares his (Babur's) justice to a palace reaching up to the very heavens, signifying thereby that the fame of that justice had not only spread in the wide world but had gone up to the heavens.

2nd couplet:—In the second couplet, the poet tells who was entrusted with the work of construction. Mir Baqi was evidently some nobleman of distinction at Babur's Court.—The noble height, the pure religious atmosphere, and the scrupulous cleanliness and neatness of the mosque are beautifully suggested by saying that it was to be the abode of angels.

3rd couplet:—The third couplet begins and ends with the expression *Buvad khair baqi*. The letters forming it by their numerical values represent the number 935, thus:—

$B = 2, v = 6, d = 4$	total	12
$Kh = 600, ai = 10, r = 200$	,,	810
$B = 2, a = 1, q = 100, i = 10$	,,	113
	Total	935

The poet indirectly refers to a religious commandment (*dictum?*) of the Qoran that a man's good deeds live after his death, and signifies that this noble mosque is verily such a one.

b. The inscription outside the Mosque is as follows:—

١. بنام انکه دانا هست اکبر * که خالق جمله غالم لامکانی

٢. درود مصطفی' بعد از ستایش * که سرور انبیائی دو جهانی

٣. فسانه در جهان بابر قلندر * که شد در دور گیتی کامرانی

---

1 Presumably the order for building the mosque was given during Babur's stay in Aud (Ajodhya) in 934 AH. at which time he would be impressed by the dignity and sanctity of the ancient Hindu shrine it (at least in part) displaced, and like the obedient follower of Muhammad he was in intolerance of another Faith, would regard the substitution of a temple by a mosque as dutiful and worthy.—The mosque was finished in 935 AH. but no mention of its completion is in the *Babur-nama*. The diary for 935 AH. has many minor *lacunae*; that of the year 934 AH. has lost much matter, breaking off before where the account of Aud might be looked for.

1. *Ba nam-i-anki dana hast akbar*
    Ki khaliq-i-jamla 'alam la-makani
2. *Durud Mustafá ba'd az sitayish*
    Ki sarwar-i-ambiya' du jahani
3. *Fasana dar jahan Babur qalandar*
    Ki shud dar daur giti kamrani.[1]

The explanation of the above is as follows:—

In the first couplet the poet praises God, in the second Muhammad, in the third Babur.—There is a peculiar literary beauty in the use of the word *la-makani* in the 1st couplet. The author hints that the mosque is meant to be the abode of God, although He has no fixed abiding-place.—In the first hemistich of the 3rd couplet the poet gives Babur the appellation of *qalandar*, which means a perfect devotee, indifferent to all worldly pleasures. In the second hemistich he gives as the reason for his being so, that Babur became and was known all the world over as a *qalandar*, because having become Emperor of India and having thus reached the summit of worldly success, he had nothing to wish for on this earth.[2]

The inscription is incomplete and the above is the plain interpretation which can be given to the couplets that are to hand. Attempts may be made to read further meaning into them but the language would not warrant it.

V.—BABUR'S GARDENS IN AND NEAR KABUL.

THE following particulars about gardens made by Babur in or near Kabul, are given in Muhammad Amir of Kazwin's *Padshah-nama* (Bib. Ind. ed. p. 585, p. 588).

1 The meaning of this couplet is incomplete without the couplet that followed it and is (now) not legible.
2 Firishta gives a different reason for Babur's sobriquet of *qalandar*, namely, that he kept for himself none of the treasure he acquired in Hindustan (Lith. ed. p. 206).

Ten gardens are mentioned as made:—the Shahr-ara (Town-adorning) which when Shah-i-jahan first visited Kabul in the 12th year of his reign (1048 AH.—1638 AD.) contained very fine plane-trees Babur had planted, beautiful trees having magnificent trunks,[1] — the Char-bagh, —the Bagh-i-jalau-khana,[2] — the Aurta-bagh (Middle-garden),—the Saurat-bagh,—the Bagh-i-mahtab (Moonlight-garden),—the Bagh-i-ahu-khana (Garden-of-the-deer-house),—and three smaller ones. Round these gardens rough-cast walls were made (renewed?) by Jahangir (1016 AH.).

The above list does not specify the garden Babur made and selected for his burial; this is described apart (*l.c.* p. 588) with details of its restoration and embellishment by Shah-i-jahan the master-builder of his time, as follows:—

The burial-garden was 500 yards (*gaz*) long; its ground was in 15 terraces, 30 yards apart (?). On the 15th terrace is the tomb of Ruqaiya Sultan Begam;[3] as a small marble platform (*chabutra*) had been made near it by Jahangir's command, Shah-i-jahan ordered (both) to be enclosed by a marble screen three yards high.—Babur's tomb is on the 14th terrace. In accordance with his will, no building was erected over it, but Shah-i-jahan built a small marble mosque on the terrace below.[4] It was begun in the 17th year (of Shah-i-jahan's reign) and was finished in the 19th, after the conquest of Balkh and Badakh-shan, at a cost of 30,000 *rupis*. It is admirably constructed.— From the 12th terrace running-water flows along the line (*rasta*) of the avenue;[5] but its 12 water-falls, because not

1 Jahangir who encamped in the Shahr-ara-garden in Safar 1016 AH. (May 1607 AD.) says it was made by Babur's aunt, Abu-sa'id's daughter Shahr-banu (Rogers and Beveridge's *Memoirs of Jahangir* i, 106).
2 A *jalau-khana* might be where horse-head-gear, bridles and reins are kept, but *Ayin* 60 (A.-i-A.) suggests there may be another interpretation.
3 She was a daughter of Hind-al, was a grand-daughter therefore of Babur, was Akbar's first wife, and brought up Shah-i-jahan. Jahangir mentions that she made her first pilgrimage to her father's tomb on the day he made his to Babur's, Friday Safar 26th 1016 AH. (June 12th 1607 AD.). She died *æt.* 84 on Jumada I. 7th 1035 AH. (Jan. 25th 1626 AD.). *Cf. Tuzuk-i-jahangiri*, Muh. Hadi's Supplement lith. ed. p.401.
4 Mr. H.H. Hayden's photograph of the mosque shows pinnacles and thus enables its corner to be identified in his second of the tomb itself.
5 One of Daniel's drawings [not reproduced here] illuminates this otherwise somewhat obscure passage, by showing the avenue, the borders of running-water and the little water-falls,—all reminding of Madeira.

constructed with cemented stone, had crumbled away and their charm was lost; orders were given therefore to renew them entirely and lastingly, to make a small reservoir below each fall, and to finish with Kabul marble the edges of the channel and the waterfalls, and the borders of the reservoirs.——And on the 9th terrace there was to be a reservoir 11 × 11 yards, bordered with Kabul marble, and on the 10th terrace one 15 × 15, and at the entrance to the garden another 15 × 15, also with a marble border.——And there was to be a gateway adorned with gilded cupolas befitting that place, and beyond (*pesh*) the gateway a square station,[1] one side of which should be the garden-wall and the other three filled with cells; that running-water should pass through the middle of it, so that the destitute and poor people who might gather there should eat their food in those cells, sheltered from the hardship of snow and rain.[2]

1 *choki*, perhaps "shelter"; *see* Hobson-Jobson *s.n.*
2 If told with leisurely context, the story of the visits of Babur's descendants to Kabul and of their pilgrimages to his tomb, could hardly fail to interest its readers.

ADDITIONAL NOTES

P. 16 L. 11.—Nizami mentions "lover's marks" where a rebel chieftain commenting on Khusrau's unfitness to rule by reason of his infatuation for Shirin, says, "*Hinoz az'ashiqbazi garm dagh ast*." (H.B.)

P. 22 N. 2.—Closer acquaintance with related books led me to delete the words "Chaghatai Mughul" from Haidar *Dughlat*'s tribal designations (p. 22, n. 2, l. 1). (1) My "Chaghatai" had warrant (now rejected) in Haidar's statement (T.R. trs. p. 3) that the Dughlat amirs were of the same stock (*abna'-i-jins*) as the Chaghatai Khaqans. But the Dughlat off-take from the common stem was of earlier date than Chingiz Khan's, hence, his son's name "Chaghatai" is a misnomer for Dughlats. (2) As for "Mughul" to designate Dughlat, and also Chaghatai chiefs—guidance for us rests with the chiefs themselves; these certainly (as did also the Begchik chiefs) held themselves apart from "Mughuls of the horde" and begs of the horde—as apart they had become by status as chiefs, by intermarriage, by education, and by observance of the amenities of civilized life. To describe Dughlat, Chaghatai and Begchik chiefs in Babur's day as Mughuls is against their self-classification and is a discourtesy. A clear instance of need of caution in the use of the word Mughul is that of 'Ali-sher *Nawa'i Chaghatai*. (Cf. Abu'l-ghazi's accounts of the formation of several tribes.) (3) That "Mughul" described for Hindustanis Babur's invading and conquering armies does not obliterate distinctions in its chiefs. Mughuls of the horde followed Timurids when to do so suited them; there were also in Babur's armies several chiefs of the ruling Chaghatai family, brothers of The Khan, Sa'id (*see* Chin-timur, Aisan-timur, Tukhta-bugha). With these must have been their following of "Mughuls of the horde".

P. 34 L. 12.—"With the goshawks" translates *qirchigha bila* of the Elph. MS. (f. 12*b*) where it is explained marginally by *ba bazi*, with the falcon or goshawk. The Hai. MS. however has, in its text, *piazi bila* which may mean with arrows having points (*Sanglakh* f. 144*b* quoting this passage). Ilminski has no answering word (*Méms.* i, 19). Muh. *Shirazi* [p. 13 l. 11 fr. ft.] writes *ba bazi miandakhtan*.

P. 39.—The *Habibu's-siyar* (lith. ed. iii, 2171.16) writes of Sayyid Murad *Aughlaqchi* (the father or g.f. of Yusuf) that he (who had, Babur says, come from the Mughul horde) held high rank under Abu-sa'id Mirza, joined Husain *Bai-qara* after the Mirza's defeat and death (873 AH.), and (p. 218) was killed in defeat by Amir 'Ali *Jalair* who was commanding for Yadgar-i-muhammad *Shah-rukhi*.

P. 49.—An *Aimaq* is a division of persons and not of territory. In Mongolia under the Chinese Government it answers to khanate. A Khan is at the head of an *aimaq*. Aimaqs are divided into *koshuug*, *i.e.* banners (*Mongolia*, N. Prejevalsky trs. E. Delmar Morgan, ii, 53).

P. 85 N. 2.—The reference to the *Habibu's-siyar* confuses two cases of parricide:— 'Abdu'l-latif's of Aulugh Beg (853–1449) to which H.S. refers [Vol. III, Part 2, p. 163, l. 13 fr. ft.] with (one of 7–628) Shiruya's of Khusrau Parviz (H.S. Vol. I, Part 2, p. 44, l. 11 fr. ft.) where the parricide's sister tells him that the murderer of his father (and 15 brothers) would eventually be punished by God, and (a little lower) the couplet Babur quotes (p. 85) is entered (H.B.).

P. 154 N. 3.—The Persian phrase in the *Siyasat-nama* which describes the numbering of the army (T. *dim kurmak*) is *ba sar-i-taziana shumurdan*. Schafer translates *taziana* by *cravache*. I have nowhere found how the whip was used; (cf. S.N. Pers. text p. 15 l. 5).

P. 171 N. 1.—Closer acquaintance with Babur's use of *darya*, *rud*, *su*, the first of which he reserves for a great river, casts doubt on my suggestion that *darya* may stand for the Kasan-water. But the narrative supports what I have noted. The "upper villages" of Akhsi might be, however, those higher up on the Saihun-darya (Sir-darya).

P. 196.—The *Habibu's-siyar* (lith. ed. iii, 250 l. 11 fr. ft.) writes of *baradaran* of Khusrau Shah, Amir Wali and Pir Wali. As it is improbable that two brothers (Anglicé) would be called Wali, it may be right to translate *baradaran* by brethren, and to understand a brother and a cousin. Babur mentions only the brother Wali.

P. 223 LL. 1–3 fr. ft.—The French translation, differing from 'Abdu'r-rahim's and Erskine's, reads Babur as saying of the ranges separating the cultivated lands of Kabul, that they are *comme des ponts de trèfle*, but this does not suit the height and sometimes permanent snows of some of the separating ranges.—My bald "(great) dams" should have been expanded to suit the meaning (as I take it to be) of the words *Yur-unchaqa pul-dik*, like embankments (*pul*) against going (*yur*) further; (so far, *uncha*). Cf. Griffiths' *Journal*, p. 431).

P. 251.—Nizami expresses the opinion that "Fate is an avenging servitor" but not in the words used by Babur (p. 251). He does this when moralizing on Farhad's death, brought about by Khusrau's trick and casting the doer into dread of vengeance (H.B.).

P. 276 para. 3.—Attention is attracted on this page to the unusual circumstance that a parent and child are both called by the same name, Junaid. One other instance is found in the *Babur-nama*, that of Babur's wife Ma'suma and her daughter. Perhaps "Junaid" like "Ma'suma" was the name given to the child because birth closely followed the death of the parent (*see s.n.* Ma'suma).

P. 277.—Concerning Bih-bud Beg the *Shaibani-nama* gives the following information :—he was in command in Khwarizm and Khiva when Shaibani moved against Chin *Sufi* (910 AH.), and spite of his name, was unpopular (Vambéry's ed. 184, 186). Vambéry's note 88 says he is mentioned in the (anonymous) prose *Shaibani-nama*, Russian trs. p. lxi.

P. 372 L. 2 fr. ft.—Where the Hai. MS. and Kasan Imp. have *mu'araz*, rival, E. and de C. translate by representative, but the following circumstances favour "rival" :—Wais was with Babur (pp. 374–6) and would need no representative. His arrival is not recorded; no introductory particulars are given of him where his name is first found (p.372); therefore he is likely to have joined Babur in the time of the gap of 924 AH. (p. 366), before the siege of Bajaur-fort and before 'Ala'u'd-din did so. The two Sawadi chiefs received gifts and left together (p. 376).

P. 393 L. 4.—In this couplet the point lies in the double-meaning of *ra'iyat*, subject and peasant.

P. 401.—Under date Thursday 25th Babur mentions an appointment to read *fiqah sabaqi* to him. Erskine translated this by "Sacred extracts from the Qoran" (I followed this). But "lessons in theology" may be a better rendering—as more literal and as allowing for the use of other writings than the Qoran. A correspondent Mr. G. Yazdani (Gov. Epigraphist for Muslim Inscriptions, Haidarabad) tells us that it is customary amongst Muslims to recite religious books on Thursdays.

P. 404 L. 7 fr. ft.—Baba Qashqa's family-group is somewhat interesting as that of loyal and capable men of Mughul birth who served Babur and Humayun. It must have joined Babur in what is now the gap between 914 and 925 AH. because not mentioned earlier and because he is first mentioned in 925 AH. without introductory particulars. The following details supplement *Babur-nama* information about the group :—(1) Of Baba Qashqa's murder by Muhammad-i-zaman *Bai-qara* Gul-hadan (f. 23) makes record, and Badayuni (Bib. Ind. ed. i, 450) says that (*cir.* 952 AH.) when Baba's son Haji Muh. Khan *Kuki* had pursued and overtaken the rebel Kamran, the Mirza asked, as though questioning the Khan's ground of hostility to himself, "But did I kill thy father Baba Qashqa?" (*Pidrat Baba Qashqa magar man kushta am*?).—(2) Of the death of Baba Qashqa's brother "Kuki", Abu'l-fazl records that he was killed in Hindustan by Muhammad Sl. M. *Bai-qara* (952 AH.), and that Kuki's nephew Shah Muh. (*see* p. 668) retaliated (955 AH.) by arrow-shooting one of Muh. Sl. Mirza's sons. This was done when Shah Muh. was crossing Minar-pass on his return journey from sharing Humayun's exile in Persia (*see* Jauhar).—(3) Haji Muh. Khan *Kuki* and Shah Muhammad Khan appear to have been sons of Baba Qashqa and nephews of "Kuki" (*supra*). They were devoted servants of Humayun but were put to death by him in 958 AH.–1551 AD. (cf. Erskine's *H. of I. Humayun*).—(4) About the word *Kuki* dictionaries afford no warrant for taking it to mean foster-brother (*kokah*). Chingiz Khan had a beg known as Kuk or Kouk (or Guk) and one of his own grandsons used the same style. It may link the Baba Qashqa group with the Chingiz Khanid Kuki, either as descendants or as hereditary adherents, or as both. (*See* Abu'l-ghazi's *Shajarat-i-Turk*, trs. Desmaisons, Index *s.n. Kouk* and also its accounts of the origin of several tribal groups.)

P. 416.—The line quoted by 'Abdu'l-lah is from the *Anwar-i-suhaili*, Book II, Story i. Eastwick translates it and its immediate context thus :—

"People follow the faith of their kings."

"My heart is like a tulip scorched and by sighings flame;

"In all thou seest, their hearts are scorched and stained the same." (H.B.)
The offence of the quotation appears to have been against Khalifa, and might be a suggestion that he followed Babur in breach of Law by using wine.

P. 487(8) N. 2.—The following passages complete the note on *wulsa* quoted by Erskine from Col. Mark Wilks' *Historical Sketches* and show how the word is used :—"During the absence of Major Lawrence from Trichinopoly, the town had been completely depopulated by the removal of the whole *Wulsa* to seek for food elsewhere, and the enemy had been earnestly occupied in endeavouring to surprise the garrison." (Here follows Erskine's quotation *see in loco* p. 487). "The people of a district thus deserting their homes are called the *Wulsa* of that district, a state of utmost misery, involving precaution against incessant war and unpitying depredation—so peculiar a description as to require in any of the languages of Europe a long circumlocution, is expressed *in all the languages of Deckan and the south of India by a single word*. No proofs can be accumulated from the most profound research which shall describe the immemorial condition of the people of India with more precision than this single word. It is a bright distinction that the *Wulsa* never departs on the approach of a British army when this is unaccompanied by Indian allies."

P. 540 N. 4.—An explanation of Babur's use of Shah-zada as Tahmasp's title may well be that this title answers to the Timurid one Mir-zada, Mirza. If so, Babur's change to "Shah" (p. 635) may recognize supremacy by victory, such as he had claimed for himself in 913 AH. when he changed his Timurid "Mirza" for "Padshah".

P. 557.—Husain *Kashifi*, also, quotes Firdausi's couplet in the *Anwar-i-suhaili* (Cap. I, Story XXI), a book dedicated to Shaikh Ahmad *Suhaili* (p. 277) and of earlier date than the *Babur-nama*. Its author died in 910 AH.–1505 AD.

P. 576 N. 1.—Tod's statement (quoted in my n. 1) that "the year of Rana Sanga's defeat (933 AH.) was the last of his existence" cannot be strictly correct because Babur's statement (p. 598) of intending attack on him in Chitor allows him to have been alive in 934 AH. (1528 AD.). The death occurred, "not without suspicion of poison," says Tod, when the Rana had moved against Irij then held for Babur; it will have been long enough before the end of 934 AH. to allow an envoy from his son Bikramajit to wait on Babur in that year (pp. 603, 612). Babur's record of it may safely be inferred lost with the once-existent matter of 934 AH.

P. 631.—My husband has ascertained that the "Sayyid Dakni" of p. 631 is Sayyid Shah Tahir *Dakni* (*Deccani*) the Shiite apostle of Southern India, who in 935 AH. was sent to Babur with a letter from Burhan Nizam Shah of Ahmad-nagar, in which (if there were not two embassies) congratulation was made on the conquest of Dihli and help asked against Bahadur Shah *Gujrati*. A second but earlier mention of "Sayyid *Dakni*" (*Zakni, Rukni*?) *Shirazi* is on p. 619. Whether the two entries refer to Shah Tahir nothing makes clear. The cognomen Shirazi disassociates them. It is always to be kept in mind that preliminary events are frequently lost in gaps; one such will be the arrivals of the various envoys, mentioned on p. 630, whose places of honour are specified on p. 631. Much is on record about Sayyid Shah Tahir *Dakni* and particulars of his life are available in the histories by Badayuni (Ranking trs.) and Firishta (Nawal Kishor ed. p. 105); B.M. Harleyan MS. No. 199 contains his letters (*see* Rieu's Pers. Cat. p. 395).

P. 699 and N. 3.—The particulars given by the *Tabaqat-i-akbari* about Multan at this date (932–4 AH.) are as follows:—After Babur took the Panj-ab, he ordered Shah Hasan *Arghun* to attempt Multan, then held by one Sl. Mahmud who, dying, was succeeded by an infant son Husain. Shah Hasan took Multan after a 16 (lunar) months' siege, at the end of 934 AH. (in a B.N. *lacuna* therefore), looted and slaughtered in it, and then returned to Tatta. On this Langar Khan took possession of it (H.B.). What part 'Askari (*æt.* 12) had in the matter is yet to learn; possibly he was nominated to its command and then recalled as Babur mentions (935 AH.).

INDEX OF PERSONS

---

1 The fist indicates Translator's matter.

'Abdu'l-karim *Ushrit* (var.) *Auighur*[1] (var.)—serving Ahmad *Miran-shahi* 40; captured by an Auzbeg (902) 65.

'Abdu'l-khaliq Beg *Isfarayini*—particulars 273–4.

Shaikh **'Abdu'l-lah** *aishik-agha*—with Jahangir (899) 32; leaves Babur for home (902) 191.

Sayyid **'Abdu'l-lah** *Andikhudi*—his Bai-qara wife Bairam-sultan and their son Barka *q.v.*

Khwaja **'Abdu'l-lah** *Ansari*—his tomb visited by Babur (912) 305; a surmised attendant on it 145 n. 1; [†481 AH.–1088 AD.].

Shaikh **'Abdu'l-lah** *bakawal*—with the Bai-qara families (913) 328.

Shaikh **'Abdu'l-lah** *Barlas*—particulars 51; excites the Tarkhan rebellion (901) 61–2; his daughter a cause of attempt on Samarkand 64; with his son-in-law Mas'ud *Miran-shahi* (903) 93.

Khwaja **'Abdu'l-lah Khwajagan Khwaja**—fifth son of 'Ubaidu'l-lah *Ahrari*—his son 'Abdu'sh-shahid, *q.v.*

Mulla **'Abdu'l-lah** *kitabdar*—one of eleven left with Babur (913) 337; given the third of a potent confection (925) 373; a drunken lapse 398; induced by Babur to restrict his drinking 399; at a party where Babur, abstaining, watches the drinkers 400–1; rebuked for an offending verse 416; joins Babur in an autumn garden 418; on service (932) 468, 530; in the right centre at Panipat (932) 472, 473, and at Kanwa (933) 565, 569; sent to take possession of Agra 475; is sarcastic 581; in attendance on Auzbeg envoys (935) 631; sent to take charge of Sambhal (935) 675, 687; conveys orders 676; sends news of Biban and Bayazid 679; arrives in Agra, 687.

Khwaja **'Abdu'l-lah** *Marwarid*—particulars 278–9: preeminent on the dulcimer 291; [†922 AH.–1516 AD.].

'Abdu'l-lah Mirza *Shah-rukhi Timurid, Barlas Turk*—succeeds his father, Ibrahim, in Shiraz (838) 20, and his cousin 'Abdu'l-latif in Transoxiana (854) 85–6; Yunas Khan his retainer *q.v.*; [† Jumada I. 22, 855 AH.–1450 AD.].

Khwaja **'Abdu'l-lah Qazi**, see Khwaja Maulana-i-qazi.

---

1 See Abu'l-ghazi's *Shajarat-i-turki* on the origin and characteristics of the tribe (Desmaisons trs. Index *s.n.* Ouighur, especially pp. 16, 37, 39).

---

1 The date 935 AH. is inferred from p. 483.
2 Cf. Badayuni's *Muntakhabu't-tawarikh* and Ranking's trs. i, 616 and n. 4, 617.
3 Ferté translates this sobriquet by *le dévoué* (*Vie de Sl. Hossein Baikara* p. 40 n. 3).

courier to him 25; joined by the Black-sheep Turkmans (872) 49; orders the Hindustan army mobilized 46; defeated and killed by the White-sheep Turkmans (873) 25, 46, 49; appointments named 24,37; his banishment of Nawa'i 271; reserves a Chaghatai wife for a son 21, 36; his Badakhshi wife and their son 22, 260; his Tarkhan *Arghun* wife and their sons, 33, 45; his mistress Khadija *q.v.*; his daughters Payanda-sultan, Shahr-banu, Rabi'a-sultan, Khadija-sultan, Fakhr-i-jahan, Apaq-sultan, Aq Begim *q.v.*; retainers named as his 'Ali-dost *Sagharichi*, Muhammad Baranduq, Aurus, and Zu'n-nun *Arghun q.v.*; his marriage connection Nuyan *Tirmizi q.v.*; [†873 AH.–1469 AD.].

Abu-sa'id Puran, see Jamalu'd-din.

Abu-sa'id Sultan *Auzbeg-Shaiban, Chingiz-khanid*, son of Kuchum—☞ at Ghaj-davan (918) 360; at Jam (935) 622, 636; sends an envoy to Babur 631, 632, 641; [†940 AH.–1533–4 AD.].

Shaikh **Abu-sa'id Tarkhan** (var. Bu-sa'id)—his house Mirza Khan's loot in Qandahar (913) 338.

Abu-turab Mirza *Bai-qara Timurid, Barlas Turk*, son of Husain and Mingli—particulars 262, 269; his son Sohrab *q.v.*; [† before 911 AH.–1505–6 AD.].

Adik Sultan *Qazzaq, Juji Chingiz-khanid* (var. Aung Sultan), son of Jani Beg Khan (T.R. trs. 373)—husband of Sultan-nigar *Chaghatai q.v.*

'Adil Sultan *Auzbeg-Shaiban*(?), *Chingiz-khanid*(?), son of Mahdi and a Bai-qara begim—marries Shad *Bai-qara* 263; suggestions as to his descent 264 n. 1; waits on Babur at Kalanur (932) 458; on Babur's service 468, 471, 475, 530; in the left wing at Panipat 472, and at Kanwa (933) 567, 570; ordered against Baluchis (935) 638; ☞ mentioned as a landless man 706.

Sayyida **Afaq**, a legendary wife of Babur 358 n. 2; her son and grandson *ib.*

Afghani Aghacha, see Mubarika.

Sayyid **Afzal Beg**, son of 'Ali *Khwab-bin*—conveys Husain *Bai-qara*'s summons to Babur for help against Shaibani (911) 255; particulars 282; takes news to Herat of Babur's start from Kabul (912) 294; sends him news of Husain's death 295; [†921 AH.–1516 AD.].

Ahmadi *parwanchi*—on service (925) 377, (932) 458, 460, (933) 540; sent to surprise Ibrahim *Ludi* (932) 468; in the left centre at Panipat 472, 473; his ill-behaviour in the heats 524.

Sultan **Ahmad Khan**—**Alacha Khan**—*Chaghatai Chingiz-khanid*, son of Yunas and Shah Begim—particulars 23, 160; meaning of his sobriquet Alacha Khan 23; younger Khandada, Babur's name for him 129; considered as a refuge for Babur (899) 29, (903) 92, (906) 129, (908) 158; visits Tashkint (908) 159; ceremonies of meeting 160–1, 171–2; moves with his elder brother Mahmud against Tambal 161, 168, 171; his kindness to Babur 159, 166–7, 169, 171; is given Babur's lands and why 168; retires from Andijan in fear of Shaibani 172; defeated by Shaibani at Archian (908 or 909) 7, 23, ☞ 182–3; his death (909) reported to Babur (911) 246 and n. 4: his sons Mansur, Sa'id, Baba (T.R. trs. 160, Babajak), Chin-timur, Tukhta-bugha, and Aisan-timur *q.v.*; his grandson Baba *q.v.*; ☞ followers of his return from forced migration (908) when Shaibani is killed (916) 351; [† end of 909 AH.–1504 AD.].

Ahmad Khan *Haji-tarkhani* (*Astrakhani*)—marries Badi'u'l-jamal (Badka) *Bai-qara* (899?) 257, 258; their sons (Mahmud and Bahadur) 258; their daughter Khan-zada *q.v.*

Sultan **Ahmad Mirza** *Dughlat*—sent by The Khan (Mahmud) to help Babur (908) 161.

Sultan **Ahmad Mirza** *Miran-shahi Timurid, Barlas Turk*, son of Abu-sa'id—the lands his father gave him 35, 86; his brother Mahmud taken to his care (873 or 4) 46; his disaster on the Chir (895) 17, 25, 31, 34; a swift courier to him 25; defeats 'Umar Shaikh 17, 34; 12 n. 2; 53; invades Farghana (899) 13, 30; given Aura-tipa 27; dreaded for Babur 29; retires and dies 31, 33; particulars 33, 40; referred to by Husain *Bai-qara* (910) 190; his wives and children 35–6; an honoured Beg Nuyan *Tirmizi* q.v.; [†899 AH.–1494 AD.].

Sultan **Ahmad Mirza** *Miran-shahi Timurid, Barlas Turk*, son of Mirza Sayyidi Ahmad—particulars 257 n. 5; his wife Aka Begim *Bai-qara* and their son Kichik Mirza *q.v.*; 266 n. 6; a building of his at Heri 305.

Ahmad *mushtaq, Turkman*—takes Mahmud *Miran-shahi* to Hisar (873 or 4) 46–7.

Sultan **Ahmad** *qarawal*, father of Quch (Quj) Beg, Tardi Beg and Sher-afgan Beg *q.v.*—defends Hisar (901) 58; enters Babur's service (905) 112; in the left wing at Khuban (905) 113; holds Marghinan 123.

Ahmad-i-qasim *Kohbur Chaghatai*, son of Haidar-i-qasim—with Babur (906) 133; invited to a disastrous entertainment (907) 152; joins Jahangir and Tambal 156; in Akhsi (908) 171; defeats an Auzbeg raider (910) 195; helps to hold Kabul for Babur (912) 313; pursues Mirza Khan 317, 320; holding Tashkint against Auzbegs (918) 356, 358, 396, 397; a Kabuli servant of his 351.

Ahmad-i-qasim *Qibchaq Turk*, (grand-?) son of Baqi *Chaghaniani* and a sister of Khusrau Shah, perhaps son of Baqi's son Muhammad-i-qasim (189 n. 3)—holding Kahmard and Bamian (910) 189; given charge of the families of Babur's expeditionary force 189; ill-treats them and is forced to flee 197, 243; goes to Husain *Bai-qara ib.*; killed at Qunduz 244; [†910 AH.–1505 AD.].

Sultan **Ahmad Qazi** *Qilich*—particulars 29; his son Khwaja Maulana-i-qazi *q.v.*

Ahmad *qushchi*—seen by the fugitive Babur (908) 180.

Khwaja **Ahmad** *Sajawandi*—his birthplace 217.

Ahmad Shah *Khilji Turk*—dispossessed of Chandiri by Ibrahim *Ludi* 593; restored by Babur (934) 598.

Ahmad Shah *Durrani, Abdali Afghan*—his victory at Panipat (1174) 472; [†1182 AH.–1772 AD.].

Ahmad Tarkhan *Arghun Chingiz-khanid* (?)—joins Babur in Samarkand (906) 133; loses Dabusi to Shaibani 137; [†906 AH.–1500 AD.].

Ahmad (son of) Tawakkal *Barlas*, amir of Husain *Bai-qara* —particulars 272.

Ahmad *yasawal*—conveys a message from Babur to the begs of Kabul Fort (912) 314.

Khwaja **Ahmad** *Yasawi*—**Sayyid Ata**—Shaibani's vow at his shrine 348, 356; [†514 AH.–1120–1 AD.].[1]

Ahmad-i-yusuf Beg *Aughlaqchi*, son of Hasan, nephew of Yusuf—managing Yar-yilaq for 'Ali *Miran-shahi* (904) 98; dismissed on suspicion of favouring Babur 98; probably joins

---

1 For an account of his tomb see Schuyler's *Turkistan*, I, 70–72.

---

1 Or Aigu (Ayagu) from *ayagh*, foot, perhaps expressing close following of Timur, whose friend the Beg was.

Babur (935) 654; in the battle of the Ghogra 672, 673; thanked 677; angers Babur 684.

Aka Begim *Barlas Turk*, daughter of Timur—an ancestress of Husain *Bai-qara* 256.

Aka Begim *Bai-qara Timurid*, daughter of Mansur and Firuza—particulars 257; her husband Ahmad and their son Kichik Mirza *q.v.*

Abu'l-fath Jalalu'd-din Muhammad **Akbar** *Miran-shahi Timurid, Barlas Turk*, grandson of Babur and Mahim—☞ 184; ☞ an addition about him made to the Chihilzina inscription 432; ☞ his visit to Panipat (963) 472; his change in the name of the cherry explained by Babur's words 501, n. 6; [†1014 AH.–1605 AD.].

Alacha Khan, see Ahmad *Chaghatai*.

Al-aman, son of Humayun—his birth and name (935) 621, 624, 642; [† in infancy].

'Alam Khan *Kalpi*, son of Jalal Khan *Jik-hat* (or *Jig-hat*)—holding Kalpi and not submissive to Babur (932) 523; goes to Court (933) 544; disobeys orders 557; is Babur's host in Kalpi (934) 590; on service (935) 682; an order about him 684.

'Alau'u'd-din **'Alam Khan** *Ludi Afghan*, son of Buhlul—☞ a principal actor between 926–32 AH. 428; ☞ asks and obtains Babur's help against his nephew Ibrahim (929) 439–441: placed by Babur in charge of Dibalpur (930) 442; ☞ defeated by Daulat Khan *Yusuf-khail* (931) 444; flees to Kabul and is again set forth 444, 455; defeated by Ibrahim and returns to Babur (932) 454–8; his relations with Babur reviewed 455, n. 1; in Fort Ginguta 457, 463; in the left centre at Kanwa (933) 565; his sons Jalal, Kamal, and Sher Khan (*Ludi*) *q.v.*

Sultan 'Alau'u'd-din **'Alam Khan** *Sayyidi*—holding Dihli 481; [†855 AH.–1451 AD.].

'Alam Khan *Tahangari*, brother of Nizam Khan of Biana—works badly with Babur's force (933) 538; defeated by his brother 539; sent out of the way before Kanwa 547.

'Alau'u'd-din Husain Shah, ruler in Bengal—the circumstances of his succession 483; his son Nasrat *q.v.*; [†925 AH.–1518 AD. ?].

'Alau'u'd-din Husain *Jahan-soz Ghuri*—his destruction in Ghazni (550) 219; [†556 AH.–1161 AD. ?].

Sultan **'Alau'u'd-din Muhammad Shah** *Khilji Turk*—
Babur visits his tomb and minar (932) 476; his bringing of the
Koh-i-nur from the Dakkhin 477; [†715 AH.–1315 AD.].

Sultan **'Alau'u'd-din** *Sawadi*—waits on Babur (925) 372, 375–6.

'Alaul Khan *Sur Afghan*—writes dutifully to Babur (935) 659.

'Alaul Khan *Nuhani Afghan*—his waitings on Babur (934, 935)
677, 680.

Sharafu'd-din Muhammad **al Busiri**—his *Qasidatu'l-burda* an
example for the *Walidiyyah-risala* 620; [†cir. 693 AH.–1294 AD.].

Alexander of Macedon, see Iskandar *Filqus* (*Failaqus*).

Sayyid **'Ali**—escapes from a defeat (909) 102; out with Babur (925)
403; sent against Baluchis (935) 638.

Sultan **'Ali** *asghar* Mirza *Shah-rukhi Timurid, Barlas Turk*,
son of Mas'ud *Kabuli*—particulars 382.

'Ali Ataka, servant of Khalifa—reinforces the right wing (*tulghuma*) at Kanwa (933) 569.

Shaikh **'Ali Bahadur,** one of Timur's chiefs—his descendant
Baba 'Ali 27.

Khwaja **'Ali Bai**—mentioned (906) 127; fights for Babur at Sar-i-
pul (Khwaja Kardzan) 139; his son Jan-i-'ali *q.v.*

Shaikh **'Ali** *Barin Mughul*, son of Shaikh Jamal—in the left wing
(*tulghuma*) at Panipat (932) 473; sent against Baluchis (935) 638.

'Ali *Barlas Turk*—his son Muhammad Baranduq *q.v.*

'Ali Beg *Jalair Chaghatai*, father of Hasan-i-'Ali and Apaq Bega—
his Shah-rukhi service 278.[1]

Mir (Shaikh) **'Ali Beg** *Turk* (inferred 389), governor of Kabul for
Shah-rukh *Timurid*—his sons Baba Kabuli, Darya Khan, and
Ghazi (Apaq) Khan (*q.v.*) cherished by Mas'ud *Shah-rukhi* 382;
(see his son Ghazi's grandson Minuchihr for a Turk relation
386).

Sultan **'Ali** *chuhra, Chaghatai*—his loyalty to Babur doubted (910)
239; rebels (914) 345.

Sayyid **'Ali-darwesh Beg** *Khurasani*—particulars 28; with
Jahangir (*æt.* 8), in Akhsi (899) 32, leaves Babur for home (903)
91; on Babur's service (904) 106, (905) 28, 118.

---

1 Daulat-shah celebrates the renown of the Jalair section (*farqa*) of the Chaghatai
tribes (*aqwam*) of the Mughul horde (*aulus, ulus*), styles the above-entered 'Ali Beg
a veteran hero, and links his family with that of the Jalair Sultans of Baghdad
(Browne's ed. p. 519).

Mir **'Ali-dost Taghai** *Kunji Mughul*, a Sagharichi-*tuman* beg—
particulars 27–8; his appointment on Babur's accession (899) 32;
has part in a conference (900) 43; surrenders Andijan (903)
88–9; asks Babur's pardon (904) 99; gives him Marghinan 100;
defeated by Tambal 106; in the right wing at Khuban (905) 113;
his ill-timed pacifism 118; his self-aggrandizement 119, 123;
joins Babur against Samarkand 123; in fear of his victims, goes
to Tambal 125; his death *ib.*; his brother Ghiyas, his son Muhammad-dost, and his servant Yul-chuq *q.v.*; [†a few years after
05 AH.–1500 AD.].

Mir Sayyid **'Ali** *Hamadani*—his death and burial 211; [†786 AH.–
1384 AD.].

Mulla **'Ali-jan** (var. Khan)—fetches his wife from Samarkand
(925) 403; is taught a rain-spell (926) 423; makes verse on the
Kabul-river (932) 448; a satirical couplet on him made and repented by Babur 448; host of Mulla Mahmud *Farabi* (935) 653.

'Ali Khan *Bayandar, Aq-quiluq Turkman*—joins Husain *Bai-qara*
(873) 279.

Shaikh-zada **'Ali Khan** *Farmuli Afghan*—his family-train captured
(932) 526; waits on Babur 526–7; in the left wing at Kanwa
(933) 567; on service 576, 582, 678.

'Ali Khan *Istilju*—leads Isma'il *Safawi's* reinforcement to Babur
(917) 353.

Sayyid **'Ali Khan** *Turk*, son of Ghazi (Apaq) Khan and grandson
of Mir (Shaikh) 'Ali Beg—one of Sikandar *Ludi's* Governors in
the Panjab (910) 382; leaves Bhira on Babur's approach *ib.*; his
lands made over by him to Daulat Khan *Yusuf-khail* 382–3; his
son Minuchihr and their Turk relation (389) *q.v.*

'Ali Khan *Turkman*, son of 'Umar Beg—defends the Bai-qara
families against Shaibani (913) 328.

'Ali Khan *Yusuf-khail Ludi Afghan*—eldest son of Daulat Khan—
his servants wait on Babur (925) 382; comes out of Milwat
(Malot) to Babur (932) 459–60; sent under guard to Bhira 461;
his son Isma'il *q.v.*

Sayyid **'Ali** *Khwab-bin*, father of Sayyid Afzal *q.v.* (cf. H.S. lith. ed. iii,
346.

Mulla Sultan **'Ali** *khwush-nawis*, calligrapher of Husain *Bai-qara*—
particulars 291; given lessons in penmanship by Shaibani
(913) 329; [†919 AH.–1513 AD.].

'Ali-mazid Beg *quchin*—particulars 26; leaves Babur for home (903) 91.

Mir **'Ali** *mir-akhwur*[1]—particulars 279; helps Husain *Bai-qara* to surprise Yadgar-i-muhammad *Shah-rukhi* in Heri (875) 134, 279.

Sultan **'Ali Mirza** *Miran-shahi Timurid, Barlas Turk*, son of Mahmud and Zuhra—particulars 47; serving his half-brother Bai-sung-har (900) 27, 55; made *padshah* in Samarkand by the Tarkhans (901) 62–3, 86; meets Babur 64; their arrangement 66; (902) 65, 82, 86; gives no protection to his blind half-brother Mas'ud (903) 95; suspects a favoured beg (904) 98; quarrels with the Tarkhans (905) 121; desertions from him 122; defeats Mirza Khan's Mughuls *ib.*; is warned of Babur's approach 125; gives Samarkand to Shaibani and by him is murdered (906) 125–7; his wife Sultanim *Miran-shahi* and sister Makhdum-sultan *q.v.*; [†906 AH.–1500 AD.].

Sultan **'Ali Mirza Taghai** *Begchik* (Mirza Beg Taghai), brother(?) of Babur's wife Gul-rukh—movements of his which bear on the *lacuna* of 914–924 AH. 408; arrives in Kabul (925) *ib.*; Kamran marries his daughter (934) 619; conveys Babur's wedding gifts to Kamran (935) 642; takes also a copy of the *Walidiyyah-risala* and of the Hindustan poems, with writings (*sar-khatt*) in the Baburi script 642.

Ustad **'Ali-quli**—his match-lock shooting at Bajaur (925) 369; shoots prisoners (932) 466; ordered to make Rumi defences at Panipat 469; fires *firingis* from the front of the centre 473; casts a large mortar (933) 536, 547; his jealousy of Mustafa *Rumi* 550; his post previous to Kanwa 558; his valiant deeds in the battle 570–1; a new mortar bursts (934) 588; his choice of ground at Chandiri 593; his stone-discharge interests Babur 595, 670–1–2; uses the Ghazi mortar while the Ganges bridge is in building 599; a gift to his son (935) 633; his post in the battle of the Ghogra 667, 668, 669.

'Ali-quli *Hamadani*—☞ sent by Babur to punish the Mundahirs, and fails (936) 700.

---

1 See H. S. lith. ed. iii, 224, for three men who conveyed helpful information to Husain.

Mir **'Ali** *qurchi*—conveys playing-cards to Shah Hasan *Arghun* (933) 584.

Malik **'Ali** *qutni*(?)—in the left centre at Bajaur (925) 369.

'Ali Sayyid *Mughul*—in the right wing at Qandahar (913) 334; rebels (914) 345; his connection Aurus-i'Ali Sayyid 335.

'Ali *shab-kur* (night-blind)—one of five champions defeated in single combat by Babur (914) 349.

Mir **'Ali-sher Beg** *Chaghatai*, pen-names Nawa'i and Fana'i —his obligations to Ahmad Haji Beg and return to Herat 38; fails in a mission of Husain *Bai-qara*'s (902) 69; his Turki that of Andijan 4; checks Husain in Shi'a action 258; opposes administrative reform 282; particulars 271–2; his relations with Bana'i 286–7, 648; corresponds with Babur (906) 106; exchanges quatrains with Pahlawan Bu-sa'id 292; some of his poems transcribed by Babur (925) 419; his restoration of the Rabat-i-sangbast 301 n. 1; his flower-garden (*baghcha*) and buildings visited or occupied by Babur (912) 301, 305, 306; his brother Darwesh-i-'ali *q.v.*; a favoured person 278; a mystic of his circle 280–1; his scribe 271; [†906 AH.–Dec. 1500 AD.].

'Ali-shukr Beg of the Baharlu, aimaq of the Aq-quiluq Turkmans—his daughter Pasha, grandson Yar-i-'ali *Balal*, and descendant Bairam Khan-i-khanan *q.v.*

Sultan **'Ali Sistani** *Arghun*—his help against Shaibani counselled (913) 326; ☛ one of five champions worsted by Babur in single combat (914) 349; with Babur and chops at a tiger (925) 393.

Shaikh **'Ali Taghai** *Mervi*(?)—holding Balkh for Badi'u'z-zaman *Bai-qara* (902) 70; joint-darogha in Heri (911) 293.

Allah-birdi (var. quli)—serving Babur (910) 234.

Allah-wairan *Turkman*—in the van at Qandahar (913) 335.

Alur or Alwar,[1] son of Babur and Dil-dar—mentioned 689 n. 5. ☛ 712; [† died an infant].

Amin Mirza—an Auzbeg envoy to Babur (935) 631; receives gifts 632, 641.

Amin-i-muhammad Tarkhan *Arghun*—punished for disobedience (925) 390–1; deals with a drunken companion 415.

---

1 Like his brother Hind-al's name, Alur's may be due to the taking (*al*) of Hind.

Khwaja and Khwajagi **Asadu'l-lah** *Jan-dar, Khawafi*—with Babur
    in Dikh-kat (907) 150; envoy to Tahmasp *Safawi* (933) 540, 583;
    has charge of Ibrahim *Ludi*'s mother 543; in the right wing at
    Kanwa 566, 569.

Khwaja **Asafi**—particulars 286; waits on Babur (912) 286: [†920 or
    926 AH.–1514 or 1520 AD.].

'Asas, see Khwaja Muhammad 'Ali *'asas*.

'Ashiq *bakawal*—with advance-troops for Chandiri (934) 590;
    ordered on service (935) 638.

'Ashiq-i-muhammad Kukuldash *Arghun*, son of "Amir
    Tarkhan Junaid" (H.S. lith. ed. iii, 359)—defends Alaqurghan
    against Shaibani (913) 328; his brother Mazid Beg *q.v.*

'Ashiqu'l-lah *Arghun*—killed fighting against Babur at Qandahar
    (913) 333.

Asiru'd-din *Akhsikiti*, a poet—his birthplace Akhsi-village (kit-
    kint) 9–10; [†608 AH.–1211–2 AD.].

Muhammad **'Askari** *Miran-shahi Timurid, Barlas Turk*, son of Babur
    and Gul-rukh—☛ his birth (922) 364; gifts to him (932) 523,
    (933) 628; ☛ his recall from Multan (934) 603–4–5, 699¹; waits
    on his father (935) 605; made Commander of the army of the
    East 628, 637; at a feast 631; takes leave 634; waits on his father at
    Dugdugi 651; east of the Ganges 654; in the battle of the Ghogra
    668–9, 671–3; waits on Babur after the victory 674; [†965 AH.–
    1557–8 AD.].

Asuk Mal *Rajput*—negotiates with Babur for Sanga's son (934–5)
    612–3.

Sayyid **'Ata**, see Khwaja Ahmad *Yasawi*.

Khwaja Jamalu'd-din **'Ata**—particulars 282.

Ataka *bakhshi* (var. Atika, Pers. Atka)—a surgeon who dresses a
    wound of Babur's (908) 169.

Ata *mir-akhwur*—gives Babur a meal (925) 418.

Mir Burhanu'd-din **'Ata'u'l-lah** *Mashhadi*—particulars 285
    (H.S. iii, 345); [†926 AH.–1520 AD.].

Atun Mama, a governess—walks from Samarkand to Pashaghar
    (907) 148; mentioned? (925) 407 l. 4.

Aughan-birdi *Mughul* (var. Afghan-birdi and -tardi)—on service

---

1 See the *Tabaqat-i-akbari* account of the rulers of Multan.

(925) 376, 377; of a boat-party 387; in the battle of the Ghogra (935) 671, 672.

Sayyid *Aughlaqchi*, see Murad.

Auliya Khan *Ishraqi*—waits on Babur (935) 677.

Aulugh Beg Mirza *Bai-qara Timurid, Barlas Turk*, son of Muhammad Sultan Mirza—his (?) journey to Hindustan (933) 265.

Aulugh Beg Mirza *Kabuli, Miran-shahi, ut supra*, son of Abu-sa'id —particulars 95; his earliest guardians amusingly frustrate his designs against them 270; his dealings with the Yusuf-zai App. K. 752; his co-operation with Husain *Bai-qara* against the Auzbegs 190; his praise of Istalif 216; his death (907) 185; gardens of his bought by Babur (perhaps one only) 216, (911) 246; another garden 315; houses of his 247, 251; his Almshouse 315; referred to 284; his joint-guardians Muhammad Baranduq and Jahangir *Barlas*, his later one Wais Ataka *q.v.*; his sons 'Abdu'r-razzaq and Miran-shah, his daughter Bega Begim and daughter-in-law Manauwar *q.v.*; [†907 AH.–1501–2 AD.].

Aulugh Beg Mirza *Shah-rukhi, ut supra* (Ulugh), son of Shah-rukh—his Trans-oxus rule 85; receives Yunas *Chaghatai* badly (832–3?) 19–20; defeated by Aba-bikr *Miran-shahi* 260; his family dissensions 20; his constructions, Astronomical and other 74, 77, 78–9; his sportsmanship 34[1]; his murder and its chronograms 85; Babur resides in his College (906) 142; his sons 'Abdu'l-latif and 'Abdu'l-'aziz *q.v.*; a favoured beg Yusuf *Aughlaqchi q.v.* [†853 AH.–1449 AD.].

Aulus Agha (Ulus), daughter of Khwaja Husain *q.v.*—particulars 24.

Aurdu-bugha Tarkhan *Arghun* (Urdu)—his son-in-law Abu-sa'id *Miran-shahi* and son Darwesh-i-muhammad *q.v.*

Aurdu-shah—murdered as an envoy (923) 463 n. 3.

Aurang-zib Padshah *Miran-shahi Timurid, Barlas Turk*— ☛ referred to as of Babur's line 184; [†1118 AH.–O.S. 1707 AD.].

Amir **Aurus**—☛ flees from his post on Shaibani's death (916) 350.

Aurus-i 'Ali Sayyid *Mughul*, son? of 'Ali Sayyid—in the centre at Qandahar (913) 335.

1 See Daulat-shah (Browne's ed. p. 362) for an entertaining record of the Mirza's zeal as a sportsman and an illustrative anecdote by Shaikh 'Arif '*azari q.v.* (H.B.).

Aurus *Arghun*—his son Muhammad-i-aurus *q.v.*

Auzbeg Bahadur (Uzbeg)—☞ one of five champions worsted in single combat by Babur (914) 349 n. 1.

Auzun Hasan Beg *Aq-quiluq Turkman*—his defeat of the Qara-quiluq Turkmans and of Abu-sa'id *Miran-shahi* 49; [†883 AH.—1478 AD.].

Khwaja **Auzun Hasan** (Uzun)¹—negotiates for Babur (899) 30; his appointment 32; confers in Babur's interests (900) 43; acts for Jahangir against Babur (903) 87, 88, 91, (904) 100, 101, 102; his servant's mischievous report of Babur's illness (903) 89; his men defeated by Babur's allies 102; loses Akhsi and Andijan 102–3; captured and released by Babur 104; goes into Samarkand to help Babur (907) 146; his brother Husain and adopted son Mirim *q.v.*

'Ayisha-sultan Begim *Bai-qara Timurid, Barlas Turk*, daughter of Husain—particulars 267; her husbands Qasim *Auzbeg Shaiban* and Buran, her sons Qasim-i-husain and 'Abdu'l-lah *q.v.*

'Ayisha-sultan Begim *Miran-shahi, ut supra*, daughter of Ahmad (Alacha Khan) and first wife of Babur—particulars 35, 36; married (905) 35, 120, 711; joins Babur in Samarkand (906) 135–6; her child 136; leaves Babur 36.

Mir **Ayub Beg** *Begchik*—particulars 50; sent by The Khan (Mahmud) to help Babur (903) 92, (906) 138, 161, 170; his Mughuls misbehave at Sar-i-pul (Khwaja Kardzan) 140; claims post in the right wing (*tulghuma*) 155; his Mughuls confuse passwords 164; in the right wing at Qandahar (913) 334; ☞ vainly tempts Sa'id *Chaghatai* to betray Babur (916) 351; ☞ does not then desert 352, 362; ☞ rebels in Hisar (918) 362; ☞ dying, repents his disloyalty (920) 362; his sons Buhlul-i-ayub, Ya'qub-i-ayub and Yusuf-i-ayub *q.v.*; (†920 AH.—1514 AD.].

'Azim Humayun *Sarwani*—invests Gualiar 477; his title changed and why (933) 537; his son Fath Khan *q.v.*

Mir **'Azu**, a musical composer—particulars 292.

Baba 'Ali *aishik-agha* (*ishik*), a Lord-of-the-Gate of Husain

---

1 I have found no statement of his tribe or race; he and his brother are styled Khwaja (H.S. lith. ed. iii, 272); he is associated closely with Ahmad Tambal *Mughul* and Mughuls of the Horde; also his niece's name Aulus Agha translates as Lady of the Horde (*ulus, aulus*). But he may have been a Turkman.

Bai-qara—particulars 278; his son Yunas-i-'ali and friend Badru'd-din *q.v.*

Baba-quli's Sultan **Baba 'Ali Beg**[1]—particulars 27; his sons Baba-quli, Sayyidim 'Ali and Dost-i-anju (?) Shaikh *q.v.*; [†900 AH.—1495 AD.].

Baba-aughuli, see Papa-aughuli.

Baba Chuhra, a household brave—reprieved from death (914) 344; on Babur's service (932) 474, 534, (934) 590, 602; does well in the battle of the Ghogra (935) 671.

Baba Husain, see Husain.

Baba Jan *akhtachi*, a groom or squire—Babur dislocates his own thumb in striking him (925) 409.

Baba Jan *qabuzi*—musician at entertainments (925) 386–7, 388.

Baba Kabuli *Turk*, son of Mir 'Ali, Shah-rukh (*Timurid*)'s Governor of Kabul—nominated 'Umar Shaikh's guardian when Kabul was allotted to the boy 14; particulars 382; his brothers Darya Khan and Ghazi (Apaq) Khan *q.v.*

Baba Khan Sultan *Chaghatai Chingiz-khanid*, (Babajak), son of Ahmad (Alacha Khan)—his ceremonious meeting with Babur (908) 159; [living in 948 Ali.—1542—T.R.].

Baba Khan *Chaghatai*, son of The Khan (Mahmud)—murdered with his father and brothers by Shaibani (914) 35.

Baba Qashqa *Mughul* (perhaps identical with Qashqa Mahmud *Chiras q.v.*)—out with Babur (925) 404, 405; in charge of Dibalpur (930) 442; his brothers Malik Qasim and Kuki; his sons Shah Muhammad, Dost-i-muhammad and Kuki *q.v.*; [†*cir.* 940 AH.—1553 AD.].[2]

Sultan **Baba-quli Beg**, son of Sultan Baba 'Ali Beg—serving under Khusrau Shah (901) 60, 61; with Babur and captured (903) 72; staunch to him 91; in the centre at Qandahar (913) 335; conveys royal letters (932) 529.[3]

---

1 The MS. variants between 'Ali and -quli are confusing. What stands in my text (p. 27) may be less safe than the above.

2 Baba Qashqa was murdered by Muhammad-i-zaman *Bai-qara*. For further particulars of his family group see Add. Notes under p. 404.

3 Sultan Baba-quli Beg is found variously designated Quli Beg, Quli Baba, Sl. 'Ali Baba-quli, Sultan-quli Baba and Baba-quli Beg. Several forms appear to express his filial relationship with Sultan Baba 'Ali (*q.v.*).

Baba Sairami—pursues Babur in his flight from Akhsi (908) 178; promised fidelity but seems to have been false 179–182.

Baba Shaikh *Chaghatai*, brother of Mulla Baba *Pashaghari*—in the left centre at Qandahar (913) 335; ☞ rebels at Ghazni (921) 363; forgiven (925) 397; deserts Humayun (932) 546; his capture and death 545; a reward given for his head *id.*; [†932 or 933 AH.–1526 AD.].

Baba Shaikh—sent out for news (935) 661.

Baba Sher-zad—one of three with Babur against Tambal (908) 163; does well at Akhsi 174; fights against rebels at Kabul (912) 315; at Qandahar (913) 335.

Baba Sultan *Chaghatai Chingiz-khanid*, son of Khalil son of Ahmad (Alacha Khan)—waits on Babur near Kalpi (934) 590; particulars 590; on service 318, (934) 599; not at his post (935) 672.

Baba Yasawal—at the siege of Bajaur (925) 370; chops at a tiger's head 393.

Babu Khan—holding Kalanjar and looking towards Hati *Kakar* (925) 387.

Zahiru'd-din Muhammad **Babur Padshah** *Miran–shahi Timurid, Barlas Turk*—b. Muharram 6th 888 AH.–Feb. 14th 1483 AD. p. 1; †Jumada I, 6th 937 AH.–Dec. 26th 1530 AD. 708;

Parentage:—paternal 13, maternal 19, 21;

Titles:—Mirza (inherited) Padshah (taken) 344, Ghazi (won) 574, Firdaus-makani (Dweller-in-paradise, posthumous) see Gladwin's Revenue Accounts;

Religion:—[1] belief in God's guidance 31, 72–3, 103–13–37–94–99; in His intervention 73, 247, 316, 446–51–74–79, 525–96, 620; that His will was done 55, 100–16–32–34–35–67, 269, 316–22–23–36–37–70, 454–70–71–80, 542–94, 627–28–70, that He has pleasure in good 331; that to die is to go to His mercy 67; reliance on Him 100–08–16–32, 311, 463, 678; God called to witness 254 and invoked to bless 624; His punishment of sin 42–5, 449–77 (Hell), and of breach of Law 449; His visitation of a father's sins on children 45; His predestination of

---

1 Down to p. 346 Babur's statements are retrospective; after p. 346 they are mostly contemporary with the dates of his diary—when not so are in supplementing passages of later data.

events 128, 243–46–53, 469, 594;—prayer to Him for a sign of victory 440, for the dead 246, against a bad wife 258; a life-saving prayer 316;

Characteristics:—ambition 92–7; admiration of high character 27, 67, 89, 90; bitterness and depression (in youth) 91, 130–52–57–78; consideration for dependants 91–9, 158–78–96, 469; distrust of the world 95, 144–56; silent humiliation 119; fairness 15, 24, 91, 105, 469; fearlessness 163–5–73; fidelity:—to word 104, 129 (see 118–9), 172–3, 194, to salt 125, to family-relation,—filial 88–9, 135–49–57–58–88,—fraternal see Jahangir and Nasir,—Timurid 41, 149–57–68, Chaghatai 54, 169–72, Mughul 27, 119–25, Auzbeg 37; friendship see Nuyan and Khw. Kalan; good judgment 43, 87, 91, 134–37–55; gratitude 99, 633; insouciance 150; joy at release from stress 99, 134–35–48–81; bashfulness and passion 120; persistence 92–7 and *passim*; promptitude 117, 170; reprobation of vice, tyranny and cruelty 42–5–6, 50, 66, 70, 90–6, 102–10–25–97, 290 and of an unmotherly woman 125–28; self-reproach 147; self-comment on inexperienced action 165–67–73; dislike of talkativeness 28, 97, 143–92–93; vexation at loss of rule 90–1–9, 129–30–57; truth for truth sake 135, 318; seeking and weighing counsel 73, 100–14–31–41–65–70–73–97–98, 229–30–31–48, 340–76–78, 410–12–69, 524–30–77, 628–39–67–69–82; enjoins Humayun to take counsel 627;

Occupations (non-military):—archery 175; calligraphy see *infra*; literary composition see *infra*; metrical amusements see *infra*; Natural History *passim*; travel, excursions, sight-seeing, social intercourse *passim*; building 5, 217–9, 375–98, in Dulpur 585, 606–07–42, in Agra 642, in Kabul 646–7, in Sikri 588, Ajodhya mosque 656 n. 3, App. U, Panipat mosque 472 n. 1; gardening and garden-making *passim*;—Babur's script (*Baburi-khatt*) devised 910 AH. 228, Qoran transcribed by him in it 228 n. 3; studied by an enquirer 285; alphabet and specimens sent to Babur's sons 642; *Abushqa* account of, App. Q, 777 to 780;

Observance and breaches of Muh. Law:—signs of his Sunni mind *e.g.* 25, 44, 111, 262, 370–7, 483, 547–51–74–89–96, in the *Mubin* and *Walidiyyah-risala q.v.*; his orthodox reputation 711; his heterodox seeming 354, and arrow-sped disclaimer 361;—his boyish obedience as to wine 302, up to his 23rd year

Badi'u'l-jamal **Badka Begim** *Bai-qara, ut supra,* daughter of Mansur and Firuza—particulars 257, 258; her husband Ahmad *Haji-tarkhani,* their sons Mahmud and Bahadur and daughter Khan-zada *q.v.*

Badi'u'z-zaman Mirza *Bai-qara, ut supra,* son of Husain and Bega *Mervi*—serving his father against Khusrau Shah (901) 57; defeated 61; takes offence with his father 61, 69; in arms and defeated by his father 69, 70; his retort on Nawa'i (*q.v.*); goes destitute to Khusrau Shah and is well-treated 70, 130; on Khusrau Shah's service 71; moves with Arghun chiefs against his father (903) 95, 261; gives Babur no help against Shaibani (906) 138; his co-operation sought by his father (910) 190, 191; takes refuge with his father 243; has fear for himself (911) 292–3; joint-ruler in Heri 293; concerts and abandons action against Shaibani (912) 296–7, 301; his social relations with Babur 297–8–9, 300–2–4; courteous to Babur as a non-drinker 303; a false report of him in Kabul (912) 313; irresolute against Shaibani (913) 326; his army defeated 275, 327; abandons his family and flees (1) to Shah Beg *Arghun,* (2) to Isma'il *Safawi* 327; captured in Tabriz by Sultan Salim *Rumi* (920) and dies in Constantinople (923) 327 n. 5; a couplet on his name 201–2; musicians compete in his presence 291; his host-facility 304; his son Muhammad-i-zaman, his begs Jahangir *Barlas* and Zu'n-nun *Arghun q.v.*; joined by Sayyidim *Darban q.v.*; his College in Heri 306; [†923 AH.–1517 AD.].

Sayyid **Badr**—particulars 276; safe-guards Mahmud *Miran-shahi* 46–7; seen by Babur in Herat (912) 299; (see H.S. lith. ed. iii, 233).

Badru'd-din—particulars 278; his friend Baba 'Ali *q.v.*; his son (?) receives Kachwa (934) 590.

Maulana **Badru'd-din** *Hilali, Chaghatai*—particulars 290; his poet-daughter 286 n. 1; [†939 AH.–1532–3 AD.].

Bahadur Khan *Sarwani*—Babur halts at his tomb (935) 686.

Bahadur Khan *Gujrati, Tank Rajput*—ill-received by Ibrahim *Ludi* (932); exchanges friendly letters with Babur 534; becomes Shah in Gujrat 535; is given the Khilji jewels 613 n. 1; [†943 AH.–1547 AD.].

Bahjat Khan (or Bihjat), a Governor of Chandiri—Babur halts near his tank (934) 592, 594.

Bai-qara Mirza *'Umar-shaikhi Timurid, Barlas Turk,* grandson of Timur—mentioned in a genealogy 256; a grandson 'Abdu'l-lah *Andikhudi q.v.*

Bai-qara Mirza *'Umar-shaikhi, ut supra,* son of Mansur and Firuza—particulars 257; his brother Husain, and sons Wais and Iskandar *q.v.*

Bairam Beg[1]—☞ reinforces Babur from Balkh (918) 359; serving Najm *Sani* 360.

Bairam Khan *Baharlu-Qara-quiluq Turkman* (Akbar's Khani-khanan), son of Saif-'ali—his ancestry 91 n. 3, 109 n. 5; ☞ mention of a witness of his assassination 348; quotation of his remarks on Hasan Khan *Mewati* 523 n. 3; [†968 AH.–1561 AD.].

Bairam-sultan Begim *Bai-qara Timurid, Barlas Turk,* daughter of Husain and Mingli—particulars 266; her husband 'Abdu'l-lah *Andikhudi,* their son Barka *q.v.*

Bai-sunghar Mirza *Miran-shahi, ut supra,* son of Mahmud and Pasha—particulars 47, 110–112; succeeds in Samarkand (900) 52, 86; withstands The Khan (Mahmud) 52; the *khutba* read for him in Babur's lands 52; his man surrenders Aura-tipa 55–6; his favouritism incites the Tarkhan rebellion (901) 38, 61; escapes from Tarkhan imprisonment 62, 86; defeated by his half-brother 'Ali 38, 63; prosperous (902) 65; moves against 'Ali 65; retires before Babur 66; at grips with him 67; asks Shaibani's help (903) 73; goes to Khusrau Shah 74; made ruler in Hisar 93, 5, 6, 261; murdered (905) 110; his death referred to 50, 112; his pen-name 'Adili 111; his sister's marriage 41; his brother Mas'ud, his guardian Ayub *q.v.*; [†905 AH.–1499 AD.].

Bai-sunghar Mirza *Shah-rukhi Timurid,* son of Shah-rukh—his servant Yusuf *Andijani* 4; [†837 AH.–1433–4 AD.].

Balkhi *faliz-kari*—grows melons in Agra (935) 686.

Baltu—rescues Khalifa's son Muhibb-i-'ali (933) 550.

Mulla Bana'i—Maulana Jamalu'd-din *Bana'i*—in Khwaja Yahya's service and seen by Babur (901) 64, in Shaibani's (906) 136, in Babur's 64, 136; particulars 286–7; given the Heri's authors to loot (913) 328; Babur recalls a joke of his (935) 648; two of his

---

1 He may be the father of Mun'im Khan (Blochmann's Biographies A.-i-A. trs. 317 and n. 2).

quatrains quoted 137; his musical composition 286, 292; [murdered 918 AH.–1512 AD.].

Banda-i'ali, *darogha* of Karnan—pursues Babur from Akhsi (908) 178–9, 180, 181.

Banda-i-'ali *Yaragi Mughul*, son of Haidar Kukuldash—sent to reinforce Babur (904) 101; in the van at Sar-i-pul (906) 139; his mistimed zeal (908) 176; his son-in-law Qasim Beg quchin *q.v.*

Baqi Beg *Chaghamani, Qibchaq Turk*—his influence on Mas'ud *Miran-shahi* (901) 57, (903) 95; defends Hisar for him (901) 58; acts against him (902) 71; joins Babur (910) 48, 188–9; advises sensibly 190, 197; leaves his family with Babur's 191; dislikes Qambar-i-'ali *Silakh* 192; helps his brother Khusrau to make favourable terms with Babur 192–3; quotes a couplet on seeing Suhail 195; his Mughuls oppose Khusrau 197; mediates for Muqim (910) 199; Babur acts on his advice 230–1, 239, (911) 246, 249; particulars 249–50; dismissed towards Hindustan 250; killed on his road 231, 251; his son Muhammad-i-qasim and grandson (?) Ahmad-i-qasim *q.v.*; [†911 AH.–1505–6 AD.].

Baqi *Gagiani Afghan*—his caravan through the Khaibar (911) 250.

Baqi (*khiz*) *hiz*—opposes Babur (908) 174, 396.

Khwaja **Baqi**, son of Yahya son of Ahrari—murdered 128; [†906 AH.–1500 AD.].[1]

Baqi Beg *Tashkindi, shaghawal* and (later) *ming-bashi* (= *hazari*)— sent to Balkh with promise of head-money (932) 463, 546; on service (934) 590, 601–2; reports from Aud (Oudh) (935) 679; on service with the Aud (Oudh) army 684, 5; leave given him for home 685.

Baqi Tarkhan *Arghun Chingiz-khanid*, son of 'Abdu'l-'ali and a daughter of Aurdu-bugha—particulars 38, 40; consumes the Bukhara revenues (905) 121; defeated by Shaibani 124; occupies Qarshi (? Kesh) (906) 135; plans to join Babur 138; goes to Shai-bani and dies in misery 40.

Baraq Khan *Chaghatai Chingiz-khanid*—mentioned in the gene-alogy of Yunas 19.

Baraq Sultan *Auzbeg-Shaiban, Chingiz-khanid*, son of Siunjuk —at Jam (934) 622.

---

1 See note, Index, *s.n.* Muhammad Zakariya.

1 He is likely to have been introduced with some particulars of tribe, in one of the now unchronicled years after Babur's return from his Trans-oxus campaign.
2 His wife, daughter of a wealthy man and on the mother's side niece of Sultan Buhlul *Ludi*, financed the military efforts of Bayazid and Biban (*Tarikh-i-sher-shahi*, E. and D. iv, 353 ff.).

Bega Begim (5)—Haji Begim—daughter of Yadgar Taghai, wife of Humayun—her son Al-aman *q.v.*

Bega Begim (6)—"the Bibi"—, see Mubarika.

Bega Sultan Begim *Mervi*, wife of Husain *Bai-qara*— particulars 261, 7, 8; divorced 268; her son Badi'u'z-zaman *q.v.*; [893 AH.– 1488 AD.].

Wais *Laghari's* **Beg-gina**—brings Babur news of Al-aman's birth (935) 621, 4.[1]

The **Begims**, Babur's paternal aunts—waited on by him 301, 616, 686.

Begim Sultan, see Sa'adat-bakht.

Begi Sultan Aghacha, *ghunchachi* of Husain *Bai-qara*—particulars 269.

Beg Mirak *Mughul*—brings Babur good news (932) 466; on service (933) 548.

Beg Mirak *Turkman*, a beg of the Chiras (Mughul) *tuman*—acts for Yunas Khan 191; [†832 AH.–1428–9 AD.].

Beg Tilba *Itarachi Mughul*, brother of Ahmad Tambal—induces the Khan (Mahmud) not to help Babur (903) 91, (905) 115; his light departure perplexes his brother 116; invites Shaibani into Farghana (908) 172.

Bhupat Rao, son of Salahu'd-din—killed at Kanwa 573; [†933 AH.–1527 AD.].

Bian Shaikh (Biyan)—his rapid journeys 621, 624; brings news of the battle of Jam (935) 622, 623 n. 3; the source of his news 624 n. 1; hurried back 624, 627.

Bian-quli—his son Khan-quli *q.v.*

Malik **Biban** *Jilwani?*[2] *Afghan*—deserts 'Alam Khan *Ludi* (932) 457 and n. 2; writes dutifully to Babur 464; is presuming at an audience 466; deserts Babur 468, 528; is defeated 528–9; with Bayazid, besieges Luknur (933) 582; defeats Babur's troops 594, 598; opposes Babur in person (934) 598–601; referred to as a rebel (935) 638; serving Mahmud *Ludi* 652, 675; Babur resolves to crush him 677–8; mentioned 679 n. 7, 692; takes Luknur (?)

1 My translation on p. 621 l. 12 is inaccurate inasmuch as it hides the circumstance that Beg-gina alone was the "messenger of good tidings".

2 In taking Biban for a Jilwani, I follow Erskine (as inferences also warrant) but he may be a Ludi.

681, App. T; action taken against him 681–2–5; his constant associate Bayazid *Farmuli q.v.*

Muhammad Shah, **Bihar Khan** *Bihari, Nuhani Afghan,* son of Dar-ya Khan—declared independent in Bihar (932) 523; particulars 664; his widow Dudu and son Jalal *q.v.*; [†934 AH.–1527 AD.].

Bihar Khan *Ludi* (or Pahar Khan,[1] a Panj-ab amir of Ibrahim Ludi's in 930 AH.—[2] defeated by Babur (930) 208, 441 (where add "or Pahar"), 578; a chronogram which fixes the date 575.

Bihjat, see Bahjat.

Bih-bud Beg—particulars 277, App. H, and Additional Notes under p. 277.

Ustad Kamalu'd-din **Bih-zad**—particulars 291; his training due to Nawa'i 272; is instructed in drawing by Shaibani (913) 329.

Raja of Bijanagar (Vijayanagar)—mentioned as ruling in 932 AH. 483.

Raja Bikam-deo, named in the Hindustan Revenue List.

Raja Bikam-chand, *ut supra.*

Raja Bikramajit, *ut supra.*

Bi-khub Sultan (var. Ni- or Nai-khub) ? *Auzbeg-Shaiban*—on Babur's service (934) 589, 602, (935) 651, 682; in the battle of the Ghogra 669.

Rana **Bikramajit**, son of Sanga and Padmawati—negotiations for him with Babur (934) ☛ 603, 612, (935) 612–3, 615, 616; pact made with him 616–7; possessor of Khilji jewels 613; his mother Padmawati and her kinsman Asuk Mal *q.v.*

Raja **Bikramajit** *Gualiari, Tunwar Rajput*—his ancestral fortress 477; his Koh-i-nur (932) 477; his buildings 607–610 and nn.; his palace Babur's quarters (935) 607; his death (932) 477; [†932 AH.–1526 AD.].

Raja **Bikramajit** (Vikramaditya)—his Observatory and Tables 79.

Birim Deo *Malinhas*—on Babur's service (932) 462.

Raja **Bir-sing Deo**—named in the Revenue List (935) 521; his force at Kanwa (933) 562; serving Babur 639.

Khalifa's **Bishka** (?)—a woman who leaves Samarkand with Babur's mother (907) 147.

---

1 For the same uncertainty between Bihar and Pahar see E. and D.'s History of India iv, 352 n. 2.

2 Firishta lith. ed. i, 202.

Bishka Mirza *Itarachi Mughul*—brings and receives gifts (925) 415, 416.

Brethren of Babur—removal of their opposition to his aim on Hindustan 478.

Buhlul-i-ayub *Begchik*, son of Ayub—Babur warned against him (910) 190; joins Babur 196; his misconduct 241, (911) 254.

Sultan **Buhlul**, **Sahu-khail Ludi**, *Afghan*—grandfather of Ibrahim 463; his treasure 470; his tomb visited by Babur 476; his capture of Junpur and Dihli 481; his sons Sikandar and 'Alau'u'd-din *q.v.*; [†894 AH.–1488 AD.].

Pahlawan **Buhlul**, *tufang-andazi*—receives gifts (935) 633.

Bujka, a household bravo—on Babur's service (932) 458, 474, 534, (933) 545; his success at Biana 547.

Malik **Bu Khan** *Dilah-zak (Dilazak) Afghan*—receives gifts from Babur (925) 394; brings tribute 409.

Buran Sultan *Auzbeg-Shaiban*—his marriage with 'Ayisha-sultan *Bai-qara* 267; their son 'Abdu'l-lah *q.v.*

Shaikh **Burhanu'd-din 'Ali Qilich**, *Marghinani*, author of the *Hidayat*—his birthplace Rashdan 7; a descendant 29, 89; [†593 AH.–1197 AD.].

Malik **Bu-sa'id** *Kamari*—a guide (910) 230, 231; doubted 233.

Chaghatai Khan, second son of Chingiz Khan—his *yurt* (camping-ground) occupied by his descendant Yunas 12; mentioned in the genealogy of Yunas 19; [†638 AH.–1241 AD.].

Chaku *Barlas*, one of Timur's noted men—an ancestor of Muhammad Baranduq 270; descent of his line to Akbar's day 270 n. 2.

Rai **Chandraban** *Chauhan Rajput*—killed at Kanwa (933) 573; [†933 AH.–1527 A.D.].

Chapuq (Slash-face), see Ibrahim *Begchik*.

Sultan Ahmad **Char-shamba**—unhorses Muhammad Mumin *Bai-qara* (902) 71; coincident occurrences of "Char-shamba" 71.

Isma'il **Chilma** (or Chalma), son of Ibrahim *Jani*—writes particulars of the battle of Jam (935) 624.

Chilma *Mughul* (or Chalma)—in the centre at Qandahar (913) 335; rebels in Kabul (914) 345.

Chilma *taghchi Mughul* (? shoeing-smith)—in the centre at Qandahar (913) 335.

Chingiz Khan *Mughul*—counted back to in Yunas Khan's genealogy 12, 19; his capture of Samarkand (619 AH.–1222 AD.) 75; referred to concerning the name Qarshi 84; his Rules (*Tura*) 155, 298; [†624 AH.–1227 AD.].

Chin *Sufi*—defends Khwarizm for Husain *Bai-qara* against Shaibani (910) 242 n. 3, 244; killed in the surrender 255–6; [†911 AH.–1505–6 AD.].

Chin-timur Sultan *Chaghatai Chingiz-khanid,* son of Ahmad—mentioned *s.a.* 912 as serving Babur 318; succeeds against Ibrahim *Ludi's* advance (932) 467; in the right centre at Panipat 472, and at Kanwa (933) 565, 568; rewarded 527, 578–9; on service (933) 540; at Chandiri (934) 590; pursues Biban and Bayazid 601, 602; in command against Baluchis (935) 638, 676; met on a journey 639; writes of loss of reinforcement 675; ordered to Agra 676; waits on Babur 688; his brothers Mansur, Aisan-timur, Tukhta-bugha, Sa'id, Khalil *q.v.*; [†936 AH.–1530 AD.].

Chiqmaq Beg—sent on road-surveyor's work (935) 629–30; the *Mubin* quoted in connection with his orders 630; his clerk Shahi *q.v.*

Chirkas qizlar (Circassian girls), see Gulnar and Nar-gul.

Chuli Begim *Azaq Turkman*—particulars 265, 268; her husband Husain *Bai-qara* and their daughter Sultanim *q.v.*; [†before 911 AH.–1505 AD.].

Damachi *Mughul*—in the centre at Qandahar (913) 335.

Dankusi var. Nigarsi—killed at Kanwa 573; [†933 AH.–1527 AD.].

Darwesh-i-'ali—serving Humayun in Sambhal (934) 587.

Darwesh-i-'ali Beg *Chaghatai,* brother of Nawa'i—particulars 275; in Babur's service (916) 275 and (917) 277; his poet-wife Apaq Bega *q.v.*

Darwesh-i-'ali *piada* and, later, *tufang-andaz*—takes news of Hindal's birth to Babur (925) 385.

Darwesh-i 'Ali Sayyid *Mughul*—in the centre at Qandahar (913) 335.

Darwesh Beg Tarkhan, *Arghun*—particulars 39; [†895 AH.–1490 AD.].

Baba Dost—put in charge of Humayun's Trans-Indus district (925) 391; conveys wine to Babur's camp (933) 551 (here *suchi*).[1]

Dost, son of Muhammad Baqir—drunk (925) 415.

Dost-anju?[2] **Shaikh,** son of Baba 'Ali—left in charge of Ghazni (911) 307.

Dost Beg *Mughul*, son of Baba Qashqa and brother (p. 588) of Shah Muhammad—at a social gathering and sent to Bhira 388 (here *muhrdar*); made a *diwan* (932) 476; in charge of Biana (933) 539 and made its *shiqdar* 579 (here Lord-of-the Gate); in the right centre at Kanwa 565, 569; waits on Babur 581; pursues rebels (934) 601 (here Dost-i-muhammad); in the battle of the Ghogra (935) 673; for his kinsmen see *s.n.* Baba Qashqa.

Khwaja **Dost-i-khawand**—lets himself down over the wall of Qandahar (913) 343; at boat-parties (925) 385, 388; comes from Kabul to Agra (933) 544; in the left centre at Kanwa 565; ☞ sent on Babur's family affairs to Humayun in Badakhshan (934) 603; delayed in Kabul till Kamran's arrival 618 and nn. 2–6; his letters reach Babur (935) 618.

Dost-kildi *Mughul*—in the centre at Qandahar (913) 335.

Dost-i-nasir Beg—Dost Beg—(Nasir's Dost), son of Nasir—enters Babur's service (904) 103; on service (906) 131, (908) 163, 165; one of three standing by Babur 166, 167, 396; with him at Akhsi 174, 396; one of the eight in the flight 177, 396; at the recapture of Kabul (912) 315; in the left centre at Qandahar (913) 335, 338; at Tashkint (918) ☞ 356 n. 1, ☞ 358, 396–7; opposing rebels (921) ☞ 364, 397; leading the left at Bajaur (925) 368 (here first styled Beg), 369, 370, 397; his revenue work 384; at wine parties 387, 388; at Parhala 390; attacked by fever 394; his death and his burial at Ghazni 395–6; his brother Mirim *q.v.*; particulars 395–7; [†925 AH.–1519 AD.].

Dost *Sar-i-puli, piada* and (later) *kotwal*—attacks Babur blindly (912) 316–7; wounded (913) 324; [†913 AH.–1507 AD.].

Dost-i-yasin-khair—wrestles well with eight in succession (935) 653; 656.

Dudu Bibi, widow of Bihar Khan *Bihari*—news of her bringing

---

1 He may be Hamida-banu's father and, if so, became grandfather of Akbar.
2 Ilminsky, *anlu*, Erskine, *angu*. Daulat-shah mentions a Muhammad Shah *anju* (see Brown's ed. Index *s.n.*).

Fatima-sultan Begim *Bai-qara Timurid, Barlas Turk*, daughter of Husain and Mingli—particulars 266; her husband Yadgar-i-farrukh *Miran-shahi q.v.*; [†before 911 AH.–1505 AD.].

Fazil Kukuldash—serving Shah Beg *Arghun* (910) 238; ☞ a good account of him named 443; his death a crushing grief to Shah Beg *ib.*; [†930 AH.–1514 AD.].

Fazil Tarkhan—a Turkistan merchant created a Tarkhan by Shaibani, [Author's Note] 133; his death *ib.*; [906 AH.–1500 AD.].

Fazli, see Darwesh-i-muhammad.

Ferdinand the Catholic—his action in 1504 (910 AH.) 187 n. 2 (Erskine).

Firuza Begim *Qanjut*, wife of Mansur *Bai-qara* her Timurid ancestry 256; her children Bai-qara (II), Husain, Aka and Badka *q.v.*; ([†874 AH.–1469–70 AD.].

Firuz Khan *Mewati*—reprieved (932) 477–8.

Firuz Khan, *Sarang-khani, Afghan*—on Ibrahim *Ludi's* service 527; waits on Babur (932) 527, and on his service 530.

Sultan **Firuz Shah**, *Tughluq Turk*—his servants' dynasties 481, 482; his relations with the rulers of Malwa 482; [†790 AH.–1388 AD.].

Firuz Shah Beg—his grandson 'Abdu'l-khaliq *q.v.*

Gadai *Balal*—rejoins Babur (913) 330–1.

Gadai *bihjat*—misbehaves (925) 414.

Gadai Taghai—shares a confection (925) 375; at social gatherings 385, 7, 8, 400, 412; rides carrying a full pitcher 386; out with Babur 404; removes a misbehaving namesake 414.

Gauhar-shad Begim, wife of Shah-rukh *Timurid*—Babur visits her college and tomb (912) 305; [†861 AH.–1457 AD.].

Gauhar-shad Begim *Miran-shahi Timurid, Barlas Turk*, daughter of Abu-sa'id—visited by Babur (935) 616.

Mir **Gesu**—finds chronogram identical with Shaikh Zain's 575.

Apaq **Ghazi Khan** *Turk*, son of Mir (Shaikh) 'Ali Beg—particulars 382; his brothers Baba Kabuli and Darya Khan, his son 'Ali and his relation Nazar-i-'ali *Turk q.v.*

Apaq **Ghazi Khan** *Yusuf-khail Ludi Afghan*, son of Daulat Khan— ☞ arrested by Babur (930) 442; moves against Babur (932) 451, 453; not trusted 455; agrees to help 'Alani Khan 455–6; receives him ill on defeat 457–8; pursued for Babur 458, 460, 461, 462, 463; Babur's reproach for his abandonment of his family 460–1; his forts in the Dun 462; his library less valuable than was expected by Babur 460; his kinsman Haji Khan and his own son 465.

Ghiyas, a buffoon 400.

Mir **Ghiyas**, building entrusted to him (935) 642.

Mir **Ghiyas Taghai** *Kunji Maghul*, brother of 'Ali-dost—particulars 28; enters the Khan (Mahmud)'s service (899) 28, 32; [† before 914 AH.–1507–8 AD.].

Amir **Ghiyasu'd-din**, ☞ patron of Khwand-amir and supposed ally of Babur—killed in Herat (927) 432.

Ghiyasu'd-din, nephew of Khwand-amir—☞ conveys the keys of Qandahar to Babur (928) 432, 435, 436.

Sultan **Ghiyasu'd-din** *Balban*—Babur visits his tomb (932) 475; [†686 AH.–1287 AD.].

Ghiyasu'd-din *qurchi*—takes campaigning orders to Junaid *Barlas* (935) 628; returns to Court 636; takes orders to the Eastern amirs 638.

Ghulam-i-'ali—returns from taking Babur's three articles to Nasrat Shah (935) 676.

Ghulam bacha, a musician—heard by Babur in Herat (912) 303.

Ghulam-i-shadi, a musician—particulars 292; his younger brother Ghulam bacha *q.v.*

Mulla **Ghulam** *Yasawal*—makes an emplacement for the Ghazi mortar (935) 670; sent to collect the Bihar tribute 676.

Ghuri *Barlas*—on Babur's service (905) 125; in the left wing at Qandahar (913) 334; wounded 336; [†919 AH.–1513 AD.].

Gujur Khan—ordered on service (935) 638.

Gul-badan Begim *Miran-shahi Timurid, Barlas Turk*, daughter of Babur and Dil-dar—☞ her birth (929 or 930) and her book (*cir.* 995) 441; her journey to Agra (935) 650 n. 2; ☞ her parentage 712; [†1011 AH.–1603 AD.].

Gul-barg *Barlas Turk*, daughter of Khalifa—☞ betrothed (?) to Shah Hasan *Arghun* (924–5) 366; ☞ married (930) 443.

Gul-chihra Begim, full sister of Gul-badan *supra*—her marriage with Tukhta-bugha *Chaghatai* 705 n. 1, 708; her parentage 712; ☞ perhaps the mother of Salima *Chaqaniani* 713.

Gul-rang Begim *Miran-shahi Timurid, Barlas Turk*, daughter of Babur and Dil-dar—☞ born in Khwast (920) 363; ☞ married to Aisan-timur *Chaghatai* (937) 705 n. 1, 708; parentage 712.

Gul-rukh Begim *Begchik*, wife of Babur—☞ with Babur on the Trans-oxus campaign (916–20) 358; particulars 712;her sons Kamran and 'Askari and her brother (?) Sultan 'Ali Mirza Taghai *q.v.*

Mirak **Gur** *diwan* (or Kur)—captured by Shaibani (913) 328.

Shaikh Abu'l-fath **Guran** (G'huran)—serving Babur (932) 526, 528–9, (933) 539, 567, (934) 590; in the right wing at Kanwa (933) 567; host to Babur in Kul (Koel) (934) 587; takes lotus-seeds to him 666; sends him grapes (935) 686; given Gualiar (936) 688, 690; ☞ holds it till Babur's death 692 n. 1.

Habiba-sultan Begim *Arghun*, wife of Ahmad *Miran-shahi* —particulars 36, 37; arranges her daughter Ma'suma's marriage with Babur (912) 306, (913) 330.

Habiba-sultan Khanish *Dughlat*, daughter of Muhammad Husain and Khub-nigar *Chaghatai*—her marriages 21-2; depends on Babur (917) 22.

Hafiz Haji, a musician—heard by Babur in Heri (912) 303.

Hafiz *kabar-katib*—his brother conveys Babur's earliest Diwan to Samarkand (925) 482; at a feast (935) 631, 632.

Hafiz Mirak—composes an inscription (913) 343.

Hafiz-i-muhammad Beg *Duldai Barlas*—particulars 25; in Aura-tipa (893) 17, 25; ☞ joint-guardian of Mirza Khan (905) 25, 122; his death 26; his sons Muhammad *miskin* and Tahir *q.v.*; his (?) Char-bagh 108; [†*cir.* 909–10 AH.–1504 AD.].

Khwaja Shamsu'd-din Muhammad **Hafiz** *Shirazi*—parodied (910) 201; [†791 AH.–1389 AD.].

Hafiz *Tashkindi*—gifts made to him (935) 632.

Haibat Khan *karg-andaz, Hindustani*—leaves Babur (933) 557.

Haibat Khan *Samana'i*—☞ perhaps the provider of matter to fill the *lacuna* of 936 AH., 693.

Mulla **Haidar**—his sons 'Abdu'l-minan and Mumin *q.v.*

Haidar '*Alamdar*—on Babur's service (925) 383, (926) 421.

Haidar-'ali Sultan *Bajauri*—obeys custom in testing his dead mother's virtue 212; ☞ his Gibri fort taken by Babur (924) 366, 7, 8.

Haidar Kukuldash *Yaragi Mughul,* Mahmud Khan's "looser and binder"—defeated 35, (900) and killed 52, 111–2; his garden 54; his son Banda-i-'ali and a descendant (?) Husain *Yaraji q.v.*

Haidar-Mirza *Bai-qara Timurid, Barlas Turk,* son of Husain and Payanda-sultan—his Miran-shahi betrothal at Hisar (901) 48, 61; rejoins his father opportunely (903) 261; particulars 263; his wife Bega *q.v.*; [†908 AH.–1502–3 AD.].

Muhammad **Haidar Mirza Kurkan** *Dughlat,* author of the *Tarikh-i-rashidi*—particulars 21–2, 348, 797; ☛ takes refuge with Babur (916) 350; ☛ his first battle (917) 353; ☛ ill when Kul-i-malik was fought (918) 357–8; goes to Sa'id Khan in Kashgar 22, 362; on Sa'id's service (933) 590, (936) 695–6; [†958 AH.–1 551 AD.].

Haidar-i-qasim Beg *Kohbur Chaghatai*—father of Abu'l-qasim, Ahmad-i-qasim and Quch (Quj) Beg *q.v.*

Haidar-quli—on Auzun Hasan's service (904) 102.

Haidar-quli, servant of Khwaja Kalan—on service (932) 467; mentioned by Babur in writing to the Khwaja (935) 648.

Haidar *rikabdar*—stays with Babur at a crisis (903) 91; his son Muhammad 'Ali *q.v.*

Haidar *taqi*—his garden near Kabul 198 n. 1.

Haji Ghazi *Manghit*—sent to help Babur (904) 101.

Haji ('Ali) Khan *Yusuf-khail Ludi Afghan*—acting with 'Alam Khan *Ludi* (932) 445–6–7.

Haji piada—killed at the Lovers'-cave 68; [902 AH.–1497 AD.].

Haji Pir *bakawal*—negotiates for Husain *Bai-qara* with the Hisar begs (901) 61.

Halahil—on service (925) 391, (925) 638.

Halwachi Tarkhan *Arghun*—engages Babur's left wing at Qandahar (913) 336.

Sayyid Mir **Hamah**—gets the better of two traitors (932–3) 546; receives head-money (933) 546; in the right wing at Kanwa 566.

Hamid Khan *Khasa-khail Sarang-khani Ludi*—opposes Babur (932) 465; defeated by Humayun 466; defeated (633) 540; sent out of the way before Kanwa 547.

Hamusi, son of Diwa—sent to make a Hindu pact with Sanga's son (935) 616.

Hati *Kakar*—particulars 387; his misdeeds provoke punishment (925) 387, 9, 91; abandons Parhala 390; sends Babur tribute and is sent an envoy 391–2; referred to 452.

'Abdu'l-lah **Hatifi**, nephew of Jami—particulars 288.

Hatim *qurchi*—promoted to be *qur-begi* (911) 252; in the centre at Qandahar (913) 335.

Hazaraspi, see Pir-i-muhammad.

Henry VII of England—his *Intercursus malus* contemporary with 910 AH. 187 n. 2.

Henry of Navarre—☛ his difficulties, as to creed, less than those of Babur in 917 AH.–1511 AD., 356.

Hilali, see Badru'd-din *Hilali*.

Abu'l-nasir Muhammad **Hind-al Mirza** *Miran-shahi Timurid, Barlas Turk,* son of Babur and Dil-dar—his pre-natal adoption (925) 374; meaning of his name Hind-al 385; gifts to him or his servants 522, (935) 633, 642; the *Walidiyyah-risala* and Hindustan verses sent to him 642; under summons to Hind 645, ☛ 696; ☛ sent by Humayun to Qila'-i-zafar (936) 695; referred to 697; ☛ waits on his father in Lahor 699; ☛ his dying father's wish to see him (937) 708; his escort of Babur's family in 946 AH. referred to 710; [†958 AH.–1551 AD.].

Hindi—Mindi,—Mahndi, see Mahndi.

Hindu Beg *quchin*—leaves 'Ali *Miran-shahi* for Mirza Khan (905) 122; sent to raid Panj-kura (925) 374; in Bhira 386–8; leaves it 399; out with Babur 403; serving under Humayun (932) 465–6, 528–9; in the right wing at Panipat 472 and at Kanwa (933) 566 and n. 2, 569; escorts Mahim from Kabul (935) 687; sent to Sambhal *ib.*; waits on Babur *ib.* and n. 2, 689; his mosque in Sambhal 687 n. 2.

☛ **Hulaku Khan** *Ail-khani (Il-khani)*—referred to 79; [†663 AH.–1264 AD.].

Hul-hul Aniga—a woman drinker 417.

Nasiru'd-din Muhammad **Humayun Mirza** *Miran-shahi Timurid, Barlas Turk,* son of Babur and Mahim—his birth (913) 344; his mother's parentage 344 n. 3, ☛ 712–3; death of elder brethren referred to 374; a Trans-indus district given to him (925) 391; carried in haste to meet his father 395; makes a good shot 417; prefers not to go to Lamghan (926) 421; ☛ appointed to

with the Tarkhans (905) 121; fights for Babur at Sar-i-pul (Khwaja Kardzan) (906) 139; his great-niece Ma'suma a wife of Babur 36.

Husain Aqa *Sistani*—in the right wing at Kanwa (933) 566.

Husain '*audi,* lutanist of Husain *Bai-qara*—particulars 292; owed his training to 'Ali-sher *Nawa'i* 272.

Shah **Husain** *bakhshi*—brings Babur news of a success (935)685.

Khwaja **Husain Beg,** brother of Auzun Hasan—particulars 26; his daughter a wife of 'Umar Shaikh 24, 146 n. 3; leaves Samarkand with the Tarkhans (905) 121; fights for Babur at Sar-i-pul (Khwaja Kardzan) (906) 139; one of eight in the flight from Akhsi (908) 177 (here Khwaja Husaini); his lameness causes him to leave Babur 178; sends Lahor revenues to Kabul (932) 446; waits on Babur 458; on service (933) 549 (here Mulla Husain); in the left centre at Kanwa 566.

Shah **Husain** *chuhra,* a brave of Husain *Bai-qara*—left in Balkh (902) 70.

Sultan **Husain** *Dughlat*—joins Babur (901) 58–9; conspires against Tambal (907) 154; sent by The Khan (Mahmud) to help Babur (908) 161.

Husain *Ghaini*—a punitive force sent against him (911) 253.

Husain-i-hasan—out with Babur (925) 403; killed and avenged 404, 405; [†925 AH.-1519 AD.].

Maulana Shäh **Husain** *Kami,* a poet—particulars 290.

Husain Kashifi—his omission from Babur's list of Herat celebrities 283 n. 1.

Husain Khan *Lashkar* (?) *Wazir*—writes from Nasrat Shah, accepting Babur's three articles (935) 676.

Sultan **Husain Mirza** *Bai-qara Timurid, Barlas Turk,* son of Mansur—defeats Mahmud *Miran-shahi* (865) 46, 259 and (876) 260; his relations with Nawa'i 33, 272; his campaign against Khusrau Shah (901) 57, 58–61, 130; his dissensions with his sons 61, 69, (902) 68–70, 260, (903) 94–5; his capture of Heri (875) compared with Babur's of Samarkand (906) 134–5; does not help Babur against Shaibani 138, 145; asks Babur's help against him (910) 190–1, (911) 255; his death 256, and burial 293; particulars of his life and court 256–292:—(personal 256—amirs 270—sadurs 280—wazirs, etc. 281—poets 286—artists 291)—his

Isma'il *Safawi 'Arab,* Shah of Persia—reference to his capture of 'Iraq (*cir.* 906) 280, 336; gives refuge to a fugitive Bai-qara (913) 327 n.5; ☞ hostilities begin between him and Shaibani (915) 350; defeats Shaibani at Merv (916) 18, 318, ☞ 350; sends Khan-zada back to Babur 18, 352; ☞ asked by Babur for reinforcement (917) 352–4; ☞ his alliance dangerous for Babur 355; ☞ indication of his suzerain relation with Babur 355; ☞ a principal actor in the *lacuna* years from 926–930, 427; ☞ his relations with Shah Beg *Arghun* 430; relations with Babur (927) 433–4; ☞ his death after defeat (930) 443; ☞ Lord Bacon on his personal beauty 443 n. 1; his son Tahmasp *q.v.*; his (presumed) Bai-qara disciple in Shi'a heresy 262; [†930 AH.–1524 AD.].

Ja'far Khwaja, son of Mahdi Khwaja and step-son of Babur's sister Khan-zada—fills his father's place in Etawa (933) 579, 582; sent to collect boats (934) 598; pursues Biban and Bayazid (935) 682.

Jahangir *Barlas,* son of Ibrahim and a Badakhshi Begim (T.R. trs. p. 108)—particulars 273; joint-governor of Kabul for Abu-sa'id 270, 273.

Jahangir Mirza *Barlas Turk,* eldest son of Timur—named in Abu-sa'id's genealogy 14; is given Samarkand by Timur 85; his tomb in Kesh 83; his son Muhammad 78, 85; [†776 AH.–1374–5 AD.].

Jahangir Mirza *Miran-shahi Timurid, Barlas Turk,* son of 'Umar Shaikh and Fatima *Mughul*—particulars 17; sent (a child) to reinforce an uncle (*cir.* 895) and then betrothed 48, 189; comes to Andijan after his father's death (899) 32; Mughul support for him against Babur (900) 43–4, (903) 87–8, (904) 101; joins Tambal 103; a "worry" 104; defeated at Khuban (905) 113; waits on Babur 119; summoned for a Samarkand expedition 122; reinforces Babur (906) 138; a gift to him from the exiled Babur (907) 150; joins Babur (908) 173; acts against Babur's wishes 173–4; flees in panic 174–5; rumoured a prisoner 176; ☞ his occupation of Khujand (909?) 182; Babur rejects advice to dismiss him (910) 191; deference to him from Khusrau Shah 193; his part in occupying Kabul 198, 199; receives Ghazni 227; out with Babur 233–4, 235–6, 239; rejects counsel to betray him 239; is Babur's host in Ghazni

240; his experiences in an earthquake (911) 247; insists on a move for Qalat-i-ghilzai 248; waits on Babur and does service 252–3; his misconduct 254; causes Babur to mobilize his troops 255; goes to Yakaaulang (912) 294; the clans not supporting him, he goes to Heri with Babur 295–6; at social gatherings 298, 302; defeats his half-brother Nasir 321; his death 331 n. 3, 345; his widow brings their son Pir-i-muhammad to Babur (913) 331; [†912 or 913 AH.–1507–8 AD.].

Nuru'd-din Muhammad **Jahangir Padshah** *Miran-shahi Timurid, Barlas Turk,* son of Akbar—his work in Babur's burial-ground 710; words of his made clear by Babur's 501 n.6; mentioned concerning the *tamgha* 553 n.1; [†1037 AH.–1627 AD.].

Jahangir *Turkman*—revolts in Badakhshan against the Auzbegs (910) 242; keeping his head up (913) 340.

Jahan-shah *Barlas,* son of Chaku—mentioned in his son Muhammad Baranduq's genealogy 270.

Jahan-shah Mirza *Barani, Qara-quiluq Turkman*—ruling in Tabriz while Yunas *Chaghatai* stayed there 20; his sons defeated by the Aq-quiluq (872) 49; his son Muhammadi's wife Pasha 49; [†872 AH.–1467–8 AD.].

Rai **Jaipal** *Lahori*—a legend of his siege of Ghazni 219; [†*cir.* 392 AH.–1002 AD.].

Raja **Jai-singh** *Jaipuri*—his astronomical instruments 79 n. 4; [†1156 AH.–1743 AD.].

Jalal Khan *Jig-hat*—waits on 'Alam Khan *Ludi* (932) 456 and n. 4; his house in Dihli Babur's quarters 476; his son 'Alam Khan *Kalpi q.v.*

Jalal Khan *Ludi,* son of 'Alam Khan—deserts his father (932) 457; in the left wing at Kanwa (933) 567.

Jalal *Tashkindi*—brings Babur news of Biban and Bayazid (935) 685.

Jalalu'd-din Mahmud *nai*—a flautist, heard in Herat (912) 303.

Sultan **Jalalu'd-din** *Nuhani*—Jalal Khan, son of Bihar Khan and Dudu—one of three competitors for rule (935) 651 n. 5; writes dutifully to Babur 659; news of his and his mother's coming 664; waits on Babur 676; receives revenue from Bihar 676.

Maulana **Jalalu'd-din** *Purani*—origin of his cognomen 306; his descendant Jamalu'd-din Abu-sa'id *Puran q.v.*; [†862 AH.–1458 AD.].

Sultan **Jalalu'd-din** *Sharqi,* son of Husain Shah—waits on Babur (935) 651; particulars 651 n. 5; his man abandons Benares 652; entertains Babur 652; his son styled Sultan *ib.*; his gift of a boat to Babur 663; in the battle of the Ghogra 669; on service 678.

Shaikh **Jamal** *Barin Mughul*—his son (?) Shaikh 'Ali *q.v.*

Shaikh **Jamal** *Farmuli Afghan*—deserts 'Alam Khan (932) 457; serving Babur (933) 551.

Shaikh **Jamali**—at a feast (935) 631; conveys encouragement to Dudu Bibi 665–6.

Shaikh **Jamalu'd-din Abu-sa'id** *Puran*—particulars 306 n. 2; ill-treated by Shaibani (913) 306 n. 2, 328; [†921 AH.–1515 AD.].

Shaikh **Jamalu'd-din** *khar, Arghun*—captor of Yunas Khan and Aisan-daulat Begim (T.R. trs. p. 94)—slain 35; [†877 AH.–1472–3 AD.].

Mir **Jamalu'd-din** *muhaddas*—particulars 284; [living 934–7 AH.–1527–31 AD.].

Shaikh **Jami**—ancestor of Akbar's mother 623 n. 8.

Jami, see 'Abdu'r-rahman *Jami.*

Jamshid (an ancient ruler of Persia)—mentioned 85, 152.

Mir **Jan-airdi,** retainer of Zu'n-nun *Arghun*—sells provisions to Babur (912) 308.

Janak—recites in Turki (912) 304.

Janaka Kukuldash (or Khanika)—escapes after Sar-i-pul (906) 141.

Jan-i-'ali—murdered by Shaibani (906) 127, 128; [†906 AH.–1500 AD.].

Jan Beg—in charge of *impedimenta* (932) 458; allowed leave for a raid 464; in a night-attack 471; in the left wing at Panipat 472 and at Kanwa (933) 567 (here Jan-i-muhammad Beg Ataka); on service (935) 682 (here Jani Beg).

Mir **Jan** *Diwan*—his house in Qandahar reserved as loot for Nasir *Miran-shahi* (913) 338.

Jani Beg *Duldai Barlas Turk*—particulars 37.

Jani Beg Sultan Khan, *Auzbeg-Shaiban, Chingiz-khanid*—his two Miran-shahi marriages of conquest 18, 35; fights for Shaibani at Sar-i-pul (906) 139; he and his sons at Jam (935) 622; flees to Merv 636 n. 2.

Jan-i-hasan, *Barin Mughul*—sent to reinforce Babur (903) 92, (908) 161, 170.

shahi, wife of Husain *Bai-qara*—particulars 262, 268; her dominance 268,292;visited in Heri by Babur (912) 301;at an entertainment to him 302; a suspicion against her 302 n. 1; captured by Shaibani (913) 327; given for a traitor to loot 328; her daughter Aq Begim and sons Shah-i-gharib and Muzaffar-i-husain *q.v.*

Khadija–sultan Begim *Miran-shahi Timurid, Barlas Turk,* daughter of Abu'sa'id—(probably) seen by Babur in Heri (912) 301; Babur visits her near Agra (934) 588 and in Agra Fort (935) 606, 616.

Khaldar *Yaragi Mughul,* son of Haidar Kukuldash—fights for Babur at Sar-i-pul (Khwaja Kardzan) (906) 139.

Khalifa, see Nizamu'd-din 'Ali *Barlas.*

Khalil *chuhra*—a brave who fought well for Babur (904) 101.

Khalil *diwana*—on Auzun Hasan's service (904) 102.

Sultan **Khalil Mirza**, *Miran-shahi Timurid, Barlas Turk,* son of Miran-shah—mentioned 262 n. 2; [†814 AH.–1411–2 AD.].

Sultan **Khalil Mirza** *Miran-shahi (ut supra),* son of Abu-sa'id —his daughter sole wife of Bai-sunghar *Miran-shahi* 112.

Khalil Sultan *Chaghatai Chingiz-khanid,* son of Ahmad, (Alacha Khan), full brother of Sa'id—his son Baba Sultan *q.v.*

Khalil Sultan *Itaraji Mughul,* brother of Ahmad Tambal— holding Madu for Tambal (905) 109; captured *id.,* and released 119; surprises Aush 125; helps Babur against Shaibani (906) 138; killed at Sar-i-pul 141; [†906 AH.–1501 AD.].

Khalwi *piada* (or Khalwa)—his spear-head bitten off by a tiger (925) 393.

The **Khatib of Qarshi**—an envoy to Babur (910) 188.

Khan-i-jahan, see Fath Khan *Sarwani.*

Khan-i-jahan, a "pagan"—opposes Babur (933) 539.

Khan-quli, son of Bian-quli—leaves Babur in Samarkand (903) 86; at a household party (906) 131; gives ground for suspicion (907) 156; one of eight in the flight from Akhsi (908) 176, 177; in the right centre at Qandahar (913) 335.

Khan-zada Begim (1), *Miran-shahi Timurid, Barlas Turk,* daughter of Mahmud—particulars 48.

Khan-zada Begim (2), *ut supra,* daughter of Mas'ud and Sa'adat-bakht—particulars 267; visited by Babur near Agra (935) 616.

Khan-zada Begim (3), *ut supra,* daughter of 'Umar Shaikh and

Qutluq-nigar—particulars 17; her marriage with Shaibani (907) 18, 147, ☞ 184; her divorce and remarriage with Sayyid Hadi Khwaja 352 [H.S. iii], 364; her reunion with Babur (916) 18, 352, 356; her marriage with Mahdi Khwaja *q.v.*; her summons to Hindustan (935) 647; her son Khurram Shah *q.v.*; [†952 AH.–1545 AD.].

Khan-zada Begim (4), *Tirmizi,* wife of Mahmud *Miran-shahi*— particulars 48; her son Mas'ud *q.v.*; her niece 48.

Khan-zada Begim (5), *Tirmizi,* niece of the above, wife of Mahmud—particulars 48, 9; her son Husain *q.v.*; her five daughters 47–8.

Khan-zada Begim (6), *Tirmizi,* wife of Ahmad *Miran-shahi*— particulars 37; Babur, a child, pulls off her wedding veil (893) 37.

Khan-zada Khanim *Haji-tarkhani,* daughter of Ahmad and Badi'u'l-jamal (Badka)—particulars 329; illegally married by Shaibani (913) 329; her husband Muzaffar-i-husain *Bai-qara q.v.*

Khawand Shah Amir, ("Mirkhond"), author of the *Rauzatu's-safa*—omitted (or lost) from Babur's list of Herat celebrities 283 n. 1; [†903 AH.–1498 AD.].

Khizr Khwaja Khan *Chaghatai Chingiz-khanid*—mentioned in Yunas Khan's genealogy 19.

Khwaja **Khizr** *Nuhani,* a merchant—killed by a Mughul (910) 235.

Khub-nigar Khanim *Chaghatai Chingiz-khanid,* daughter of Yunas and Aisan-daulat—particulars 21, 22; her death announced to Babur (907) 148, 149; her rebel husband forgiven for her sake (912) 319; her husband Muhammad Husain *Dughlat,* their son Haidar and daughter Habiba *q.v.*; [†907 AH.–1501–2 AD.].

Khuda-bakhsh *Chaghatai,* retainer, (1) of Khusrau Shah, (2) of Babur—in the right wing at Qandahar (913) 334; rebels against Babur (914) 345.

Khudal-birdi Beg *tughchi, Mughul*—stays with Babur at a crisis (903) 91; made a beg and on service 110; killed at Sar-i-pul 141; [†906 AH.–1501 AD.].

Khudai-birdi *buqaq, Mughul*—killed at Asfara (900) 53 (here *atakam,* my guardian); his favour from Babur 105; his son Quli *chunaq q.v.*; [†900 AH.–1495 AD.].

Khudai-birdi *tughchi Timur-tash*—made 'Umar Shaikh's Lord-of-the-Gate (*cir.* 870) 14; particulars 24–5; [†a few years after 870 AH.–1466 AD.].

Khurram Shah *Auzbeg-Shaiban, Chingiz-khanid,* son of Shaibani and Khan-zada—particulars 18; [†a few years after 916 AH.– 1510–11 AD.].

Khush-kildi[1] *Mughul*—in the centre at Qandahar (913) 335.

Khusrau, an ancient ruler of Persia—mentioned in a couplet 85.

Khusrau *Gagiani*—waits on Babur (910) 230; taken as a guide 231.

Khusrau Kukuldash—at a household party (906) 131; captured by Tambal (908) 168; rejoins Babur (913) 330–1; in the right centre at Qandahar 335; out with Babur (925) 377, 403; an enquiry 405; ☞ posted in Sialkot (930) 442; seeming still to hold it (932) 453; on service 465, 471; in the van at Pani-pat 472; in the right wing at Kanwa (933) 566, 568; given Alur (Alwar) by mistake 578; sent against Baluchis (935) 638; at social gatherings 385–7–8.

Amir Khwaja **Khusrau** *Lachin Turk*—a couplet of his quoted 503; [†725 AH.–1325 AD.].

Khusrau Shah[2] *Turkistani, Qibchaq Turk,*—particulars 49–50; takes Mahmud *Miran-shahi (cet.* 17) to Hisar (*cir.* 873) 46–7; referred to as a rival 50; his tolerance of Hisari ill-conduct (899) 41–2; ex-pelled from Samarkand on Mahmud's death (900) 51–2; opposes Husain *Bai-qara* (901) 57, 60–1; his rise helped by Bai-qara fail-ures 61; supports Mas'ud *Miran-shahi* 64; falls out with him 71, 93; blinds him (903) 95; defeats Badi'u'-zaman *Bai-qara* 60–1; re-equips him defeated by his father (902) 70; receives well the fugitive Bai-sunghar *Miran-shahi* (903) 74; makes him *padshah* in Hisar 93; strangles him (905) 110; a fugitive Tarkhan goes to him (906) 120, 141; his niggardliness to Babur 129, 130; gives him no help against Shaibani 138, ☞ 183; Qasim Beg *quchin* takes refuge with him (907) 27; his position less secure (910) 188; followers of his join Babur 189, 192, 196, 227 n. 3; invited to co-operate with the Timurid Mirzas against Shaibani 190; takes the Kabul road on Babur's approach 192, 244; offers him service 192; the interview of his submission 193–4; allowed to go towards Khurasan 194, 195; breaks his pact and is put to flight 197, 243;

1 His name might mean Welcome, *Bien-venu.*
2 Khusrau-shah may be the more correct form.

gets sensible counsel in Herat 243; makes trouble for Nasir *Miran-shahi* in Badakhshan 244–5; beheaded at Qunduz by the Auzbegs 244; good results from his death for Babur 245; Babur's reflections on the indiscipline of his followers 199, 230 n. 5, 239, 244–5; his former following rebels (914) 335; his brothers Wali and Baqi, and nephew Ahmad-i-qasim *q.v.*; [†910 AH.–1505 AD.].

Khwaja Chishti var. Husaini—at a feast (935) 631.

'Abdu'l-lah **Khwajagan-khwaja**, fifth son of 'Ubaidu'l-lah *Ahrari*—his son 'Abdu'sh-shahid 653 n. 4.

Khwajaka Khwaja, Muhammad-i-'ubaidu'l-lah, eldest son of Ahrari—protects Bai-sunghar *Miran-shahi* in the Tarkhan rebellion (901) 62; becomes his spiritual guide 63; visited in Farkat by Babur (907) 149; his brother Yahya *q.v.*

Khwaja Kalan, descendant of 'Ubaidu'l-lah *Ahrari*—☞ a likely recipient of the *Mubin* 438, 631 n. 3; at a feast in Agra (935) 631; gifts and leave given 632, 641–2; a copy of *Babur-nama* writings sent to him 653.

Mir **Khwaja Kalan**, son of Maulana Muhammad Sadru'd-din —receives Bajaur (925) 370; particulars 370 n. 3; prisoners pardoned at his request 371; out with Babur 372; returns to Bajaur 376; is recalled on grounds given (926) 422–3; joins Babur for Hindustan (932) 447; on service 465–6; in the right wing at Panipat 472; helps to secure Agra 475; of his leaving Hindustan 520, 531; his offending couplet about leaving, and Babur's reply 525–6; has charge of Kabul and Ghazni 524; conveys money to repair the Ghazni dam 219, 647 n. 1; requests leave to depart after capture of Agra 524; Babur's various writings sent to him, quatrains (925) 372, (932) 525–6, (935) the *Walidiyyah-risala* and Hindustan poems 642—letters (925) 411, (935) 604, 618 n. 2, quoted 645–8; commended to Humayun as a friend 627; a letter of his mentioned 644; wine parties in his house (925) 371–2, 375; has Ghazni wine at Milwat (932) 461; urged to renounce wine 648; tells Babur of a fruitful orange-tree (935) 510; ☞ quotation from his ode on Babur's death 709.

'Abdu'l-lah **Khwaja Maulana-i-qazi**—particulars 29, 89–90; supports Babur (899) 30; chases off an invader 32; confers with other well-wishers of the boy (900) 43; mediates for Ibrahim *Saru* 53, for Aurgutis (902) 68; envoy to Auzun Hasan (903) 87;

open-handed to Babur's followers 88; entreats him to save Andijan 88–9; Mir Mughul aids him in its defence 122; hanged by Tambal and Auzun Hasan 89; 'Ali-dost fears retaliation for his death (905) 119; his right guidance recalled by Babur (912) 303; [†903 AH.–1498 AD.].

Khwajaki Mulla-i-sadr, son of Maulana Muhammad Sadru'd-din, and elder brother of Khwaja Kalan—particulars 67; killed near Yam 67; [†902 AH.–1497 AD.].

Khwaja Mir-i-miran—speaks boldly at Akhsi (908) 174; in charge of baggage camels (925) 376, 377, and of Babur's camp 389, 391; Babur halts near his Lamghan village (926) 424; given charge of Daulat Khan *Yusuf-khail* (932) 459–60; in the left centre at Panipat 973; entrusted with gifts for Kabul 525.

Khwaja Mir Sultan—he and his son receive gifts (935) 632.

Khwand-amir, grandson of Khawand Shah Amir ("Mirkhond") —☞ associated with Muhammad-i-zaman *Bai-qara* (923) 364–5, 463 n. 3; fleeced by Shaibani's order (913) 328 n. 3; his discomforts in Herat 617 n. 2; waits on Babur (935) 605; Babur invites him in verse 693; completes the *Habibu's-siyar* while at Tir-muhani with Babur 687 n. 3; his omission (or loss) from Babur's list of Herat celebrities 283 n. 1; his and Babur's varied choice of details 328 n. 2; ☞ his patron Amir Ghiyasu'd-din and nephew Ghiyasu'd-din 436; [†942 AH.–1535 AD.].

Khwaja **Khwand-sa'id**—Babur visits his tomb (925) 407.

Mir **Khawand**—Shah Amir ("Mirkhond")—author of the *Rauzatu's-safa*, grandfather of Khwand-amir—his omission (or loss) from Babur's list of Herat celebrities 283 n. 1; [†903 AH.–1498 AD.].

Kichik 'Ali—his courage (908) 176; made prisoner (933) 557, 576; *shiqdar* of Koel 176.

Kichik Baqi *diwana*—suspended (911) 248; killed at Qalat-i-ghilzai 248; [†911 AH.–1505 AD.].

Kichik Begim *Bai-qara Timurid, Barlas Turk*, daughter of Husain and Payanda-sultan—refused in marriage to Mas'ud *Miran-shahi* 265; "afterwards" marries Multa Khwaja 266.[1]

1 The "afterwards" points to an omission which Khwand-amir's account of Husain's daughters fills (lith. ed. iii, 327).

Kichik Khwaja—on ʿAskari's service (935) 681, 682.

Kichik Khwaja Beg, son of Maulana Muhammad Sadruʾd-din and elder brother of Khwaja Kalan—in the left wing at Khuban (905) 113; killed at Qalat-i-ghilzal 248[1]; [†911 AH.–1505 AD.].

Kichik Mirza *Miran-shahi Timurid, Barlas Turk*, son of Ahmad (Mirza Sayyidi) and Aka *Bai-qara*—particulars 257.

Kichkina *tunqtar*—sent with orders to Tramontane begs (925) 406.

Kipa and **Kipik**, see Kupuk.

Raja **Kirti** *Gualiari*, see Karna.

Kitin-qara Sultan *Auzbeg*—in Balkh (932) 545–6; at Jam (935) 622; makes complaint to Babur 649, 645 n. 1.

Kitta Beg *Kohbur Chaghatai*, son of Sayyidi Qara—convoys Yusuf-khail chiefs to Bhira (932) 461; on Babur's service 465–6, 468, 528, (933) 545, (935) 638; wounded at Biana (933) 548.

Kitta Mali and **Kichik Mah**, slaves of Muzaffar-i-husain *Bai-qara*—offend Babur by their performance (912) 304.

Kuchum Khan Sultan—Kuchkunji—*Auzbeg-Shaiban, Chin-qiz-khanid*—particulars 632 n. 3; ☞ his force gathered at Qarshi (917) 353; ☞ a principal actor between 926 and 932 AH. 427; his position in relation to ʿUbaiduʾl-lah (935) 618 n. 6; in the battle of Jam 622; various accounts of his escape or death 623, 636; his envoy to Babur 631, 632; his sons Abu-saʿid and Pulad *q.v.*; [†937 AH.–1530–1 AD.].

Kuki[2] (Haji Muhammad Khan *kuki*), son of Baba Qashqa—601, 669, 673–4, 679.

Kuki,[2] paternal-uncle of the last-entered—on Babur's service (934) 589, (935) 674, 679; in the battle of the Ghogra 673; [†940 AH.–1553 AD.?].

Kupuk Beg, var. Kipik, Kipa (hunchbacked)—in Babur's service (910) 237; promoted (911) 253; frost-bitten (912) 311; in the centre at Qandahar (913) 335; envoy to Mirza Khan (925) 405.

Kupuk Bi *Auzbeg* var. *ut supra*—blamed for three murders (906) 128; given Khwarizm by Shaibani (911) 256; his son Qambar-i-ʿali *q.v.*

---

1 No record survives of the Khwaja's deeds of daring other than those entered above; perhaps the other instances Babur refers to occurred during the gap 908–9 AH.
2 This may be a tribal or a family name. Abuʾl-ghazi mentions two individuals named "Kouk". One was Chingiz Khan's grandson who is likely to have had descendants or followers distinguishable as *Kuki*. See Add. Note (to p. 404) on pp. 798–9 on Kuki fate.

Makhdum-i-'alam, Nasrat Shah's Governor in Hajipur—his defences on the Gandak (935) 663.

Hazrat **Makhdumi Nura**—mentioned 641 n. 1.

Makhdum-sultan Begim *Miran-shahi Timurid, Barlas Turk*, daughter of Mahmud and Zuhra—in Badakhshan (*cir.* 935) 48.

Makhdum-sultan Begim *Qara-guz*, wife of 'Umar Shaikh—particulars 18, 24.

Malik-dad *Kararani (Karani)*[1]—reprieved (932) 477-8; on service (933) 540, 582, (935) 682; in the right wing at Kanwa (933) 557.

Malik-i-muhammad Mirza *Miran-shahi*, nephew of Abu-sa'id—aspires to rule (899) 41; murdered 41; his wife 47; his house 146; [†899 AH.–1494 AD.].

Maliks of Alangar—their garden a halting-place (926) 424.

Malik of Fan—stingy to Babur (906) 130.

Malik-quli *Kunari*—Babur halts at his son's house (926) 423.

Malik Sharq—returns from service (935) 683.

Mallu Khan of Malwa—his tank at Chandiri 597 and n. 8, 598.

Mamaq Sultan *Auzbeg-Shaiban, Chingiz-khanid*, son of Hamza—takes service with Babur (901) 58, 59; ☛ his death 353; [†917 AH.–1511–2 AD.].

Mamum Khalifa *'Abbasi*, son of Harunu'r-rashid—his Observatory and Tables, Author's Note 79; [†218 AH.–833 AD.].

Manik-chand *Chauhan Rajput*—killed at Kanwa 573; [†933 AH. –1527 AD.].

Raja **Man-sing** *Gualiari, Tunwar Rajput*—his buildings 607, 608; his son Bikramajit *q.v.*; [†924 AH.–1518 AD.].

Shah **Mansur** *bakhshi*—helps Shaibani to take Herat (913) 325; given Khadija Begim to loot 326.

Shah **Mansur** *Barlas*—on service (932) 465–6, 475, 530, (933) 545; in the right centre at Panipat (932) 472, 473, and at Kanwa (933) 565, 569; his untimely praise of the Rajput army 548, 550.

Sultan **Mansur Khan** *Chaghatai Chingiz-khanid*, eldest son of Ahmad, Alacha Khan—☛ defeats his half-brother Sa'id (914) 349; ☛ mentioned as Khaqan of the Mughuls, Sa'id as Khan in Kashghar 427; [†950 AH.–1543 AD.].

---

1 Cf. E. and D. for "Karani" (*e.g.* vol. iv, 530). The Hai. MS. sometimes doubles the *r*, sometimes not.

Mansur Mirza *Bai-qara*, '*Umar-shaikhi Timurid, Barlas Turk*
—mentioned in his son Husain's genealogy 256; his not-
reigning 256; his wife Firuza and their children 256, 257;
his beg Wali *q.v.*

Mansur *Turkman*—in the centre at Qandahar (913) 335.

Malik Shah **Mansur** *Yusuf-zai Afghan*, son of Sulaiman—envoy of
his tribe to Babur (924) 371; his daughter's marriage with Babur
(925) 375, App. K; waits on him 399, 400; his brother Taus
Khan and cousin Ahmad *q.v.*; a follower 377.

Maqsud *suchi, sharbatchi, karg*—in the left centre at Qandahar (913)
335, 338; his tossing by a rhinoceros (*karg*) 400.

Marghub *qul*—in Mahawin (932) 523.

Mian **Ma'ruf** *Farmuli Afghan*[1]—disaffected to Ibrahim and (later)
to Babur (932) 523; his opposition 530; flees 533–4; his son
Muhammad (?) leaves him (934) 598; his sons Muhammad and
Musa *q.v.*

Ma'ruf *Yaq'ub-khail Dilah-zak (Dilazak) Afghan*—waits on Babur
at 'Ali-masjid (925) 394.

Shaikh **Maslahat** *Khujandi*—his birthplace 8; dreamed of by Babur
(906) 132; his tomb visited by Timur (790) 132 n. 2.

Masti *chuhra*—deals with a drunken man (925) 415; intoxicated by
beer (926) 423.

Sultan **Mas'ud** *Ghaznawi*—his tomb 218.

Sultan **Mas'ud Mirza** *Miran-shahi Timurid, Barlas Turk*, son of
Mahmud and Khan-zada I—particulars 47, 48; holding Hisar
(900) 52; opposes Husain *Bai-qara* and flees (901) 57–8, 130; one
of three besieging Samarkand; retires with his desired Barlas
bride 64; quarrels with Khusrau Shah (902) 71, and with the
Hisar begs (903) 93; takes refuge with Husain *Bai-qara* 93, 95,
261, 265; returns to Khusrau and is blinded by him 95, 50; goes
back to Husain 95, 266; mentioned as older than Bai-sunghar
110; meets Babur in Herat (912) 302; murdered by Auzbegs
(913) 267; his wives Saliha-sultan *Miran-shahi*, and Sa'adat-bakht
Bai-qara q.v.; his betrothed (?) Kichik Begim *Bai-qara q.v.*;
[†913 AH.–1507 AD.].

Sultan **Mas'ud Mirza** *Kabuli, Shah-rukhi, ut supra*—particulars

---

1 See *Waqi'at-i-mushtaqi*, E. and D. iv, 548.

382; his cherished followers, sons of Mir 'Ali Beg *q.v.*; his son 'Ali *asghar q.v.*; [deposed 843 AH.–1439–40 AD.].

Mulla **Mas'ud** *Sherwani*, of Husain *Bai-qara*'s Court—no particulars 284.

Ma'suma-sultan Begim *Miran-shahi Timurid, Barlas Turk*, daughter of Ahmad and Habiba-sultan, and wife of Babur—particulars 36, ☛ 711; her marriage arranged (912) 306, ☛ 714; brought from Herat (913) 330; married 339; dies in child-bed and her name at once given to her child 36; [†*cir.* 915 AH.–1509 AD.].

Ma'suma-sultan Begim, *ut supra*, daughter of Babur and Ma'suma-sultan (*supra*)—her birth 36; with her father in the Trans-oxus campaign (916–920) 358; her marriage (or betrothal) to Muhammad-i-zaman *Bai-qara* (923 or 924) 365; gifts made to her servants (935) 633; ☛ in the family-list 705, 706.

Maulana Sayyidi, or *Mashhadi*—his chronogram on Humayun's birth (913) 344.

Shaikh **Mazid Beg**, Babur's first guardian—particulars 26, 27, [† before 899 AH.–1494 AD.].

Mir **Mazid Taghai** *Kunji Mughul*, brother or uncle of Aisan-daulat—takes part in a sally from Samarkand (906) 142; wounded at Akhsi (908) 168; rebels (921) 363, 397; his relations, 'Ali-dost, Sherim, Qul-nazr *q.v.*; [†*cir.* 923 AH.–1517 AD.].

Mazid Beg Tarkhan *Arghun*, son of Amir Tarkhan Junaid (H.S. lith. ed. iii, 359)—his retainer Khusrau Shah 49; his action in 873 AH. 51; his brother 'Ashiq-i-muhammad *q.v.*

Shaikh **Mazid Kukuldash**—envoy of Muhammad-i-zaman to Babur (925) 402.

Medini Rao var. Mindi *etc.*—particulars 593 n. 5; his force at Kanwa (933) 562; holding Chanderi (934) 483, 593; Babur negotiates with him 594; his house the scene of a supreme rite 595.

Mihr-angez Begim *Bai-qara Timurid, Barlas Turk*—married as a captive (913) 329 n. 1.

Mihr-ban Khanim (see *infra*)—gifts to and from Babur (935) 631, 632, 641; her husband Kuchum *Auzbeg* and their son Pulad *q.v.*; a verse seeming to be addressed to her (925) 402.

Mihr-banu Begim *Miran-shahi*, half-sister of Babur (perhaps the Khanim last entered)—particulars 18.

Mihr-nigar Khanim *Chaghatai Chingiz-khanid*, daughter of Yunas—particulars 21, 149; joins Babur in Kabul (911) 246; visited by him after her disloyalty (912) 315; goes to Badakhshan (913) 341; dies a prisoner 21.

Milli Surduk—reprieved from death (932) 477, 478.

Mingli Bi Aghacha, a mistress of Husain *Bai-qara*—particulars 269; her sons and daughters 262–3, 266.

Minglik Kukuldash—leaves Samarkand (907) 147.

Minuchihr Mirza *Miran-shahi Timurid, Barlas Turk*, brother of Abu-sa'id—an attributed descendant 24; his son Malik-i-muhammad *q.v.*

Minuchihr Khan *Turk*—delayed in waiting on Babur by a forcible marriage (925) 386, 388; on Babur's service in Bhira 389; leading Darya-khanis (934) 589; his relation Nazar-i-'ali *Turk q.v.*

Mirak—entrusted with building work (935) 642.

Mirak Kur Diwan (or Gur)—in Ala-qurghan when Shaibani took Herat (913) 328.

Miran-shah Mirza *Miran-shahi Timurid, Barlas Turk*, son of Aulugh Beg *Kabuli*—rebels against his father and goes to Khusrau Shah 95; sent to Bamian 96.

Miran-shah Sultan Mirza *Timurid, Barlas Turk*, 3rd son of Timur—mentioned in a genealogy 14; his daughter's son Ahmad *Bai-qara q.v.*; [†810 AH.–1407–8 AD.].

Mir Buzurg *Tirmizi*—his daughter and granddaughter, wives of Mahmud *Miran-shahi* 47–8, 49.

Mirim—Mir Muhammad ?[1]—adopted son of Auzun Hasan—killed fighting against Babur 170; [†908 AH.–1502 AD.].

Mirim Diwan—*ut supra*—captured serving Babur (904) 106; released (905) 119; discovers a rebel (912) 319.

Mirim Laghari—*ut supra*—leaves Babur for home (903) 91; captured serving Babur (904) 106; killed 167; [†904 AH.–1499 AD.].

Mirim-i-nasir Beg—*ut supra*—enters Babur's service (904) 103; one of a household-party (906) 131; in the left centre at Qandahar (913) 335, 338; at social gatherings (925) 385, 388; on service 389, 391; receives his dead brother's district 397.

Mirim Tarkhan—*ut supra*—drowned while serving Bai-sunghar *Miran-shahi* 74; [†903 AH.–1497 AD.].

---

1 Shaikhim *Suhaili* however was named Ahmad (277) not Muhammad.

Muhammad 'Ali *bakhshi*—on Abu-sa'id's service and defeated by Husain *Bai-qara* (868) 259.

Muhammad 'Ali *Jang-jang*—in the centre at Bajaur (925) 370; at boat-parties 387, 388; his servant's service 391, 392; his districts 392–3, 530; reinforced 412; waits on Babur 403, 419, (932) 458; at Milwat (932) 460, 461; at Hisar-firuza 465–6; wounded 471; in the van at Panipat 472; on service 530, (933) 549, 550, 576, 582; in the left wing at Kanwa 557; acts unsuccessfully against Biban and Bayazid (934) 589, 594, 598; pursues from near Qanuj 601; sent against Baluchis (935) 638; his brother Arghun and sons Tardi-muhammad and Nau-roz *q.v.*

Khwaja **Muhammad 'Ali** *kitabdar*—messenger to Khwaja Yahya (905) 124; confuses a pass word (908) 164 (here *sairt-kishi* = sart); captured by Tambal 168; fights against rebels (912) 315; in the left centre at Qandahar (913) 335; in charge of treasure 338; at entertainments (925) 410, 411, 413; ☞ at Kalanur (930) 442 (here Tajik = Sart).

Muhammad 'Ali *Mubashir-beg*—stays with Babur at a crisis (903) 91; at Khuban (905) 113; in the flight from Akhsi (908) 163; captured by Tambal 168; killed on service 252; his servant Sulaiman 175; [†911 AH.–1506 AD.].

Muhammad 'Ali *piada*—deserts Nasir *Miran-shahi* (913) 343.

Khwaja **Muhammad 'Ali Taghai**—'Asas—brother of Mahim Begim?—in the van at Qandahar (913) 335; meets Babur at a crisis (914) 346; waits on Babur (925) 399, 403; answers a military summons 408; the first to follow Babur in renouncing wine (933) 552; at various entertainments (925) 387, 388, 400, 412, (926) 423, (935) 683; on his identity 522 n. 4; ☞ in charge of Babur's Agra tomb (937) 709.

Khwaja **Muhammad-amin**—out with Babur (910)230; deserts from Qandahar (913) 343; at a garden-wine-party (925) 418; his servant Imam-i-muhammad *ib.*

Muhammad-amin Khan *Qazani, Jugi Chingiz-khanid*—Shaibani sends him a Herat musician 292; [†925 AH.–1519 AD.].

Ustad **Muhammad-amin** *jibachi*—attention for him desired from Khwaja Kalan (935) 647.

Muhammad *Andijani*—sent to Kabul (912) 313–4.

Muhammad *Arghun*—with Mughuls against Babur (904) 106.

the right wing at Kanwa (933) 566, 569, 576; sends news of a second[1] Baluchi incursion (935) 638; reports action 675; ordered to Agra 676; at various entertainments (925) 385, 388, 412.

Muhammad-i-makhdumi—his son Mahmud *q.v.*

Muhammad Ma'sum Mirza, *Bai-qara Timurid, Barlas Turk*, son of Husain and Mingli—particulars 264, 269; his wife Bega *Miran-shahi q.v.*; [†907 AH.–1501–2 AD. See HS. iii, 290].

Mulla **Muhammad** *Mazhab*—profers support to Babur (932) 463; Babur's envoy to Bengal (935) 637.

Muhammad Mazid Tarkhan *Arghun Chingiz-khanid*, son of Aurdu-bugha—particulars 39; has charge of Nasir *Miran-shahi* (899) 32; leaves Samarkand after the Tarkhan rebellion (901) 62; displeases 'Ali *Miran-shahi* (905) 121; plotted against *ib.*: invites Mirza Khan and Babur 122, 123; welcomes Babur 40, 124; joins Khusrau Shah (906) 129; fights for Babur at Sar-i-pul (Khwaja Kardzan) 139; takes refuge with Khusrau Shah 141; at Kul-i-malik (918) ☛ 357; killed there 39; his house a post of Babur's 143; [†918 AH.–1512 AD.].

Sultan **Muhammad Mirza** *Bai-qara Timurid, Barlas Turk*—parentage 257.

Sayyid **Muhammad Mirza** *Dughlat*, uncle of Haidar—sent to help Babur (906) 139; envoy of Sa'id *Chaghatai* to him (917) 22; escorts his niece to Kashghar *ib.*

Sultan **Muhammad Mirza** *Miran-shahi*, grandson of Timur—his son Abu-sa'id *q.v.*

Sultan **Muhammad Mirza** *Miran-shahi Timurid*—his father Abu-sa'id *q.v.*

Muhammad *miskin, Duldai Barlas*, son of Hafiz—captured by Babur's men (903) 72.

Muhammad Muhsin *Bai-qara*, see Kupuk.

Muhammad Muqim Beg *Arghun*, son of Zu'n-nun—takes possession of Kabul (908) 195 n. 3; loses it to Babur (910) 198, 199, 227, 246 n. 3; loses Qalat-i-ghilzai to him (911) 248–9; seeks his co-operation against Shaibani (913) 330; withdraws and fails in etiquette 331–2; opposed to Babur at Qandahar 333–7; flees in defeat 339.

---

1 The record of the first appears likely to be lost in the *lacuna* of 934 AH.

Khwaja **Muhammad Muqim** *Harawi*, father of Nizamu'd-din Ahmad the historian—☞ mentioned 691 n. 1, ☞ 692; ☞ his story of a plan to supersede Humayun as Padshah in 937 AH. 703; discussion of it 704–7; its incredibility as told 704–5.

Muhammad Mumin *Bai-qara Timurid, Barlas Turk*, son of Badi'u'z-zaman—Astarabad claimed for him (902) 69; defeated by an uncle 71; his murder attributed to Khadija Begim 268.

Shaikh **Muhammad** *Musalman*, ancestor of the Farmuli Shaikh-zadas—his tomb and descendants 220.

Sultan **Muhammad Muzaffar** *Gujrati, Tank Rajput*—particulars 481–2; his death 481; his sons Sikandar Shah and Bahadur Khan *q.v.*; [†932 AH.–1526 AD.].

Muhammad *Nuhani*, see Bihar Khan.

Mulla **Muhammad** *Parghari*—loquacious (932) 453.

Muhammad-i-qasim *Barlas*—comes accidentally on Babur (925) 417.

Muhammad-i-qasim Mirza *Arlat*, son of Abu'l-qasim (H.S. iii, 327)—his Bai-qara wife and their child 265; his sons (?) Babur and Murad *q.v.*

Muhammad-i-qasim Mirza *Bai-qara Timurid*, son of Husain and Papa—parentage 265.

Muhammad-i-qasim *Nabira*, grandson of Muhammad *Sighal* —made prisoner when opposing Babur (903) 72.

Muhammad-i-qasim *Qibchaq Turk*, son of Baqi *Chaghaniani*—leaves his family in Ajar (910) 191; father (?) of Ahmad-i-qasim *q.v.*

Muhammad-quli *quchin* (Mir Shah *quchin*)—helps Bai-sunghar's escape from Samarkand (901) 62; with Babur at Samarkand and wounded (902) 68; stays with him at a crisis (903) 91; captured (904) and released by Tambal (905) 119; in the van at Sar-i-pul (Khwaja Kardzan) (906) 139; besieged in Samarkand 142–144; with Babur when surprised by Tambal (908) 163; in the left wing at Qandahar (913) 334; in a raid (925) 403.

Muhammad *qurchi*, retainer of Khusrau Shah—rises against the Auzbeg occupation of Badakhshan (910) 242; expels Nasir *Miran-shahi* (912) 321; keeping up his head (913) 340.

Ustad **Muhammad** *sabz-bana*—his son Bana'i *q.v.*

Maulana **Muhammad Sadru'd-din** *Andijani*—his six sons'

service to Babur 370 n. 2; his sons Khwajaka Mulla-i-sadr, Kichik Khwaja, Khwaja Kalan *q.v.*

Muhammad Salih Mirza *Khwarizmi*, author of the *Shaibani-nama*—in Khwaja Yahya's service[1] and waits on Babur (901) 64; leaves Samarkand with the Tarkhans (905) 121; enters Shaibani's service 65 n. 3; on Shaibani's service (910) 196 n. 6; couplets of his quoted by Babur 120–1, 448; [†941 AH.–1534–5 AD.].

Ustad Shah **Muhammad** *sang-tarash*—cuts an inscription (913) 343; receives orders for work (933) 585, 606, (935) 642.

Muhammad Shah *Khilji Turk*, son of Nasiru'd-din of Malwa —takes Chanderi and seeks Ibrahim *Ludi*'s protection (916) 593; his young son Ahmad *q.v.*; [†931 AH.–1524 AD.?].

Muhammad Shah Padshah *Miran-shahi Timurid, Barlas Turk*—his change of name for an orange 511 n. 4; [†1161 AH.–1748 AD.].

Muhammad *Shaibani*, see Shaibani.

Shaikh **Muhammad-i Shaikh Bhakari** (?)—on service (933) 382.

Shah **Muhammad Shaikh-zada** *Farmuli Afghan*, son of Ma'ruf— leaves his Afghan associates (934) 598 (no name here); favoured by Babur 603, 675; compelled to act with Biban and Bayazid (935) 675; writes dutifully to Babur *ib.*; waits on 'Askari and Babur *ib.* and 679.

Muhammad Sharif *munajjim* (astrologer)—comes to Kabul (925) 399 and to Agra (933) 551; augurs defeat at Kanwa 551, 576; offers congratulations on victory, blamed and banished with a gift 576.

Sultan **Muhammad** *Sighal*, *Chaghatai*—his descendants Muhammad-i-qasim and Hasan *q.v.* (Cf. 66 n. 4 and H.S. lith. ed. iii, 275 for tribe and title resp.).

Muhammad Sultan *bakhshi*—left behind to catch pheasants (925) 404; in a night-attack on Ibrahim's camp (932) 471; in the left wing at Panipat 472; has custody of the cook who poisoned Babur (933) 542; staff-officers at Kanwa 568; host to Babur (935) 629; introduces a Kabul messenger 644; brings news of Mahmud *Ludi* 653–4; writes that Babur's family is on

---

1 See *Shaibani-nama*, Vambéry's ed. Cap. xv, l. 12, for his changes of service, and Sam Mirza's *Tuhfa-i-sami* for various particulars including his classification as a Chaghatai.

its way from Kabul 657; waits on Babur 606; his servant Shah Qasim *q.v.*

Sultan **Muhammad Sultan** *Chaghatai Chingiz-khanid*— Sultanim and Khanika—eldest son of The Khan (Mahmud) —sent to help Babur (903) 92; his guardian and he oppose Babur (905) 116; his part in acclaiming the standards (907) 155; goes out to meet his uncle Ahmad (Alacha Khan) (908) 159; ☛ murdered 350; [†914 AH.–1508 AD.].

Muhammad Sultan-i-jahangir Mirza *Jahangiri Timurid, Barlas Turk*—Samarkand given to him by his grandfather Timur 85; his college 78.

Muhammad Sultan Mirza *Bai-qara Timurid, Barlas Turk*, son of Wais and Sultanim—particulars 265; waits on Babur at Kalanur (932) 458; on Babur's service 468, 471, 475, 530, 534, (933) 545, 548, 582, (934) 589, (935) 682; in the left wing at Panipat (932) 472 and at Kanwa (933) 567, 570; gifts to him 527; given Qanuj 582; joins Babur (935) 651; in the battle of the Ghogra 671, 672, 674; ☛ mentioned 706 (where wrongly classed with half-Timurids); once owner of the Elphinstone Codex 706 n. 3.

Beg **Muhammad** *ta'alluqchi*—conveys gifts to Humayun (Muh. 934) and returns (Rabi' I, 935) 621; Babur complains of his detention.

Muhammad Tahir—captured (903) 74.

Muhammad **Timur Sultan** *Auzbeg-Shaiban, Chingiz-khanid*, son of Shaibani—at Samarkand (906) 128; at Sar-i-pul (Khwaja Kardzan) 139; defeats and kills two Bai-qara Mirzas (913) 263, 329–30; leaves Samarkand on Babur's approach (917) 354; at Ghaj-davan (918) 360; his marriages with captives 24, 36, 328 n. 1.

Mulla **Muhammad** *talib-mu'ammai*—an enigmatist of Husain *Bai-qara*'s Court—particulars 201 n. 7[1]; a couplet of his quoted 201–2; [†918 AH.–1512 AD.].

Pahlawan Haji **Muhammad** *tufang-andazi*—receives gifts (935) 633.

---

1 He died serving Babur, at Kul-i-malik (H.S. iii, 344).—Further information negatives my suggestion (201 n. 7) that he and Mir Husain (p. 288 and n. 7) were one.

Mulla **Muhammad** *Turkistani*, retainer of Khusrau Shah—makes Qunduz safe for Shaibani Khan (910) 192.

Muhammad-i-'ubaidu'l-lah, son of Ahrari, see Khwajaka Khwaja.

Sultan **Muhammad Wais**—waits on Babur (902) 66; runs away and is suspected (907) 156; serving Babur at Akhsi (908) 174; his retainer Kichik 'Ali *q.v.*

Muhammad Wali Beg—particulars 277; on Husain *Bai-qara's* service (901) 57, (902) 70, (903) 94.

Muhammad-i-yusuf *Aughlaqchi*, elder son of Yusuf—waits on Babur (905) 125.

Mir **Muhammad-i-yusuf**—particulars 285; waits on Babur in Herat (912) 285; Shaibani instructs him in exposition (913) 329.

Muhammad *Zaitun*[1]—opposing Babur (932) 523; written to and makes false excuse 529, 530; waits on Babur (933) 540; sent out of the way before Kanwa 547.

Khwaja **Muhammad Zakariya**,[2] son of Yahya—murdered 128; [906 AH.–1500 AD.].

Muhammad-i-zaman Mirza *Bai-qara Timurid*, *Barlas Turk*, grandson and last surviving heir of Husain—particulars 261, 269 n. 6, 279; spared by Shaibani 263; his wanderings and association with Khwand-amir 364–5, 463 n. 3; sent to Babur and married to his daughter Ma'suma-sultan (923–4) 365; in Balkh 365, 522; dutiful letters and tribute sent by him to Babur (925) 385, 402, ☛ 427, ☛ (926–932) 428; with Babur (935) 606, 631, 639, 659; objects to the Bihar command 661–2; does homage for it and is given *insignia* of royalty 662, ☛ 706; starts for Bihar but is recalled 663, 664; in the battle of the Ghogra 668, 669, 671; ☛ given Junpur 682; pursues Biban and Bayazid 682; grounds for surmising in Babur the intention to leave him as ruler in Hindustan 705–7; ☛ of his later uprisings against Humayun 714 n. 1; [†drowned at Chausa 946 AH.–1539 AD.].

Muhibb-i-'ali Khan *Barlas Turk*, son of Khalifa—☛ marries

---

1 "Zaitun is the name of the Chinese city from which satin was brought *(hodie* Thsiuancheu or Chincheu) and my belief is that our word satin came from it" (Col. H.Yule, E. and D. iv, 514).

2 My text omits to translate *yigit* (*aughul*) and thus loses the information that Yahya's sons Baqi and Zakariya were above childhood, were grown to fighting age—braves—but not yet begs.

troops (933) 538–9; waits on Babur 539; in the left wing at Kanwa 567; on service (935) 678.

Khwaja **Nizamu'd-din Ahmad**, the author of the *Tabaqat-i-akbari*, son of Muhammad Muqim—☞ discussion of his story of the intended supersession of Babur's sons 702–8; [†1003 AH.–1594 AD.].

Sayyid **Nizamu'd-din 'Ali Khalifa** *Marghilani, Barlas Turk,* son of Junaid—escapes from prison and death (900) 55; driven from Babur's presence (903) 90, (905) 119; defends Kabul (912) 313; mediates (914) 345; hears rumours of Mughul revolt 346; in the left centre at Bajaur (925) 369 and at Panipat (932) 473; given charge of Ibrahim's corpse 474 n. 1; at Kanwa (933) 556, 558, 564–5; on service 384, 395, 666; communicates bad news at Chandiri (934) 594 and (935) 639; mediates for Rahim-dad 689; ☞ declines the Badakhshan government (936) 697; ☞ discussion of his plan to set Humayun aside (in Hindustan?) 702–8; his seat at a feast 631; host to Babur 408; his sons Muhibb-i-'ali, Husamu'd-din-i-'ali, Hamza and daughter Gul-barg *q.v.*

Shaikh **Nizamu'd-din Auliya**—his tomb visited by Babur (932) 475; [†725 AH.–1325 AD.].

Nizamu'l-mulk *Khawafi,* Diwan in Heri—arrested and put to death 282; [†903 AH.–1497–8 AD.].

Hazrat **Nuh** (Noah)—his father Lam *q.v.*

Nur Beg (perhaps Sayyid Nuru'd-din *Chaghaniani infra*)—disobeys the Law, plays the lute (925) 395; joins Babur in an autumn garden 418; his brethren on service (932) 446; with Babur in the East (935) 653; in the battle of the Ghogra 673; sent to allay Rahim-dad's fears 688–9; his brother Shaham *q.v.*

Sayyid **Nuru'd-din** *Chaghaniani*—Sayyid Amir—a son-in-law of Babur and father of Salima-sultan ☞ 713; perhaps Nur Beg *supra.*

Shaikh **Nuru'd-din Beg** *Turkistani, Qibchaq Turk*—grandfather, through a daughter, of Yunas *Chaghatai* 19 (see T.R. trs. p. 64).

Nuru'l-lah *tamburchi*—his experience in an earthquake (911) 247.

Sayyid **Nuyan Beg** *Tirmizi*—particulars 273; his son Hasan-i-ya'qub *q.v.*

Nuyan Kukuldash *Tirmizi*—makes a right guess (906) 131–2; on service against Shaibani 142; his sword sent as a gift to Tambal

(907) 150; that sword wounds Babur's head (908) 151, 167, 396; his suspicious death 151–152; Babur's grief 152; Nuyan's uncle Haq-nazar *q.v.*; [†907 AH.–1502 AD.].

Padmawati, wife of Rana Sanga—in Rantanbhur (935) 612; mentioned 613 n. 1; her son Bikramajit and kinsman Asuk Mal *q.v.*

Pahar Khan *Ludi,* see Bihar.

Pahar Mirza, a father-in-law of Jahangir *Miran-shahi*—his daughter brings her son Pir-i-muhammad to Babur (913) 331.

Pahlawan *Audi (Oudhi)*—wrestles (935) 683, 688.

Pahlawan *Lahori*, a boatman—wrestles (935) 656.

Papa Aghacha, a mistress of Husain *Bai-qara*—particulars 266, 268–9; her five sons and three daughters *ib.*

Papa-aughuli, of Babur's household—out with Babur (910) 234; at Qandahar (913) 335.

Parbat *Kakar*—conveys tribute to Babur (925) 391, 392, 393.

Pasha Begim *Baharlu, Aq-quiluq Turkman*, daughter of 'Ali-shukr Beg—particulars 49; her nephew Yar-'ali *Balal q.v.*

Payanda-muhammad *Qiplan*—out with Babur (925) 404.

Payanda-sultan Begim *Miran-shahi Timurid, Barlas Turk*, daughter of Abu-sa'id and wife of Husain *Bai-qara*—particulars 263, 265, 268; her son Haidar and her daughters *ib.*; visited in Herat by Babur (912) 301; arranges a marriage for him 306; captured by Shaibani (913) 327.

Pietro della Vallé—an illustration drawn from his recorded morning-draught (1623 AD.) 395.

Khwaja **Pir Ahmad** *Khawafi*—his son 281.

Pir Budagh Sultan, Khaqan in Desht Qibchaq (H.S. iii, 232) —his Bai-qara marriage 258 n. 3.

Mir **Pir Darwesh** *Hazar-aspi*—in charge of Balkh (857) 50; fights there *ib.*

Piri Beg *Turkman*—joins Babur (913) 336; particulars Author's Note, 336.

Pir Kanu of Sakhi-sarwar—Babur halts at his tomb (910) 238.

Pir-i-Muhammad *Ailchi-bugha, quchin*—particulars 50 and nn.; drowned 48 n. 4, 50; [895 AH.–1490 AD.].

Pir Muhammad *Miran-shahi Timurid, Barlas Turk*, son of Jahangir—

brought by his widowed mother to Babur (913) 331.

Pir-quli *Sistani*—in the right wing at Panipat (932) 472, and at Kanwa (933) 566; on service (932) 530.

Pir Sultan *Pashai*—one of Babur's guides (912) 308.

Prester John, Wang Khan [T.R. trs. 16], Ong Khan [Abu'l-ghazi, Desmaisons' trs. p. 55]—his title 23 n. 3.

Pulad Sultan *Auzbeg-Shaiban, Chingiz-khanid*—son of Kuchum—Babur sends him his earliest-mentioned Diwan (925) 402, 632 n. 3; at Jam (934) 622; an envoy goes from him to Babur (935) 631, 632, 641.

Puran (Allah-birdi or Allah-quli)—out with Babur (910) 234; wounded (913) 342; his father-in-law Qasim *quchin q.v.*

Qabil (Cain)—Babur goes alone to his tomb (925) 415.

Qadir-birdi *Ghaini*—spoken to by Babur when in hiding (908) 180–1.

Qaitmas *Turkman*, retainer of Jahangir—drowned (910) 237.[1]

Qalandar *piada*—on Babur's service (932) 529.

Qambar-i-'ali *Arghun*—on Babur's service (935) 688.

Qambar-i-'ali Beg—mobilizes the Hindustan army by Abu-sa'id's order (873?) 46; expelled from Khurasan with Mahmud *Miran-shahi* 47.

Qambar-i-'ali Beg *quchin*, son of Qasim—races with Babur (?) (907) 147; wounded, brings Babur a message (908) 174; one of the eight in flight from Akhsi 177; gives Babur his horse 177–8; beats down snow for a road (912) 308–9; fights rebels in Kabul 315; at Qandahar (913) 334; wounded 336; hurries from Qunduz against rebels in Ghazni (921) 364; brings Babur a letter from Balkh (?) (925) 385.

Qambar-'ali Beg *Silakh, Mughul*—particulars 28; his inconvenient absence (904) 106; recalled (905) 108; goes away 110; returns 112; in the van at Khuban 113; goes away 115; returns and is ill-tempered 117; his districts 115, 124; his ill-timed pacificism 118; his misconduct 123; goes to Tambal, made prisoner, escapes to Babur 124; on Babur's service (906) 130, 131; at Sar-i-pul 138, 139; sends his family out of Samarkand 141; ? races with Babur

---

1 Cf. H.S. Ferti's trs. p. 70 for the same name Qaitmas.

---

1 His capture is not recorded.

service (925) 377, (933) 538; in the *tulghuma* of the left wing at Kanwa 568, 569.

Rustam Khan—Ilias (p. 576)—captures Babur's commander at Kul (Koel) (933) 557, 576; captured and flayed alive 576.

Sa'adat-bakht Begim—Begim Sultan—*Bai-qara Timurid, Barlas Turk*, daughter of Husain—particulars 266–7.

Nasiru'd-din **Sabuktigin** *Ghaznawi Turk*—the humble status of his capital 217; a legend concerning him 219; his son Mahmud *q.v.*; [†387 AH.–997 AD.].

Sadharan *Tank Rajput*—his acceptance of Islam 481 n. 5.

Pahlawan **Sadiq**—made to wrestle (935) 650; forbidden as an antagonist 653; wrestles 688.

Mulla **Sa'du'd-din Mas'ud** *Taftazani*—a descendant of 283; [†792 AH.–1390 AD.].

Sultan **Sa'id Khan** *Ghazi, Chaghatai Chinqiz-khanid*, son of Ahmad—particulars 698 nn. 2, 3, 349; meets Babur (908) 159; stays with him in Kabul (914) 318, 349–50; receives Andijan from him (916) 318, 357; loyal to him 344 n. 2, ☛ 351–2; sends an envoy to him (917) 22; Haidar *Dughlat* goes from Babur to Sa'id (918) 362; two kinswomen take refuge with him (923 and 924) 24; reported to have designs on Badakhshan (925) 412; an envoy to him returns 415; ☛ named as a principal actor between 926 and 932 AH. 427; writes and sends gifts to Babur (932) 446; ☛ invades Badakhshan (936) 695–6; ☛ gist of a letter from Babur to him 697–8; ☛ Babur moves menacingly for the North-west 698; his full-brother Khalil, his son Rashid, his wife Habiba, and *kukuldash* Yangi Beg *q.v.*; [†939 AH.–1533 AD.].

Sa'idliq Sa'd *Turkman*—defeated by Husain *Bai-qara* (873?) 260.

Saif-i-'ali Beg *Baharlu Qara-quiluq Turkman*, father of Bairam Khan-i-khanan—particulars 91 n. 3.[1]

Maulana **Saifi** *Bukhari*—'Aruzi—particulars 288; [†909 AH.–1503–4 AD.].

Saif Khan *Nuhani*, son of Darya Khan—deserts 'Alam Khan *Ludi* (932) 457.

1 He joined Babur with his father Yar-i-'ali *Balal* (*q.v.*) in 910 AH. (Blochmann's 'Biographies,' A.-i-A. trs. 315).

frustrated (934) 598; his wife Padmawati and sons Ratan-si and Bikramajit *q.v.*; his trusted man Medini Rao *q.v.*; [†934 AH.–1528 AD.].[1]

Sangur Khan *Janjuha*—waits on Babur (925) 383; on service 389, 419; killed in a sally from Biana 548; [†933 AH.–1527 AD.].

Mir **Sar-i-barhana**, see Shamsu'd-din Muhammad.

Sarigh-bash Mirza *Itarachi*—sent by The Khan (Mahmud) to help Babur (908) 161, 170.

Mulla **Sarsan**—Kamran's messenger and custodian of Ibrahim *Ludi*'s son (933) 544.

Sar-u-pa *Gujur*—Babur's guide to Parhala (925) 389, 391.

Satrvi Kachi—his force at Kanwa (933) 562.

Sultan **Satuq-bughra Khan Ghazi Padshah** (b. 384 AH.–994 AD.).—a surmised descendant 29 n. 8; his style Padshah 344 n. 2.

Sayyid Amir, see Nuru'd-din *Chaghaniani*.

Sayyid Dakkani—Shah Tahir *Khwandi Dakkani*—present at a feast (935) 631.[2]

Sayyid Dakni *Shirazi*, or Rukni, or Zakni—receives honours and orders (935) 619; on his name and work *ib.* n. 2, 634 n. 1; (see *supra*).

Sayyidi Beg Taghai, see Sherim Taghai.

Sayyidim 'Ali *darban* (? Muhammad-'ali), son of Baba 'Ali Beg—particulars 307; serving Khusrau Shah (901) 60–1; leads the Rusta-hazara to join Babur (910) 196; a follower punished 197; takes Bai-qara service (912) 307; drowned by Badi'u'z-zaman 307–8; [†*cir.* 913 AH.–1507 AD.].

Sayyid Mashhadi (var. Masnadi)—brings Babur news of Khwaja Rahimdad's sedition (935) 688.

Sayyid Mirza *Andikhudi*, ? brother of Apaq Begim—his two Bai-qara marriages 267.

Sayyid Rumi—at a feast (935) 631.

---

1 Concerning the date of his death, see Additional Notes under p. 576.

2 Since my text was printed, my husband has lighted upon what shows that the guest at the feast was an ambassador sent by Burhan Nizam Shab of Ahmadnagar to congratulate Babur on his conquest of Dihli, namely, Shah Tahir the apostle of Shiism in the Dakkan. He is thus distinguished from Sayyid Dakni, (Rukni, Zakni) *infra*. (See Add. Notes under p. 631 for further particulars of the Sayyid and his embassy.)

Shahi *qalandar*—plays the *ribab* (925) 417.

Shahi *tamghachi*—appointed clerk (935) 629.

Shahim (Shah Muhammad?)—sent for news (932) 454; climbs into Chandiri (934) 595 (here *yuz-bashi)*; his brother Nur Beg *q.v.*

Shahim-i-nasir—one of eight fugitives from Akhsi (908) 177.

Shah-jahan Padshah *Miran-shahi Timurid, Barlas Turk*— 184; his imitation of Babur (1030) 298 n. 3; his work in Babur's burial-garden 710, App. V, 795, [†1076 AH.–1666 AD.].

Shah Muhammad *muhrdar*, son of Baba Qashqa—on Babur's service (925) 388, (935) 688; his kinsmen *see s.n.* Baba Qashqa; [†958 AH.–1551 AD.].

Shah-quli *ghichaki*—a guitar-player—particulars 291.

Shah-quli *Kul-abi*—goes into Hisat (935) 640; his brother Wais *q.v.*

Shah-quli, ? servant of Div Sultan (p. 635)—sent to give Babur a report of the battle of Jam (935) 649; conveys from Babur an acceptance of excuse to Tahmasp *Safawi* 649.

Shahrak—conveys letters and a copy of Babur-nama writings (935) 652, 653.

Shahr-banu Begim *Miran-shahi Timurid, Barlas Turk*, daughter of Abu-sa'id—particulars 268; married to Husain *Bai-qara* (*cir.* 873) and divorced (876) 268.

Shahr-banu Begim *Miran-shahi, (ut supra)*, daughter of 'Umar Shaikh, wife of Junaid *Barlas*—particulars 18.

Shahrukh Mirza *Barlas Turk*, son of Timur—mentioned in a genealogy 14; ruling in Herat when Husain *Bai-qara* was born there (842) 256; his wazir serves Husain (after 873) 281; [†850 AH.–1447 AD.].

Shahrukh-Sultan *Afshar Turk*—commands a reinforcement for Babur from Isma'il *Safawi* (917) 354.

Shah Sufi—does well in Samarkand (906) 144.

Shah Sultan Begim (? *Arghun*), wife of Abu-sa'id *Miran-shahi* and mother of 'Umar Shaikh—her parentage not stated 13 n. 5, 45 n. 1; goes from Akhsi to Andijan when widowed (899) 32; a mediator (905) 113; her death announced (907) 149; [†906 AH.– 1501 AD.].

1 Down to p. 131 the Hai. MS. uses the name Shaibani or Shaibani Khan; from that page onwards it writes Shaibaq Khan, in agreement with the Elphinstone MS. —Other names found are *e.g.* Gulbadan's Shahi Beg Khan and Shah-bakht.

---

1 The title "Aughlan" (child, boy) indicates that the bearer died without ruling.

---

1 This cognomen was given because the bearer was born during an eclipse of the moon (*ai*, moon and the root *al* taking away); *see* Badayuni Bib. Ind. ed. i, 62.

---

1 Concerning this title, see Add. Notes under p. 540.

Tang-atmish Sultan *Auzbeg-Shaiban?*—at a feast (935) 631; his descent 631 n. 4; in the battle of the Ghogra 669.

Tardi Beg, brother of Quj (Quch) and Sher-afgan—in the left centre at Panipat (932) 472, 473, and at Kanwa (933) 565; on service 538–9, 582, (934) 590, 602; [†946 AH.–1539 AD.].

Tardi Beg *khaksar*—Babur visits him (925) 417–8; makes verse dropping down the Kabul-river (932) 448; praises a spring and receives a district 467, 581; returns to the darwesh-life (933) 583; conveys a gift to Kamran in Qandahar 583.

Tardika—Tardi *yakka* (568 n. 1)—on service (932) 462; in the right wing [*tulghuma*] at Kanwa (933) 568, 579; joins Babur at Dugdugi (935) 651; on service 678.

Tardi-muhammad *Jang-jang*, son of Muhammad *Jang-jang*—sent into Bhira (935) 661, 664.

Tardi-muhammad *Qibchaq*—at entertainments (925) 386, 400.

Tarkhan Begim *Arghun Chingiz-khanid*, daughter of 'Abdu'l-'ali—particulars 36.

Tarsam Bahadur—punishes the Mundahirs (936) 700–1.

Tarsun-muhammad Sultan—serving Humayun (935) 640.

Malik **Taus** *Yusuf-zai Afghan*—escorts his sister Mubaraka to her wedding with Babur (925) 375.

Tatar Khan *Kakar* (or *Gakar*)—particulars 387; detains one travelling to Babur (925) 386; killed by his cousin Hati 387, 389; Babur dismounts at his house in Pauhala 390; [†925 AH.–1519 AD.].

Tatar Khan *Sarang-kham Afghan*—Khan-i-jahan—in Gualiar and not submissive to Babur (932) 523; surrenders (933) 539–40; on Babur's service (935) 582 (here Khan-i-jahan).

Tatar Khan *Yusuf-khail Ludi Afghan*—particulars 382, 383; his son Daulat Khan *q.v.*; [†a few years before 910 AH.–1504–5 AD.].

Amir **Timur Beg** *Barlas Turk*—Sahib-i-qiran—mentioned in genealogies 14, 256; his birthplace Kesli 83; Samarkand his capital 75, 77, 78; his description of Soghd 84; his removal of the body of Sayyid Barka to Samarkand 266 n. 4; circumambulates Shaikh Maslahat's tomb (790) 132 n. 2; and Ahmad *Yassawi's* (799) 356; captures of Qarshi 134 n. 1; his example followed in the bestowal of Farghana 14; his gifts of the governments of

Dihli 487 and Samarkand 85; his descendants styled Mirza down to 913 AH. 344; Husain *Bai-qara* the best swordsman of his line 259 and greatest in his lands 191; a descendant 567; favoured begs 19, 39; one of his old soldiers 150; a descendant effects the migration of fowlers to Multan 225; Babur's victor where his had been at Pul-i-sangin 352; his and his descendants rule in Hindustan 382; their loss of lands to the Auzbegs 340; his builders and Babur's numerically compared 520; [†807 AH.– 1405 AD.].

Timur 'Usman *Miran-shahi Timurid, Barlas Turk*—mentioned 280.

Tingri-birdi *Bashaghi* (?) *Mughul*—in the left wing [*tulghuma*] at Panipat (932) 473.

Tingri-birdi Beg, son of Qasim *quchin*—helps to beat down snow for a road (912) 308–9; in the left wing at Qandahar (913) 334, 336; his servant at Bajaur (925) 361; entertains Babur 401; returns to his districts Khwast and Andar-ab 403; overtakes Babur at Jul-shahi 410; acts swiftly for him (932–3) 546.

Tingri-quli, a musician—plays at Babur's entertainments (925) 385, 386, 388; upset into the Parwan-water 407; first given wine 415.

Tirahi Sultan—takes a letter to Khwaja Kalan (925) 411.

Mulla **Tirik-i-'ali** (= Pers. Jan-i-'ali?)—fights for Babur at Bajaur (925) 368 and (on his name) n. 5; on service (933) 551.

Tizak, son of Qul-i-bayazid *bakawal*—captured as a child and kept 4 years (910) 197.

Tufan *Arghun*—joins Babur and so creates a good omen (913) 333.

Sayyid **Tufan**—on Babur's service (932) 453.

Tughluq-timur Khan *Chaghatai Chingiz-khanid*—mentioned in Yunas Khan's genealogy 19.

Tuka *Hindu* (var. Nau-kar)—given charge of gifts for Kabul (932) 525.

Tukhta-bugha Sultan *Chaghatai Chingiz-khanid*, son of Ahmad (Alacha Khan)—waits on Babur (934) 601; at a feast (935) 631; referred to as serving Babur 318; works magic 654; in the battle of the Ghogra 672, 673; receives praise, thanks, and guerdon 674, 677; on service 682; [†*cir.* 940 AH.–1533– 4 AD.].

Tulik Kukuldash[1]—Tambal strikes him with Babur's sword (912) 316; defeats Auzbegs in Badakhshan (925) 408; on Humayun's service (935) 640; his servant Barlas Juki *q.v.*

Tulmish *Auzbeg*—in the battle of the Ghogra (935) 669; on service 678.

Tulun Khwaja Beg, *Barin Mughul*—particulars 87; on Babur's service (902) 66, (903) 88; killed 88; [†903 AH.–1498 AD.].

Tun-sultan (var. Yun) *Mughul*—*ghunchachi* of 'Umar Shaikh 24.

Tuqa Beg, son of Sherim Taghai—captured by Tambal when serving Babur (904) 106; killed as a prisoner 107; [†904 AH.– 1499 AD.].

Khwaja **'Ubaidu'l-lah** *Ahrari Naqshbandi*—his righteous influence in Samarkand 42; his intervention for peace between 'Umar Shaikh and kinsmen 62 and n. 1; Pashaghar once his village 97; disciples named by Babur, Ahmad and 'Umar Shaikh *Miran-shahi*, Darwesh Beg Tarkhan, and Maulana-i-qazi *q.v.*; held in slight esteem by Mahmud *Miran-shahi* 46; his family ill-treated by Mahmud (899) 41; dreamed of by Babur (906) 132; his *Walidiyyah-risala* versified by Babur 619–20, 631 n. 3, 648 n. 4, ☞ 604, 775; his sons [Muhammad 'Ubaidu'l-lah] Khwajaka Khwaja and Yahya *q.v.*; [†895 AH.–1491 AD.].

'Ubaidu'l-lah Sultan Khan *Auzbeg-Shaiban, Chingiz-khanid*, son of Mahmud and nephew of Shaibani—defeats two pairs of Bai-qara Mirzas (913) 263, 329–30; defeated at Merv (917) 354; defeated north of Bukhara *ib.*; his vow and return to obedience 348, 356; victorious over Babur at Kul-i-malik (918) 201 n. 7, 357–8; routs Najm Sani at Ghaj-davan 360–1; avenges Mughul tyranny in Hisar 362; attacks Herat (927) 434; takes Merv (932) 534, 617 n. 2; takes Mashhad (933) 534, 623 n. 3; attacked by Tahmasp *Safawi* (934) 618, 622; defeated at Jam (935) 622, 635–6; Tahmasp's description of him 636 n. 2[2]; his wives by capture Habiba *Dughlat* and Mihr-angez *Bai-qara q.v.*; [†946 AH.– 1539 AD.].

---

1 He may be the Tulik Khan *quchin* of the *Ma'asiru'l-umra* i, 475.
2 Haidar Mirza gives an interesting account of his character and attainments (T.R. trs. p. 283).

Sultan **Wais** *Kulabi*—his friendship recommended to Humayun (935) 627; ☛ reinforces Qila'-i-zafar (935 or 936) 696; his daughter Haram Begim *q.v.*

Wais *Laghari* **Beg** *tughchi*—particulars 28; joins The Khan (Mahmud) (899) 32; safe-guards his ward Nasir *Miran-shahi ib.*; on service for Bai-sunghar (902) 65; waits on Babur 66; stays with him at a crisis (903) 91; on his service (904) 98, 100, 101, 106; at Khuban (905) 113; advises 117; plundered by 'Ali-dost 119; leaves Samarkand during the siege (906–7) 146; his son (?) Beggina *q.v.*

Wais *Miran-shahi*, see Mirza Khan.

Sultan **Wais Mirza** *Bai-qara Timurid, Barlas Turk*, son of Bai-qara II—parentage 257; his cousin and wife Sultanim *q.v.*

Sultan **Wais** *Sawadi*—mentioned 372; sent to collect a tax he had fixed (925) 374; receives gifts and leave 376.[1]

Sultan **Walama** *Taklu*—mentioned in Shah Tahmasp's account of the battle of Jam (935) 636 n. 2.

Pir **Wali** *Barlas Turk*—☛ loses Siwistan to Shah Beg (*cir.* 917) 429 n. 1.

Wali Beg *Barlas*—particulars 272–3; his son Muhammad-i-Wali *q.v.*; [†973 AH.].

Wali Beg *Qibchaq Turk*, brother of Khusrau Shah[2]—particulars 51; on his brother's service (901) 60, 64, (902) 71, (903) 93–4; mentioned (906) 129, (910) 191 by Husain *Bai-qara*; inquired for from Khusrau by Babur 193; defeated by Aimaqs 196; his death 51, 196; his former followers gathered together 242; [†910 AH.– 1504 AD.].

Wali *khazanchi, Qara-quzi*—captured by Tambal in Akhsi (908) 181; in the left centre at Qandahar (913) 335; his matchlock shooting at Bajaur (925) 369; on service 391, (932) 458, 465–6, 471; in the right wing at Panipat 472, 475, and at Kanwa (933) 566; his ill-behaviour in the heats 524.

Wali *parschi* (cheeta-keeper)—receives a gift (935) 633.

Wali Qizil *Mughul*—rebuked (932) 453; in the right wing [*tulghuma*] at Panipat 473; made *shiq-dar* of Dihli 476; on service (934) 601, (935) 638.

1 See Additional Note under p. 372.
2 See Additional Notes under p. 196.

Yadgar-i-muhammad[1] **Mirza** *Shah-rukhi Timurid, Barlas Turk,* son of Muhammad—his capture of Herat referred to 278; his defeat by Husain *Bai-qara* at Chanaran (874) 260; his loss of Herat to Husain (875) 260, 279, compared with Shaibani's of Samarkand to Babur (906) 134–5; the date of his death referred to 259 n. 1; his Master-of-horse Mir (Qambar-i-)'ali *q.v.*; [†875 AH.–1470–1 AD.].

Yadgar-i-nasir Mirza *Miran-shahi Timurid, Barlas Turk,* son of Nasir—gifts made to him (935) 632; [†953 AH.–1546 AD.].

Yadgar-i-sultan Begim *Miran-shahi (ut supra),* daughter of 'Umar Shaikh—particulars 18; her Auzbeg marriage (908) 18, 356; her return to Babur (917) 356.

Yadgar Taghai—his daughter Bega Begim *q.v.*

Khwaja **Yahya**, younger son of 'Ubaidu'l-lah *Ahrari*—his part in the Tarkhan revolt (901) 63; treats with Babur (904) 98; welcomes him to Samarkand (905) 124; waits on Shaibani (906) 127; banished by him and murdered with two sons 128, 147 n. 4; his house mentioned 133; his sons Muhammad Zakariya and Baqi, his grandsons 'Abdu'sh-shahid and Khwaja Kalan *q.v.*; [†906 AH.–1500 AD.].

Shaikh **Yahya** *Chishti*—his tomb visited by Babur (935) 666; his son Sharafu'd-din *Muniri q.v.*

Yahya *Nuhani,* at the head of Hindustan traders—allowed to leave Kabul (925) 416.

Yahya Nuhani (perhaps the man last entered)—waits on Babur (935) 676; a grant and leave given 683; his younger brother (no name) 683.

Yakka Khwaja—on Babur's service (934) 598; in the battle of the Ghogra (935) 671; drowned 674; his brother Qasim *q.v.*; [†935 AH.–1529 AD.].

Yangi Beg Kukuldash—brings Babur letters and gifts from Kashghar (932) 445–6.

Ya'qub-i-ayub *Begchik,* son of Ayub—on Husain Bai-qara's service (901) 58; proffers Khusrau Shah's service to Babur (910) 192–3.

Sultan **Ya'qub Beg** *Aq-quiluq Turkman*—a desertion to him 275;

---

1 Here the Hai. MS. and Ilminsky's Imprint add "Nasir".

affords refuge to Bana'i 287; his beg Timur 'Usman *Miran-shahi*
q.v.; [†896 AH.–1491 AD.].

Maulana **Ya'qub** *Naqshbandi*—his birthplace Chirkh 217; [†851
AH.–1447 AD.].

Ya'qub *tez-jang*—☛ one of five champions defeated in single
combat by Babur (914) 349 n. 1.

Ya'qub Sultan—mentioned as at Jam 636 n. 2.

Mulla **Yarak**—plays one of his compositions and incites Babur to
compose (926) 422.

Yarak Taghai (var. Yarik)—stays with Babur at a crisis (903) 91;
locum tenens in Akhsi (905) 116; retaliates on Turkman Hazaras
(911) 253; takes charge of sheep raided by Babur (912) 313; in
the right wing at Qandahar (913) 334.

Yar-i-'ali *Balal, Baharlu Qara-quiluq Turkman*, grandfather of
Bairam Khan-i-khanan—stays with Babur at a crisis (903) 91;
wounded (905) 109; rejoins Babur (910) 189; on his Tramontane
service (932–3) 546.

Yar-i-husain, grandson of Mir (Shaikh) 'Ali Beg—waits on Babur
(910) 228; asks permission to raise a force in Babur's name 231;
kills Baqi *Chaghaniani* (911) 250–1.

Yarim Beg—Yar-i-muhammad?—on Babur's service (913) 337.

Yili-pars Sultan *Auzbeg-shaiban*—his brother Aisan-quli (*q.v.*)
265.

Yisun-tawa Khan *Chaghatai Chingiz-khanid*—mentioned in
Yunas Khan's genealogy 19.

Yul-chuq—conveys a message to Babur (904) 99.

Yunas-i-'ali, son of Baba 'Ali Lord-of-the-Gate—surprised at a
Tuesday's fast (925) 398; on Babur's service 278, 468, 475, 521; in
the right centre at Panipat (932) 472, 473 and at Kanwa (933)
565, 569; has charge of Ibrahim's mother 543, 545; makes a garden (932) 532; in social charge of Tahmasp *Safawi*'s envoys (935)
631; inquires into Muhammad-i-zaman *Bai-qara*'s objections to
Bihar 661, 662; in the battle of the Ghogra 671; at entertainments
(925) 400, (935) 683; his kinsman Ibrahim *qanuni q.v.*

Yunas Khan *Chaghatai Chingiz-khanid*, Babur's maternal grandfather—particulars[1] 19–24; made Khan of the Mughuls by

1 The natural place for this Section of record is at the first mention of Yunas
Khan (p. 12) and not, as now found, interrupting another Section. See p. 678 and
n. 4 as to "Sections".

Babur's grandfather 20, 344 n. 2, 352; his friendly relations with
Babur's father 12; receives Tashkint from him 13; defeats him 16;
his sons Mahmud and Ahmad *q.v.* and daughters 21–4; his
servant Qambar-i-'ali *q.v.* mentioned 92 n. 1, 149, 565 n. 1;
[†892 AH.–1487 AD.].

Khwaja **Yunas** *Sajawandi*—his birthplace in Luhugur (Logar) 217.

Yusuf-i-'ali—musician at entertainments (925) 385, 387, 388; 418.

Yusuf-i-'ali *bakawal*—on Babur's service in Bajaur (925) 375.

Yusuf-i-'ali Kukuldash—made joint-*darogha* in Herat (911) 293;
Babur's cicerone in Herat (912) 304; his good dancing 303.

Yusuf-i-'ali *rikabdar*—conveys a letter concerning Hind-al's
pre-natal adoption (925) 374; receives a gift for swimming 401;
meets Babur 418; (?) in Sambhal (934) 587; (?) dies there 675,
687 (here 'Ali-i-yusuf); [†935 AH.–1529 AD.].[1]

Khwaja **Yusuf** *Andijani*, a musician—particulars 4.

Yusuf-i-ayub *Begchik*, son of Ayub—Babur warned against him
(910) 190; takes service with Babur 196; winters with Nasir 241;
leaves Babur for Jahangir (911) 190, 254.

Yusuf *badi*[2]— particulars 289; [†897 AH.–1492].

Sayyid **Yusuf Beg** *Aughlaqchi*, son of Murad—particulars 39; waits
on Babur from Samarkand (903) 72; holding Yar-yilaq for 'Ali
Miran-shahi (904) 98; dismissed from Khurasan on suspicion 98;
joins Babur (910) 196; advises him 197; his death 241; his
brother Hasan and sons Muhammad-i-yusuf and Ahmad-i-
yusuf *q.v.*; [†910 AH.–1505 AD.].

Yusuf darogha of Akhsi?—interviews Babur during the flight
(908) 181–2.

Sayyid **Yusuf** *Machami*—particulars 118; opposes Babur (905) 118,
117 n. 2.

Zahid Khwaja—abandons Sambhal (933) 557; on service (935)
682; [†953 AH.–1546 AD.].

Shaikh **Zain** *Khawafi*—verse-making on the Kabul-river (932)
448; his account of Babur's regretted couplet 448 n. 5; goes into
Dihli for the Congregational Prayer 476; makes a garden at

---

1 The entries of 934 and 935 may concern a second man 'Ali-i-yusuf.
2 Perhaps skilled in the art of metaphors and tropes (*'ilmu'l-badi'*).

GEOGRAPHICAL INDEX

---

1 KPK, Khyber Pakhtunkhwa, is the former North-West Frontier Province.

Baksara (U.P. India), Babur at *603, 660.

Baladar, Biladar (U.P. India), Babur at 686.

Bala-hisar (Kabul), present site of 198 n. 4; (*see* Citadel).

Bala-jui (Kabul), maker and name of 200 and n. 5.

Ballia (U.P. India), sub-divisions of 637 n. 1, 664 n. 8, 667 n. 2.

Balkh (Oxus valley), border-countries of 76, 261, 204; heat in 520; a melon-grower of 686; its trade with Kabul 202; holders of 18, 61–9, 257, 263, 275; exploits at 50, 93, 270; Husain *Bai-qara* and 70, 191; Khusrau Shah and 93–4, 110, 270; Shaibani and 294–6, 300, *363; Kitin-qara and 545.6; 'Ubaid and 622; *Isma'il *Safawi* and 359, 363; Muhammad-i-zaman and *364, 385, *428; Babur and 220, *359, *426–7, *442–4–5–6, 463 and n. 1, 625.

Balkh-ab, headwaters of 216; Babur crosses 295.

Balnath Jogi's hill (Punjab), Babur near 452.

Bamian (Khurasan? w. of Ghur-bund, Kabul), mountains of 215; how reached from Kabul 205; Khusrau Shah and 96; Babur and 189, 311, *351, 409.

Bam-valley (Herat), a *langar* in 308 n. 1; Babur in 296, 297 n. 1.

Banakat, Fanakat = Shahrukhiya (Tashkent) 2 n. 5, 76.

Banaras, Benares (U.P. India), crocodiles near 502; threatened 652–4; Babur near 657.

Banas-river (India), course of 485.

Bandir, Bhander (C. India), a fruit of 507; Babur at 590–8.

Band-i-salar Road (Ferghana), Babur on 55, 116.

Bangarmawu, Bangarmau (U.P. India), Babur near 601.

Bangash *tuman* (Kabul), described 220, 209, 233, 405; a holder of 27, 252; plan of attack on 229, 231–3, 382.

Bannu plain (KPK, Pakistan), a limit of Kabul territory 200; a waterless plain

near 234; date of the modern town 232 n. 5; Babur and 218, 231–2, 382, 394.

Banswara (Rajasthan), an old name of 573 n. 1.

Banur (Patiala, Punjab), Babur on (Ghaggar) torrent of 464.

(The) Bar (Punjab), 380 n. 4.

Baraich (U.P.), *see* Bahraich.

Barak or Birk (? KPK, Pakistan), mentioned as between Dasht and Farmul 235.

Barakistan, Birkistan (Zurmut, Kabul), a tomb in 220; ? tongue of 207.

Bara-koh (Ferghana) described 5; position of 5 n. 2.

Baramula (Kashmir), a limit of Sawad territory 372 n. 3.

Baran-su,[1] Panjhir-su (Kabul), affluents to 210–1; the bird-migrants' road 224; migration of fish in 225; bird-catching on 228; routes crossing 209, 342; locates various places 207 n. 5, 215, App. E, 733;—passers along 195, 242; Babur and 254, 420, *see* Koh-daman.

Baran *wilayat* (Kohistan, Kabul), Babur in 253, 320, 405.

Bara (KPK, Pakistan), road of 411; Babur fords the water of 230.

Bari (Rajasthan), hills of 486; hunting-grounds in 509 n. 1; Babur at 509, 585.

Barik-ab (affluent of the "Kabul-river"), Babur on 409, 414, 446.

Bast, Bost, Bust (on the Helmand, Afghanistan), Husain *Bai-qara's* affairs at 94, 260.

Bastam ('Iraq), a w. limit of Khurasan 261 (where read Bastam); captured 622.

Bateswar (U.P. India), ferry of 643 n. 3.

Bazar and Taq (India), *see* Dasht.

Bazarak (Hindu-kush), described 205.

Beg-tut (Kabul), earthquake action near 247.

Benares (India), *see* Banaras.

Bengal, Bangala (India), particulars of the rules and customs in 482; envoys to and from 637, 640, 665; army of 663; Babur at ease about 677, 679 n. 7; traversed by the Ganges 485; a bird of 495; fruits of 504.

---

1 Babur uses this name for the Kabul-river as low as nearly to Dakka.

---

1 "The Dara-i-suf, often mentioned by the Arabian writers, seems to lie west of Bamian" (Erskine, Memoirs p. 152 n. 1).

Irij or Irich (C. India), Babur at 590.

Ishkimish (Kunduz?), not in Badakhshan 288; on a named route 321; military action at 60, 192, 243.

Ispahan, Isfahan (Persia), a governor of 635 n. 6.

Istalif (Kabul), described 216; a garden at 246; fishing at 226; Babur at 246, 406, 416–8.

Jagdalik pass (Kabul), Babur crosses 229, 341, 414.

Jahan-nama fort (Bhira, Punjab), Babur in 384.

Jahan-nama hill (Delhi district), 485.

Jahan-nama'i (Kabul), Babur at 421; see Jui-shahi.

Jajmau or Jajmawa (U.P. India), rebels in 533; a submission near 534.

Jakin *pargana* (U.P. India), Babur in 644.

Jalandhar (Punjab), an appointment to 442.

Jalisar, Jalesar (on the Jumna, U.P. India), Humayun at 531; Babur at 589, 640.

Jalisar, Jalesar (on the Ghogra, U.P. India), Babur at 681; perhaps Chaksar 681 n.4.

Jalmish (w. frontier, Kabul), 205 n. 2.

Jal-tu var. Cha-tu (Kabul), Babur at 228.

Jam, mod. Jamrud (KPK, Pakistan), Babur at 229, 230, 412.

Jam (Khurasan), Hatifi's birthplace 288; how marked in maps 623 n. 8, *714; Jami the cognomen of Maulana 'Abdu'r-rahman *q.v.*; Auzbeg defeat near 622 n. 1, 625 n. 4, 635, 636 n. 2, details as to location of the battle 623 n. 8, 635 n. 4.

Janglik (Kabul), Babur at 251–3, 311–14 n. 1.

Jaswan-dun (Punjab), described 462; Babur in 461–3.

Jaunpur (U.P. India), see Junpur.

Jauz-wilayat (Khurasan), 46 n. 3.

Jihlam, Jilam, Jhelum (Punjab), Babur near 453; see Bahat for Jhelum river.

Jud mountains (Punjab), see Koh-i-jud.

Juduk (Samarkand), Babur at 147.

Jui-shahi (Kabul), Babur at 229, 394, 410, 422; (see Jahan-nama'i).

Jumandna, "Jumoheen"? (U.P. India), Babur at 649.

Jun-river, Jumna (India), course of 485; locates a place 532; a drowning in 582; Babur on or crossing 467, 475, 531, 605, 616, 638–9, 640, 650–5, 684–6; he bathes in 644; orders his officers to cross 684; in flood 685.

Junahpur, Junapur (U.P. India), an old form of Junpur or Jaunpur 676 n. 4; used by Babur 276, 544, 636, 676, 682; see *infra* Junpur.

Junpur, Jaunpur (U.P. India), water of 658; formerly a Sharqi possession 481; revenue of 521; taken by Humayun 544; an assignment on 527; appointments to 276, 538, 544, 676, 682; arrivals from 636, 667.

Jurgha-tu (Kabul), see Qurgha-tu.

Jusa or Chausa (C.P. India), Babur at 581.

Kabul town and country, description of 199 to 227,—position and boundaries 199, 481, town and environs 200, fort 201, 344, bridges 198, 314, 417, trade 202, climate 77, 201–3, 223, 314, 584, snow in 208–9, 223, 314, dividing line between hot and cold climates 208, 220, 229, fruits 202, 510, cultivated lands 243, meadows 204, Hindu-kush roads 204, Lamghanat roads 201, Khurasan road 205, Hindustan roads 205, 206, 231, 308, 629; highwaymen 205, 341, peoples 207, 221, subdivisions 207 to 221, dependencies 214–5, revenue 221, mountain-tracts 221, firewood 223, fauna 223, 496–8, bird-catching 224, fishing 225;—rivers of, Baran *q.v.*— Kabul, Luhugur (Logar); *garm-sil* 208, 484; unfitness for nomads 228, 402; use "Hindu-kush" in 485; use of "Kabul" in Agra 532; a mulla 284;—given to 'Umar Shaikh 14; Aulugh Beg *Kabuli* and 95 and n. 2; *185; Ababikr and 260; 'Abdu-r-razzaq and 195; Muqim *Arghun* and 195, 198–9, 227; Khusrau Shah and 192;—Babur's move to win it 7, 189, 191–7; his capture of 198–9; dates fixed, by the capture of, 19 n. 1,

ABOUT THE INTRODUCER

WILLIAM DALRYMPLE is a writer and historian. His books include *The Anarchy: The Relentless Rise of the East India Company*, *Koh-i-Noor* (with Anita Anand), *Return of a King: The Battle for Afghanistan*, *The Last Mughal*, *Nine Lives*, *White Mughals*, *From the Holy Mountain*, *City of Djinns* and *In Xanadu*. He lives in Delhi.

ABOUT THE TRANSLATOR

ANNETTE BEVERIDGE (1842–1929) has been described as one of the most outstanding oriental scholars of the early twentieth century. Her first work on Indian history was a translation from German of Count Noer's *Emperor Akbar* (1890); her translation from Persian (the first) of the then little-known *History of Humayun* by the princess Gulbadan followed in 1902. Beveridge was unassuming about her scholarship but her monumental work on the *Babur Nama* (1912–21) was all the more remarkable for having been achieved when Chaghatai studies were in their infancy. Her life was as compelling as her work, as documented by her son William Beveridge in a joint biography of his parents, *India Called Them* (1947). Stronger on her intellectual achievements is *Annette Akroyd Beveridge: Victorian Reformer, Oriental Scholar* by M. A. Scherer (Ohio State University, 1995), online at etd.ohiolink.edu. She was an indomitable character who refused to allow the onset of deafness in early middle age to cramp her style. Bernard Shaw described her as 'the cleverest woman of my acquaintance and the wickedest in her opinions'.

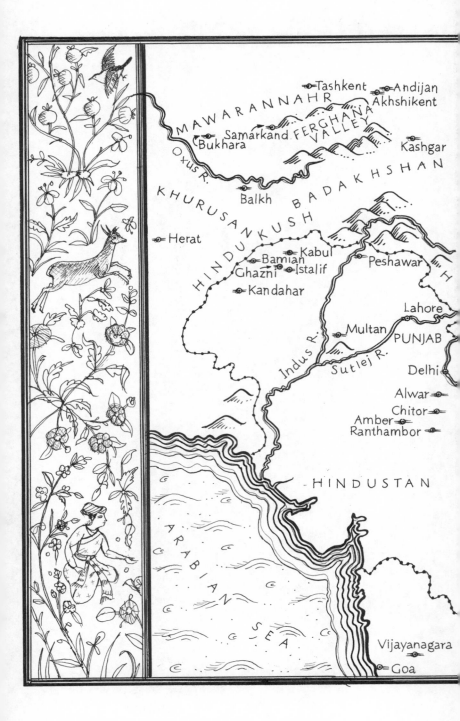

THE TRAVELS OF BABUR

MALAYAS

Ganges
Yamuna
Faizabad
Ayodhya
Patna
Gwalior
Allahabad
Chanderi
Varana
Jaunpur
Ganges R.

Bijapur

BAY OF BENGAL

This book is set in BEMBO which was cut
by the punch-cutter Francesco Griffo
for the Venetian printer-publisher
Aldus Manutius in early 1495
and first used in a pamphlet
by a young scholar
named Pietro
Bembo.